FOR REFERENCE

Do Not Take From This Room

Twentieth-Century Literary Criticism

Guide to Gale Literary Criticism Series

For criticism on	Consult these Gale series
Authors now living or who died after December 31, 1959	*CONTEMPORARY LITERARY CRITICISM (CLC)*
Authors who died between 1900 and 1959	*TWENTIETH-CENTURY LITERARY CRITICISM (TCLC)*
Authors who died between 1800 and 1899	*NINETEENTH-CENTURY LITERATURE CRITICISM (NCLC)*
Authors who died between 1400 and 1799	*LITERATURE CRITICISM FROM 1400 TO 1800 (LC)* *SHAKESPEAREAN CRITICISM (SC)*
Authors who died before 1400	*CLASSICAL AND MEDIEVAL LITERATURE CRITICISM (CMLC)*
Black writers of the past two hundred years	*BLACK LITERATURE CRITICISM (BLC)*
Authors of books for children and young adults	*CHILDREN'S LITERATURE REVIEW (CLR)*
Dramatists	*DRAMA CRITICISM (DC)*
Hispanic writers of the late nineteenth and twentieth centuries	*HISPANIC LITERATURE CRITICISM (HLC)*
Native North American writers and orators of the eighteenth, nineteenth, and twentieth centuries	*NATIVE NORTH AMERICAN LITERATURE (NNAL)*
Poets	*POETRY CRITICISM (PC)*
Short story writers	*SHORT STORY CRITICISM (SSC)*
Major authors from the Renaissance to the present	*WORLD LITERATURE CRITICISM, 1500 TO THE PRESENT (WLC)*

ISSN 0276-8178

Volume 69

Twentieth-Century Literary Criticism

**Excerpts from Criticism of the
Works of Novelists, Poets, Playwrights,
Short Story Writers, and Other Creative Writers
Who Lived between 1900 and 1960,
from the First Published Critical
Appraisals to Current Evaluations**

Scot Peacock
Editor

Thomas Ligotti
Associate Editor

GALE

DETROIT • NEW YORK • TORONTO • LONDON

STAFF

Scot Peacock, *Editor*

Thomas Ligotti, *Associate Editor*

Susan Trosky, *Permissions Manager*
Kimberly F. Smilay, *Permissions Specialist*
Sarah A. Chesney, *Permissions Associate*
Steve Cusack, Kelly A. Quin, *Permissions Assistant*

Victoria B. Cariappa, *Research Manager*
Andrew Guy Malonis, *Research Manager*
Tamara C. Nott, Michele P. LaMeau, Tracie A. Richardson,
Cheryl L. Warnock,
Research Associates
Alfred A. Gardner, I, *Research Assistants*

Mary Beth Trimper, *Production Director*
Deborah L. Milliken, *Production Assistant*

Sherrell Hobbs, *Macintosh Artist*
Randy Bassett, *Image Database Supervisor*
Robert Duncan, *Imaging Specialist*
Pamela Hayes, *Photography Coordinator*

Library of Congress Catalog Card Number 76-46132
ISBN 0-7876-1169-7
ISSN 0276-8178

Printed in the United States of America
10 9 8 7 6 5 4 3 2 1

Contents

Preface vii

Acknowledgments xi

Preface

Since its inception more than fifteen years ago, *Twentieth-Century Literary Criticism* has been purchased and used by nearly 10,000 school, public, and college or university libraries. *TCLC* has covered more than 500 authors, representing 58 nationalities, and over 25,000 titles. No other reference source has surveyed the critical response to twentieth-century authors and literature as thoroughly as *TCLC*. In the words of one reviewer, "there is nothing comparable available." *TCLC* "is a gold mine of information—dates, pseudonyms, biographical information, and criticism from books and periodicals—which many libraries would have difficulty assembling on their own."

Scope of the Series

TCLC is designed to serve as an introduction to authors who died between 1900 and 1960 and to the most significant interpretations of these author's works. The great poets, novelists, short story writers, playwrights, and philosophers of this period are frequently studied in high school and college literature courses. In organizing and excerpting the vast amount of critical material written on these authors, *TCLC* helps students develop valuable insight into literary history, promotes a better understanding of the texts, and sparks ideas for papers and assignments. Each entry in *TCLC* presents a comprehensive survey of an author's career or an individual work of literature and provides the user with a multiplicity of interpretations and assessments. Such variety allows students to pursue their own interests; furthermore, it fosters an awareness that literature is dynamic and responsive to many different opinions.

Every fourth volume of *TCLC* is devoted to literary topics. These topic entries widen the focus of the series from individual authors to such broader subjects as literary movements, prominent themes in twentieth-century literature, literary reaction to political and historical events, significant eras in literary history, prominent literary anniversaries, and the literatures of cultures that are often overlooked by English-speaking readers.

TCLC is designed as a companion series to Gale's *Contemporary Literary Criticism,* which reprints commentary on authors now living or who have died since 1960. Because of the different periods under consideration, there is no duplication of material between *CLC* and *TCLC.* For additional information about *CLC* and Gale's other criticism titles, users should consult the Guide to Gale Literary Criticism Series preceding the title page in this volume.

Coverage

Each volume of *TCLC* is carefully compiled to present:

- criticism of authors, or literary topics, representing a variety of genres and nationalities

- both major and lesser-known writers and literary works of the period

- 6-12 authors or 3-6 topics per volume

- individual entries that survey critical response to each author's work or each topic in literary history, including early criticism to reflect initial reactions; later criticism to represent any rise or decline in reputation; and current retrospective analyses.

Organization of This Book

An author entry consists of the following elements: author heading, biographical and critical introduction, list of principal works, excerpts of criticism (each preceded by an annotation and a bibliographic citation), and a bibliography of further reading.

- The **Author Heading** consists of the name under which the author most commonly wrote, followed by birth and death dates. If an author wrote consistently under a pseudonym, the pseudonym will be listed in the author heading and the real name given in parentheses on the first line of the biographical and critical introduction. Also located at the beginning of the introduction to the author entry are any name variations under which an author wrote, including transliterated forms for authors whose languages use nonroman alphabets.

- The **Biographical and Critical Introduction** outlines the author's life and career, as well as the critical issues surrounding his or her work. References to past volumes of *TCLC* are provided at the beginning of the introduction. Additional sources of information in other biographical and critical reference series published by Gale, including *Short Story Criticism, Children's Literature Review, Contemporary Authors, Dictionary of Literary Biography,* and *Something about the Author,* are listed in a box at the end of the entry.

- Some *TCLC* entries include **Portraits** of the author. Entries also may contain reproductions of materials pertinent to an author's career, including manuscript pages, title pages, dust jackets, letters, and drawings, as well as photographs of important people, places, and events in an author's life.

- The **List of Principal Works** is chronological by date of first book publication and identifies the genre of each work. In the case of foreign authors with both foreign-language publications and English translations, the title and date of the first English-language edition are given in brackets. Unless otherwise indicated, dramas are dated by first performance, not first publication.

- Critical excerpts are prefaced by **Annotations** providing the reader with information about both the critic and the criticism that follows. Included are the critic's reputation, individual approach to literary criticism, and particular expertise in an author's works. Also noted are the relative importance of a work of criticism, the scope of the excerpt, and the growth of critical controversy or changes in critical trends regarding an author. In some cases, these annotations cross-reference excerpts by critics who discuss each other's commentary.

- A complete **Bibliographic Citation** designed to facilitate location of the original essay or book precedes each piece of criticism.

- **Criticism** is arranged chronologically in each author entry to provide a perspective on changes in critical evaluation over the years. All titles of works by the author featured in the entry are printed in boldface type to enable the user to easily locate discussion of particular works. Also for purposes of easier identification, the critic's name and the publication date of the essay are given at the beginning of each piece of criticism. Unsigned criticism is preceded by the title of the journal in which it appeared. Some of the excerpts in *TCLC* also contain translated material. Unless otherwise noted, translations in brackets are by the editors; translations in parentheses or continuous with the text are by the critic. Publication information (such as footnotes or page and line references to specific editions of works) have been deleted at the editor's discretion to provide smoother reading of the text.

- An annotated list of **Further Reading** appearing at the end of each author entry suggests secondary sources on the author. In some cases it includes essays for which the editors could not obtain reprint rights.

Cumulative Indexes

- Each volume of *TCLC* contains a cumulative **Author Index** listing all authors who have appeared in Gale's Literary Criticism Series, along with cross references to such biographical series as *Contemporary Authors* and *Dictionary of Literary Biography*. For readers' convenience, a complete list of Gale titles included appears on the first page of the author index. Useful for locating authors within the various series, this index is particularly valuable for those authors who are identified by a certain period but who, because of their death dates, are placed in another, or for those authors whose careers span two periods. For example, F. Scott Fitzgerald is found in *TCLC*, yet a writer often associated with him, Ernest Hemingway, is found in *CLC*.

- Each *TCLC* volume includes a cumulative **Nationality Index** which lists all authors who have appeared in *TCLC* volumes, arranged alphabetically under their respective nationalities, as well as Topics volume entries devoted to particular national literatures.

- Each new volume in Gale's Literary Criticism Series includes a cumulative **Topic Index,** which lists all literary topics treated in *NCLC, TCLC, LC 1400-1800,* and the *CLC* yearbook.

- Each new volume of *TCLC,* with the exception of the Topics volumes, includes a **Title Index** listing the titles of all literary works discussed in the volume. In response to numerous suggestions from librarians, Gale has also produced a **Special Paperbound Edition** of the *TCLC* title index. This annual cumulation lists all titles discussed in the series since its inception and is issued with the first volume of *TCLC* published each year. Additional copies of the index are available on request. Librarians and patrons will welcome this separate index; it saves shelf space, is easy to use, and is recyclable upon receipt of the following year's cumulation. Titles discussed in the Topics volume entries are not included *TCLC* cumulative index.

Citing *Twentieth-Century Literary Criticism*

When writing papers, students who quote directly from any volume in Gale's literary Criticism Series may use the following general forms to footnote reprinted criticism. The first example pertains to materials drawn from periodicals, the second to material reprinted from books.

[1]William H. Slavick, "Going to School to DuBose Heyward," *The Harlem Renaissance Re-examined,* (AMS Press, 1987); excerpted and reprinted in *Twentieth-Century Literary Criticism,* Vol. 59, ed. Jennifer Gariepy (Detroit: Gale Research, 1995), pp. 94-105.

[2]George Orwell, "Reflections on Gandhi," *Partisan Review,* 6 (Winter 1949), pp. 85-92; excerpted and reprinted in *Twentieth-Century Literary Criticism,* Vol. 59, ed. Jennifer Gariepy (Detroit: Gale Research, 1995), pp. 40-3.

Suggestions Are Welcome

In response to suggestions, several features have been added to *TCLC* since the series began, including annotations to excerpted criticism, a cumulative index to authors in all Gale literary criticism series, entries devoted to criticism on a single work by a major author, more extensive illustrations, and a title index listing all literary works discussed in the series since its inception.

Readers who wish to suggest authors or topics to appear in future volumes, or who have other suggestions, are cordially invited to write the editors.

Acknowledgments

The editors wish to thank the copyright holders of the excerpted criticism included in this volume and the permissions managers of many book and magazine publishing companies for assisting us in securing reproduction rights. We are also grateful to the staffs of the Detroit Public Library, the Library of Congress, the University of Detroit Mercy Library, Wayne State University Purdy/Kresge Library Complex, and the University of Michigan Libraries for making their resources available to us. Following is a list of the copyright holders who have granted us permission to reproduce material in this volume of *TCLC*. Every effort has been made to trace copyright, but if omissions have been made, please let us know.

Joris-Karl Huysmans

1848-1907

(Born Charles-Mark-Georges Huysmans) French novelist, critic, essayist, and short story writer.

INTRODUCTION

Although Huysmans began his career as a strict naturalist and ended it as one of the most important Catholic novelists of the nineteenth century, his most influential work is *A rebours* (*Against the Grain*), which became a manifesto of the decadent movement in European literature. A catalogue of the exquisite and bizarre tastes of its protagonist, Duke Jean Floressas des Esseintes, this book not only served to define an already existing artistic trend but also encouraged and gave direction to its progress. A proliferation of literature exploring perversity and the cult of sensation followed, reaching a high point in such *fin de siècle* figures as Oscar Wilde and Aubrey Beardsley. Huysmans's later study of satanism in *La-bas* (*Down There*) contributed to his reputation as an analyst of moral decay. These works, however, are equally significant as Huysmans's reaction against his naturalist beginnings and as stylistic experiments pointing toward later developments in modern fiction.

Biographical Information

Huysmans was born in Paris, the only child of a French mother and Dutch father. His childhood was upset by the death of his father and the remarriage of his mother in the following year. Huysmans resented his mother for what he felt was a premature second marriage. After earning his degree under private tutorship, he studied law at the University of Paris and went to work as a civil servant in the Ministry of the Interior, where he remained for the next thirty-two years. He died in 1907.

Major Works

Huysmans's early novels are notable for their acute observations conveyed with a stylistic precision and originality which he practiced throughout his career. His first novel, *Marthe*, was inspired by the works of Edmond de Goncourt, following the popular Realist trend of minute psychological portraiture. Like Huysmans's other early novels, *Marthe* is devoted to the faithful rendering of the banality and desperation of daily life. In the foreword to this book the author states: "I write what I see, what I feel, and what I have lived through, the best I can, and that is all there is to it." This credo of the Naturalist writer also pervades *Les soeurs vatard*, which Huysmans dedicated to Emile Zola. The short story "Sac au dos" ("Knapsack"), based on Huysmans's military experience during the Franco-Prussian War, was published by Zola

in his anthology of Naturalist fiction, *Les soirées de Médan*. Gustave Flaubert's *L'éducation sentimentale* influenced Huysmans's depiction of romantic discontents in his next work, *En ménage* (*Living Together*). With *A vau-l'eau* (*Downstream*) Huysmans introduced the kind of hypersensitive, tortured protagonist that critics have frequently identified as being patterned after the author himself. He also began moving away from the rigid objectivity of Naturalism, which he described as "suffocating," in favor of a more subjective and literary style.

Against the Grain was Huysmans's experiment in a new form, a work dubbed by Remy de Gourmont as "the consecration of a new literature" and by Arthur Symons as "a breviary of the decadence." Rather than describing the outward conflicts common to Naturalism, *Against the Grain* portrays the inward struggle of a spiritual crisis. The neurotic hero of the book is known as the prototype of the decadent connoisseur of new sensations, celebrating the superiority of imagination to reality. Des Esseintes's exotic tastes in literature, art, romance, and decor defined him as a new character type, one whose successors appear in such works of European decadence as Oscar Wilde's *Picture of Dorian Gray* and George Moore's *Confessions of a Young Man*. Some critics, however, have read *Against the Grain* as a parody of the decadent sensibility, intended to ridicule not glorify. But the likeness des Esseintes bears to his author, particularly in his desperate religious conflict, is submitted as evidence of Huysmans's seriousness.

The concern with religious questions again appears in *Down There*, which introduces Durtal, Huysmans's fictional alter ego who returns in the later Catholic novels. The novel opens with a dialogue on the inadequacy of Naturalism to portray the inner mysteries of the mind and soul with the same detailed analysis as is given to the outer world of human society. Durtal, while working on a biography of the murderer and convert Gilles de Rais, seeks a new "spiritual naturalism." The study of satanism eventually leads Durtal to the Catholic religion and the arduous process of conversion depicted in *En route, La cathédrale (The Cathedral)*, and *L'oblat (The Oblate)*. These works-while sometimes criticized for their erudite digressions on art, architecture, and ecclesiastical history-are considered among Huysmans's best. In them the author details the progress of his own conversion to Catholicism. While not questioning his sincerity, a number of critics have pointed out that Huysmans's Catholicism displays many of the characteristics of his decadence, taking the form of a world-rejecting aestheticism rather than conventional Christian virtue. The equivocal nature of Huysmans's conversion, however, is of less importance to his stature as a writer than his certain achievements in artistic form and his contribution to an important movement in literature.

PRINCIPAL WORKS

Le drageoir à épices [*A Dish of Spices*] (prose poems) 1874
Marthe [*Marthe*] (novel) 1876
Les soeurs vatard (novel) 1879
Croquis Parisiens [*Parisian Sketches*] (prose poems) 1880
"*Sac au dos*" ["*Knapsack*"] (short story) 1880
En ménage [*Living Together*] (novel) 1881
A vau-l'eau [*Downstream*] (novel) 1882
L'art moderne (criticism) 1883
A rebours [*Against the Grain*] (novel) 1884
En rade (novel) 1887
Certains (criticism) 1889
Là-bas [*Down There*] (novel) 1891
En route [*En Route*] (novel) 1895
La cathédrale [*The Cathedral*] (novel) 1898
De tout (essays) 1902
L'oblat [*The Oblate*] (novel) 1903
Les foules de Lourdes [*Crowds of Lourdes*] (nonfiction) 1906

Downstream (A vau-l'eau), and Other Works (prose poems and novels) 1927

CRITICISM

Anne Hudson Jones and Karen Kingsley (essay date 1981)

SOURCE: "Salome: The Decadent Ideal," in *Comparative Literature Studies*, Vol. XVIII, No. 3, September, 1981, pp. 344-52.

[*In the following essay, Jones and Kingsley focus on Huysmans's descriptions in* Against the Grain *of paintings by Gustave Moreau in which the biblical figure of Salome is depicted as the epitome of Decadence.*]

The Salome story has undergone many changes in its retellings over the centuries. In the Biblical versions, Salome is not even named and is presented as an innocent, if not unwilling, instrument of her mother's revenge against John the Baptist. In the following centuries, the dancing daughter became known as Salome and assumed more importance in the story as attempts were made to assign motivation to her. The Salome figure reappeared sporadically in art and literature for several centuries but emerged as an obsessive motif for artists and writers only in the late nineteenth century. She became a favorite figure for the Symbolists and Decadents who, in their obsession with the *femme fatale*, saw in her the exotic and erotic Decadent ideal.

The portrayals of Salome in the works of Gustave Moreau and Joris-Karl Huysmans are among the most remarkable of the time although they are not as well known as those of Aubrey Beardsley and Oscar Wilde. Moreau painted many versions of Salome, but the best known are two that were exhibited in the Paris Salon of 1876: *Salomé dansant devant Hérode* and *L'Apparition*. Both were purchased and described by Des Esseintes, the hero of Huysmans' Decadent novel *A Rebours*, published in 1884. Analysis of Des Esseintes' lengthy commentary on the paintings provides insight into the Decadent sensibility, both as Huysmans understood it in Moreau's works and as he expressed it in his novel. We will compare the stylistic qualities of Moreau's Salome paintings with Huysmans' style in *A Rebours* to help elucidate the aesthetics of Decadence that informs both the art and the literature of the period. Although the influence of Moreau on Huysmans and the similarity of *A Rebours* to Moreau's Salome paintings have been often remarked, the components of the similarity have gone largely unexamined. Our analysis will not include an explication of the iconography of the paintings because that has already been offered by several other critics.

In *A Rebours,* readers are told that the artist who most ravishes Des Esseintes' senses is Gustave Moreau. Des Esseintes' extravagant descriptions of the two Salome paintings demonstrate both his transcendence into realms beyond sensual pleasure and also the Decadent style Huysmans used in his novel. Des Esseintes' first description is of *Salomé dansant devant Hérode,* and it begins straightforwardly enough:

> . . . le tableau de la Salomé, ainsi conçu:

> Un trône se dressait, pareil au maître-autel d'une cathédrale, sous d'innombrables voûtes jaillissant de colonnes trapues ainsi que des piliers romans, émaillées de briques polychrômes, serties de mosaïques, incrustées de lapis et de sardoines, dans un palais semblable à une basilique d'une architecture tout à la fois musulmane et byzantine.

Moreau stages the scene in a vast hall of eclectic design but with definite Islamic details, an architectural style historically impossible for the event, but which adds a certain exotic Eastern ambience. Des Esseintes describes the setting as both Islamic and Christian, an even more outrageous construction since it is ideologically unfeasible. Already we can begin to see the contradictions inherent in both Moreau's and Huysmans' works, as well as the piling up of details in them. Moreau carefully builds up the content of the painting through repetition of visual details. In the vast hall, there is the repetition of arch after arch, column after column, and flower after flower across the floor. Small dots of paint are applied in long series to represent Salome's jewels. In addition to the repetition of single visual motifs, Moreau's method of applying paint so thickly that the surface of the painting is highly encrusted and textured and his use of a profusion of small details, especially the sensuous details, combine to produce "la richesse necessaire" that was one of the aesthetic principles of his art. All of these techniques are matched in Des Esseintes' description by the accumulation of series of adjective phrases that so much marks Huysmans' style:

> Au centre du tabernacle surmontant l'autel précédé de marches en forme de demi-vasques, le Tétrarque Hérode était assis, coiffé d'une tiare, les jambes rapprochées, les mains sur les genoux.

> La figure était jaune, parcheminée, annelée de rides, décimée par l'âge; sa longue barbe flottait comme un nuage blanc sur les étoiles en pierreries qui constellaient la robe d'orfroi plaquée sur sa poitrine,

> Autour de cette statue, immobile, figée dans une pose hiératique de dieu Hindou, des parfums brûlaient, dégorgeant des nuées de vapeurs que trouaient, de même que des yeux phosphorés de bêtes, les feux des pierres enchâssées dans les parois du trône; puis la vapeur montait, se déroulait sous les arcades où la fumée bleue se mêlait à la poudre d'or des grands rayons de jour, tombés des dômes.

The texture of the description, like that of the painting, is built up by accretions of layers of verbal detail as thickly encrusted as Moreau's paint. All senses are aroused: sight, smell, touch, and even hearing—by the guitarist in the painting and by the repeated *é*'s of Huysmans' many adjective endings.

Moreau's painting is bathed in light and dark, an illusion created in part by the lack of any single or rational light source. Light enters the great hall from in front (the viewer's space), from behind, and from the lamps within. The light seems mysteriously to shift and alter, thereby transforming both the architectural space and its inhabitants from natural to supernatural. Moreau's technique of sharply delineating some objects while leaving others obscure or unclear in their outline adds to the mystic, indefinable quality of the scene. The most important effect of the painting is its elusiveness; what is suggested is more important than what is stated. The unidentifiable, timeless, exotic setting; the diffuse light; and the figure of Salome create ambiguities between what is seen and what imagined. The sheer profusion of details allows the viewer to move beyond the world of normal experience and natural forms into the world of imagination and surreality. In his description, Des Esseintes emphasizes these qualities of the painting by focusing on the brilliant flashes and beams of light and on the misty, smoky vapors scenting the air with perfumes that can only be inferred from the painting.

But Des Esseintes' description does more than just emphasize the elements of the painting; it begins to add elements—especially motion and visual detail—that are not in the painting. For example, writing of Salome's motion as she begins her dance, he goes far beyond what Moreau presents in the painting:

> Dans l'odeur perverse des parfums, dans l'atmosphère surchauffée de cette église, Salomé, le bras gauche étendu, en un geste de commandement, le bras droit replié, tenant à la hauteur du visage, un grand lotus, s'avance lentement sur les pointes, aux accords d'une guitare dont une femme accroupie pince les cordes.

> La face recueillie, solennelle, presque auguste, elle commence la lubrique danse qui doit réveiller les sens assoupis du vieil Hérode; ses seins ondulent et, au frottement de ses colliers qui tourbillonnent, leurs bouts se dressent; sur la moiteur de sa peau les diamants, attachés, scintillent; ses bracelets, ses ceintures, ses bagues, crachent des étincelles; sur sa robe triomphale, couturée de perles, ramagée d'argent, lamée d'or, la cuirasse des orfèvreries dont chaque maille est une pierre, entre en combustion, croise des serpenteaux de feu, grouille sur la chair mate, sur la peau rose thé, ainsi que des insectes splendides aux élytres éblouissants, marbrés de carmin, ponctués de jaune aurore, diaprés de bleu d'acier, tigrés de vert paon.

Salome *is* on the points of her toes, but she does not glide forward; her breasts do not quiver; her nipples are not even visible. Only her veils and jewels, painted in small touches or slashes of brilliant color that contrast with her pale smooth skin, suggest movement. But these undulating spirals of jewels and veils are not, as Des Esseintes says, creeping and crawling over her flesh. Moreau's Salome is static, anchored to the ground by the weight of her costume. Her rigid body is arrested in space and time: the moment is eternal. Des Esseintes adds motion and time, moving his description towards an act only partially implied in Moreau's painting. Again, the description itself is typical of Huysmans' style: the entire paragraph is one sentence listing item after item, modifying each in series of adjective phrases. And on a small scale, this represents the style of the entire novel, which reads like a series of catalogs, listing, for example, all the colors Des Esseintes considered for his room, all the liqueurs for his "mouth organ," all his mistresses, and so forth.

But there is an aspect of Des Esseintes' description that is ironic. In the chapter of the novel immediately preceding the one about paintings, Des Esseintes recounts how he had a living tortoise gilded and encrusted with gems so that it could add the proper adornment to the carpet in one of his rooms. Analogously, even a woman as voluptuous as Salome would—in her natural, unadorned state—be unable to rouse Des Esseintes jaded passions. She must be encrusted, like the tortoise, with jewels of many colors. Yet when Des Esseintes tries to describe these jewels in their shimmering beauty, he goes back to the world of nature for his metaphors and describes them as serpents and insects, coiling, crawling, swarming over her flesh, glittering with brilliant colors, like those of the dawn, of steel, of a peacock. Aroused at first only by the artificial, Des Esseintes exhausts its possibilities and reverts to the natural world in his attempt to describe the creature who will dance before him in the painting.

Nonetheless, it is the artificiality, the surreality, of the *Salomé dansant devant Hérode* that most attracts Des Esseintes. He writes of her as a figure "surhumaine et étrange qu'il avait rêvée". No longer the simple dancing girl of St. Matthew or St. Mark, she has been transformed by Moreau and then by Huysmans into "la déité symbolique de l'indestructible Luxure, la déesse de l'immortelle Hystérie, la Beauté maudite, . . . la Bête monstrueuse, indifférente, irresponsable, insensible, empoisonnant, de même que l'Hélène antique, tout ce qui l'approche, tout ce qui la voit, tout ce qu'elle touche". Looking at her, Des Esseintes is transported beyond the everyday world and even far beyond the surface statement of Moreau's painting.

Des Esseintes' reaction to *L'Apparition* is similar, yet different in one important respect. Huysmans compares Des Esseintes' reaction to the one he imagines for Herod: "écrasé, anéanti, pris de vertige . . ." But the effect of this painting comes more from the suggestion of Salome's dreadful act—by the floating head—than from any supernatural quality of Salome's figure itself. In fact, the relative simplicity of Salome's figure, the

increased nudity, the reduced complexity of the setting, and the changed medium—watercolor instead of oil—all work to emphasize what fascinates Des Esseintes the most about this representation of her: the depravity of the human woman. Des Esseintes describes her this way:

> D'un geste d'épouvante, Salomé repousse la ter-
> rifiante vision qui la cloue, immobile, sur les
> pointes; ses yeux se dilatent, sa main étreint con-
> vulsivement sa gorge.
>
> Elle est presque nue; dans l'ardeur de la danse, les
> voiles se sont défaits, les brocarts ont croulé; elle
> n'est plus vêtue que de matières orfévries et de
> minéraux lucides; un gorgerin lui serre de même
> qu'un corselet la taille, et, ainsi qu'une agrafe
> superbe, un merveilleux joyau darde des éclairs
> dans la rainure de ses deux seins; plus bas, aux
> hanches, une ceinture l'entoure, cache le haut de
> ses cuisses que bat une gigantesque pendeloque
> où coule une rivière d'escarboucles et d'émeraudes;
> enfin, sur le corps resté nu, entre le gorgerin et la
> ceinture, le ventre bombe, creusé d'un nombril dont
> le trou semble un cachet gravé d'onyx, aux tons
> laiteux, aux teintes de rose d'ongle.

Again, Des Esseintes has added elements not in the painting. Salome does not gesture with horror, nor does she convulsively grip her throat. Rather than repulsed, she seems almost enamoured of the floating head. With her body exposed from her fallen veils, her slightly arched back, her lassitude, and her somnambulistic air, she appears to offer herself to the head. Her body, not clearly outlined, looks soft and voluptuous; it invites touch. Yet the pallor and icy smooth surface of her flesh suggest death. The superhuman, surreal goddess has disappeared. The act of cutting off John the Baptist's head cannot have really grotesque effect as long as it is performed by a creature not human. Its depravity depends upon its having been done by a human woman, and its depravity is what is so arousing for Des Esseintes.

Thus, the tension present in the second description Des Esseintes gives of Salome—she is at the same time "plus raffinée et plus sauvage, plus exécrable et plus exquise"—is important on the larger scale as well. Salome must be artificial and natural, unreal and real, inhuman and human, existing in a realm between life and death. The artificial, pushed to its extreme, can end only in death, as did the gilded, encrusted tortoise; yet the natural, when it is the everyday or ordinary, cannot arouse Des Esseintes' imagination or passions. The delicate balance between the two—the artificial and the natural—is established by the two paintings: one taking the image beyond the human, the other bringing it back.

Decadence, implying a decay or falling away from something—some standard of style—can be fully understood only when contrasted with the standard it opposes. The best way of demonstrating the Decadent style of Moreau's paintings is to contrast the Salome of a finished painting like *Salomé dansant devant Hérode* with one of the many studies Moreau made for the figure of

Salome in preparation for the painting. In the studies, the nude female form is drawn with a classic naturalness and simplicity. In the finished work, the female form is painted in elaborate detail, with artificial and complex gilding and encrustation. Analogously, in the literature, the original scriptural story of the dance, which does not even mention Salome by name, is classic in its simple unadorned and unelaborated statement. Des Esseintes includes it in his long description of the first painting:

> Combien de fois avait-il [Des Esseintes] lu dans la vieille bible de Pierre Variquet, traduite par les docteurs en théologie de l'Université de Louvain, l'évangile de saint Mathieu qui raconte en de naïves et brèves phrases, la décollation du Précurseur; combien de fois avait-il rêvé, entre ces lignes:
>
> "Au jour du festin de la Nativité d'Hérode, la fille d'Hérodias dansa au milieu et plut à Hérode.
>
> "Dont lui promit, avec serment, de lui donner tout ce qu'elle lui demanderait.
>
> "Elle donc, induite par sa mère, dit: Donne moi, en un plat, la tête de Jean Baptiste.
>
> "Et le roi fut marri, mais à cause du serment et de ceux qui étaient assis à table avec lui, il commanda qu'elle lui fût baillée.
>
> "Et envoya décapiter Jean, en la prison.
>
> "Et fut la tête d'icelui apportée dans un plat et donnée à la fille; et elle la présenta à sa mère."
>
> Mais ni saint Mathieu, ni saint Marc, ni saint Luc, ni les autres évangélistes ne s'étendaient sur les charmes délirants, sur les actives dépravations de la danseuse. . . .

The contrast between the simple Biblical statement and Des Esseintes' prolonged, elaborate description of her dance parallels the contrast between the nude studies for Salome and the finished figure in the painting.

Salome is the ideal choice for Decadent artists and writers for two important reasons. First, her story is only outlined in the Biblical account, suggesting but not elaborating sexual enticement and incest. Only enough is given to whet the imagination; later artists can add their own details. Salome's character, nature, and motivation are unknown; she can become anything. If her story had been more detailed, it would have worked less well. Salome's act seems almost gratuitous and thus more grotesque. Second, the Biblical origin of Salome's story helps Moreau and Huysmans maintain a sense of the religious and transcendent element in their works even while they explore human sexuality and depravity.

Stylistically, Moreau's paintings and Huysmans' novel are remarkably similar in technique. They bombard the senses with as many sensuous details as possible, to create a dizzying effect and provide the overstimulation necessary to evoke any response from jaded Decadent heroes who can no longer respond to ordinary stimuli. The desired result is disorientation, to free the mind from the reality of the everyday world; the goal is escape—transcendence—into imaginary realms beyond present reality. Thus, the profusion of sensuous details is absolutely necessary to create the desired effect, but so is the contradiction within the details themselves that maintains the necessary tension between the human world and the one beyond.

Des Esseintes' descriptions are Huysmans' testimony to the success of Moreau's paintings. They chronicle Des Esseintes' progressive dizziness, overstimulation, disorientation, and transcendence from the surface reality in front of him into a surreality of his own creating. Huysmans attempts the same effect in his novel and uses the verbal equivalent of Moreau's techniques. But Huysmans' medium—fiction—is a temporal one, unlike painting, which is static. A novel can bombard the senses only cumulatively, over time, as the reader progresses through the text. A painting can bombard the senses all at once. Although it may take time for a viewer to analyze the parts of a painting, still all the parts are static in time and function simultaneously to elicit the desired response. Painting, then, seems to have an inherent advantage over fiction in achieving the effect Huysmans sought with his novel.

Annette Kahn (essay date 1987)

SOURCE: "The Aesthetic Development of a Novelist Art Critic," in *J. K. Huysmans: Novelist, Poet, and Art Critic,* UMI Research Press, 1987, pp. 11-32.

[*In the following essay, Kahn examines the aesthetic and psychological principles underlying Huysmans's art criticism.*]

Huysmans wrote during a time of profound debate and fundamental changes in the arts. He experienced and influenced the end of Naturalism and saw the proliferation of many experimental groups of writers and painters. The lack of a confident direction which typified the arts in general at this time is reflected in Huysmans' perpetual search for the "true" aesthetic formula and his resultant changes of taste. Huysmans' unusually desperate attempt to understand the meaning and aim of art and literature stems largely from the fact that he was so dissatisfied with his own life that he turned to the world of the arts to fill a personal void.

Huysmans' literary works are uniformly depressing, revealing a pessimistic view of life, characterized by melancholy, disgust, and despair. He was irresistibly drawn to the sensual pleasures available in Paris, yet was always revolted by the experience; he had highly developed erotic tendencies yet feared and disdained women, seeing in them an embodiment of evil; he found little joy in nature and in travel; he respected very few people and showed contempt for the masses. Yet his works express, with great enthusiasm and an original, sardonic style, a passion for art which became both an escape and a guiding force for him.

Huysmans showed a love of painting from his earliest childhood. So it was natural for him to try his luck in art criticism for journals and newspapers to earn a little money while he began his more serious writing of fiction. Art criticism was a great source of pleasure to him and he approached it with less self-doubt than he did his literary writing. Moreover, it put him in touch with the work of many artists he would otherwise not have encountered and it gave him time to study certain paintings at length. This provided a rich source of material for his prose poems and novels, in which descriptions of art are frequently a focal point. Huysmans' criticism contains fine writing and original, perceptive views, and his collected articles lend valuable historical insight into the artistic debates of the eighties and nineties, in which Huysmans was a very active and influential participant. At present, however, his art criticism and its relationship to the rest of his writing are a much neglected aspect of his work.

In his own time Huysmans was known as a critic to be reckoned with and many of his contemporaries considered Huysmans to be an important figure in the development of artistic taste. Roger Marx, for instance, himself a distinguished critic, wrote in 1893:

> There is certainly no dearth, nowadays, of either erudite historians or of reporters on the lookout for news of the day . . . but J.-K. Huysmans' supremacy remains unchallenged. Whether or not it cares to admit it, very nearly all of today's criticism is descended from him. . . . Not since Thoré had one encountered so unerring an analysis, nor, since Baudelaire, the double gifts of intuition and expression, which make of their author at this time, not merely a judge among judges, but a unique personage, *the* critic of modern art.
>
> Certes, l'heure présente ne manque ni d'historiens érudits, ni de reporters à l'affût de l'actualité . . . mais la suprématie de J.-K. Huysmans demeure inattaquée. Qu'elle le veuille ou non confesser, la critique de maintenant descend de lui, à bien peu près, tout. . . . Il n'était pas arrivé de rencontrer depuis Thoré un diagnostic aussi peu faillible, depuis Baudelaire, le double don de la divination et de l'espression, qui fait de leur auteur, en ce temps, non point un juge parmi les juges, mais une personnalité unique, le critique le l'art moderne. [*Etude sur Huysmans*]

The English critic Arthur Symons wrote [in *Figures of Several Centuries*], "No literary artist since Baudelaire has made so valuable a contribution to art criticism, and the *Curiosités esthétiques* are, after all, less exact in their actual study, less revolutionary, and less significant in their critical judgments than *L'Art moderne*." Félix Fénéon, a critic of more lasting importance than Huysmans, after reading *Certains* wrote more flatteringly of his colleague that

> His two books of criticism are, by their sureness of judgment and their firm execution, the only ones to have been written on modern art.
>
> Ses deux livres de critique sont, pour leur sûreté de verdict et leur ferme exécution, les seuls qui aient été faits sur l'art moderne. [*Art et Critique*]

Huysmans' criticism includes studies of individual artists, paintings, and exhibitions, and comprehensive accounts of the Paris Salons. He began his career as a writer on art in 1867 with a piece on contemporary landscape painting and he continued to submit art studies, in both French and Belgian newspapers and periodicals until 1904.

The articles can be divided roughly into four periods. The first, between 1867 and 1878, consists of sixteen articles, mainly on contemporary exhibitions, of which none were published in his collected works. They lack the originality, confidence, and stylistic excellence of his later articles. In **"Le Salon de 1876: natures mortes"** and **"Notes sur le Salon de 1877: portraits et natures mortes,"** for instance, he even uses the identical text for the introduction and conclusion and simply changes the names of the pictures he is discussing. They are important, however, because they contain, in simple and tentative form, many of the ideas Huysmans developed in his mature work.

From 1879 to 1882, the second period, Huysmans wrote regular accounts of the Paris Salons for *Le Voltaire* and *La Réforme*. These articles were collected and published in 1883 in **L'Art moderne,** the book which established Huysmans as an important critic of contemporary art. It contains lengthy, sarcastic attacks on the Academic painters and enthusiastic praise for the Independents and the Impressionists.

The third period, from 1882 to 1889, is one of transition, corresponding to a similar phase in Huysmans' fiction, in which he turns from a confident Naturalism to a greater interest in human psychology. In art he becomes increasingly concerned with the emotional content of a work and less interested in its subject matter or its formal aspects. Huysmans collected the most important parts of these articles and published them, in 1889, together with some new essays, in **Certains,** which was his favorite among his books, not only because it deals with many of his favorite painters such as Degas, Moreau, Redon, Puvis de Chavannes, and Whistler, but because of its format—essays on individual artists. Huysmans was sceptical about schools of thought and general movements and was more interested in discussing individuals, a feeling expressed by des Esseintes in **A Rebours,** for whom "les écoles n'existaient point."

The fourth and last period of Huysmans' criticism, 1889 to 1899, is devoted entirely to the study of religious art, both historical and contemporary. Most of these articles, all of which appeared first in *L'Echo de Paris*, were either published in **De Tout,** 1902, or used as material in

La Cathédrale. After 1899 Huysmans wrote only one article, in 1904, on the Grünewalds in the Colmar Museum for *Le Mois Littéraire et Pittoresque.* Adding notes he took on a journey to Germany, Belgium and Switzerland in 1903, Huysmans developed this article into a larger study which he published in 1905 under the title *Trois Primitifs.*

Huysmans' aim in his art criticism was to give an honest account of what he saw at exhibitions. He was always very thorough and his honesty often resulted in angering and offending his more conservative readers. For Huysmans' tastes were always aggressively individualistic and he believed firmly, like Baudelaire, that a good critic must have strong, personal opinions—"unless one either loves passionately or hates passionately, one has no talent" ("l'on n'a pas de talent si l'on n'aime avec passion ou si l'on ne hait de même") (*Certains,*). He never held his tongue and as he proudly told Camille Lemonnier in a letter of August 1880, "because of my violent criticism of the people I hate, you can trust my sincerity in matters of art" ("Vous pouvez, étant donné la violence de ma critique contre les gens que je hais, au point de vue de l'art croire à ma sincérité").

Huysmans did not have a well-developed general theory of art. He held strong views on particular issues such as Impressionism, Naturalism, and Catholic art and on particular artists such as Degas and Moreau, and he often provides perceptive analyses of the style and general direction of a work or movement. He certainly tried to evaluate paintings dispassionately and never lost sight of their objective qualities. He does not, however, claim to take an objective approach to aesthetic problems in general and throughout his criticism one finds the expression "my needs" ("mes besoins"); his is a self-centered kind of criticism. Despite a professional commitment to writing comprehensive accounts of the works on exhibit, Huysmans seems to be using his critical writings as a creative experiment, as a way of solving emotional and artistic problems of his own. This accounts for the large degree of interaction between his art criticism and his fiction. Huysmans himself was well aware that his tastes and his approach to art were very subjective and this consciousness is reflected by des Esseintes in *A Rebours:*

> Yet his literary opinions had started from a very simple point of view. For him, there were no such things as schools; the only thing that mattered to him was the writer's personality, and the only thing that interested him was the working of the writer's brain, no matter what subject he was tackling. Unfortunately this criterion of appreciation . . . was practically impossible to apply, for the simple reason that, however much a reader wants to rid himself of prejudice and refrain from passion, he naturally prefers those works which correspond most intimately with his own personality, and ends by relegating all the rest to limbo.

> En art, ses idées étaient pourtant parties d'un point de vue simple; pour lui, les écoles n'existaient point; seul le tempérament de sa cervelle intéressait

> quelque fût le sujet qu'il abordât. Malheureusement, cette vérité d'appréciation . . . était à peu près inapplicable, par ce simple motif que, tout en désirant se dégager des préjugés, s'abstenir de toute passion, chacun va de préférence aux oeuvres qui correspondent le plus intimement à son propre tempérament et finit par reléguer en arrière toutes les autres.

Huysmans' career is characterized by remarkable changes in artistic taste. His devotion to Grünewald and Chartres Cathedral is far removed from his love of the Independent Parisian artists of the eighties, just as his novel *Sainte Lydwine de Schiedam,* the story of a saint, could hardly have been anticipated by *Marthe,* the story of a prostitute. In his later years Huysmans was embarrassed by his youthful enthusiasms and, in spite of the obvious passion and sincerity of his early writing, he often claimed that his opinions had not been serious. These changes in taste are not surprising, however, when one recognizes that Huysmans looked to art as a substitute for life. This attitude resulted in a fundamental confusion, in his mind, between art and reality, with ensuing disappointments and a constant reevaluation of his tastes.

The powerful influence which art exerted on Huysmans can be seen from the very inception of his literary career. As a law student he spent a great deal of time in the Louvre, often accompanied by his close friend Ludovic de Francmesnil. He was attracted by the Dutch and Flemish masters of the seventeenth century and found in them an inspiration for his own writing. In a letter to Verhaeren of 1881 he wrote,

> The idea of writing no doubt came to me when, just out of school, I used to stroll through the Louvre; there, I ignored all the other rooms, to linger in those containing the Flemish and Dutch school.

> L'idée d'écrire m'est certainement venue, alors que sorti du collège, j'allais me promener au Louvre, où négligeant toutes les autres salles, je m'arrêtais devant celles renfermant l'école flamande et hollandaise.

These paintings appealed to him because of the *joie de vivre* they seemed to portray, in painful contrast with Huysmans' own existence; and he tried to relive some of the experiences seen in the paintings through his first book of prose poems *Le Drageoir aux épices,* which appeared in 1874. Four of the eighteen poems are based on Dutch and Flemish works he had seen in the Louvre. They are the first examples of his experimentation with the integration of a visual experience into writing. He shows here a charming playfulness with the reader which he loses in his later works.

One of the poems based on works seen at the Louvre is **"Le Hareng saur,"** a *transposition d'art* inspired by a Rembrandt still life. Foreshadowing his interpretation of Moreau, Huysmans uses mineral imagery to describe the herring:

The patina of old bronze, the burnished gold of Cordovan leathers . . . one might say that your eyes were black nails driven into copper spheres.

La patine du vieux cuivre, le ton d'or bruni des cuirs de Cordoue . . . l'on dirait de tes yeux des clous noirs plantés dans des cercles de cuivre.

In **"Adrien Brauwer"** Huysmans incorporates into a ten-page anecdote about the painter Brauwer a one-page *transposition d'art*. It is a description of a painting Brauwer paints to pay for his drinks. Huysmans breaks the fiction of the story by bringing the reader back to reality with "You know this canvas. It is in the Louvre" ("Ce tableau, vous le connaissez. Il est au Louvre"). This poem also contains a discussion between Brauwer and his patron about his reasons for leaving Rubens' atelier to spend most of his time in brothels and cafés. Couched in a story about seventeenth-century Holland, this discussion is really about the contemporary debate between the Academics and the Independents, who believed that a studio portrait could never achieve the veracity of a painting executed with natural models in natural surroundings.

In **"Claudine"** Huysmans develops further this device of inserting a *transposition d'art* into a narrative. Incorporated into a story of sixteen pages about Les Halles, which was the topic of Zola's *Le Ventre de Paris*, is a half-page description of Rembrandt's *Flayed Ox* in the Louvre. In this poem Huysmans is not explicit about his source but the change from the banal, everyday vocabulary of the narrative to the dense physiological and plant vocabulary of the *transposition* clearly sets it apart from the rest of the prose poem. The type of vocabulary Huysmans uses here typifies his descriptions of Redon and certain nightmare episodes in *En Rade* and *A Rebours*:

> The carcass of a great ox exuded . . . the monstrous jewel box of his viscera. The head had been torn violently from the trunk and some of the nerve endings still twitched, convulsed . . . twisted. . . . The stomach . . . yawned horribly and disgorged from its large cavity pendants of red entrails. As though in some hothouse, a wondrous vegetation blossomed in that carcass.

> Le cadavre d'un grand boeuf étalait . . . le monstrueux écrin de ses viscères. La tête avait été violemment arrachée du tronc et des bouts de nerfs palpitaient encore, convulsés . . . tortillés. . . . L'estomac . . . baîllait atrocement et dégorgeait de sa large fosse des pendeloques d'entrailles rouges. Comme en une serre chaude, une végétation merveilleuse s'épanouissait dans ce cadavre.

Huysmans confirms the fact that the description of the ox is of a special nature by commenting that the butcher was amazed at the sight of the ox, a sight with which one would expect him to be familiar: "Le boucher semblait *émerveillé* par ce *spectacle*" [my italics].

"La Kermesse de Rubens" is a further example of a *Transposition d'art* incorporated into a narrative. It be-

gins with the words "The following evening, I was wandering through the streets of a small village . . ." ("Le lendemain soir, j'errais dans les rues d'un petit village . . ."), as if the poem were a continuation of an episode. The description of the countryside is interrupted by the phrase "I noticed a faint glimmer gleaming red in the window of a barn" ("j'aperçus une faible lueur qui rougeoyait à la fenêtre d'une grange"). This window acts as a frame for a painting Huysmans is describing. At the end of the description Huysmans gives a more explicit hint that he has just described a painting when he says, "It looked like one of Teniers' paintings" ("On eût dit un tableau de Teniers"). The scene changes and Huysmans modifies his explanation—"It was no longer one of Teniers' village dances, it was Rubens' village fair" ("Ce n'était plus une danse villageoise de Teniers, c'était la kermesse de Rubens"). These identifications bring the reader sharply back from the *rêverie* created by the *transposition* and prepare him for the important final paragraph which shows the extent to which the life described in these paintings afforded an escape for Huysmans:

> Well, I swear to you that it was good to see such joy; I swear to you that I was charmed by the naive simplicity of those fat sailors' wives and that I detested all the more those Paris dens where a crowd of sewer nymphs and ghastly boozers carry on frantically, as though lashed by hysteria's whip!

> Eh bien! je vous jure que cette joie était bonne à voir, je vous jure que la naïve simplesse de ces grosses matelotes m'a ravi et que j'ai détesté plus encore des bauges de Paris où s'agitent, comme cinglés par le fouet de l'hystérie, un ramassis de naïades d'égout et de sinistres riboteurs!

That Huysmans had a naive view of Holland is seen again in a prose poem called **"La Tulipe,"** written in 1875 but never published in his collected works. He sings the praises of the tulip as if addressing a lover and paints a conventional picture of Holland with cows, windmills, red houses, women in lace headdresses, all images gleaned from the paintings he saw in the Louvre. In the final paragraph, in which he recalls the smells and noises of the countryside, Huysmans writes: "I once again see Holland, land of village fairs and of great painters, of flowers and of skies . . ." ("Je revois la Hollande, pays des kermesses et des grandes peintres, des fleurs et des ciels . . .").

Apart from short visits as a child to relatives in Breda, Tilburg, and Ginnik between 1850 and 1856, Huysmans as far as we know did not visit Holland or Belgium until 1876, when he had to go to Brussels for the publication of *Marthe*. He expected to find the way of life he had found so appealing in the Dutch and Flemish paintings in the Louvre and he was sadly disappointed. Contrary to his expectations, he found Holland to be a dull, puritanical country which did not live up to its rich and joyous past. He visited a great many museums, where his love for the Dutch and Flemish masters was confirmed. He wrote about some of these works, as of his personal dis-appointment, in an article called **"En Hollande"** which first appeared in the *Musée des Deux-Mondes* on February 15, 1877 and was reprinted in a longer version, in *La Revue Illustrée* ten years later. Huysmans ends the article by dolefully bemoaning the future of Holland, which confirms his admiration for the art and his frustration with the fact that it is not an accurate representation of reality:

> Yes, Holland is the land of the arts! but, oh, you artists, . . . soon the homeland of Rembrandt and Steen will no longer be Holland the joyous and the picturesque.

> Ah, la Hollande est le pays des arts! oui, mais, vous les artistes . . . la patrie de Rembrandt et de Steen ne sera bientôt plus la joyeuse et la pit-toresque Hollande.

Seven years later, in *A Rebours,* Huysmans makes use of this first experience of being deceived by art and ex-presses, in clearer and more explicit terms, the problem arising from the confusion of art and reality:

> On the whole, this tour had proved a bitter disappointment to him. He had pictured to himself a Holland such as Teniers and Jan Steen, Rembrandt and Ostade had painted . . . he had to admit that the paintings of the Dutch School exhibited in the Louvre had led him astray. They had in fact served as a springboard from which he had soared into a dream world of false trails and impossible ambitions, for nowhere in this world had he found the fairyland of which he had dreamt.

> Somme toute, il était résulté de cruelles désillusions de ce voyage. Il [des Esseintes] s'était figuré une Hollande, d'après les oeuvres de Teniers et de Steen, de Rembrandt et d'Ostade . . . en résumé, il devait le reconnaître, l'école hollandaise du Louvre l'avait égaré; elle avait simplement servi de tremplin à ses rêves; il s'était élancé, avait bondi sur une fausse piste et erré dans des visions inégalables, ne découvrant nullement sur la terre ce pays magique et réel qu'il espérait.

Huysmans' love for the Dutch and Flemish paintings of the seventeenth century was based on their realism. Like Baudelaire, whom he greatly admired and sought to emulate in many ways, he believed in "la modernité," that in art "one must be of one's time" ("il faut être de son temps"). This meant a rejection of all ideas of classical, universal beauty, an acceptance of a variety of beauties peculiar to each age. New styles and new subject matter were essential elements of any important artistic movement. In keeping with this theory, Huysmans rejected any moralistic, didactic intention in art. In an 1875 article on *La Cruche cassée* by Greuze, for instance, he takes the opportunity to attack "this deplorable aesthetic whose spokesman Diderot had become; the regeneration of society by art" ("cette esthétique déplorable dont Diderot s'était fait le porte-voix; la régénération de la société par l'art").

Huysmans' very first piece of art criticism was a simple exposé of this theory that one of the aims of good art is to express the spirit of the time, and in this he felt the Dutch seventeenth-century painters had been eminently successful:

> Ruysdael, Berchem, Swanevelt van Artois, Hob-béma and our immortal Claude Gelée understood landscape, just as Rembrandt did the dim interiors that he lit with dazzling rays, as Brauwer did the taverns, Van Goyen the sea in repose, Van de Velde the raging waves. . . .

> Ruysdaël, Berchem, Swanevelt van Artois, Hob-béma et notre immortel Claude Gelée ont compris le paysage comme Rembrandt les intérieurs sombres, qu'il illuminait d'éblouissants rayons, comme Brauwer les tabagies, Van Goyen la mer en repos, Van de Velde les flots en courroux. . . . [**"Des Paysagistes contemporains"**]

Huysmans' disappointment in Holland was shattering in that he did not find a place where he could feel at ease. At the same time, however, it was a valuable learning experience for him. It forced him to face the fact that life was not so different elsewhere and that he had to come to terms with his own immediate environment and, above all, himself. Fortunately, one of Huysmans' greatest qualities was an ability to "change gear" and to allow himself to be guided by his very receptive artistic sensibility. In the very year he went to Holland he discovered Degas, and this discovery radically changed his whole outlook on modern art and contemporary life.

Degas awakened Huysmans' interest in the Impressionists and they quickly replaced the Dutch and Flemish painters in his affections. As he wrote in *L'Art moderne,*

> [they] bring with them a new technique, the scent of an art that is singular and true; [they] distill the essence of their time, as the Dutch Naturalists expressed the aroma of theirs.

> [ils] apportent une méthode nouvelle, une senteur d'art singulière et vraie, [ils] distillent l'essence de leur temps comme les naturalistes hollandais exprimaient l'arôme du leur.

The "essence" and "aroma," words typical of Huysmans' olfactory vocabulary, are none other than the spirit of the age to which Huysmans felt art should address itself. There is a certain irony, however, in the fact that Huysmans suddenly embraced an artistic movement which chose to depict aspects of Parisian life that he had been trying to escape. However, his appreciation of the Impressionists soon became very selective and he concentrated on those artists who seemed to him to express his own cynical and melancholy view of the world.

Huysmans was introduced to Degas the same year he published *Marthe,* his first Naturalist novel, and in his art criticism he emphasized the comparison between Impressionism and Naturalism. Huysmans was emotionally drawn to Baudelaire yet was a great admirer of Zola with his staunch defense of an objective reality. Huysmans contributed a story to *Les Soirées de Médan* and worked within the current theoretical framework of Naturalist doctrine.

In 1876 he wrote a lengthy article on Zola in *L'Actualité* which clarifies his general aesthetic views at this important junction in his career. He ignores the scientific premise of Zola's Naturalism and writes primarily of the type of subject matter he and his colleagues consider appropriate for literature, underlining the importance of accurate and detailed observation. Echoing his reasons for liking Degas and the Dutch and Flemish masters, and revealing his constant awareness of the art of painting, he writes that "a writer, just as much as any painter, must move with the times; we are artists thirsting for modernity" ("un écrivain aussi bien qu'un peintre doit être de son temps, nous sommes des artistes assoiffés de modernité"). ["**Emile Zola et *L'Assommoir***"] He proudly claims that the Naturalist authors are comprehensive in their subject matter: "Society has two faces: we show these two faces" ("La société a deux faces: nous montrons ces deux faces"). This statement typifies Huysmans' tendency to conceptualize in opposites or dualities and it is this approach which explains his subsequent rejection of the subject matter of the earthy Naturalist novels in favor of more spiritual topics. The one aspect of Naturalism to which Huysmans remained faithful, however, was honesty and truth of observation. As he writes in the 1876 article on Zola, "Naturalism is . . . the patient study of reality, the whole obtained by the observation of details" ("le naturalisme c'est . . . l'étude patiente de la réalité, l'ensemble obtenu par l'observation des détails"). He frequently uses the words "vrai" and "vérité" such as in the expressions "to make it true is to make it moral" ("faire vrai, c'est faire moral") and "he achieves the artist's highest purpose: truth, life" ("il atteint le but suprême de l'artiste; la vérité, la vie"). Similarly, in *L'Art moderne* Huysmans talks scathingly of academic painters for "not bringing to life and not making true" ("ne pas faire vivant et ne pas faire vrai") and admires Degas for having painted "de vraies danseuses".

Huysmans, like all defenders of realism, understood "true" ("vrai") not in opposition to "ideal" but to false. So whether he is talking here about the Naturalist novel, the Dutch and Flemish masters, the Impressionists, or, as he was to later, about Moreau, Redon, and the medieval Primitives, Huysmans is looking for art based on direct, precise, and detailed observation. At the same time, however, Huysmans, like Zola, was fully aware that if one took Naturalism, which aimed, as they both believed, at the objective rendering of contemporary life to its logical limits, art could be replaced by photography. They recognized the degree of personal vision in every work and they therefore introduced the concept of temperament so that a work of art was, as Zola put it, "a pocket of creation seen through a temperament" ("un coin de la création vu à travers un tempérament"). Huysmans follows Zola completely in his division between "the real

element, which is Nature" ("l'élément réel, qui est la nature") and "the individual element, which is Man" ("l'élément individuel, qui est l'homme"), so that, in *L'Art moderne,* he writes apropos of Dutch seventeenth-century paintings that

> although they are exact, almost photographic reproductions of Nature, they are yet marked by particular accents determined by each painter's temperament.

> tout en étant une reproduction exacte, presque photographique de la nature, elles sont néanmoins empreintes d'un accent particulier déterminé par le tempérament de chacun de ces peintres.

As a result, Huysmans became increasingly interested in the attitude of the artist towards his subject, preferring figure painters who portrayed the sordid aspects of women, such as provocative stances and vulgar clothes, and landscapists who conveyed the melancholy of the Parisian suburbs. He especially loved Degas, Forain, and Raffaëlli because their works reflected a pessimistic view of life similar to his own, but by the middle of the eighties he began to tire of the type of art which portrayed contemporary Paris, where he found only manifestations of man's limitations. He was bored by the Post-Impressionists such as the Pointillists and the Synthetists because they were more concerned with form than with subject matter. He began to express a general lack of faith in the future of painting.

He needed an escape and turned more and more to artists such as Moreau and Redon to satisfy his growing need for the fantastic, the mystical, and the occult. Zola's aesthetics had at first been very appealing to Huysmans because of their involvement with the contemporary, but Zola's writing lacked a metaphysical dimension and Huysmans began, by the late eighties, to express an overwhelming "need for the supernatural" ("besoin de surnaturel") (*Là-Bas*). Huysmans was reflecting a general shift of emphasis from the realist to the imaginative type of art, described as follows by Marcel Schwob:

> We had ended up in an extraordinary time: the novelists had shown us every aspect of human life and all the undersides of thought. We were tired of many feelings before experiencing them; many had allowed themselves to be drawn toward a chasm of mystical and unknown shadows; others were possessed by a passion for the strange, by the search for the quintessence of new sensations; and still others melted away into a vast compassion that swept across everything. . . .

> Nous étions arrivés dans un temps extraordinaire où les romanciers nous avaient montré toutes les faces de la vie humaine et tous les dessous des pensées. On était lassé de bien des sentiments avant de les avoir éprouvés; plusieurs se laissaient attirer vers un gouffre d'ombres mystiques et inconnues; d'autres étaient possédés par la passion de l'étrange, par la recherche du quintessencié de sensations nouvelles; d'autres enfin, se fondaient dans une

large pitié qui s'étendait sur toute chose. . . . ["Les Portes de l'oplum"]

A Rebours, 1884, marked Huysmans' first step away from Naturalist topics by entering into a whole new world of unusual sensations and unorthodox tastes, but his first attempt to broaden the psychological scope of his novels was *En Rade,* 1887, in which the soul was given as much importance as the body. He did this by incorporating substantial dream chapters into the realistic narrative. He felt, however, that the novel was unsuccessful and he lost faith in his own ability as a writer and became increasingly convinced that literature, especially the novel, had reached a total impasse.

Huysmans' first lucid explanation of his dissatisfaction with Naturalism is in the opening of *Là-Bas:*

> I do not really care how the naturalists maltreat language, but I do strenuously object to the earthiness of their ideas. . . . Filth and the flesh are their domain. They deny wonder, reject the extrasensual, and don't even understand that artistic curiosity begins at the very point where the senses leave off!

> ce que je reproche au naturalisme, ce n'est pas le lourd badigeon de son gros style, c'est l'immondice de ses idées. . . . Vouloir se confiner dans les buanderies de la chair, rejeter le suprasensible, dénier le rêve, ne pas même comprendre que la curiosité de l'art commence là où les sens cessent de servir!

In spite of his instinct that art begins where the senses end, Huysmans was still committed to the values of realist description and thus conceived of a modern novel in the following way:

> We must [thought Durtal] retain the documentary veracity, the precision of detail, the compact and sinewy language of realism, but we must also dig down into the soul and cease trying to explain mystery in terms of our sick senses. If possible the novel ought to be compounded of two elements, that of the soul and that of the body, and these ought to be inextricably bound together as in life. Their interreactions, their conflicts, their reconciliation, ought to furnish the dramatic interest. In a word, we must follow the road laid out once and for all by Zola, but at the same time we must trace a parallel route in the air by which we may go above and beyond, and create, in a word, *a spiritual naturalism!* It must be complete, powerful, daring in a different way from anything that is being attempted at present.

> Il faudrait, se disait [Durtal], garder la véracité du document, la précision du détail, la langue étoffée et nerveuse du réalisme, mais il faudrait aussi se faire puisatier d'âme et ne pas vouloir expliquer le mystère par les maladies des sens; le roman, si cela se pouvait, devrait se diviser de lui-même en deux parts, néanmoins soudées ou plutôt confondues, comme elles le sont dans la vie, celle

> de l'âme, celle du corps, et s'occuper de leurs réactifs, de leurs conflits, de leur entente. Il faudrait, en un mot, suivre la grande voie si profondément creusée par Zola, mais il serait nécessaire aussi de tracer en l'air un chemin parallèle, une autre route, d'atteindre les en deça et les après, de faire, en un mot, un *naturalisme spiritualiste*; ce serait autrement fier, autrement complet, autrement fort! [my italics]

Just as Huysmans had originally been inspired to write when he saw the seventeenth-century Dutch paintings in the Louvre, it was painting, once again, which helped him out of the impasse he believed literature to be in, by showing him the possibilities of his new aesthetic of spiritual naturalism:

> [He began to think that Des Hermies] was right. In the present disorganized state of letters there was but one tendency which seemed to promise better things: the need for the supernatural. . . . Now his thoughts carried him away from his dissatisfaction with literature to the satisfaction he had found in another art, in painting.

> C'était vrai, il n'y avait plus rien debout dans les lettres en désarroi; rien, sinon un besoin de surnaturel. . . . En s'acculant ainsi à ces pensées, il finissait, pour se rapprocher de cet idéal qu'il voulait quand même joindre, par louvoyer, par bifurquer et s'arrêter à un autre art, à la peinture.

In the summer of 1888 Huysmans' doctor had recommended a trip to help his "dreadful nervous complaint." Prompted by Verhaeren's article on the German Primitives in *Société Nouvelle,* August 15, 1886, Huysmans finally decided to accept a long-standing invitation from Arij Prins to visit him in Hamburg and continue with him to visit several museums throughout Germany. Their trip took them to Cologne, Berlin, Weimar, Lübeck, Gotha, and Cassel. It was in the Cassel museum that Huysmans saw the *Crucifixion* by Grünewald, which was a revelation to him on two levels. It led him one step closer to the Catholic faith, towards which he had gradually been groping, and also to a solution of his aesthetic problems. As he wrote to Jules Destrée on December 12, 1890,

> All art was within them, the Supernaturalism that is the only truthful and great art. The only and true formula, so sought after, is in Roger van der Weyden, Metsys, Grünewald—absolute Realism with spurts of soul, what material Naturalism has not understood . . . and thereby collapsed!—despite all the services it rendered.

> Tout l'art était en eux, le surnaturalisme qui est le seul art véridique et grand. La seule et vraie formule tant cherchée est dans Roger van der Weyden, Metsys, Grünewald—le réalisme absolu avec des jets d'âme; ce que le naturalisme matérialiste n'a pas compris . . . et il en est crevé!—malgré tous les services qu'il a rendus.

Huysmans' impressions of Cologne, Hamburg, Lübeck, Berlin, and Gotha were introduced, years later, into *La*

Cathédrale and *De Tout*. But the impact of the Grünewald *Crucifixion* was so enormous that it was given a place of honor in the opening chapter of *Là-Bas*, in which Durtal and Des Hermies discuss the problem of contemporary literature. The painting is introduced into the novel as part of Durtal's personal experience: "Durtal's introduction to this Naturalism had come as a revelation the year before" ("La révélation de ce naturalisme, Durtal l'avait eue, l'an passé") (XII, 13). In order to create the impression that he is in the presence of the painting, as des Esseintes is in the presence of Moreau's *Salomé,* Durtal closes his eyes and relives the experience:

> He shuddered in his armchair and closed his eyes as if in pain. With extraordinary lucidity he saw the picture again, there, in front of him, as he evoked it.

> Et il frissonna dans son fauteuil et ferma presque douloureusement les yeux. Avec une extraordinaire lucidité, il revoyait ce tableau, là, devant lui, maintenant qu'il l'évoquait.

He even repeats the scream he let out when he first saw the painting in the museum: "He screamed again, mentally, as here, in his study, the Christ rose before him, formidable, on his cross" ("Il le hurlait mentalement encore, alors que, dans sa chambre, le Christ se dressait, formidable, sur sa croix")

The description reveals that Durtal is at first totally absorbed by the realism and the physicality of the Christ figure. Indeed there is a marked similarity between the portrayal of Christ and the *Flayed Ox* which forms part of the prose poem **"Claudine,"** and Huysmans' viewpoint is still clearly guided by Zola's tenets of Naturalism which demand a faithful, honest, detailed rendering of external appearances. He uses a mixture of plant, kitchen, and medical terminology which typifies much of his writing:

> The trembling chest was greasy with sweat. . . . the flesh swollen, blue, mottled with flea-bites, specked as with pin-pricks by spines broken off from the rods of the scourging and now festering beneath the skin where they had penetrated.

> Purulence was at hand. The fluvial wound in the side . . . inundated the thigh with blood that was like congealing blackberry juice . . . the flesh tumefied. . . .

> Les pectoraux tremblaient, beurrés par les sueurs . . . les chair gonflaient, salpêtrées et bleuies, persillées de morsures de puces, mouchetées comme de coups d'aiguilles par les pointes des verges qui, brisées sous la peau, la lardaient encore, çà et là, d'échardes.

> L'heure des sanies était venue; la plaie fluviale du flanc . . . inondait la hanche d'un sang pareil au jus foncé des mûres . . . la chair bourgeonnait. . . .

The power of Grünewald's descriptive ability overwhelms Durtal and he judges that "Grünewald was the most daring of realists" ("Grünewald était le plus forcené des réalistes"). Yet he quickly modifies that comment and explains that the earthly figures in the painting all exude a spiritual quality: "Thief, pauper, and peasant had vanished and given place to supraterrestrial creatures in the presence of their God" ("Il n'y avait plus de brigand, plus de pauvresse, plus de rustre, mais des êtres supraterrestres auprès d'un Dieu"). To complete his description of Grünewald as a great realist he adds the seemingly antithetical judgment that

> Grünewald was the most daring of idealists. Never had an artist known such magnificent exaltation, nor so resolutely jumped from the heights of the soul to the rapt orb of heaven.

> Grünewald était le plus forcené des idéalistes. Jamais peintre n'avait si magnifiquement exalté l'altitude et si résolument bondi de la cime de l'âme dans l'orbe éperdu du ciel.

Grünewald thus fulfills the two requirements of Huysmans' "naturalisme spiritualiste."

Huysmans' admiration for Grünewald, based on the dichotomy of matter and spirit, led him to do further research into the life of the painter, and he published a study of the Grünewalds in the Colmar museum in *Trois Primitifs* in 1905, two years before his death. Unlike the dramatic description in *La-Bas,* this study is a less emotional and more objective work of art criticism. Huysmans is primarily concerned with the history of the painter, the problems of identification and the analysis of picture space and color. Not that Huysmans was less impressed by the Isenheim Crucifixion than the one in Cassel, for "It looms up fiercely, as soon as one enters, and it overwhelms you instantly with the dreadful nightmare of a Calvary" ("Il surgit, dès qu'on entre, farouche, et il vous abasourdit aussitôt avec l'effroyable cauchemar d'un Calvaire") (*Trois Primitifs*). And it was the unique contradictions in Grünewald's work, the mixture of Naturalism and spiritualism, which continued to fascinate Huysmans. He seemed to find in Grünewald the combination of contrasts to which he himself aspired:

> He is, in fact, all paradoxes, all contrasts; this furious Orlando of painting leaps without respite from one extravagance to another, but this demoniac is, when the occasion requires, a very skilled painter, a master of every trick of the trade. Though he may go mad for the dazzling clash of colors, he also possesses, on his good days, a very refined sense of hue—his *Resurrection* proves it— and he can join the most hostile colors by coaxing them, by drawing them together little by little, by adroitly negotiating the tints.

> He is at the same time Naturalist and mystic, savage and civilized, frank and devious.

> Il est, en effet, tout en antinomies, tout en contrastes; ce Roland furieux de la peinture bondit sans cesse d'une outrance dans une autre, mais l'énergumène est, quand il le faut, un peintre fort

habile et connaissant à fond les ruses du métier.
S'il raffole du fracas éblouissant des tons, il
possède aussi, dans ses bons jours, le sens très
affiné des nuances—sa *Résurrection* l'atteste—et
il sait unir les couleurs les plus hostiles, en les
sollicitant, en les rapprochant peu à peu par d'adroites
diplomaties de teintes.

Il est à la fois naturaliste et mystique, sauvage et
civilisé, franc et retors.

As Huysmans explains in the opening chapter of *Là-Bas,*
he had been searching for a formula which would resolve
the contradiction between his respect for the documentary method of the Naturalists, and his dislike for their
crude, materialistic subject matter. Having found the
answer in medieval painting, Huysmans naturally turned
to the Middle Ages as a source for his contemporary
novel which would put into practice his new theory. In
contradiction to the nineteenth century which Huysmans
now regarded as mediocre and materialistic, he viewed
the reign of Charles VII as an age of high villainy and
high virtue, in which rich and poor seemed to dedicate
themselves wholeheartedly to God or to Satan. It was
also natural that Huysmans chose as his hero Gilles de
Rais, the antithesis of the nineteenth-century Naturalist
protagonist, who had touched the extremes of human
experience, from satanic vice to Christian fervor.

Reflected in the story of Gilles de Rais and in Durtal's
study of contemporary satanism is Huysmans' own spiritual anguish. Huysmans was spending part of his free
time in the company of prostitutes and petty criminals
and at the same time was beginning to attend Church and
to find, to his surprise, that it held increasing fascination
and consolation for him. The discovery of Grünewald
and other medieval mystical artists had first awakened in
him the possibilities of a return to a Catholic faith:

"But then," said Durtal to himself, awakening from
his reverie, "if I am consistent, I shall end up at
the Catholicism of the Middle Ages, to mystical
naturalism. Ah, no I will not—and yet perhaps I
may!"

Mais alors . . . se dit Durtal, qui s'éveillait de sa
songerie, mais alors, si je suis logique, j'aboutis
au catholicisme du Moyen Age, au naturalisme
mystique; ah non, par exemple, et si pourtant!

and the peace and serenity he found when attending
Church services persuaded him to seek help from a
priest. On May 28, 1891 he met for the first time with
the Abbé Mugnier and his conversion was completed by
1892. This reversion to organized religion ended
Huysmans' trend away from contemporary art and he
turned wholeheartedly now to a comprehensive study of
medieval art.

Huysmans' conversion to Catholicism has been the subject of much debate, both at the time and after, many
people arguing that it represented a genuine return to the
religion of his childhood, others that it was merely an

escape from the literary life of Paris. Some people see in
it a mere fascination with the occultism practiced at that
time by some Catholic sects; others explain it purely by
Huysmans' love of Catholic art and liturgy.

Huysmans himself was troubled by doubts and confusion
about his conversion and recognized that he was being
pulled in many directions. In *En Route,* 1895, the account of his conversion, as told through Durtal, he certainly puts art first in the list of motives leading him to
the Church:

his love of art, his heritage, his weariness of
living. . . . It was art that brought Durtal back to
religion. More than his disgust for life itself, art was
the irresistible lover that had drawn him toward God.

l'amour de l'art, l'hérédité, l'ennui de vivre. . . .
Durtal avait été ramené à la religion par l'art. Plus
que son dégoût de la vie même, l'art avait été
l'irrésistible aimant qui l'avait attiré vers Dieu.

Durtal recalls, for instance, how

he used to take refuge—during his idle days, after
coming out of the Louvre, where he had drifted
for a long time in front of the canvases of the
Primitives—in the old Church of Saint Séverin,
tucked away in a corner of the poor section of
Paris. He brought there with him the visions of
the canvases that he had admired in the Louvre
and he contemplated them anew in those surroundings, where they were truly at home. Then
he knew moments of delight.

il se réfugiait, les jours de flâne, en sortant du
Louvre où il s'était longuement évagué devant les
toiles des Primitifs, dans la vieille Eglise de Saint
Séverin, enfouie en un coin du Paris pauvre. Il y
apportait les visions des toiles qu'il avait admirées
au Louvre et il les contemplait à nouveau dans ce
milieu où elles se trouvaient vraiment chez elles.
Puis c'étaient des moments délicieux.

His greatest fear remained, however, that his love for
medieval art was a substitute for true faith:

He wore himself out in arguments, to the point
that he doubted the sincerity of his conversion,
telling himself, when all is said and done, I'm
only interested in the Church for its art; I only go
to see or hear, not to pray; I'm not seeking the
Lord, but my own pleasure.

Il s'usait en disputes, en arrivant à douter de la
sincérité de sa conversion, se disait, en fin de
compte, je ne me suis emballé à l'église que par
l'art; je n'y vais que pour voir ou pour entendre et
non pour prier; je ne cherche pas le Seigneur, mais
mon plaisir.

Whatever the role of art in Huysmans' conversion and
his post-conversion years, his return to faith cannot be
dismissed as a dilettantish flirtation with Catholicism.
The life he chose to lead as a result of his beliefs was by

no means an easy one and the faith he displayed during the years he suffered from his own illness and endless misfortunes among his friends is ample proof of a genuine commitment to Catholicism. It is too easy to accuse Huysmans derogatively of "aesthetic Catholicism," implying that love of Catholic art precluded genuine beliefs. As T. S. Eliot writes in a study of Pater:

> When religion is in a flourishing state, when the whole mind of society is moderately healthy and in order, there is an easy and natural association between religion and art. Only when religion has been partly retired and confined, when an Arnold can sternly remind us that Culture is wider than Religion, do we get "religious art" and in due course "aesthetic religion". Pater undoubtedly had from childhood a religious bent naturally to all that was liturgical and ceremonious. Certainly this is a real and important part of religion and Pater cannot thereby be accused of insincerity and "aestheticism". ["The Place of Pater"]

Marcel Proust, in the introduction to his translation of John Ruskin, shows great sensitivity about the process whereby works of religious art awaken a latent faith:

> He [Ruskin] will be able to speak of the years in which the Gothic appeared to him with the same gravity, the same emotional remembrance, the same serenity with which a Christian speaks of the day the truth was revealed to him. The events of his life are intellectual and the important periods are those in which he understands a new art form. . . . Just so did his religious feeling guide his aesthetic feeling. . . . That divine something that Ruskin felt at the heart of the feeling that works of art inspired in him was precisely what, in that feeling, was profound and original and thrust itself upon his taste without possibility of modification. And the religious respect that he brought to the expression of that feeling, his fear that translating it would subject it to the least deformation, prevented him—contrary to what has often been believed—from ever adulterating his responses to works of art with any alien tricks of reason. Thus, those who see in him a moralist and an apostle who loved in art what was not of art, are as mistaken as those who, ignoring the deepest essence of his aesthetic feeling, confuse it with a sensual dilettantism.

> Il [Ruskin] pourra parler des années où le gothique lui apparut avec la même gravité, le même retour ému, la même sérénité qu'un chrétien parle du jour où la vérité lui fut révélée. Les événements de sa vie sont intellectuels et les dates importantes sont celles où il pénètre une nouvelle forme d'art. . . . C'est ainsi que son sentiment religieux a dirigé son sentiment esthétique. . . . Ce quelque chose de divin que Ruskin sentait au fond du sentiment que lui inspiraient les oeuvres d'art, c'était précisément ce que ce sentiment avait de profond, d'original et qui s'imposait à son goût sans être susceptible d'être modifié. Et le respect religieux qu'il apportait à l'expression de ce sentiment, sa peur de lui faire subir en la traduisant la moindre déformation,

l'empêcha, au contraire de ce qu'on a souvent pensé, de mêler jamais à ses impressions devant les oeuvres d'art aucun artifice de raisonne-ment qui leur fût étranger. De sorte que ceux qui voient en lui un moraliste et un apôtre aimant dans l'art ce qui n'est pas l'art, se trompent à l'égal de ceux qui, négligeant l'essence profonde de son sentiment esthétique, le confondent avec un dilet-tantisme voluptueux.

Whereas Huysmans' initial appreciation of medieval art had been emotional in this way, and in his art criticism he analyzes works from an aesthetic viewpoint, his interest became increasingly ethical. In *La Cathédrale,* 1898, he defines Christian symbolism in art as "The allegorical representation of a Christian principle, in a perceptible form" ("La représentation allégorique d'un principe chrétien, sous une forme sensible"), and in this novel he was intent on comprehending and explaining this symbolism. For he believed that the Gothic period marked the height of truth and that all periods since then were morally inferior and their art less significant. Already in 1879 he had written that

> Religious painting has been floundering in its rut for centuries. Aside from the murals executed by Delacroix at Saint-Sulpice, we find only a precise formula scrupulously respected by all the chrism-mongers.

> La peinture religieuse patauge dans l'ornière depuis des siècles. Ecartons les peintures murales exécutées par Delacroix, à Saint-Sulpice, et nous ne trouvons qu'une précise formule scrupuleusement respectée par tous les batteurs de saint-chrême.

And in *La Cathédrale* he confirms that

> after Rembrandt. . . . There follows the irreparable decay of religious impression in art. . . . As for the eighteenth century, there wasn't even any to speak of; that century was an age of belly and bidet, and whenever it sought to approach worship, it turned a holy-water font into a wash basin.

> après Rembrandt. . . . C'est l'irrémédiable déchéance de l'impression religieuse dans l'art. . . . Quant au dix-huitième siècle, il n'y avait même pas à s'en occuper; ce siècle fut une époque de bedon et de bidet et, dès qu'il voulut toucher au culte, il fit d'un bénitier une cuvette.

Huysmans thus became committed to the idea, expressed later by the sculptor Rodin in his book on the French Cathedrals, that "if we could manage to understand Gothic art, we would be irresistibly brought back to the truth" ("si nous parvenions à comprendre l'art gothique, nous serions irrésistiblement ramenés à la vérité"). [*Les Cathédrales de France*]

Unfortunately, Huysmans' Catholic novels, sincere as they are in their attempt to investigate Church art, make for tedious reading. They are lengthy and didactic and lack the humor and imaginative treatment of his earlier novels and prose poems. It is indeed ironical and pathetic that after Huysmans felt he had discovered a new aesthetic formula to spur him on to new creative endeavors, he felt less confident than ever in his work. On April 3, 1893, for instance, he wrote to Arij Prins:

> I am working in disgust—and I have strong urges to toss every damn thing into the fire, for what I am writing at the moment seems to me mediocre indeed. I have lived for art—and—now that I am forty-five years old, I realize its emptiness
>
> Je travaille avec dégoût—et j'ai de fortes envies de tout foutre au feu, car ça me paraît bien médiocre, ce que j'écris pour l'instant. J'ai vécu pour l'art—et—aujourd'hui que j'ai quarante-cinq ans, j'aperçois son néant [*Le Journal d'En Route*]

and after the publication of *La Cathédrale* he wrote despondently to Abbé Ferret on March 7, 1897:

> It's a pot of erudition, a concentrated bouillon of Church art, but it seems to have been pasted together with albumin; these enumerations and these quotations are not really springboards for writing, packed as though by a hydraulic press, compressed into chapters. Well, anyway. That completes *En Route*.
>
> C'est un réceptacle d'érudition, un bouillon consommé de l'art de l'Eglise, mais ça a l'air d'être écrit avec de l'albumine; ce ne sont vraiment pas des tremplins à phrases que ces énumérations et ces citations, tassées comme à la presse hydraulique, comprimées dans des chapitres. Enfin! Cela complète *En Route*.

Huysmans' realization of his own creative problems are all the more painful when one remembers the criticism he levelled at his own mentor Zola years earlier. Attacking Zola's systematic method of writing a certain number of pages each day, he wrote that "his novels are not works of art, but works of ideas" ("ses romans ne sont pas des oeuvres d'art, mais des oeuvres d'idées").

Aware of artistic failure in himself yet still determined to recreate the moral and spiritual character of medieval art, Huysmans began to work towards the founding of an artistic monastery where talented Catholic artists, himself included, could live together according to Christian principles. He had first felt this strong need to escape bureaucratic life in 1893 and, as he expresses it in *La Cathédrale,*

> he envisioned himself a monk in an accommodating monastery inhabited by a lenient order, one that loved the liturgies and was enamored of art.
>
> il se voyait moine dans un couvent débonnaire, desservi par un ordre clément, amoureux de liturgies et épris d'art.

In *L'Oblat,* 1903, the novel in which Huysmans attempts to present an accurate account of life in a French reli-

gious community at the beginning of the century, he lays great stress on the role of art in maintaining true religious practice:

> One has, moreover, to be ignorant indeed to deny the power of art, even if only from the standpoint of practicality. It was the surest aid to mysticism and liturgy during the Middle Ages. . . . If the Benedictine rule has an objective, it is precisely to create it anew and to promote it.
>
> Il faut être bien ignorant, du reste, pour nier, en ne se plaçant même qu'au point de vue pratique, la puissance de l'art. Il a été l'auxiliaire le plus sûr de la mystique et de la liturgie, pendant le Moyen Age. . . . Si l'oblature Bénédictine a une raison d'être, c'est précisément de le créer à nouveau et de l'élever.

Huysmans was not alone in his ideas of setting up a religious artistic community. He knew that there were similar attempts being made all over Europe, notably by the Rosicrucians and by Lenz and his followers at Beuron, Germany. In England, the writer Rolfe, whose life is described by A. J. A. Symons in his novel *The Quest for Corvo,* was asked by a friend whether he was interested in taking part in such a plan: "This ambitious project was the founding of a secular semi-monastic order which, by joint studies, should, in a spirit of disinterestedness, add to the learning of the world." It was Rolfe's belief, as it was also Huysmans' that "it is desirable to revive the virtues of that period of the World's history commonly called the Middle Ages, and to practice them, in the hope that we may thereby the better pursue wisdom."

The overwhelming problem which faced Huysmans, however, was the lack of what he considered gifted and genuine Catholic artists. As he wrote in *La Cathédrale,*

> There is no point in seeking among modern artists either; painters like Overbeck, Ingres, and Flandrin were wan old nags harnessed to commissioned works of piety; in the church of Saint-Sulpice, Delacroix crushes all the daubers around him, but his feeling for Catholic art is nonexistent. And the same is true of our contemporary artists.
>
> Dans le moderne, il n'y a non plus à chercher; les Overbeck, les Ingres, les Flandrin furent de blèmes haridelles attelées à des subjects de commande pieux; dans l'église Saint-Sulpice, Delacroix écrase tous les peinturleurs qui l'entourent, mais son sentiment de l'art catholique est nul. Et il est de même de ceux de nos artistes contemporains.

In spite of the fact that Huysmans' aesthetic aims seemed to correspond to the ideas of the Rosicrucians, as set out in Péladan's *Comment on devient artiste,* 1874, Huysmans dismisses that group as fake mystics. He is no kinder towards the artists at Beuron and describes some of their work as follows:

> Those frescos refer back to the imagery of Assyria and Egypt. . . . Beuron's ideal had become a

mixture of French art of the First Empire and modern English art.

> Ces fresques reportaient à l'imagerie de l'Assyrie et de l'Egypte. . . . L'idéal de Beuron était alors devenu un alliage de l'art français du Premier Empire et de l'art anglais moderne.

In contrast, many of the Synthetists, such as Emile Bernard, Paul Sérusier and Maurice Denis, were in close contact with Beuron and were much inspired by its art. Sérusier even translated Lenz's book into French and Denis wrote an introduction to it, mentioning what he considered the unfounded judgment of Huysmans in *La Cathédrale*. Huysmans' lack of sympathy with these artists was, of course, grounded in his belief that realism was still a fundamental part of symbolism and that true-to-nature description was still the starting point of all art. He could therefore understand and support the theoretical thrust of the Synthetists and the Rosicrucians, among others, but totally rejected their style. As he writes in *La Cathédrale:*

> To stop working from nature, to impose an unvarying ritual of colors and line . . . indicated an absolute incomprehension of art in anyone who took such a chance. This system was destined to end in the ossification, the paralysis of painting, and indeed these were the results achieved.

> Supprimer l'étude d'après nature, exiger un rituel uniforme de couleurs et de lignes . . . dénotait chez celui qui risqua cet effort, une incompréhension absolue de l'art. Ce système devait aboutir à l'ankylose, à la paralysie de la peinture et tels furent, en effet, les résultats atteints.

Since Huysmans did not feel at ease with any of the existing artistic communities but was more and more determined to leave Paris for a sheltered existence in the country, he made attempts to set up his own artistic monastery, where he could write better in the presence of religious artists. His first hopes were raised in 1894 when he was introduced to a certain Dom Besse, who had similar ideas about an artistic retreat and told Huysmans of his plans to restore the Benedictine Abbey of Saint-Wandrille. When Huysmans heard that Dom Besse had been sent to Spain and had to drop any thought of Saint-Wandrille, he fell into despair.

His hopes were raised again in 1895 when Antoinette Donavie, a seventy-year-old nun, wrote him about setting up an artistic cloister in the convent of Fiancey near Valence. On May 29 Huysmans wrote about it to Abbé Moeller:

> The joy—in an abbey where there would be nothing but plainsong and clean things—of being able to work in peace on a life of the good Lydwine! This attempt to renew religious art in truly propitious surroundings would be so beautiful.

> La joie, dans une abbaye où il n'y aurait que du plain-chant et des objects propres, de pouvoir travailler en paix à une vie de la bonne Lydwine! Ce serait si beau cette tentative de rénover l'art religieux dans un milieu réellement propice.

However, when Huysmans visited the nun at Fiancey, he realized that the plans would never materialize because Mother Célestine, as she was known, was more concerned with her hydrotherapy clinic than with artistic projects.

Huysmans' third hope of joining an artist's community was also frustrated. Knowing of his desire of retreating to a monastery, Abbé Mugnier suggested to Huysmans that he should spend some time at the Abbey of Saint-Maur de Glanfeuil, in Anjou. On visiting he decided that he was probably unsuited to the life of the cloister and he accepted the advice that he would be happier as an oblate. On July 8 he wrote his close friend Léon Leclaire, with whom he had hoped to set up an artistic community: "Cloisters are fine in dreams, but dreadful in reality; and one certainly finds one's savation less there than in the world" ("Les cloîtres, c'est beau en rêve, mais affreux en réalité; et l'on y fait certainement moins son salut que dans le monde").

The idea of oblature became more attractive in August of that year, when Huysmans spent a very happy time at Ligugé near Poitiers and even found a perfect plot of land for building a house. He incited the Leclaires with the same enthusiasm and after some negotiation they decided to build a shared house at Ligugé in which they could be joined by other oblates with similar tastes and aims. Huysmans did not intend to have much connection with the monks, because he had a very low opinion of most clergymen's aesthetic judgment and believed they would only interfere with his plans. Huysmans greatly hoped that he could persuade Marie-Charles Dulac to join this community. Dulac was a young painter whom he had singled out in *La Cathédrale* as the most talented of all contemporary Catholic artists. Dulac approached Huysmans in January 1898 to thank him for the favorable criticism of his work in *La Cathédrale* and to discuss the possibilities of setting up an artistic community. At no time had Huysmans been more optimistic, but then, one by one, the prospective members of the project backed out. The plans were given their final blow when Dulac, the cornerstone of it all, died after Christmas 1898. After this failure to set up his community, Huysmans never mustered the courage again. He isolated himself for two years at Ligugé to write *Sainte Lydwine de Schiedam,* but gradually the unpleasant atmosphere created by impending government legislation directed against Catholic associations, combined with his ill health, made life unbearable. In 1901 he left Ligugé and returned to his lonely and miserable life in Paris.

Huysmans never saw the revival of Catholic art but, in spite of great suffering, he died in peace in 1907. In the painting, architecture, sculpture, and music of the Middle Ages he had found an expression of spiritualism, anguish, and faith which gave meaning to his life. Inspired by the beliefs expressed in these works, he was able to dedicate the last years of his life to the account of his own conversion, the explanation of Church symbolism and the story of a saint who personified the suffering Huysmans had first seen in the Grünewald *Crucifixion* and who could now inspire him with the faith he needed to endure his own painful illness.

We have seen how Huysmans had difficulty dealing with reality and therefore looked to art as a substitute. He often found it easier to find inspiration in paintings than in people or nature and sublimated many of his deepest feelings in art, often mistaking art for reality. This accounts, to a large degree, for the impact of the visual arts on his aesthetic development and the influence of specific paintings on his literary imagination and language.

Carol A. Mossman (essay date 1988)

SOURCE: "Gastro-Exorcism: J. K. Huysmans and the Anatomy of Conversion," in *Compromise Formations: Current Directions in Psychoanalytic Criticism,* edited by Vera L. Camden, Kent State University Press, 1988, pp. 113-27.

[*I the following essay, Mossman argues that the neur tic personality of the central character of* Against the Grain *reveals elements of Huysmans's own psyche that eventually led to his religious conversion to Catholicism.*]

The Catholic church made a prestigious conversion in the case of J.-K. Huysmans. In his 1903 preface to *A rebours* (1884), the converted author attempts to explain, as much to himself as to his readers, the curiously monkish tastes of the novel's neurotic hero, des Esseintes, who is nothing if not a dyed-in-the-wool hedonist bent on exploring the limits of sensual experience. Far from repudiating this earlier product of an "un-Christian" phase, as one might have expected him to do, Huysmans maintains that "all the novels which I have written since *A rebours* are contained in embryonic form in that book."

Thus a continuity is postulated throughout the work in spite of a radical shift in state of mind occurring somewhere within the span. Nonetheless it is a troubled continuity, one which is (to use the phraseology of conversion) not without lapses: "I understand . . . up to a certain point," proffers Huysmans, "what happened between the year 1891 and the year 1895, between *Là-bas* and *En route,* but nothing at all about what happened between 1884 and 1891, between *A rebours* and *Là-bas*".

How, then, might one account for Huysmans's celebrated passage from the profane to the mystical, for that shift which is merely apparent since *A rebours* is an embryonic form of all future creations? Referring to des Esseintes, Huysmans advances the following: "It seems in fact that the neuroses open up fissures in the soul

through which the Spirit of Evil penetrates". The conversion which took place at an indeterminate point in the erstwhile naturalist's career was already manifest in some form in the illness which is the subject of *A rebours*. Looking backward in 1903, Huysmans affirms a kinship between mind and soul, between the self-divisive attacks of neurosis and infiltrations diabolical.

One is tempted to wonder whether this soul, evidently prone to fracture and highly vulnerable to exterior forces, can be situated in some specific locus, as Descartes had placed it, for instance, in the pineal gland? By way of response, we can turn to the final sentence of *Là-bas,* the second way station cited by Huysmans in his spiritual itinerary. There the misanthropic protagonist Durtal, having finished his novel on satanist Gilles de Rais, muses on the future awaiting the offspring of what he views as an abject modernity, devoid of spiritual values. These children "will do as their fathers and mothers . . . they will fill their guts and empty out their souls through the lower abdomen!"

The soul, it would seem, must be sought somewhere in the digestive tract whence it apparently runs the unorthodox risk of being flushed out. It follows from this that spiritual therapy might best be envisaged in terms of containment or retention, an inference borne out, indeed, by the obvious attraction which reclusion and claustration exercise over many of Huysmans's characters, and which the monastic temptation exercised over Huysmans himself [Robert Baldick, *The Life of J.-K. Huysmans*]. In *En route,* the third and final stage of the itinerary, Durtal (again the novel's protagonist) explains that his conversion occurred in a manner redolent of the digestive process: "For God acts as He pleases. . . . [The method] he used in my case . . . was something analogous to a stomach digesting without my feeling it".

Clearly, then, the continuity which joins the sacred to the profane is alimentary in nature. However, the profile of conversion is by no means a simple one. Overlaying the gastroreligious fundament and infusing it to a rather remarkable extent are two alternate systems which seek to explain disorders, be they religious or digestive: neuropathology and demonology. Throughout these three key works which Huysmans named as milestones on his personal road to Damascus, the discourses of the divine, the demonic, the digestive, and the neurotic intertwine. The depiction of salvation and the resultant state of grace is problematic, to say the least. In this study, I shall argue that for J.-K. Huysmans, good, evil, and insanity cohabit the self-same space in the body.

In May 1884 Huysmans wrote to Emile Zola explaining his struggle writing a novel which featured a single character, with no love interest—in short, a book lacking traditional narrative structure. If the master was later to chastise his "disciple" for overturning the naturalist canon in his novel, *A rebours,* an entire generation would find that it spoke directly to their sensibilities. For it was perhaps the first novel to draw on a genre which, however appreciated, had not yet crossed over into the French literary camp: the case history. It is well known that Huysmans based the narrative progression of *A rebours* on the etiology of "nervosisme" as elaborated by Bouchut in his 1877 edition of *Du nervosisme aigu et chronique et des maladies nerveuses*. This is the documentary aspect of the novel through which its links to Naturalism are retained.

Françoise Gaillard has brilliantly argued that the very scrupulousness with which Huysmans adheres to Bouchut's narrative gives the lie to the medical myth by exposing the gaps in a doctrine which fails to establish convincing links between the cause (heredity) and the disease itself. I shall return to this point later insofar as it relates to Huysmans's own diversion from the neuropathological and his conversion to another mode of explanation.

Meanwhile, it is perversion which prevails in *A rebours*. *Webster's New International Dictionary* defines "perversion" as a "deviation from the right, true or regular course . . . as, to *pervert* the order of nature," and it is certain that *A rebours* flaunts the unnatural, including the pathological, with perverse relishment. Nor, it has been observed, does des Esseintes seem to want to seek a cure to his malady. (Gaillard goes so far as to say that illness is the essence of the character.) This indulgence can doubtless be ascribed to the fact that what the exaltation of neurosis secures, at the expense of all that is "normal" and "natural," is access to privileged zones of the mind open to the irrational, the suprasensible, the unconscious, and the demonic. It thus comes as no surprise that this aesthetic of pathology should take as its principal devices of expression dreams, involuntary memory, and hallucinatory descriptions of paintings, all activated through the senses and set against a Baudelairean metaphysical backdrop of correspondences.

Central, then, to Huysmans's aesthetic is communication with a beyond lying, vaguely, *là-bas,* However, there is a disturbing aspect to this contact, for in order to move in and out of these zones of revelation, there must be passage points. Victor Brombert has demonstrated the Huysmansian hero's unending quest for hermetic reclusion. Perhaps equally revealing, I would suggest, is the corollary to this penchant for sequestration—the terror of leakage. Therein lies the anguish and the interest of this writer's universe. For it stands to reason that try as one may, a perfect sealing off can never be achieved: madness can always seep in through some crack (*A rebours*), or "le Démon" can penetrate through one of the soul's fissures (*Là-bas*), and, more disquieting still, grace always runs the risk of escaping through the bowels ("they will empty out their souls through the lower abdomen").

As we shall see, throughout Huysmans's works, the dread of puncture and penetration translates into a discourse which is riddled with holes, scars, orifices, and wounds being sutured up. Yet as fear-inspiring as the prospect of invasion seems to be, the anxiety of penetra-

tion is, at the very least, an equivocal one. After all, it seems only fair that the "Divinity" should have an equal right of access to the soul as "le Malin." Indeed, the conversion/digestion operated in *En route* began with an aperture: "Christ opened, little by little, the shuttered lodging of his [Durtal's] soul, and light came streaming in" (cited by Baldick). Neoplatonic metaphors aside, in Huysmans's novels the struggle of madness versus sanity, of possession versus grace is won or lost in the openings.

With these various equivalences provisionally set forth, let me examine *A rebours* in greater detail. It begins, as a nineteenth-century case history should, with the genealogy of the family des Esseintes, the underlying assumption being that the young Duke Jean's nervous malady has been transmitted to him hereditarily. The hereditary solution, forged into literary doctrine by Zola, enjoyed the credibility of the evolving community of neurologists, as was pointed out earlier. Not only had Bouchut grounded his nosology of "nervosisme" in heredity (see Gaillard), but it also provided Charcot, Huysmans's celebrated medical contemporary, with the theoretical base for his own more systematic study of the neuroses. (Charcot's Tuesday Lessons almost invariably began by tracing the hereditary pathological "antecedents" of his patients.)

Thus the gallery of ancestral portraits exhibited at the beginning of *A rebours* as a mode of scientific explanation of des Esseintes's physical and mental degeneration is true to genre. Striking, however, is the fact that on closer scrutiny, one notices that Jean des Esseintes's most direct "racial" forebear, if such it can be called, is none other than a hole: "a hole existed in the lineage of this race". This interruption of the family chain is itself subsequently interrupted and patched over by the insertion of one "mysterious" head which "was a suture between the past and the present". If the missing link has been restored, the gap in the family tree has merely been filled in. As a weak spot, it still bodes a potential for rupture.

Clearly, the "mysterious other" with the "ambiguous expression" who is associated with openings is to be regarded as des Esseintes's most direct hereditary influence. It is with some interest, then, that we perceive this ancestor's relation to orificial irregularity as being *double,* since his one most noteworthy function in life lay in serving as one of Henri III's celebrated minions. Through the discourse of heredity and neuropathology, one is returned to the bottom end of the alimentary canal.

It is scarcely a matter of returning to the repressed, however, because it is precisely in terms of gastric dysfunction which the progress of des Esseintes's neurosis is measured. He begins his "refined Thebaid" with modest, mild menus suited to a stomach which, in the past, had already proven itself rebellious. Des Esseintes, like any human being, must bodily take in nourishment from the exterior. This limited dependence on nature and the outside world finds its parallel at the plot level, since the erudite recluse is still able to derive spiritual nourishment from books.

As des Esseintes's health deteriorates, the reader is treated to a succession of essays on the virtues of artifice, Latin authors of the Decadent period, the significance of gemstones through history, and the art of Moreau and Redon, to name a few. The delirious description of the "erudite hysterias" captured in the Salome painting marks a crucial point in the evolution of des Esseintes's illness, for following it, the protagonist ceases to draw on the outside world for sustenance: "He lived off himself, took nourishment from his own substance, like a sluggish animal nestled in his hole for the winter . . ." The hibernal period of feeding off one's reserves cannot go on indefinitely; sooner or later des Esseintes, whose intellectual and gastrointestinal systems are no longer digesting material, is bound to become an empty shell, incapable either of ingesting at one end or producing at the other. But the greatest danger resides in the fact that the vacating of this internal space renders it vulnerable to assault, all the more so because access to the mind/stomach can always be gained through an aperture.

In fact, that is precisely what does happen at this point in the narrative. The hollowed-out des Esseintes relinquishes all control over his environment and becomes a passive receiver, submitting to the vagaries of uncontrollable exterior forces: solitude "guided a stream of dreams to which he submitted passively without even trying to escape them". "Morbid" symptoms appear as des Esseintes is assailed by thoughts of "le Démon" and by "the madness of magic, black masses, sabbaths, possessions and exorcism . . ." And it is as if these thoughts of the demonic, relishing that vacuum which nature is said to abhor, have penetrated through some crack into des Esseintes's stomach regions. In spite of the sick man's attempt to evict the alien pressures through "vain and urgent efforts," his belly bloats ("il gonflait"), and no manner of effort can exorcize the "gaseous heartburn" from the vulnerable region.

When des Esseintes realizes that his stomach is temporarily dysfunctional, he turns to the outside world to divert his attention. He purchases ornamental plants which, assembled together "as in a hospital," form a forest of gaping, syphilitic apertures. Although the collection is primarily genital in character (as has often been noted), at least two of these floral monstrosities represent the alimentary openings. In fact, the cypripedium orchids even combine madness and digestion. As if "imagined by a demented inventor," they resemble human tongues "as one sees these rendered in the illustrations of works treating disorders of the throat and mouth . . ." The nidularium fungi, on the other hand, display "raw and gaping fundaments". The promenade through the forest of scar tissue masquerading as plants gives way to the famous nightmare, a sort of allegory of the ravages of

Syphilis, in which Huysmans's misogyny is very much in evidence.

It is one of those remarkable conjunctures of science and literature that, writing in Paris one year before Freud was to embark upon his decisive course of study under Charcot in that very city, Huysmans should give us a masterpiece which focuses nearly its entire attention on the divagations of the unconscious mind. In fact, certain of these oneiric meanderings so clearly constitute a system, having deep structures, a syntax, and so on, that they virtually beckon for interpretation. Nor has that beck gone unheeded by critics, particularly in the case of the nightmare. Charles Bernheimer, for instance, sees in these dream sequences appearing throughout Huysmans's works a textual site which privileges the articulation of psychoconstructs: "These dream narratives open up onto a fantasy space and allow Huysmans complete freedom . . . to recreate his personal obsessions". I would like to examine two other such episodes, less explicitly unconscious since they both take place in des Esseintes's waking life, which demonstrate the extent to which the gastrointestinal discourse presides over the narrative structure and the unconscious psychological content of *A rebours*.

When des Esseintes's illness progresses to the point where he begins to hallucinate smells and wonders if he might not be "under the influence of one of those possessions that they exorcized in the Middle Ages". he determines to take a trip to London. Every reader of the novel knows that the voyage remains an imaginary one, since the would-be traveller contents himself, Baedecker in hand, with an excursion into a pub and, later, an English eating establishment. Another victory of mind over matter is proclaimed. Or so it would seem. Yet nothing is more physical than des Esseintes's visit to the Bodega which takes on all the allegorical flavor of a descent into the human belly. The pub into which des Esseintes slips is described as a "belly decorated in crenellated wood".

Making his way further into this medieval abdomen, our hero pursues his architectural observations, noting that in "the lower abdomen" of the building there is a "hole connected to a pipe". Will des Esseintes be flushed out of this clearly rectal nether exit, just as the souls of the plebeian children were imagined to do in *Là-bas*? No, instead, des Esseintes watches the operations of this bowel with a fascination that suggests he is observing the functioning of his own poor stopped-up organism, which at this point, it will be recalled, will receive almost no foreign matter. The "explosive sodas" which the bartender is opening are redolent of that "gaseous heartburn" which agitates his own digesting machine.

At length, the general ambiance combined with the sight of a "cigar planted in the hairy hole of [the] mouth" of one client, has a relaxing effect on des Esseintes, who surrenders himself to "a certain softening". Evidently the quest in this journey to the center of the organism has been therapeutic in nature. With the gastric juices stirred into movement, des Esseintes is subsequently able to consume a hearty meal for the first time in months.

One of the most intriguing aspects of *A rebours* is not only that it stages a series of forays into the beyond, but also that these take place at different levels of unconsciousness. The more lucid episodes, such as the descent into the abdominal cavity, can be read as allegories. It is, in fact, probably no accident that the decor of this journey is medieval, and it is by reading this episode in terms of genre that one is led to conclude that what is at issue is a quest, albeit one whose goal ("a certain softening") can hardly be called lofty. Interpretation takes place at a fairly rational level through substitution of whole blocks of the narrative. The syntax of the tale thus remains intact. By comparison, the syphilis nightmare operates according to a more complex logic in which the smooth seams of allegory are occasionally torn through by occurrences of signifiers felt to be out of place. Reading through a generic screen will not satisfactorily decode this episode.

Let me turn to another of those texts which seems to articulate unconscious desires, this time at the level of the daydream. I am referring to des Esseintes's memory of his visit to the dentist. Proustian *avant la lettre,* the act of recollecting is triggered by the "music" which des Esseintes composes on his mouth organ through various blends of arcane liqueurs. From the palate to the tooth, the associational device linking the two experiences is thus the mouth. But here it is worth interjecting that with Huysmans, there is more to the mouth than meets the eye. For at its simplest, the mouth merely represents a point of access into the alimentary canal and is, as such, interchangeable with the anus. (In fact, des Esseintes's ultimate triumph over nature at the end of the novel results from precisely this reversal, as will be seen.) Actually, the anal/buccal permutation was already suggested in the pub adventure when des Esseintes, at his ease in the nether extreme of abdomen-pub, had noted the man with an (excremental) cigar "planted in the hairy hole of [the] mouth."

That one orifice can stand for another is nowhere more clear than during the hero's visit to the terrible Doctor Gatonax. The dentist's extraction of the troublesome tooth takes on the aura of a forcible and painful penetration. When, at first, "having stuck an enormous index finger into his mouth", only half the tooth is recovered, the practitioner renews his assault: "The man . . . again flung himself upon him [des Esseintes] as if he wanted to plunge his arm to the far end of the abdomen . . . ." And the result of the penetration through this equivocal mouth into the "abdomen" most often associated with the bowel is that des Esseintes feels bestialized: he "began . . . to kick and squeal like an animal being killed". Just as a sense of relief came to des Esseintes in his therapeutic journey into his own internalia, here the grisly experience leaves him, a trifle oddly, "happy, feeling ten years younger".

Des Esseintes's terrifying encounter with the dentist and the operation which the latter performs is further linked to the discourse of neuro-pathology. Somehow the penetration of an orifice entails the advent of madness. The suffering protagonist exhibits behavior "similar to a madman's." On the threshold of the office "a horrible fear overcame him," and during the scene, his reason deserts him.

If forcing an opening of the "mouth" is related to the puncture of the rational mind, the last-recourse visit to the dentist also takes on the allure of a degrading visit to a low-class brothel: "He decided to go to the first one he came upon, to a vulgar tooth-puller." These sorts "know how to extract, with unmatched speed, the most tenacious stumps; they are open early in the morning and one is not kept waiting". By this time one suspects that a discourse which allies a vocabulary of mental alienation to a passive sexuality operated upon by a male dentist will probably also insist on those orifices which point both to digestion and the demonic. In fact, the text is quite explicit to the effect that vulgar practitioners of this ilk "know how to extirpate" and not how to "fill cavities and seal up holes". Their function is thus to exorcize, to vacate, and not to heal. It will be seen that terms relating to healing through blocking the apertures (the word "panser" occurs with persistence in Huysmans's prose) constitute references to divine operations. Leaks in the bottom are more the Devil's handiwork.

Now it is very much to our point that the various excursions into the realm of the unconscious are initiated in a similar manner, namely when des Esseintes has somehow come into contact with that exterior he so dreads. The terrifying remembrance of the visit to the dentist, for instance, is preceded by des Esseintes's opening the window: "This abrupt passage with no transition from torrid heat to a wintry chill had taken its toll on him . . . ." The syphilis nightmare was similarly inspired: "The *passage* from the outside air to the warmth of his dwelling, from his static, reclusive life to the mobility of a liberated existence had been too abrupt . . . soon he fell prey to the somber *madness* of a nightmare" (emphasis added). His ventures into the English bookstore and the Bodega are marked by identical assaults perpetrated by an inclement Mother Nature. In all these cases, ravings, deliria, and pure dementia are felt to be the results of invasions wrought by an exterior which has managed to force itself into the hero's mind through a "passage."

As des Esseintes's health begins to decline more and more rapidly, his throat becomes obstructed. At length, he is reduced to digesting food outside his body with a "sustenteur" and then ingesting it: "He drank a spoonful of muddy, salty juice deposited at the bottom of a pot. Then he felt a warm presence descend like a velvety caress". The coprophagic tenor of this ingestion finds its "unnatural" echo in the final phase of his illness which des Esseintes sees as his ultimate triumph over nature: his feeding through enemas. Nature has at last been turned upside down, one orifice replacing another: "[D]es

Esseintes could not help secretly congratulating himself on the event which was the crowning triumph . . . of the life he had contrived for himself . . . nourishment thus absorbed was surely the last aberration of the natural that could be committed". Exultant and carrying the inversion of nature to its extreme, des Esseintes regales this "strange palate" with liquified three-course "meals."

Earlier it was suggested that the dramas of Huysmans's plots are played out in the apertures. It is this final joke on Mother Nature in *A rebours* which signals that the narrative—and des Esseintes's life—have reached, quite literally, an impasse, for with the orificial inversion, no future writing can be produced, no material excreted. Surely it can be no coincidence that the moment of organic shutdown is also that of des Esseintes's celebrated prayer (addressee unknown) imploring that an unbeliever be shown the faith. Nor is it coincidental that the formulation of this plea should betray an anguish at the thought that faith, even if arrived at, can always leak out: des Esseintes "would have liked to have forced himself to possess faith . . . to have been able to secure it to his soul with clamps . . ." *A rebours* comes to rest unresolved, and its final dilemma can be formulated (as one might by now have suspected) in alimentary terms: therapy of an exorcistic nature can indeed be effected in the lower gastrointestinal zones (the mouth having been sealed off); however, it is within the logic of this gastrotheology that faith can make its exit through the same passages.

Durtal, the hero of *Là-bas*, takes over where des Esseintes left off. Early in this novel, which explores the relationship of satanism to insanity, Durtal also expresses a desire to believe. Unfortunately, muses he, what is wanting is "a naked soul and his was obstructed with filth, soaking in the concentrated juices of old guano". This view of the soul as cesspool, a respiratory of fecal matter, besides being related to neurosis as we saw in *A rebours*, is intimately linked to the notion of erotic visitation of incubi and succubi, a topic which the novel explores in considerable detail. For not only is this brand of diabolic possession frankly sexual, but it includes one element which distinguishes it from the "natural." Gévingey, the astrologer and one of the work's several occultists, informs Durtal: "You must know that the member of the incubus splits and penetrates both the openings at the same time".

Thus it is that the Devil gains a rear access to the soul, and it is not hard to imagine that Durtal's soul is a cesspool for the good reason that it harbors the "Demon." What is troubling in this theology *par derrière* is that the divine soul, that is, the state of grace, can also be evacuated from below as was noted earlier. This suggests an uneasy equivalence of God and Devil, of good and evil, which, in fact, is entirely consistent with Huysmans's own beliefs. Inasmuch as both partake of the supernatural, both may penetrate by the same entrances. (In this

connection one thinks immediately of Freud's analysis of Chief Justice Schreber who, in one phase of his illness, assumed a passive sexual position vis-à-vis divine penetration.)

Huysmans's remark to the effect that nothing much occurred in matters of religious conversion between *A rebours* (1884) and *Là-bas* (1891) is not entirely accurate. True, the preoccupations of the two novels remain similar, but in the interim separating them an important inversion has nonetheless been operated. The discourse of neuropathology, dominant in *A rebours*, has become explicitly subservient to the theme of thaumaturgy in *Là-bas*. This coup de théâtre is crucial because no longer will mental illness be accorded the status of prime cause, but rather it will be invoked as a *manifestation* of the occult, indeed much as it was in the Middle Ages. The genre to which *Là-bas* adheres is still that of the case history since one of the two principal narratives is a clinical discussion of the pathological Gilles de Rais complete with documentary evidence. Now, however, it has become a matter of diagnosing the ills of the spirit. In this way, in the seven-year gap which separates these novels, the two-headed monster of materialism and positivism has been vanquished. Henceforth in Huysmans's work, the spiritual will reign.

Of course the irony of this shift lies in the fact that neuropathology now assumes an adversarial posture. And the proponent of this scientific mode of explanation in *Là-bas* is none other than Doctor Charcot in person. Now, what Huysmans finds repugnant in the discipline which was then emergent at the Salpêtrière Hospital is Charcot's reduction of demonic presence to mere symptoms of hysteria. In *Là-bas*, des Hermies, the doctor who has lost his medical faith through contact with the "Inexplicable," declares that the notion of hysteria is secondary and in itself explains nothing: "Yes, without doubt Charcot is good at pinpointing the phases of the attack . . . he finds the hysterogenic zones and, by adroitly manipulating the ovaries, can slow down or speed up the crises, but . . . as for knowing their sources and causes, as for curing them—that's another matter!"

There is some truth to this Pascalian sulk. Like Bouchut before him, Charcot does establish a nosology of hysteria, but he fails to explain it except in terms of heredity. It will, in fact, take Freud to remove the neuroses from the materialist arena through postulation of an unconscious. Meanwhile, as Gaillard observes apropos of *A rebours*: "Just as a photograph at the moment of development, it [the fiction] will reveal, in the very processes through which it takes form, that which it does not suspect itself of knowing: *medicine's blind spots*". If Huysmans has unwittingly uncovered and displayed the holes in the neuropathological edifice (and Charcot's caustic remarks against des Esseintes-like creatures seem to bear out Gaillard's argument), then perhaps this text worked similar unconscious magic on its own author, by turning him away—perverting him—from his old patterns of predilection.

A satisfactory cause of hysteria thus lacking, at least for the time being, Huysmans is free to turn the tables on science as he had earlier done on nature in *A rebours*, in a movement from perversion toward conversion. Madness becomes a mere symptom of diabolic presence which is now promoted to the status of prime mover. Victims of possession, advances des Hermies of *Là-bas*, "end up mad. The insane asylums are overflowing with them. The doctors, even most of the priests do not understand the causes of their dementia . . ." If all of science remains powerless to determine the true cause of the disorder, as does most of the religious community, Huysmans has left himself one critical loophole: mysticism. The Church may be the "hospital of souls" (*En route*), but Durtal diagnoses his own ill as (inevitably) "dyspepsia of the soul," and his case of digestion/conversion requires more esoteric attentions which can only be dispensed at a Trappist monastery.

After sniffing about the robes of the Church for two novels already, it is hardly surprising that the Huysmansian protagonist balks considerably at such a dire solution. Urging—indeed almost forcing—Durtal to come to this decision is the good priest Gévresin, who exhibits monastic tendencies himself. What is remarkable is that the act of persuasion which takes place against Durtal's will resembles des Esseintes's encounter with the dentist to an uncanny degree. Gévresin, "hitherto so discreet, suddenly flung himself on Durtal's being and *opened it violently*. . . . And Durtal . . . agreed that the priest was right and that he had to *stop up* the pus of his senses and expiate for . . . their abominable desires; their *decayed* tastes [goûts cariés]; and he was overcome by an intense, irrational fear (emphasis added).

Reading across these two texts which define each pole of the author's conversion, one does indeed find the continuity which he proclaimed in the 1903 preface to *A rebours*. The forcible sodomy performed by the dentist on des Esseintes ("the man . . . flung himself upon him [des Esseintes] as if he wanted to plunge his arm to the far end of the abdomen") is repeated here in the same terms. The rape perpetrated by Gévresin may well be a spiritual one, but it is wise to bear in mind what I have been at pains to demonstrate: namely, that at all times the Huysmansian discourse equates dyspepsia, mental pathology, and disorders of the soul. In Huysmans's case, it is abundantly clear that the body's stigmata are irremediably branded onto the representation of the soul, or, perhaps more accurately, the text of the flesh is inscribed forever in the language of the soul.

The two quotations above indicate that both des Esseintes and Durtal have been forcibly penetrated for therapeutic purposes. At this point, however, important differences between the twin operations emerge. The dentist, it will be recalled, was but a vulgar practitioner. Thus his function—limited to ridding the organism of an undesirable presence—could be termed exorcistic in nature. He lacked the ability to "fill the cavities and seal up the holes," and, anyhow, at that stage on life's way, the Huysmansian hero has no intention of rendering his stomach/mind/soul hermetic because it is precisely the access to an elsewhere which he holds dear and on which his art depends. In contrast, the Durtal of *En route* has acquiesced to the idea ("convenait") that the cavities must be filled if conversion is to take place. It has become apparent that sealing the apertures is the only guarantee against the Devil.

Unfortunately the horns of the Devil are also the horns of a dilemma. It has been seen that good and evil penetrate the body in identical ways, often rectally. (The privileging of one alimentary aperture seems to carry with it a closing off of the other: in *A rebours*, des Esseintes rarely speaks, and at last, his mouth becomes useless for feeding purposes, while the miracles of *En route* can only be accomplished under a Trappist rule of silence.) How is one to know which supernatural power has penetrated, which words "emanate from God and not from our imagination or even from the Devil"? The evil Demon, brushed aside by Descartes in a similar formulation of the problem, is not so easily dispatched by Huysmans, who realizes full well that "from lofty Mysticism to frustrated Satanism, there is but one step. In the beyond, everything touches" (*Là-bas*). Furthermore, divine invasion as Durtal experiences it is not unequivocably pleasurable: "It must be admitted that it is most disturbing to feel that infusion of an invisible being into one's being, and to know that it could nearly evict you, if it so chose, from the domain of your own person" (*En route*).

The dilemma alluded to earlier is the following: openings permit supernatural penetration, although one can never be sure of the identity of the occupying force, but closing the holes could entail sealing in Satan and thus the soul's perpetual annexation by the Devil. Besides making the state of grace uncomfortably analogous to a state of constipation, Huysmans's peculiar representation of religion in gastrointestinal terms has led him to a theological impasse.

Indeed, in the course of these three key works, J.-K. Huysmans has ensnared himself in a web of his own spinning. The contrapuntal play of discourses in *A rebours* (neurological, digestive, and demonic) is reinforced and embroidered upon in *Là-bas*. With devilish force and by dint of accumulated metaphor, the text turns against its maker in *En route*, which spends many an anguished page wrestling with the Demon. The final solution—something of a *truquage*—lies outside, in the doctrine of mystical substitution.

Ironically enough, for Huysmans, the author of interiors if ever there was one, no help can be sought from within. Mystical substitution allows the expulsion of diabolic influence from weaker souls by projecting it onto consenting "victims" who compose certain contemplative orders such as the Poor Clares. The Poor Clare, weak of body but staid of soul, thus serves as a decoy, substituting herself for the intended victim of the attack. As Gévresin explains in *En route*, "They draw the demonic fluid upon themselves" and Durtal benefits from their intercession during his own arduous conversion.

The Huysmansian gastrointestinal representation of soul may strike one as idiosyncratic, if not downright obscene. Yet it is important to realize that this highly personal *vision du monde* poses the larger problem of man's linguistic relation to the divine. In what language, code, or system of signs, through which incantations, prayers, or ritual acts can the sacred by grasped from out of the profane? Yea—how can the discourse of mysticism *not* be forged out of the flesh forever to bear its imprint? From Huysmans's case we stand to learn that all language, however exalted, is grounded in the body.

Brian R. Banks   (essay date 1990)

SOURCE: "The Works," in *The Image of Huysmans,* edited by Brian R. Banks, AMS Press, 1990, pp. 83-139.

[*In the following essay, Banks provides a survey of Huysmans's fiction written during his Naturalist, Decadent, and Catholic phases.*]

LE DRAGEOIR À ÉPICES, 1874

On October 10, 1874, Huysmans published at his own expense through the Dentu house a series of prose poems that marked not only his debut, but also something of a signpost for his whole life work. From the two known manuscript states and various notebooks together with newspaper files and personal anecdotes, we know that the material was not only used for articles throughout the formative years of the 1870s, but also as a touchstone for ideas on a larger scale. Apart from the reprinting of **"The Herring"** and **"Ritornello"** in *Croquis Parisiens* (1880), many of the elements that run through his work may find their embryonic seeds here, including *A Rebours* (1884). Such works grew from the same stem.

The powerfully scented, overloaded fruits are generally traced to the Romantic Aloysius Bertrand and Charles Baudelaire, and, as with those two poets, gamy decadence mingles with an earthy realism. Bertrand's famous *Gaspard de la Nuit* was subtitled "Fantasies in the manner of Rembrandt and Callot," which finds echo in Huysmans's dedication "Aux vieux amis j'offre ce drageoir fantasque et ces menus bibelots et fanfreluches." Here he is the tapestry rack-master of Baudelaire's themes woven into little, piquant tales. **"Repeated Theme"** could serve as a synopsis of the bulk of Realist/Naturalist literature, where a street-seller with three children is freed from her bullying drunkard of a husband only to end up after his death with another just the same, but with six children and the same lamentable refrain. It is extended, with Villonesque flavor, in **"Chlorotic Ballad"** and **"Ecstasy"** where an idyllic tryst is broken by the natural functions of the protagonist's lover! "Ballad in honour of

my so sweet torment" is a paean upon the beauty of precious gems, and with **"The Enameller"** might have been written at the time of *A Rebours*, just as **"The Left Bank"** in his series of Paris quarters in the 1890s, and **"Claudine"** in *The Vatard Sisters*. The descriptions of fêtes first shown here was constant throughout his later novels, and to add *spice* the sketches of Flemish artists alternate with pen-portraits of a prostitute and a Japanese geisha, a butcher's window and a vegetable market. Huysmans certainly took the smoke of Bertrand and Baudelaire, yet filtered through the prism of his heritage he crafted something fine and original, in spite of its limitations and the author's own view fifteen years later that it was "mediocre" in hindsight.

The originality of this "Comfit-dish of Spices" is often overlooked and invariably overshadowed by academic interest in the following works with their relationship to Naturalism (this being somewhat ironical, as the story goes that he spent what trifling profits there were on Zola's Rougon-Macquart novels to supplement his reading of Murger and Heine). As a slim, grey volume of just over a hundred pages it remained unsold until published orthodoxly (with a slight spelling change in the title and also his name) the following year.

In his diary dated 23 March 1886, Edmond de Goncourt noted a conversation he had with Huysmans in a café regarding these beginnings, when a publisher and some time author of children's books informed him that ". . . he had no talent whatever . . . wrote in an execrable style, and that he was starting a revolutionary Commune in the French language [for] he was mad to think that one word was better than another, to believe in the existence of superior epithets. . . ." He had been warned by this friend in his mother's initial letter inviting a meeting in the rue Jacob, which spoke of things probably unpleasant to hear and not "entirely complimentary," but afterwards his friends urged private publication.

It did not go entirely unnoticed. Théodore de Banville, a devout Hugoist and friend of Baudelaire who actually lived long enough to review *A Rebours*, was a critic of some eminence when he received a special copy of this work at his house. This somewhat smug, thin-lipped, completely bald old gentleman dressed in old fashioned clothes including a woollen waistcoat, called it in his review a "jewel of a master goldsmith, chiselled with a hand firm and light" and compared the author to Bertrand, Baudelaire, Flaubert, and the Goncourts—even if he did misspell Huysmans's name!

MARTHE, HISTOIRE D'UNE FILLE, 1876

On September 12, *Marthe* was published in Belgium, signifying the first appearance of Huysmans as one of his characters (Léo), which is to remain a leitmotif throughout his career as a novelist. In some instances, this work is the only source of information regarding his early years. *Marthe* is also the first of his characters to go *downstream*, another knot in the continuous thread of his works, for it develops certain themes from his first book in realistically treating the subject of relations between man and woman in an artistic setting, namely the theater and journalism. The "heroine" is a small-part actress in student revues, and the self-character is appositely a journalist working for shortlived periodicals, who enters as a spur and deviation from her normal circle of friends. One singular but constantly personal trait of these early novels is humor, sardonic and at times malicious; here, it is black as jet.

It had to be hurriedly completed, literally in a matter of weeks, when Huysmans heard of Goncourt's similar theme, eventually published as *La Fille Élisa*. Smuggled copies from Belgium sold for fantastic sums due to the misinterpretation of the title, and the edition was soon exhausted. It was republished in Paris three years later illustrated by Forain. There is actually nothing immoral in the book, and only one mention of a brothel. Huysmans spoke at the time in private that he had created a work of art because it was moral, and therefore anti-erotic. If there is any literary link, it is with Murger's *Vie de Bohème* and the Goncourts.

LES SOEURS VATARD, 1879

At the end of February, **The Vatard Sisters** was published and dedicated to his friend Émile Zola, whose own publisher brought it out. It was written somewhat under the Zolaist banner, who was "ravished" by it as well as critical of the depiction of the setting and characters and the style. It went to a second edition two days later.

Revolving around two sisters and their different views toward men and love, the novel enabled the author to utilise the family bookbindery where he lived and also his taste for the seedier adventures of Paris life. One contemporary French critic thought it little more than the portrayal of gutter vice, costing three francs fifty like his books, which is like blaming the engineer who lays the tracks for the pollution of the locomotive. It was actually watered-down in revision.

The descriptive passages are pure Huysmans: the Third Republic fairground, workshop world and poor districts of Nanaesque Paris, a music hall (resurrected from his first novel) as well as very probably the first description of a railway in French literature. All are admirably evoked in cameo. For the student there is a self-portrait (Cyprien), prototype of Folantin, des Esseintes, and Durtal later, the street where he lived over twenty years above the inherited bookbindery, and also the only portrayal of a mother-type not summarily dismissed in the first chapter. His sardonic view of mistresses and general disillusion with life are constant refrains in the early novels, and nowhere else more so than here, but it is description rather than characterization that is the forte.

It has been said that the novel was written in the first flush of the sensation of Zola's *L'Assommoir* (1877), and certainly there is the same innovative use of street language through the voice of the narrator, but there are also very definite links with the Goncourts and Flaubert. In a pseudonymous self-portrait in 1885, Huysmans called it a discovery of the bizarre temperament of the writer, an inexplicable amalgam of a Parisian sophisticate and a Flemish painter, fused with a pinch of black humor and rough English comedy, a chant of nihilism, a filthy, exact slice of life worthy of Steen (with beautiful pages, but he prefers **En Ménage**!) It confirmed him as a novelist, rather than a poetic disciple.

SAC AU DOS, 1880

Although this was published in *Les Soirées de Medan*, the collection of war stories by friends of Zola, there were various states in the preceding years successively called "Le Chant du Départ" and "Leproserie," as well as the variations under the same title. It seems, therefore, to have been a work more important than the place it eventually took, and certainly parallels another piece on the same theme of the 1870 Prussian war that was returned to throughout his life and eventually burned at his death: **"La Faim" ("The Hunger")**.

His war adventures were very probably a painful recollection, and not for the obvious reason of spending the duration in various hospitals because of stomach ailments. It is a vivid memoir, heightened following revision that eroded the cruder aspect of war in favor of sharpened observation. The autobiographical aspect also shows certain religious undertones, a profoundly touching episode of a nun's chaste ministerings and a singing of the Te Deum in celebration of his return. This exactly true account of an inauspicious time shows traces of his pessimism as a critic, a Rabelaisian tour de force of ferocious irony in its satire of patriotism not a little surprising in view of his daily tasks.

CROQUIS PARISIENS, 1880

This work, varied and multi-form and therefore because of its lack of classification a true Huysmans example, was revised and enlarged six years later with pieces from his first book and new poetical still lifes published in Bohemian journals like *La Cravache* since 1874. Due to its position chronologically, it has been labelled Naturalist, but this was discounted by Zola himself in his review of 15 June 1880 in *Le Voltaire*. Huysmans wished it to be a little more pungent, ". . . to create little sonnets, small ballads, tiny poems, without the jingle of rhyme, but in language as singing as verse," he wrote to that author a month before, in the decadent ethos of the *Abbé Mouret*. It is like a book of etchings with Villonesque refrains. Reviewing the later edition, Léo Trezenick in the weekly journal appropriately called *Le Lutèce*, wished to cure himself of the disgust brought about by reading Zola's *L'Oeuvre* "by means of some kind of stimulant. And, on the most frequently visited shelf in my library my hand found a little flask covered with the dust of years, one of those whose contents are to be tasted with the tiny, expert sips of an epicure." An interesting view from a Decadent journal! François Coppée, on the other hand, believed it would be consigned to the lock-up section of public libraries, a view he more appropriately expressed regarding Loüys's *Aphrodite* in *Le Journal* of April, 1896.

This slim volume contains almost every subject that occurred in his novels, in microcosm. The Marthesque **"Folies Bergère"** with its brothel-like decor and humorous asides, when among the program's notices even for fencing schools, "for such fools do exist!", there is one upon sewing machines, "implements not normally used by girls who work in this place; unless it was placed there as a symbol of decency . . . perhaps, in another form, the equivalent of the moral pamphlets distributed by the English to bring corrupt creatures back to virtue." In the same vein is the series *Parisian Types,* where we find among others **"The Journeyman Baker"** fallen from a Watteau canvas, and the hairdresser's salon seen as a torture chamber with the heroism of monks and their horsehair shirts coming to mind on the way home (there is a parallel in *A Rebours* at a two-franc dentist, also seen in terms of nightmare). In the section "Fantasies and Forgotten Corners" a throwback to his first book, a strange piece entitled **"Damiens"** occurs where he imagines himself a tortured regicide about to be quartered by horses, presumably, for money is mentioned, to atone for sins of the flesh. **"The Washerwoman"** also has religious undertones, but that is just one of numerous threads here.

An air of Schopenhauerean world-weariness, a whiff of Mephistophelean smoke clings to the very fibers of these vignettes, which undoubtedly colored the famous *A Rebours* very soon after. In the first section (it is the first person singular employed) he dreams of Antwerp and how strange that one evokes in the place where one is the pleasures of the place where one is not, for "imagination is certainly a wonderful thing; it allows you to credit people with ideas even more foolish than those which they doubtless had"! This, of course, recalls the episode in that novel where des Esseintes decides not to trouble himself with the visit to England after sampling its atmosphere in an English tavern at Paris. Imagination, therefore, suffices both aesthetically and realistically.

The forward projection of ideas first encountered here is almost limitless. "Similitudes" overpowers the senses like *En Rade,* in the manner of his article on "the prince of mysterious dreams," Odilon Redon, which was later included in the enlarged 1886 version of *Croquis Parisiens*. The latter contains an extraordinarily wide field of reference, including Egyptian and Assyrian history, marine biology, ancient and medieval astronomy, while his review of a Wagner concert shows a growing interest in the religious Middle Ages (the early Christian poet Prudentius, for example, was discussed here rather than in *A Rebours,* which shows that Huysmans's tastes were wider and of longer duration than the later published material might indicate).

After Baudelaire, there is a "poem" to a dressmaker's dummy shop (**"Low Tide"**), a discourse on the Wandering Jew, the much-reprinted and quoted **"The Herring."** There is a transitory form of impressionistic decadence mirrored in his volumes of art criticism, especially on artists like Degas, Forain, and Rops where verbal paraphrasing of the pictures produces a heightened effect reminiscent of the "slashings" of Expressionism. It is realism brutal and stark, seen here in his views of women like the pitiful street-walker on her way to the workhouse or hospital for incurables. **"The Washerwoman"** shows a Baudelairean contrast between physical and spiritual decay on their road to the Cross. The **"Folies-Bergère"** is a caustic analysis of depravity, where one finds creatures stinking "deliciously" of the cosmetics of paid caresses, wearily motivated either by lucre or lust. One particular dancer is almost a Commune in herself, such are the passions aroused by her projected image of heavy paint and showy clothes. *Croquis Parisiens* caused quite a scandal, and had to sustain outraged attacks due to the risqué nature of some of the sketches such as **"The Armpit."**

In spite of its magic and glory, for Huysmans the beauty of a landscape was composed fundamentally of melancholy, and it tinges his Parisian view of **"The rue de la Chine," "The View from the Northern Ramparts,"** and **"The Bièvre,"** the latter returned to as a theme on several later occasions. It is another branch of his realism, no doubt inspired by the work of Raffaëlli. As in the earlier novels where the depiction of fairgrounds showed the course of his eye, so here we find the first chapter of an aborted novel planned as a study of tobacco girls in the working class district of Grenelle. Even his archetypal hero from *Downstream,* Jean Folantin, seems to have been pre-incarnated in **"The Prose Poem of Roast Meat"** (dedicated to a Government friend who lunched with him), where he muses that it is the "deceptive beef steaks and illusory chops served in public restaurants that foster the ferments of concubinage in the embittered minds of old bachelors."

Perhaps it is not surprising that such a volume should provoke the very first mention of the author in English— Paul Bourget's review in *The Academy* of July, 1880. Certainly, it was Baudelaire's poetry and poetical prose that touched Huysmans more than any work of the Realists; his favorite Zola work was the atypical *La Faute de l'Abbé Mouret.* It may have rung the bells of a time when he briefly contemplated becoming a poet at the outset of his career. There are various works later that show the same atmosphere as here, too diverse even to be seen as variations of a theme or as a clear definition of one particular artistic school.

EN MÉNAGE, 1881

There are glimpses again of Huysmans's love of Paris under certain of its guises in this novel, published less than a year after *Parisian Sketches.* The landscapes of the city's melancholy suburbs under different aspects, the bars and night zones, railway stations and gardens, buildings he loved or loved to hate, all reappear as by a refined and morbid colorist, whether rain or shine, dawn or dusk.

It revolves around yet another Baudelairean choice, that between Art (as Religion) and bourgeois cosiness as exemplified in the ideal of marriage, which ends by the creative impulse being drained or mocked on one side, and a critical eye being cast on the vanities and vulgarities of the other. It was a very real dilemma in the author's life. It was also his first novel to shift the emphasis from description—although there are some powerful scenes—to characterization.

For example, the two friends André Jayant and Cyprien Tibaille, who are an amalgam of the author, Jeanne (his long-time mistress Anna Meunier), the servants and various families, all intertwine through interior dialogue and psychological insights in a very personal manner, and decades before Proust. There is also a long description of his unhappy schooldays that is generally considered to be fairly accurate. While his personal *bête noire* of complaints about food hardly shows, that concerning the stupidity of people certainly does. A re-engaged housekeeper, for example, provokes satisfaction when he notes that her faults have neither increased nor decreased but remained stationary with the passing of time.

The pivot of the novel—André coming home to find his wife in bed with a stranger, in spite of her pretense at bourgeois respectability in the manner of Madame Bovary—actually occurs in the first chapter. His leaving her allows the author to philosophize on the relationship most suitable for a creative artist; but if that were all, it would just be another "modern" novel. It is the manner, through the whole repertoire of his unique style, as well as its faithfulness to true life, that lifts the work above the genre. Its pessimism and spleen toward the taedium vitae exemplified in bourgeois values is all the more surprising for its accuracy of a role the author never played in real life. The chronic melancholia crackles across the pages.

One French critic, borrowing the views of Bloy without acknowledgment in the L'Herne dossier on Huysmans recently published in Paris, considered the originality of *En Ménage* to be its treatment of the double nature of man: his body and its needs, his soul and its desires struggling to achieve quasi-equilibrium and quietude in the face of modern living for a sensitive individual. Life is viewed as an illness, a malady of which needs and desires are the symptoms, *à la Baudelaire.* The original title was to be *Un Bon Ménage,* a happy marriage, almost painful in its sarcasm in this context. *Living Together,* as it was called in M. Sandiford Pelle's translation, is a valuable and interesting document today as then, while the style proves the author to be one of the prose masters of Realism.

A VAU-L'EAU, 1882

This novel, one of the shortest by the author, also signifies the first appearance of one of his self-characters due to attain immortality in French literature (the others being des Esseintes and Durtal). They are all protagonists in the Greek sense, rather than heroes, with varying degrees only of his true character and environment. There is much here that points to the author's future as well as his past, from the echoes of *Marthe* to *The Crowds of Lourdes.*

Jean Folantin (Zola suggested the change of title from "M. Folantin" to *Downstream*) is slightly older, at 40, but the material is consistent with the real life civil servant in the 1870s. The fusty office with its stupid colleagues, a subsistence salary reducing him to respectable poverty (without the "basic luxury" of a housekeeper), the father's death when young, religious relatives in the "provinces" (Belgium in real life), nostalgia for the Saint-Sulpice area where he actually grew up, all are sealed here. Likewise, he wanders the quays and bookshops between the rue du Bac and rue Dauphine—before M. Eiffel crowned the landscape—overwhelmed by the new buildings and brightly-lit shops, regretting the destruction of old streets and forgotten lanes and loathing the omnibuses. The Right Bank fills him with nausea, its "vague suggestion of prostitution" viewed contemptuously as the invasion from the New World.

Folantin sees his life as a Way of the Cross, halting at each station in despair and self-pity, a sort of bookkeeper of petty miseries and ironies who could say that the inventor of card games ought to be blessed because such activity kept shut the mouths of imbeciles! (in *En Ménage* the variation went along the lines of the free trade of stupidity being suppressed). The reader is almost made to feel a victim, drinking the bitter lees of existence from this particular cracked vessel.

Yet in spite of Huysmans's reading and interest in Schopenhauer's nihilistic philosophy, religion is interestingly seen as an antidote to the misery of life, with certain reservations. He envied that calm life and the faith he had lost: "What better occupation, he thought, than prayer, what better employment of one's time than confession, what better outlet for one's energies than the practise of religion? You go to church, bury yourself in meditation, and the cares of this world become as nothing." Pious souls, he muses, are never bored and in their acceptance of life's trials are happy. But then, Folantin/ Huysmans harbors certain doubts as to their intelligence in accepting church dogma and the intolerance of priests, whom he views ironically but unbelligerently. Yet ". . . religion alone could heal the wound that plagues me."

In this "stomachic, bitter as wormwood" (in the words of Villiers de L'Isle Adam) barren as the plains of the Bièvre, the central character shows a surprising self-acceptance in allowing the annihilation of his health by such as café cooks, housekeepers, and concièrges. The author admits, in a different context, in the preface to *A Rebours* in 1903, to a lack of tenacity of purpose in worldly matters, which is a corollary to the passive receptivity of his art, put down in his own opinion to some unknown element and trace of direction outside of himself. One might say that his conscience is his art, and in *Downstream* it is stripped raw.

A manuscript was published in France in 1964 as a slim, 12mo volume with a two-page variant entitled "La Retraite de M. Bougran" (which R. Baldick thought lost after an auction sale). The original idea surfaced in a notebook of the author in 1886, probably earmarked for a persistent American journal. It describes a "functionaire" whose life becomes empty after retirement from the civil service. He decides to furnish his flat as an office, hire a messenger, and spend the rest of his days writing official letters to himself. And it is, of course, Huysmans's sardonic view of Huysmans at his daily tasks, another side of Folantin.

The anti-hero of *Downstream* was apparently modelled partly on Restif de la Bretonne's Monsieur Nicolas and Guy de Maupassant's Monsieur Patissot ("Dimanches d'un bourgeois de Paris"), in addition to Huysmans himself. It was also said to have been the inspiration for J. -P. Sartre's Roquentin in *La Nausée* and Duhamel's Salavin from the cycle *Vie et aventures de Salavin*. Folantin's existence is an odyssey of a dyspeptic, overwhelmingly sad in his dreary, respectable drifting *downstream,* life in *naturalibus veritas*. The subject, intensely drawn, is universal and undoubtedly successful within the narrow Naturalistic frame it is set in.

L'ART MODERNE, 1883

Huysmans's Naturalist phase is brought to a close with this volume, a collection of his essays from various journals, although it does not contain all his critical papers, for example, those that appeared in Belgium. In the foreword, Huysmans says that for the most part he is gathering articles that have already appeared in certain journals, and contrary to recognized opinion, believes it is good for the truth to be told. His stressing of the value and importance of Impressionism was roundly attacked by "official" critics, while his analysis of Decadent/Symbolist artists like Moreau and Redon was considerably ahead of its time (an interesting parallel because there are religious elements in his "Salon of 1879" essay). It is not exaggerating to say that these essays changed contemporary views toward art and brought the epoch, at last, face to face with modernity and the changing world.

The work consists of six essays on the official and unofficial exhibitions between 1879 and 1881, with the final one on the art and artists of 1882. The latter exhibitions, incidentally, were the ones where such art was forced to show itself, being beyond critical acceptance until this breath of change was blown. He poured scorn on the art Establishment in a revolutionary and unorthodox style, as did his friend Gustave Geffroy, although for different reasons, in his universality of art theory with its socialist implications. ("Art is the visible sign of the life of the spirit [consciousness] . . . the representation of the world by images reflected in us and of Man with everything

that exists" ("**La Vie Artistique**"). But Huysmans was non-political, with no particular axe to grind except a defence of true art, and with a curiously singular, overloaded style was incomprehensible to the crowd and "official" criticism.

In his self-portrait in 1885 under the pseudonym of A. Meunier, Huysmans believed *L'Art Moderne* the first book to seriously explain the Impressionists and assign to Degas the high place he deserves. He went on to say that having substituted the pen for the brush of his ancestors, this work had fallen among the young artists like a grenade—but its *repercussions* were wider than that. Huysmans, along with very few others, championed the movement from the beginning, as the Goncourts had done for Watteau and other eighteenth-century masters, and both directly through his essays and indirectly by using similar methods in his books. It caused one fellow-critic, Félix Fénéon, to dub Huysmans the "inventor of Impressionism," perhaps a little too generously.

While his enthusiasm was genuinely ardent, it was by no means uncritical, as faults were highlighted and deplored also. Huysmans regretted that the Impressionists did not turn their eyes away from the dazzling picnic fields and not so dazzling rustics (whom Francis Thompson thought "sprung from the illicit union of a mowing-machine and a turnip," in a Huysmansian vein!) toward the city districts, railway stations, abattoirs, brothels, and bars. Too often they recorded the merely incidental: a poppy field in 1868 does not differ intrinsically from any other, except according to the season. Degas, Forain, and Raffaëlli, the pictorial equivalents of Huysmans's and the Goncourts' novels, were praised for their "relentless abuse of humanity" in depicting their models/types in the starker moments of privacy and weakness. Renoir, Monet, Pissarro, Gauguin, Moreau, and Redon were all enthusiastically reviewed (as were certain English illustrators including Crane, Greenaway, and Caldecott at a time when Anglo-French interest was going the opposite way; Hogarth's realism had been praised some years before in *Marthe*). However, Courbet, Millet, and Chavannes were less kindly treated.

Huysmans's critiques are of the same atmosphere as his descriptive writings in the novels and prose poems, which have been seen as a straight development of Baudelaire and Gautier's prose sketches of nineteenth-century industrial and suburban life. The position he is given by today's historians, as for Baudelaire earlier, is that of the finest art critic of his generation, and only relegated perhaps when measured against the whole nineteenth century. His opinions are a barometer for art evaluation a full century later, with little if any modification.

A REBOURS, 1884

This was the power drill Huysmans used to blast himself from the cul-de-sac of Naturalism (and Zola's tutelage, in spite of Huysmans's comments to that author stating the contrary), and which he thought would find favor with only a few of his close friends. It turned out to be an incendiary device that would not only light the course of all his later work, but all the prose of the Decadent period from Lorrain to Gourmont, Wilde, D'Annunzio, Mallarmé, George Moore, and many others. A segment of the artistic age contemplated itself in the mirror held to it by the central character, des Esseintes. Overnight, this prototype anti-hero became immortal and one of literature's classic characters.

The Duc Jean des Esseintes was modelled partly on Folantin from *Downstream* as his first self-character, on King Ludwig II of Bavaria (who was allegedly the most happy when in an artificial indoor forest where mechanical lizards crawled through the painted foliage), partly also on Edmond de Goncourt, the dandy Barbey D'Aurevilly, and Baudelaire, and on the more commonly cited Comte Robert de Montesquiou, as noted in the Goncourt Journal soon after the novel's publication. Montesquiou apparently never met Huysmans, but admired his "great talent and unusual books," and it was the poet Stephane Mallarmé who told Huysmans about the inner secrets of the Comte's strange house, where each room was carefully fitted out like a film set before the invention of the cinema. The Comte was none too pleased with this violation, yet he was later to serve as the model for Proust's Baron de Charlus and probably Wilde's Dorian Gray. Another possible influence, although tenuous, is that of Wilkie Collins's *The Woman in White,* with its atrophic recluse Mr. Fairlie. The Duc has also been seen as an Edgar Allan Poe character (presumably after Roderick Usher), and certainly Huysmans read him, as Poe appears in both *A Rebours* and *La Cathédrale*. There is reason to believe that the American's reputation was at least considerably enhanced, if not established in France, by *A Rebours* in the wake of the earlier efforts of Baudelaire and Mallarmé, who translated his work. But such a writer as Poe was both "fascinating" and a "moral poison" Huysmans believed, and would only have had a limited or restricted influence in the making of such a complex, composite character.

Des Esseintes is a type, a self-creation of the art he adores. Moreover he is undoubtedly the repository of the author's secret tastes and untold dreams, to the extent of being unionized in their sickly sensibility and thirst for new and bizarre sensations, their yearning for solitude and abhorrence of human mediocrity. Only in reality was the wealth and the aristocratic breeding lacking, for it is Huysmans's first character who is not a diminution of himself. Certain characteristics and life paths bear resemblance, aside from the artistic tastes, even allowing for a novelist's licence: age around thirty, blue eyes and bearded, hollow cheeks, bad nerves and general health, straight nose and long, slender hands. An unhappy school life, confirmed through the earlier novels, and a father who was rarely around (probably due in real life to the difficulty finding commissions for his art work). Both parents were also dead by approximately the

same time as in the novel, with little known about the circumstances. Finally, a religious ancestry also coincides.

Unquestionably there is a good deal of the author invested in the work, as well as various excursions in "mental tourism." Huysmans is the essence of Esseintes, the emblematic shield of his opus up to that time, wherein the individualist broke the fetters and was successful, in literary terms, in the process. This atrophic, aristocratic scion is Folantin magically invested with the means for escape, which only really results in material agonies becoming spiritualized agonies. Both, indeed, were, actually christianized Jean (the religious name he took when becoming an oblate, although there is definitely no conscious connection in this point), while the Duc's house was in reality a place where he vacationed in 1881 for health reasons, namely nervous exhaustion.

As a Romantic hero may die from his artistic creativity, the gravest of mortal ills, so des Esseintes ebbs through his sensibilities. On one level, his agony is the inversion of Romantic idealism. The retreat from society was a dilemma very much realized by the Romantic hero-type and its creators: to associate with society produced pain, but to live like a hermit and forego ordinary pleasures resulted in the agony of solitude. The traits are in this character also: cosmological fatalism; Pessimism; aristocratic stoicism in the face of suffering and death, which may or may not be the pleasure substitute; hypersensitivity between self and society/cosmos; egomania or outcast syndrome, due to the notion of self-superiority; pathological rather than logical thought processes.

The Decadent is but the Romantic at the end of his road, and to some degree, Huysmans accepted where Esseintes drew back. His books are mosaics and masks behind which burns life; his taste for human sores and the tang of hospital, kitchen, and brothel, as Baldick put it, exists in the subconscious of *A Rebours*. No other novel weighs so heavily on the reader than this case history. It is the ethos of Baudelaire's "Anywhere out of the World," that decorated des Esseintes's wall. Léon Bloy was one of the most perceptive of the early critics of Huysmans's work (before the bile took over), and describes him through *A Rebours* as "formerly a Naturalist, but now an Idealist capable of the most exalted mysticism, and as far removed from the crapulous Zola as if all the interplanetary spaces had suddenly accumulated between them." He obviously ignored the realism there, even if it was idealized, indeed was at that time the secretary of that most anti of anti-Naturalists, Barbey D'Aurevilly. He, in turn, thought the work decadent, not because of its talent, but the way that talent was used, with its profusion of ideas and precious, overloaded style "[like] the precious stones in the shell of the tortoise . . . which kill it." (This strange episode, probably after Montesquiou's example, is even stranger in English—the tortoise becomes a turtle, with no mention of the need for water!).

But D'Aurevilly sees the suffering in the book, thereby exalting it beyond its talent, a moral anguish and despair as the rebel anti-hero realizes his own nothingness:

> "Des Esseintes is no longer an organic being in the same way as Obermann, René, Adolphe, those heroes of human, passionate, and guilty novels. He is a mechanism breaking down. Nothing more. . . . Huysmans has not just given us the confessions of a particular depraved and solitary personality, but he has at the same time written the nosography of a society destroyed by the rot of materialism. . . . Make no mistake! For a Decadent of this power to appear, and for a book such as M. Huysmans's to take root inside a human skull, we must truly have become what we in fact are—a race at its last gasp."

This invoking of Romantic hero-types from Senancour, Chateaubriand, and Constant was deliberate of course, but shows how rarely (if ever) the voyeur can be the voyant. Originally conceived as, in some sense, a Zola-like treatment of a town-dweller transposed to the country, a victim of race and environment that had affected the family blood (to be called "Alone"), the definitive version with its influx of wealth to satisfy the fantasies becomes de-naturalized, to become the "quintessence of everything under the sun", as the author's researches became the "extract of specialities, the sublimate of a different art" (Huysmans).

The result was a richly colored and fashioned Persian carpet, with a beautiful, complicated melody full of morbidezza, played to the sound of a single viol string. Edmond de Goncourt must have read the book immediately, for on 16 May 1884 his journal comments that it is as if written by a favorite son, the hero of which is ". . . a wonderful neurotic. They may say what they like against the book, it brings a little fever to the brain, and books that do that are the work of men of talent. And it is written in an artistic style to boot. . . . Yes, literature is making progress." And that was by a mentor, one who doubted Mallarmé's sanity!

And yet, the paradoxes remain. *Against Nature* or *Against the Grain,* to give its English titles, was written for a few friends, like Balzac's *Louis Lambert,* and as a means of breaking with the past, not as a credo for a movement, however nebulous. The follow-up novel was even more fantastic and picturesque, and yet as Naturalistic as the next work *Un Dilemme,* also in 1887. The aestheticism, with the walls bound like rich books and Latin authors specially printed and cased, servants dressed as Contemplatives, the tortoise which incidentally sparked a female fashion in live broaches etc., did not preclude a place among Moreau, Luyken, and Redon for Zola, Forain, and Raffaëlli. Do the historians consider such Realists as these "decadent," or the Catholic mystics like Bloy, Hello, and Bossuet whose works are discussed?

It is true that certain religious motifs or themes are decadent within the context that they are expressed, e.g., the church furniture and decorations, the "dim, religious light" and monasticism of certain rooms, the triptych of Baudelaire pieces ("The Lovers' Death"; "The Enemy"; "Anywhere out of the World") like an icon, Luyken's macabre torture scenes more a sadist's martyrology than a sanctified pictorial hagiography, even the Scriptural quotation in chapter five illustrating Moreau's art. Yet, Father Lacordaire's famous letters (in Paris, at least, after that Dominican's series of lectures at Notre Dame) do not suffer in their comparison with Schopenhauer's nihilist aphorisms, and des Esseintes "could never forget Catholicism, so poetical, so touching . . . whose essence he had absorbed through every pore."

The scene of the bedroom turned into a monastic cell has a monologue on the virtues of monasticism which would probably have been beyond Montesquiou's imagination, while most of Chapter 13 is spent dreaming of Benedictine monks and their life, which, through the subsequent chapters, culminates in a dissertation on the merits of pure plainchant against the latter-day church adulterations that come almost straight out of his *L'Oblat* twenty years later. Similarly, passages exist on the tampering with the species of Holy Communion that roundly turns on condemnation of the modern clergy—mixed in with criticism of the commercial ventures of the Orders—as he sees the Church as the only repository of the heritage of art through the ages, which is an interesting conjunction of the rituals with the art. Heresy, sacrilege, symbology, etc., all point to parallels or expansions found in his post-conversion work, showing the transitional element of that book.

The examples that academics of Decadence highlight are, of course, also fascinating, but they usually neglect the facets just outlined. As seen, the famous gem-encrusted tortoise may have died more from lack of water than the aesthetic weight it carried, the mouth organ of symphonic music on the palate, the sinister black banquet where the food, drink, ornaments and even servants are black, adds up to a very small amount of space—and sometimes only a paragraph!—compared to the Library, the voyage experiences including the Poesque cabin-room, the nervous disorders or disquiet, even the weather. The isolation of material in relation to the total proportion, coupled with the neglect of other areas, is ironically in its own way decadent!

However, the matter of Grace showing as early as *A Rebours* can also be overstretched. After all, several works including *Là-Bas* followed before the novel of conversion, and the author himself could not explain the reasoning behind the religious elements or the famous prayer-like ending that recalls Baudelaire's "Spleen de Paris." As early as *En Ménage,* his library contained Jansenist works among Charpentier's canary-yellow books of realism and Hachette's red foreign novels. Certain episodes can be traced to fairly contemporary secular sources. For example, the library divarications recall both the Goncourts' *La Maison d'un Artiste* and Cervantes's *Don Quixote,* where the barber and priest decide which books are more deserving of the fire. Rollinat's notorious *Les Nevroses* (1883) has a grotesque mistress who's also a ventriloquist ("**La Voix**"), just as des Esseintes has one miming the sphinx and chimaera to Flaubert's prose while in bed. Baudelaire's prose poem "Les Projets," which celebrates the making of plans rather than their execution, was probably transposed into his English tavern scene (after sketching it in **En Ménage** and **Downstream**), and the theme was very real in both writers lives. Two works by Villiers de L'Isle Adam that actually were published after the novel, may have been seen or heard about earlier (or influenced by *A Rebours*!) e.g., *Axel,* especially the last act, and *L'Eve Future* contain an artificial underground world. Older and more obscure sources have been cited earlier in the present work, in the bibliographical section.

A Rebours employs only a linear plot, and narration is relegated and deemed less important to the overall tone and theory. The tension exists between the art of decadence, in its historical as much as contemporary sense, and the demands of naturalism seen through the writer's own individual artistic temperament (the Zolaist aspect is absented via the use of dream and the strategy of memory, which also fulfills the role of action usually employed in novel forms). It is an internal quest through external influence like some flamboyantly realistic stained glass window, a record of aesthetic stimuli and responses to the sensations of the world in the manner of a far-seeing medieval hermit of the blood of Nostradamus. And it changed the course of literature, both French and European, both for its style and influence on artists and writers including Gustave Moreau, Redon, Forain, Bresdin, Carrière, Mallarmé, Villiers de L'Isle Adam, Verlaine, Corbière, championed as well as resurrected to influence every strand of modern literature as we now know it.

EN RADE, 1887

The follow-up novel to *A Rebours* might be seen to contain a hidden message in its title, which is impossible to translate with sufficient accuracy. One American biographer called it "At Harbor," a rather free rendering which misses the import of storm damage of the original, a nautical term. It also signified the longest gap between publications, as Huysmans sought a vehicle to carry his shift of attitude toward art and life. There is now a preoccupation with dreams and the invisible world.

This can be seen in an interest in the art of Odilon Redon, who became a close friend and lived nearby. Huysmans's review of the artist's series of lithographs entitled "**Hommage à Goya,**" reprinted in the revised edition of *Parisian Sketches* (1886), became as "Cauchemar" (Nightmare) a fantasia of his own. Five years earlier in his critique of the Independents, the artist's work was "a veritable transposition of one art into another" and "nightmare transported into art," and the illustrations to such literary material as Flaubert and Baudelaire found a ready kinship that was only severed

after *En Route*. Redon's art was, to a limited degree, what the man-of-letters wanted to do in his own art.

En Rade was the attempt, but deemed not totally successful in its results, although in truth it did have to be rushed to meet a serial deadline. The dream-blending, or synthesis, of the visible and invisible realities recalls Nerval in some respects, but without the "logic of the insane" that makes the Romantic's achievement more homogeneous with its aims. The contrived and somewhat inartistic separation of dream and reality was not only criticized by Zola, for the author in his reply agreed about this "two legs of a pair of trousers, one down-to-earth and the other up-in-the-air." While there is the torturous death of a cat and cattlemating, "enough to make a cowman blush" in Baldick's phrase, to show that Naturalism still found a place in his work, dreams and the world of the unseen are given equal weight and value.

The setting is a long-neglected, decaying chateau and the portrayal of the no less decrepit and depraved rustics of the immediate region. He believes the harvest, dirty and orange-colored, does not compare in effect with the beauty of a factory or steelworks, in a rather strained attempt to dispel and shatter people's illusion of the romantic countryside where the painted and idealized farmers in truth only stank of sweat and carousing. The astonishing descriptions of the house combine both arch-realism and a fulgent, decadent style almost too rich for *A Rebours*. There are dream sequences, including a lunar visit and a vast palace scene, where a slave girl is presented to a potentate amidst overwhelming surroundings. Jacques Marles, the central character whose wife is considered a true likeness of Huysmans's mistress, contains little or none of the author in his make-up, except perhaps in his anguish at the world, which is unusual in his work.

This novel, as much as its predecessor, greatly influenced the Surrealists and in particular André Breton, who considered Huysmans a precursor of their movement only a short way behind Rimbaud and Lautréamont. The sharp juxtaposition of dream with recognized reality counted with them as much as the art of Moreau and Redon (although the author's dissatisfaction seems as unimportant to them as to the Symbolists, even if it was a singular and constant trait). As with the Symbolists before him, Breton considered it the duty of the artist to rise above "bric-a-brac realism," a feat Huysmans later achieved in his eyes, for all would have agreed in viewing the mere portrayal of realism as mediocrity.

Breton, as father of that movement, much admired Huysmans who "shared with me that vibrant boredom which almost every sight caused him." In *Nadja* (1928), he says that although he never met Huysmans, "he still is, perhaps, the least alien of my friends," while earlier in a 1917 conversation Breton professed admiration for Huysmans as well as for the more obvious links of Jarry,

Mallarmé, and Rimbaud, according to J. Pierrot's *The Decadent Imagination* (1981). One can only speculate how far the bizarre imagery in fact travelled into the works of that artistic theory.

The influences upon Huysmans's somewhat uncharacteristic book might be seen in two sources mentioned in the famous Manifesto of Surrealism, Baudelaire's *Paradis artificiels* and Lautréamont's *Chants de Maldoror* (one French critic compared it with *le roman noir anglais,* the Gothic novels of Lewis and Radcliffe!). Huysmans certainly read the obscure Isidore Ducasse—"Comte de Lautréamont" was a pseudonym of the South American emigré—and privately praised the work in a letter to Jules Destreé in September, 1885, after receiving that scatologically satanic book when it was reissued in Belgium. Bloy had also reviewed it at the same time.

En Rade is generally described by historians as regressive, an opinion in sharp contrast to Bloy's contemporary review claiming it signified a new course for its author, even for one who acknowledged Charles Baudelaire, Flaubert, and Schopenhauer as his masters. Both opinions are extremes, for it was more a marking of time, taking stock of the situation to date, yet in its way the nearest amalgamation of a poem-in-prose, using the techniques of naturalism, that was to reach its zenith a few years later in *Là-Bas,* with the descriptively memorable word-painting upon the Grünewald Christ abandoned in a neglected Church as symbol of Christ's body under modern decay. It confirmed his evacuation from the pit of Zola's brand of Naturalism (and his publisher!) toward a framework that did not preclude the Imagination, and contained the sky and heavens in its perspective.

It is, therefore, to some degree an inversion of realism, practicing surrealistic methods involuntarily in its contrast of the real and fantasy worlds. In a revealing train of thought in the novel that was to be taken up again in chapter ten of *La Cathédrale,* Huysmans asks if, "in their hermetic madness did the dreams have a meaning? Was Artemidorus right when he maintained that the dream is a working of the imagination of the soul, signifying a good or an evil omen, and did old Porphyrus see correctly when he attributed the elements of dreaming to a spirit which warned us, during sleep, of the pitfalls which awakened life prepares?" This pungent, overloaded and overcharged atmospheric work was a virtuoso performance that culminated all his skills and artifices, and showed him setting out toward the new explorations that were to intertwine both his art and life. The central character's final departure might echo des Esseintes, but the attempt to assuage his distressing melancholy simply prefigures Huysmans taking his own road to Damascus, and it was a return.

UN DILEMME, 1887

This work should be seen rather as a nouvelle than a novel, which as a long short story is a definite genre in France, conforming to strict rules regarding length and format. It should be, traditionally, a narrative of a single and usually everyday situation and its characters with an element of the tragic, which leads to some sort of dramatic conclusion. Its exponents have included Voltaire, Vigny, Nerval, Flaubert, Camus, and perhaps most successfully Villiers de L'Isle Adam and Maupassant.

Although *A Dilemma* was dated 1887, it did not appear until February, 1888, but again was actually written in the Spring of 1884 as "a kind of antidote" in the author's mind to *A Rebours*. It first appeared in a journal in September, six months after the sensation created by that "poisonous" book, as a matter-of-fact account and explication of the moral duplicity and turpitude of the bourgeois, as it was understood by that great slayer of important nonentities, Ernest Hello. The setting is a small village in the Marne. Two of the central characters of the plot, such as it is within the nouvelle form, are types that Huysmans detested for their petty criminality or moral negligence: the lawyer and the politician, in this case his son. But the latter dutifully dies, leaving the father and son-in-law as sole heirs to the family fortune.

Yet, before he died, the son was cared for by a woman who is carrying his child. She appeals to the heirs for assistance, but is summarily dismissed with mutterings about the waste of postage in arranging the interview, only to die herself in childbirth. Her only friend petitions the same relatives for the burial expenses, who instead present the dilemma: either she was the son's servant, in which case there is a payment of wages due, or if simply a mistress she is "legitimately" entitled to nothing. She is the kind of creature that ". . . throws her hooks upon some family or sows discord in some home," as Huysmans has the bourgeois say.

The characters, or more exactly types, are drawn with that bitter sharp black humour that marked the Naturalistic *En Ménage* a few years earlier. The plot is the interrelationship of these men and women, living types but sketched as in a preliminary for an oil portrait. Outside France, it has been called Naturalistic (by Brandreth) and neither Naturalistic or Decadent (by Ridge), but a notable addition to that very French genre by both. It is only twice glancingly referred to by Baldick, perhaps because, unusually, Huysmans does not appear there.

A Dilemma is difficult to quantify, except perhaps in terms of seeing the author as still searching for the ideal subject and vehicle for his new direction. The book was virtually ignored by contemporary critics and did not sell. As with *En Rade,* there has never been a translation in part or whole of these works which, interestingly, are both set in a milieu that he detested. It falls in a period difficult to classify, the so-called middle period between *A Rebours* and *Là-Bas,* 1884-1891, which is also the least discussed by English commentators excluding the art criticism. If *A Dilemma* is Naturalistic, it owes more to Maupassant than Zola.

CERTAINS, 1889

This is a miscellaneous collection of critical papers on art and artists that is usually associated with the earlier *L'Art Moderne* in the minds of historians. This can lead to certain, subtle flaws, for **Certains** contains more of Huysmans's philosophical world view than the 1883 anthology of his art journalism. It also shows the spiritual turmoil he was passing through, with the answer to his quest very near at hand.

The book clearly is a defence of his opinions and a desire to "throw a lance" on behalf of emotional subjectivity for the evaluating of art. The role of art critic in a bourgeois world was not to his liking, as in the essay "Of Dilettantism" which is a virulent attack on materialistic "art lovers" and their press attendants. And he has this to say regarding the position of a true artist like Degas:

> I am not a prophet, but if I am to judge by the ineptitude of the enlightened classes, who, after having for long condemned Delacroix, do not yet suspect that Baudelaire is the poet of genius of the nineteenth century, that he towers a hundred metres above all the others, including Hugo, and that the masterpiece of the modern novel is the *Sentimental Education* of Flaubert—and yet, literature is said to be the one art that is most accessible to the masses!—if I am to judge by this, I can believe that this truth, which I am the only one to write today concerning M. Degas, will probably not be recognised until after an unlimited period of years.

His views on Degas are worth quoting more fully, not just for their original defence of an artist who was by no means near to public acceptance at this time, but also because they afford an insight into the development of Huysmans's own personality:

> M. Degas, who in his admirable pictures of dancers had so implacably rendered the moral decay of the mercenary female, her mind dulled by mechanical gambollings and monotonous jumping about, has on this occasion with his nude studies, contributed a lingering cruelty, a patient hatred. It seems as though, exasperated by the baseness of his surroundings, he has resolved to proceed to reprisals and fling in the face of his century the grossest insult, by overthrowing Woman, the idol which has always been so gently treated and whom he degrades by showing her naked in the humiliating and intimate positions of her private toilette. And the better to recapitulate her origins, he selects a women who is fat, drum-bellied and short, burying all grace of outline under tubular rolls of skin, losing from the plastic point of view all dignity; making her, in fact, regardless of the class to which she belongs, a pork-butcher's wife, a female butcher, in short a creature whose vulgar shape and coarseness suggest her countenance and determine her horribleness!

> . . . Such are the merciless positions assigned by this iconoclast to the being usually inanely showered

with fulsome gallanteries. In these pastels there is a suggestion of mutilated stumps, of the rolling motion of a cripple—a whole series of attitudes inherent even when she is young and pretty, adorable when reclining or standing up; but froglike and simian when, like these women, she has to stoop to masking her deterioration by this grooming.

But in addition to this special accent of contempt and hatred, the most obvious thing in these works is the unforgettable veracity of types caught with a simple, basic draughtsmanship with lucid, controlled passion coldly but feverishly . . . the warm, veiled color of these scenes, their rich, mysterious tone, the supreme beauty of flesh turning to blue or pink under the water, lit by closed, muslin-draped windows in sombre rooms where the dim light from a courtyard reveals wash-basins and bathtubs, bottles and combs, the glazed boxwood backs of brushes.

This is no longer the smooth, slippery, eternally naked flesh of goddesses, the flesh seen in its most inexorable formula in a picture by Regnault—a picture in which one of the three Graces displays a pair of buttocks made of pink, oiled muslin and lit from inside by a night-light; this is real living unclothed flesh, turned in its ablutions to goose-pimples which will gradually soften away.

Of the people who visited this exhibition, some, confronted by the woman squatting full-face, her belly disclaiming the usual deceptions, would exclaim aloud, indignant at such frankness, yet gripped by the life that emanates from these pastels, they would end by exchanging some shamefaced or disgusted remarks and move away, uttering as their last word: "It's obscene!" But never was work less obscene, never was work so free from precautionary tricks and ruses, so entirely, decisively chaste. Indeed, it glorifies the disdain of the flesh as no artist has ventured to do since the Middle Ages. . . .

Huysmans would go out on a limb whenever his views were felt strongly enough, even to the point of contradicting accepted mores. And so also with regards to Gustave Moreau and Felicien Rops, although the reasons for conducting their defence may be more ambiguous, for they also served as useful foils for syntactical swordplay. Havelock Ellis in *The Dance of Life* thought that Huysmans was only really attracted to their programs because they produced a stimulus for his own special art, and private comments by Huysmans seems to bear this out. But there is the subtlety mentioned earlier. The first collection of art essays which looked at the same artists spanned several years of his early Naturalist period—the embryo of his critical achievement—that was simply given their seal of approval in *A Rebours* (with additions, like Bresdin), where the author condensed his loves and hates in chapter form. In *L'Art Moderne,* artists were chosen for their stand and quality of vision, almost independent of the writer, but in *Certains* they were chosen for their kinship, their searchings that paralleled his own among every spiritual pharmacy known to artistic addicts.

He was on the path to a stern, medieval Catholicism through the back door and by way of the fire escape. The shift of attitude cannot be overstressed as profound literary and psychological symbols combined with deep ideals now entered the arena. Even the avowedly erotico-satanic art of Rops provided an opportunity to give the Catholic position toward sin, just as Moreau had for rituals and prayer, Whistler and Redon for the part-veiled world of the spirit. Unlike his predecessors, Felicien Rops did not confine himself.

> to rendering the attitudes of bodies swayed by passion, but has elicited from ignited flesh the sorrows of fever-stricken souls and the joys of warped minds, painting demonic rapture as others have painted mystical yearnings. Remote from his century, from an age when materialistic art can see nothing but hysterics eaten up by their ovaries or nymphomaniacs whose brains beat in the regions of their belly, he has celebrated not contemporary woman, not the Parisienne, whose simpering graces and dubious finery are not for him, but the essential and timeless Woman, the naked malignant Beast, the mercenary handmaid of Darkness, the absolute bonded slave of the Devil.

Huysmans thought that the theory of environment so famously posited by Taine worked effectively in reverse for such artists, filling them with hatred and revulsion that acted as an irritant to their artistic sensibility, a seed for their isolation. The results are seen in Poe, Baudelaire, Flaubert, the Goncourts, Moreau, Redon, and Rops (i.e., all of his personal likes!), "exceptional beings who retrace their steps down the centuries and, out of disgust for the shameful promiscuities which they are forced to suffer, throw themselves into the abyss of the ages, into the tumultuous spaces of dream and nightmare." Purity was dead and inaccessible to art since the time of Grünewald and Roger Van Der Weyden, he believed, while his style seems to show traces of his outcast friends Bloy and Villiers as he becomes almost expressionist in views and taste—virulent, excessive, bizarre in the spirit of Munch, Rouault, and Ensor, rejecting not only staid classicism and the merely anecdotal methods of Academics, but also art that was avant-garde for its own sake.

Art became all-consuming in *Certains,* rather than the hitherto all-pervading, and, mingled with Huysmans's slowly developing religiosity, the ordinary world became even more unbearable than ever. Its symbols were an opportunity for derision, like the Exposition as the Mecca of Mugwumpery and the newly-built "gravy-colored ironmongery" of M. Eiffel, that was simply "infundibuliform lattice-work, that bottle wickered in painted straw, that solitary suppository riddled with holes." He was seeking through art a means of escape from modernity, into various forms of vagueness such as fantasy, mysticism, the Middle Ages, and the occult. And within ten years, he would deplore the nullity of modern

art and regret the time of Moreau and Degas, that "most original and daring of Impressionists" who had accompanied the author in far-off days to the theater to study circus performers.

Most art historians in English dislike where these essays lead, but it is contentious to hold that he ignored the "best" of contemporary art, because it oversimplifies the fact that he was not a critic by trade. He only wrote about things he loved or hated, according to his own lights (moreover, there is a good deal of material uncollected, especially upon individual artists). Some may regret that he did not turn his pen to, say, Van Gogh or Lautrec (he would not have looked kindly on noisy cabaret life, with its vulgar patriotic ditties paralleling academic military art), but a case might also be made for the Nabis that included Denis and Vuillard whom his friend Paul Valéry championed later, and whose paths were not dissimilar. Still, there is much to savor in *Certains,* and readers today might well be surprised that the valuations were made a hundred years ago. For, with the possible exception of a rather narrow view toward Cézanne that was perhaps over-influenced by Zola, the present status of his loves and hates have moved very little, if at all, from the time they were made. And on the biographical side, it importantly provides an insight into his spiritual development, for here Huysmans sees, if dimly and unclearly, the light at the end of his journey, prefiguring *Là-Bas.* It is almost as revealing as any of his novelistic self-portraits, with the exception of Durtal in the subsequent novels.

LA BIÈVRE, 1890

Although this work extends the hiatus away from his novels, it is also undoubtedly part of the true Huysmans as he wished to project himself. A gamy, Goncourtian sketch of a poor Parisian working district becomes an ideal subject and vehicle for this sharp impressionist. He had read the evocations of that river district by Balzac, Hugo, the Goncourts, and Baudelaire in "Parisian Dream." The subject initially found expression in his very first book, where he leaves the noisy Boulevard Montparnasse to wander the lanes around the meandering rivulet, "framed by bizarrely melancholy prospects, which have on me something of the effect of distant memories or of the desolating rhythms of Schubert's music."

There is another piece of the same atmosphere in *Parisian Sketches* and this had appeared earlier in an 1877 periodical. This in turn was a preliminary version for the essay that appeared in a Dutch journal in April, 1886, which was published in its own right by Genonceaux four years later. The history shows the durability and depth of interest the subject held for Huysmans, yet it became naturally colored by his shifting attitude toward life itself: it became a symbol.

This work on one level describes the pitiful condition to which modern industry had reduced the second river of

Paris, the river that had provoked a famous anecdote of Rabelais, but by Huysmans's time had partly become a section of the municipal underground sewage system. Then, something more like a miserable, degraded half-sewer and half-canal, full of dead cats and floating abominations, winding a slow way through the backs of slums and the noisome yards of tanneries and dyeworks. It was formerly a prairie-like region, in winter a vast plain of ice inaccessible as the arctic, but the broken, narrow lanes had their cabarets and *guinguettes* (small, surburban taverns with music) where children played and hunted wild rabbits in the beer-gardens. But industrialization turned it into a "lost quarter," dangerous at night and out of bounds to the solitary wanderer. For Huysmans, it became no longer one of the old districts which he and his friends could explore on Sundays—in spite of its having escaped Haussmannization—smoking endless cigarettes and breathing the distinctive air beneath skies that rarely met with approval. Landscape became as changed for them as the dedications in *Parisian Sketches* became discolored by age.

By the time of World War I, one would need his book in hand even to try to resuscitate the streets and alleyways around the Gobelins and the orchards belonging to that factory, according to the Académie Goncourt book *The Colour of Paris,* where the hovels elbowed each other beside the bank of the muddy, rust-colored stream, and the beflaked workers and washhouse queens wended their way beneath original street oil lamps. Nature, for Huysmans, was only interesting when weak and distressful:

> I do not deny her magic and glory when her great laugh bursts her corsage of dark rocks, and she brandishes in the sun her green-tipped bosom. But I confess I do not feel before her displays of vigor that tender charm which is produced in me by a desolate spot in a great town, a bare mound, a little stream weeping between two frail trees. Fundamentally, the beauty of a landscape is made up of melancholy.

It is in the later version of 1890 (but to be returned to twice more in 1898 and 1901) that he introduced the spiritual element into this prose poem: later French publishers, indeed, include this volume in his oeuvre Catholique. The river becomes a girl fresh and innocent from the country, who, as soon as she approaches the city, is forced to exchange her rural finery for the garb of a slattern, to be imprisoned in drab, grey walls and brow-beaten, over-worked and eventually corrupted by her employers, for industrialism is seen as synonymous with pimpery. If the author was constantly criticized for his realism, he in some ways sought escape whenever possible with the aid of symbols. He magnifies the sadness of the spot, but is violently indifferent to the possible municipal idea of alleviation:

> The Bièvre, with its desperate attitude and reflective, suffering air, delights me more than any other, and I deplore the destruction of its trees and

gullies as the greatest of crimes! This suffering landscape, this ragged stream, these broken plains were all that was left to us, and now they are going to be dismembered! Every section of land will be put up for sale, every bowlful of water auctioned off, the marshes will be filled in, the roads will be levelled, and the dandelions, the brambles, and all the flora of the rubbish heaps and the waste land will be torn up . . . disappear, together with the heathland, choked up with slag and rubbish, broken up by old pipes and flower pots, scattered here and there with puddles, piles of ashes, and rotten, fly-blown fruit, and filled with the stench from the wet mattress-straw and the piles of filth gradually gathering in the porridgy mire; and the melancholy view of an Artesian well and the Butte aux Cailles and the distant prospects in which the Panthéon and the Val-de-Grâce, separated by factory chimneys, raise their violet domes against the glowing embers of the clouds, will soon give way to the foolish joys and banal delights of new houses!

Huysmans continues in this strain and builds to a fine crescendo as he laments in true Romantic fashion such desecration of nostalgia, which he knows will only end in various forms of whitewash. A fugitive artistic impression allows him to disregard the arguments in favor of hygiene, embroidering the rags with a pen of gold and retouching the crumbling walls with the magic of his style.

As the dedicatee of the 1886 version, Henry Céard provides an important and evocative memory of these excursions:

> We used to wander along in the fetid summer twilight, admiring the reflection of the setting sun in the brown waters dotted with green weeds. Ah! the rue Croulebarbe and the Passage Moret—how well he has described them! And when we came to the end of the long lane skirting the Gobelins factory, we would make for a restaurant on the Avenue d'Italie, the Restaurant de l'homme decore. This was not its real name, but an allusion to Coppée who was then the only one among us who wore a red ribbon. . . .

> After dinner, in a night full of the sounds of children at play and of washing flapping against the windows of sordid laundries, we would continue our explorations of districts that are now neither accessible nor recognisable—for the Highways Department has diverted the Bièvre from its course, dried it up and disinfected it, while the Orléans Railway Co. has filled in its leprous swamps in order to lay the foundations of its locomotive depots. Nothing now remains but Huysmans's pages illustrated by Raffaelli. . . .

François Coppée also wrote affectionately, in gratitude this time, probably for being sent a copy of the 1890 edition:

> I knew her when she was still something of a rustic . . . this Bièvre to whom you have devoted such

intensely artistic pages. How right you are to compare her to a girl of the fields debauched by the big city! To think that perhaps at her source, she sets the water cress a-quivering, and that she dies in squalor, like a beggar woman of the Faubourg Saint Marcel! You have put this into the most marvellous words, and all Parisians who truly love their Paris will be grateful to you for your work.

And so, in spite of not being one of the better known titles and in a minor key, boasting less than fifty pages, it was probably closer to the author's heart than the bulky, erudite work he consecrated to Decadence. In its poetry and melancholy view, *La Bièvre* is quintessentially Huysmans. It marks the end of his so-called middle period and its searching, yet is something of a relaxation from the intense progression of his novels and their psychological analysis, at once a throwback to the time of Naturalism with its grimy descriptions, and a foreshadowing of his later spiritualism with its concern for the eternal problems of the human soul, in short, a compressed tour de force with the heady, extracted juice in combination with carefully selected illustrations, producing a powerful sense-impression. The renowned Edwardian traveller E. V. Lucas, thought it one of the best examples of imaginative topography he knew.

LÀ-BAS, 1891

Of all Huysmans's works, this is the one that critics and historians in English attack the most sharply, even at times wishing it was not written (in agreement with the English civil courts in the 1930s). Yet, the opposite view was taken in France at the time. Edmond de Goncourt was as enthusiastic as when *A Rebours* appeared. His diary, written during the serialization in February, 1891, thought the prose too good for a newspaper and a joy to wake up to, containing rich writing with some bold thinking behind it. But not even he could know where the book was taking its author.

The work is complex and interweaving, with sub-narratives adding to the fascination. It opens with an argument for and against Naturalism, a "blind alley [of] romances without doors or windows." After paying respect to Balzac, he sees the main highway as Zola, but importantly with a parallel one in the sky, to take account of the soul as well as the flesh and senses, to be called spiritual-realism, not unlike Dostoevsky but without the politics. Grünewald and the Primitives are deemed the supreme example in art, and mystics like Ruysbroeck and Emmerich in "literature."

This is linked to his views upon history and its importance over and above not only science, which he has no faith in, but also the novel, in its role as an important medium for men of talent. Personally, he was rejuvenated by his new study of the Middle Ages and such characters as Gilles de Rais, the satanic child-torturer and murderer who laid whole regions waste with his insatiable crimes. This is an important sub-plot throughout, a novel within a novel, for he sees the Middle Ages as only understandable by its individuals. Ordinary historians, those without talent, cannot even explain such recent events as the Commune or Revolution, let alone such a period of wild extremes. It needs an historian of the caliber of Michelet to use history as a springboard for ideas and style, to render the battles in space between science and faith, for even now positivists and atheists have not succeeded in overthrowing Satanism. Now, "men believe in nothing and swallow everything. Every morning they invent a new science. . . ." The end of medieval wisdom, now almost forgotten, was put into motion by the systematic and hostile indifference of a godless people, he believes, who tore the soul from France, with nothing left for them to do but to fold their arms and listen to the "insipid twaddlings" of a society that can only grouse and frivol its life away. Successive centuries have destroyed instead of mending, and amidst "all the lunacy of a people ill-fed, overfull of alcohol and armed" only the monks and demoniacs now join us to the Middle Ages, "the only decent era humanity has known." It is a major shift in attitude, for in his first book the period was not at all seen in terms of a "lost paradise."

It is probable that a new edition of the abbé Bossard's biography in 1886 set Huysmans off in search of Gilles de Rais, the Bluebeard of legendary history. He was of that type most interesting to the author, by virtue of being outside or beyond their time, although firmly rooted there. He was a monster, a hybrid creature of contrasts, the ultimate archetype, and only extremes interested Huysmans. This former fighter beside Joan of Arc went to the opposite pole and became "the most artistic and most refined, most cruel and most abominable" of human beings who ever lived. The first phase is examined from chapter four onward, when his great taste and refinement made him a "des Esseintes of the fifteenth century," until in subsequent, alternate chapters his alchemical and diabolical studies lead him to be outlawed by king and pope, culminating with the view that he makes de Sade seem but a "timorous bourgeois and paltry dilettant beside him." Chapter eleven is the much-censored "terrible chapter," wherein Huysmans recounts Bluebeard's pact with the Devil and lists his awful crimes and sins, and using the full battery of his realism to produce in the reader absolute nausea. In the last chapters, the arrest, trial, and execution are retold, which allows Huysmans to aim some shots at the stupidity of crowds, for in Bluebeard's time the reaction of people was "a long way from the Lynch Law" of the American Wild West, which he must have read about, and becomes a parallel for the mob cheering General Boulanger's election in the Place Saint-Sulpice, beneath the Church bell tower where he is discussing such matters. Huysmans also recounts (chapter eight) a visit he made to Gilles de Rais's ruined castle at Tiffauges, the unchanged landscape and local costumes, and in a fine prose poem imagines the interior, the feasts, etc. in a manner reminiscent of *A Rebours*.

Among some passages of the novel that recall the naturalism of **Downstream**—anti-concièrge views, restaurants and kitchen stoves, pessimism about the future and what will happen to the children, his cat seen as a bachelor's "spiritual discharge-tube of loneliness and celibacy"—Huysmans weaves his subtle and complicated thread around the central themes which are the import of the book. But one of them is a hangover from the earlier period, and is the only tiresome aspect: the slow development of the identity of a female admirer, together with the intrigue and subsequent love-making with the woman he calls Madame Chantelouve. One must assume it is a novelist's device to render a mundane counterpart to the Mysteries (which she initiates) and the supra-terrestrial activities of Gilles de Rais, as well as provide reasons for his misogyny.

Another theme is the unifying treatment of historical and modern Satanism, which is usually a matter of debate in Saint-Sulpice's tower. The exception to the rule is when he witnesses a Black Mass with Mme. Chantelouve. With the fictitious bell-ringer Carhaix, the latter's library becomes an opportunity to recount his documentary sources and love of ancient books, reveal his antipathies to modern medicine in the light of the healing powers of magic and cures of Lourdes, the symbolism and hierarchy of bells and the miracles attributed to them, the history of spiritual phenomena including the Fox family in America and W. Crookes, the views of Paracelcus, even rebel and renegade priests together with what sanctions they might incur from the Church—just as Chantelouve's house library was a passport to discuss certain extraordinary saints.

The contemporary Satanists that figure in **Là-Bas** were, however, quite known to him in real life. Peladan, "cheap-jack magician and mountebank of the Midi," Papus and the Rosicrucians who used to frequent Montmartre cabarets like the Chat Noir are ridiculed as old journalists, charlatans, and plagiarists who have gone to seed, exploiting the tastes of a public harassed by positivism. One of the only Satanists of his time who was considered genuine, is under the name of Dr. Johannes but in actuality was the ex-abbé Joseph-Antoine Boullan of Lyons.

In the novel there is a little licence given, for Boullan becomes a doctor of theology and "miracle-worker," but he did neutralize satanic threats and announce the Second Coming of the Paraclete in Bloy-like fashion. He is highly praised, as was his living counterpart. Boullan was born in a small French village in 1824 and died in early 1893 (an obituary appeared in *The Nation*), but his miracles and theology brought censure from Rome and eventually both holy and civil imprisonment. Because his activities were cloaked in secrecy and behind noble names like the Society for the Reparation of Souls, Huysmans did not discover the truth of Boullan's diabolism until he came into possession of his papers after Boullan's death (which passed from Huysmans to L. Massignon and then back to where they were written, the

vaults of the Vatican, in 1930; *The Tablet* review of Laver's biography claims they were "part-published").

Boullan was ordained the year of Huysmans's birth, but after being forced to leave the Church in 1875, became the head of the Vintrasian sect that indulged in heretical rites including "spiritual attainment" via incest, bestiality, and incubism. But when the author first wrote in early 1890, all this was unknown, so that Boullan's portrait in **Là-Bas** becomes itself unintentional fiction. The book's other characters are composite pictures, but all with some basis in people of his acquaintance.

Mme. Chantelouve is a group portrait of four women: the mistress of a Marseilles painter, the wife of a Catholic journalist friend, Charles Buet, Henriette Maillat (the source of the lengthy correspondence), and Berthe Courrière, an unbalanced occultist who was also the mistress of the sculptor Clésinger and then Remy de Gourmont, appearing in *Sixtine* among others. It was she who introduced Huysmans to his first confessor, the abbé Mugnier. Carhaix the bell-ringer is pure fiction (the real Saint-Sulpice servant thought Huysmans was after his daughter!) and a vehicle for discussion only, to some degree a symbol of medievalism. The astrologer Gevingey was an adept called Eugène Ledos, of whom very little is known, although Jules Bois is believed to have seen him living above the Café Voltaire! The Canon Docre is said to be Louis Van Haecke, Chaplain of the Bruges Church of the Precious Blood (the ceremony for which is still viewable today). Huysmans believed the real man was also an observer at the Black Mass he attended, which occurs in the novel. Finally, Huysmans himself is split between the characters des Hermies, who is soon discarded, and Durtal, the future mouthpiece of his Catholic novels and last great self-character.

Like the originally-named Runan of the novel's first draft, the name Durtal came from a railway timetable during a café conversation. He immediately pencilled it in a memorandum book, and asked for more information on this market town situated on the Angers line, being singularly struck by how unFrench it sounded (there was also the constant problem of finding names for his characters). He thought it meant, in the languages of the North, the Valley of the Door, and repeated the word as if struck by its symbolism. It was certainly portentous, for as his religious novels are shorn of the usual incidents of fiction, they become entirely devoted to what the main character thinks, feels, and sees of life, faith, and art.

Down There crystallizes the world-weariness and frustration, the time when he discovered the questions but not the answers: "Conversations not of religion or art are so sordid and futile," as persons of common sense simply reiterate the everlasting anthem of their tiresome existences, which weary Huysmans "to extinction." Even certain occult and spiritualist personal experiences were used, by association, in an attempt to understand the artistic impulse. Some of his most flamboyantly extravagant views find expression here, in tones of surprise or disbelief that are either made or broken by argumentation.

As *A Rebours* had highlighted his dissatisfaction with the novel as an art form of any depth, so he breaks the mould by introducing an interior-novel with various interwoven digressions, in some ways a prefigurement of the journal style in the next, and most of the subsequent, work. The cataloguing of the faults and limitations inherent in Naturalism shows an interior reassessment of personal theories and an intuition of the end of his search. It allowed the chance to ridicule the Positivist hero Taine, who painted history with a made-up face and pinned-down facts as dead insects on a sheet of cardboard, like the "flea-bite tones" of some modern painters. Biographers of this approach, Huysmans concludes, would prefer their subjects to be "tradesmen like themselves." He also puts the Decadent-Satanist vogue in its true historical perspective, as a minor and superficial trend. Of a more general, and positive, nature, he revived the powerful art of Grünewald and the Primitives, who had become overshadowed by such contemporaries as Dürer and Holbein.

The atmosphere of Paris, the novel's setting, becomes almost Gothic, bathed in mists of sinister, almost evil, mystery. A modern Babylon, conjured up in a pungent style that has by no means dated. The historical data, excepting that upon Boullan, is true and real enough to send one into cobweb-libraries and shadow-castle ruins, in quest of the ghosts of such a rich, vibrantly alive tapestry.

EN ROUTE, 1895

This was the novel that set Huysmans free and onwards to his new Catholic life and work. In some ways it springs from *Là-Bas*—a "white book" written as an antidote to that satanic examination. It was originally planned to be a study of the miracle-center of La Salette, but this was abandoned and only fragments appeared in *La Cathédrale*. Almost from the beginning, *En Route* was announced as the first installment of a trilogy, a grouping that was never to be given an overall title. But it also proceeds from *A Rebours,* in its absolute depth of despair, which renders *En Route* the only logical path and way of escape.

It is, therefore, a culmination of all his various searchings in both art and life, signifying the spirituality attained, with the result that he becomes almost exclusively concerned with religious problems and how they affect his soul. *En Route* is subdivided into two parts, the first recounting Durtal/Huysmans's vacillations and ultimate preparation for a first retreat. This includes the very painful act of confession, as it encompasses the activities described in *Là-Bas* Additionally, there are certain other obvious parallels with *A Rebours,* even if subconscious and simply part of his technique as a novelist.

For instance, a guide to his library recurs (chapter 10), but in keeping with the shift of attitude, it includes mystics like Ruysbroeck, Saints Angela of Foligno and Bonaventure, with their pious but rarely readable hagiographies. There is a long, warm discussion of the stigmatic visionary Catherine Emmerich, as well as high praise for the English theologian and Oratory priest, Father Faber, author of *The Precious Blood*. The analogy with *A Rebours* is extended by the denouement to Part One, the preparations for the departure (among his favorite books, packets of cigarettes, and emergency chocolate!) and the lamentations of foreboding.

Part Two sees the symbolical journey to the valley of Notre Dame de l'Atre (i.e., Igny) and being set down in front of the daunting entrance. When the time comes for confession, Durtal notes what was to become a constant personal characteristic: he believes that a combination of events that was to end by his first act of faith made before just that brand of clergy he detested and thought he had escaped from, actually turned out to be received by the ailing abbot who had heard miraculously a voice saying he should rise from his sick bed. This leads into fascinating digressions upon the miracles of saints, such as stigmata, bilocation, mystical scent and heat, etc., the Devil in the world and monasteries in particular, how they used mystical substitution to offset the sins of the nearby towns and beyond, and the question of Faith.

Importantly, Huysmans thinks that perhaps the stricter rules and exercises of piety restricted his outlook, and prefers the approach of Saint Bernard and Saint Angela to such Church Fathers as Ignatius, Francis de Sales, and Vincent de Paul. A little surprisingly, the view toward the "terrible" Bossuet is not quite as one might expect. Towards the end, there is a paean to the beauties of plainchant, the liturgical year compared to a crown with its encrusted gems and precious metals (the Miserere is deemed the most perfect example of the Church's music).

Durtal is a masterpiece of self-analysis, a character both true and yet always surprisingly interesting. He lives as a creation, and somehow *built-in* carries the traits of his creator that led him to the point of existence: the ancestral piety, the spleen and disgust with life aggravated by artistic isolation (yet, only in *Là-Bas* does he carry the pretence of plying the same trade), a deep-rooted passion for religious art, fascination with the priesthood and monasticism (especially the atmosphere of medievalism), the lost art of plainchant and hagiography ("an unplumbed branch of literature"), which thereby overpowers all the senses simultaneously. The Church is a haven, an escape from the sins of the flesh just as it had conquered the heresies and set a true course in its own history.

He says that to cross the distance separating us from our Creator in life, we must pass through three stages toward Perfection: Purification, Illumination, and Unity, depending on the individual and Will of God. The first is like a "perpendicular and breakneck road," the next a considerably narrower pathway, and the last consisting of a wide and almost smooth route. It is the journey of Huysmans and the story of Durtal in the trilogy. The change was enough for this Parisian sophisticate to view his beloved and keenly observed city in a totally new and perhaps even less favorable light upon return: his life was literally transfigured.

From the literary point of view, it is a confessional journal, stark and simple, with little of the usual novelistic devices like plot structure or character interplay, while the action is of an internal nature with the external elements cut to a minimum. Notwithstanding, there are scenes that will remain in the memory: the powerful, symbolical realization of his place at the monastery entrance; the dawn "battlefield" of monks lost in their ecstasies; the beauties of the liturgy, among others. Again, the analogies with *A Rebours* present themselves—not, be it said, in the Decadent sense, but regarding the overall state of the author's conscience and consciousness. As he broke with Naturalism with the former work, so here he breaks with the Darkness of occultism. And there is the music, the art and literature, the soul-searching and moving invocations, the mundane details of cataloguing, the awesome dreams and nightmares (of a man with supposedly no imagination!). After *En Route,* it was the culture of the mind seen as nothing compared to the culture of the soul, and the body was a charnel house to be fled from. This masterpiece encapsulated the state of soul of modern man.

LA CATHÉDRALE, 1898

The second part of his trilogy was completed by a study of Chartres Cathedral, but more generally it is an expansion of his studies upon the whole range of Catholic art, starting from the time of *A Rebours*. The highest form of a Christian place of worship is seen as a synthesis, a unity in fact, which included everything for the author. It was a bible, a catechism, an ethics class, a history course, and for the unlettered it replaced the written text by the visual image.

It was also a living, dynamic entity within which Huysmans sought the soul beneath the body of that edifice of love. The style of the concept was important. As the Romanesque was the equivalent of the Old Testament so the Gothic style was of the New Testament, and there is no doubt that he preferred the latter. A clash of approaches would render it a monster (Mainz cathedral, for example, with its hodgepodge influences and hemmed in by rows of houses, was a "lunatic they've had to shut up!"). A visit to Rome, in this context, was never on his agenda!

The opening pages investigate the claims of Lourdes and La Salette, in the latter case it was the extract from a projected novel that was superseded by *En Route*. He also examines the message and how it was publicized, but sarcastically compares the principal Catholic de-

fender of Lourdes, Henri Lasserre, with the opposition's Émile Zola. As to be expected, there are long meditations (and catalogues) upon mystics like Jeanne de Matel and those lives worthy of hagiography, which in turn allows for discussions of sin and the "chambers of the soul." He mentions desire to one day write a biography of Lydwine of Schiedam and in fact undertook this a few years later. For Durtal/Huysmans is strongly critical of traditional pious literature, written he feels with bird-lime instead of ink, as well as so-called Church music (laments the absence of plainchant, a little unreasonably, for a church as opposed to an abbey) at Chartres and some of its ignoble sub-art.

In spite of his criticisms, moreover justified from the purely artistic viewpoint, there are countless positive aspects in his attitude. The historical cathedral, the fifth to be built on the site of a druidical cave, must be one of the most lightning-struck places in the world, yet with the exception of the fourteenth century not a generation passed without some additions or embellishments made to the edifice. There is lyricism, as when comparing in two different passages the achievement to Nature and to manmade beauty:

> And there is not a park, whether older or more recent than the groves of Jumièges, which does not exhibit the same forms with equal exactitude; but what Nature could not give was the prodigious art, the deep symbolical knowledge, the overstrung but tranquil mysticism of the believers who erected cathedrals. But for them the church in its rough-hewn state, as Nature had formed it, was but a soulless thing, a sketch, rudimentary; the embryo only of a basilica, varying with the seasons and the days, at once living and inert, awaking only to the roaring organ of the wind, the swaying roof of boughs wrung with the slightest breath; it was lax and often sullen; the yielding victim of the breeze, the resigned slave of the rain; it was lighted only by the sunshine that filtered between the diamond and heartshaped leaves, as if through the meshes of a green network. Man's genius collected the scattered gleams, condensed them in roses and broad blades, to pour it into his avenues of white shafts; and even in the darkest weather the glass was splendid, catching the very last rays of sunset, dressing Christ and the Virgin in the most fabulous magnificence, and almost realizing on earth the only attire that beseems the glorified Body, a robe of mingled flame . . . a cathedral is a superhuman thing!

> With its ship-like character, [it] strikes me as amazingly like a motionless vessel with spires for masts and the clouds for sails, spread or furled by the wind as the weather changes; it remains the eternal image of Peter's boat which Jesus guided through the storm.

For Huysmans, of all cathedrals it is *the* mystical one, that which best suggests the idea of a delicate, saintly woman emaciated by prayer and almost transparent by fasting. In chapter one he paints it at dawn, and in chapter eight at twilight and night, which are classic forms of descriptive writing, a new unexplored medium for *Parisian Sketches*. It teaches us the catechism by means of "stone sentences."

He completes the education by explication of the symbolism of numbers and color, of animals that includes mythology, of flora (only white and blue are non-vice), of odors and the virtuous gems, sublime meditations upon the statuary, etc. But among the mystics, apostolic studies, and Scripture (an evocation of a palace recalls *En Rade*), one finds Mallarmé, Verlaine, as well as Flaubert, Ernest Hello, and Gustave Moreau, in short comparisons overall. One finds in the last chapters a certain *en routian* dilemma regarding his own personal style toward the subjects treated, as he attempts to reconcile his past with a new direction. The recent trend of Catholic Symbolists like the Rosicrucians are "simpletons," the Beuron experiment is dismissed, Tissot only an illustrator for that "joker" Renan as Huysmans's faith makes him more discerning than ever in proportion to the importance of the subject matter. Only two little-known religious artists are praised, Paul Borel and his later friend Charles Dulac, who was soon to be cut down in his prime.

Historical art shows his breadth of taste or interest, as he looks at German, Flemish, Italian, Spanish, and English examples. He praises Roger van der Weyden as always, a Rembrandt and a Zurbaran (whom his father liked and copied), but is disappointed by Ingres and even Delacroix from the religious point of view, admittedly above the usual in his field but whose Catholicism is considered nil. There is no doubt that Huysmans's approach is considerably less open to the art that is not to his taste, probably due to his newly-won faith being so hard to attain that it is absolutely supported by the Church's art and world view, but there are discussions worthy of comparison to his previous volumes of criticism. He admits in chapter four that his character is "cross-grained," which makes his observations the more difficult to formulate.

Contemporary Catholics could not reconcile themselves with his stressing of the beauty (and therefore their neglect) of medievalism, the time when martyrs rightly trusted to the Will of God rather than physick, when life was seen in either black or white according to its value for the soul. Saint Gregory, the restorer of plainsong and for whom the author must have had a special place, regarded it "as a temptation of the devil that made the bigots, the pharisees of his day determined not to read profane literature, for he said it aids our understanding of what is sacred." Huysmans therefore could do little else than criticize modern Catholics, for they challenged his own deep-seated convictions. And specifically, he was still the Parisian sophisticate who found himself in a provincial "hole," as when the town "bigwigs" celebrate a new bishop and all the various nuns' coifs remind him of the Paris roofs!

As Paul Valéry wrote somewhere, this book contains the whole tremendous store of medieval erudition like a chart of the world of mysticism, and it is opened with the first blaze of Chartres's rose windows. The host of saints come to life and mingle with the vague misfits of the town, the somnolent priests, and timid scholars. Unusually for Huysmans, the actual facts within the novel very rarely coincide with his life, but this is incidental. Still, we come across many of his favorite themes like familiar memories, allusions to *A Rebours* and *Downstream,* the bells of St. Sulpice from *Là-Bas,* the Bièvre itself flowing as far as the cathedral door. There are very few characters, Madame Bavoil part-nun, part-peasant who quotes Jeanne de Matel, and the abbé Gevresin, who is considered to be based more on the ex-abbé Boullan than abbé Mugnier, in spite of his role, both appearing in *En Route* but not developed. Surprisingly, we find a certain bitterness toward the setting of that novel, the monastery of La Trappe. Contrary to impressions, his memories are of the discipline which made life the more difficult after returning to Paris. It may be merely a novelistic device to "put the hounds off his scent" after the storm created in the journalist press, for inconsistently he calls the cloister "a health resort for the soul," with its "splendid completeness."

So the book was the summation of his long researches, by which he wished to render a service by glorifying the Church's art, but on his own terms. Hence the emphasis on medieval symbolism and piety. A sub-strata is the theme of Durtal/Huysmans's growing religious sense, although when focused it cannot be ignored, and coincides with the time when retirement from his employment meant the possibility of permanent retirement to the cloister. It should not be overlooked that it was written when secular symbolism in the art world held sway. He takes something often taken for granted, and by extension to infinity through his personal vision, creates beauty out of beauty. Chartres Cathedral is the hero of this work. In the French edition, an appendix was deemed necessary to accommodate the endless, encyclopedic supply of sources. In spite of Huysmans's qualms, *Cathédral* became the most successful of all his books, the stupendous achievement in modern times of rendering the concept and ideal of medieval times, separated from our age as if they all occurred on a different planet.

LA BIÈVRE ET SAINT-SÉVERIN, 1898

The first part of this work was a revised version of the study that was published in 1890, although the viewpoint remained unchanged. The second section looks at another district close to the author's heart, and not just because he lived most of his life thereabouts. In Huysmans's time, for it has considerably changed in subsequent years, there was a medieval atmosphere within the environs of the church, flanked by the boulevards St. Michel and St. Germain, the rue St. Jacob and the Seine embankment. Time moved slowly here, if it had moved at all. The destruction of the area for its own sake and the satisfaction of those who wish to eradicate any sign of artistic value in the environment, is deemed a folly bordering on crime. He devotes some impassioned prose in this, by far, the largest part of the book.

The old church, set amidst dark, narrow streets was like a diamond of the Middle Ages in its black vein of rock, this area "the exact image, when reproduced, of a slice of Brie cheese." He had already witnessed the disappearance of the Place Maubert and part of the rue Galande, where stood the notorious Chateau rouge, a tavern dive used by burglars and assassins which he had visited. The area had become one of ill-fame and misery as well as a time capsule. He had also wished to write of the Abbaye aux Bois before that, too, was condemned. In the words of the English review in *The Spectator* (January, 1899) it was a return to the picturesque where he had won his earliest glory, and the mark that set him aside.

It was reissued in 1901 with a new section on Les Gobelins, the factory that occupies the Bièvre land, and is itself an extension of that essay. It shows his abiding love and interest in the area, for the Bièvre River is mentioned in *La Cathédrale* and the Gobelins has several pages in *De Tout*. The gardens there were a delight for the wandering author, whose overhanging alleys were a simulacrum of the countryside for artists, lovers, and workers to pass through.

LA MAGIE EN POITOU: GILLES DE RAIS,
1899

A brochure in two parts, published while at Ligugé monastery. It shows in the first section, on the occult practices of the area, that the subject had by no means been totally left behind by his conversion. But it is localized, and the work as a whole is but an interlude, reflecting a new period of calm and study. Gilles de Rais is looked at in this new light, away from the shadows of Parisian spiritualists and Satanists. More importantly, in the total context of his work, it shows that Huysmans had set aside the novel as a means of conveying his thought, and, latterly, his faith. Although several works were to follow, only one was to be a novel.

SAINTE LYDWINE DE SCHIEDAM, 1901

After many years, Huysmans finally fulfilled his desire to write a biography of this martyr who was not only from the land of his ancestry but also was a symbol of his beloved Middle Ages. She was also one of the greatest sufferers in expiation the world has ever seen. Medievalism is seen to triumph over Science and Progress, not only in the sphere of medicinal impotence but in terms of reconciling the sufferer to the point where joy finally supersedes pain. More than a hagiography, it turns to the realm of legendary biography, as powerful and harrowingly real as the supranaturalist art of Grünewald and the Primitives.

There has been some controversy as to whether his subject was a saint in the strictest sense, or a beata—the preliminary stage to canonization. At the close of chapter fifteen, Huysmans states that the cult of veneration was officially started in 1616, and by decree of Pope Leo XIII in 1890 Lydwine was elevated to the rank of saint, the *cultus ab immemorabili tempore* being proved as fact. This is also verified by the English translator to Thomas à Kempis's biography of Lydwine in 1912.

The short preface lists the documents consulted and also the difficulty this raises, for Thomas à Kempis and two other principal works do not present the facts chronologically, but according to themes and related matters. Huysmans, therefore, compares the texts detective-fashion and seeks to clarify. Chapter one is an astonishing panorama of the state of Europe around the year 1400, and the picture is by no means rosy: war, plague, barbarism, heresy, witchcraft, etc., are rife. Yet, Joan of Arc was Lydwine's exact contemporary, and died but two years before the saint. The faithful were seeking their true way, until succumbing to the "sewer" disinterred by Paganism, the Renaissance. Heresies were "like the fungus growths in vegetation, or those parasites which flourish in the darkness of drains," in this time of the three popes, which two successive saints tried to reconcile.

This sets the scene for one of Huysmans's central arguments, that of the law of equilibrium, or mystical substitution, between good and evil, literally between Satan and God (for whom capitals are used throughout). The punishments by human suffering (epidemics, earthquakes, famines, war) can only be counterbalanced by the suffering saints who take on the burden of the world's sins by their own example and courage. This "army of militants" also includes the enclosed religious orders, the lightning conductors of faith. The author's style here is reminiscent of Léon Bloy with its metaphors of balance, cohorts of hell, and so forth, and who indeed was a tangible influence in helping Huysmans to form his views on the subject. This "army" also included the recluses and hermits, whom he lists, who suffered for the crimes of the universe, the souls in Purgatory, the abominations of schism, the excesses of monks, the delinquencies of kings and people alike.

The following chapters are specific to Lydwine, and her family that included a grandfather "assailed by Satan," in Huysmans's phrase, by which he means psychic phenomena—a conjunction no doubt arrived at through the author's seances with occultists. Lydwine's name, symbolically, is derived from the Flemish *lyden,* to suffer, and certainly the extent of her burden and its duration is unsurpassed in the annals of the saints. She was racked by every disease known to Man, except leprosy (interestingly, the only one that would have required intervention by civil law). And what she endured was increased by tumors and infestation of worms to the extent that handfuls could be extracted at will. Yet, despite her nonhuman appearance she exhaled a sweet scent.

Lydwine, whose martyrdom began when as a child she had a simple accident while skating on ice, certainly did not see her situation in terms of expiation at the beginning. Huysmans says she despaired, and the local priest was too worldly and indifferent to think about consolation (the reason for her spiritual "anaemia," says Huysmans). A visiting priest told her of Christ, the first example of mystical substitution, who suffered by seeing the centuries before him. Huysmans recounts, in true Naturalistic manner, the full unexpurgated detail of her horrific torture, the culmination of which included the detail that Lydwine had to be bound when moved, lest her body physically separate.

Huysmans provides data from every source, as he had in *La Cathédrale* but in a more simple style. What may seem the minutiae of biography have a wider and more subtle application here, as an argument taught by example. For example, Lydwine "loved humiliations as others love honors", for when a madwoman came and spat at her the saint sent a gift in gratitude. She was subjected to endless disturbances by the curious, but she gave counsel, for "grief is a portion of one's heritage taken in advance from Purgatory." It can be a substitution of those already in Purgatory by loved ones left behind, although human love is called a "parody of God's love" because it excludes the Divine. Such traits obviously found sympathy in the author's subconscious, as his faith was built on a reaction in extremis, after Satanism.

Lydwine was also less and less of this world, otherworldly to the extent of receiving visions of angels (warning her regarding the tricks of an unbelieving priest, whom the town folk wished to destroy for his sacrilege), and then by Christ Himself. She could predict somebody's death to the hour, was the recipient of apports (i.e., gifts from the spirit world, including money, which she distributed as alms) and journey astrally into all three spheres of the afterlife (recorded by Huysmans in chapter eight and compared to the art of Van Eyck), as well as the rare, high mystical gift of bilocation. As Huysmans recounts, this is almost the surest sign of ultimate spiritual grace, and in Lydwine's case she also gave physical after-signs of her experience, verified independently by unimpeachable witnesses. The astonishing catalogue continues with the account of her only food as the Eucharist, the total absence of sleep, physical meditation on the Passion of Christ with the wounds as "thuribles of perfume," and so forth.

Not unexpectedly, Lydwine predicted her own death in 1433, at the age of 53. After almost her whole life spent in agony, the body returned to beauty the perfume of which was enough to sustain anyone present—including arch-sceptics—for three days without nourishment or sleep. There were three verified miracles following specific intercession, as Kempis relates in the second part of his work. Such was her wide appeal that her relics were preserved (including some tears of blood) which Huysmans may also have obtained by unknown means when visiting the town for the purposes of collecting information. The total number of pilgrims were "several millions" in Huysmans's account, although Kempis actually gives "beyond many thousands."

As with all his books that wished to state the author's position and world view, especially after conversion, *Sainte Lydwine* is a complete dossier of all known facts and their sources, which in this case is rendered even more difficult by the fact that the medieval chroniclers worked in their own, individual system and, in Brugman's case, a "biography" was written that was in reality a translation of German into (old) Latin with certain additions. The subject was interesting for him in several ways and on different levels. Lydwine was a true Medieval and contemporary of Joan of Arc, with some of her purest characteristics, a female to some degree *beyond* Woman, so pure as to be almost a paradox of her true species in Huysmans's mind. An extreme type, therefore, to the extent that the natural and the invisible world become merged and interlaced so as almost to enter the domain of dream, even when actual events are retold. Fact tries to interpret the super-legendary. Religion then is of a nature unknowable by the common mass of people, especially the modern bourgeoisie who believed it their private estate. On a literary level, it was a subject ready-made, naturalistically decadent with a small "d," where the sheer immensity of detail and the gut-horror it engenders allows for the *luxury,* in Huysmans's case, of a simple style, overloaded as if of its own accord. It is certainly central to the tenor and ethos of the later writer, for it encapsulated his world view and art, thereby changing yet completing him as he revived the lost art of hagiography in a single flame.

According to Huysmans in the book, there were two purposes, although the first is implicit. It is didactic in wishing to give by example—and it had to be extreme—a personal yet historically true perspective of Faith, that upon which the Church is based in its heritage by the saints, stigmatized martyrs and the enclosed Orders, who form a rampart against the Devil or the wrath of God's punishment. Such an example as the recent fire at a charity bazaar in Paris, when a number of middle-class charity helpers lost their lives, makes it, in Huysmans's words, "very difficult to believe that there was nothing more in it than the material causes enumerated in the magistrates report" (Chapter 15), a view echoed by Bloy. Lydwine and her fellow expiatory victims linked in history to this mission are a weight in the hands of Christ, which he uses to counterbalance the crimes of the world and the disorders of the Church (in Huysmans's time, the latter means the rationalists and Modernists, historically the Jansenists and schismatics, of Catholicism). It is, therefore, a signpost for a truer, more vital faith. The second intention was to render a service to the suffering themselves, especially those who are not aware that they may well be accomplishing the work of reparation; it provides a framework of meaning and possible rejoicing, although Huysmans was well aware how little the lesson will probably be heeded.

Huysmans gives an appendix to his work that charts the liturgical status of the saint. As the translator of Thomas à Kempis's work in 1912 states, Huysmans's "very original and intensely interesting" hagiography in translation is the only modern English study of the saint. The fact of when it was published is purely a coincidental accident.

DE TOUT, 1902

This volume, fascinating as it is, yet again highlights Huysmans's apparent wish to confound his historians. After the preceding works of intense Catholicism, he returns to the era of **Parisian Sketches** but with even more of a desire to show catholic, in the sense of eclectic, taste. There are twenty-four essays, unconnected in three sections, although an appendix is really only another section. If there is any leitmotif, the second is travel impressions, the third and appendix have religious subjects, while the opener is miscellaneous.

It is a wide, amorphous, yet intensely artistic sketch pad on diverse subjects: saints, monks, barbers, painters, sleeping-cars, railway refreshment rooms, Paris cafés, impressions of Germany and Belgium that were originally planned ten years before as a book in their own right, of the Nôtre-Dame quarter of Paris that was issued three years later, and also upon Ligugé abbey. In like manner, Huysmans also writes upon the history of his former family home for more than a quarter of a century, No. 11 rue de Sèvres. A relaxed atmosphere permeates the book, as when describing the historic Dark Virgin [La Vièrge noire de Paris], a statue housed at the Convent of the Ladies of Saint-Thomas-de-Villeneuve also in the rue de Sèvres, where

> . . . to the works of vanity of the great industries in the neighborhood, it opposes the works of Mercy. A crowd made up of sick people and of ragamuffins are ingulfed through its doors; and the sisters dress wounds, cure whitlows without operation and ease old sores with white linen; then all these unfortunates pass through a wicket where the *cashier* is a nun paler than the sacred wafers that she cuts, paler than the tapers that surround her, and this nun, instead of receiving money, gives it and distributes bread to all who enter . . .

> Our Lady reveals herself here as a Virgin *familière,* benign to all who enter. She has not the slightly disdainful pout of Our Lady of Victories who is a queen, and the customary service of her temples, the subalterns disguised as beadles and flunkeys in chains of office, are lacking in her little church in the rue de Sèvres. She is a sister of the Black Virgins of Moulins, of Dijon, of Bourg, of Chartres, and it would seem that the Virgins of this color, who are the ancestors of our white Madonnas, are grandmothers rather than mothers to us; we count on their faculty for spoiling us, and on the weakness of their good nature; we feel that they are more indulgent, more ready to pardon, and we would sooner recount our iniquities to them than to the Mother who would grumble a little and to the Father who might be angry.

> Before our Lady of Deliverance, then, we somehow fancy that we must try to become children again and to pray more with the beads than by the book. She is so rustic, so often besought by candid women, that she has grown used to naive prayers and simple supplications!

Such is a prose poem from his religious period. The Naturalism had not left this keenest of observers, who affords a penetrating insight into such Parisian institutions as the café, *les habitués de café* of the old fashioned, sedately semi-clerical café Caron in the rue des Saints-Pères, as if the road from Chartres was ineluctably joined to the inner boulevards. He sees always the same shopkeepers at their coffee break, financiers and merchants between deals, employees full of laments, journalists in their quest for articles, bohemians on the look-out for credit, all searching the clinging smoke for the waiter whom they only know by his first name to place orders. All submit to a certain polite etiquette, except the broker from the Bourse who, upon entering, does not even say good day and afterwards, without even moving his hand to his hat, leaves without closing the door! Huysmans delineates, and de-masks as an artist would for a group portrait. He continues:

> The appeal exercised by the café upon this kind of customer is easily explained, for it consists of schemes being hatched, of profit motivation, of intoxicated repose, of bestial pleasures. But in addition to these customers whose psychology is infantile and whose refinement is zero, there are still others upon whom a tyrannical influence acts: rich or broadly experienced customers, unconquered bachelors without a home to flee to, abstemious people decrying the game, not speaking at all, scarcely reading the newspapers. Those are the disinterested amateurs, frequenters who enjoy the café beyond any other preoccupation, beyond any consideration of profit, just for itself . . .

> At first glance, this café does not seem different from the good old clubs of the provinces, but its clientele which is oldish and strange, and which includes neither the gossip nor the shabby idler of the provinces, has affected its physiognomy and marked with a particular stamp the senility of its rooms.

> Abolished manners survive there; hoary-headed waiters, turned grey in their very old harness, serve in silence, thank you for their tip, assist you with your overcoat, precede you when you leave, open and close the door, and render gratitude to you for having come. Do not these customs seem strange in a period when all café waiters either do not answer your call or boom at you, juggle carafes and cups, cut capers with trays and glasses, and fly when you demand a paper!

Such an extract shows the masterly analysis, restrained but biting, and a welcome variation on the aspect usually projected by his Symbolist and Decadent contemporaries. But the book as a whole undoubtedly represents and culminates Huysmans the journalist, the observer, as

Certains does for the art critic. To some degree, *De Tout* is a continuation of that role, for its diversity is a mirror held to his artistic vision and critical panorama. Yet, it closes with a reminder that it is Huysmans the Catholic now writing, now giving evidence, for he has been dispossessed—yet again—by the hated world around him. **"Un Mot,"** dated in the last days of the religious community whose life he had shared for over two years, comments on the result of the government's anti-religious Laws of Association. Their political action, Huysmans writes, should focus readers' attention on what the monasteries of the great orders were like "before the scum of the lodges polluted what was still healthy in the soul, the sickly soul, alas! of this shameful country." The subject was to provide a depth of feeling in his last novel, and final part of the trilogy, soon afterwards.

ESQUISSE BIOGRAPHIQUE SUR DON BOSCO, 1902

This biographical sketch, or draft, upon the life of the nineteenth century founder of the Salesian Order, is without doubt the only one of his works that should not have been published. He wrote it only after repeated requests, including that of the poet François Coppée, as a defence of their charitable work then under attack by a government that wished to separate church and state.

Giovanni Bosco had died in 1888, after instigating a great and difficult program of child care in the form of orphanages for the poor. He has affectionately been called the Apostle of Youth, and was canonized as soon after as 1934. Although some historians have seen him as the greatest religious figure of the time (biographies have been written by such as Lancelot Sheppard and Jorgensen), for various reasons it was not a subject suited to Huysmans.

The eighty-page essay should have numbered eighty-one, but the printers forgot a page, according to Huysmans in a letter dated 30 August 1902, and they "couldn't bother about a little thing like that." He tried to keep its publication quiet, and though he sent a copy to his correspondent, he asks that it be put in the privy afterwards! It included amateurish illustrations with similar captions, and an uninspiring sonnet by Coppée. In truth, the subject deserved more.

L'OBLAT, 1903

This novel marks the final journey of Huysmans as a novelist, and as a self-analyzer that started with *Marthe* more than a quarter of a century before. The subject, quality, and even world view may have changed or improved, but the intrinsic techniques of his trade remained the same. *The Oblate* actually has the same number of chapters as *The Cathedral, Lydwine*—and *A Rebours!* The vivid, vibrant style forged under Naturalism had not left him, nor had its documentary methods.

It is set a Val-des-Saints, which is Ligué abbey, but there are basic differences between his life and the infor-mation given in the novel. For example, he rents a house there when in actuality he had bought land and had it built; he moves there with Mme. Bavoil (Julie Thibault, a woman with her own very singular form of piety) who also appeared in earlier novels, but this housekeeper was removed from her position before leaving for Ligugé; the reason for leaving Chartres, that is the narrative as it was left at the end of *Cathedral,* was the death of the abbé Gevresin (Boullan/Mugnier) instead of simply the author's wish to make a permanent retreat; the lower floor is damp, so only the upper is used, again ficti-tiously, for he shared the whole house with his friends M. and Mme. Leclaire; finally, the idealized monk Dom Felletin is considered as a portrait of his friend Dom Besse, although it is also true that Besse is mentioned by his real name—as is Ligugé itself. But more importantly, the closing scenes of evacuation are accurate.

There are similar themes to those seen in the other two instalments of the trilogy, as he gives a fascinating his-tory of oblatehood (i.e., those who take vows of monas-tic allegiance but remain outside the stricter observances of the order, if required) which leads to an inquiry into the nature of sin and saintliness seen through the ex-ample of hermits, who, as the rules relaxed, became equivalent to oblates. They were founded before lay-brothers but after recluses, therefore, and attached to monasteries and churches through ritual and ceremony. Huysmans compares the various rules of the Orders with details of the ceremony, together with his own prepara-tions to enter that service.

But there are, of course, subjects that are given more weight or space than previously thereby highlighting his own spiritual development. There are several passages of Scriptural exegesis, including that of the symbolical comparison between the rising sun and the Resurrection that was, incidentally, used as a famous poetical analogy by Francis Thompson. *The Oblate* also gives more analysis to artistic subjects than *En Route* or *The Cathe-dral* (not a paradox in the latter example, for there it was historical analysis and merely mentioned artists individu-ally according to their relative importance), while artists he finds sympathy for are looked at on a wider scale, in the manner of *Certains*. This may arise from an increas-ing feeling of isolation after the failure of his artistic community venture. One example is the praising of the fourteenth-century sculptor Claus Sluter who worked at Dijon and was himself an oblate. Huysmans admits to Sluter's personality haunting him, for he is seen as an artist among artisans. Although little about him is known, he gives an amusing anecdote about when he sent to Dijon for a pair of spectacles—which were for his statue of Jeremiah!

Of course, the Middle Ages was a time that had captured the author's imagination, the "ages of faith" here (in *A Rebours* they were "the only really characteristic eras humanity has ever known"), so it is not surprising that we find lengthy discussions of the Cathedral and Carmelite Chapel at Dijon, as well as other churches and the museum of that ancient town. There is a history of the lost art of Illumination, "a delightfully frail, blue-eyed, golden-haired little girl who, in giving birth to her big daughter Painting, was fated to die!" A study also of another almost-lost *cultivation,* the liturgical garden with its des Esseintes-like invoking of sense-sensations (celandine is his favorite), and the symbology of precious gems is as if continued from *Là-Bas* while the almost obligatory library scene is re-introduced.

But the novel is more often remembered for its treatment of the liturgy, the Church's high contribution to the world's treasure house of religious music. So it is praised in the highest terms, "a glimpse of Heaven as in an ideal picture by some old Flemish master," scarcely able to contain itself when joyful as if composed under the inspiration of the Holy Ghost himself. Several chapters return to the subject, a golden thread throughout intertwined with the noble Benedictine way of life:

> What a beautiful life that good monk leads, a life of study and prayer! And what a beautiful life, too, is this Benedictine life, which soars so high above the centuries and beyond the ages! Indeed, how could one well travel heavenwards with firmer step and marching to better music? Such a life as theirs is the realization upon earth of the life of angels above in which we, too, shall have our share hereafter. When our march is ended we come before the Throne, not as novices but as souls already trained by careful study for the duties which we are for ever to perform in the eternal bliss of His Presence. In comparison to this, how turbulent and how vain seem the lives of other men!

Not for the first time, there is praise of Dom Gueranger as a true Benedictine, for his revival of plainsong (Durtal's favorite is Epiphany) and lesser-known revivalists whose works, in their own way, are as "clever as any of Balzac's." But the reader finds also a newer, sharper emotion in *The Oblate* that is more prominent than previously: an unwillingness to accept the Faith as it is generally meted out to believers, and a desire to criticize where he feels it due. This had not shown itself since *En Route,* moreover it was invariably limited to his private letters and diaries, but it reached its height (or nadir, for the victims) in his last book *The Crowds of Lourdes*. His contempt for priests and modernist piety, synonymous with decaying faith, the Republic motivated by greed and atheism and led by scheming, hypocritical politicians, is given full rein here.

Rarely, almost as an interlude, the author returns to mundane topics like the weather, landscape, the ordinary people around him, as if pulled back to his lower duties as a novelist. But this takes a sharp turn from chapter thirteen on, whereafter looking at the cult of Mary and the religious significance of pain and sorrow, Huysmans suddenly mentions the preparations of the community for evacuation ahead of the deadline set by the Laws of Association. As Durtal/Huysmans says to a monk, "In the eyes of those who condemn you, you have committed the most unpardonable of crimes, that of not sinning against God." He still dreams of an artistic community, but is increasingly pessimistic, and as he would put it, one has to pay nowadays even for dreaming. It prompts a melancholy look at the garden, and some study of the hierarchy of saints. The world has its revenge on the time-traveller.

A feeling of bitterness then permeates, justified as it is, but some of his close friends believe the return to Paris was inevitable and something of a relief to the author, and certainly the view in chapter fourteen that a characteristic dislike of the country (and its inhabitants) means there is little point in staying after the departure of the monks carries verisimilitude. The abbot actually suggests the convent in the rue Monsieur, where Huysmans did indeed install himself. But it was a torturous decision, for he had left Paris with the intention of not returning. His inner desolation is mirrored by the disintegrating monastery, when he is down to his "last bottle of plainchant, and tomorrow the cellar of Gregorian melodies will be empty. . . ."

The last pages are a mournful prayer made public, for as Durtal says, he had only taken a chair to sit down and rest awhile, which now gives way and lands him on the floor: "I am wondering whether the same dishonesty prevails in the Heavenly workshops as in the earthly ones? Whether the celestial cabinet-makers also manufacture cheap and nasty chairs, the legs of which give way as soon as you sit on them?" Such poignant scenes as the abbot's leaving, the symbolical end, certainly add to the powerful sense of despair that the novel leaves in the reader's imagination.

Life there in the shadow of a simple, medieval-like monastery, is a poem which he recites and bathes in, exalted in its pure mysticism. Paris then becomes something like a necropolis, with only the artistic distractions and near-submerged places of plainchant to interest him. Huysmans is very much Durtal at this point in the book's evolution, in spite of a rare exploitation of the first person singular, mostly in conversation. There is, in addition, no mention of Durtal being a writer (projects, note collecting, etc.) whereas in *The Cathedral* Durtal has an "article used before." One might wonder if Huysmans realized that he had achieved most everything he had set out to do, and that the return to Paris was only an antechamber to the Beyond. His whole spiritual and artistic attainment is reflected in *The Oblate,* and it remains an important document eighty years afterwards, both for the author and for modern man generally, who spends his days bartering his soul and is ever further removed from the light of an ancient but timeless wisdom.

TROIS PRIMITIFS, 1905

As the title says, it is a study on the work of three primitive artists of the Middle Ages: Grünewald, the Master of

Flemalle, and the Florentine, all housed at German museums at Colmar and Frankfurt-on-Main. That, in fact, is the basis of the book, consisting of two essays on the museums, with black-and-white reproductions of their paintings.

The ninety-four pages are typical of the author, for it is a throwback to the period of *Certains* and *Là-Bas* both in subject matter and general views, colored by his deeper faith (the Master of Flemalle's "Nativity" at Dijon Museum was mentioned in *The Oblate,* Huysmans reminds us). His love of their artistic vision is therefore constant, especially for the work of Grünewald, a painter born between 1470 and 1475 in Germany and who died in 1528. The work is realistic yet mystical, savage and civilized to a high degree of refinement. In some ways, this Medieval was the pictorial precursor of the Frenchman; certainly Huysmans wished his own art to attain the same level of spiritualrealism, after first discovering Grünewald during the gestation period of *Là-Bas*. Huysmans tells us himself, in the opening line, of his fascination over many years.

The moment one sees "the fearsome nightmare" of Grünewald's "Calvary," "it is as if a typhoon of art had been let loose . . . striking you dumb [then] sweeping you away." Huysmans wonders whether the artist, about whom so little is known, was involved in the emotional religious battles of the Reformation, "which was to end in the most austere coldness of the heart, once the Protestant swamp had frozen over." Grünewald's art has its own severe fervor and rawness of faith which might prompt such an interpretation. Huysmans sees him as personifying the religious piety of the sick and poor, "art made in the image of the ergotics who prayed to [Grünewald's] altarpiece of Christ," perhaps explaining why the artist was not commissioned by lay royalty, although he was by an Archbishop and a Cardinal. He concluded by believing that Grünewald could only be understood by "the sick, the unhappy and the monks, by the suffering members of Christ."

Huysmans's narrative is a tour de force, and certainly his power of description had not diminished since the astonishing passage on the primitive in the opening chapter of *Là-Bas* fifteen years before. The subject was close to his heart during the difficult years of conversion, and remained so to his death—it was to be reprinted in the last posthumous work to carry the author's signature.

LES FOULES DE LOURDES, 1906

The Crowds of Lourdes, to give its English title, has little to do with the standard pattern of novels: there is no named protagonist, the first person singular is employed, and no plot or character development. It is hardly a chronicle, but, in Huysmans's words, simply sketches and notes. After his introduction, the author gives a brief history of the miracle center that he had first discussed in *La Cathédrale.* Somewhat surprisingly, we find it is not unique in France, for several such places

existed before the cult achieved its height at Lourdes, and even in the same region.

There were known miracles at Montousse in 1848, for example, and at Medoux exactly two hundred years before a plague was sent for unrepentant villagers who did not heed the call. Like Lourdes, it had its processions and pilgrimages until the time of the Revolution, while Garaison could actually have rivalled the scale of its modern equivalent during the sixteenth and seventeenth centuries. Indeed, Huysmans shows that there is a discernible pattern in French historical examples (which has only been enhanced in our own time by examples like Knock and Fatima): visions or apparitions first appeared, usually to simple folk like children, peasants, or shepherds, with messages of an eschatological import and a sign of wonder as proof—in Lourdes's case, of course, the new source of spring water which resulted in cures (as doctors and scientists on the spot have testified). Many of these principal witnesses became nuns.

As the Lourdes case is unique for promoting a doctrine of the Church that was not in general currency among the faithful, especially the rural poor, Huysmans gives the details of the Immaculate Conception that was defined as a dogma by Pope Pius IX in an encyclical of 1849, but had been witnessed by Catherine Laboure as recently as 1830, in Huysmans's beloved rue du Bac at Paris (his favorite church, Saint-Severin, was the first in Paris to celebrate the dogma). Before Lourdes, the principal place of pilgrimage was La Salette, but the former dealt a death-blow to that site which was so symbolically important to Léon Bloy later.

The second and further chapters are concerned with Huysmans's own views and impressions of a place he originally had no desire to visit, for he agrees with Saint John of the Cross regarding the unbalancing effect of crowds upon an individual. He arrives, therefore, some weeks before the "mass-attack" of what turns out to be a record pilgrimage. But it might surprise some readers to hear Huysmans speak kindly of the "comradeship of a bivouac" among the pious strangers there, just as later he recites prayers for the sick and their helpers when almost breaking down with pity at the sights he witnesses, the admirable communion of souls, as it is termed.

Unlike his old, late friend Zola, the arch-Naturalist whose work on Lourdes in 1894 this book seeks to refute both in overall terms and specifically, for he is mentioned on almost a dozen different occasions and never favorably, Huysmans went with a ready-made framework of inner belief regarding the truth of miracles. It was built upon the solid knowledge that mysticism was an exact science, irrespective of the opinion in which it might be held in more modern times. The Huysmansian twist comes when he juxtaposes the orthodox miracles with ones less obvious: the charity of good will and human pity for fellow-sufferers, or the fact that worst illnesses are not contracted from the over-used baths. With a twinge of shame, he confesses to eventually being interested only in the unusual, or "exotic" disorders, the "runaways from leper asylums and monstrosities," which is really enervation. For it is a "milieu destitute of all proportion, in the extreme of joy and sorrow," a losing of one's self from the outside world. But this feeling is simultaneous with a personal despair and frustration at those he noticed who were not cured. This turns to a need for penance and a belief in the divine value of vicarious suffering, as it was propounded in *Sainte Lydwine*.

A second motif here and again one that modern Catholics found insupportable—was the view he held upon the pious "art" found at such religious places, from the inexcusable ugliness of devotional wares to the cathedral that reminds one of "the cork models of churches used for window-dressing in certain trades; it takes its cue from the aesthetics of cork-merchants." Huysmans lets fly on this subject with the full force of his sarcasm and invective, for he believed such ugliness, far from being uplifted by fervor of piety, could only be inspired by the devil as his revenge on earth. Regarding such a supreme example of faith as the Basilica, "the least of village chapels erected in the Middle Ages, compared with such contraband Gothic, looks like a masterpiece of delicacy and strength," with its roof "shaped on the colossal mould of a Savoy cake, flanked with three domed boiler covers, made of zinc. Seen sideways . . . this rotunda, with its double-sloping terrace undulating downwards from the roof to the ground, looks like an enormous crab extending its long pincers toward the old town." Within, Huysmans is almost petrified by what greets him, so truly inconceivable is the "heap of trashy bric-à-brac and variegated tatters used to adorn it," the votive offerings of the faithful. It is incoherent and incongruous, an irrelevance like the ornamentation, of which its proper place is the salon, just as the former belongs to the stable. The Church of the Rosary fares on better. This "dropsical circus" is more of a puzzle, for "we should like to hear what style it belongs to, as it contains something of everything, the Byzantine and the Romanesque, the Hippodrome and the Casino; but if we look closer there is above all else something of the machinery store and the housing for locomotives; only the rails and the central turntable are wanting, instead of the high altar, to enable the engines to come out of the side wings and to perform their evolutions on the broad walks of the Esplanade."

But, instead of finding the place smoky and pitch-black with soot, he is even more surprised to find it decorated like a provincial theater. He invariably makes first for the nave and crypt, but one shrinks from so naming these queerly shaped halls, "clearly the product of the imagination of a gambler in luck and a beadle in delirium. . . . The builder of this religious casino was a man of genius compared with the artists [who] have surpassed one's wildest dreams. Art, even at its lowest, has nothing to do with what is here." It is not even bad art, for that implies some sort of standard and criteria. The ugliness of everything at Lourdes starts to become unnatural, for it falls below the lowest watermarks of taste, to the point where

not even man in his most dismal state could inflict such an insult on God; there is some other agent, the intervention of the Most Base, Huysmans concludes, the "vindictive pranks" of the devil. When ugliness comes to be applied to such subjects that are due veneration, it becomes blasphemy and sacrilege. With power and emotion, this is then contrasted almost inevitably with the Middle Ages, when flocks of the faithful were given beauty instead of ugliness to feed their faith upon (Huysmans cites Lamennais, of all people, who said that Beauty, by definition, could only be related to God.) Huysmans sums up this point at the close, when warning that healthy visitors who also are lovers of the artistic, will suffer and be stirred to holy wrath at what is inflicted upon them by "the degeneracy of churchmen." But, and most importantly, this must be balanced by the spiritual and moral beauty illumined by the raptures of the sufferers' Faith, Hope, and Charity, as vouchsafed by the Virgin Mary.

These extreme reactions are also turned back upon those people who make their living from the various forms of products sold at Lourdes. The candle-sellers, whose wares symbolize the communion of souls, are like the population of the old town in Huysmans's eyes, who fleece the pilgrims and are only civilized by having to buy and sell. The candles mirror those souls who take them out, the humbler ones all together and the "aristocratic" variety apart. One of the exceptions to his view of the local inhabitants is the candle-attendant, who is something of a parallel to the simple swineherd in *En Route*. Their unreason or indifference to the miracles is shared by the priests, who are generally seen in a poor light, although a slight change is noticeable in his view of confession: instead of lamenting about the confessor he bemoans the penitents, for while the men simply go to be cleansed, the women not only want to be starched but ironed afterwards as well! The attitude toward these "laundrymen," or at least the benefits derived, shows a marked development from the outset of his career as a Catholic writer. He reserves his highest praise for the selfless helpers, who by their actions transcend the generally low depths of devotion found around him.

It is only when the pilgrimage really begins, with the candle-lit processions giving the impression of golden moths, that Huysmans loses himself for a moment and leaves behind the awful catalogue of ills witnessed at the hospital and grotto. But in spite of the examples used to illustrate his faith and artistic attitude—an individuality defended as necessary—at the time, they are also proof that the Naturalist was not buried. Even the digressions upon symbolism take a minor role here, and are limited to short discussions upon candles, water, and the liturgy. A rare topic after conversion was that of looking at his surroundings in a straightforward, realist mode. In *The Crowds of Lourdes*, Huysmans does look at the landscape, but puts down his dislike of mountain scenery to his ancestry from his father's side (though he cannot speak Dutch, or understand the "countrymen of St. Lydwine"). It is worth noting that his descriptions of the various nationalities and groups recalls the finest passages from *Parisian Sketches* and *En Ménage* at the height of the Naturalist period. One step further, there is, if unmentioned, a recollection of *A Rebours* when he "wouldn't give a penny to be an Alpinist," for the peaks instead of giving the impression of infinitude merely stifle—his imagination is quite strong enough while sitting in an armchair!

As this, of course, is not a novel, it allows Huysmans as an observer to analyze externals to a greater degree than hitherto, although this in turn gives us an insight into his character make-up through what he sees, feels, and says in reaction to the external world around him. He analyzes, that is, tries to come to terms with, all the influencing data which as an artist means everything that is extreme and out of the ordinary. He therefore discounts Zola's hysteria theory, for example, which does not hold water in the face of such extraordinary—indeed, anti-scientific—examples of miracles, some applying to very young children and others to atheists. It is patently absurd to believe such cures are of nature, and he adopts a line once taken by Bishop Berkeley (without attributions) that as they are beyond any level of our understanding they must be the actions of an intelligence greater than ourselves, or "divine dynamics" as Huysmans terms it in the concluding pages. (Belgium is cited, where the "most unheard of cure that has ever been witnessed in the memory of man" took place, that of bone-joining in a leg that was almost severed and beyond surgery. In the same medical circumstances, needles literally dropped from the flesh.)

In the East the cult of the Virgin Mary is earlier and of a higher brand. At Constantinople in 1880, the Georgian Fathers, who had been sent a statue and miracle water from Lourdes, had to be expelled due to the extreme results. The miracles were real and completely verified, which prompted Huysmans to show theories like auto-suggestion and "nervous wounds" in their true light. Pure miracles like those at Lourdes were a vindication of his faith, and a confirmation of its timelessness through the Middle Ages and the depths of modern life. It cemented his beliefs, as did the discovery that the Apparitions "coincided" with the liturgical feasts and festivals of the Church in that region.

The thought of returning to Paris comes as something of a relief, for Lourdes is like a distant dream-city where life is intense, with its extremes of religious intoxication interrupted by fits of revulsion, yet infinitely sweet at times with an atmosphere of divinity through the close proximity of the miraculous. It is important to visit, but not for any length of time, as the dramatic nature of the cures starts by exciting, then dulls the senses, until only the extremes of hideousness cause interest or reaction. Then, also, his "implacable disgust for [his] own era" sees only a Lourdes "reared in the unwholesome cradle of our times exhaling the fetid odor of the industries which weigh it down." The clownishly stupid architecture and outbursts of debased piety that results in a

"Satanism of ugliness" vies with a massed faith not seen since the Middle Ages, fusing all classes with a single unparalleled love and hope, a return to the Gospels in this "lazaretto for souls" where one is "disinfected with the antiseptic of charity."

In short, two impressions are created, and both are mutually hostile: the repulsive and the divine. In spite of himself, Huysmans does become involved in the environment around him, although he must have been surprised by the scale. Yet, unlike ordinary tourists, he is completely unmoved by the "breath-taking" scenery. The book does include, of course, a history of Saint Bernadette—for so she became, in 1933, seventy-five years afterwards—but it is Lourdes as it was then that he investigates and dissects. For a few weeks a year, society becomes Utopian through the classless practice of virtue. The constant use of the word "witness" is important, for it shows that the author believed himself to be in a human drama, or passion play, with the stage directions coming from on high. It also explains the vehemence of his criticisms of those he believed did not even try to be worthy of this honor.

All these facets contribute to impress how important the work is, not just because it is the last book to be published during his lifetime, nor even because of the subject and its obvious didactic value. It specifically gives an insight into the development and maturity of a singular artistic faith, and that belonging to an ex-decadent and onetime Zolaist whose conversion was seen as little more than a ruse and ploy. In its vibrant, ennobling style and powerful imagery, there is a sacred feeling throughout that shows the height of his personal religion and art. *The Crowds of Lourdes* knots the thread of his quest, and with its final lines of invocation to the Immaculate Conception, shows a constant and parallel characteristic that began with the despairing, agnostic *A Rebours* and was to continue, like a prayer, in the ending of all his subsequent major works throughout the span of his Catholicism.

TROIS EGLISES ET TROIS PRIMITIFS,
1908

This work was posthumous, a collection of five essays upon subjects that are not unexpected. They are almost like stray leaves that could find no previous place in works like *Là-Bas, La Cathédrale,* and *De Tout.* Indeed, the section upon the three primitives—actually in only two essays: "Les Grünewald du Musée de Colmar" and "Francfort-sur-le-Mein"—is a reprint of the book with the same title, published in 1905.

The three churches, Notre-Dame, Saint-Germain-l'Auxerrois, and Saint-Merry, are of course all Parisian, but none is chosen for its location, itself a shift of attitude from earlier studies. It is now the interior that interests Huysmans, in every sense of the word. "The Symbolism of Notre-Dame of Paris" develops the framework first built in his book on Chartres; indeed, it was a possible choice as **The Cathedral,** we were told there. Every facet of its structure is explained in terms of symbology, even down to its tiles and cornerstone, for it is seen in terms of a science employing an image that represents something else, like a sign, deemed the greatest idea of the Middle Ages. And it was in Huysmans's favorite style, the Gothic.

Saint-Germain-l'Auxerrois, in spite of being directly opposite the Louvre, at that time was suffering from the indifference of a people living under an anti-clerical Government. It was more often than not deserted, even at high mass on Sunday, and consequently its interior had been neglected. In spite of giving its history, including the time during the Revolution when it was taken over by the sacrilegious, revelling mob, it was probably for its peace and calm that the author had visited it (he could have taken a slightly longer way home from his Ministry job, a few years earlier).

Saint-Merry, or Merri, allows for a study of that saint, or at least what little is known, as well as the adjacent streets that can be compared to the ancient histories of Paris, a positive gold mine for Huysmans's love of the extraordinary and bizarre. Overall, the various essays, excluding the reprinted ones on the primitives previously discussed, show an unusually restrained Huysmans, but still a deeply religious man. There is also a feeling of melancholy, as no doubt the book reflects the sad, dispossessed medievalist wandering dark streets in search of pure angel music, as close to the end of the world as he wished to go.

Christopher Lloyd (essay date 1990)

SOURCE: "J. K. Huysmans," in *J. K. Huysmans and the Fin-de-siécle Novel,* Edinburgh University Press, 1990, pp.1-18.

[*In the following essay, Lloyd discusses Huysmans's works in the context of French literary trends of the late nineteenth century, particularly Naturalism and Decadence.*]

Finding a reliable, unadulterated source of nourishment is a constant preoccupation of the heroes of Huysmans' novels. Nowadays we know that lightly boiled eggs have certainly not escaped contamination by the century. Solipsistically retiring into one's shell brings no escape from the pressures of the world. Huysmans' name is most frequently linked with that of his great contemporary Zola—as disciple, or as renegade disciple—even though Huysmans turns inward, and Zola outward, the first producing the private fantasy world of **A rebours,** the second the massive social documentary of *Germinal,* within a year of each other in 1884-85. But there is no paradox in the yoking of their names: both focused their disturbing and disturbed imaginations on the moral, social and linguistic taboos of the late nineteenth century and created literature which was deemed scandalous and

excessive in form and content. Yet as Huysmans carefully noted in an enthusiastic essay written in defence of *L'Assommoir* (1877), Zola was, like himself, a highly private individual, perfectly content to lead a respectable, mundane bourgeois existence among his books.

Unlike Huysmans, however, twenty years after *L'Assommoir,* Zola did achieve a notoriety of a political rather than a literary kind by his public intervention in the Dreyfus Affair, which resulted in his prosecution and year-long exile in England. By this time Huysmans was no longer his ally, a naturalist neophyte, but an enemy, a Catholic reactionary prepared to dismiss Zola's sacrifice of his hard-won personal security as a dubious publicity stunt. Similarly, the event which in preceding years had most disturbed Zola's private life, his adulterous liaison with Jeanne Rozerot, and the birth of their two children, had also aroused Huysmans' derision: 'Vous ai-je dit que Zola avait enlevé la femme de chambre de sa femme et qu'il était père d'un enfant!!! Il en a pleuré d'attendrissement, paraît-il. La joie d'avoir engendré le délectait a écrit Flaubert dans l'Education Sentimentale' (to Prins, 7 April 1890). Huysmans was fond of this sarcastic allusion to Flaubert's novel (although the phrase 'L'idée d'avoir engendré le délectait' actually occurs in *Madame Bovary,* and refers to the future paternal bliss of Charles Bovary). He had used it on a previous occasion when describing the paternal bliss of Léon Bloy, another friend turned enemy, whose offspring Huysmans referred to as 'le misérable foetus issu de ses répugnants spermatozoïdes' (to Prins, 3 September 1888).

Huysmans himself remained childless and unwed throughout a life whose main events were largely unremarkable. He was born in Paris on 5 February 1848, the only child of Elisabeth-Malvina Badin and Victor-Godfried Huysmans, a commercial artist who was born in Holland in 1815 and emigrated to France as a young man. Their son was baptised Charles-Marie-Georges: the famous initials 'J.-K.' were an invention of his own at a later date, when, in an attempt to re-assert his Dutch ancestry, he signed his first book, **Le Drageoir à épices** (1874), 'Jorris-Karl Huysmans' (although 'Karel' is the more appropriate Dutch version of Charles). Subsequently, for literary purposes, these forenames were reduced to the bare initials J.-K. While Huysmans usually signed his name 'Georges Hüysmans' in personal life and was known as 'Georges' to family and intimate acquaintances, his more deferential literary associates took to calling him 'J.-K.', or 'Jika'. (One unfriendly reviewer, noticing the author's scatological manner, remarked that 'K.-K.' would be more suitable.)

This inaccurate onomastic tribute to Victor-Godfried and the fact that Huysmans faithfully kept some of his paintings are the only clues to the son's relations with his father, who died aged forty-one when Huysmans was eight. A year later, in 1857, his mother married Jules Og, a Protestant businessman, with whom she had two daughters. Ten years later Og died, though he too was only in his forties, having invested his capital in a book-bindery, a share in which enterprise Huysmans was to inherit another ten years later when his mother died in 1876, aged fifty. Since the age of eighteen, having passed the first part of the baccalauréat, Huysmans had been earning his living as a minor civil servant, and was to do so until the age of fifty. He began his career as an 'employé de sixième classe' at the Ministry of the Interior; after the Franco-Prussian War, during which he spent August and September 1870 as a reluctant conscript in the sixth battalion of the Garde nationale mobile de la Seine, he was transferred to the Ministry of War in Versailles. Following the death of his mother he was able to transfer back to Paris, and for twenty-two years worked in the Sûreté Générale, part of the Ministry of the Interior on the rue des Saussaies.

The remainder of Huysmans' life, at least as a chronicle of publicly known facts, is largely an account of the publication of his books: a struggle for fame in the 1870s and 1880s, marked of course by his masterpiece *A rebours,* which appeared in 1884 when he was thirty-six. Popular rather than literary acclaim, however, came to him over a decade later. In July 1892, he undertook a retreat to a Trappist monastery, Notre-Dame d'Igny (near Reims), where he took communion for the first time since childhood, thus officially marking his return to the Catholic Church, though he had been flirting with religion for a number of years. Much to his surprise, the books he then wrote about his religious experiences sold increasingly well. Although Huysmans made no attempt to court popularity in these works, he seemed to have captured some of the yearning for spiritual certainly of his age. Ironically, too, his attempts to retire from the Parisian literary scene were thwarted. He spent two years as a Benedictine oblate in a monastery at Ligugé in Poitou, but was obliged to return to Paris in 1901 when the monks chose to leave France, following the enactment of draconian laws controlling religious and other associations. In 1900 he had been elected the first president of the Académie Goncourt, which had finally been founded after several years of prolonged litigation, and thus he had been forced to play a central and continuing part in the literary intrigues of the day.

Throughout his life, Huysmans was dogged by apparently interminable illnesses: dysentery, gonorrhoea, sundry nervous ailments, rheumatism, to name only a few. For six months in the winter of 1905-06 he became almost totally blind, following an attack of facial shingles. After his recovery from this disabling disease, the agonising toothaches from which he had increasingly suffered over a number of years were finally diagnosed as incurable cancer of the jaw and mouth. He died on 12 May 1907 after a protracted and lucid agony, heroically borne and sustained by his peculiarly grim brand of Catholicism in which the willing acceptance of suffering and physical pain played a central role.

Such are the bare facts of Huysmans' life, which offer a useful chronological peg with which to insert him into a wider view of French life and letters in the second half of the nineteenth century, but tell us little about his character, his inner world, and almost nothing about the world created by his books, for which he is remembered. Do we need such biographical details at all if our main aim is to explore this entirely fictitious universe, in terms of themes, functions, the development of the French novel? The old-fashioned approach through "l'homme et l'oeuvre', where the second is seen in a crudely deterministic and reductivist way as a product of the first, has long since been discredited. Thus Leo Bersani, attempting to pin down the notion of 'the author', states that 'biography is no help at all to us in our efforts to know that mysterious figure somehow different both from the stories of his novels and from the man who once lived and for whom the novels were only a part of his existence'. Certainly, the critics who refer interchangeably to Huysmans and 'Durtal' (the autobiographical hero of the last four novels) seem to be making a somewhat facile and ingenuous identification between biographical and fictional, with the result that our perspectives on both are blurred rather than sharpened. On the other hand, the rigorous textual analysis of some modern criticism, which expels any referential allusion to biographical or historical data, adopting instead linguistic or philosophical models and presenting them in a technical vocabulary largely unintelligible to the layman, seems to reduce the serious study of literature to the specialised concern of a handful of 'professional' readers.

Significantly, perhaps, the most substantial book on J.-K. Huysmans is Robert Baldick's biography (referred to here in the French version published in 1958). All subsequent studies and revaluations owe an immense debt to Baldick [who died in 1972 while still in his mid-forties), and through Baldick to Pierre Lambert, if only as a source of impeccably accurate and thorough information. Nevertheless, the most interesting interpretations of Huysmans written in the last thirty years have generally tried to move away from the tendency enshrined in Baldick's book, where the writings are unashamedly seen as autobiographical statements plain and simple. The fact is, for instance, that we know very little about Huysmans' childhood or youth in the period before 1870. Biographers have assumed perhaps somewhat glibly that when the 'vert paradis' of the Huysmans household was disrupted by the death of Godfried and the intrusive arrival of the stepfather Og, the boy Georges received an emotional shock from which he never recovered. It is true that, describing the house situated at 11, rue de Sèvres where the new family lived, Huysmans remarked in a telling phrase 'je me souviens d'y avoir passé, dans un immense appartement de premier, toute une enfance à la glace' (*De tout*). The caustic comments about the procreative achievements of Zola and Bloy quoted earlier also show a jaundiced and joyless view of family life. But is it legitimate to supplement the gaps in our knowledge by plundering the novels, as Baldick does, for example, in presenting his supposed account of Huysmans' gruesome sexual initiation at the age of sixteen?

Anyone familiar with Huysmans' tone and manner in his novels will however have recognised the same distinctive voice in those comments on Zola and Bloy—negative, truculently cynical, but at the same time essentially comic, its perception of the ridiculous and clever choice of a satirical epithet or allusion redeeming what might otherwise seem a gloomily monotonous fondness for disparaging the achievements of other people. Jean Bellemin-Noël remarks that, 'd'une manière générale le travail du critique littéraire n'a à prendre en considération que *l'auteur devenu texte'*. But clearly, when revealing his opinions and actions in a letter, particularly to one of his more intimate correspondents, Huysmans is creating a text just as much as he is when writing a novel, and allowing us to glimpse his inner life in a much more naked fashion. Some awareness of this inner life must surely add to our understanding of the imaginary world which is projected from this life in his fictional writing. Besides, it seems more fruitful to see an author as a totality than to compartmentalise our knowledge about him, provided we are sensitive enough to read public and published literary texts in a different (if parallel) way to private autobiographical writings.

Strictly speaking, Huysmans wrote very little autobiographical material, apart from a tongue-in-cheek article published under the pseudonym' A. Meunier' in 1885 (Anna Meunier was the name of his long-standing female companion), and a number of unpublished notebooks, the fullest of which is usually known as 'le carnet vert'. Like many nineteenth-century writers, however, he was an assiduous and voluminous correspondent, and two thousand or more of his letters have been preserved (largely thanks to the efforts of Pierre Lambert). Like Flaubert and Maupassant, Huysmans seems to have found that letter-writing fulfilled a deep-seated emotional need for which perhaps he had no other real outlet. As a result, he could write with a frankness which certainly scandalised the first scholarly readers of his more private letters and even today may still shock, though for less obviously Victorian reasons. Huysmans' uninhibited manner is conveyed with a great deal of bravado and gusto, and the best collections of his letters make for stimulating and informative reading. Yet we have had to wait for the less prudish (or more subtly prurient) climate of the post-permissive age for the letters to Hannon (1985) and Prins (1977) to be published complete. Though Huysmans probably wrote more letters to the Leclaires, a boring Catholic couple he met after his conversion, than to anyone else, his extensive correspondence with the Dutch writer and businessman Arij Prins is undoubtedly the best document we possess about his day-to-day life over a period of twenty-two years, from 1885 to his death.

Curiously, though, Robert Baldick not only took no account of the then unpublished letters to Prins in his admirable biography, which was forgivable, but also chose to remark that they were of little interest, which was rather less so. Subsequent commentators have also paid little attention to Huysmans as a letter-writer, with the worthy exception of Pierre Cogny. Thus the author of a recent book on Huysmans and decadence does not even cite the various editions of his correspondence as a source in her bibliography (Birkett, 1986), although one could build up an interesting picture of Huysmans as 'decadent' in theory and practice from his letters. Another of Huysmans' correspondents, for ten years between 1876 and 1886, was the Belgian poet Théodore Hannon. A letter to the latter of 18 April 1882 presents a familiar impression of overstated world-weariness: 'A part tout cela, rien de neuf, ici—la vie continue sa monotonie, sa pluie fine échappée d'une tinette. Il faudrait inventer quelque vice nouveau pour se divertir, malheureusement la série des vices est encore plus restreinte que celle des vertus . . .' Huysmans tends to over-use the cloacal image of the 'tinette' (a septic tank) in his urge to give concrete weight to his ennui ('la tinette liquide qu'est l'abominable vie': to Bloy and Landry, 26 August 1885); but here his juxtaposition of material grossness and the 'spiritual' quest for a new vice typifies a certain *fin-de-siècle* manner, exemplified in his own novel *Là-bas* or in the very title of a book like Péladan's *Le Vice suprême* (1884).

Sometimes the 'decadent' went beyond complaints to action, with results that could be embarrassing:

> Je suis décidément dans une veine de saletés pour l'instant. J'apprends, avant hier, samedi, qu'un grand marchand d'antiquités de la rue Laffitte, près du boulevard, un juif appelé Meyer possède 60 lettres autographes de moi, dans lesquelles il est question de pédérastie, de baisage, et d'opinions sur des livres. Ce juif veut vendre la collection complète.

> Ce sont mes lettres intimes à Caze!!!—la famille—riche—les a vendues pour se faire de l'argent . . .
> (To Prins, 19 October 1887)

Even in his lifetime, the private missives of a moderately famous person could thus become public property, with a commercial value enhanced by their potentially pornographic qualities. In this case, Huysmans appears to have bought back and destroyed the letters. But commentators who solemnly expose the author's supposedly hidden perversities and homosexual tendencies in their critical readings of *A rebours* ought to take into account the fact that pederasty, fucking, and opinions on books' are dealt with quite openly in his letters to Hannon and Prins. One does not want to present a caricature of Huysmans as decadent poseur and pervert beneath the cloak of bourgeois respectability mentioned at the beginning of this chapter (if one lumps together contemporaries like, say, Huysmans, Lorrain, Péladan and Mirbeau under the catchy title 'decadence', there is a high risk of simply obscuring their most distinctive individual qualities). Nor does one want to convey the impression of Huysmans as compulsive pornographer by excessively highlighting the salacious passages of his correspondence. Nevertheless, it is particularly the surprising but deliberate juxtaposition of comments on writing and sexual 'confessions' which gives certain letters their tone, a tone both engaging and at times disturbing.

Huysmans is of course a highly self-conscious writer, and it would be naive to assume that all his observations were spontaneous outpourings to be taken at face value. An element of calculation is often present. Writing to Prins about his excursions into the Paris underworld of prostitutes and their unsavoury protectors, Huysmans describes a vicious fight in a café in which he claims he was lucky to escape alive and another victim was murdered. But he lets slip the tell-tale comment: 'J'ai heureusement toutes mes notes' (11 February 1891). Collecting copy is all for the lowlifer' who refuses personal or moral involvement with the subjects of his observations. In fact, he seems greatly to have exaggerated this bloodcurdling incident, which was probably no more than a drunken brawl. Elsewhere, however, the exaggeration is intentional:

> En fait de cochoncetés. Je suis assez calme. De temps à autre une minette et une succion—mais l'art se perd!—Il n'y a plus que des ouvrières, des mécaniques, aucune femme d'art, c'est le triomphe de l'Industrie! . . quel siècle d'américanisme abject! (to Prins, 30 August 1886)

Huysmans is often at his best when complaining about something (as Paul Valery astutely noted: 'On eût dit [. . .] que les abominations de toute espèce eussent pour effet d'engendrer un artiste spécialement fait pour les peindre dans un homme créé spécialement pour en souffrir' Here, the comic effect is achieved less by the smutty boast—in poor taste in every sense of the word, given his oral practices—than by the metaphor which shifts the lament for a dying art to the social and economic plane, allowing a familiar jibe at an industrialised, Americanised age of uniform mediocrity, a jibe revitalised however by the unlikely circumstances which provoke it.

Most of the uninhibited references to sex, it should be noted, are either to what at one time would have been called perversions or else to impotence. Huysmans of course writes in a spirit of male camaraderie, of a sexual culture highly dependent on brothels and prostitution, and to correspondents who share both his tastes and excursions in these areas. At the same time, these correspondents are also men of letters, unhampered by middle-class linguistic taboos, aware no doubt that writing brings its own 'jouissance'. Huysmans, interestingly enough, draws attention to what we might regard as a typical piece of nineteenth-century hypocrisy, the objection to seeing others call a spade a spade, the objectors of course being quite prepared to use the spade provided it remains unnamed. Thus he observes that the sanctimonious 'vieux cochons à air grave qui vomissent de dégoût sur nos livres' are precisely those who 'tous les soirs, se livrent à des exercices de langue' (to Prins, 6 September 1886).

The modern reader is unlikely to be offended by Huysmans' own linguistic or lingual exercises and may

grant him credit for turning acts into writing with a certain inventiveness; on the other hand, the social context behind these exploits may seem more troubling. For example:

> . . . J'ai découvert une superbe fille dans mon quartier. Elle m'use la langue—elle est trés jolie et a la peau qui dégage l'odeur canaille d'une pastille du sérail, du benjoin et de l'encens—c'est bizarre et excitant. D'autre part, j'ai trouvé, dans une famille de musiciens tziganes, une petite fille qui joue du xylophone et qui me branle assez bien. C'est très montant. Je ne puis faire plus avec elle, l'honnêteté de sa famille s'y opposant. (To Prins, 2 December 1886)

Here the air of complicity with a fellow debauchee takes on a rather sinister aspect as we glimpse a world of male aggressors and repressed females, of a grim commerce in flesh, especially young flesh, a callous corruption of innocence and exploitation of poverty by privilege. Normally Huysmans affects a schoolboyish jocularity when expatiating upon his erotic achievements, as a means no doubt of diverting attention from such sordid mercenary details. Indeed, abetted by his colleague Alexis Orsat, known for various reasons as 'the Professor', he enjoys playing the schoolmaster with Prins and Hannon, offering them detailed anatomical advice for the best way to perform a 'minette' or a 'feuille de rose' (cunnilingus and anilingus), berating his pupils for their recalcitrance, and jovially excusing his outrageousness ('Mais tonnerre et hémorroïdes! je deviens d'une indécence rare!': to Hannon, 15 April 1878).

But it would be a mistake to see in Huysmans a cynical if unashamed sensualist. The complaints about the failure of sexual experience, about the gloomy betrayals, compromises and disappointments which invariably define the relationship between the sexes are to be found not only in the novels but also in his personal writing. The emotionally bleak childhood he probably suffered seems to have led to an equally unsatisfactory adulthood. Though Huysmans never married, alongside the references to anonymous prostitutes we find references throughout the letters to Anna Meunier, usually described as 'ma femme'. Anna was born in 1851 and earned her living as a seamstress. She probably met Huysmans after the Franco-Prussian War, in 1872, and at this stage their liaison was short-lived; she had two daughters by another man in 1874 and 1877. A letter to Hannon of 12 November 1877 tells us that Anna renewed contact with Huysmans at this time, and their relationship then continued for eighteen years until her death in 1895.

Huysmans pretends a certain reluctance to pick up this relationship in his letter to Hannon, claiming that his flagging appetites need more exotic stimulation (perfumes and silk stockings played a large part in Huysmans' erotic imagination, as the editors of these letters note). Nevertheless, the earliest references suggest a certain sensual joy, even if Huysmans cannot resist a burlesque note: 'En folatrant avec ma jeune personne j'ai détraqué le sommier de mon lit blanc [. . .] la nuit va être dure, sur ce sacré sommier détraqué!' (To Hannon, 15 April 1878). At the same time, however, Huysmans and Anna never actually lived together; he continued to frequent prostitutes, enjoyed a number of liaisons with other women, and occasionally ventured into the homosexual underworld (he expresses some distaste for the hirsute muscle-men he found there in his letters to Prins, while teasingly trying to persuade his Dutch correspondent to satisfy his pederastic fancies with a youth the latter had met at an ice-rink). One reason for this promiscuity was that by 1887 Anna was seriously ill: a year later Huysmans writes bluntly to Prins 'elle se paralyse et devient folle!' (18 June 1888). Innumerable doctors were consulted, in vain (including Dr Pierre Marie, an eminent colleague of Charcot at La Salpêtrière). Gradually Anna declined to a state of infantilism, leading to her eventual internment in the lunatic asylum of Sainte-Anne, where she lingered on wretchedly for two years (suffering the same grim fate as had Maupassant shortly before her). Small wonder that Huysmans was driven to observe bitterly: 'Il n'y a décidément de vrai que le bordel; c'est au moins terminé après' (to Prins, 8 September 1888). In effect, as the editor of the Prins letters remarks, Huysmans eventually was forced to accept all the burdens of marriage with Anna Meunier with few of the rewards.

The brief portraits of her drawn by visitors to Huysmans' household suggest a rather wan and self-effacing young woman, clearly overshadowed by the writer and his circle of artistic and intellectual associates. In the novels, if we accept that they have an autobiographical basis, the ebullient and sensual Jeanne of *En ménage* is replaced six years later by Louise in *En rade,* hag-ridden by creeping paralysis and financial worries. As Huysmans said, the relationship became a cross he bore loyally to the end, which in part explains the jaundiced eye he turned on most marital or extra-marital relationships. Three years after Anna Meunier's death, Huysmans at the age of fifty noted in his diary with gloomy laconicism: 'les femmes, tout raté', elliptically enumerating a number of abortive affairs. After the carnal torments which beset him as he hesitated on the threshold of Catholicism (one possible title for *En route* was 'la bataille charnelle'), in the last fifteen years of his life he seems to have practised total chastity. Maupassant, famed for his sexual athleticism, claimed he received innumerable unsolicited letters and offers from female admirers. On a lesser scale, Huysmans found himself in a similar position, when such escapades no longer interested him: 'Depuis que je suis vieux, les jeunes filles s'emballent. J'ai des histoires inouïes à ce point de vue . . .' (to Prins, 25 July 1902). One of these episodes with a young Catholic girl of aristocratic origins has a rather sad charm—a recent biographer has chosen to resuscitate it, in a manner some readers may find embarrassingly sentimental (Pevel, 1984). Given the chance to seduce or marry Henriette du Fresnel, Huysmans opted instead to remain with his solitary existence, and persuaded her to

become a nun—a strange alternative, one might think. But human love, as we have seen, had never meant very much more for Huysmans than rather grotesque gymnastics stimulated by oral-genital contact and bizarre accoutrements. Real love was spiritual, and the cloister was the only place to tap it successfully. Thus in a fashion more medieval than modern, Huysmans would have genuinely believed that to consign his protégée to a nunnery for thirty-four years did not represent the waste but the ultimate fulfilment of a life. If nothing else, he behaved decently and without duplicity in extremely trying circumstances.

So far, the image I have evoked of Huysmans suggests a depraved misogynist turned reactionary Catholic, a man perhaps stunted in his emotional existence turning to religion in order simultaneously to fill this affective vacuum and to satisfy some of his masochistic impulses. His writing too gives the impression of a somewhat cold-blooded character, if one looks beneath the outrageousness and verbal fireworks and notes the cruel ease with which he can turn out grotesque caricatures of others and himself. When Léon Bloy had to be circumcised, Huysmans viewed this operation with a certain relish: 'On lui a coupé le prépuce et tailladé sa pauvre pine.[. . .] Le revoilà vierge, car son phimosis de naissance lui avait toujours interdit un contact réel avec la femme' (to Prins, 24 October 1887). Huysmans summed up Bloy's notoriously ugly Danish spouse as 'la grenouille-girafe qui lui sert de femme' (to Prins, 20 December 1894). Here too, however, we may run the risk of replacing the hackneyed notion of the 'decadent' with a rather prissy notion of a 'pauvre type'—Huysmans, like the pathetically frustrated bureaucrat M. Folantin in his story *A vau-l'eau,* with an additional sprinkling of literary talent.

In fact, despite his barbs (and they are funny, after all), Huysmans was not mean-spirited. The awful, or god-awful, Léon Bloy he dubbed 'ce pou de lettres!': (to Prins, September 1897), but never ceased to send the lousy mendicant money, which was rarely if ever returned, even in the form of thanks. Remy de Gourmont remarked that Huysmans was the victim of his verbal sharpness: 'Il resta jusqu'au bout méchant en paroles et bon en actions'. Intruders could be faced with a hostile exterior: those who visited him at the office were confronted with two files prominently displayed on the desk, one marked 'bores' and the other 'spongers'. Biographers who favour a physiognomical approach may attempt to penetrate this exterior by inspecting photographs of the subject, though one often suspects that this tells us more about their imagination than anything else. An early photograph of Huysmans in his late twenties shows him full-bearded and with a surprisingly large amount of romantically flowing hair. This virile-looking customer one could imagine as youthful law student, spending his time and money with an actress rather than his books, writing a romantic verse drama (called *La Comédie humaine* and presumably burnt), and ingratiating himself with the up-and-coming Zola.

A better-known photograph shows him a few years later, aged thirty-three. Disillusionment has set in; the hair has been cropped back, Samson-like, to produce the familiar crew-cut. The body too seems to have shrunk; the high-buttoned jacket suggests a frame sheltering against the chilly outer world. The neck pokes out scrawnily from a collar of over-generous dimensions. Much of the face still hides behind a beard and unruly moustache. The sitter gazes with earnest melancholy at the camera. The best-known images of Huysmans picture him twenty years on. He is in his mid-fifties; the convert has shrunk still more, his diminution further emphasised by the enormous tomes he is often wielding, as he hunts down 'documents' to display in the pages of those indigestible final novels. The hair has gone—the tonsured cleric replacing the hirsute sensualist. He looks prematurely aged, pedantic, not very happy. The beard has been trimmed to a Mephistophelian point, while the curving bony nose is ever ready to sniff out some of the stranger heresies or doctrines of Christianity and its adjuncts past and present.

All this is somewhat fanciful. Huysmans' 'livret de garde mobile' adopts a more neutral manner: 'taille de 1m 73, visage ovale, front ordinaire, yeux gris, nez aquilin, bouche moyenne, menton rond, cheveux châtains, sourcils idem' (Cogny). An ordinary forehead and an average mouth: the military imagination does not rise to great heights. Huysmans, for whom domestic comforts seem to have had a sort of metaphysical status (he makes as much fuss about an overnight train journey as a more adventurous spirit might about a trip to the Hindu Kush), was a lover of cats. He frequented a brothel known as 'La Botte de paille', where he was called 'mon oncle', but complained that his interest in the 'minettes' (or pussies) there was waning: 'Alors qu'est-ce qu'il reste? mon chat qui est une bête aimable, mais insuffisante au point de vue intellectuel et charnel' (to Prins, 25 November 1890). A recent biographer remarks: 'J'aurais pu tenter de faire un Portrait de l'Artiste en vieux chat' (Audoin). But the artist had already had this idea himself. His alter ego, A. Meunier, observed that 'Il me faisait l'effet d'un chat courtois, très poli, presque aimable, mais nerveux, prêt á sortir ses griffes au moindre mot'. The famous ginger cat Barre-de-Rouille used to catch bats on the balcony, and developed a neurotic obsession with straightening pictures and crooked objects on the writer's desk. But following a fall from a window-ledge, his back legs became paralysed, and Huysmans was obliged to have the vet despatch what Anna called her 'enfant rouge' with strychnine. This cat's life and death were however celebrated in *En ménage* and *En rade,* forming the third side of the domestic triangle with the women based on Anna and the male protagonists. Durtal in *Là-bas* tells his feline companion: 'tu es l'exutoire spirituel de la solitude et du célibat'.

Edmond de Goncourt recorded an account given him by the painter Raffaelli of Huysmans' strange physical mannerisms (15 April 1894). He was seen to close his um-

brella in an idiosyncratic fashion, to rub his hands compulsively against the top of his chest, to have a jerky, inhibited gait as though his legs were chained together. All this was 'moitié d'un prêtre, moitié d'un aliéné'. Not so much a tomcat, more a clerical grasshopper. There were those who doubted both Huysmans' sanity and his sincerity after the conversion. Zola, for instance, as the abbé Mugnier noted, 'croit que son disciple de Médan est "toqué" et a quelque "fêlure"' (27 April 1892). Both an orthodox Catholic like the abbé Belleville and a writer like the uncharitable Jules Renard thought Huysmans a charlatan, 'un Léo Taxil plus lettré' as Renard put it in his journal on 11 August 1902. (Léo Taxil, real name G.-A. Jogand-Pagès, 1854-1907, wrote numerous anti-clerical works, simulated a conversion in 1885, and then publicly admitted this was a mystification.)

Huysmans, of course, was unlikely to win himself many allies and sympathisers outside his immediate circle of acquaintances, thanks to his truculent and dismissive conversational manner. Most other writers were 'raseurs' (especially famous foreign ones like Goethe, whose birthplace Huysmans refused to visit when passing through Frankfurt-am-Main). Gustave Guiches depicts him unsuccessfully rolling cigarettes or fiddling with nail scissors while holding forth:

> il émet d'une voix grêle et nasale, avec de petits nuages bleus, s'il fume, ou, si non, avec accompagnement de ses ciseaux, des jugements si stupéfiants d'arbitraire injustice, d'illogisme, de platitude et de grossiéreté, sur les hommes, les femmes, sur l'art, même sur la température, qu'on finirait par se demander s'il ne voudrait pas, par hasard, faire rire.
>
> Les appellations préférées de son mépris et de son indignation sont 'Salopiot, sagouin, voyou, muffeton, gouape, galapiat, etc.', et ses formules de prédilection 'Il m'indiffère . . . il est infoutu d'écrire . . . c'est des glaires . . . de la lavasse . . .' et les plus aimees de toutes 'C'est du pipi de mouche ou c'est de la sous-m. . . .'

If Lamartine was 'une infusion de fleur d'oranger qui ferait mal au coeur', Musset was 'un rinceur de cuvettes'. Even at one remove, we sense that Huysmans possessed an admirable polemical verve and impressive range of invective. But such practitioners of 'la parole pamphlétaire' always run the risk of being exposed as toothless tigers; beneath the pose of philistinism and ready command of abusive formulas one may suspect a narrow-minded and timorous desire to hide within an armoured suit of prejudices, a suit which soon begins to ring rather hollow.

Huysmans' eccentricity and mystifying posture were in any case exacerbated in the period 1885 to 1893 by his choice of an unlikely set of bedfellows and mentors. Before this period, most of his immediate friends were writers and journalists, while in the last fifteen years of his life, priests, monks and other reasonably conventional Catholics were probably closer to him than any of his literary associates. Whatever his amorous vicissitudes and moments of despair (he told Myriam Harry he considered suicide after his enforced return to Paris from Ligugé in 1901), for most of the time Huysmans seems to have led a busy social and professional life. He was certainly not the solitary hermit whom he chose to portray in *A vau-l'eau* and *A rebours*. In the late 1870s, for instance, he was actively involved in the naturalist literary scene around Zola and the publisher Charpentier, with its innumerable meals, soirées and journalistic activities. Thus in a letter to Hannon of 10 April 1878, he writes:

> Je suis bien en retard avec vous, mais oyez!samedi dr—soirée chez Montrosier, dimanche, chez Coppée, lundi, chez la mére de Charpentier, mardi, diner du boeuf nature et ce soir mercredi, dîner chez un ami et demain dîner de *L'Assommoir* et dimanche chez Flaubert!!!!! C'est tuant et idiot.

In the winter of 1901-02, as a minor celebrity newly back in Paris, he was bombarded with unwanted invitations, which he was able to refuse diplomatically since the doors of the annexe of the Benedictine convent on the rue Monsieur where he was temporarily living were locked at nine in the evening.

The story of Huysmans' conversion is well known. His period as an 'occultist' is rich in bizarre and farcical episodes, episodes enriched in some cases by the dubious character of some of those witnesses who chose to record them for posterity. One of these is Joanny Bricaud, who is eager to tell us about the writer's attendance at a Black Mass and the magical rites by which the ex-abbé Boullan preserved Huysmans from the spells cast on him by the Rosicrucians. Bricaud's veracity can be gauged from the fact that, while employed in a humble position in a bank in Lyon, he granted himself various high-sounding titles for the purposes of his occult existence and claimed to have met Boullan in the course of this second career, forgetting perhaps that he had been only twelve years old when Boullan died in 1893. While Bricaud never met Huysmans, another chronicler, Gustave Boucher, certainly did, and produced a pamphlet entitled 'Une séance de spiritisme chez J.-K. Huysmans' shortly after the latter's death. The highlight of the séance, held in the writer's flat on the rue de Sévres in January 1892, proved to be the evocation of the fantom of the recently deceased General Boulanger, a sort of poor man's version of the figure of Napoleon who often appears on such occasions. Boulanger had disappointed those of his supporters who hoped he would follow the example of Napoleon III by seizing power in a *coup d'état* by choosing instead to flee the country on 1 April 1889 and committing suicide on his mistress's grave in September 1891. Though largely indifferent to the General's political aspirations, Huysmans had had the task at the Sûreté Générale of reading the unlucky Boulanger's love letters to the aptly named comtesse de Bonnemains. It is unclear what the participants in the séance learned from

their ghostly visitor, and how seriously Huysmans really took such antics. The fact remains, however, that on other occasions he was eager to display to sceptical enquirers like Jules Huret or Myriam Harry his 'exorcism paste' and the innumerable evil spirits swarming in the room which the paste helped dispel.

The most notorious charlatan with whom Huysmans became involved was Joseph-Antoine Boullan. Boullan would doubtless have liked to be remembered as an unorthodox theologian and thaumaturge who had fallen foul of the dogmatic conservatism of the Church's hierarchy. This is certainly the picture painted of 'Dr Johannés' in *Là-bas*. Huysmans heard of Boullan's reputation as a specialist on occult matters while searching for 'authentic' documents for this novel, and eventually made contact with him in February 1890, through the intermediary of a strange Catholic lady, Berthe Courriére, whom he had met a few months earlier. It is often assumed that Huysmans was completely bamboozled by Boullan, perhaps because the fictional Dr Johannés is presented as a whiter-than-white magician who does epic battle with the satanic Canon Docre in *Là-bas*. In fact, whatever the simplified contrast between good and evil presented in the novel, Huysmans was attracted to Boullan precisely because he seemed to be, not a conventional priest, but a magician whose views were somewhat heterodox, to say the least, and whose activities irregular, if not criminal. Thus the day after his initial letter to Boullan, he writes to Prins: 'Je suis plongé dans des courses, á la recherche d'un prêtre démoniaque et sodomite qui dit la messe noire. J'en ai besoin pour mon livre. J'ai dû pénétrer dans le monde des occultistes pour tout cela—quels jobards et quels cons!' (6 February 1890). By the end of the month, the prêtre sacrilége' had already supplied Huysmans with a whole battery of documents on contemporary Satanism, causing the writer to exclaim 'C'est un homme délicieux que ce vieux monstre' (to Prins, 26 February 1890).

In other words, Huysmans was quite prepared to suspend conventional moral judgements when dealing with this delicious monster, just as he does in the portrait of Gilles de Rais in *Là-bas*. In Boullan's community of visionaries and heretics in Lyon, he discovered 'le Moyen-âge en plein': 'le Moyen-âge en plein, c'est à rêver, à cette époque!' (to Prins, 24 July 1890). It is true that Huysmans probably only discovered the full extent of Boullan's iniquity after the latter's sudden death on 3 January 1893. In 1861, he had been sentenced to three years' imprisonment for fraud with his associate Adèle Chevalier, a former nun. He was finally expelled from the Church in 1875, mainly because his concept of 'l'oeuvre de réparation' and the sects he founded to pursue it involved a mixture of magical and orgiastic practices. His most serious crime remained undiscovered, however, until he admitted it to the Church authorities: in December 1860 he had murdered the child he had had with Adèle Chevalier. He was not prosecuted for this offence.

Huysmans, then, was not deceived by Boullan, although he clearly found in him a fascinating living example of the morally ambiguous, larger-than-life figures he created in his best novels; *A rebours* and *Lá-bas*. Even the death of the defrocked abbé managed to combine the fantastical with the farcical, as the Lyon Vintrasians accused the Paris Rosicrucians of murdering their self-proclaimed leader with black magic. These living occultists, however, used the more conventional means of newspaper columns and the duelling ground to continue their campaign. Nevertheless, Boullan's influence on Huysmans was undoubtedly powerful, and not merely in the paradoxical sense that he drove the writer from the marginal fringes of the occult to a more reputable brand of Christianity, from 'là-bas' to 'là-haut'. Whatever the scepticism he affected to outsiders like Prins, the supernatural milieu in which Boullan and his acolytes lived clearly changed the writer's perception of daily reality, and the abbé's peculiarly carnal, materialistic concept of mysticism was incorporated into Huysmans' own highly literal—minded conception of Christian mystery and doctrine. To the curses of rheumatism and colic were added the nefarious attacks of succubi and other spirit presences.

Yet it would be wrong to assume from this that the converted Huysmans lapsed into crankiness or underwent a radical change of character. Some years before, he had distanced himself from the crazier notions and behaviour of his friends Villiers de l'Isle-Adam and Bloy, observing 'Ce ne sont point précisément des cerveaux équilibrés' (to Prins, 6 July 1886). As one might expect of a conscientious, life-long civil servant, Huysmans was regular in his habits and responsible in his actions. Following the publication of *A rebours,* Huysmans began receiving a series of enthusiastic anonymous letters. Their author, as he informed Prins, proved to be a 'bizarre dame catholique qui [. . .] avait absolument voulu se faire baiser' (8 September 1888). She was Henriette Maillat, a former mistress of Bloy and Péladan. Huysmans carefully copied her correspondence and subsequently used some of her letters in *Là-bas,* citing them almost verbatim. But her extravagant demands for satisfaction and money did not arouse his enthusiasm. Faced with the prospect of a rendezvous, he remarked to Prins: 'Je vais être, lundi soir, obligé de garer ma pauvre queue et de subir le grand jeu des fureurs et des larmes'. (8 September 1888). Huysmans' attempts to regulate the relationship in a more economical fashion did not suit Mme Maillat, who did not appreciate what Baldick calls his 'bureaucratic' conception of love. 'Merci, néanmoins, de cette bonne petite affection réglée par le calendrier que vous m' offrez', she wrote, '—mais ce n'est pas ma mesure, mon coeur *gante* plus grand'.

Another commentator has noted a similar bureaucratic side to Huysmans' Christianity. He (or his characters) are forever drawing up statements of profit and loss, taking stock of their situation, seeking out documents which give quantifiable proof of their beliefs (Bessède,). While a more boisterous and extravagant character like Maupassant seems genuinely to have loathed the ten years of petty drudgery he spent as a minor civil servant, Huysmans was reluctant to follow the former's example and abandon the office for the more independent but hazardous existence of daily journalism. Of course, he complains frequently about 'la boîte infamante qui me détient pour 200F par mois au milieu de ses paperasses et de ses cartons' (to Hannon, 20 November 1877). He is aware, too, of the apparent paradox of an aggressively innovative author living a double existence as a writer of official letters and minutes: 'Comme c'est drôle tout de même quand on songe que c'est moi qui manie cette langue sévère de l'adm[inistration]' (to Hannon, 20 August 1877). The Byzantine niceties of official rhetoric are parodied in the story **"La Retraite de M. Bougran,"** as is the obsessive punctiliousness of the petty functionary in the character Désableau in *En ménage*. The wretched M. Folantin in *A vau-l'eau* is bullied by his chief and has little chance of advancement without protection from influential people.

The fact is, however, that the predictable routine of the office seems perfectly to have suited Huysmans' stay-at-home temperament. When he is compulsorily pensioned off, the character M. Bougran discovers belatedly that his office has been a womb-like refuge and source of security. For once Zola and Bloy were in agreement, in seeing Huysmans' career at the Ministry as a convict's ball-and-chain which he should make every effort to shake off. But Huysmans despised the feckless way in which Bloy, who rarely had a permanent source of income, allowed his dependants to live in squalor and supported them with hand-outs from obliging friends. At the same time, he despised what he saw as Zola's increasing commercialism and the compromises this entailed, such as the adaptation of his novels in the theatre as trashy melodramas. Huysmans was not a successful businessman: far from supplementing his income as an author and civil servant, the bookbindery seems to have run at a loss, bringing him perilously close to bankruptcy in the mid-1880s. If he had abandoned his career as a bureaucrat as others had suggested, he observed, 'je serais dans la boue, á la merci du premier venu [. . .] Je suis bien gênè.d' argent, depuis que les affaires ne marchent plus, mais enfin, j'ai toujours avec le Ministére, un fixe par mois '(to Prins, 19 March 1888).

Was the office, for that matter, simply a comfortable sinecure, as is sometimes assumed? For six days of the week, so the story goes, except for official holidays, his annual period of one month's leave, and any time he managed to claim for sickness, Huysmans would arrive at the rue des Saussaies between ten and eleven in the morning and remain there for about six hours. During this time, his official tasks were sufficiently light to allow him to devote most of his energy to writing his personal correspondence and even his novels; much of the manuscript of *A rebours* is written on paper headed 'Ministére de l'Intérieur'. A careful reading of the letters to Prins over more than a decade indicates that this picture is not so far from the truth. The pressures of the job seem to have depended both on Huysmans' immediate superiors and the stability of the Minister himself, whose downfall could bring with it the dismissal of his underlings. Huysmans protests bitterly on the relatively few occasions when he is obliged actually to work for ten hours a day, with the implication that this is an uncommon state of affairs.

It should be pointed out too that, unlike the fictional M. Folantin, and given his relative lack of ambition in this domain, Huysmans was quite successful as a civil servant. Folantin is an *employé* on an income of 3,000 francs per annum: Huysmans' own situation in 1881 (his salary had doubled since 1866). Six years later, however, Huysmans was promoted to the post of *sous-chef,* which gave him the right to a private office and an income of 4,500 francs a year. On his retirement in February 1898, he earned 6,000 francs, and was entitled to a pension of 2,800 francs. Furthermore, in September 1893 he had been made a Chevalier de la Légion d'honneur (he was promoted to the rank of Officier in 1907), not for his services to literature, but, ironically, for those given to the administration. The publicity created by this decoration he regarded characteristically as un embêtement á haute dose qui n'est même pas compensé par la joie du ruban rouge dont je me fous' (to Prins, 8 September 1893). A few years earlier he had diplomatically refused the offer of the Palmes académiques, an award usually granted to minor functionaries and second-rate academics.

As we have already seen, literary celebrity and substantial sales also came to Huysmans relatively late in life, and did not coincide with his greatest creative achievements. A simple but effective gauge of his popularity and reputation as a writer can be made by studying the books of press cuttings which he assiduously collected throughout his career. These seven large volumes are now kept in the Fonds Lambert of the Bibliothèque de l'Arsenal. While the nineteen years between 1874 and 1893 (from *Le Drageoir à épices* to *Lá-bas*) are covered in the 474 pages of the first volume, the remaining 1,275 pages of the other volumes are devoted to Huysmans' last fourteen years as a Catholic writer. In fact the turning point was *Là-bas,* which attracted over a hundred reviews, both inside and outside France. In an age where literary figures played a significant role in journalism, even the *Liverpool Mercury* expressed interest in the writer's sojourn at Notre-Dame d'Igny: 'M. Huysmans has just made a "retreat", it is said, to a Trappist monastery in France, lives on bread, radishes, and water, and even sleeps on the floor' (11 August 1892). Such anecdotal details may, individually, seem rather trivial or ridiculous; yet to confront the whole mass of the thousands of articles about himself which Huysmans gathered in from his press agencies is to gain an impression in a very concrete sense of the weight and achievement of a career, of a writer making his particular mark on a historical epoch, itself recaptured in these pages of cuttings.

One of the most interesting accounts of the material conditions of writers in nineteenth-century France is given by Emile Zola in an essay entitled 'L'Argent dans la littérature'. Zola himself became a rich man through the sales of his novels from the late 1870s onwards, but was well aware that his situation was exceptional. A 'good' sale for a novel in 1880, he says, would be 3,000 or 4,000 copies, which on royalties of 50 centimes a copy would bring an author 1,500 or 2,000 francs (rather less than the average annual wage of an urban working man). Writing for the theatre was far more profitable, on the whole, since authors received a percentage of the takings of their plays. And journalism could be even more lucrative: a debutant might earn 200 or 300 francs a month for his articles. With some of the smugness of the self-made man, Zola sees in money a force which emancipates the modern writer from the patronage of private individuals or the state. There is a certain ingenuousness in this view, since anyone who chose to live through journalism was in effect obliged to accept the patronage of editors and directors and to make the appropriate compromises (as Maupassant's novel *Bel-Ami* amply demonstrates).

Hence the dream of so many writers of founding and directing their own review or newspaper. The most famous example in mid-nineteenth-century France is perhaps Jules Vallès. Even Huysmans had played with this idea, at the time of his collaboration with Zola, Maupassant and the other authors of *Les Soirées de Médan* (a collection of stories which they published in 1880, and which is often seen as marking the arrival of naturalism as a literary movement). Predictably, perhaps, the project to establish *La Comédie humaine* as an organ to proclaim the naturalist cause petered out amid venomous bickering between the writers themselves, and lawsuits between the writers and their potential publisher. Such an episode helps explain Huysmans' reluctance thereafter to commit himself wholeheartedly to journalism, although despite the outrage caused by his polemical art criticism (in *Le Voltaire* in 1879, for instance), throughout his career he earned quite large sums from his contributions of both articles and the serial rights of his novels to a variety of journals.

This had certainly not been the case at first with his novels. He told an interviewer from *Le Journal* on 6 September 1893 that the four editions of *A rebours* had earned 1,600 francs, and the two editions of *En rade* 1,000 francs. But in two years *Là-bas* had earned him 10,000 francs—hardly a fortune, but still 'une des stupeurs de ma vie'. The sales of the Catholic works were to surpass this success: *Les Foules de Lourdes* sold 21,000 copies within a month of publication in 1906, by which time *En route* and *La Cathédrale* had reached figures of about 30,000 copies each. (In other words, Huysmans would have earned the equivalent of at least six times his annual salary with these three books.) Such achievements are, naturally, relative: one of Zola's less well-known novels, *L'Argent,* sold 50,000 copies in a few days in 1891. Nevertheless, at the end of his life Huysmans was an established literary figure, who enjoyed a reasonable financial independence and was perhaps more respected as President of the Académie Goncourt than as a Catholic proselyte, since the outspoken nature of his views inevitably offended many conventionally minded members of the Church.

So much for this biographical sketch of J.-K. Huysmans, which has I hope gone beyond the cursory and constraining form of the chronologies found in many editions of his works, and given some impression of the writer's most pressing personal preoccupations, of the incidents banal or bizarre which shaped the course of his life, and of the manner in which Huysmans himself chose to describe such inner preoccupations and outer incidents. The time has come to turn to Huysmans as a writer, a writer of books, and in the first place to look at that confrontation with the French language which has caused every commentator on his writing to draw attention to his extraordinary stylistic virtuosity.

Camille Paglia   (excerpt date 1990)

SOURCE: "Cults of Sex and Beauty: Gautier, Baudelaire, and Huysmans," in *Sexual Personae: Art and Decadence from Nefertiti to Emily Dickinson,* Yale University Press, 1990, pp. 408-38.

[*In the following excerpt, Paglia views Huysmans, Charles Baudelaire, and Théophile Gautier as the three principal French authors whose works defined characteristically Decadent ideals of eroticism and physical beauty.*]

Joris-Karl Huysmans' novel *A Rebours* (1884) expands the Decadent innovations of Balzac, Gautier, Poe, and Baudelaire. The title means "against nature" or "against the grain." Des Esseintes, the epicene hero, is product of an incest-degenerated aristocratic line, like Poe's Usher. Romantic solipsism contracts to its ultimate Decadent closure. Renouncing social relationships, Des Esseintes withdraws into the self-embowered world of his ornate mansion. Surrounded by curios and art works, he is like a Pharaoh entombed with his possessions. He is both priest and idol of his own cult. But his dream of perfect freedom is defeated by humiliating dependency on others—servants, doctors, dentists, horticulturists. *A Rebours* contains its own ironic self-deflation. Like *Madame Bovary,* it shows reality comically frustrating the lofty ideals of an author-identified protagonist. Des Esseintes wants life entirely artistic and artificial. But nature takes her revenge, tormenting him with toothache, nauseating him with his rare perfumes, disordering his delicacy-sated stomach. Unable to eat, Des Esseintes is fed by enema, "the ultimate deviation from the norm" which he relishes as "a happy affront against nature": "What a slap in the face for old Mother Nature!" The novel ends with the ailing aesthete forced to return to society and nature. So the Decadent enterprise fails.

A Rebours is a novel without a plot, consistent with the Romantic withdrawal from action. It is spiritual autobiography, recording a journey not through space but through modes of perception and experience. The chapters, containing few events, are meditations on *things*: books, flowers, antiques. Persons are also things. Des Esseintes performs a botched Sadean experiment on a boy by trying to turn him into a criminal. Des Esseintes has the Decadent sexual recessiveness. He trifles, with poor results, with two masculine women he hopes will give him a new sensation. Miss Urania, an American acrobat with boy's hair and "arms of iron," is really an automaton, slow and witless. When her oscillating gender turns feminine, Des Esseintes drops her like a hot potato. Reality always falls short of imagination. Miss Urania is all muscle and no mystique. She exasperatingly refuses to take charge. Without Baudelairean sexual subordination, Des Esseintes is impotent (apparently like Huysmans himself). But potency belongs to the realm of vulgar acts. Decadent eroticism is perceptual or cerebral.

Unlike Poe, Baudelaire, and Swinburne, Huysmans has no *anima* or projected female spirit. Even Roderick Usher is immured with a sister. Des Esseintes' lavish mansion may be Huysmans' attempt to construct a male house, a mental space excluding the female. But the repressed always returns with redoubled force. The aesthete's buried affect toward women produces the horrors of Chapter Eight, a spectacular flight of imagination. Over ten astonishing pages, woman appears in stages of increasing sexual clarity. It is Huysmans' metamorphoses of the vampire. The process begins as another exercise in Decadent connoisseurship. Des Esseintes has been a collector of artificial flowers that look real, nature of course being inadequate: "Nature, he used to say, has had her day; she has finally and utterly exhausted the patience of sensitive observers by the revolting uniformity of her landscapes and skyscapes." But Chapter Eight advances past this Baudelairean position into new Decadent terrain: "Tired of artificial flowers aping real ones, he wanted some natural flowers that would look like fakes." He will force nature into art's frame.

Des Esseintes inspects cartloads of hothouse specimens, lurid flowers of evil. There are Caladiums with "swollen, hairy stems" and "huge heart-shaped leaves." Aurora Borealis with "leaves the colour of raw meat." Echinopsis with "ghastly pink blossoms" like "the stumps of amputated limbs." Nidularium, with "sword-shaped petals" and "gaping flesh-wounds." Cypripedium like a diseased, bent-back "human tongue" in a medical text. Some flowers seem "ravaged by syphilis or leprosy," others "blistered by burns" or "pitted with ulcers." To make these "monstrosities," nature borrows tints of rotting flesh and the "hideous splendours" of gangrene. Muses Des Esseintes, "It all comes down to syphilis in the end."

Huysmans' fantastic catalog is a meditation on Romantic nature. It is an anti-Rousseauist polemic, where not society but nature is shown as deeply corrupt. Organic life is in advanced disease, clotted with mutilations insulting beauty and form. We seem to be in a brand-new genre, science fiction, transporting us to a Venusian jungle of half-animal plant creatures. This is Huysmans' voyage to Cythera, Venus' isle. Baudelaire's syphilitic hanged man is infected by Huysmans' noxious blooms, the ulcerated genitals of mother nature. Syphilis, which Des Esseintes sees devastating every generation "since the beginning of the world," is like Poe's red death invading the prince's castle and annihilating humanity. The flowers are a Trojan Horse bringing deadly freight into Des Esseintes' walled city: the daemonic female of chthonian nature.

Adam in the primeval garden falls asleep for the birth of woman. Exhausted, Des Esseintes dreams a series of weird female androgynes, first a tall, thin woman in Prussian soldier's boots, then a haggard "sexless creature" on horseback, her green skin studded with pustules. He recognizes her as "the Pox," a female version of Poe's ghoulish masquer. The dream shifts to "a hideous mineral landscape," surely Baudelaire's rocky Cythera. Here Des Esseintes has one of the most horrifying archetypal experiences in literature. Something stirs on the ground, "an ashen-faced woman, naked but for a pair of green silk stockings." Nepenthes pitchers hang from her ears; "tints of boiled veal" show in her flaring nostrils. As she calls to him, her eyes glow, her lips redden, and her nipples shine like "two red peppers." He recoils in horror from her spotted skin.

> But the woman's eyes fascinated him, and he went slowly towards her, trying to dig his heels into the ground to hold himself back, and falling over deliberately, only to pick himself up again and go on. He was almost touching her when black Amorphophalli sprang up on every side and stabbed at her belly, which was rising and falling like a sea. He thrust them aside and pushed them back, utterly nauseated by the sight of these hot, firm stems twisting and turning between his fingers.

Her arms reach toward him. He panics as her eyes turn a terrible "clear, cold blue." "He made a superhuman effort to free himself from her embrace, but with an irresistible movement she clutched him and held him, and pale with horror, he saw the savage Nidularium blossoming between her uplifted thighs, with its swordblades gaping open to expose the bloody depths." Just before he touches the plant's "hideous flesh-wound," he wakes up, choking with fear. "'Thank God,' he sobbed, 'it was only a dream.'"

Thus Chapter Eight ends, with Des Esseintes having escaped, like Poe's hero in the maelstrom, from a forcible return to female origins, sucked into the womb of the rapacious all-mother. The woman in green stockings is a syphilitic whore, like Blake's Harlot. Her earrings of carnivorous plants symbolize her command over nature. The boiled veal of her nostrils is the fetid grossness of biology, to which the female always resummons the male. Her nipples are red peppers because they scald the lips of every infant and perforate the chest of every man. Her eyes fascinate because she is the vampire hypnotiz-

ing by eye-contact. Des Esseintes is magnetically drawn to her even in his terror because she exerts earth's malign gravitation, which we saw at work in Michelangelo.

Amorphophallus is, incredibly, a real flowering plant of great height; the name means "shapeless" or "misshapen penises." The black fronds springing up and stabbing at the woman's belly are her self-generated male organs, by which she pleasures and fecundates herself. Her belly "rising and falling like a sea" contracts in orgasm and labor: she is Baudelaire's parkside carcass billowing with maggots. The swordblades ringing her vulval "bloody depths" reproduce mythology's vagina dentata. Female genitals perceived as a wound are a commonplace of psychoanalytic literature. That they can be a diseased flower we know from Blake's "Sick Rose." Tennessee Williams told Elizabeth Ashley about being taken to a brothel for his "initiation into manhood." A prostitute forced him to look between her legs: "'All I could see was somethin' that looked like a dyin' orchid. Consequently I have never been comfortable either with orchids or women.'" In *A Rebours,* female genitalia are flower and wound, because this is the place where man is born and from which he must tear himself away. Des Esseintes builds a palace of art against nature, but in his dreams nature comes to reclaim and devour him.

Huysmans' poisonous genital flowers are botanic androgynes, like Lewis Carroll's shrewish rose and tigerlily. "Androgynous" is actually a scientific term for plants with staminate and pistillate flowers in one cluster. The female vegetation of *A Rebours* relates to some amazingly misogynous remarks Huysmans made about Degas' paintings of bathing women. He speaks of "the humid horror of a body which no washing can purify." Humid horror: here is that inescapable connection I find between female physiology and the chthonian liquid realm. Certain male celibates or homosexuals express their phobic attitude toward the female body in a nervous fastidiousness, a compulsive cleanliness manifested in small well-scrubbed hands, punctilious dress, and aridity of manner and speech. In the old days, such men were the petty tyrants of musty midlevel civic, bank, and library bureaucracies. The female, with her dark, dank inwardness, is visually unintelligible. Medusa's pubic head is the plant world of writhing stems and vines; she is artistic disorder, the breakdown of form. Liquidity plus vegetative overgrowth equals the chthonian swamp of female nature. The male homosexual, the most active dissenter from female dominance, rebels against the marshy organicism of the female pudendum and the cushy softness of the female body, which he perceives as irresolution of silhouette. This is one reason why, in America, so many gay men are reed-thin, while so many gay women are fat. When women stop trying to please the harsh male eye, the female body just drifts right back to oceanic nature. In *A Rebours,* written by an idealizing celibate, the connoisseur Des Esseintes creates a ritual cult of sharply defined objects d'art, because Decadent aestheticism is the most comprehensive system of aversion to female nature devised by western culture.

Tennessee Williams' memory of his traumatic initiation confirms my chthonian reading of *Suddenly Last Summer*. The play originally appeared with another in *Garden District* (1958), a New Orleans place name that Williams makes a metaphor of rapacious nature. The brilliant movie of *Suddenly Last Summer* (1960), directed by Joseph L. Mankiewicz with a screenplay by Gore Vidal, was a critical disaster. It shows mother nature as a Sadean and Darwinian vortex where the weak are devoured by the strong. In an incantatory scene of expressionistic horror, straining at the emotional limits of film, Katharine Hepburn as Violet Venable narrates the annual assault of birds of the Encantadas on newborn turtles as they race for the sea.

Suddenly Last Summer is *A Rebours* turned inside out. Instead of a chthonian cubicle (Huysmans' horticultural Chapter Eight) inside an aesthetic domain, there is an aesthetic cubicle inside a chthonian domain. Williams' aesthetic cubicle is a votive shrine preserved by a despotic *mater dolorosa* in honor of her son/lover, the homosexual aesthete Sebastian Venable, who produced one perfect poem per year, in a fancy private edition worthy of Des Esseintes. Wealthy mother and son were "a famous couple," touring fashionable Europe. In the inseparable Violet and Sebastian, Williams sexually updates Shakespeare's hermaphrodite twins, Viola and Sebastian. Modernization here, as in Picasso, means a return to primitive archetype. Violet and Sebastian are the Great Mother and her ritually slain son. He is killed by a pack of predatory beggar boys, who hack and eat his flesh in ritual *sparagmos*. She cultivates insectivorous plants in a steaming "jungle-garden," which the play describes with language straight from *A Rebours*. The sinister garden is cinema's most potent evocation of the primeval swamp-world, rivalled only by the dinosaur saga of Disney's *Fantasia*. Mankiewicz' film is sophisticated and learned: hanging in the son's chamber is a Renaissance painting of St. Sebastian, the bleeding beautiful boy. Sebastian Venable belongs to the tradition of homoerotic martyr, to which Oscar Wilde contributed by taking the name Sebastian Melmoth after his release from prison.

Des Esseintes' aesthetic ambition is to discriminate, to use Pater's word, every thing and every experience. This scholarly process secures the identity of objects against nature. Ironically, in *A Rebours* discrimination collapses back into nondifferentiation. All the aesthete's exotic fragrances begin to smell disgustingly alike. Language alone retains its Decadent separateness. Gautier says imperial late Latin was "an ingenious, complex, learned style," which Baudelaire drew upon for inspiration, since "the fourteen hundred words in Racine's vocabulary" are inadequate for complex modern ideas. Hugo's *Hernani*, whose defense Gautier led, defied the Racinian canon with its eccentric locutions in the Shakespearean manner. *A Rebours* culminates this movement to broaden the rationalist French language. Huysmans' rich, bizarre vocabulary is both antiquarian and futurist. Symons said, "He could describe the inside of a cow hanging in a butcher's shop as beautifully as if it were a casket of jewels."

The diversification of Huysmans' language is a psychic and therefore sexual self-development. *A Rebours* has few characters, for words substitute for persons. Des Esseintes admires imperial Latin because "it was rotten through and through and hung like a decaying carcass, losing its limbs, oozing pus, barely keeping, in the general corruption of its body, a few sound parts." Language becomes Baudelaire's crucified corpse. I said the body in Spenser is a social integer. The paradigm in Baudelaire is the alienated body: each poem is a corrupted object, a mirror of the self. Baudelaire made lyric a reliquary of decay. In Huysmans, with his glut of rare words, language generates dense new personae. *A Rebours* (originally called *Alone*) is Romantically self-contained, its linguistic energy invested in internal sexual differentiation. Its words are thronging multiples, spores of competitive identity. The whole, subdividing into fractious parts, makes love to itself.

Rita Felski (essay date 1991)

SOURCE: "The Counterdiscourse of the Feminine in Three Texts by Wilde, Huysmans, and Sacher-Masoch," in *PMLA*, Vol. 106, No. 5, October, 1991, pp. 1094-1104.

[*In the following essay, Felski considers depictions of gender roles in novels by Huysmans, Oscar Wilde, and Leopold von Sacher-Masoch.*]

An imaginary identification with the feminine permeates much of the writing of the male European avant-garde in the late nineteenth century, a period in which gender norms were being protested and redefined from a variety of standpoints. This "feminization" of literature, exemplified in a destabilization of traditional models of male bourgeois identity, was linked to an emerging self-conscious aestheticism that set itself in opposition to realist and naturalist conventions. Seeking to expose the seemingly natural features of the dominant culture as simulacra, the male artist drew upon stylistic and thematic motifs codified as feminine, thereby challenging both sexual and textual norms. Thus a complex array of alignments and contradictions among the structures of gender, class, and commodity culture both shaped and constrained the contestatory "textual politics" of the fin de siècle cult of art and artifice.

The feminization of male avant-garde texts was, of course, only one of the ways in which gender identities were being reconstituted during the period. Most obviously, feminist movements in various European countries were becoming increasingly vocal in their organized demands that women be allowed access to the public sphere. Indeed, late-nineteenth-century discourses often linked the feminized aesthete and the New Woman, twin symbols of the "decadence" of the age and focal points of contemporary anxiety about changing gender roles. Yet one can debate the assumption—shared by a number of present-day critics—that this early-modernist appropriation of metaphors of femininity was aligned with the feminist project. I hope to show, to the contrary, that the parodic subversion of gender norms reinscribes more insistently the divisions that the text ostensibly calls into question, revealing deep-seated anxieties about both gender and class in the strenuous repudiation of a vulgar and sentimental aesthetic.

I explore this logic through an analysis of three prose texts: *Against the Grain* (*A rebours*), by J. K. Huysmans (1884); *The Picture of Dorian Gray,* by Oscar Wilde (1890); and *Venus in Furs* (*Venus im Pelz*), by Leopold von Sacher-Masoch (1870). The first two are often yoked together as exemplary illustrations of decadent and aestheticist trends in the French and English fin de siècle, while Sacher-Masoch's work, although widely translated and known in Europe in the 1870s and 1880s, has been largely ignored by literary historians and read primarily for its clinical interest as one of the first detailed representations of male masochistic fantasy. All three texts, however, share a number of distinctive stylistic and thematic motifs that can be drawn out through comparative analysis. Each bears witness to the artist's sense of alienation from dominant social structures and his own class identity, an alienation that in turn affects his literary representation of gender. Yet the preoccupation with femininity in late-nineteenth-century writing should not therefore be seen as epiphenomenal, deflecting attention from latent but fundamental antagonisms of class. On the contrary, a feminist reading casts another light on recent leftist interpretations of the nineteenth-century avant-garde as the self-critique of modernity, as the articulation of a counterdiscourse of symbolic resistance to the commodification and technical rationality of modern capitalism (see, e.g., Terdiman; [*Discourse/ Counter-discourse: The Practice of Symbolic Resistance in Nineteenth-Century France*] my source for the term *counterdiscourse*). Without denying the contradictions and tensions in the artistic expressions of a patriarchal culture, such a reading qualifies the adversarial status of early-modernist texts by revealing that their models of male subjectivity are intimately connected to, rather than at odds with, the espousal of a self-reflexive and parodistic aesthetic.

Naomi Schor has pointed out the long-standing and often pejorative association of femininity with ornamentation and detail in Western culture. Further elaboration is required, however, to explain the specific late-nineteenth-century nexus among femininity, decadence, and a self-consciously decorative and antirealist aesthetic. Such an association is by no means self-evident, since the equation of women with the natural and the organic is well established in bourgeois ideology. In Goethe's *Sorrows of Young Werther,* for instance, woman is nostalgically identified with a harmonious plenitude, exemplifying a sphere of organic community that compensates man for the alienating experience of modernity. There is a clear difference between this set of symbolic configurations, which remains influential throughout the nineteenth century, and the later identification of femininity with artifice, exhaustion, and decadence. Whereas in sentimental and early Romantic literature the feminine is linked with an expressive aesthetic, providing a vehicle for the cultivation and articulation of feeling, in the late nineteenth century it also becomes associated with aestheticism, parody, and the preoccupation with surface and style. Femininity is now appropriated by the male artist as emblematic of the modern, rather than as standing in opposition to it.

In the three novels under discussion, this motif is exemplified most obviously in the explicitly feminized male protagonists, who are identified with love of artifice, excess, and everything unnatural. Significantly, each is an aristocrat and thus a figure outside the cycle of production and the male bourgeois ethos of individual achievement; in *Venus in Furs,* for example, the hero, Severin, defines himself as "nothing but a dilettante . . . an amateur in life" 'nichts weiter, als ein Dilettant . . . ein Dilettant im Leben.' Renouncing the struggle for active self-realization in the world, the aesthete displays traits the dominant ideologies of his day identified with women: passivity, languidness, vanity, hypersensitivity, a love of fashion and ornamentation. Spending much of his time in an interior, private space codified as feminine rather than in the public sphere of work and politics, he devotes himself to the cultivation of style and to the appreciation of life as an aesthetic phenomenon. None of these men considers himself an artist; the Romantic myth of the creative genius has become exhausted, and aesthetic pleasure is now located in consumption, in the exercise of taste through the collection and enjoyment of beautiful objects. Given the bourgeois encoding of production as masculine and consumption as feminine, this inclination accentuates the aesthete's feminized status. So too does his fascination with the decorative as well as the "high" arts: the exercise of style manifests itself in his delight in the details of decor and costume, and the evocation of elaborately furnished interiors and glamorous fashions plays an important part in all three texts. Such concerns were of course more usually associated with the middle-class woman, who, while denied the possibility of creating great art, was encouraged to exercise her aesthetic sense in decorating herself and the interior of the bourgeois household (Saisselin).

Against the Grain, for example, details the aesthetic experiments of the jaded aristocrat des Esseintes, the last scion of a family marked by a progressive "effemination" of its male members. Huysmans's protagonist abandons Parisian society to pursue the isolated cultivation of refined and artificial pleasures: almost the entire text is committed to descriptions of his collections of esoteric and exotic objets d'art; his fastidious discriminations among colors, fabrics, and styles of furnishings; and his elaborate experiments with liqueurs and perfumes. In *The Picture of Dorian Gray,* Wilde depicts the aesthetes of English high society, for whom "[l]ife itself

[is] the first, the greatest, of the arts" and who share des Esseintes's contempt for vulgar bourgeois social norms. The dandy, the prototype of both des Esseintes and Dorian Gray, devotes himself to the production of the self as an aesthetic artifact; he is the ultimate representative of fashion, the embodiment of what Wilde, following Baudelaire, calls the "absolute modernity of beauty." Like woman and like the work of art, the dandy can be perceived in aestheticist doctrine as quite useless; exalting appearance over essence, decoration over function, he voices a protest against prevailing bourgeois values that associate masculinity with rationality, industry, utility, and thrift. The dandy's transformation of the self into a work of art is symbolized by Dorian, who assumes the qualities of his own portrait; enclosed within an invisible frame that separates him from the continuum of history, he presents an image of static and unchanging physical perfection. An "excessively developed aestheticism" 'auf das Höchste getriebener Schönheitssinn' also characterizes the hero of *Venus in Furs,* causing him to flee modern society in order to worship the ideal, embodied in the imperious Countess Wanda. Severin is both feminized and infantilized in his role as slave; whipped and humiliated by his mistress, he must listen to her taunt: "you are not a man" 'du bist kein Mann'. Sacher-Masoch's text depicts the ritualistic enactment of an elaborately staged and costumed erotic drama; life is made art through a highly stylized and deliberately anachronistic relationship between mistress and masochistic slave that constantly comments on its own status as performance.

The narcissistic dimension of the feminized male is epitomized most clearly in Dorian Gray, whose androgynous qualities are evoked in descriptions of his scarlet lips, golden hair, and eternal youth. If, as Rachel Bowlby points out, his yearning to retain the flawless and ageless qualities of his own portrait uncannily preempts the narcissistic fantasies inspired by the dream-world of contemporary advertising ("Dorian Gray"), this trait also accentuates his feminized status, since it is, above all, images of women that circulate in commodity culture as objects of identification and desire. Moreover, Dorian's preoccupation with the portrait carries broader resonances in symbolizing the construction of identity through representation. He only begins to develop a sense of self-consciousness after viewing his idealized image in the painting by his friend, the artist Basil Hallward: "A look of joy came into his eyes, as if he had recognized himself for the first time. . . . The sense of his own beauty came on him like a revelation." As Ed Cohen argues in a reading that draws implicitly on the Lacanian theory of the mirror stage: "Looking on his completed portrait for the first time, Dorian encounters himself as reflected in the 'magical mirror' of Basil's desire. This image organizes the disparate perceptions of his body into an apparently self-contained whole and reorients Dorian in relation both to his own identity and to his social context."

The point here, then, is that Dorian's narcissism, as exemplified in his fascination with a self-image generated by another's desire, relates to the novel's more general emphasis on the textual mediation of identity. The figure of Dorian Gray is in fact explicitly defined as a product of various textual influences—Hallward's painting, the "evil book," Wotton's aphorisms—and Wilde's text constantly calls into question the distinction between original and copy, the real Dorian Gray and the imitation. With identity revealed as artifice and rendered indeterminate and unstable, Romantic notions of the organic subject are undermined: "Is insincerity such a terrible thing? I think not. It is merely a method by which we can multiply our personalities." Similarly, des Esseintes in *Against the Grain* aspires to a completely artificial existence, where experience can be translated into style. In his secluded retreat, he can simulate the austere severity of a monastery cell through a skillful combination of fabrics and furnishings, without the necessity for either physical hardship or religious conviction. A judicious selection of images, smells, and objects replicates in his own dining room the sensations of a maritime voyage, precluding any need for actual travel. For Huysmans's hero, techniques of illusion and artifice, made possible through a combination of aesthetic sophistication and technological expertise, have conspired to make nature itself anachronistic.

Thus the blurring of gender roles evident in the texts under discussion forms part of a larger destabilization of conceptions of authenticity within a society whose cultural expressions are increasingly shaped by commodity aesthetics and the logic of technological reproduction. The fin de siècle preoccupation with style and appearance underlines the aestheticization of everyday life, the mediation of experience and identity through the consumption of mass-produced images, texts, and commodities that renders any appeal to a true self merely another fiction. "Being natural is simply a pose" (Wilde). This insistence on the artificiality of the real can thus be read as a critical response to the presentation of bourgeois values and beliefs as rooted in an organic and unchanging reality. The authority of nature is exposed as nothing but art, reality as simulation—an insight that contains an emancipatory moment in its recognition that identity is constructed and hence changeable. At the same time, the aesthete's preference for art over nature carries with it, as I hope to show, another, more problematic meaning in relation to gender politics.

One of the most common ways to signal gender ambiguity is in the sphere of sexuality, and these texts explore a variety of sexual roles and options: male masochism, homosexuality, transvestism, voyeurism, and fetishism. Des Esseintes, for example, reminisces about his own infatuation with a sturdy athletic American acrobat called Miss Urania, an erotic attraction linked to his perception of her latent masculinity. In the grips of this desire, "he presently arrived at the conclusion that, on his side, he was himself getting nearer and nearer the female type" 'il en vint à éprouver, de son côté, l'impression que lui-même se féminisait,' that he was "craving for her as an anaemic young girl will for some great, rough Hercules whose arms can crush her to a jelly in their embrace" 'aspirant ainsi qu'une fillette chlorotique, après le grossier hercule dont les bras la peuvent broyer dans une étreinte'. This desire to be dominated by a woman is associated with the thrill of perversity, the defiant exploration of "unnatural" and artificial pleasures. The Romantic yearning for unmediated pleasure, beyond symbolization, is radically undermined in these late-nineteenth-century texts; desire, instead of being repressed by the constraints of the symbolic order, is constituted through it. The aestheticization of the erotic is particularly apparent in *Venus in Furs,* where sexual desire is generated and mediated through diverse forms of textuality: letters, contracts, books, paintings, statues, and elaborate theatrical rituals. As Gilles Deleuze observes, it is not the sexual act that is portrayed as exciting but the elaborately posed image of the fur-clad woman: "The woman torturer freezes into postures that identify her with a statue, a painting or a photograph. She suspends her gestures in the act of bringing down the whip or removing her furs; her movement is arrested as she turns to look at herself in a mirror". In a suggestive reading of Sacher-Masoch's work, Deleuze establishes a number of links between the formal logic of the texts and their defining theme of male passivity and masochism. In *Venus in Furs* the fetishistic fixation on costumes, the ritualized representation of static erotic tableaux, derives from the pleasures of suspense, waiting, and disavowal in the masochistic fantasy, which, as Deleuze convincingly argues, differs fundamentally from sadism in its self-conscious and contemplative aestheticism.

Deleuze's reading offers a psychoanalytic explanation of Sacher-Masoch's art, but it is also clear that the distinctive textual features of *Venus in Furs* are historically overdetermined and that the late nineteenth century saw a proliferation of works linking the realm of the aesthetic to passive, feminized male subjects. One of the most obvious factors contributing to this phenomenon was the symbolic polarization of science and art through gender dualisms drawn from the division of private and public spheres; in the social imaginary, the aesthetic became increasingly feminized in relation to the "objectivity" and "rationality" of a scientific worldview. Both art and women could be seen as decorative, functionless, linked to the world of appearance and illusion and divorced from the work ethic and the reality principle. As Saisselin notes, "The realm of art was the realm of women; it answers to the feminine principle while the battle of the streets exemplifies the male principle". This feminization of the aesthetic ran parallel to the aestheticization of women, evident in the expansion of consumerism, the "democratization of luxury" resulting from the establishment of the department store and the increasing importance placed on women's fashion and display as conspicuous consumption [Rachel Bowlby, *Just Looking: Consumer Culture in Dreiser, Gissing, and Zola*]. At the same time, health, nationalism, and masculinity became closely intertwined in the late-nineteenth-century imagination; the motif of the feminized male

thus came to function as a symbol of decadence that could be counterposed against models of bourgeois optimism and progress. While contemporary reviewers criticized *The Picture of Dorian Gray* for its unmanliness and "effeminate frivolity" [Regenia Gagnier, *Idylls of the Marketplace: Oscar Wilde and the Victorian Public*], self-identified decadents found "man . . . growing more refined, more feminine, more divine" [George L. Mosse, *Nationalism and Sexuality: Middle Class Morality and Sexual Norms in Modern Europe*]. Both acolytes and critics of decadence and aestheticism drew on a common vocabulary of such binary oppositions as normal/abnormal, natural/unnatural, masculine/feminine, healthy/diseased; though disdaining the rationalist claims of science, aestheticism was nevertheless deeply suffused by its organicist and pathological metaphors and by Darwinian notions of evolutionary development. Thus the distinctive features of late-nineteenth-century aestheticism—the decomposition of "organic" narrative into detail, the preference for exotic and perverse subject matter over social realism, the acute linguistic self-consciousness—could be condemned by writers like Max Nordau as a cultural symptom of a pervasive degeneration and hysteria. For supporters, however, the very modernity of aestheticism lay, paradoxically, in proclaiming the exhaustion of the modern, in rejecting middle-class ideals of reason, progress, and industrious masculinity and defiantly celebrating perversity.

This refusal of history and of the concomitant mimetic claims and sociopolitical concerns of realist aesthetics manifests itself formally in a spatial and atemporal structure through which literature seeks to approach the condition of painting. Description takes precedence over narration; movement and action give way to an at times claustrophobic sense of immobility and ahistoricity; and the aestheticist text reveals a self-reflexive preoccupation with the surface of language, with the grain and texture of the word. *Against the Grain,* for example, can be seen as one of the first modernist novels, a text that is, notoriously, "without a plot" (Wilde) and that is structured around fetishistic, quasi-pornographic descriptions of works of art, bibelots, and interior furnishings. Huysmans's fascination with the materiality of language, which is at one point likened to a decaying carcass and at another to precious metals, enamels, and jewels, is reflected in a self-consciously decadent style of sinuous distortions and exotic references that aspires to material opacity. *Venus in Furs* follows a dreamlike logic of association—dreams in fact play a crucial role in the text— and imitates the qualities of the uncanny, fantastic, and ahistorical images it constantly evokes. As the text's geographical and temporal vagueness suggests, its true locus is the imagination of the fantasizing subject, resulting in the ritualistic and self-referential logic of constantly repeating the same images of the cruel woman. Sacher-Masoch's formulaic style, its reliance on cliché and stereotype, causes language to become solidified and unreal and hence to undermine any putative referential dimension. *Dorian Gray* remains closest to the conventions of realistic narrative and Victorian melodrama; yet here too an acute linguistic self-consciousness manifests itself in elaborate descriptions, in parodies and borrowings from such texts as *Against the Grain* and Pater's *Studies in the History of the Renaissance,* and above all in the aphorisms and paradoxes that implicitly subvert the novel's ostensible moral ending. Thus all three texts replicate in various ways the feminine preference for form over function, for style over history, that characterizes their languid heroes.

Accordingly, it can be argued, the topos of the feminine serves a specific function in the counterdiscourse of late-nineteenth-century literature, signaling a formal as well as a thematic refusal of an entire cluster of values associated with bourgeois masculinity: the narrative of history as progress, the valorization of function over form, the sovereignty of the reality principle. From an antinaturalist standpoint, gender, as one of the central categories of social and symbolic organization, provides a key terrain on which to challenge dominant definitions of the real. Feminine traits, when adopted by a man, are defamiliarized, placed in quotation marks, recognized as free-floating signifiers rather than as natural, God-given, and immutable attributes. Defamiliarization through quotation in an incongruous context is of course the defining characteristic of parody, and the relation between parody and male femininity here assumes the form of a dialectic. If the hero's preoccupation with style, quotation, and linguistic play testifies to his femininity, so in turn his mimicry of femininity confirms the authority of a parodistic worldview. The feminized male deconstructs conventional oppositions between the "modern" bourgeois man and the "natural" domestic woman; he is male, yet disassociated from masculine rationality, utility, and progress; feminine, yet profoundly unnatural. Whether hailed as subversive or condemned as pathological, his femininity signifies an unsettling of automatized perceptions of gender, whereas feminine qualities in a woman merely confirm her incapacity to escape her natural condition. Krafft-Ebing, for example, claims that masochism can only be seen as a true perversion in men, for nature has given women "an instinctive inclination to voluntary subordination" [Bram Dijkstra, *Idols of Perversity: Fantasies of Feminine Evil in Fin de Siècle Culture*]. The semiotic significance of feminine characteristics is, in other words, fundamentally altered when appropriated by the male aesthete.

It is not surprising that some critics have related this antinaturalist strain in nineteenth-century aestheticism to the interests of contemporary poststructuralist theory. Deleuze, for instance, suggests that the masochistic fantasy functions as a form of demystification, revealing the absurdity of the law through techniques of exaggeration and humor. Jonathan Dollimore argues similarly that Wilde's "transgressive aesthetic" is intimately related to a transgressive sexuality, constituting a radical subversion of organicist ideals of the authentic and natural self. Yet while the texts of Wilde, Huysmans, and Sacher-Masoch subvert established distinctions between art and life, nature and culture, masculinity and femininity, this

very process can reveal an investment in the creation and maintenance of new boundaries. Just as class identity is not transcended by the counterdiscourse of the avant-garde, so too is gendered subjectivity implicated in, rather than dissolved by, the espousal of a self-reflexive and parodistic consciousness.

The logic of exclusion operative in an aestheticist or decadent work centers on the repudiation of vulgarity, which is defined as explicitly antithetical to the text's own literary project. Wilde's aristocrat Henry Wotton refers to "an age so limited and vulgar as our own" and speaks dismissively of "vulgar realism in literature" Severin describes his own disgust, "for everything base, common and ugly" 'gegen alles Niedere, Gemeine, Unschöne'. Des Esseintes condemns "the vulgar reality of actual, prosaic facts" 'la vulgaire réalité des faits' and defines his aesthetic preferences in explicit opposition to the coarseness of popular taste:

> [T]he work of art that has appealed to the sham connoisseurs, that is admired by the uncritical, that is not content to rouse the enthusiasm of only a chosen few, becomes for this very reason, in the eyes of the elect, a thing polluted, commonplace, almost repulsive.

> [L]'oeuvre d'art qui ne demeure pas indifférente aux faux artistes, qui n'est point contestée par les sots, qui ne se contente pas de susciter l'enthousiasme de quelques-uns, devient, elle aussi, par cela même, pour les initiés, polluée, banale, presque repoussante.

The parodistic consciousness freely subverts a number of oppositions, including, as I have shown, traditional distinctions between masculinity and femininity; this act of subversion, however, both presumes and reinforces a primary division between the refined and the vulgar, a division that separates the self-conscious aesthete from the common and sentimental herd, which is by definition incapable of this kind of irony. This metadistinction is, in other words, simultaneously aesthetic and political; it affirms the superiority of a particular interpretative mode (self-conscious, antiutilitarian, ironic) that is in turn inflected by class and gender interests. In holding vulgarity in contempt, the aesthete voices a protest against the materialism, hypocrisy, and conventionality of bourgeois culture; viewed from another angle, however (the two readings are not of course mutually exclusive), this act of negation expresses an elitist disdain for the non-intellectual majority, who are perceived to adhere unthinkingly to a naive and nonparodic aesthetic. In this context, women and the masses are often blurred together as symbols of the democratizing vulgarity of modern life, embodying a murky and ill-defined contaminating influence that threatens the precarious superiority of the artist. As Andreas Huyssen has shown, the vanguard consciousness of male modernism has historically grounded itself in a gendering of mass culture as feminine and inferior, exemplifying a kitsch and sentimental aesthetic antithetical to the self-conscious and ironic experimentalism of high art.

Thus the male aesthete's playful subversion of gender norms, his adoption of feminine traits, paradoxically re-inforces his distance from and elevation above women, who are by nature incapable of such intellectual mobility and aesthetic sophistication. This hierarchization is apparent in the texts under discussion. On the one hand, Rachel Bowlby suggests the late-nineteenth-century aesthete foreshadows the replacement of the ascetic bourgeois of early capitalism by a "feminized" and narcissistic subject engendered by a mass-culture society of image consumption (*Just Looking*). Yet, on the other hand, this feminized aesthete takes great pains to define himself in explicit opposition to the prototype of the vulgar female consumer. Des Esseintes, for example, is no longer able to gain pleasure from certain objects, like specific kinds of flowers and jewels, that have become sullied by their association with feminine middle-class taste. In his consumption of literature, Huysmans's hero, "whose mind was naturally sophisticated and unsentimental" 'qui avait l'âme peu fraîche et qui était peu sentimental de sa nature', is unable to tolerate the works of women writers, whose "wretched prattlings" 'misérables bavardages' are couched in a style of nauseating triviality. If the aesthete and dandy shares with women an identity as consumer, it becomes imperative for him to signal the superior taste and the qualitative difference of his own aesthetic response. As A. E. Carter has pointed out, decadence differs most significantly from the Romantic tradition in enacting a dual negation, condemning not only a tawdry modern urban culture but also the nostalgic yearning for an idyll of unmediated nature. In this pessimistic vision, women stand for the most despised aspects of both culture and nature, exemplifying the crass vulgarity and emptiness of modern bourgeois society (woman as archetypal consumer) as well as a natural sentimentality coded as specific to women, an inclination to outpourings of uncontrolled feeling that threaten the disengaged stance of the male aesthete.

Thus the dandy, in pursuit of uniqueness through the narcissistic cult of self, sees women as exemplifying the uniformity and standardization of modern life that he most abhors. Des Esseintes reflects on these qualities in the prostitutes he has known: "all, like so many automata wound up at the same time with the same key, uttered in the same tone the same invitations, lavished the same smiles, talked in the same silly phrases, indulged in the same absurd reflexions" 'toutes, pareilles à des automates remontés à la fois par la même clef, lançaient du même ton les mêmes invites, débitaient avec le même sourire les mêmes propos biscornus, les mêmes réflexions baroques'. Similarly, Dorian Gray explains his passion for Sybil Vane by contrasting the glamour of the actress with the mundaneness of ordinary women: "They are limited to their century. No glamour ever transfigures them. One knows their minds as easily as one knows their bonnets. One can always find them. There is no mystery in any of them. . . . They have their stereotyped smile, and their fashionable manner. They are quite obvious". In both examples, the superficiality and interchangeability of women symbolize an abstract identity

and an economy of sameness, an all-pervasive disenchantment of the world in which sexuality, like art, has been deprived of its aura, contaminated by the rationalization of everyday life.

Yet while such descriptions emphasize the mechanical, depersonalized, and ultimately soulless quality of modern femininity, women are simultaneously seen to embody the "innate folly" 'bêtise innée' of their sex, a natural and excessive emotionality antithetical to the controlled consciousness of the aesthete. *Dorian Gray*, for example, includes frequent jibes about women's tiresome sentimentality, their subjection to feelings beyond their control. "Women . . . lived on their emotions. They only thought of their emotions". The point is echoed by Wanda in *Venus in Furs:* "In spite of all the advances of civilization, woman has remained as she was the day Nature's hands shaped her. . . . Man, even when he is selfish or wicked, lives by principles; woman only obeys her feelings" 'Das Weib ist eben, trotz allen Fortschritten der Zivilisation, so geblieben, wie es aus der Hand der Natur hervorgegangen ist . . . so folgt der Mann, auch wenn selbstsüchtig, wenn er böswilling ist, stets *Prinzipien*, das Weib aber folgt immer nur *Regungen*'. Severin's memories of his youth reveal a clearly established chain of associations linking vulgarity, women, and the fear of sexual and emotional intimacy: "When I first began to think about love, it seemed to my raw adolescent's eyes particularly crude and vulgar; I avoided all contact with the fair sex" 'Als etwas ganze besonders Niederes und Unschönes erschien jedoch dem reifenden Jüngling die Liebe zum Weibe, so wie sie sich ihm zuerst in ihrer vollen Gewöhnlichkeit zeigte. Ich mied jede Berührung mit dem schönen Geschlechte'.

The male aesthete thus explicitly defines his identity in opposition to all womanly inclinations to sentimental excess. Dorian Gray, for example, articulates his desire for mastery over feeling: "A man who is master of himself can end a sorrow as easily as he can invent a pleasure. I don't want to be at the mercy of my emotions. I want to use them, to enjoy them, and to dominate them." In this yearning for self-sufficiency and control, the aestheticist standpoint demonstrates its underlying identity with the rationalist, scientific worldview against which it defines itself. Thus Henry Wotton's purely aesthetic appreciation of life is compared, in its disinterestedness and detachment, to the experimental method of science and the dissecting gaze of the surgeon:

> He had been always enthralled by the methods of natural science, but the ordinary subject-matter of that science had seemed to him trivial and of no import. And so he had begun by vivisecting himself, as he had ended by vivisecting others. . . . What matter what the cost was? One could never pay too high a price for any sensation.

In a similar fashion, des Esseintes positions himself as an ironic and detached observer, not only of his own inner psychological processes but of the lives of others, which under his weary scrutiny seem nothing more than badly plotted and cliché-ridden works of art.

In this context Baudelaire's assertion that the artist "stems only from himself" can be read as symptomatic of a general repression of infantile dependency and emotional connectedness, a repression implicit in the ideology of the self-sufficient male bourgeois subject and echoed essentially unchanged in the disengaged sensibility of the detached aesthete. This fear of emotional ties as a potential threat to autonomous subjectivity suggests deeper anxieties about sexuality and the body; a sublimating impulse is apparent in the fantasy of transcending a sexual and mortal body associated with putrefaction and decay. The theme is evident in *Against the Grain,* where, as Rodolphe Gasché notes, des Esseintes lives against nature as a means of transcending nature, "to achieve a purity independent from the senses, and, thus, a life of spirituality exclusively concerned with simulacra of nature in the shape of artefacts, memories or essences". A similar desire to escape the limitations of the body reveals itself in the aestheticization of Dorian Gray, his transformation into an unblemished icon that defies—if only temporarily—the "hideousness of age" and the reality of his own mortal condition. Sacher-Masoch's apparently erotic texts are also paradoxically preoccupied with asceticism, embodying an aspiration to the ideal by spiritualizing the senses and transcending the flesh. In all three novels the fascination with the trappings of religious ritual reflects a deeper allegiance to a Christian conception of nature as fundamentally base and corrupt, with art now taking on the sublimating function previously ascribed to religion.

Such anxieties about sexuality, of course, are frequently projected onto women, so that the female body functions as a primary symbolic site for confronting and controlling the threat of an unruly nature. If the dandy and the aesthete aspire to the ideal, then women, according to the dualisms of nineteenth-century thought, represent materiality and corporeality, the "triumph of matter over mind" (Wilde). In the same way that the "objectivity" of scientific discourse relies, as feminist theorists have shown, on metaphors of subjugating and dominating a feminized nature, so too the disinterested contemplation of the world as an aesthetic phenomenon conceals a subtext of anxiety and repressed violence. Calinescu's description of des Esseintes's aestheticism as a "violation of nature," a consuming desire to "thwart, chastise and finally *humiliate* nature", hints at the psychosexual aggression underlying the persistent association of women and nature in late-nineteenth-century writing. Charles Bernheimer identifies obsessive fear of the female body as an insistent subtext in Huysmans's work and detects castration anxiety in the association of female sexuality with pervasive corruption and decay. Huysmans's preoccupation with artifice in both the style and the content of his writing, Bernheimer argues, is intimately related to this concern; the creation and manipulation of simulacra offer the illusion of control, operating as a form of sublimation by denying the organic,

that is, the female body ["Huysmans: Writing against (Female) Nature"].

This insight is confirmed in the texts under discussion, where a self-conscious aestheticism reifies the female body. The overt fetishism evident in *Venus in Furs,* bearing witness to the "sex-appeal of the inorganic" [Walter Benjamin, *Charles Baudelaire: A Lyric Poetin the Age of High Capitalism*], erases the materiality of the naked female body to relocate erotic excitement in an exotic apparatus of whips, furs, and elaborate costumes. The idealization of the "cold, cruel beloved" requires her decorporealization, since she symbolizes the divine law in relation to the male aspiration to transcendence through martyrdom (a function underlined by the biblical epigraph to *Venus in Furs:* "The Lord hath smitten him by the hand of a woman" 'Gott hat ihn gestraft und hat ihn in eines Weibes Hände gegeben'). In the dreamlike structure of the novel, the body of the cruel mistress frequently merges into the image of a white statue made of marble or stone, offering a clear example of what Buci-Glucksmann describes as "the masculine desire to immobilize, to *petrify* the feminine body" ["Catastrophic Utopia: The Feminine as Allegory of the Modern"]. Thus a symptomatic double strategy of projection and denial manifests itself with particular clarity in Sacher-Masoch's narrative. Woman is identified with the primitive, uncontrollable forces of nature—"She is like a wild animal, faithful or faithless, kindly or cruel, depending on the impulse that rules her" 'es hat den Charakter des *Wilden,* welcher sich treu und treulos, grossmütig und grausam zeigt, je nach der Regung, die ihn gerade beherrscht'—yet at the same time she is aestheticized, so that the threat of the natural is negated by being turned into art; the female body is transformed into a visually pleasing play of surfaces and textures under the scrutiny of the male gaze. Whereas in *Venus in Furs* woman is frozen into a painting or statue, Dorian Gray and Henry Wotton prefer to reduce the actress Sybil Vane to a collection of dramatic performances, a collection of texts acknowledged to be more real than the performer herself: "The girl never really lived, and so she has never really died."

Against the Grain also offers numerous examples of such reification techniques. In one notorious passage, des Esseintes reflects on man's creation of the locomotive as an achievement superior to nature's creation of woman, describing one railroad engine as "an adorable blonde, shrill-voiced, slender-waisted, with her glittering corset of polished brass, her supple catlike grace" 'une adorable blonde, à la voix aiguë, à la grande taille frêle, emprisonnée dans un étincelant corset de cuivre, au souple et nerveux allongement de chatte', and another as "a massively built, dark-browed brunette, of harsh, hoarse-toned utterance, with thick-set loins" 'une monumentale et sombre brune aux cris sourds et rauques, aux reins trapus'. This blurring of the distinction between machine and woman is a recurring motif in nineteenth-century writing; as Huyssen suggests, in the image of the woman as machine the bourgeois desire for control over nature through technological invention meshes with the male libidinal fantasy of creating and hence controlling woman, thus depriving her of her otherness. At this juncture, *Against the Grain* establishes a clear link between des Esseintes's love of artifice, as "the distinctive mark of human genius" 'la marque distinctive du génie de l'homme', and his contempt for a nature explicitly identified with and represented by woman.

From this perspective, it becomes possible to understand the emblematic significance of certain "deviant" female figures in the literature of the nineteenth-century European avant-garde. The prostitute has fascinated numerous male writers, from Büchner to Baudelaire to the German naturalists, because as a blatant embodiment of the commercialization of sexuality she can symbolize the commodification of the artist in the marketplace. Her extensive use of fashion and cosmetics underscores the artificiality of conventional gender roles, exaggerating femininity to the level of parody, and in her dual role as seller and commodity she is seen to expose and subvert the hypocrisy of the bourgeois ideology of romantic love. For similar reasons, the actress can represent the modern; "a creature of show, an object of public pleasure", she owes her allure to the distance between her and the spectator, attesting the power of image, illusion, and publicity to generate desire. The figure of the cosmetic, artificial woman is easily appropriated to the cause of a textualist philosophy, confirming a perception of existence as performance and parody, as an acting of multiple roles, while her ambiguous social position makes her attractive to artists in revolt against bourgeois mores. In the Baudelairean text this identification extends to the lesbian and the androgyne, "heroines of modernity" who, in their rejection of feminine roles closely identified with reproduction, can be linked to the decadent's cause in a common refusal of nature and bourgeois respectability (Buci-Glucksmann, *La raison baroque: De Baudelaire á Benjamin*).

Unlike the dandy, however, women themselves lack the ironic self-consciousness that their presence inspires in others. They embody artifice naively, as it were, without being able to raise it to the level of philosophical reflection: women "are charmingly artificial, but they have no sense of art" (Wilde). Wotton's aperçu is emphatically vindicated in the Sybil Vane episode of *Dorian Gray*. Having become infatuated with the actress after seeing her in a variety of roles, Dorian Gray is half aware that his passion is inspired by the multiple identities of her performances rather than by any interest in the history and identity of the performer. In contrast, Sybil Vane herself, on learning of his adulation, loses all interest in her acting, which she now decries as false and illusory, and reverts to a sentimental aesthetic of romantic love grounded in an ingenuous belief in the authentic subject. As a result, of course, her erotic appeal is eradicated, and Dorian's abandonment of her and her subsequent suicide provide an appropriately melodramatic conclusion. So too, des Esseintes's hopes of experiments in erotic per-

versity with the athletic Miss Urania end in disappointment when, unlike the male aesthete, she proves unable to transgress the limits of her own gender:

> He had pictured the pretty American athlete to be as stolid and brutal as the strong man at a fair, but her stupidity, alas! was purely feminine in its nature . . . all the childish weaknesses of a woman were there in full force; she had all the love of chatter and finery that marks the sex specially given up to trivialities; any such thing as a transmutation of masculine ideas into her feminine person was a pure figment of the imagination.

> Il s'était imaginé l'Américaine, stupide et bestiale comme un lutteur de foire, et sa bêtise était malheureusement toute féminine . . . tous les sentiments enfantins de la femme subsistaient en elle; elle possédait le caquet et la coquetterie des filles entichées de balivernes; les transmutations des idées masculines dans son corps de femme n'existait pas.

Women's association with performance thus does not signal any deeper commitment to or comprehension of a parodistic vision; women are "sphinxes without secrets" (Wilde), their enigmatic aura purely superficial, exemplifying conventionality without aesthetic self-consciousness. The female character who comes closest to attaining the ironic detachment of the aesthete is Wanda in *Venus in Furs* when she acts the part of the cruel mistress whom Severin yearns to have dominate him "in a serene and fully conscious manner" 'ruhig und selbstbewusst'. Yet she, too, continually lapses out of her role and needs his guidance and instruction to fulfill its requirements. Thus, while the text ostensibly places the man in the role of victim, it is his desire that in fact controls the fantasy: the tormenting woman functions as his double or reflection, speaking the words he wishes to hear. The demonic femme fatale of the late-nineteenth-century cultural imagination is revealed as a projection of male fantasy; the writer's identification with the "deviant" woman denies her identity and agency in the very process of idealizing her. The narcissistic vision of the aesthete negates the possibility of female self-consciousness; women can only function as the other of a male subject, a stimulus to his pursuit of the ideal. The representations of despotic, phallic women that permeate the literature and art of the period (Salomé, Judith, Delilah) can be seen in this context as yet another facet of the anxiety with which the male European intelligentsia responded to contemporary debates about the "woman question" and the increasing urgency of feminist demands.

The appeal to the feminine in late-nineteenth-century writing entails a fundamental ambiguity; underlying the apparent subversion of gender norms is a persistent identification of women with vulgarity, corporeality, and the tyranny of nature, allowing the male aesthete to define his own identity in explicit opposition to these attributes. Such an analysis in turn throws light on the contradictory and many-sided relation between symbolic and political transgressions: while the cult of aestheticism challenges repressive norms of bourgeois masculinity, it contains a misogynistic dimension that is closely related to, rather than dissolved by, an antirepresentationalism and anti-naturalism. The appropriation of femininity as sign through the parodistic citation of gender codes is inextricably intertwined with the denial and repression of woman. In the context of our own "postmodern" fin de siècle, which reveals some striking parallels with its nineteenth-century predecessor, it may be pertinent to consider the potential relevance that aspects of this discussion have for current theoretical and political debates. Is it possible to detect any similarity between the topos of the feminine in late-nineteenth-century modernism and the recent French poststructuralist fascination with woman as a metaphor for subversion—a fascination that is, in at least some instances, accompanied by an explicit disavowal of the vulgar essentialism of feminist thought? My analysis suggests that to dematerialize the natural by insisting on the totalizing claims of the textual may be to echo rather than challenge a long-standing aesthetic tradition that has sought transcendence through a denial and repression of the (female) body.

Donald Leach   (essay date 1995)

SOURCE: "Sexual Conflict and Self Disintegration in the Work of J. K. Huysmans," in *Literature and Psychology*, Vol. 41, No. 1, 2, 1995, pp. 37-51.

[*In the following essay, Leach uses three of Huysmans's novels to illustrate aspects of the psychological theories of Heinz Kohut, contrasting these with traditional Freudian psychoanalysis.*]

In spite of the fact that Freudian concepts such as penis envy in women and the equation of possessing a female body to the state of being castrated are clearly antithetical to feminist values, Freudian psychoanalysis continues to play a central role in the critique of gender and sexuality. It is becoming increasingly clear, however, that psychoanalytic theory is in need of a tool allowing for the separation of the necessary from the unacceptable. As long as this is not found, psychoanalysis will continue to polarize the larger intellectual community into two groups. On the one side are those who make use of Freudian insights, fully aware that in so doing they are allying themselves with a conception of human nature which is, at least in certain respects, unacceptable. On the other side are those who refuse this alliance and resolve instead to do without psychoanalytic insights. It must be said that it is easier to make such a resolution than to carry it out. It is practically impossible to discuss themes related to sexuality without explicit or implicit reference to psychoanalysis.

In the early sixties Paul Tillich began a critique of psychoanalysis by first discussing the dependence of the analysis of psychological processes on a doctrine of man. Insight into psychological processes can only occur on the basis of some conception of man's essence. Tillich argued that the Freudian conception of man did not fit the immense contribution Freud had made to our understanding and that if psychoanalysis wished to arrive at new understanding, it was necessary to correct the Freudian conception of human nature. It is in this context that I intend to present the self psychology of Heinz Kohut and its relation to Freudian psychoanalysis. I will demonstrate this relation by studying the case of the late nineteenth-century French novelist: J.-K. Huysmans. Huysmans's decadent novels have been analyzed by Charles Bernheimer, whose analysis appeared in its most classically Freudian form in his 1985 article: "Huysmans: Writing Against (Female) Nature."

The self psychological conception of human nature is fundamentally different from that upon which Freudian psychoanalysis is based. Kohut refers to classical psychoanalysis as "conflict psychology." This is to be taken in two senses. On the one hand, the pathology of those whom it studies is defined in terms of conflict. Freudian psychoanalysis situates the origin of pathology in the conflict between cultural directives and the biological imperatives deriving from man's existence as an animal. Classical psychoanalysis can also be referred to as "conflict psychology" in the sense that it sees itself as a participant in the conflict it identifies in its patients. The goal of Freudian psychoanalysis is to make man aware of his animal essence so that he will be free to behave in a manner consistent with cultural ideals. Freudian psychoanalysis takes the side of culture and participates in the struggle to dominate the instincts.

Self psychology defines man in terms of his capacity to behave in a manner characterized by freedom and creativity. The conflicts which Freud believed to be fundamental to human nature are considered to be the manifestations of a defective self. Self psychology posits that the drives of aggression and sexuality are not primary structures. When they are allowed to become central, it is in response to a desperate need to hold together a fragmenting self. Whereas the patient of classical psychoanalysis finds natural that he should be the object of drives and condemnation, the patient of self psychology is beset with profound doubts as to his own significance. He spends his life trying to establish and maintain the sense of selfhood which the patient analyzed by Freudian psychoanalysis takes for granted.

Kohut argues for equal recognition for both conceptions of man and frequently illustrates the feasibility of making use of self psychology within the framework of Freudian psychoanalysis. In *The Restoration of the Self,* Kohut's final and most important work, he refers to this as "self psychology in the narrower sense of the term." In this perspective the Freudian conception of human nature remains the basis of interpretation, and self psychology is used only in cases which do not respond well to classical psychoanalysis. The principal purpose of *The Restoration of the Self,* however, is self psychology in the broader sense. In this case, the self-psychological conception of man is taken as the basis of interpretation. This does not require that one reject the findings of Freudian psychoanalysis. It does require redefining their importance.

The work of Kohut represents an attempt to distance psychoanalysis from nineteenth-century idealism and to redefine human nature in terms of experiences which can be recognized and confirmed by all. Kohut's definition of the self is the result of a return to the direct observation of clinical phenomena. The self, as defined by Kohut, is created and maintained from birth to death through its relationships with self-objects. There are two types of self-objects corresponding to two basic experiences of the self: 1) the experience of participating in the ideals and dreams of a powerful external force and 2) the experience of being the object of a gaze which admires its creativity and independence. Kohut refers to the parental figure which responds to the child and adult need to share power as the "idealized self-object." The parental figure which responds to the child and adult need to be admired is referred to as the "mirroring self-object." In order to provide an image of a successful encounter with the idealized self-object, Kohut describes the harmony of the child as it stands by its father's side, sharing in his work. There is no better example of a relation to an idealized self-object, than that of the classical psychoanalyst to the person of Freud and to the ideals of psychoanalysis. The father accepts the child's contribution with pride and joy, but does not gaze upon it. If he were to do so, he would be forced to recognize its imperfection. The gaze of the idealized self-object perceives the world as an object to be categorized and evaluated. While it is constructive to consider the idealized self-object as a refinement on Freud's conception of the superego, the mirroring self-object has no significance in the Freudian conception of human nature. As an image of a successful encounter with the mirroring self-object, Kohut describes the gleam in the mother's eye as she joyfully gazes at the creativity of her naked child and accepts his assertiveness as being good. The mirroring self-object provides the child with a feeling that the mind and body are united and whole. Defective mirroring is associated with a feeling that the body is mutilated and inadequate.

J.-K. Huysmans began his career as a naturalist and until 1884 was considered a faithful disciple of Emile Zola. In the early 1890s he converted to Catholicism and all his later works are dedicated to glorifying an austere, latently violent form of medieval mysticism. The novels published between these dates, a period which has come to be referred to as Huysmans's decadent period, are known for their scenes of perverse, occasionally violent eroticism. Of particular interest to Charles Bernheimer and other psychoanalytic literary critics have been the dream sequences of *A rebours* (*Against the Grain* 1884) and *En rade* (*In Harbor* 1887). In the third and final dream of *En rade*, the dreaming Jacques Marles observes through a glass wall the naked body of a young woman as it emerges into a pool of water. Jacques soon per-

ceives that the woman is bleeding from the grasping steel "beaks" of a crane, which is said to "peck" deeper and deeper into her body. Jacques is attracted by the woman's body and wishes to save her. But the woman's image does not remain stable. As Jacques hurries to help the woman, he hears her beautiful eyes falling out like marbles, but as Jacques in disgust stops his movement towards her, the beautiful eyes return and he is again attracted. Bernheimer's description of this passage is precise and deserves to be reproduced here. It will be possible to build upon it later in this article, when this same passage will be considered from the perspective of self psychology:

> The imagery of castration is unmistakable here. Woman lures man with the illusion of her being intact, complete, inviolate. In this state she invites the male to phantasize that she is no different than he. Indeed, the attributes of the adolescent body emerging from the water (tiny breasts with rigid nipples, a firm torso, a flat stomach, a slightly lifted leg that hides the sexual organs) all suggest a disguised phallic image. However, the attraction of sameness is destroyed with the discovery of woman's gaping wound, the hideously bloody sign of her lack. ("Huysmans: Writing Against (Female) Nature")

The problematics of what Bernheimer defines in terms of castration are also at work in the dream of Chapter 8 of *A rebours*. While awake, Des Esseintes arrogantly enjoys reflecting on his successful replacement of nature with artifice. But when he falls asleep, Syphilis appears as a character in a nightmare. Syphilis is without sex, green like a plant and mounted on a horse. Its clear blue eyes fix upon Des Esseintes who is filled with panic and attempts to escape. The galloping hooves of the horse of Syphilis are heard beating the ground as Des Esseintes attempts pitifully to protect the mutilated feminine figure (she has lost her teeth) who is said to belong to him. The figure of Syphilis disappears, and Des Esseintes is in the presence of a naked plant-woman he intuitively calls "the Flower." Des Esseintes's attraction and subsequent horror correspond very closely to Jacques Marles's relation to the woman being mutilated by the crane in *En rade*. Des Esseintes finds himself attracted and advances slowly, frightened at the possible consequences, when suddenly her eyes turn clear and blue, just like the eyes of Syphilis on horseback. Des Esseintes wishes to flee, but the arms of "the Flower" seize him and as it draws him towards it he sees beneath its vertical thighs a blooming Nidularium plant with its gaping, bloody wound filled with sword blades. Des Esseintes senses that he is dying and awakes.

Reference to the Freudian master plot by which the child is traumatized by his perception of the mother's missing penis, allows Bernheimer to introduce the concept of fetishism. Reacting with horror and dread that he also might be the object of mutilation, the fetishist seeks to replace the unpleasant reality he has perceived with an object: a fetish, which is under his control. In the case of Huysmans, it is Huysmans's writing which serves as a fetish. The fetish must contain those elements of reality which are held to constitute a threat and, at the same time, control it. The title of Bernheimer's article: "Huysmans: Writing Against (Female) Nature," reflects the conflicts fundamental to his critical approach. Huysmans's writing, which is gendered male, is set against nature, which is gendered female. Central to Bernheimer's analysis, is the concept of denial. In the same way that Freud's fetishist attempts to deny the reality of the physical mutilation he perceived in his mother, the writing of Huysmans attempts to deny the reality of the physical mutilation he perceives in both woman and nature. This is a precise description of the central conflict of *A rebours* in which Des Esseintes attempts to avoid all contact with woman and the biological world by establishing an interior space totally dominated by art. It also corresponds to the action of *En rade,* whose central character Jacques Marles, strives in vain to keep nature from invading his home, his marriage, and finally his mind.

Bernheimer's concept of fetishism also allows him to accurately describe the evolution of Huysmans's writing through each stage of his career. In naturalism, the language of science serves the role of the fetish by transforming the perceived chaos of nature into the continuity of scientific description. In his decadent period, artistic language becomes the means of defending against the threat of mutilation. The discontinuity of Huysmans's narrative structure, his obscure vocabulary and distorted syntax all serve to displace concern for the disorder of nature. Finally, Bernheimer provides insight into Huysmans's conversion. The horror of Huysmans's depiction of the mutilated body of Saint Lydwine in *Sainte Lydwine de Schiedam* (1901) equals or exceeds anything written by Huysmans. In the scheme of Huysmans's Catholicism, God is the one who protects against the threat of mutilation.

With regard to the phenomenon he identifies: the fact of Huysmans's perception of nature and woman as mutilated and mutilating, Bernheimer's analysis is undisputable. But what is the origin of Huysmans's vision of women? In standard classical psychoanalytic fashion, Bernheimer situates this origin in an oedipal trauma: his perception of the absence of the mother's penis. In more recent articles, Bernheimer has stated his wish to correct Freud on this point. Freud spoke in a way that makes it clear that he himself equated the woman's non-possession of a penis to the state of being castrated. The function of analysis, according to Freud, was to lead the child to accept as fact that women are castrated. Freud defined fetishism as the denial of an unpleasant truth. Bernheimer redefines it as the denial of an unpleasant, but self-serving, misogynist phantasy. Both the theory and the practice of fetishism are built on a: "phallocentric deceit: woman can not be deprived of an organ that was not hers to begin with" ("Fetishism and Decadence: Salome's Severed Heads"). But Bernheimer's criticism of Freud really does nothing to resolve the problem of origins. Freud's fetishist seeks to deny the

truth of nature. Bernheimer's fetishist seeks to deny the truth of difference. What remains in Bernheimer's analysis is the quintessentially Freudian belief that the perception of truth is traumatic to the human being and that he or she will react by trying to deny it. Bernheimer's psychoanalysis retains the Freudian vision of a universal conflict between man and nature; between man's sense of his own importance and the menace represented by knowledge that his behavior is determined by nature.

The goal of self psychology is to go beyond the Freudian conclusion that the desire to deny truth is fundamental to human nature. Self psychology believes that an inability to accept truth must be considered the by-product of a self self-object constellation which is functioning abnormally. By making use of self psychology, I will now show that behind the naturalist story of man versus (female) nature, there is a drama of self disintegration. Symptoms of self pathology are clearly present in Huysmans's life and work in the 1880s. Huysmans's earlier adherence to the naturalist movement of Emile Zola is an excellent example of an individual founding self cohesion by sharing the ideals of a powerful leader. By 1884, the year *A rebours* was published, naturalism was no longer satisfying this need. In his 1903 preface to *A rebours,* Huysmans describes Zola as a "massive" artist, "endowed with powerful lungs and big fists," but whose work had ceased to be compelling. Huysmans's description of the sense of dread which he felt besieging him and other naturalists corresponds to the "ill-defined and yet pervasive anxiety" (*The Restoration of the Self*) which Kohut says is characteristic of a disintegrating self: "The rest of us . . . were left to wonder if Naturalism was trapped in a dead-end street and if we were not about to slam into the wall at the end. . . . I was somehow seeking to escape from an impasse in which I was suffocating" (*A rebours*).

The novel's protagonist: Des Esseintes, suffers from the same pervasive anxiety. The opening chapter of *A rebours,* entitled "Notice," describes a childhood in which Des Esseintes is surrounded by self-objects who do not include him and do not admire him. In the rare moments he is present, his father has nothing to say to him. When he goes to school, the priests categorize him as recalcitrant and abandon him to his solitude. His mother's disinterest is interrupted only by an apparent sense of pity for her child: "His vacations, in the summer, were spent at the Chateau of Lourps. His presence did not distract his mother from her thoughts; she rarely noticed him, or would gaze at him for a few seconds with an almost pained smile, then busy herself again in the artificial night created by the window curtains enveloping the room." When Des Esseintes leaves school he feels he has nothing in common with those classes of people the most capable of providing ideals and recognizing his uniqueness: "He could entertain no hope of discovering in another the same aspirations and the same hatreds, no hope of coupling with an intelligence which took pleasure, like he did, in a studious decrepitude, no hope of joining his fretful and jigsawed mind to that of a writer or a man of learning."

The "Notice" concludes with another description of ill-defined anxiety. Self dissolution is described reaching its conclusion, a moment when the self's energy will reach zero or when violence will erupt. An end is said to be immanent, though the exact nature of this end is vague. The first use of the word seems to imply that he is about to die a natural death, but the second contradicts this interpretation by implying that he is considering suicide: "Whatever he tried, an immense ennui oppressed him. . . . Then, it was the end; as if satisfied that everything had been tried, as if exhausted from fatigue, his senses fell into a state of lethargy, he would soon be powerless. He was out on the road, with no illusions, alone, horribly weary, imploring an end that his cowardly flesh kept him from reaching." No longer willing or able to tolerate the absent or alien gaze of those whose approval and support he desperately needs, Des Esseintes reacts with hatred and withdrawal. In order to replace the missing admiration of others, Des Esseintes activates a fantasy in which he becomes his own mirroring self-object. He creates a world of objects which are the incarnation of what he perceives as his own beauty: favorite paintings and books, objects referring to significant events in his past, demonstrations of personal fantasies; and then gazes upon them with the joyful admiration and understanding which the outside world has denied him.

In *En rade,* Jacques Marles has fled Paris following a financial disaster. The banks which in Paris served the function of idealized self-objects, have now turned their power upon him. As reflected in the novel's title: *En rade,* or "In Harbor," Jacques's intention is to seek shelter. But Jacques's relatives serve neither as idealized self-objects nor as mirroring self-objects. They use their power to exploit him financially, and are ill prepared to understand the human qualities of their book-loving nephew. They seek instead to take advantage of his ignorance. The disintegration of Jacques's self is described in terms similar to those describing Des Esseintes. Threatened by total submersion, Jacques feels his humanity escaping from him: "He tried to analyze himself, admitted that his soul was in an out of orbit state, subjected to exterior impressions opposed to any will, dominated by skinned nerves revolting against his sanity."

Returning now to the dreams, it can be seen that they reflect the self pathology characteristic of both Huysmans and his protagonists. The figures representative of power: Syphilis in *A rebours* and the crane in *En rade,* are alien and incomprehensible. Des Esseintes seeks to hide from Syphilis, but there is no reason to believe that Syphilis even recognizes his presence. The same can be said concerning Jacques Marles's relation to the crane. Jacques can neither participate in nor act against it. He has no knowledge as to its origin or its purpose. The comrades whom Des Esseintes and Jacques Marles do possess are singularly lacking in power. When Syphilis approaches, the woman accompanying Des Esseintes screams hysterically and her teeth fall out. Jacques is accompanied by an old lady and a legless cripple.

It is with reference to the mirroring self-object, that self psychology can make use of Bernheimer's description of castration imagery. Throughout the work of Huysmans, the self presents itself to the gaze of the world, confident of its perfection, vigor and unity. This is the case of the beautiful woman being lifted by the crane in the dream of *En rade*. It is the story of Christ's perfection being mutilated on the cross. It is the story of the youthful Saint Lydwine before she has been informed of God's desire that she should suffer. The violence which Freudian psychoanalysis relates to the necessary pain of realizing others are different, self psychology relates to the unnecessary pain experienced by the child or adult whose autonomous existence goes unrecognized. In each of the dreams, the protagonist perceives a figure with beautiful eyes gazing upon him and spontaneously advances towards it. But in each case, the object perceived as a potential mirror responds in a disappointing or aggressive manner. At the very moment that Jacques is about to touch the woman being lifted by the crane, her eyes fall out. At the very moment that Des Esseintes is about to touch "the Flower," disgusting branches suddenly spring from everywhere and threaten him with annihilation.

Failed mirroring is also central to the story in *En rade* of Jacques Marles's relation to his wife: Louise. While this story may lack the mystery and drama of the nightmares, the fact that it brings analysis back into the realm of common experience makes its relevance undeniable. Traditional marital roles would lead us to expect Jacques to look to his wife for mirroring. But, in a manner characteristic of Huysmans, he perceives of her as a source of power. He defines his relationship with her in terms of an alliance against material difficulty: "What he had wanted, was . . . the skirt to chase away like flies all concern about senseless worries, to preserve him like a mosquito net from the sting of little nothings, to keep the room at a regulated, even temperature." To Jacques, Louise is an idealized self-object, and as such his main concern is that her power be directed in a way which will assist him. Instead of conceiving of her in terms of a presence which would accept his human limitations, Jacques relates the past success of their relationship to the fact that she has never perceived what he himself believes to be his fundamental guilt. At a key moment in the novel, Jacques realizes that: "During the three years they had been married, neither of them had known each other." The narrator describes Jacques's vision of his wife as she coldly and objectively judges his weakness: "She suddenly discovered a nervous defect in her husband, a weakness characteristic of refined souls which when agitated are unbearable to women."

The evolution of Huysmans's career from naturalism, through decadence to Catholicism is characterized by exclusive reliance on the idealized self-object. When his idealization of naturalism is no longer possible, Huysmans does not turn to the mirroring self-object to compensate. He instead engages in a search for an alternative idealized self-object. At the end of *A rebours* Des Esseintes accepts the advice of one idealized figure of authority: the doctor. But before abandoning his retreat, he expresses his rage at the inadequacy of two others. The aristocracy has become decomposed and dead. The Church is powerless to resist the material concerns of the bourgeoisie. A decade later, Huysmans succeeds in locating the idealized self-object he can not do without. Huysmans's God is the ultimate judge and the ultimate source of power. The model and co-worker of the monks in *En route* (1895) is Jesus Christ: "Only the Church . . . has known how to trace for us a plan of necessary occupations, of useful ends. It has given us the means to walk forever side by side with Jesus" (*En route*).

The fact that the culture of Huysmans (and Freud) conceives of the human being almost exclusively in terms of idealized power has a profound effect on the perception of women. In the culture of Huysmans (and Freud), and to a perhaps lesser extent in our culture, the role of serving as self-object tends to be attributed according to gender. Women are more likely to serve as mirroring self-objects and to seek the support of mirroring self-objects. Men, on the other hand, are more likely to serve as idealized self-objects and to seek the support of idealized self-objects. This has to do with the differing material situations of men and women. Women are smaller and possess a voice which is less frightening. Women have the capacity to nurse, which leads them to be particularly intimate with the child at an age in which the child is particularly in need of a mirroring self-object. It has to do with historical factors: men are taught to identify with work and women are taught to identify with beauty. Men are taught to judge and women are taught to support.

Statements of feminine inferiority are to be found throughout Huysmans's writing, but they are particularly prevalent in Huysmans's Catholic novels. They are invariably based on the fact that the mirroring function associated with women is attributed no value. The accepting gaze of the mirroring self-object is perceived in terms of what it lacks. Women are associated with a lack of strength and an absence of orientation toward a goal. This is reflected in Father Gévresin's description of Saint John of the Cross: "Saint John forces more deeply than the others into the depths of the mystic origin. . . . He does not have the natural weakness of women, he does not get lost in digressions, is not constantly turning back, he always walks with a sense of purpose" (*En route*). Because women do not identify with the power of the idealized object, they are referred to in terms of a lack of aggressivity. They are said to be passive. In the context of the Christian valorization of self-effacement, this makes them naturally more gifted for being the object of God's will, as does their familiarity with the sensation of being looked at. As the Oblate Bruno says: "The woman usually appears more passive, more reserved, while man reacts more violently against the wishes of heaven".

In response to statements such as these, Freudian psychoanalysis and self psychology respond in fundamentally different ways. Consistent with the Freudian conception of human nature, classical psychoanalysis would consider such statements to be the expression of the male's desire for mastery. In the perspective of Kohut, a wish to believe in one's own mastery is based not on human nature, but is the result of a faulty sense of self. These two manners of responding to pathology are mutually exclusive. From the perspective of self psychology the Freudian conclusion is false. From the perspective of Freudian psychoanalysis the self psychological perspective is inconceivable. In addition, neither form of psychoanalysis can criticize the other's conclusions. This is due to the circular relationship at work in all criticism between insight and presuppositions. Freudian psychoanalysis presupposes that human psychology involves a struggle between the forces of culture and the forces of nature. This is the presupposition which informs its critical attitude. It takes part in this struggle on the side of culture and finds that the philosophical presuppositions which define its own mission also define the work of Huysmans. This does not in any way invalidate the analysis undertaken. Indeed, the same circularity is at work in self psychology. Starting from a conception of human nature in which normality is defined in terms of healthy self acceptance, self psychology reaches its conclusion when it locates the factors which have perverted the original health it believes in.

That self psychology could not be integrated with classical psychoanalytic theory is a realization that Kohut arrived at belatedly. In his first systematic presentation of self psychology: *The Analysis of the Self,* published in 1971, Kohut attempted to make self-psychology consistent with Freudian theory by basing it on Freud's conception of primary narcissism. Six years later, however, in *The Restoration of the Self,* Kohut rejected both the concept of primary narcissism and the relevance of the drives to understanding pathologies of the self. This led Kohut to suggest what he termed a "principle of complementarity," according to which two forms of psychoanalysis: "conflict psychology" and "self psychology," would "accommodate, side by side, both major aspects of man's total psychology."

The validity of each form of psychoanalysis must be recognized, but only within the parameters of its presuppositions. Self psychology believes that there are vital issues which the presuppositions of Freudian psychoanalysis make it incapable of addressing. It was in order to refer to the Freudian attitude toward human failing that Kohut coined the term: "Guilty Man." Classical psychoanalysis strives to locate and condemn the pathology it sees resulting from man's animal nature. It does not and can not prescribe a solution to evil. In reference to the self psychological attitude toward human failing, Kohut coined the term: "Tragic Man". The term Tragic

Man has been criticized by Steven Marcus on the basis that tragedy is no more essential to the psychology of Tragic Man than it is to the psychology of Guilty Man. This is true, but it fails to understand the logic informing Kohut's choice of terms. Guilty Man and Tragic Man are intended to reflect opposing critical attitudes toward pathology. Self psychology calls for a different relation between therapist and patient and, by extension, between literary critic and literary work. Self psychology sees human failing as an unnecessary tragedy. Starting from the belief that man by nature admires difference, it can only look with sorrow upon Huysmans's recourse to conflict.

By situating the origin of pathology in common experience, self psychology allows us to see pathology in terms of the individual's present and past relationships to those close to him. Sexual conflict is posited with an origin which can and must be analyzed. Whereas human nature can not be changed, human relationships are the product of human freedom and creativity. By recognizing creativity self psychology empowers the individual. I believe that this is a compelling reason for allowing self psychology to assume the autonomous status Kohut sought for it.

FURTHER READING

Bibliography

Cevasco, G. A. *J.-K. Huysmans: A Reference Guide.* Boston: G. K. Hall & Co., 1980, 155 p.
    Annotated bibliography of criticism in English.

Biography

Baldick, Robert. *The Life of J.-K. Huysmans.* Oxford: Clarendon Press, 1955. 425 p.
    Most comprehensive biography in English.

Laver, James. *The First Decadent: Being the Strange Life of J. K. Huysmans.* London: Faber & Faber, 1954. 283 p.
    Popular biography.

Criticism

Brandreth, Henry R. T. *Huysmans.* London: Bowes & Bowes, 1963, 127 p.
    Introductory critical study.

Brombert, Victor. "Huysmans: The Prison House of Decadence." In his *The Romantic Prison: The French Tradition,* pp. 149-223. Princeton: Princeton University Press, 1978.
    Study of the theme of isolation in Huysmans's works and the symbolic connection between "images of enclosure and reveries of impotence and eroticism."

Brookner, Anita. "Huysmans." In her *The Genius of the Future: Studies in French Art Criticism,* pp. 147-67. London, New York: Phaidon, 1971.
    Finds Huysmans's art criticism increasingly concerned with theme and meaning rather than strictly artistic qualities.

Cevasco, George A. "Huysmans: Fifty Years After." *Renascence* IX, No. 3 (Spring 1957): 115-19.
    Defense of Huysmans during a period when his works had fallen into neglect, with an overview of his writings and their critical reception.

Frost, Mary D. "J. K. Huysmans." In her *Contemporary French Novelists,* pp. 351-73. New York, Boston: Thomas Y. Crowell & Co., 1899.
    Sees Huysmans's conversion, along with that of his literary alter ego Durtal, as more aesthetic than religious.

Highet, Gilbert. "The Decadent." In his *Talents and Geniuses: The Pleasures of Appreciation,* pp. 92-9. New York: Oxford University Press, 1957.
    Portrays Huysmans as a supersensitive artist of ugliness and a "mystic of suffering."

Krutch, Joseph Wood. "Making Good." *The Nation* 119, No. 3099 (26 November 1924): 575-76.
    Finds *The Oblate* "the least interesting of the tetralogy of which *Là-bas* is the first volume."

Lavrin, Janko. "Huysmans and Strindberg." In his *Studies in European Literature,* pp. 118-30. London: Constable & Co., 1929.
    Connects the two writers as representatives in European literature of the "curious transition from naturalism to extreme mystic symbolism."

Nordau, Max. "Decadents and Aesthetes." In his *Degeneration,* pp. 296-337. New York: Howard Fertig, 1968.
    Diatribe against late nineteenth-century art, first published in English in 1895. Nordau describes Huysmans as "the classical type of the hysterical mind without originality."

Ridge, George Ross. *Joris-Karl Huysmans.* New York: Twayne Publishers, 1968, 123 p.
    Critical study examining Huysmans in turn as Naturalist, Decadent, and spiritual writer.

Shenton, C. G. "'A vau-l'eau': A Naturalist *Sotie.*" *The Modern Language Review* 72, No. 2 (April 1977): 300-09.
    Reads *A vau-l'eau* as a comic novel which derives its humor "from the farcical application of the naturalist-realist manner."

Taylor, John. "Joris-Karl Huysmans as Impressionist in Prose." *Papers on Language & Literature* VIII, supp. (Fall 1972): 67-78.

Demonstrates the influence on Huysmans's prose style of the French impressionist school of painting, particularly its emphasis on subjective experience.

Turnell, Martin. "Romantics and Decadents." *The Spectator,* No. 6567 (7 May 1954): 559-60.
    Classifies Huysmans as a minor writer whose novels are "not creative" but "simply an account of his own spiritual ordeal cast in the form of fiction."

Van Roosbroeck, G. L. "Huysmans the Sphinx: The Riddle of *A Rebours*." In his *The Legend of the Decadents,* pp. 40-70. New York: Institut des Etudes Françaises, Columbia University, 1927.
    Interprets *Against the Grain* as a satire on the decadent movement.

Additional coverage of Huysmans's life and career is contained in the following sources published by Gale Research: *Contemporary Authors* **Vol. 104;** *Dictionary of Literary Biography* **Vol. 123;** *Twentieth-Century Literary Criticism* **Vol. 7.**

Robert Johnson

1911(?)-1938

American songwriter.

INTRODUCTION

Johnson is generally considered the archetypal influence on the blues as both a musical form and as an American mythology. His mastery of the guitar as a fully articulated counterpart to the singing voice, not simply a rhythmic background accompaniment to it, inspired his contemporaries and influenced generations of later musicians, notably Eric Clapton and Jimi Hendrix. The combination of his prodigious musical ability and the paucity of information regarding his brief life and violent death has made John-son's one of the most enduring legends in American music.

Biographical Information

Johnson was born in Hazelhurst, Mississippi, the son of Julia Ann Majors and Noah Johnson. Julia was married to Charles Dodds, Jr., a successful farmer, carpenter, and furniture maker who, because of a dispute with a prominent white family, was forced to flee to Memphis, Tennessee, where he took the name Charles Spencer. Johnson was conceived and born in Spencer's absence, and his first years were spent traveling with his mother between various labor camps and plantations in the search for work. Julia and her son eventually moved to Memphis and lived with Spencer, his mistress, and their children. Julia left after a time, and her son, then known as Robert Spencer, stayed until 1918. He then left to rejoin his mother, who had married Willie "Dusty" Willis, in Robinsonville, in northwestern Mississippi. After learning of his real father when he was in his early teens, he became Robert Johnson. His interest in music apparently developed around this time. He mastered the Jew's harp and the harmonica and then started learning the guitar. While local bluesman Willie Brown gave him some informal lessons, it was Brown's friend Charlie Patton who probably exerted the most profound early influence on Johnson; Patton is regarded as a virtuoso guitarist and singer who played a combination of gospel, spiritual, and popular music that critics cite as instrumental to the birth of the blues. Johnson followed these men to the juke joints and barrelhouses where they played, and learned by studying their performances. In early 1929 Johnson married Virginia Travis, and the two lived with his half-sister on the Klein plantation near Robinson-ville. Accounts suggest that Johnson was an attentive husband and proud expectant father; Virginia died during childbirth in 1930, however, and Johnson resumed his musical apprenticeship with Brown, Patton, and now Son House, a bluesman and fallen preacher whose intensely emotional songs soon became Johnson's favorites. House has recalled that at that time Johnson was only an average guitar player, and that he, Brown, and Patton would occasionally make fun of him. In 1931, he married Calletta Craft, an older woman with three small children, near Hazelhurst in southern Mississippi. He stayed for a time, but soon abandoned Calletta, who was in frail health and died several months later. Johnson traveled north, appearing in Robinsonville with preternatural abilities on the guitar and letting it be known that he had sold his soul to the devil. Johnson did not invent the story that one's soul could be sold at "the crossroads"—it was an established part of local lore and earlier musicians had claimed to have done so. But John-son's claim appears to have been believed more than anyone else's. For, in a relatively short period of time, his playing had improved from unremarkable to astounding; he had not only mastered and expanded on the styles represented by Brown, Patton, and House, but also had assimilated the techniques of other, non-local musicians. He was playing in a way no one had heard before. In addition, acquaintances noted a sinister quality to his demeanor. Muddy Waters, who had seen him play at this time and who was a much larger man than the rather slightly-built Johnson, recalled him with awe and fear, saying that he was widely perceived to be "a *dangerous* man." Johnson's reputation spread quickly and he became the most popular blues performer in Mississippi and the surrounding states. In a hotel room in San Antonio, Texas, on the 23rd, 26th, and 27th of November 1936, Johnson held the first of his two recording sessions; the second took place in Dallas on the 19th and 20th of June 1937. He recorded 29 songs all together. In August 1938, Johnson was back in Mississippi, an itinerant musician. Past accounts of his death have been sketchy. The latest and apparently most reliable is related by Stephen C. LaVere in his liner notes to *Robert Johnson: The Complete Recordings* (1990). Johnson and Sonny Boy Williamson (Alec Miller), the famed blues harmonica player, were performing at a house party in Greenwood, Mississippi. Johnson was lavishing attention on a woman he knew, who happened to be the wife of the man who was hosting the party. During the evening someone handed Johnson an opened bottle of whisky, which Williamson—who had been noticing the effect of Johnson's actions on some of the men at the party—promptly knocked from his hands, warning him never to drink from an open bottle. LaVere writes that Johnson responded "'Man, don't never knock a bottle of whisky outta my hand.'" Another bottle was offered to Johnson, which he drank, and which was laced with strychnine. Johnson became violently ill, contracted pneumonia, and died three days later.

Major Works

As LaVere notes, Johnson's songwriting reflects four basic themes: unrequited love; traveling; evil thoughts; and intense, serious concentration and self reflection. For example, in "Kindhearted Woman Blues" he poetically articulates what became a staple preoccupation of blues songs: "I love my baby, ooh / my baby don't love me / But I really love that woman / can't stand to leave her be / A-ain't but the one thing / makes Mister Johnson drink / I's worried 'bout how you treat me, baby / I begin to think / Oh babe, my life don't feel the same / You breaks my heart / when you call Mister So-and-So's name. . . ." The urge to travel was as prominent in his songs as it was in his life. In "Hellhound On My Trail" he says "I've got to keep movin' / blues fallin' down like hail. . . / And the days keeps on worryin' me / there's a hellhound on my trail. . . ." In one of his most famous verses, from "Me and the Devil Blues," he suggests that his restless ways will continue even after death: "You may bury my body, ooh / down by the highway side / So my old evil spirit / can catch a Greyhound bus and ride." Critic Robert Palmer states that the inspiration for this lyric may have been a song by Peetie Wheatstraw, in which he sings "When I die, ooh, well, please bury my body low / So, now, that my old evil spirit, mama, now, won't hang around your door." Palmer argues that a comparison of Wheatstraw's and Johnson's words "makes a telling case for Johnson's genius, for while Wheatstraw's image is a fairly straightforward rendering of a prevalent black folk belief, Johnson seizes on the Greyhound buses that were beginning to crisscross the Delta's growing network of two-lane highways for a contemporary, strikingly specific image." A major thematic concern of Johnson's was the contemplation of evil and, sometimes, the remorse it can cause. In one of his most vicious songs, "32-20 Blues" (a 32-20 was a powerful gun), he considers what to do "if she gets unruly and / thinks she don't wan' do": "Take my 32-20, now, and / cut her half in two / She got a .38 special but I b'lieve it's most too light. . . / I got a 32-20, got to make the camps alright. . . ." On the other hand, suggesting that Johnson was aware that his actions had serious consequences, he wrote in "When You Got A Good Friend" that "I mistreated my baby / but I can't see no reason why / Everytime I think about it / I just wring my hands and cry. . . ." And in "Preachin' Blues (Up Jumped the Devil)" he presents a touching image of lonely self-reflection and determination: ". . .the blues / is a low-down achin' heart disease / Like consumption / killing me by degrees / I can study rain / oh, oh, drive, oh, oh, drive my blues / I been studyin' the rain and / I'm 'on' [going to] drive my blues away."

PRINCIPAL WORKS

Robert Johnson: King of the Delta Blues Singers, Vol. 1
   (songs) 1961

Robert Johnson: King of the Delta Blues Singers, Vol. 2
   (songs) 1970
Robert Johnson: The Complete Recordings (songs)
1990

CRITICISM

Paul Garon (essay date 1971)

SOURCE: "Robert Johnson: A Perpetuation of A Myth," in *Living Blues*, Vol. 94, 1971, pp. 34-6.

[*In the following essay, Garon attempts to provide a balanced estimate of Johnson's talent and influence as a blues musician.*]

". . . Robert Johnson is acknowledged as perhaps the most accomplished and certainly the most influential of all bluesmen. . . ." This overwhelmingly biased opinion, dressed as "acknowledged" fact, not only appears in a rock magazine whose readers are in dire need of real information about the blues, but it was written by someone whose familiarity with the blues is more than superficial; someone who, indeed, should have known better.

That a writer with much more than a passing acquaintance with the blues should continue to perpetuate the Robert Johnson myth is evidence only of how firmly the myth is entrenched. The purpose of this article is not at all to denigrate Robert Johnson, who really was one of the finer bluesmen, but to discuss the implications of the myth as well as some general problems centered around the concept of "influence."

But first, the myth itself: "acknowledged as perhaps the most accomplished [bluesman]." Whether we read "accomplished" in the sense of "dynamic" or "effective," there is considerable disagreement among those enthusiasts who have been listening to the blues for years; few of them would name Robert Johnson as their favorite country bluesman. The names one might hear would be Charlie Patton, Tommy Johnson, Skip James, Son House, or maybe William Harris or Garfield Akers. And since Johnson is not usually mentioned in this context, it is rather a misrepresentation to suggest his superior accomplishments are acknowledged facts. Yet we might add that the writer mentioned above did say "perhaps" in the matter of accomplishment, and not press the case any further.

But I consider the next clause, ". . . certainly the most influential of all bluesmen," to be stretching the facts to the point of fabrication. How one decides how influential someone is is no doubt a problem of considerable difficulty, but since everyone seems to ignore it, it's best that we now take it up.

Johnson's influence, as well as that of other performers, is usually discussed in terms of who sings like him, who plays like him, and what songs of his are sung by others. What is not usually discussed is, how did the performer affect the evolution of blues as a whole? Clearly, taking this last question into account makes the matter more difficult, but there are many who would still feel that the effect of Johnson has been supreme.

I think this latter view is narrow and erroneous, but it is worth investigating nonetheless. Why is Robert Johnson felt to be influential, especially by those whose introduction to the blues is comparatively recent (the above writer and a few others excepted)? First, influence is not synonymous with publicity, and whereas the degree of influence that can be credited to Johnson is a matter of dispute, there is no question that he has posthumously been enveloped by an enormous amount of publicity, not all of it undeserved, beginning with the publication of *The Country Blues* and the release of the first Robert Johnson LP a few years later. His life and accomplishments indeed became legend, and the romanticism of the tale of the intensely passionate but shy youth who was poisoned while still young did not fail to exert a certain amount of attraction for its own sake. Rock groups not only helped perpetuate the myth, but seemed to swallow it whole, for although many city blues artists exerted a powerful influence on latter-day rock, Johnson was one of the few country blues artists to have had his songs adopted. Since the songs were really no more suitable for adaptation than countless others, and since every positive attribute of a Johnson performance was lost when transferred to the rock mold, why were Johnson's songs chosen, aside from the legend and romance which surrounded them? Simply because the rock groups were attracted by Johnson's intensity, passion, and power—all qualities which were, unfortunately, not transferable.

Another answer to why Johnson seems so influential is that to the beginner, the bluesmen who influenced Johnson are virtually unknown. Many people knew that Son House had great influence on Johnson, but they never seem to really appreciate the meaning of it all. One is ultimately misled into thinking that ideas developed elsewhere actually originated with Johnson. Additionally, certain artists, Muddy Waters and Johnny Shines, for example, who are popular and held in high esteem today, actually were influenced by Johnson. Yet the esteem in which these artists are held tends to de-emphasize the importance of their contemporaries who were not influenced by Johnson. Howlin' Wolf, for example, owes much to Patton and Tommy Johnson (and maybe Robert Johnson, too), but B.B. King's style evolved out of an amalgam of Lonnie Johnson, Django Reinhardt, Dr. Clayton, and T-Bone Walker. To trace the Robert Johnson influence in Muddy Waters, Elmore James, or Johnny Shines is indeed worthwhile, but it has usually had the effect of underestimating the importance of every other artist who ever lived.

There is also a tendency to lump all slide guitarists into the category of "artists influenced by Robert Johnson" where clearly a magnificent slide guitarist like Robert Nighthawk owed his heaviest stylistic debt to Tampa Red.

My personal feeling is that Robert Johnson was not nearly as exposed to the public or other artists as dozens of his contemporaries or predecessors were, either personally or on records, and that it is only the high position to which several of his followers have risen that distorts his actual effect on the blues. One might advance the argument that it is simply because Johnson influenced those artists who later became noteworthy that we must say his influence was great, but I can only disagree: once again, we are left with hundreds of performers, uninfluenced by Johnson, who are totally, and unjustifiably, ignored.

In discussing those performers who influenced Johnson, we are presented with a new difficulty. We know who influenced Johnson: Patton, House, Skip James, Lonnie Johnson, and '30s performers like Kokomo Arnold and Peetie Wheatstraw, yet it is nearly impossible to trace those artists who influenced Patton, House, and the other singers from the '20s. We know some names, but we've never heard the music as it was played and sung by the bluesmen of 1900. Without debating the issue of whether the blues of 1900 was really the "blues" or whether it was some earlier, more loosely-developed form, the Pattons and other singers of the '20s appear more original because so few of their influences are traceable. (One can, however, find slight influence of earlier singers on Patton's records).

Originality itself is not the sole criterion, of course, for the tracing of influences proves only that an artist was part of the continuum along which the blues developed—it is hardly demeaning to have evolved out of something. Yet those musical factors which influenced Muddy Waters are often traced to Robert Johnson and no further. For certain purposes, this may be acceptable, but in general, a researcher should be thorough enough to trace these factors as far as he can—it may be regrettable that we cannot very well penetrate the early 1900s, but there is no reason for stopping at 1936.

One of the most glaring examples of the perpetuation of this error is the tendency to credit Robert Johnson as the originator of the "Rolling and Tumbling" theme. Musically, it is the melody and guitar line used by Johnson in his **"If I Had Possession over Judgment Day"**—it is also used at a greatly de-accelerated pace for his **"Traveling Riverside Blues."** This melody was used later by Muddy Waters "Down South Blues," "Rollin' and Tumblin'" with Baby Face Leroy), Howlin' Wolf, Big Joe Williams, Sunnyland Slim, Elmore James, and others. The tune predates Johnson by nearly ten years, however, being done most identifiably by Hambone Willie Newbern's piece, but the melody is also associated with what other singers call "Brownsville Blues," recorded in

1929 by Sleepy John Estes as "The Girl I Love, She Got Long Curly Hair."

The song "Baby Don't You Want to Go" or "Sweet Home Chicago" has been performed by artists like Magic Sam, Junior Parker, Bobo Jenkins, and Jimmy McCracklin, and it is easily traced to Johnson's **"Sweet Home Chicago,"** but Kokomo Arnold made it popular in 1934, before Johnson as "Old Original Kokomo Blues." An earlier recording, however, was Scrapper Blackwell's "Kokomo Blues" (1928), a slightly different song, but still the prototype.

Muddy Waters' "Walking Blues" and "I Feel Like Going Home" are easily traceable to Johnson's **"Walking Blues,"** but to fully appreciate the evolution of the piece, it must be understood that Johnson got the melody and rhythm from Son House's "My Black Mama."

At this point we are confronted with the question, where did Muddy Waters and Johnny Shines learn the song? From Johnson or from House? The answer is that for all practical purposes, they learned it from Johnson, and because of this, Johnson must be given a certain amount of credit. We have mentioned that there are other ways of evaluating performers besides originality, and this is one of those ways. While Robert Johnson might have learned things from other singers, many later singers learned from Johnson. It is possible that Johnson might have been effective in rescuing a song like "Roll and Tumble Blues" from undeserved obscurity, and although it seems likely that the song would have carried on without Johnson's help, through Estes, Furry Lewis, etc., we have no way of knowing whether Muddy Waters would ever have heard it, or in what form it would have ultimately survived. In the case of "Baby Don't You Want to Go" it would seem that Kokomo Arnold's version was more popular than Johnson's, and that it was he and not Johnson who exerted the strongest influence on many of the later artists who performed the song. It is senseless to engage in too much speculation about the effects of broken links in the chain of evolution, but it is necessary to realize that Johnson's role in a link in that chain may still assure him of a vital position, even when his originality, or the preposterous amount of influence he is assumed to have, is subjected to questioning.

Besides, influence must also be placed on those songs of Johnson which were entirely (or largely) original; songs like **"Hellhound On My Trail,"** or songs like **"Dust My Broom"** which have indeed become blues standards.

Perhaps the most difficult task is articulating what it is that makes Johnson so popular today; in some sense it is involved with his dynamism, his intensity, and his poetry, all difficult subjects to analyze. For me, he is one of the great ones—but not the greatest. I've listened to him for many years, but it is the other singers I discovered at the same time (Patton, Tommy Johnson, William Harris) that have maintained the intensity of their original attraction. To answer the question I introduced earlier, regarding the effect of the performers on the blues as a whole I have to say that for many different purposes, I would discover different answers. But my answer for the most influential, from any point of view, would never be Robert Johnson. One must consider those artists like Big Bill Broonzy who wrote hundreds of blues songs, dozens of which became standards in the repertoires of later artists. Or artists like Leroy Carr, or to a lesser extent, Peetie Wheatstraw, whose influence seems to cover a more broader range than Johnson's; and even contemporary performers like B.B. King who seems to have affected the styles of many younger artists.

But not Robert Johnson. There seems to have been something unusual about Johnson, both in his style and his position. In many ways, he was out of his time, echoing the tone of the blues of earlier years. Not really the greatest, but a performer magnificently powerful, poetic, and unique, an artist whose enduring vitality inescapably draws our attention, just as it must have attracted Muddy Waters, Johnny Shines, and Elmore James, dozens of years ago.

Peter Guralnick (essay date 1982)

SOURCE: "Searching for Robert Johnson," in *Living Blues,* Vol. 53, 1982, pp. 27-41.

[*In the following excerpt, Guralnick presents an evaluation of Johnson's achievements as a blues artist.*]

The sources of [Robert Johnson's] art will . . . remain a mystery. The parallels to Shakespeare are in many ways striking. The towering achievement. The shadowy presence. The critical dissent that great art cannot come from a person so uneducated. The way in which each could cannibalize tradition and create a synthesis that is certainly recognizable in its sources and yet somehow altogether and wholly original. I am not arguing that Robert Johnson's art has a Shakespearean scope, nor is he a lost figure in an epic tradition, as some romanticists would suggest. As a lyric poet, though, he occupies a unique position where he can very much stand on his own.

His music remains equally unique. Not that it cannot be placed within a definable tradition, still forcefully represented by Muddy Waters and Johnny Shines today. But there was something about his music that seemed to strike all who listened, so that even a professional musician like Henry Townsend—on friendly terms with recording stars like Roosevelt Sykes and Lonnie Johnson— would express his awe at Robert's technique and execution. Most accounts agree he rarely practiced. "When he picked up his guitar, he picked it up for business," says Johnny Shines. According to Shines and Robert Lockwood he never sang his own songs in public before he recorded them. Women with whom he stayed described to [Johnson biographer] Mack McCormick how they would wake up in the middle of the night to discover him fingering the guitar strings almost soundlessly at the window by the light of the moon. If he realized that they were awake, he would stop almost immediately, a detail which corresponds with the many accounts of how he would shield his hands or turn away if he felt that another musician's eyes were on him while he was playing. He liked to play solo for the most part, though Townsend describes working out parts with him and Johnny Shines says that on certain songs he welcomed a complement and had decided ideas of what part he wanted the second guitar to play. Most observers agree that he generally played his songs the same way each time; it might be that before he had a song worked out he would experiment with different voicings, but for the most part, once the song was set, neither accompaniment nor vocal effects varied a great deal. His was a very clearly thought out approach, then, but where he got his initial conception from no one seems to know. "He was a great guy for plain inspiration," Henry Townsend told Pete Welding. "He'd get a feeling, and out of nowhere he could put a song together . . . I remember asking him about songs he had sung two or three nights before, and tell me, well, he wouldn't, he couldn't do that one again. And I'd ask him why. He'd say, 'Well, that was just a feeling. I was just, just . . . reciting from a feeling.'"

What made his music so different from that of his contemporaries is equally a mystery. You can point to Hambone Willie Newbern, whose "Rollin' and Tumblin'" melody (actually a traditional piece, which was first recorded by Newbern) was the inspiration for many of Johnson's songs; you can point to Son House, Johnson's closest influence, or Charley Patton, an equally emotive performer. The music of more apparently sophisticated guitarists like Scrapper Blackwell and, of course, Lonnie Johnson, shows up again and again in his work, and his style of slide guitar playing was a commonplace in the Delta. And yet there was something altogether unique and immediately recognizable about the way in which Robert Johnson transmuted all these familiar elements, adapted them to the nervous, edgy style which critic Whitney Balliett once called "rough" and "wild-animal"-like. Perhaps this was the very source of his attraction: the seeming tension between a fiery emotionalism barely on the edge of control and a masterful sense of technique. Johnny Shines has been most eloquent in describing the effect of his music as well as its accomplishments. According to Shines: "Robert came along with the walking bass, the boogie bass, and using diminished chords that were not built in one form. He'd do rundowns and turnbacks, going down to the sixth and seventh. He'd do repeats. None of this was being done . . . I guess the guitar players before Robert come along just picked up what their daddies had done. It was like father, like son. Robert said, to heck with father, he'd do it the way he wanted to." And yet for all of his regard for Robert's technical accomplishments, which, while undoubtedly real, could very likely have been duplicated by any number of guitar adepts, even Johnny Shines recognizes that the real uniqueness of his music lay in its emotional appeal.

"He was a guy," Johnny wrote in his own reminiscence of Robert, "that could find a way to make a song sound good with a slide regardless of its contents or nature. His guitar seemed to talk—repeat and say words with him like no one else in the world could . . . This sound affected most women in a way that I could never understand. One time in St. Louis we were playing one of the songs that Robert would like to play with someone once in a great while, **"Come on in My Kitchen."** He was playing very slow and passionately, and when we had quit, I noticed no one was saying anything. Then I realized they were crying—both women and men."

His voice, too, served as the ideal emotional conveyance. Not as heavy as House's or Muddy Waters', for example, nor as forceful as Johnny Shines', Robert Johnson's voice possessed a plasticity and an adaptability that lent itself to every variety of emotional effect. "It was not particularly strong," Johnny Shines says, "but it carried very well, he would sing loud and soft just for the effect of the song." You can hear this over and over in the recordings, which demonstrate a grasp of dynamics, a range of vocal effects that eludes attempts at electronic duplication. At times he seems virtually to be impersonating another, rougher singer, as he interjects a rough growl or aside; at other times he croons like the Bing Crosby records that he evidently admired, but with a sexual intensity that makes it seem as if he is crooning obscenities. What makes his work so unrepeatable is the way in which he intermixes all his approaches. At times his voice cracks, as if it really were slipping out of control; often he employs a tight, constricted vocal tone that effectively conveys this same tension. In one song he sings, "I been stuttering, oh-oh d-drive, oh oh d-drive my blues away." Occasionally you will hear a more full-throated vocal. At times he seems as free as Aretha Franklin or James Brown at their best, at other times as controlled as the most metronomic blues singer. Always, it seems, he is searching for a conscious effect.

Perhaps this very facility, this openness to new sounds and experimentation, would have led to a new kind of fusion music in the '40s and '50s. Johnny Shines is convinced of it. "Robert's material was way ahead of his time," says Shines. "He was already trying to play jazz, you see, diminished sixths, diminished sevenths, all that kind of stuff that you *still* won't hear today. A lot of people think that if Robert was around today he'd still be playing the same thing, but he was playing stuff then that they're only catching up to now. If he was around today, you can't *imagine* what he'd be doing." Shines envisions a kind of Wes Montgomery progression, or perhaps something close to what Robert Jr. Lockwood plays today—a mix of swing, be-bop and traditional blues—and perhaps this would have been the case. Or perhaps, like some of the less fortunate blues singers rediscovered in the '60s, in middle age he would have lost the edge off his singing voice, his playing would have become clumsy and conventional, and he would have appeared a sad reminder, a near-parody of the great artist he once had been. Unlike Shines and Lockwood he may not have been stable enough to have survived the rigors and disloca-tions of meeting a whole new audience which knew noth-ing, save what it had read, of the background of his music. And yet in the end none of this speculation really matters for Robert Johnson, like Housman's athlete, like Orpheus, Keats and James Dean, was kissed by the flame of youth and never lived to see the effects of the infatu-ation wear off.

The news of his death hit the blues community hard. Shines heard of it from Sonny Boy Williamson (Rice Miller), who claimed that Johnson had died in his arms. Son House obviously saw it as an inevitable denouement for a protege who simply would not take good advice. Robert Jr. Lockwood gave up playing the guitar for a long time because he was so affected and "because I didn't know nothing else but his songs to play." And yet the songs were kept alive, in many cases by musicians who had only casually known Robert Johnson or—in the case of Muddy Waters—known *of* Johnson. Did they speak of him? I ask Robert Jr. and Johnny Shines. When they sang his songs, did they unconsciously nod towards his memory? Did friends ever get together in the course of an evening and exchange reminiscences? "Some did, some didn't," Shines says, but, from what he and Robert say, for the most part they didn't. Robert Johnson's mu-sic was an unacknowledged presence in the lives of a whole generation of Mississippi-born musicians. They in turn passed it on to the world. Robert Jr. Lockwood re-corded **"Dust My Broom"** for Mercury in November 1951, several months before Elmore James, another of Johnson's disciples, had a national hit with the same song (with Sonny Boy Williamson accompanying him on har-monica) on the Trumpet label. Johnny Shines did an unreleased session for Columbia in 1946 which featured several songs very much in the Robert Johnson tradition. Baby Boy Warren, who knew Johnson in Memphis, re-corded **"Stop Breakin' Down"** around 1954, though a good part of the inspiration may have come from the first Sonny Boy Williamson's well-known adaptation. Honeyboy Edwards, along with a whole raft of others, recorded **"Sweet Home Chicago"** in 1952 and continued to mine the vein of Robert Johnson material available to him. And, of course, Muddy Waters, through his popular Chess recordings, constantly drew upon the inspiration ("Mean Red Spider,") "Streamline" Woman) and reper-toire ("Walkin' Blues," "Kind Hearted Woman") of Rob-ert Johnson.

Just how unaware this school of blues singers, in touch with each other yet only tangentially, was of the massive interest building in the outside world is indicated by the response of Calvin Frazier, Johnny Shines' cousin (with whom Shines and Johnson traveled to Detroit and broad-cast on the Elder Moten Hour in 1937-38), when collec-tor George Paulus found him still living in Detroit in the late '60s. "Did you ever hear of Robert Johnson?" Frazier asked Paulus then. "Calvin's description of Rob-ert," Paulus wrote, "was of a man who was moody and quickly changing emotions. Robert, he said, was crazy, because he was so involved with music . . . Calvin said

he never heard any of Robert's records, so on a following visit I brought along an LP. 'Motherfucker . . . that Rob-ert!' Calvin explained, as the disc played on, he did not even know there was an LP of a little-known figure like Johnson. He said he did not imagine I had ever known about Johnson; so he thought he would tell me about his favorite musician."

Like Joe Hill, in a sense, Robert Johnson never died, he simply became an idea. Robert Jr. Lockwood had one last flash of Johnson after his death. He was playing in Handy Park in Memphis one day probably a couple of years after Johnson had died, and a man walked up to him "and stood and just looked at me play and just stood there, and I knew he must have been doing that, you know, from some sort of concern. So finally I stopped playing, and he said, 'You're Robert Jr., aren't you?' I said, 'Yes.' He said, 'I live right around the corner. Would you go home with me? I got something I want to show you.' Well, I told him, 'Yeah,' and I walked around there, and he reached in the closet and got out a guitar. It was a Kalamazoo, big round-hole, made by Gibson. He said, 'You know this guitar?' I said, 'Yeah. It look like Robert's.' He said, 'It is.' And he told me he was one of Robert's brothers. I took the guitar and set down and played it and handed it back to him. I ain't seen him since."

T. Coraghessan Boyle (essay 1985)

SOURCE: "Stones in My Passway, Hellhound on My Trail," in *Greasy Lake & Other Stories*, Penguin Books, 1985, pp. 146-52.

[*The following is a short story based on Johnson's life.*]

> I got stones in my passway
> and my road seems black as night.
> I have pains in my heart,
> they have taken my appetite.
>   —Robert Johnson (1914?-1938)

Saturday night. He's playing the House Party Club in Dallas, singing his blues, picking notes with a penknife. His voice rides up to a reedy falsetto that gets the men hooting and then down to the cavernous growl that chills the women, the hard chords driving behind it, his left foot beating like a hammer. The club's patrons—field hands and laborers—pound over the floorboards like the start of the derby, stamping along with him. Skirts fly, straw hats slump over eyebrows, drinks spill, ironed hair goes wiry. Overhead two dim yellow bulbs sway on their cords; the light is suffused with cigarette smoke, dingy and brown. The floor is wet with spittle and tobacco juice. From the back room, a smell of eggs frying. And beans.

Huddie Doss, the proprietor, has set up a bar in the cor-ner: two barrels of roofing nails and a pine plank. The plank supports a cluster of gallon jugs, a bottle of Mexi-can rum, a pewter jigger, and three lemons. Robert sits on a stool at the far end of the room, boxed in by men in kerchiefs, women in calico. The men watch his fingers, the women look into his eyes.

It is 1938, dust bowl, New Deal. FDR is on the radio, and somebody in Robinsonville is naming a baby after Jesse Owens. Once, on the road to Natchez, Robert saw a Pierce Arrow and talked about it for a week. Another time he spent six weeks in Chicago and didn't know the World's Fair was going on. Now he plays his guitar up and down the Mississippi, and in Louisiana, Texas, and Arkansas. He's never heard of Hitler and he hasn't eaten in two days.

When he was fifteen he watched a poisoned dog tear out its entrails. It was like this:

They were out in the fields when a voice shouted, "Loup's gone mad!," and then he was running with the rest of them, down the slope and across the red dust road, past the shanties and into the gully where they dumped their trash, the dog crying high over the sun and then baying deep as craters in the moon. It was a coonhound, tawny, big-boned, the color of a lion. Robert pushed through the gathering crowd and stood watching as the animal dragged its hindquarters along the ground like a birthing bitch, the ropy testicles strung out behind. It was mewling now, the high-pitched cries sawing away at each breath, and then it was baying again, howling death until the day was filled with it, their ears and the pits of their stomachs soured with it. One of the men said in a terse, angry voice, "Go get Turkey Nason to come on down here with his gun," and a boy detached himself from the crowd and darted up the rise.

It was then that the dog fell heavily to its side, ribs heaving, and began to dig at its stomach with long racing thrusts of the rear legs. There was yellow foam on the black muzzle, blood bright in the nostrils. The dog screamed and dug, dug until the flesh was raw and its teeth could puncture the cavity to get at the gray intestine, tugging first at a bulb of it and then fastening on a lank strand like dirty wash. There was no sign of the gun. The woman beside Robert began to cry, a sound like crumpling paper. Then one of the men stepped in with a shovel in his hand. He hit the dog once across the eyes and the animal lunged for him. the shovel fell twice more and the dog stiffened, its yellow eyes gazing round the circle of men, the litter of bottles and cans and rusted machinery, its head lolling on the lean, muscular neck, poised for one terrible moment, and then it was over. Afterward Robert came close: to look at the frozen teeth, the thin, rigid limbs, the green flies on the pink organs.

Between sets Robert has been out back with a girl named Beatrice, and Ida Mae Doss, Huddie's daughter, is not happy about it. As he settles back down on the stool and reaches for his guitar, he looks up at the pine plank, the barrels, Ida Mae stationed behind the bar. She is staring at him—cold, hard, her eyes like razors. What can he do? He grins, sheepish. But then Beatrice steams in, per-

fumed in sweat, the blue print shift clinging like a wet sheet. She sashays through the knot of men milling around Robert and says, "Why don't you play something sweet?" Robert pumps the neck of the guitar, strikes the strings twice, and then breaks into **"Phonograph Blues"**:

> And we played it on the sofa and we played it
> 'side the wall,
> But, boys, my needle point got rusty and it will
> not play at all.

The men nudge one another. Ida Mae looks daggers. Beatrice flounces to the center of the floor, raises her arms above her head, and begins a slow grinding shuffle to the pulse of the guitar.

No one knows how Robert got his guitar. He left Letterman's farm when he was sixteen, showed up a year and a half later with a new Harmony Sovereign. He walked into the Rooster Club in Robinsonville, Mississippi, and leaned against the wall while Walter Satter finished out his set. When Satter stepped up to the bar, Robert was at his elbow. "I heard your record," Robert said. He was short, skinny, looked closer to twelve than eighteen.

"You like it?"

"Taught me a lot."

Satter grinned.

"Mind if I sit in on the next set?"

"Sure—if you think you can go on that thing."

Robert sat in. His voice was a shower, his guitar a storm. The sweet slide leads cut the atmosphere like lightning at dusk. Satter played rhythm behind him for a while, then stepped down.

The lemons are pulp, the rum decimated, jugs lighter. Voices drift through the open door, fireflies perforate the dark rafters. It is hot as a jungle, dark as a cave. The club's patrons are quieter now—some slouched against the walls, others leaning on the bar, their fingers tapping like batons. Beatrice is an exception. She's still out in the center of the floor, head swaying to the music, heels kicking, face bright with perspiration—dancing. A glass in her hand. But suddenly she lurches to the left, her leg buckles, and she goes down. There is the shrill of breaking glass, and then silence. Robert has stopped playing. The final chord rings in the air, decapitated; a sudden unnatural silence filters through the smoke haze, descending like a judgment. Robert sets the guitar across the stool and shuffles out to where Beatrice lies on the floor. She rolls heavily to her side, laughing, muttering to herself. Robert catches her under the arms, helps her up, and guides her to a chair in the corner—and then it's over. The men start joking again, the bar gets buys, women tell stories, laugh.

Beatrice slumps in the chair, chin to chest, and begins to snore—delicate, jagged, the purr of a cat. Robert grins and pats her head—then turns to the bar. Ida Mae is there, measuring out drinks. Her eyes are moist. Robert squeezes the husk of a lemon over his glass, half fills it with rum, and presses a nickel into her palm. "What you got cooking, Ida Mae?" he says.

A thin silver chain hangs between her breasts, beneath the neckline of her cotton dress. It is ornamented with a wooden guitar pick, highly varnished, the shape of a seed.

"Got eggs," she says. "And beans."

Lubbock, Natchez, Pascagoula, Dallas, Eudora, Rosedale, Baton Rouge, Memphis, Friars Point, Vicksburg, Jonesboro, Mooringsport, Edwards, Chattanooga, Rolling Fork, Commerce, Itta Bena. Thelma, Betty Mae, Adeline, Harriet, Bernice, Ida Bell, Bertha Lee, Winifred, Maggie, Willie Mae. "Robert been driving too hard," people said. "Got to stumble."

In 1937 Franco laid siege to Madrid, the Japanese invaded Nanking, Amelia Earhart lost herself in the Pacific, and Robert made a series of recordings for Victrix Records. He was twenty-three at the time. Or twenty-two. A man from Victrix sent him train fare to New Orleans in care of the High Times Club in Biloxi. Robert slit the envelope with his penknife and ran his thumb over the green-and-silver singles while the bartender read him the letter. Robert was ecstatic. He kissed women, danced on the tables, bought a Havana cigar—but the bills whispered in his palm and he never made it to the station. A week later the man sent him a nonrefundable one-way ticket.

The man was waiting for him when the train pulled into the New Orleans station. Robert stepped off the day coach with his battered Harmony Sovereign and a cardboard valise. The stink of kerosene and coal blistered the air. Outside, automobiles stood at the curb like a dream of the twentieth century. "Walter Fagen," the man said, holding out his hand. Robert looked up at the wisps of white-blond hair, the pale irises, the red tie, and then down at a torn ticket stub on the platform. "Pleased to meet you," he mumbled. One hand was on the neck of the guitar, the other in his pocket. "Go ahead, shake," Fagen said. Robert shook.

Fagen took him to a boardinghouse, paid the big kerchief-headed woman at the door, instructed Robert to come around to the Arlington Hotel in the morning. Then he gave him a two-dollar advance. Three hours later Fagen's dinner was interrupted by a phone call from the New Orleans police: Robert was being held for disorderly conduct. Fagen hired a taxi, drove to the jailhouse, laid five silver dollars on the desk, and walked out with his recording artist. Robert's right eye was swollen closed; the guitar was gone. Robert had nothing to say. When the taxi stopped in front of the boardinghouse, Fagen gave him thirty-five cents for breakfast and told him to get a good night's sleep.

Back at the Arlington, Fagen took a seat in the dining room and reordered. He was sipping a gimlet when a boy paged him to the phone. It was Robert. "I'm lonesome," he said.

"Lonesome?"

"Yeah—there's a woman here wants forty cents and I'm a nickel short."

The voices wash around her like birds at dawn, a Greek chorus gone mad. Smoke and stale sweat, the smell of lemon. She grits her teeth. "Give me a plate of it, then, girl," he is saying. "Haven't eat in two days." Then she's in the back room, stirring beans, cracking eggs, a woman scorned. The eggs, four of them, stare up at her like eyes. Tiny embryos. On the shelf above the stove: can of pepper, saltcellar, a knife, the powder they use for rats and roaches.

Agamemnon, watch out!

Robert's dream is thick with the things of women, the liquid image of songs sung and songs to come, bright wire wheels and sloping fenders, swamps, trees, power lines, and the road, the road spinning out like string from a spool, like veins, blood and heart, distance without end, without horizon.

It is the last set. Things are winding down. Beatrice sags in the chair, skirt pulled up over her knees, her chest rising and falling with the soft rhythm of sleep. Beside her, a man in red suspenders presses a woman against the wall. Robert watches the woman's hands like dark animals on the man's hips. Earlier, a picker had been stabbed in the neck after a dispute over dice or women or liquor, and an old woman had fallen, drunk, and cut her head on the edge of a bench. But now things are winding down. Voices are hushed, cigarettes burn unattended, moonlight limns the windows.

Robert rests the guitar on his knee and does a song about a train station, a suitcase, and the eyes of a woman. His voice is mournful, sad as a steady rain, the guitar whining above it like a cry in the distance. "Yes!" they call out. "Robert!" Somebody whistles. Then they applaud, waves on the rocks, smoke rising as if from a rent in the earth. In response, the guitar reaches low for the opening bars of Robert's signature tune, his finale, but there is something wrong—the chords staggering like a seizure, stumbling, finally breaking off cold.

Cramps. A spasm so violent it jerks his fingers from the strings. He begins again, his voice quavering, shivered: "Got to keep moving, got to keep moving, / Hellhound on my trail." And then suddenly the voice chokes off, gags, the guitar slips to the floor with a percussive shock. His bowels are on fire. He stands, clutches his abdomen, drops to hands and knees. "Boy's had too much of that Mexican," someone says. He looks up, a sword run through him, panting, the shock waves pounding through his frame, looks up at the pine plank, the barrels, the cold, hard features of the girl with the silver necklace in her hand. Looks up, and snarls.

Sebastian Junger   (essay date 1991)

SOURCE: "Last Fair Deal Gone Down," in *Michigan Quarterly Review*, Vol. 30, No. 2, 1991, pp. 323-33.

[*In the following essay, Junger offers an account of his research into Johnson's life in Mississippi.*]

The drug dealer is my age but broke and black and missing two fingers. He wants to do business but I want to hear about growing up poor in Greenville, Mississippi; we end up just driving around town in the heat of the day. After a while he says he owes too much money to be just sittin' around talking. I don't believe him—who ever heard of a broke drug dealer?—but I take him to his old neighborhood to pay off one of the debts. The kid he owes spots him a block away and chases the car on foot down the street. I pull over and my friend jumps out and hands over nine dollars, a good-faith payment on two hundred, then slaps some hands and gets back inside.

"I got to get out of this business," he says. "But I don't even have a dollar."

We drive around some more as the sun sets and the afternoon cools off. People are filling the street corners and front porches in loose gangs, family groups. I ask him when crack hit the little towns of the Mississippi Delta. He says a few years back.

"It's everywhere," he says somberly. "I won't say I'll never do it again because I don't want to lie; but someday I will clean myself up. I know the Lord does not visit a defiled temple."

"Do you know Booba Barnes?" I ask. Booba (his real name is Roosevelt; Booba comes from booby-trap, spelled phonetically from a Southern accent) is a local musician who I interviewed about blues in the Delta.

"Yeah I know Booba," he says.

"Why don't you get a job? Booba says there's lots of jobs."

"Look," he says, getting not quite unfriendly but suddenly very serious. "I did have a job. I grew up working in the cotton fields for twenty dollars a day. Don't tell me about no job."

The Delta starts in Greenwood, Mississippi. Route 82 humps through the rolling country to the east and then, bang, tumbles out of the hills on a last downgrade and the Delta spreads out before you, flat, hazy, fertile. I'm here to research blues singer Robert Johnson, who died mysteriously in 1938 at the very pinnacle of his career. He wrote many of the classic blues songs—**"Crossroads Blues," "Love In Vain," "Dust My Broom"**—and mastered the slide guitar as no one had before. He was recorded once in a hotel in San Antonio, Texas, and once above a Buick showroom in the same town. Forrest Gander has written a collection of verse about him. Johnson was playing in a Greenwood juke joint when someone, probably a jealous husband, killed him with a drink of poisoned whiskey. He was 27. Rumor had it he made a deal with the Devil in return for his unheard-of wizardry on the guitar ("Hello Satan, I believe it's time to go . . ." he sang in **"Me and the Devil Blues"**); rumor also had it he spent his last hours crawling around the juke joint yard in agony, barking like a dog.

Greenwood is shadowless and still in the midday sun, a hot wind blowing that has been blowing for days. It is one of the towns where Johnson is supposed to have been buried and I am here to look for his grave. I am not the first to look and I certainly don't expect to find it—or even want to find it. Try to love the questions themselves, as the poet Rilke said. Mississippi's sharecroppers' shacks and lonely crossroads don't give up their secrets easily and I eventually realize that the importance is in the search itself. No pile of bones could teach me more about this land than the places I have been to find them. Bones, after all, are just bones; but myths live forever. Or for as long as one needs them to.

Local history is written all over the streets of the town: Cotton Street, River Road. I park in front of the Greenwood library and go in through the double glass doors. The building is over-air-conditioned like every modern building in the South. I ask the young woman at the front desk for the whereabouts of the Three Forks Cemetery. She says she doesn't know.

"Who's buried there, anyway? People have been here looking for that cemetery before," she says.

I tell her about Johnson. The story seems to ring a bell. She rummages around in the vertical file for a few minutes and comes up with a typed letter from the "Cemeteries" folder, dated July, 1988. "To the best of our knowledge no one has found the grave of Robert Johnson," the letter reads; "although we believe that he is buried near Morgan City, MS—some say at the Four Corners Cemetery near a highway."

The Four Corners Cemetery is a desolate piece of land near an old wooden church at a crossroads and I have been there—there is no grave for Robert Johnson, just a dozen handmade headstones sticking up at angles from the long grass. I tell the librarian this and, to get rid of me, she sends me to the Town Hall.

It's lunch hour and the Town Hall is nearly empty. I eventually find several older women in the Clerk's Office, all of whom recognize Robert Johnson's name. Some have even dealt with out-of-towners like me. One thinks the place I'm looking for might be near the junction of the Yazoo River and the Yalobusha River, just west of town ("There's an old church and a cemetery and a whole, you know . . . *black* thing down there," she says).

Then another woman gets the director of the local funeral home on the phone. He can tell me where the place is—he has, he says, encountered this question before. I take careful notes and soon I'm back in my car, crossing the Yalobusha, heading west.

The cemetery, when I finally find it, is pretty much what I expect: a half-dozen graves under a big shade tree at a T-intersection in the road. Nearby is an old farm and a scatter of shacks and rusting machinery. There's not a soul in sight and no sound except the birds and the hot May wind. James Horton, 1943-1974, reads one stone. Mother Ellen Freeman, 1899-1977, says another. Johnson's grave, I realize, could just as easily be in this cemetery as any of the hundreds like it in the Delta. He roamed from Ontario, Canada, to Texas (often at a moment's notice; one fellow performer recalls Johnson leaving in the middle of a song and the man didn't see him again for weeks) and the fact that we can't find his remains is, ultimately, just an extension of the man.

I get back in my car, thinking about things in this new light, and head for Oxford, the next stop in this land where Johnson learned and sang his blues.

Oxford is the home of Ole Miss, the University of Mississippi, the last bastion of the Old South. The sons and daughters of many "Delta Planters," as they are called, prepare for life among the university's grand brick buildings and sweeping lawns. Sorority sisters are "dropped, pinned and engaged," by fraternity brothers—a three-step courtship that sounds more like a gear mechanism than something that would happen to a young woman. Among other worthy things, Ole Miss is the location of the Center for the Study of Southern Culture, *Living Blues* Magazine, and the Blues Archives.

The Center for the Study of Southern Culture is in a once-elegant wooden house that now has holes in the porch and shutters that hang off their hinges. It would be an appropriate place for a blues archives but I am directed across the street to the second floor of a much larger, more imposing building. The woman in charge there laughs and says, "Oh, something new," when I ask her for the folder on Robert Johnson. Others, obviously, have been here before me—many British musicians digging up their roots, says the woman. She also tells me that a journalist from Jackson, Mississippi, spent a year trying to find Johnson's grave before finally giving up.

"The grave's probably just jungle by now," she says. "Blacks here often just put a wooden marker on a grave, or the paper card provided by the funeral home. Those things don't last."

I sit down at a long table with the Robert Johnson folder, several books on the man, and a 1986 issue of *Rolling Stone* Magazine that published a rare photograph of him. I look at the photograph for a long time. I see a cocky, handsome young man with closely-cut hair and two cigarettes hanging out of his mouth. He wears a pressed white shirt and suspenders, and the tell-tale cataract is clearly visible in his right eye. Thrust across the frame of the camera is the neck of his guitar, and a portion of the body. Clamped to the neck—in a chord that no guitarist I know can identify—is one graceful, elongated, spidery hand.

Johnson's Mississippi Delta is a two-hundred mile swath of flood-plain whose rich alluvial deposits and plentiful rainfall make it perfect for growing cotton. It was first settled in the 1830s and largely farmed by slaves until Reconstruction, when a sharecropping system developed that amounted to little more than serfdom for the local blacks. Today the poverty is crushing: Unemployment in some counties is as high as 18 percent, and the number of working farms has dropped by a factor of five since 1960. (The size of the average farm, however, has gone up by a factor of four; in other words, only the big operations survive). Technology has eliminated many of the field labor jobs, and "white flight" has drained the local towns of resources and capital.

For all the poverty, or perhaps because of it, music welled up from the rich Delta soil like so much crude oil. Sharecroppers played the one string—a piece of wire strung between two nails on a cabin wall. Itinerant musicians were brought out to the plantations on weekends to play for the fieldhands. Young hopefuls like Johnson cut their teeth on rough-and-tumble juke joints where drinks were served in tin cups to keep injuries at a minimum. Playing the juke joints offered an alternative to farm work but it could also—for Johnson, crawling around on his hands and knees outside a shack in a Greenwood cotton field while the dancing continued inside—exact a terrible price.

Johnson began his musical career innocently enough, watching old masters such as Charlie Patton and Son House play at the Saturday plantation parties. He would borrow their guitars when they went on break and, as he was far from accomplished, endure their ridicule. Then at age 19 he suddenly disappeared from the Robinsonville area. The story goes that he showed up a year later at a club in Banks, Mississippi, where Son House and Willie Brown were playing. He asked if he could sit in and the two musicians agreed, assuming Johnson was just going to embarrass himself. He didn't. House and Brown listened, slack-jawed, as Johnson conjured up from his guitar some of the most advanced playing they had ever heard.

"Robert came along with the walking bass, the boogie bass, and using diminished chords that were not built in one form," said guitarist Johnny Shines, who occasionally played with Johnson. "He'd do rundowns, turnarounds, going down to the sixth and seventh. None of this was being done."

Johnson could hear a song once on a juke box and then pick up his guitar and play it note for note. He could make his guitar sound as if it were talking, or produce the big, full sound of an entire band. His girlfriends would wake up in the middle of the night to see him sitting by the window, quietly picking his guitar in the moonlight.

"One time in St. Louis we were playing **"Come On In My Kitchen,"** said Shines. "He was playing very slow and passionately, and when he quit, I noticed no one was saying anything. Then I realized they were crying . . ."

Rumors immediately circulated that Johnson made a deal with the Devil in return for his stunning new ability. (In reality he moved to his hometown of Hazlehurst, Mississippi, married an older woman who supported him, and practiced every moment he could). In an area steeped in voodoo and superstition, this was not a surprising assumption. Besides, other musicians had claimed similar deals—including Tommy Johnson, a contemporary of Robert's who lived near Hazlehurst and drank a can of Sterno a day.

"Take your guitar and go to where a crossroads is," Tommy's brother LeDell told a later researcher. "Get there just a little before twelve that night. Play a piece there by yourself. . . . A big black man will walk up there and take your guitar, and he'll tune it. And then he'll play a piece and hand it back to you." Tommy told LeDell: "That's how I learned to play anything I want."

Whatever the methods, Johnson was quick to enjoy the rewards. He became chronically footloose, roaming as far away as the East Coast to play the bars and even the sidewalks. He had an endless succession of girlfriends ("Women, for Robert, were like motel rooms," wrote Johnny Shines). And he had more money in his pocket than any common fieldhand would ever have.

Johnson, in other words, lived a life—albeit a brief one, perhaps part of the deal—of freedom, fame, and relative wealth that musicians have been living and dying for ever since. One of the songs he recorded above the Buick showroom in San Antonio was called **"The Last Fair Deal Gone Down."** For the son of a poor black field hand from Mississippi, that may well have been true.

In the small town of Friar's Point, a pickup truck pulls up in front of Hersberg's Drugstore and three dusty black men get out, waving their weekly paychecks. They stomp into an adjacent shanty (it turns out to be a liquor store; there's no sign) and soon emerge with bottles of Thunderbird and Old Grand-Dad. The Thunderbird and Old Grand-Dad are the beginning of an evening that will end some twelve hours later, possibly at daybreak, in the Black Cat Lounge or the White Castle or any of the nameless joints on nearby Sheriff's Ridge Rd. It's a Friday evening that can't be much different from countless

ones Johnson witnessed during his musical career; Johnson, in fact, performed in front of the very Hersberg's Drugstore that is still there today.

Friar's Point is so small you can see the cotton fields through the houses a quarter mile away. There is a modern brick post office and the tiny North Delta Museum, which has a tank, an old red tractor, and an anti-aircraft gun on its front lawn. Across from the museum is Hersberg's, a place that sells everything from BB guns to fountain drinks. Johnson was paid to play on the sidewalk there and collect a crowd, which he probably managed to do. Around the corner from Hersberg's is the Black Cat Lounge where, as advertised by a handwritten cardboard sign in a store window ("Come jam with us," it says), a large, rough musician named Smokey Joe does essentially the same thing Johnson used to do fifty-odd years ago.

"Smokey Joe's a dangerous man," one of the black kids on the street corner advises me, using a word Muddy Waters once used to describe Johnson. "He's big and you can't stay in there too long. Women just pile themselves on him when he plays."

We are standing on the corner in front of the Black Cat and everyone seems a little uneasy.

"Hey, do you want to buy some crack?" someone finally asks.

Through the houses I can look out into the cotton fields. The question seems grotesquely out of place.

I shake my head.

"Just as well," the seller says. "But remember, you gotta die of something."

Crack in the Delta—and there's a lot of it, don't be fooled by the country air—is, depending on who you talk to, either the Scourge of the Century or the Last Fair Deal Gone Down. The rewards are the same ones that Johnson bargained for in the '30's: money, girlfriends, local notoriety. The result is a powderflash of fast life that is almost sure to end badly ("What's he going to do with all the money?" I asked the girlfriend of a New Orleans drug dealer who had $50,000 in the bank. "Pay bail," she said. "Or start a real business if he gets out of this in time.") The economic situation in the Delta, particularly for blacks, makes crack a tempting business. And the white establishment sees both drugs and blues with the same kind—though very different degrees—of mistrust. ("Well don't get carried away," said the matronly, white-haired owner of The Den, a Clarksdale restaurant, when I told her I was in town to hear some music.)

Crack is a new twist on an old theme. Traditionally crime, music and sports have been the three avenues of success that don't depend on privilege; and, traditionally, the price has been steep. Muhammad Ali has a hard time speaking coherently. Jimi Hendrix, Janis Joplin, Elvis Presley—the list is long—made early death practically *de rigueur* for young stars. And crack dealers, convicted under recent legislation, can face life imprisonment with no hope of parole for certain offenses.

The economics of the area are easy to blame for the "crack epidemic," though the problem runs much deeper. There are jobs to be had in the Delta, but they exist in a context of such hopelessness that young black men need a nearly blind optimism to take advantage of them. Conventional routes to success simply don't exist. In the absence of such things as adequate education, the racism inherent in the welfare state becomes a racism not of laws, as during Jim Crow, but of opportunities. What inducement can there be to work for $3.35 an hour? What hope can there be of a $3.35-an-hour job turning into something better?

"Racism is a very expensive state of mind," says community organizer Malcolm Walls. (Expensive not just in terms of tax dollars, which it is—keeping a population economically dysfunctional can't be cheap—but in terms of lives wasted, of futures denied). "You can go into the drug business with a welfare check and suddenly be making 1,000 dollars a week. People here are going to have to die and die and die before the racism is gone."

Walls has pointed out that one of the flaws of the welfare system is that it's based on power, not money. Flimsy housing projects are built when the same money could be used to guarantee loans for individual families to buy their own houses—which, finally, would put people in control of their lives. Control is the key. A proposed bill in the Louisiana state legislature required welfare recipients to undergo regular drug tests to receive their checks (on the elegant equation that the poor receive welfare, the poor take drugs, so the poor spend their welfare money on drugs. Actually, it's grandmothers and unwed mothers—hardly the big crack users—who receive most of the welfare.) The law, of course, would not prevent anyone from *investing* in drugs, which is more of a problem; all it would do is demonstrate to the poor how those in power can turn the money off and on.

Malcolm Walls is the director of the Mississippi Action for Community Education in Greenville; he is also, no less importantly, the organizer of the Delta Blues Festival, which takes place in a field outside of town every fall. Although the Festival brings in some of the biggest blues musicians in the country, it also draws on a rich pool of local talent. ("I want this to stay a picnic," says Walls; "when it becomes a concert they can kiss my ass goodbye.") One of the best-known locals is Roosevelt "Booba" Barnes, a guitarist, singer and harmonica player who weekly rocks a little cement-floored juke joint on Nelson Street in the best Delta fashion.

Greenville's Nelson Street is, for most whites in town and probably for a lot of blacks, a frankly scary stretch of asphalt where young drug dealers chase cars on foot down the street, hoping to make a sale ("Whadda you need? Whadda you need?" they yell). It's also, perhaps not coincidentally, the home of some of the best blues in the area. The street has its respectable parts but the "bad stretch"—literally on the other side of the railroad tracks— is a row of ramshackle juke joints with hand-painted signs or no signs at all: The Scorpio Club, The New Club Sade, LakeSlaughter's Club, Eugene's Basement. Crowds shuffle endlessly from place to place on Saturday nights, ducking into doorways that give no clue of the bar within: a glimpse of dancing, the clack of a pool ball, and then the door swings shut.

Barnes' Playboy Club is a stone's throw from the tracks at the edge of the bad stretch. It's a low, crumbling building with industrial fans the size of DC-3 propellers bricked into the walls and a patchwork of plywood boards facing the street. In the back of the room are ladders, car tires, and a jumble of old sound equipment. There is a juke box with titles from former Delta singers—Bobby "Blue" Bland, B.B. King, Little Milton—and a precarious-looking bar where Barnes sells, mostly, quart-bottles of Miller and 25-cent setups for those who bring their own booze.

The Playboy Club has the only regular live music on the street. Every weekend Barnes and his band play a driving, hoarse-voiced blues that may be the closest thing to Howlin' Wolf, now dead, the world is ever going to hear. The atmosphere in the bar ranges from well-lit and calm, early-on, to a dark crush of bodies by the end of the night. People stand shakily on chairs yelling, "Sing the blues, Booba! Sing the blues!" Old ladies dance out in front of him and lift their skirts, swivel their hips. A man who has been unconscious on the pool table for two hours suddenly finds new strength in the music and bounds to the dance floor in a frenzy. People literally climb the walls, or anything they can grab onto. One night the lights went out while Barnes was singing "my baby bought a ticket, long as my right arm . . ." The band kept playing, the people kept dancing, and all that could be seen was the red cigarette tips that swirled like fireflies in the dark.

One hot, windy Friday afternoon I had a chance to talk to Barnes about the music he plays and the tradition he preserves. He is, he says, one of the last musicians to play "out in the country" (at a place called The Tin House on Sunday nights). It was in a country juke joint at age seventeen that he got his start, playing for the workers on the Leroy Grace plantation outside Greenville.

"We'd start up late and catch the people leaving town at two o'clock when the bars closed. We'd play till five or six in the morning."

Barnes was born in 1936 in Longwood, Mississippi. He's not an imposing man, physically, but his self-assurance and the rough edges of his voice command respect from the most unruly drunk. Born two years before Robert

Johnson died, Barnes knew personally Sonny Boy Williamson and other early blues singers. He has a family and does not touch alcohol; he is a man, one feels, who has made no deals at all. When he was young he played in bars that allowed no blacks except the members of the band. "I was there to play my music—I just held my head up and kept going," he says of that experience. The blues he has played since age seven may be on the wane, he admits, but will never vanish completely.

"The juke joints are dying out, and I know the young kids are into other stuff. But they'll always sit and listen to the blues. And, you know, you never hear about no disco festival anywhere."

Barnes can't talk long because he's got to fill the ice bin and pick up his bartender at her house. He leaves me to finish my beer in the welcome blast of one of the industrial fans. I finally get up and go outside, squinting in the sunlight. Whirlwinds of dust hurry down the street. On the sidewalk, clusters of young men wait and watch, pass a bottle or count their change.

Many of them are drug dealers (you can tell by the way they try to catch your eye) and, if asked, many of them would express envy at Barnes's success. The broke dealer I toured Greenville with seemed to think Barnes simply had a God-given talent that he trotted out on stage from time to time. He didn't realize Barnes plays three, sometimes four nights a week, every week of the year, and that his ability on guitar is the result of nearly forty years of practice. ("It's been nice workin' for you all," an elderly blues singer once said to a white, college-educated audience in Boston, and Barnes is similarly humble: "Let's have a hand for the people because without them there wouldn't be no stars," he says on stage). The debt of the musician to his fans, and the labor, even drudgery involved in a rise to the top is something that the fans generally don't want to know about. It ruins, perhaps, the idea of easy success, and the hope that the same success could visit them.

Robert Johnson got a lot of mileage out of the misconception that there are shortcuts available to musicians. The truth of the matter is he spent a year supported by an older woman so that he could, in all likelihood, work his long fingers to the bone to learn guitar. He traded the hours of his day for status and money as any good office professional would do today.

Then, after his apprenticeship, came a life of wandering that obviously caused Johnson pain and regret. Underneath the bravado of his lyrics is a despair that turns the blood cold: "Standin' at the crossroads, I tried to flag a ride / Didn't nobody seem to know me, everybody passed me by. . . . I've got to keep movin', blues fallin' down like hail / And the days keep worryin' me, there's a Hellhound on my trail."

The fact that his life precluded what the poorest field-hand had—a home, a family—may ultimately be the Deal

Johnson so often referred to. The hellhound that pursued him would be the anguish of watching a conventional domestic life slip further and further from his grasp. And in his loneliness he would hit the road again, guitar in hand, to play the music that was supposed to have made it all worthwhile.

The Yoruba of Africa believed in a trickster God, Legba, who was associated with crossroads and who provided a conduit for supernatural powers. Suicides in England were traditionally buried at crossroads because that was a suitably lonely resting place for those who had severed their ties with God and community. It is interesting, given Robert Johnson's life, that the names of his two possible grave-sites reek of similar banishment: Three Fork Cemetery and Four Corners Cemetery. It is also interesting—given these two grave-sites—how Johnson ended **"Me And The Devil Blues,"** one of his most damning songs: "You can bury my body down by the highway side / So my old evil spirit can catch a Greyhound bus and ride."

It's as if he had an inkling of what sort of death his life would produce. It's as if he knew the outcome of saying, too loudly or bitterly, "I grew up working in cotton fields. Don't tell me about no damn job."

Bennett Siems   (essay date 1991)

SOURCE: "Brer Robert: The Bluesman and the African American Trickster Tale Tradition," in *Southern Folklore*, Vol. 48, No. 2, 1991, pp. 141-57.

[*In the following essay, Siems discusses parallels between African-American folktales and accounts of the lives of famous blues musicians.*]

Many of the African American musicians who helped to create the blues have left behind colorful tales of their lives and careers. The narratives told by a particular group of these musicians—male "downhome," or "rural" blues artists—have received a great deal of scholarly attention, primarily because rural artists were thought to be closest to the roots of the blues. Whatever their factual accuracy, the tales told by these men represent artistic oral performances which are at times as entertaining as the bluesmen's music. And as oral performances, the stories of the bluesmen draw heavily on themes and character traits which have existed for centuries in African American narrative tradition.

Although commercial recordings from the 1920s and 1930s reveal many of the musical and lyrical elements which made up the rural blues styles, they provide little information on how those styles developed or on how the obscure performers of those styles actually lived. To obtain information of that sort, scholars searched the communities from which the first rural blues recording artists came in the hope of finding living artists and the relatives and friends of artists who had died before such research began. Scholars, ranging from John and Alan

Lomax in the forties through Samuel Charters in the fifties to David Evans and a host of other researchers in the sixties, collected the stories these people had to tell. Such efforts were intended to enable the scholars to reconstruct both the true lives of the blues musicians and the true history of the blues.

The interviews with living musicians and their relatives and friends, as well as those with relatives and acquaintances of deceased musicians, contain observations, recollections, and stories. Hoping to determine the factual accuracy of the conversations and to produce a comprehensive history of the blues, over the years folklorists compiled and compared these recorded conversations, along with a very few written items offered by literate musicians such as Johnny Shines from Memphis. As a result of the efforts to analyze this material, it gradually became clear that uncovering the facts of the lives of the first country blues recording artists through the interview process was not at all easy. John Fahey offers this description of the frustrations involved in creating a brief biography of Mississippi Delta blues musician Charley Patton:

> In the first place, no one sought to unearth any of the facts of Patton's life until 1958, when the author first visited Clarksdale and Greenwood, Mississippi, although Patton had died twenty-four years earlier. No one recalled anything about Patton except that he was a great musician and songster, indeed the most popular blues-singer living in the Yazoo Basin [the "Delta"] during the last twenty years of his life. People remembered that he drank a lot and 'lived a rough life' . . . and that his last record was "There Ain't No Grave Gonna Hold My Body Down," which he recorded a few days before he was stabbed to death or poisoned by a jealous woman. The first two of these 'facts' which many Delta Negroes 'remember' appear to be true. The third is easily disproved and the fourth is only half true.

As a biographer and historian, Fahey was primarily concerned with the "reliability" of his informants—the factual accuracy of the stories they told. But the goals of the folklorist are not always shared by the folk artist. Searching for blues history and the facts of the bluesman's lives, scholars like Fahey collected storytelling performances which represented a mixture of history and oral tradition, fact and creative expression. Certainly, some informants seemed more reliable than others; Fahey was particularly impressed by bluesman Sam Chatmon, whom he judged to be "entirely honest" and to have "an excellent memory." But over the years, it would become clear that the bluesmen-informants who appeared most reliable and honest may simply have been the most talented storytellers.

In *"Sounds So Good to Me": The Bluesman's Story* (1984), Barry Lee Pearson demonstrates that the stories bluesmen have left behind in interviews cannot be viewed simply as historical documents. By the time of Pearson's writing in the late 1970s and early 1980s, many blues historians had realized that the "life stories" of a variety of blues musicians (the collection of tales in which they told of their musical careers and those of deceased fellow musicians) showed remarkable similarities, to the point where many of the stories seemed to be variants of the same tale. Pearson realized that the musicians' tales were not merely recollections but stylized oral performances. Furthermore, the performances appeared to draw on certain artistic techniques of blues singing. In short, the bluesman telling his tales, while not in general trying to deceive his audience, was nonetheless involved in a creative act.

Before attempting to analyze the tales which grew out of such creative acts, it is necessary to consider the methods by which the texts were collected. With a very few exceptions, the tales were collected in an interview format with the interviewer helping to shape the resulting dialogue with questions. Unfortunately, in an effort to let the musicians "tell their own stories," the interviewers—Pearson is a noteworthy exception here—have generally failed to transcribe the interviews in full. Jeff Titon points out that the musicians' statements have often been edited to remove "embarrassing" errors in factual accuracy and rearranged in chronological order, the interviewer's questions deleted, and the resulting overhauled text printed as the "bluesman's own story." It would be a mistake, then, to regard such "autobiographical" articles and books as unified oral narrative performances. However, embedded in those long texts one often finds shorter, self-contained narratives which were apparently told as complete stories by the musician without interruption from the interviewer. These relatively short texts, focusing on a single event or a brief period of time in the bluesmen's lives, are the focus of my attention in this paper.

Not surprisingly, blues musicians have tended to tell complete stories only when recalling pivotal events in the bluesman's development: learning to play guitar, coming to grips with religion, joining the ranks of the professional bluesmen, encountering fellow musicians. These stories in particular caught Pearson's attention. Realizing that the similarities in a vast range of musicians' stories indicate that those stories have a common, traditional basis, Pearson suggests that that basis lies in a stereotypical image of the blues singer: "trickster, hoodoo man, lone wolf, the devil's son-in-law, too lazy and too proud to work for a living." But if Pearson is right, where did that stereotype come from? Did it originate with the blues, which just happened to be a popular folk music with African Americans at the time when businessmen began exploring the prospect of selling records in black communities? Or had the image pre-existed the bluesman, to whom it eventually clung?

Pearson writes that "Black folk culture provides the primary source of the bluesmen's reputation, as it does the subjects of his story." Although he fails to elaborate, Pearson has suggested a starting point for the study of the narratives of the bluesmen. Those narratives are worthy of study not only as items in an isolated storytelling genre but also as contributions to the larger body of African American folk narrative. When the bluesmen's stories are viewed from this perspective, it becomes clear that they derive from tales, themes, and conceptions of character which were common in African American oral tradition long before the first blues recording artists were even born. Within the African American tradition, the tales which most directly influenced the twentieth century bluesmen's tales were those tales which featured a character variously portrayed as a spider, a rabbit, a crafty slave, or an ugly witch boy. Whatever his form, the character was, first and foremost, the Trickster.

In *Big Bill Blues,* a book-length "autobiography" which resulted from Big Bill Broonzy's conversations with Yannick Bruynoghe, Broonzy provides a number of stories closely related to prior African American narrative traditions. For example, Broonzy tells the following story of his days working on a rail-lining gang whose caller (the gang leader whose musical chants coordinated the laborers' work) was a future bluesman, "Sleepy" John Estes:

> One day we had stopped to let a train pass. The boss always stopped us from work about ten minutes before the train got to us, so we could get all the bars out the track and he would tell us to stand back from the track. John Estes was asleep, and when the train got to us it blowed. He got scared when he heard it and he ran off. After the train had passed the boss said: "Where's John Estes at?" We said we didn't know.

> "I'll be damned," said the boss, "there's always something wrong with him, if he ain't sleeping he has run off. All you Negroes get out in the woods and don't come back until you find John Estes."

> Of course we was glad because we couldn't work without John Estes. So we went looking for him and found him about three miles away dead asleep. We didn't wake him up. We just sat down on a log under a big tree and went to sleep, too.

> About three hours later, one boy woke up and said: "We'd better go." So we woke John Estes up and we went back to where we was working at, and on our way we made up a good lie to tell the boss where we had been. John Estes had it fixed for us because the boss didn't think John would lie or would lie to him, and we all knew that. So John said: "I'll tell him a bear had run me up a tree and you all had to run the bear away before I could come down out the tree." So when we all got back to our place to work we saw the boss lying down under a tree and John Estes said: "That's one lie I won't have to tell old boss because he's asleep now and it's time to go home, so I'll just wake him up."

> So John Estes called the boss. He woke up and said: "Where have you been?"

> "Right here boss, right here beside you."

> So we put the hand car on the track and all of us went home together. The boss didn't say a word all the way.

In the tale, the character of Estes displays the most important traits which the traditional African American Trickster possesses in his various forms: the ability to disappear in an instant; a desire to avoid work; a reputation for "always being up to something," and yet an ability to appear trustworthy and sincere; a quick wit that allows him to lie his way out of trouble, improvising new lies on the spot when unanticipated events occur. Had Broonzy substituted the name Slave John, or even Brer Rabbit, for Sleepy John Estes, scholars would no doubt have treated the tale as an authentic and artistic contribution to the body of African American Trickster tales, without pausing to question its value as a historical-biographical document.

Why should Trickster tales—rather than some other traditional genre of tales—have a particularly strong influence on the storytelling of the bluesmen? First of all, Trickster tales have been the most consistently popular oral narratives within African American tradition from North Carolina to Surinam for centuries; that good storytellers would draw on such popular tales in crafting their own is not surprising. Moreover, certain characteristics of the real lives of African American folk musicians made an identification of the secular musician with Trickster natural. For one thing, in at least three of his forms, Trickster was known to be a secular musician himself, and a good one.

In 1882, before most of the future rural blues recording artists were even born, Joel Chandler Harris's Uncle Remus said of Brer Rabbit: "Now, everyone knew that Brer Rabbit was quite a musician, because he was always singing or patting or doing some other kind of dance to get himself out of trouble. In fact, there wasn't any tune that Brer Rabbit couldn't pat." In a similar fashion, Caribbean taletellers have said of Brer Rabbit's more African cousin, Anansi the spider, "Anansi is a wonderful singer and dancer, you know."

When he takes human form, Trickster's involvement with music often involves a violation of rules set down by responsible adults. The beginning of a famous Bahaman tale features a Trickster character in the form of a young boy (probably a relative of Witch Boy) going behind his father's back to join the ranks of secular, string-playing musicians: "There was once an old man who had a son, and he taught him to play the fiddle. This was an amazing, magic fiddle, though, and in the hands of a small boy it could really lead him into some bad, bad trouble. So the father told the boy, 'Whatever you do, don't touch my fiddle!' The boy said, 'No sir, I won't do that.' But you know how these boys are, and as soon as his father was gone he went and took down the fiddle and he went down to the crossroad and just started to play."

The image of a musician getting his start by sneaking around the rules and playing a forbidden instrument pervades the tales of bluesmen. Barry Lee Pearson collected the following variations on this theme, told by bluesmen from different generations and different parts of the country. The first was told by John Cephas of Virginia:

> This is a very true story. When my father first bought a guitar he was an adult man and he was kind of fascinated with a guitar and he had aspirations of playing guitar, of being a blues musician.
>
> So at that time, I had already been exposed to the blues. I was actually playing a little bit of open key stuff and slide that he didn't know anything about. So he went out and bought himself a guitar. I didn't have a guitar. He went out and bought himself a guitar and he used to hide his guitar in the closet. And he would not allow me to play his guitar, wouldn't allow me to touch it.
>
> Well, when he wasn't home I would go and get his guitar and I would play his guitar. And almost every time he would catch me. He would come home and catch me and I got many a licking because of his guitar.
>
> And finally, he never did learn how to play the guitar. So when he just finally got disgusted with his efforts to play the guitar he just told me, he say, "Well, you—I can't stop you." He said, "There's the guitar if you want to play it. There it is." Said, "You can have it, you can play it." So then I was kind of home free with the guitar then, and that really gave me a chance to play it as much as I wanted after he almost killed me trying to keep me from playing it.

Mississippi bluesman Sam Chatmon, a generation older than Cephas and one of Fahey's "reliable" informants, offered this version of the "forbidden instrument" tale:

> People ask places I learned how to pick the guitar. They ask and I told the truth, told them I learned to play by lying. I—soon as I would pull that guitar off the wall—see there wasn't no cases in them days—I'd get that guitar off the wall and I'd wind it until I broke a string and I'd slip back in and I'd put it back up there. They come in and say, "Who had my guitar?" And I'd say, "I didn't." So you see I had lied and that's the way I learned to pick.

A third variant came from Virginia bluesman Archie Edwards:

> I started playing when I was six or seven years old. See, I—my father played when I was a kid you know. He had some friends that played the guitar and on Saturday night back in those days people didn't have nothin' to do but walk five or ten miles and come by his house, you know, and eat dinner, drink whiskey, and play the guitar. So my father had a buddy that would do that quite often.
>
> So one Saturday night in March of I reckon around the early thirties—I was a little child. So my father

and this fellow was playing the guitar and my mother fixed dinner, so when they went to eat dinner the fellow left the guitar on the bed there in the living room.

> So there was one note that was ringing like crazy in my mind, in my head, you know. So in those days, you know, children were taught not to touch anything that belonged to anyone else. If you did you just got torn up. But this note that this guy had made on the guitar it sounded so pretty and one mind told me, "Say, man, if you can just get over there to that bed and make that note just one time real low you'll have it made." So I finally got the courage to sneak over there to the bed and I picked up the guitar and I made the note. [Plays.] I think I dropped down a little too heavy with that and my daddy hear it.
>
> He says, "Who's that in there playing that guitar?" and that fellow said, "Uncle Roy, that's your boy playing that guitar." Says, well, he's right it was Uncle Roy's boy and Uncle Roy been playing, Uncle Roy's boy been playing ever since. But I just knew if I could just make that one note I could do it. So that's when I started. When I was about six or seven years old. But I knew if I could just get that one note I'd have it. That's what you call the old "Red River Blues," but when I dropped down, uh oh, I got it, now, but I didn't get the whipping either. That's one thing I did my father did not whip me for: "Now, wait a minute as young as he is he done made that note like that."

All three musicians placed their beginnings as musicians in the context of trickster-like disobedience, even outright lying. In addition to this basic theme, the narrative of Edwards presents images which suggest that the bluesman's music possesses remarkable power: the one note he just had to play even though his conscience told him to leave the guitar alone and his father's leniency based on the revelation that the boy had a special gift for playing music. The belief that music can have magical powers runs deep in folk traditions throughout the world. In the African American communities of the United States South, that belief developed a peculiar importance, stemming from the conflict between Christianity and African philosophies about music and dance. A strict line dividing the Lord's music and the Devil's music was drawn long before the first blues song was played. Spirituals and sanctified songs brought people closer to the Lord; music for recreational dancing, such as fiddle tunes, drew people away. And in the African American mind, the line of division was inflexible. One "got religion" or one "lost religion." There was no halfway point spiritually and so no halfway point in the realm of music and dance. These beliefs were expressed artistically in the tales of Brer Rabbit, for the Trickster was renowned for the mysterious powers of his pre-blues folk music: "Now Brer Rabbit worked the fiddle in his own devilish way at all the dances and picnics in the country, and made people lose their religion. And a whole lot of them had been turned out of their churches because they had crossed their feet to his dancing tunes, because when

Brer Rabbit played, there aren't any feet around that can take any notice whether they are crossing or not!"

The early bluesmen, and other African Americans of their time, inherited traditional beliefs about the conflict between religion and secular dance music—and the blues was unquestionably secular dance music. Those beliefs had a profound effect on the bluesmen's storytelling. Son House explains his first decision to give up religion in favor of secular music and the blues: "I says, well, I got to do something, 'cause I can't hold God in one hand and the Devil in the other one. Them two guys don't get along together too well. I got to turn one of them loose. So I got out of the pulpit." Bill Broonzy's variant of the same tale begins, "This is the reason why I stopped preaching and went back to playing the fiddle: one day I was sitting astride a fence and my Uncle came up to me and said, 'That's the way you's living: straddle the fence,' he said. 'Get on one side or the other of the fence.' That's what he said, and he meant preach or play the fiddle, one at the time. Don't try to be both at the same time. Just be what you are: a preacher or a fiddler." Having made the decision to lose his religion, the bluesman was ready to tap into the mysterious powers of dance music which Brer Rabbit exploited and so draw others to "cross their feet" to the music.

A few very striking and peculiar tales focus on the young musician's first contact with those supernatural powers. This narrative, told by Reverend LeDell Johnson about his bluesman-brother, Tommy, has become a popular American legend:

> Now if Tom was living, he'd tell you. He said the reason he knowed so much, said he sold hisself to the devil. I asked him how. He said, "If you want to learn how to play anything you want to play and learn how to make songs yourself, you take your guitar and you go to where a road crosses that way, where a crossroad is. Get there, be sure to get there just a little 'fore twelve o'clock that night so you'll know you'll be there. You have your guitar and be playing a piece there by yourself. You have to go by yourself and be sitting there playing a piece. A big black man will walk up there and take your guitar, and he'll tune it. And then he'll play a piece and hand it back to you. That's the way I learned to play anything I want." And he could. He used to play anything, don't care what it was. Church song. You could sing any kind of tangled up song you want to, and I'll bet you he would play it.

Such dramatic tales are rare, however. More often, a simple statement or two accounts for the blues artists' ability to play irresistible, devilish music in the tradition of the trickster heroes. Johnny Shines gave this description of his boyhood impression of Howlin' Wolf (Chester Burnett): "People back then thought about magic and all such things as that. I didn't know it at the time, but Wolf was a tractor driver. As far as I knew, he could have crawled out of a cave, a place of solitude, after a full week's rest, to serenade us. I thought he was a magic man, he looked different than anyone I'd seen, and I come along and say, a guy that played like Wolf, he'd sold his soul to the devil."

Yet it was not simply their role as semi-supernatural performers of secular dance music that led to the identification of blues musicians with traditional trickster characters. Many, if not most, members of southern African American communities participated in the making of such music on occasion, but the lifestyle of those who actually attempted to make their living by playing dance music had several distinctive elements. The first of these was the musicians' trickster-like rejection of honest work; given a choice, Brer Rabbit would certainly prefer to fiddle a few dance tunes to trick other animals out of their food rather than growing his own. In addition, the constant travel associated with the lives of professional bluesmen led them to encounter situations where a quick getaway was necessary. Trickster tales naturally shaped bluesmen's stories of such events, for Trickster's single most important attribute was his ability to realize when he had stirred up a little too much trouble and to make tracks in a hurry when that realization came. Consider this ending to a tale in which Brer Rabbit tricks Brer Wolf into eating his own grandmother:

> So Brer Rabbit knew he was going to get caught and he scampered away from there. But he hollered back, "Brer Wolf, you just ate Grinny Granny."
>
> Brer Wolf got so mad. He heard Brer Rabbit holler and he tried to catch him. His feet just tore up the grass the way he was running along. Finally, he ran down Brer Rabbit, he was pushing himself so hard. Brer Rabbit had run and run till he couldn't run any more, so he hid underneath a leaning tree. Brer Wolf found him there, but couldn't get to him. Brer Rabbit hollered, "Hi, Brer Wolf, come quickly and hold up this tree before it falls down, for the world is coming down. Come on and hold it up and I'll run and get a prop for it." Brer Wolf was scared now, so he held up that tree for Brer Rabbit; he held it until he got tired, and Brer Rabbit was gone.

In all of his forms, Trickster made numerous such narrow escapes. In a Jamaican tale, Anansi stirred up a ruckus by eating Brer Tiger's testicles and framing a group of monkeys for the crime. Confusion escalated until things reached the boiling point, and "when Brer Tiger and Brer Anansi saw how it was going, Brer Tiger took to the bush and Brer Anansi to the housetop. And that's where they lived ever since." Slave John, too, knew to disappear quickly when his tricks against Old Master backfired, as when the master came to the big house in disguise while John was throwing an unauthorized party: "Now it came to him (John) what he was seeing. John said, 'Oh, Master, is that you?' and he kept singing that over and over. Next thing you knew, John was in the next county, and he didn't stop there either."

Such traditional tales of Trickster's timely escapes left their mark on some of the most colorful tales bluesmen told of themselves and of each other. Pearson hints at this influence on bluesmen's tales when he states that "musicians admire those who break conventional taboos and get away with it because of their wit. They may laugh at their colleagues' discomfort, but they respect the improvised escape." Trickster's influence on the following tale told by Arthur Crudup about Sonny Boy Williamson is hard to miss:

> Sonny Boy would get to advanced. This white woman in Little Rock, she like him, and he was in her house taking it easy. He had his shoes off, and a white man came by. Sonny Boy, he left there running. Me and Elmo (Elmore James) was going back home in my old car and we ain't seen Sonny Boy. Elmo was saying, "Where's Sonny Boy?" And I was saying, "I don't know." My radiator was leaking and I stopped by a ditch to get a little water. Sonny Boy calls, "Motherfucker, open the trunk and let me get in!" He was hiding in the ditch there.

In a conversation with fellow bluesmen, recorded by Pearson, Howlin' Wolf described his own ability to get out of a bad situation, with a clear reference to a trickster character of traditional tales: "Now when the Wolf leave a place, he lifts both foots like a rabbit. Nobody can see where he go."

The scrapes which inspired trickster-like escapes often developed in the setting of a country ball, the setting in which rural blues musicians most often performed. With alcohol generally present, the power of the bluesmen's music made people "cross their feet," drawing women from their men and creating the sort of chaos which demanded an imitation of traditional trickster-heroes: "Them country balls were rough! They were critical, man! They'd start off good, you know. Everybody happy, dancing and some guy would be outside selling his corn whiskey and they'd be going backwards and forwards getting them a bottle—you could get a little small bottle for a quarter—and then they'd start to getting louder and louder. The women would be dipping that snuff and swallowing that snuff spit along with that corn whiskey, and they'd start to mixing fast, and oh, brother! Be some running done! Sometimes we'd almost leave our guitars behind."

This description of the chaos of the country balls, stirred up in part by the music of the ones who ended up on the run, was given by Son House. He followed the description with a narrative about Charley Patton who, having died long before bluesmen's tales were collected, was an ideal candidate for the role of Trickster in stories:

> I remember one night Willie (Brown) and I and Charlie were to play at the same place and Willie and I were late, but Charlie had gotten there kind of early. And the guys got off the center kind of early, too. Got to fighting and shooting off those old owl-head pistols. Well, Willie and I got near to the house and we heard such a gruntin' and a rattlin' coming up through the stalks, and I said,

"Wait a minute, Willie. Hold it. I hear something coming up through the cotton field. Don't you hear it?" He said, "Yeah, it's something." We were always suspicious, you know, about animals. Out in the country around there, it wouldn't be anything to see a teddy-bear or something. So we got the idea we wanted to hurry up and get to the road where we could see it. Finally, who should pop out to the roadside but Charlie! He looked and saw us and said, "I'll kill 'em all. I'll kill 'em all." Me and Willie started laughing and told him, "How you gon' kill 'em all? We heard you running."

During their escapes from the trouble which they helped to create, the characters of Patton and Sonny Boy Williamson hid out and popped up in some unusual locations: Williamson in the roadside ditch and the car trunk, Patton in the "stalks." This, too, is a character trait of Trickster. Several Anansi stories end with the spider making for the rooftops, the rafters, or the remote corners of a house "where he has been ever since." A tale from St. Vincent explains that Witch Boy, who lived with a king and "did all the nasty stuff around the palace," had to stay hidden under a bed because he was dirty. Bluesman Eddie Taylor provides an unusual tale which revolves around Trickster's tendency to appear in, or disappear into, strange or obscure places. Taylor tells of how he used to go under his house and listen through the floor when music and dancing were on hand. In response to the question, "Do people dance to the blues?," he built the following story out of that image: "Yeah, whoo! Break the house down. I was under the house one night and the snakes, cats, dogs, chickens came out from under the house with me, running, POW! I didn't know what it was, a bomb or something, but it was the house broke down, right in the middle of the floor. You know, the truth is the truth. The only thing saved me, I was sitting over in the chimney corner, right up under the piano."

The young Taylor's hidden location and his survival of the disaster through a combination of cleverness, good luck, and fast feet make for an entertaining story. It would be foolish to worry excessively about whether or not that story presents accurate "facts" about Taylor's life or about the blues. Certainly, it provides a great deal of insight into the bluesmen's conception of the power and the popularity of their music. Beyond that, the folklorist ought to heed Taylor's words: the truth is the truth. It is true that the events of bluesmen's tales are based on important events in the bluesmen's life and also true that the tradition of African American Trickster tales provided the bluesmen with an artistic medium through which to convey the meanings they attached to such events.

One bluesman about whom a great many narratives have been collected is Robert Johnson, the great Mississippi Delta musician who recorded in 1936 and 1937. As a musician whose work was greatly admired both by black musicians and by white researchers, and as a man who died young within several months of his second and final recording session, Johnson was, like Patton, an ideal character around whom to build bluesmen's narratives. One of the most often-quoted of these "biographical" narratives about Robert Johnson is the following one told by Son House in the mid-1960s:

> But we'd all play for the Saturday night balls and there'd be this little boy standing around. That was Robert Johnson. He was just a little boy then. He blew a harmonica and he was pretty good with that, but he wanted to play a guitar. When we'd leave at night to go play for the balls, he'd slip off and come over to where we were. His mother and step-father didn't like for him to go out to those Saturday night balls because the guys were so rough. But he'd slip away anyway. Sometimes he'd even wait until his mother went to bed and then he'd get out the window and make it to where we were. He'd get where Willie and I were and sit right down on the floor and watch from one to the other. And when we'd get a break and want to rest some, we'd set the guitars up in the corner and go out in the cool. Robert would watch and see which way we'd gone and he would pick one of them up. And such another racket you never heard! It'd make the people say, "Why don't y'all go in there and get that guitar away from that boy! He's running people crazy with it." I'd come back in and I'd scold him about it. "Don't do that, Robert. You drive the people nuts. You can't play nothing. Why don't you blow the harmonica for 'em?" But he didn't want to blow that. Still, he didn't care how I'd get after him about it. He'd do it anyway.
>
> Well, he didn't care anything about working in the fields and his father was so tight on him about slipping out and coming where we were, so he just got the idea he'd run away from home. He was living on a plantation out from Robinsonville. On a man's place called Mr. Richard Lellman. And he ran away. Didn't want to work on any farms.
>
> He stayed, looked like to me, about six months. Willie and I were playing again out at a little place east of Robinsonville called Banks, Mississippi. We were playing there one Saturday night and, all of a sudden, somebody came in through the door. Who but him! He had a guitar swinging on his back. I said, "Bill!" He said, "Huh?" I said, "Look who's coming in the door." He looked and said, "Yeah. Little Robert." And Willie and I laughed about it. Robert finally wiggled through the crowd and got where we were. He spoke, and I said, 'Well, boy, you still got a guitar, huh? What do you do with that thing? You can't do nothing with it." He said, "Well, I'll tell you what." I said, "What?" He said, "Let me have your seat a minute." So I said, "All right, and you better do something with it, too," and I winked my eye at Willie. So he sat down there and finally got started. And man! He was so good! When he finished, all our mouths were standing open. I said, "Well, ain't that fast! He's gone now!"

Slipping out the window and escaping from his parents, disregarding the orders of an elder to leave alone the precious guitars, "Little Robert" behaves according to the habits of the trickster characters who influenced Son House's tale. Johnson shirks honest work and disappears in order to avoid it. He reappears "all of a sudden," as if by magic, and then performs music which leaves the people spellbound, even though he could produce nothing but noise only six months before. To account for Johnson's transformation, Son House later relied on another motif in the trickster-bluesman tale complex: Little Robert had "sold his soul to the devil in exchange for learning to play like that." House's tale had a profound influence on the process of creating a character to fit the name of the recording star Robert Johnson, even as it was profoundly influenced by preexisting African American narrative traditions.

Several other bluesmen have offered brief narratives or sketches which have further developed the character of the trickster-like Robert Johnson. Like the fiddler/dancer/ "patter" Brer Rabbit, Johnson could rapidly sway a crowd in his favor with his devilish music. As Johnny Shines explains, "Robert was a natural showman; he didn't need no guitar—he could be clapping his hands and have a crowd around him in no time. And they'd give him their money too." His semi-supernatural power, combined with that of his guitar, produced musical results that no mortal could resist:

> His guitar seemed to talk—repeat and say words with him like no one else in the world could. I said he had a talking guitar, and many a person agreed with me. This sound affected most women in a way that I could never understand. One time in St. Louis we were playing one of the songs that Robert would like to play with someone once in a great while, **"Come on in My Kitchen."** He was playing very slow and passionately, and when we had quit, I noticed no one was saying anything. Then I realized they were crying—both women and men.

Possessing these near-magical musical abilities, Johnson was often portrayed as one who attempted to hide his techniques. Peter Guralnick states that both Johnny Shines and Robert Lockwood tell tales of Johnson "turning away from other musicians if he felt their eyes upon him, as if . . . he had some dark secret to hide." Guralnick adds, "Women with whom he stayed described to Mack McCormick how they would wake up in the middle of the night to discover him fingering the guitar strings almost soundlessly at the window by the light of the moon. If he realized that they were awake, he would stop almost immediately . . ." Such accounts show Johnson keeping ahead of those who might threaten him, maintaining his competitive edge in true Trickster fashion.

The resemblance of the character of Robert Johnson to traditional trickster characters goes beyond the bizarre power of Johnson's music. Though Guralnick does not identify his source, he includes a portrayal of Brer Robert's ability to slip out of town or out of sight in an instant, while always demonstrating his mysterious, magical abilities: "See, he was a peculiar kind of fellow.

Robert'd be standing up playing some place, you know, just playing like nobody's business, but Robert'd just pick up and walk off and leave you standing there playing. And you wouldn't see Robert no more maybe in two or three weeks." Another comment describes his uncanny ability to remain clean even when others could not: "But Robert was always neat. Robert could ride highways and things like that all day long, and you'd look down at yourself and you'd be as filthy as a pig and Robert'd be clean—how, I don't know."

Johnson's unexplained absences at times led to the traditional narrow escape:

> One day we missed Robert and thought he was on 8th Street with a girl that he gave quite a bit of attention to. We were satisfied with this explanation until the girl we thought he was with came over with food for Robert, and the rest of us too, but when she didn't find Robert we had to make a quick guess as to where he was regardless of what we really thought. So we said he was in Memphis, but she wanted no part of this and was getting quite angry. So somebody had to find him. Well, I knew this little girl always was up and around early and she might just know where Robert was—and she did. One guess, and I bet you are right! He was there in her bed. She only had one room and since it would have looked kind of foolish to ask her to go out of her own room so I could talk to Robert, I told her what had happened, and she was very broad-minded about the whole thing. She in turn told Robert as though he weren't listening and showed him a way to get out of the hotel without being seen, and it worked. After that, Robert used this exit quite often, but he was not always coming from the little girl's room!

And as quick as he could disappear, Brer Robert could turn up in a strange, unexpected place: "Once night I came in and was putting my guitar away when a girl came up to me and told me that a fellow was in my bed who said he knew me real well and could play like she had never heard before. I asked what did he play? When she said guitar, that did it! I knew it was Robert." Above all, Johnson excelled at the activities which were the basis of all of Trickster's traditional antics—stirring up trouble and then getting out fast when things started boiling over. Robert Lockwood has said that "Robert would do some funny things that I didn't like. Things would just create around him . . ." Shines offers a tale which illustrates what Lockwood means: "One time we were in Wickliffe, Kentucky, and met some girls that I liked very much. They were a dance team that had never been no place and wanted to be seen and heard. I should have said a song-and-dance team of four people. They could really go to town, and I wanted to take them with us when we left and had it all arranged, but Bob, he would slip from one girl to the other until he had them all fighting among themselves. Now he was ready to give them the slip, and we did."

What emerges from the few complete bluesmen's narratives about Robert Johnson, such as that of Son House,

and the many other narrative fragments which have been transcribed, is not, then, simply an expression of a stereotype. It is also not primarily a factual account of Johnson's life. Rather, these stories represent the creation of an oral-literary character derived in part from the facts of a man's life and in part from traditional African American Trickster characters. Brer Robert played magically irresistible dance music which was the descendant of the fiddle-and-pat music which Brer Rabbit once played. And as they had done in the cases of Brer Rabbit and the other Trickster characters, storytellers implied that Johnson's secular music was truly "devilish"; he lost his religion and jumped down squarely on the Devil's side of the fence. This character lived with trouble all around him—trouble which he helped to create but trouble which he always managed to keep at bay long enough to make his getaway, only to reappear later in some unexpected place.

Admittedly, the case of Robert Johnson is an extreme one. His tragic early death and the tremendous interest in his music on the part of white scholars led to the collection of a particularly rich body of tales. Narratives focusing on the lives of other bluesmen reveal more balanced mixtures of tradition, history, and artistic storytelling. What the Brer Robert tales demonstrate is not so much the general patterns of bluesmen's tales but the tremendous potential for creative expression which those tales embody. Hopefully, blues scholars who have preserved their tape recordings of interviews will continue to publish faithful transcriptions of the bluesmen's many tales so that those tales may assume their rightful place within the African American oral narrative tradition. Such work would not only help to make a large body of entertaining stories available to the public but would also lead to a deeper understanding of African American conceptions of heroism, mystery, and, best of all, humor.

Barry Lee Pearson   (essay date 1992)

SOURCE: "Standing at the Crossroads Between Vinyl and Compact Discs: Reissue Blues Recordings in the 1990s," in *Journal of American Folklore*, Vol. 105, No. 416, 1992, pp. 215-26.

[*In the following essay, Pearson discusses the "Robert Johnson myth" and examines the reception of Johnson's work as a recording artist.*]

Thinking about Robert Johnson generates questions about the impact of phonograph recordings on folk tradition. After all, Robert Johnson is characterized as a bellwether—the artist who represents the transition from country-dance musicians limited to local influences to a new breed of professionals whose technique and repertoire were influenced by phonograph recordings. Fairly or not, Johnson is portrayed as an innovator who conceptualized and shaped his songs in a modern way, as preformed units conditioned not by the needs of an audience of dancers but by the limitations of recordings.

To a certain degree, the strange career of Robert Johnson has been shaped by three manifestations of his recordings that reflect the major changes in commercial sound recording formats. The first few 78s issued in his lifetime brought him the status and notoriety of a recording artist. David "Honeyboy" Edwards, who knew Johnson, provided an anecdote illustrating the prestige of recordings. A Delta woman offered Johnson a dime to play **"Terraplane Blues"** on a street corner in Greenwood, Mississippi. When Johnson replied "Miss, that's my record," and played it, the crowd agreed, and rewarded him with nickels, dimes, and quarters, proud to hear a recording star in person.

As much as his early recordings augmented his local reputation, they also paved the way for his eventual national recognition, spurring John Hammond and Alan Lomax to search for him. Then as the 1960s ended, Frank Driggs and Columbia reissued his 78s on an LP, *King of the Delta Blues Singers* (CL 1654), later followed by *King of the Delta Blues Singers: Volume II* (C 30034). These albums made a terrific impact on the folk- and blues-revival audience and countless coming-of-age musicians, including me. Robert Johnson's songs obviously spoke to alienated '60s youth culture, providing strangers to the blues tradition the opportunity to filter Johnson's potent lyrics through their own imaginations. On the surface it seemed a perfect union. He was, after all, dead, and his new fans could safely re-create meaning in his songs at their own convenience. These new devotees did not share a cultural frame of reference with Johnson, yet they firmly believed his blues songs to be literally autobiographical. Any one of them could smoke a joint, listen to the songs, and puzzle out their interpretation of his life based on the images in his compositions. Johnson's most successful biographer, Peter Guralnick, characterized this romantic approach to the blues: "Blues offered the perfect vehicle for our romanticism. What's more, it offered boundless opportunities and certain characteristics associated with the music itself."

Justin O'Brien, reacting to the publication of the first Robert Johnson photograph (now familiar because of its use in the *Complete Recordings* and related publicity), also reflected back to his teenage encounter with the first Columbia LP, and its impact on him and his friends.

> We became the cognoscenti, sharing a fascination with this mysterious man and his equally mysterious music. It seemed it was ours to mythologize, a man and his music who we thought were long forgotten by any admirers and also culturally neglected by blacks who by the '60s had largely rejected the blues as a musical expression.

Other critics echo recurring themes: how hearing Johnson changed their lives and how their own reading of his song lyrics allowed them to put together their very own personal Robert Johnson. The process of romanticizing and appropriating his songs continues with today's new format, whether vinyl, tape, or disc. Today, however, he is much less of a stranger, thanks to lots of fieldwork, sev-

eral recently released photographs, and the commentary of people who knew him. But even with the excellent supporting data documenting the new boxed set [*Robert Johnson: The Complete Recordings*], we find that today's critics and reviewers continue to prefer the mythic Robert Johnson to the human blues artist.

How do we explain why we consistently mythologize Robert Johnson? First, there's the hype, partially fanned by Columbia's promotion and partly self-perpetuating, which has generated an incredible volume of misinformation. Granted, the average journalist, like the average reader, should not be expected to command in-depth knowledge of African-American folk belief, the blues as a traditional system, or the history of white perceptions of the blues. But if most writers and readers simply started from scratch, and not Old Scratch either, we would be better served by, and in a position to learn something about, the life and art of the long deceased man of the hour.

However, this has not been the case, and an unfortunate, deeply fixed set of misconceptions has been brought to bear at the beginning of any discourse related to Johnson. These include the pernicious notions that tie his musical personality to the devil, and that credit him with inventing rock and roll. Granted, both ideas connect generally with the blues as a whole and certainly make for good copy. The former idea comes from methodological errors in the reconstruction of Johnson's life in which Johnson's few references to the devil are interpreted literally by an audience eager to accept the more exotic elements of African-American folk belief.

The development of white America's version of the Robert Johnson myth—and I see it more as myth than legend—dates back to John Hammond's appreciation for producer Don Law's "tall tales" of Johnson's recording session. Even here misinterpretation abounds. Johnson's turning his back to an informal audience of Mexican musicians is read as an example of extreme shyness rather than the more typical musician's desire to guard his instrumental techniques. Anecdotes that came to light circa 1938 were rehashed and fleshed out as Johnson's posthumous fame spread via his limited 78 rpm records. By the time *King of the Delta Blues* was issued, these stories had become fixed as gospel.

Only more recently, with the boxed set and with the opportunity to interview rock stars who listened to the first LP, has the retrospective connection between Johnson and rock and roll surfaced. Actually, his first wave of folk-revival fans would have disputed this contention tooth and nail, although in a broad sense Johnson's music fits into a continuum of many blues artists who set the stage for rhythm and blues, including Louis Jordan, the personal choice of Johnson's stepson, Robert Junior Lockwood, as the inventor of rock and roll.

Who talks about Robert and the devil? Maybe it's more a question of "who asks." When I interviewed Lockwood,

"Honeyboy" Edwards, Johnny Shines, and Henry Townsend, as long ago as 1979, they spoke of him at some length but never *offered* any comment about a deal with the devil. In 1991, these same living experts who traveled with, and learned from, Robert Johnson all ridiculed the idea of a deal with the devil. Robert Junior Lockwood told Worth Long,

> There are some people who want to try to get some glory because Robert is so popular. They say they knew Robert and they don't know a damn thing. They talked about him selling his soul to the devil. I want to know how you do that—I don't like the way they are trying to label him. He was a blues musician just like the rest of us.

During a 1991 Festival of American Folklife workshop, Johnny Shines responded,

> I want anybody that believes in that, bring me your soul up here and lay it on the stage. I want to see it. If you can sell your soul you got to have control over it—if you can't do that, you can't sell your soul. I don't believe those lies. I never did believe it.

At the same workshop, "Honeyboy" Edwards acknowledged the crossroads but shifted focus to a separate folk belief:

> I walked them old country roads and get to them old dirt crossroads. I'd sit there at the fork and I'd play my guitar. And my father told me said "Honey, you want to learn to play guitar hang it over your head at night."

Another workshop participant, Henry Townsend, also heard about the crossroads.

> Indeed I did. I heard at the end of the rainbow there's a pot of gold. But I was smart enough even when I was a kid . . . I would make a little mist of rain and you could see a little rainbow is in there. And I knew there wasn't any pot of gold right there in the yard. So I believe in selling your soul to the devil in the same way I believe in the pot of gold at the end of the rainbow.

What Townsend did say of Johnson was more to the point: "He was one of those people if you played it right, he could play with you, if you played it wrong, he could play it with you and whatever you do, it was right for him because he was just so bright—I thought he was brilliant."

If his peers deny the story, who then seems committed to equating Johnson's skills with the devil? Delta resident and former *Living Blues* editor Jim O'Neal surmises: "The mythic proportions of the Johnson legend are largely the product of modern day white audiences as well as writers' enthusiasm." Perhaps, but not exclusively. African-American expatriate bluesman Julio Finn proves as guilty as his white counterparts when it comes to creating his own version of Robert Johnson: "The devil became his excuse for being a genius—a word by the way, none of his white biographers has used to de-

scribe him—having made his pact he felt that it was all right to see things in a way no one had seen them before."

Finn, who knows more about neo-African belief systems than most writers, stakes the ranch on the devil deal, positing two opposing camps of Johnson biographers: "the bluesmen who knew him and believe he made a pact with the devil at the crossroads; and the folklorists who don't."

Finn's assessment obviously doesn't include the musicians who knew him best, but to be fair, his argument implies blues people could accept the devil reference because it was part of their overall folk belief system. As to the folklorists, I'm not sure whom he is referring to, although it certainly fits me.

Although Finn is nice enough to acknowledge folklorists and knows Chicago blues artists intimately, he casts his lot with the romantics, and even though his version of the devil is slightly more African, his method, like that of his white counterparts, remains based in projecting, on the basis of textual analysis, what Robert Johnson thought. Here again, Johnson's power to elicit a sense of connection that allows people to flatly state what he was thinking, let alone what he did, never fails to amaze me. More than 14 years ago I complained about the process of constructing biography from repertoire, warning that the result would be part tradition and part the biographer's fantasy. Apparently, it is impossible to convince anyone that blues songs do not mirror the singer's own experience; nor is it possible to deter people from nurturing their own image of Johnson as satanist, genius, outsider, and inventor of rock and roll. So why should I spoil the fun? Isn't it reward enough that great traditional music can break into the charts? Maybe so. But I worry that misconceptions about Robert Johnson and his art, which once only affected a few, may now have a much broader impact on the way a popular audience thinks about blues.

From another perspective, I'm sorry the media hype obscures Johnson's gifts, which were those of synthesizer as well as innovator, a creative individual working within a tradition yet able to mold it into his own personal vehicle. His voice is a great blues voice—in fact, if you listen closely you will hear several voices because he had yet to find a single voice for all his work. Perhaps the best entrée into his music is *The Roots of Robert Johnson* (Yazoo L 1073), a compilation that, although it lionizes the individual, at least provides a sense of the sources of his musical vocabulary by presenting the work of the artists he emulated and with whom he shared a tradition. Historically, it also begins the odd story of his relation to phonograph recordings, demonstrating that he learned from the records of stars like Lonnie Johnson and Leroy Carr.

It's also worth noting that his fans prefer the excitement of experimentation, and possible indecision, in his work compared to the mature confidence of Lonnie Johnson, Big Bill Broonzy, Memphis Minnie, or even Blind Boy Fuller, who to my mind was much like Johnson in his skills as a synthesizer or cover artist. Perhaps I feel out of sorts because Johnson's notoriety, as opposed to his skills, has obscured the presence of the other major artists in the, [CBS's] "Roots n' Blues" series whose records initially far outsold those of Robert Johnson.

Then, again, America can only handle one star at a time. This applies particularly to roots music, especially at the crossover level. We tend to simplify traditions by proclaiming single fountainheads, the so-called kings or queens of bluegrass, zydeco, or western swing, rather than muddling through the maze of traditional influence. Current pop history now dubs Johnson innovator, the source, so to speak, of the music of the Rolling Stones and other blues rock contingents. The cover of *Musician* (January 1991) magazine proclaims Johnson "The Father of Rock and Roll." I understand rock and roll, bastard that it is, to have many parents.

Without discounting Johnson's musical gift and the innovations his fellow musicians credit him with, the statement that he was the father of rock and roll is incorrect and has political ramifications. To my mind it is insulting and deliberately evasive to credit a single outsider genius with something produced by a culture, including the countless recorded and unrecorded musicians who shaped the blues over the last 100 years. As I see it, the line is now supposed to read that Robert Johnson invented rock and roll. He was unique, different from his contemporaries, an aberrant outsider with supernatural connections. Then he up and died, leaving his music in the hands of today's inheritors, including Eric Clapton and Keith Richards. Clapton's fans have become Johnson's fans and, for what it's worth, have appropriated Johnson and his music for their own ends.

Obviously Robert Johnson has already outlived most pop groups even after his death. Still the hype keeps coming. But then again blues as commercial music is no stranger to hype.

FURTHER READING

Charters, Samuel. *Robert Johnson.* New York: Oak Publications, 1973, 87 p.
  Includes commentary on Johnson's life and work as well as transcriptions with brief analysis of his twenty-nine songs.

Greenberg, Alan. *Love In Vain: The Life and Legend of Robert Johnson.* Garden City, NY: Doubleday and Company, 1983, 252 p.
  Screenplay to the fictionalized narrative film directed by Greenberg.

LaVere, Steve. "Tying Up a Few Loose Ends." *Living Blues* 94 (November-December 1990): 31-3.
  Corrects some errors in the liner notes to the reissue of *The Complete Robert Johnson.*

"The Death of Robert Johnson." *Living Blues* 94 (November-December 1990): 8-20.
  Various articles and reminiscences by musicians, scholars, and acquaintances of Johnson's.

O'Neal, Jim. "A Travelers Guide to the Crossroads." *Living Blues* 94 (November-December 1990): 21-4.
  Presents various accounts of where the "crossroads" in Johnson's music may be located .

Rubin, Dave. "Robert Johnson: The First Guitar Hero." *Living Blues* 94 (November-December 1990): 38-9.
  Overview of Johnson's guitar-playing technique.

Shines, Johnny. "The Robert Johnson I Knew." *American Folk Music Occasional* (1970): 30-3.
  Reminiscence by a fellow musician and traveling partner of Johnson's.

Vilfredo Pareto

1848–1923

Italian sociologist, economist, and political theorist.

INTRODUCTION

One of the preeminent figures of modern social science, Pareto was among the first to unite the discipline of mathematics with the sciences of sociology and political economics. Throughout his career, Pareto strove to develop an inductive sociological system based upon "logico-experimental reason." The most enduring example of his efforts, his four-volume treatise *Trattato di sociologica generale* (1916, *The Mind and Society*), contains Pareto's controversial contributions to the field, including his theories of nonrational motivation and of the circulation of elites. The former theory schematizes the interior and exterior forces that influence human behavior. According to the latter theory, the rulers of society attempt to legitimize their authority by masking imbalances of power with a veneer of reason; when the deception is revealed a new elite takes power, displacing the old. In the view of many early commentators, Pareto's political beliefs—which favored absolutism and opposed democracy—allied him with fascism. Critics have since acknowledged that Pareto, rather than laying the groundwork for fascism, outlined a thoroughly individual and iconoclastic theory of social behavior. A prominent economist as well as a sociologist, Pareto is also remembered for his ideal model of economic efficiency and for his law of the distribution of wealth, which notes the invariability of income inequality in all economic systems.

Biographical Information

Pareto was born in Paris, France, on August 15, 1848. His father was an Italian aristocrat whose sympathies with the democratic movement in Italy forced him to flee his homeland and live in exile for more than two decades. In 1858 Pareto returned with his parents to Italy. There he was educated in mathematics and classical literature. Graduating from the Polytechnic Institute of Turin in 1870, Pareto embarked on an engineering career, and eventually rose to the position of Director of National Railways in Rome in 1874. Later, he served as the superintendent of Florence's iron mines, and in the 1880s undertook an ill-fated political career. Meanwhile, he accepted the position of lecturer in mathematics and engineering at Florence and Fiesole, and in 1889 married Alessandra Bakunin, daughter of the renowned Russian political theorist. In 1893 Pareto was selected by the economist Leon Walras to fill his vacated post as professor of political economy at the University of Lausanne in Switzerland. He moved with his wife to nearby Céligny.

Several years later Pareto published the *Cours d' économie politique* (1896-97), his first significant work on the subject of economics. In 1900, after inheriting a large sum of money from an uncle, Pareto limited his teaching activities and withdrew to his villa at Céligny in order to write. In 1907 he retired from his professorship and, now separated from his wife and largely reclusive, devoted himself to his sociological studies, which culminated in his *Trattato di sociologica generale*. In 1922, during the rise of fascism in Italy, Pareto was appointed a senator by Benito Mussolini, who considered the aging sociologist the father of fascist ideology. Pareto reluctantly accepted the post but died shortly after the appointment, on August 19, 1923, of heart disease.

Major Works

Trattato de sociologica generale contains most of the salient elements of Pareto's sociological thought. In it he constructed a general theory of social behavior based upon what he called sentiments, residues, and derivations. According to Pareto's definitions, most human behavior is determined by nonrational and typically unobservable qualities of the mind called sentiments, though vestiges of these sentiments can be observed in a more concrete manifestation as residues. In light of what Pareto observed as the nonlogical basis of social behavior, human beings have developed a tendency to rationalize their actions whenever possible, employing a variety of rhetorical structures, or derivations, to do so. Elsewhere in his treatise, Pareto elucidated his theory of the circulation of elites. Beginning with the observation that all advanced cultures in history have demonstrated some form of social hierarchy in which an elite group wields authority, Pareto argued that the elite class justifies its non-rational authority over the lower classes by employing rationalizing derivations. The process is continued into perpetuity as one group of elites is expelled when its derivations are exposed and a new elite class takes its place. As a political economist, Pareto's priniciples are contained in his *Manuale di economica politica* (1906, *Manual of Political Economy*), which includes the *Cours d' économie politique* and his article "Economie mathématique," published in the *Encyclopédie des sciences mathématique*.

Critical Reception

Commentators on Pareto's *Trattato di sociologica generale* have noted that the chaotic style of this massive work has made it difficult to understand, and have criticized its sometimes imprecise vocabulary. Also, his sociological writings have been interpreted as proto-fascist, though most scholars now agree that this is not the case. Additionally, many of his works have not been translated, and consequently his overall influence outside of France and Italy has been relatively limited. Still, his methods, economic ideas, and theories on nonrational behavior have enjoyed considerable critical attention in Europe and America, leading many to place him next to Max Weber and Émile Durkheim as one of the fathers of modern sociological thought.

PRINCIPAL WORKS

Il portezionismo in Italia ed i suoi effetti (sociology) 1891

Programme d' économie politique (economics) 1892

Théorie mathématique des changes étrangers (economics) 1895

Cours d' économie politique (economics) 1896-97

La Liberté économique et les événements d'Italie (sociology) 1898

Les Systémes socialistes (sociology) 1901-02

Manuale di economica politica [*Manual of Political Economy*] (economics) 1906

La Mythe vertuiste et la littérature immorale (sociology) 1911

Trattato di sociologica generale [*The Mind and Society*] (sociology) 1916

I sistemi socialisti (sociology) 1917-20

Compendio di sociologica generale (sociology) 1920

Fatti e teorie (sociology) 1920

Il problema dei cambi e l'industria nazionale (sociology) 1920

Transformazione della democrazia [*The Transformation of Democracy*] (sociology) 1921

Alcune lettere di Vilfredo Pareto (letters) 1938

Corrispondenza (letters) 1948

The Ruling Class in Italy Before 1900 (sociology) 1950

Scritti teorici (sociology) 1952

Pareto-Walras da un carteggio inedito (1891-1901) (economics) 1957

Mon journal (diary) 1958

Lettere a Maffeo Panteleoni 1890-1923, 3 vols. (letters) 1960

Carteggi paretiani 1892-1923 (economics and sociology) 1962

Oeuvres complètes (economics and sociology) 1964

Cronache italiane (sociology) 1965

Scritti sociologici [*Sociological Writings*] (sociology) 1966

Socialismo e democrazia nel pensiero di Vilfredo Pareto (sociology) 1966

Lettere ai Peruzzi 1872-1900, 2 vols. (letters) 1968

The Rise and Fall of the Elites (sociology) 1968

Principi fondamentali della teoria della elasticità de corpi solidi e ricerche sulla integrazione differenziali che ne definiscono l'equi-librio (economics) 1969

Lettere ad Arturo Linaker 1885-1923 (letters) 1972

Scritti politici (sociology) 1974

Battaglie liberiste: Raccolta di articoli e saggi comparsi sulla stampa italiana (sociology) 1975

Guida a Pareto: Un'antologia: Per una teoria critica della scienza della società (sociology) 1975

Lo sviluppo economico italiano (economics) 1975

The Other Pareto (sociology) 1980

CRITICISM

Talcott Parsons (essay date 1935)

SOURCE: "General Works, Theory and Its History," in *The American Economic Review*, Vol. 25, No. 3, 1935, pp. 502-8.

[*In the following essay, Parsons reviews the English-language translation of* Trattato di sociologia generale.]

The final appearance, after being heralded for so many years, of the English translation of Pareto's **Trattato di Sociologia Generale** is surely an event of the first importance for the social sciences of the English-speaking world, though perhaps not altogether for the reasons most generally heralded. The editor, his collaborators and the publishers are to be congratulated upon the successful completion of so monumental a task.

The particular form which Pareto's venture into sociology takes happens to be of the greatest importance to all economists who are interested in the general status of their science relative to the other social sciences. Pareto's experience has a peculiar relevance to the current methodological controversies in American economics between "orthodox" and "institutionalist" schools. For he took a way out of the situation underlying the controversy which is not very widely accepted, at least in any systematic, methodologically self-conscious form, but which is in my opinion exceedingly fruitful.

In this connection Pareto's personal history is interesting. His concern with economic problems began from a practical, political point of view. He became involved as a popular writer in the protectionist controversy in Italy in the eighties on the free trade side. From here he turned to economic theory as a "pure" science, linking it up with his previous training in mathematics and the physical sciences. Finally to supplement his economic theory, in part in an attempt to understand the same concrete problems of protectionism with which he started, he turned to the immense task of formulating a treatise on general sociology.

This personal experience is formulated in the *Treatise* in his extremely interesting discussion of the relation of protection to the general cycles of social change with which he is there concerned. Here he carefully distinguishes three things: (a) the direct economic effects of a protectionist measure, (b) the indirect economic effects and (c) the social effects. To get an accurate picture of the concrete results all three must be considered together in close interdependence with each other.

The direct economic effect is in general a "destruction of wealth." But this *may* (not must) be counterbalanced by the indirect effects *through* the relation to other than economic elements of the social situation. This comes about above all through the fact that protection puts into the hands of government a very far-reaching control over economic opportunity. Under certain circumstances this may be used in such a way as to favor the entrance to such opportunities of a certain type of persons, the "speculators" who would otherwise be denied the opportunity to rise to positions of influence. The result of this transfer of control over enterprise *may,* on account of the productiveness of this group, be an augmentation of wealth in the community more than sufficient to counterbalance the direct economic effects.

But under the third heading Pareto puts the question into a still wider perspective. The relation of protection to a process of "circulation of the élite" is part of the general alternation between relative predominance of the first two classes of "residues" in the governing classes. That is, it is part of the process by which men of "faith," of strong moral character, who are willing and able to use force to defend their faith and their position, are gradually displaced by men facile in "combinations" who govern by "ruse" but who are in general unable to use force,

of whom the "speculators" are one sub-type. This process, proceeding far enough, eventually creates an unstable situation in which the governing class can be easily overthrown by persons organized to employ force to attain their ends. Such a revolution will result in the end of the previous cycle, including that of increasing economic prosperity. To this result protection contributes its quota. It is itself in turn, of course, in part a function of the other elements. A certain type of governing class, in command at a certain phase of Pareto's cycle, will tend to turn to protectionist policies on account of the exigencies of its own position—it has need of the "speculators" and protection offers an immensely powerful means of winning their support.

This example may serve as an introduction to the general issue of the relations of economics and sociology in Pareto's thought. What impressed him were above all three facts: (1) That the teaching of "pure" economic theory was in general that protection would lead to a "destruction of wealth"—the exceptions were of quite minor importance; (2) that the protectionist movement had, in continental Europe, steadily gained ground in spite of this fact, and (3) that the immediate result had not been detrimental to economic prosperity but rather the reverse. The third fact, as we have seen, he explained by the *indirect* economic effects of protection, the second by the situation of the governing classes.

Most economists may be presumed to be familiar with Pareto's work in economic theory which attained its most comprehensive formulation in his *Manuale d'Economia Politica*. In spite of its mathematical formulation, its general tone is "orthodox" or "neo-classical." But from the above consideration of the question of protectionism, and similar treatments of other problems, Pareto did not conclude that the inability of economic theory alone to give a satisfactory solution of a concrete "economic" problem (*e.g.,* to explain the effects of a given protective measure) was a reason for discarding the economic theory. He concluded rather that the economic theory was correct, but abstract, dealing with only one element of a complex situation. To get a satisfactory solution of the concrete problem it is necessary to synthesize the results of economic theory with those of other theories dealing with the other elements in the same situation. It is this, above all, which his sociology is meant to do—to provide a theory, analogous to the economic, of these other elements.

In this review it is possible to give only the barest sketch of the structure of his general theory. Its genesis from the problem of the scope of economics is evident in the fact that the point of departure is from a distinction between the "logical" and the "non-logical" elements of action and the fact that only the former is positively defined, leaving the latter as a residual category. Logical action includes the economic element but is a broader category including also the technological, political and other elements. It is defined as actions consisting of "operations logically united to their end" from the point of view both of the person performing them and of an observer having "a more extensive knowledge" of the circumstances—the former being the "subjective," the latter the "objective" aspect. This is essentially the familiar postulate of "economic rationality." Insofar as it departs from this standard for any reason whatever, action is non-logical, which Pareto explicitly states "does not necessarily mean illogical."

Since the "logical" elements of action are in his opinion fairly adequately analyzed by other sciences, especially economics, Pareto devotes his analytical attention in the treatise to the non-logical element. Here he follows a peculiar method which has not been very generally understood. There are, he says, two roughly distinguishable sets of concrete data which may be studied—"overt acts" (B) and the linguistic expressions or "theories" associated with them (C). Both may be regarded as causally connected with a non-observable "state of mind" (A) from which on the whole they result. Now the "theories" (C) may be regarded as a more accurate index of (A) than can (B), which is more influenced by the external circumstances of the situation, etc. Hence he *confines* his analytical attention to (C), the "theories" associated with non-logical action.

Insofar as action is logical it may be regarded as "resulting from a process of reasoning." This process of reasoning, the "theory" associated with logical action takes the form of a scientific theory, a "logico-experimental" theory as Pareto calls it. Non-logical action, on the other hand, proceeds from "a certain state of mind," "sentiment," etc. While scientific theories reflect external facts, those associated with non-logical action, which are "theories" current in society departing from the scientific standard, are, as Pareto generally puts it, "manifestations of sentiments."

To the study of these non-scientific theories, or more accurately theories *insofar as* they are non-scientific, Pareto then addresses himself by the inductive method. The result of his induction is the distinction of two elements *in these theories,* a relatively constant and a relatively variable. The former he calls "residues," the latter "derivations."

Thus the famous category of "residues" is not an "instinct" or "drive" or any other psychological element, but the constant element in non-scientific *theories.* The residues are not themselves the "forces" which determine non-logical action but are rather "manifestations" of them in much the same sense as a thermometer-reading manifests the thermal state of a substance. The real forces lie in the "state of mind" or more specifically the "sentiments."

The question of the kind of doctrine Pareto is advancing when he lays such great stress on the residues becomes then a matter of what is included in this category of "sentiments." It will be remembered that the concept of non-logical action was in the first place a residual category

and it follows that this character is shared by that of sentiment. It is not surprising, therefore, that further analysis, beyond the point to which Pareto himself explicitly carried it, reveals more than one element. In fact as ultimate non-logical elements in action we find two main categories emerging. One is the "non-rational" psychological factor of instinct or drive, the other that of "ultimate value-attitudes" (my own, not Pareto's term).

The latter form the source of the *ultimate* ends of action even though the adaptation of means to end is "logical." That is, in this case even though there is a logical element, the means-end relationship, there is also in concrete action a non-logical element, that of ultimate ends. The residues, the "major premises" of non-scientific theories, contain as *one* element these ultimate ends. They are not "statements of fact" but "manifestations of sentiments" because the ultimate ends of action are not determined by the exigencies of the conditions of action but form a separate element.

These value-attitudes are expressed not only in the form of ultimate ends of "logical" means-end relationships, but constitute at least the main basis of another extremely important class of actions namely "ritual" actions, both magical and religious. The discovery of the immense social importance of ritual and not its dismissal as the result of mere "ignorance" and "superstition" may be regarded as one of the most important results of Pareto's explicit study of the "non-logical" elements of action—a distinct improvement on the type of economist who tends to generalize his postulate of economic rationality to cover human action as a whole.

I have dwelt at some length upon this central logical structure of Pareto's sociological thought for two reasons—because it is one of the best examples available of the way a realization of the limitations of economic theory in the solution of concrete problems may lead directly from a consideration of the place of the economic element in human action to a consideration of the other elements in relation to it. In this respect Pareto's experience is highly instructive. It is of the greatest interest to economists as a means of placing their discipline in its wider perspective, and to sociologists since the path from the economic (more broadly "rational" in Pareto's "logical" sense) element of action into the sociological is *one* of the main paths by which a science of sociology has been emerging in the recent development of European social thought. In that development Pareto deserves for this reason alone an important place. The second reason for emphasizing his theoretical analysis is that it has been very generally misinterpreted in the discussion in such a way as seriously to obscure the questions here discussed.

This theory does not, however, remain hanging in the air, as it were. Pareto uses it in the latter part of the book to develop a most interesting theory of cycles of social change of which I have given a bare hint in the discussion of protection above. There is no space to go further into it here. It represents, however, one instance of a highly significant type of turning point in the interpretation of the general trend of contemporary social change. The slackening of economic "progress," the resurgence of violence, and of nationalism and other "irrational" faiths all find a place which it is difficult to find for them in the theories of orthodox liberalism. In his interpretation of some of these concrete phenomena Pareto advances views which have provided the main subject matter of the popular discussion of his work. I do not propose to enter upon that discussion here. Suffice it to say that though he is doubtless open to criticism at many points, and, like almost all writers, probably exaggerates the importance of certain aspects, nevertheless his work will well repay careful consideration along with other interpretations. But equally his concrete theories should be interpreted in the light of his general theoretical problems, which many have failed to do.

I have not discussed Pareto's views on general scientific methodology because it seemed to me that other aspects were of greater interest to economists. Pareto was himself trained in mathematics and physical science. Both in economics and in sociology he always had in mind the methodology of the physical sciences as a model. In this respect, however, his work was much more sophisticated than that of the earlier "positivists" in the social sciences. He is far less open to the charge of importing physical science concepts into fields of phenomena not adapted to their use.

On this aspect of Pareto's work Professor Henderson's little book should prove an indispensable guide to the serious student. It is written by a man who is a careful, thorough and penetrating student of Pareto's work and at the same time an eminent scholar in some of the natural sciences on the background of which Pareto would like to have his own work projected. It stands out head and shoulders above every other secondary attempt with which I am acquainted to interpret Pareto's methodological position.

For the most part I think there is to be accorded high praise and little criticism for Pareto's "natural science" methodology of sociology. His sceptical and sophisticated form of it divests it of most of the objectionable features of "positivism," reducing it to the methodological fundamentals of science in general, natural or social. It need only be said, I think, that Pareto's general preoccupation with the natural science model rather closes his mind to the importance of some methodological questions *peculiar* to the sciences dealing with human action, notably those pertaining to the status of the "subjective aspect" of action and the interpretation of forms of "symbolic expression." Such questions arise, however, in an acute form only at a relatively advanced stage in the analysis on the frontiers of Pareto's own theory. This disadvantage is much more than counterbalanced by the clarity and cogency of Pareto's argument on the more general level. One who has gone through his work thoroughly certainly *should* be forever cured of many of the most common and—alas—still prevalent errors.

In conclusion let me state—Pareto's *Treatise* was not written as and should not be taken as the bible of a new religion—for the worship of "science" is just as much a religion as any other. It is a scientific treatise written by a great scientist for scientists; it is unquestionably one of the few most eminent works of its kind in its time in the social sciences. Its eminence, however, does not lie so much in its final systematization of the pioneer work of others, but in itself being a pioneer work, pushing the boundaries of systematic scientific theory into regions which though by no means uncharted in human experience have been none the less highly inadequately subjected to rigorous scientific analysis. It stands by no means alone in this attempt. The approximately contemporary works of Durkheim and Max Weber furnish two other instances. But it is one of the few most important of its kind.

Morris Ginsberg (essay date 1936)

SOURCE: "The Sociology of Pareto," in *Reason and Unreason in Society: Essays in Sociology and Social Philosophy*, Harvard University Press, 1948, pp. 84-103.

[*In the following essay, which was first published in 1936, Ginsberg challenges the central points of Pareto's sociological theories.*]

Pareto's sociology falls naturally into two parts. The first is devoted to an analysis and classification of the elementary constituents of human nature as manifested in social life. The second is concerned with the interactions of these elementary traits and the changes which occur in their distribution in the different classes of society. The method followed is inductive and comparative, that is to say, it starts with empirical facts such as beliefs actually held in different societies, maxims of conduct accepted by them and the like, and it seeks to analyse out the constant and variable elements in these forms of behaviour and to discover the laws or uniformities which determine their mutual relations. Incidentally, Pareto discusses at great length the nature and importance of what he calls the "logico-experimental" method in social science, but he hardly lives up to his own requirements. The definitions given of fundamental terms are obscure, and they are not, as they might be expected to be, gradually clarified by "successive approximations." Further, what appears to me the most interesting portions of the treatise, namely, those devoted to the dynamics of social change, are very inadequately supported by empirical evidence, the facts given being hardly more than illustrative of the hypotheses put forward. The plan of the work is conceived on an imposing scale and it is carried out with great independence and a wealth of learning. It is therefore worthy of the serious consideration of sociologists.

The analysis of the fundamental forces of social life is carried out mainly by means of a classification of human actions into logical and non-logical, and by a more detailed account of the non-logical acts which brings out their overwhelming preponderance in human affairs. In this account Pareto pays no attention to the work of psychologists, but proceeds to put forward independent hypotheses suggested, as he thinks, by direct inspection of the facts. His neglect of psychology has resulted in an extremely vague use of such terms as "sentiments," "instincts," "interests," which has made a proper understanding of his views more difficult than it needs to be. But shed of technicalities and expressed as a first approximation, his conclusions are hardly revolutionary. They amount to this: that people perform and always have performed many acts without knowing why they do them (i.e. by habit and instinct); that the real drives of action are often quite different from the purposes which the agents consciously entertain; that in the pursuit of given conscious ends people often attain quite other ends than those aimed at, either because they adopt the wrong means, or because they do not foresee the remoter consequences of their acts; that men, having a hunger for logic or reason, will try to give a reasoned explanation or justification of acts they do from obscure or unconscious motives. The bulk of the treatise is devoted to an analysis of the non-rational elements in human conduct and of the fictions which are invented to give a flavour of rationality to conduct that is really the result of feeling and impulse.

The classification of acts into rational and non-rational, or in Pareto's not very happy terminology, logical and non-logical, turns upon the distinction between means and ends which he assumes without further inquiry to be applicable to all human behaviour. Briefly, acts are non-logical (i) when they serve no end subjective or objective, e.g. futile or non-adaptive instinctive acts, if such there be; (ii) when the agent thinks a particular end is being realized but nothing is in fact achieved through the act as judged in the light of wider knowledge, e.g. in magical operations; (iii) when there is an objective end but the subject is not consciously aiming at it, e.g. in theoretically "pure" instinct; (iv) when an end is actually achieved which differs from the end the subject sets to himself, whether the objective end would or would not have been acceptable to him could he have foreseen it. Briefly, acts are non-logical when the subject acts without explicit knowledge of the purpose of his action, or, having such knowledge, chooses means which in the light of better grounded information are either not likely to achieve the purpose, or to achieve something else. By contrast acts are logical when the consequences anticipated by the subject are identical with the consequences that might reasonably be anticipated in the light of wider knowledge. So far logic, or rather rational reflection, is not concerned with ends at all, save perhaps that in order to act rationally you must know what you want. Logic is concerned rather with the appropriate linking of means and ends. But this position is not consistently maintained. Unfortunately, Pareto makes no attempt to classify the ends of conduct or to relate them to the fundamental drives. These are said to consist of sentiments, tastes, proclivities, inclinations, instincts, residues, and interests. The residues are said to include neither the simple appetites or instincts nor the interests, but to "correspond

to" instincts or appetites. By this, as we shall see later, appears to be meant that there is a residue when an appetite or instinct does not act itself out simply but finds expression in an indirect or disguised form. Thus sex conceived as mere union of the sexes is not a residue, but it is residual, for example, in the behaviour of people who preach virtue as a way of lingering in their thoughts on sex matters. If this is the correct interpretation, the residues are not themselves drives, but rather ways in which the fundamental drives disguise themselves, and they are thus non-logical in the sense of obscuring the nature of the impulses really at work. So far it would seem that the adequate fulfilment of *any* impulse, provided it is conscious and direct, is logical. But there are many passages in which it seems to be suggested that it is more logical to act in accordance with one's interests than in accordance with other drives. What, then, are the interests? They are said to consist in impulses to acquire material goods, whether "useful" or merely pleasurable, and to seek consideration and honour. It is not easy to see why these goods are singled out as rational, why, for instance, it is more logical to pursue honour and consideration than to satisfy other social impulses, or let us say, the desire for knowledge. Or is the pursuit of interests regarded as logical not because of the particular ends involved, but because in achieving them men can be shown to act with greater circumspection than in other activities in the choice of appropriate means?

The difficulty may be illustrated by reference to the frequent description of economic activity as typical of logical behaviour. It is easy to see that economic activity contains a logical element in so far as the means chosen are technically appropriate to given ends. But economic behaviour is clearly non-rational in so far as men acting economically are not aware of the motives which impel them. A man's choice of profession may be as an intention clearly envisaged. But the motives of the choice are often obscure and even unconscious. It may be influenced by all Pareto's residues, for example, by authority and prestige, by sociability, by the persistence of abstractions and what not. Further, it is clear that men in seeking economic satisfaction attain ends which they did not foresee and do not want. Men do not want war, but their behaviour leads to it. Business men and workers do not want unemployment, but the outcome of their linked activities is to produce it. If success in the fulfilment of impulses is the criterion of logical behaviour, economic activity must be largely non-logical, since it fails to secure for the masses of men the conditions of a purposeful life. In short, without an examination of the ends of human endeavour and of their relations to each other as well as to the means available for their realization, it is impossible to throw much light on the rational elements in behaviour, or on the relation of economic to other activities in human life.

There is a further complication which must now be considered. In the later portions of the treatise a person is said to act logically in so far as he tries to secure a maximum of individual utility. This means action in accordance with what is "advantageous" or "beneficial" to him and involves a comparison of different satisfactions in accordance with some norm. Presumably a logic is required for making these comparisons, but this line of thought is not pursued. In economics it would seem the individual is assumed to be the best judge of his own interests or utility and to act rationally in regard to it. But outside economics there may be an infinite number of norms and therefore an infinite number of possible maxima of utility. The choice of the norm itself is arbitrary and non-logical. Thus we cannot say whether it is to the advantage of the individual to suffer physically for the sake of a moral satisfaction, or whether it is better for him to seek wealth or to apply himself to some other pursuits. Despite the elaborate discussion of utility, there is extraordinarily little to be gained from it. Since the norm is arbitrarily chosen we can only determine the maximum utility for an individual from the line of conduct that he actually adopts. That is the maximum which in fact appears to him to be such and that appears to be the maximum which in fact he pursues. Or is it possible for the individual to make mistakes regarding what is to his advantage apart from the mistakes he may make in the choice of means? If so, a logic of ends is required which would enable the individual to distinguish apparent and real advantage, and that would soon lead to an ethics of the teleological kind which Pareto despises along with all other brands of ethics. In brief, Pareto's treatment of the logic of behaviour leaves out of consideration what to most people will appear essential to it. Rational behaviour no doubt requires us to know what we want and to choose means in a manner which will stand the test of empirical verification. But a logic of behaviour would also have to discover whether the norms that individuals adopt in relation to the ends that they pursue are self-consistent, and whether they form part, or can be made to form part, of a systematic and ordered whole. Such a logic obviously could not be confined to the norms governing the acts of particular individuals, since it is equally or more important to inquire how far the norms of different individuals or groups are or can be made to be compatible and perhaps harmonious. Pareto makes no attempt whatever to deal with these problems and asserts as a self-evident dogma that norms are just the expression of "sentiments." There is, for example, no criterion save sentiment for choosing between a society based on large inequalities of income and one based on approximately equal incomes. If we admire supermen we will assign zero utility to the lower classes; if we love equality we will prefer the type of society which secures to the lower classes an equal share in the goods of life. Is reason really helpless in the face of such a problem?

It may be suggested that before dealing with the ultimate problems of valuation here involved there is a good deal that reason can do by way of clarifying the issues and settling questions of fact. Pareto, together with other anti-egalitarians, assigns a meaning to the principle of equality which egalitarians are not concerned to defend. The principle does not assert either that men are equal in endowment or that they should be treated equally. It is

concerned, negatively, to exclude arbitrary assignments and, positively, to base distribution on a general rule impartially applied. If for the sake of argument it be agreed that this rule is that distribution should be in proportion to the needs of individuals with a view to the realization of such capacity in them as they have, it will be seen that this does not involve equality of treatment. Certain questions of fact then become very important. Firstly, what is the extent of the differences in capacity between individuals, and are these so great as to justify us in regarding some of them as supermen and large numbers of the masses of men as having zero value? Secondly, how great are the differences in external conditions which are really required in order to enable the alleged supermen to fulfil their capacities, and can these differences in conditions only be assured them by a system of private property, involving the amount of inequality that now prevails? Thirdly, we need to know what effects upon the total available for distribution will be produced by adopting the principle of equality, and this raises questions not only of economics but of psychology also; since we need to know how incentives work in different economic systems. Ultimately, no doubt, when these questions of fact have been answered, value judgments will have to be discussed, but it may be doubted whether they would then loom so large in the minds of the disputants. Pareto, at any rate, does not discuss the nature of value judgments, but merely asserts dogmatically that they express nothing but "sentiments." He is impressed by the fact that in moral judgments, for example, people are swayed by superstitions and prejudices which deceive themselves and others. But this applies to all human thought and action and if seriously pressed would lead inevitably to the conclusion that there can be no logical thought or action at all. Pareto also makes much of the argument that if ethical judgments permitted of rational examination, ethics would have made greater progress than it appears to have made since the days of Aristotle. This, however, is not substantiated by any examination of ethical systems. Moreover, it would apply with equal force to, say, economics right up to the eighteenth or nineteenth century, since it is by no means certain that any great advances were made in it in the interval between these periods and Aristotle's discussion of economic problems. Curiously enough, Pareto thinks that ethical discussions, though logically futile, have had great influence on social life: "they are forever shaking the foundations of the social order." A philosopher might say that this was no mean achievement for mere "derivations."

The difficulties in Pareto's theory of non-logical actions are due ultimately to his failure to inquire more fully into the nature of logical, or as I should prefer to say, rational action. The function of reason is, according to him, exhausted in linking means and ends appropriately. But even Hume, who held a similar view, admitted that thought can influence action by disclosing the hollowness of objects of desire which before reflection excited lively passions, and it is clear further that many of our most passionate devotions are only possible on the reflective level. Thought and impulse cannot, in fact, be sharply dissevered and the ends of life cannot therefore be relegated to the sphere of impulse alone. Ends and means again profoundly affect one another, and it is impossible to deal logically with means without clarification of the nature of the ends. Reason, too, is concerned with the relations of the various ends to each other, with the possibility of their mutual consistency or harmony, and in cases of conflict with the grounds of preference. An element of generality in preferences cannot surely be denied. We prefer not only particular things to other particular things, but kinds of things to other kinds, and our orders of preference have a certain constancy; the business of reason is to reflect on the standards which are implicit in these intuitive judgments. If action can be rational at all, such reflection on values and standards of values must be able to claim validity. If, on the other hand, our choices and preferences are utterly arbitrary, there can be no sense in speaking of any action as rational or as logically justifiable. All that we could then do in a theory of conduct would be to describe and classify human actions as sheer matters of fact, and at most to inquire into the relations which men subjectively set themselves and the ends which are in fact attained by them. In such a theory of human conduct the belief that some acts are "logical" would only be one fact among others, and to deal with it "logico-experimentally" would mean to inquire whether it in fact satisfies the queer hunger for logic that men appear to have, or whether it is useful as a means to other ends. Its power to satisfy the demands of logic at any rate does not seem to be very great.

The theory of non-logical actions is further elaborated by Pareto in his doctrine of the residues and derivations. Formal definition of the residues is lacking and we can only rely upon an analysis of the very numerous examples given and the classification offered of the principal types. To begin with, the residues are not identical with what psychologists call instincts. They are expressly said not to reflect all the instincts, and to include neither the simple appetites, tastes or inclinations, nor what he understands by interests. Yet the residues "correspond to" the instincts, and it is pointed out that there may be residues corresponding also to other impulses, though these are not further dealt with. The meaning seems to be this. In so far as the fundamental impulses are realized directly without diversion or substitution of object they do not give rise to residues. Animals who are supposed to act on pure instinct can have no residues, and in human beings the simple satisfaction of food or sex impulses is not residual. The sex residue becomes important when we recognize its influence in such phenomena as asceticism. Only creatures capable of theorizing and therefore of deceiving themselves can have residues. A classification of the residues would thus be a classification of the different ways in which the fundamental impulses realize themselves in human behaviour, excluding, on the one hand, fully conscious and experimentally directed behaviour, and on the other, behaviour which is based on simple and direct impulse. If this is the right interpreta-

tion, the ultimate dynamic elements in human nature are not to be found in the residues but rather in what Pareto calls the sentiments. The residues are the patterns or principles in accordance with which the sentiments work, and they can only be discovered by an analytic and comparative study of complex acts, in which the influence of the sentiments may not at first sight be at all obvious. In studying them Pareto is thus trying to discover the different ways in which the "sentiments" unconsciously affect belief and action.

Pareto does not undertake, as might have been expected, an analysis of such processes as repression, projection, aim inhibition, substitution or sublimation, symbolization, dramatization, and the like. Of the work done in this connection he appears to have no knowledge. Yet despite his repudiation of psychological methods, what he here attempts to do is psychological and not sociological. He does not endeavour to study the social influences affecting belief and behaviour, but on the contrary finds the explanation of social behaviour in the permanent underlying psychological elements and their varying combinations in different societies, and his conclusions must be therefore tested from the point of view of their adequacy in the light of psychology. Thus regarded, his account is not very impressive. He gives six classes of residues with numerous subdivisions, namely, combinations, persistent aggregates, sociability, activity, the integrity of the individual, and sex.

The residue of combinations is of such wide scope that it really includes the whole synthetic activity of the mind, the operations of science and of constructive imagination, and, indeed, all forms of association. Behind all these there is apparently a single drive to combine elements into aggregates. That the mind has a tendency to combine or synthesize is true, though it is equally true that it has a tendency to break up or analyse, and no account of mental activity can be given unless both these tendencies are taken into consideration. But in any case the resort to such general tendencies takes us but a little way, and it is important to discover the principles in accordance with which the various forms of analysis and synthesis are effected. As far as the underlying motive is concerned it cannot be assumed that it is just an urge to combine. This is certainly not the case either in purely theoretical or practical activity. When Pareto comes to distinguish the different types of combination he is far too ready to rely on his assumed general tendency just to combine. This leads him to stress unduly the arbitrariness of the combinations, as in his account of magical operations, or to adopt familiar principles of association such as of similars or opposites which permit of more refined psychological analysis. Magical practices, for example, do not rest upon a general tendency to combine anything and everything, but upon a readiness, under the stress of practical needs and in the absence of a critical method, to rely on coincidences. There is always an element of experience behind them, though this is too readily generalized and no adequate means are available for disentangling the subjective and objective factors. The tendency to generalize on a slender basis has a much better claim to be called a residue than the tendency to arbitrary combinations. No doubt the experiences underlying a particular belief may be difficult to detect, and Pareto is undoubtedly right in stressing the difficulty of tracing the historical origins of ancient or primitive magical beliefs. Yet occasionally what appears to be an arbitrary association can be shown by historical analysis to be based on intelligible, though of course not scientifically founded, associations. To say "five" in order to avert the evil eye may seem hopelessly arbitrary. Yet in Morocco, according to Westermarck, this is a remnant of the ancient practice of throwing the hand forward with outspread fingers and saying "five in your eyes"; which has now become attenuated to just saying "five" or even "Thursday." Here the original practice requires examination in accordance with the psychology of the magic of gestures, and is in line with much else of the pantomimic or dramatic in magic. In all cases an analysis of the objective and subjective conditions determining belief in particular connections is necessary. It is mere evasion of the issue to appeal to purely general tendencies capable of explaining all connections, and therefore not specially helpful in dealing with any of them.

Under the heading of the persistence of aggregates Pareto brings together a number of interesting facts, but here again the analysis is not very illuminating from the psychological point of view. At least two rather different things are here confused. One is the tendency for sets of psychological dispositions which have grown up between a person and other persons or things to cohere and persist in time. This requires analysis in terms of Shand's doctrine of the sentiments and the theory of complexes. The other is the tendency to individualize or to regard as single entities groups of experiences in relation to which sentiments have grown up, and to attribute to these entities, real or imaginary, any further attributes which our emotional attitude to them requires. The phenomena here included have usually been studied under the headings of animism, animatism, personification, and the like, and to their elucidation, I should say, Pareto makes very little contribution, except perhaps in the stress he lays on the influence of personified or reified abstractions on social life.

Under the residue of activity Pareto discusses facts which are usually treated by psychologists under the heading of the expression of the emotions and other drives and the pleasure taken in the exercise of faculty. He rightly stresses the part played by fantasy or imagination in providing symbolic expression of the emotions, but does not further analyse symbolism, nor does he inquire into the reasons why symbolic substitution is needed. The principal examples that he uses are taken from the phenomena of religious exaltation, such as revivals, mystical ecstasies, and the like. But his interpretations of these phenomena are of very doubtful value. There is much to be said for the view that ecstatic manifestations are due not so much, as he thinks, to a sheer need for activity as to the need for relaxation from the strain and monotony of

ordinary life and for release from repression and conflict. In political agitation, which is another of his examples, the feeling that "something must be done" is hardly due to a desire for activity as such. On the contrary, in the case of leaders and agitators it is rooted in deep conflicts, and in the masses the readiness to yield to leaders who claim to get things done is a reflection of their own apathetic anxiety and the disinclination or inability to do anything effective themselves. The whole discussion is extraordinarily vague. It is not at all clear whether the residue of activity is a specific tendency to act, or whether it is a collective term for the need of expressing all the emotions and impulses in outward acts. In any event, to find the residual, that is to say, the constant and invariable elements in religious manifestations in bare activity without any attention to the nature of the emotions and needs which are at work can hardly be said to constitute a profound contribution to the psychology of religion.

The residues of sociability include a number of tendencies, principally the desire for uniformity, the desire to impose uniformity on others, the hatred of the new, counterbalanced by interest in novel combinations, the tendency to pity balanced by cruelty, the tendency to share with others, to suffer for them even to the extent of self-sacrifice, the need for the approval of others, the compound of submission, fear, respect, pride, and domination which constitutes the psychological basis of hierarchical organization, and others. The account given of these tendencies, and especially the discussion of asceticism, is of great interest, but it is not very precise or systematic, and there is too great a readiness to invent instincts *ad hoc*. The desire for uniformity, for example, is hardly to be accounted for in terms of a general instinct to imitate. Psychologists are not agreed that such an instinct exists, and, in any case, the respect for rules *qua* rules is very complex. There is a rational element in it based on the recognition that for societies to cohere there must be a readiness on the part of individuals to conform to rules without insisting on a reasoned justification on every occasion of their application. Such recognition may not be very clearly present to the minds of all members, but there is always present a feeling that order must be maintained and that there must be rules. Whether rational or not, the feeling of respect for accepted rules does not rest on sheer imitativeness, but on deeper social bonds. The purest form of the tendency to imitate Pareto sees in fashion; but here again the analysis strikes me as superficial. Fashion is not based on a tendency to imitate anything and everything, but rather upon an identification with those who have social prestige, and thus involves at least as much desire to be distinguished from others as to be like them. In regard to his account of the other social tendencies, it may be noted that Pareto owes much of his recent popularity to the cynical account he gives of humanitarianism. Anything more remote from logico-experimental evidence can hardly be imagined. He imputes all sorts of motives to humanitarians without the slightest attempt at proof, and indulges in vast historical generalizations without anything like adequate inductive verification. It is one of his favourite generalizations that repugnance to suffering and the tendency to pacifism are characteristic of *élites* in decadence. One might counter this by formulating *ad hoc* the parallel generalization that brutality and war-mongering are characteristic of *élites* uncertain of their power. For neither generalization is there adequate evidence of the "logico-experimental" kind that Pareto considers essential for a scientific sociology.

The treatment of asceticism as a residue of sociability is striking. Pareto interprets ascetic behaviour as in the main due to a hypertrophy or perversion of the social instincts, or, as it might perhaps be better put, as an exaggeration of the need to control and master the self-assertive impulses. The interpretation is worked out with much insight, but perhaps insufficient attention is paid, especially in the elaborate discussion of flagellation and allied phenomena, to the sado-masochistic elements in asceticism.

The residue of the integrity of the individual broadly includes all reactions tending to maintain equilibrium or to restore a violated equilibrium. It is not at all clear whether this is a specific tendency, how it is related to what psychologists call the self-regarding sentiment, and whether it is not merely a collective term for a group of reactions. In a sense all responses whatever may be brought under it, since they may all be interpreted as the result of a disturbance due to inner or outer stimuli. The examples that Pareto gives here are mainly derived from ritual. Thus purificatory rites are regarded as efforts to restore the integrity of the individual which has been disturbed by pollution. But here, as in the case of the residue of combinations, the tendency appealed to is so general that it would explain all ritual whatever and therefore throws but little light on any. Why is the integrity of the individual endangered by contact with blood, and why is the malaise produced by this pollution got rid of just by this or that form of purificatory ritual? To say that these are just arbitrary combinations is surely to abandon the problem. There is, I think, a somewhat similar difficulty in Lévy-Bruhl's treatment of what he calls "transgressions," with which Pareto's discussion has some affinity. For example, it is not an explanation but only a restatement of the problem to say that the horror of incest is due to the fact that it is treated as a transgression.

Somewhat unexpectedly, Pareto brings under the residue of the integrity of the individual the demand for equality by inferiors. He interprets this demand as really a hidden desire for another kind of inequality or selfish privilege. Perhaps this is not as pessimistic a view as that of Freud, who suggests that social justice means that we are ready to deny ourselves many things so that others may have to do without them as well. But what direct evidence is there of the real motives which inspired the leaders of humanitarianism or the mass of their followers? In general, Pareto's attack on humanitarian ethics hardly calls for detailed analysis here. His arguments are very far

from being presented with the detachment which he considers so necessary in a logico-experimental sociology and they abound in value judgments. Since such judgments are in Pareto's view nothing but the expression of "sentiments," his discussion has merely biographical interest in so far as it throws light on Pareto's own mentality.

In his treatment of the residue of sex Pareto brings out with great gusto the vagaries and inconsistencies of sexual morality and he stresses the well-known fact that behind the condemnation of sex there is often hidden an excessive preoccupation with it. He might have generalized this and shown how in the case of other impulses the repression of self takes revenge in the reprobation of others. In this discussion even more than elsewhere the fundamental weakness of his method is revealed. In his anxiety to stress the constant and invariable elements in sex he fails to come to grips with the medley of social forces affecting the morals of sex-relationships and to deal with the variations that have been observed in them. One almost gets the impression that the rules regulating the relations between the sexes and the respect for chastity are based on nothing but disguised sexual greed and jealousy. There is no study of the need to canalize and control the sexual impulses in view of the manifold derangements of which they are susceptible, no examination of the relation of sex to tenderness and affection and the social impulses, or of the problems connected with precocious sexuality, or of the influence on sex relationships of the institutions of property and the family. In short, there is no treatment of the numerous factors, sociological and psychological, which must be taken into consideration in a just estimate of sex regarded as a constant and invariable drive.

The theory of the derivations is intended to furnish a psychology rather than a logic of error, that is, to reveal the hidden forces which lead to error and make it acceptable rather than to disclose the logical structure of erroneous reasoning. Clearly the derivations must be rooted in the residues. There is, in fact, a double connection between them. Firstly, men have a strange hankering after logic and they are not satisfied unless they can give reasons for their actions and beliefs. This Pareto regards as being one form of the residue of combinations which supplies the drive both for logical and non-logical reasoning. But, secondly, particular derivations owe their strength and influence to other residues and the "sentiments" underlying them. That the ultimate driving power lies in the sentiments or their residual manifestations and not in the theories which are offered to account for behaviour can be seen, Pareto argues, from the fact that the feelings or sentiments remain essentially unaltered despite changes in derivations and theories. He is fond of using in this connection examples derived from the history of morals. "A Chinese, a Moslem, a Calvinist, a Catholic, a Kantian, a Hegelian, a Materialist, all refrain from stealing; but each gives a different explanation for his conduct." Strangely enough, Pareto claims greater constancy for moral rules than is needed for a rationalist ethics, and he makes no attempt whatever to account for the variability of the moral judgment. The residue of the integrity of the individual will account for the laws of theft, but only if you are content to neglect the enormous variations that are found in the laws of property and consequently in what is regarded as theft, and so with other institutions. While both the varying and constant elements in morals contain both rational and non-rational elements, I do not think that Pareto provides any method for estimating their relative strength, for determining, for example, the rôle of reason in the history of law or indeed of any social or political movement; though nowadays no one would be concerned to deny the importance of the irrational or even unconscious factors in human life.

The interest of Pareto's treatment of the derivations lies largely in his acute and penetrating criticism of many famous social theories, for example of Benthamism or of the General Will, for which it provides an occasion. It is not particularly successful as a systematic exposition of the sources of prejudice and modes of sophistication. The derivations are grouped under four headings: affirmation, authority, accord with sentiments, and verbal arguments. Under the first are included assertions claiming authority simply as assertions. The examples that he gives are maxims such as "Silence is an ornament to all women"; "Neither do nor learn aught that is shameful." These correspond, I think, to what Mill calls fallacies *a priori,* mere assertions claiming to be self-evident. It is not easy to see where derivation comes in here, since by definition no reason is given for the assertion, unless what is meant is that if challenged the answer will be just their indisputability. Pareto does not discuss the psychological factors which produce the feeling of self-evidence, nor why assertions that are regarded as self-evident in one age are considered nonsensical or false in another. Occasionally the examples chosen beg important questions of theory, as when æsthetic judgments are interpreted as unconscious conversions of subjective likings into assertions of objective fact. I doubt whether the derivations of affirmation form a distinct class, and in most instances they pass readily into those resting on authority or verbal argument. The derivations of authority have long been familiar, and among the writers whom Pareto quotes in other connections, he might here have referred to Bentham who has given an elaborate discussion of them. The derivations of accord with feeling present a good opportunity for a consideration of the subjective factors of belief, and Pareto has much of interest to say on the influence of the self-assertive and the social tendencies upon belief. Here his analysis would have been greatly improved had he paid attention to the work of modern psychology and especially the psychology of the unconscious. In his discussion of the derivations of verbal argument the logical aspect is not kept very distinct from the psychological. Perhaps the most valuable part of his exposition is his insistence on the tendency of abstractions to persist and to become the nuclei of powerful emotional dispositions.

Pareto has no doubt that the residues remain constant or undergo only slight and slow change even over long periods. But though this may be true in a sense the proof offered is not very convincing. The residues are so vaguely defined that it is easy to find what is alleged to be the same residue in what are apparently very different social movements. In this way it is argued, for example, that behind Ancestor worship, Polytheism, Catholicism, Protestantism, Nationalism, Socialism, Humanitarianism there is the same residue of group-persistence. So again the residue of individual integrity is regarded as constant, because though it is not so strong in the modern plutocracy as it was, say, in the feudal nobility, the loss is made up by the growth of self-respect on the part of the lower classes and in the recognition that even criminals have a personality deserving of consideration. A humanitarian may be pardoned for thinking this "compensation" a matter of some importance. Even more surprising is the claim that the residues of combination have not changed much if the class is considered as a whole; on the ground that territory formerly occupied by magic, theology, and metaphysics is now increasingly occupied by experimental science which is also a product of the residue of combinations. Units of comparison so pliable and interchangeable are hardly what one would expect to find in a logico-experimental sociology.

The most interesting and suggestive part of Pareto's treatise is that concerned with the dynamics of social change and the factors determining social equilibrium at any one time. The social system is conceived as made up of the elements which have hitherto been considered in abstraction but which in fact are in a relation of mutual dependence. The elements in question are the residues, the derivations and the interests, and since these are differently distributed in the population, account has to be taken of individual differences and of the amount of circulation or movement from one group to another that occurs in given societies. The important influences he thinks are those exerted by the interests, that is, broadly, of economic factors on the residues and upon their distribution in the different social classes and the converse influence of the changing distribution of the residues on the interests. On the other hand, the influence of theories or derivations on the residues is slight, if not negligible. The interaction of these elements is such as to result in undulations or oscillations, movement in one direction usually setting up compensatory movements in the opposite direction, with the result that change is not in a straight line but is cyclical in character.

The individual differences that Pareto considers at length are those in the intensity or strength of the residues of combinations and persistent aggregates. He lays special stress on one particular classification. In both the ruling classes or *élite* and in the masses, though in different proportions, two types are to be found. There are, on the one hand, individuals of the speculator type, enterprising, eager for new experiences, imaginative, expansive, fertile in new ideas. Contrasted with them are people of the *rentier* type, timid, conservative, anxious to preserve what has been won, averse to anything new. The differing relative proportions in which these two types are combined in the governing class and the extent to which recruitment from below is permitted determine the different types of social structure and civilization. In the political sphere, for example, if the governing class consists of individuals in whom Class II residues predominate over Class I residues, we find types of government which rely chiefly on physical force and on religious and similar sentiments; on the other hand, if the ruling class is chiefly of the speculator type, we find types of government relying chiefly on intelligence and cunning, and appealing either to the sentiments of the multitude, as in the theocratic forms of government, or else playing upon the interests, as in the demagogic plutocracies of modern times. The changes that occur as a result of the predominance of one or other of these types are not, however, in a continuous direction. Compensatory movements occur, whether as a result of internal changes or of war, and oscillations of varying length are thus produced. It is to be noted that the distinction between the speculator and *rentier* types does not quite correspond to that between liberal and conservative in the political sense, since the speculators will ally themselves with or make use of liberals and conservatives alike, and even of anarchists if it suits their purpose. Revolutions occur mainly when the ruling class, relying too much on the combination residues, develops an enervating humanitarianism and is disinclined to use force, especially if it cultivates a policy of exclusiveness and does not find ways of assimilating the exceptional individuals who come to the front in the subject classes. On the other hand, a governing class may also encompass its own ruin by accepting, for their economic value, individuals who are well endowed with Class I residues, and this may end in the government passing from the lions to the foxes. History shows, Pareto thinks, that changes in the proportions between Class I and Class II residues in the *élite* do not continue indefinitely in one direction, but are sooner or later checked by movements in a counter-direction. In this way the modifications in the *élite* are shown to be among the major factors determining the undulatory form of social change. They are correlated, it is claimed, not only with political transformations but also with economic cycles and with oscillations in thought and culture. Thus in periods of rapidly increasing economic prosperity the governing class comes to contain greater numbers of individuals of the speculator type, rich in Class I residues, and fewer of the opposite type; while the converse is the case in periods of economic depression or retrogression. With these alternations are connected also the oscillations that Pareto traces in the history of thought, expressed roughly in the conflict between "reason" and "superstition," scepticism and faith.

It will be noted that in this theory Pareto is not merely replacing the "Marxist" conception of a struggle between bourgeoisie and proletariat by that of a struggle between speculators and *rentiers*. It is essential to his thesis that the residues are differently distributed in the ruling and ruled groups, and it is on the balance of the residues in both groups that social equilibrium depends. Further, it is in this part of his inquiry that Pareto makes the transition from individual psychology to sociology proper, that is to say to a study of interactions between individuals. His view does not imply that the course of events is determined by the schemes of individual speculators who rule the world by deliberate and concerted stratagem. Their policy is the resultant of a complex set of forces and an infinite number of acts each initiated by the particular circumstances of the time, but leading collectively to results which individually they do not foresee, despite the fact that they may have a clearer conception of their own interests than the masses have of theirs. Here as elsewhere in the *Treatise* Pareto insists on the great complexity of social interactions and on the need for replacing the notion of one-sided causality by that of mutual dependence of the factors involved.

How far the theory of the circulation of the *élites* is to be interpreted in biological or genetic terms is not very clear. Pareto undoubtedly thinks that the residues are determined by inherited constitution. Further, it would seem that in his view "aristocracies" tend to die out in the sense of leaving no descendants: "History is the graveyard of aristocracies." On the other hand, one gets the impression that according to him the residues are remarkably constant in a given society taken as a whole apart from infiltration of individuals from other societies. The changes that occur are rather in the distribution of the residues in the different portions of the population and the opportunities offered for their manifestation. Such changes might well occur without involving any genetic changes in the stock and be largely socially conditioned. Pareto refers now and again to the work of the Anthroposociologists, e.g. Lapouge and Ammon, but he seems to have paid little attention to modern studies of individual differences and the effects of differential fertility, and one cannot be sure of his attitude to them. As the residues clearly involve temperamental traits in addition to cognitive ones, and as the evidence of individual differences in temperamental traits is very slight, perhaps he would not have been able to get much help from these studies.

Pareto supports his theory of social change by numerous examples derived from the history of Græco-Roman civilization and of modern Europe. Brilliant as the exposition is, it is hardly adequate to establish the periodicity of social and political movements as a regular law, or the correlations alleged between these movements and the history of thought and culture. The proof of such a law would require a much more exact social morphology than he provides and an extension of the inquiry to non-European civilizations. It would also require independent evidence of the mental make-up of the different social groups, especially of the individuals directly concerned in social movements, and a more exact determination of the nature and extent of what he calls the circulation of *élites*. It may be remarked that he makes very little use of the work of others. Occasionally he might have found support for some of his theories. It is worth mentioning that Pirenne's later study of European capitalism, and the explanation that he gives of the alternations traced by him between periods of innovation and periods of stabilization, appear to be in line with Pareto's views.

If the occurrence of undulatory movements in history be granted, there remains the important problem of their significance from the point of view of long-range trends. Pareto himself grants that in economic production and in the arts and sciences there has been on the whole a movement forward, or as he expresses it, Class I residues and the conclusions of logico-experimental science have forced a retreat on group persistences. But he insists that this growth in the power of reason has not affected political and social activities to any great extent, and that in any case there is no ground for the belief in continuous progress. The notion of progress is never mentioned by him without bitter derision. But it will be noticed that, though according to him there can be no reliable criteria of progress he does not hesitate to speak of decadence which requires criteria of the same kind. To me it is clear that Pareto has developed no adequate method for estimating the rôle of reason in law, morals, and politics, and that he vastly under-estimates what has on the whole been achieved in these directions. The growing interconnection between economic and social and political movements which he himself stresses is an important phenomenon and one which may compel humanity to make increasing use of rational agencies. The fact also that the notion of conscious control of social change in its application to humanity as a whole is relatively new must be taken into consideration in estimating future trends. No one nowadays believes in automatic progress or in indefinite and unlimited perfectibility. What is asserted is that it is theoretically possible to formulate a coherent ideal of human endeavour, and that from a study of the failures as well as the successes of mankind in dealing with its problems, there is ground for the belief that such an ideal permits of realization if men are prepared to work for it. Pareto's denial of human progress rests upon (*a*) his disbelief in any rational ethics; (*b*) his view that history so far has disclosed no significant changes but only oscillations. As to (*a*), I do not find that he provides any reasoned justification for his disbelief. As to (*b*), it seems to me that he greatly exaggerates the constant elements in human history, and that if there is no law of human progress neither is there any law of cyclical recurrence. From the point of view of policy, in any event, if a choice is to be made between persistent aggregates and combinations, I see no reason for not choosing combinations.

Max Lerner (essay date 1939)

SOURCE: "Pareto's Republic," in *Ideas Are Weapons: The History and Uses of Ideas,* The Viking Press, 1939, pp. 348-55.

[*In the following essay, Lerner offers a highly critical view of Pareto's sociological thought.*]

Take a Machiavelli, with his amazing sense of the springs of human conduct and his cynicism about ethics; soak him in the modern worship of scientific method; hard-boil him in a hatred for democracy in all its manifesta-

tions; fill him with an intense animus against proletarian movements and Marxian theory; add a few dashes of economic fundamentalism; stir it all with a poetic feeling about the ruling élite; sprinkle thoroughly with out-of-the-way erudition; season with a good deal of acuteness and homely wisdom; and serve at interminable length. If you follow this recipe you should have something that resembles Pareto's treatise on *The Mind and Society*.

I do not want to underestimate the personal achievement that these four volumes represent. Here is prodigality—of ideas, of learning, of spleen. Here is a far-flung exploration of history and human foibles, in two thousand pages with an enormous footnotage. Here are a million words, and many of them not at all foolish, poured into the huge mold of an argument. Pareto was an old man, well on toward seventy, when he wrote this work. He could look back on a career in which he had been successively mathematician, engineer, political journalist, professor of economics at Lausanne. Now, almost alone on his large Swiss estate, suffering from heart disease and insomnia, surrounded by his cats whom he adored and relatively unmolested by the pallid democratic beings whom he despised, he gathered his strength for his greatest effort. It would chart human history and social behavior, as cold and unswerving in its course as the calculations of the movements of the heavenly bodies.

Although he failed (as anyone would fail in such an effort) his failure has a ring of greatness in it. But over this greatness there hangs the pall of death. Written on the eve of the World War, in the midst of class tensions such as the great strikes in France and the Red Week in Italy, this book bears on it marks of the death agony of a culture.

Pareto seeks to apply the logico-experimental method of celestial mechanics to the very uncelestial events of this planet. Nothing will be held valid except what can, if necessary, be reduced to graphs and algebraic symbols. As though by a compulsion neurosis he plasters almost every page with manifestoes of this intent. His search for purity of method takes on the aspect of a religious quest. The reader stands uncomfortably in the presence of someone who is being washed of all bias in the blood of the scientific lamb.

Let it be said unmistakably that such a logico-experimental man as Pareto sets himself up for, squeezed dry of all emotion and values, never existed except possibly on Swift's island of Laputa, where the inhabitants cut their clothes by trigonometry. Everything valid in Pareto's method can be summed up in the injunction that applies in every field to think as rigorously, honestly, realistically as possible. The rest is mumbo-jumbo. When a social scientist seeks to wrap himself in a divine objectivity you can make a shrewd guess that he is either naïve and is looking for a false sense of security, or that he has his tongue in his cheek and is trying to hide something, or else that he is more or less willfully obscuring the basic issues of social policy involved.

Pareto's central theory, that of residues and derivations, is in reality a brilliant intuition. Stated baldly it holds that human behavior is irrational (non-logical); that it is based on certain deep-lying drives (residues) in human nature; and that theories, theologies, programs, faiths are so many variable expressions (derivations) of these underlying drives. But before he is through with his theory Pareto has analyzed, classified, and subclassified these residues and derivations until he has made the whole thing cumbersome, arbitrary, and just a bit absurd. He groups the residues into six general classes; of these I take it that the "instinct of combinations" covers the drive toward inventiveness and intelligence, and that "group persistences" are what American social thought has termed, with a varying emphasis, traditions, folkways, institutions. The derivations are grouped into four classes. Each of the classes is minutely subdivided. The entire structure is a triumph of ingenuity and shows a taxonomic talent of the first order. But when you try to use it bewilderment turns into chagrin and finally into despair.

I do not mean that the game lacks its attractiveness. Take any item of behavior on the part of your pet aversion in politics, and place its various elements in Pareto's tables of residues and derivations. It can become a fine art of annihilation. It is the Benthamite calculus of today. A Pareto scholar should not lack for mental stimulus the rest of his life, and there will be so many amateur Paretians among American intellectuals that I make bold to prophesy a seven-year plague of residues and derivations. But as a working instrument of analysis Pareto's scheme has some essential defects. He has not decided in what sense his residues are basic and in what sense his derivations are derivative. At times he seems to regard the residues as instincts, at other times as deep-lying "hungers" or human tendencies of an ever-vaguer character; often (as in the case of many of the group persistences) they are only socially conditioned folkways or traditions. The derivations are sometimes the logical coating that we apply to our own non-logical actions in order to save face, and sometimes the tricks and stereotypes by which we manipulate the actions of others. The whole scheme suffers from being a classification on a single plane rather than an analysis on various planes, and leaves in darkness the basic problem of sociology—the relation of invariant traits to the variable conditionings of cultures and institutions.

Pareto's emphasis on the irrational mind will, however, have an abiding influence. He is, in a sense, the Bentham of the irrational. In fact, he is strikingly like Bentham in many of his mental traits—his narrowness, his formalism of reasoning, his crotchets and obsessions, his Linnaean bent of mind, his barbarous terminology. Somewhere during his life he picked up a corrosive realism which eats through surfaces to reveal non-logical traits in man that are unlovely to those who believe in *Homo rationalis*. But the theory of residues is one of the few glimpses of this sort into the depths of life that the reader gets from Pareto. He is otherwise dismally bare of the

sudden insights that one finds in Swift or Nietzsche. What Pareto gives best is not a rigorously valid analysis of the irrational, or an artistic probing of it, but a fascinating travelogue through its darkest Africas. He roams through history and ethnology, a rather ponderous Frazer, finding instances of how men have used magic and it has passed for reason.

Clearly Pareto must be seen as part of the revolt against reason, swelling the anti-intellectualist currents of the past half-century. He must therefore be related to Nietzsche, Bergson, Sorel, Freud, Lawrence, and Spengler. What partly obscures this connection with them is that while they celebrate man's irrationality, he is content to lay it bare; and while they throw scientism overboard, he holds onto it, and in fact celebrates it. In this respect Pareto, despite his merciless attacks on Comte, Buckle, and Mill, represents a carry-over from the positivist thought of what John Strachey has called "the century of the great hope."

But this attempt to reconcile a current of intellectualism with a current of anti-intellectualism pervades the whole school of social psychology. Pareto's book was contemporary with Graham Wallas's *Great Society,* Trotter's once-famous herd books, Le Bon's crowd books, and McDougall's instinct books, as well as a host of lesser siblings. It shares their loose and ramshackle instinct psychology, and it shares also their sense of how blind or stupid or animal-like the masses of men are when they vote or fight or unite to revolt. The Pareto vogue, on account of the peculiar translation lag, comes fifteen years after the social-psychology vogue. But the generation that feels itself on the brink of revolutions should accept the emphasis on the irrational as eagerly as the generation that felt itself on the brink of a catastrophic war.

Unlike his theory of how we think, Pareto's social theory is like an iceberg: much the greater and more sinister portion of it lies beneath the surface. It is most clearly intelligible if it is referred back to the outlines of Marxian thought, for its underlying intention is to build a counter-system to Marxism. Marxian social economics and its theory of surplus (exploited) value are matched (as developed in Pareto's earlier books) by a "pure" economics with its famous Paretian law of the distribution of income, in which income distribution is shown to follow the same curve as the distribution of ability traits. The Marxian doctrine of the class struggle is matched by the Paretian theory (borrowed from Mosca) of the circulation of the élite. Marxian economic determinism as a theory of social causation is confronted by a theory of society as a web of interdependent and mutual relations. The Paretian theory of revolution ignores the Marxian emphasis on the movement of economic forces which prepare the ground, and concentrates on the resistance that the élite can offer through their morale, and on the weakening of proletarian leadership by class circulation. Finally the Marxian dialectic of history is matched by a semi-Spenglerian theory of rhythmical undulations in history, in which the moving forces are not the changes in the materialist basis of society but the waxing and waning of group persistences.

The central thread that runs through this network of theory is the notion of a militant élite. In the theory of class circulation the men of strength and intelligence come to the top; but there is a continuing process of decadence among them, a sloughing off of the old rot and a drawing upon new vigor. Their susceptibility to the residue of combinations weakens the élite, while the masses are retaining their stamina because of their susceptibility to the group-persistence residue. Thus the matter of relative stamina in the ruling and the underlying class at any time furnishes the rationale of revolutionary success or failure. It is the militant and cohesive élite that can become the decisive force in history. Pareto seems to have been influenced, through his friend Sorel, not only by the Bergsonian *élan vital* (in the form of class stamina) but also by Sorel's theory of violence. To Sorel violence had a transcendent and cleansing virtue, and helped to keep the body politic sturdy. Pareto's ultimate exhortation to the élite is to keep its spinal column straight and its fighting instincts in trim—and the ruling classes in Italy and Germany have illustrated his thesis.

This confronts us with the much debated question of Pareto's relation to fascism. In any sense of direct participation or influence, Pareto's fascism has been negligible. Mussolini's insistence that his mind was shaped as a student under Pareto at Lausanne, and his offer (unrejected) of senatorial honors to Pareto after his march on Rome, are inconclusive. They prove less about Pareto than they do about Mussolini's desperate efforts to rig up a respectable intellectual lineage for his own fascism.

What is much more to the point is that Pareto's theory and his preconceptions follow the approved pattern of fascist thought as we have come to recognize it. At the core of Pareto's attitude is a hatred of socialism and a contempt for democracy. He uses the epithet "socialist" vaguely, as many Americans do today with "communist," to describe anything from unemployment insurance to feminism and the new criminology; but he never utters it without a hiss. In his earlier book, *Les Systémes Socialistes,* he was chiefly concerned to show socialist doctrine to be fallacious, crotchety, millennial; but in this book, more than a decade later, it is hard to find even a vestigial scholarly urbanity in discussing it. He seems to regard socialism as the final term in democratic degradation, since it has not only given a new messianism to labor movements but has even corrupted the élite.

But it is democracy that is the principal target. Pareto regards it, with humanitarianism, as the central deity of the new Pantheon that includes all the "modern Gods"—Progress, Tolerance, Democracy, Humanitarianism, Universal Suffrage, Solidarism, Pacifism, Tolstoyism. Against these reigning divinities he hurls his Promethean defiance. He reveals the plutocratic character of modern democracy, in which cowardice skulks behind money to buy votes and bribe legislators. His rather unalgebraic symbolism to convey the temper of plutocratic democracy rests on the distinction between the Lions and the Foxes. The Foxes are the men of craft who replace the Lions, the men of force, in governmental posts in an attempt to buy off mass unrest instead of suppressing it. Being himself (to use William James's phrase) tough-minded, Pareto has an admiration not only for tough-minded thinkers such as Aristophanes, Machiavelli, Nietzsche, and Sorel, but also for ruthless leonine men such as Bismarck. The Foxes are eating away at the morale of the élite. They form an unholy alliance with plutocrats and trade-union leaders in order to keep peace and divide the spoils, and their method of keeping peace is direct bribery and social reform.

This raises the question of the exact nature of Pareto's class attitudes. An obituary notice called him "the bourgeois Karl Marx," and several American critics have taken up the expression and dubbed him the Marx of the middle class. In our American sense of middle class this would of course be wide of the mark. Pareto despised the indecisiveness of the middle class, its humanitarianism, its vulnerability to all the new modern cults and mass religions, its swarming democracy. If to be a fascist theorist is to be a theorist of middle-class revolt against the capitalists, as is sometimes asserted, Pareto does not fit the formula. Nor can he be called the theorist of the capitalist bourgeoisie, using the term in its stricter Marxian sense. Pareto draws a distinction in his thinking between the Speculators (whom he calls the S's) and the investors or *Rentiers* (the R's). In its European context this is a distinction between the predatory restlessness of the new plutocratic bourgeoisie, and the sturdy group persistences of the more conservative industrialists and the large landowners. I take it also that this is not very far from Feder's distinction in the early Hitlerite ideology between the interest slavery imposed by unproductive (Jewish) capital and the social beneficence of productive (Junker and Thyssen) capital.

Thus, the essence of Pareto's position is that of a capitalist-aristocrat who despises democratic equalitarianism and who seeks within capitalist society the more exclusive and traditional forces that will renew its vigor and steel its resistance to the proletarian thrusts. Pareto was writing in a Europe that was already on the brink of the precipice. These volumes give evidence that he was quite realistically aware of the meaning of the deepening crisis, with its heightened nationalist feeling, its conflicting imperialisms, its huge scandals of political corruption, its class tensions. That meaning lay not in the road to war but in the road to fascism. Quite strikingly the pattern of Pareto's thought reveals that fascism was not merely a post-war growth but was already integral in the European situation in 1914. If Pareto was not a fascist theorist, then fascism may be said to have cast its shadow before in the shape of Pareto's treatise.

All this leads quite obviously to the conclusion that Pareto has not so much written a scientific work as a very able and vigorous polemic in defense of the traditional forces within capitalist society. And in doing so he has given us, as Plato did, a picture of his republic. Every social theorist gives his vision of the world, whether he presents it as scientific reality or Utopian dream. Even when he seeks to thrust his own values into the background, they operate just as effectively as preconceptions. Pareto's values burst the mold of his elaborate scientific categories with an emotional force all the greater for his attempt at suppression. Every scientist is at bottom a poet, and any analysis of a society implies, on the writer's part, an ideal society. Dig deep into any social theory and you will strike a poetic myth.

What was Pareto's republic like? It must be remembered that Pareto's own origins were those of a capitalist-aristocrat. He was descended from a family of Genoese merchant princes whom Bonaparte elevated to the nobility and who afterward fought in the cause of Italian nationalist liberties. He learned to hate, with an inverted Mazzinian intensity, the compromises of Italian and French democracy. His book seeks to evoke a polity in which the older aristocracy will come back to strengthen a decadent capitalist élite, and together the landed aristocracy, the *rentier* class, the army, and the most militant of the industrialists will carve out their world. They will sweep plutocratic democracy aside, suppress the proletarian rabble, and replace the false humanitarianism of the middle class by derivations from real group persistences.

It will be a republic ruled by fierce young conquering gods, continually renewed by fresh blood. And the ruling gods will not hesitate to use force, both as a way of holding the masses in their place and as a way of maintaining their fighting instincts. The trade unions will no longer be allowed to keep labor in feudal darkness. The masses will be so much material to be shaped in the image of the desires of the ruling gods: they will be valuable for harboring the group traditions and for their hatred of novelty, but the only art they need to know is the art of being ruled. As for the rest of the population, a Catonian severity will prevail toward anything humanitarian (even Christianity) that may weaken their primitive stamina. Criminals, pacifists, and socialists will be hunted down like disease-bearing rats. In war and in foreign affairs it will be the courage of the Lions that will be the glory of the republic.

But enough. It must be clear by now that if the real test of the validity of a republic is its capacity to get itself enacted, Pareto has the advantage. "That illustrious Greek dreamer," as he calls Plato, had to be content with his book. But Pareto's republic is now a reality: it is Hitler's totalitarian state.

Giovanni Demaria (essay date 1949)

SOURCE: "Demaria on Pareto," in *The Development of Economic Thought: Great Economists in Perspective,* J. Wiley, 1952, pp. 628-51.

[*In the following essay, which originally appeared in an Italian economic journal in 1949, Demaria examines Pareto's economic writings.*]

I

By a consent which is nearly unanimous, Pareto has been given the honor title, "father of contemporary economic science." In order to appreciate the significance of the work of the great Italian thinker, we must pause for a moment to examine the stage at which economic science had arrived during the third quarter of the past century. At this period, economics abounded with historical interpretations which emphasized certain historical factors, claiming a fundamental character for each of these. This was often done in an arbitrary manner, on the basis of simple intuition, and in complete disregard of theoretical considerations. But during this period the reviewer also meets at every turn quantitative postulates and purely mathematical, that is, exclusively hypothetical, formulations. These were usually expressed in the form of pseudo-universal absolutes, such as the doctrines advanced by English classical economics, and the doctrines of the continental hedonists, which were based on the assumption of personal interest, considered as *causa causarum* of economic activity, of cost as well as of utility.

We do not intend to discuss, in the present context, the original contributions which Pareto made in the realm of historical interpretations, such as his greatly admired **Systèmes socialistes**. However, it seems to us that the scientific appraisal of the position and even the general conceptual limitations of Pareto's original work in economics call for attention to the central point of his sociological system. The equilibrium of economic quantities, in its most general aspects, is interpreted as a historical phenomenon, which is not exclusively economic but political and sociological as well, based, in other words, on meta-economic judgments. From this it follows that the deductive discipline of economics requires postulates and value scales of economic as well as sociological character, and that these in turn need to be supplemented, with the help of the method of successive approximation, by research of the empirical, inductive, statistical, and historical variety. The old-line economic theorists, for the sake of clear exposition and coherent interpretation, had neglected the development of sociological categories designed to interpret the reality of economic life. It does not suffice, in fact, to speak intuitively of legal institutions, moral beliefs, and sentiments, which dominate the various social spheres, and to say that all this is closely related to the hedonistic springs of action. In order to avoid a uniform and undifferentiated interpretation, it is also necessary to establish a classificatory scheme which embraces these matters. The empirical concepts of history and the no less inductive concepts of the old science of politics must be segregated and then re-aligned in coherent units. Only in this manner can the complete truth be revealed. As Pareto indicated on the occasion of his anniversary at the University of Lausanne in July

1917, these sociological concepts make it possible to attain experimental truth and to find a way out of the impasse to which exclusive reliance on pure economics leads.

The two large volumes of Pareto's *Trattato di sociologia generale* constitute the first contribution to the creation of a system, formed by theorems of mathematical precision, in which the elements of the sociological phenomena are considered by themselves. They also contain, and this concerns economics, a theoretical scheme, unequalled to the present day, for limited competition, oligopoly, and voluntary associations such as industrial combinations and labor unions—configurations which the recent economic theory, especially the English and American, misinterprets rashly in terms of "bargaining strength," "strategies," "minimax," and uncertainty, instead of interpreting them exclusively, as Pareto did, in terms of social causation, "non-logical actions," "derivations," "residues," "combinations," and "persistence of aggregates."

The specific as well as general economic policies pursued by oligopolists, polypolists, and combinations appear undoubtedly as a perpetual search for maximum conditions. Nevertheless, their dynamics, and even their statics, must be brought into close relation to sociological forces, more so, perhaps, than to purely economic forces. From this point of view, it is unfortunate indeed that Pareto's sociological work continues to be badly neglected by the pure economists. They fail to be aware of the hierarchy of sociological and economic values, concentrating their attention, as they do, on purely hedonistic behavior or, at best, limiting themselves to simple historical excursions—whenever they fail to rely exclusively on their precious gift of intuition. No doubt, this part of Pareto's work has a claim to definitiveness. The fundamental sociological categories which he reveals lead in a rational manner to the economic equilibrium of markets where exchangers are few. They present also characteristics so general that it is difficult to understand how they could have been neglected, in the absence of other investigations of similar profundity or of the formation of sociological rival systems. If they would not exist, it would be necessary to create them. Whatever their qualities, they constitute to this day doctrinal advances of the highest order. It seems indispensable for economists to understand them and to derive from them all conclusions which they are capable of yielding.

After having taken cognizance of the need for sociological expansion of economics along the lines developed by Pareto's genius, we shall now investigate the impetus given by his work to pure and applied economics. In this respect, as we shall see, all his fundamental contributions were published for the first time in the *Giornale degli economisti*, in numerous articles very characteristic for their intellectual strength. These writings were then reformulated in his three radically different books: *Cours d'économie politique* (Lausanne, 1896-1897); *Manuale di economia politica* (Milan, 1906); and *Manuel*

d'économie politique (Paris, 1909). The French edition of the *Manuale* differs considerably from the Italian edition in the Mathematical Appendix. A remarkable summary of Pareto's economics is contained in his forty-page article in the *Encyclopédie des sciences mathématiques*.

II

As we have noted, Pareto's economic work made its appearance toward the end of the nineteenth century, at a stage of development of economic science of which the doctrines of the English classicists and the continental hedonists were characteristic. It is well known that these doctrines had arrived at a point at which they had become particular and specific, having turned, in the last analysis, into a mere series of dissociated problems which were integrated in a singularly formal manner. The doctrines of the English classicists had been made comprehensive with the help of a pretentious generalization which presented every economic fact as a phenomenon of absolute cost and the whole of economic facts as a comparative table of absolute costs. The doctrines of the continental hedonists had been made comprehensive with the help of a no less trite panutilitarianism which vested exclusive power of explanation in a neat and subtle theory of utility. These two constructions attach an exaggerated significance to a few economic phenomena, whereas other factors, much more numerous and important, are either relegated to a shadowy existence or cast out altogether from the conceptual framework of the doctrine.

The scientific position of the two doctrines has so often been examined that it would not be interesting to resume the discussion in the present context. It is equally well known that the germ of the concept of general economic equilibrium existed already in the theories of the classical economists and utilitarian authors, and that the first, highly ingenious attempt at the coordination of the classical and utilitarian doctrines was undertaken by Alfred Marshall, dating from the period of his two widely studied works, *The Economics of Industry* (1879), and *Principles of Economics* (1890). But, in reality, there had been no "coordination." The classical doctrine of cost is an empirical universe which denies the utilitarian solution. The hedonistic doctrine itself must also be characterized as a pseudo-logical concept, excluding, as it does, the historical reality of cost. How can one talk of coordination when the problem of the unity of the two explanations claiming universality is resolved by a mere juxtaposition, exclusively empirical, full of precarious casuistry—when it is impossible to say which of the two spheres of judgment is the decisive one?

No doubt, intuition, which infers general conclusions *ex posteriori* on the basis of observed facts, comparing and assembling partial truths, is an artificial construction. Practical, as it is, it nevertheless is a psuedo-concept, leading to a mirage and to deceptive reasoning—as is always true of *a posteriori* rather than theoretical reasoning. This was indeed the path followed by Cournot,

Marshall, and Edgeworth, which led to laws—and this is important to note—valid only under the *ceteris paribus* condition, "others being equal."

It was Walras who cast light on the fundamental aspect of economic equilibrium—the mutual dependence of a series of closely aligned relations. As Enrico Barone has pointed out, this construction was not a mere continuation of the first attempts, highly meritorious as they were, of Cournot and Marshall. Instead, it was a veritable jump forward, accomplished in an original and masterly fashion, in the field of pure economics. It is the imperishable merit of Leon Walras—which Pareto in no way shares— of having applied his powerful mind to the development of the framework of the relations of general interdependence. But it is fitting—and this observation is of major importance—to underline the decisive character of the advance of the problem of interdependence due to Pareto's work. The classical economists, and, before them, the authors of fragmentary works written in the course of the seventeenth and eighteenth centuries, had a clear perception of economic interdependence but were unable to visualize it as a whole, even in the form of a rough sketch. To present it as the momentous discovery of Pareto would thus contradict a variety of testimony. It is true indeed that the great Walras was the first to give a demonstration of it in mathematical language and that he incorporated it safely into his own theoretical system. But Pareto, by insisting on the subjective character of interdependence, went farther. And he also may claim technical priority for having presented, for the first time, competitive and purely monopolistic relationships under the same head in an interdependent system, although he overlooked the problem of a larger number of dependent monopolies. But, apart from this, it must be emphasized that Pareto always interpreted his system as a complex of necessarily individual relations. To him, all relations which appear as aggregate today but not from today on— and which lead to the so-called macro-economics—are considered as accidental, ephemeral, and impermanent, only approximately universal or not universal at all.

It is not intended to repeat here what has been said a hundred times about Pareto's work in the histories of economic thought and elsewhere. Instead, we shall try to go beyond the limits of the traditional appraisals of Pareto's work. It seems that nobody has ever observed, or, at least, has paid adequate attention to the fact that Pareto always presents interdependence as a subjective datum, that is, that the activities and value judgments of individuals, not the activities and judgments of the mass, constitute the economic problem. To be sure, numerous economists do not deny this principle, but they believe that in practice they can neglect it with impunity. It suffices to recall only two readily available interpretations, those of Marshall and Walras. In the first edition of his *Principles* Marshall points out that the many subtle points which are required for giving precision to the most general and abstract economic doctrines have only a very limited practical significance. He thereby intended to defend the methodological legitimacy of partial equilib-

ria, of the notions of aggregate demand and supply, and of the representative firm. In the work of the Cambridge school, the idea of general equilibrium ends up in an empirical and approximative formula. If economic analysis progresses in this direction, it will never emancipate itself from Marshall's empirical and, thus, alogical foundation. Partial equilibria provide insight into detail, useful, no doubt, but unable to open up an exact view of the economic system as a whole: the observer is faced by problems which all are indeterminate. Partial-equilibrium analysis obscures the facts and leads to sophisms and erroneous conclusions. Pareto always considered Marshall a great man, because, "on the basis of a small number of principles, he constructed economic science." This is as far as his admiration went. He immediately emphasizes that "Walras and his school had gone very much farther."

Pareto did not endorse the assumption of constant marginal utility of money, perfectly arbitrary as it is, although convenient and necessary for operations with two-dimensional curves. These times "have passed." In an essay published in 1892 he stated, in connection with arguments based on constant marginal utility of money, and in opposition to Jevons' point of view: "It is peculiar that he made this assumption, since he himself had correctly emphasized the necessity of regarding it as variable. If one considers it as constant, one is unable to deal properly with the most important points of economic science."

Similar observations can be found in an earlier study relating to Auspitz and Lieben's theory of prices: "To start out with an examination of certain aspects, while assuming other economic quantities as constant—this is not merely a question of method. Such a method conforms to the disposition of the human mind; but it is a mistake nevertheless because it promotes the search for a simple expression of phenomena which are so highly complex that one cannot represent them with the help of a curve." It is indeed impossible to draw the curve of the production cost of a commodity on the assumption that equilibrium continues to prevail with respect to other goods. Effects which appear as secondary may be essential; variations of the value of one element may not only modify the value of all unknown quantities but may also change the known quantities in the equations. The dependence among economic quantities is so pronounced that each degree of utility depends upon several quantities. Moreover, in order to carry studies of this sort to their successful conclusion, it is necessary always to observe that the degrees of utility are related to the costs. Thus, the *ceteris paribus* method will never result in an appropriate treatment, not even in a coherent treatment, because it never leads to theorems and rigorous corollaries.

It was the highest aim of Pareto's speculation to retrace all relations and correlations among the economic facts, to cast light on the real economic process from its beginning to its end, and to reveal the successive movements which never terminate, which cannot be separated from each other, and which reappear incessantly. In comparison with the thought of Walras, this aim was achieved in an even more complete and masterly fashion.

These are the words with which Pareto honored the memory of Walras shortly after the latter's death:

> Walras' name will endure in science, and his reputation will continuously grow. The evolution which tends to turn political economy into an exact science is not going to be stopped, just as the parallel movements have not been stopped which wrested all modern sciences from empiricism. Once a true science has emerged from literary economics, one will not fail to go back to Walras' work when dating its origin.
>
> The principal merit of this scientist, his very great merit, is based on the study, which he undertook as the first, of a general case of economic equilibrium. Thereby he led economic science on a path which can best be compared with the path opened up to rational mechanics by Lagrange.
>
> Jevons, and later Marshall and Edgeworth, applied mathematics to political economy at the same time as this was done by Walras. But, unlike Walras, these authors did not consider the general hypothesis of economic equilibrium. It is exactly in this case that the application of mathematics becomes useful. If the investigator restricts himself to particular problems, the use of mathematics can lead to interesting results but it cannot cause the science to advance.
>
> General economic equilibrium, on the other hand, casts light upon the great principle of mutual dependence, which requires the use of a special logic, that is, of mathematical logic. In the works of Walras we find the first comprehensive conception of the economic phenomenon, just as the theory of universal attraction entailed, for the first time, a comprehensive conception of the movements of the celestial bodies.

There is, perhaps, no other statement by Pareto which would illustrate better and more succinctly the historical significance of the Walrasian construction. What then is this general hypothesis of economic equilibrium which was studied by Walras for the first time? Pareto surely did not intend to allude to the general assumption of competition, or of constant coefficients of production. Pareto's words, uttered under delicate circumstances, are not of the type employed in a common-place judgment. Having to attach himself to the Walrasian tradition and to emphasize his personal affinity with it, he had to place in bold relief the point where his own system diverged from that of Walras. Everything finds an explanation if we recall what we have noted before: Pareto presents the fact of interdependence as a complex of necessarily individual relations. To be sure, Walras had considered and systematized the individualistic aspect of reality. But he did so with the view of deriving therefrom the aggregative or synthetic categories of total demand, total supply, and total saving, adding up the algebraic sums of

the various partial supplies and demands. The Walrasian system does not always rest on the double foundation of individual valuations and individual actions. In certain moments it is based directly on mass actions. It suffices to open up the definitive edition of Walras' *Éléments* to demonstrate this and to appreciate the change brought about by Pareto. At a certain stage of his construction, Walras' work ceases to be theoretical and becomes mere description. Walras does not always recognize that the individual, and his relationships, must invariably remain the primary element. He yields to the mechanism of synthetic functions or synthetic methodological procedures. He considers it legitimate to add up the algebraic sum of the various partial supplies and demands. At this stage, a break, in the nature of a genuine discontinuity, occurs in his system. Before long, the consequences of this were to make themselves felt in the scientific development of the schools of thought which do not belong to the Lausanne group. These were to refer to the high authority of Walras in order to justify systematically what today tends to become a universally fashionable approach to economic science—a fashionable approach but not an essential method.

One can understand the temptation created by the employment of mass categories. The human mind is easily thrown into confusion when confronted by an infinitely complex reality. It feels the spontaneous need for representative schemes which are as simple as possible, that is, synthetic. But what is the result of this? One enters the realm of the deceptive mechanism of synthetic economics, presented at one time in the form of the naive constructions of Moore or Cassel, generated by massive trends which are surreptitiously or openly introduced as assumptions or as *a priori* historical postulates. Similar considerations apply to later developments, such as the "condensed" functions of Keynes and his school, and the functions based on the distinction between wage goods and non-wage goods, elaborated by Pigou and his followers. These constructions are the most formal and the most empirical ones which one can imagine. In a first stage they favor explicative clarification, but they are dialectically erroneous, leading, as they do, to conclusions which are contained in the basic assumptions themselves: within the realm of the hypothesis one moves from the prologue to the epilogue, traversing the whole development from the statement of the problem to its solution. This is true of the hypotheses of extrapolated trends, of algebraic sums, of *ex ante* collective propensities to save and to invest, of discounted profit rates, of the *ex ante* behavior of the interest rate, etc., which lose themselves in precarious casuistry. The march of science eventually comes to a standstill. Science finds itself abandoned to intuition rather than to logic, and confusion results, since only practice, not theory, can determine which of the different hypotheses is the correct one. An irreconcilable opposition arises between the various constructions and potential reality, with the latter continuously and inexorably contradicting the former. True science does not artificially smooth the difficult points in order to resolve them. True science proceeds with the help of pure rather than statistical hypotheses, of hypotheses which do not need to be modified every moment. Pure hypotheses do not need to be changed—otherwise one faces mere pseudo-concepts, arbitrary constructions, sophisms.

Pareto indeed does appreciate the importance of the hypotheses. He recognizes that the conclusions can only be functions of the hypotheses. For this reason his hypotheses are truly universal, being based on the elementary activities of individuals and kept free from historical qualifications. Specific qualifications are provided only in the light of a sociological system. Pareto thus maintains neatly the difference between science and history, insisting that the equilibrium is always and exclusively a complex of relations among individuals. Since contents which are so divers—and lacking in homogeneity, as is the case of individuals, their actions and evaluations—cannot be measured and enumerated, the synthetic categories are not the result of proper reasoning and cannot be universal. In brief, the synthetic categories either serve to express an *a posteriori* synthesis of historical character, or they are intellectual manipulations of reality, helpful, perhaps, in the explanation of reality but without ever shedding the character of arbitrary exteriority.

It is our opinion that the absolute and fundamental character of the individual element, which Pareto places at the basis of his general construction of equilibrium and which he consistently retains, constitutes the major contribution of Paretian scientific speculation. After this contribution was made, it failed to yield all the fruit it is capable of bearing. Only those economists who understand its message will know how to reap this rich harvest. All other theorems discovered by Pareto are only of relatively secondary importance if compared with this foremost and most profound contribution.

III

It is much less difficult now than it was in 1924 to indicate which of Pareto's secondary contributions are the most important ones and how they are to be ranked according to their systematic significance. This is much easier now than it was at the time of Maffeo Pantaleoni, when he refused to indicate the influence of these contributions on subsequent studies. In Pantaleoni's opinion, Pareto's sociological studies represented an alpha, whereas his work in pure economics was in the nature of an omega, bringing a cycle to conclusion and terminating all opportunities for further research aiming at higher generalization. After the passage of a quarter century this judgment seems an inadequate half-truth. Today, mathematical generalization is a sovereign fact, advancing, as it does, irrepressibly in the modern economic literature, which is so rich of controversy rather than of conclusions. At a certain point even the most capable "literary" economists lose heart in the face of so complex a play of economic activities, and feel the spontaneous need for recourse to mathematics, being unable to resign themselves to the historical method with its mere registration of events. Pareto's merit does not rest upon the fact that

he expressed himself in the language of mathematics, with the power of one who

sopra gli altri come aquila vola.

There were other powerful minds, Cournot and Edgeworth, for example, who were his equals in the use of mathematics. But, to Pareto, the use of mathematics did not serve exclusively as a means to satisfy the desire to give greater precision to concepts and to delineate the meaning of assumptions with the view of producing a more rigorous demonstration. His use of mathematics was equally inspired by the intention to prove that all economic problems are determinate and determinable. As he put it, "in nature there is no indeterminateness. If we say that a problem is not determinate, then a well-constructed theory must indicate that there was occasion to take into account certain circumstances which were neglected."

With respect to the determinateness of economic problems, the proof produced by Walras and Pareto can surely not be considered as definitive. The Walrasian concept of *tâtonnements*—"gropings"—cannot stand up under a rigorous examination since it does not lead to a unique equilibrium position. As the Italian mathematician Gaetano Scorza has shown in a famous polemic with Pareto, there may be more than one equilibrium price even in the case of an exchange of only two quantities between two groups of buyers and sellers. In the case of a larger number of commodities the problem becomes still more complicated. There may be an infinite number of systems of equilibrium prices.

In this connection very difficult problems arise, which in the Paretian analysis are treated with the help of the theory of "closed and open cycles." Aside from an additive constant which determines the unity of measure, an unequivocal correspondence between the quantities of goods combined in the indifference curves and the utilities enjoyed by each individual exists in two cases: (1) when the cycle is closed, that is, when the order of consumption is indifferent, and the pleasure resulting from the incremental consumption of each commodity depends only on the quantity of that commodity; (2) when the pleasure is different, depending on the order of consumption, that is, when the cycle is open. There remains excluded the case of closed cycles when the basic utilities are functions of more than one variable.

Unfortunately, this ingenious theory was met with silence by the contemporary critique. For further penetration into this mysterious realm, the Paretian theory of open and closed cycles does not suffice. A distinction of this type does not adequately exhaust the profundity of the problem. If one has to accept the *consensus auctorum,* it is convenient to take equal account of divergence of opinion. Moreover, the paths should be laid out along which a choice must be made among the infinite number of systems providing solutions and the infinite number of constants and arbitrary integration functions which can be adapted to economic reality. This could be done with the help of certain criteria which satisfy the integrability conditions from the point of view of economic reality. With the form of the basic functions known, one can choose one of the infinite number of positions covered by the functions. In the third place, it seems necessary to abandon certain absolute references if the functions or arbitrary constants are to be determined in advance on the basis of economic reality. This does not mean that one should proceed in accordance with partial equilibrium theory—where the form of the curves is ingeniously presupposed—but, on the contrary, that attention be given to some indisputable empirical truths, the distribution of income, for example; or that an inductive criterion, uncertain as it is, be adopted consisting of the system of prices as it existed a moment before; or that a relationship be established with the concrete mechanism of price-level determination as controlled by the monetary authorities. The ultimate goal, remote as it may seem, consists of the transformation of problems posed in terms of differential equations into simple algebraic problems.

Whatever the future development of these investigations may be, they will have to resume the basic themes of Pareto's thought. The participants in this dialogue will all stand in the same light, as it were. The public of today, the literary economists, and the exponents of the various partial-equilibrium theories do not have the slightest idea of this dialogue about an issue on which the future of scientific economics depends.

The importance of pure hypotheses has been pointed out in the preceding paragraphs. When these are rigorously defined—as Pareto wanted them to be—and when the integration of the differential equations and the determination of arbitrary constants and functions have finally taken place, the economist of later times will truly be in a position where he can advance to the exploration of the future. He will attain this position when the material for his constructions has become coherent—under the same conditions as those which have enabled the modern scientist to determine thousands of years in advance the movements of the stars and the eclipses on the basis of the law of gravitation. Compared with literary economics and the theories of partial equilibrium—based, to the present, on a series of artifices and on a world of conventions and subterfuges—Pareto's work has broken the path which leads to the proper appreciation of the problem.

IV

The study of the interrelation between demand (or supply), price, and income is equally remarkable among Pareto's relatively secondary contributions. This well-known study takes its origin from the Walrasian system of equations of general equilibrium, and centers around the search for the sign of a double series of partial derivatives. These partial derivatives bring into a precise relationship the small variations of the demand (or of the supply) of different goods, small variations of the income of the exchanger, and small variations of different prices.

At the time of Pareto, everything in this field was still to be accomplished. Although his work left a notable mark, much remains to be done. In any event, Pareto pointed out the direction into which, according to his own prediction, "the economists must move if they aim at the true progress of science." The road laid out by Pareto in 1892, four years before the publication of the *Cours,* was again taken by Slutzky in 1915, and later on has been widely travelled by English and American economists. These applied his method to a number of practical problems, including the statistical derivation of collective demand and supply. Unfortunately there were neglected in their work certain basic objections which can be raised from a heuristic point of view. The theory of the partial derivatives of incomes and prices has for all practical purposes remained at the stage of *cogitationes privatae*. The knowledge of it has, however, spread more widely than is true of the matters discussed in the preceding paragraph, since it has become more widely known in the form of special theories of income and substitution effects and of the multidirectional character of demand and supply.

We shall limit ourselves to a single observation. The theory of partial derivatives concentrates on movements around a point. It would seem desirable to arrive at a complete solution, represented by finite rather than by point variations. This is a problem in dynamics—also studied by Pareto as will be seen shortly.

V

In the Walrasian fortress with its complex of exchanges, consumption, savings, investments, and mutually dependent production, there is one element which was destined to provoke the most profound discord with Pareto's speculation. This is the production function, represented by coefficients of production which are axiomatically assumed as constant. These functions have no roots because they assume empirically known data—but, on the other hand, these data must be considered unknown, especially since the dynamic succession can only be explained in this manner. The difference between theory and reality is not considerable, however, since the dynamic succession—in the case of the assumption of an uniformly progressive society—is hardly pronounced. But, in a clearly dynamic situation, the coefficients of production cannot figure among the given data. The idea of passive coefficients of production is untenable in every respect whenever they constitute active agents in the production function. The theory of variable coefficients of production constitutes perhaps Pareto's greatest merit in the field of the representation of the equilibrium of production.

The distinction between constant and variable coefficients of production is fundamental for two reasons.

First, from the point of view of political economy: Pareto was the first who demonstrated that the coefficients have the same value under competition and under state socialism. This was done in 1894, fourteen years before the publication of Enrico Barone's famous essay on this subject. Walras, on the other hand, considered the coefficients of production as determined in a manner designed to realize minimum cost. In contrast therewith, Pareto proposes to examine how they should be determined in order to obtain the maximum of utility for society, and he studies the relation between the two types of coefficients. The state should adopt this value as coefficient of production, regardless of a subsequent redistribution of the goods turned out. When it is desired to guarantee the workers a certain income irrespective of their productive contribution, it is preferable to grant them directly a certain amount of goods, or a certain amount of money taken from other citizens, and thus leave undisturbed the coefficients of production which assure maximum utility at least cost.

We shall not enter into a detailed critique of Pareto's formulation of the problem. Objections may be based on the fact that the prices, by which the coefficients of production are multiplied in order to obtain the costs, cannot be considered as constants. The unknowns of the equations of instantaneous exchange undergo variations in conjunction with the modification of the distribution of goods or money brought about by the public authority. We want to state, nevertheless, that Pareto has posed a true problem of pure economics such as crude observation cannot solve. At the time of Pareto's article, mathematical economics was barely born. Even if his study impresses us as imperfect, as much from the mathematical as from the economic point of view, it nevertheless constitutes one of the very first objective studies. One does not know whether to think more highly of the unruffled calmness of his research, of the mathematical preparation, or of the admirable scientific intuition.

There exists, however, a second reason for the fundamental importance of the distinction between fixed and variable coefficients of production. The coefficients of production which are placed under the sign of the integral representing cost of production, are not independent of the limits of the integrals themselves. This is always true in the case of monopoly, and it is true also in the case of competition, but only for one of the numerous firms in existence—unless the whole question of minimum cost is restricted to the moment when all enterprises attain the equilibrium position, considering only small variations around a point.

These observations confirm the conclusion that it is necessary to solve a system of equations which are not only differential but integro-differential as well as related to the time interval. However, even if the variable coefficients of production are considered from this point of view, the movements occur again around the equilibrium point.

VI

Pareto, like Walras, worked primarily in the realm of statics. He barely touched upon the question of how to elaborate a theoretical apparatus which would approach as closely as possible the concrete phenomena, that is, the question of rational dependencies of the dynamic variety. Pareto recognized this himself: "Enormously much remains to be done in this direction."

Although the present sketch must necessarily be brief, a few references are in order to that part of Pareto's work which contains the equations of dynamic equilibrium.

It is true that Pareto's dynamic equations offer only a broad outline. The values of various economic quantities are considered at the time $t1$ and then brought into a relationship with the corresponding values at time $t0$, the intervening period being very short. The diversity between the two values rests entirely upon the predetermined variation of the coefficients of production. There is implied the assumption of certain innovations, or changes, attributable to outside forces, in the equilibrium of tastes and obstacles. Walras himself had formulated this hypothesis, ascribing the existence of uniformly progressive societies to the variation of the coefficients of production. But Walras had only affirmed that there would be re-equilibrating tendencies as long as the economic quantities had not reached previously established levels. If Pareto's theory would have been restricted in this manner, it would have been rather inconsequential. In the last analysis it would have been reduced to a new form of scholasticism connected with the formulation of certain hypotheses concerning the teleology of the coefficients of production. In effect, the system would not have been dynamic but only static or quasi-static at best, since it would simply contain an explanation of what happens during the time interval. New savings, new capital accumulations, new interest payments, and new production would all have been taken into account, with time considered in physical rather than in dynamic terms. But the essential difficulty would have been passed over with the help of a hypothetical instead of a rational "bridge."

The integration, over time, of the differential equations would simply have been a hypothetical integration, in other words, a science of the possible and virtual, based on certain hypothetical movements arising from the outside.

The real problem, on the other hand, would call for the removal of the indeterminateness which arises from exogenous factors, for the exploration of the roots of these factors. Sooner or later, all problems of pure economics run in this direction. If this decisive turning point is missed, the platform "time" has no significance at all.

In the first paragraph of this study we have come across the problem whether it is possible, by means of a theoretical construction of sociological character, to formulate a theory of these exogenous factors. It was Pareto's idea to develop such a theory through experimentation. He adopted a method of reasoning which had been characteristic of the greatest scientists of his time, for example, of Vito Volterra, who had stated the problem in these terms:

Begin with the formulation of concepts which lend themselves to measurement. Then measure. Then deduce laws. Return from these to the assumptions, and deduce, with the help of analysis, a science, ideal in character but rigorously logical. Compare it with reality. Reject or transform the basic assumptions which you have used, if there are contradictions between the results of the calculation and the real world. Arrive in this manner at the discovery of new facts and analogies. Then deduce, from the present status, what has happened in the past and what will happen in the future. This is a summary, as brief as possible, of the birth and evolution of a science mathematical in character.

In substance, the "bridge" over time must be constructed with the help of inductive knowledge. To Pareto, merely hypothetical knowledge has no value, and he brings the experimental part into the foreground of the science. "We do not know," he said, "the rational laws of movement of the planets, due probably to an infinite number of causes which only God can know. But we do know that it approximates an elliptical movement." One can approach the economic phenomena over time in a similar fashion. They, too, are extraordinarily complex, so much so that at a certain point nobody can have precise knowledge of them. That is why it is necessary to have recourse to empirical expressions which help to reveal approximative stability in time and space.

VII

We shall now briefly review Pareto's practical researches. Having discovered the law of income distribution, and having sharply delineated various types of interpolation, he did much to advance the experimental part of economics.

Pareto's theory of income distribution is a contribution of such momentous importance that its author, had he left nothing else behind, could claim rank among the most outstanding masters of human thought. The curve of "total receipts," as Pareto calls it, virtually is in the nature of an *a priori* axiom. An abundance of data confirm it. "When exceptions emerge in the future (as they surely will do sooner or later), investigations must be undertaken to search for the special cause responsible for the deviation of the new phenomena from a form which so many facts have proved to be the normal one." If Pareto's law can be considered as pertaining to inductive, quantitative economics, his theoretical results indicate, however, that the mechanism of income distribution forms one of the most important properties of the economic system *vis-à-vis* the budget constraint.

The second contribution is less widely known, although Pareto had devoted much work to this question. He does not just construct a method of interpolation but of interpolations which are adapted to distinctly different types of oscillations. With the help of a principle similar to Alembert's, the oscillations are distinguished in accordance with the tangents drawn to the curves. In a way, this theory is a forerunner of the modern statistical theories of the decomposition of historical series, containing,

as it does, their limitations and imperfections. The arbitrary element in the establishment of different points of discontinuity can in part be avoided by the use of a single mathematical criterion, tempered either by *a priori* reasoning aiming at the rational determination of the necessity of maxima and minima and of the length of the various periods, or by unsophisticated historical investigations of the type of Thorp's *Business Annals*.

VIII

Let us return to the topic considered in Section VI. Nobody can say for sure what the content of the treatise on economic dynamics would have been, which Pareto mentioned so often in his correspondence as well as in public statements, and in which the exogenous factors were to be systematically related to the representation of the equations of dynamic equilibrium.

It may be that Pareto's grandiose construction was stopped by the lack of statistical material of the type which is becoming available only now and to whose collection he gave such a powerful impetus. It surely is true that the hypothetical "bridge" for dynamic work is better marked today than it was at the time of Pareto. This is due to the gradual introduction, during the past 25 years, of the Bergsonian concept of evolution, as well as to the investigations of variables and strategic relations through time.

In the light of these investigations, the Paretian method of dynamic abstraction lacks acuity. This criticism does not detract from the honor and recognition which are due to the most illustrious exponent of the Italian school. He considers dynamic abstraction as a mere problem of averages. Today, however, dynamic abstraction has become more specific. The emphasis has become more concrete and more general as well, as witnessed by investigations into the "order of infinitesimals" or by statistical calculations of strategic variables, as done, for example, by J. M. Clark. These studies are still tentative, because, in this realm, the phase of fragmentary equilibria, or, at most, of particular equilibria, has barely been reached. At the moment, these are highly artificial, but they promise more than a merely generic formulation à la Moore. There is agreement that a synthesis must be worked out at the end, and that one or more links must be forged to connect the dynamic partial equilibria obtained from slices of space with economic time. Valuable tools, which can become a lasting component of the alphabet of dynamics, have been made available, at the very first, by Pantaleoni with his dynamic theory of instrumental, complementary, substitute, and joint relations among families of goods and economic agents, then by Keynes and other well-known authors, such as Haberler, with the dynamic theories based on the principle of acceleration and the multiplier.

IX

In the preceding paragraphs we have tried to cast light on the most remarkable parts of Pareto's work. But, side by side with these, there are others which perhaps impressed their author as still more important, at least in view of the length of time which it took to develop them. Nevertheless, these parts do not enable us to separate neatly the Walrasian and Paretian formulations of the problem and to establish the original character of the latter. We have in mind the arrangement of the theory of general equilibrium and the theory of the maximum total utility of a collective entity.

The relationship between the Walrasian and Paretian positions is very close. Pareto's system of equations is divided into two parts, and so is that of Walras. The first part treats of instantaneous exchange, with a complex of given data which in the second part—relating to capital accumulation and production—figure as many unknowns. Walras has the same immense conception. Both have pushed the search for equilibrium positions to the maximum of generality. Pareto's synthesis is more complete, however, since monopoly and exchange are considered as one special case of the general theory; since the mathematical argument can be applied equally to societies based on individualism or on socialism; and since the Paretian language utilizes simultaneously a variety of forms of expressions: utility, indifference curves, and index functions. Such a wealth of vistas and of new perspectives, added to the gigantic analytical design, constitutes a grandiose spectacle, fascinating to followers and opponents alike. We do not intend here to pass judgment on Pareto's exposition. We only wish to refer in passing to the fact that Pareto eliminated psychological analysis from economics, by rejecting such concepts as the final degree of utility, rarity, and ophelimity, the corner stones of hedonistic economics, and by retaining only the pure and simple fact registered by indifference curves which are derived from experience and which Pareto presents as an authentic discovery. In our opinion, however, all this is less decisive from the scientific point of view than Pareto believed. In any event—and this applies equally to the theory of "obstacles" which technology puts in the way of various transformations or which result, for each individual, from the attitude adopted by his partners—this approach does not raise intrinsically new problems. To Pareto, the theory of indifference curves was destined to enlarge the world of theory. He repeatedly found occasion to recommend their application and never tired in his efforts at their improvement.

In connection with the deduction of the law of demand, he considered as real progress the passing from independent utilities—as formulated already by Dupuit, Gossen, Jevons, Menger, Launhardt, and Pantaleoni—to complementary utilities—as they can be found also in the Walrasian equations—and from there to the indifference series, to the choices among goods, visualized in pairs, and to choices considered as effects of resistances. From choices he deduced not only the law of demand but all conditions of economic equilibrium. This procedure was considered by Pareto as a great advance because it dispensed with the need for knowing whether utility is measurable and for examining total utilities and their partial

derivatives. From an analytical point of view, the procedure was entirely new. However, the assumption of known choices is a hypothesis equivalent to the assumption that utility is known. In the theory based on choices, the projections of the indifference curves are considered as known. The other theory, on the other hand, assumes that the pleasure surface is known. In reality, very little is gained in precision, since the empirical knowledge assumed in the two cases remains nearly the same. For this reason the distinction is not as interesting on the practical as on the conceptual level. But, even in the latter realm, the definitions of equilibrium remain identical; only two different ways are selected. Instead of a relation between the intensities of wants there is one between the partial derivatives of the ordinate expressing the equation of choices. The equivalence of the two procedures is sufficiently demonstrated also by the fact that Edgeworth had arrived at the equation of indifference curves by taking knowledge of the pleasure surface as a point of departure. Remaining always on the same conceptual level, there is no obstacle to the formulation of the problem in still other terms, for example, with the help of marginal rates of substitution—as was done by Hicks, using a concept implied by Walras as well as Pareto—or with the help of other concepts such as the Walrasian "transformed utilities" and those which can be derived from certain properties of the determinants. All this does not involve a new idea—unless the new speculation receives a decisive experimental content.

In expressing these thoughts, we do in no way intend to regard the new orientations as rationally unjustified or illegitimate. They illustrate the aptitude of Paretian thought to express the same problem in different formulations. Nobody has had on hand a similar wealth of formulations.

What is the most important conclusion which can be derived from the theory of general equilibrium? In an approximative manner, it was already known in the light of the theory of partial equilibria that a competitive order entails the maximum of total utility for society. Walras had expressed this thought in a general manner, but only in the language of utilities. This procedure could not fail to raise suspicion, operating, as it did, with non-homogeneous quantities. This breach in the Walrasian edifice was repaired in a general manner by Pareto, who multiplied the variations of total ophelimity—pertaining to each individual—by certain coefficients with the view of rendering them homogeneous. In economic equilibrium, the variations of the quantities of goods are multiplied by prices. These products correspond to the relations between the derivative of total utility and marginal utility. In the sociological equilibrium, the Paretian procedure is even more daring. The coefficients in question are determined in the light of an objective goal, such as the prosperity of the collective entity.

Pareto then went on to demonstrate that the problem of the maximum is a problem of production, not of distribution. The variation of a coefficient of production will bring forth increases or reductions of utility for different individuals. When the sum of the increments exceeds the sum of the decrements, it is possible to transfer from the individuals who receive increments such a quantity of goods as is required for the reduction of the decrements to zero, and still have an excess of increments. Society, considered as a whole, thus receives a benefit. In this manner, the search for the value of the coefficient of production guarantees production in such quantities as, if properly redistributed, will assure for each individual maximum utility, expressed as the algebraic sum of the positive and negative utilities.

We do not intend to discuss here whether this procedure is entirely legitimate. Reference has been made to the polemic between Scorza and Pareto, which is of relevance in the present context. Scorza had estimated that the derivatives of total utilities cannot all be positive or negative unless special restrictions prevailed. But even in this case the procedure is not complete, since Pareto's maximum condition can equally be applied to monopoly and imperfect competition. In any event, however, Pareto deserves credit for having arrived, on a road which never was used before, at a new formula, which expresses, imperfectly but in scientific terms, a concept which until his time was discussed only in metaphysics.

X

Pareto belonged to those thinkers who are unable to resign themselves to a single direction in their scientific work. Incessantly he related his own central concepts to a whole world of special studies, covering the vast realm of applied economics. He aimed at the fundamental revision of current principles, traditional concepts, and generally accepted interpretations, with the help of daring speculations which to this day deserve close attention. This applies to the theories of circulation in Pareto's writings, to the theory of international trade, and to the inexhaustible historical documentation with which he enriched and supported his theoretical demonstrations. One cannot with advantage neglect his caustic critique of the political and economic regime of his own country as illustrated by the chronicles published by him in the *Giornale degli economisti* and in a number of political dailies. In this critique he is inspired by the principle requiring that all economic activities, public and private, be appraised in the light of experimental logic, abstracting from all idealistic and spiritual premises. In this respect one could correctly speak of a Paretism, that is, of a new pedagogy, a new doctrine of politico-economic education, applied to all interventions of the government in the economic sphere.

A. J. Jaffe (essay date 1960)

SOURCE: "Pareto and Fascism Reconsidered," in *The American Journal of Economics and Sociology*, Vol. 19, No. 4, July, 1960, pp. 399-411.

[In the following essay, Jaffe reconsiders the basis for Pareto's reputation as a fascist ideologue.]

From time to time various writers have linked the name of the Italian economist and sociologist, Vilfredo Pareto, with fascism. He has been portrayed by some as the ideological father of fascism ("Marx of the bourgeoisie"), by still others as a precursor of fascism. Accordingly, it would seem well systematically to appraise Pareto's work, especially as it relates to fascist ideology. Here we will attempt this task, singling out four aspects of his work: first, his anti-intellectualism and anti-rationalism; second, his quasi-biological theory of the elite third; his vilification and hatred of democracy; and fourth, his glorification of force as an instrument of rule.

A good many definitions have been advanced for fascism. Most of them have reflected their authors' proclivity for some particular theory seeking to explain the rise of fascism, theories ranging from the revolt of the middle class to the domination of the militaristic caste. Here we will treat fascism broadly, referring to it primarily in terms of the regimes that characterized Italy under Mussolini and Germany under Hitler.

I

PARETO'S ANTI-INTELLECTUALISM AND ANTI-RATIONALISM

Central to Pareto's theoretical work is his conception of logical and non-logical actions. By logical actions Pareto means those actions which use means appropriate to ends as judged by logic and experience. They are actions determined by some real aim. He singles out scientific and economic activities as illustrative of such actions. Although Pareto does not explicitly include the well-considered struggle for political power in this category, nevertheless it can be surmised from his work that he so included it.

Non-logical actions, on the other hand, are those actions which do not use means appropriate to ends. They are actions opposed to science, to economic activities and to the real interests of the individual as interpreted by experience and logic. As Pareto views non-logical actions, they are determined simply by some impulse which is inaccessible to any further explanation. Thus non-logical actions, since they do not use means appropriate to ends, and since they are governed by some unexplainable impulse, are essentially irrational. According to Pareto, non-logical actions overwhelmingly predominate in social life; thus in the last analysis human behavior is irrational. And it is against rationalism which Pareto directs his thrusts in the three early chapters of *Mind and Society*.

In short, Pareto perceives man as an irrational and non-logical entity propelled onward by mysterious, mystical impulses which are inaccessible to explanation. Except for certain economic and scientific activities and the struggle for political power on the part of his elites, he denies to man the ability to act with some real aim or to use means appropriate to gaining his ends. Man is a bundle of irrational sentiments and instincts. And as we shall see, the sentiment and instinct glorified by Pareto above all others, as indicative of strength, virility and excellence, was brute force—force used by an elite as an instrument of gaining and exercising power.

Pareto's theory of non-logical actions is in profound agreement with the trend prevailing in fascist movements and regimes against intellectualism and in favor of vigorous and natural sentiments. It found expression in official fascist ideology, and more particularly and importantly it was carried into practice. Lederer in his study of fascism characterizes it as revering the irrational, exalting the *élan vital,* idealizing the hero and glorifying its own self-proclaimed destiny. Borkenau points to such attributes of fascism as its emphasis upon uncontrolled sentiments, its acceptance of authority instead of rational consideration, its eulogy of activity in the place of thought, its unconsidered acceptance of a few meta-physical principles taken for granted, its rejection of any "problems" not solved by its official axioms, and its banishment of rationalism from the most important spheres of human life. Fascism was indeed the logical fulfillment of Pareto's system from its militant anti-rationalism to its limitation of the rational to science, and we might add to the science and technology of war, to economics with its corporate states and managed economies, and to the fascist struggle for political power.

Eberstein summarizes the anti-intellectualism and anti-rationalism of fascism in these words:

> . . . obedience, discipline, faith and a religious belief in the cardinal tenets of the Fascist creed are put forth as the supreme values of a perfect Fascist. Individual thinking along independent lines is discouraged. What is wanted is not brains, daring ideas, or speculative faculties, but character pressed in the mold of Fascism.

A similar situation existed in Germany. Anti-rationalism, anti-intellectualism and the favoring of vigorous and natural sentiments, when carried to their logical culmination, are epitomized by a fascist regime. It is reflected in its purging of the faculties and student bodies of anti-Fascist elements, its gang attacks on the persons and homes of prominent educators, its hounding and persecution of intellectuals, its loyalty oaths, its militarization of the universities and schools, its racist ideologies and the burning of books.

Perhaps had Pareto lived longer than 1923 he would have himself revolted at this phenomenon because although he disliked political liberty he loved economic and intellectual liberty. But be this as it may, it has nevertheless been true that in contemporary democratic history political liberty has been inextricably bound up with economic and intellectual liberty. This, to be sure, is a contradiction in

Pareto's thinking, and is evidence which can be used to buttress our later conclusion, that although Pareto cannot be characterized as a fascist, he can best be understood as a precursor of fascism. For the logical fulfillment of Pareto's thought would be that system which has since become known to us as "fascism."

Pareto was likewise contemptuous of intellectuals, who are a frequent source of his sneers and barbs. No one can read Pareto without feeling this antipathy. He identifies intellectuals with that group in which Class I residues predominate, a group he characterizes as weak, degenerate and reluctant to use force. At one point he writes:

> The "intellectuals" in Europe, like the mandarins of China, are the worst of rulers, and the fact that our "intellectuals" have played a less extensive role than the mandarins in the conduct of public affairs is one of the many reasons why the lots of European peoples and the Chinese have been different, just as it explains in part why the Japanese, led by their feudal chieftains, are so much stronger than the Chinese.

II

PARETO'S THEORY OF THE ELITES AND THEIR CIRCULATION

The second great cornerstone of Pareto's theoretical system is his theory of the elites. Except in a number of secondary aspects, this theory is an independent body of concepts distinguished from his other work. Thus there is no serious obstacle to discussing these two aspects separately. The extent of Pareto's indebtedness to Gaetano Mosca, Italian sociologist and author of *The Ruling Class* (1896), for his ideas concerning elites remains considerably clouded in controversy.

Pareto's theory of the elites can be summarized as follows: People in any society are characterized by differentiated innate abilities, from which there arises domination of one group by another. The group which dominates possesses a special talent for ruling, a talent which is a natural, quasi-biological fact. This group is the elite. They exhibit natural, biological traits which are lacking in the masses.

Pareto differentiates between two types of elites, the speculator and the rentier. These two terms are not used in the literal sense of the word, although the choice of terms is one of many cases where Pareto's violent passions appear behind his quiet formulae. In this instance, the "speculator" is evaluated as the least desirable of the two. Governments with speculators in power are characterized by many democratic features, features for which Pareto periodically indicates his hatred and contempt. The speculators, according to Pareto, are a weak lot who rule by cunning and cleverness rather than by might and force (the methods esteemed by Pareto). Humanitarians and intellectuals are likely to be found in such governments, which only serves to intensify Pareto's hostility.

The rentiers, on the other hand, are a virile, vigorous group, as contrasted with the weak, cowardly, humanitarian speculators. They are not afraid of force and violence, which are their chief instruments of rule. Found in this group are the conservative industrialists, the bureaucrats, the real rentier and like groups, all of which are jumbled together.

These elites rotate in power. The rule of the one cannot last forever, since, according to Pareto, there is no new influx of fresh blood into the ruling group, admission to it being barred. In the long run, the ruling group contains an increasing percentage of unfit members as it fails to draw the innately talented from the masses. In effect, as Meisel points out, we have no way of judging the relative superiority or inferiority of an elite other than the factual one of success.

Pareto further traces the division of society into the elite and the ruled to an inherent residue or instinct, namely "the sentiment of hierarchy." Included in this category is the "sentiment of superiors" and the "sentiment of inferiors." In short, Pareto makes his division between the ruled and the rulers one which ultimately rests upon certain mystical, unexplained instincts of a biological character.

The parallels between Pareto's thought in this connection and fascism are striking. The fascist parties of Germany and Italy laid claim to being an elite. Hitler declared the National Socialists to be "racially the most valuable section of the German nation," a party which "represents an elite, a natural aristocracy." In his speech in Nuremberg on September 16, 1935, Hitler asserted that the National Socialist Party must see to it "that all Germans are ideally educated to be National Socialists; that the best National Socialists become Party members; and that the best Party members take the lead in the state." In short, there must be exclusiveness and hierarchy.

Inextricably tied to this notion of the elite is that of the leader or hero. Palmieri in his *The Philosophy of Fascism* (a work bearing the seal of the fascist "Dante" organization and endorsed by Mussolini) gives a clear and articulate insight into the fascist definition of the "hero." He writes:

> Fascism holds, in fact, that the State must be a social, political, economic, moral and religious organism built as a pyramid at whose vertex is the national hero, the greatest man of his time and his nation, and leading to this national hero by an uninterrupted series of continuously widening powers arranged in hierarchies.

> The hierarchy becomes thus the very essence of Authority and the hierarchical arrangement of Society its truest expression in the world of man.

Indeed, this is the logical culmination of Pareto's system. Here is the epitome of the "elite," with lesser men of the elite grading down from the hero in hierarchical order.

Still again Palmieri writes:

> The day may come, perhaps, and we all sincerely hope and pray for it, when all men will be heroes, but at the present stage of human evolution, let only the greatest among the great rule and govern, because he sees deeper and further than we shall ever be able to see, because he knows what we shall never be able to know, because he is gift from God.

In Germany, likewise, the supreme authority of the Führer appears again and again in the writings and propaganda of the Nazi.

To those who object that the quotations cited point to the worship of a hero and not to a ruling elite as Pareto perceived it, it might be well to recall the following words of Pareto:

> The governing class is not a homogeneous body. It too has a government—a smaller, choicer class (or else a leader, or a committee) that effectively and practically exercises control.

Fascism is the logical culmination and fulfillment of Pareto's thought in practice, fascism with its exaltation of the hero, with its elite of the party, in particular the officialdom, and with its Italian Black Shirts and German S.A. (Stormtroopers—Sturm Abteilung) and S.S. (Schutz Staffel—Himmler's Black Shirts), the elite of masculinity. It is the embodiment not alone of the elite, but of the elite most desired by Pareto, those who have no humanitarian or democratic compulsions about the use of force and violence.

And like Pareto, Palmieri sees the elite as constituted by a special sort of men, men endowed with special biological talents:

> Vainly we offer knowledge, education, wisdom to the common man. He cannot benefit of our offer. Mother nature dotes her human children very sparingly of the higher gifts of intelligence, understanding, spirituality. Once in a long time she gives birth to Buddha, a Confucius, a Plato, a Jesus, filling the whole world with visions of a high life opening its realm to the access of man.

III

PARETO'S ANTIPATHY TO DEMOCRACY

As Borkenau aptly puts it: "Pareto's sociology is first and foremost a violent manifesto against democracy; and assertions as to its scientific character change nothing in that respect." At the very core of Pareto's work is a most violent, passionate hatred and contempt for democracy, and with it humanitarianism, as the central deity of Pareto's despised Pantheon that includes all the "modern Gods"—Progress, Tolerance, Universal Suffrage, Pacifism and Women's Rights. He seldom mentions these terms without indicating a sneer or hurling a barb. In particular he had a mortal fear of socialism and believed that society stood on the brink of a trade union despotism.

Against democracy Pareto exalted authoritarianism, traditionalism, patriotism, military spirit and physical courage. Disparagingly he refers to ". . . the devout democrat who bows reverent head and submits judgments and will to the oracles of suffrage, universal or limited, or what is worse, to the pronouncements of parliaments and legislatures, though they are known to house not a few politicians of unsavoury reputations."

Singled out for special vilification are parliamentary forms of government. These too are condemned as modern Gods in these terms:

> The ancient Romans credited the gods with the success of their Republic. Modern peoples attribute their economic betterment to corrupt ignorant, altogether contemptible parliaments.

Pareto repeatedly hammers away at the plutocratic character of modern democracy, in which corruption and bribery reign supreme.

The following expression by Pareto of his sentiments on parliamentary systems is not too distant from that of Mussolini:

> A governing class is present everywhere, even where there is a despot, but the forms under which it appears are widely variable. In absolute governments a sovereign occupies the stage alone. In so-called democratic governments it is the parliament. But behind the scenes in both cases there are always people who play a very important role in actual government. To be sure they must now and again bend the knee to the whims of ignorant and domineering sovereigns or parliaments, but they are soon back at their tenacious, patient, never-ending work, which is of much the greater consequence.

Mussolini writes:

> Democratic regimes may be described as those under which the people are, from time to time, deluded into the belief that they exercise sovereignty, while all the time real sovereignty resides in and is exercised by other and sometimes irresponsible and secret forces.

Similar sentiments are expressed by National Socialist writers for whom democracy, parliament, stupidity and cowardice became synonymous terms. "How nice must it be," Hitler writes, "to hide one's self behind the coatskirts of a so-called 'majority' in front of all real decisions of some importance!" Alfred Rosenberg referred to democratic rule as *Massen-vernebelung*" (translation: causing fogs through a dull mediocrity of plebeianism) and equated democracy with money-rule: "Democracy is not the rule of character, but of money."

Some of us may object that some of these expressions are to a degree actual, realistic characterizations of the functioning of parliamentary systems. But the question then arises, if this is indeed the case, what is the answer? The democrat and the fascist would respond quite differently, the fascist calling for the destruction of parliament, and here Pareto, Mussolini and the National Socialists are in agreement. Not alone in word but in action the fascists moved. By 1928, Mussolini, by virtue of the Laws of May 17th and September 2nd, robbed parliament of all functions through which it reflected the will of the people. Hitler upon coming to power quickly moved in a like direction.

Turning again to Palmieri, we find strong shades of Pareto in this statement:

> Fascism recognizes therefore at the outset that Democracy cannot be realized and that whenever and wherever it has been tried, it has degenerated sooner or later into an oligarchy of tyrannical autocrats—be they military, as of old, or financial, as of modern times.

> To a bastard form of social and political organization [democracy—JVZ], which like all bastard things, cannot last because of its inherent falsehood, Fascism substitutes a genuine life-enhancing organization sprung from the recognition of the fundamental truth of life: the truth that the mass of men is created to be governed and not to govern; is created to be led and not to lead, and is created, finally, to be slaves and not masters: slaves of their animal instincts, their physiological needs, their emotions, and their passions.

Alas, in this statement by Palmieri, we find a striking similarity with Pareto's thought—from the vilification of democracy, to the glorification of the elite, and to the blind irrationalism of instincts, needs, emotions and passions. Nor does Palmieri neglect in the course of his work to vent his wrath upon Progress, Universal Suffrage and the other gods of Pareto's Pantheon of abuse and ridicule.

IV

PARETO'S GLORIFICATION OF FORCE

Pareto makes the utilization of force in the acquisition and maintenance of power his chief criterion of a vigorous, virile elite. He was firmly convinced that force was a much more useful instrument for a sound society than parliamentary democracy. He exalted political suppression as a necessity for social stability, and was critical of the reluctance with which it was employed by contemporary governmental authorities.

Pareto viewed the slaughter and pillaging attendant upon revolution as a healthy phenomenon. Slaughter and robbery were perceived as "signs that those who were called upon to commit them deserved power for the good of society" and ". . . slaughter and rapine are external symptoms indicating the advent of strong and courageous people to places formerly held by weaklings and cowards."

Pareto was alarmed lest the speculator-type governments of his day (that class which has "contributed to the triumph of the regime that is called democracy [and might better be called pluto-demagogic]") would prepare the ruin of their respective nations. And why the alarm? Because the speculator elite was "divesting the class of individuals who are rich in Class I residues and [who] have an aptitude for using force." Nor had Pareto any use for humanitarians, at one point calling upon the rentier elite to kill them as no better than "a baneful animal pest." Elsewhere Pareto laments the fact that:

> . . . the notion is coming to the fore that an existing government may make some slight use of force against its enemies, but no great amount of force, and that it is under all circumstances to be condemned if it carries the use of force so far as to cause the death of considerable numbers, of a small number, a single one, of its enemies; nor can it rid itself of them, either, by putting them in prison or otherwise.

And Pareto believed despotic governments showed the right instinct when they outlawed all independent associations of their subjects.

Pareto's ideal of rule based upon force found its embodiment in the fascist regimes of Europe. "Certainly a government needs power, it needs strength. It must, I might also say, with brutal ruthlessness press through the ideas which it has recognized to be right, trusting to the actual authority of its strength in the State." Violence was glorified and extolled and the governments were premised upon its systematic use. Ashton writes: "From the castor-oil therapy invented by Mussolini's lieutenants to the beatings within an inch of the victim's life, which for some time were a regular feature in Hitler's concentration camps, arbitrary seizures and bodily maltreatment of prisoners characterized the known instances of Fascist rule."

Fascism was conceived, born and reared in force and violence, in the Italian Black Shirts, in the Nazi S.A., S.S. and Gestapo (*Geheime Staats Polizei*), in the murder and assaults upon political opponents and intellectuals, in the extermination of millions of Jews, in concentration camps, in the militarization of the youth, and in the culminating stage—in an aggressive imperial program. In a word fascism was characterized by terror. Mussolini's Italy and Hitler's Germany were the realization in actual life of Pareto's thought.

V

PARETO'S RELATION TO FASCISM

As Borkenau points out, Pareto's sociology can best be understood as simply a political manifesto in scientific guise. It is a philosophy of society, a social creed, determined mainly by violent political and ever purely personal passions. The logical fulfillment of this political manifesto is fascism. The chief ingredients in Pareto's work, his anti-intellectualism and anti-rationalism, his theory of the elite, his militant hatred and contempt for democracy and his glorification of force, reached their logical culmination in Hitlerite Germany and Fascist Italy.

It is questionable, however, if Pareto can be viewed as the intellectual father of fascism. It would be more correct to suggest that Pareto was himself a product of the same political, economic and social forces and the intellectual climate which gave birth to fascism. As Bernard De Voto observes, ". . . to find Fascist dogma in the *Traité* [*The Mind and Society*] itself is equivalent to finding defense of the Immaculate Conception in Willard Gibbs's *Statistical Mechanics,* or a tract on Christian Science in Newton's *Principia.*" In fact, it is questionable whether any one individual can be singled out as the ideological father of fascism. One of the earliest acts of Mussolini upon coming to power was to call for the writing of a philosophical work laying the ideological basis for fascism. Fascism unlike Communism never had its *Communist Manifesto,* its *Das Kapital,* or its *State and Revolution* prior to coming to power. Perhaps Germany was the exception with Hitler's *Mein Kampf,* but fascism was already in the ascendancy in Italy.

What can be said with greater accuracy is that fascism drew upon and was the intellectual heir of Machiavelli and the neo-Machiavellian writers, of the German Storm and Stress literature with its appeal to violence and passion and its disdain for rule and reason, of Nietzsche and Sorel, of Gobineau and the racists, and of writers in similar veins. And in this category Pareto must be included. The insistence by Mussolini that his mind was shaped by Pareto as a student at Lausanne and his offer to Pareto of numerous honors prove less that Pareto was the intellectual father of fascism than that Mussolini was desperate to rig up a respectable intellectual lineage for his own fascism. In this sense Pareto can best be understood as a precursor of fascism.

Little can be said regarding Pareto's attitude toward the fascist regimes as he died on August 19, 1923, less than a year after the advent of fascism in Italy. However, the available evidence points to the fact that Pareto welcomed fascism only hesitatingly. Borkenau characterizes the matter as follows:

> In the first years of his rule Mussolini literally executed the policy prescribed by Pareto, destroying political liberalism, but at the same time largely replacing state management by private enterprise, diminishing taxes on property, favouring industrial development, imposing a religious education in dogmas, which he did not himself believe in. Moreover, Pareto was loaded with the highest honours available. He was designated as a delegate to the Disarmament Conference at Geneva but excused himself on account of his poor health; this was

indeed a fact, but he perhaps utilized it as a pretext as well. Then he was made Senator of the Kingdom of Italy and a contributor to Mussolini's personal periodical *Gerarchia*. Here his scientific career with its many contradictory views finished on a characteristic note. Praising the government of Mussolini for its achievements he at the same time asked for liberty of opinion, liberty of university teaching and pronounced a warning against any alliance with the Papal See.

Reflected in this analysis are some of the contradictions that characterized Pareto's thought. But it is interesting to note that these contradictions were resolved in practice not in a democratic, but in an authoritarian direction. This is seen as well in Pareto's reaction to a series of Royal Decrees, drastically cutting down governmental expenses and suppressing a number of offices, which appears in the April 1923 issue of *Gerarchia*. There had been much discussion about the "legality" or "illegality" of these measures. Pareto took the position that measures of this sort could not be carried out through the normal workings of parliamentary institutions, yet they were necessary for the safety of the country; in any event, the pre-Mussolini governments had been equally guilty of "illegal" acts which, instead of benefiting the country, brought it to the verge of disaster.

The source of the contradictions in Pareto's thinking can perhaps best be understood in terms of Pareto's social position as it has been analyzed by Max Lerner. Lerner views Pareto not as a spokesman for the middleclass revolt against capitalism as has sometimes been asserted. Pareto despised the indecisiveness, the humanitarianism, the democracy and the mass religions of the middle class. Nor does Lerner believe that Pareto can be viewed as the theorist of the capitalist bourgeoisie in the Marxian sense. Rather his theoretical work is consistent with his position as a member of a family of Genoese merchant princes whom Bonaparte elevated to the nobility.

Lerner concludes:

> Thus, the essence of Pareto's position is that of a capitalist-aristocrat who despises democratic equalitarianism and who seeks within capitalist society the more exclusive and traditional forces that will renew its vigor and steel its resistance to the proletarian thrusts.

and

> His book seeks to evoke a policy in which the older aristocracy will come back to strengthen a decadent capitalist elite, and together the landed aristocracy, the rentier class, the army, and the most militant of the industrialists will carve out their world. They will sweep plutocratic democracy aside, suppress the proletarian rabble, and replace the false humanitarianism of the middle class by derivations from real group persistences.

In summary, Pareto can best be understood as a precursor of fascism. In particular, four main aspects of his work

stand out conspicuously in this regard: first, his intense anti-intellectualism and anti-rationalism; second, his quasi-biological theory of the elite; third, his militant vilification and hatred of democracy; and fourth, his glorification of force as an instrument of acquiring and maintaining power.

Norberto Bobbio (essay date 1964)

SOURCE: "Introduction to Pareto's Sociology," in *On Mosca and Pareto*, Librairie Droz, 1972, pp. 55-78.

[*In the following essay, which was originally published in Italian in 1964, Bobbio examines the formal structure of* Trattato di sociologia generale.]

As is known, the ***Trattato di sociologia generale*** was born after a long gestation as a work which can only be described as "monstrous," the word "monster" being used in the triple sense of "prodigy", "deformed creature" and, neutrally, "unusual event". Prodigious in the *Trattato* is the breadth of design and research; from an introduction to economics, the sociology, as a result of subsequent additions, became a detailed analysis and a complete reconstruction of social equilibrium and of the factors which determine it. The analysis is based on a mass of facts, particularly of ancient and modern history, which have been gathered as a result of a varied and haphazard reading of classics and newspapers. The reconstruction is entrusted to an ambitious description and classification of the constant motives of social action and to a testing based on ample passages of historical interpretation. Pareto put into the *Trattato,* seemingly in utter confusion, but in reality by following an ideal order whose design was clearly impressed in his mind, everything that happened to occupy his thoughts concerning the vicissitudes of human society and the meaning of history in the most intense period of his intellectual activity. The exposition is continually interrupted by digressions, and by digressions within digressions, some of which are small treatises in themselves. We find in them, for instance, a minute description of the magic practices for causing or preventing storms, a long and sharp criticism of natural law, an analysis of Bentham's utilitarian theories and of Kant's categorical imperative. Pareto accumulated like a miser and spent like a megalomaniac. He possessed to an exceptional degree two qualities which are usually divorced from each other and which characterize two different types of researchers: an analytical talent bordering on pedantry, a curiosity for facts (helped by an exceptional memory) akin to gossip. He had the passion of the collector as well as that of the classifier: one helped the other, and both contributed towards producing a work which astounds and tires the ordinary reader and frequently arouses two contrasting attitudes among the critics of Pareto's works, that of the most naïve enthusiasm and that of the most deep-seated aversion.

The deformity of the *Trattato* is so obvious that there is no need to dwell on it: moreover, all has been said about it. To put things in a nutshell, the *Trattato* conveys an impression of great slovenliness. Pareto was well aware of this, but being the obstinate man he was, pretended not to attach any importance to the matter and became annoyed when his attention was drawn to it. On being shown a review which deplored the bad distribution of matter between text and footnotes, he unburdened himself to Sensini in this way: "I am anxious to find those uniformities, but I could not care less about putting them in the text, or in the footnotes, in chapters which are 'mastodontic' or of the right length, in 'digressions' or eloquent speeches. Luckily no one has yet criticized the format of the book, the paper, the print, the type etc." It is not as though he had no continuous thread, but he willingly lost sight of it in order to follow his inspiration, his moods, his resentments, or merely his mania for collecting outstanding episodes, with the result that he was forced every now and then to revert to his theme by recapitulation, to dot the text with references to the ground already covered and to that still to be covered, to draw up those long tables of contents which are an indispensable guide to the rational perusal of the work. Pareto was wrong in taking offence at the pin-pricks he had received from those who had criticized the formal structure of the *Trattato*: the *Trattato* is and remains a work which ruins weak stomachs and paralyses the strong, and has, by the very reason of this unpleasant aspect, been more tasted than assimilated, more sniffed at than tasted, and almost fifty years since it was first published parts of it still remain to be rediscovered.

The aspect worth dwelling upon at greater length is that indicated by the third meaning of *monstrum*: the *Trattato* is unlike any other book bearing the same title, and it cannot be included, except with a certain effort, in the classical way of thinking through which sociological research has developed in Europe and America in the last hundred years. It was no mere coincidence that the "guild" of sociologists, with few exceptions, repeatedly repudiated him. Traces remain in the *Trattato* of two classical problems of nineteenth-century sociology (and which nineteenth-century sociology had inherited from the philosophy of history), the problems of factors and progress, even if Pareto prefers to refer in a less compromising manner to elements rather than to factors; as to progress, he disavows it completely by conceiving the historical movement as a wave-motion. On the other hand, the problem of the nature of social life is completely alien to him, together with the connected problem of the typology of the various forms of society, which are the two problems by means of which sociology, in particular, had been building and rebuilding its own autonomy. The only time the problem arose of distinguishing between the individual and the social was when he agreed to discuss the compulsory theme of the 1904 Philosophical Congress; but he glided over the basic question by showing clearly that he had no specific interest in the problem. In the *Trattato*, the problem of the nature of social life which is the problem of the objective delimitation of the field of sociology, is not even touched upon: starting from the mechanistic instead of the

organistic model, Pareto regards society as a system in equilibrium of which it is essential to seek the forces that compose, decompose and recompose it; these forces are always manifestations of inclinations, or instincts, or individual sentiments, that is, of separate individuals taken singly. As to social morphology, Pareto takes no interest in it because the only type of society he has in mind is the political society, characterized by relations between rulers and the ruled, to the extent that nowadays he appears to be far more a continuator of Machiavelli than a contemporary of Durkheim. As has already been pointed out by Schumpeter, among others, his sociology was mainly "a sociology of the political process." He conceived sociology as an elaboration of categories, schemes, concepts for a more adequate interpretation of past history (meaning political history, of course) and, whatever his protestations of lofty unconcern, for a more honest approach to the political struggle of which he was a spectator. This explains why he preferred the company of historians to that of sociologists: a glance at the indices of names which he himself had insisted upon is enough to make one realize that his sources, besides the theologians, who will be mentioned later, are the great historians, from Thucydides to Mommsen. On reaching the last chapter, he makes an attempt (and a rather questionable one at that, to tell the truth), at providing an empirical (Pareto, mistakenly, always uses the word "experimental") verification of previously assumed and illustrated hypotheses by means of a lengthy analysis of Roman history.

Moreover, as is known, the analysis of the social system occupies only the last two chapters, or approximately one fourth of the *Trattato*. The subject matter of the other ten chapters has nothing in common with what is normally studied by sociologists, and if anything, it comes nearer to social psychology: the analysis of the motivations of man's behaviour in society. Furthermore, the material used by Pareto in elaborating a theory of motivations consists not so much of individual social behaviours as of theories concerning social behaviours which have been elaborated by means of non-logico-experimental procedures. The *Trattato*, not unlike *Systèmes socialistes* (and in this one is able to discern the continuation of a dominant motive), is mainly a critical analysis of ideologies chosen at random in the enormous field of religious, philosophical, political, juridical and social thought. What had impressed Pareto in observing the social behaviour of mankind and induced him to take up sociology (or at least what he understood by sociology) was the prevalence of non-logical actions over logical ones. In the wide sphere of non-logical actions Pareto included what an old moralist would have described as the world of passions. Hobbes, in *Leviathan*, had likewise preceded the study of society and of the State by an analysis of passions. Pareto's work is primarily a treatise of passions, brought up-to-date as far as methodology and nomenclature are concerned, and written by a firm believer in the experimental method. As has been pointed out frequently, and particularly so by La Ferla, who described Pareto as a Voltairian character, Pareto had the unpleasant scoffing habit of the moralist who scrutinizes human beings and lays bare their vices rather than their virtues, their weaknesses, their vanity and stupidity, not in order to disprove or flay them, but in order to enjoy the spectacle from above. He did not have the makings of a moral reformer, nor those of a preacher, but he did have those of a moralist in the classical sense of the word, i.e. of the dispassionate investigator of other people's passions. And if it is true, as has been pointed out, that moralists are born "when confidence in mankind starts to dwindle," Pareto's vocation as a moralist was born when political delusions had caused him to lose all hope that human nature could be improved. He knows his Montaigne well, and whereas he normally quotes his sociologist colleagues merely in order to make fun of them, he willingly has recourse to the common sense of a practical man like Montaigne, "an antidote against the faulty reasoning of authors who write disconnectedly about natural rights. The first and major source of the theory of non-logical actions was not provided by the psychologists of his time, whom he had never read, and even less so by Freud, of whom he has no notion and to whom he was likened on many occasions for the theory of "residues" but by Pierre Bayle, whom he regards as superior to Rousseau as Kepler's astronomy is superior to that of Cosma Indicopleuste. He assures us that in Bayle's works there are "various theories of non-logical actions, and it is surprising to read in this author truths which are ignored even today."

Between the moralists' analysis and that of Pareto there was nevertheless a difference in the observation material used. Pareto neglected literary works; he did, it is true, examine theories in which men appear as the direct protagonists with their actions and feelings, sometimes openly confessed, sometimes only implied, but he was fond above all af examining the works of reflected thought, from the ancient cosmogonies to the theologies of the Cristian era, to the modern philosophies of history, from the theories of natural right to the recent theories of utilitarianism, socialism, solidarity, in which human action is the subject of a more or less rational interpretation and justification. Pareto had been struck, not only by the agitated play of passions in the theatre of history, but also by the varying and captious way in which these passions had been hidden, simulated, masked by pseudo-rational constructions. The classical contrast between passion and reason no longer appeared to him as a contrast between the inferior and the superior part of the human soul, but between natural instinct and its falsification, between spontaneousness and fabrication. The function of reason was by no means that of dominating the passions, regarded as the servile part of man, but merely of disguising them in order to make them more acceptable (but not less offensive). In studying the social theories of his time, he had been forced to convince himself that even doctrines which proclaimed themselves to be scientifically founded, such as that of Comte, or Spencer, or Marx, were inspired by certain sentiments, that their ultimate aim was to inculcate them in others, that in the final resort they had placed reason at the service of pas-

sion. In examining closely the rôle of reason in history, one could only be struck by the small part it played in the task, usually considered to be of primary importance by the incorrigible or interested exalters of the rational human animal, of collaborating with the senses for the discovery of truth. This small part it played solely in connection with the logico-experimental theories, which had made some progress in the study of nature, but little or none in the study of mankind and society. Into the heterogeneous, badly defined category of non-logico-experimental theories, defined, moreover, like the non-logical actions, only negatively, Pareto put a considerable part of the products of human thought, from theology to metaphysics, from philosophy to pseudoscience. And he prepared himself for the task of investigating its intimate structure in order to extort its secret, and in so doing he went back from the pseudological justifications to the motives which had caused them, from manifest reason to hidden sentiment. The analysis of the non-logico-experimental theories was one way, even if it meant a detour, of arriving at the analysis of sentiments. Hitherto the moralists had faced the enemy in the open field; Pareto meant to outflank him and attack him in the rear with a better chance of success.

Pareto devotes two chapters, the fourth and fifth, to the study of the non-logico-experimental theories. This detailed examination may seem out of all proportion to the nature and purpose of the work if one fails to understand that it is not its purpose to clear the ground for the theory it is proposed to champion after having criticized the theories it is proposed to reject, and hence it is by no means the *pars destruens* of the *Trattato*; its aim is rather to arrive at the root of the problem, i.e. to grasp the nature of the forces that move society through ascertainable facts which reveal these forces with greater clarity. And these facts, these "experimental facts", as Pareto calls them, are precisely the non-logico-experimental theories "by means of which we can have full knowledge of the forces which exert their influence on society, i.e. of the dispositions and inclinations of mankind." The non-logico-experimental theories are, as has been stressed with particular insistence by Parsons, the research datum itself, i.e. the prime or raw material from which inductive analysis starts in order to arrive at the uniformities. Only this can explain the very special construction of a work so different from other sociological works. Pareto, in the development of the *Trattato*, himself draws a distinction between the inductive and the deductive method; the inductive method is the method which, by analysing the non-logico-experimental theories, discovers the forces operating in society and permits of the elaboration of the theory of "residues" and "derivations", which occupies the greater and central part of the *Trattato*; the deductive method is the method which, once it has established the nature of these forces and suggested their classification, turns to the study of history in order to verify their validity. Thus the study of history, which in traditional political science comes first, is last in this case, in consequence of the fact that the primary source of research are not historical narratives, but the so-called non-logico-experimental theories. Among the latter an important position is occupied by books on theology, which, incredible though it may seem, end up by becoming, side by side with a number of historiographical classics, the main source of the *Trattato,* that is, the first being the source of the initial movement (the search for uniformities and work hypotheses), the second, of the final movement (confirmation of the uniformities and empirical verification of the hypotheses).

Notwithstanding the abundance of material and the irregularity of the layout, it must be admitted that the design of the work is fairly clear and, as has been repeatedly pointed out by Bousquet, extremely simple. After a preliminary chapter on method, the research is developed through six logically connected stages. *First stage*: distinction between logical and non-logical actions (to which the second and third chapters are devoted). The term logical actions is applied to actions which have the dual characteristic of establishing a link which is objectively adequate for the purpose, and of being achieved with the awareness of this adequacy. All the others are non-logical actions. Non-logical actions therefore include actions which establish means that are objectively inadequate for the purpose, as for example making sacrifices to Neptune in order to have a smooth passage, and those which establish adequate means but of which the agent has no awareness (these are instinctive actions typical of the animal world). This distinction is important, because only the discovery that the world of human actions which determine the social movement is of the second type opens the door to a real, or even realistic analysis, of society. *Second stage*: the best way to arrive at the enucleation and description of non-logical actions is to commence with the study of their verbal manifestations, i.e. with the non-logico-experimental theories, which are divided into theories that transcend experience (fourth chapter) and into pseudo-scientific theories (fifth chapter), according to whether the intervention of the non-experimental principles is explicit or merely implicit, and hence more or less disguised. It is perhaps needless to point out that the distinction between logico-experimental and non-logico-experimental theories is a duplication of the distinction between logical and non-logical actions, although it is not quite the same thing: the non-logico-experimental theories are the verbal manifestations of the non-logical actions, but it does not follow that they themselves are non-logical actions, i.e. subjectively and objectively inadequate for the purpose it is proposed to achieve. Unfortunately, the problem of the relationship between the two basic distinctions of the *Trattato* has not been discussed expressly by Pareto, who seems not to realize the dual plane on which his work is constantly moving: the analysis of the social forces, including the theories, and the analysis of theories only as material for the study of social forces. *Third stage*: the analysis of non-logico-experimental theories has served to underline the two elements of which they are composed: the slightly variable part, which is a manifestation of basic sentiments, and the more variable part, which includes the sum total of all the more or less logical rea-

soning with which man attempts to rationalize his impulses or instincts, or interests, or inclinations (Pareto's language in this very delicate and fundamental matter is, as has been pointed out on more than one occasion by his critics, indecisive and not very precise). The first part consists of the "residues", which are divided into six classes (to which are devoted three chapters—the sixth, seventh and eighth); the second part consists of the "derivations", which are divided into four classes (to which are devoted two chapters—the ninth and the tenth). These five chapters represent the heart of the work, i.e. the systematic analysis of the forces which act in human society, i.e. in a society of beings who are both instinctive and symbolic (in the sense that they adopt symbols to communicate with each other). *Fourth stage*: the principal outward expressions of the forces which act in a social system having been recognized as "residues" and "derivations", their way of acting must be conclusively examined by studying their respective importance, the relationship of their reciprocal influence and the effects of their varied combination on the composition and development of a social system. The eleventh chapter dealing with this matter is the longest and also the most confused: it represents a bridge between the analysis of the simple elements of every social system and their recomposition in the theory of social equilibrium; its main purpose seems to be to prove, by means of the varied distribution and the complex integration of these simple elements, that every system is heterogeneous (theory of social heterogeneity) and that the more striking and permanent aspect of this heterogeneity is the distinction and the continuous interchange between the rulers and the ruled (theory of the *élites* and of their circulation). *Fifth stage*: the preceding study of the various forces acting in a social system permits of the construction of a theory of social equilibrium in which the elements (to which must be added the self-interest category typical of economic action) so far examined operate in various ways and can be reduced to the following four: (a) "residues"; (b) self-interests; (c) "derivations"; (d) heterogeneity and social circulation. The theory of the general form of society is dealt with in the twelfth chapter, which is likewise long and composite and contains various treatments badly connected with each other, the best-known of which (not for its scientific value, but because it reveals the author's political moods) is the one concerning the nature of political power, which is a diagnosis as well as a judgment of contemporary society. *Sixth stage*: after the construction of the theoretic model we have the empirical verification, which in this case becomes the historical test (thirteenth and last chapter).

The formal structure of the *Trattato* can be condensed even more concisely into the following traits and links: a basic observation (the prevalence of non-logical actions), or moment of *hypothesis,* is verified by examining a material to which sociologists have hitherto devoted little attention (the non-logico-experimental theories), or *critical* moment; this examination permits of the identification and classification of the original elements of a social system, or moment of *analysis,* which is followed by the construction of a theoretic model of social equilibrium, or moment of *synthesis,* and, lastly, by historical test, or moment of *verification.* It is obvious that this separation into moments is approximate and must be accepted with considerable caution: its faults are over-simplification (the subject-matter of the *Trattato* is overflowingly vast; and there is no dam that will contain it), and exaggerated schematization (the *Trattato* is one of the most untidy, convulsive and farraginous books ever written).

What the recapitulation and the brief outline adequately reveal is the novelty of the book to which Pareto devoted himself for years in the isolation and solitude of Céligny. As we have seen, he waged war on the sociology of his time from the very start. He was never on good terms with official sociology. Of the great German sociologists of his time, from Ferdinand Tonnies to Max Weber, there is no trace either in the letters or in the *Trattato.* We know that he did not read German, notwithstanding Eisermann's assumption to the contrary, and despised everything German. The greatest of French sociologists and a contemporary of his, Emile Durkheim, is never quoted; but a recently published letter to Claparède reveals fairly clearly what he thought about him: "Il est pourtant de mon devoir de vous avertir que je crains fort ne pas me trouver d'accord sur ce sujet avec Mr. E. Durkheim." Of Lévy-Bruhl he recalls with praise, in an article published in 1907, *La morale et la science des moeurs,* but in the *Trattato* this work is not mentioned. In his sociological readings he went little farther than the hardly very recent sociologists writing in French, Letourneau (born 1831), Le Bon (born 1841), De Greef (born 1842) and Tarde (born 1842). He occupied himself with the latter in his very first articles on sociological matters, which appeared in 1897 and 1899. In the *Manuale d'economia politica,* quoting two of this author's books, *Les lois de l'imitation* (1890) and *L'opposition universelle* (1897), he says: ". . . they are lacking in scientific precision to a very extraordinary degree." Le Bon is often quoted in *Systèmes Socialistes.* He does Letourneau the great honour of quoting him together with Comte and Spencer, as one of those who passes off his personal religion as scientific sociology. Of the English-speaking sociologists, in addition to Spencer he had read Giddings (born 1855), whose main work, *The Principles of Sociology,* had moreover been translated into French by one of Pantaleoni's friends, Viscount Gaëtan-Guillaume Combes de Lestrade.

As to the two fathers of sociology, Comte and Spencer, he must have known them, particularly the latter, fairly well. Pantaleoni wrote in the obituary: "If we were to attempt to discover some of the main sources of Pareto's culture—apart from mathematics—we would have to quote, in addition to Comte, three writers whose works he always liked to have within his reach: H. Spencer, Darwin and Bain." But in the *Trattato* he repeatedly pointed to them as outstanding examples of non-scientific sociology. His philosophical and methodological leanings he undoubtedly derived from Comte, as was revealed by Pantaleoni in the article quoted above. But

already in *Systèmes Socialistes* he had dwelt at length of the *Système de politique positive* in a critical and caustic spirit. In the *Trattato* he casts off Comte's philosophy with this amusing utterance: from *Cours* to *Système,* to *Synthèse,* Comte gradually proceeds from experimental to metaphysical and theological explanations, thereby revealing "an evolution in direct contrast with the one he supposes in human societies." For several years he had counted Spencer among his favourite authors, but subsequently he changed his mind, to the great disappointment of Pantaleoni. Frequent traces of his old predilection are found in the earlier letters he wrote to Pantaleoni. Writing to his friend in 1897 about what he had been reading, he observed that "Spencer soared above all the others like an eagle"; in January 1898 he repeated that "he is the only writer who has turned out a really scientific work in sociology"; in the 1899 article he speaks of the evolution of political society "so skilfully expounded by Spencer." But already in *Systèmes Socialistes,* even amid much praise and in spite of the statement that from the scientific point of view he is "tellement au-dessus de Comte qu'il ne peut en aucune sorte lui être comparé," Pareto insinuates that Spencer, too, like John Stuart Mill, after criticizing Comte as not being sufficiently positivist, ends by embracing a kind of metaphysical religion. His shafts are directed primarily against the work *La Morale des différents peuples* (this is how Pareto cites it in the French edition), which does not seem to have been written by the author of *Principes de sociologie* (as he terms it), packed as it is with moral precepts and thus absolutely incompatible with the scientific spirit. In another place he complains that the scientist gradually disappears in Spencer "pour faire place au moraliste dogmatique." A few years later he severely criticizes in the *Manuale* the *Morale evoluzionista* (sic) as well, and accuses its author of having betrayed the ideal of science in order to chase after the moralist's ideal. In the *Trattato* the idol is definitely shattered. Paragraph 112 begins like this: "Herbert Spencer's positivism is simply metaphysics". There is no longer any difference between Comte and Spencer: the identical criticism is levelled against both of them. Their alleged scientific systems are "different religions, but even so are always religions."

Separate treatment could be accorded to Pareto's relations with Darwin, referred to by Pantaleoni in the piece quoted earlier, or to describe them more exactly, to his relations with social Darwinism which, with the predominance it gave to instincts in the phenomenology of society, and with its doctrine of evolution through struggle, had opened up a vein of realistic social thought, for the use of strong minds, which has much in common with Pareto's crude, sometimes ruthless conception of social development. Pareto speaks of social Darwinism, on the whole with sympathy, at several points of the *Trattato;* he regards it as a corpus of doctrines "very well put together" but incomplete (and, what is more, with the pretension that it is complete) because it does not determine the forms of institutions but only the limits that the latter must not overstep, and ambiguous because it does not make clear the difference between the "fittest" for individual welfare and the "fittest" for the welfare of the species. But in a footnote added to the French edition, Pareto points out that the criticisms made of this theory were by no means intended to deny its importance.

Those who wish to discover the sources of Pareto's inspiration must seek them rather a long way from the paths trodden by official sociology. His greatest sources of inspiration were Machiavelli, Marx and Sorel. Griziotti relates that when he reached Lausanne in 1907, Pareto was giving sociology lessons on Machiavelli explaining the scientific value of *Il Principe*. Pareto says of Machiavelli, who is often given honourable mention in the *Trattato,* that "he soars like an eagle over the multitudes of ethical historians," a compliment which, as we have seen, he had reserved for Spencer in the years of his fervour for the English sociologist. Marx and historical materialism had been amply dealt with by Pareto in *Systèmes Socialistes,* where he affirmed that he preferred Marx's sociology to his economic theory: having rejected the common interpretation of historical materialism according to which the economic factor would by itself and in the end determine the whole movement of history, he had accepted the learned (*savante*) interpretation according to which history is a quest for facts and for relations between facts, which can be objectively determined; and not for the notions which men form about them (the ideologies). The theory and the critique of "derivations", which take up so much of the *Trattato,* are simultaneously an interpretation and an extension of the Marxian critique of ideologies. He likewise shared the Marxian interpretation of history as the scene of the class struggle, even while mistaking it for and confusing it with Darwinism (a confusion which, for that matter, was a commonplace with both the defenders and the detractors of the latter). In connection with that interpretation he declares that one must "admirer l'énergie et la force de caractère que Marx a deployées pour la défendre envers et contre tous." In two paragraphs of the *Trattato* he clearly summarizes his attitude towards historical materialism and the class struggle: he launches against them the same reproach already directed against the majority of the theories—that they had made complex phenomena far too simple. In opposition to the thesis of the single factor and the dependence upon the economic phenomenon of the other phenomena, he upholds the thesis of the plurality of factors and of their mutual interdependence. But he gives to historical materialism that praise of which usually he was very sparing: ". . . it marked a noteworthy scientific step forward, since it has helped to underline the contingent character of certain phenomena, such as the moral phenomenon and the religious phenomenon, to which was attached, as is largely true still today, an absolute character." Pareto had a long and close friendship with Georges Sorel, documented by, among other things, Sorel's letters recently published by De Rosa, who prefaces them with an instructive parallel between the two men, who resembled each other in many of their external features, their moods, their likes and dislikes, opinions on contemporary society, and were unanimous on how to interpret Marxism, even if they disagreed about the way of utiliz-

ing it, both of them as much ruthless destroyers of old (and often beneficial) myths as they were indefatigable inventors of new (and harmful) myths, iconoclasts, prophets of doom, interpreters and at the same time architects of the "destruction of reason". Like Machiavelli and Marx, Sorel is regarded by Pareto as one of the few sages who have approached the study of social facts without prejudice but in a scientific spirit, leaving all empty talk to preachers and politicians. A note in the *Trattato* reads: "Certain university professors . . . who confuse science with pedantry . . . who when dealing with a theory do not go beyond insignificant details or other similar stupidities, completely lack the intellectual capacity necessary to understand the work of a scientist such as Sorel is." Pareto, in his speech of thanks on the occasion of the honours paid to him by the Lausanne University in 1917, after expressing the debt of gratitude he owed to Italian and foreign economists, from whom he had drawn inspiration and guidance, mentions one name only of the sociologists and economists, Georges Sorel, on account of his works that were "si puissamment scientifiques." Pareto was not fond of wasting time in quoting sources and cheerfully ridiculed the mania of compiling complete bibliographies. After Sorel he recalls several sociologists, among whom there is not one of the great names of the sociology of his day. He cites Ostrogorski and Michels for the political parties, Lombroso and Ferri for criminal sociology, Colajanni and then the old Fustel de Coulanges and Henry Sumner Maine for what he calls "sociologie historique". And he ends up by actually eulogizing that great foe of sociology, Benedetto Croce, who, although himself a "metaphysician", had contributed to scientific progress in Italy "débarassant le terrain des idéologies positivistes et humanitaires."

According to Parsons, when Sorokin was once questioned at a meeting of eminent scholars of social science, he declared that the greatest contemporary sociologists had been Max Weber, Durkheim and Pareto. But unlike the first two, whose authority has never been challenged, Pareto the sociologist (his fame as an economist has never been questioned) was the object of the most conflicting opinions. Pareto, praised, exalted, eulogized by enthusiastic—and generally mediocre—disciples who had to disturb the shades of the great such as Aristotle or Machiavelli or Vico to find terms of comparison sufficiently worthy of their teacher, while ignored by the philosophers whom he had derided, was kept at a respectful distance by the scholars of social science, whose labours he had almost always thought he could disregard. Even though Croce appreciated Pareto the economist, his opinion is well known: when the *Trattato* appeared he defined it as "a case of scientific teratology." It is less known that more than 30 years later Croce, now an old man but no less pugnacious, during a series of lectures given at Naples between 1948 and 1950, speaking of sociology and the scanty interest displayed in it in Italy, re-stated his old opinion that a reader of the *Trattato* could exclaim in Baconian style *numeratae pecuniae nihil* "because no truth could be got out of it that was not some tautology or other." As to the sociologists, whose interest in the *Trattato* was aroused only when the English translation appeared at New York in 1935, (in Italy the tradition of sociological studies had by then been interrupted, while in France, where a French translation had appeared as early as 1917, the *Trattato* was an utter failure, from what Bousquet tells us), Leopold von Wiese, in Germany, reacting violently to the "Pareto-fever" of certain American circles, demolished the *Trattato* as the work of a bright amateur and called Pareto, not altogether without reasons, "Philosoph der Rebarbarisierung"; Ellsworth Faris, in the United States, considered Pareto's attempt to construct a scientific sociology a miserable failure and praised in comparison Sumner's work; William McDougall, who in 1908 had published his *Introduction to Social Psychology,* which in certain respects may be compared to the *Trattato,* after accusing Pareto of being behind the times—"midvictorian"—of having written a treatise on sociology with a psychological basis (the theory of "residues") without possessing a knowledge of psychology, of not having defined the principal terms of his construction and of having transformed the classification of the "residues" into a "hodgepodge" of heterogeneous items, accused Pareto's admirers of inducing young people to waste one or two years of their life in an endeavour to extract "some grain of wisdom from a crazy book"; Raymond Aron, in France, bluntly defined the *Trattato* as "une immense dérivation, dont les résidus sont les haines politiques et le souci exclusif des relations entre gouvernants et gouvernés."

More balanced and substantially fairer opinions were not lacking, as that of Morris Ginsberg in England, and well-argued apologias like that of the American physiologist, L. J. Henderson, who held for a time at Harvard a seminar for advanced students on Pareto and wrote a long essay with the aim of demonstrating the originality, the brilliance, and what is more, the high scientific value of the *Trattato*. But in the United States about 1936, as for that matter in Italy about 20 years before, the virulence of the attacks was often a reaction to the exaggerated tone of the panegyrics, which laid emphasis on the more striking and disconcerting (even detestable) aspects of the *Trattato,* the daring nature of its political views, the discovery of the irrational forces that make history, the necessity to meet violence with violence, the result being that Pareto was variously described as another Machiavelli, the Nietzsche of sociology or the Marx of the middle classes (or of fascism). Certainly no good was done to Pareto's scientific standing (nor, for that matter, to Nietzsche's fame of philosopher) by the curious attraction he exercized through the intemperance of his polemics upon a few queer personages of the intellectual world, who were eager to give a welcome to his doctrines and hand them on. Among the personages who cannot be classified as mediocre (no matter what opinions may be held about their work and their highly diverse personalities) it is sufficient to recall Giovanni Papíni, who according to Pareto himself was one of the few who had understood the *Trattato,* and Filippo Burzio, a fervent disciple of Pareto.

Pareto's not always very clear relations with fascism were likewise of no help in ensuring a calm discussion of his thought. His champions try to show, by quoting from documents (his last articles and a few letters), that his adherence to fascism was circumspect and full of reservations; but the question is not as simple as this. Pareto died too soon—only a few months after the march on Rome—to be able to give a conclusive opinion on the new political regime. Many authoritative representatives of Italian culture, beginning with Croce, who were later to become stern opponents of fascism, were in those early months more inclined towards adherence than towards aversion. The problem is a different one: was there any connection between the political conceptions often expressed by Pareto, right from the years of his contributions to *Regno,* and fascist ideology? This connection is undeniable: Pareto missed no opportunity of lashing democratic ideals, humanitarianism, pacifism, regarding them as hypocritical expressions of less noble interests or sentiments; he extolled the force that dominates the world; convinced that in history the bellicose aristocracies are destined to prevail, the weak to succumb, he foresaw that the European bourgeoisie, that of Italy in particular, tyrannized over by the "speculators" (the breed he detested most), would be overthrown if they did not meet violence by violence. The kernel of fascist ideology was the historical and moral legitimization of bourgeois violence. [Paragraph 2480] of the *Trattato* has several times been cited from the fascist side as a possible source of its doctrine: "It can be said that the ruling class's resistance is effective only if it is ready to carry it to extremes, regardless of everything whatsoever, using when necessary force and arms, otherwise it is not only ineffective but can, indeed, help, and sometimes greatly help, its adversaries". But Pareto's thought was ambiguous, like that of Machiavelli, and provided answers that differed according to whether it was accepted purely and simply as a salutary lesson of political realism (which is equally useful to either side engaged) or as a factional system of precepts. The fact is that Pareto repeatedly declared he was an impassive spectator of the political struggle that was developing before his eyes, almost as if he wished it to be believed that he was indifferent to the *élites* happening to be in power, content to know and reveal the secret of their rise and their fall. Certain it is that his teachings were accepted by both the parties engaged and there were fervent Paretoians on both sides: fascists such as Fani, De Stefani, Morselli, Scalfati; antifascists like several contributors to *Rivoluzione liberale,* Gobetti, Dorso, Burzio himself. The Piero Gobetti publishing firm printed in 1924 the first monograph on Pareto, by Alberto Cappa, who strove to show that Pareto was really neutral in face of the vicissitudes of his time and how impossible it was to find in this any confirmation that he favoured authoritarianism. The editor of a combative antifascist review of the 'twenties, Oliviero Zuccarini, has written recently, on the occasion of the publication of Pareto's letters to Maffeo Pantaleoni, a true and proper *apologia pro Pareto,* defending him against all posthumous accusations and generously presenting him as a faithful friend of democracy.

Hitherto the *Trattato* has been a subject for apologias and denigration rather than an object for critical studies. Of the great contemporary sociologists, one of the few who have openly admitted owing a debt of gratitude to Pareto is Sorokin; the only one who has attempted to penetrate the clouds of incense raised by the disciples in an effort to make a critical study of the *Trattato* and extract from it an analytical scheme, is Talcott Parsons. His studies, however, date back to almost 30 years ago. Perhaps it is only now, with the gradual fading of the clamour raised by political controversy, that a propitious time has come for a discussion at once calmer and deeper from the critical point of view. Two balanced and simultaneously authoritative articles by Schumpeter and Jannaccone, published on the occasion of the centenary of Pareto's birth, may be regarded as premonitory signs of a new turn, the introduction to which could be an article of 1952 by Demaria, which suggests that economists should study Pareto's sociology and affirms that in order to understand the scientific fertility of Pareto's contributions to economics it is necessary to go back "to the kernel of his sociological conception." Meanwhile the path towards a critical re-examination has been opened, as always happens, by the discovery and publication of unpublished material, particularly frequent in recent years, the greatest credit for which is due to Gabriele De Rosa (though the contributions in previous years of Giacalone-Monaco must not be forgotten, and now that of Busino, who has brought out the "Cahiers Vilfredo Pareto", published by the Librairie Droz of Geneva, which have already devoted, and will in the future continue to devote, still more space to the study of Pareto's personality). The time is ripe for a complete new edition of his works, both the greater and the lesser, and to this end the new Italian edition of the *Trattato* by *Comunità* appears as a forerunner and a stimulus.

The *Trattato* still today makes irksome, often irritating reading, but now it can be read with greater detachment and in a cooler frame of mind. For that matter, the theories that made it famous and aroused love and hate are perhaps the most transient. There remains the rare example of a lucidity so ruthless as to border on perversion. But in face of the rhetoric of ideals, the triumphs of misrepresentation, and the treacheries of the "fausse conscience," the perverse is better than the falsely naïve. The desecration of ideals is the price that a corrupt society pays for the nonchalant practice of their persistent abuse. The *Trattato* has also been described as a guide for those who wish to find their bearings in the domain of human folly. For the men of my generation, at least, Pareto was not the inventor of human folly: had he lived another ten years he would, if at all, have had to blame himself for having been too moderate. Further, in spite of the agitation that his anti-humanitarian outbursts arouse in the reader who does not penetrate beyond the surface, the *Trattato* should not be read under the misconception that its author is Machiavellian, a cynic, since this approach to the work, while the most frequent, will in the end be found a mistaken one. The true and proper monument of the *Trattato* is the theory and critique of ideologies, in

the sense that has been grasped and developed in recent years, for example by Topitsch. Lévi-Strauss recently declared that he had learned from Marx that "men are always the victims of their own and others' deceits, and that if one wants to study the humanities, one must begin by refusing to allow oneself to be deceived." Well, Pareto, following Marx's footsteps, has with his *Trattato* carried out the first grandiose attempt to elaborate a phenomenology and a typology of the various "disguises" behind which man hides his instincts, and to indicate the ways and effects of the "unmasking". His famous realism is not only a mood, but the basis of a theory and of a new science.

Except in the last two chapters where, as Pareto himself observed, a study is made of the social effects of the elements, found to exist by their appearance in the non-logico-experimental theories, the real object of the *Trattato* is man as an "ideological animal". Right from the beginning Pareto is at pains to point out that the theories can be studied from three different standpoints: from the standpoint of their truth or falsity, from the standpoint of their persuasive power, and from the standpoint of their social utility. The systematic design of most of the work is contained in 15 where the first eleven chapters are arranged on the basis of an outline focusing on the theories and nothing but the theories.

That Pareto began with the idea of writing a book on social equilibrium in the image and likeness of the one he had already written on economic equilibrium cannot be doubted. But from the start of his researches on society he encountered the difficulty—to which other sociologists, Marx excepted, had not paid sufficient attention—of separating verbal statements from real motivations in the documents that the sociologist must take into account. As he progressed with his researches, this procedural difficulty grew to gigantic proportions, to the point of becoming the dominant stimulus and the principal object of his reflections. While the social equilibrium theory underwent no radical changes from the first writings on it, the study of the non-logico-experimental theories grew beyond measure, was the origin of the two great themes of "residues" and "derivations", of which there is almost no trace in the first writings, and ended by forming the quantitatively most conspicuous and the qualitatively most original part of the *Trattato*. With regard to the persuasive power of the theories, Pareto offered us also a first, ample outline of a true and proper theory of argumentation, which is the most interesting historical precedent of today's *nouvelle rhétorique* movement. There is this difference, however, that while the present rediscovery of rhetoric is being made under the banner of a new rationalism, the theory of "derivations" meant for Pareto a confirmation, however paradoxical, of the intrinsic irrationality of history.

Pareto himself had provided the key to the way in which he wished the work to be read, when he said: "The whole of the present work is a search for the reality that is concealed behind the derivations, revealed to us by the documents." But for some odd ~~reason or because~~ of an inadvertence he buried the key in the *Index to the Contents* under a sub-heading of the item *Derivatives and derivations,* from where no one has ever unearthed it. Not that the wish here is to throw a veil over the social equilibrium theory. The only aim is simply to turn the attention of new readers, especially those who belong to the new generation, to the theory and critique of ideologies, a subject that stands on its own and is susceptible of further development. I believe that only those who turn to the *Trattato* bearing this interpretative approach in mind will realise that far from being a field that has been over-ploughed, the work is a still unexplored mine.

Joseph A. Schumpeter (essay date 1965)

SOURCE: "Vilfredo Pareto, 1848-1923," in *Ten Great Economists: From Marx to Keynes,* Oxford University Press, 1965, pp. 110-42.

[*In the following essay, which first appeared in the* Quarterly Review of Economics *in 1949, Schumpeter focuses on Pareto's economic theories.*]

In a volume devoted to Pareto's life and work, Professor Bousquet relates that the obituary article devoted to Pareto in the socialist daily, *Avanti,* described him as the 'bourgeois Karl Marx.' I do not know that a man can rightly be called 'bourgeois' who never missed an opportunity to pour contempt on *la bourgeoisie ignorante et lâche.* But for the rest, the analogy conveys very well the impression that Pareto had made upon his countrymen: they had in fact raised him to an eminence that was unique among the economists and sociologists of his time. No other country erected a similar pedestal for his statue, and in the Anglo-American world both the man and the thinker have remained strangers to this day. There was, indeed, a short Pareto vogue in this country that followed upon the translation of his sociological treatise. But it died out soon in an uncongenial atmosphere. Moreover, so far as the small circle of pure theorists is concerned, Pareto came to exert considerable influence on Anglo-American economics in the 1920's and 1930's, that is, after the publication of Professor Bowley's *Groundwork.* But both in England and the United States, Marshallian and post-Marshallian economics offered enough in the line in which Pareto excelled to prevent him from gaining much ground of his own even before other tendencies took away whatever he had gained.

This might seem surprising owing to the fact that several important developments in theoretical economics are now seen to stem from him. But it is not difficult to explain. Pareto was the product of a sector of the Franco-Italian civilization that is far removed from English and American currents of thought. Even within that sector his towering figure stood almost alone. Pareto cannot be pigeon-holed. He paid court to no 'ism.' No creed or party can claim him as its own, although many creeds and parties

appropriated fragments of the vast intellectual realm over which he held sway. He seems to have taken pleasure in running counter to ruling humors and slogans. Votaries of extreme laissez-faire may cull plenty of passages from his writings in support of their views. Yet there was nothing he despised so thoroughly as the 'pluto-democracy' or 'plutocratic demagogy' of liberalism. Socialists are under obligation to him for rendering, as we shall see, a very important service to socialist doctrine, and also for his protests against the anti-socialist measures that the Italian government took in 1898. Yet he was not only an anti-socialist but one of that type whose criticism derives sting from contempt. French Catholics might thank him for his attacks upon the persecution of the French clergy that was so unedifying a sequel to the Dreyfus affair. Yet he attacked the 'laicist' policies of the Combes ministry because he was a gentleman, and not because he believed either in the mission of the Catholic Church or in her teaching.

A gentleman of such independence and pugnacity who is in the habit of dealing vigorous blows right in the midst of arguments that might in themselves be agreeable to some party or another has little chance of being popular. By now he is a figure of the past. But even in the epoch of his prime the political and social slogans with which we are all familiar controlled official phraseology, the press, party programs, and popular literature including its economic sector. The wrapping in which he presented his strictly scientific results were then not much more popular than they would be now. One has only to imbue oneself with the spirit that pervades an American textbook and then open Pareto's *Manuel* in order to realize what I mean: the naïve lover of modern social creeds and slogans must feel himself driven with clubs from Pareto's threshold; he reads what he is firmly resolved never to admit to be true and he reads it together with a disconcerting wealth of practical examples. Therefore it seems that the problem is not to explain why Pareto did not exert influence more widely; the problem is rather to explain how he came to exert as much as he did.

Could we confine ourselves to Pareto's contributions to pure theory, there would be little need for glancing at the man and his social background and location. But into everything that was not a theorem in the pure logic of economics the whole man and all the forces that conditioned him entered so unmistakably that it is more necessary than it usually is in an appraisal of scientific performance to convey an idea of that man and of those forces. I shall make an attempt to do so first (I). Then I shall briefly survey Pareto's work in pure theory (II). And I shall end up with a glance at his conception of society that has found so inadequate an expression in his *General Sociology* (III).

I. THE MAN

Pareto's father, the Genoese Marchese Raffaele Pareto, seems to have been a typical product of the Italian Risorgimento of the first half of the nineteenth century, an ardent adherent of Mazzini—perhaps more from national than from social reasons—an uncompromising enemy of all the governments that barred Italy's way toward national unity, and a revolutionary in this if in no other sense. Accordingly, he exiled himself to Paris where Vilfredo, the subject of this memoir, was born of a French mother: if General Galliéni once described himself as 'Francese ma anche Italiano,' Vilfredo Pareto might have described himself as 'Italiano ma anche Francese.' He was taken to Italy in 1858 and there went through the usual course of studies that issued in a Doctor's degree in engineering in 1869. He immediately embarked upon engineering and industrial management as a profession and after various other appointments rose to be manager general—we should say 'president'—of the Italian Iron Works. It was only in 1893 that he was appointed successor to Walras in the University of Lausanne, although he may be considered as a full-time economist a few years before that. Thus, the span during which he was primarily engaged in economic research extends from about 1892 to about 1912—practically all his later work is sociological in nature. He resigned his chair in 1906 and then retired to his home, a country place on the lake of Geneva, to grow in the course of a vigorous and fertile old age into the 'lone thinker of Céligny.'

Substantially, this suffices for our purpose: we have to underline a few of these facts rather than to add others. First, theorists will note that owing to his training as an engineer—and he seems to have cultivated theoretical aspects—he acquired at an early age command of mathematics on a professional level. Second, it is worth while to notice that, to a degree quite unusual with scientific economists, Pareto was thoroughly familiar with industrial practice—familiar in a sense which is quite different from the kind of familiarity that may be acquired by the means available to the academic economist, the public servant, the politician. But, third, it was his passionate interest in the current issues of economic and general policy, presently to be commented on in another connection, which made him something of an economist long before he started his own creative work. Francesco Ferrara was then at the height of his fame and influence, and the frosts had not yet fallen upon a theoretical structure glorified by uncritical liberalism. His writings, especially his famous introductions (*prefazioni*) to the classics published in the *Biblioteca dell' economista*, served Pareto as well as, or better than, any of the university courses could have done that were available in his student days. His way to Walras, however, was chalked out later on by Maffeo Pantaleoni.

None of the facts above will account completely for Pareto's vision of society and politics, or even for his attitudes to the practical problems of his age and country. Nor do I believe for a moment that the deep pool of personality can ever be drained so as to show what is at the bottom of it. But there is the patrician background which, I am sure all who knew him will agree, meant much more in his case than it usually does. In particular

it prevented him from becoming a brother in spirit to the men—and a fully accepted member of the various groups—with whom life threw him. It also prevented him from establishing *emotional* relations with the creations of the bourgeois mind, such as the twins that are called democracy and capitalism. Acting upon this background, his financial independence—a bare independence at first, something like affluence later on—helped to isolate him still further by offering the possibility of his isolating himself.

Still acting upon this background, his classical scholarship worked the same way. I do not mean that part of it which he shared with every educated person of his time, but that part which he conquered himself through incessant study of the Greek and Roman classics during his sleepless nights. The ancient world is a museum, not a laboratory of applied science, and he who trusts too much to the wisdom to be gathered there is bound to stray from every group of men that was in existence either in 1890 or 1920. Isolation was made complete by the result of his participation in the debates on the policies and politics of his country—so complete that he had decided to emigrate to Switzerland even before he received the call to Lausanne. And isolation had its effects—soothed only late in life by a second marriage that brought domestic peace (see the dedication of the *Trattato*)—upon a fiery temperament that was not really made to stand it.

But why should he have left his country in wrathful exasperation—the country that he loved from the bottom of his heart and whose national rebirth he had not only yearned for but witnessed? The detached observer is all the more likely to ask this question because it will seem to him that the new national kingdom did not do so badly in the thirty years that preceded Pareto's emigration. Besides progressing economically at a considerable rate and growing out of financial disorders—*pace* our Keynesians—it took its first steps in social legislation and established itself successfully as one of what then were called the great powers. Looking at things in this light, our observer will develop a good deal of respect for a régime such as that of Agostino Depretis. And, considering the difficulties incident to the beginnings of the new national state, he will make allowances for the less exhilarating parts of the picture. But Pareto made no such allowances. He saw nothing but incompetence and corruption. He fought with impartial ferocity the governments that succeeded one another, and it was then that he became known as an ultraliberal—in the nineteenth-century sense of uncompromising advocate of laissez-fire—and that he helped to create, among the German New-Dealers of that period, the impression that marginal utility was just a wicked trick with which to thwart reformers. Possibly this is all there is to say about Pareto's attitude in matters of economic policy and the strong traces it left upon his scientific writing before 1900. But even then there was something in that ultraliberalism of his that points in a direction exactly opposite to the creeds and slogans of official liberalism. He certainly was *anti-étatiste*, but for political reasons rather than for purely economic ones: unlike the English classics, he did not fight against government activity *per se* but against the governments of parliamentary democracy, of the very parliamentary democracy that commanded the fervent allegiance of the English classics. Viewed from this angle, his type of laissez-faire acquires a connotation that is entirely at variance with the laissez-faire of the English type. And once we realize this, the rest is easy to understand.

Toward the end of the nineteenth and during the first two decades of the twentieth century, an increasing number of Frenchmen and Italians began to voice dissatisfaction that varied from mere disappointment to violent disgust at the manner in which the *cotillon* of parliamentary democracy functioned and at the results it produced in France and Italy. Such sentiments were shared by men as different as E. Faguet and G. Sorel, and they were not confined to any one party. This is not the place to analyze let alone to pass judgment upon them. All that matters for us is their existence and the fact that the later Pareto stands out from this current of thought only because he himself stood out from his contemporaries and because he wrote a sociology that was—along with those of Sorel and Mosca—to rationalize it.

Englishmen and Americans, oblivious of the particular and historically unique circumstances that have developed in their minds an equally particular and unique attitude toward parliamentary democracy, have wondered about the possible meaning of Pareto's attitude toward Fascism. But this attitude is not problematical in the least. No theory is necessary in order to explain it. The events of 1914-22 had called him back to the arena of political debate. The masterly analyses he published on the origins of the First World War, on the miscarriage of Versailles, and on the futility of the League are among his strongest performances although they found no answering echo outside of Italy. But above all he witnessed with something like horror the social disorganization in Italy which it is necessary to have seen in order to believe. Attributing all the troubles of those years to the weakness of the political system of a decadent bourgeoisie, the student of Roman history may have thought of the formula by which, in republican Rome, the senate, in order to deal with an emergency, used to direct the consuls to appoint an officer of practically unlimited though temporary power, the dictator: *videant consules ne quid detrimenti res publica capiat.* But there was no such provision in the Italian constitution, and it would not have done any good if there had been one. So the dictator had to appoint himself. Beyond this and beyond approval of the success with which Mussolini restored order, Pareto never went. Mussolini honored himself by conferring senatorial rank on the man who kept on preaching moderation and who stood throughout for the freedom of the press and of academic teaching. But to his last day Pareto refused to embrace this 'ism' as he had refused to embrace any other. There is no point whatever in judging his action—or, indeed, any action or sentiment of his—from the standpoint of Anglo-American tradition.

Everything else is at the bottom of the pool.

II. THE THEORIST

Any appraisal of Pareto's contribution to economics must first of all give due credit to a feat of leadership. He never taught in Italy. The Faculty of Law in the University of Lausanne did not make very favorable headquarters for a campaign of intellectual conquest. The country house in Céligny looked like a *buen retiro.* Yet he did what Walras had not been able to do: he formed a school in the full sense of the word. An inner circle of eminent economists, a wider circle of followers of less eminence, and beyond this a broad fringe of more or less definite adherents emerged soon after 1900. They co-operated in positive work. They cultivated personal contact. They stood for one another in controversy. They recognized One Master and One Doctrine.

This school was specifically Italian. As has been pointed out already, there were but few foreign adherents, though individual pieces of Paretian teaching eventually gained acceptance both in England and in the United States. Nor did the Pareto school ever dominate Italian economics. No school ever does dominate its own country. Impressions to the contrary, e.g. the impression that the Ricardo school ever dominated English economics, are due to nothing but unrealistic historiography. Several other Italian leaders, like Einaudi, held their own ground entirely, and others, like Del Vecchio, while recognizing Pareto's eminence and adopting this or that of his doctrines, thought and wrote pretty much as they would have done had Pareto never lived. Still, there remains the fact that was a school did emerge on the basis of a theoretical structure that was inaccessible not only to the general reader but, in some of its most original parts, also to students of economics, students moreover who had never heard or seen the master.

But once we have duly recognized and thereupon discarded this feat of leadership, we see a theorist who continued the work of Walras. Nobody, of course, ever denied this, not even the most ardent disciple and, least of all, Pareto himself. Difference of opinion on this point is inevitably confined to the extent to which he surpassed the great pioneer and to the relative mental statures of the two men. There are several reasons why disciples will never agree on this either with outsiders or among themselves. One of these reasons must be noticed at once. Walras presented his immortal theory in the garb of a political philosophy that is extra-scientific in nature and, moreover, not to everyone's taste. I am afraid that there is no better way of conveying what that philosophy was than to call it the philosophy of petty-bourgeois radicalism. He felt called upon to preach an *idéal social* that hails from the semi-socialist French writers of the first half of the nineteenth century or, as we may say with equal justice, from utilitarianism. He looked upon the nationalization of land as an essential item in his teaching, and he was a monetary reformer whose plans have a strikingly modern ring. All this was gall and wormwood to Pareto. It was just metaphysical speculation and metaphysical speculation of a very unsympathetic kind. Their common ground was confined to pure theory and specifically to Walras' equations of equilibrium. But in every other respect they were as different as two men can be, and even their companionship in arms in the fight for mathematical economics and Pareto's obligation to Walras in the matter of the Lausanne professorship did not prevent their deep-seated mutual dislike from asserting itself or even from spilling over in conversation with third persons. While their pure theories are cast in the same mould, their systems of thought taken as wholes and their visions of the social process are not. And all those economists who are not disposed to neglect a man's philosophy and practical recommendations completely, that is to say the majority of the profession, will, for this reason alone, consider the Paretian structure to be something completely different from that of Walras.

In any case—we are neglecting sociology for the moment—it was, with one exception, in pure theory alone that he made scientific history. Let us note this exception first. In the *Cours* and also in a separate memoir of 1896 Pareto published a highly original pioneer achievement in econometrics that first established his international reputation and, under the title of 'Pareto's Law,' created what may be fairly called a whole literature devoted to its critical discussion. Call N the number of income receivers who receive incomes higher than x, and A and m two constants; then Pareto's 'Law' asserts that

$$\log N = \log A + m \log x$$

Chapter 7 of the *Manuel* contains Pareto's most mature interpretation of this generalization. We must confine ourselves here to noticing the two classes of problems which it raises. There is, first, the question of fit. Numerous investigations have been made, some of which were held by their authors either to refute the Law completely or else to establish the superiority of other methods of describing the inequality of incomes. The reader will observe that the central issue turns on the approximate constancy of the m. However, by and large, the 'Law' has stood fire rather well as the fact that it is sometimes used by competent statisticians even now suffices to prove. But there is, second, the question of interpretation. Granted that up to quite recent times the distribution of incomes according to brackets has been remarkably stable, what are we to infer from this? This problem has never been attacked successfully. Most participants in the discussion, Pigou among them, have confined themselves to criticizing Pareto's own interpretation—which, to say the least, was in fact open to objection at first—and, like so many of our controversies, this one has petered out without yielding a definite result. Few if any economists seem to have realized the possibilities that such invariants hold out for the future of our science. Viewed from this standpoint, Pareto's 'Law' is path-breaking in the literal sense even though in the end nothing whatever is left of its particular form.

I take this opportunity to dispose of another matter. In the *Manuel,* Pareto dealt with his 'Law' of Income Distribution in the chapter on Population. So far as the topics are concerned that are usually dealt with under this heading, this chapter does not contain much that would call for notice. But it contains a number of other things which, like the 'Law,' are not usually included in the theory of population, and it is these items which liven up this chapter and impart to it its freshness and originality. Pareto's theory of the *circulation of the élite* is an example (see below, section III). Most of them are sociological rather than economic in nature, and some of them bring out sharply, indeed almost naïvely, certain prejudices that sat so incongruously upon the great analyst of human prejudice.

In the field of pure theory, properly so called, Pareto's thought developed slowly and in fact retained certain pre-Paretian features to the end. In addition to the early influences of Ferrara and of the English and French economists of the 'classic period,' he had Walras' equations of static equilibrium to start from—after having realized, not without considerable initial resistance, that they were in fact the keys to everything else. He was further stimulated by all the suggestions that no competent theorist could have helped receiving in the decade from 1885 to 1895. Finally, he was acutely aware of the technical shortcomings and other limitations of his immediate predecessors. Thus his own theoretical work was cut out for him—most of it, indeed, by Walras himself. But his earlier work, such as his **'Considerazioni sui principi fondamentali dell' economia politica pura'** (*Giornale degli Economisti*, 1892-3), never went beyond the range of the Walrasian signposts. This is also true, and emphatically so, of his *Cours.* Some economists who respected Pareto but were not strictly Paretians have paid him the dubious compliment of calling the *Cours* his masterpiece. It is, indeed, a striking performance enlivened throughout by a strong temperament that imparts sparkle even to conventional passages. But Pareto was right in refusing to sanction a reprint or a second edition. For, so far as pure theory is concerned, there was nothing specifically Paretian about it. It was only after 1897 that he rose to heights of his own. The first major publications that testify to his progress are the **'Sunto di alcuni capitoli di un nuovo trattato di economia pura'** (*Giornale degli Economisti,* 1900) and the **Résumé** of his Paris course. The *Manuale* or rather, because of the appendix, the *Manuel* (1909), then marks the point of highest elevation that he reached.

The structure of the tower he erected on that spot is far from faultless. Many things that are essential in a comprehensive treatise received but scant attention. I do not mean merely that Pareto's work cannot stand comparison with Marshall's in those qualities that are ordinarily looked for in a 'manual.' Much more serious is it that important parts of the *theoretical* organon are inadequately thought out. Pareto's theory of money, for instance, is on the whole inferior to that of Walras. His theory of capital and interest derives all its merits from that of Walras. As regards interest he seems to have been content to rely for explanation on the fact that items of physical capital, hence their services, are not free goods. His theory of monopoly cannot, I believe, be salvaged by even the most generous interpretation. In spite of all this, the adverse judgment arrived at by some critics is completely wrong. For it neglects not only many individual strong points but, much more important, the essence of the achievement. The most important of those strong points, the theories of value and of production, will be discussed presently. But first we must try to define that achievement itself of which these two theories were but applications.

The first idea that must occur, from a purely theoretical point of view, to anyone who has mastered Walras's system is to raise it to a still higher level of generality. When we follow Walras and, indeed, all the marginal utility theorists on their progress through the phenomena of exchange, production, and so on, we discover that they are trying to solve problems that in ultimate logic reduce to one only: *all* their problems—not only the problems of production—are problems in the transformation of economic quantities and formally alike, the differences consisting merely in the different restrictions to which economic action is subject in different fields. Suppose we decide to do what we do in all the sciences, that is, to separate out the common core of all economic problems and to build a theory of this common core once and for all. The point of view of 'mental economy' (E. Mach's *Denkökonomie*) will justify this endeavor to utilitarians. A theory of this kind will work with quite general indices, such as 'tastes' and 'obstacles,' and need not stop at the specifically economic meanings that we may assign to these words. We may transcend economics and rise to the conception of a system of undefined 'things' that are simply subject to certain restrictions and then try to develop a perfectly general mathematical *logic of systems*. Stretches of this road should be quite familiar to economists who have for generations used primitive devices, such as our venerable friend Crusoe, for the purpose of displaying certain features of economic logic. Pareto simply did the same on a much higher level and on a much broader front. But in these altitudes it is difficult to breathe and still more difficult to gain ground. Critics as competent as the late A. A. Young have been of the opinion that Pareto achieved nothing but 'arid generalizations.' But only the future can tell whether this is so. Meanwhile we should recognize the greatness of the attempt.

An example will show that such a 'rush for generality' may produce not only logical stones but also economic bread, though it suffers from the weakness that it still moves on a relatively low level of generality and, indeed, dates from the *Cours*. As everyone knows, Marx's work is an analysis of the capitalist process, no doubt geared to the purpose of showing that this process will issue in a socialist society but entirely free from any attempt at blocking out the economics of this society. And there are a number of Marxist and Neo-Marxist contributions to

the latter problem that can be described only as complete failures. As everyone also knows by now, the service to socialist doctrine that Marxist theories have been unable to render has been rendered by E. Barone, whose famous paper on the subject ('Il Ministro della produzione nello stato colletivista,' *Giornale degli Economisti,* 1908) has been surpassed by modern writers only in secondary details. But the essential idea of Barone's argument is clearly indicated in the second volume of Pareto's *Cours* and in his *Manuel,* namely the idea to lift, as it were, the logical core of the economic process above the ground of the institutional garb in which it is given to observation. The reader will observe how easily this idea suggests itself, as a special case, once we place ourselves on the standpoint of Pareto's general theory of tastes and obstacles, although it also suggested itself to Wieser.

In this special case, Pareto has nearly lost his claims to priority—at least among Anglo-American economists—although he had not only posited the problem but also pointed out the way to its solution. In other cases, he lost them completely because he confined himself to mere suggestions. Thus, assisted by hindsight, we may discern in the *Manuel* many pointers toward the later economic dynamics. However, none of them, such as his reference to a form of adaptation similar to a *courbe de poursuite* (dog-and-his-master problem, see e.g. p. 289) and to the presence of *vibration continuelle,* was put to any use other than the negative one of showing that the economic system's tendency toward a unique and stable 'solution' (i.e. a unique set of values that will satisfy its conditions) is a much more doubtful matter than the economists of that period, including Walras, supposed. No positive use was made of these suggestions, and no method was indicated for attacking these problems. I think therefore that we should not hesitate to describe Pareto's work as static theory, and that substantial justice is done if we add that he, more than others, was aware of its limitations and of the call of the problems beyond.

We now proceed to a brief discussion of Pareto's work in the fields of value and production keeping in mind that, from the standpoint adumbrated above, they really merge into a single theory.

Most modern theorists, although not all, will agree that the historical importance of the utility and marginal utility theory of Jevons, Menger, and Walras rests mainly upon the fact that it served as the ladder by which these economists climbed up to the conception of general economic equilibrium, although this conception was much more clearly perceived and much more fully developed by Walras than it was by either the Austrians or Jevons. In other words, the utility and marginal utility theory was one of several possible avenues to the thing that really mattered and, besides offering an excellent method for demonstrating in an easily understandable way the relations that hold the economic system together and, in fact, make a unified system out of the mass of economic phenomena which departmentalize so easily, had no great importance in itself. Or, to put it still differently, utility theory was an extremely useful heuristic hypothesis and nothing more. But neither Walras nor the Austrians were of this opinion. On the contrary, for them the utility theory was nothing less than ultimate truth, the discovery of the key to all the secrets of pure economics. In consequence, they placed an emphasis upon it that in turn induced Pareto and the Paretians to place undue emphasis upon their renunciation of it. Authors in the English-speaking world, particularly Professors Allen and Hicks, followed suit and very generously congratulated Pareto on what to them also seemed a new departure of first-rate importance. In fact, there is a widespread opinion to the effect that this new departure constitutes Pareto's main contribution.

There are indications in the *Cours* that Pareto was not quite satisfied with the Walrasian theory of value from the first. But his amendments, either insignificant or not original, remained within the precincts of the principle itself. Of the insignificant amendments, we merely mention the introduction of the term *ophélimité* in the place of the term utility (*ophélimité élémentaire* for marginal utility or Walras' *rareté*) on the ground that the latter carried too many misleading associations. Of those that are not original with Pareto I mention the conception of utility and marginal utility as functions of all the commodities that the consuming unit possesses or consumes in an appropriately chosen period of time, instead of Walras' conception of total and marginal utility of every commodity as function of the quantity of that commodity alone. This obvious improvement is due to Edgeworth, but I confess to some doubt whether Edgeworth was fully aware of the theoretical difficulties this improvement would cause, for it turns the final degree of utility that was simply an ordinary differential coefficient with Jevons, Walras, and also with Marshall, into a partial differential coefficient and this greatly increases the mathematical difficulties we encounter when trying to prove the determinateness of the economic system even in its most simplified form.

Before long, however, and certainly before 1900, the year in which he delivered his Paris lectures that made his change of standpoint publicly known, Pareto realized that, for his purposes at least, the concept of measurable utility (cardinal utility) might be safely abandoned or that, in any case, it would have to be abandoned for reasons that were first stated exactly in the second part of Irving Fisher's *Mathematical Investigations into the Theory of Value and Price* (1892). To save the situation he appealed to the indifference and preference curves that had been first introduced by Edgeworth. But, whereas Edgeworth still started from a measurable total utility from which he deduced the definition of these lines, Pareto inverted the process. He took the indifference lines as the given thing to start from and showed that it was possible to arrive from them at the determination of economic equilibrium in pure competition and also to proceed to certain functions which might be identical with utility if it exists. In any case, it was possible to obtain (ordinal) *indices* of utility or what Pareto called index functions.

I wish to bring out two points quite clearly. The first is that Pareto, though he may have adapted an invention of Edgeworth's to his own use, imparted to the indifference varieties a meaning that they do not carry in Edgeworth's *Mathematical Psychics*. They are quite divested of any utility connotation, and what the concept of utility had done for the theory of economic equilibrium was now to be done by certain assumptions about the form of these indifference curves. The new idea was to replace utility postulates by postulates about observable behavior and thus to base economic theory on what seemed to Pareto to be more secure foundations. It might be urged of course that in spite of several attempts nobody has as yet succeeded in carrying out such observations and that it is difficult to indulge in the hope that we might construct them from objective data *in their whole extent* so as to derive a complete empirical indifference map. Let us call them, therefore, potentially empirical or, to misuse a Kantian term, 'referring to possible experience.' In any case, their introduction for a purpose entirely foreign to Edgeworth's might be called a truly original achievement were it not for the fact that this achievement had been, as Pareto recognized, foreshadowed in Fisher's work mentioned above.

The second point is that Pareto's own argument brings out the difficulty he experienced in disentangling himself entirely from the old utility theory. He always kept an eye on the cases in which it might be possible to speak of utility and even of cardinal utility, the existence of which—hence the question of integrability—continued to interest him very much. And his index functions bear after all a pretty close similarity to the old concept. In fact, as has been pointed out by Allen and Hicks, he never succeeded quite in disentangling himself entirely, and he continued to use concepts such as the Edgeworthian definitions of rivalry and complementarity that do not go well with his fundamental idea. This fundamental idea, let us add, was developed and defended as early as 1902 by P. Boninsegni. By 1908, Enrico Barone, in the paper mentioned already, definitely went beyond Pareto by confining his fundamental assumptions in the matter of value theory to what he called the *fact* that, confronted with given prices of products and productive services, every individual distributes his receipts from the sale of his services between expenditures on consumption goods and saving in a certain unique manner 'of which we are not going to investigate the motives.' This, so he pointed out, does away with any concept of either utility or indifference functions. The rest of the story is too well known to detain us. I shall merely mention the papers of Johnson and Slutsky that for the time being remained practically unnoticed; the important reformulation of Bowley in his *Groundwork* that was more influential; and the work of Allen and Hicks, Georgescu-Roegen, Samuelson, and H. Wold. If we accept the present situations as 'provisionally final,' we must indeed salute either Fisher or Pareto as the patron saint of the modern theory of value.

But, still more definitely than patron saint of the modern theory of value is Pareto the patron saint of the 'New

Welfare Economics.' The story of how, once more, he came to render a service to a cause with which he was—or would be—completely out of sympathy is not without its humor. From the very beginnings of economics, a loosely defined public welfare played a great role in the writings of economists. The familiar slogans of utilitarianism (Beccaria, Bentham) did something toward rationalizing the concept, and the utility theory of value seemed admirably qualified to implement it: in fact it was promptly harnessed to the task, e.g. in the field of taxation. The Fisher-Pareto theory of indifference varieties, destroying as it did the bases of arguments that worked with cardinal utility or even with interpersonal comparison of utility (satisfaction), should, so we might think at first blush, have done away with all this. But instead of drawing this conclusion—and in spite of his contempt for the political humanitarianism of our age—Pareto immediately went on to attack the problem of maxima of *collective* satisfaction afresh. The definitive formulation was left for Barone, but the main idea is again Pareto's. He observed, first, that all changes imposed upon any given economic pattern may be said to increase welfare or collective satisfaction in a perfectly objective sense if those who gain in terms of *numéraire* could compensate those who lose in terms of *numéraire* and still have some gain left. This criterion will in fact salvage some though not all of the welfare judgments usually passed by economists. Second, Pareto pointed out that welfare judgments that cannot be salvaged in this manner must be explicitly based on extra-economic, e.g. 'ethical,' considerations. And third, he showed that the criterion may be used in order to establish that *l'état collectiviste* may improve upon the level of welfare that is practically attainable under perfect competition. But, barring developments, these points are pretty much what the New Welfare Economics amounts to.

That part of Pareto's welfare economics which deals with the logic of production provides a convenient transition to his second great contribution to pure theory, his theory of production. Approaching the problem from the side of the theory of choice and applying to the producer's case the general apparatus of indifference curves and derivative concepts (*lignes du plus grand profit, lignes de transformations complètes et incomplètes* etc.), he sketched out a comprehensive structure only parts of which are explicitly present in the literature of his time and which may be said to constitute the foundation of the mathematical theory of production of our own age or, at all events, of its statics. In particular, its very generality leaves room for all the special cases that we may wish to treat without placing exclusive emphasis on any one of them: the 'obstacles' may be anything at first, and can then assume any of the forms that occur more commonly in practice—the factors that are required in fixed quantities irrespective of output, the factors that are required in technologically determined quantities per unit of output, the 'compensatory' factors, and so on, all take their places in a theoretically complete schema of possibilities. In appraising this achievement, we must keep in mind that Pareto was primarily concerned with generalizing

and otherwise improving the work of his great predecessor. Again his work may be divided into a first part that culminated in the *Cours* and a second part that culminated in the *Manuel,* though some minor touches were added in the article in the *Encyclopédie des Sciences Mathématiques* (Volume 1, 1911).

Originally, Walras had expounded his theory of production on the assumption of fixed coefficients of production—fixed (average) inputs per units of output—not because he believed that this was the only or even a very important case but because he thought himself justified in adopting what he considered to be a simplification. His reply to private criticisms that poured in on him was that 'the economists who will come after me are free to insert one by one all the complications they please. They and I, so I think, will then have done everything that it was our duty to do'. So far as this goes Pareto cannot be said to have done more than take Walras' advice. In addition, when the *Cours* appeared, Walras had already introduced variable coefficients, on a suggestion of Barone's that reached him in 1894, though without altering the argument of the fundamental section on production. In the same year (1894) appeared Wicksteed's *Essay on the Coordination of the Laws of Distribution.* Finally, variable coefficients of production were no novelty in any case after all that Jevons, Menger, and Marshall had said on the subject. Pareto's *Cours* added only an elegant formulation and a number of reasons—not all of them convincing—why the case of compensatory coefficients should not be treated as the only or the fundamental one either.

It is of course a mere matter of terminological taste whether or not we are to confine the phrase 'marginal productivity theory' to this case. Pareto did so confine it and, in the years following upon the publication of the *Cours,* grew increasingly hostile to it, declaring it definitely 'erroneous.' He was evidently under the impression that he had refuted or, at any rate, outgrown it in the same sense in which he felt that he had refuted or outgrown the marginal utility theory. His brilliant theory of cost—which, among other things, withdraws from their dangerously exposed positions the textbook theorems that, in perfect equilibrium of pure competition, price should equal marginal cost and total receipts should at the same time equal total cost—permit us to test this claim. So far as productive combinations depend on economic considerations—and, after all, it is the economic considerations which it is the economists' task to clear up—the difference, as compared with straight marginal productivity theory, is not great. But Pareto does teach us how to handle the deviations from it that technological and social restrictions impose. And, here as elsewhere, he does something else: he always points beyond himself.

III. THE SOCIOLOGIST

There is nothing surprising in the habit of economists to invade the sociological field. A large part of their work—

practically the whole of what they have to say on institutions and on the forces that shape economic behavior—inevitably overlaps the sociologist's preserves. In consequence, a no-man's land or everyman's land has developed that might conveniently be called economic sociology. More or less important elements that hail from that land are to be found in practically every economic treatise or textbook. But beyond this many economists, and especially those who define economics proper rather strictly, have done sociological work. A. Smith's *Moral Sentiments* and Wieser's *Gesetz der Macht* are both outstanding instances of a large genus. But few if any men in the list of great economists have devoted so large a part of their energy as has Pareto to what at first sight seems to be an extra-curricular activity, and few if any owe so much of their international reputation to what they have done in that field. But his achievement is not easy to characterize and to appraise. The enthusiastic applause of some and the hostility of others are both understandable but neither can be taken quite seriously because the non-scientific sources of both are painfully obvious in most cases. Although several minor works and a large number of newspaper articles would have to be considered in order to give a satisfactory picture, we need not go beyond the *Systèmes socialistes,* the *Manuel* (especially Chapters II and VII), and the *Trattato di Sociologia Generale*.

Let us begin with two aspects of Pareto's sociology that are perfectly obvious and the reverse of difficult to characterize. First, although Pareto the economist touched upon a large number of extremely concrete and practical problems throughout his long life, his purely scientific contribution is in the realm of the most abstract economic logic. It is, therefore, quite understandable that he should have experienced a wish and, in fact, a need to erect alongside his pure theory another building that would shelter facts and reasonings of a different kind, facts and reasonings that would do something toward answering the question how the elements taken care of by his economic theory might be expected to work out in practical life. Second, we have seen that in his earlier days, at least as long as he lived in Italy, he had taken a passionate interest in the debates on questions of economic and general policy. The born thinker that he was must have been struck by the impotence of the rational argument, and the question must have intruded upon him of what it really is that determines political action and the fate of states and civilizations. Again, it is quite understandable that, so soon as he had settled down to a life of thought, this question should have emerged from the sphere of easy and superficial answers that all of us are prone to give when immersed in our daily work, and that he should have attempted to raise it to the plane of scientific analysis. This amounts to saying that primarily and fundamentally his sociology was a sociology of the political process. Of course, everything that man does or thinks or feels and all his cultural creations and his attitudes toward cultural creations are bound to come in somehow or other when we think about the political process which then becomes but a special case. But it was this special case which fascinated Pareto and for the sake of which he erected and adorned a much larger structure.

Next, still moving on ground that is relatively easy to survey, we shall consider his method. Pareto himself emphasized again and again that he simply applied the same 'logico-experimental' methods that had served him for the purposes of economic theory to the task of analyzing the 'experimentally' verifiable reality of other aspects of social life, allowing himself to be guided here as elsewhere by the example of the physical sciences. This was, of course, a complete delusion. It is easy to observe, for instance, that he made large and in part illegitimate use of psychological interpretations for which there is no analogy in the physical sciences and that his material, such as it was, was the product of observation and not of experiment—a difference which is fundamental from the standpoint of method. I am afraid that what he really meant to emphasize when trying to formulate his rules of procedure was simply the detachment of the philosopher who does not identify himself with any party, interest, or creed. The possibility of such detachment raises, of course, a very well-known fundamental difficulty and one that Pareto was the less qualified to overcome because he failed to see it. Actually he used two different analytic schemata: one that may be called a morphology of society and does invite the use of facts that are, potentially at least, amenable to observation as are the facts of anatomy or biology in a similar sense; and another that pertains to social psychology. Both schemata are indeed *illustrated* or even, to some extent, *verified* by historical and contemporaneous instances, but neither is *derived* from them by anything like a 'logico-experimental' method: both are reflexes of a highly personal vision of the social process that owes much to Pareto's background, practical experience—and resentments. The affinity of the morphological schema with Darwinian selection and of the socio-psychological schema with parts of the teaching of Tarde, Dürkheim, Lévy-Bruhl, and Th. Ribto is obvious. Still more so is the relation of both with the current of thought glanced at in the first section of this essay that issued in derogatory criticism of the doings of parliamentary democracy—the current that was anti-intellectualist, anti-utilitarian, anti-equalitarian and, *in the special sense defined by these terms,* anti-liberal. But the force of the man created from these materials something that was nevertheless specifically his own.

The morphological schema centers in the proposition that all societies consist of heterogeneous masses of members—individuals or families—and are structured according to the aptitudes of these members for the relevant social function: in a society of thieves, the *ex hypothesi* widely varying ability to steal would determine social rank, and hence influence upon the government of the society. Pareto seems to assume that these abilities, while capable of improvement and of decay, are substantially innate, though he makes little effort to establish this. Moreover, though distributed continuously in the population, they lead to the formation of classes, the 'higher' ones of which have and use the means of buttressing their position and of separating themselves from the lower strata. In consequence, there is in the lowest strata a tendency to accumulate superior ability that is prevented from rising, and in the topmost stratum, in the aristocracy or *élite,* a tendency to decumulate energy through disuse—with resulting tension and ultimate replacement of the ruling minority by another ruling minority that is drawn from the superior elements in the *couches inférieures.* This *circulation des élites* does not, however, affect the principle that it is always *some* minority which rules, and does not do anything to bring any given society nearer to the ideal of equality, though it does produce equalitarian philosophies or slogans in the course of the struggles that ensue. With a turn of phrase that recalls the first sentence of the *Communist Manifesto,* Pareto proclaimed that history is essentially a history *de la succession des aristocracies.* But his presentation of this part of his argument is so very sketchy and he leaves his readers with so much to interpolate that I am not at all sure that I have rendered justice to his thought. Nevertheless, I had to make the attempt. For some such argument is necessary in order to put his social psychology into its proper light.

The socio-psychological schema centers in the concept of the non-logical (not necessarily illogical) action. This concept recognizes the well-known fact—well known, in particular, to economists—that the great mass of our everyday actions is not the result of rational reasoning on rationally performed observations, but simply of habit, impulse, sense of duty, imitation, and so on, although many of them admit of satisfactory rationalization *ex post* either by the observer or the actor. So far there is nothing in Pareto's psycho-sociology that could be unfamiliar to anyone. What is unfamiliar, however, is his tremendous emphasis upon the additional facts that a great number of actions—and let us add at once, beliefs—are being rationalized, both by actors and by observers, in ways that will not stand up under scientific analysis and, more important, that some actions and beliefs are altogether incapable of being rationalized in any way that will. The importance of this second step for a sociology of the political process becomes obvious if we take a third one: Pareto maintained that the large majority of all the actions and beliefs that make up that process are of the type mentioned last. Take, as an instance on which we all agree, the idea of the Social Compact or, as an instance on which most of us agree, Rousseau's theory of the *volonté générale.* Only, according to Pareto, practically all the actions, principles, beliefs, and so on prevailing in the collective mind of electorates belong in the same category. And a large part of the *Trattato* consists in illustrating this, often amusingly, sometimes instructively.

It will serve our purpose to put this point strongly, more strongly than Pareto himself ever put it. The masses of thought and the conceptual structures that form the conscious surface of the social and in particular of the political process have no empirical validity whatever. They work with entities such as liberty, democracy, equality, that are as imaginary as were the gods and goddesses who fought for and against Greeks and Trojans in the *Iliad,* and are connected by reasonings that habitually violate the rules of logic. In other words, from a logical standpoint, they are nonsense unalloyed. This makes a political philosophy that is best described by its diametrical opposition to that of Jeremy Bentham. It should be observed, however, that this diagnosis of the political myths (Sorel) did not induce Pareto to overlook the function that this logical nonsense may fill in national life. After having gone through with an analysis that is severely positivist in nature, he refused to draw the conclusion that would seem the obvious one to the positivist. While political creeds and social religions—with Pareto there is very little difference between these two—contribute to dissolution in dissolving civilizations, they also contribute to effective organization and action in vital civilizations. This is a very curious attitude for a thorough-going positivist to take and will perhaps be cited at some future time as an outstanding example of the mentality of an epoch that destroyed one type of metaphysical beliefs while ushering in another. It reminds me of the advice which I have heard some psychoanalysts give to some of their patients, namely the advice to cultivate with a view to possible remedial effects a sort of synthetic belief in God. There is of course no contradiction between maintaining that social and political creeds have no empirical significance and admitting that some of them may make for social cohesion and efficiency. But the social philosopher who should thereupon undertake to advise the adoption of the latter would run into the same difficulty as our psychoanalyst: so long as his *analysis* is being accepted his advice must be ineffective, for no synthetic God can be trusted to help; so soon as his *advice* is accepted his analysis will have to be rejected.

That tissue of creations of our imagination Pareto called *dérivations.* The argument adumbrated in the preceding paragraph abundantly shows that they are not without importance as factors that help to shape the historical process. It was Pareto's opinion, however, that this importance is relatively small and that substantially these *dérivations* do no more than verbalize something more fundamental that comes much nearer to determining actual political behavior and the sum total of non-logical actions. Now if we defined this more fundamental something in terms of group interests, and if we then went on to define these group interests in terms of the social location of groups within a society's productive organization, we should be, to say the least, very near Karl Marx's view of the matter, and there is in this point actually a strong affinity which I think it important to emphasize. In fact, if we adopted this line of reasoning, there would be only two major points of difference left between Marxian and Paretian political sociology. On the one hand, Pareto introduced explicitly an element that is only implicitly present in the Marxist analysis: the importance for the explanation of an actual stretch of history, of the greater or smaller degree of social flexibility that a given society displays, or, in other words, the importance of the fact that there exists an optimum or vertical mobility and of resistance to it that will better than others guarantee what might be termed stability of political change. On the other hand, we need only recall our sketch of Pareto's social morphology in order to realize that with Pareto the historical process is not so much the result of the conflict of comprehensive social classes as it is the result of the conflict of their ruling minorities. It is submitted that, while both differences are to the credit of Paretian sociology, they do not amount to more than corrective improvements upon the Marxist schema. I might add the fact that property relations *per se* are much less in evidence with Pareto than they are with Marx, and that this also constitutes a claim to superiority of the Paretian analysis. But it will be readily seen, that this point is really implied in the other two.

Actually, however, Pareto did not follow up this line of analysis. With him the link between the tissue of delusions which he called *dérivations* and the objective determinants of actual behavior was supplied by what he called the *résidus*. I am conscious of the danger of being unfair if, for the sake of brevity, I define these *résidus* as impulses generally found to be present with human beings that revive, and not in a very inviting manner, the old psychology of 'instincts.' We need not discuss the list that Pareto drew up—and which contains such items as an instinct of combinations, the sexual impulse, and so on—especially as Pareto himself does not seem to have been very satisfied with it. It is sufficient to point out the obvious methodological objection to any such procedure; even if Pareto's *résidus* and the 'laws' of their association and persistence were much more satisfactorily analyzed than they are, they would still be labels rather than solutions of problems, and call for professional investigation of a kind for which Pareto lacked the equipment. It is therefore quite understandable that Pareto's work has exerted so little influence upon professional sociology and social psychology, and that professional sociologists and social-psychologists have but rarely displayed a sense of the greatness of the structure as a whole.

But those and other shortcomings are not decisive. Pareto's work is more than a research program. Also, it is more than mere analysis. The fundamental principle that what individuals, groups, and nations actually do must find its explanation in something much deeper than the creeds and slogans that are used in order to verbalize action, conveys a lesson of which modern men—and none more than we economists—stand much in need. We are in the habit when discussing questions of policy of accepting at face value the slogans of our own and, indeed, of a by-gone time. We reason exactly as if the Benthamite creed of the eighteenth century had ever been valid. We refuse to realize that policies are politics and to admit to ourselves what politics are. We cultivate the subnormal and do our best to suppress whatever there is of strength and sparkle. In conditions such as these, Pareto's message, however one-sided, is a healthy antidote. It is not, like his economics, a technical achievement of the first order. It is something quite different. It is an attempt to preach a sermon.

Joseph Lopreato and Robert C. Ness (essay date 1966)

SOURCE: "Vilfredo Pareto: Sociologist or Ideologist?," in *The Sociological Quarterly,* Vol. 7, No. 1, 1966, pp. 21-38.

[*In the following essay, Lopreato and Ness dismiss the view of Pareto as a forerunner of modern fascist ideology.*]

In the history of science it has often happened that a scholar's ideas are denied full recognition because of that scholar's real or assumed connection to some controversial ideology. The position accorded to Vilfredo Pareto is one illustration of such practice in present-day sociology. This scholar is often said to have been a "Newton of the Moral World," or altogether a fascist ideologist. So Faris informs us that "The book [*The Mind and Society*] formulates the implicit philosophy of Italian Fascism, advocating the right of the strong to take what they want without apology or appeal to moral principles." In tracing the development of social thought, Bogardus devotes an entire chapter to "Pareto and Fascist Thought," and authoritatively argues that "While fascism has some of its roots in Nietzsche's concepts and other roots in Machiavellianism, yet Pareto's ideas come even closer to giving an adequate basis." Zanden, in turn, interprets Pareto's sociology to be "a philosophy of society, a social creed, determined mainly by violent and ever purely personal passions. The logical fulfillment of this political manifesto is fascism."

We need not continue further; analogous affirmations are bountiful in the literature. To be sure, not all sociologists accept this view, but to date little or no systematic effort has been made to resolve the controversy, with the result that many students of sociology are unwitting victims of one of the most cruel intellectual hoaxes perpetrated against their discipline and one of their kind. The present paper proposes to offer a clarification with respect to the alleged connection between Pareto's sociology and fascist ideology. Our approach takes us in two major directions: first, an examination of Pareto's *Treatise,* his chief sociological work, and second, an examination of a series of letters written to his great friend Pantaleoni during the period when fascism was a political reality in Italy.

Before proceeding to present our argument, it may be useful to inquire briefly about the meaning of "fascism," as his critics tend to use that word. A rapid glance at the literature reveals that the following are generally believed to be among the chief characteristics of fascist ideology: distrust of reason, a code of behavior based on "race" and violence, belligerent nationalism, government by an elite, and totalitarianism. Characteristically, these then provide the basis for accusing Pareto of "antirationalism," "anti-intellectualism," "contempt for democracy," and approval of the use of force at all costs. The major portion of this paper will be concerned, therefore, with explicating Pareto's position on these four issues. We shall begin by considering Pareto's alleged antirationalism.

PARETO'S "ANTIRATIONALISM"

Although it is difficult to determine the exact source of this label, it appears to us that fundamentally it is rooted in a widespread misunderstanding of Pareto's analysis of human conduct. It will be recalled that in analyzing human action, Pareto uncovers three major types: the logical, the nonlogical, and the illogical. To act logically in Pareto's sense would be to select, consciously and deliberately, goals which are not metaphysical or impossible, and then to take the appropriate steps as dictated by logic and scientific experience, toward reaching those goals. Other types of actions, on the other hand, originate chiefly in "psychic states, sentiments, and subconscious feelings"; they are actions in which men often use entirely inappropriate means, according to the criteria of logico-experimental science, to achieve their goals.

Pareto argues that much of human behavior is nonlogical. Because of this fact, the social scientist must pay particular attention to the role of nonlogical actions if he is to understand the social phenomenon. The conclusion, however, cannot be drawn (as it often is) that because Pareto emphasized the significance of nonlogical actions he was an antirationalist. He did not distrust reason or even suggest that men are totally incapable of rational behavior. On the contrary, in his search for "scientific truth," Pareto strongly argued that it was a product of man's reasoning power. Indeed, within this context, his positive emphasis on rationality includes the important desideratum of "freedom of inquiry." Thus,

> before a theory [and this includes ideologies] can be considered true, it is virtually indispensable that there be perfect freedom to impugn it. Any limitation, even indirect and however remote, imposed on anyone choosing to contradict it is enough to cast suspicion upon it. Hence freedom to express one's thought, even counter to the opinion of the majority or of all, even when it offends the sentiments of the few or of the many, even when it is generally reputed absurd or criminal, always proves favorable to the discovery of the objective truth.

Statements such as these (which are legion in the *Treatise*) have strangely escaped the attention of Pareto's critics, especially those who might profit from a consideration of what such statements imply for fascist or any other totalitarian ideology. What has not escaped their attention, however, is Pareto's scientifically merciless critique of the pseudological theories of what he called "the worshippers of the Goddess Reason," namely those luminaries of Western thought who have emphasized "reason," "free will," and such other metaphysical concepts. As A. G. Keller once said of Pareto, "it is hard to call to mind any other critic who has nailed more hides stripped from such oracles [as Rousseau] to the barn door."

There is no one, to our knowledge, who has attempted to prove Pareto wrong in this connection. Many of his critics have merely reacted to him as if he were an iconoclast, committing an abominable heresy. Thus, his argument that nonrational behavior is more prevalent than heretofore suspected is translated by them into "antirationalism," but what they are really doing is to object to an intellectual posture contrary to that of Rousseau, Aristotle, and the like.

There is, however, one sense in which Pareto might be called an antirationalist, and that is in the sense that he was forever skeptical of all rationalizations and pseudological explanations of human behavior. In Pareto's view, "human beings have a conspicuous tendency to paint a varnish of logic over their conduct." Accordingly, he constantly probed this "varnish of logic," or "derivation" as he called it, attempting to uncover and clarify the fundamental forces behind human behavior. But assuming a skeptical attitude does not make one an antirationalist in any sense attributed to Pareto by his critics. This form of skepticism, as Merton among others has pointed out, is an integral part of a truly scientific approach, and "the institution of science makes skepticism a virtue."

There is another and related respect in which Pareto might conceivably be called an antirationalist, although in this case we would prefer the term "irrationalist" in order to avoid the insidiously ideological connotations of the former term. Here we enter more directly the realm of the sociology of knowledge. According to Hartung, an irrationalist is one who, lacking the criteria for determining the validity of a doctrine of the existential determination of thought and action, is forced to resort to intuitive understanding in order to apprehend knowledge. In this sense, Pareto's theory of the "sentiments" or "residues" may be said to be irrational. It may be recalled that for Pareto these theoretical elements imply no psychological processes, but are "abstractions" or convenient makeshifts which help the observer to organize social facts, just as these suggest the residues to him. But the isolation of the residue is an act of intuition precisely because, as an "abstraction," it does not refer the scientist to an actual phenomenological unit of reality. In this sense, however, to be an antirationalist is in no particular way blameworthy, and Hartung correctly puts Pareto in the company of Marx, Nietzsche, Freud, and Mannheim himself.

PARETO'S "ANTI-INTELLECTUALISM"

We would maintain that the criticism of antirationalism advanced against Pareto results from a misunderstanding of his general intellectual position. It is no accident that, in an attempt to prove Pareto an antirationalist, several critics have argued that he was contemptuous of intellectuals. They have failed, however, to appreciate the connotations of the term "intellectual" as Pareto uses it. Specifically, they have confused his attitude toward the "intellectual" with his position on what we might call "intelligent" activity in general. This problem, too, is very closely related to Pareto's discussion of the three major types of conduct mentioned above. His often forceful critique of intellectuals is directed only toward those "so-called intellectuals" who are inclined to explain social phenomena in terms of derivations rather than residues. Hence, throughout the *Treatise* the term "intellectual" is placed in quotation marks to suggest the real nature of many of those who imagine themselves to be critical, objective thinkers. About these Pareto had this to say:

> A . . . judgement may be passed upon the work of our "intellectuals" as leading to few results that are beneficial and to many that are very bad; because, from the standpoint of sentiments, they shut their eyes to realities as the latter stand reflected in many sentiments that they condemn from failure to grasp their role in society; and because, from the standpoint of logico-experimental science, they reason not on facts but on derivations, and from the latter draw, by a logic inopportunely thorough-going, inferences that are altogether at war with the facts.

So, for instance, in discussing "sentiments of equality" Pareto argues, in a fashion familiar to most present-day students of social stratification, that the "sentiment of equality . . . is not related to any abstraction, as a few naive 'intellectuals' still believe," but to direct interests of individuals who are bent on escaping certain inequalities not in their favor, and setting up new inequalities that will be in their favor, this latter being their chief concern. What happens in the concrete is that people agitate for equality to get equality in general, and then go on to make countless distinctions to deny it in the particular. "Equality is to belong to all—but it is granted only to the few."

If Pareto sometimes seems to be unduly forceful in his criticism of "intellectuals," it is because he thinks that as self-appointed practitioners of social science they should make a greater effort to divorce the residue from the logico-experimental fact. But instead, as he states in his discussion of the residue of "hunger for combining residues," in "intellectuals" this impulse goes beyond the ordinary. So it is that they make one general blend of "well-being," "the true," "the good," "the broadly human," and "solidarity," forming a "simple complex" gratifying as a whole to their sentimentality. The complex then may acquire an independent existence, and in some cases may even be personified as Progress, Democracy, Reason, and the like.

But even in view of this argument, is Pareto completely opposed to such "intellectuals"? The answer is very much in the negative. On the contrary, he holds that even the wildest and most untenable speculations often perform the very useful function of leading to the discovery of real facts and scientific laws. Indeed, "if one were to assert that but for theology and metaphysics experimental science would not even exist, one could not be easily confuted. Those three kinds of activity are probably

manifestations of one same psychic state, on the extinction of which they would vanish simultaneously." He found it worthy of note, however, that an "intellectual," like Theodore Roosevelt, despite his tenuous knowledge of the historical and social sciences, was able to keep audiences spellbound at the universities of Berlin and Cambridge, which conferred on him the title of Doctor *honoris causa,* while the French Institute of Moral and Political Sciences elected him a corresponding member. Pareto recognized that the public attentions showered on Roosevelt were to a certain extent logical actions, in the sense that they were intended to obtain favors from him, but they were anchored in "the feeling also that a man who is competent in one thing is competent in everything." Since Pareto's days this phenomenon has come to be known as the "halo effect," and considerations of it produce no particular cries of anti-intellectualism. In Pareto's sociology, the phenomenon is classified among the derivations of "authority."

We must, therefore, conclude that Pareto was not at all an anti-intellectualist in the derogatory sense in which this term is most frequently used. There is, however, one respect in which Pareto may properly be judged an anti-intellectualist, but this is a methodological question that should excite no strong reaction on the part of his critics. As Parsons has fittingly noted, the problem again arises because of Pareto's particular position on the distinction between logical and nonlogical action. Setting out from the vantage point of the methodology of positive science, Pareto argues that "theories" accompanying logical action can be understood in their own terms. That is, a theory in this context is a scientifically verifiable explanation of the actions to which it refers. Such is not the case with theories that are grounded in nonlogical action. Here Pareto has found it necessary to introduce the notion of "state of mind," which is the real independent factor in the theory, and which must be clearly distinguished from the theory as a *manifestation* of the state of mind. This is to say that the explanation of the theory must be sought by reference not to it as an intellectual product but to the "psychic state," the pre-intellectual and amotivational state of the individual who advances the theory. In effect, what we have here is a crude typology of theories into what we might call "intellectual" ones, being those which are of a logico-experimental character, and "pre-intellectual" ones (though not anti-intellectual) referring to those that are of a sentimental nature. Pareto may be judged an anti-intellectualist only in the sense that he focused on "pre-intellectual" as well as "intellectual" theories.

THE USE OF FORCE IN SOCIETY

Perhaps the most frequent, and at the same time the least justifiable, criticism leveled against Pareto would have us believe that Pareto "approves the forceful tactics of the conservative 'lions' who do not hesitate to use the most ruthless means to keep themselves in power." From such a position it is an easy step to say that Pareto provided the intellectual justification for the fascists, and more disastrously, for the Nazis. Thus it is, according to Zanden, that "Pareto's ideal of rule based upon force found its embodiment in the fascist regimes of Europe. . . . his glorification of force reached [its] logical culmination in Hitlerite Germany and Fascist Italy." This author then goes on to argue that

> Pareto viewed the slaughter and pillaging attendant upon revolution as a healthy phenomenon. Slaughter and robbery were perceived as "signs that those who were called upon to commit them deserved power for the good of society" and "slaughter and rapine are external symptoms indicating the advent of strong and courageous people to places formerly held by weaklings and cowards."

Unfortunately, this author is badly misinterpreting or altogether misrepresenting Pareto. In fact, Pareto did not judge "slaughter and pillaging" a "healthy phenomenon": he merely argued that such phenomena should not be judged superficially, and that the sociologist, qua analyst of what today we call the "latent functions" of social phenomena, should consider the possibility that "slaughter and pillaging" are "manifestations—as regrettable as one may wish—of sentiments, of social forces, that are very salutary." But the question of whether or not the use of such force is a healthy phenomenon is entirely problematic for Pareto, "for there is no relationship of cause and effect, *nor any close and indispensable correlation, between such outrages and social utility*"(—emphasis provided). Moreover, if such correlation exists, it can be ascertained only through a strict functional analysis. Formally speaking, the correlation exists only in those cases in which the "utility" would be a "manifest function" directly linked to an intended "state of equilibrium" in a given system. Thus, for instance,

> when a governing class divests itself too completely of the sentiments of group-persistence, it easily reaches a point where it is unfit to defend, let alone its power, what is far worse, the independence of its country. In such a case, *if the independence is to be deemed an advantage,* it must also be deemed an advantage to be rid of a class that has become incompetent to perform the functions of defence (—emphasis provided).

Rebus sic stantibus, the careful, unbiased, and dispassionate reader will notice that there is no question of Pareto's "approving" the use of the most ruthless force in society. The use of force *may* have positive functions only under special circumstances. Never, however, does Pareto take an ideological position in this respect. The closest he comes to doing so is when he considers the type of utility that may properly be called societal: specifically, when he considers the question of order and "protection of the citizen" in the society. In this connection Pareto appears to some to be arguing in favor of the type of ruling elite that is capable of using force to maintain itself in power. This is, however, a totally unwarranted interpretation of his position, for his focus is not on power maintenance per se but on social order. To be sure, power maintenance by the ruling elite is a crucial

expression of social order, but one must understand that, for Pareto the continuing maintenance of power depends also upon the circulation of the elite. For the most stable, the most effective, and the most legitimate ruling elite is that which is open and allows a free flow of talent into it from the governed masses.

That Pareto's focus is ultimately on social order and citizen protection should be readily evident; otherwise, we could not explain the fact that his strongest *theoretical* commitment to the use of force occurs when he focuses on the governed masses vis-à-vis the ruling class, a fact, incidentally, that Martindale fails entirely to understand. This fact, in turn, clarifies another that should be kept in mind; the "ultimate good" or utility—if we may speak of such—is not social order per se but rather a political and social organization in which the sentiments of the masses are properly represented. The governed class rebels—and from the viewpoint of collective utility, justifiably—when "the differences in temperament," namely sentiments and values, between itself and the ruling class, "become sufficiently great." In this sense, if it be at all necessary to have recourse to political labels to make our point, it is entirely possible to conclude that Pareto was an "apostle of political democracy" rather than a fascist ideologist.

Two critical observations remain to be made in concluding this section of our paper. First, for Vilfredo Pareto the use of force in society was an inescapable and universal datum, subject to sociological analysis like every other recurrent social phenomenon. To ask whether or not force ought to be used in a society was for him "a question that has no meaning; for force is used by those who wish to preserve certain uniformities and by those who wish to overstep them; and the violence of the ones stands in contrast and in conflict with the violence of the others." Nor indeed is it meaningful to ask whether the use of force in society is beneficial or detrimental unless such a question specifies also the particular aim that the use of force is designed to achieve. And even in such instances, it is never easy to "compute all the advantages and all the drawbacks, direct and indirect" in the society, taken as a collectivity of heterogeneous groups and individuals.

Second, in his study of order in society, Pareto, the sociological realist, sought to synthesize the two prevailing metatheories that more recently Dahrendorf has referred to as the "Utopian" or "integration" and the "Rationalist" or "coercion theory of society." As Lopreato has recently demonstrated, Pareto viewed both consensus and coercion as inseparable properties in the function of order maintenance. Pareto's synthesis of the two theories comes about in his discussion of "the use of force in society" in terms of the residues of "individual integrity" and "sociality," particularly the subresidue within the latter class referred to as the "need of uniformity." In its irreducible form, Pareto's argument is as follows. The need of uniformity is not equally strong in all members of a society, for societies are "heterogeneous affairs." This differential potency of the sentiments of uniformity will result in a "number of centers of similarity." But for purposes of facilitating the analysis, Pareto reduces these into "two theologies," "one of which will glorify the immobility of one or another uniformity, real or imaginary, the other of which will glorify movement, progress, in one direction or another." The result is potential, and oftentimes real, conflict between the different "sets," the one trying to extend its own particular uniformity to the other. This tendency to impose conformity is, in turn, related to the class of residues that Pareto discusses under the name of "integrity of the individual and his appurtenances." Specifically, Pareto argues that when a person departs from the common standards, his conduct seems to jar and produces a sense of discomfort in the persons associated with him. As a consequence, "an effort is made to eliminate the jar, now by persuasion, more often by censure, more often still by force."

In conclusion, the basic forces of integration and consensus are also the ultimate causes of conflict and coercion. Indeed, as Lopreato has stated in an analogous context, there is a reciprocal relationship between consensus and coercion that might be expressed in the following terms: just as the requirement of uniformity (and thus consensus) is the ultimate cause of coercion, so the use of force is, in some unspecified degree and for an unspecified period of time, also the cause of consensus; for coercion, as a response to the need of uniformity, tends to strengthen conformity and, therefore, integration and consensus in society.

PARETO AND DEMOCRACY

Before turning to the next and final topic of this paper, in order to more directly answer the question of whether or not Pareto was a fascist, it will be useful to present Pareto's position with respect to "democracy," for it is indubitable that whatever ideological charges are made against him are linked to certain arguments that Pareto wove around this political phenomenon. It has been argued that "Pareto's sociology is first and foremost a violent manifesto against democracy; and assertions as to its scientific character change nothing in that respect."

Pareto was indeed critical of "democracy," but most decidedly he was *not against* democracy. The problem of interpretation here arises from the fact that while Pareto was concerned with "discovering the substance underlying outward forms," some of his readers have accepted as a definition of democracy that given to it by polities calling themselves democratic. This is to say that, while Pareto operated on the basis of an ideal type of democracy and sought to point out how far actual "democratic systems" depart from that type, those who would accuse Pareto of "totalitarianism" insist on defining democracy with reference to actual "democracies," dear perhaps to their own little hearts.

In discussing "government and its forms," Pareto raises the old question, "What is the best form of government?"

and argues, in a manner reminiscent of many contemporary "liberals," that such a question "has little or no meaning unless the society to which the government is to be applied is specified and unless some explanation is given of the term 'best,' which alludes in a very indefinite way to the various individual and social utilities." Unless specifications of this sort are clearly made, statements about the best form of government as well as the relative worth of various political doctrines, "religions," or "faiths," "have not the slightest experimental validity," although this does not "in any way impugn the utility to society with which [they] may be credited."

But what is the exact meaning of the term "democracy"? Pareto asks. In view of its vagueness, let us turn to the facts that it covers. One observes at the outset a pronounced tendency on the part of modern countries to organize governmental forms in which (1) "legislative power rests largely with an assembly elected by a part at least of the citizens," and (2) a tendency predominates "to augment that power and increase the number of citizens electing the assembly." By way of exception, there are also cases in which the legislative powers of the elective assemblies tend to be limited. Such, for instance, is the function of the popular referendum in Switzerland and the federal courts and the presidency in the United States, so that "the power of the legislative assembly varies all the way from a maximum to a minimum." But when all considerations are made, and

> Ignoring exceptions, which are few in number and of short duration, one finds everywhere a governing class of relatively few individuals that keeps itself in power partly by force and partly by consensus of the subject class, which is much more populous. The differences lie principally, as regards substance, in the relative proportions of force and consent; and as regards forms, in the manners in which the force is used and the consent obtained.

Indeed, whatever the form of government, the rulers are inclined to use their power "to keep themselves in the saddle, and to abuse it to secure personal gains and advantages." Moreover, "behind the scenes" there are always people, invariably "at their tenacious, patient, never-ending work," who play a very important role in actual government. "King Demos, good soul, thinks he is following his own devices," but from the days of Aristotle down to our own, he has always been effectively "bamboozled."

In view of these arguments, a careful examination of Pareto's thought will reveal that his attacks—if such they were—were directed only against a particular form of democracy. His position in this respect is analogous to his position on "science," which more often than not refers only to a mixture of magico-religious practices, often engaged in to "exploit the poor in spirit under the kindly eye of the legislator." The superficial reader might, then, infer that Pareto, "the scientific fanatic," also had a peculiar aversion to science! The truth is that Pareto's "aversion" to "democracy" was based on the conviction that "democracy" hides despotism under policies and acts of fraudulence and deception. But does this mean that Pareto was against democracy in principle? The answer is forthright and unambiguous. In a moment of enthusiasm, Pareto did set forth, in a footnote, a value judgment which revealed his personal preference concerning political systems, but which has remained strangely unnoticed by those who would have us believe that he was antidemocratic. It is difficult to imagine a "fascist sympathizer" writing this:

> The best government now in existence, and also better than countless others that have so far been observable in history, is the government of Switzerland, especially in the forms it takes on in the small cantons—forms of direct democracy. It is a democratic government, but it has nothing but the name in common with the governments, also called democratic, of other countries such as France or the United States.

Now the serious scholar may, of course, disagree with Pareto's analysis of democracy, but it is difficult to find anywhere in Pareto's work "a violent manifesto against democracy."

PARETO AND THE FASCIST PARTY

Let us now conclude by raising an historical question. Pareto lived scarcely ten months after fascism came to power in Italy. Did he, during this period, say or do anything that justifies the label of "fascist" frequently pinned upon him?

Surveying the literature on Pareto, we find that, in the concrete, his reputation as a fascist rests largely on the fact that early in 1923 he was appointed to the Italian senate. Typically, it is maintained that "in accepting the honor [of senator], Pareto showed himself not averse to the fact that this doctrine provided the perfect intellectual justification for Fascism." But on what grounds would we be justified in condemning Pareto, or any other scholar, for lending his services (if this had been the case) to a government in the very period of its birth? Have students of political phenomena achieved the level of theoretical development that will permit them to predict the future behavior of newly arisen political leaders as well as the direction of the government they represent? How many present-day "liberals," we must ask, would have made common cause with the Bolsheviks against the "tyranny" of the Russian Czars.

Any scholar familiar with Italian history must know that the Fascist regime, whatever its later development, was constituted within a context of political chaos. Pareto, or any one else, could have had no way of assessing the political worth of a Mussolini, then a moderate Socialist, other than on the basis that, for the moment at least, he provided a degree of social order and political rationality for his country. When a governing class is incapable of providing its citizens with the protection that it was allegedly organized to give, the plain probability is that any

new governing class will constitute an improvement. Yet it is of the utmost importance to remember that for Pareto the greater utility of the new class would not last forever. Eventually, this class too would be corrupted, would lose its utility, and would consequently give way to still another class, which in turn would do likewise. Indeed, the victory of Italian fascism in 1922 constituted for Pareto a validation of his theory of elite circulation and, what is better still, the expression of a theoretical prediction come true. Writing to his friend Pantaleoni, on August 11, 1922, Pareto could say:

> When I was writing the *Treatise,* no one foresaw Fascism; and yet I demonstrated how a historical uniformity [law] has it that, when a government neglects the protection of the citizenry, private forces emerge and take over. Was I not right?

Indeed, the failure of the pre-fascist ruling class in Italy seemed so evident to Pareto that he was convinced that ten men of courage could at any time march on Rome and put to rout the clique of "speculators" that were filling their pockets and leading the collectivity to economic and political disaster. When, therefore, the "March on Rome" was smoothly consummated, Pareto was able, as Livingston correctly points out, to "rise from a sick-bed and utter a triumphant 'I told you so!'—the bitter exultance of the justified prophet, not the assertion, and by far, of a wish."

But let us now consider the circumstances under which Pareto became a "Fascist" senator. One could hardly say that these included genuine sympathy for Mussolini and his party. On June 17, 1921, Pareto had written to Pantaleoni:

> I am pleased to learn that your great trust in the Fascists has now abated. Try to understand that, as I have always told you, they will not be a party till they have an ideal, a myth, a program. . . . As to Mussolino [spelling intended to recall the Calabrian brigand to mind], remember what I said when you were last here. . . . He is a busybody.

Just the same, considering the existing alternatives, Mussolini appeared to Pareto to be "a statesman of more than common merit," but he did wonder if Mussolini would succeed in "getting rid of the rubbish of his followers." Furthermore, Pareto, the eternal skeptic, argued that "economic and financial problems are not solved with hymns and cries of 'Long Live Italy' [*Viva l'Italia!*]."

The plain fact is that neither Mussolini nor fascism received Pareto's favor. Pareto had little or no faith in politicians and parties of any kind. In being approached with political honors, time and again he expressed a desire to be left alone to his studies. Mussolini, however, was not a man to be refused. His insistence on this score can be best illustrated by reference to a letter by Pantaleoni, in which this scholar writes to Pareto, "Mussolini is obsessed with the idea of our being senators, together with Corradini, Martini, and the Bishop of Trento. But can you not see the black balls? . . . Tell me, whom have we not attacked?"

At the time of his death, Pareto had indeed accepted a *royal* appointment to the Italian senate, but the senatorship was bestowed upon him with an insistence and a perseverance that defied any protestation on his part. When the official channels came to naught, Mussolini was clever enough to turn to more informal and disarming techniques by approaching Pareto through the agency of dear and trusted friends. Eventually he gave in, but it is important to know his reasons. Writing to Pantaleoni on December 23, 1922, Pareto stated:

> . . . you must know that time and again I begged them ["the friends"] to drop the whole matter [of his appointment to the senatorship]. They may have believed that my refusal was one of those that are not truly intended. Please tell them that on the contrary it is genuine, sincere, and represents my deepest intention. [Finally] I said that I would accept a purely honorary appointment, without stipend (about this I am inflexible). The idea of a Fiuman senator [strictly speaking, Pareto was not an Italian] who lives in Céligny is ridiculous, but it is not ridiculous for a scholar—whatever his nationality or residence—to do whatever he can for a country.

What conclusions can be drawn from all this? Pareto accepted the principle that a scholar should render a service to the collectivity, and he was fully aware that Italy could use such service; but he knew full well that he would not render it. He was a sick man and had no intention of leaving his beloved Switzerland. Furthermore, he had deep misgivings about the possibility of ever leading a peaceful and comfortable life in Italy. Writing to Pantaleoni on May 22, 1921, he had complained thus:

> If I returned to Italy, I should be compelled to go hunting grasshoppers for a living. . . . And then I fear that my cats would incur the hatred of union leaders, or of the Fascists, and would be killed like vile human beings. But tell me: do you not see in the newspapers that there is not a day without murders and woundings? In Switzerland, one does not see such things.

Considering "Senator" Pareto a fascist without considering the circumstances and the time of his appointment would seem to amount to the kind of "mud-slinging" that social scientists should be particularly diligent to avoid. Beyond this, there is still an important question to be answered, one which further reveals the injustice and the uncritical character of Pareto's critics. Let us take his senatorship as given and examine the advice and warnings Pareto gave to the fascist regime.

We find immediately an incessant, relentless insistence on those very aspects which democratic governments purport to foster, and which the fascist regime went on to

utterly neglect. In numerous newspaper articles, interviews, and letters Pareto fought for freedom of speech, restrictions on the use of force, freedom of coalition, and the abolition of racial prejudice. Thus, in the very letter in which he explains to Pantaleoni his reluctant acceptance of the "honorific title," he writes:

> In Italy one can already see signs—albeit very slight—of a future less good than what could be hoped for. The danger of the use of force consists in slipping into abuse. . . . It would be especially unfortunate to limit freedom of thought, even if factious! Let the government of Napoleon III and innumerable similar cases be a lesson.

On May 17, 1923, Pareto warns that "To govern is the art of acting on the basis of prevailing sentiments." In July, 1923, while admitting the apparent benefits of fascism at the time, he warns against the "abuse of force," "oppressive and arbitrary actions," restrictions on "freedom of the press" and "foreign adventures." On January 10, 1923, he had added to these the warning against restrictions on "economic syndicalism."

Concerning the question of "foreign adventures," already in the *Treatise*, Pareto had isolated "appeals to patriotism" as a cause of war. Furthermore, he had made a statement, concerning European colonialism, that could hardly be pleasing to Mussolini, or distasteful to his critics, if they had bothered to read it. Pareto wrote:

> . . . if an Englishman, a German, a Frenchman, a Belgian, an Italian, fights and dies for his country, he is a hero; but if an African dares defend his homeland against any one of those nations, he is a contemptible rebel and traitor. So the Europeans are performing a sacrosanct duty in exterminating Africans in an effort to teach them to be civilized. . . . With a hypocrisy truly admirable, these blessed civilized peoples claim to be acting for the good of their subject races in oppressing and exterminating them, indeed so dearly do they love them that they would have them "free" by force.

And what about the question of racial prejudice? Here is an interesting example of Pareto's intellectual sanity, his deep sense of justice, his boundless objectivity. Having received from Pantaleoni an antisemitic book, he writes to his friend on May 22, 1921:

> Have you become antisemitic? Once, if I do not err, you were Dreyfusard. There are those who accuse the Jews of all manner of evils; others so accuse the Masons, still others accuse the clericals (once they were called Jesuits), or the militarists, the Socialists, the reactionaries, and so forth. The only truth in all this is that men are inclined to form cliques in order to seek an advantage at the expense of others.

Pareto never compromised with the facts, as he saw them, even at the cost of chastising in a superior and condescending way his very best friend. And he saw the facts as a detached, objective, skeptic thinker.

CONCLUSION

It should by now be clear that no political label for Vilfredo Pareto would have a valid basis. The social phenomena that attracted his attention were analyzed sociologically rather than ideologically. As James Burnham, once a student of Marx, has rightly and dispassionately observed, Pareto tried "merely to describe what society is like, and to discover some of the general laws in terms of which society operates." The advancing of knowledge without consideration of its consequences is a methodological view intrinsic to the institution of science in general. Students of social phenomena may disagree with this scientific ethos, but it behooves them not to chastise Pareto for political views he never held, or for political actions which he himself would never have condoned.

To ignore or condemn Pareto is convenient, but it is also naive and irresponsible. We hold that this would be true even if Pareto could indeed be considered, in some degree, an ideologist. To accept Pareto *spiritu et corde* would be scientifically fruitless and dangerous, but no serious scientist can ignore or condemn one of his kind because he does not approve of his political attitude or some aspects of his theories. Yet—we emphatically reiterate this point—Pareto's political attitudes cannot be reprehensible simply because, as a sociologist, he expressed none. His dispassionate analysis may have been misinterpreted, but as Sidney Hook, himself hardly a fascist, has aptly stated,

> Many of Pareto's doctrines [could not] be defended in Italy or Germany without bringing their professors into concentration camps. No matter how many honors Mussolini may have heaped upon Pareto in *absentia,* any talk about Pareto being the ideologist or prophetic apologist of fascism is sheer poppycock.

R. Cirillo   (essay date 1979)

SOURCE: "Vilfredo Pareto: His Life and His Economic Theories," in *The Economics of Vilfredo Pareto,* Frank Cass, 1979, pp. 7-25.

[*In the following excerpt, Cirillo provides a biographical and historical perspective for an examination of Pareto's economic writings.*]

THE MAN

Vilfredo Pareto was born in Paris on July 15, 1848 and died at Céligny, in the Canton of Geneva, on August 19, 1923. His family belonged to the Genoese nobility which governed the Republic till it was conquered by Napoleon. His father, Marchese Raffaele Pareto, typical of the youth of the Italian Risorgimento of the first half of the nineteenth century, was involved in a Mazzinian conspiracy, and at the age of twenty-four as a result was forced to leave Italy and live in Paris. Here he took a job as a civil engineer and married Marie Metenier who bore him two daughters and one son, Vilfredo. One of the daughters, Cristina, died in 1893 of meningitis; the other, Nina, died of heart disease in 1906.

Due to a political change and also because of his proficiency in hydraulics, the Marchese Pareto was recalled to Italy. A few years later Pareto took a five year course in civil engineering at the University and the Polytechnical Institute of Turin and the first two years were mostly devoted to mathematics. This training was to serve him exceedingly well when he later undertook to work out his economic theories. The thesis for which he received a doctor's degree was a study of the fundamental principles of equilibrium in solid bodies. This was a treatise in mechanical equilibrium, but it also proved later to be the cornerstone of his fundamental conception of economics, and of his sociology as well. It seems that it was also at this time that he acquired a prodigious knowledge of Greek and Latin culture. He showed an even stronger passion for Greek as his footnotes to the *Cours* and *Il trattato* testify.

Soon after he graduated, he accepted the post of railway engineer with a company in Rome. Later he became manager general of an iron-works enterprise, the *Ferriere Italiane,* which the Banca Generale had under its control in the Val d'Arno. After his father's death in 1882, Pareto relinquished his last job and became a consultant. In 1889 he married a girl from Venice, Alessandrina (Dina) Bakounine, daughter of a modest Russian family. She was quite an educated girl and knew German and English well; she even translated an article written by her husband into English.

From the start of his public life, Pareto manifested strong liberal feelings. He believed not only in economic liberalism, which was evident in his many writings advocating free trade, but also in other tenets of liberalism, such as the freedom of the press, universal suffrage and free primary education for all. He intervened frequently to voice these feelings in the meetings of the Georgophiles and the Adam Smith Society. There is enough evidence to show that till the end of the 19th century he was a great supporter of the opponents of the doctrine of the supremacy of the state (*l'étatisme*) which was prevalent in Italy during the last quarter of the nineteenth century. A self-confessed unbeliever throughout his life, Pareto embraced liberalism as a sort of religion and worshipped G. de Molinari as one of his gods. But he was also a humanist and a very active pacifist.

1876 was a turning point in the political history of Italy. The leftist party managed to overcome the rightists and drive them out of power which they had enjoyed for a long time. Many of the reforms of the new government (such as universal suffrage and free primary education) satisfied his aspirations; but after a wave of enthusiasm he soon became disenchanted with the party, mainly because the party chiefs, Depretis and Crispi, showed lack of principle and were in fact plain opportunists.

The party embarked on a policy of protectionism which resulted in various tariff wars with France. Pareto attacked this policy severely in the *Giornale degli Economisti* and the *Monde Economique* of Paris.

As years went by he got more and more involved in politics, so much so that in 1882 he presented himself as candidate for parliament, but suffered a crushing defeat. From that time he was not sure any more that the people knew best!

His lack of popularity in government circles became more evident in 1891 when the police stopped him from giving some public talks in Milan. As a result his disenchantment with Italian politics became stronger. He could accept many of the socialist ideas, but could not favour any form of intervention on the part of the state which he believed could be advantageous only to the bourgeoisie. In an article entitled **'Parliamentary Regime in Italy'** which appeared in 1893 in the *Political Science Quarterly* he complained: '. . . there is no true political party in this country but groups of people without convictions'.

Already at the time of the Milan incident he was contemplating leaving Italy for good. His frustration was complete. In that same year he wrote to Léon Walras: 'I wanted to give without remuneration a course in mathematical economics, but the government opposed it'.

This was the political Pareto, but what sort of man was the *real* Pareto during this period? He was definitely a man of contradictions. He remained essentially an aristocrat, even though his views on democracy, free trade and republicanism did not agree with those of the nobility. He even despised the aristocratic class for exploiting the poor. But he could not digest socialism either. He despised the socialists as well, yet he sympathized with the persecuted socialists, in the same fashion as when in spite of his anticlericalism he always defended the clergy and the Church when they were seriously attacked. He was essentially a social misfit; some even considered him a misanthropist. He isolated himself first from the aristocratic classes and then from the masses.

One of Pareto's most admirable qualities was that he could not stand corruption and incompetence, and he became involved in politics precisely because he thought that his intervention could help to lessen corruption in Italian political life. When he failed, he became disenchanted with parliamentary democracy and became adverse to any form of interference on the part of the government. His opposition stemmed mainly from his liberal philosophy though later on in his life he modified his views. But Pareto's laisser-faire type of liberalism was political rather than economic even though he tried to justify it on economic grounds. His was certainly different from the economic liberalism of his English contemporaries even though he thought otherwise. To voice adequately his philosophy he became an active member of the Adam Smith Society of Ferrara which fought

against protective tariffs. It was also at this time that he took charge of the monthly publication called *Cronache Italiane*.

Between 1889 and 1893 he wrote about 167 articles, some of a scholarly nature but largely consisting of anti-government polemics. Though this made him unpopular in government circles, it also brought him friends from the circle of free trade writers. Among these was Maffeo Pantaleoni who became his life-long friend. It was after reading Pantaleoni's *Elementi di economia pura* that Pareto became interested in pure economics. And it was Pantaleoni who insisted that he contact Walras.

Léon Walras (1834-1910) was French and an engineer like Pareto, though his engineering career was mediocre. In 1870 Walras was appointed to the chair of economics in the Academy, known later as the University of Lausanne. His first ideas about general economic equilibrium go back to 1874 but, for about thirty years, his work, particularly in France, was largely ignored. Pareto was the first economist to appreciate Walras's outstanding pioneering contribution to economic thought. Walras was mainly concerned with social reform and economic theory was simply a tool for this end. At one time he even advocated land nationalization on the lines of Henry George. His enthusiasm for social reforms and peace even earned him a nomination for the Nobel prize for peace.

His contacts with Walras aroused a genuine interest in him for the mathematical treatment of the equilibrium system already developed by his predecessor, and stimulated him to make the first real contribution to economic theory.

Though Pareto appears for the first time as an economist at the age of fifty, we must recall that for many years he was working as an engineer and during this time he was solving many practical problems and digesting techniques which he later embodied in economic thought. His case, in fact, is not dissimilar from that of David Ricardo who went to economics after years of experience in the London Stock Exchange.

Pareto's first letter to Léon Walras was written on July 23, 1891. It seems that Walras was much impressed by the potentialities of the younger man, for on November 7, 1892 he offered to recommend him for the Chair of Economics which he was about to relinquish. In 1893 Pareto was officially approached by the University of Lausanne and was offered the Chair, which he accepted after some anxious days when he seriously feared that by going to Lausanne without the permission of the Italian government he might lose his Italian nationality. But, as a matter of fact, he managed to keep it till the end of his life.

To the teaching of political economy he soon added a course in sociology. This was his most fruitful period. It was in Switzerland that he published his four major works that were to establish his reputation:

Cours d'économie politique in two volumes (1896, 1897). This included most of the lectures he delivered during his first years at Lausanne. Next he published *Les systèmes socialistes* (1902); *Manuale d'economia politica* (1907), more commonly known as the *Manuel* after the French edition in 1909; and *Il trattato di sociologia generale* (1915), later translated into French and called *Traité de sociologie générale* (1917).

He worked intensely, so much so that his first wife complained on various occasions that she had 'to meow with the cats being unable to chat with her too busy husband'. Though he was a good teacher, he was more concerned with research. 'Lecturing is a wasted time for science', he complained to Pantaleoni. The fact that he found out that the students were not interested in mathematical economics did not help his urge for lecturing. In fact, everyone, including Walras, urged him to put as little mathematics as possible in his course—advice he accepted readily.

Because of his heart condition, he was already planning to retire in 1900. An unexpected event was also influencing his decision by then for in 1898 his uncle Dominique died and left him a considerable fortune. He became a rich man overnight. Unfortunately he invested most of this fortune in gold bought from the Bank of England. He lost most of this during the first World War when gold was requisitioned, and also because he made some bad investments. But he lived in luxury for quite some time with a big retinue of servants.

Meanwhile in 1901 his wife Dina ran away with the cook and went to Russia. She refused to join him in Paris where he went to give some important lectures. This made him so furious that he took immediate steps for a legal separation. Within a short time of his separation from Dina (she died in 1940) another woman came into his life who was to become his second wife—a French girl called Jeanine Regis (Jane, as he used to call her). She was 31 years his junior, but she managed to give him much more than his first wife. If there was not much love between them there was certainly companionship and understanding. Pareto, in fact, dedicated the *Trattato* to her.

Because of his Italian nationality he could not obtain a divorce from Dina. However, much later the Italian city of Fiume, which belonged to Hungary (a country which had divorce laws), became independent for a short time, thanks to Gabriele D'Annunzio, the poet-soldier, and many Italians took advantage of the situation to obtain a divorce; so did Pareto. Thus, a few days before he died, on June 19, 1923, Pareto legally married Jane.

It was around 1900 that a change in Pareto took place. From that time he became more interested in mathematical economics and pure theory and less interested in reforms, much to the disappointment of Léon Walras. He stopped being a fervent supporter of free competition and started modifying his opinion of protection. He also became more and more the hermit of Céligny. Though he decided to give up lecturing in 1906, he continued to give courses from time to time, and it was in May, 1916 that he gave a last series of lectures on sociology. Yet this was the period during which he reached the peak of his intellectual activity.

In the last years of his life he was a bitter man. He resented particularly the treatment he received from his country. In 1906 he was asked to teach a course in sociology for a few weeks at the University of Bologna—a gesture which pleased him immensely. He was looking forward to being offered a professorship at that time but when the offer came he was too sick to accept it.

During the last six years of his life he hardly left the villa because of his heart ailment. His only joy was his cats which numbered a score at one time. They had precedence over anyone else and were given food before his visitors. His irony and sarcasm, which alienated many of his friends, became more pronounced as is evident from his later writings. One can say that his life was over even before his death. 'I want to follow events without wishing to take the least part in them', was one of the last statements he made to Pantaleoni.

Pareto and Fascism

During the crucial period 1914-1922 Pareto witnessed the social and political disorganization of Italy with dismay, and once more he became involved in politics. When fascism triumphed in Italy, Mussolini made him, together with Maffeo Pantaleoni, who was definitely a fascist, one of the first senators of Italy. Much has been written on what sort of a 'fascist' Pareto was, if he ever was one.

It seems that he underwent a change in his feelings towards fascism. Before it came to power, he was sceptical as to its purpose, and even more so as to its ability to create the kind of Italy he dreamed of. Thus, in a letter to Giacalone Monaco (June, 1921) he wrote: 'I may be wrong, but I don't see in fascism a permanent and profound force'.

When fascism gained power he seemed to be more favourable towards it but he kept insisting that the fundamental freedoms be safeguarded and warned the fascist hierarchy not to enter into an alliance with the Church. One cannot help recalling that when fascism triumphed in Italy, Pareto had only ten months to live. It must have seemed to him, after a life-time of disappointment with the politics of his country, that a sort of messianic revolution was taking place. But anyone who knew Pareto well would have bet that later, when fascism became as corrupt and despotic as the previous regimes, he would have attacked it as bitterly as he attacked the previous parties and governments.

There is no doubt that the new fascist government regarded with sympathy the man whose sociological theories could be interpreted as favouring the new doctrine.

In December, 1922 Pareto was asked to represent Italy on the Commission of Disarmament at the League of Nations in Geneva. He had to decline for health reasons. But when in March, 1923 he was named senator, he accepted.

THE ECONOMIST

One cannot really understand adequately a thinker of the calibre of Pareto without some knowledge of the intellectual climate in which he lived. I am here limiting myself to the more relevant characteristics of his times and the conditions under which his thought was developing.

By the second half of the nineteenth century most of Europe had already entered an advanced stage of industrialization. Admittedly progress was uneven and some countries, particularly Britain and France, were ahead of other countries not only industrially but economically and politically as well. No country, however, was immune to the challenge of the new age. The new techniques and innovations were having a lasting effect not just on the political structure of Europe, but also on every aspect of its cultural and social life as well. Hence, the social disciplines, particularly social philosophy, sociology and economics were sensitive to the radical changes that were taking place. At the same time they were facing the supreme challenge in that in a predominantly scientific age they could not survive if they failed to become true sciences.

It was during this period that Pareto was actively engaged in his economic studies which lasted till 1912, when he turned to sociological research. This was also the time when the theories of the Classical School were being constantly attacked by the adherents of Marxism as well as by the members of the German Historical School. Defending the Classicists were the English and French liberal economists. But most of the arguments advanced on both sides were basically ethical in nature. Hence, there was no way of defending economics on its own grounds.

Pareto, who started his career as a champion of a laissez-faire type of liberalism, soon realized that political economy as it was then with all its ethical connotations, could not command respectability, much less win the argument against the Marxists. He became fully aware of the paramount need to establish ethical neutrality in the social disciplines for without it there was no chance of their ever being accepted as sciences. To achieve this the scope of economics and sociology needed to be clearly defined. There was much sociology that was being labelled economics and vice versa. By defining the respective fields of the two disciplines and clearly marking their boundaries, they could be set on the way to the progress which so far had been denied them. Beside these considerations, Pareto's mind was preoccupied with the significance of empirical research and the impact it could have on theory.

These were the preoccupations that engaged his mind, and by the time he was writing the *Manuel* he felt confident enough to advance solutions to the problems which were troubling him. Even if his efforts were not as successful as he thought, Pareto should earn the admiration if not the gratitude at least of those who appreciate the efforts of his contemporaries, such as the Austrian economists, and Jevons, Marshall, Wicksteed, Edgeworth and Wicksell.

When he started corresponding with Maffeo Pantaleoni at the age of 42 he was already familiar with the works of Cournot, Walras and Marshall. He had a long way to go before he wrote the *Manuel,* but by the time he came to write it his break with the past was complete. By then he had rejected the marginal utility theories of Walras, Menger and Jevons and at the same time became an ardent proponent of ethical neutrality. In the process he also turned his back on the English economists with their emphasis on partial equilibrium analysis and developed the theory of general economic equilibrium of his predecessor.

Pareto's contributions to economics are numerous and varied, but they are also of uneven quality. Nevertheless they all reflect not only his mind but his personality as well. They are striking in many respects, so much so that, unlike Léon Walras, he managed to form a school of devoted disciples and followers.

One or two qualities he possessed could throw some light on the inconsistencies and contradictions which sometimes are evident in his thought to the dismay of his admirers and students alike. One such quality, which made him unpopular in his life and sometimes affected his scientific outlook, was that he could not stand adverse criticism. He resented intensely his critics and this led him to despise their works irrespective of their merits. The only exception he made was in the case of Léon Walras, whose basic theories at least he continued to admire even when he stopped admiring the man because of his approach to applied economics and his socialistic tendencies. But he had little sympathy for either Marshall, Edgeworth or Fisher.

His attitude towards Alfred Marshall was typical. He never appreciated Marshall's use of partial equilibrium analysis. Thus he expressed his feelings: 'Marshall has not yet managed to grasp the idea of economic equilibrium . . . He adds nothing remarkable to our knowledge'. On another occasion he wrote: 'But I must say that the English proposition of the constant utility of money is asinine. . . . I keep on saying that the theories of the classical economists are better than those of Marshall with their mathematical frills'.

One wonders how Pareto could be not only ungenerous but also ignorant of such important contributions as Marshall's. The true reason can only be found in his impetuous passionate character which at times blinded his deep sense of perception and appreciation and made him fall into all sorts of contradictions. In the case of Marshall this contradiction is evident when one compares the above utterances to what he wrote one day about Walras:

> He (Walras) insists at length on the points separating him from Aupitz and Lieben, because, according to him one must take account of the prices of all goods. In theory he is right, but in practice it would no longer be possible to solve a single problem.

It is hard to believe that Pareto could not sense that this was the best defence he could make for Marshallian analysis. It seems that by the time he was criticizing Walras, his mind had no place for Marshall or anyone else!

Sometimes his hostility for an economist grew progressively so that he became more and more suspicious that the latter was his declared or undeclared enemy. This is what happened in the case of Edgeworth. First, he resented Edgeworth because he ignored him; later, when he criticized him Pareto became furious and called him 'a real Jesuit [who] could only show how to solve the equations of exchange. These are the only ones he knows'. Ironically this happened to be the man from whom Pareto borrowed so much for his theory of utility!

He was also obsessed with the ignorance not only of people in general, but in particular with that displayed by his contemporary economists. This made him at one time doubt whether economic science should be taught at all!

It might be interesting to answer the question why Pareto, who made few original contributions to economic theory, should have left such a mark on economic thought. I think the secret of Pareto's greatness lies in the fact that he had such a wide vision of social life and society. His interest in economics was never exclusive; his works on sociology are ample evidence of this vision. Even his obsession with general equilibrium was derived from his determination to use it as a tool of analysis to be applied not just to economics but all the other social sciences as well. He was convinced that society encountered so many problems and with such frequency because it swerved very often from positions of stable equilibrium. To Pareto these problems involved and affected not only the 'homo oeconomicus' but also the 'homo politicus, religiosus, ethicus'.

Another reason for his distinction in the history of thought is that Pareto was, as has been rightly called, a competent artisan. He knew which tools to borrow from other economists and handled them extremely well. When in the process he discovered new ideas he worked on them and managed to produce new techniques. Moreover, Pareto always looked and thought beyond his immediate task. Unfortunately his wealth of ideas sometimes prevented him from developing the more promising ones. Thus, some ideas remained in an embryonic state only to be discovered from time to time in his rather obscurer statements.

THE *COURS* AND THE *MANUEL*

Pareto was not satisfied with his first major work, *Cours d'économie politique*. As a matter of fact, he never agreed to see it reprinted because he intended to make some important changes in it. It seems that when the *Manuel* was published he was satisfied that it had replaced the *Cours*. In the 'proemio' to the *Manuel* he did criticize the *Cours,* particularly for 'some subjective considerations' which he made in it, and also because he had professed too much faith in economic freedom.

It is strange that Bousquet, his biographer, thinks that the *Cours* looks mainly to the future, and that it is such a contribution to economics that this work alone 'could have been sufficient to make Pareto a great economist'. This opinion is not at all shared by other scholars. There is, of course, agreement that in the *Cours* Pareto gives a much clearer version of Walras's theory, the exposition of which in the *Eléments* Bousquet describes as 'detestable, tedious, prolix and such that it turns away men of good will'. No doubt Pareto had the advantage of explaining the theory to his students and in the process he rendered it more intelligible.

Yet, on the whole the *Cours* makes little contribution to economic theory. Out of about 800 pages not more than 75 are concerned with pure theory. The presentation is chaotic; for example, it is hard to understand why production is treated after banking and social evolution. There are also some blaring contradictions—the more serious being that, while Pareto expresses himself strongly in favour of a positive theory, the work abounds with normative statements. Also, no one has so far given a satisfactory explanation as to why he calls the second part 'applied economics'.

There are, of course, positive elements in the *Cours*. In it he already visualizes general equilibrium as the result of the interdependence of all the economic elements within the system. Consequently, he emphasizes complementarity and substitution between all these elements. As in the *Manuel,* the *Cours* contains many concepts and hypotheses which are never completely worked out. Among these one comes across his theories of rent and economic crises; and in the treatment of the latter he seems to foreshadow Schumpeter.

It is in the *Cours* that Pareto introduces the 'law' of income distribution. Though it is a pioneering example of economic investigation, it is also an apologia for the inequality of wealth. He attributes this inequality strangely enough to the varying capabilities of men in society. But in the *Manuel* he qualifies this statement by pointing out that inequality is due to 'other facts which are related to these qualities' (Chap. VII, sec. 13).

Manuel

This work consists of nine chapters: the first one deals with general principles; the second is largely an introduction to sociology; chapters three to six deal with general economic equilibrium. A study on population is reserved for chapter seven; the next chapter treats of capital, whilst the last chapter is devoted to 'concrete economic phenomena' (rent, savings, international trade and economic crises). The work closes with a mathematical appendix.

Schumpeter who, unlike Bousquet and others, thought little of the *Cours,* was strongly of the opinion that Pareto made the first step that was to take him up the ladder of success in the *Sunto* (which appeared in the *Giornale* in 1900); next came the publication of a *Résumé* of a course of lectures he delivered in Paris. But 'the highest elevation in Pareto's claim to immortality' was reached in the *Manuel* in 1909, particularly because of the mathematical appendix.

The Italian original called *Manuale di economia politica* was completed in 1904. When the French translation was being prepared (1906-7) Pareto revised it and added the mathematical appendix. He also made some corrections mostly concerning the style, but left untouched the substance of the original work.

By the time he wrote the *Manuel* much change had taken place in his mind. For one thing he became a lukewarm liberal and even accepted protection under certain conditions. He also manifested a sort of neutral attitude on most social questions.

The main theme of the *Manuel* is general equilibrium—a notion he applies to almost all sections of the work including the one dealing with sociology. But while the *internal* forces within the economic system, such as individual and group interests, receive a great deal of attention, the *external* forces (such as climate and race) which are amply discussed in the *Cours,* no longer find a place in the *Manuel*. Interests, on the contrary, play a secondary and unimportant role in his sociological works because, as we shall see in the chapter on methodology, sociology, according to Pareto, should be concerned mainly with the non-rational actions of men in society.

Other important contributions in the *Manuel* consist of pioneering statements in the field of welfare, his theories of utility and production and the theory of international trade. The chapter on concrete economic phenomena is also of interest because of the attempt Pareto makes to confront real situations with the theoretical model.

There seem to be two schools of thought with regard to the merits of the *Manuel*. Those who subscribe to Pareto's ideas about economics as a positive science share the views of Schumpeter and think highly of this work. On the other hand, others such as Pirou and those economists who accept the views of the 'second' School of Lausanne, approve of it with reservations and, in some respects, believe it marks a retrograde step.

A Note on the 'Marché Financier Italien' *(1891-1899)*

This is the second volume in the *Oeuvres complètes de Vilfredo Pareto* edited by Professor G. Busino of the University of Lausanne. This volume consists of a valuable collection of articles and other minor works which Pareto published during the period 1891-1899. These contributions should help the reader to understand the *Cours* better. The matters they deal with range from money and banking to the role of savings in economic growth. But they are also invaluable for the wealth of information they contain about the economic and social life of Italy at the end of the nineteenth century. These writings help the reader to get an insight into the nature and goals of the free trade movement as well as its weakness (e.g. the anti-protectionists were few and disorganized). They also contain a detailed account of the financial events that took place in Italy during the period.

This collection throws much light on Pareto's economic thinking, particularly on the role of the banks in an expanding economy and the misuse of credit as a cause of business fluctuations.

PARETO'S MAJOR CONTRIBUTIONS TO ECONOMICS

Pareto's main contributions to economic theory consist of a novel approach to utility theory, a reformulation of general economic equilibrium theory and the laying of the foundations of modern welfare economics. To these one must add his unique pioneering work in the field of income distribution.

Utility Theory

From the very start of his career as an economist, Pareto was worried about 'this wretched utility'. He could not understand how it could ever be measured. He coined the word *ophelimité* from the Greek root 'ophelimos' with the purpose of departing completely from the traditional notion of utility. In the *Cours,* however, it was still a subjective quality of the individual consumer even though he tried hard to give to ophelimity a meaning different from the one usually implied by utility. It was a convenient way of expressing the satisfaction one derived from the use of a commodity without the need of measuring its intensity. Thus, though utility was 'utilitarian' in the Benthamite sense, ophelimity was not necessarily so.

This distinction is not perhaps substantial enough, but it is a sure indication of Pareto's intention of moving away from measurable utility. It was in the *Manuel,* however, that Pareto abandoned this concept when he made full use of Edgeworth's indifference curves, though he reversed the process in the sense that he regarded the indifference map as given, thus discarding the need of measuring utility. This process had already been used by Irving Fisher, but Pareto used it more forcefully and turned it into a more efficient tool for his own purpose.

His reaction against the marginalist theory which had dominated economic theory since 1870 was directed mainly against a trend of thought which moved farther away from production, as emphasized in Classical thought, to theories which to Pareto seemed too individualistic and gave excessive importance to consumption. Hence, in his quest to give more meaning to the theory of general equilibrium, he produced an analysis which he could apply not only to consumption but to other sectors, particularly to production, as well.

General Equilibrium Theory

There is no doubt that for his theory of general economic equilibrium Pareto owed much to Léon Walras, but he managed to refine it and bring it to a higher level of generalization. His analysis was simpler than that of Walras. By reducing all the opposite forces to the simple indices of *tastes* and *obstacles* he produced an analysis which was applicable not only to the study of economic equilibrium, but to other social equilibria as well. At first sight the analysis may appear too general to be conducive to meaningful results, but one must keep in mind that Pareto never meant to confine it only to the determination of economic equilibrium.

His method was aimed at generalizing Walras's theory and he succeeded in producing an analysis which could be applicable to the economic process not subject to an institutional constraint.

In spite of his efforts to transform the system and make it dynamic, Pareto's treatment of general economic equilibrium remained static. Sometimes he seemed to confuse comparative statics with dynamics and, in fact, the whole analysis was concerned with a succession of static states. Yet, in the **Manuel** one can discover various dynamic elements which are an essential part of the apparatus of economic models which appeared much later.

This failure on the part of Pareto was also largely the result of his conviction that social reality cannot be confined within the realms of economics alone. This point was made quite clear in the **Cours** and was emphasized in the **Traité**. In the **Manuel** he reiterated the conviction that economic theory alone could not take account of what he called the undulations of the system. Given his mind regarding the nature and role of sociology, it seems, then, that Pareto was inclined to think that economics without the help of sociology was incapable of taking into account sufficient dynamic elements to render it significant.

Pareto gave special importance to the theory of production in his system of general equilibrium and his treatment of the theory is superior to that of Walras. The indifference curve techniques which he applied to the problem of choice confronting the consumer in the theory of demand, he also applied to the same problem facing the producer. He was the first to use this approach. He also introduced variable co-efficients of production, thus making the theory more realistic, whereas Walras at first worked on the assumption that these coefficients were fixed.

In connection with his equilibrium analysis one should mention a curious attitude on the part of Pareto to mathematics. Not only was he apologetic whenever he felt the need to make use of them, such as when he introduced calculus to give more precision to his theories and analytical work, but he also expressed a strange conviction that the use of mathematics should be confined only to general equilibrium analysis. This was apparently his more mature opinion, for earlier in his correspondence with Pantaleoni he made the unconditional statement that 'sooner or later mathematics will be the basis of economics'. It seems that he took this stand at the time when he criticized Marshall for giving so much importance to partial equilibrium analysis. He found Marshall's use of mathematics as 'useless and harmful', because, to Pareto's mind, 'only the need to solve this system of equations which expresses the interdependence of the phenomena justifies the use of mathematics'.

It is, of course, not easy to read Pareto's mind on this matter, but one could venture one or two suggestions. Either his prejudice against Marshall became so strong that he sought to deprive Marshallian theory of any scientific content, even to the extent of making him look foolish for using mathematics as a scientific garb to theories 'which add very little to our knowledge'. Or he genuinely believed that only in the case of general economic equilibrium analysis, on account of the system of equations involved, did one need mathematics. According to Pareto, the use of mathematics was being confused with the use of symbols. Of one thing, however, we may rest assured: to Pareto mathematics was only *one* of the ways of ensuring the progress of political economy, but not the only way of treating the science. He was not in favour of the exclusive use of any one method and considered discussions as to which method he used, as a sheer waste of time.

Welfare Economics

If all these contributions left a mark on subsequent economic thought, in the field of welfare, Pareto was the founder of modern welfare economics. So whilst in other fields he made unique contributions to a body of thought which already existed, in welfare economy he was definitely a pioneer.

According to Pareto, for a maximum welfare position to be reached, society has to act in such a way that the ophelimity of some could not be increased to the detriment of others. Only if all the members of the community gained, could we be sure that welfare was enhanced. This optimal solution presupposes some arguable assumptions: that there should be a simultaneous achievement of both the subjective optimum and a physical optimum, that the distribution of income is ideal, that a position of equilibrium under conditions of perfect equilibrium is not only possible but a most desirable one for society, and other assumptions which we shall discuss later. But the Pareto criterion has been found quite useful in judging whether a proposed change in a policy is an improvement or not. Even some important analytical results have been achieved with the use of this criterion. Of course, it has its limitations particularly since it does not apply in the case of a policy by which some could gain and others lose.

In this regard it is interesting to note that though Pareto intended to establish a neutral standard of welfare, it became essentially a matter of value judgments with ethical overtones. Yet his approach to the theory of general welfare is essentially different from that of Edgeworth, Sidgwick, Marshall and especially Pigou who constructed a utilitarian theory which derived its inspiration from Bentham. The same was done by Walras who was concerned with 'the most equitable distribution possible of social wealth among men in society'. Pareto, on the contrary, refused to discuss redistribution of wealth and was not at all concerned about maximum satisfaction. In this respect he managed to build a collective optimum on very strong grounds.

The Pareto Law

The other pioneering work by Pareto is his 'law' of income distribution, which he discovered empirically and which, more than any other of his achievements, enhanced his reputation. Pareto argued that above a certain level, the distribution of incomes was rigid and followed a definite pattern. This implied the existence of a natural economic law according to which inequality could never be reduced simply by tampering with the distribution of incomes, but rather by making production grow faster than population. At first when he discovered the 'law' Pareto concluded that it was valid only for those countries whose data he studied; later, however, he expressed the belief that it could be applied to all countries.

This unscientific generalization was partly motivated by the fact that Pareto was delighted to have found an answer to the socialist attack on the distribution of wealth. The only hope for the working class to attain a higher standard of living and get closer to the better-off classes lay in an overall increase in production.

Though Pareto's law was subjected to much criticism and was received with scepticism by quite a few; many others found out that income data supported it. Even today from time to time one notices renewed interest in it, and in the possibilities it offers. All agree that one definite merit of the law is that it focussed the attention on minimum incomes. However, irrespective of its merits, it will always remain a unique pioneering work of econometric investigation.

Renato Cirillo (essay date 1983)

SOURCE: "Was Vilfredo Pareto Really a 'Precursor' of Fascism?," in *American Journal Of Economics and Sociology*, Vol. 42, No. 12, April, 1983, pp. 235-44.

[*In the following essay, Cirillo investigates whether or not Pareto was in fact, as is often contended, a "precursor of fascism."*]

I

INTRODUCTION

The fact that Vilfredo Pareto embraced fascism during the last months of his life generated enough prejudice against the man that even scholars sometimes approach his works with an initial bias. Readers will recall that when Arthur Livingston published the English translation of *Trattato di sociologia generale* in 1935, *The New Republic* of New York reacted predictably and *Mind and Society* languished on the bookshelves. Labelling great thinkers fascists, communists, anarchists, panacea-mongers or whatever has always had the unfortunate effect of casting doubts on the integrity and validity of their thoughts. Pareto's great predecessor at the University of Lausanne suffered from a similar fate. Léon Walras' works were ignored for quite a time, particularly by French economists, partly because he preferred to call himself socialist, even though his brand of socialism would not be acknowledged as such by any genuine Marxist socialist and was characterized by Karl Marx himself as "utopianism." Our generation knows it as libertarianism.

Few have bothered so far to put Pareto on trial and see to what extent he rightly deserved to be called fascist; whether he subscribed unconditionally to such a doctrine and system, and in particular whether his works contributed substantially, directly or indirectly, to the philosophy of fascism. I have already dealt summarily with this question in my book on Pareto, and on both counts I reached the verdict of 'not guilty'. This time, however, I intend to produce as much evidence as possible on that question and the much broader one whether Pareto was really a precursor of fascism—and thereby help the reader to reach his or her own conclusion.

II

A GREAT LIBERTARIAN

In all his writings, from his major works on economics and sociology to the many articles he contributed to the learned journals as well as those appearing in the popular press, Vilfredo Pareto manifested consistently a strong attachment to a type of liberalism not dissimilar to the one later attributed to Mises and Hayek. His liberalism was so uncompromising that for the last twenty years or so of his life he doubted whether any political system was capable of rising up to its lofty aspirations. His belief in man's freedom of thought and action, whether in the marketplace, in the press or in the university lecture halls remained unshaken till the end of his life. His economic liberalism was similar to that of the classical school; he upheld the freedom of markets, defended the merits of a free competitive system and was responsible more than any other economist for turning economics into a positive science, devoid of ethical considerations. He did this mainly by neutralizing utility theory, but he also stressed that the economist, *qua* economist, has no business to deal with the ethical and moral aspects of economic problems. However, unlike Walras, Pareto analyzed monopoly and condemned the practises of big monopolies. As a result of research he carried on in the income statistics of various countries, he concluded that any change in income distribution would increase welfare to a very small extent *unless* production would also increase at the same time. This neutral stand by Pareto in purely economic matters is nowhere more evident than in the use present-day economists have made of the Pareto optimum and the Pareto optimality conditions in modern welfare theory. The limited usefulness of this theory is due precisely to the nature of the economic principles of Pareto from which it derives. Thus, there is no doubt whatsoever that the main concern of Pareto's economics is exclusively with the *homo economicus,* even though Pareto himself never believed that that construct was realistic.

Economics was Pareto's first love for it satisfied his scientific disposition and he saw much merit in the theory of general equilibrium which became the core of his economics. But he also recognized its limitations, particularly as a guide for social policy. He hoped that sociology could provide such a guide since it was the social science eminently concerned with social relations and the interaction of people in society. In this sense he was close in spirit to another great positivist thinker, Auguste Comte. It is such concern that prompted him to build up his sociology, but unfortunately he did not come up with the answers he sought. Admittedly he introduced such notions as the predominant role of sentiments in social life, the distinction between the logical and non-logical actions, the theories of residues and the circulation of elites. These were exciting notions but their value was limited only to an *explanation* of the dynamic changes in society. Nevertheless, they established Pareto's fame as a sociologist even before he became accepted as an important economist.

III

WHAT FASCISTS THOUGHT OF HIS WORKS

It is important to recall this body of thought created by Pareto in order to judge correctly whether he was truly a precursor of fascism. It was fascist propaganda that depicted him as such, for fascism needed an intellectual of the calibre of Pareto to lend prestige and credibility to its cause. But is it fair to regard him as its precursor? The truth is that there is nothing in his writings that could even remotely make Pareto responsible for the body of doctrines that came to constitute fascism.

Some writers have suggested that the notion of the circulation of elites must have pleased Mussolini and his henchmen. But surely other leaders of whichever revolutionary movement would be equally pleased, for the no-

tion has universal application and in no way must it necessarily result in a fascist dictatorship. Nor is there any reason why the movement of elites should stop with the advent of fascism!

One could argue for a long time as to the relevance of Pareto's sociology to fascism. There are admittedly enough elements in Pareto's thoughts which, particularly if viewed separately from his particular view of society, would not be alien to the nature and spirit of fascism. I am alluding to his acceptance of the rule of force in order to displace a decadent elite, to Pareto's anti-intellectualism and particularly to his hostility to democracy, whilst championing at the same time a hierarchical State ruled by a strong elite. I will return to these elements at the end of this study. Meanwhile, I believe nothing better could settle the argument than to find out what the fascist writers themselves thought of Pareto's works. As a matter of fact, they did not think much of them and they all but condemned them.

Let us examine the evidence. A. Rocco, who was considered to be one of the principal theoreticians of fascism, revealed the stand taken by him and his associates in an interview he gave to M. Rosentock-Franck in 1924. In this interview Rocco stressed that fascism was equally opposed to both liberalism and socialism for they were in effect "the two faces of the same coin" since both had their common origin in materialism. As an example, he referred to the fact that both gave preeminence to the labor theory of value which, according to him, was imbued with the spirit of materialism. In contrast to these doctrines he exalted the corporative conscience which "was ingrained in the freedom of individuals, consciously guided by the State to serve the interests of society and the nation as a whole." In this he echoed the view of another prominent fascist writer, Gino Arias, who held that the political economy of fascism reached back to the spirit of the economy of medieval times which was based on the Thomistic doctrine of the supremacy of the common good.

It is evident that within such a philosophical context there was no place for Pareto's liberalism. This point was made quite clear by Ugo Spirito, the respected editor of the review *Nuovi Studi*. A collection of his articles was published in 1930 in three volumes. The first of these contains articles in which he attacked viciously Enrico Barone, the eminent contemporary of Pareto, for building up an economic science on the "false premise" of a free competitive economy, thus "reducing economics to an empty science." In the volume entitled *La critica dell'economia liberale* he equally criticized Pareto's economics, but used softer gloves since by that time the fascists had elevated Pareto to the honors of a patron saint of their movement. Nonetheless, Spirito had harsh words for "the theoretician of the mathematical method who succeeded no less than Barone in separating economics from the world of reality." What saved Pareto, according to Spirito, was his sociology because this gave him the opportunity of showing the complexity of social life and helped him to produce the real man, "who is by no means the *homo economicus*." This was the only concession he made in favor of Pareto because in the same breath he concluded that, in spite of his good intentions, Pareto did not succeed in building up a new sociology!

Ugo Spirito rejected wholeheartedly the distinction between the logical and non-logical actions, and the theory of residues as well. This negative attitude on the part of a convinced fascist to the theories of Pareto's sociology makes sense when one recalls what inspired Pareto in the first instance to formulate his fundamental theory. He came to the conclusion that most human activity was not the result of a rational process but rather of irrational sentiment, when he reflected on the reason why Marxism, which he considered to be a false and nefarious doctrine, managed to fire the imagination of the Italian youths. Later, with the advent of fascism Pareto could clearly see a verification of his cherished theory, but no one should expect a fascist to manifest the same enthusiasm!

There is little in Pareto's sociological works that could even remotely have been an inspiration to fascism, *even though much of his analysis could have predicted the phenomenon.* In no way therefore could Pareto, the economist and sociologist, be regarded as the precursor of fascism. Even the fascist intellectual elite never made that claim.

IV

THE POLITICAL PARETO

What remains to be seen now is whether the political Pareto ever became a true fascist. Even though he remained a fanatic libertarian to the end, his political beliefs underwent some drastic changes. When he was growing up, the climate of opinion, which influenced his thought, was conducive to a liberal utopia. There was genuine belief in human progress in all spheres of life; there was also faith in scientific positivism. It was universally held that democracy was the only system that could guarantee the basic freedoms and that it promoted pacifism and humanitarianism. It was also under democracy that free trade and a competitive market economy could be promoted and preserved. It is not surprising, then, that during his first period as a writer which ran from 1876 to 1893, Pareto adhered to such beliefs.

He also expressed strong patriotic and radical ideals. But soon he became a passionate critic of the Italian government. For two years (1896-1898) he used his monthly 'Cronache,' which were published in *Giornale degli economisti,* as a platform to attack prevalent policies such as protectionism, and excessive military expenditures; he also fought incessantly corruption in high official circles. So far he was a critic of a democratic government, but not of democracy.

By 1900, however, his views changed and from a radical democrat he turned into an anti-democrat. He finally lost hope in the democratic system and as the years went by his feelings became more hostile. His scorn for parliamentary democracy became so pervasive that his scientific works finished by mirroring these feelings. Parliamentary democracy was not a vague concept, for he was directing his attacks against the two democratic regimes with which he was most familiar, those of Italy and France. There was much intrigue and corruption in both, but what bothered him most was the 'plutocratic character' of these 'demagogic democracies.' The class in power did not change this 'character,' so much so that when the French working class got the upper hand, to Pareto it simply looked as if a bourgeois oppression was being replaced by a working class oppression.

In time his contempt for these democracies extended to all other countries which had parliamentary governments. Thus, when the first World War broke out he had no sympathy for the Allies. In a note prefacing *Mon Journal,* Giuseppe La Ferla had this to say about his feelings at that time:

> The war appeared to him, as a sordid Carthagenian war, a war of different plutocracies: on one side Germany with a plutocracy based on military power and on the other, the allies with their demagogic plutocracies.

V

PARETO'S OPPOSITION TO SOCIALISM

Pareto's opposition to socialism was equally strong. As a libertarian he naturally felt no affinity to socialism because of its authoritarian philosophy; also, he was convinced that it was no less immune to demagogy than political liberalism. Yet, in spite of his bitter and scornful criticism of the founder of socialism, he felt close to Marx, the agitator. He also shared quite a few feelings with him. For different reasons both were hostile to democratic capitalism and both condemned its corruption and its insatiable quest for power embodied in the big monopolies. Like Marx, Pareto despised the bourgeoisie particularly for its hypocrisy, often appearing behind the cloak of humanitarianism. (Humanitarians were for Pareto "animal pests.") What is perhaps even more significant is that he also shared Marx's belief about the illusory elements in the liberal ideology, which he equally scorned.

The similarity between these two great thinkers ends here. Pareto could not agree with Marx on other fundamental points and denied all validity to the theory of class struggle which he considered irrelevant and simplistic. Yet, whilst Marx followed his critique of capitalism by laying the foundations of 'scientific' socialism, Pareto did not succeed in providing a new system to replace the old. He had no real solutions to offer.

VI

HIS BRAND OF FASCISM

The last questions we must ask: did Pareto foresee the coming of fascism? Did he embrace it unconditionally?

As to the first question, the evidence is preponderant that until the end he was not fully aware of its existence and showed much skepticism as to its ultimate success. Even as late as June, 1922, his lack of faith in fascism is manifest in a letter to his friend Tommaso Giacalone-Monaco:

> I may be wrong, but I don't see fascism as a profound and permanent force.

His foremost biographer, G. H. Bousquet, has quoted many instances which prove that before the March on Rome in October, 1922, Pareto gave little thought to fascism, whilst his opinion of Benito Mussolini, its founder and leader, was not too flattering. Writing to Maffeo Pantaleoni, his friend of many years and a confirmed fascist, he reminded him of what he had told him earlier, that "Mussolini was an intriguer and void of ideals." These were strong words which no 'precursor of fascism' would ever have written. It is also interesting to note that for quite some time Pareto could not spell correctly the dictator's name (he referred to him as Mussolin*o*).

Again, much has been written about Mussolini attending Pareto's lectures during his stay in Lausanne in 1902, almost creating the impression that Pareto indoctrinated Mussolini and that they were buddies. No one knows for sure whether Mussolini did attend his lectures, but it is a fact that there was no personal contact between the two. This we know from Pareto's letter to Placci in January, 1923.

The answer to the second question: yes, he showed enough sympathy for fascism once it gained power, but his support was conditional. I also believe that this support would have been withdrawn had he lived long enough to see fascism in its true colors. One of the most explicit statements of approval Pareto gave to fascism is contained in another letter to Placci in July, 1923 and yet it carries with it a note of caution:

> Your *liberals* talk a lot and conclude little except when it suits their particular interests—It is good for you to be a fascist partisan; fascism might be the salvation of Italy, *but there are precipices on both sides of the road which it still has to tread.*

What made Pareto accept fascism even conditionally? Like many Italians he had hoped for a radical change for a long time. To him as to the others fascism during its first stage had much appeal. Its strong patriotic propaganda and its condemnation of corruption seemed to promise a new era. Respectable intellectuals, such as the philosopher Benedetto Croce and Luigi Einaudi, the finance expert and later president of post-war Italy, welcomed it with some reservations. Pareto had even stronger reasons to manifest both his sympathy and hopes for the future of fascism. In a way he saw in it the vindication of his theories and prophecies. Fascism marked the end of a degenerate demagogic plutocracy and a transition from sheer individualism to a form of collective government. Moreover, as a man of authoritarian temperament he admired the sense of authority and discipline in fascism, whilst his strong patriotic passion inclined him to see in the new movement a force which could help Italy recover its pride and turn it into a truly dynamic country.

VII

CONCLUSION

It is all part of history now how the fascists exploited Pareto for their own ends. Mussolini, who lacked a *Das Kapital* or even a *Mein Kampf,* needed badly the intellectual support of Pareto, the famous sociologist. The honors bestowed on Pareto within a few months of the triumph of fascism, culminating in his nomination as a senator of Italy, unfortunately more than confirmed in the minds of many the impression that Pareto, if not the precursor, must have been a godfather of fascism.

To prove, however, that such an accusation is unfounded, I wish to refer to two more documents. The first is an excerpt from a letter to Bousquet which shows once more how skeptical of fascism he remained till the end of his life. On October 31, 1922 he wrote that "the program of fascism is one thing; the goal which it will attain may be completely different." Later on December 16 of the same year, in an article in the newspaper *Il Secolo* he made a statement which is good enough to be included in his obituary:

> I am a scholar. I assist at the game and I mark the shots. (But) I never liked nor will I ever like to join the noisy chorus of the flatterers.

I need to add one final note to explain what makes me conclude that he would never have condoned the sins of fascism which became evident at a later stage. First of all, he could never agree with the politics of corporativism for it ran against all the cherished principles he upheld all his life both as an economist and as a sociologist. Moreover, even after the triumph of fascism he kept on insisting that it was the responsibility of the State to guarantee basic freedoms, such as religious freedom (he warned the government not to enter into an alliance with the Church), the freedom of electors to vote according to their conscience, and in particular the freedom of the press and of teaching. Academic freedom was so important to him that he urged the fascist government to allow the teaching of Marx's theories in the universities!

I agree with Borkenau, Vander Zandem and others that Pareto was a child of his times; he was the product of the same social, economic and political forces that gave birth to fascism. But he was no more a fascist than Léon Walras was a socialist.

In an article in which Vander Zandem reached a conclusion totally opposite to mine, it is stated that "fascism was indeed the logical fulfilment of Pareto's system," even to the extent of providing economic justification for its corporate State. This is, of course, untrue, as I have pointed out already. There is nothing in Pareto's economics to support such a State. On the contrary his economic thought is the negation of corporativism, as fascist writers were quick to discover.

In summing up why Pareto should be considered "a precursor of fascism," the same writer points to four main aspects of his work, namely (a) "his intense anti-intellectualism and anti-rationalism," (b) his theory of the elites, (c) his anti-democratic stand, and (d) "his glorification of force as an instrument of acquiring and sustaining power."

I would like first to make a couple of general remarks on this statement. Even if all the above aspects of Pareto's work were irrefutably correct, they would not necessarily make him a precursor of fascism, for he could equally be considered a precursor of *any* other revolutionary movement which subscribed to his theory. Moreover, a political movement needs badly a suitable economic program and, as we have seen, Pareto never provided one for fascism. Lastly, a precursor is a *forerunner,* whose works and words must directly and positively pave the way to a doctrine or a movement. This was not true of Pareto either. On the contrary he always complained that his works were often ignored or misinterpreted. Fascist writers and thinkers were never influenced by Pareto before the March on Rome in 1922, and only later did they discover that certain aspects of his sociology were agreeable to their doctrine.

Pareto was too spiritually independent to belong to any party, and it was alien to his character to lay the ground for any revolutionary movement. He considered himself first and foremost a scientist. Thus he expressed his perception of himself:

> My purpose is not to defend a doctrine, a tendency or to attack those doctrines to which I do not subscribe. Nor do I wish to persuade anybody. I have only one wish, namely, to search objectively for truth.

So, who was the true Pareto? We have seen what an ardent liberal he was at first, and how he shared the beliefs of his peers in social and material progress and in human perfectibility. We also noticed how Pareto, later, began to manifest strong hostility towards democracy, largely as a result of his own experience with a corrupt Italian regime which was run by a clique of mediocre politicians. It was in this same period that he became part of the revolt against reason and an anti-intellectualist. But unlike Nietzsche, Bergson, Freud and others, he did not revel in man's irrationality; he simply exposed it and analyzed it. Furthermore, he kept on holding to scientism even when the others rejected it.

Pareto was always intellectually honest. Admittedly the *Treatise* represents a sarcastic delusion, but he believed in his social theories. His aim was to warn genuine libertarians not to believe in a utopian society. Thus, he argued, man seldom acted rationally, hence only a few have

the ability and the power to influence society's destiny. These were men of authority and discipline; the rest were followers. When they failed through corruption or decadence, another breed of special men had the right to displace them. The task of the libertarian, according to Pareto, is to face this reality and to ensure the preservation of basic freedoms even under such essentially authoritarian regimes. Thus, whilst he was concerned to dispel the illusions of utopian libertarians, Pareto himself became the victim of a delusion in believing that in the absence of democracy liberalism could continue to survive! But was Pareto really different from present-day libertarians who confuse their system with anti-libertarian ideas?

Pareto was not an architect of revolutions; he was simply a spectator of man's conduct in society. He was no one's precursor. Sidney Hook, reviewing Pareto's *Treatise* in *The Nation* of New York in the same year in which Lerner's virulent attack appeared in *The New Republic,* declared:

> Many of Pareto's doctrines cannot be defended in Italy and Germany without bringing their professors into concentration camps. No matter how many honors Mussolini may have heaped upon Pareto in absentia, any talk about Pareto being the ideologist or prophetic apologist of fascism is sheer poppycock.

To this unambiguous verdict I wholeheartedly subscribe.

Richard Bellamy (essay date 1987)

SOURCE: "Vilfredo Pareto," in *Modern Italian Social Theory: Ideology and Politics from Pareto to the Present,* Polity Press, 1987, pp. 12-33.

[*In the following essay, Bellamy takes issue with critics who perceive a significant ideological discontinuity between Pareto's earlier and later writings.*]

Pareto, when studied at all, is generally interpreted in two apparently mutually exclusive ways. Economists regard him as a classical liberal, who made important contributions to the theory of rational choice underlying the defence and analysis of market mechanisms. Sociologists and political theorists, by contrast, tend to dismiss his ideas as crude and illiberal—as attacking the role of reason and democracy in politics, and exalting the use of force by an elite to impose its will on the populace. The two images are said to correspond to different periods of his life. The first belongs to the early phase when, as an engineer and later a captain of industry, he threw himself into the movement for free trade. The second resulted from disillusionment at the frustration of his early hopes. An exile and recluse in Switzerland, he became the bitter and cynical commentator and dissector of contemporary events. The two divergent views are thereby reconciled by the thesis of an historical break between the early and the late Pareto.

This [essay] challenges this view by exploring the development of his sociology in the context of his political opinions and involvements. If disappointment with Italian politics is indeed the key to his sociological thought, then the ideals of the early period repay study by providing the background to his later criticisms. This constitutes the first section of this [essay]. I then turn, in section two, to the examination of his system to show how the principles of his economic liberalism governed those of his sociology. Finally, in section three, I demonstrate the continuity between the supposed two Paretos, revealing how his use of the insights of the *Trattato* to describe political developments from the First World War to his death in 1923, echoes his analysis of events before the war.

I claim that the similarity between Pareto's earlier and later views derives from the conceptual scheme he employed to interpret human behaviour. Pareto's liberal principles led him to shrink the political spectrum drastically, reducing all human activity to certain sharply defined and contestable types—essentially 'rational' or 'irrational'. These categories were then enshrined within his sociology. This, in turn, had the effect of legitimizing a particular form of political practice—namely fascism. Pareto's development thereby illustrates the central issue of this book—namely, the nature of the relationship between social theory and political action.

THE POLITICS OF PARETO'S SOCIOLOGY

Pareto was born in Paris in the year of liberal revolutions, 1848. His father, the Marquis Raffaello Pareto, had been exiled from Genoa to France in 1835 or 1836 for his Mazzinian opinions, and had taken a French wife. An amnesty enabled him to return in 1855. A civil engineer, he rose to high rank in the service of the Piedmontese (later Italian) government. Pareto followed his father's career, graduating in engineering in 1869 with a thesis on 'The fundamental principles of equilibrium in solid bodies', which inspired a number of his later ideas on economics and sociology. He was appointed a director of the Florence branch of the Rome Railway Company in 1870 and held this post until 1874, when he became managing director of the Società Ferriere d'Italia.

During these years he increasingly took part in political debates as an ardent supporter of universal suffrage, republicanism, free trade and disarmament. Borkenau and H. Stuart Hughes regard his later debunking of humanitarian and democratic ideas as a reaction to his father's Mazzinian beliefs. Yet, as Finer has pointed out, there is no evidence for this interpretation. On the contrary, he was plainly attracted by these ideas, regretting the 'inauspicious circumstances' that led to his being born in France rather than Italy, and regarding someone opposed to the goals of the Risorgimento as a 'bad citizen' and 'a disgraceful being who lacks one of the prime qualities of man: patriotism and the love of liberty. Far from rejecting his paternal heritage, Pareto's writings, in both economics and sociology, have their roots in his attempt to analyse the conditions governing the development of democracy in post-unification Italy, and to struggle for its realization in an uncorrupted form.

The difficulties confronting such schemes can be imagined by anyone with a cursory knowledge of Italian history. The moderate conservatives, the 'Historical Right', who ruled Italy from 1861 to 1876, were obsessed with reducing the debts incurred by the Risorgimento, the Italians becoming the most heavily taxed populace in Europe as a result. This was combined with a centralized and heavily bureaucratic administration, distant and remote from the people, only 2 per cent of whom had the franchise in any case. As attention was focused increasingly on internal problems, the right's inability to stimulate the economy or ameliorate the social conditions of the masses drew increased criticism. Popular unrest manifested itself in violent mass movements—Bakunin's anarchism enjoying a spectacular new lease of life—and culminating in an attempted insurrectional *putsch* in 1874. Unfortunately the parliamentary opposition did little to solve these problems either. The 'Young Left' dropped the Mazzinian programme for the privileged of office, seeking little more than a reduction of taxation and a small increase of the electorate (to 7 per cent of the population) to ensure their continued stay in office. Under their leader Depretis, Italian politics became a matter of bargaining and the exploitation of government patronage to obtain the necessary balance between northern and southern interests by the various party or faction leaders to maintain their administration power. This policy of *trasformismo* characterized public life for the next fifty years, and effectively blocked any radical change in government.

Pareto's first political writings were primarily directed against the abuses of the Italian parliamentary system and the ruling classes' lack of concern for the plight of the people. An admirer of Mill and Spencer and the British political system generally, he argued from the principle of individual liberty for a policy of universal suffrage and free trade. Pareto contended that the opposition of the bourgeoisie to both of these policies was motivated by the desire to protect their privileges, rather than a principled defence of freedom, as they maintained. They argued that the franchise must remain limited, because only those who paid taxes had a stake in the nation, adding that the illiterate masses were unable to make a reasoned decision in any case. Pareto retorted that responsible government would only result when all, through elections, were involved in it. The vote was not, he wrote, a right, but 'the exercise of a necessary function for the good working of civil society.' The voter required, as 'a first and indispensable quality', the possession of 'the culture and the necessary knowledge to fulfil adequately his task.' Compulsory education was therefore a prerequisite in a country where 78 per cent of the people were illiterate, if universal suffrage was to become not just 'an empty word, but a beneficial reality.'

Following Mill, he defined liberty as 'the faculty of doing everything which in a direct and immediate way does not harm others.' Like Mill, however, some of the conclusions he drew from this principle which have more in common with T. H. Green's 'new liberalism' than 'classical liberalism'. For example, he argued that compulsory education, far from conflicting with liberty, was essential for its exercise:

> Now it is manifestly clear that compulsory education should rather be called freedom of education, since the parent who does not educate his son harms him greatly and in a direct way . . . The new born son is a citizen to whom the law owes guardianship and protection, and in fact this principle prevails in the modern legislation of civilised peoples . . . even taking away the father's right to dispose of his entire estate in his will. In virtue of what principle, I ask, must this guardianship, which is exercised over material goods, be diminished when treating that other patrimony, education, which is indispensable to all but above all to those, and they are the majority, who have no other?

Pareto defended the workers' right to combine and strike on analogous grounds. The innovative studies of Franchetti, Sonnino, Fortunato and Villari, from 1874 onwards, had already revealed the abject poverty oppressing the southern peasantry. Pareto's own experience made him aware of the similar conditions prevailing amongst factory workers in the north. Commenting on a proposal to set a minimum wage and a maximum margin of profit, he sarcastically speculated on where the 'lovers of liberty', who opposed it, had been hiding

> when the tide of government interference was growing, instituting monopolies of every sort. It must be because of my weak mental faculties that I can't understand such a subtle distinction, but I fail to understand . . . how the principles of economics are unhurt when one punishes a citizen who does not want, either in agreement with others or alone, to sell his labour for a supposedly fair price and are mortally wounded when one imposes this just wage not on the worker but on the person who exploits him. For my own part I believe that justice leaves open only two paths: either the state does not meddle either in this nor in many other even graver ways in the relations between capital and labour and only exercises the office of maintaining free competition, or if it intervenes, it does so impartially, in everyone's favour, and not constantly for one side and to the detriment of the other. Either the state protects nobody or it protects everybody; beyond this there are only arbitrary acts, injustice and damage to national prosperity.

Pareto argued that if there were really uncorrupt elections and free competition then everyone's welfare would improve, because the opinions and talents of the best would prevail to the advantage of the whole community. In many respects this remained his conviction. Yet it was equally clear to him that, given the current state of affairs, the workers' use of extreme tactics to get their grievances heard was both justified and reasonable.

Increased familiarity with parliamentary politics did little to improve his poor view of it. He stood twice as a candidate, in 1880 and 1882, and declined a third opportunity in 1886 in no uncertain terms: 'I've already had too many opportunities for seeing at close quarters the bad faith and cowardice of certain people without seeking out other ones. I'm content with the satisfaction of despising them and of saying it loudly to everyone.' He withdrew increasingly from active participation in politics and business, resigning as managing director of the Italian Iron and Steel Company in 1889 in order to devote himself to writing.

His career as an economist and political journalist took off in these years, and be began to develop many of the core ideas of his sociology. His liberal convictions and his growing cynicism were fuelled by a deterioration, even by Italian standards, of the political climate. Depretis died in 1887 and was succeeded as Prime Minister by Francesco Crispi. Originally a Mazzinian Republican and a follower of Garibaldi, in power he became an authoritarian demagogue. An admirer of Bismark, he mixed repressive domestic measures with abortive schemes for colonial expansion, whilst continuing to exploit the system of *transformismo* to retain his parliamentary support. A disastrous economic and foreign policy, combined with government corruption, produced a number of financial scandals which supplied Pareto's caustic pen with plenty of material.

He had become friendly with the liberal economist Maffeo Pantaleoni, and began to gain a reputation as an economic theorist because of his development of the market theories of Walras and Edgeworth through the application of sophisticated mathematical techniques. He combined the two activities of polemicist and economist when, at Pantaleoni's invitation, he began to contribute numerous comments on contemporary politics ('*cronache*') to the *Giornali degli Economisti* from 1891 to 1897. The themes noted in his earlier polemics continued to predominate. Pareto retained his commitment to individual liberty, and his conviction that militarism and protectionism originated from the selfish and ultimately shortsighted desire of the bourgeoisie to keep their dominant position. This led him to express sympathy for the socialist cause—a fact which may surprise those who only know him for the ridicule he poured on the 'socialist myth' in *Les Systèmes Socialistes* (1901). Pareto's early support was, however, not inconsistent with his later scorn for the doctrine, which he never accepted.

Pareto had already warned the middle classes that 'it is to count over much on human ignorance, to expect that one can persuade the workers of the inefficiency, or worse the damage, that would come from measures wholly analogous to those adopted by the wealthy for their own ends'. The protectionist policies subsequent on Italy's joining the Triple Alliance, which led to a drop of 40 per cent in exports previously secured by a free trade agreement with France, seemed to confirm his worst fears. 'Popular socialism', he now argued, was but the natural response to 'bourgeois socialism', the only difference being that the latter pursued the less laudable aim of favouring the haves rather than the have-nots. Pareto bemoaned the lack of scientific judgement amongst the populace which could allow two such erroneous doctrines to hold sway, because once in power the socialists acted no differently from the others. Even 'if power should pass into the hands of the masses, they would make no better use of it, on the contrary, as they are still more ignorant and brutal than the *bourgeoisie*, their oppression would be worse.' The remedy was not in a change of masters, though that might be necessary by way of transition:

> [A]s I look at it, the only way of diminishing the sum total of suffering in the country is to withdraw the individual as far as possible from the power of the government or of the commune,—that is, to follow a path opposite to that which has led us to the existing *bourgeois* socialism, and which will lead us, in the future, to popular socialism.

The problem lay 'not with the men', or not only with them, but with the system of ideas they espoused. He greatly admired individual socialists, such as Napoleone Colajanni, who risked prison by denouncing the wrongs of contemporary politics. Moreover, he appreciated that it was faith in a socialist future which gave them the strength to risk their personal liberty in so doing. This position is well expressed in the following passage from a letter to Colajanni:

> I am not a socialist, and I'm saddened by that, because if I could have that faith I would see a better moral reward for the work of those who fight to better the lot of the people than can be expected from Political Economy. But it seems to me that socialists and economists should be able to travel some way along the same road, to oppose the evil ways of our rulers.

Pareto remarked that he felt his position 'in comparison to the socialists and supporters of our governments is similar to that occupied by the positivists with respect to the various religious beliefs.' Indeed, anticipating his later theory of ideologies and his use of Sorel's theory of myths, he maintained that socialism and reactionary conservatism had exactly the same attraction as Christianity, from which they derived their form. However, whilst they undoubtedly appealed to genuine emotional needs, and had a practical value in inspiring people to act, their 'scientific' value was nullatory, 'unfortunately lacking the use of the experimental method to make them profitable, the sole secure guide to human reason'.

Pareto contended that the attempt to define the best society for humankind was inherently authoritarian, since the possibilities for human expression and fulfillment defy classification. As a result freedom, even occasionally to make mistakes, must be conceded so that full scope could be given to human diversity. Mill and Spencer were still very much at the forefront of his thinking, and he demonstrated a faith in the progress of reason worthy of these heirs of the Enlightenment. He exhorted the liberals to employ rational argument, rather than force or deception, to make their case, 'thereby paving a way down which

they cannot be followed or blocked by those who derive their power from lies and fraud.'

Pareto succeeded Walras as professor of political economy at Lausanne in 1893. Here he took on the task of laying the foundations for a science of society, grounded on the 'sure basis' of the logico-empirical method of the natural sciences, in his lectures on economics. The *Cours d'Economie Politique* of 1896 are perfectly consonant with the liberal principles of the youthful social reformer. He aimed to expound the 'uniformities' underlying human behaviour, 'stripping man of a large number of accretions, ignoring his passions, whether good or bad, and reducing him eventually to a sort of molecule, susceptible solely to the influence of the forces of ophelimity [self-satisfaction].' Drawing on Spencer, Pareto argued that society evolved through the progressive development of needs and desires as individuals sought ever more varied and higher forms of self-satisfaction. Societies consequently ceased to be simple homogeneous units and diversified into a heterogeneous organic community. He asserted that an ideal equilibrium between different individuals pursuing their divergent but ultimately compatible projects, could be discovered by a 'science of utility'. However, given the current state of our knowledge, he argued, the presumption must be in favour of individual liberty and the free market, and all attempts at intervention, be it from socialists or protectionists, strongly resisted.

Discussion of the important innovations in econometrics made by Pareto in pursuit of this goal are beyond both the competence of the author and the present study. However, he saw fit to expound his theories in a sociological rather than a purely economic context in two chapters of the *Cours*—on 'social evolution' and 'social physiology' respectively. The argument of the first has already been outlined above; the second is more innovatory. Numerous scandals during Crispi's second administration, from 1893 to 1896, convinced him that the ruling classes were willing to use any expedient other than free and open government to preserve their interests. His friend Pantaleoni's resignation from his post at the Scuola Superiore di Commercio at Bari, due to government pressure after he had criticized their policy of a customs duty on wine, symbolized this further decay of public morality. Pareto felt particularly bitter since he had drawn attention to this paper in an article in the *Revue des deux mondes*. The bank crises led to the further smothering of criticism by free-trade economists. More than ever before, Pareto shared common cause with the socialists, whose followers in the Sicilian *Fasci* were brutally suppressed and the party forcibly dissolved in 1894. This sympathy is reflected in the *Cours* in Pareto's first sketch of what later became his theory of the circulation of elites.

As Finer has pointed out, Pareto neither adopted nor rejected Marxism; he absorbed certain salient features into his own theory and thereby denatured it. Acknowledging a debt to Marx and the *soi disant* Italian Marxist Achille

Loria, Pareto agreed that 'class struggle . . . is the great dominant fact in history', but argued that it took two forms. In the first, beneficial form, it was equivalent to economic competition and produced maximum ophelimity. Usually, though, it took the second, harmful form, 'whereby each class endeavours to get control of the government so as to make it an instrument for spoliation.' Pareto argued that it mattered little what the declared principles of the government might be—democratic, socialist or liberal—the effect was the same: the exploitation of the poor for the benefit of whoever was in power. Class war in the healthy sense, he believed, originated from the natural differences and inequalities obtaining between individuals, and was therefore an ineradicable aspect of all societies, the Marxist dream of an egalitarian communist community being a dangerous utopia. However, the class war justifiably attacked by Marx arose not from differences of ability, which might ultimately serve the good of all, but as a result of differential access to the organs of power. In this latter instance, the governing class abused its position in order to serve its own narrow ends. The only solution was to reduce drastically the capacity for governments, of whatever political disposition, from intervening to curtail individual or economic freedom.

The *Cours* puts Pareto's subsequent desire to unmask the irrational and essentially self-interested origins of political behaviour into perspective. His later attacks on humanitarian and democratic arguments did not indicate an aristocratic lack of concern with the plight of the people. On the contrary, they were motivated by a profound sympathy with their condition. He directed his cynicism against those whom he regarded as hiding self-interest behind a veneer of false altruism, not those who had a genuine interest in helping their fellow citizens. However, this reveals a contradiction in Pareto's own analysis and remedy—namely between his belief that efficiency, in the sense of optimal individual utility, could be attained in a perfectly competitive market composed of egoistic individuals, and the need for an assumption of altruism if the necessary redistribution of rights and power which would allow the market to operate in the desired manner were to occur. As we shall see later, a number of problems related to Pareto's defence of individual liberty follow from this paradox.

Government oppression steadily increased in the last years of the 1890s, culminating in an attempted palace *coup d'état* in 1898 when reactionary liberals, led by Sidney Sonnino, attempted to invoke the royal power to exact legislation directly by statute, rather than through parliament. In a series of articles in the socialist journal *Critica Sociale,* Pareto urged genuine liberals to unite with the socialists in their fight against the growing authoritarianism of the state. He remained a fervent opponent of socialist theories, 'but the fact is, that throughout Europe the socialists are almost alone in effectively resisting government oppression and fighting superstitious patriotism, which should not be confused with a healthy love of one's country . . .' This and similar state-

ments, written as late as 1899, might well seem to render Pareto's massive attack on *Les Systèmes Socialistes,* only two years later, inexplicable. Indeed, a change of tone is present only months afterwards in a number of academic articles warning of 'the dangers of socialism', and elaborating his theory of ideology.

This change can partly be accounted for by political developments. On 29 July 1900 Umberto I was assassinated by an anarchist. Instead of inaugurating an even darker period of reaction, this event lent authority to the warnings of the liberal parliamentary opposition, forming under Zanardelli and Giolitti, of the need to conciliate the new social forces or be destroyed by them, a point emphasized by a crippling general strike in Geona in December 1900. Giolitti heralded the new mood in a speech which was to bring the conservative rule of Crispi's successors, Pelloux and Saracco, to an end:

> For a long time attempts have been made to obstruct the organisation of workers. By this stage anyone who knows the conditions of our country . . . must be convinced that this is absolutely impossible . . . The rising movement of the ordinary people accelerates daily; it is an invincible movement common to all civilised countries, because it is based on the principle of equality between men . . . Friends of institutions have one duty above all: to persuade these classes, and persuade them with deeds, that they can hope for far more from existing institutions than from dreams of the future.

This passage neatly sums up the policy followed during the next fifteen years of largely Giolitti-led administrations. He added a new element to the *trasformismo* of his predecessors—that of reformism. He aimed to woo the socialists gradually with piecemeal social legislation and bring them into the existing system, disarming their revolutionary potential by 'putting Marx in the attic.'

Pareto's attack on the socialists should be examined in this context. The period from 1900 to 1902, when *Les Systèmes* was composed, witnessed an unprecedented number of strikes—1,034 in 1901, and 801 in 1902 respectively. To many commentators it appeared that the leniency of Giolitti was to blame. Pareto's analysis went deeper, fully according with the earlier castigation of the right-wing government and his sympathy for the left. Part of the answer lay in the fact that the strikes were an understandable backlash after years of repression and exploitation. To this extent he still supported the workers. What disturbed him was the manner in which they turned on their fellows who had declined from joining their action, accusing them of a lack of solidarity. This seemed to him to reflect the authoritarian measures of the right. Even worse, though, was Giolitti's connivance at this in order to retain the political support of the PSI (*Partito Socialista Italiano*) and organized labour. Clearly a new elite or aristocracy of power-brokers and 'spoilators' was forming, even more adept at manipulating the institutions of government than the reactionary bourgeoisie had been. Their influence was all the more persuasive, since socialism acted like a new religion and diverted the people's attention away from their true interests with the hope of a mystical and totally illusory future paradise.

Les Systèmes Socialistes did not signify the historical break between the young liberal and the future fascist. It sprang from the same liberal belief in the rights of the individual against all forms of authority and the claims of reason against those of religion and tradition. However, Pareto was now convinced that pure economic analysis was incapable of explaining human behaviour. As he wrote in the introduction, it ascribed too much importance to human reason, forgetting that 'Man is not a being of pure reason, he is also a being of sentiment and faith.' Pareto aimed to place the study of these latter elements on a scientific basis in order to build a complete picture of political economy. Yet instead of complementing each other, his sociology became the inverted image of his economics—describing the pursuit of self-interest by irrational rather than rational means.

To the extent that Marxism and socialism had a similar enlightenment heritage, Pareto continued to sympathize with them. He distinguished the 'learned interpretation' (*l'interpretation savante*) from the 'popular' view of Marx: 'The learned interpretation of the materialist conception of history is close to reality and has all the characteristics of a scientific theory'. However, in this form, Marxism was 'at bottom, no more favourable to socialism than to any other doctrine; it is even absolutely opposed to sentimental and ethical socialism . . .' Rather, class war, properly considered, was simply an aspect of the Darwinian struggle for the survival of the fittest. Contemporary politics had quite convinced Pareto of the plausibility of Marx's thesis, but the fight was not just between capitalists and workers, nor could it ever be overcome in a communist society. It was inherent in the essential inequalities prevailing amongst human beings. He still retained his liberal belief that in a free market these differences were mutually enhancing. But in a society which enabled the ruling group to extend its privilege and power, it inevitably led to the exploitation of the weak. Pareto had yet to elaborate his notion of the circulation of elites into its developed form, largely attributing the rise and fall of 'aristocracies', as he here calls them, to natural selection. His firm conviction of the rather brutal reality underlying social processes had nevertheless toned down his crusading liberal zeal, though it derived from similar premises concerning the nature of human action. This thesis, though, was only the background to the principal theme of the *Systèmes*—the demolition of the 'popular interpretation of socialism.'

Influenced by Sorel, whom he came to admire and correspond with, Pareto developed his comparison between socialism and religion. He distinguished 'between the concrete *objective* phenomenon and the [*subjective*] form in which our mind perceives it. . . .' The first corresponded to our 'scientific' knowledge of an object or of society. The second, on the other hand, often gave quite

a different picture and could be found in most of our theories and beliefs. Pareto wished to discover why the subjective viewpoint held such sway over men's minds. The main source of error, he contended, 'lies in the fact that a very large number of human actions are not the outcome of reasoning. They are purely instinctive actions, although the man performing them experiences a feeling of pleasure in giving them, quite arbitrarily, logical causes.' As a result, there were two aspects to any doctrine: 'the real facts' which gave rise to it, and 'the methods of reasoning employed in their justification.' Pareto applied this dual perspective to socialism and argued that whilst the 'scientific' theory corresponded to the 'objective' reality of the struggle for survival, 'popular socialism' covered this up in a mass of high-sounding, humanitarian language. The task of sociology was to classify the 'hard core of sentiments' from which the various and often seemingly contradictory beliefs and theories derived.

This task was only sketched out in the *Systèmes* and formed the subject of the *Treatise of General Sociology* of 1916. His concern for the moment was to show that however well-intentioned 'popular socialists' might be, their ideas had but one consequence—the expropriation of one part of the nation by the other, ruling section. The motivation for his attack on communist ideals has often been misinterpreted as a desire to bolster the power of the bourgeoisie. This interpretation mistakes Pareto's purpose entirely. He did not attack those who genuinely felt for the poor and oppressed, and supported individual freedom, but maintained that those who argued for these causes on socialist grounds were either deluded or charletons. Politicians like Giolitti claimed to be working a peaceful social revolution, Pareto regarded this as simply a cover for their own ends. They hoped to retain political power by meeting the workers' demands, but he saw it as the last desperate effort of an exhausted class. 'Bourgeois socialism' was being replaced by the new leaders of 'popular socialism'. The bourgeoisie's new-found enthusiasm for liberty, democracy and equality was indicative of its inability to oppose the new social forces. When this became apparent he believed a direct clash would occur and the new elite of workers' leaders would take over. This would not inaugurate the communist utopia, but another era of oppressors and oppressed. The struggle between different individuals he concluded could not be abolished. Indeed, even in a free market system only the harmful consequences of this struggle were prevented, since it was instrumental to the progress of society. Socialists who ignored this reality would become its victims. As his favourite Genoese saying expressed it: 'Play the sheep and you will meet the butcher.'

Les Systèmes Socialistes was the work of an entrenched economic liberal, not a die-hard reactionary. Pareto was not alone in his disillusionment with Giolitti's regime. Young intellectuals of both left and right castigated his system of compromise as corrupt. Radical socialists believed Giolitti had undermined the revolutionary potential of the proletariat, buying them off with transient material benefits; and nationalists bemoaned his abandoning the creation of an Italian Empire. As we shall see, a similar anger towards this belittling of their hopes for a revived new Italy expressed itself in all the major theorists of this period.

Compared with many of the accusations and fantastic projects of his contemporaries, Pareto's work seems both restrained and reasonable. A well-known review of *Les Systèmes Socialistes,* by the intellectual entrepreneur Giuseppe Prezzolini, illustrates this contrast. Like most of his generation, Prezzolini was somewhat maverick in his political allegiances, regarding himself as part of an intellectual elite which praised creativity and individuality, and damned conformity and the second-rate. He regarded Pareto's book as a warning to the bourgeoisie not to become the dupes of the socialists, whose leaders sought to replace their benign rule and set up as an 'aristocracy of brigands.' Pareto responded that he had not taken sides on the issue, showing if anything more sympathy for the socialists' energy than for the pathetic acquiescence of the middle classes. As he had made plain in the *Cours,* he viewed Prezzolini's elitist nationalism with a distaste matching his aversion to socialism, regarding it as 'equally exaggerated, only in the opposite direction'. The 'neo-aristocrats' had simply reversed the socialist 'gospel of complete equality . . . According to them, the whole human race existed merely in order to produce a few superior men; it was only compost for some flowers'. Prezzolini captured the difference of their approaches in his reply: 'In a word, you see in the theory of aristocracies a scientific theory; I see it instead as a scientific justification of my present political needs.'

If Pareto desired to write 'scientifically' on the subject, this did not entail an absence of political passion. In fact, this ambition was the expression of his point of view. He had long divorced himself from the existing parties and decided to limit his own political activity to his study. His bitterness at the political scene was no more a sign of support for the bourgeoisie than it had previously been for the socialists. He opposed oppression from either side, but the hope that the socialists would be more tolerant than their adversaries seemed to have become a chimera. He succinctly expressed his position in the following passage from an article of 1905:

> Before, the restrictive legislation was all to the advantage of the bourgeoisie, and against the people; whoever fought it, therefore, could honestly believe he was working to create a just regime, which would not favour either side with privileges. I do not see how you can demonstrate such a conception to be erroneous *a priori,* and it seems to me that only subsequent events have the power to give such a demonstration, as they have done. They have shown that we have not stopped even for a moment at a mid-point, where there are no privileges; instead the bourgeois privileges have been abolished only to make way for the popular privileges, so that he who fought all privilege, in reality and contrary to his intention has succeeded only in substituting one kind for another.

The *Trattato* originated as an indictment of human cupidity and foolishness, rather than a Machiavellian handbook on how to use irrationality and force to undermine the aspiration to set up a humanitarian and democratic society. On the contrary, Pareto shared this goal, but despaired of its ever being realized. His ideal liberal polity assumed that individuals acted as rational calculators, able to work out where their self-interest lay. Unfortunately, as he had written to Pantaleoni, the study of society had convinced him that 'reason is of little worth in giving form to social phenomena. Quite different forces are at work. This is what I want to demonstrate in my sociology . . .' He thus ignored the exhortations of his friend, and gave up what he now viewed as the utopian study of economics for the real world of society. However, by turning the political practices of contemporary Italy into universal laws of human behaviour, he had the effect of legitimizing the very attitudes which he had previously sought to condemn. In the next two sections I shall show, first, how Pareto transformed his bitter characterization of Italian politics into a general sociology; and, second, demonstrate that this led to an endorsement of fascism.

PARETO'S SOCIOLOGY OF POLITICS

Although not published until 1916, the *Trattato* was the product of 'twenty years of study'. Vast and 'monstrous' as it is, a guiding thread can nevertheless be discerned. Pareto desired to unmask ideologies of all kinds, and reveal the true structure of society. He aimed at separating factual analysis from evaluation. He achieved this by denying the validity of discussing the ultimate value of any political system. Politics consisted of necessarily subjective emotional responses, conditioned by our nature and social experience. All science could do, he argued, was describe those psychological states which correspond to particular values, and show how people attained their goals. But the worthiness of aspirations and ends could not be judged. He consequently made an important distinction, implicit in his earlier work, between the claims people make for their acts and the real motivations behind their behaviour, and he attempted to show that there was no necessary connection between the two.

Pareto divided actions into 'logical' and 'non-logical'. The former adhered to the criterion of scientific rationality he had outlined in *Les Systèmes*. He defined them as actions 'logically linked to an end, not only in respect to the person performing them, but also for those who have a more extensive knowledge . . .' The latter consisted of all the remaining actions, which failed to adopt 'logico-experimental' modes of reasoning. These 'other actions' were 'non-logical; which does not mean illogical.' Pareto noted that the subject believed most of his deeds belonged to the first category—'For Greek mariners, sacrifices to Poseidon and rowing with oars were equally logical means of navigation.' However, he argued that because only the second belief was susceptible to empirical verification, it alone was 'logical'. Regrettably most human behaviour therefore belonged to the 'non-logical' class.

This rather narrow definition of rationality led Pareto into a number of difficulties, since almost no normative proposition is of this nature. Yet axioms such as 'Do as you would be done by' form part of the moral fabric of any society. Pareto, by suggesting that only action towards a definite and attainable end was valuable and meaningful, risked undermining the complex web of tacit understandings that make up social life, and replacing it with a crude utilitarian rationalism. This danger was signalled by Croce who, in a review of the **Manuale,** argued that Pareto's instrumentalism turned men into machines.

The justice of this criticism became clear in Pareto's analysis of 'non-logical' actions, which he held to govern the vast majority of human activity. Pareto maintained that most behaviour of this class emanated from certain 'non-rational' states of mind. The theories which apparently guided action were a 'logical veneer', subsequent to the original motivation to act. The operative forces in society were not ideas, therefore, but the psychic states and dispositions of which these ideas were manifestations. The social scientist's task consisted of elaborating the 'residues', the constant element, of which theories were the 'derivations'. Pareto discovered some fifty-two residues, which he broke down into six classes.

In spite of this diversity, he explained most political conduct in terms of the first two classes of residue. Class I he called the 'instinct of combinations'. The Italian word, *combinazione,* connotes a range of meanings suggesting shrewdness and wit, as well as the usual English sense of the term. According to Pareto, it functioned as an intellectual and imaginative attribute, employed equally by the scientist using the logico-experimental method, the poet in his creative fantasy, and the schemer playing on the sentiments of others. Class II was the 'persistence of aggregates'. This was a conservative tendency, which held on to conventional ways of seeing the world and resisted the establishment of new combinations. Each category corresponded to a broad set of attitudes and behaviour on the part of all human beings.

Pareto claimed that his framework provided a scientific, value-free description of social activity. Yet, though Pareto swamped his readers with a mass of anecdotes and recondite facts, he was not content to remain at the level of simply describing the external aspects of events. Appearances to the contrary, he goes beyond the random collection of facts. Instead of simply stating, for example, that Prussia defeated France in 1870, he provided an explanation of the course of events in terms of his theory of human motivation. However, as Croce was to show, any attempt to go beyond crude empiricism introduces innumerable conflicts of interpretation over the choice of facts and the attribution of motives to the agents involved. I shall argue below, that far from providing a 'neutral' description of human behaviour, Pareto merely endowed his own ideological leanings with a spurious scientific status.

Pareto held that all societies were governed by an elite, the composition of which was constantly changing. The rise and fall of governing classes he put down to the alternation within them of the proportions of Class I and Class II residues. Government, he maintained, required both qualities: the invention, cunning and persuasiveness of the 'foxes', in whom the combining instinct predominated; and the strength of purpose and willingness to use force of the 'lions', moved more by the 'persistence of aggregates'. He classified different types of polity according to the proportions of the two different classes present in the governing elite. Moreover, there was no perfect balance which would keep an elite in power for ever. History showed a constant circulation between these two types of ruling class. 'Foxes' gained power in civilized countries, manipulating the political machine to their advantage to obtain the consent of the populace. But ultimately they would give too much away to the opposition, in order to appease them, and were incapable of wielding force to protect their position. The 'lions', who replaced them, willingly employed coercion and even violence to obtain their ends, but their rule would become stultified and mechanical, and they in turn would fall to the 'foxes', who cleverly exploited them for their own ends. Finally, the political cycle was paralleled by changes in the economy between two similarly-motivated economic groups—the speculators and the *rentiers* respectively.

Although Pareto tended to draw on ancient history for his examples, his theory was clearly inspired by his interpretation of contemporary Italian politics, examined in the previous section. This need not invalidate his position; indeed if his view of events was correct it would tend to support it. However, not content with limiting his thesis to an explanation of the current political situation, he elevated it into a universal law of social behaviour, valid for all times and places. Pareto professed to have tested his system by an appeal to the 'facts of history'. He implied that he could provide empirical evidence of the presence of classes I and II and then show an event to be produced by them—a claim he illustrated with the equation

$$q \text{ (event)} = \frac{A \text{ (Class I)}}{B \text{ (Class II)}}$$

However, he then admitted that such a procedure was next to impossible, and that we must infer the presence of A and B from variations in q. Thus, he first described historical events in terms of his theory of residues, e.g. Bismark's victory over the French in 1870 as the result of his combination of cunning and force. He then explained and purportedly verified his thesis by explaining Bismark's conduct by the existence of the appropriate balance of Class I and Class II residues! By this method Pareto could make any event fit his scheme.

Pareto desired to render the study of human kind scientific in the manner of the natural sciences. The meaning agents ascribed to their acts was taken as a potentially verifiable fact about the presence of certain residues within them. This procedure was entirely arbitrary, since the very choice of which features to study was prejudiced by the interpretative framework Pareto employed in the first place. He ignored differences of scale, organization, economic structure and systems of belief between societies throughout history. However these might vary, he believed, the underlying political reality of the circulation of elites had always been the same. The protagonists of the Franco-Prussian war of 1870 displayed identical characteristics to those of the Athenians and Spartans during the Pelopennesian war, whilst socialists and liberals in modern Italy relived the conflicts between rival factions in ancient Rome.

Yet there are clearly important differences between classical and contemporary politics, for example in the social composition of their democracies, which Pareto dismissed because of his obsession with discovering elites. In particular, two quite different conceptual schemes governed political behaviour in the respective periods. The Greeks regarded the human world as displaying an inherently rational order, as the embodiment of an underlying meaningful scheme in nature. The modern view rejects this parallel between the natural macrocosom and the social microcosm. This produces two divergent notions of personal identity. The ancients regarded themselves as part of a larger order, to which they must become attuned; moderns see themselves as characterized by a private set of drives and goals. Clearly Pareto adopted the latter view, but he thereby missed the point that the political practices of ancient Greece were quite different from those of today. For example, he stated that 'the controversies that raged at Athens over the profanation of the Hermic pillars and the Eleusinian mysteries, and the quarrels that raged in France over the Dreyfus affair, were largely masks and pretexts to cover passions and interests'. This conclusion only seemed plausible because, in his account of the two affairs, Pareto attributed modern drives to the ancient Greeks. Yet the self-interested desire for power and wealth, in many guises quite acceptable today (as in the successful entrepreneur), was universally condemned as a kind of madness by Greek moralists. He criticized the Athenians for recalling Alcibiades from command of the fleet because of 'superstitious' beliefs, at a time when his skills were required against the Spartans. But to describe the act in these terms gives an inaccurate picture of what was involved, since in Greek eyes someone who defied the Gods was *ipso facto* a disastrous leader of men. By attributing the decision to a preponderence of conservative Class II residues over the more realistic Class I, Pareto superimposed a parochial view of the nature of politics, totally at odds with that available to the agents at the time. He treated their religious beliefs as if they could be adopted or dropped at will, as simply the private opinions of the individuals concerned. But this was a presupposition of his sociology, not of those who actually held them. For the Greeks, these ideas and norms were rooted in their social relations, they constituted the practices they adopted and provided guidance about the appropriate attitude to take in a given situation.

Pareto believed he was providing a factual account of Greek and French politics respectively. In fact, he was redescribing them in a fashion which misconstrued the motives of the principle actors so that they conformed to his scheme. However, he went further than this, to impose an image of politics in which anyone who did not seek to serve his or her own narrowly-defined egotistical interests was either a fool or a charleton. Little surprise then, that Pareto should have fallen into the role of the advocate of the Machiavellian use of force and persuasion to maintain oneself in power. Since no political goal could be regarded as more rational than any other, success became the only measure.

This conclusion has led many commentators to attribute a change of political allegiance to Pareto, from liberal to proto-fascist. However, the assumptions behind his sociology were clearly the same as those inspiring his earlier liberalism. He retained the atomistic model of society, as made up of independent individual units continuously seeking different states of equilibrium. He was equally committed to the belief that the best balance of forces was that which yielded the greatest social utility, in terms of the maximum want-satisfaction of each individual, and that this would be achieved in a libertarian free-market society. Pareto's hostility towards ideologies expressed his frustration at what he deemed the irrationality of humankind. But arguing for his own case involved him in a paradox. For all people to adopt the free market and accept the redistribution of rights necessary for the system to work optimally, there must be a prior commitment on their part to the type of society it entails. However, this conflicts with the advantage claimed for free markets over centralized allocation—that they function by leaving the actor as the ultimate judge of his or her own preferences and projects. In fact the necessary measures would have to be imposed, or a sudden single flash of altruism be presumed, if those currently benefiting from the injustices of society were to accept a more equitable division of power. This provides a further explanation for Pareto's later endorsement of fascism. Authoritarian politics appeared to be the only way to free the market from the political spoilation of a democratic order. In this respect he remained perfectly consistent, carrying through to the 1920s his convictions about the proper relation between the market and the state developed in the 1890s. Had he lived long enough to see Mussolini's economic policy, he would undoubtedly have withdrawn his support.

Pareto's programme had two serious and interrelated drawbacks.

i The attempt to construct a science of society based on certain constant phenomena is vitiated by the relation between thought and action. Changes in how we define ourselves produce changes in how we act. Since the conceptual scheme governing human behaviour has not been the same throughout history, no sociological system can fail to take philosophical and ideological mutations into account and accurately describe past acts.

ii Pareto's understanding of his own society was similarly affected. By reducing politics to the circulation of elites, Pareto effectively closed the door on other political options, such as democracy or socialism. Statecraft, according to his theory, consisted solely in the manipulation of sentiments and the presence of the requisite balance of residues amongst the ruling group. Instead of creating a new 'value free' science of society, Pareto constructed a justification of the corrupt practices he had previously criticized. As the next section shows, this conception of politics was easily amenable to fascism.

THE TRANSFORMATION OF DEMOCRACY

Pareto's methodology hinged on establishing certain polarities between 'objective', 'scientific' thought and action, and 'subjective', 'non-logical' modes of conduct. This epistemological position had consequences in his social and political thought extending beyond the immediate domain of sociological method. According to his scheme, the moral and the rational were quite distinct, the former simply being certain ends particular to the individual who held them. The conflict between competing ethical systems could not be solved by the growth of rationality. For Pareto, reason corresponded to what Weber meant by *zweckrational*—that is, action to attain a given practical end by the most appropriate means.

Since values were largely subjective illusions, politics was the art of the practicable rather than the desirable. The struggle between different individuals could not be transcended, because the goals people pursued were irreducibly diverse. Conflict is therefore endemic to the human condition and the 'scientific' politician could appreciate this. Democracy, in Rousseau's sense of leading to a general will of the people, was impracticable, as no genuine intersubjective values were possible. Instead politics consisted of battling interest groups. Thus 'humanitarianism' was not a true expression of concern for your fellow human beings, but a rationalization of self-interest. When expressed by socialists it was used to weaken the strength of the elite in power. Bourgeois politicians, on the other hand, used it in the hope that piecemeal reform would prevent their overthrow by a violent revolution.

A rational consensus between rival groups being impossible, Pareto put forward two alternative strategies. The first was the use of manipulative technique, appealing to the irrational sentiments of some groups and to the self-seeking greed of others. This was the tactic of the 'foxes' and, he believed, of the Italian middle-class policy of *trasformismo*. However, this approach could only work whilst economic growth kept the populace largely aquiescent and allowed opponents to be bought off. The system broke down in a time of crisis, when the governing class had to use force to remain in power. In such a situation the 'lions' would have their day.

Examining post-war events in Italy, Pareto saw the government as a weak and outmoded party of 'foxes' attacked by socialist 'lions'. The *biennio rosso,* of 1919 to 1920, produced a fresh wave of strikes, far better organized than ever before. The government's attempts to appease the workers, rather than tackle them head on, convinced Pareto of their imminent demise. These events provide the context in which Pareto's appraisal of fascism should be viewed. Mussolini was the man of the moment because, whilst not devoid of the cunning of a 'fox', he could apply force with the strength of a 'lion'. From a 'scientific' point of view, therefore, he was Pareto's consummate politician. What purpose he put these skills to, though, is a matter of personal opinion.

This quandary bedevils Pareto's last writings. Initially he claimed he had simply described the conditions which had given rise to fascism. However it is clear from his letters, and his remarks about the 'red tyranny' of 1919 to 1920, that he welcomed it. He saw it as ending the stranglehold of the two power-blocks of producers and organized labour, who he believed had despoiled Italy before and since the war. His motivation was thus that of the early agitator, appealing to the petit bourgeoisie, whom he regarded as having lost most from the situation.

The only difficulties arose from fascism's lack of an alternative ideology to arouse the sentiments of the people sufficiently to make it a lasting political force. Pareto feared that Mussolini was simply doing Giolitti's dirty work for him, and that nothing would change as a result. His initial support, therefore, differed from that of Croce and other moderate conservatives, who hoped Mussolini would strengthen the liberal regime without destroying it. If fascism failed to establish itself as a new elite, which required fox-like cunning as well as leonine strength, violent anarchy would result. As he warned Pantaleoni, an earlier enthusiast of Mussolini than himself, 'There are growing signs in Italy, very slight it is true, of a worse future than one ever could have imagined. The danger of using force is of slipping into abusing it.' Unfortunately, Pareto had deprived himself of any grounds for isolating what was or was not an abuse.

Efficacy or social utility was the only standard by which he could judge a particular regime. Without further defining an objective standard of human happiness, a claim at variance with his liberalism, this depended solely on whether a group could persuade people that their rule was better than another. The veracity of the claim was immaterial. Pareto could not appeal to our 'real' interests when evaluating the policies of different parties, because this would have infringed the liberal belief that people should be free to decide for themselves what their wants were. Thus once Mussolini had successfully seized power, after the march on Rome, Pareto's earlier doubts faded completely. He applauded the use of force and fascism's anti-democratic stance for only in this manner 'could a radical change in Italian politics take place.' Whereas 'Italian bolshevism' had exhausted itself in sporadic violence, Mussolini had laid the foundations for a new regime via a fox-like appeal to conservative sentiments. 'The victory of fascism', Pareto wrote to Lello

Gangemi, 'confirms splendidly the previsions of my *Sociology* and many of my articles. I can therefore rejoice both personally and as a scientist.' He now hailed Mussolini as 'a statesman of the first rank', who would be a historical figure 'worthy of ancient Rome.' He was his Machiavellian Prince—'the man the *Sociology* can invoke', who would bring about 'the resurgence of Italy'.

There is therefore a certain circularity in the reasoning behind Pareto's sociology. Disillusionment at the frustration of his liberal ideals led to a cynical view of politics as the preserve of various elites composed of 'foxes' and 'lions'. His sociology then elaborated upon this jaundiced interpretation. Finally, the application of these categories to the study of contemporary politics actually confirmed his thesis, though in a manner he would have repudiated. For his theory provided a re-conceptualization of politics which made fascist practice respectable. As Adrian Lyttleton has remarked, 'if Pareto's theory had not existed, fascism would have had to invent it.'

FURTHER READING

Aron, Raymond. "Vilfredo Pareto." In *Main Currents in Sociological Thought, Volume II: Durkheim/Pareto/Weber*, translated by Richard Howard and Helen Weaver, pp. 99-176. New York: Basic Books, Inc., 1967.
>   Analysis of Pareto's theories of logical and non-logical actions within the framework of western thought.

Ascoli, Max. "Society through Pareto's Mind." *Social Research: An International Quarterly of Political and Social Science* 3, No. 1 (February 1936): 78-89.
>   Critique of Pareto's theories as found in *The Mind and Society*. Ascoli takes exception to Pareto's loose definitions, vague terminology, pretense of objectivity, and detached use of "logico-experimental reason."

Berger, Brigitte. "Vilfredo Pareto and the Sociology of Knowledge." *Social Research: An International Quarterly of Political and Social Science* 34, No. 2 (Summer 1967): 265-81.
>   Examines Pareto's thought, especially his sociological theory of history, as a useful adjunct to American sociological theory.

Blaug, Mark, ed. *Vilfredo Pareto (1848-1923)*. Aldershot, England: Edward Elgar Publishing Ltd., 1992, 381 p.
>   Collection of twenty-three essays from the years 1933-1984 on Pareto's social, economic, and political theory.

Bogardus, Emory S. "Pareto and Fascist Thought." In *The Development of Social Thought*, pp. 505-22. New York: Longmans, Green and Co., 1940.
>   Surveys the basic tenets of Pareto's *Trattato de sociologica generale* and the relation of these ideas to fascist thought.

Burnham, James. "Pareto: The Nature of Social Action." In *The Machiavellians: Defenders of Freedom*, pp. 171-220. New York: The John Day Company, Inc., 1943.
>   Analysis of Pareto's theories of logical and non-logical conduct, residues and derivations, social utility, and the circulation of the elites as part of a larger study of sociological thought since Dante.

Coser, Lewis A. "Vilfredo Pareto, 1848-1923." In *Masters of Sociological Thought: Ideas in Historical and Social Context*, pp. 386-426. New York: Harcourt Brace Jovanovich, 1977.
>   Overview of the main points of Pareto's sociological theories.

Faris, Ellsworth. "An Estimate of Pareto." In *The Nature of Human Nature and Other Essays in Social Psychology*, pp. 190-201. New York: McGraw-Hill Book Company, Inc., 1937.
>   Claims that Pareto's *Trattato de sociologica generale* has little or no value for the American student of sociology.

Finer, S. E. Introduction to *Vilfredo Pareto: Sociological Writings*, translated by Derick Mirfin, pp. 3-95. London: Pall Mall Press, 1966.
>   Includes a biographical summary, along with an examination of the development of Pareto's theoretical system and a critique of his overall contribution to sociology.

———. "Pareto and Pluto-Democracy: The Retreat to Galapagos." *The American Political Science Review* LXII, No. 2 (June 1968): 440-50.
>   Investigates the reasons why Pareto developed his theories, reexamines his views on pluto-democracy and the elite, and argues that he has been misinterpreted as a proto-fascist.

Harrington, John. "Vilfredo Pareto." In *Social Theorists*, edited by Clement S. Mihanovich, pp. 174-200. Milwaukee, Wisc.: The Bruce Publishing Company, 1953.
>   Outlines the framework of Pareto's sociological theory and highlights its influence on American sociology.

Henderson, Lawrence J. *Pareto's General Sociology: A Physiologist's Interpretation*. New York: Russell & Russell, 1935, 119 p.
>   Book-length study of the scientific aspects of Pareto's sociological system. Half of the text is organized into notes dealing with specific points of Pareto's theory.

Homans, George C. and Charles P. Curtis, Jr. *An Introduction to Pareto: His Sociology*. New York: Howard Fertig, 1970, 299 p.
>   Detailed exploration of Pareto's sociology and his place in the development of the field.

Hook, Sidney. "Pareto's Sociological System." *The Nation* (New York) CXL, No. 3651 (June 26, 1935): 747-48.

Review of *The Mind and Society* that calls the work "the most ambitious attempt of the twentieth century to construct a scientific system of sociology."

Meisel, James H., ed. *Pareto & Mosca*. Englewood Cliffs, N. J.: Prentice-Hall, Inc., 1965, 184 p.
    Contains essays on Pareto's sociological system by various contributors, including articles on the relation of his thought to that of Gaetano Mosca.

Nye, Robert A. "Pareto." In *The Anti-Democratic Sources of Elite Theory: Pareto, Mosca, Michels,* pp. 20-5. London: SAGE Publications, 1977.
    Discusses the social and political context in which Pareto developed his theory of elite social classes.

Perry, Charner. "Pareto's Contribution to Social Science." *International Journal of Ethics* 46, No. 1 (October 1935): 96-107.
    Remarks on flaws in Pareto's sociological theory, while noting the importance of his observations on the non-logical factors in human behavior.

Ricci, Umberto. "Pareto and Pure Economics." *Review of Economic Studies* 1, No. 1 (1933): 3-21.
    Evaluation of Pareto's theories on the sources of economic equilibrium: consumption, production, and exchange.

Samuels, Warren J. *Pareto on Policy*. Amsterdam: Elsevier Scientific Publishing Company, 1974, 232 p.
    Examines Pareto's contribution to a general equilibrium economic policy and his influence on the science of policy analysis.

Tarascio, Vincent J. "Pareto on Political Economy." *History of Political Economy* 6, No. 4 (Winter 1974): 361-80.
    Extracts a theory of political economy from Pareto's sociological, economic, and political writings.

————. "Pareto: A View of the Present through the Past." *Journal of Political Economy* 84, No. 1 (February 1976): 109-22.
    Biographical interpretation of Pareto's philosophical principles.

Theodore Roosevelt

1858–1919

American politician, historian, naturalist, biographer, essayist, journalist, and orator.

INTRODUCTION

The twenty-sixth president of the United States of America, Roosevelt is largely remembered as a politician and speech-maker, but he is also a respected man of letters who left behind a considerable literary corpus. His political record reflects the ideals of Progressivism which marked the era of his presidency in the years 1901-1908. An active domestic reformer, Roosevelt fought for social justice, especially on the side of labor, against the abuses of the wealthy and of big business, helping to forge the modern welfare state in America. A naturalist and staunch conservationist, he sought to preserve the na-tion's natural resources from exploitation by the private sector, nearly doubling the amount of land set aside for national parks during his administration. In foreign policy, Roosevelt combined an interest in military affairs and a belief in expansionism with a great degree of political acumen, particularly in his Far Eastern diplomacy. He strengthened the U.S. army and expanded the navy to protect America's presence in the Pacific and the Caribbean. In addition, he was awarded the Nobel Peace Prize in 1906 for mediating an end to the Russo-Japanese war. As a writer, Roosevelt is remembered for his historical accounts of American exploration, especially *The Winning of the West; An Account of the Exploration and Settlement of Our Country from the Alleghanies to the Pacific* (1889-1896).

Biographical Information

Roosevelt was born on October 27, 1858, in New York City into a prestigious and wealthy family. Afflicted with asthma and weak eyesight, he actively engaged in sports such as boxing and horseback riding in order to strengthen himself. Likewise, his youthful fascination with nature led him to spend as much time as possible outdoors. Educated by private tutors until entering Har-vard University, Roosevelt graduated in 1880, and while there had begun work on his first historical work, *The Naval War of 1812* (1882). Beginning in 1881 he served three consecutive one-year terms as a member of the New York legislature, but left his home state for the Dakota territory soon after the deaths of his wife and mother in 1884. Two years of writing and research ended in 1886 with a return to New York City and a failed campaign for mayor. Roosevelt's return to politics came in 1889, however, with his appointment to the Civil Service Commission by then-president Benjamin Harrison. He quickly rose to the position of commission head and served for

six years. His next office was that of New York City's police board president during the years 1895 to 1897. Named Assistant Secretary to the Navy by president William McKinley in 1897, Roosevelt resigned his post the following year to organize the 1st Regiment of U. S. Cavalry Volunteers, the "Rough Riders," during the Spanish-American War. As colonel of the force Roosevelt led the now famous charge up San Juan Hill and returned to New York a war hero. Elected governor in November of 1898, he launched a campaign of social reform that would later be reflected on a wider scale in his presidency. In 1900 he appeared as McKinley's vice-presidential running mate, and became president in September of 1901 when McKinley was assassinated. In his first term, Roosevelt used his powers to increase the size of the U.S. military and applied the Sherman Antitrust Act against the Northern Securities Company in February of 1902 to destroy its railroad monopoly. That year Roosevelt also interceded in the national coal strike on the behalf of labor, forcing the coal companies to arbitrate. Reelected in 1904 by an overwhelming popular majority, Roosevelt continued to implement his Progressivist ideas on social reform, and to pursue his foreign policy, expanding U. S. protective influence in Latin America by invoking the so-called Roosevelt Corollary to the Monroe Doctrine. In the election of 1908 Roosevelt gave his support to the successful campaign of William H. Taft, and left for an extended African safari in early 1909. In the following presidential election, Roosevelt, feeling that Taft's conservatism had grown excessive, ran as a member of the independent Progressive or "Bull Moose" Party. The resulting split in the republican vote gave Woodrow Wilson, the democratic candidate, victory in 1912. For the next several years Roosevelt remained a vocal part of public life—he called for U. S. military involvement on the side of the Allies at the outbreak of World War I in 1914—and continued to travel and write until his death on January 6, 1919.

Major Works

Among Roosevelt's earliest writings are several works of naturalism on highly specific subjects, such as *The Summer Birds of the Adirondacks in Franklin County, N.Y.* (1877). His first significant work, *The Naval War of 1812*, was published in 1882 and elicited modest but favorable reviews. In this essentially patriotic monograph, Roosevelt offers his esteem for the courageousness of U.S. naval officers and sailors who fought in the conflict, while criticizing the lack of military astuteness he observed in Thomas Jefferson and James Madison. As an historical biographer, Roosevelt produced works on *Thomas Hart Benton* (1886) and *Oliver Cromwell* (1900) among others. His literary representations of the American senator and the Puritan leader, however, have been observed by critics to lack depth and verve. *The Winning of the West* remains one of Roosevelt's most highly esteemed works. Covering the period from Daniel Boone's crossing of the Appalachian range in 1767 to Zebulon Pike's expedition to the Rocky Mountain region (1807) in its four volumes, the work's strengths are said to lie in its personality sketches, accounts of Native American culture, and socioeconomic analysis of historical events. Roosevelt's history of *New York* (1891) represents an early concern with the varied ethnic character of the city and the sociological dynamics of immigration and economic inequality operating there. Another of his favorite topics, exploring, hunting, and general outdoor life, appeared as the subject of several works including *Ranch Life and the Hunting-trail* (1888), *The Wilderness Hunter* (1893), and *Through the Brazilian Wilderness* (1914). Lastly, Roosevelt's essays and oratory, from fiery political speeches to literary reviews, have been published separately and in collections, among them, *The Strenuous Life: Essays and Addresses* (1900) and *Social Justice and Popular Rule: Essays, Addresses, and Public Statements Relating to the Progressive Movement* (1926).

Critical Reception

Theodore Roosevelt's character and reputation have been the subject of much critical attention, in large part due to his long and varied political career. An immensely popular politician typically associated with the reforms of Progressivism, he is often remembered for his rugged individualism and personal integrity. His literary works, though generally well accepted in his day, have been lauded for their patriotic evocations of historical figures, but have typically been criticized for excessive moralizing. Nevertheless, Roosevelt remains a compelling subject for historians and biographers, and is widely considered an outstanding figure in twentieth-century American politics.

PRINCIPAL WORKS

The Summer Birds of the Adirondacks in Franklin County, N.Y. (naturalism) 1877
Notes on Some of the Birds of Oyster Bay, Long Island (naturalism) 1879
The Naval War of 1812; or, The History of the United States Navy during the Last War with Great Britain [republished as *The Naval Operations of the War Between Great Britain and the United States*] (history) 1882
Hunting Trips of a Ranchman (essays) 1885
Thomas Hart Benton (biography) 1886
Essays on Practical Politics (essays) 1888
Gouverneur Morris (biography) 1888
Ranch Life and the Hunting-trail (essays) 1888
The Winning of the West; An Account of the Exploration and Settlement of Our Country from the Alleghanies to the Pacific (history) 1889-1896
New York (history) 1891
The Wilderness Hunter: An Account of the Big Game of the United States and Its Chase With Horse (naturalism) 1893
Hero Tales from American History (history) 1895
American Ideals, and Other Essays, Social and Political (essays) 1897
The Rough Riders (personal history) 1899
Oliver Cromwell (biography) 1900
The Strenuous Life: Essays and Addresses (essays and speeches) 1900
California Addresses (speeches) 1903
Outdoor Pastimes of an American Hunter (essays) 1903
Addresses and Presidential Messages of Theodore Roosevelt, 1902-1904 (speeches) 1904
Good Hunting (essays) 1907
Addresses and Papers (speeches and essays) 1908
The Roosevelt Policy; Speeches, Letters and State Papers, Relating to Corporate Wealth and Closely Allied Topics, of Theodore Roosevelt (speeches, letters, and essays) 1908
Outlook Editorials (journalism) 1909
African and European Addresses (speeches) 1910
African Game Trails, An Account of the African Wanderings of an American Hunter-Naturalist (essay) 1910
Realizable Goals (The Earl Lectures) (speeches) 1912

CRITICISM

Gansey R. Johnston (essay date 1899)

SOURCE: "The Writings of Theodore Roosevelt," in *Book Buyer,* Vol. xviii, No. 1, 1899, pp. 5-10.

[*In the following essay, Johnston considers the varied subject matter of Roosevelt's writings.*]

As a man of action rather than a man of letters, Colonel Roosevelt has in our American year of 1898 appeared in the public eye. Some of his deeds have been so dramatic that when we come to view his books it will no doubt be difficult to place them in proper perspective. We cannot separate them from the man, whose character is stamped upon all their pages, of whose faults and virtues they partake, of whom, indeed, they have much to say; but by the association we should not be led to under-estimate their inherent value. If the man could maintain his place in the rough democracy of the frontier, where only the individual virtues find recognition, his books may not fear competition on the same ground.

He is in reality a man of many sides. One might follow his political or military career without guessing his quali-

ties as an historian; join in his hunting without knowing his politics; read his political biographies without suspecting that he ever held an office or fired a gun. He writes the story of New York as though he had spent his life (and as a spectator) on Manhattan Island. Mr. Roosevelt's own books on western life of this generation are three: *The Hunting Trips of a Ranchman* (1885), *Ranch Life and the Hunting Trail* (1888), and *The Wilderness Hunter* (1893). The first and third of these are primarily books of the chase. Their author is a great lover of the sport of which he says: "The chase is among the best of all national pastimes; it cultivates that vigorous manliness for the lack of which in a nation as in an individual the possession of no other qualities can possibly atone."

He is much more than a killer of game. If he is an enthusiastic sportsman, he is a careful zoölogist as well. The big game of the United States is rapidly disappearing; those animals which have not become extinct have had their habits modified by the presence of man; and such records as these have a scientific value. In no other books of the class that I know is there less of what scientists call the "personal equation." The statements may be taken as they stand. The author is writing of his own experiences and observations, and necessarily the capital I's are plentiful. His modesty, however, deserves mention; steering clear of deprecation on the one hand and of conceit on the other. A hunter once expressed it to me thus: "I like Roosevelt's books; the other fellow gets as much game as he does."

The reader is carried along with their spirit. He breathes with the writer the free air; views with him the rolling prairies, the buttes and gullies of the Bad Lands, the grand peaks of the Rockies; lives with his people; shares in his hardships and exposure; creeps with him in tiresome labor on the stalk, or pants with his footrace; rejoices in his success, is humiliated with his failure. An interesting comparison might be drawn between *The Wilderness Hunter* and *The Workers.* Wyekoff is writing of men, and Roosevelt for the most part of beasts; they both have a keen, true observation, a power of description in meaning and unwasteful language; they both are content with a small proportion of philosophy.

Ranch Life and the Hunting Trail deals largely with the highly interesting human life of a passing epoch. The Indian fighter, the trapper, the ground-breaker, the cowboy, the ranchman, of the Great West, will soon be displaced. They are especially fortunate in having their story told by one who has lived their lives with them, and who yet can study them from the older civilization.

A thorough knowledge and a just appreciation of the men who won the continent lying behind the Alleghanies must give high rank in historical writings for the four volumes of *The Winning of the West.* Undoubtedly, too little attention has been paid, in the study of our history, to the events west of the mountains. It is a piece of rare good fortune that the story is told by one who combines the historian's studiousness and judgment with heartfelt sympathy with the movement, and the skill to relate the living details with ability to place his epoch in the world's history. Mr. Roosevelt knows the meaning of this mighty movement of the English race, displacing French, Spanish and Indian claimants to so vast a space of the fairest ground under the skies. He knows the backwoodsmen, brave, strong and often noble, if sometimes unrestrainable and cruel, who fought their way west to found homes and independence. He knows their hard sense and their capacity for self-government. He knows little of good and much of evil of the Indian, doomed to succumb in fearful death-struggle before the advance of the superior race. He knows the treachery of the Spaniards, the fickleness of the French, the unavailing bravery and the hideous alliances of the British. He knows the wilderness, its enemies in thickets and floods and fires, in cold and storms, in savage beasts and not less savage men, its promise in land and fertility and freedom.

His attitude towards the Indians' rights is summed up briefly in his sentence: "The most ultimately righteous of all wars is a war with savages." Had that sentence been placed at the beginning of the work it might have saved the reiteration that the Indians owned the enormous territory over which their scanty tribes roamed, only by virtue of dispossessing rival claimants—the very title of the white settlers.

The *Life of Thomas Benton* speaks the spirit of the West. The period of rapid expansion is one of the most interesting in our annals: when the young West, with its glories, its faults, its contradictions, was beginning to feel its political power; when Webster and Calhoun and Clay, with Benton—in some respects most admirable of them all—gave the Senate a mighty name; when glimmered the first signs of the split on Mason and Dixon's line, and it seemed that the inevitable conflict might be stayed by compromise. So long as men care for the past and the present history of their country, they will consider the failings and the merits of the great party led so differently by Jefferson and Jackson. To Mr. Roosevelt our thanks are due for his clear outline of Jackson's great lieutenant, and for the fresh thought he brings into the discussion of his period. The sturdy Benton, brave, boastful, persevering, opinionated, partisan, broadening, national, even in his independence, which at last cost him his seat, was a type of the people from whose loins he sprang. Roosevelt's greatest books are those which throw the true light upon the essential manhood of the pioneers whose uncouth and passionate qualities had shadowed their better natures. As a concentrated, intense thinker, Mr. Roosevelt tends to overlook the minor features of his topic, and the qualifications which a wider view might give his statements. His enthusiasm sometimes carries him further than cold judgment would do, and his antipathies are perhaps too pronounced. This is but saying that some allowance must be made in his histories for the personal equation; "biased" is entirely too strong a word to apply to any of his phrases. It is one of his merits that he has due regard for both the strength and weakness of

every character; he knows that we can love a man of many faults as well as despise one with marked virtues; and he does not fear to present the traits of the whole man. We cannot think he estimates every one at his true worth; but we cannot call this the error of his method. Intense as is his patriotism (to my mind, *because* of its intensity), his denunciation of those actors and actions that have made for national shame is only less severe than his censure of those creatures of colonial habit unable to appreciate their country at its real grandeur. He is a stanch believer in party politics, but is no partisan in his thinking.

The *Life of Gouverneur Morris* must take its place as one of the lesser volumes of an admirable series, even as its subject was one of the lesser American statesmen. Mr. Roosevelt has the honesty not to magnify the men who really did much excellent work for the new nation both at home and abroad; and he has the art to delineate a clean-cut complete character, whom we are glad thus to know. The French, among whom Morris spent several years before and in their revolution, receive considerable attention in this book. Between the contemporary recorder, who was one of the most brilliant of observers and writers, and the historian at long range, we feel that we approach near to the heart of that terrible storm, of the sufferers by whom it was raised, and of the poor-spirited nobles swept before its violence.

The Story of New York, though brief and containing little of special note, is more than a well-written perfunctory history. Into the political life of his city, Mr. Roosevelt has entered with as much zeal as into the wild life of the West, and its treatment of its government has the same vital touch. The best features of this book, relating to the Revolution and to the local government, we can find in more extended form in the *Gouverneur Morris* and in various essays.

The Naval War of 1812 was written rather for the student than the popular reader. On account of inaccuracies and misrepresentations of previous historians the work is controversial and much of its space is given to the weighing of evidence. It also abounds in technicalities, so that only by study can a landsman make progress in its reading. He will find himself rewarded, however, when the sea fights warm his pulses and renew his admiration for his country's heroes. To a later edition is appended an account of the battle of New Orleans, which is full of fire. It is a real omission that the political history of the war and its causes is scarcely mentioned—the more so as Mr. Roosevelt has written of the periods that might have been connected by this link. Possibly his lack of sympathy with the Jeffersonians has been the cause of the omission.

The introduction of the later editions has something to say of the lesson of unpreparedness—a warning emphasized by the Assistant Secretary of the Navy in 1897, and by the events of 1898. Until in the certainty of perpetual peace all war preparations are obsolete, there is certainly need for the best mechanisms. The spirit of battle may spring up in a breath, but not so its machinery. Sailors may be promptly recruited, but battle-ships require years to construct. A thousand soldiers may be gathered in a day, but it takes months to make a regiment. A Secretary of War may be appointed off-hand, but some apprenticeship is necessary to learn the trade. As one of the earliest works, this volume shows the defects of the author's style—defects not entirely outgrown. It is often a disappointment in falling just short of excellence. Frequently it appears that a little more attention would have given the language the finish that it elsewhere displays. Many parts of *The Hunting Trips of a Ranchman* present the appearance of having been taken straight from notes day by day; and perhaps in an outdoor book this is a gain. In political discussion, too, we are glad to get a writer's first vigorous thought, that might be tamed by revision. In such a work as *The Winning of the West,* however, we cannot but regret the occasional evidences of haste.

Hero Tales of American History, the joint work of Theodore Roosevelt and Henry Cabot Lodge, deserves more than passing mention. I trust that the parents of the boys and girls of the present generation may be mindful of their advantages over us, but few years older. For us such books as Fiske's *War of Independence* and these "Hero Tales" did not exist. Historians have here a field for whose cultivation they might well pause in their other work, for by it they may make their names honored by the youngsters whose intellects are quicker to respond to the best than to guess the vapidity of the mediocre.

Periodical literature has caught much of Mr. Roosevelt's writings. Questions of politics—using the word in its proper sense—of immediate and of more lasting interest, have called from him many papers. Books of sociological and other topics have found him a thoughtful and suggestive reviewer. To the periodical *Science* he gave "**A Layman's Views on Scientific Nomenclature.**" From a literary point of view, it is interesting to note the varying ways in which, in half a dozen magazines, he defended his actions as Civil Service Commissioner, and as the renewer of the New York police force.

A goodly number of the political articles and reviews have been gathered into his latest volume, *American Ideals and Other Essays.* This book so well displays the many-sidedness of his political life, that it is a bit of self-denial not to turn through it piece by piece. The spirit of all the chapters is the same, and we can best consider it as a whole. The fundamental lesson is the need of energy and manly character and intelligence in the conduct of public life. Colonel Roosevelt has had much to say of the soldierly virtues, and is frank to place them at the head of his list. Yet it shows little discrimination to say, as has been said, that fighting is the highest of his American ideals. Personally, he may enjoy battle for its own sake, even as he enjoys the chase, but this is not the spirit of his call. In the public life, as an officer of the city, the state, the nation, through active experience with realities, the conviction has been forced upon him that not alone

eternal vigilance but also eternal work and eternal battle is the price of liberty. The fact is that more or less conflict is a necessary *condition* of the world's progress. In such peace and in such of the peaceful virtues as we enjoy to-day, we are but reaping what has been sown by the sacrifices of the past. We shall make an ill return of our harvest if we sow no seed for the betterment of generations to come. Peace, when it means acquiescence in wrong, is the poorest of doctrines to preach in a democracy, whose very foundation is the virility of its people. It is not to be said of Americans that courage in battle is incompatible with mercy and justice and love and peace. But it may be said that these cannot coexist with cowardice. Of the chronic peacemakers, Colonel Roosevelt might say, as he has said of sheep: No man can associate with them and retain his self-respect.

The conflict into which he calls the honest men of the nation is not always a pleasant one. Some of his exhortations would be unacceptable from a weaker man. Once in writing of the ferocity of the grizzly he mentioned the habit of a certain hunter to seek refuge in a tree from the bear's charge, and parenthetically remarked that he "did not approve of this, however." He had shown his own valor with the rifle. So may he call upon others to take their part in the fiercest of civic conflicts.

That this book contains propositions with which the present writer disagrees is not to the point, when it will be impossible in short space to touch a fraction of its excellences. There is one phrase, however, which should not be overlooked, because it is so inconsistent with the colonel's own deeds, and because of the possibilities of evil that it contains. I do not think he has elsewhere struck so false a note.

In the noble panegyric on **"True Americanism,"** it is a surprise to find the unqualified endorsement of a paragraph (the words of naturalized Germans) in which appears the sentiment "America, right or wrong." We have seen Mr. Roosevelt fighting the internal as well as the external enemies of his country. He could suffer on the battlefield for America right, but could lead a brave protest against needless suffering permitted by the administration wrong. His comparison of patriotism with monogamous marriage is not the best; though little could be said for marriage right or wrong. A better comparison would be of the national with the religious life. Christianity has had an influence in the world's advance surely not less than that of the United States; but I cannot believe Mr. Roosevelt's religion is so poor that it would let him toast "Christianity right or wrong." Certainly he has scant sympathy for those who prate of "Protestantism right or wrong." Indeed, his own words in this same plea for unselfish love of country forbid the belief that under the standard "Our country right or wrong" he would condone any concrete evil. The one-idea'd man has accomplished much in this world; the discriminating, more.

"Phases of State Legislation" and **"Machine Politics in New York City"** are the two articles making up the thin volume published in 1885, under the title *Essays on Practical Politics*. Mr. Roosevelt has much to say in criticism of the legislative body in which he did some active work in the early eighties—criticism of a robust sort that gives credit where credit is due. It is his perception that the evil is weaker than the good, even in machine politics, if the good but rouse itself, that keeps his energies active and maintains his hopefulness. It is noteworthy that in reprinting these essays he points out some real reforms that have been established since they were first published.

He is especially emphatic in his demand upon the educated men to take their part in the political work of the day. Criticism combined with earnest effort to set up the good is to his taste; criticism that is cynical and undoing has his contempt. Practical as opposed to merely theoretical politics is his keynote. The sentimental humanitarians and the timid good receive about equal portions of his denunciation. It is the lesson taught over and over by his experience that good intentions are potent only for harm unless roused to activity intelligent and unwavering. The workers for honest and efficient government have found the inertia of friends scarcely less inimical than the action of enemies.

Colonel Roosevelt's tendency is toward optimism, but not an optimism based on unreason. He has little in common with those who would make the world over, and who, with the inevitable discovery that the world is not a mechanism to be reconstructed at will, lose spirit and balance. He believes that the need is for a little more work in the way in which work has been done; and a man of his energy cannot fail to have faith in the energy of other men. The following paragraph, from the review of Mr. Pearson's *National Life and Character*, well expresses his attitude toward the world:—

> We ourselves are not certain that progress is assured; we only assert that it may be assured if we but live wise, brave, and upright lives. We do not know whether the future has in store for us calm or unrest. We cannot know beyond peradventure whether we can prevent the higher races from losing their nobler traits and from being overwhelmed by the lower races. On the whole we think that the greatest victories are yet to be won, and that there are yet in store for our peoples and for the causes that we uphold grander triumphs than have ever yet been scored. But be this as it may, we gladly agree that the one plain duty of every man is to face the future as he faces the present, regardless of what it may have in store for him, and, turning toward the light as he sees the light, to play his part manfully, as a man among men.

He who would learn of the character, the ideals, the purposes of one who seems destined to have a growing influence in the affairs of the nation he loves so well and has served with high courage and unselfishness, may well take his inspiration from the writings of Theodore Roosevelt.

Theodore Roosevelt (essay date 1913)

SOURCE: "Theodore Roosevelt: From History As Literature," in *Style*, Vol. 13, No. 1, winter, 1979, pp. 1-4.

[*In the following essay, originally published in* History as Literature *in 1913, Roosevelt argues that historical writing should retain a distinct literary aspect as exemplified by the works of the great historians of the past.*]

Because history, science, and literature have all become specialized, the theory now is that science is definitely severed from literature and that history must follow suit. Not only do I refuse to accept this as true for history but I do not even accept it as true for science.

Literature may be defined as that which has permanent interest because both of its substance and its form, aside from the mere technical value that inheres in a special treatise for specialists. For a great work of literature there is the same demand now that there always has been; and in any great work of literature the first element is great imaginative power. The imaginative power demanded for a great historian is different from that demanded for a great poet; but it is no less marked. Such imaginative power is in no sense incompatible with minute accuracy. On the contrary, very accurate, very real and vivid, presentation of the past, can come only from one in whom the imaginative gift is strong. The industrious collector of dead facts bears to such a man precisely the relation that a photographer bears to Rembrandt. There are innumerable books, that is, innumerable volumes of printed matter between covers, which are excellent for their own purposes, but in which imagination would be as wholly out of place as in the blue prints of a sewer system or in the photographs taken to illustrate a work on comparative osteology. But the vitally necessary sewer system does not take the place of the cathedral of Rheims or of the Parthenon; no quantity of photographs will ever be equivalent to one Rembrandt; and the greatest mass of data, although indispensable to the work of a great historian, is in no shape or way a substitute for that work.

History, taught for a directly and immediately useful purpose to pupils and the teachers of pupils, is one of the necessary features of a sound education in democratic citizenship. A book containing such sound teaching, even if without any literary quality, may be as useful to the student and as creditable to the writer, as a similar book on medicine. I am not slighting such a book when I say that once it has achieved its worthy purpose, it can be permitted to lapse from human memory as a good book on medicine, which has outlived its usefulness, lapses from memory. But the historical work which does possess literary quality may be a permanent contribution to the sum of man's wisdom, enjoyment, and inspiration. The writer of such a book must add wisdom to knowledge, and the gift of expression to the gift of imagination.

It is a shallow criticism to assert that imagination tends to inaccuracy. Only a distorted imagination tends to inaccuracy. Vast and fundamental truths can be discerned and interpreted only by one whose imagination is as lofty as the soul of a Hebrew prophet. When we say that the great historian must be a man of imagination, we use the word as we use it when we say that the great statesman must be a man of imagination. Moreover, together with imagination must go the power of expression. The great speeches of statesmen and the great writings of historians can live only if they possess the deathless quality that inheres in all great literature. The greatest literary historian must of necessity be a master of the science of history, a man who has at his fingertips all the accumulated facts from the treasure-houses of the dead past. But he must also possess the power to marshal what is dead so that before our eyes it lives again.

. . . . In the field of historical research an immense amount can be done by men who have no literary power whatever. Moreover, the most painstaking and laborious research, covering long periods of years, is necessary in order to accumulate the material for any history worth writing at all. There are important by-paths of history, moreover, which hardly admit of treatment that would make them of interest to any but specialists. All this I fully admit. In particular I pay high honor to the patient and truthful investigator. He does an indispensable work. My claim is merely that such work should not exclude the work of the great master who can use the materials gathered, who has the gift of vision, the quality of the seer, the power himself to see what has happened and to make what he has seen clear to the vision of others. My only protest is against those who believe that the extension of the activities of the most competent mason and most energetic contractor will supply the lack of great architects. If, as in the Middle Ages, the journeymen builders are themselves artists, why this is the best possible solution of the problem. But if they are not artists, then their work, however much it represents of praiseworthy industry, and of positive usefulness, does not take the place of the work of a great artist.

. . . . So far from ignoring science, the great historian of the future can do nothing unless he is steeped in science. He can never equal what has been done by the great historians of the past unless he writes not merely with full knowledge, but with an intensely vivid consciousness, of all that of which they were necessarily ignorant. He must realize that man has been on this earth for a period of such incalculable length that, from the standpoint of the student of his development through time, what our ancestors used to call "antiquity" is almost indistinguishable from the present day.

. . . . The great historian of the future cannot be excused if he fails to draw on the vast storehouses of knowledge that have been accumulated, if he fails to profit by the wisdom and work of other men, which are now the common property of all intelligent men. He must use the instruments which the historians of the past did not have ready to hand. Yet even with these instruments he cannot do as good work as the best of the elder historians unless he has vision and imagination, the power to grasp what is essential and to reject the infinitely more numerous non-essentials, the power to embody ghosts, to put flesh and blood on dry bones, to make dead men living before our eyes. In short he must have the power to take the science of history and turn it into literature.

. . . . Beyond all question the great historian of the future must keep ever in mind the relative importance of the usual and the unusual. If he is a really great historian, if he possesses the highest imaginative and literary quality, he will be able to interest us in the gray tints of the general landscape no less than in the flame hues of the jutting peaks. It is even more essential to have such quality in writing of the commonplace than in writing of the exceptional. Otherwise no profit will come from study of the ordinary; for writings are useless unless they are read, and they cannot be read unless they are readable. Furthermore, while doing full justice to the importance of the usual, of the commonplace, the great historian will not lose sight of the importance of the heroic.

. . . . History which is not professedly utilitarian, history which is didactic only as great poetry is unconsciously didactic, may yet possess that highest form of usefulness, the power to thrill the souls of men with stories of strength and craft and daring, and to lift them out of their common selves to the heights of high endeavor. . . . the service done is immeasurably increased in value when the man arises who from his study of a myriad [of] dead fragments is able to paint some living picture of the past.

This is why the record as great writers preserve it has a value immeasurable beyond what is merely lifeless. Such a record pulses with immortal life. It may recount the deed or the thought of a hero at some supreme moment. It may be merely the portrayal of homely every-day life. This matters not so long as in either even the genius of the historian enables him to paint in colors that do not fade. . . . Only a great historian can fittingly deal with a very great subject; yet because the qualities of chief interest in human history can be shown on a small field no less than on a large one, some of the greatest historians have treated subjects that only their own genius rendered great.

So true is this that if great events lack a great historian and a great poet writes about them, it is the poet who fixes them in the mind of mankind, so that in aftertime importance the real has become the shadow and the shadow the reality. . . .

When, however, the great historian has spoken, his work will never be undone. No poet can ever supersede what Napier wrote of the storming of Badajoz, of the British infantry at Albuera, and of the light artillery at Fuentes d'Oñoro. After Parkman had written of Montcalm and Wolfe there was left for other writers only what Fitzgerald left for other translators of Omar Khayyam. Much new light has been thrown on the history of the Byzantine Empire by the many men who have studied it of recent years; we read each new writer with pleasure and profit; and after reading each we take down a volume of Gibbon, with renewed thankfulness that a great writer was moved to do a great task.

The great historian must be able to paint for us the life of the plain people, the ordinary men and women, of the time of which he writes. He can do this only if he possesses the highest kind of imagination. . . . The great historian will in as full measure as possible present to us the every-day life of the men and women of the age which he describes. Nothing that tells of this life will come amiss to him. The instruments of their labor and the weapons of their warfare, the wills that they wrote, the bargains that they made, and the songs that they sang when they feasted and made love; he must use them all. He must tell us of the toil of the ordinary man in ordinary times, and of the play by which that ordinary toil was broken. He must never forget that no event stands out entirely isolated. He must trace from its obscure and humble beginnings each of the movements that in its hour of triumph has shaken the world.

. . . . He must ever remember that while the worst offense of which he can be guilty is to write vividly and inaccurately, yet that unless he writes vividly he cannot write truthfully; for no amount of dull painstaking detail will sum up as the whole truth unless the genius is there to paint the truth.

Henry A. Beers (essay date 1919)

SOURCE: "Roosevelt as Man of Letters," in *Four Americans: Roosevelt, Hawthorne, Emerson, Whitman,* Yale University Press, 1919, pp. 7-31.

[*In the following essay, Beers praises Roosevelt for his ability to translate his experiences as a man of action into a body of literary works.*]

In a club corner, just after Roosevelt's death, the question was asked whether his memory would not fade away, when the living man, with his vivid personality, had gone. But no: that personality had stamped itself too deeply on the mind of his generation to be forgotten. Too many observers have recorded their impressions; and already a dozen biographies and memoirs have appeared. Besides, he is his own recorder. He published twenty-six books, a catalogue of which any professional author might be proud; and a really wonderful feat when it is remembered that he wrote them in the intervals of an active public career as Civil Service Commissioner, Police Commissioner, member of his state legislature, Governor of New York, delegate to the National Republican Convention, Colonel of Rough Riders, Assistant Secretary of the Navy, Vice-President and President of the United States.

Perhaps in some distant future he may become a myth or symbol, like other mighty hunters of the beast, Nimrod

and Orion and Tristram of Lyonesse. Yet not so long as *African Game Trails* and the *Hunting Trips of a Ranchman* endure, to lift the imagination to those noble sports denied to the run of mortals by poverty, feebleness, timidity, the engrossments of the humdrum, everyday life, or lack of enterprise and opportunity. Old scraps of hunting song thrill us with the great adventure: "In the wild chamois' track at break of day"; "We'll chase the antelope over the plain"; "Afar in the desert I love to ride"; and then we go out and shoot at a woodchuck, with an old double-barrelled shotgun—and miss! If Roosevelt ever becomes a poet, it is while he is among the wild creatures and wild landscapes that he loved: in the gigantic forests of Brazil, or the almost unnatural nature of the Rockies and the huge cattle ranches of the plains, or on the limitless South African veldt, which is said to give a greater feeling of infinity than the ocean even.

Roosevelt was so active a person—not to say so noisy and conspicuous; he so occupied the centre of every stage, that, when he died, it was as though a wind had fallen, a light had gone out, a military band had stopped playing. It was not so much the death of an individual as a general lowering in the vitality of the nation. America was less America, because he was no longer here. He should have lived twenty years more had he been willing to go slow, to loaf and invite his soul, to feed that mind of his in a wise passiveness. But there was no repose about him, and his pleasures were as strenuous as his toils. John Burroughs tells us that he did not care for fishing, the contemplative man's recreation. No contemplation for him, but action; no angling in a clear stream for a trout or grayling; but the glorious, dangerous excitement of killing big game—grizzlies, lions, African buffaloes, mountain sheep, rhinoceroses, elephants. He never spared himself: he wore himself out. But doubtless he would have chosen the crowded hour of glorious life—or strife, for life and strife were with him the same.

He was above all things a fighter, and the favorite objects of his denunciation were professional pacifists, nice little men who had let their muscles get soft, and nations that had lost their fighting edge. Aggressive war, he tells us in *The Winning of the West,* is not always bad. "Americans need to keep in mind the fact that, as a nation, they have erred far more often in not being willing enough to fight than in being too willing." "Cowardice," he writes elsewhere, "in a race, as in an individual, is the unpardonable sin." Is this true? Cowardice is a weakness, perhaps a disgraceful weakness: a defect of character which makes a man contemptible, just as foolishness does. But it is not a sin at all, and surely not an unpardonable one. Cruelty, treachery, and ingratitude are much worse traits, and selfishness is as bad. I have known very good men who were cowards; men that I liked and trusted but who, from weakness of nerves or other physical causes—perhaps from prenatal influences—were easily frightened and always constitutionally timid. The Colonel was a very pugnacious man: he professed himself to be a lover of peace—and so did the Kaiser—but really he enjoyed the *gaudium certaminis,* as all bold spirits do.

In the world-wide sense of loss which followed his death, some rather exaggerated estimates made themselves heard. A preacher announced that there had been only two great Americans, one of whom was Theodore Roosevelt. An editor declared that the three greatest Americans were Washington, Lincoln, and Roosevelt. But not all great Americans have been in public life; and, of those who have, very few have been Presidents of the United States. What is greatness? Roosevelt himself rightly insists on character as the root of the matter. Still character alone does not make a man great. There are thousands of men in common life, of sound and forceful character, who never become great, who are not even potentially great. To make them such, great abilities are needed, as well as favoring circumstances. In his absolute manner—a manner caught perhaps partly from Macaulay, for whose qualities as a writer he had a high and, I think, well-justified regard—he pronounces Cromwell the greatest Englishman of the seventeenth century. Was he so? He was the greatest English soldier and magistrate of that century; but how about Bacon and Newton, about Shakespeare and Milton?

Let us think of a few other Americans who, in their various fields, might perhaps deserve to be entitled great. Shall we say Jonathan Edwards, Benjamin Franklin, Alexander Hamilton, John Marshall, Robert Fulton, S. F. B. Morse, Ralph Waldo Emerson, Daniel Webster, Horace Greeley, Henry Ward Beecher, Admiral Farragut, General W. T. Sherman, James Russell Lowell, Nathaniel Hawthorne, General Robert E. Lee? None of these people were Presidents of the United States. But to the man in the street there is something imposing about the office and title of a chief magistrate, be he emperor, king, or elected head of a republic. It sets him apart. Look at the crowds that swarm to get a glimpse of the President when he passes through, no matter whether it is George Washington or Franklin Pierce.

It might be safer, on the whole, to say that the three names in question are those of our greatest presidents, not of the greatest Americans. And even this comparison might be questioned. Some, for example, might assert the claims of Thomas Jefferson to rank with the others. Jefferson was a man of ideas who made a strong impression on his generation. He composed the Declaration of Independence and founded the Democratic party and the University of Virginia. He had a more flexible mind than Washington, though not such good judgment; and he had something of Roosevelt's alert interest in a wide and diversified range of subjects. But the latter had little patience with Jefferson. He may have respected him as the best rider and pistol shot in Virginia; but in politics he thought him a theorist and doctrinaire imbued with the abstract notions of the French philosophical deists and democrats. Jefferson, he thought, knew nothing and cared nothing about military affairs. He let the army run down and preferred to buy Louisiana rather than conquer it, while he dreamed of universal fraternity and was the forerunner of the Dove of Peace and the League of Nations.

Roosevelt, in fact, had no use for philosophy or speculative thought which could not be reduced to useful action. He was an eminently practical thinker. His mind was without subtlety, and he had little imagination. A life of thought for its own sake; the life of a dreamer or idealist; a life like that of Coleridge, with his paralysis of will and abnormal activity of the speculative faculty, eternally spinning metaphysical cobwebs, doubtless seemed to the author of *The Strenuous Life* a career of mere self-indulgence. It is not without significance that, with all his passion for out of doors, for wild life and the study of bird and beast, he nowhere, so far as I can remember, mentions Thoreau, who is far and away our greatest nature writer. Doubtless he may have esteemed him as a naturalist, but not as a transcendentalist or as an impracticable faddist who refused to pay taxes because Massachusetts enforced the fugitive slave law. We are told that his fellow historian, Francis Parkman, had a contempt for philosophers like Emerson and Thoreau and an admiration for writers such as Scott and Cooper who depicted scenes of bold adventure. The author of *The Oregon Trail* and the author of *African Game Trails* had a good deal in common, especially great force of will—you see it in Parkman's jaw. He was a physical wreck and did his work under almost impossible conditions; while Roosevelt had built up an originally sickly constitution into a physique of splendid vigor.

Towards the critical intellect, as towards the speculative, Roosevelt felt an instinctive antagonism. One of his most characteristic utterances is the address delivered at the Sorbonne, April 30, 1910, **"Citizenship in a Republic."** Here, amidst a good deal of moral commonplace—wise and sensible for the most part, but sufficiently platitudinous—occurs a burst of angry eloquence. For he was always at his strongest when scolding somebody. His audience included the intellectual *élite* of France; and he warns it against the besetting sin of university dons and the learned and lettered class in general, a supercilious, patronizing attitude towards the men of action who are doing the rough work of the world. Critics are the object of his fiercest denunciation. "A cynical habit of thought and speech, a readiness to criticise work which the critic himself never tries to perform, an intellectual aloofness which will not accept contact with life's realities—all these are marks, not, as the possessor would fain think, of superiority, but of weakness. . . . It is not the critic who counts; not the man who points out how the strong man stumbles, or where the doer of deeds could have done them better. . . . Shame on the man of cultivated taste who permits refinement to develop into a fastidiousness that unfits him for doing the rough work of a workaday world. Among the free peoples who govern themselves there is but a small field of usefulness open for the men of cloistered life who shrink from contact with their fellows."

The speaker had seemingly himself been stung by criticism; or he was reacting against Matthew Arnold, the celebrated "Harvard indifference," and the cynical talk of the clubs.

We do not expect our Presidents to be literary men and are correspondingly gratified when any of them shows signs of almost human intelligence in spheres outside of politics. Of them all, none touched life at so many points, or was so versatile, picturesque, and generally interesting a figure as the one who has just passed away. Washington was not a man of books. A country gentleman, a Virginia planter and slaveowner, member of a landed aristocracy, he had the limited education of his class and period. Rumor said that he did not write his own messages. And there is a story that John Quincy Adams, regarding a portrait of the father of his country, exclaimed, "To think that that old wooden head will go down in history as a great man!" But this was the comment of a Boston Brahmin, and all the Adamses had bitter tongues. Washington was, of course, a very great man, though not by virtue of any intellectual brilliancy, but of his strong character, his immense practical sagacity and common sense, his leadership of men.

As to Lincoln, we know through what cold obstruction he struggled up into the light, educating himself to be one of the soundest statesmen and most effective public speakers of his day—or any day. There was an inborn fineness or sensitiveness in Lincoln, a touch of the artist (he even wrote verses) which contrasts with the phlegm of his illustrious contemporary, General Grant. The latter had a vein of coarseness, of commonness rather, in his nature; evidenced by his choice of associates and his entire indifference to "the things of the mind." He was almost illiterate and only just a gentleman. Yet by reason of his dignified modesty and simplicity, he contrived to write one of the best of autobiographies.

Roosevelt had many advantages over his eminent predecessors. Of old Knickerbocker stock, with a Harvard education, and the habit of good society, he had means enough to indulge in his favorite pastimes. To run a cattle ranch in Dakota, lead a hunting party in Africa and an exploring expedition in Brazil, these were wide opportunities, but he fully measured up to them. Mr. W. H. Hays, chairman of the Republican National Committee, said of him, "He had more knowledge about more things than any other man." Well, not quite that. We have all known people who made a specialty of omniscience. If a man can speak two languages besides his own and can read two more fairly well, he is at once credited with knowing half a dozen foreign tongues as well as he knows English. Let us agree, however, that Roosevelt knew a lot about a lot of things. He was a rapid and omnivorous reader, reading a book with his finger tips, gutting it of its contents, as he did the birds that he shot, stuffed, and mounted; yet not inappreciative of form, and accustomed to recommend much good literature to his countrymen. He took an eager interest in a large variety of subjects, from Celtic poetry and the fauna and flora of many regions to simplified spelling and the split infinitive.

A young friend of mine was bringing out, for the use of schools and colleges, a volume of selections from the English poets, all learnedly annotated, and sent me his manuscript to look over. On a passage about the bittern bird he had made this note, "The bittern has a harsh, throaty cry." Whereupon I addressed him thus: "Throaty nothing! You are guessing, man. If Teddy Roosevelt reads your book—and he reads everything—he will denounce you as a nature faker and put you down for membership in the Ananias Club. Recall what he did to Ernest Seton-Thompson and to that minister in Stamford, Connecticut. Remember how he crossed swords with Mr. Scully touching the alleged dangerous nature of the ostrich and the early domestication of the peacock. So far as I know, the bittern thing has no voice at all. His real stunt is as follows. He puts his beak down into the swamp, in search of insects and snails or other marine life—*est-ce que je sais?*—and drawing in the bog-water through holes in his beak, makes a booming sound which is most impressive. Now do not think me an ornithologist or a bird sharp. Personally I do not know a bittern from an olive-backed thrush. But I have read some poetry, and I remember what Thomson says in 'The Seasons':

> The bittern knows his time with bill ingulf'd
> To shake the sounding marsh.

See also 'The Lady of the Lake':

> And the bittern sound his drum,
> Booming from the sedgy shallow.

See even old Chaucer who knew a thing or two about birds, *teste* his 'Parlament of Foules,' admirably but strangely edited by Lounsbury, whose indifference to art was only surpassed by his hostility to nature. Says Chaucer:

> And as a bytoure bumblith in the myre."

My friend canceled his note. It is, of course, now established that the bittern "booms"—not in the mud—but in the air.

Mr. Roosevelt was historian, biographer, essayist, and writer of narrative papers on hunting, outdoor life, and natural history, and in all these departments did solid, important work. His ***Winning of the West*** is little, if at all, inferior in historical interest to the similar writings of Parkman and John Fiske. His ***History of the Naval War of 1812*** is an astonishing performance for a young man of twenty-four, only two years out of college. For it required a careful sifting of evidence and weighing of authorities. The job was done with patient thoroughness, and the book is accepted, I believe, as authoritative. It is to me a somewhat tedious tale. One sea fight is much like another, a record of meaningless slaughter.

Of the three lives, those of Gouverneur Morris, T. H. Benton, and Oliver Cromwell, I cannot speak with confidence, having read only the last. I should guess that the life of Benton was written more *con amore* than the others, for the frontier was this historian's favorite scene. The life of Cromwell is not so much a formal biography as a continuous essay in interpretation of a character still partly enigmatic in spite of all the light that so many acute psychologists have shed upon it. It is a relief to read for once a book which is without preface, footnote, or reference. It cannot be said that the biographer contributes anything very new to our knowledge of his subject. The most novel features of his work are the analogies that he draws between situations in English and American political history. These are usually ingenious and illuminating, sometimes a little misleading; as where he praises Lincoln's readiness to acquiesce in the result of the election in 1864 and to retire peaceably in favor of McClellan; contrasting it with Cromwell's dissolution of his Parliaments and usurpation of the supreme power. There was a certain likeness in the exigencies, to be sure, but a broad difference between the problems confronting the two rulers. Lincoln was a constitutional President with strictly limited powers, bound by usage and precedent. For him to have kept his seat by military force, in defiance of a Democratic majority, would have been an act of treason. But the Lord Protector held a new office, unknown to the old constitution of England and with ill-defined powers. A revolution had tossed him to the top and made him dictator. He was bound to keep the peace in unsettled times, to keep out the Stuarts, to keep down the unruly factions. If Parliament would not help, he must govern without it. Carlyle thought that he had no choice.

Roosevelt's addresses, essays, editorials, and miscellaneous papers, which fill many volumes, are seldom literary in subject, and certainly not in manner. He was an effective speaker and writer, using plain, direct, forcible English, without any graces of style. In these papers he is always the moralist, earnest, high-minded, and the preacher of many gospels: the gospel of the strenuous life; the gospel of what used to be called "muscular Christianity"; the gospel of large families; of hundred per cent Americanism; and, above all, of military preparedness. I am not here concerned with the President's political principles, nor with the specific measures that he advocated. I will only say, to guard against suspicion of unfair prejudice, that, as a Democrat, a free-trader, a state-rights man, individualist, and anti-imperialist, I naturally disapproved of many acts of his administration, of the administration of his predecessor, and of his party in general. I disapproved, and still do, of the McKinley and Payne-Aldrich tariffs; of the Spanish war—most avoidable of wars—with its sequel, the conquest of the Philippines; above all, of the seizure of the Panama Canal zone.

But let all that pass: I am supposed to be dealing with my subject as man of letters. As such the Colonel of the Rough Riders was the high commander-in-chief of rough writers. He never persuaded his readers into an opinion—he bullied them into it. When he gnashed his big teeth and shook his big stick,

> . . . The bold Ascalonite
> Fled from his iron ramp; old warriors turned
> Their plated backs under his heel;

mollycoddles, pussy-footers, professional pacifists, and nice little men who had lost their fighting edge, all

scuttled to cover. He called names, he used great violence of language. For instance, a certain president of a woman's college had "fatuously announced . . . that it was better to have one child brought up in the best way than several not thus brought up." The woman making this statement, wrote the Colonel, "is not only unfit to be at the head of a female college, but is not fit to teach the lowest class in a kindergarten; for such teaching is not merely folly, but a peculiarly repulsive type of mean and selfish wickedness." And again: "The man or woman who deliberately avoids marriage . . . is in effect a criminal against the race and should be an object of contemptuous abhorrence by all healthy people."

Now, I am not myself an advocate of race suicide but I confess to a feeling of sympathy with the lady thus denounced, whose point of view is, at least, comprehensible. Old Malthus was not such an ass as some folks think. It is impossible not to admire Roosevelt's courage, honesty, and wonderful energy: impossible to keep from liking the man for his boyish impulsiveness, camaraderie, sporting blood, and hatred of a rascal. But it is equally impossible for a man of any spirit to keep from resenting his bullying ways, his intolerance of quiet, peaceable people and persons of an opposite temperament to his own. Even nice, timid little men who have let their bodies get soft do not like to be bullied. It puts their backs up. His ideal of character was manliness, a sound ideal, but he insisted too much upon the physical side of it, "red-bloodedness" and all that. Those poor old fat generals in Washington who had been enjoying themselves at their clubs, playing bridge and drinking Scotch highballs! He made them all turn out and ride fifty miles a day.

Mr. Roosevelt produced much excellent literature, but no masterpieces like Lincoln's Gettysburg Address and Second Inaugural. Probably his sketches of ranch life and of hunting trips in three continents will be read longest and will keep their freshness after the public questions which he discussed have lost interest and his historical works have been in part rewritten. In these outdoor papers, besides the thrilling adventures which they—very modestly—record, there are even passages of descriptive beauty and chapters of graphic narrative, like the tale of the pursuit and capture of the three robbers who stole the boats on the Missouri River, which belonged to the Roosevelt ranch. This last would be a capital addition to school readers and books of selected standard prose.

Senator Lodge and other friends emphasize the President's sense of humor. He had it, of course. He took pains to establish the true reading of that famous retort, "All I want out of you is common civility and damned little of that." He used to repeat with glee Lounsbury's witticism about "the infinite capability of the human mind to resist the introduction of knowledge." I wonder whether he knew of that other good saying of Lounsbury's about the historian Freeman's being, in his own person, a proof of the necessity of the Norman Conquest. He had, at all events, a just and high estimate of the merits of my brilliant colleague. "Heu quanto minus est cum reliquis versari quam tui meminisse!" But Roosevelt was not himself a humorist, and his writings give little evidence of his possession of the faculty. Lincoln, now, was one of the foremost American humorists. But Roosevelt was too strenuous for the practice of humor, which implies a certain relaxation of mind: a detachment from the object of immediate pursuit: a superiority to practical interests which indulges itself in the play of thought; and, in the peculiarly American form of it, a humility which inclines one to laugh at himself. Impossible to fancy T. R. making the answer that Lincoln made to an applicant for office: "I haven't much influence with this administration." As for that variety of humor that is called irony, it demands a duplicity which the straight-out-speaking Roosevelt could not practise. He was like Epaminondas in the Latin prose composition book, who was such a lover of truth that he never told a falsehood even in jest—*ne joco quidem.*

The only instance of his irony that I recall—there may be others—is the one recorded by Mr. Leupp in his reply to Senator Gorman, who had charged that the examiners of the Civil Service Commission had turned down "a bright young man" in the city of Baltimore, an applicant for the position of letter-carrier, "because he could not tell the most direct route from Baltimore to Japan." Hereupon the young Civil Service Commissioner challenged the senator to verify his statement, but Mr. Gorman preserved a dignified silence. Then the Commissioner overwhelmed him in a public letter from which Mr. Leupp quotes the closing passage, beginning thus: "High-minded, sensitive Mr. Gorman! Clinging, trustful Mr. Gorman! Nothing could shake his belief in that 'bright young man.' Apparently he did not even yet try to find out his name—if he had a name," and so on for nearly a page. Excellent fooling, but a bit too long and heavy-handed for the truest ironic effect.

Many of our Presidents, however little given to the use of the pen, have been successful coiners of phrases—phrases that have stuck: "entangling alliances," "era of good feeling," "innocuous desuetude," "a condition, not a theory." Lincoln was happiest at this art, and there is no need to mention any of the scores of pungent sayings which he added to the language and which are in daily use. President Roosevelt was no whit behind in this regard. All recognize and remember the many phrases to which he gave birth or currency: "predatory wealth," "bull moose," "hit the line hard," "weasel words," "my hat is in the ring," and so on. He took a humorous delight in mystifying the public with recondite allusions, sending everyone to the dictionary to look out "Byzantine logothete," and to the Bible and cyclopedia to find Armageddon.

Roosevelt is alleged to have had a larger personal following than any other man lately in public life. What a testimony to his popularity is the "teddy bear"; and what a sign of the universal interest, hostile or friendly, which he excited in his contemporaries, is the fact that Mr. Albert Shaw was able to compile a caricature life of him pre-

senting many hundred pictures! There was something German about Roosevelt's standards. In this last war he stood heart and soul for America and her allies against Germany's misconduct. But he admired the Germans' efficiency, their highly organized society, their subordination of the individual to the state. He wanted to Prussianize this great peaceful republic by introducing universal obligatory military service. He insisted, like the Germans, upon the *Hausfrau's* duty to bear and rear many children. If he had been a German, it seems possible that, with his views as to the right of strong races to expand, by force if necessary, he might have justified the seizure of Silesia, the partition of Poland, the *Drang nach Osten,* and maybe even the invasion of Belgium—as a military measure.

And so of religion and the church, which Germans regard as a department of government. Our American statesman, of course, was firmly in favor of the separation of church and state and of universal toleration. But he advises everyone to join the church, some church, any old church; not because one shares its beliefs—creeds are increasingly unimportant—but because the church is an instrument of social welfare, and a man can do more good in combination with his fellows than when he stands alone. There is much truth in this doctrine, though it has a certain naïveté, when looked at from the standpoint of the private soul and its spiritual needs.

As in the church, so in the state, he stood for the associative principle as opposed to an extreme individualism. He was a practical politician and therefore an honest partisan, feeling that he could work more efficiently for good government within party lines than outside them. He resigned from the Free Trade League because his party was committed to the policy of protection. In 1884 he supported his party's platform and candidate, instead of joining the Mugwumps and voting for Cleveland, though at the National Republican Convention, to which he went as a delegate, he had opposed the nomination of Blaine. I do not believe that his motive in this decision was selfish, or that he quailed under the snap of the party lash because he was threatened with political death in case he disobeyed. Theodore Roosevelt was nobody's man. He thought, as he frankly explained, that one who leaves his faction for every slight occasion, loses his influence and his power for good. Better to compromise, to swallow some differences and to stick to the crowd which, upon the whole and in the long run, embodies one's convictions. This is a comprehensible attitude, and possibly it is the correct one for the man in public life who is frequently a candidate for office. Yet I wish he could have broken with his party and voted for Cleveland. For, ironically enough, it was Roosevelt himself who afterward split his party and brought in Wilson and the Democrats.

Disregarding his political side and considering him simply as man of letters, one seeks for comparisons with other men of letters who were at once big sportsmen and big writers; Christopher North, for example: "Christopher in his Aviary" and "Christopher in his Shooting Jacket." The likeness here is only a very partial one, to be sure. The American was like the Scotchman in his athleticism, high spirits, breezy optimism, love of the open air, intense enjoyment of life. But he had not North's roystering conviviality and uproarious Toryism; and the kinds of literature that they cultivated were quite unlike.

Charles Kingsley offers a closer resemblance, though the differences here are as numerous as the analogies. Roosevelt was not a clergyman, and not a creative writer, a novelist, or poet. His temperament was not very similar to Kingsley's. Yet the two shared a love for bold adventure, a passion for sport, and an eager interest in the life of animals and plants. Sport with Kingsley took the shape of trout fishing and of riding to hounds, not of killing lions with the rifle. He was fond of horses and dogs; associated democratically with gamekeepers, grooms, whippers-in, poachers even; as Roosevelt did with cowboys, tarpon fishers, wilderness guides, beaters, trappers, and all whom Walt Whitman calls "powerful uneducated persons," loving them for their pluck, coolness, strength, and skill. Kingsley's "At Last, a Christmas in the West Indies," exhibits the same curiosity as to tropical botany and zoölogy that Roosevelt shows in his African and Brazilian journeys. Not only tastes, but many ideals and opinions the two men had in common. "Parson Lot," the Chartist and Christian Socialist, had the same sympathy with the poor and the same desire to improve the condition of agricultural laborers and London artisans which led Roosevelt to promote employers' liability laws and other legislation to protect the workingman from exploitation by conscienceless wealth. Kingsley, like Roosevelt, was essentially Protestant. Neither he nor Mr. Roosevelt liked asceticism or celibacy. As a historian, Kingsley did not rank at all with the author of *The Winning of the West* and the *Naval War of 1812*. On the other hand, if Roosevelt had written novels and poetry, I think he would have rejoiced greatly to write *Westward Ho, The Last Buccaneer,* and *Ode to the North-East Wind*.

In fine, whatever lasting fortune may be in store for Roosevelt's writings, the disappearance of his vivid figure leaves a blank in the contemporary scene. And those who were against him can join with those who were for him in slightly paraphrasing Carlyle's words of dismissal to Walter Scott, "Theodore Roosevelt, pride of all Americans, take our proud and sad farewell."

Brander Matthews (essay date 1919)

SOURCE: "Theodore Roosevelt as a Man of Letters," in *The Tocsin of Revolt and Other Essays,* edited by Brander Matthews, Charles Scribner's Sons, 1919, pp. 229-50.

[*An American critic, playwright, novelist, and educator, Matthews wrote extensively on world drama. In the following essay, originally published in 1919, he examines* Roosevelt's multifaceted character as expressed in his writings.]

I

The more closely we scrutinize Theodore Roosevelt's life and the more carefully we consider his many ventures in many totally different fields of human activity, the less likely we are to challenge the assertion that his was the most interesting career ever vouchsafed to any American,—more interesting even than Benjamin Franklin's, fuller, richer and more varied. Like Franklin, Roosevelt enjoyed life intensely. He was frank in declaring that he had been happy beyond the common lot of man; and we cannot doubt that Franklin had the same feeling. The most obvious cause of the happiness and of the interest of their contrasting careers, is that they had each of them an incessant and insatiable curiosity, which kept forcing them to push their inquiries into a variety of subjects wholly unrelated one to another. The 'Many-sided Franklin' was the title which Paul Leicester Ford gave to his biography; and Roosevelt was even more polygonal.

Like Franklin again, Roosevelt will hold a secure place among our statesmen, our men of science and our men of letters, demanding due appraisal by experts in statecraft, in natural history and in literature. But they differ in this, that Roosevelt was an author by profession, and Franklin was an author by accident. Roosevelt had looked forward to literature as a calling, whereas Franklin produced literature only as a by-product. Excepting *Poor Richard's Almanack* Franklin never composed anything in the hope or desire for fame or for money, or even in response to a need for self-expression. He never published a book; and if he could return to earth he would indubitably be surprised to discover that he held an important place in the histories of American literature. Roosevelt was as distinctly a man of letters as he was a man of action. He made himself known to the public, first of all, as the historian of the American navy in the War of 1812; he followed this up with the four strenuously documented volumes of his *Winning of the West*; and amid all the multiplied activities of his later years he made leisure for the appreciation of one or another of the books he had found to his taste.

II

It must be admitted that in the decade which elapsed after he left the White House his intense interest in public affairs led him to devote a large part of his energy to the consideration of the pressing problems of the hour, to topics of immediate importance, to themes of only an ephemeral value, sufficient unto the day. In three or four different periodicals he served as "contributing editor"; in other words, he was a writer of signed editorials, in which he was always free to express his own views frankly and fully without undue regard for that mysterious entity, the "policy of the paper." These contemporary contributions to dailies and weeklies and monthlies are journalism rather than literature; and the more completely they fulfill the purpose of the moment the less do they demand preservation; now and again they have the over-emphatic repetitions which are more or less justified by the conditions of journalism. But in these same ten years Roosevelt wrote also his two books of travel in Africa and in South America, as vivacious as they are conscientious, his alluring and self-revelatory autobiography, his two volumes of essays and addresses, *History as Literature* and *A Booklover's Holidays in the Open,* both of them pungent with his individuality.

It is not always—in fact it is not often—that the accomplished man of letters has the essential equipment of the journalist; he is likely to be more or less "academic" and to lack the simplicity, the singleness of purpose, the directness of statement demanded in the discussion of the events of the moment. The editorial stands in the same relation to literature that the stump-speech does to the stately oration. The editorial, like the stump-speech, aims at immediate effect; and it is privileged to be more emphatic than might be becoming in a more permanent effort. It was perhaps Roosevelt's wide experience in addressing the public from the platform which made it easier for him to qualify as a contributing editor and to master the method of the newspaper.

In his state-papers and in his messages he had already proved that he had the gift of the winged phrase, keenly pointed and barbed to flesh itself in the memory. He had preached the doctrine of the Strenuous Life and he had expounded the policy of the Square Deal. He had denounced some men as Undesirable Citizens and others as Malefactors of Large Wealth. And when he took up the task of journalism he was happily inspired to the minting of other memorable phrases. There was, for example, an unforgettable felicity in his characterization of the Weasel Words that sometimes suck the life out of a phrase, seemingly strong and bold. Never did he use smooth and sleek rhetoric to disguise vagueness of thought. In the periodical as on the platform he spoke out of the fulness of his heart, after his mind had clarified his emotion so that it poured forth with crystalline lucidity.

There was no mistaking the full intent of his own words. He knew what he meant to say, and he knew how to say it with simple sincerity and with vigorous vivacity. His straightforwardness prevented his ever employing phrases that faced both ways and that provided rat-holes from which he might crawl out. His style was tinglingly alive; it was masculine and vascular; and it was always the style of a gentleman and a scholar. He could puncture with a rapier and he could smash with a sledge-hammer; and if he used the latter more often than the former it was because of his consuming hatred of things "unmanly, ignominious, infamous."

Journalism was young, indeed, one might say that it was still waiting to be born, when Franklin put forth his pamphlets appealing to the scattered colonies to get together and to make common cause against the French who had let loose the Indians to harry our borders. Franklin was

cannily persuasive, making use of no drum-like words, empty, loud-sounding and monotonous. But there burnt in his pages the same pure fire of patriotism that lighted Roosevelt's more impassioned exhortations for us to arouse ourselves from lethargy, that we might do our full duty in the war which saved civilization from the barbarian. Where Franklin addressed himself to common sense, Roosevelt called upon the imagination. Perhaps Franklin, as is the tendency of a practical man, a little distrusted the imagination; but Roosevelt, as practical as Franklin, had imagination himself, and he knew that the American people also had it.

It is by imagination, by the vision and the faculty divine, that now and again an occasional address, like Lincoln's at Gettysburg, or a contributed editorial, like Roosevelt's on the **'Great Adventure,'** transcends its immediate and temporary purpose, and is lifted aloft up to the serener heights of pure literature. It is not without intention that the **'Great Adventure'** has been set by the side of the Gettysburg address; they are akin, and there is in Roosevelt's paragraphs not a little of the poetic elevation and of the exalted dignity of phrase which combine to make the address a masterpiece of English prose. Consider the opening words of the **'Great Adventure'** and take note of the concision, like that of a Greek inscription:

> Only those are fit to live who do not fear to die, and none are fit to die who have shrunk from the joy of life and the duty of life. Both life and death are parts of the same Great Adventure. Never yet was worthy adventure worthily carried through by the man who put his personal safety first. Never yet was a country worth living in unless its sons and daughters were of that stern stuff which bade them die for it at need; and never yet was a country worth dying for unless its sons and daughters thought of life as something not concerned only with the selfish evanescence of the individual, but as a link in the great chain of creation and causation, so that each person is seen in his true relations as an essential part of the whole, whose life must be made to serve the larger and continuing life of the whole.

Consider also these words a little later in the same article:

> If the only son who is killed at the front has no brother because his parents coldly dreaded to play their part in the Great Adventure of Life, then our sorrow is not for them, but solely for the son who himself dared the Great Adventure of Death. If, however, he is the only son because the Unseen Powers denied others to the love of his father and mother, then we mourn doubly with them, because their darling went up to the sword of Azrael, because he drank the dark drink proffered by the Death Angel.

III

Roosevelt's style is firm and forthright; and its excellence is due to his having learnt the lesson of the masters of English. He wrote well because he had read widely and deeply,—because he had absorbed good literature for the sheer delight he took in it. Consciously or unconsciously he enriched his vocabulary, accumulating a store of strong words which he made flexible, bending them to do his bidding. But he was never bookish in his diction; he never went in quest of recondite vocables, partly because his taste was refined but chiefly because he was ever seeking to be "understood of the people." Like Lord Morley, he had little of the verbal curiosity contemned by Milton as "toilsome vanity"; and he was ready with Montaigne to laugh "at fools who will go a quarter of a league to run after a fine word."

To him life was more important than literature, and what he was forever seeking to put into his literature was life itself. He was a nature-lover, but what he loved best was human nature. Yet his relish for life was scarcely keener than his relish for literature. We may think of him as preeminently an outdoors man, and such he was, of course; but he was also an indoors man, a denizen of the library as he was an explorer of the forest. Indoors and out he was forever reading; and he could not venture into the wilds of Africa in search of big game without taking along with him the volumes of the Pigskin Library, which testified at once to the persistence and to the diversity of his tastes as a reader.

He devoured books voraciously, all sorts of books, old and new, established classics, and evanescent "best sellers," history and fiction, poetry and criticism, travels on land and voyages by sea. To use an apt phrase of Dr. Holmes, he was at home with books "as a stable boy is with horses." He might have echoed Lowell's declaration that he was a bookman. The title of one of his later collections of essays is revelatory of his attitude toward himself,—*A Booklover's Holidays in the Open,* for even when he went into the open he wanted to have a book within reach. Of course, he enjoyed certain books, and certain kinds of books better than others. Of all Shakespeare's tragedies he best liked the martial *Macbeth,* preferring it to the more introspective *Hamlet.* He was not unlike the lad who was laid up and whose mother proposed to read the Bible to him, whereupon he asked her to pick out "the fightingest parts." He had a special regard for the masculine writers, for Malory, more particularly, holding the *Morte d'Arthur* to be a better piece of work than the more delicately decorated *Idylls of the King* which Tennyson made out of it. In fact, Roosevelt once went so far as to dismiss Tennyson's elaborate transpositions as "tales of blameless curates, clad in tinmail."

He enjoyed writing as much as he did reading, and as a result his works go far to fill a five-foot shelf of their own. When the man of action that he was had been out in search of new experiences and in the hunt for new knowledge, the man of letters that he was also, impelled him to lose no time in setting down the story of his wanderings that others might share in the pleasure of his adventure without undergoing its perils. Being a normal human being he liked to celebrate himself and to be his own Boswell; but he was never vain or conceited in his record of his own sayings and doings. He had the saving sense of humor, delighting in nothing more than to tell a tale against himself. He was not self-conscious nor thin-skinned; and he laughed as heartily as anyone when Mr. Dooley pretended to mistake the title of his account of the work of the Rough Riders, calling it 'Alone in Cubia.' Perhaps it was because he was so abundantly gifted with the sense of humor that he had a shrewd insight into character and that he could depict it incisively by the aid of a single significant anecdote. In sketching the many strange creatures with whom he was associated in the Far West, in South America and in Africa, he showed that he had the kodak eye of the born reporter.

So it is that he gave us the two delightful volumes for which he drew upon his experiences as a rancher in the West, the stirring book devoted to the deeds of his dearly beloved Rough Riders ("my regiment"), and the solid tomes in which he set down the story of his trips as a faunal naturalist in Africa and in South America. They are all books pulsing with life, vibrating with vitality, and they are all books unfailingly interesting to the reader because whatever is narrated in them has been unfailingly interesting to the writer. Walter Bagehot once suggested that the reason why there are so few really good books out of all the immense multitude which pour forth from the press, is that the men who have seen things and done things cannot write, whereas the men who can write have not done anything or seen anything. Roosevelt's adventure books are really good, because, after having seen many things and done many things, he could write about them so vividly and so sharply as to make his readers see them.

Perhaps the *Autobiography* ought to be classed with the earlier adventure books, since they also were autobiographic. It is a candid book; it puts before us the man himself as reflected in his own mirror; but it is not complete, since it was composed, not in the retrospective serenity of old age, but while the autobiographer was in the thick of the fight, compelled to silence about many of the events of his career which we should like to see elucidated. It was published serially month by month; and, perhaps because of the pressure under which it was undertaken, it seems to have a vague air of improvisation, as tho it had not been as solidly thought out and as cautiously written out as one or another of the earlier books, the *Hunting Trips of a Ranchman,* for example, or the *Rough Riders.* But it abides as a human document; and it explains why the autobiographer's buoyant personality appealed so intimately to the American people.

IV

A Booklover's Holidays in the Open contains two characteristic essays, both of them delightful in their zest and in their individuality. One is on **'Books for Holidays in the Open'** and the other is about the author's **'Wild Hunting Companions,'** a searching and sympathetic appreciation of the human types developed by the wild life of the lessening wild places still uninvaded by advancing civilization. In *History as Literature and Other Essays,* there are other papers as characteristic and as attractive. Three of them are the addresses which he delivered (on his triumphant return from his African journeys) at the Universities of Oxford and Berlin and at the Sorbonne in Paris. They represent the high-water mark of his work as a constructive thinker. They are the lofty and dignified utterances of a statesman who was a practical politician of immense experience in the conduct of public affairs, and who was also a man of letters ambitious to present worthily the results of his experience and of his meditation. These disquisitions on themes seemingly so remote from his special fields of activity as the biological analogies of history, for example, have been called daring; and in fact they are daring. But they justify themselves, since they disclose Roosevelt's possession of the assimilated information and the interpreting imagination which could survey the whole field of history, past and present, using the present to illuminate the past and the past as a beacon to the present, and calling upon natural history to shed light upon the evolution of human history.

These addresses are representative of Roosevelt when he chose to indulge himself in historic speculation; and in the same volume there is an essay, less ambitious but highly individual in theme and in treatment, and quite as characteristic as its stately companions. This is the discussion at once scholarly and playful of **'Dante in the Bowery'**—a paper which could have been written only by a lover of lofty poetry who had been a practical politician in New York. To Roosevelt Dante's mighty vision is not a frigid classic demanding formal lip-service but a living poem with a voice as warm as if it had been born only yesterday. To him the figures who pass along Dante's pages are not graven images, tagged with explanatory foot-notes; they are human beings like unto us, the men of today and of New York.

Thus it is that Roosevelt is led to dwell on the unaffectedness with which Dante dares to be of his own town and of his own time, and the simplicity with which Dante, wishing to assail those guilty of crimes of violence, mentions in one stanza Attila and in the next two local highwaymen "by no means as important as Jesse James and Billy the Kid," less formidable as fighting men and with adventures less startling and less varied. Roosevelt called attention to the fact that "of all the poets of the nineteenth century, Walt Whitman was the only one who dared to use the Bowery,—that is, use anything that was striking and vividly typical of the humanity around him—as Dante used the ordinary humanity of his day; and even Whitman was not quite natural in doing so, for he always felt that he was defying conventions and prejudices of his neighbors; and his self-consciousness made him a little defiant." Roosevelt asked why it is that to us moderns in the twentieth century it should seem improper, and even ludicrous, to illustrate human nature by examples chosen alike from Castle Garden and the Piræus, "from Tammany and the Roman mob organized by the foes of

friends of Cæsar. To Dante such feeling itself would have been inexplicable."

V

Varied and brilliant as were Roosevelt's contributions to other departments of literature, it is more than probable that his ultimate reputation as a man of letters will most securely rest upon his stern labors as a historian,—not on the brisk and lively little book on New York which, he contributed to Freeman's 'Historic Towns' series, not on the biographies of Benton and Gouverneur Morris which he wrote for the 'American Statesmen' series, not on the shrewd and sympathetic life of Cromwell, not on the stirring and picturesque *Hero Tales of American History,* which he prepared in collaboration with Henry Cabot Lodge, but on the four stately volumes of his most energetic and ambitious undertaking, the story of the *Winning of the West,* which he began early in his manhood and which he was always hoping to carry further. Macaulay once praised the work of one of his contemporaries because it exhibited the most valuable qualities of the historian,—"perspicuousness, conciseness, great diligence in examining authorities, great judgment in weighing testimony, and great impartiality in estimating characters"; and no competent reader of the *Winning of the West* could fail to find all these qualities in its pages. A later historian, Professor Morse Stephens, set up four tests for the valuation of historical writing; first, the modern historian must have "conscientiously mastered all the documents relating to his period at first hand"; secondly, he must appreciate all accessible primary material "with careful weighing of evidence and trained faculty of judgment"; thirdly, he must possess absolute impartiality, "in intention as well as in act"; and fourthly, he must also possess "the one necessary feature of literary style" in a history, "clearness of statement." And the *Winning of the West* can withstand the application of all four of these tests. In other words, it is scientific in the collection and comparison and analysis of the accessible facts, and it is artistic in its presentation to the reader of the results of the writer's indefatigable research.

As the *Winning of the West* was written by Roosevelt it could not help being readable. Every chapter and every page is alive and alert with his own forceful and enthusiastic personality. This readability is not attained by any facile eloquence or any glitter of rhetoric, altho it has passages, and not a few of them, which linger in the memory because of their felicitous phrasing. The book is abidingly readable because it is the result of deliberate literary art employed to present honestly the result of honest, scientific inquiry. This is his sterling virtue as a historian, fittingly acknowledged by his fellow-workers in this field when they elected him to the presidency of the American Historical Association.

In an evaluation of the final volumes of Parkman's fascinating record of the fateful struggle between the French and the English for the control of North America, an article written in 1892 while that great historian was still living, Roosevelt remarked that "modern historians always lay great stress upon visiting the places where the events they described occurred"; and he commented that, altho this is advisable, it is far less important than the acquisition of an intimate acquaintance "with the people and the life described." Then he asserted that "it is precisely this experience which Mr. Parkman has had, and which renders his work so especially valuable. He knows the Indian character and the character of the white frontiersman, by personal observation as well as by books; neither knowledge by itself being of much value for a historian. In consequence he writes with a clear and keen understanding of the conditions." Roosevelt himself had the clear and keen understanding of the conditions with which he credited Parkman, in whose footsteps he was following, since the *Winning of the West* may be called a continuation of 'France and England in North America.' Like Parkman, Roosevelt was a severely trained scientific investigator, who was also a born story-teller. If the historian is only an investigator, the result is likely to be a justification of the old jibe which defined history as "an arid region abounding in dates"; and if he is only a story-teller his narrative will speedily disintegrate.

"The true historian," Roosevelt asserted in *History as Literature,* his presidential address to the American Historical Association, "will bring the past before our eyes as if it were the present. He will make us see as living men the hard-faced archers of Agincourt, and the war-worn spearmen who followed Alexander down beyond the rim of the known world. We shall hear grate on the coast of Britain the keels of the Low-Dutch sea-thieves whose children's children were to inherit unknown continents. . . . We shall see conquerors riding forward to victories that have changed the course of time. . . . We shall see the terrible horsemen of Timur the Lame ride over the roof of the world; we shall hear the drums beat as the armies of Gustavus and Frederick and Napoleon drive forward to victory. . . . We shall see the glory of triumphant violence and the revel of those who do wrong in high places; and the broken-hearted despair that lies beneath the glory and the revel. We shall also see the supreme righteousness of the wars for freedom and justice, and know that the men who fell in those wars made all mankind their debtors."

VI

At the end of the Foreword to *A Booklover's Holidays,* there is a noble passage which calls for quotation here as an example of Roosevelt's command of nervous English, measured and cadenced. It is proposed in proof of the assertion that the joy of living is his who has the heart to demand it:

> The beauty and charm of the wilderness are his for the asking, for the edges of the wilderness lie close beside the beaten roads of present travel. He can see the red splendor of desert sunsets, and the unearthly glory of the afterglow on the battlements of desolate mountains. In sapphire gulfs of ocean he can visit islets, above which the wings of myriads

of sea-fowl make a kind of shifting cuneiform script in the air. He can ride along the brink of the stupendous cliff-walled canyon, where eagles soar below him, and cougars make their lairs on the edges and harry the big-horned sheep. He can journey through the northern forests, the home of the giant moose, the forests of fragrant and murmuring life in summer, the iron-bound and melancholy forests of winter.

Theodore Roosevelt had the heart to demand it, and the joy of living was his.

H. L. Mencken (essay date 1920)

SOURCE: "Roosevelt: An Autopsy," in *Prejudices: Second Series,* edited by H. L. Mencken, Alfred A. Knopf, 1920, pp.102-35.

[*Mencken was one of the most influential figures in American literature from the First World War until the early years of the Great Depression. His strongly individualistic, irreverent outlook on life and his vigorous, invective-charged writing style helped establish the iconoclastic spirit of the Jazz Age and significantly shaped the direction of American literature. In the following essay, Mencken condemns what he considers unjustifiably favorable portrayals of Roosevelt by his early biographers.*]

One thinks of Dr. Woodrow Wilson's biography of George Washington as of one of the strangest of all the world's books. Washington: the first, and perhaps also the last American gentleman. Wilson: the self-bamboozled Presbyterian, the right-thinker, the great moral statesman, the perfect model of the Christian cad. It is as if the Rev. Dr. Billy Sunday should do a biography of Charles Darwin—almost as if Dr. Wilson himself should dedicate his senility to a life of the Chevalier Bayard, or the Cid, or Christ. . . . But such phenomena, of course, are not actually rare in the republic; here everything happens that is forbidden by the probabilities and the decencies. The chief native critic of beautiful letters, for a whole generation, was a Baptist clergyman; he was succeeded by a literary Wall Street man, who gave way, in turn, to a soviet of ninth-rate pedagogues; this very curious apostolic succession I have already discussed. The dean of the music critics, even to-day, is a translator of grand opera libretti, and probably one of the worst that ever lived. Return, now, to political biography. Who can think of anything in American literature comparable to Morley's life of Gladstone, or Trevelyan's life of Macaulay, or Carlyle's Frederick, or even Winston Churchill's life of his father? I dredge my memory hopelessly; only William Graham Sumner's study of Andrew Jackson emerges—an extraordinarily astute and careful piece of work by one of the two most underestimated Americans of his generation, the other being Daniel Coit Gilman. But where is the first-rate biography of Washington—sound, fair, penetrating, honest, done by a man capable of comprehending the English gentry of the eighteenth century? And how long must we wait for adequate treatises upon Jefferson, Hamilton, Sam Adams, Aaron Burr, Henry Clay, Calhoun, Webster, Sumner, Grant, Sherman, Lee?

Even Lincoln is yet to be got vividly between the covers of a book. The Nicolay-Hay work is quite impossible; it is not a biography, but simply a huge storehouse of biographical raw materials; whoever can read it can also read the official Records of the Rebellion. All the other standard lives of old Abe—for instance, those of Lamon, Herndon and Weil, Stoddard, Morse and Miss Tarbell— fail still worse; when they are not grossly preachy and disingenuous they are trivial. So far as I can make out, no genuinely scientific study of the man has ever been attempted. The amazing conflict of testimony about him remains a conflict; the most elemental facts are yet to be established; he grows vaguer and more fabulous as year follows year. One would think that, by this time, the question of his religious views (to take one example) ought to be settled, but apparently it is not, for no longer than a year ago there came a reverend author, Dr. William E. Barton, with a whole volume upon the subject, and I was as much in the dark after reading it as I had been before I opened it. All previous biographers, it appeared by this author's evidence, had either dodged the problem, or lied. The official doctrine, in this as in other departments, is obviously quite unsound. One hears in the Sunday-schools that Abe was an austere and pious fellow, constantly taking the name of God in whispers, just as one reads in the school history-books that he was a shining idealist, holding all his vast powers by the magic of an inner and ineffable virtue. Imagine a man getting on in American politics, interesting and enchanting the boobery, sawing off the horns of other politicians, elbowing his way through primaries and conventions, by the magic of virtue! As well talk of fetching the mob by hawking exact and arctic justice! Abe, in fact, must have been a fellow highly skilled at the great democratic art of gum-shoeing. I like to think of him as one who defeated such politicians as Stanton, Douglas and Sumner with their own weapons—deftly leading them into ambuscades, boldly pulling their noses, magnificently hamstringing and horn-swoggling them—in brief, as a politician of extraordinary talents, who loved the game for its own sake, and had the measure of the crowd. His official portraits, both in prose and in daguerreotype, show him wearing the mien of a man about to be hanged; one never sees him smiling. Nevertheless, one hears that, until he emerged from Illinois, they always put the women, children and clergy to bed when he got a few gourds of corn aboard, and it is a matter of unescapable record that his career in the State Legislature was indistinguishable from that of a Tammany Nietzsche.

But, as I say, it is hopeless to look for the real man in the biographies of him: they are all full of distortion, chiefly pious and sentimental. The defect runs through the whole of American political biography, and even through the whole of American history. Nearly all our professional historians are poor men holding college posts, and they are ten times more cruelly beset by the ruling politico-plutocraticsocial oligarchy than ever the Prussian professors were by the Hohenzollerns. Let them diverge in the slightest from what is the current official doctrine, and they are turned out of their chairs with a ceremony suitable for the expulsion of a drunken valet. During the recent war a herd of two thousand and five hundred such miserable slaves was organized by Dr. Creel to lie for their country, and they at once fell upon the congenial task of rewriting American history to make it accord with the ideas of H. P. Davison, Admiral Sims, Nicholas Murray Butler, the Astors, Barney Baruch and Lord Northcliffe. It was a committee of this herd that solemnly pledged the honor of American scholarship to the authenticity of the celebrated Sisson documents. . . .

In the face of such acute military imbecility it is not surprising to discover that all of the existing biographies of the late Colonel Roosevelt—and they have been rolling off the presses at a dizzy rate since his death—are feeble, inaccurate, ignorant and preposterous. I have read, I suppose, at least ten of these tomes during the past year or so, and in all of them I have found vastly more gush than sense. Lawrence Abbott's *Impressions of Theodore Roosevelt* and William Roscoe Thayer's *Theodore Roosevelt* may well serve as specimens. Abbott's book is the composition, not of an unbiased student of the man, but of a sort of groom of the hero. He is so extremely eager to prove that Roosevelt was the perfect right-thinker, according to the transient definitions of right-thinking, that he manages to get a flavor of dubiousness into his whole chronicle. I find myself doubting him even when I know that he is honest and suspect that he is right. As for Thayer, all he offers is a hasty and hollow pot-boiler—such a work as might have been well within the talents of, say, the late Murat Halstead or the editor of the New York *Times*. This Thayer has been heavily praised of late as the Leading American Biographer, and one constantly hears that some new university has made him *Legum Doctor,* or that he has been awarded a medal by this or that learned society, or that the post has brought him a new ribbon from some literary potentate in foreign parts. If, in fact, he is actually the cock of the walk in biography, then all I have said against American biographers is too mild and mellow. What one finds in his book is simply the third-rate correctness of a Boston colonial. Consider, for example, his frequent discussions of the war—a necessity in any work on Roosevelt. In England there is the mob's view of the war, and there is the view of civilized and intelligent men, *e. g.,* Lansdowne, Loreburn, Austin Harrison, Morel, Keynes, Haldane, Hirst, Balfour, Robert Cecil. In New England, it would appear, the two views coalesce, with the first outside. There is scarcely a line on the subject in Thayer's book that might not have been written by Horatio Bottomley. . . .

Obviously, Roosevelt's reaction to the war must occupy a large part of any adequate biography of him, for that reaction was probably more comprehensively typical of the man than any other business of his life. It displayed not only his whole stock of political principles, but also his whole stock of political tricks. It plumbed, on the one hand, the depths of his sagacity, and on the other hand the depths of his insincerity. Fundamentally, I am convinced, he was quite out of sympathy with, and even quite unable to comprehend the body of doctrine upon which the Allies, and later the United States, based their case. To him it must have seemed insane when it was not hypocritical, and hypocritical when it was not insane. His instincts were profoundly against a new loosing of democratic fustian upon the world; he believed in strongly centralized states, founded upon power and devoted to enterprises far transcending mere internal government; he was an imperialist of the type of Cecil Rhodes, Treitschke and Delcassé. But the fortunes of domestic politics jockeyed him into the position of standing as the spokesman of an almost exactly contrary philosophy. The visible enemy before him was Wilson. What he wanted as a politician was something that he could get only by wresting it from Wilson, and Wilson was too cunning to yield it without making a tremendous fight, chiefly by chicane—whooping for peace while preparing for war, playing mob fear against mob fear, concealing all his genuine motives and desires beneath clouds of chautauqual rhetoric, leading a mad dance whose tune changed at every swing. Here was an opponent that more than once puzzled Roosevelt, and in the end flatly dismayed him. Here was a mob-master with a technique infinitely more subtle and effective than his own. So lured into an unequal combat, the Rough Rider got bogged in absurdities so immense that only the democratic anæsthesia to absurdity saved him. To make any progress at all he was forced into fighting against his own side. He passed from the scene bawling piteously for a cause that, at bottom, it is impossible to imagine him believing in, and in terms of a philosophy that was as foreign to his true faith as it was to the faith of Wilson. In the whole affair there was a colossal irony. Both contestants were intrinsically frauds.

The fraudulence of Wilson is now admitted by all save a few survivors of the old corps of official press-agents, most of them devoid of both honesty and intelligence. No unbiased man, in the presence of the revelations of Bullitt, Keynes and a hundred other witnesses, and of the Russian and Shantung performances, and of innumerable salient domestic phenomena, can now believe that the *Doctor dulcifluus* was ever actually in favor of any of the brummagem ideals he once wept for, to the edification of a moral universe. They were, at best, no more than ingenious *ruses de guerre*, and even in the day of their widest credit it was the Espionage Act and the Solicitor-General to the Postoffice, rather than any plausibility in their substance, that got them their credit. In Roosevelt's case the imposture is less patent; he died before it was fully unmasked. What is more, his death put an end to whatever investigation of it was under way, for American sentimentality holds that it is indecent to inquire into the weaknesses of the dead, at least until all the flowers have withered on their tombs. When, a year ago, I ventured in

a magazine article to call attention to Roosevelt's philosophical kinship to the Kaiser I received letters of denunciation from all parts of the United States, and not a few forthright demands that I recant on penalty of lynch law. Prudence demanded that I heed these demands. We live in a curious and often unsafe country. Haled before a Roosevelt judge for speeding my automobile, or spitting on the sidewalk, or carrying a jug, I might have been railroaded for ten years under some constructive corollary of the Espionage Act. But there were two things that supported me in my contumacy to the departed. One was a profound reverence for and fidelity to the truth, sometimes almost amounting to fanaticism. The other was the support of my venerable brother in epistemology, the eminent Iowa right-thinker and patriot, Prof. Dr. S. P. Sherman. Writing in the *Nation,* where he survives from more seemly days than these, Prof. Dr. Sherman put the thing in plain terms. "With the essentials in the religion of the militarists of Germany," he said, "Roosevelt was utterly in sympathy."

Utterly? Perhaps the adverb is a bit too strong. There was in the man a certain instinctive antipathy to the concrete aristocrat and in particular to the aristocrat's private code—the product, no doubt, of his essentially *bourgeois* origin and training. But if he could not go with the Junkers all the way, he could at least go the whole length of their distrust of the third order—the undifferentiated masses of men below. Here, I daresay, he owed a lot to Nietzsche. He was always reading German books, and among them, no doubt, were *Also sprach Zarathustra* and *Jenseits von Gut und Böse*. In fact, the echoes were constantly sounding in his own harangues. Years ago, as an intellectual exercise while confined to hospital, I devised and printed a give-away of the Rooseveltian philosophy in parallel columns—in one column, extracts from *The Strenuous Life*; in the other, extracts from Nietzsche. The borrowings were numerous and unescapable. Theodore had swallowed Friedrich as a peasant swallows Peruna—bottle, cork, label and testimonials. Worse, the draft whetted his appetite, and soon he was swallowing the Kaiser of the *Garde-Kavallerie*-mess and battleship-launching speeches—another somewhat defective Junker. In his palmy days it was often impossible to distinguish his politico-theological bulls from those of Wilhelm; during the war, indeed, I suspect that some of them were boldly lifted by the British press bureau, and palmed off as felonious imprudences out of Potsdam. Wilhelm was his model in *Weltpolitik,* and in sociology, exegetics, administration, law, sport and connubial polity no less. Both roared for doughty armies, eternally prepared—for the theory that the way to prevent war is to make all conceivable enemies think twice, thrice, ten times. Both dreamed of gigantic navies, with battleships as long as Brooklyn Bridge. Both preached incessantly the duty of the citizen to the state, with the soft pedal upon the duty of the state to the citizen. Both praised the habitually gravid wife. Both delighted in the armed pursuit of the lower fauna. Both heavily patronized the fine arts. Both were intimates of God, and announced His desires with authority. Both believed that all men who stood opposed to them were prompted by the devil and would suffer for it in hell.

If, in fact, there was any difference between them, it was all in favor of Wilhelm. For one thing, he made very much fewer speeches; it took some colossal event, such as the launching of a dreadnaught or the birthday of a colonel-general, to get him upon his legs; the Reichstag was not constantly deluged with his advice and upbraiding. For another thing, he was a milder and more modest man—one more accustomed, let us say, to circumstance and authority, and hence less intoxicated by the greatness of his state. Finally, he had been trained to think, not only of his own immediate fortunes, but also of the remote interests of a family that, in his most expansive days, promised to hold the throne for many years, and so he cultivated a certain prudence, and even a certain ingratiating suavity. He could, on occasion, be extremely polite to an opponent. But Roosevelt was never polite to an opponent; perhaps a gentleman, by American standards, he was surely never a gentle man. In a political career of nearly forty years he was never even fair to an opponent. All of his gabble about the square deal was merely so much protective coloration, easily explicable on elementary Freudian grounds. No man, facing Roosevelt in the heat of controversy, ever actually got a square deal. He took extravagant advantages; he played to the worst idiocies of the mob; he hit below the belt almost habitually. One never thinks of him as a duelist, say of the school of Disraeli, Palmerston and, to drop a bit, Blaine. One always thinks of him as a glorified longshoreman engaged eternally in cleaning out bar-rooms—and not too proud to gouge when the inspiration came to him, or to bite in the clinches, or to oppose the relatively fragile brass knuckles of the code with chair-legs, bung-starters, cuspidors, demijohns, and ice-picks.

Abbott and Thayer, in their books, make elaborate efforts to depict their hero as one born with a deep loathing of the whole Prussian scheme of things, and particularly of the Prussian technique in combat. Abbott even goes so far as to hint that the attentions of the Kaiser, during Roosevelt's historic tour of Europe on his return from Africa, were subtly revolting to him. Nothing could be more absurd. Prof. Dr. Sherman, in the article I have mentioned, blows up that nonsense by quoting from a speech made by the tourist in Berlin—a speech arguing for the most extreme sort of militarism in a manner that must have made even some of the Junkers blow their noses dubiously. The disproof need not be piled up; the America that Roosevelt dreamed of was always a sort of swollen Prussia, truculent without and regimented within. There was always a clank of the saber in his discourse; he could not discuss the tamest matter without swaggering in the best dragoon fashion. Abbott gets into yet deeper waters when he sets up the doctrine that the invasion of Belgium threw his darling into an instantaneous and tremendous fit of moral indignation, and that the curious delay in the public exhibition thereof, so much discussed since, was due to his (Abbott's) fatuous interference—a *faux pas* later regretted with much bitterness. Unluckily,

the evidence he offers leaves me full of doubts. What the doctrine demands that one believe is simply this: that the man who, for mere commercial advantage and (in Frederick's famous phrase) "to make himself talked of in the world," tore up the treaty of 1848 between the United States and Colombia (*geb.* New Granada), whereby the United States forever guaranteed the "sovereignty and ownership" of the Colombians in the isthmus of Panama— that this same man, thirteen years later, was horrified into a fever when Germany, facing powerful foes on two fronts, tore up the treaty of 1832, guaranteeing, not the sovereignty, but the bald neutrality of Belgium—a neutrality already destroyed, according to the evidence before the Germans, by Belgium's own acts.

It is hard, without an inordinate strain upon the credulity, to believe any such thing, particularly in view of the fact that this instantaneous indignation of the most impulsive and vocal of men was diligently concealed for at least six weeks, with reporters camped upon his doorstep day and night, begging him to say the very thing that he left so darkly unsaid. Can one imagine Roosevelt, with red-fire raging within him and sky-rockets bursting in his veins, holding his peace for a month and a half? I have no doubt whatever that Abbott, as he says, desired to avoid embarrassing Dr. Wilson—but think of Roosevelt showing any such delicacy! For one, I am not equal to the feat. All that unprecedented reticence, in fact, is far more readily explicable on other and less lofty grounds. What really happened I presume to guess. My guess is that Roosevelt, like the great majority of other Americans, was *not* instantly and automatically outraged by the invasion of Belgium. On the contrary, he probably viewed it as a regrettable, but not unexpected or unparalleled device of war—if anything, as something rather thrillingly gaudy and effective—a fine piece of virtuosity, pleasing to a military connoisseur. But then came the deluge of Belgian atrocity stories, and the organized campaign to enlist American sympathies. It succeeded very quickly. By the middle of August the British press bureau was in full swing; by the beginning of September the country was flooded with inflammatory stuff; six weeks after the war opened it was already hazardous for a German in America to state his country's case. Meanwhile, the Wilson administration had declared for neutrality, and was still making a more or less sincere effort to practice it, at least on the surface. Here was Roosevelt's opportunity, and he leaped to it with sure instinct. On the one side was the administration that he detested, and that all his self-interest (*e.g.*, his yearning to get back his old leadership and to become President again in 1917) prompted him to deal a mortal blow, and on the other side was a ready-made issue, full of emotional possibilities, stupendously pumped up by extremely clever propaganda, and so far unembraced by any other rabble-rouser of the first magnitude. Is it any wonder that he gave a whoop, jumped upon his cayuse, and began screaming for war? In war lay the greatest chance of his life. In war lay the confusion and destruction of Wilson, and the melodramatic renaissance of the Rough Rider, the professional hero, the national Barbarossa.

In all this, of course, I strip the process of its plumes and spangles, and expose a chain of causes and effects that Roosevelt himself, if he were alive, would denounce as grossly contumelious to his native purity of spirit—and perhaps in all honesty. It is not necessary to raise any doubts as to that honesty. No one who has given any study to the development and propagation of political doctrine in the United States can have failed to notice how the belief in issues among politicians tends to run in exact ratio to the popularity of those issues. Let the populace begin suddenly to swallow a new panacea or to take fright at a new bugaboo, and almost instantly nine-tenths of the master-minds of politics begin to believe that the panacea is a sure cure for all the malaises of the republic, and the bugaboo an immediate and unbearable menace to all law, order and domestic tranquillity. At the bottom of this singular intellectual resilience, of course, there is a good deal of hard calculation; a man must keep up with the procession of crazes, or his day is swiftly done. But in it there are also considerations a good deal more subtle, and maybe less discreditable. For one thing, a man devoted professionally to patriotism and the wisdom of the fathers is very apt to come to a resigned sort of acquiescence in all the doctrinaire rubbish that lies beneath the national scheme of things—to believe, let us say, if not that the plain people are gifted with an infallible sagacity, then at least that they have an inalienable right to see their follies executed. Poll-parroting nonsense as a matter of daily routine, the politician ends by assuming that it is sense, even though he doesn't believe it. For another thing, there is the contagion of mob enthusiasm—a much underestimated murrain. We all saw what it could do during the war—college professors taking their tune from the yellow journals, the rev. clergy performing in the pulpit like so many Liberty Loan orators in five-cent moving-picture houses, hysteria grown epidemic like the influenza. No man is so remote and arctic that he is wholly safe from that contamination; it explains many extravagant phenomena of a democratic society; in particular, it explains why the mob leader is so often a victim to his mob.

Roosevelt, a perfectly typical politician, devoted to the trade, not primarily because he was gnawed by ideals, but because he frankly enjoyed its rough-and-tumble encounters and its gaudy rewards, was probably moved in both ways—and also by the hard calculation that I have mentioned. If, by any ineptness of the British press-agents, tear-squeezers and orphan-exhibitors, indignation over the invasion of Belgium had failed to materialize—if, worse still, some gross infringement of American rights by the English had caused it to be forgotten completely—if, finally, Dr. Wilson had been whooping for war with the populace firmly against him—in such event it goes without saying that the moral horror of Dr. Roosevelt would have stopped short at a very low amperage, and that he would have refrained from making it the center of his polity. But with things as they were, lying neatly to his hand, he permitted it to take on an extraordinary virulence, and before long all his old delight in German militarism had been converted into a lofty detestation of

German militarism, and its chief spokesman on this side of the Atlantic became its chief opponent. Getting rid of that old delight, of course, was not easily achieved. The concrete enthusiasm could be throttled, but the habit of mind remained. Thus one beheld the curious spectacle of militarism belabored in terms of militarism—of the Kaiser arraigned in unmistakably *kaiserliche* tones.

Such violent swallowings and regurgitations were no novelties to the man. His whole political career was marked, in fact, by performances of the same sort. The issues that won him most votes were issues that, at bottom, he didn't believe in; there was always a mental reservation in his rhetoric. He got into politics, not as a tribune of the plain people, but as an amateur reformer of the snobbish type common in the eighties, by the *Nation* out of the Social Register. He was a young Harvard man scandalized by the discovery that his town was run by men with such names as Michael O'Shaunnessy and Terence Googan—that his social inferiors were his political superiors. His sympathies were essentially anti-democratic. He had a high view of his private position as a young fellow of wealth and education. He believed in strong centralization—the concentration of power in a few hands, the strict regimentation of the nether herd, the abandonment of democratic platitudes. His heroes were such Federalists as Morris and Hamilton; he made his first splash in the world by writing about them and praising them. Worse, his daily associations were with the old Union League crowd of high-tariff Republicans—men almost apoplectically opposed to every movement from below—safe and sane men, highly conservative and suspicious men—the profiteers of peace, as they afterward became the profiteers of war. His early adventures in politics were not very fortunate, nor did they reveal any capacity for leadership. The bosses of the day took him in rather humorously, played him for what they could get out of him, and then turned him loose. In a few years he became disgusted and went West. Returning after a bit, he encountered catastrophe: as a candidate for Mayor of New York he was drubbed unmercifully. He went back to the West. He was, up to this time, a comic figure—an anti-politician victimized by politicians, a pseudo-aristocrat made ridiculous by the mob-masters he detested.

But meanwhile something was happening that changed the whole color of the political scene, and was destined, eventually, to give Roosevelt his chance. That something was a shifting in what might be called the foundations of reform. Up to now it had been an essentially aristocratic movement—superior, sniffish and anti-democratic. But hereafter it took on a strongly democratic color and began to adopt democratic methods. More, the change gave it new life. What Harvard, the Union League Club and the *Nation* had failed to accomplish, the plain people now undertook to accomplish. This invasion of the old citadel of virtue was first observed in the West, and its manifestations out there must have given Roosevelt a good deal more disquiet than satisfaction. It is impossible to imagine him finding anything to his taste in the outlandish doings of the Populists, the wild schemes of the pre-

Bryan dervishes. His instincts were against all that sort of thing. But as the movement spread toward the East it took on a certain urbanity, and by the time it reached the seaboard it had begun to be quite civilized. With this new brand of reform Roosevelt now made terms. It was full of principles that outraged all his pruderies, but it at least promised to work. His entire political history thereafter, down to the day of his death, was a history of compromises with the new forces—of a gradual yielding, for strategic purposes, to ideas that were intrinsically at odds with his congenital prejudices. When, after a generation of that sort of compromising, the so-called Progressive party was organized and he seized the leadership of it from the Westerners who had founded it, he performed a feat of wholesale englutination that must forever hold a high place upon the roll of political prodigies. That is to say, he swallowed at one gigantic gulp, and out of the same herculean jug, the most amazing mixture of social, political and economic perunas ever got down by one hero, however valiant, however athirst—a cocktail made up of all the elixirs hawked among the boobery in his time, from woman suffrage to the direct primary, and from the initiative and referendum to the short ballot, and from prohibition to public ownership, and from trust-busting to the recall of judges.

This homeric achievement made him the head of the most tatterdemalion party ever seen in American politics—a party composed of such incompatible ingredients and hung together so loosely that it began to disintegrate the moment it was born. In part it was made up of mere disordered enthusiasts—believers in anything and everything, pathetic victims of the credulity complex, habitual followers of jitney messiahs, incurable hopers and snufflers. But in part it was also made up of rice converts like Roosevelt himself—men eager for office, disappointed by the old parties, and now quite willing to accept any aid that half-idiot doctrinaires could give them. I have no doubt that Roosevelt himself, carried away by the emotional storms of the moment and especially by the quasi-religious monkey-shines that marked the first Progressive convention, gradually convinced himself that at least some of the doctrinaires, in the midst of all their imbecility, yet preached a few ideas that were workable, and perhaps even sound. But at bottom he was against them, and not only in the matter of their specific sure cures, but also in the larger matter of their childish faith in the wisdom and virtue of the plain people. Roosevelt, for all his fluent mastery of democratic counter-words, democratic gestures and all the rest of the armamentarium of the mob-master, had no such faith in his heart of hearts. He didn't believe in democracy; he believed simply in government. His remedy for all the great pangs and longings of existence was not a dispersion of authority, but a hard concentration of authority. He was not in favor of unlimited experiment; he was in favor of a rigid control from above, a despotism of inspired prophets and policemen. He was not for democracy as his followers understood democracy, and as it actually is and must be; he was for a paternalism of the true Bismarckian pattern, almost of the Napoleonic or Ludendorffian pattern—a paternalism concerning itself with all things, from the regulation of coal-mining and meat-packing to the regulation of spelling and marital rights. His instincts were always those of the property-owning Tory, not those of the romantic Liberal. All the fundamental objects of Liberalism—free speech, unhampered enterprise, the least possible governmental interference—were abhorrent to him. Even when, for campaign purposes, he came to terms with the Liberals his thoughts always ranged far afield. When he tackled the trusts the thing that he had in his mind's eye was not the restoration of competition but the subordination of all private trusts to one great national trust, with himself at its head. And when he attacked the courts it was not because they put their own prejudice before the law but because they refused to put *his* prejudices before the law.

In all his career no one ever heard him make an argument for the rights of the citizen; his eloquence was always expended in expounding the duties of the citizen. I have before me a speech in which he pleaded for "a spirit of kindly justice toward every man and woman," but that seems to be as far as he ever got in that direction—and it was the gratuitous justice of the absolute monarch that he apparently had in mind, not the autonomous and inalienable justice of a free society. The duties of the citizen, as he understood them, related not only to acts, but also to thoughts. There was, to his mind, a simple body of primary doctrine, and dissent from it was the foulest of crimes. No man could have been more bitter against opponents, or more unfair to them, or more ungenerous. In this department, indeed, even so gifted a specialist in dishonorable controversy as Dr. Wilson has seldom surpassed him. He never stood up to a frank and chivalrous debate. He dragged herrings across the trail. He made seductive faces at the gallery. He capitalized his enormous talents as an entertainer, his rank as a national hero, his public influence and consequence. The two great lawsuits in which he was engaged were screaming burlesques upon justice. He tried them in the newspapers before ever they were called; he befogged them with irrelevant issues; his appearances in court were not the appearances of a witness standing on a level with other witnesses, but those of a comedian sure of his crowd. He was, in his dealings with concrete men as in his dealings with men in the mass, a charlatan of the very highest skill—and there was in him, it goes without saying, the persuasive charm of the charlatan as well as the daring deviousness, the humanness of naïveté as well as the humanness of chicane. He knew how to woo—and not only boobs. He was, for all his ruses and ambuscades, a jolly fellow.

It seems to be forgotten that the current American theory that political heresy should be put down by force, that a man who disputes whatever is official has no rights in law or equity, that he is lucky if he fares no worse than to lose his constitutional benefits of free speech, free assemblage and the use of the mails—it seems to be forgotten that this theory was invented, not by Dr. Wilson, but by Roosevelt. Most Liberals, I suppose, would credit it, if asked, to Wilson. He has carried it to extravagant lengths; he is the father superior of all the present advocates of it; he will probably go down into American history as its greatest prophet. But it was first clearly stated, not in any Wilsonian bull to the right-thinkers of all lands, but in Roosevelt's proceedings against the so-called Paterson anarchists. You will find it set forth at length in an opinion prepared for him by his Attorney-General, Charles J. Bonaparte, another curious and almost fabulous character, also an absolutist wearing the false whiskers of a democrat. Bonaparte furnished the law, and Roosevelt furnished the blood and iron. It was an almost ideal combination; Bonaparte had precisely the touch of Italian finesse that the Rough Rider always lacked. Roosevelt believed in the Paterson doctrine—in brief, that the Constitution does not throw its cloak around heretics—to the end of his days. In the face of what he conceived to be contumacy to revelation his fury took on a sort of lyrical grandeur. There was nothing too awful for the culprit in the dock. Upon his head were poured denunciations as violent as the wildest interdicts of a mediæval pope.

The appearance of such men, of course, is inevitable under a democracy. Consummate showmen, they arrest the wonder of the mob, and so put its suspicions to sleep. What they actually believe is of secondary consequence; the main thing is what they say; even more, the way they say it. Obviously, their activity does a great deal of damage to the democratic theory, for they are standing refutations of the primary doctrine that the common folk choose their leaders wisely. They damage it again in another and more subtle way. That is to say, their ineradicable contempt for the minds they must heat up and bamboozle leads them into a fatalism that shows itself in a cynical and opportunistic politics, a deliberate avoidance of fundamentals. The policy of a democracy thus becomes an eternal improvisation, changing with the private ambitions of its leaders and the transient and often unintelligible emotions of its rank and file. Roosevelt, incurably undemocratic in his habits of mind, often found it difficult to gauge those emotional oscillations. The fact explains his frequent loss of mob support, his periodical journeys into Coventry. There were times when his magnificent talents as a public comedian brought the proletariat to an almost unanimous groveling at his feet, but there were also times when he puzzled and dismayed it, and so awakened its hostility. When he assaulted Wilson on the neutrality issue, early in 1915, he made a quite typical mistake. That mistake consisted in assuming that public indignation over the wrongs of the Belgians would maintain itself at a high temperature—that it would develop rapidly into a demand for intervention. Roosevelt made himself the spokesman of that demand, and then found to his consternation that it was waning—that the great masses of the plain people, prospering under the Wilsonian neutrality, were inclined to preserve it, at no matter what cost to the Belgians. In 1915, after the *Lusitania* affair, things seemed to swing his way again, and he got vigorous support from the British press bureau. But in a few months he found himself once more attempting to lead a mob that was fast slipping away.

Wilson, a very much shrewder politician, with little of Roosevelt's weakness for succumbing to his own rhetoric, discerned the truth much more quickly and clearly. In 1916 he made his campaign for reëlection on a flatly anti-Roosevelt peace issue, and not only got himself reëlected, but also drove Roosevelt out of the ring.

What happened thereafter deserves a great deal more careful study than it will ever get from the timorous eunuchs who posture as American historians. At the moment, it is the official doctrine in England, where the thing is more freely discussed than at home, that Wilson was forced into the war by an irresistible movement from below—that the plain people compelled him to abandon neutrality and move reluctantly upon the Germans. Nothing could be more untrue. The plain people, at the end of 1916, were in favor of peace, and they believed that Wilson was in favor of peace. How they were gradually worked up to complaisance and then to enthusiasm and then to hysteria and then to acute mania—this is a tale to be told in more leisurely days and by historians without boards of trustees on their necks. For the present purpose it is sufficient to note that the whole thing was achieved so quickly and so neatly that its success left Roosevelt surprised and helpless. His issue had been stolen from directly under his nose. He was left standing daunted and alone, a boy upon a burning deck. It took him months to collect his scattered wits, and even then his attack upon the administration was feeble and ineffective. To the plain people it seemed a mere ill-natured snapping at a successful rival, which in fact it was, and so they paid no heed to it, and Roosevelt found himself isolated once more. Thus he passed from the scene in the shadows, a broken politician and a disappointed man.

I have a notion that he died too soon. His best days were probably not behind him, but ahead of him. Had he lived ten years longer, he might have enjoyed a great rehabilitation, and exchanged his old false leadership of the inflammatory and fickle mob for a sound and true leadership of the civilized minority. For the more one studies his mountebankeries as mob-master, the more one is convinced that there was a shrewd man beneath the motley, and that his actual beliefs were anything but nonsensical. The truth of them, indeed, emerges more clearly day by day. The old theory of a federation of free and autonomous states has broken down by its own weight, and we are moved toward centralization by forces that have long been powerful and are now quite irresistible. So with the old theory of national isolation: it, too, has fallen to pieces. The United States can no longer hope to lead a separate life in the world, undisturbed by the pressure of foreign aspirations. We came out of the war to find ourselves hemmed in by hostilities that no longer troubled to conceal themselves, and if they are not as close and menacing today as those that have hemmed in Germany for centuries they are none the less plainly there and plainly growing. Roosevelt, by whatever route of reflection or intuition, arrived at a sense of these facts at a time when it was still somewhat scandalous to state them, and it was the capital effort of his life to reconcile them, in some dark way or other, to the prevailing platitudes, and so get them heeded. Today no one seriously maintains, as all Americans once maintained, that the states can go on existing together as independent commonwealths, each with its own laws, its own legal theory and its own view of the common constitutional bond. And today no one seriously maintains, as all Americans once maintained, that the nation may safely potter on without adequate means of defense. However unpleasant it may be to contemplate, the fact is plain that the American people, during the next century, will have to fight to maintain their place in the sun.

Roosevelt lived just long enough to see his notions in these directions take on life, but not long enough to see them openly adopted. To the extent of his prevision he was a genuine leader of the nation, and perhaps in the years to come, when his actual ideas are disentangled from the demagogic fustian in which he had to wrap them, his more honest pronunciamentoes will be given canonical honors, and he will be ranked among the prophets. He saw clearly more than one other thing that was by no means obvious to his age—for example, the inevitability of frequent wars under the new world-system of extreme nationalism; again, the urgent necessity, for primary police ends, of organizing the backward nations into groups of vassals, each under the hoof of some first-rate power; yet again, the probability of the breakdown of the old system of free competition; once more, the high social utility of the Spartan virtues and the grave dangers of sloth and ease; finally, the incompatibility of free speech and democracy. I do not say that he was always quite honest, even when he was most indubitably right. But in so far as it was possible for him to be honest and exist at all politically, he inclined toward the straightforward thought and the candid word. That is to say, his instinct prompted him to tell the truth, just as the instinct of Dr. Wilson prompts him to shift and dissimulate. What ailed him was the fact that his lust for glory, when it came to a struggle, was always vastly more powerful than his lust for the eternal verities. Tempted sufficiently, he would sacrifice anything and everything to get applause. Thus the statesman was debauched by the politician, and the philosopher was elbowed out of sight by the popinjay.

Where he failed most miserably was in his remedies. A remarkably penetrating diagnostician, well-read, unprejudiced and with a touch of genuine scientific passion, he always stooped to quackery when he prescribed a course of treatment. For all his sensational attacks upon the trusts, he never managed to devise a scheme to curb them—and even when he sought to apply the schemes of other men he invariably corrupted the business with timorousness and insincerity. So with his campaign for national preparedness. He displayed the disease magnificently, but the course of medication that he proposed was vague and unconvincing; it was not, indeed, without justification that the plain people mistook his advocacy of an adequate army for a mere secret yearning to prance upon a charger at the head of huge hordes. So, again,

with his eloquent plea for national solidarity and an end of hyphenism. The dangers that he pointed out were very real and very menacing, but his plan for abating them only made them worse. His objurgations against the Germans surely accomplished nothing; the hyphenate of 1915 is still a hyphenate in his heart—with bitter and unforgettable grievances to support him. Roosevelt, very characteristically, swung too far. In denouncing German hyphenism so extravagantly he contrived to give an enormous impetus to English hyphenism, a far older and more perilous malady. It has already gone so far that a large and influential party endeavors almost openly to convert the United States into a mere vassal state of England's. Instead of national solidarity following the war, we have only a revival of Know-Nothingism; one faction of hyphenates tries to exterminate another faction. Roosevelt's error here was one that he was always making. Carried away by the ease with which he could heat up the mob, he tried to accomplish instantly and by *force majeure* what could only be accomplished by a long and complex process, with more good will on both sides than ever so opinionated and melodramatic a pseudo-Junker was capable of. But though he thus made a mess of the cure, he was undoubtedly right about the disease.

The talented Sherman, in the monograph that I have praised, argues that the chief contribution of the dead gladiator to American life was the example of his gigantic gusto, his delight in toil and struggle, his superb aliveness. The fact is plain. What he stood most clearly in opposition to was the superior pessimism of the three Adams brothers—the notion that the public problems of a democracy are unworthy the thought and effort of a civilized and self-respecting man—the sad error that lies in wait for all of us who hold ourselves above the general. Against this suicidal aloofness Roosevelt always hurled himself with brave effect. Enormously sensitive and resilient, almost pathological in his appetite for activity, he made it plain to every one that the most stimulating sort of sport imaginable was to be obtained in fighting, not for mere money, but for ideas. There was no aristocratic reserve about him. He was not, in fact, an aristocrat at all, but a quite typical member of the upper *bourgeoisie;* his people were not *patroons* in New Amsterdam, but simple traders; he was himself a social pusher, and eternally tickled by the thought that he had had a Bonaparte in his cabinet. The marks of the thoroughbred were simply not there. The man was blatant, crude, overly confidential, devious, tyrannical, vainglorious, sometimes quite childish. One often observed in him a certain pathetic wistfulness, a reaching out for a grand manner that was utterly beyond him. But the sweet went with the bitter. He had all the virtues of the fat and complacent burgher. His disdain of affectation and prudery was magnificent. He hated all pretension save his own pretension. He had a sound respect for hard effort, for loyalty, for thrift, for honest achievement.

His worst defects, it seems to me, were the defects of his race and time. Aspiring to be the leader of a nation of third-rate men, he had to stoop to the common level.

When he struck out for realms above that level he always came to grief: this was the "unsafe" Roosevelt, the Roosevelt who was laughed at, the Roosevelt retired suddenly to cold storage. This was the Roosevelt who, in happier times and a better place, might have been. Well, one does what one can.

Raymond C. Miller (essay date 1938)

SOURCE: "Theodore Roosevelt, Historian," in *Medieval and Historiographical Essays in Honor of James Westfall Thompson*, edited by James Lea Cate and Eugene N. Anderson, Kennikat Press, Inc. 1966, pp. 423-38.

[*In the following essay, Miller offers a critical view of Roosevelt's historical works.*]

The career of historian was the first to which young Roosevelt, newly graduated from Harvard, turned his attention. He had considered the life of a naturalist, but reasons either sentimental or temperamental led him to abandon it. Probably it was a fortunate decision, for the earlier impulse came more from a healthy love of outdoors and an extension of his boyhood collecting habits than from any real interest in science as such. The older naturalist-philosopher on the bank of the lily pond was giving place to the scientist-technician with his laboratory and his microscope, and for that Roosevelt had no taste. He chose history.

He knew little or nothing of this new field—not enough to recognize that this same transition was occurring there. The masters whose gallant treatment of great sweeps of history, the Bancrofts, the Parkmans, were giving place to craftsmen of a different sort. Even in Roosevelt's day in Harvard, the seminar in medieval history which Henry Adams had instituted, preceded and echoed by similar work elsewhere, was a clear indication of the change, and the organization of the American Historical Association so soon thereafter shows how widely spread was the idea that history was not a ranging field for individual literati but a realm of human knowledge to be developed by the co-operative work of individual specialists.

These things the young graduate did not know. He had avoided the Harvard seminar as he had avoided the laboratories; in his Sophomore year he had had one course in history, which had little effect on his historical career. From some outside source, however, he developed a personal interest in the naval aspects of the War of 1812, and when graduated he had already done some work on the subject. It dragged on, interrupted by some perfunctory study of law, a little dabbling in practical politics, and a honeymoon in Europe.

In 1882 *The Naval War of 1812* was published and provoked no sensation; Roosevelt himself subsequently referred to it as being "dry as a dictionary." The style is choppy, excessively nautical, sometimes almost unintelligible, and marked with frequent and not always well-mannered contradictions of other authors; the tiresome repetitions of conclusions and lessons justify the author's worst criticisms. More serious flaws appear in the organization; a clear recognition of the purpose or objective of a navy in the war would offer not only a standard by which its success could be measured but also a meaningful plan about which the account could be organized. This book has no such coherence and remains a disorganized story of a succession of individual encounters, unrelated except in time.

The original purpose seems to have been to write a companion work about the war on land. Abandoning the idea as not worth doing, Roosevelt appended to the *Naval War* one chapter on the Battle of New Orleans which contradicts all these criticisms. It is a swift, graphic, vigorous narrative of a battle which roused his interest, provoked an avowed partisanship, and stimulated him with its setting and importance. The account is clear, the style simple and direct, and the entire story is moving and dramatic.

In *The Naval War* the sources used were to some extent secondary, especially on the English side, though the author made the effort to obtain from the Navy Department such material as was available and took time from his honeymoon trip to gain access to some British material. The form of documentation, if it leaves something to be desired, is still understandable.

The next two works, *Thomas Hart Benton* (1886) and *Gouveneur Morris* (1888), both in John T. Morse's "American Statesmen" series, lack formal documentation altogether. The greater part of the first was written at the ranch house of the Bad Lands, by the author's own confession largely in a period of three months, and shows prominent evidence of the careless haste with which it was produced. Nowhere in the book does the author discuss his sources, but aside from general knowledge he seems to have depended almost exclusively on Benton's political autobiography. [Roosevelt to Lodge, June 7, 1886. "Now I hesitate to give him (Benton) a wholly fictitious date of death, and to invent all of the work of his later years. Would it be too infernal a nuisance for you to hire some one on the *Advertiser*. . . . to look up, in a biographical dictionary or elsewhere, his life after he left the Senate in 1850? He was elected once to Congress; who beat him when he ran the second time? What was the issue? Who beat him, and why, when he ran for Governor of Missouri? and the date of his death. . . . . As soon as I can get these dates I can send Morse the manuscript." Evidently Lodge sent the information with a horrified letter of protest, for the next Roosevelt letter, of June 19, promised not to send the manuscript; he only "wanted to get it so far done that a week's hard work when I get East near the Public Libraries would finish it" (*Selections from the Correspondence of Theodore Roosevelt and Henry Cabot Lodge*)]

The volume on Morris is more carefully prepared, and the author used, in addition to Morris' own published writings, a little monographic material and some manuscripts. [Morris mss were not available; the Jay and Pickering collections are mentioned. In a letter to Lodge, who had suggested the Pickering papers, dated August 20, 1887, Roosevelt asked whether they were published and, if not, whether Lodge could have copied the letters from Morris among them. A letter two weeks later (September 5, 1887) announced that the book had just gone to Houghton Mifflin Co., publishers.]

The Winning of the West is the most pretentious historical production Roosevelt attempted. The years between the first volume (1889) and the fourth (1896) mark the limits of his most vigorous research. He used the considerable body of documents published by the government, some archival material, and a number of private and semipublic collections of papers and manuscripts. It was manifestly impossible for him in so few years to become a complete master of the field on which he chose to write, but the work was a pioneer task, opening up an area in history which was important, and the performance of the task was more than creditable.

In these same years Roosevelt was working on a brief history of New York, which may be dismissed, and a biography of Oliver Cromwell, which is of equal importance. The last volume mentioned (1900) marked the close of the purely historical work of the man who so soon thereafter became president.

It is an astonishing list of books. Since 1880, in twenty years, Roosevelt had written his *Naval War,* three biographies, a four-volume history of the West, two other historical works, and at least three volumes on hunting and ranching. [A number of magazine articles appeared subsequently in book form.] It is a list so extensive as to sound like the work of an industrious lifetime rather than the product of a man forty-three years old; but this remarkable individual found time also to be New York legislator, civil service commissioner, assistant secretary of the navy, governor of New York, and to fight in five presidential campaigns and one war.

Haste and frequent superficiality in the work were inevitable, of course, but there are flashes of insight and brilliance of understanding which are as unexpected as they are penetrating. In the day when historical convention described the Revolution as a struggle of the all good against the all bad, Roosevelt discovered a revolutionary America, discordant and disunited, in which the cleavage was more often than not social or economic, and in which good men were torn in the agony of conflicting loyalties. That the right cause triumphed inevitably, Roosevelt leaves one no doubt; but behind the conventional conclusion there is presented a glimpse of a stratified America which a more leisurely worker would have followed to important results.

When he wrote his *Benton,* American history was still under the shadow of the Civil War, with its emphasis on the national division north and south, and on the enlarge-

ment of the slavery struggle. Roosevelt correctly argued that slavery as an issue did not appear before the fifth decade of the century and, refusing to make Benton either northern or southern, talked of him and his West as distinct and different from either. So sharp is the statement, so definite is the description of western characteristics, that one cannot resist wondering whether this work may not have been the conscious or unconscious suggestion which directed the thought of Turner into his fruitful studies of the West as a section. [It is not intended here to suggest that the essentials of the Turner ideas are to be found in Roosevelt's work. Roosevelt emphasized the individual so strongly as to make his history almost biographical episodes and could not thus sense the larger implications of western characteristics which Turner emphasized.] These and similar suggestions indicate an unconventionality of approach and a flair for stimulating generalization of a high order: Roosevelt's failure was the failure to test and confirm through adequate research and to correlate and complete into a reintegrated whole.

Frequently, indeed almost by compulsion, the choice of a topic by a historian carried implicit in it an interpretation of history which underlies and colors his entire work. When Roosevelt wrote *The Winning of the West,* it was not a mere local or sectional history he had in mind, and certainly not an addition to local antiquarian lore. He had caught a glimpse, foreshadowed in his *Benton,* of the role of the West in American history, and his major work was dedicated to that West and the nation it would explain.

The greatness of the American nation, as he saw it at the close of the century, was the result of the westward movement of the people, and their conquest of that vast region. That concept, once accepted, enabled Roosevelt to cut himself clear from the ties of political history and opened the way for a complete reorientation, if he could make it. His was a story of people, not government. Government did nothing for them. Even the matchless American political institutions aided not at all, for in the early years a kind of perverted blindness to needs and possibilities handicapped the actions of the Federalists, and, after the turn of the century, authority was in the hands of the spineless Jefferson and his successors.

Roosevelt sensed, somehow, the importance of the West, but between that uncertain and almost intuitive hint and the completed concept of a West within the framework of a national development lay a chasm too broad to be crossed by mere inspiration. The only relationship of this West to the United States, as he developed it, was the mere physical expansion of the geographic limits; in place of a conquest directed from Washington and politically explained, he described a conquest directed from nowhere and unexplained.

Unsupported, the pioneers moved into the dangerous distance of Kentucky and Tennessee, fought their battles, and lived their lives, as unconscious of their import as were their contemporaries, but with the destiny of the nation in their hands. The westward movement was a folk movement, a nineteenth-century migration of a German tribe, a new Norse conquest; behind it was only the drive of the inevitable. ["It (the winning of Louisiana) followed inevitably upon the great westward thrust of the settler-fold; a thrust which was delivered blindly, but which no rival race could parry, until it was stopped by the ocean itself" (*The Winning of the West*).]

The result was foredetermined. Titular claims to at least part of the region rested in three European nations, but governments with their conversations and diplomatic engagements are present only in the background, belatedly confirming in the transfer of title what the movement of conquest had already made an actuality. The claim of the Indian, except when vigorously defended in battle, is here brushed aside. The race was doomed, and only a quibbler would worry over where or how destruction came; Roosevelt was not one to talk of morals to destiny.

Thus treated, *The Winning of the West* was the work of the extreme frontier alone, and the account was reduced to the story of the doings of those local and sometimes half-mythical heroes by whose daring some minute point was held or some lives rescued. The construction of government as told is purely a local venturing under local leadership. Those larger implications, the creative impacts of social and economic forces generated in the West back upon the United States as a whole, Roosevelt did not see. It is the absence of any real idea of the role of the West which reduces the first two volumes to a series of microscopic biographies, almost as episodic as *The Naval War,* with only the uncertain unity given by time and geography.

The third and fourth volumes, covering the period after the Revolution and particularly after the Constitution, include in the narrative the settlement north of the Ohio. It is perhaps true, as Roosevelt suggests, that there was a larger measure of governmental direction in this settlement and thus a greater degree of order to it, but that is not the chief reason for the improved coherence of the history. There was a larger amount of monographic work available, and Roosevelt used it freely, to the noticeable improvement of his own work.

But even with this aid, the account remained a narrative of events essentially heroic. Perhaps Roosevelt was conscious of the weaknesses of the first work; but, if so, the effort made to improve it did not take the direction of more careful study with limited and supportable generalization. He only transferred his drama to a grander stage. The fourth volume opens with a long discussion of those race characteristics which make for empire-building, bestowed freely and positively, and with illustrations and comparisons impressed from his wide reading to prove the permanent validity of assertions made.

> The people that for one or more generations finds
> its alloted task in the conquest of a continent, has
> before it the possibility of splendid victory, and

the certainty of incredible toil, suffering, and hardship. . . . As it is in a battle, so it is in the infinitely greater contests where the fields of fight are continents, and the ages form the measure of time. . . . Of those who venture in the contest some achieve success: others strive feebly and fail ignobly. If the race is weak, if it is lacking in the physical and moral traits which go to the makeup of a conquering people, it cannot succeed. . . . The task must be given the race just at the time when it is ready for the undertaking. . . . Even a strong race, in its prime, and given the task at the right moment, usually fails to perform it. . . . Only the most far-seeing and high minded statesmen can grasp the real weight, from the race standpoint, of the possibilities which to the men of their day seem so trivial. [*The Winning of the West*]

Here, indeed, was the skeleton of an epic. Whole races fought and suffered for the dominion of a whole continent and for a victory which only subsequent ages could understand. It was no mere local affair, with individual contests and heroes; it was larger even than the nation. Cleveland had only recently defied the British power in the Venezuela affair; Cuba and its excitements were current topics; men were talking of Hawaii and the Pacific. The nation was moving out of its accustomed place to play on the world-stage a new and active and perhaps a controlling role. In this heady prospect, the work of those men who had made the West and the nation took on a new importance. The epic of the West broadened until all mankind was involved, its future hanging breathless on this American venture, and its fate tied in the outcome. American history, as Roosevelt read it, was no paltry affair.

This interpretation, striking though it was, probably colored his work less than those convictions and attitudes of which he was less aware. The world to which the young historian introduced himself was filled with certainties. There had been problems of a political nature in the past, it is true, but the war and its associated contests had settled them, and all correctly. The days to come might bring troubles, but they would not invoke intellectual uncertainties, and all would be solved if men had intelligence and honesty enough to think them through along the paths which the intellectuals, of whom Roosevelt was one, were eager to point out.

Indeed, that was his function as a historian. History had as its task so to unfold the truth about the past that its lessons would be learned; they were lessons of a direct and immediate nature, and, when Roosevelt pointed them out, he wrote large so that no man could miss them. The obligation resting on the historian was to find and tell the truth, of course, and Roosevelt poured scorn on those men who, calling themselves historian, perverted their work to special pleading. That was the trouble with so many men with whom Roosevelt disagreed. His distress at this evident error was equal to his disdain of those "small men in the universities" who, pretending in their preposterous association that their work was "scientific," refused to find lessons at all, or who insisted that the lessons found were purely subjective, read into the facts at the will of the historian. [Joseph B. Bishop, *Theodore Roosevelt and His Time*] Roosevelt knew better, for history as he studied it showed clearly the universality of the lessons to be learned—lessons which by fortunate coincidence were those most needed by contemporary American society.

The ideas were those of his contemporary liberals, translated in whole from English and Continental sources and publicized here most completely and purely by Curtis and Schurz and, above all, by Godkin of *The Nation*. The economics were those of the enlightened British school; individual enterprise, operating in a freely competitive society, responded to "laws" which were as understandable but as inevitable as those which ruled the swing of the planets or the movements of the tides. The laws of business—by which the intellectual meant no man-made statutes—were thus akin to those "laws of nature" by which the scientific seventeenth and eighteenth centuries had sought to rule its conduct, and perchance even to peer into the purposes of the infinite. In business, as in physics, they were inexorable, but, fortunately for mankind, they operated with such harmony under the beneficent foresight of Providence as to produce the "just" distribution of economic rewards and the ultimate good of mankind.

Laissez faire was thus a comfortable doctrine; those business men who gave hardly a grateful thought to the doctrine were freed from all limitation and responsibility by it, and the guardians of the public good were relieved of the necessity of battling on this particular front. If these new-found laws fought inevitably on the side of public good, what was there for reformers to do but keep the road clear and prevent artificial and inevitably unwise interference with destiny.

In government the British liberals had to trust their fortunes to some broad-base franchised group as the foundation of their constitutional institutions, but they did it with obvious reluctance inspired by fear of democracy. In America the tradition of democracy was translated slowly but smoothly into a tradition of constitutionalism, and the political institutions cushioned the shock of too much democracy. The complex federal system, the cumbersome and delaying check and balance system, the written constitution, all promised procrastination and even inaction. The Supreme Court was a wonderful comfort to timorous democrats. [This doubt of democracy, as reflected by Roosevelt, appears in *Morris*]

Thus economic laissez faire and political constitutionalism were the foundations of American liberalism. When evils appeared, and the decades before Roosevelt had had their share, they were explained to the satisfaction of the believers by the failure not of their principles but in the application of their principles. The leaders of men, the "scholars in politics" whose task was to point the inevitable way onward, understood clearly the road to reform and progress. Reform meant return to those fixed principles when the nation wandered and a holding fast to them when error threatened.

The field of politics was the field of reform, for here, unfortunately, flourished most of those pernicious panaceas by which embittered farmers and laborers sought to improve their lot, in ignorant disregard of this economic law and its ultimate justice. Reform would fight them off, sternly and implacably, whether the demand for wages above the level set by supply and demand (and no tinkering with that supply by unions or strikers), for monetary juggling, or for special tariff protection. Thus it was said, government, separate from business, would give no favors in the competitive struggle. [Roosevelt persistently expressed this idea when he talked of the "duty" of public officials as if their acts were completely disassociated from any economic connection and operated in a separate sphere. The concept of duty is, of course, highly subjective and can hardly be assumed as clear or definite under all circumstances alike. One illustration of this naïve use of the word appears in *Thomas Hart Benton*.]

But that program of disassociation demanded in government men of honesty and intelligent foresight and gave small comfort to those who saw contemporary politics with open eyes. If government itself was corrupt, there was small hope left for disinterested aloofness in economic dealings. A cynic might forthwith have abandoned democracy as hopeless, but the liberal could no more do that than he could abandon laissez faire, and he must hold that the trouble lay in some interference with the working of constitutional democracy. Casting about for the evil influence, the reformer hit on the political boss and made his elimination the basis of the program which would restore government to its sphere and permit economy to work out its good.

The merit system of political appointment might bring incidental benefits in economy and improved civil service, but far more important than either was the removal of the patronage from the boss and the cutting of the foundation from beneath the whole political machine. The entire arch of reform depended on this keystone, and this explains the tremendous emphasis which reformers place on it, in the day when to the casual observer other things seemed more important. It even justified the final point in reform politics, independency in voting, though that part was perhaps hardest of all. But if a boss ruled one party, with dishonesty apparent, special privilege flaunted, and the merit system scorned, inevitable logic drove reformers to the ultimate necessity of independency.

Theoretical free trade, or at least tariff reform, sound money, civil service reform, unhampered competition, and independency in voting—these are the ideas of the liberal, and to them young Roosevelt gave unquestioning acceptance. It is not surprising that they should be the lessons which history taught him as eternal verities.

But the young politician-historian did not live in complete isolation from the rest of the world. The student of political affairs from the safe seclusion of the academic study, or the editorial chair, could maintain such positions regardless of events, but the active participant who made politics a deliberate life-profession came into contact with external realities so forcefully that he was compelled to reconsider those eternal truths in the light of his own experiences.

In New York, before his progress in politics had carried him beyond the state legislature, Roosevelt had been a member and at least once a speaker for a free-trade club. But the tariff, though not a dominant issue, ran as a disturbing note through the campaign of 1884, and the rising politician allowed his contacts with the club to lapse. Pringle implies that it was merely a clever about-face, deftly accomplished before damage was done, but it was more than that. Almost immediately after the campaign, he wrote his **Benton,** and the discussion of the tariff has in it a new note. Elsewhere he dashed off sweeping generalities, pronouncements of right against wrong in cavalier style, but on the tariff, even when South Carolina nullifiers appear to add emotional attitudes, the treatment is a careful statement of rival interests involved, with such a balancing of opinion as to make the contest almost one of right against right. The young historian had been thrown into the necessity of just such a decision, not in the abstract but in real politics, had discovered the nature of the conflicting pressures out of which decisions must come, and had lost the certainty of eternal rightness. History ceased to teach him much about the tariff.

That same campaign of 1884 destroyed another conventional notion of liberalism for him—the acceptance of independency as a method. Blaine's personal record seemed to mark him as an object of special detestation to the reformers, and the accidents of domestic politics in New York threw unexpected weight behind their opinions in that state. Roosevelt joined his friends in opposing him for nomination; but, when that effort proved vain, and they went on to independency, Roosevelt could not follow them. To a hopeful politician such a move would have been suicide. His own uncertainty probably added acid to his defense of his conduct, and the denunciation he poured on his late associates, the Mugwumps, was increased by the tone of complacent superiority with which they referred to him.

Roosevelt in this campaign and again in 1888 worked out the notion of party entity, independent of, and superior to, personalities in control of the party and used this ancient defense to justify his conduct to himself. The road to reform must be through the party and not independent of it. As he became increasingly a part of the party and, finally as president, its leader, this naturally grew on him, until it became almost one of the certainties, a lesson which history should teach. As president he referred to independency as a "fool attitude," but even as early as **Benton** he scolded the Abolitionists for taking this position politically, on the ground that they thus aided the enemy, and he devoted an entire chapter to the title "The Abolitionists Dance to the Slave Baron's Piping." Having started out convinced of the values of independency, Roosevelt found that history had reversed itself and now taught as clearly the virtues of party loyalty and disciplined obedience.

In common with his fellows, Roosevelt exaggerated beyond reason the hoped-for results of civil service reform. Ignoring all the other things which the election of Jackson meant, Roosevelt insisted that his election was "one for the worse" on the sole ground of an alleged spoils activity, "a debasement and deterioration which has only been checked in our own days." [**Benton**] But civil service reform came, and the dreamed-of utopia did not come. Machines still flourished in politics, and only Roosevelt's biographer, from academic seclusion, could say "the big boss is no more." [Bishop] Surely Roosevelt would never have said it. Indeed, this reform actually increased the much denounced interference of business in government, since it made the machine dependent on business for contributions. Roosevelt continued to be a believer in civil service, but the dependence on it as the universal solvent of all ills was gone, with other certainties.

The presidency demolished more of those ideas with which the young man began. On money, he would instruct the world, in the eighties and nineties; as president, he confessed he knew nothing of it. The sovereign benefits of unregulated competition were sufficient creed for the liberal, but the president faced circumstances where competition destroyed rather than regulated, and where, in the world of practical affairs, laissez faire was a joke. Lawsuits, he discovered, could not prevent monopoly, and, when "natural" processes failed, governmental interference seemed essential to maintain that just distribution of economic rewards. And 1912, with all its disasters, left small remainders of the virtue of party loyalty and discipline. [In **Oliver Cromwell** Roosevelt had referred to those men who "run small, separate tickets on election day, thereby giving aid, comfort, and amusement to the totally unregenerate."]

Yet that year, 1912, brought him the presidency of the American Historical Association and the obligation and opportunity of the annual address. Roosevelt lacked time, inclination, and perhaps the analytical objectivity which would produce from this complex of experiences and defaults a new and conscious historical philosophy, but he had too keen a grasp of realities not to know that the assumptions with which he had begun were no longer tenable. Perhaps it was that disconcerting confusion and distasteful uncertainty which made him approach that address with such reluctance.

Roosevelt had nothing to say. There were pleas for a breadth of vision and a vividness of writing which were undebatable. He caught at the new history to urge a point not new. He used a wealth of illustration and eulogy to forward the cause of historical classics which needed no such advertising. The only hint of the old certainties appear in the pronouncement that the historian must be a moralist and in the assertion that American history would prove the eternal righteous progress of the nation; the decade of the twenties was still ahead.

Roosevelt had nothing to say. He knew the truth of his assertion that "the wisdom of one generation may seem the folly of the next." There is even a note of aspersion used toward those who talk of a "purely utilitarian history." It was a nicely worded address, but the things left unsaid were far more eloquent than those things said. For a title, Roosevelt chose "**History as Literature.**"

Arthur Schlesinger, Jr. (essay date 1951)

SOURCE: "The Pragmatic Hero," in *Partisan Review,* Vol. 18, No. 4, July/Aug., 1951, pp. 466-71.

[*Schlesinger is a prominent American historian and an influential figure in liberal politics. As a special assistant to Presidents John F. Kennedy and Lyndon Johnson, he was instrumental in formulating the "New Frontier" and the "Great Society," the two major social reform movements of the 1960s, which promoted Medicare, the war on poverty, and extensive civil rights legislation. Schlesinger has twice been the recipient of the Pulitzer Prize: the first for* The Age of Jackson *(1945), an examination of Jacksonian democracy as the genesis of American liberalism, and the second for* A Thousand Days: John F. Kennedy in the White House *(1965), an overview of the Kennedy administration. In the following essay, Schlesinger reviews a two-volume edition of Roosevelt's collected letters for the years preceding his term as president.*]

"These, then, are my last words to you," said William James to the Harvard chapter of the Young Men's Christian Association in 1895: "Be not afraid of life. Believe that life *is* worth living, and your belief will help create the fact." He was expressing what would become a basic aspect of the ethics of pragmatism; he was expressing too what was, on many levels, a characteristic faith of his time—the faith in the capacity of the will to achieve anything. Orison Swett Marden's *Pushing to the Front: or Success under Difficulties* had begun its enormous popular success the year before; William Makepeace Thayer's *Turning Points in Successful Careers* was published the same year. They all praised the "iron will." "Life," said Marden, "is what we make it. . . . Give a youth resolution and the alphabet, and who shall place limits to his career?" James called it "the will to believe" and Marden "the will to succeed": strictly, they were talking about quite different things, but in a significant sense too they were interpreting a central impulse of the times. The great exponent of this impulse in practice was Theodore Roosevelt.

For Theodore Roosevelt his whole life—his style of personality, his very physique—was a triumph of the will. He was a spindly boy, nearsighted and asthmatic, interested in reading and in the study of nature; but his physi-

cal weakness, he came to feel, invited aggression; so he remade himself by sheer force of will, teaching himself to ride and box and be tough. "I went in for boxing and wrestling a good deal," he writes in a letter of 1900, "and I really think that while this was partly because I liked them as sports, it was even more because I intended to be a middling decent fellow, and I did not intend that anyone should laugh at me with impunity because I was decent." A deep interior anxiety made him forever apprehensive over the possibility of ridicule; a deep interior violence shaped his response.

He thus redesigned his personality; he wanted to do good and feared being a sissy, and this was his solution. "My ordinary companions in college would I think have had a tendency to look down upon me for doing Sunday school work if I had not also been a corking boxer, a good runner, and a genial member of the Porcellian Club." But Roosevelt did not stop at being a muscular Christian, given to pugilism and good works; he had a large vision. "It is exactly the same thing with history," he continues in a strikingly characteristic vein. "In most countries the 'Bourgeoisie'—the moral, respectable, commercial, middle class—is looked upon with a certain contempt which is justified by their timidity and unwarlikeness. But the minute a middle class produces men like Hawkins and Frobisher on the seas, or men such as the average Union soldier in the civil war, it acquires the hearty respect of others."

This introduces the second theme in the life of Roosevelt: the dilemma of an aristocrat in a plutocracy. It obsessed his historical speculation, dominated his politics and colored his personal relations. He hated "the commercial and cheap altruistic spirit, the spirit of the Birmingham school, the spirit of the banker, the broker, the mere manufacturer, and mere merchant"; he detested "the stock-jobbing timidity, the Baboo kind of statesmanship, which is clamored for . . . by the men who put monetary gain before national honor." Possessing himself the security of family and status, he was deeply affronted by the domination in society of the men of business.

This was, of course, a predicament of the highest importance in the intellectual life of late nineteenth-century America. The descendants of the mild, settled and relatively cultured men of wealth of the pre-Civil War period now found themselves confronted by the crude and fierce world of the "robber barons." Their varied responses to this new world supplied pervading themes for the writing and behavior of the time. James Russell Lowell sought refuge in good old books; Henry Adams in cynicism and disillusion; Oliver Wendell Holmes, Jr., in skepticism and detachment; Henry James, Jr., in Europe. For all of them, a sense of affirmative social function had waned, yet they would not yield to the new forces. Others yielded, and became the agents, the front men, the sages and instructors for the new masters.

Of those who would neither yield nor seek refuge, who sought to confront their predicament squarely and directly, William James and Theodore Roosevelt were clearly the most successful. Both their reputations have suffered perhaps as a result; their very attempts to come to terms with their times produced in each a certain jocosity and even vulgarity which, if for James an obvious rhetorical tactic, appears for Roosevelt to have been an abiding and much-relished personal impulse. Roosevelt's bluster and brag were increasingly offensive to later generations which had abandoned the big words and the manly virtues. By 1931, Henry Pringle's brilliant and devastating biography seemed permanently to diminish Roosevelt's place in history.

The new edition of Roosevelt's letters provides documentation for all Henry Pringle's astringencies about the man. There is the intolerable rhetoric of manliness: the praise for the rough, the virile, the clean-living, the constant desire to administer a "sound drubbing" to the "cowardly" and the "sentimental." "If we ever come to nothing as a nation it will be because the teaching of Carl Schurz, President Eliot, the *Evening Post* and the futile sentimentalists of the international arbitration type, bears its legitimate fruit in producing a flabby, timid type of character, which eats away the great fighting features of our race."

This is all, of course, very funny, and it reaches its strident and supposedly hilarious climax at San Juan Hill. Yet it must be remembered that the Spanish were not shooting blank cartridges in Cuba, that men were killed, and that Roosevelt at least had the courage to apply his doctrine of the "strenuous life" to himself. And when Mr. Dooley suggested that Roosevelt's book *The Rough Riders* should have been called *Alone in Cubia* or *Th' Biography iv a Hero be Wan who Knows,* Roosevelt could hardly have been more disarming. I "regret to state," he wrote Finley Peter Dunne, "that my family and intimate friends are delighted with your review of my book."

These Roosevelt letters remind us vividly of the exuberance, the inextinguishable vitality, and the keen, animal instinct of the man. He was, of course, voracious in his interests; except for Jefferson, no American president has ever known so much, read so widely, or dogmatized so freely in so fantastic a variety of fields. If his opinions of Henry James seem cheap and stupid today, how many active politicians, then or now, have read Henry James at all? And the more striking thing is the number of new men and ideas Theodore Roosevelt recognized and encouraged. He instantly perceived the importance of Mahan on the influence of sea power in history; he sensed, less sharply, that of Turner on the frontier. He singled out the bright young men of the day: William Allen White, Jacob Riis and Lincoln Steffens were his friends; Stephen Crane dined with him; he entertained Hamlin Garland in Washington, introducing him to Brooks Adams and Cabot Lodge; he responded, coarsely but positively, to a whole range of new sensations, from Tolstoy (reading *Anna Karenina* on a western trip in between rounding up cattle thieves) to Professor Langley's flying machine.

More important was his sense for the grand movements of the time. He had no original ideas; but his instinct for historical tendencies drove him to seize upon the big issues. His letters in these two volumes show him edging into the trust agitation, scenting the unrest and knowing that something had to be done. Even more striking is his understanding that the days of American isolation were over, that the U.S. was irrevocably condemned to competition among the great world powers. The Germans and, in the longer perspective, the Russians stood athwart his conception of American interests. "I look upon them," he wrote in 1897 of the Russians, "as a people . . . with a great future, as we have; but a people with poisons working in it." If Russia continues in its despotic way, "she may put off the day of reckoning; but she cannot ultimately avert it, and instead of occasionally having to go through what Kansas has gone through with the populists she will sometime experience a red terror which will make the French Revolution pale." And he understood too the new strategic significance of the Pacific; if Russia "ever does take possession of Northern China and drill the Northern Chinese to serve as her Army, she will indeed be a formidable power."

America could not last in this dangerous new world, Roosevelt felt, so long as bourgeois timidity and avarice prevailed over the martial qualities indispensable for survival. Here, again, he called for a triumph of will. If he could rebuild his own body by personal moral determination, could not the nation be restored by an invocation of the "strenuous life"? In the end, he was a moralist in politics, a great political educator, and, though his significant career lay largely beyond the two volumes under review, we can see in these letters the essential stirrings of preparation.

The two volumes, it should be added, are a triumph of the editorial art. The notes of identification are compact, discreet and often witty; and the essays on Roosevelt by Elting E. Morison and John M. Blum have a penetration and detachment which put them in the same class with the brilliant earlier essays by Stuart P. Sherman and Richard Hofstadter. The only failure is the index, which for some reason does not list all proper names mentioned in the letters and therefore will be much less useful than an index should be.

Out of these volumes emerges above all a pragmatist's sense of the power of will. T.R. and William James never had much personal contact. Roosevelt's political and historical interests and his active dislike of business domination drew him much more to Henry and Brooks Adams. James, it is true, had been Roosevelt's anatomy instructor at Harvard (where, a classmate later recalled, "T.R. *always* had the last word"); but the two men later differed bitterly over the policy of expansionism. Yet in 1905 James supported Roosevelt for the presidency of Harvard. "Think of the mighty good will of him," he wrote, "of his enjoyment of his post, of his power as a preacher, of the number of things to which he gives his attention, of the safety of his second thoughts, of the increased courage he is showing, and above all of the fact that he is an open, instead of an underground leader. . . . Bless him—and damn all his detractors!"

"Anaesthesia," James wrote on another occasion, "is the watchword of the moral sceptic. . . . *Energy* is that of the moralist. Act on my creed, cries the latter, and the results of your action will prove the creed true." In this sense, Theodore Roosevelt was the pragmatist in politics (as, in the sense of the word favored by the followers of Robert M. Hutchins, he was doubtless the "pragmatist" in diplomacy—Panama—and the "pragmatist" in reform). The volcanic Rooseveltian energy performed a magnificent service in its day. "Thousands of innocent magazine readers," said James in 1882, "lie paralyzed and terrified in the network of shallow negations which the leaders of opinion have thrown over their souls. All they need to be free and hearty again in the exercise of their birthright is that these fastidious vetoes should be swept away. All that the human heart wants is its chance." In his brawling and offensive way, Theodore Roosevelt swept away many fastidious vetoes. The human heart in America, on the whole, benefited from his violent energy, though T.R., for whom energy became almost an end in itself, concluded as his own major casualty.

Merrill E. Lewis (essay date 1963)

SOURCE: "History as Melodrama: Theodore Roosevelt's *The Winning of the West*," in *The American West: An Appraisal,* edited by Robert G. Ferris, Museum of New Mexico Press, 1963, pp. 201-10.

[*In the following essay, Lewis explains his reasons for considering* The Winning of the West *a failure both as literature and as history.*]

The incongruity of Harvard-educated Theodore Roosevelt in the Bad Lands of North Dakota has been the source of numerous stories. As one of his biographers said: "His somewhat precise tones still flavored by exposure to Harvard culture rang strangely in [the ears of westerners]. He did not smoke or drink. His worst profanity was an infrequent 'Damn!' and his usual ejaculation was 'By Godfrey!' The first time he took part in a round up, sometime during the summer of 1885, one or two hardened cowboys nearly fell from their saddles as he called in his high voice to one of the men: 'Hasten forward quickly there!'" The phrase became a classic in the Bad Lands to express the westerner's view of eastern greenhorns.

Conscious of some need to adjust to an image, Roosevelt worked hard at playing the role of the westerner, just as he had previously worked hard at playing the role of political reformer, and later would work hard at playing that of the African big-game hunter. In the Bad Lands, he dressed like a cowboy dandy, wearing a buckskin shirt and sporting a pearl-handled revolver. As a deputy sheriff, he prepared on one occasion to trail some thieves

who had stolen his boat. The evening before leaving a friend overheard him in the kitchen practicing the lines he would use the next day: "I've got the gun on you," he repeated over and over. "I know you stole my boat and I'm here to claim it." Paradoxically, he planned to take along on the chase Matthew Arnold to read for relaxation. If Roosevelt, finally, out of dogged persistence and a sort of naive courage, succeeded in gaining acceptance as a westerner, his figure still remained essentially incongruous, even theatrical, against the western landscape.

He was saved from uniqueness only because role playing was becoming more and more the pattern in the West of the 1880's. He actually played many roles: cowboy, member of the cattlemen's association, deputy sheriff, chivalric gallant, and man of letters. All of them were dominated by the same general characteristics: a boyish robustness and athletic vigor of mind and body coupled with a sentimental attachment to the West as a place and with morality as a sentiment. All the roles championed Roosevelt's philosophy of the strenuous but moral life.

Most scholars conclude that Roosevelt's inveterate play acting merely illustrated his innate adolescence. Even Roosevelt's contemporaries saw him in this light. When he was elected to the White House for a second term in 1904, Cecil Spring Rice, an Englishman, wrote of him, "You must always remember that the President is about six." And Elihu Root wrote to Roosevelt on his forty-sixth birthday, "You have made a good start in life, and your friends have great hopes for you when you grow up." To his friend Henry Adams, Roosevelt was exasperating. "What annoys me," Adams said, "is his childlike and infantile superficiality with his boyish dogmatism of assertion. He lectures me on history as though he were a high school pedagogue." Dixon Wecter has summed up the nature of Roosevelt's private world in these words: "Like the world of adolescence, [it] was a place of high adventure, swagger, conspiracies, with a touch of melodrama, fierce loyalties, and equally fierce hates."

Roosevelt the actor became Roosevelt the mythmaker. The kind of myths he was content to create is a fair measure of his intellectual achievements as well as his psychological makeup. More specifically, the philosophy of the strenuous life, filled as it was with strenuous loyalties to the West and the wilderness, suggests a mixing of matters subjective and objective, imaginative and factual. But sometimes the boundary line was fuzzy. At one of his interviews with Roosevelt, Hermann Hagedorn said, "I referred to his life in the Bad Lands as 'a kind of idyl.' 'That's it!' he exclaimed. 'That's it! That's exactly what it was!'" Of course, Roosevelt's life in the Bad Lands was an idyl only in a highly subjective sense.

On yet another occasion, when there was talk of renominating him for President in 1916, he stated: "It would be a mistake . . . to nominate me unless the country has in its mood something of the heroic." In light of such remarks, it is not surprising that, within a year after he left the ranch in North Dakota, he was at work on a history of the American West, as he announced to Lyman Copeland Draper, "from the days when Boone crossed the Alleghenies to the days of the Alamo and San Jacinto." The first volume of *The Winning of the West* was published the next year. It was clearly an attempt to find a vehicle for the myth—to substantiate it in the solid matter of history. The result was a "literary" history.

Roosevelt had been formulating his views on the relationship of history and literature for some time. In a review of Francis Parkman's just-completed *France and England in North America* in 1892, he wrote, "Mr. Parkman would have been quite unequal to his task if he had not appreciated its romance as well as its importance." The importance which Roosevelt noted, of course, was the irrevocable march of the civilization of the Anglo-Saxon people against the lands of barbarism and savagery. The romance and color were to be found in the "incidents of wild and picturesque adventure" that accompanied the march. Coming as it did in the year that the second volume of *The Winning of the West* was published, the review is a candid confession of Roosevelt's own intellectual and emotional involvement in the westward movement. The wilderness, he said, "appeals to Parkman's very inmost soul." The same could be said for Roosevelt. He even obtained permission to dedicate *The Winning of the West* to Parkman.

But a full development of Roosevelt's ideas had to await the famous presidential address, **"History as Literature,"** before the American Historical Association on December 22, 1912. Roosevelt reaffirmed that history was devoted to actual facts, but he saw nothing incompatible between truthfulness and color. History must be scientific and "accept what we now know of man's place in nature." But it should also be imaginative. The great historians must have the power to grasp "what is essential and to reject the infinitely more numerous non-essentials, the power to embody ghosts, to put flesh and blood on dry bones, to make dead men living before our eyes." A "literary" history would not only render the scene, the incidents, and the characters of history, but it would also analyze their relative significance.

Yet history should also be moral. "It is no proof of impartiality," Roosevelt assured his audience, "to treat wickedness and goodness as on the same level." So literature also became the vehicle for educating its readers to "a broad human sympathy" and lifting them "out of their common selves to the heights of high endeavor." High moral truth could be taught only through concrete instances, and literature had the power to render life in concrete terms. No contradiction existed between moral truth and colorful adventure. It was only in some literary form that encompassed those elements that history "[pulsed] with immortal life."

Roosevelt viewed the westward movement as a conquest—an epic struggle—that pulsed with this "immortal life." In a letter to Frederic Remington, on December 28, 1897, he complimented Remington for his sketches of the

West, and added that they, along with "the very best," would live on as the "cantos in the last Epic of the Western Wilderness."

Roosevelt tried to capture the history of the West in epic terms in *The Winning of the West*. It was a heroic age, he stated in the opening volume. But a history which merely renders the scene and elevates the soul cannot be epic; in *The Winning of the West,* Roosevelt did not render the scene, let alone write an epic or elevate the soul.

Certain limitations in Roosevelt's own literary taste foreshadowed the literary failure of *The Winning of the West*. Reading literature was, Roosevelt felt, a matter of taste. He liked books in which "something happened." He disliked introspective ones that were psychologically oriented or dealt with subtle social relationships. This may explain why he avidly read *Macbeth* and *Othello* and disliked *Hamlet* and *King Lear,* even though he knew "perfectly well the latter were wonderful." He felt that the novels of Henry James were "diseased"—nothing but "polished, pointless, uninteresting stories" that made "one blush to think that James was once an American." He enjoyed Chaucer, but found some of the tales "needlessly filthy," even unreadable; and he considered Tolstoi a great but decadent writer.

Many of these attitudes simply show not only a lack of good judgment, but, even more important, a lack of sensibility. Roosevelt was contemptuous of the intellectual and esthetic in literature. One of his problems as a writer was that he lacked any sense of literary esthetics. He could tolerate tragedy in certain of the great dramas and in some poetry, but not, he insisted somewhat unintelligibly "in good, readable novels of sufficient length to enable me to get interested in the hero and heroine." He read "to lose all memory of everything grimy" and did not "care to study suffering unless for some sufficient purpose." He further stated, "It is only a very exceptional novel which I will read if He does not marry Her; and even in exceptional novels I much prefer this consummation."

His distaste for sordid details led him to censure his good friend Owen Wister for allowing Balaam, in the short story "Balaam and Pedro," to gouge out one of the eyes of Pedro, his horse, in a fit of violent anger. When Wister rewrote the scene for *The Virginian,* leaving that detail out, it lost what "meaning" it might have had and became a scene of melodramatic violence, in which the Virginian's "sledgehammer blows of justice" revenge the act and pound Balaam into "a blurred, dingy, wet pulp." Roosevelt did not object to the new version.

The Winning of the West reflects Roosevelt's lack of literary sensibility. The participants in the action of the history are nothing less than the forces of good and the forces of evil—the forces of civilization and the forces of savagery. Good is personified in the deeds of the heroic Anglo-Saxon backwoodsman, and evil is personified in the Indian, his French and British allies, the Spanish, and such backwoodsmen as Simon Girty—all who turn their backs on destiny and side either directly or indirectly with savagery. On such a grandiose scale, the conquest of the West was "in its essence just and righteous." War was inevitable. Providence predestined victory.

"It is indeed," said Roosevelt, without a hint of irony, "a warped, perverse, and silly morality which would forbid a course of conquest that has turned whole continents into the seats of mighty and flourishing civilized nations." The crises created by the conquest "demanded that the [backwoodsmen] should be both strong and good; but, above all things, it demanded that they should be strong." Because justice must prevail before mercy, it was the warlike qualities of the Long Knives that were truly admirable. Under existing conditions, it was perfectly proper for Bible-reading backwoodsmen to take Indian scalps.

This confusion of muscle-flexing with moral righteousness turns *The Winning of the West* into a cosmic melodrama in which the forces of "dark death," "butchery," wantonness, and cruelty fight "ferocious wars" with the "hardy [and] strenuous band" of frontier Vikings in the midst of "dark and gloomy woods" and along "blood-stained rivers." The situations in the history contain stock elements of melodrama: bloodshed, revenge, capture, escape, deception, and intrigue. Despite the appearance of realism—the attempt at the verisimilitude of historical facts—Roosevelt was often frustratingly vague and even ambiguous about significant events. He recommended to his friend Owen Wister in a letter: "Throw a veil over what Balaam did to Pedro, leave that to the reader's imagination, and you will greatly strengthen your effect." The statement accurately describes Roosevelt's method in *The Winning of the West*. The history leaves all "conscientious descriptions of the unspeakable" to the reader's imagination. Like all melodramatists, Roosevelt relied on the imagination of his reader to supply the unpleasant details. Even when he narrated grotesque events, emotional and moral conviction was lacking.

Roosevelt's awareness of the mind of his audience was a trait that his friend Brander Matthews admired: "Roosevelt . . . had imagination, and he knew that the American people also had it." Though this trait may have made him a successful politician, it proved his undoing as a writer. He failed to discriminate between the masses' supposed awareness of high moral truth and elevated emotion, and their stock responses to patriotism, honor, race superiority, bravery, and women. He confused the triumph of virtue with "blood and thunder," and consequently was guilty of a series of literary and historical hypocrisies that mark his own peculiar insensibility to the absurd.

A passage describing the Indians during Clark's conquest of the Northwest illustrates Roosevelt's emotional treatment of his subject matter: "The darkbrowed, sullen-looking savages, grotesque in look and terrible in possi-bility . . . strutted to and fro in their dirty finery or lounged round the houses, inquisitive, importunate, and insolent, hardly concealing a lust for bloodshed and plunder that the slightest mishap was certain to render ungovernable." A more open invitation to the imagination than "grotesque in look and terrible in possibility" cannot be imagined.

Despite these basic deficiencies in the history, Roosevelt seriously attempted to explain frontier character. He wrote to Frederick Jackson Turner, following Turner's review of *The Winning of the West,* that his purpose in writing the history was to "show who the frontiersmen were and what they did." In reply to Turner's specific criticism that he had failed to recognize the regional unity of the West, Roosevelt stated that separatist feeling made the various communities indifferent to one another, though "in type the men were the same." It was a favorite theme with Roosevelt. In *Ranch Life and the Hunting Trail,* he distinguished between the cowboy and bad-man types in the prairie West. And, in his "Letter to John Hay," he wrote of possible new types developing in the Pacific coast regions. Daniel Boone is described as the archetype of the "hunter and wilderness wanderer," a rather vague figure, in both *Hero Tales from American History* and *The Winning of the West*. The latter book further identifies a distinctively American type, a strongly individualistic, self-reliant freeman, who is "produced" or "molded" by his frontier environment. A series of other types are also presented: hunter, hunter-settler, settler, and the like. The book also states that the frontier offered, pre-eminently, a "contrast in types."

Roosevelt felt that the pressures of the frontier experience intensified and accentuated the qualities of "good" and "bad" (he often used just these terms). Though in *The Winning of the West* some attempt is made to render the Indian as a noble figure, as in the characterization of Cornstalk, and though savagery is presented in a repetitious catalogue of atrocities, the Indian is usually presented as a foil for the exploration of the character of the backwoodsmen. His fickleness, for example, is meant to stand in clear contrast to the unwavering steadfastness of the white man. The pressure of Indian actions, like the primitiveness of the environment, accentuate the backwoodsman's tendencies toward good and evil and make him act in heroic or villainous fashion—in a rationale for melodrama.

Though Roosevelt examined the frontiersman in the traditions of the romantic hero-villain, in no sense did he seriously explore the real nature of heroism or villainy. His statement that "sharp dealing" in the East became "highway robbery" in the West appears to have been only an excuse for stressing the more colorful elements of the West. When Roosevelt treated men whom he was forced both to admire and damn, such as George Rogers Clark and John Sevier, he actually created two characters to play each role, each representing the extremes he wished to portray. He could not wholly conceive Sevier because he did not understand him and could not accept him:

"Sevier must be judged by another standard [than John Kirk, the brutal murderer of friendly Indians]. He was a member of the Cincinnati, a correspondent of Franklin, a follower of Washington. He sinned against the light, and must be condemned accordingly." Clark was "undone by his fondness for strong drink."

Roosevelt clearly wrote in a literary as well as a historical tradition, owing as much to his literary predecessors James Fenimore Cooper and Sir Walter Scott as he did to the manuscripts and state papers which he studied. Early in the first volume of *The Winning of the West,* he describes a levy of frontier soldiers as "composed of men of the type of Leatherstocking, Ishmael Bush, Tom Hutter, Harry March, Bill Kirby, and Aaron Thousandacres." In the second volume, he compares Captain Kenton's running of the Indian gauntlet with *The Last of the Mohicans.* He refers to Cooper again when he sums up a few of the most typical examples of frontier heroics from among the hundreds he has read about in contemporary manuscripts. The battle of the two Poe brothers with the seven Wyandot warriors is clearly told in the Cooper style. Unlike Cooper, Roosevelt cannot be defended on the grounds of innovation.

At the ending of his account of the Poe-Wyandot episode, Roosevelt states: "It is curious how faithfully, as well as vividly, Cooper has reproduced these incidents. His pictures of the white frontiersmen are generally true to life; in his most noted Indian characters he is much less fortunate. But his 'Indian John' in *The Pioneers* is one of his best portraits; almost equal praise can be given to 'Susquesus' in the *Chainbearer.*" It is no wonder that many parts of *The Winning of the West* strongly resemble Cooper.

Allusions are also made to Scott. For example, Roosevelt compares the skirmishes between Indians and whites to the English-Scottish border wars fought two centuries before. Because *Rob Roy* was one of his favorite novels, such allusions are not surprising.

Striving to make his history colorful and his color authentic, Roosevelt naively regarded the conflict between history and literature as potential rather than actual. He insists that the "silence . . . cunning and stealth . . . terrible prowess and merciless cruelty" of the Indians makes it no figure of speech to call them "the tigers of the human race." Elsewhere, he says that it is not a fanciful expression to say that Logan went for help with the "tireless speed of a wolf" because you cannot tire wolves. In fact, "too horrible to mention" was not a figurative expression because every white captive of the Indians suffered torture. Certainly Roosevelt had a gross misunderstanding of the nature of figurative language.

He had two mistresses when he wrote *The Winning of the West*—history and literature—and his pleasures with one could not easily be reconciled with his pleasures with the other. For one thing, he was not very apt at telling them apart. Early in the history, Roosevelt makes it plain

that he wishes to correct the inaccuracies of earlier writers like Haywood and Kirke. Kirke is criticized for stating that 15,000 Indians fought a single battle with the settlers. Yet only a few pages later Roosevelt tells a highly implausible story of the rescue of Kate Sherrill by her fiancé, John Sevier. Within the matter of a few pages, then, Roosevelt defends authenticity and destroys plausibility.

Equally glaring is Roosevelt's failure to face the problem of sentimentalism squarely. Some of his most caustic criticism is aimed at Helen Hunt Jackson and all "sentimental" historians because they apologized for the conquest of the West. His own assertions that the white man had a legal and moral right to the West are tedious, repetitive, and in themselves sentimental. But, while he exhibits such seeming tough-mindedness as a historian, he indulges in the most blatant sentimentalism as a creator of character and situation. To create the Indian in the role of villain, he stresses his indiscriminate cruelty to women and children—"the helpless non-combatants." He also dwells on emotional and spiritual dilemmas of the white captives, the situations arising from the marriage of Indian warriors and white women, and the tragedy of "half-breed" children.

Frequently, he insists, during the Indian retreats the captive women and children—and particularly "the women heavy with child"—were "tomahawked and scalped as soon as their steps faltered." After narrating the Battle of Blue Licks, he indulges in bathos: "In every stockade, in almost every cabin, there was weeping for husband or father, son, brother or lover. The best and bravest in the land had been shed like water. There was no one who had not lost some close and dear friend, and the heads of all the people were bowed and their hearts sore stricken." Here, as elsewhere, the sentimental bias is inherent in the sometimes trite, sometimes stilted rhetoric. An additional example of sentimentalism is Roosevelt's reiteration of the "settler's fondness" for the "lonely life of the woods."

Certainly Roosevelt lost many literary and historical opportunities. He could not conceive a complex character who had several sets of values, although he realized values clashed on the frontier. His own attraction to lawlessness was purely romantic. Temperamentally, he was drawn to admire physical prowess in any colorful form, but he could not conceive with any coherence or depth the conflict of values inherent in what he called savagery and civilization. He always felt most at ease characterizing men he could classify as pure villains—men like Aaron Burr. He did not explore the paradox of Boone the Empire Builder and Boone the primitivistic child of nature. In fact, he did not even indicate that he was aware of the paradox, although he attributed both qualities to Boone.

A greater literary capability would not have been enough to insure consideration of these themes; Roosevelt would have had to conceive a society much more complex than that described in *The Winning of the West*. When the pattern of history shifted away from the frontiersmen toward the settlers, he lost interest, though admitting that the settlers were "the only part [of the community] worth taking into account" and that the "drifting element" was essentially unimportant.

But did Roosevelt write good history? Macaulay, who defended "literary" histories, wrote that the historian who stated only facts might "produce the effect of grossest falsehood" unless he understood the "art of selection" and could, like the painter or writer, produce the effect of truth as well as the authenticity of truth. Roosevelt tried to follow Macaulay's advice. He conceived an epic: the history of the westward movement illustrated the providential victory of civilization over savagery. But, when these abstractions were applied to the events and characters of history, history became melodrama. It is satisfying, he said, to find the stories of the prowess of heroes "attested by contemporary records."

The very theories and principles propounded in Roosevelt's philosophy of history are literary as well as historical. But Roosevelt did not have the imaginative power—let alone the command of literary technique—to make *The Winning of the West* a notable literary achievement. Its failure as literature also accounts in part for its failure as history.

Ellen Moers (essay date 1963)

SOURCE: "Teddy Roosevelt: Literary Feller," in *Columbia University Forum*, Vol. 6, No. 3, Summer, 1963, pp. 10-16.

[*An American educator and critic, Moers is the author of* The Dandy: Brummel to Beerbohm *(1960) and* Literary Women *(1976). In the following essay, she documents Roosevelt's relationship to New York's literati during his term as police commissioner of that city.*]

In the 1890s New York became the literary center of America as it had never been before and perhaps would never be so effectively again. As the center of a publishing revolution, the city could offer three things to men of talent: a living (on newspapers and magazines), an apprenticeship (via journalism to all the arts and idealisms), and a subject matter: the urban poor. This last New York possessed in greater abundance and variety and showed off to greater effect (by contrast with its flashy plutocracy) than any other American city.

The great new subject was summarized by the nineties under the catchall heading of "the Bowery": slum streets and tenements, immigrants and policemen, sweatshops and strikes, corruption, vice, disease, and vagrancy. Everyone went down to the Bowery to have a look, and "slumming" became in that decade obligatory for novelists, painters, photographers, critics, historians, reporters, sociologists, settlement workers, politicians, ministers, and plain reformers. The interchange of methods and

ideas, over the counter of journalism, and all in the Bowery line of business, was what gave New York its special quality as an intellectual center, in marked contrast to its old rival, literary Boston, to the north.

New York also had Theodore Roosevelt. From 1895 to 1897 the relatively young and untried politician served the city officially as Police Commissioner, and unofficially as social commissioner to the literati. Stationed on that block of the Bowery called Mulberry Street, where police headquarters was (and is), Roosevelt brushed against journalists, writers, and artists, learning from them and giving them something in return. William Dean Howells, Hamlin Garland, Stephen Crane, Richard Harding Davis, Lincoln Steffens, Jacob Riis, and Brander Matthews all moved into Roosevelt's orbit in the 1890s, and he into theirs; they were all working in New York, all studying the Bowery subject matter, all involved with the newspapers and magazines that gave New York its special place in American publishing. In view of the traditional complaint about the historic alienation of the American writer, it is regrettable that Roosevelt's relationship with the Bowery school has left barely a trace on the standard Roosevelt biographies (or on his autobiography, for that matter); it is only partially documented in the Elting Morison edition of Roosevelt's letters.

Roosevelt linked old New York to the young New York of the 1890s. If he shared the curiosity, enthusiasm, and even irresponsibility of his literary friends, he clearly represented inherited wealth, family, and position. Though his ascent to the White House was an improbable five years away, Roosevelt's intrepidity and energy also suggested power (even, to the sophisticated noses of journalists like Steffens and Riis, the faint, intoxicating aroma of Presidential aspirations). By any standard Roosevelt was a voracious reader; by the standard of successful American politicians, before and after his time, he was an absolute glutton for books and the people who wrote them. His appetite for friendships with men of talent was hearty and genuine—more genuine, perhaps, than the generation of the New Frontier can credit.

Well before he became Police Commissioner, Roosevelt had dreamed of a "far distant salon" in his own home that would include "society men who take part in politics, literature, and art, and politicians, authors, and artists whose bringing up and personal habits do not disqualify them for society." The last clause testifies to Roosevelt's sincerity, not the reverse; his standards were not so high as to exclude from his acquaintance Riis the immigrant or Crane the shabby, scandal-prone Bohemian. "I never can . . . be intimate," he had written in 1890, "with that enormous proportion of sentient beings who are respectable but dull. I will work with them, or for them; but for pleasure and instruction I go elsewhere."

Official history has for some reason obscured the fact that Roosevelt in his early years was as active an author as he was a politician. If he pretended, when among writers, to be one of their own, it was not all affectation.

He knew the pains and pleasures of the craft, as his early letters charmingly testify. Richard Hofstadter has pointed out that a political career was then an unlikely choice for a college man of good family, and Roosevelt in fact began to work at writing (history) before the end of his Harvard years. Though he enrolled at Columbia Law School after graduation, he grew more and more determined on a "literary" career and went so far as to buy a partnership in the publishing house of Putnam. Years later Major Putnam would reminisce sourly about young Theodore's enthusiastic impracticality as a publisher, and would even claim to have recommended T. R. to Republican bigwigs as a nominee for the state Assembly, simply to get him away from G. P. Putnam's Sons. "And then during the sessions of the Legislature," Major Putnam wrote, "I had, for five days of the week, a comparatively quiet time in the office. On Saturdays, Theodore would return to his publishing desk. . . ."

However he got there, it is clear that from the day of his election to the Legislature in 1881, Roosevelt adored politics, the more "practical" the better. But it is equally clear that until he felt his political future secure (until as late as his election to the Governorship in 1898), he clung to literature as his *pis aller*. The writing of both articles and books contributed in a significant way to Roosevelt's income. In the 15 years between 1882 and 1897 he published almost a book a year, if we count separately the four volumes of *The Winning of the West*. These were works of history, biography, politics, and travel; not "literature," if you will, but they certainly entitled Roosevelt to think of himself as a professional writer. He did, too—whenever he lost an election. Defeated for Mayor of New York, he wrote Brander Matthews: "I'm a literary feller, not a politician, nowadays." Writing to Lodge of his yearning for office, he said that if unsuccessful he would "go in for literature." Even after his appointment as Civil Service Commissioner Roosevelt wrote to Francis Parkman, who had praised a book of his, that "literature must be my mistress perforce, for though I really enjoy politics, I appreciate perfectly the exceedingly short nature of my tenure."

Of all the evidence of Roosevelt's dalliance with his muse (for if literature was a sometime mistress, politics was surely his legal wife) the most amusing comes in a letter to Frederic Remington. Roosevelt never so wished to be a millionaire, he wrote, as when Remington had pictures to sell; indeed, it was the only time he wished to be "any person other than a literary man with a large family of small children and a taste for practical politics and bear hunting." Roosevelt was writing from New York in 1895, some months after he took office as Police Commissioner. There on Mulberry Street this literary man with many small children and many odd tastes was busy making front-page headlines—the headlines that first made Roosevelt a figure of national prominence and started him on the road to the Presidency.

As Police Commissioner T. R., with his eminently caricaturable hat, spectacles, and huge, gleaming teeth,

was the journalist's dream. For his part, he played the role as if he had studied it in a novel by Richard Harding Davis, who made the colorful, reckless newspaper sleuth the idol of the generation. Roosevelt was no genteel reformer safe behind a desk. His "beat" was the Bowery streets, where he would go late at night to shake the police out of the quiet accomplishment of their nightly round of corruption. He liked to walk out of a late party in evening dress, throw a cape and sombrero over him for "disguise," and sneak up on a delinquent policeman found dozing, boozing, or taking bribes in a dark alley. The reporters called him Haroun al Roosevelt. At least one of them put on a sombrero to roam the same beat and frighten policemen, as Henry Pringle says, "by chattering his teeth at them."

The warmth and informality of Roosevelt's manner, the famous energy and enthusiasm, the breezy way he had of snubbing dignitaries while deferring to reporters, the impatience and irresponsibility that were always good for a front-page story: these were the reasons why writers and journalists adored Roosevelt. They are evoked by Lincoln Steffens' classic description of Roosevelt's accession to the Police Commission and to the world of literary journalism.

> . . . T. R. ran. He came ahead down the street; he yelled, "Hello, Jake," to Riis, and running up the stairs to the front door of police headquarters, he waved us reporters to follow. . . . T. R. seized Riis, who introduced me, and still running, he asked questions: "Where are our offices? Where is the board room? What do we do first?" . . . The old commissioners waited, like three of the new commissioners, stiff, formal, dignified. Not T. R. He . . . called a meeting of the new board; had himself elected president . . . and then adjourned to pull Riis and me with him into his office.

> "Now, then, what'll we do?"

> It was all breathless and sudden, but Riis and I were soon describing the situation to him, telling him which higher officers to consult, which to ignore and punish; what the forms were, the customs, rules, methods. It was just as if we three were the police board, T. R., Riis, and I. . . .

The school of Bowery realism, which Stephen Crane would credit later for his whole "artistic education," was officially opened up for literary men by William Dean Howells, who began his move from Boston to New York in the late eighties. The subject of Howells' first New York novel, *A Hazard of New Fortunes* (1889), was the impact of New York's poverty-stricken underworld on a literary Bostonian of taste and sensibility who moves to New York to edit a magazine. But if young realists took inspiration from Basil March, the hero of Howells' novel, they took guidance from Jacob Riis, the Virgil of the 1890s. Less than a year after the publication of *A Hazard of New Fortunes*, Riis brought out his passionate, documentary account of New York's tenement streets, *How the Other Half Lives*. Its publication was a catalyst to the intellectual melting pot of the New York nineties, an event in journalism, in sociology, in politics, in reform, in art. The brilliant photographs, taken by Riis himself, marked a major step toward the development of photography as an art in America—a movement that Steiglitz would bring to fruition in New York before the end of the decade. *The Other Half* was also a literary event. The first important imaginative work to come out of Bowery materials was *Maggie: A Girl of the Streets,* by Stephen Crane, in 1893. The summer before, Crane had "covered" for the *Tribune* an illustrated lecture delivered by Riis, with slum photographs and slum statistics.

Now Theodore Roosevelt was hardly fitted by temperament, social background, or political bias to welcome the new Bowery realists. Roosevelt knew and admired Howells; he was one of the young New York writers to whom Howells assigned articles when Howells took over the editorial post at *The Cosmopolitan* in 1892. But Roosevelt was alarmed by the increasing "morbidity" of Howells' fiction, which he rightly associated with the novelist's move toward the political left. Howells had suffered, T. R. wrote his friend Brander Matthews at Columbia, by taking a "jaundiced view of life. This is not an uncommon development of the reform spirit."

With even greater suspicion Roosevelt at first approached Howells' leading critical disciple, Hamlin Garland. Following Howells from Boston to New York in the 1890s, Garland was preaching the literary gospel of "veritism"—and the political gospel of Henry George (the "utterly cheap reformer" whose campaign for the New York mayoralty Roosevelt had opposed by running himself). In critical pieces (1890-93) and then in the manifesto *Crumbling Idols* (1894), Garland proclaimed an extreme relativism of literary forms and methods, to cut loose the young from their terror of the (European) classics. He transformed the stigma of provincialism, so damaging to American literary self-confidence, into the glamorous blush of "local color."

Brander Matthews was always urging Hamlin Garland on Roosevelt, and it was rough riding. Garland's facts were sometimes wobbly, his style rough, and his enthusiasm rather juvenile; these defects seemed to bother T. R. more than they did Professor Matthews. "After receiving your letter," Roosevelt wrote Matthews, "I got Hamlin Garland's book [*Crumbling Idols*] and read it. . . . I think that his ignorance, crudity, and utter lack of cultivation make him entirely unfit to understand the effect of the great masters. . . . Nevertheless, in his main thought, as you say, he is entirely right. We must strike out for ourselves."

At this period, Brander Matthews was Roosevelt's closest literary friend. A professor at Columbia, a member of the best clubs, a contributor of urbane reviews and sketches to the magazines of prestige, and furthermore the son of a millionaire, Matthews was as fine a representative of the "genteel" tradition as New York could boast. Roosevelt regarded Matthews as representative of a more

safe and civilized literary school than Howells' or Garland's; yet it was Matthews, curiously, who was always urging Roosevelt toward the literary left. For Matthews, though cosmopolitan in his habits and tastes, was also an ardent literary nationalist and a passionate New-Yorkophile. And he had caught the local color fever. When Stephen Crane had some shabby, privately printed copies of *Maggie* to distribute, he sent one of the first to Brander Matthews, along with a note describing the novel as "a very small book which Mr. Hamlin Garland thinks will interest you." Meanwhile, Matthews was bringing out his own sketches of the New York scene, which, when collected under the title of *Vignettes of Manhattan* in 1894, bore a dedication to Theodore Roosevelt.

Matthews' *Vignettes,* a pallid, pleasant little volume, Roosevelt thought "really admirable." It was a somewhat ambivalent, somewhat wry, tribute from gentility and academia to the new spirit abroad in New York of the nineties. The sketches bore traces of Matthews' admiring yet not quite committed reading of Garland and Crane. One of them is called "In Search of Local Color." An elegant New York novelist (with the delectable name of Rupert de Ruyter) finds that, though he knows the fashionable 400 inside out, he needs new material, fashionable in another sense, from the slums. Therefore he goes down to the Bowery and, in the company of a genteel young social worker (a Columbia graduate, of course), he peers fastidiously into foul streets and dank tenements. "Yes!" cries the novelist. "Local color—that's what I want—fresh impressions."

In another of the sketches, "Before the Break of Day," Matthews either follows or spoofs or mildly corrects (I cannot tell which) the new novel by Stephen Crane. He tells the story of a girl of the tenements who, like Crane's Maggie, is reared in an atmosphere of profanity and degradation. Like Crane's Maggie, she has drunken parents. Like Crane's Maggie, she is put out of her home when she loses her virtue. Like Crane's Maggie, she falls in love with a bartender—but *her* bartender (unlike Crane's, who is horrid) is a splendid young fellow who saves up enough money to buy his own saloon, and rescues the girl from the dance halls, the streets, and the specter of the morgue. She ends not as a prostitute, but as a loyal, heroic wife. Matthews' girl, incidentally, is named Maggie.

Roosevelt and Matthews argued back and forth in their letters about the new literature and the new criticism. Hamlin Garland, in particular, was often a subject for their debate. It should be remembered that Garland's special brand of realism, the presentation of the boredom and meanness of the lives of people performing heavy outdoor chores somewhere in the west, was just the sort of thing to rub Roosevelt the wrong way. In one of the more amusing of these letters, T. R. snorts at Garland's pathetic account of the hardships of the lumberjack. (Why, Teddy himself had lived in just such a lumber camp and loved it—all the men did; good hearty outdoor life even if a bit rough—best thing for a man who's not "overcivilized"—snort, snort.)

Nevertheless, somewhere in the mid-nineties Roosevelt met Garland and learned to respect him; years later he would write a eulogistic preface to one of Garland's books. By 1897 Roosevelt was inviting Garland most cordially to a lunch and to a dinner, to meet Brooks Adams and Senator Lodge, "for both of them are men you ought to know." But it may not have been Brander Matthews, after all, who succeeded in bringing Roosevelt and Garland together. In the summer of 1896 Stephen Crane urged Garland to come to dinner at Crane's Bohemian hangout, the Lantern Club, because "Roosevelt expects to be there. He wants to meet you." Roosevelt missed that dinner because of a western trip, but "I wish," he wrote Crane, "I could have seen Hamlin Garland."

Police matters rather than literary concerns brought Roosevelt and Crane together. During the years of Roosevelt's Commissionership, Crane was also engaging in front-page skirmishes with the New York police. While T. R. would slither up one Bowery Street in search of bad cops to terrify and good cops to promote, Crane might be slinking down another with an eye out for deceitful cops carting off honorable chorus girls to the station house, under trumped-up charges of prostitution. (In fact, Crane's testimony against the villainous Charles Becker—who twenty-five years later was the first member of the New York force to be sent to the electric chair—brought him into a drawn-out vendetta with the police that had something to do with driving Crane abroad in the last years of his life.) The next day, Citizen Crane and Commissioner Roosevelt might meet or exchange telegrams to argue the pros and cons of the New York police. In 1896 Crane announced that he was planning a new book—about "the life of the metropolitan policeman."

Roosevelt read Crane's *Maggie* (perhaps at Brander Matthews' urging) and indeed asked Crane to call because "I have much to discuss with you about 'Madge.'" Roosevelt read Crane's cowboy and Mexican stories, and asked for more. Crane inscribed for Roosevelt a copy of his second Bowery novel, *George's Mother*, and Roosevelt wrote back that what he would dearly like was a similar autograph in his *Red Badge of Courage*, "for much though I like your other books, I think I like that book the best." Certainly a shared enthusiasm for the Bowery (and playing policeman), for the West (and playing cowboy), for war (and playing soldier) brought together two such unlikely contemporaries as Theodore Roosevelt and Stephen Crane.

But it was God, according to Jacob Riis, who brought together Roosevelt and Riis, by personally bringing Roosevelt to the Police Commission. T. R. gave *How the Other Half Lives* some of the credit. Shortly after that book came out, Roosevelt had gone around to the *Evening Sun* office and left a note for Riis saying that he

had read it and had "come to help." "When I went to the Police Department," he wrote Riis later, "it was on your book that I had built, and it was on you yourself that I continued to build." The friendship between the two men was warm and lasting. They often met socially as well as professionally. On one occasion, a notable one, Roosevelt had Riis to dine along with Stephen Crane, and they spent the evening with a society matron discussing "a girl's library in the Jewish quarter."

Roosevelt also considered Lincoln Steffens "a personal friend of mine," as he wrote in a letter introducing Steffens to the editor of the *Atlantic*. Steffens had come to New York in 1892 and gone to work for the *Evening Post*, where he soon was specializing in police news under the tutelage of Jacob Riis, who, on the *Evening Sun*, was the dean of New York's police reporters. Steffens' interest in the police and municipal corruption predated his meeting with Roosevelt; before Crane he had planned and then actually written half of a novel about a policeman. But surely no other practical politician than Theodore Roosevelt would have let Steffens listen to the gossip of detectives in the basement of police headquarters, after Steffens' articles based on that gossip had proved damaging to Roosevelt's office. Steffens was welcome to police gossip, T. R. said, on the condition that he would use it "only to collect local color for fiction or data for the scientific purposes of [his] studies in sociology and ethics." For his part, Steffens eagerly followed Roosevelt around when he was commissioned later to write his life for Doubleday Page. (Jacob Riis, however, was the one who actually produced a book on Roosevelt.) It was to Steffens that Roosevelt wrote the extraordinarily tasteless envoy to his role as Police Commissioner. "I am going to do what I can for the man behind the gun now," he wrote in 1897, "just as I used to do for the man with the night stick."

That letter was written from the Navy Department, whence Roosevelt would write on another occasion to someone else, "The Secretary is away, and I am having immense fun running the Navy." Roosevelt's enthusiasm for playing navy probably led to another interesting nineties friendship, with a young New York artist named Louis Sonntag. A talented painter then doing his apprenticeship as a magazine illustrator, Sonntag might well have made a lasting name for himself as a member of the "Ashcan" group if he had lived on into the new century, but he is remembered today only for his importance to Theodore Dreiser. During Roosevelt's term as Police Commissioner, Dreiser was in New York editing a magazine, and his eye was caught by Sonntag's illustrations in one of the Sunday papers of "the spectacular scenes which the citizen and the stranger most delight in—Madison Square in a drizzle; the Bowery lighted by a thousand lamps and crowded with 'L' and surface cars; Sixth Avenue looking north from Fourteenth Street."

Dreiser went after Sonntag to illustrate Bowery scenes, and the two men became close friends, but for magazines like *Harper's* Sonntag was increasingly called upon as a naval illustrator. When Roosevelt dropped in at Sonntag's studio to talk and play chess, which, according to Dreiser, he often did, the talk probably centered on battleships. Sonntag was something of an engineering genius. He made fantastically accurate model ships, which he sailed and fought, most realistically, on Long Island ponds. This kind of naval play, which Roosevelt must have admired and Crane might have understood, was the source of Sonntag's expertise as a naval illustrator, though it meant little to Dreiser, who did not share the current fondness for playing war. Warships turned out to be a fortunate specialty for Sonntag after the sinking of the *Maine*. Fortunate up to a point, that is; on assignment in Cuban waters, Sonntag caught a fever and died in 1898.

The *fin de siècle* everywhere was greedy for sensation. Across the ocean there were self-conscious dramatics about the decline of the West, but the sensationalism of the American nineties was modified by the adolescent play-acting of a nation coming to maturity. Hamlin Garland's "local color" theories had as much to do with a craving for novelty as with a demand for realism. As Lincoln Steffens pointed out, his own infatuation with the Ghetto was simply the Californian's equivalent to the "Eastern boys'" craving for the Wild West. The ultimate sensation yearned after, and indeed gratified, by the generation of the nineties was war—a war whose consequences we of the middle-aged midcentury are still suffering. Roosevelt, of course, among the war fanciers and warmongers, was one of the worst offenders.

The last picture we have of Roosevelt in the world of the talented nineties is a tragic one—though not without the comedy in which that decade was rich. In the advance through the jungle to Las Guasimas, General Young led the regulars on the right while Roosevelt and Wood led the Rough Riders (that implausible collection of cowboys, playboys, and bums) on the left. Richard Harding Davis stuck to Roosevelt and reported to the New York *Herald* that the Rough Riders were ambushed. (This account, though it explained why Roosevelt's looses were much greater than the Spanish, Davis later retracted, for he came to admire T. R. greatly. And Roosevelt, for his part, tried to make Davis a captain for bravery under fire—much as he had turned two reporters into a kitchen police board.) Meanwhile, Stephen Crane, a less efficient correspondent than Davis, attached himself to Young, a less newsworthy, if more efficient, commander than Roosevelt. Under the influence of fever—or liquor, or concern for a wounded friend, or the general psychological malaise that clouded his mind in 1898—Crane seems to have staggered through the brush, back to the beach, forward again and back again, missing Roosevelt's Rough Riders and a front-page story. Crane did see Roosevelt in Cuba—he reported T. R.'s consideration for his men *after* the battle—but that was certainly their last meeting. Crane died in 1900 after Roosevelt had been elected Governor with, it might be added, the writer's blessing. "Let him be a politician if he likes," Crane said. "He was a gentleman, down there."

If Colonel Roosevelt as a soldier was something of a gentleman, Police Commissioner Roosevelt was something of a "literary feller." There was too much of dilettantism and playing for journalistic effect to make Roosevelt's term of office a permanent contribution to reform. Oddly enough, however, Roosevelt's relationships with the Bowery literati may have had lasting political consequences. At the outset of his political career in the 1880s, Roosevelt had been more or less willing and eager to lynch all anarchists, fire on the unemployed, and ignore the tenements. By the time he reached the White House he had acquired a degree of understanding of the poor that modified his native, muscular conservatism. To some extent he merely moved with the times. But there is little doubt that his experiences down on Mulberry Street opened his eyes, and considerable likelihood that his friends among the literary journalists taught him to use them.

"The midnight trips Riis and I took," he said later, "gave me personal insight into some of the problems of city life. It is one thing to listen in perfunctory fashion to tales of overcrowded tenements, and it is quite another actually to see what that overcrowding means, some hot summer night."

James W. Tuttleton   (essay date 1965)

SOURCE: "The President and the Lady: Edith Wharton and Theodore Roosevelt," in *Bulletin of The New York Public Library*, Vol. 69, Jan/Dec., 1965, pp. 49-57.

[*In the following essay, Tuttleton investigates the significance of a reference to Theodore Roosevelt in Edith Wharton's novel* The Age of Innocence *as well as the author's lifelong acquaintanceship with Roosevelt.*]

The facts of our literary history suggest that, in general, the American novelist has not been absorbingly concerned with the interaction of politics and society. Very few American writers, as Irving Howe has rightly observed, "have tried to see politics as a distinctive mode of social existence, with values and manners of its own. Even those who understood that a fruitful subject for the novel might be the *idea* of politics," he has argued, "could not find enough supporting material in their experience or their environment with which to give this theme a full embodiment."

Howe's assertion about the infrequency of politics as an important theme in American fiction is particularly true of Edith Wharton's novels. Primarily a novelist of manners rather than a propagandist, reformer, or muckraker, Mrs Wharton was committed to a detailed, realistic representation of the manners and customs of a specific nineteenth- and early twentieth-century American social class in New York City. Little of political interest appears in her fiction because this social class, old New York "high society," deprived her of a basis in actuality for exploring the relations of politics and society.

The people she wrote about were what she called the "best class of New Yorkers." Essentially merchants who settled in New York during colonial days, the ancestors of her class pursued their mercantile objectives in silent opposition to the growing tide of Jacksonian democracy and westward expansion. Her own New York and Philadelphia relatives—the Schermerhorns, the Newbolds, the Pendletons, the Ledyards, Gallatins, Rhinelanders, and the Jonesses—eventually became close associates with the families of European aristocratic origin who had settled in New York—the Duers, the Livingstons, the Rutherfurds, the de Grasses, and the Van Rensselaers. Eventually the group assumed the distinction of a local aristocracy. These families had a great deal of social power, but their influence was not directly expressed in politics. Like the Ralston family of *Old New York: The Old Maid (The 'Fifties)*, who "had not come to the colonies to die for a creed but to live for a bank account," Mrs Wharton's antecedents were purely middle-class—a fact she dwells on in her memoirs, *A Backward Glance*, as if she were refuting a popular error. Like the Ralston family, her ancestors (with a few notable exceptions) did "little to shape the destiny of their country, except to finance the Cause when it had become safe to do so. They are related to many of the great men who had built the Republic," she wrote of the Ralstons, "but no Ralston had so far committed himself to be great. As old John Frederick said, it was safer to be satisfied with three percent: they regarded heroism as a form of gambling."

I

But politics in a work of literature, as Stendhal has somewhere observed, is like a pistol shot in the middle of a concert, something loud and vulgar yet a thing to which it is not possible to refuse one's attention. And when, in the epilogue of *The Age of Innocence*, Edith Wharton tells us that Newland Archer ran for the State Assembly of New York at Theodore Roosevelt's suggestion, we are faced with some curious questions about Mrs Wharton's intentions: Why does she have Archer enter politics, and what is the significance of her reference to Roosevelt?

At least three reasons, it seems to me, lie beneath this passage in the epilogue. On the surface, it is clear that Mrs Wharton intends Archer's behavior to reflect a transition in the opinion of conservative old New Yorkers about involvement in the political life of the times. After the Civil War, as Mrs Wharton was later to write, the best class of New Yorkers finally began to develop a municipal conscience, but it took the rather secure form of administering museums, libraries, and "approved" New York charities. The idea "that gentlemen could stoop to meddle with politics had hardly begun to make its way, and none of my friends," Mrs Wharton wrote, "rendered the public services that a more enlightened social system would have exacted of them." [*A Backward Glance*] Only later in the history of old New York, about 1900, as she observed in *The Age of Innocence* (1920), did young men begin to emancipate themselves from the traditional pursuits of the leisure class. A few of them even broke with the values of the past and entered state politics and municipal reforms. Newland Archer's personal friendship with Governor Theodore Roosevelt was ostensibly the basis for Roosevelt's saying, "'Hang the professional politician! You're the kind of man the country wants, Archer. If the stable's ever to be cleaned out, men like you have got to lend a hand in the cleaning.'" In response to this call, Archer therefore enters politics.

In addition to dramatizing in fiction this shift in old New York's attitude toward active political involvement, this passage in the epilogue also tells us a great deal about Mrs Wharton's ambivalent attitude toward Newland Archer's character—if we are not already quite sure by this time what kind of man he is. Although Archer is a major character for whom we always retain a great deal of sympathy, Mrs Wharton suggests as early as the first chapter of *The Age of Innocence* that Archer is a dilettante who prides himself on his penchant for contemplative thought and cultivated inaction. Archer, in fact, luxuriates in his patrician fragility. In the middle chapters of the book, however, as the love of Archer and the Countess Ellen Olenska grows and as Archer dimly discerns and longs for a freedom society denies him, we may tend to forget that, being the kind of man he is, Archer will never be able to give up New York values for Ellen's love. He capitulates to the marital mores of the tribe, surrenders Ellen, and remains with his wife May. In a biological phrase which Mrs Wharton often used to define the character of such aristocrats, Archer "reverts to type." His political career is, then, such as we might expect from a man who had been brought up to believe that active political life is a vulgar pursuit. Although elected to the State Assembly of New York, Archer must have offered little distinguished service, for he failed to be returned to office. His own retrospective view of this political venture confirms the view of old New York that Edith Wharton presents in *A Backward Glance* and that we have seen dramatized in *Old New York*. For Archer, finally, "was not sure that men like himself *were* what the country needed, at least in the active service to which Theodore Roosevelt had pointed." Both his affair with Ellen and his political venture are abortive character mutations, followed by a reversion to type. His political experience and Mrs Wharton's commentary upon it are thus a means of further characterizing Archer.

To vivify the social ineffectuality of this aristocratic class, Mrs Wharton needed a striking contrast. And herein lies the third reason: Theodore Roosevelt offered the perfect antithesis to everything that Mrs Wharton wished to say about both Archer and the *haut monde* of which he was typical. Moreover, Roosevelt's term as Governor of New York (1898-1900) exactly fitted the chronology of her narrative: the epilogue is set at about 1900. Her attitude toward Roosevelt, however, has so many unexplored personal implications that to understand the full irony of the contrast between him and Archer, her relationship to Roosevelt deserves our scrutiny.

II

In the first place, Edith Newbold Jones Wharton had known Roosevelt nearly all her life. Although their meetings were not frequent—Mrs Wharton lived most of her adult years in France—they did enjoy each other's company at the homes of Bay Lodge, J. J. Jusserand, and her sister-in-law, Mary Cadwalader Jones. When Roosevelt remarried in 1886, it was a distant cousin of Mrs Wharton, Edith Kermit Carow, whom he married. Too, they were sometimes together in Europe when Roosevelt went abroad. And they were frequent correspondents.

That the Jones family and the Roosevelt family were thus socially intimate is not surprising. Both Teddy Roosevelt and Edith Wharton claimed descent from immigrant Holland-Dutch families who had founded great estates in New York—he from Nicholas Van Rosenvelt, who came to this country in 1658 and she from the Schermerhorns and Rhinelanders. Their families thus moved together in the highest New York social circles. The Roosevelts and the Joneses, moreover, were business associates as well as friends. Much of the wealth of both families derived from the Chemical Bank of New York, a conservative banking house created for chemical manufactories. Matthew Hale Smith in his *Twenty Years Among the Bulls and Bears of Wall Street* wrote in 1870 that while the Chemical Bank had "none of the North River steamboat style," "it is the most profitable banking house, with the most valuable franchise in the city." The stockholders of the bank, he went on, "are John I. Jones, the president, who has been at the head of the institution twenty-five years, and the Rosevelts [sic] and their relatives, who with a few friends, own the institution." If we may trust Smith's accounting, the bank was indeed profitable. It started with a capital of $300,000, which never increased, and by 1870 had a surplus of two million dollars. It paid a dividend on eight times the capital of the bank. "All the stockholders," Smith remarked casually, "are wealthy." And of John I. Jones, Smith concluded: "The president is a careful, quiet, prudent man, with little to do, and large pay."

The personal friendship and business association of the two families, then, brought Edith and Theodore into contact. He represented to her a member of the social aristocracy with which she was intimately familiar. Yet unlike the Newland Archers of their class, Theodore Roosevelt had a strenuous social conscience. As Mrs Wharton wrote in *The Age of Innocence,* most of the young men of Archer's generation looked forward only to "the narrow groove of money-making, sport and society to which their vision had been limited." Very few of them entered politics, and of those few in the real world of New York, Roosevelt was by far the most energetic. Paradoxically, despite his social position as a member of one of the "best families" of New York, he got down in the muck and tried to reform corrupt social conditions. Roosevelt was successively United States Civil Service Commissioner, Police Commissioner of New York City, Assistant Secretary of the Navy, Lieutenant Colonel of the First U. S. Volunteer Cavalry (the Rough Riders), Governor of New York, Vice President and President of the United States—a remarkable public career in view of old New York's political attitudes, as Mrs Wharton defines them in *The Age of Innocence.* Looking back upon his active career in public life as she concluded the novel, Edith Wharton saw Roosevelt as the perfect contrast to the ineffectual Archers of their youth.

In addition to admiring Roosevelt's career as a public servant, however, Mrs Wharton also treasured his highly cultivated mind, for he was widely read in history, science, and literature. When Mrs Wharton visited the Roosevelts in Washington shortly after his election to the presidency in 1904, for example, his first words to her were, "'Well, I *am* glad to welcome to the White House someone to whom I can quote "The Hunting of the Snark" without being asked what I mean!'" If he valued her knowledge of literature, she appreciated not only his gift for political action but also his range of subjects, his "intellectual curiosity almost as fervent as his moral ardours," his gift for mimicry, his skill as a *raconteur,* and his wit. "In looking back over my memories of Theodore Roosevelt," she wrote a few years before her death, "I am surprised to find how very seldom I saw him, and yet how sure I am that he was my friend. He had the rare gift of bridging over in an instant those long intervals between meetings that so often benumb even the best of friends, and he was so alive at all points, and so gifted with the rare faculty of living intensely and entirely in every moment as it passed, that each of those encounters glows in me like a tiny morsel of radium."

III

Roosevelt's entry into public life in order to realize his social ideal has a striking parallel in the life of Edith Wharton. Like Roosevelt, she broke with the proprieties of her class and became a public figure—even worse, a professional writer. Her rebellion against the artificial standards of old New York's aristocracy is singularly reflected in her fiction—particularly in the devastating portraits of the young men of her class. The portrayal of characters like Newland Archer of *The Age of Innocence,* Peter Van Degen and Ralph Marvell of *The Custom of the Country,* Louis Tarrant of *Hudson River Bracketed* and *The Gods Arrive,* and Fraser Leath of *The Reef* is often so unrelieved in its sustained irony that some critics have concluded that Mrs Wharton was so embittered a feminist that she could not create a convincing male. But Edith Wharton had always wanted the aristocracy of her youth to be something better than a merely superficial society, and she was too clear-sighted to ignore its failures. When she saw young aristocrats "going in for" Central American archaeology, landscape-engineering, and pre-revolutionary architecture—frivolous pastimes in her view—she railed at them because she had no other way to resolve her ambivalence.

To compensate for her class guilt, Mrs Wharton, like Roosevelt, involved herself in public issues. She did not of course run for public office. But during World War I she personally organized and supervised the relief of French and Belgian refugees. When in 1916 the Children of Flanders Rescue Committee desperately needed money to continue its refugee work, Mrs Wharton edited an anthology of prose, poetry, and music intended to raise money to further its war work.

Because of the seriousness of her cause and the similarity of their views, Mrs Wharton asked Theodore Roosevelt to write the introduction to this anthology, *The Book of the Homeless (Le Livre Des Sans Foyer)*, which was primarily intended for sale in America. His introduction explains the purpose of the book and of the Children of Flanders Rescue Committee and extols the heroic activities of Mrs Wharton in her relief work during the war. Like Edith Wharton, Roosevelt was frustrated at America's failure to join immediately with the Allies in defeating the Germans. Thus he wrote (1916): "The part that America has played in this great tragedy is not an exalted part; and there is all the more reason why Americans should hold up the hands of those of their number who, like Mrs. Wharton, are endeavoring to some extent to remedy the national shortcomings. We owe to Mrs. Wharton all the assistance we can give."

Roosevelt's comments on the failure of the American government to declare war on Germany paralleled the views of Edith Wharton, who regarded the posture of the American government as "supine." When America finally entered the war, Roosevelt vainly begged Woodrow Wilson, then President, to allow him to raise two to four divisions of volunteers and lead them to France. Meanwhile, Mrs Wharton was deeply disturbed by the course of the war. France symbolized everything worth living—and dying—for. She believed it to be the focus of spiritual and aesthetic values. "If France went, western civilization went with her," she wrote in *A Son at the Front*. Like Roosevelt, she repeatedly called for the intervention of the United States in behalf of the Allies. In addition, she traveled to the front lines and observed actual battles in order to write *Fighting France: From Dunkerque to Belfort*. Meanwhile she redoubled her efforts in behalf of the refugees and children pouring out of Ypres and Poperinghe. Her mood toward America during the first three years of the war was like that of Henry James, who renounced his American citizenship as a gesture of protest at America's seeming indifference to the collapse of civilization.

In July 1918 Roosevelt's son Quentin was shot down behind the German lines. When Mrs Wharton tried to console him, Roosevelt replied: "I value your letter, and naturally I am pleased at what you say about Quentin. . . . His death is heartbreaking. But it would have been far worse if he had lived at the cost of the slightest failure to perform his duty." Many of her own young friends were killed at the front. Like Quentin Roosevelt, Mrs Wharton's young cousin Newbold Rhinelander was shot down by the Germans in September 1917. Appointed later a Chevalier and Officer of the Legion of Honor by

France, and a Chevalier of the Order of Leopold by Belgium, Mrs Wharton never recovered from the awful personal, social, and cultural consequences of World War I. Neither did Roosevelt.

In a sense it is almost certainly true that the principles of Edith Wharton's social criticism of the New York aristocracy are not unlike those reflected in Theodore Roosevelt's life and writing. These principles, expressed in the irony of her fictional portraitures, in her critical articles, and indeed even in the example of her life, were to generate in the aristocracy a sense of its responsibility in shaping an enlightened social system in which its talents could be fully put to use; to bring about a closer relationship between the aristocracy and the centers of artistic and intellectual life; to promote the idea of culture, much as she had experienced it in the prose of Matthew Arnold and William Crary Brownell, her Scribner editor; and, in the words of E. K. Brown, to "broaden and deepen and diversify the currents of aristocratic life so that instead of the 'innocence' of the Seventies and the animality of the Twenties there should be conscience and balance."

At Roosevelt's death, Mrs Wharton wrote perhaps the most moving elegy to his memory. "With the Tide," written on January 7, 1919, at Hyeres, France, is based on the legend that when the days of a man are counted, a boat comes at evening, with the tide, to where he is, and in the boat he sees the faces of friends long dead. In lines which are highly reminiscent of both Arnold and Whitman, Mrs Wharton wrote:

> But never
> To worker summoned when his day was done
> Did mounting tide bring in such freight of friends
> As stole to you up the white wintry shingle
> That night while they that watched you thought
>   you slept.
> Softly they came, and beached the boat, and
>   gathered
> In the still cove under the icy stars,
> Your last-born, and the dear loves of your heart,
> And all men that have loved right more than ease,
> And honor above honors; all who gave
> Free-handed of their best for other men,
> And thought their giving taking: they who knew
> Man's natural state is effort, up and up—
> All these were there, so great a company
> Perchance you marveled, wondering what great
>   ship
> Had brought that through unnumbered to the cove
> Where the boys used to beach their light canoe
> After old happy picnics—

She called Roosevelt a "great American" and foresaw his ebbing with the tide "on some farther quest."

In the epilogue of *The Age of Innocence*, Newland Archer finds himself suddenly saying, "'But I'm only fifty-seven—' and then he turned away. For such summer dreams it was too late; but surely not for a quiet harvest of friendship, of comradeship, in the blessed hush of

[Ellen's] nearness." Archer's situation in the epilogue of the novel deserves comparison to the conditions of Mrs Wharton's life as she concluded the novel. Archer's sudden perception of how the passage of time had altered his life, and his realization of the need for comradeship with a friend whom he would never see again, derive from Mrs Wharton's meditation of her own losses. Alone, like Archer, in France, she too was fifty-seven years old when she wrote those lines. Alone, like Archer, she too had "high things to contemplate, great things to delight in; and one great man's friendship to be [her] strength and pride." Not to perceive, in this epilogue, the implications of her relationship to Roosevelt is not only to miss the power of Mrs Wharton's irony in contrasting Archer with Roosevelt but also to miss the affection for Roosevelt she wished to memorialize in Archer's friendship with him. For Theodore Roosevelt died in 1919, the year she finished writing *The Age of Innocence.*

David H. Burton　(review date 1968)

SOURCE: "Theodore Roosevelt and Edwin Arlington Robinson: A Common...," in *The Personalist,* Vol. 49, No. 3, Summer, 1968, pp. 331-50.

[*In the following review, Burton discusses a likeness he perceives in the attitudes and ideas of Roosevelt and the poet Edward Arlington Robinson.*]

Theodore Roosevelt's chance reading in 1905 of Edwin Arlington Robinson's *The Children of the Night* was the occasion of a well-known episode in the lives of both men. The President liked what he read in Robinson, though he had to admit there was that in the poet's work which eluded him, and when he learned of his dire financial need provided a position for him at the New York Customs Office. The job was an ideal sinecure. The pay proved sufficient for a modest way of life and Robinson was required to spend no hours at his desk. Despite some pressing family obligations he was free, really for the first time in his life, to write. Strangely or not, Robinson produced none of his great verse while under this official patronage which lasted until 1909. But it may not be too much to believe that T. R. had rescued the poet from literary obscurity in his own time. It was under presidential pressure that Scribner's issued a second edition of *The Children of the Night,* thus establishing the author with a major publishing house.

A comparison of Roosevelt's public mind and that particular portion of Robinson's work which can be termed "socio-historical" poetry cannot but underscore, however, that the president and the poet had much more in common than this incidental relationship suggests. Their spiritual affinity, moreover, went well beyond the aestheticism of the creative artist echoing the public man's love of nature and his sponsorship of conservation legislation. It was a kinship drawing heavily on the American sense of mission, a feeling for its high destiny rooted in the national consciousness and manifested in its national

history. And so, coming to maturity in an America that was experiencing unexampled material achievement and with it an alteration of its traditional moral commitment, neither man was left undisturbed by the advance of a new morality. While it is an easy matter to point out that Robinson and Roosevelt disagreed on certain large issues facing the nation—American expansion overseas after 1898 is the most persuasive example—it is well to emphasize that they were possessed of a common awareness of what they considered to be the besetting illness of their times and a common vision of what would heal that illness. Roosevelt and Robinson, the tough-minded public man and the tender-minded poet, displayed a singular reaction to what they spoke of as the materialization of American life, and in their own ways they sought to make common cause against it. Surely neither the historical reputation of Theodore Roosevelt nor the poetic stature of Edwin Arlington Robinson can be said to rest only on their opposition to the materialization of American society. But just as certainly the evidence of their opposition argues the persistence of the conservative strain in the American temper.

Both Roosevelt and Robinson were born to a tradition of individualism, but for each of them it was an individualism antithetical to the harsh postulates of Herbert Spencer's *Social Statics,* for it spoke of responsibility and service as integral parts of striving for success. Theirs was a moral world of absolutes, not precisely defined, but commanding their adherence nonetheless. And in so far as each managed to insist upon the individual's integrity as the foundation of a sound political life, or of life itself, their resolution of the problem of man in society ought to be appreciated as emerging from congeries of contending and in some ways conflicting moralities. For Robinson this inner contention included a Puritan heritage that was real enough, traces and more of Emerson and Royce, and the lessons offered by the economic consolidations and scientific speculations that were helping to shape America in the latter half of the nineteenth century. Roosevelt's adherence to the old-fashioned individualism survived the assaults of social Darwinism and the magnetic appeal of power for its own sake that American nationalism sometimes cloaked. The intellectual formation of these two men, when taken together, would seem to mirror their generation faithfully enough to view the results as portraying some significant portion of that generations's moral doubt and its idealized resolution.

Theodore Roosevelt was an enormously popular figure in his own era and he has been a fascination for later Americans as well. Contemporaries applauded him for his zest for living and for his ability to accomplish much, and historians and writers have not yet tired of telling of him. But his advocacy of the strenuous life even as he lived it should not be permitted to obscure or to detract from his vision. Behind action there lay principles, derived from a view of man that appealed to him at once as natural and workable. This view was best expressed by T.R. when he spoke, as he often did, of the need of character in man's personal habits and in his social life. His own definition of character needs little elaboration. "By character I mean the sum of qualities essential to moral efficiency. Among them are resolution, courage, energy, self-control, fearlessness in taking the initiative and in assuming responsibility, and a just regard for the rights of others." The value of character in the individual was quite transcendent, becoming "the foundation-stone of national life." In terms of political considerations in the United States, Roosevelt treated character as the critical link between private and public life. ". . . No man can lead a public career really worth leading, no man can act with rugged independence in serious crisis, nor strike out at great abuses, nor afford to make powerful and unscrupulous foes, if he himself is vulnerable in his private character." Nor should there be any doubt that Roosevelt was thinking of moral and not intellectual qualities. Writing in 1895 he had observed that "character is far more important than intellect to the race and to the individual. We need intelligence and there is no reason why we should not have it together with character, but if we must choose between the two we choose character without a moment's hesitation." Nothing he was to experience during the presidency or afterwards caused him to change his judgment.

The place of character in Roosevelt's thought is of especial value also for understanding the nature and purpose of his imperialism. If he judged his own country's moral health by its fulfillment of what he termed character, he was prepared to measure other countries and other peoples by standards that were no less exacting. This is a critical consideration for seeing through to the center of his justification for the so-called backward races remaining under the control and tutelage of the Powers. For the United States, as for Roosevelt himself, the Philippine Islands came to represent the fullest expression of American imperialism. The ability of one of the world's lesser peoples, like the Filipinos, to learn to rule themselves soberly and responsibly, amounted to the development of character in that race. As he pointed out, "our people are now successfully governing themselves because for more than a thousand years they have been slowly fitting themselves, sometimes consciously, sometimes unconsciously, toward this end." A similar gradual unfolding of character in the Filipino people would signal an end of American control in the Islands for it would disclose the absence of any further need of American mentorship. "I would certainly try to prove to the islanders," he told one friend in 1900, "that we intend not merely to treat them [the Filipinos] well, but to give them a constantly increasing measure of self-government, and we should be only too delighted when they are able to stand alone." But he also wrote more soberly to President Eliot in reference to the political realities being encountered by the United States in the Philippines, the people there must be shown that "freedom does not mean the absence of all restraint. It merely means the substitution of self-restraint for external restraint." This moral proposition was the same for the individual and for the nation; it remained a constant virtue in the superior nation, as well as an ideal

for the race striving to become superior by means of demonstrating its political stability.

If Roosevelt lived in a time when there was an increasing awareness of the contributions of society itself to the evils men endured, he retained an insistence that men as individuals were ultimately responsible for the conditions in which they found themselves. Though not indifferent to the social inferences, he maintained that character in the person was the beginning of reform in the group. The effort to reconcile the place of character and the function of law as an instrument designed to promote social betterment, an effort of special importance as Roosevelt was fighting for his political life in the Progressive election of 1912, is well summarized in the following passage taken from one of his campaign addresses.

> We are not proposing to substitute law for character. We are merely proposing to buttress character by law. . . . In civil life, as in the every day life of the nation, it is individual character which counts most; and yet this individual character can not avail unless in addition thereto there lie ready to hand the social weapons which can be forged only by law and by public opinion operating through and operated upon by law.

Yet with the election lost, and the need to appear more a Progressive than he actually was no longer felt, Roosevelt seemed willing to return to an unambiguous statement of the primacy of character. Writing in 1913, by which time Progressive journalists like George Kibbe Turner had exposed the social side of the causes of prostitution, the ex-president, nonetheless, continued to judge the matter as a personal defect of character.

> As with so many other problems, while there must be government action there must also be strengthening of character in the average individual in order to achieve the desired end. Even where economic conditions are bad, girls who are both strong and pure will remain unaffected by temptations to which girls of weak character or lax moral standards readily yield. It is out of the question to treat economic conditions as the sole conditions or even the chief conditions that determine this.

A somewhat ingenuous set of remarks perhaps, but a steadfast reminder of the traditionalism of Roosevelt's moral world.

One of the most frequently noted criticisms of Theodore Roosevelt is the disparity that seemed to exist between his preachments and certain of his opinions and policies, the kind of criticism that poet-moralists rarely have to endure. The failure of T.R. to live up to many of his professed ideals, often for no better reason than that it was politically expedient to do otherwise, has left him open to the charge of hypocrisy, or at least of insincerity. One unfortunate result has been to render difficult an appreciation of the genuineness of his belief in the old-fashioned morality. In a comparison of Roosevelt's vision and that of Edwin Arlington Robinson a like obstacle is to be encountered. Because these two different men responded in different fashion to the same issues, the common bond of respect for the individual which they shared and the numerous instances of their agreement are not readily apparent. It is to be totally unexpected that two persons of such diverse temperament, even granting their concurring traditionalism, should always arrive at the self-same conclusions. What is more illuminating is that the traditional ways of looking at men persisted in both the tough public man and the tender poet to a degree that traces a remarkable contour in one of the major patterns of the American mind.

The pattern is discernible in much of the socio-historical poetry of Edwin Arlington Robinson. A line that proposes to demarcate the social poetry from the general body of his work may appear a tenuous one in that a social message of greater or lesser clarity suffused all the major divisions of his verse. His answers to the perplexities of life of whatever kind, like those of Roosevelt, went straight to the individual. But he composed a small, noteworthy number of poems which criticized society as an institution and, by indirection, men as social beings. In this group of poems very often he made use of figures and episodes drawn from American history, or the contemporary national scene, to foil his moralizing. He never came to grips with those peculiar concepts that are the stock-in-trade of the sociologist, however, nor did he find it congenial to reduce his criticism to merely "social significance". This is a necessary distinction for an understanding of Robinson's social commentary. For him society before all else was composed of men as individuals and the environment they were placed in could not be thought of as determining them in questions of right and wrong. In view of this most all his poetry might be said to possess social overtones, while his socio-historical verse speaks a traditional estimate of man in society simply and purposefully. Even in his early years with their distinctly Idealistic propensities, Robinson could not bring himself to abandon the world to its own devices. In a letter to Daniel Gregory Mason, in commenting on Thoreau's essay, "Walking," he wrote:

> I stretched out yesterday and read "Walking", but did not quite relish what seemed to be to me a sort of glorified world-cowardice all through the thing. For God's sake, says the sage, let me get away into the wilderness where I shall not have a single responsibility or the first symptom of social discipline. Let me be a pickerel or a skunk cabbage, or anything that will not have to meet the realities of civilization.

For Robinson personally, in even his incidental dealings with people, "to do a little spiritual good in this world" was the fuel that kept him going.

The total of his verse likewise displayed a spiritual concern. From the first songs of the fledgling muse to the final drama of the major poet, Robinson rarely departed from the fundamental purpose of his art: to reflect on and to interpret the meaning of life. His criticism of life was

relentlessly pursued, it was a criticism nearly always subtle, often elusive, sometimes ambivalent. The burden of his poetry was his intent curiosity about the final purpose of human existence, and knowingly did he with peculiar indirection muse that

> God has been very good to him
> Whose end is not an asking why.

Robinson sought out man as might a scientist in the laboratory delineating him in his essential relationships. His was a dissection of man *qua* man, proposing to judge him as a being ruled by a scheme of spiritual values. The poetry resulting carried with it a moral, it was fashioned out of ethical terms, and the sanctions of the ethics were such as to give significance to life. Judging him on the totality of his work, Robinson insisted on adherence to the ethical postulates that were common to Western Man, but as a child of his times he remained reluctant to be very specific about the kind of God his ethical system seemed to demand.

The nature of the commentary on life which provided the motif of Robinson's work suggests the sources of his heritage as an American and as a New Englander, at the same time as it blends with the contemporary emergence of scientific speculation on society. His criticism was of a varied content, and if it records the poet's sustained struggle to come to a knowledge of life, it reflects faithfully the influential elements in his spiritual background. Inherited traditionalism lost some of its immediacy when paralleled by the philosophical appeals of Emerson and Royce, while scientific skepticism introduced a quality of doubt that was with Robinson to the last. Such a cultural complex explains in part the distinctive variations which mark the answers to the large moral questions which troubled this sensitive man. The result is something of an unevenness in Robinson's views on God, man, and society which underlines certain contradictions of thought, typical of him as a commentator on man in society as his America portrayed the human problem to him. It is unprofitable to seek in Robinson's poetry a consistent philosophy of life, or for that matter an inconsistent philosophy fully developed. The man was wholly artist, the philosophy of his poetry was not consciously or deliberately wrought. Yet in his socio-historical verse, dealing as it did with concrete episodes, the very tangibleness of the subject matter may have encouraged him to avow, as clearly as he has done, the basis of his value system. Elusiveness was all but gone, ambivalence had been put away, as he confronted the historical past to know better the social present.

"Cassandra" is a good example of Robinson's distress over the materialization of society. It also typifies the parallel, though not the identical, reaction that he and Roosevelt experienced when considering the same eventful crisis. "Cassandra" was written while Robinson watched the disastrous War of 1914 engulf Europe and eventually involve the United States. According to Hermann Hagedorn, "he was appalled by the easy optimism of the average American, the cheap idealism, the faith in phrases and gestures, the waves of fear and greed, the spiritual inadequacy to meet the challenge of world catastrophe." The War, thought Robinson, was the product of rampant selfishness on a personal as on a nationalist scale. In "Cassandra" he stressed the fact of personal responsibility for what the social scientist might choose to describe as pressures, or forces, or long-term trends.

> Think you to tread forever down
>   The merciless old verities?
> And are you never to have eyes
>   To see the world for what it is?

Yet without doubt there were tones emanating from the poet's strictures on the War which were sharply at odds with Roosevelt's feelings about it. Robinson was bitterly critical of the smugness of American nationalism.

> What lost eclipse of history,
>   What bivouac of the marching stars,
> Has given the sign for you to see
>   Milleniums and the last great wars?

In contrast it must be said that the War provided Theodore Roosevelt the occasion for some of the worst kind of jingoistic demogogy, even as he sorrowed over the War itself.

World War I, it must be remembered, was an intellectual catastrophe for Roosevelt. According to his mature version of history, since 1500 progress had been possible for mankind because the superior peoples of western Europe, and especially the Anglo-Americans, had developed stable systems of government for themselves along with enormously productive economies. The benefits of their political forms and their economic enterprize, in a word—Civilization—had been brought to backward areas of the earth by the world movement of imperialism. As this imperialism extended itself under various national auspices, and often the use of military force was needed to effect expansion, civilization advanced. Roosevelt believed that the United States had to enter into the competition for empire as part of its responsibility as an advanced or superior nation. In fact, he conceived of it as nothing less than a rightful continuation of the classic American frontier movement, now rendered transmarine in scope by the circumstances of the time. English control in Egypt and in Burma, German colonies in Africa, Russian penetration of Turkestan, American supervision of the Philippines, even Austro-Hungarian absorption of Bosnia and Herzegovina, were all estimated as parts of this process of human betterment through imperialism. When these same imperialist Powers collided in the War of 1914 Roosevelt's theory of modern history was exploded, and he was driven to re-think the nature of international political development. In his re-analysis, though it was strongly colored by American nationalism and obviously swayed by war-time propaganda, he did, at the last, re-assert the proposition that the welfare of mankind as proposed by the traditional morality was what counted most for him. He might well have agreed with some lines

characteristic of Robinson's judgment of man in respect to his fellowmen:

> There's a contentious kingdom in myself
> For me to rule before I shall rule others.

Thus while it would be inaccurate to contend that Roosevelt rose above many blatant aspects of war-time nationalism bred so profusely by World War I, it would be equally unfair not to recognize that in the post-war era he looked forward to a time of greater individual fulfillment for the peoples of Europe within the framework of new nation-states modeled on Western democracy.

As though to supply a convenient guide to his awareness of the American dream and the troubles it had encountered, Robinson wrote a series of interpretative poetic sketches of figures prominent in American history. These constitute settings for the statement of certain of his socio-political convictions. While in one sense his moral precepts need not be thought of as confined to any one national experience, still America was his country and he was deeply aware of it. As with Roosevelt, Lincoln was an outstanding hero to Robinson. The viewpoint of the two might differ, though their final estimates of him were similar. Robinson saw in Lincoln "The Master," the spokesman of a great moral cause, the leader of a nation enduring its moment of agony that men might be free. And what were the qualities the poet discovered in Lincoln? Leadership, he wrote, asks meekness and patience, endurance and humility. Lincoln became the "Titan" of his time, possessing these virtues in full measure. As might be expected, Roosevelt's response to Lincoln was more hard-nosed. He inclined to esteem him primarily for his political astuteness. "Lincoln was a great radical. He was of course a wise and cautious radical—otherwise he could have done nothing for the forward movement." But Roosevelt too could catch a poetic mood when at times he mused on Lincoln.

> He grew to greatness, but never to ease. . . . Power was his, but not pleasure. The furrows deepened on his brow, but his eyes were undimmed by either hate or fear. Disaster saddened but never dismayed him. Unbroken by hatred, unshaken by scorn, he worked and suffered for the people. Triumph was his at the last.

It may not be enough to observe that Roosevelt and Robinson grew up in an America which remembered its Civil War only too well, and for whom the memory of Lincoln was very meaningful. It is helpful to add that the respect in which Lincoln was held was made possible, in large part, by the persistence of the "merciless old verities", despite the appearance of new, conflicting values. Both Roosevelt and Robinson in their own ways helped to sustain the old values by accepting them and, in so far as they were able, by exemplifying them. Their common moral reflexes may be gauged also by their estimation of another Civil War figure, John Brown at Harper's Ferry. Robinson undoubtedly was attracted to the wild idealism of the man—"there was a time for service and he served"—

yet he saw that the humanity of Lincoln was to be more effective than the violence of lesser men. He agreed with Roosevelt's judgment of Brown, that he was deluded by his own vision and a faith in violence.

Robinson possessed a kind of Hamiltonian faith in democracy. In "On The Way" he tells of an imaginary dialogue between Hamilton and Aaron Burr. Burr is presented as an adventurer and opportunist, annoyed both by Washington's regal manner and by the incongruity of a people ruling itself. How "are men to dance/ When all men are musicians?", he wonders. He whispers overtures to Hamilton to join him in his half-hatched plots for power, but Hamilton turns the temptation aside. "We are done with ermine," he says. Yet Hamilton's decision is made to appear as resting as much on his faith in Washington's leadership as in his trust of the people. And so it was with Robinson. He felt that leadership in a democracy, and in particular in a democratic government needing reform, as was the case in the United States at the turn of the century, was indispensable. The poem, "The Revealer", which was dedicated to Theodore Roosevelt himself, conveyed this thought in a manner akin to T.R.'s own pronouncements. In the poem Robinson argued that the need for democratic leadership was very great, yet limited by the nature of democracy. It was the function of the leader to reveal to his fellow citizens the mistakes and attendant evils in public policy: ". . . the combs of long defended hives / . . . dishonored and unclean." But for a free people, reform of abuses rested finally with the citizens. The leader could only serve as their conscience-guide. It was the people who had to act.

> What you and I and Anderson
> Are still to do is his reward;
> If we go back when he is gone—
> There is an Angel with a Sword.

The lesson seems clear enough. The effectiveness of a leader is finally determined by the willingness of the people to follow him, in the recognition of the role that they themselves must act out in the continuing process of moral renewal. Yet all this implies that the people must be capable somehow of a constructive reaction to a leader; otherwise, the leadership of the sort described in "The Revealer" would have little relevance. Roosevelt, for his part, was to sum up these ideas in what he termed "the Lincoln school of American political thought." By this he meant a government strong and efficient in the Hamiltonian style, but Jeffersonian in a belief in the people as the ultimate authority and in the welfare of the people as the end of government.

Theodore Roosevelt died in 1919 and so he was not witness to the social conformity and the moral confusion that featured the 1920's in the United States. But it was during these years that Robinson explored some of the problems and dangers that caused him deep concern for the future good health of American democracy. His views were expressed in a series of three "Demos" poems:

"Demos" (1920), "Dionysius in Doubt" and "Demos and Dionysius" (1925). More or less abstract in character, all of them voiced the identical theme: Robinson's misgivings about a democracy in which the simple canon of majority rule might conspire the ruin of the individual. His partizanship, if it can be called that, was his insistence on personal choice even when the word freedom was invoked as a reason for its infringement. In an overall estimate of Robinson's poetry these "Demos" pieces form a political corollary to his perennial concern for man as an individual.

Fundamental aspects of his political outlook were given expression in "Demos." In it there was an essentially Augustinian conception of human nature. The design of democracy, happiness for all, and the inclination of selfish men were judged to be opposites difficult of reconciliation because in the equality of democracy happiness was "not equal to the envy it creates." Thus if democracy was to be workable the separate selfish desires of the citizens had to be drastically curtailed. A democracy that promised absolute equality was dismissed as contradictory. Even in a democracy, if it were to provide an ordered society, there must be some to lead and some to follow. Robinson displayed alarm because he worried about the lack of a mechanism built into democracy to help it avoid excesses. The old-fashioned morality, as far as he could tell, had lost too much ground to enable it to function as a brake on the will of the majority.

The poem in which Robinson explored more fully the abstractions of his political philosophy was occasioned by that puzzling American law, the Eighteenth Amendment. Not only did he regard it as being a "fundamentally evil and arbitrary" invasion of his personal freedom so that he started drinking again "almost as a matter of principle", but he proceeded also to protest the injustice in the best way he knew how, his verse. The results were contained in two poems, "Dionysius in Doubt" and "Demos and Dionysius", the former "about prohibition" and the latter about "spurious democracy."

In "Dionysius in Doubt" Robinson warned America that it might become the victim of standardized servitude which many would mistake for a highly satisfactory form of liberty, merely because it suited them personally. Americans were somehow convinced, he wrote, that in legislation they had discovered the magic wand of happiness and equality. But to the poet's mind liberty based on the legislative process alone was not rule by the majority but tyranny by the majority, and

> . . . and insecure delight
> For man's prolonged abode,
> And the wrong thing for him to meet at night
> On a wrong road.

The danger of this conception of liberty was that it knew no bounds; it derived its energy from legislation which of itself had no inherent limitations. Legislation, rather, was always ready for "the infliction of more liberty." Under this dispensation a majority of the people, he thought, had every right to suborn all citizens of the republic in such wise as it felt might conduce to the greatest good of the greatest number. There existed no authority beyond the will of the people to which a minority, or a single individual, might appeal. The result Robinson feared was a standard of liberty that would "moronize the millions for a few." He likened this situation to playing with fire in the dry season. There were three kinds of people whose attitudes gave birth to a standardized servitude. There were those who bowed to the commands of the state out of timidity or expediency; there were those asleep; and finally there were those to whom liberty was only an empty phrase for an empty gesture. Robinson thought he found evidence of all three such enemies of human dignity in the America of the 1920's. It was these several attitudes as they acted collectively to weaken the ideal of liberty that seemed to him to threaten to effect "complacency and joy / Of uniform size and strength." In "Dionysius in Doubt" there was revolt against a middle class tyranny that could be as frightening in its effects on individual men as a totalitarian dictatorship, and Robinson saw it as being more perilous because it paraded disguised as liberty.

"Demos and Dionysius" exposed "spurious democracy" even more forcefully than the other of the "Demos" pieces. If Demos was the social device that proposed to make all men equal and happy, and thus equally happy, Dionysius was represented as the embodiment of man's immortal vision, the expression of all that was noble in him. Indeed, the very idea of freedom Demos owed to ideals proposed by Dionysius. Once again Robinson recounted the contrariety that exists between freedom and equality. He reproached Reason for having reduced everything to its own dimensions, thus conjuring up the absurdity of equality:

> . . . Reason and Equality, like strong twins
> Will soon be brother giants, overseeing
> Incessantly the welfare of . . . all.

In the poem this kind of equality was seen as issuing solely from Reason, uninstructed by morality. It was not really a moral equality at all. Robinson was fearful that enforced equality, without regard for man's nobility—Dionysius—might deceive by its feigned liberty. Reason and Equality might reduce men's souls to common fuel and "the obedient selves of men to poor machines." In the end man would live a hive-life where art would be "a thing remembered as a toy" and the "infirmity that you name love / . . . subdued to a studious procreation." But, as Dionysius is made to ask, "Where would be the purpose or the need of such a hive?" Men existing in a hive-life would no longer be free, and no longer truly men. This denial of freedom to act, and for men a moral freedom to choose between right and wrong was the most meaningful of acts, deleted the distinguishing trait of the culture Robinson wished to preserve. Man's moral freedom was what gave significance to life, as Robinson in so much of his poetry acknowledged clearly. With a sus-

tained argument he contended that the worst of all tyrannies could confront men in the guise of Demos. He was not in this poem attacking democracy "properly understood", as he might have said, but what has been termed "directed democracy." "There *is* a Demos" that he believed in. It was erected on a recognition and an avowal that personal integrity was inviolable and as a consequence could not be subordinated to the interests of the state. Robinson was opposed not to democracy, but he was truly fearful of the dangers in it when it was based on what he thought of as a spurious notion of man's nature.

The views of Edwin Arlington Robinson on the operation of the American democracy in the 1920's are well documented, but one can only speculate, of course, on the reaction of Theodore Roosevelt had he lived into the period. Having been caught up by the passions unleashed during the first World War, conceivably he could have come to advocate less freedom for the individual and more authority in the hands of the state in order to reestablish the old-fashioned morality. This moral order appealed to him as a pre-supposition to the maintenance of the best interests of the individual. Nor is it quite certain that he would have grasped the irony of such a position. More importantly, it would have been inconsistent with some of his previously voiced estimates of democracy that carry phrases suggestive of Robinson's Demos trilogy. "The distinctive features of the American system are its guarantees of personal independence and individual freedom," he once wrote. "That is, as far as possible it guarantees to each man his right to live as he chooses and to regulate his own private affairs as he wishes, without being interfered with or tyrannized over by an individual, or by an oligarchic minority, or by a democratic majority." As he was to tell a Progressive rally in 1912, "We stand against all tyranny, by the few or by the many." Yet it is hard to forget that under wartime pressures Roosevelt also described "the democratic ideal [as] that of subordinating the individual to the community, of subordinating individual selfishness to collective sacrifice for a lofty purpose." And he talked darkly of democracy "going down" "if it once demonstrated that it was incompatible with national security." The result is that there can be as little certainty as there can be much provocative speculation on Roosevelt's position with respect to the sharply debated issues of the 1920's.

The possibility of divergence between Robinson and Roosevelt, and to some it must appear more as a likelihood, may serve to a degree to illustrate the historic and continuing distinctions and contradictions within the conservative tradition in America as in Europe. Robinson's concern for the inviolability of the individual person from the will of the majority has roots that go back to Edmund Burke. And Roosevelt's susceptibility to the charms of authority, as a way of recalling into respect the old moral order, is reminiscent of de Tocqueville addressing himself to a responsible upper class, or even of Joseph de Maistre, postulating an absolute sanction for nationalism as de Maistre did for monarchy. The differences of opinion and judgment expressed by Roosevelt and Robinson remind us of the variety of viewpoints, some mutually antagonistic, that claim their source in the conviction that the rights of the person can be guaranteed best within a prescriptive framework of custom and tradition—political, ethical, moral. Certainly both men could have agreed with many of the thoughts of leading conservative intellectual spokesmen of the 1920's, critics like Irving Babbitt and Paul Elmer More while still retaining distinctive attitudes on specific issues. Nor has the conservative problem of preserving individual rights in an authoritarian state moved much closer to resolution today than it had attained in the era of Roosevelt and Robinson. What transcended that dilemma, then as now, was the vision of man both held in common. Only a continuing assessment of the future will tell if this common vision is enough.

Harold Zyskind   (essay date 1968)

SOURCE: "A Case Study In Philosophical Rhetoric: Theodore Roosevelt," in *Philosophy and Rhetoric,* Vol. 1, No. 1, 1968, pp. 228-54.

[*In the following essay, Zyskind studies Roosevelt as an example of a public figure who embodied conflicting views and qualities whose source of may be found in the nature of philosophic rhetoric.*]

I. INTRODUCTION

The minds of many men of action are opaque, or so they seem when we seek their logic. It is reasonable and important to ask whether the thought of a political figure had an intelligible pattern; but the question seems to admit of opposed answers. Plato shows this in his treatment of Pericles: In the *Phaedrus* Pericles is an exemplar of intellectual coherence. But in the *Gorgias* he exemplifies irrationality. What makes him subject to this variable treatment is that he was so excellent a rhetorician; the problem of intellectual integrity is nowhere more acute than in those men of action who owe most to their hold on the people.

Is it possible to grasp and formulate how such a mind works—does it indeed have a way of working? This paper is a case study of Theodore Roosevelt, whom I have chosen in the belief that he is a near-ideal instance of such a mind.

Herbert Agar argues persuasively that Roosevelt "seems never to have thought at all," confirming the view even of an admirer, Lincoln Steffens, that Roosevelt was a careerist who "thought with his hips." To an intellectual such as Richard Hofstadter, Roosevelt could be ultimately farcical for he went "exploding in every direction at once." The annoying point is that this man of action ("pure act" to the cloistered Henry Adams) was not only effective in his day but time has shown him to have been remarkably attuned to the long-range trends

seen later by scholars and intellectuals. Thus, Clinton Rossiter says,

> To be a great President a man must think like a great President; he must follow Theodore Roosevelt and choose to be a "Jackson-Lincoln." [the quoted phrase is from Roosevelt's *Autobiography*]

There is a double irony here. Roosevelt's giant stride in bringing the Presidency closer to its modern magnitude may be attributed simply to his vigorous disposition—to exploding rather than thinking, to a preference for action over theory. But the alternative irony is then that men such as Rossiter and Sidney Hyman take him as a theorist or formulator of the policy—and they have ample warrant for doing so. Roosevelt wrote reflectively and in general terms on most of his policies.

What adds to the perplexity and makes Roosevelt's case particularly instructive is that he was himself, even more than Winston Churchill, the sort of man of action who also produces in intellectual areas. Historian, biographer, field biologist, critic and reviewer in art, literature, and other fields, Roosevelt read widely enough to challenge Eliot's choice of the hundred great books by specific and public argument; and he produced more works than most intellectuals. Nearly all his writings are competent, and at least some are retaining a place in the literature of their respective field.

How does this side of Roosevelt relate to his political career? Edward Wagenknecht answers principally by separating the several "worlds of Theodore Roosevelt," and Henry Pringle dismisses the problem by calling him polygonal. But it seems unlikely that his intellectual world could be as remote from his life as Pringle's biography makes it. William Harbaugh's otherwise illuminating recent biography is little better on this point. It is astonishing how disinterested are Roosevelt's biographers in the biographies *he* wrote. As P. R. Cutright says, "Only the political facet of his career has been reasonably lighted. The others are in shadow."

But the search for connections has not been abandoned. John Blum's study is perhaps the single most penetrating attempt. He found that if Roosevelt had a "supreme belief," it was in "character." But there is no clear ground for elevating this concept above other terms Roosevelt variously elevated; Blum also concludes that Roosevelt's intellectual home was "eclectic . . . more comfortable than integrated." Hermann Hagedorn explored the doctrine of unity as itself the unity of Roosevelt's thought. David Burton discovers at best a "composite of faiths"—Darwinism and morality.

Such searches try to discover how close Roosevelt's thought came to fitting the model of a systematic intellectual position, grounded if possible in a "supreme belief," and taking form in a "body of doctrine." But "body of doctrine" may be the wrong model, as Blum suggests. Why could not a method, a stance, a *modus operandi,* be prior? I assume it could be. This is my first hypothesis.

This hypothesis reverses the usual direction of search for the starting point of his thought. His intellectual writings would be the place to start if his thought were patterned by doctrines; but if by method, his politics seem more inviting. It is possible indeed that his intellectual writings get their pattern from his use in them of the same method that governed his politics, *mutatis mutandis*. I assume this to be so, as my second hypothesis.

Everyone recognizes what Roosevelt repeatedly said his method was: to assimilate theory to practice, the ideal to the real, altruism to success. In broad terms applicable to thought and action alike, this is an operational rhetoric: a rhetoric because the end is to do and say what has impact on the minds of men, and operational because the "what" is conceived in terms of effect achieved by altering or adjusting to actual circumstances.

In politics the stance was present consciously in what has been called Roosevelt's careerism (or showmanship), but also, often perhaps unconsciously, in virtually every turn of phrase. This latter perhaps gives the flavor better. Consider his explanation of the statement of the Declaration of Independence on the equality of men in the inalienable right to life, liberty, and the pursuit of happiness. In his paraphrase this becomes the "ideal that each man shall have an equal opportunity to show the stuff that is in him." He has here converted an *ethical* concept (the right) into its *operational* condition (the opportunity) and has similarly replaced the *natural ground* of the right (its inalienability) with its *rhetorical* counterpart (showing).

What was in his hips was this stance. It is the same as that of traditional (Aristotelian) rhetoric in this: that they both rest on the view that ideas are relative to man and action. But there is a difference which is critical. In Aristotle two speakers, though opposed, are conceived as having the same underlying art; both are rhetoricians, grounded in opinion and the practical. Their disputes and reasonings occur in a realm separable from that of theory and philosophy, and concern matters similarly separable. In Roosevelt this separation tends to disappear. The reason he did not call his approach rhetorical is that he did not restrict it to the political platform, but saw in it the key to judging the significance of the problems, culture, and bodies of knowledge of the day. It is as if Aristotle's rhetorician refurbished and expanded his art to enable him to deal not with other rhetoricians merely, but with all thinkers—generating ideas in any area by their persuasive as distinct from their theoretic warrant. My third hypothesis then is that Roosevelt's thought and action alike exemplify such usurpatory rhetoric—usurpatory, that is, in the sense that it takes over philosophy's office of judging the bases and values of the various fields of action and thought—in brief, a philosophic rhetoric. These hypotheses are explored below in Roosevelt's Criteria of Thought (Section II); Science (III); History (IV); and Action (V).

II. CRITERIA OF THOUGHT

The rhetorician has a pair of needs which may seem incompatible. On the one hand he purports to speak on a subject such as war without being an expert in it, and so needs to cast some doubt on the knowledge the expert claims to have acquired through full inquiry. But the rhetorician depends for his existence on open discussion, and so must uphold the values and needs of full inquiry. Roosevelt met both needs simultaneously by putting his focus and emphasis on the necessity of testing expert knowledge, scientific reasoning, and linguistic precision by all available non-theoretical means.

In part he was directly countering professionalism for its tendency to push beyond its proper limits. So strong was the tendency, he thought, and so definite the limits even of science, that the errors of Darwin and his more dogmatic followers "were left to be exposed by men who were not professional scientists." Similarly, he attacked legalism in law, traditionalism in literature, intellectualization in ethics, universal humanitarianism in politics, technical proficiency in oratory—even professionalism in sports. He called for the freedom of the inquirer (especially in history) to pursue his interests without being constrained by some narrow notion of the kind of data which qualified as scientific. He argued too against specialization itself so far as it implied a separation of the sciences; the boundaries among them should be fluid and the great work of any field should be valuable both to other specialists and to the cultivated layman. Roosevelt's friend Arthur Lee found him "equally at home with the experts" in many fields from political economy to the Greek drama and Irish sagas. The vigor of Roosevelt's interchanges with them in conversation and in print did not turn on an effort to be a part-time expert but on his method of applying to technical knowledge criteria outside its technical bases.

His attitude towards knowledge applied also to reason and reasoning. Roosevelt's emphasis fell on the power and insight of the other faculties of the mind: those which are not strictly rule-governed and which can accordingly be seen as testing or transcending reasoning. He urged their importance within the methods of science and theory: in discussing the nature of history with those who thought it should be a science, he highlighted imagination and prophetic vision, making the historian a greater poet. In field biology he put the stress on authentic observation undistorted by a preconceived theory; in pure science, on experience and spirit as the needed stimulus and check to logic; and in poetry and literature, on the possession of feelings and experience in tune with the national "soul." Even Roosevelt's attitude on methods of debate reflects the same pattern: he censured Harvard's practice of assigning students to defend a given position which the student might not believe. Such a practice wrongfully separated one's logic from one's feeling. In area after area Roosevelt thus saw himself as exposing those whose commitment to a rigid method inhibited the responses they could make as men with experiential, imaginative, and emotional powers.

The same method of using every available means to prevent the separation of theory from its human and experiential context appears in Roosevelt's treatment of linguistic precision specifically and of style generally. He was tolerant but disparaging of much professional terminology as a special sort of "slang," and argued that for significant purposes the portrait was truer than the photograph, the drawing than the blueprint. He emphasized the need for expressive style, in all areas, since on it depends the extent to which a theory comes alive in the minds of men. To Roosevelt Darwin's theory of evolution, for example, was not appreciably superior to that of Lamarck or of others; the greater acceptance of Darwin's theory resulted rather from his greater power of expression.

When rhetoric is basic, this stylistic point is of critical importance; and Roosevelt was explicit about it:

> In the last analysis all that distinguishes civilization from savagery rests on the written word.

The foundations of institutions, the development of knowledge and technology, the natural tendencies of man to society—all such features which theorists could advance as bases of civilization are here seen as dependent in turn on the means of communication and persuasion. This is why the problem of language is not seen as precision of terminology but power of expression.

(In application of his views, when Roosevelt in 1897 revised his youthful (1882) but much respected *Naval War of 1812,* he did a painstakingly extensive stylistic overhauling; he replaced statistical tables and technical descriptions with vivid accounts which shrewdly embodied the same historical truth in action, and he replaced the loglike sequences with a patterned narrative which gave the log its meaning.)

It should be evident from what I have reported that Roosevelt's attitude to the scientific, the logical, and the precise was not negative—*not* anti-intellectual. On the contrary, he sought to apply his extra-theoretic criteria to the enrichment of the several disciplines. The trouble with most historians for him was not that they were restricted by history, but that history was restricted by them. He did not turn from monographic history to current politics but from monographic history to Herodotus, Thucydides, and Gibbon. He did not turn from highly specialized biological monographs to horseback riding simply, but to the work of men whose competence spanned the data of both laboratory and field (and who had literary ability). Similarly, he did not turn from formalistic poetry to merely didactic works, but to Edward Arlington Robinson for "the light that was never on land or sea." The ideal of the liberal life for Roosevelt assumed both that the cultivated man should be engaged by the thought and art of his time and that, accordingly, the best of such work would be oriented to the liberal mind rather than to a specialized audience.

We can summarize the point thus far in the statement that Roosevelt sought to assimilate the theoretic to what could be called the practical in the large sense—the sense that includes whatever works an effect on the minds of men. But just because of this use of the practical in the large sense as his general touchstone, the ultimate touchstone is the practical in the narrow sense of the actions, institutions, and circumstances which shape economic and political life; for on it all else depends. Yet even when Roosevelt came upon this ultimate touchstone of the practical, he did not treat theory negatively. He did not turn from political theorists to political manipulators, but, for example, from the sort of unrealistic theorists who (like Wilson) worked out the advantages for America of the Cabinet form of government, to the *Federalist,* and he explained:

> It is a misfortune for any people when the paths of the practical and the theoretical politicians diverge so widely that they have no common standing ground. When the Greek thinkers began to devote their attention to purely visionary politics of the kind found in Plato's *Republic,* while the Greek practical politicians simply exploited the quarrelsome little commonwealths in their own interests, then the end of Greek liberty was at hand. . . . The ideal to be set before the student of politics and the practical politician alike is the ideal of the *Federalist.*

So to conceive political theory in the form it takes in practice (rather than, say, as a "pure" formulation distinct from its "applications") not only brings the theory into the vicissitudes of office-holding but also, conversely, credits the persuasiveness of the policies of the office-holder—their rhetoric—with the force of theory.

III. SCIENCE

The rhetorician as such can support either side of a dispute—and so remains under a cloud: How can a committed position be derived from an intellectually indifferent approach? One way out is to see rhetoric univocally as a technique separable from one's principles. Thus Bishop Whately has us first decide logically what our position is and then afterwards bring rhetoric in to make it persuasive. Or, if rhetoric considers its own ability to generate counter-arguments, there is a tendency to various forms of scepticism or Machiavellian cynicism.

Roosevelt took neither way out, at least in any simple sense. He attacked cynics: A man had to take a stand. But we have seen that, on the other hand, his general stance was based on distrust of stands strictly reasoned from determinate doctrines. The question then is how that approach could enter into the fabric of thought which determined his *specific* position on a specific issue.

Looking at the same photograph of a chipmunk among twigs and leaves, Roosevelt and Abbott H. Thayer, the expert on cryptic coloration of animals, disagreed on whether the chipmunk's striping made it easier to see.

This difference typified the dispute which Roosevelt and Thayer carried on from 1910 to 1918 in both scientific and popular media, and which in principle was carried *forward practically* into issues of military camouflage as the difference between zigzag striping and battleship gray, and *backward theoretically* into the role of coloration in natural selection. I here examine only enough of their complex quarrel to bring out its philosophic roots—and to argue that it was Roosevelt's general stance which pushed him to the view that the chipmunk was easier to see than, say, a weasel (unstriped) would be.

Thayer began with axioms of what he called optical science, applicable to every case of the sighting of an object: The universal primary factors are light-and-shade and lines of perspective. These show the presence (solidity), shape, and position of an object. Color as such is secondary. But the graduated light-dark pigment of animals imitates natural light-and-shade, thereby normally off-setting it. Again, the outlines of color stripes and patches can give the illusion of a real object's boundaries. Hence

> All markings and patterns whatsoever are, under ordinary outdoor conditions, unfavorable to the conspicuousness of the thing.

Whereas Thayer here deduces from the universals of optical theory the visibility-values of particular markings, Roosevelt conversely bases his position on the facts of visual experience which must serve as the practical touchstones of theory.

> The facts as regards these [sc. birds and mammals] are so obvious that any man of common sense *must* realize them, if he wishes to translate his theory into action.
>
> . . . . .
>
> There must be a foundation of common sense for every scientific structure.

Accordingly Roosevelt multiplied particular field perceptions (e.g., that ordinarily a crow is conspicuous and a wood frog virtually invisible) and generalized on the conditions of success and failure in identifications as thus experienced.

It was plausible therefore for differences between the two men to reflect disagreement on what features were identifying. For Thayer, it is because the essentially identifying feature is contour or silhouette that the zebra's striping, for example, is concealing. It "cuts up" the zebra's true contour into reed-like shapes seen in relief, thus obliterating it except against a "perfectly plain background.,, But Roosevelt would report seeing the zebra's coat, thus making the coloration itself the identifying feature.

Thayer thus could prove the coloration was a disguise; to which Roosevelt replied in effect that it was just this permanent disguise by which he identified the animal. Similarly, Thayer showed how white rump patches against the sky distort true silhouettes. Roosevelt replied that often at night the (moving) patch is the cause of the animal's being seen.

In general, Roosevelt treated the visual identity of an animal opportunistically as any kind of feature that on occasion can be singled out and made to serve pragmatically as a sign of the animal's presence (in the case of the zebra, color pattern; of the giraffe, odd shape; of the bull sable "the intensity" of color). Thayer conceived its identity as the universally most reliable kind of feature (its true shape and place in visual space) and analyzed the extent to which special markings interfered with this or offered inferior substitutes. Hence while Roosevelt could shift his criteria from case to case, according to what was rewarding (even if with difficulty), Thayer's descriptions always rested ultimately on the same kind of analysis. For example, when both reported on a herd of zebras, Thayer treated the scene atomistically as a collection of instances of a single, visually fixed set of strips of such and such shape, while Roosevelt treated it holistically as a visually *moving herd.*

Roosevelt did not confine his attack to particular cases, however. He made generalizations descriptive of the most frequent cases, exceptions freely admitted. What is normally basic, for him, apart from motion, is bold (black, white), bright color patterns—these being visually conspicuous; at the other end of the continuum are neutral, dull color patterns. Thus for Roosevelt colors rather than light and shade are normally primary in identification.

Thayer, it will be recalled, worked on precisely the *contrary* optical weighting, colors being last in importance. Where Thayer talked of coloration which gives the effect of actual light-and-shade, imitating shape and solidity, Roosevelt talked of the way actual light and shade brings out or obscures color patterns.

The result of these reversed priorities was that for Thayer the field of vision is made up ideally of an assemblage of geometrical objects in distinct spatial relations, while for Roosevelt the primary field of vision is a scene ranging from brilliant or otherwise prominent features (e.g., foreground) to dull or otherwise neutral features (e.g., background).

This difference in their sense of the field of vision reflects directly Thayer's specialized and Roosevelt's rhetorical approach. The geometric features of Thayer's field were deducible, or explicable, by the particular combination in it of the three universal visual elements. On the other hand, to conceive the features as a range from bold to dull, as Roosevelt does, is to conceive them just in terms of their attention-getting power; Roosevelt's descriptions abound with references to what "catches the eye" or "advertises" a presence or makes a "leap to the eye"—in brief, to the rhetoric of vision (as neon flashers constitute the rhetoric of roadside vision, while they distract from the clarity of shapes). The color markings, unlike the contour features, may not be *essentially* characterizing features but they are serviceable as immediate *signs* and signals, and these have always been of peculiar use in rhetoric since they are guides to a mind rather than simply objective existants. Thus by making color basic Roosevelt oriented the issue to the rhetorical problems of attention-getting and sign-interpretation.

There was a corresponding difference in the *act* of seeing (rather than simply in the field of vision). Roosevelt's approach would make it a *development* from an unorganized encounter with a scene to the (successful or unsuccessful) identification or emergence of an object; i.e., since he is responding to signals, seeing is an act of bringing the field of vision into focus around a selected object; e.g., by peering at a yellow patch he came to realize "that the dim yellow smear in the yellow brown grass was a lion." What is finally seen depends on his responsive operation on the cues, as in this 3-stage identification:

> Glancing towards this, my eye was at once caught by a row of white objects . . . another look showed they were snow-geese.

In Thayer's approach what is seen is separable in analysis from its visual emergence. He tells what a hunter sees, now in the far view, now in the near, independently of the process of taking in the scene. His tendency is to play down the process even in watching motion; e.g., he breaks down the flight of a butterfly into a sequence of frames or "stills." His observer thus fixes objects as distinctly as possible in their spatial relations.

These differences are reflected, finally and more philosophically, in the structure of the visual experience in the sense of the relation between seeing and interpreting what is seen. For Thayer the two are sharply distinct: volumes and shapes are seen; these are then interpreted into animals which have been pegged as having such features. For Roosevelt the two are inseparable; one does not see a solid and then translate it into an animal; Roosevelt sees *animals,* not geometrical objects. Accordingly Thayer's expert see-er is the artist who can distinguish what we really see from what we think we see (e.g., if a colored solid is totally unshaded, it looks flat to the expert, but the layman falsely thinks it *looks* solid because he knows it is solid), while Roosevelt's expert is a long-practiced guide who can spot a Colobus monkey in the trees before anyone else can. An optical science must separate out all non-optical features; a rhetoric must include whatever can function to convince oneself that a lion stands before him.

It seems possible, then, that both Roosevelt and Thayer were right about the chipmunk mentioned earlier. Could not Thayer, with his geometricizing eye, after he had first surveyed the photograph and begun identifying shapes, be more likely to see that of a weasel because its unbro-ken coloring was co-terminous with that shape, thereby defining and enhancing it, while Roosevelt, with his practical eye, could (1) be attracted to and fasten first on the stronger signals, including that of the chipmunk's bold white striping, and (2) then follow up that eyehold to the discrimination of the chipmunk before his eye ever stopped on the un-arresting distant-like tint of the weasel shape? If this is so, we have before us a concrete instance of a specific rhetorical position which is generated by the neutral art of arguing for either of opposed positions. Roosevelt argues from the effects animals produce on men as the latter interpret scenes from the perspective of their own interest or attention. Within the boundaries of this approach, there inevitably is room for opposed interpretations (and interest). But Thayer's position is not just an opposed interpretation; it is rather an opposed *basis* of interpretation: indeed he could eliminate interpretation from the arena, since he argues from the geometry of visible objects. That view is what the art of arguing for either of opposed interpretations must and did oppose.

In its broader context Roosevelt's position on cryptic color was explicitly an attack on over-use of natural selection as explanation. Since natural selection was the keystone of the law-like and hence theoretic character of Darwinian evolution, Roosevelt was detheorizing the doctrine. This same de-theorizing constituted the dominant impulse of his other treatments of biological Darwinism. For example:

> (i) He divested evolution's content of any certain direction, since every true evolutionist must admit the possibility of retrogression no less than of progress.

> (ii) He shunned universal explanations in favor of what he called "causes which we see actually at work around us"—i.e., local, observable variables such as "a change in the amount of moisture in climate" or "a great period of cold."

> (iii) He opposed inferences of a sort essential to most theories—i.e., those based on a hypothetical isolability of the effects of a given cause.

> Other things being equal, the species where this rivalry [of natural selection] is keenest will make most progress; but then 'other things' never are equal.

> (iv) Finally, he emphasized the limits both of knowledge and of the rational method of biology, stressing (a) the "growing impression that there are forces at work which our blinded eyes wholly fail to apprehend," and (b) our ability to "show with flawless logic that something cannot occur when, as a matter of fact, it does occur."

When it is argued that Darwinism was the starting point of Roosevelt's thought, or that he accepted Darwinism without question within the sub-human realm, the interpretation is weak: not because Roosevelt was not an evolutionist but because he was a Rooseveltian rather than a

Darwinian one. As we have seen, this rhetorical dimension determined, not a simple ability to argue on any side, but a commitment to those probabilistic positions which were closest to what could be exhibited and used.

IV. HISTORY

When rhetoric operates as a socio-historical method, a critical development beyond the biological type of analysis may be expected. Whereas in biology the subject matter is treated as relative to the inquirer, in history not only is the past as subject matter relative to the historian but the past itself is made up of the men or inquirers to whom things are relative. Thus the subject matter of history would become, not simply something relative to man, but that relativity itself. This too Roosevelt illustrates and illuminates, by his treatment of causation in history.

For him, the "ideal" (but in fact unrealized) case of a fully deterministic course of events would be a sequence in which a population is fully directed by a farseeing leader; i.e., there would be *necessity* in history so far as a great *individual* was genuinely causal. (This correlation of necessity with great men reverses the more usual correlation of it with universal factors distributed through whole populations and nations.) Roosevelt found that in fact, however, individual leaders were rarely able to achieve total control; as a result history tended to lack even the practical determinateness great men could impose: Roosevelt's emphasis fell accordingly on history as a contingent process whose chief feature was its precariousness. This feature is what emerges as persuasive in history when the sweep of events is seen to be, like rhetoric, relative to the invention of agents rather than set by nature.

This can be illustrated even by the work of Roosevelt's which is an apparent exception—*The Winning of the West*. W. H. Harbaugh says that in it Roosevelt stresses the "deterministic" character of the Western advance, "'the thrust which . . . no rival race could parry until it was stopped by the ocean itself.'" But even in the account of this movement the emphasis on the precarious pushes through. There is Roosevelt's insistence that the "chance of failure" was "very great." Further, because of the interdependence among the Westerners' three "tasks"— to drive out the foe, settle the land, and consolidate politically—if the Westerners had failed in any *one* of the three, the result would have been "utter failure." Nor is it only the tasks which are contingently related; the succession of events is equally susceptible: if

> the chain of events by which the winning was achieved . . . had . . . snapped, it is likely that the final result would have been failure.

From this perspective Roosevelt saw the emergence of the United States in its amplitude, power, and unity as a rare and precarious development; one infers this not only from his persistent emphases but also from his explana-

tion that these awesome results were brought about not by the plans of a far-sighted leader but rather by a "fortunate" and "seldom-occurring" concurrence of the private interests of men with the good of the whole.

The key explanation in Roosevelt's treatment may be specified more sharply by comparison with F. J. Turner. Turner's specific view was that

> the West, at bottom, is a form of society . . . whose social conditions result from the application of older institutions and ideas to the transforming influences of free land.

The reason is that "free lands meant free opportunities," and the "fundamental traits of the man of the interior were due to the free lands of the West."

Turner's account thus locates the evolutionary opportunity primarily in an *environment* or external circumstance—free land—and this functions as an overarching cause. Roosevelt on the other hand shifts the focus from the environmental cause or "surroundings" to the near-uniqueness of the *agent*:

> It has often been said that we owe all our success to our surroundings; that any race with our opportunities could have done as well. . . . The Spaniards, the Portugese, and the French, not to speak of the Russians in Siberia, have all enjoyed, and yet have failed to make good use of, the same advantages which we have turned to good account.

To restate: an opportunity for Turner is an environmental condition which brings evolutionary laws into operation, and the Western advance is thus "a history of the evolution and adaptation of organs in response to a changed environment." An opportunity for Roosevelt is rather a challenge to the genius or character of the agent, and the results reflect *his* merits rather than the operation of institutional regularities and powers. An open continent

> is an opportunity such as is offered to an army by a struggle against a powerful foe; only by great effort can defeat be avoided, but triumph means lasting honor and renown.

Thus, though both men see the situation as an opportunity (bringing Turner close to Roosevelt's actional mode of interpretation), yet Turner analyzes it on the model of stimulus-and-response mechanisms, while Roosevelt analyses on the model of strategy and character. (As a result Turner felt that the passing of free land was a lamentable terminus—"Never again can such an opportunity come to the sons of man"—while Roosevelt, with his emphasis on the agent's invention, argued that the greatest opportunities in national life might well lie in the future.)

It is this ultimacy of the agent as cause in Roosevelt—an agent, moreover, defined by his power to seize and exploit the opportunity rather than by the effects on his institutions and fundamental traits of a single external factor—it is this which underlies Roosevelt's interpretation. Turner's purpose was to *explain* the institutions and basic human traits by reference to a key external factor; Roosevelt's was to *assess* different types of men by their ability to take advantage of an opportunity and set up an actional model. In response to Turner's friendly criticisms, Roosevelt shrewdly pointed out that, unlike Turner's aim to explain institutions, his own "aim is especially to show who the frontiersmen were and what they did." *The Winning of the West* embodies the rhetoric of our expansion.

In summary, thus far it seems clear that a single general method pulsed through Roosevelt's literary, scientific, and historical works—opportunistic, relativistic, operational. This has shown the usurpatory power of rhetoric in all these fields; but it has equally shown the capacity of rhetoric to develop concrete positions and perspectives in them. Using that as warrant, we will seek now similarly for something more than showmanship in the rhetoric of politics which Roosevelt also illustrates.

V. ACTION

Rhetoric seems at best ambivalent in political action. As a manipulative art its motive is the love of power, and its modern refinement into propaganda has resulted from efforts to scientize techniques of control. One of its most effective instruments in this process, however, is the appeal to broad concepts of justice and loyalty. Accordingly the critics of rhetoric—and occasionally a Machiavelli—discount the professions of principle and discover beneath them the pursuit of immediate advantage, finding that the gentlemen speak of peace and mobilize their armies.

Here again Roosevelt's case is exemplary. From the time of his support of Blaine in 1884, Roosevelt was subject to Lincoln Steffens' charge that he was but a careerist. At the same time he was plausibly charged with believing he had invented the Ten Commandments; and eminent historians find him "moral rather than realistic." As with himself, so also with the United States in *his* conduct of its affairs. Roosevelt simply took Panama, in his own words, and yet he went back to the legalities of the Treaty of 1846 with New Granada to buttress his case. He played the power game in international affairs as he spoke out for the rule of justice among nations. Even temperamentally he illustrates the double vision of rhetoric: Richard Hofstadter cites his "penchant for violence," accompanied by the need he felt for self-restraint.

David Burton calls these two strands in Roosevelt the Darwinian and the moral. Burton resolves the problem by making the Darwinian strand only a means to the ends embodied in the moral strand. Roosevelt at times does make this claim, but rarely in the sense that power is a neutral instrument, abstractable in thought from the values bound up with the objectives of its use. Rather the use of power can take on the highest value in its own

right: "No triumph of peace is quite so great as the supreme triumphs of war." He even classified the virtues themselves in terms of their use of force—they were "positive" or "negative." And he was capable of stretching social Darwinism into the objective of action, for in rating racial expansions he prized most those which had wholly displaced native populations and secured the fairest lands for white settlement. Power is not a derivative principle in Roosevelt, generated by the demands of the ends it serves, but an end itself. Accordingly, the rhetorician's treatment of it—to which I now turn—constitutes his method, and determines the role of justice and loyalty.

This method can best be characterized in originally nonmoral terms as *the incremental interpretation of power*. To speak abstractly, though only a commonplace mode of thought is referred to and will be exemplified shortly, the principle of such a method is a literal, that is, operational, as distinct from a strictly logical, beginning—a first step rather than a comprehensive premise. The method is thereafter *incremental* because it proceeds by elaborating, building on, extending or even modifying the power or position established in the first step. The technique of elaboration is *interpretive* in the sense that it is not a way of making explicit what is implicit in the principle, or even of reasoning about and manipulating basic constants isolated by that first step; but that it is rather an extension of that beginning determined by the conceptual suggestiveness or practical momentum the first step has for the agent whose power it constitutes. The procedure is rhetorical "all the way" in its suspicion of determinate or theoretically warranted beginnings and in its capacity to develop in the direction that the first step makes persuasive rather than in some direction which it theoretically or logically implies.

In logical terms, the method is illuminated by a comparison with the way Wittgenstein develops the meaning(s) of a family concept by beginning with a particular use of it (rather than an abstractly universal definition) and progressing by adding other resembling but different (and hence incremental) uses. The process is kept moving by the suggestiveness of the first example to the language user, and is constituted by the perspicuity afforded by the juxtapositions. In Roosevelt's case we are concerned with the same problem and method in developing a network of *actions* (rather than of language uses) which as such may be connected causally rather than only conceptually.

The starting point—the "first step" need—is self-defense. This is perhaps the only or indispensable beginning for the rhetorician (as Callicles and Cicero long ago saw). For Roosevelt, from the time a boyhood defeat led him to take up boxing, through his efforts to shame Wilson into war with Germany, self-defense was that use of power without which no other use and hence no action is possible, *for it establishes an agent*.

Self-defense and self-interest so conceived expand into formulas of *domination* on the one hand (since freedom is for one who can "take his part in the rough struggle with his fellow men for political supremacy"), and, on the other, into a basis of *morality* (since "no man can take the part of anyone else unless he is able to take his own part"). The nation is analogized to the individual for similar conceptual expansions from national self-defense to international peace. Both cases thus illustrate the second trait of the method—the projection from a first step, in which power and the individual self-interest are prior, to further steps which are at once based on it and qualitatively different from it.

Perhaps the sharpest illustration of the two-moment movement from a power base is Roosevelt's treatment of exemplary cases of national growth and democracy. The first moment is characteristically that in which one man or a few generate a political reality by authoritarian control or other means of imposing their will; this makes possible the second moment in which the people, now able to see themselves as an agent in being, take their destiny into their own hands. Timoleon's career, which Roosevelt so much admired, embodies the two moments in pure form. Again, Roosevelt saw Peter the Great as accomplishing the first step for Russia. Even U.S. history follows the pattern: The birth of the Union was due to the success of *leaders* in overcoming the recalcitrance and lack of vision of the people in the Revolution; but at the time of the Civil War, with an existent Union to preserve, it was the *people* who required of the leaders the policy of its preservation.

Roosevelt adapted his two-step analysis to his platform rhetoric. He first would concede the priority of self-interest (whether of the individual or a special interest group such as labor, Negro, etc.) and then call for support of more broadly moral or nationally-oriented policies by claiming

> that the very fact that I grant this [sc. your self-interest] as the essential first need to meet, entitles me to have you accept what I say at its face value when I add that this represents only the beginning.

We have here the rhetoric of concede-and-lead: concede the priority of the audience's self-interest and then on the basis of the good faith established by the concession lead them to commitments beyond self-interest. The demagogue reduces rhetoric to the first step alone; the idealist, to the second. Roosevelt's formula was designed to correct the reductionism of each.

We have seen three key aspects of the method by which Roosevelt generated policies. We now look at some key policies generated by it:

(i) On the question of trusts, unlike Wilson who approached the problem by determining the size corporations should be restricted to for the sake of equality, Roosevelt saw rather a first-step problem of power. The primary need was not to cut corporations down to size but to establish the power of the government to control

them as it saw fit, including possible tolerance of the giants.

(ii) On the question of international organization, unlike Wilson who saw the problem as the establishment of an association of equals, Roosevelt campaigned for a league of the great powers to enforce the peace, anticipating the Security Council of the United Nations.

(iii) Roosevelt's theory of the Presidency similarly illustrated the notion of power-in-use. He conceived the office, not in terms of Constitutional specifications or of a theory of its function, but in terms rather of its *scope* of action: the President should do whatever for the general welfare he could that was not expressly forbidden by the Constitution; and Roosevelt suggested that the specific scope and force of these activities was determined operationally, i.e., that they depended on the *man who made the office:* thus he called himself a member of the Jackson-Lincoln school.

It is doubtful if mankind will ever be reconciled to the fact that the most impassioned and self-certain appeals to justice are made by those who philosophically root themselves in power and relativity. Much of the paradox is manageable, however, if we see how a strictly ethical concept and treatment of justice are in fact modified in the way the rhetorician treats it; i.e., gives it values—and problems—that arise authentically out of its involvement with power and circumstances. Three of these modifications are indicated below. (These are not always documentable by an explicit statement, but I believe anyone familiar with Roosevelt's works—or with that of comparable rhetoricians—will confirm their presence.)

(i) Even at the level of labels Roosevelt was not concerned with justice as such but always with the fate it undergoes when men defend, attack, or redefine it. This is the rhetoric of it, what it is in the thoughts and acts of men. The initial problem then is not how to determine what justice is, but whether a man is in fact concerned with it—i.e., is disinterested in motive. Roosevelt's premise here was that a man who professes idealism is probably not motivated by it unless he is either *secure* in power or at least unafraid of conflict. Praise of peace has been translated immemorially into fear or weakness. Roosevelt made just this translation in attacking first the anti-imperialists and, later, Wilson on this charge.

His position will be clearer by contrast with Kant. For Kant no man can be sure that an act which externally conforms to the moral law is in fact motivated by respect for it rather than by inclination. The distinction between respect and inclination is an analytical one which is difficult to apply. Rhetoric neglects it in favor of a distinction between *two inclinations:* fear and self-interest on the one hand and, on the other, a desire for the satisfactions that come from benefitting others. The latter is *operational* disinterest (you in fact do not act for your own interest) and can be identified fairly persuasively because it is not coerced. Roosevelt's admiration of

Timoleon must have been based on the fact that Timoleon held total power when, unsolicited, he gave it to the people. Justice and generosity "count most," he asserted, when shown by the strong.

(ii) The second proposition is that when men will not defend justice, *its* worth is diminished or brought into question. This tendency exists whether one sees other men's failure to defend it as evidence of their *disbelief* in its value or as evidence of its lack of appeal to them. Either hypothesis would explain why Roosevelt was less aroused to horror by cowardice than by the passive suffering of injustice—letting it prevail: He showed intense revulsion from the massacre of the Moravians who made a Christian virtue of not defending themselves.

(iii) As both the preceding points would suggest, the idea of justice for Roosevelt was not understandable apart from specific just actions. This did not mean for him simply that the political figure, who must get things done, has to settle for less than the best or truly just action. Rather, an unrealistic or unrealizable notion of justice tended to be an error not in tactics but in the conception of what justice is. Ineffective reformers, he thought, tended to be separated from their times, not by "longitude" (that is, not by being more advanced than others in idealism) but in "latitude."

This view meant that the criterion by which moral values were to be discovered and judged was their relevance to rules of successful action (power-in-use) in a situation. The rules themselves had to be drawn from operational models. For example, Roosevelt's moral discussions of the Western expansion were based on the "tasks" which the early settlers had shown to be essential to success (to tame the wilderness, subdue the native and foreign people, and establish self-rule). The charges of injustice made against the frontiersmen were rebutted by Roosevelt by testing the charges against these three touchstones.

It would be a serious error to see him as saying here that actional touchstones can justify a neglect of moral criteria, i.e., the doing of a necessary evil. The point rather is that the actional problem determines values in a situation. Anti-imperialism tended to reflect, not unwillingness to face a necessary evil, but a "craven fear of being great."

In effect, then, virtue itself consists in seeing and not shrinking back from the opportunity which variable circumstances offered. Roosevelt was a progressive at home and an imperialist abroad; he showed a zest for ruthless social expansion, and he insisted that the U.S. withdraw its army from Cuba; he sent the battle fleet around the world and won the Nobel Prize for peace. There are obvious points of view from which these pairs of positions are incompatible; but it is just as clear that on the basis of operational touchstones they are not only compatible but can form moments in a genetic continuity originating in self-defense.

The usurpatory rhetorician, who goes "all the way" in making persuasion and action the final touchstone of what is worth believing and respecting, encounters a special difficulty on the question of *necessity*. It is not a theoretical difficulty but a rhetorical one: He deals with the world so far as it is subject to man's manipulation. He does not want to conceal this premise, or rather he cannot, since his speeches must pulsate with the idea of how much depends on the will and efforts of man—either audience or speaker. But this makes visible the concomitant point that man is not compelled to the action in question, as the existentialists, for example, have rediscovered for philosophic purposes. For persuasive purposes, however, the point logically gives the audience its (perhaps non-conscious) sense of *its right and power to reject whatever is proposed*.

A summary indication of the nature of Roosevelt's political rhetoric as so far explored, is indicated in the way it encountered this difficulty—particularly before World War I, when he carried on a protracted and voluminous campaign for popular support of our entry into the war. I believe it is clear that, though we did finally declare war, Roosevelt was less effective here than in any other of his major campaigns. In the circumstances, against the rhetoric of Wilson, he tended to sound shrill and interminable. The difficulty, on his own analysis, was that the people could not be aroused to a "heroic mood." Nonetheless the notion that the audience could remake itself was the basis of his appeal—the rhetorical resource—in this effort to generate ideal attitudes or actions by a kind of crusade.

Contrast with this the resources available to a Lincoln for generating "ideal" attitudes or actions. Lincoln assumed, and conveyed the assumption of, human dimensions *outside* rhetoric's scope—i.e., of non-contingent moral impulses which had the force of necessity. He sought in his rhetoric, much like a Freud, to strip away the specious issues which prevented men from confronting their natural inner sentiments: he was willing, once the confrontation was effected, to leave the rest to the compelling force, the imperative quality of the inner impulse. Thus while Roosevelt's focus on the role of men made him turn so often to a *crusading* rhetoric, Lincoln's rhetoric, in times of equal stress, could have the *clinical* cut and calm of a psychological probe or a political dissection, as in the debates with Douglas and the First Inaugural. Even the "poetic" rhetoric of the Gettysburg Address seeks its effect by tying the issue and the nation to the necessities of the natural processes of generation and decay.

As our earlier analysis suggests, of course there *is* a rule which in Roosevelt's approach carries necessity with it. This is the rule embodied in his starting point—self-defense. Nations "*must* obey" the law of self preservation, he says. What Roosevelt means by this "must," however, points up how distant is his sort of necessity from Lincoln's: Roosevelt means that it is impossible for a nation to play any rôle at all should it fail to defend itself through cowardice, sloth, or folly.

Roosevelt's World War I campaign was a rhetoric of self-defense: but the actual situation did not lend itself to the argument that self-defense was here a sharp necessity: the danger was too remote. Other rhetoricians of Roosevelt's kind, however, have found themselves in "perfect" situations just for making a crusading necessity of self-defense, and the best of them have shown that the resultant call for heroism can equal any in compelling power. Winston Churchill's speeches on the Battle of Britain constitute an incomparable example of arguments in which the fact that everything from existence to value depends on his audience generates the persuasive necessity of their heroism.

We have been looking at the rhetorician as he brings thought to the test of action. Turning now to the process of thought itself, we encounter as a central feature the familiar logic of combining contraries—freedom and order, justice and power, courage and restraint, theory and practice, etc. This logic of combination was for Roosevelt so crucial a rule that he used the Foreword to his *Autobiography* to argue that the primary need of individual and nation alike was to combine qualities which merely singly were common enough.

His particular use of this rule exhibits its peculiarly rhetorical form. He does not reconcile the contraries by seeking a higher *synthesizing* concept. Neither was his avoidance of extremes a search for the middle in the sense of the *mean* which was logically distinct from either contrary. Instead of a synthesis above or a mean falling between, he rather sought the conditions of *coexistence* of the contraries. This was provided for the terms by using each as the limit of the other. The "true" meaning of freedom for him thus could be grasped (negatively) by seeing that it could not be stretched to anarchy, because this would eliminate the contrary good—order. The contraries are treated as if they were competitors— *the two sides of a question as it were*—which ideally would each limit, not destroy, the other.

The enthymematic justification for this mode of fixing the meaning of desired traits, by using their contrary as a limit to an otherwise loose definition, is that two goods are better than one. The *ultimate* proof, however, was found in the operational fact that the contraries did exist in single agents. Roosevelt was content to justify his claim that morality and the fighting edge were compatible, and that their coexistence was desirable, by simply pointing to Timoleon, Hampden, Washington, and Lincoln as men who possessed both.

That the rhetorical orientation of Roosevelt's politics carried with it its own modes of action and logic is now perhaps evident. But the question remains whether such an approach can yield a political program of significance. The charge made against it generally, as against Roosevelt's method in particular, is that it achieves nothing fundamental, does not affect the social system but employs *ad hoc* measures to treat symptoms. But, as we noted earlier, some of Roosevelt's policies and precedents turned out to have been remarkably in tune with what

at least later emerged as long-range trends: the growth of the Presidency, Federal regulation permissive of financial empires, the protection of national resources from privileged exploitation and the rise of the United States to world leadership based on power—these are examples of trends Roosevelt initiated or decisively carried forward.

The paradox is less puzzling if a mode of analyzing Roosevelt's policies is worked out from the standpoint of his approach. The preceding inquiry suggests viewing each policy at three levels: (i) the first corresponding to the first-step problem of action; (ii) the second, to its incremental interpretation; and (iii) the third, to the combinations of contraries involved in justifying it.

(i) The treatment of action as a first-step principle of power orients the initial problem in formulating policy to the opportunities at hand for making a visible impact. In this context policies necessarily become matters of an adjustment and response to the immediate pressures and vulnerabilities in the situation. The Northern Securities combine, which Roosevelt so effectively battled, was an attackable, vulnerable target; monopoly capitalism, an abstraction. Policies get their *ad hoc* character from the initial focus on problems of execution and success.

(ii) The policy is seen secondarily, however, by envisaging what can be built on it—its incremental possibilities. This is what ties it to long-range trends, if shrewdly conceived. The action against the Northern Securities combine (a) "established the power of the government to deal with all great corporations," and (b) added to instances which could support his claim of the need and possibility of extending the sphere of responsibility and action of the Presidency.

(iii) Finally, the policy is considered at the level at which it is justified: Here the ultimate appeal is to the mode of relating power and justice, freedom and order, and corollary contraries. In this context policy takes on a generality which ties it—though not rigorously—to the values and social patterns of the times. The extension of the power of the Presidency reflected for Roosevelt the necessity that, with the shift from an agrarian society, the Federal government would have to extend its power on behalf of the freedoms which local resources were no longer able to sustain (thus preserving order and freedom, collectivism and individualism).

Some of the steps of analysis are of course not so pat as indicated above, but any analysis of a Roosevelt policy will be inadequate if it fails to observe all three dimensions: the initial formulation of it by consideration of problems of *execution* and success; the interpretation of it by consideration of its *extension;* and the justification by consideration of its inclusiveness of the diverse but basic *values* of the time.

VI. CONCLUSION

We have seen that Roosevelt's several worlds are pervaded by the same general pattern of thought and action and that this pattern is less a doctrine than a method—that of seeking the means of having an effective impact on the thought and action of one's time. No doubt most men seek to make their mark. But few follow out the implications of the search as he did, to make it a principle of inquiry and basis of understanding. He is to be contrasted with those who, even having in some sense the same stance, do not push it through to the conception, for example, of field biology as based on visual opportunism, of history as a precarious process of emergent powers, even of civilization and truth as functions of the persuasive style of great men, and of one's own identity as the sum of effects one can produce. He is to be contrasted, even more determinately, with those who sharply separate the problem of determining the truth of various fields of knowledge from the rhetoric of the time, and the standards of moral and social good from the means of persuasion about them. He denied such separations, and on the basis of that sense of the incompleteness of theory, he developed both intelligible structures of thought in a variety of fields, and patterns of action with incredibly complex reach in political affairs. If so, or to the extent that it is so, these structures and patterns are the fruit and exemplification of a philosophic rhetoric.

William M. Gibson (essay date 1980)

SOURCE: "TR and Mark Twain," in *Theodore Roosevelt: Among the Humorists, W. D. Howells, Mark Twain, and Mr. Dooley,* University of Tennessee Press, Knoxville, 1980, pp. 24-42.

[*In the following essay, Gibson outlines the affinities and conflicts between Roosevelt and Mark Twain.*]

Although in 1906 Mark Twain remarked that he had known Theodore Roosevelt "for certainly twenty years," dining in his company on occasion and enjoying Roosevelt's heartiness and gusto, it was not until his return from several years of round-the-world lecturing, in the fall of 1900, that Clemens began to take a strong, lasting interest in the Vice President soon to become President. That the foremost humorist of the country should begin to follow closely the career of the President of the country is not surprising. Both men over the years had formed intense moral commitments, Clemens' often unconventional, Roosevelt's largely traditional. Thus Mark Twain, fresh from Europe in October 1900, informed a New York audience that he was maintaining strict vigilance in order to "regulate the moral and political situation on this planet." Similarly, as Owen Wister once told Mrs. Roosevelt, TR was at heart, profoundly, a "preacher militant."

But in nearly every other respect the humorist of sixty-six and the President of forty-three were almost contrapuntally different and opposed. To name only a few of the most striking differences. Roosevelt believed in and lived the "strenuous life." Mark Twain insisted that he had never taken any exercise, except sleeping and resting,

and that he never intended to take any. "Exercise," he said, "is loathsome." A part of the Strenuous Life, as TR led it, was his passion for hunting, particularly big game hunting in the West of the United States and in South America and Africa, for sport, for food, for museum collections. Mark Twain, on the other hand, hated cruelty to animals and the killing of animals and wrote *A Horse's Tale* and *A Dog's Tale* to protest bullfighting and vivisection. The depth of his hatred may be measured by the image of the town loafers at Bricksville in *Huckleberry Finn,* who amuse themselves by pouring kerosene on a stray dog and touching a match to it.

Reading the newspaper stories of how the President killed a bear in Louisiana, in the fall of 1907, Mark Twain entertained himself and Isabel Lyon, his secretary, with his own burlesque version of the hunt. Really, he insists, it was a cow that was Roosevelt's victim, who in her flight "acted just as a cow would have done . . . with a President of the United States and a squadron of bellowing dogs chasing after her." When the cow's strength was exhausted, according to the humorist, she stopped in an open spot and tearfully said to the President, "Have pity, sir, and spare me. I am alone, you are many . . . have pity, sir—there is no heroism in killing an exhausted cow." But Roosevelt, who is "still only fourteen years old after living half a century," shot the bear in an "extremely sportsmanlike manner" and hugged his guides jubilantly after the kill. He is, Mark Twain then declared, "the most formidable disaster that has befallen the country since the Civil War."

Roosevelt's taste in literature was for the romantic and the epic, and embodied reverence for "the great men and great deeds and great thoughts of a bygone time," whereas Clemens tended to love the real and especially the "irreverent" or the iconoclastic. Roosevelt's manner of speech and writing was straightforward and simple, while Clemens' was ironic.

A more complex difference, recorded in Mark Twain's autobiographical dictation, arose from the Morris episode in January 1906. A Mrs. Minor Morris had called on the President at the White House to plead the case of her husband, who had been dismissed from military service. A private secretary to the President, one Barnes, had summoned the police and had had Mrs. Morris physically ejected and taken to a local police station. From the episode Mark Twain concludes that Roosevelt, "one of the most impulsive men in existence" wrongly permits himself "impulsive secretaries." Roosevelt, he declares, is "so hearty, so straightforward, outspoken, and, for the moment, so absolutely sincere" that one finds him thoroughly likable, as a private citizen. But these traits make him a "sufficiently queer President." TR is yet "the most popular human being in the United States." The reasons for his great popularity? If the twelve apostles were to come to the White House (Clemens claims) the President would invite them in and say how much he admired their progress. "Then, if Satan should come, he would slap him on the shoulder and say, 'Why, Satan, how *do* you do? I am so glad to meet you. I've read all your books and enjoyed every one of them.'" Anybody—says Mark Twain—could be popular with a gift like that.

Only a few months later, Mark Twain's view of Roosevelt's character had darkened. Offended by TR's "scream of delight" when General Leonard Wood's men killed 600 Moros in the Philippines—men, women, and children—Clemens spoke privately of the President as "fearfully hard and coarse"; "the worst President we have ever had"; yet also "the most admired."

By 1907 Clemens was even more consistently "down on" the President, coming to regard him as a master at self-advertising. He notes the newly made charge that TR had bought the election of 1904 in the final week with money from E.H. Harriman and Standard Oil. He observes that the President is sending Secretary Taft around the world and the U.S. Navy to San Francisco, for advertisement. And he accuses Roosevelt of half-wrecking the industries of the country and reducing the value of all property therein in the Depression of 1907. In short, Mark Twain charges:

> Mr. Roosevelt is the Tom Sawyer of the political world of the twentieth century; always showing off; always hunting a chance to show off; in his frenzied imagination the Great Republic is a vast Barnum circus with him for a clown and the whole world for audience; he would go to Halifax for half a chance to show off, and he would go to hell for a whole one.

It needs to be added that the creator of Tom Sawyer was never exactly averse to the limelight, himself, and that the extravagance of his analysis of President Roosevelt's character is partly due to his dictating an autobiography that was not to be published until long after his death.

Roosevelt, the truly omnivorous reader, began to read Mark Twain early in his life. He also read him widely, taking special pleasure in *Tom Sawyer* and *Huckleberry Finn*—which he included in his own Pigskin Library as "classics"—and in *Life on the Mississippi*. TR did *not,* however, like *A Connecticut Yankee in King Arthur's Court.* He considered Mark Twain a "real genius" but wholly without cultivation or real historical knowledge, who in the book belittled the great knights of the round table. Nonetheless, in June 1904, he sent a special directive permitting Clemens and his family immediate passage through customs when they returned from Italy with the body of his wife Olivia Clemens. TR also paid a rambling, rather vague tribute in a letter to Clemens for his seventieth birthday celebration on 5 December 1905; and he eulogized him after his death as "not only a great humorist, but a great philosopher [whose] writings form one of the assets in America's contribution to the world of achievement, of which we have a right as a nation to be genuinely proud."

One area in which Mark Twain and the President came together—on a small island in a sea of disagreement—

was spelling reform. The Simplified Spelling Board was initiated by Andrew Carnegie; Brander Matthews chaired the group; Mark Twain was a prominent member; President Roosevelt endorsed it. At an Associated Press banquet in New York City in September 1906—the same month in which Howells wrote an "Easy Chair" column praising the effort—Mark Twain argued that if the Associated Press were only to adopt simplified spelling for three months, the infallible result would be victory for the forces of reason. After such an experiment, he asserted, "the present clumsy and ragged forms will be grotesque to the eye and revolting to the soul. And we shall be rid of phthisis and phthisic and pneumonia, and pneumatics, and diphtheria, and pterodactyl, and all those other insane words which no man addicted to the simple Christian life can try to spell and not lose some of the bloom of his piety in the demoralizing attempt."

In this same fall of 1906, Clemens poked fun at Roosevelt's strenuous endorsement of large families. The occasion was his speech in the company of Howells and others backing a new copyright law before a congressional hearing in Washington. "Why," he said, "if a man who is not even mad, but only strenuous—strenuous about race suicide—should come to me and try to get me to use my large political and ecclesiastical influence to get a bill passed by Congress limiting families to twenty-two children by one mother, I should try to calm him down. I should reason with him. I should say to him, 'That is the very parallel to the copyright limitation by statute. . . . Leave it alone and it will take care of itself.'" President Roosevelt is not named in the passage—but he is patently the momentary target of Mark Twain's absurd reversal of the Rooseveltian view.

The source of the most fundamental disagreement between Mark Twain and Theodore Roosevelt was the 'imperialist' or "expansionist" policy of McKinley, which TR pursued and broadened throughout his presidency. The men differed on the Boxer rebellion in China and the role of American missionaries there, on the Cuban conflict and especially the war in the Philippines that ensued, on the policy of the English in the Boer War in South Africa, on Roosevelt's "taking" of the Panama Canal, and even on his achieving peace by arbitration between Russia and Japan.

At the beginning of 1901, Mark Twain's wrath against Kaiser Wilhelm, the European powers in China, and the American missionary William S. Ament boiled over in an article called "To the Person Sitting in Darkness," one of the most powerful pieces of invective that Clemens ever wrote. Clemens even declared in an interview that he was a Boxer, and favored the Boxer policy of driving foreigners out of China. In July, Vice President Roosevelt wrote privately to a friend, "The trouble with China was, as with most great questions, that the problem was infinitely complicated; whereas all our prize idiots from Mark Twain and Godkin down airily announced that both the problem and the solution were absolutely simple." Then, in October, at the Yale Bicentennial for a degree, with

Mark Twain, President Roosevelt may well have let Clemens overhear him exclaim to a missionary back from Peiping, "When I hear what Mark Twain and others have said in criticism of the missionaries, I feel like skinning them alive!"

This rather ferocious animus in the President against Mark Twain and other anti-imperialists was in fact symptomatic. In a rising storm of popular abuse, the charge soon appeared that Mark Twain was a traitor for opposing administration policy in the Philippines. The measure of Clemens' hurt, resentment, and anger on being branded traitorous becomes clear when one considers the number and weight of the counterattacks he made, published and unpublished, throughout the last decade of his life upon Roosevelt and much of Roosevelt's "Big Stick" foreign policy.

In the first two years of the century, however, Clemens tended to condemn the McKinley administration rather than Vice President Roosevelt for certain dangerous tendencies in American life, as he viewed them. At a Lotos Club dinner in New York City in November 1900, Mark Twain spoke of the Vice President wittily: "We have," he said, "tried an illustrious rough rider for Governor and liked him so well that we made him Vice-President"—in order to "give a little needed distinction to the office." Now, for a while anyway, Clemens continued, "we shall not be stammering and embarrassed when a stranger asks us, 'What is the name of the Vice-President?' This one is known; this one is pretty well known, pretty widely known, and in some places favorably. I am a little afraid," the speaker added, "that these fulsome compliments may be misunderstood. . . . I am not used to this complimentary business; but—well, my old affectionate admiration for Governor Roosevelt has probably betrayed me into the complimentary excess; but I know him, and you know him; and if you give him rope enough. . . ." Mark Twain wound up his joshing by claiming he would have been a Rough Rider and gone to war himself—if he could have taken an automobile rather than a horse.

It was this satirical stance assumed by Mark Twain in regard to the new expansionism and Roosevelt's sudden popularity as a war hero that led the *New York Nation* in the same month, November 1900, to praise the humorist as a commentator on public affairs. Mr. Clemens, said the *Nation* editorially, with his "fatal eye for folly and humbug" has seen the new delusion of grandeur in the United States for the "vulgar hypocrisy it is." He has "even refused to fall down and worship Roosevelt" and has "actually made fun of that solemn man!" Mark Twain remains a "homely and vigorous republican," the editorial concluded, "let who will trick themselves out in the gauds and paste jewels of imperialism."

At another dinner, early in January 1901, Mark Twain explained that he had not voted for either Bryan or McKinley because Bryan was wrong on the money question and McKinley was wrong in sending "our bright boys" out to the Philippines "to fight . . . under a polluted flag." Only a few weeks later at a dinner for Governor Odell of New York, with Theodore Roosevelt on the toast list, Clemens noted that a minister, unnamed, had recently called him a traitor for not fighting in the Philippines. But declared the humorist, when the life of the nation is not in danger, then the nation may be politically divided, "half patriots and half traitors, and no man can tell which from which."

Just how differently Mark Twain and Roosevelt faced the future in America, at this juncture, Howells disclosed in his report of a friend's analysis of the current American dilemma. The friend—unnamed—was surely Clemens. Howells said:

> He is not himself one of the fatly satisfied Americans who fancy the fulfilment of our mission to mankind in our present welter of wealth and corpulent expansion. Rather he finds that . . . we stand gasping in a tide of glory and affluence that may soon or late close over the old America forever. He speaks darkly of a dying republic, and of a nascent monarchy or oligarchy.

This same friend, Howells concluded, thought it a good thing to create a hall of fame, where the names of Washington, Franklin, Jefferson, and Lincoln set on high might long challenge the eyes of the people.

Just before Christmas of 1901 Mark Twain, on an impulse presumably, wrote to Roosevelt, claiming that he spoke not as a stranger but for the whole nation, saying, "Not Duncan himself was clearer in his great office." Mark Twain presumably means that Roosevelt had done well to retain intact McKinley's cabinet and to maintain McKinley's domestic policies so faithfully. Roosevelt answered from the White House, "Praise from Sir Hubert, my dear Doctor," returning Mark Twain's compliment and alluding to Clemens' recent honorary degree from Yale. The President thanked Clemens heartily for the Christmas greeting, which "touched and pleased" him, and he said, "Approbation from Sir Hubert Stanley is praise indeed."

Before Roosevelt became President, at the death of McKinley on 14 September 1901, Mark Twain had unloosed a truly fearful barrage of criticism against the McKinley administration and the European imperialist powers. Of these blasts at Foreign Secretary Chamberlain of England; President McKinley; General Frederick Funston of the United States Army; the American missionary in China, William S. Ament; the czar of all the Russias; and King Leopold of Belgium, two will have to represent Clemens' furious long-burning wrath. The first, "A Salutation-Speech from the 19th Century to the 20th, Taken down in Shorthand by Mark Twain," appeared in the *New York Herald* on 30 December 1900. It takes the form of a toast and reads as follows:

> I bring you the stately matron named Christendom, returning bedraggled, besmirched & dishonored

from pirate-raids in Kiao-Chou, Manchuria, South Africa & the Philippines, with her soul full of meanness, her pocket full of boodle, & her mouth full of pious hypocrisies. Give her soap & a towel, but hide the looking-glass.

This carefully wrought, highly effective bit of rhetoric carries a considerable shock in cartooning the United States and other Christian nations as a drunken matron returning from a bout of debauchery, sexual and alcoholic. Clemens tried with considerable success to repeat and expand the attack in a piece which he called "The Stupendous Procession," portraying the same aggressive warring nations led by the twentieth century, "a fair young creature, drunk and disorderly. . . ." But he would not, and probably could not, publish it. The American army general, Frederick Funston, for example, marches in the procession as the Siamese twin of Judas Iscariot.

The second representative piece, like its predecessors "To the Person Sitting in Darkness" and "To My Missionary Critics," appeared in the *North American Review* but unlike them failed to hit its target dead center. By now Mark Twain's conviction that human beings were inherently limited and had no freedom of choice was so strong that he must admit it even in his ironic "A Defense of General Funston." The weight of the attack on Frederick Funston is nevertheless heavy. This American general had captured the Filipino leader Aguinaldo by what William James called "a bunco-steering trick"—by methods, that is, which Funston himself admitted were nothing to be proud of. Mark Twain "defends" Funston by asserting that to bribe a courier, to disguise one's self, to accept a courteous welcome, and even to assassinate the welcomers—all are justified by the customs of war. But to accept food when they were nearly helpless with hunger, as General Funston and four other officers did, and then to lift one's hand and weapons against one's host violates all customs pagan and civilized. It is, says Mark Twain, a uniquely base act.

Clemens had written his "Defense" by mid-April, but found it necessary to add a postscript on the fourteenth on a closely related matter, in which he declared:

> The President is speaking up, this morning, just as this goes to the printer, and there is no uncertain sound about the note. It is the speech and spirit of a President of a people, not of a party, and we all like it, Traitors and all. I think I may speak for the other traitors, for I am sure they feel as I do about it. I will explain that we get our title from the Funstonian Patriots—free of charge. . . . they are born . . . flatterers, these boys.

President Roosevelt had ordered a through investigation of charges of cruelty committed by the American army and its Macabebe scouts against captured Filipino insurgents, and of the torture known as the water-cure. According to the *New York Evening Post,* the President had declared he would personally be answerable for punishing any officers found guilty with the "hardest penalty the law allows."

This is probably the last time Mark Twain praised Roosevelt for any feature of his foreign policy. Certainly by the early fall of 1904, when he wrote "A Brief Biography of the Government" for George Harvey and *Harper's Weekly,* he was becoming persuaded that Roosevelt and the rich were creating a federal oligarchy. He was especially incensed at President Roosevelt's securing land for the Panama Canal "by methods which might have wrung a shudder out of the seasoned McKinley." Mark Twain wrote:

> The Government of the United States was born in the State of New York forty-six years ago, of an old and eminent Dutch family. In the common school, the academy and the university he acquired his civil education; he acquired his military education in the Rocky Mountains in conflicts with the bear; among the cowboys he got his training in the cautious arts of statesmanship and in the delicate etiquette of diplomacy.

> In time he became Police Commissioner of New York City, and was a good one. Later he was Governor of his State, under Mr. Platt. After a while he was made Assistant Secretary of the Navy and chief promoter of a war with Spain. Then he resigned and went to his war, and took San Juan Hill, without concealment, but in the most public manner. Nothing in history resembles this engagement. . . .

> Next he accepted the Vice-Presidency of the Republican Party, which is the United States. Presently he became President and Government by the visitation of God. By and by he took fourteen million dollars out of the public till and gave it away, dividing it among all elderly voters who had had relatives in the Civil War [a reference to Roosevelt's Executive Order 78, which extended pensions and benefits, in exchange for votes, according to TR's critics]. . . .

> When the Government of the United States wanted some territory for a canal, he took it away from the proprietor by the strong hand. The proprietor was not big and strong, like Russia or England or Germany, and in other ways was not entitled to respect.

> When Russian imperial pirates take his merchant ships away from him he tries to be patient. And succeeds.

> When Russia violates his mail-bags on the high seas he tries to forget about it. And succeeds.

> Still—among us—what he wants he takes. It will be best for us again to elect him Government of the United States on the eighth of November next. Otherwise he will take it anyhow.

The tone of Mark Twain's "biography" is jocular, but the undertone is deeply ironic, and he finally withheld the letter from publication even under the protective signature, "Constant Reader." Curiously enough, according to Harvey's biographer, when such "excellent fooling" came to Roosevelt's attention, "he hugely enjoyed it, and at this very time he accounted both Mark Twain and George Harvey his dear friends." Harvey was now in fact as much opposed to TR as Clemens.

By the time TR was elected in 1904, Clemens had come to a clearer understanding of his attitude toward the President. Just before the election, he begged his old friend, Joe Twichell, a minister, to get out of the "sewer of party politics," where McKinley and John Hay and Roosevelt had led him—soiled public men who were, Clemens insisted, "in private life spotless in character." Even more lucidly in a letter to Twichell a few months later, Mark Twain defined his mixed feelings about the President: "For twenty years I have loved Roosevelt the man and hated Roosevelt the statesman and politician." For twenty-five years, he confesses, a "wave of welcome" has streaked through him in shaking hands with the man. But the politician, vote hungry per order 78 and "ready to kick the Constitution into the back yard," he found utterly destitute of morals and not respect-worthy.

Perhaps the point of greatest revulsion in Mark Twain's view of the President came in 1906 when General Leonard Wood and 540 American soldiers killed 600 Moro guerilla fighters, including women and children, who had fortified themselves in the bowl of an extinct volcano, near Jolo. As Mark Twain recorded the event in his Autobiographical Dictation for 12 March 1906, Wood and his men had climbed the steep slope with artillery; their order had been to "Kill or capture the six hundred"; after a day and a half "battle," fifteen Americans lost their lives—but the six hundred Moros were all dead.

Mark Twain quotes figures of the killed and wounded in the Civil War, and at Waterloo, and in the "pathetic comedy" of the Cuban War—where 1 percent of the American forces had been killed or wounded, and 2 percent of the Spaniards. But in this Philippine encounter, "we abolished them utterly"—Mark Twain says, "leaving not even a baby to cry for its dead mother." He calls it "incomparably the greatest victory that was ever achieved by the Christian soldiers of the United States." The day following the cabled news from the Philippines, President Roosevelt had cabled in return, "Wood, Manila—I congratulate you and the officers and men of your command upon the brilliant feat of arms wherein you and they so well upheld the honor of the American flag." Clemens charges that Roosevelt *knew* the soldiers dishonored the flag. He adds two days later that George Harvey believed the episode might destroy the Republican party and President Roosevelt, but that "prophecies of good things rarely come true." He ends by comparing Roosevelt's joy in this victory with President McKinley's "earlier presidential ecstasy" in "motions resembling a dance" on learning the news that Funston had captured Aguinaldo.

This account of the death of six hundred Moros is unrestrainedly indignant partly perhaps because Mark Twain did not intend it for publication until long after his death. But in a speech prepared for delivery in mid-October 1907, on the occasion of a visit to the United States by the Right Reverend Winnington-Ingram, lord bishop of London, Mark Twain may have declared openly what he dictated to a secretary privately for his autobiography. His theme was "our great country," satirically treated, and he adopted the device of addressing the lord bishop directly, thus:

> Our form of government, sir, is . . . monarchy . . . like your own at home. . . . Yours is hereditary monarchy under a permanent political party. . . .
>
> You will read and hear much of the President of the United States. Dear sir, do not be deceived—there is no such person. And no such office. There is a President of the Republican party, but there has been only one President of the United States since the country lost Mr. Lincoln forty-two years ago. . . . The party, only, is hereditary now, but the headship of it will be hereditary by and by, in a single family.
>
> Pray do not overlook our patriotism, sir. There is more of it here than exists in any other country. It is all lodged in the Republican party. The party will tell you so. All others are traitors, and are long ago used to the name. . . . We are nearly ripe for a throne, here; in fact all we lack is the name.

One not familiar with the thought of Mark Twain late in his life might suspect him of mere joking in his talk of a coming monarchy under Theodore Roosevelt. But he had predicted a coming monarchy in the United States thirty-five years before—so he recalls in the Autobiographical Dictation of 16 July 1908—and he gives his reasons. Man wishes by his nature to look up to God or to King. Great republics have never lasted. Vast power incites public favorites to dangerous ambitions. The immediate startling proof of his contention is that Roosevelt has named his own successor in the presidency, William Howard Taft. Only a few months later, Mark Twain with something less than perfect logic and consistency admitted that he was going to vote for Mr. Taft, and that "The monarchy is here to stay."

Mark Twain's final word on Theodore Roosevelt, dictated to a stenographer two days after the President left office, gives thanks that the country is rid of Roosevelt the heavy burden, the incubus—though not probably forever. After four years a hostile providence may re-impose "this showy charlatan" whom our people have adored "as perhaps no impostor of his breed has been adored since the Golden Calf." The nation, Clemens predicts, will want him back after he is through with his hunting other wild animals heroically in Africa. Mark Twain died in 1910 and did not live to witness Colonel Roosevelt's effort to be re-elected on the Bull Moose platform, but one may safely guess he would have continued to oppose him in his public character.

As for Mark Twain's fear that Roosevelt might become monarch or dictator of the United States, at our distance in time the fear seems to have been groundless. In the extremely bitter contest between Roosevelt and Taft in the campaign in 1912, however, it was rumored that Roosevelt had gone mad, and that if he could seize the presidency, he would make it an hereditary office. The *Louisville Courier* could see only one issue—in Roosevelt's name and person—"life tenure in the executive office." Charles H. Dana compared TR to the Roman consul Tiberius Gracchus. Thus, Mark Twain's distrust of Roosevelt's ambition may have been groundless—but it was shared.

In the political struggles and wars of the turn of the century, none interested Mark Twain more than the conflict between czarist Russia and imperial Japan. As "The Czar's Soliloquy" published in March 1905, demonstrates, Clemens hoped for the overthrow of the czar in the defeat of the Russian forces by Japan, whereas President Roosevelt shrewdly brought the two powers together at Portsmouth, New Hampshire, and persuaded them to sign a treaty of peace. Roosevelt's intent was to maintain a balance of power in Asia and the Pacific; his reward was the Nobel Peace Prize. But the peace treaty profoundly disappointed Mark Twain. Shortly before it was signed he wrote the editor of the *Boston Globe* that Russia was "on the high road to emancipation from an insane and intolerable slavery," that it was a "holy war" with a high mission, and that that mission was now defeated. Russia's chains were re-riveted, he feared, this time to stay. One more battle would have "abolished the chains of billions of unborn Russians," but now the czar will "resume his medieval barbarisms." "I hope I am mistaken," he concluded, "yet in all sincerity I believe that this peace is entitled to rank as the most conspicuous disaster in political history." The letter to the *Globe* is all the more arresting because it strikes the single negative note in two full pages of letters approving Roosevelt's role in achieving peace. Six months later, Clemens recalled saying to an elderly Russian revolutionary, Tchaykoffsky, "when our windy and flamboyant President conceived the idea, a year ago, of advertising himself to the world as the new Angel of Peace [between Russia and Japan] . . . no one in all this nation except Doctor Seaman and myself uttered a public protest against this folly of follies." He had believed at the time that Roosevelt had "given the Russian revolution its death-blow," and he was of that opinion yet.

Mark Twain differed more often than not, vigorously, with Theodore Roosevelt on turn of the century wars and U.S. foreign policy. What Roosevelt's position was in regard to the cruel exploitation of native labor in the Congo by King Leopold of Belgium has only recently been explored. He may well have agreed with Mark Twain, privately, that the Belgian king's agents in the Congo were ruthless butchers; but for a time he accepted the views of his secretary of state—first John Hay and then Elihu Root—that any formal protest or the creation of a board of inquiry on Belgian policy would constitute interference in the domestic affairs of a friendly nation.

Mark Twain himself reluctantly came to this same view, but not until several months after he had published *King Leopold's Soliloquy,* in September 1905. This was a harsh, often brilliant, condemnation in pamphlet form of Leopold's treatment of workers in the Belgian Congo, with photographs of mutilated Congolese. The work was published by the Congo Reform Association in England and the United States. Clemens' name appeared in it as first vice president of the protest group, and he contributed all financial returns from it to the Association.

A partial solution to the question of Roosevelt's reaction lies in Mark Twain's letter to Mrs. Roosevelt of 27 November 1905. In it, thanking her for her recent "charming hospitality" in the White House, he confesses that he was troubled during the visit because he feared the President did not know that he had "come to Washington to ask for a private word on a public matter." His "citizen-conscience" had in fact forced him to unload the burden onto the President's shoulders. Then after making an elaborate joke about his hardened conscience, Mark Twain again speaks of "appeals which are not made in a personal & sordid interest but in behalf of a matter clothed in the dignity of an honorable & national importance." And he closes, most sincerely, thanking the President for remembering him "when the irremediable disaster of my life fell upon me"—a reference of course to the intervention of TR with the customs people fifteen months earlier when Clemens had returned from Italy with the body of his wife.

Nothing concerned Mark Twain more on 28 November 1905—not even his seventieth birthday, two days away—than the need to expose and to stop King Leopold's atrocities. Hence I conclude that the matter of "national importance" which Citizen Clemens raised with Theodore Roosevelt was a request that the President act openly to condemn Leopold. The same day Clemens wrote a note to Robert Bacon in the State Department, sending him "those Congo documents" and explaining the role in England of "John Morley & some strong peers and bishops" and the possibility of America's "taking a hand." In December, Clemens was planning to "give a talk on the Congo question" and still hoped "to unseat Leopold." But by 8 January, Clemens had become profoundly discouraged because "the American people unbacked by the American government cannot achieve reform in the Congo"—so he had concluded after his last visit to the State Department some weeks earlier. Moreover, he could not "make a second step" in the "Congo matter" because that would compel further steps—and unlike E.D. Morel, head of the Congo Reform Association, he was not equipped with sufficient "energy, brains, diligence, concentration, persistence." Even so, Clemens in his seventy-first year did not give up easily. As he told Dr. Thomas Barbour in a letter of early February 1906, he had visited Bacon and Root in Washington a week earlier. They had told him that the U.S. government was so entirely outside the Congo matter that it could not move, or second any other nation's move, without laying itself open to the charge of "undiplomatic intrusion." The clinching argument of the State Department people had been that John Hay, dead since July, had held this view and had left it on record. Clemens, and old friend and true admirer of Hay, unhappily agreed.

But within months of Mark Twain's giving up his campaign, so angry and frustrated that he could not bear to read or even think about King Leopold, the President quietly reversed United States policy. In December 1906 he wrote the British Foreign Secretary, Sir Edward Grey, in open support of Congo reform, saying he was "moved by the deep interest shown by all classes of the American people in the amelioration of conditions in the Congo State." Roosevelt's letter, Leopold himself believed, marked the turning point in Congo reform; the Belgian parliament took over control of the Congo from Leopold in 1908.

The supreme irony in all this is that Mark Twain seems never to have known about Roosevelt's changing U.S. policy or the eventual success of the reform movement he had so passionately committed himself to. Nor did he realize that his "fury of generous indignation" in the pamphlet and his talks with the President and the State Department people *had* truly helped to relieve Leopold's wretched Congolese subjects. Clemens was a wrathy but also a just man. Had he known about it, he would surely have esteemed Theodore Roosevelt highly for this action, no matter what else TR had done.

The Gorki affair forms a kind of pendant to any account of Mark Twain's hope for revolution in Russia. Maxim Gorki, Russian writer and revolutionary, was warmly received in the United States in the spring of 1906. Howells, Mark Twain, Finley Peter Dunne, Jane Addams, and others formed a committee to raise money for revolutionary purposes, and at a dinner for Gorki on 11 April, Mark Twain spoke briefly but fervently on helping to "give the persecuted people of the Czar's domain the same measure of freedom that we enjoy." A few days later, however, the newspapers discovered that Gorki was living not with his wife but with a Russian actress, Mme. Andreieva—and Howells and Mark Twain with some embarrassment concluded that Gorki had badly misjudged the American public and largely wrecked his mission. Gorki might just as well have appeared in public in his shirt-tail, so Clemens concluded. Theodore Roosevelt on the other hand curtly refused an audience to Gorki at the White House. He despised Gorki's political ideas as those of "the fool academic revolutionist," a revolter against order as well as tyranny in governmental matters, and in domestic matters a rebel against "ordinary decencies and moralities."

It is apparent, then, that Mark Twain differed often and sometimes violently, in print and privately, with President Roosevelt on the war of the U.S. in Cuba and the Philippines, of England against the Boer Republics of South Africa, of the European powers against China during the Boxer Rebellion, of the revolution in Panama, and of Russia and Japan. He held, extravagantly enough, that

TR was insane in several ways and "insanest upon war and its supreme glories."

Clemens was critical of TR as well on such domestic issues as the tariff, the recession of 1907, Executive Order 78, and even the coining of gold double-eagles without the inscription "In God We Trust." Most seriously, Mark Twain faulted the President for inviting the Negro educator Booker T. Washington to lunch at the White House and for prejudicing, as he saw it, the trial of a black army regiment at Brownsville, Texas.

What Mark Twain thought in 1901 at the time of Roosevelt's inviting Washington to lunch at the White House is not certain. What Mark Twain recalled in the Autobiographical Dictation of July 1908 is this: to make a big sensation Mr. Roosevelt invited a Negro to the White House—a man "worth a hundred Roosevelts"— only to face deep disapproval from the southern half of the country. When they were together a little later to receive honorary degrees from Yale, the President asked Clemens if he had not done right in inviting Booker Washington to lunch. Mark Twain had replied that it was a private citizen's right to invite whom he pleased to his table—but that a "president's liberties were more limited." The invitation, Mark Twain believed, was purely, mistakenly, political.

Shortly after it happened, in late 1906—a clash between black soldiers of the 25th Colored Infantry and white townspeople in Brownsville, Texas—Mark Twain told an interviewer that his daughter Jean had written to ask if the dishonorable discharge of all the colored soldiers was not wrong. He had replied that he had as yet no opinion because he had not mastered the facts of the case. By mid-July 1908, however, Clemens was persuaded that the President, seeking to regain favor in the South, had treated the clash of black soldiers and white civilians from the beginning as a "conspiracy" on the part of the soldiers. Unable to convict some of the soldiers, the President himself in effect convicted the entire command and discharged them from the army "without honor." Understandably, neither the White House luncheon nor Brownsville is mentioned in TR's Autobiography. But historically speaking it must be noted that in 1972, Dorsie W. Willis, one of the last surviving members of the 25th Colored Infantry, was given an honorable discharge by the army to replace the discharge "without honor." Willis also received $25,000 compensation from the Congress of the United States.

How then may we interpret and evaluate this sketch by Mark Twain of Theodore Roosevelt, his character and his career as politician and statesman? The spirit is of course the spirit of the satirist. The technique is sometimes deflationary, as in Daumier; more often broad caricature, as in the cartoons of Clemens' friend, Thomas "Nasty" Nast; rarely, grotesque and despairing, as in Goya. There are several occasions, I believe, when Mark Twain loses control, so that the reader tends to sympathize with the subject of the satirical portrait, Roosevelt, rather than the sketcher, Mark Twain. This is often due to Clemens' sense of absolute freedom in the Autobiographical Dictation, his awareness that he is writing for some future reader when the persons treated will be long since dead. The practice is of a piece with his life-long habit of writing angry letters—and then never sending them. That is, many of these excesses in Mark Twain's depiction of Roosevelt would be erased or modified in work designed for publication. Nevertheless, Clemens was a skilled rhetorician who spoke his mind rather often, publicly, about the public Roosevelt, and even his unpublished excesses are interesting. As Howells once remarked in a letter to his friend, "I never knew a man to let himself loose as you do," to the utter delight, he added, of the entire Howells family. Finally Clemens may have kept to the end some liking for Roosevelt as an individual, a private person face to face—though this on balance remains ambiguous. And it seems certain he would have praised TR for the official move against King Leopold— had he known of it. But for Roosevelt the expansionist, the big game hunter, the army colonel who could never forget San Juan Hill, the "Tom Sawyer" show-off, the ambitious politician, Mark Twain saved some of his very sharpest strokes of the pen.

Harry Gershenowitz (essay date 1981)

SOURCE: "The Natural History Controversy Between Theodore Roosevelt and Jack London...," in *Jack London Newsletter,* Vol. 14, No. 2, May-Aug., 1981, pp. 80-2.

[*In the following essay, Gershenowitz defends the authority of Jack London as a naturalist with respect to Roosevelt's criticism of him as a "Nature-Faker."*]

The controversy between President Theodore Roosevelt and Jack London concerning animal strength and ability to survive in battle has not been resolved. It is possible that the disputation was fueled by the decreasing popularity of President Roosevelt's writings dealing with his wild-life adventures and the mounting interest in London's stories of the land in the north.

Both the President and London were advocators of biological and social Darwinism. In spite of London's humanitarian philosophy and Utopian dreams, he still believed in the struggle for existence and the survival of the fittest. These basic biological principles of animal behavior and development appeared in many of London's stories.

The President's academic training in science and his travels throughout the Far West with the famous naturalists, John Burroughs (1837-1921) and John Muir (1838-1914), are well known.

The two, (Roosevelt and London), were aware of the Turnerian thesis (Frederick Jackson Turner, American historian and professor of history at the University of Wisconsin), and the social neo-Lamarckian implications

of the future development of the western part of the United States.

In Chapter IV, "Men Who Misinterpret Nature," in *Through the Brazilian Wilderness and Papers on Natural History,* Roosevelt wrote, "Take the Chapter from Jack London's 'White Fang' that tells the story of a fight between the great northern wolf, White Fang, and a bulldog. Reading this, I can't believe that Mr. London knows much about wolves, and I am certain that he knows nothing about their fighting, or as a realist he would not tell this tale . . . This thing is a very sublimity of absurdity . . .

"In the same book London describes a great dog-wolf being torn in pieces by a lucivee, a northern lynx . . . Nobody who really knew anything about either a lynx or a wolf would write such nonsense."

London, in a letter dated December 5, 1904 to George P. Brett, outlined his plan to organize and write a story with the central subject illustrating "the evolution, the civilization of a dog-development of domesticity, faithfulness, love, morality, and all the amenities and virtues." This dog-wolf character became the famous "White Fang." With characteristic historian scholarship, London researched in various libraries the history of the life cycle of the wolf.

London describes the size, weight and degree of ferocity in *White Fang* (1906) of the dog-wolf, the lynx and the sturdily built bulldog, Cherokee. He pictured White Fang as 'fully five feet in length, and standing two and one-half feet at the shoulder, he far outweighed a wolf of corresponding size . . . so that he weighed, without any fat and without an ounce of superfluous flesh, over ninety pounds. It was all muscle, bond, and sinew-fighting flesh in the finest condition." He then continued to give a detailed account of the rapidity and lightness of movement of a full-grown female lynx. London submits, "Her quickness matched his; her ferocity equalled his; while he fought with his fangs alone, and she fought with her sharp-clawed feet as well." White Fang's battle with the bulldog, Cherokee, contrary to popular opinion, did not favor the dog-wolf. He barely survived the encounter because during the conflict he was caught by the bulldog's grip even though he was "trying to shake off the fifty pound weight that dragged at his throat."

Ernest Thompson Seton (1860-1946), author of forty books on nature, and considered an authority on wild-life on the Arctic prairies, offers live accounts of the habits of animals of the Northland. In the early 1900's he enjoyed a 2,000 mile canoe-journey in search of the Caribou in the region north of Aylmer Lake. Seton observed the Northland in its natural beauty with its animal life untamed. He tells us that "the Lynx is a huge cat weighing 25 or 35 or even 40 lbs., that it is an ordinary cat multiplied by some 4 or 5 diameters, . . ."

Meanwhile, however, the naturalist, John Burroughs, accused Seton of being one of the founders of "Sham

Natural History" and not reporting the true picture of animal life in their natural habitat. Perhaps, Burroughs was over-identifying with the egotistical President Roosevelt, and, perhaps, there existed an emotional unconscious tie to curry favor. It is possible that President Roosevelt had seen full-grown members of the species Lynx rufus (Bobcat) and observed the average weight was approximately 20 pounds. These smaller Lynxes were not the larger species Lynx canadensis molliposus (Northern Canada Lynx) that London was describing.

An unresolved problem is, how much historical and biological knowledge did President Roosevelt possess about the Lynx (Felidae) and Canis (Canidea) genera and families?

In his seminal work, *The Variation of Animals and Plants Under Domestication,* Charles Darwin in precise fashion describes the power of the vice grasp of the lower jaw of a bulldog in pinning down an elephant by its trunk. The major weight of a bulldog is in its forequarters, and, hence produces a capacity for agility. The original species of bulldogs raised in England weighed almost sixty pounds, and was trained to bear-bait as well as bull-bait. The bulldog was conditioned to carry out the process of obstinately hanging on to the bull's nose in order to excite the bull.

This writer has verified London's and Seton's work through studying (1) William T. Hornaday, *The American Natural History,* (2) E. Raymond Hall and Keith R. Kelson, *The Mammals of North America,* (3) Ernest P. Walker, *Mammals Of The World,* (4) William Henry Burt, *A Field Guide to the Mammals,* and (5) R.F. Ewer, *The Carnivores.* This writer concludes that President Roosevelt was inaccurate in his charges that London was one of the "Nature-Fakers."

John Milton Cooper, Jr. (essay date 1986)

SOURCE: "Theodore Roosevelt: On Clio's Active Service," in *The Virginia Quarterly Review,* Vol. 62, No. 1, 1986, pp. 21-37.

[*In the following essay, Cooper traces Roosevelt's development as a historian.*]

The most casual visitor to Sagamore Hill, Theodore Roosevelt's home at Oyster Bay, cannot fail to grasp two of the owner's greatest interests. The most immediately striking impression of the interior of the house comes from the plethora of animal trophies—mounted heads, antlers, tusks, stuffed birds and small game, and elephants' feet made into footstools. Even someone who knows nothing about Theodore Roosevelt can see that he was an enthusiastic outdoorsman and an avid hunter. The next most striking impression is made by the books. Sagamore Hill is a house full of books. The library is one of the largest rooms, and a casual glance at the volumes, which come in all sizes and shapes and many of which

show signs of repeated use, reveals that these are not decorative sets or collectors' editions. Other bookcases filled with similar hodgepodges of well-worn volumes in several languages and on a galaxy of subjects abound in nearly every room of the house. Even an ignorant visitor can see that Roosevelt was a lover and a reader of books. Curiously, few mementos serve to recall that the owner of the house was also a state legislator and governor, military officer, federal appointee, and vice president and president of the United States.

The appearances are not really deceiving. Sagamore Hill was not just a refuge for Roosevelt. His private pursuits also profoundly shaped his public performance. More than any other president who was primarily a professional politician, Roosevelt enjoyed a rich and varied life apart from affairs of state. The hunting trophies bear witness to his love of nature and zest for physical challenge, which had important effects on such public concerns of his as conservation of natural resources, military preparedness, and health and safety in the workplace. Roosevelt's outdoor interests had an intellectual side, too. Never what he scorned as a "game butcher," he hunted as an outgrowth of the passion for animal life and the natural environment that persisted throughout his adult years. A large number of the books at Sagamore Hill treat biological and other scientific subjects. Roosevelt's original ambition as a boy and young man had been to become a biologist, specifically a faunal naturalist. Although he abandoned that ambition during his sophomore year at Harvard, he never lost the thirst for scientific knowledge which later made him the most scientifically literate president and greatest patron of science in the White House since Thomas Jefferson.

A further glance at the section of the library devoted to the many volumes published under Roosevelt's name reveals more about his interests. Of his own books, only the collections of speeches and state papers outnumber the works of history. All other interests, even science and nature, took a back seat to Roosevelt's ardor for learning the histories of myriad times, peoples, and places. No subject occupied more of his writing and intellectual interests than history. Roosevelt published nine volumes of American history: *The Naval War of 1812,* which he began during his senior year at Harvard; brief biographies of Gouverneur Morris and Thomas Hart Benton; a collection of heroic accounts which he coauthored with his friend Henry Cabot Lodge; a short treatment of his birthplace and home political base, New York City, and his largest work, the four volumes on late 18th-century expansion and settlement entitled *The Winning of the West.* Also, while he was governor of New York, he wrote a book-length essay on the political character of Oliver Cromwell. In addition, many of his shorter pieces concerned historical subjects, the best known of which was his presidential address to the American Historical Association, "History as Literature."

Roosevelt has a clear claim to the title of historian. It is true that he never did any graduate study or taught in a college or university, not even briefly, like his friends Lodge and Henry Adams. Roosevelt did not belong to the new breed of academic professionals who were emerging in the United States during his youth. He came instead toward the end of the long line of gentlemen amateurs who were best exemplified by the historian whom he admired most, Francis Parkman. Yet Roosevelt's sheer productivity should shame others who have not devoted themselves to time-consuming public careers or followed demanding outdoor pastimes but can spend most of their waking hours in uninterrupted research and writing. Some of his work did show signs of thin research and hasty composition, but the better part of it rested on a solid base of broad acquaintance with original sources, familiarity with the latest literature on his subjects, and consultation with leading academic experts. The quantity and quality of his work established Roosevelt as an able, if not a great historian. Even without the reflected luster of his public career, he might have earned the honor of becoming president of the American Historical Association.

It would be wrong, however, to try to separate the statesman from the historian. Roosevelt first became drawn to history and public affairs at the same time, and his attitudes, interests, and reflections in each field vitally affected his conduct in the other. His attraction to history and public affairs arose out of the vocational crisis that he suffered at the age of 19, during his sophomore year in college. Roosevelt forsook his scientific ambitions in part because he had grown disgusted with the German-inspired emphasis on microscopic work and minute laboratory research which dominated biological studies at Harvard. "The sound revolt against superficiality of study had been carried to an extreme," he wrote later; "thoroughness in minutiae as the only end of study had been erected into a fetich [*sic*]." The young Roosevelt renounced a scientific career not only because his interests were changing but also because he rejected an intellectual spirit that he found alien. That rejection would, in turn, have a major impact on his approach to history.

Emotional factors played an even stronger role in his renunciation of science. The death of his father in February 1878, also during his sophomore year, plunged the 19-year-old Roosevelt into a harrowing nine months of grief and turmoil. He emerged from the ordeal a changed person, with a newfound interest in public affairs and a determination to become more worldly. Shortly afterward he also began his first historical research. By his senior year at Harvard, he was at work on his first book, which was published two years after his graduation, *The Naval War of 1812*. Family background almost certainly played a part in his choosing naval history as a field. For several generations, the Roosevelts had engaged in overseas shipping, while two of his maternal uncles had seen colorful service during the Civil War as Confederate naval officers. The particular subject, naval operations during the War of 1812, attracted him, Roosevelt said, for the simple reason that historians had neglected it.

The Naval War of 1812 set the pattern for his subsequent historical work. Copious research in original sources, including material from out-of-the-way places, undergirds his narrative and interpretations. Mastery of technical matters—shipbuilding, naval tactics, and seamanship in this case—informs his account of events. Despite his admiration for Parkman, Roosevelt did not excel at description and narrative. He wrote as he spoke, in vivid, exciting bursts, but not in a rounded, crafted whole. His battle scenes are rather flat and full of distracting detail, and the overall effect of the book is one of tedious recounting. The best writing comes in passages which make assessments or render judgments. The judgments reflect a mixture of partisanship and detachment. Roosevelt left no doubt that he was an American, a white man, and a Republican nationalist of Federalist and Whig antecedents. He delights in the defeats of the British and the Indians and in the embarrassment of Thomas Jefferson's and James Madison's earlier Republicans. At the same time, he distributes praise and blame evenhandedly. American mistakes and shortcomings in battle receive censure, while virtues and accomplishments of their British and Indian foes gain commendation. New England Federalists earn condemnation for their opposition to the war, while an old nemesis of his forebears, that "master spirit" Andrew Jackson gets high marks for "his cool head and quick eye, his stout heart and strong hand" in carrying the day at New Orleans.

The blending of current public concerns with historical interests is unmistakable. Roosevelt's main reason for writing about the War of 1812, aside from its scholarly neglect, sprang from his nationalism and attraction to military life. He wanted to expose the evils of governmental fragmentation, social particularism, and military unpreparedness, and he found plenty of bad examples among the Republicans of the 1810's, in sorry contrast to the deeds of their Federalist predecessors. Naval affairs remained one of Roosevelt's main public concerns for the rest of his life. During the 1880's he joined the small band of advocates of expansion and modernization of the United States Navy. He became an early convert to the strategic and geopolitical doctrines of Alfred Thayer Mahan, and in 1890 he wrote an enthusiastic review of Mahan's *The Influence of Seapower upon History*. As assistant secretary of the Navy in 1897 and 1898, Roosevelt boosted Mahan's career as a naval officer. Both in that office and later as president, he pushed tirelessly for a bigger, stronger, more up-to-date navy. The statesman was applying the lessons learned by the historian.

One other precedent that Roosevelt established in *The Naval War of 1812* was personal involvement with his historical subjects. He wrote no other naval history except for short pieces. A different interest had already attracted him. Oddly for a book of naval history, *The Naval War of 1812* devotes a great deal of attention to events and developments on the North American mainland. Another of the author's unconcealed delights lies in his depiction of white settlers crossing the Appalachians, clearing the wilderness, and conquering and displacing "savage" natives. Roosevelt was writing about the subject that interested him most—the West. Of his remaining works of American history, only the volume on New York City failed to touch on westward expansion and settlement. The biography of Gouverneur Morris contains discussions of diplomatic negotiations about the new nation's western boundaries and deplores Federalist opposition to the Louisiana Purchase. Given its subject's Missouri residence and expansionist politics, the Benton biography offered much broader scope to Roosevelt's Western interests, and it served as a warm-up for his most ambitious undertaking, *The Winning of the West*.

II

Those four volumes, which were published in installments in 1889, 1894, and 1896, constitute Roosevelt's major bid for serious consideration as an historian. None of his other works matches it in scope and sophistication. Dedicated to Francis Parkman, "to whom Americans who feel a pride in the pioneer history of their country are so greatly indebted," *The Winning of the West* takes up where Parkman's great history leaves off, with the defeat of the French in 1763, and ends with the Louisiana Purchase in 1803, although there are also brief accounts of later trans-Mississippi exploration and Aaron Burr's conspiracy. These four volumes reflect the same balance of strengths and weaknesses as Roosevelt's previous work. Extensive research in primary materials again informs the writing. A variety of well-mastered subjects, including agriculture, transportation, social and political organization, weapons technology, and diplomacy, enter into the account of westward movement and settlement. Roosevelt showed a keen appreciation of what the frontier experience meant to the people who underwent it and to the rest of the nation. Thereby, he anticipated in his first two volumes Frederick Jackson Turner's famous thesis of 1893. Once more, the best writing is in the interpretative passages, whereas narrative and description, even of armed clashes and natural scenes, remain competent at best. As an account of what happened in the West, Roosevelt's work is good but nowhere near in the same league with Parkman.

The outstanding feature of *The Winning of the West* lies in its analysis not of what happened to people on the frontier but of what outside influences impelled them to go there. Roosevelt brought an astonishing breadth and penetration of learning to bear on his subject. He was among the first to grasp the significance of Turner's statement of the frontier thesis, and with due acknowledgment he incorporated the interpretation into the last two volumes of *The Winning of the West*. Still more remarkable is the sweep of Roosevelt's historical vision. He depicts westward settlement against the backdrop not just of three preceding centuries of transatlantic migration by Europeans but of movements of Western peoples going back a thousand years and more. He invokes mythology and literature from ancient times and diverse places to illuminate the behavior of white men and Indians in the primitive environment of the woodlands,

swamps, and prairies. The two departments in which Roosevelt does approach his idol Parkman are in conveying a sense of the literary universality of his characters and of the contending of grand cultural and geopolitical forces in the conquest of a continent.

Even more than his earlier works, *The Winning of the West* brings Roosevelt's personal engagement with his subject into sharp relief. By the time he wrote the first volume he had become, thanks to his sojourn in the Dakota Territory in the mid-1880's, a part-time Westerner by adoption. To readers of higher-toned magazines he was well known as a Western writer through his articles about ranching, hunting, and chasing outlaws. Roosevelt invoked his own experiences in *The Winning of the West* when he compared personal observations of wintering in the wilderness with Daniel Boone's exploits and when he declared in the introduction, "The men who have shared in the fast-vanishing frontier life of the present feel a peculiar sympathy with the already long-vanished frontier life of the past." Such sympathy suffuses his re-creation of soldiers, scouts, traders, and settlers enduring hardship and loneliness and resorting to violence as they make their way far beyond the fringes of settled society. In that respect as an historian, too, Roosevelt resembled Parkman, the amateur who had trekked the Oregon Trail and insisted on visiting the scenes he wrote about, more than Turner, the academic who evoked the frontier through intellectual projection.

Public concerns continued to mesh with historical writing in Roosevelt's work on the West. He saw his subject as one phase in a still unfolding drama in which he meant to play a major role himself. In his view, he asserted in December 1897 "that mighty westward thrust of our people" was but one more "part of the great movement which within three centuries has made the expansion of the English-speaking peoples infinitely the greatest feature in the world's history." Within a year, Roosevelt would personally advance that movement by helping prepare the Navy for the Spanish-American War, leading his regiment of Rough Riders in battle, advocating retention of the Philippine Islands as an American colony, and rising like a political skyrocket to become governor of New York and a likely future contender for the White House. Seldom has an historian enjoyed a clearer chance to draw on his study of the past to create and then play a leading role in the events of the present.

After 1898, the pressures of public life left little room for historical study, even for someone so preternaturally energetic. Roosevelt had originally intended to write several more volumes of *The Winning of the West,* which would carry the story through the Mexican War and the beginning of settlement of the Pacific Coast. "I believe that this summer I shall be able to break the back of the next two volumes of *The Winning of the West,*" he told his publisher in January 1898, "or at least of the next volume." But he added a caution: "I am a very busy man here." He soon became busier still, as he readied the fleet for war, fought in Cuba, and hit the campaign trail first for governor and then for vice-president in 1900, with an exciting interlude between in the statehouse in Albany. The only time Roosevelt could contemplate a return to history came during his half-year as vice president. After leaving office, he told a Harvard professor in May 1901, "There is nothing I should like more than to become a 'docent,' a professor of history who would deal only with graduate students who had a serious purpose, and who would be expected in addition himself to do, or at any rate try to do, serious scholarly work of a type which should go on the shelves at least with Henry Charles Lea and John Fiske, if not with Parkman and [John Lothrop] Motley." Four months later, William McKinley's assassination sent Roosevelt to the White House.

III

Before the preoccupations of the statesman completely overwhelmed the writing of the historian, one final work did appear. While he was governor of New York, Roosevelt wrote two books, mainly by dictating to stenographers at odd moments in the day, particularly while he was being shaved by his barber. One was his war memoir, *The Rough Riders;* the other was a 260-page volume entitled *Oliver Cromwell*. According to one recollection, a friend of Roosevelt's quipped "that it was a fine imaginative study of Cromwell's qualifications for the governorship of New York." The joke had a point. *Cromwell* suffers from the same shortcomings as Roosevelt's lesser previous works. The writing shows signs of hasty, interrupted composition, with scant reworking. No original research and not even a lot of detailed knowledge of 17th-century English history inform the study. It also appears to fall into anachronism, with repeated references to George Washington, Abraham Lincoln, the American Revolution, the Civil War, and men and events of his own time.

In another way, those drawbacks are beside the point. It would be more accurate to call the book an imaginative study of Roosevelt's qualifications for leadership of the English Civil War. In it, the statesman and the historian merge at their best. Cromwell helps Roosevelt gain his bearings as he enters the 20th century, while Roosevelt uses his experiences to place Cromwell in the 17th century. As an extended meditation by a leader on the character and performance of a great predecessor, Roosevelt's *Cromwell* contains some of the finest reflections by an American on the balance between thought and action in wielding power. "Cromwell, like so many a so-called 'practical man,'" observes Roosevelt, "would have done better if he had followed a more clearly defined theory, for though the practical man is better than the mere theorist, he cannot do the highest work unless he is a theorist also."

The references to Washington, Lincoln, and American events are hardly gratuitous, either. They spring from a comparative perspective on revolutionary movements in the modern world, through which Roosevelt reflected on the competing demands of liberty and order. The English Civil War was, he argues, "the first modern and not the last medieval, movement" and therefore "the men who figured in it and the principles for which they contended, are strictly akin to the men and the principles that have appeared in all similar great movements since: in the English Revolution of 1688; in the American Revolution of 1776; and the American Civil War of 1861." Between them, its latitude for reflections on power and for comparison of movements and its freedom from the burden of narrative make *Oliver Cromwell* Roosevelt's finest single work. The book made a fitting valedictory to Roosevelt's writing as an historian.

Although he wrote no more works of history, the subject seldom left his mind after 1900, not even amid the pressures of office or in the heat of political controversy. Patronage of art, science, and culture became the hallmark of the Roosevelt presidency. Publicly, through exhortation from his "bully pulpit" and the example of entertaining novelists, poets, scientists, explorers, and historians at the White House, he promoted excellence in intellectual pursuits. Privately, he offered comment and criticism to scholars and scientists in a variety of fields. In all these activities, Roosevelt recalled, in gentler and updated fashion, the Italian princes of the Renaissance who had made themselves cultural arbiters of their states. History occupied a prominent place in both the public and private sides of Roosevelt's role as an intellectual patron. Henry Adams and James Ford Rhodes numbered among his most frequent guests at the White House, as did other historians. Rhodes not only corresponded with the President about published volumes of his *History of the United States, 1850-1877,* but he also got him to read at least one volume in manuscript. For his part, Roosevelt felt no reticence about challenging Rhodes on facts and interpretations of Civil War military operations and politics.

The historian in the White House went beyond benign public encouragement and private exchanges. Roosevelt promulgated his own views of how history should be written and how knowledge in general should be pursued. In January 1904, he stole time from political matters to write a six-page letter commending the British historian Sir George Otto Trevelyan for his "noble" rejoinder to calls by J. B. Bury and others for a "scientific" history. Actually, the rejoinder had come from Trevelyan's son, George Macaulay Trevelyan, and Roosevelt was confusing the two in his praise. "In a very small way," he added "I have been waging war with their kind on this side of the water for a number of years. We have a preposterous little organization called the American Historical Association, which when I was just out of Harvard and very ignorant I joined." Roosevelt counted himself fortunate that "good sense, or obstinacy, or something" had inoculated him against the "distinctly noxious" conceits of the "conscientious, industrious, painstaking little pedants" who filled the ranks of his country's professional historians. Although he appreciated their "excellent revolt against superficiality and lack of research," Roosevelt scorned their delusion "that the ideal history of the future will consist not even of the work of one huge pedant but

of a multitude of articles by a multitude of small pedants." Any such historian was "a good-enough day la-
borer, trundling his barrowful of bricks," but when he
and his fellows "imagined by their activity they rendered
the work of the architect unnecessary they became both
absurd and mischievous."

If those opinions sounded familiar, it was because they
drew upon the same intellectual spirit that had earlier led
Roosevelt to forsake a scientific career. His objections
extended much further than history. "Even in science itself," Roosevelt asserted to Trevelyan, "I think we shall
see a turning back from the dry-as-dust fact-collecting
methods after a while." He deplored the lack of appreciation of faunal naturalists among American biologists,
thanks to "the Germanization of our colleges and universities." All of their minute work represented "only the
gathering of material for some man of large mind to
mould into matter of importance. But as it is treated as
the be all and end all, the result has been a lamentable
dearth in America of work in the abstract sciences which
is of notable and permanent value." American scientific
education snuffed out "any impulse toward originality,"
leaving the student "a stereotyped well-meaning little
creature, only fit for microscopic work in the laboratory.
Now such work is good, but it is chiefly good in so far
as it gives a wider and deeper foundation to the scientific
man like Darwin or Huxley. . . ." As Roosevelt made
clear to Trevelyan, his view of the proper pursuit of historical knowledge extended to all fields, especially the
sciences. In his own way, he was very much a "scientific"
historian.

Those views—which put the highest premium on imagination and synthesis in all intellectual work and on literary excellence in historical writing—remained largely
confined to private correspondence and conversation, but
not entirely. "American scholarship will be judged,"
Roosevelt asserted in a speech at Harvard in 1907, "not
by the quantity of routine work produced by routine
workers, but by the small amount of first-class output of
those who, in whatever branch, stand in the first rank. No
industry in compilation and in combination will ever take
the place of this first-hand original work, this productive
and creative work, whether in science, in art, in literature." Other hints of his views sometimes cropped up in
the speeches, essays, and presidential papers in which
Roosevelt exhorted Americans to foster a new Augustan
age. But the fullest expression of his approach to history
did not come until after he had left the White House and
reentered the political arena.

IV

In 1912, that "preposterous little organization," the
American Historical Association, elected Roosevelt its
president. He accepted the accolade and addressed the
organization's annual meeting in Boston on Dec. 27,
1912. Roosevelt's appearance signaled no softening of
his scorn for pedantry, and the title of his presidential
address, **"History as Literature,"** waved a red flag at

fact-grubbers. The address elaborated on the points he
had made to Trevelyan nearly nine years before. Though
conceding the necessity for accurate research, Roosevelt
had no patience with the notion "that science is definitely
severed from literature and that history must follow suit.
Not only do I refuse to accept this as true for history, but
I do not even accept it as true for science." Like the great
scientist, the great historian must possess "imaginative
power. The industrious collector of dead facts bears to
such a man precisely the relation that a photographer
bears to Rembrandt." Imagination is the indispensable
gift. "When we say that the great historian must be a man
of imagination, we use the word as we use it when we say
that a statesman must be a man of imagination. Moreover, together with imagination must go the power of
expression. The great speeches of statesmen and the great
writings of historians can live only if they possess the
deathless quality that inheres in all great literature."

In that quality—the power to move people through art-
istry of presentation joined to loftiness of subject—the
historian and the statesman become one to Roosevelt.
"History as Literature" concludes with injunctions to
"bring the past before our eyes as if it were the present."
Not just the deeds of great men but "the days of common
things" from countless times and places must come alive
in their sights, sounds, smells, and dreams. People must
learn from history as from other branches of literature.
"We shall see the glory of triumphant violence, and the
revel of those who do wrong in high places; and the bro-
kenhearted despair that lies beneath the glory and the
revel. We shall also see the supreme righteousness of the
wars for freedom and justice, and know that the men who
fell in these wars made all mankind their debtors."
Americans, above all others, would learn from Washington and Lincoln and the ordinary folk who fought the
Revolution and the Civil War that they "possess an emer-
gency-standard far above mere money-getting," a standard that proclaimed "our belief that righteousness
exalteth a nation."

When he delivered that address, Roosevelt remained a
man in whom the public figure and the historian reinforced each other. Like his earlier historical work, his
views on the proper pursuit of history owed much to his
advocacy of certain policies. His sneer at "mere money-
getting" near the end of "History as Literature" echoed
the political and economic reform arguments that he had
recently made when he had run again for president in
1912 at the head of the newly formed Progressive Party.
Roosevelt's historical interpretations played a critical
part in his conduct after he left the White House. His
growing admiration for Lincoln as an apostle of inspired
moderation between dangerous extremes and his analogies between his own time and the slavery and sectional
crises of the 1840's and 1850's weighed heavily in his
decisions to oppose his handpicked presidential successor, bolt the Republican party, and lead the Progressives.
More personally, his sense of having led the nation in
prosaic times with little opportunity for heroism disposed
him to see overweening significance in those later events

and in his part in them. Historical perspective served, for a change, not to induce calm and forbearance but to incite zeal and daring. For Roosevelt, unlike others, Clio was not a conservative muse.

As both historian and statesman, one field attracted Theodore Roosevelt above all others—the field of battle. Wars and smaller armed combat figured, usually to a large extent, in all his historical writing. War was the activity with which his name became most closely linked. From youth onward, Roosevelt believed that the greatest tests of human character and the greatest achievements open to men, if not to women, came in war. Intellectual reflection, particularly from historical reading and research, reinforced emotional convictions about the place of war in human affairs. For himself as ex-president, Roosevelt felt deep pangs of regret at not having had the chance to lead his nation in war. "If there is not a war, you don't get the great general," he declared in a speech in 1910; "if there is not the great occasion, you don't get the great statesman; if Lincoln had lived in times of peace, no one would have known his name now." That sense of lost personal opportunity, even more than political and strategic views, lent special fury to Roosevelt's opposition to Woodrow Wilson during World War I. That yearning to play one more great role in history lent special poignancy to his plea to Wilson to allow him to raise a division to fight on the Western Front after the United States entered the war. Once more, the public man was grasping at the part the historian had set out for him.

But Roosevelt had to stay on the sidelines. His one solace at being shunted off the historical stage came from his four sons' service in the war. All of them saw action; two were wounded; one, the youngest, Quentin, was killed when his airplane was shot down. "You are having your crowded hours of glorious life," Roosevelt exulted to his oldest son; "you have seized the great chance, as it was seized by those who fought at Gettysburg, and Agincourt, and Arbella and Marathon." Time ran out for Roosevelt himself just after World War I ended. He remained a public figure almost to his last breath, as he planned peacemaking strategy with Lodge, regained leadership among Republicans, and was probably preparing to run again for president. Death came to him unexpectedly on Jan. 6, 1919, as he slept among the trophies and the books at Sagamore Hill. The curtain had come down on a unique American career.

No one like him had risen to the top rank in American politics since long before the Civil War; no one like him would go so far after him. Roosevelt shared with Wilson the distinction of being the only genuine intellectual to become president since the first decades of the American Republic. Both he and Wilson recalled the fusion of intellect and power that had marked such early leaders as Jefferson, Madison, John and John Quincy Adams, and Alexander Hamilton. Still more striking, however, were the differences that separated Roosevelt from both his great rival and his illustrious predecessors. Not a professional academic like Wilson, he remained a gentleman-scholar and amateur, somewhat after the fashion of the bygone aristocrats who had led the new nation. Yet Roosevelt's simultaneous pursuit of public and intellectual life bore little similarity to the reasoned, enlightened assumptions that had guided his predecessors, even the fiery Hamilton and the skeptical, pessimistic Adamses. Among American writers about danger, war, and elemental challenge Roosevelt fell between Francis Parkman and Ernest Hemingway, and he embodied a sensibility somewhere between 19th-century romanticism and 20th-century existentialism. Above all, no other American before or since has combined the statesman with the historian as fruitfully as he did.

Fittingly for someone with his cosmopolitan upbringing and frame of reference, Roosevelt's closest equivalents during his lifetime and later were to be found abroad, particularly in Great Britain. Such British contemporaries as his friends Trevelyan and James Bryce, as well as John Morley, furnished comparable examples of historians-in-politics, but in their beliefs and temperament those men more strongly resembled Wilson and the earlier American intellectuals in power. Roosevelt's nearest spiritual, political, and intellectual kin was an Englishman who was born 16 years and one month after him whom he knew slightly and did not like—Winston Churchill. Dislike notwithstanding, no man resembled Theodore Roosevelt more than Churchill in the way that he fused the public man with the historian. If Roosevelt had lived to read Churchill's life of his ancestor the Duke of Marlborough, whom he also admired, or his memoirs of the World Wars or his history of the English-speaking peoples, the bonds of sympathy would have been apparent. If Roosevelt had lived to witness Churchill's war leadership, the reflection in the glass would have been unmistakable. The man of the crowded hours and the man of the finest hour would have known each other as brothers in history and statesmanship.

David H. Burton (essay date 1988)

SOURCE: "Theodore Roosevelt: Learned Style," in *The Learned Presidency*, Fairleigh Dickinson University Press, 1988, pp. 39-88.

[*In the following essay, Burton examines the influences that formed Roosevelt's prose style.*]

On 7 June 1910, in the Sheldonian Theatre of the University of Oxford, ex-President Theodore Roosevelt delivered the Romanes Lecture. He called it "**The World Movement—Biological Analogies in History**." The invitation by Lord Curzon, the chancellor of the university, to give the address was recognition accorded Roosevelt as a distinguished man of letters as well as a former American president. His reputation in each regard was understood and appreciated on both sides of the Atlantic. Roosevelt found the prospect of giving the Romanes Lecture greatly attractive. It would afford him the opportunity once more of expounding his view of modern history, the leading feature of which was the world movement of the European races across the backward areas of the world. This movement, which had been in process since 1500, he had first elaborated in writings done during the 1880s. Years later as a politician and statesman he had pursued policies that fit within this frame of historical reference. In **"Biological Analogies in History"** he proposed to relate his understanding of history to the scientific spirit of the day for the purpose of placing man in social perspective.

During the closing months of his presidency Roosevelt took time away from pressing political concerns to make a careful preparation of the text of his address. Early drafts were read and criticized by Henry Fairfield Osborn of the American Museum of Natural History in New York, while Lord Bryce, the British ambassador to Washington and sometime Regius Professor of Civil Law at Oxford, found himself at the White House, as the President put it, "to suffer the wholly unwarrantable torments which I design to inflict . . . by going over my Romanes Lecture with me." But the result was a summation of the ideas of Roosevelt himself, a major effort on his part to pronounce a view of man in history. The success of the lecture has been dimmed by the comment of Dr. Lang, the Archbishop of York. "In the way of grading which we have at Oxford," he said, "we agreed to mark the lecture Beta-minus but the lecturer Alpha-plus. While we felt that the lecture was not a very great contribution to science, we were sure the lecturer was a very great man." If anything, Roosevelt intended to illuminate not science but society, using the methods of science where they seemed applicable and rejecting them when they were not. It is on this test that the lecture should be judged.

"Biological Analogies in History" strictly qualified the role of evolution in human affairs. The address exhibited in Roosevelt a sympathy for scientific method and achievement, as he extolled the greatness of Darwin and asserted that from the biological process of birth, growth, maturation, prosperity, and death, social patterns could be better understood: "As in biology, so in human history. . . ." He also pointed up differences and the danger of deductions from facile comparisons. For example, he said that "most of the great civilizations which have developed a high civilization and have played a dominant part in the world have been, and are, artificial, not merely in social structure but in the sense of including totally different types. A great nation rarely belongs to any one race." While the important ethnic divisions of mankind could not be ignored or discounted, usually they had not remained unified, and, accordingly, had not produced cultures that could be defined as purely ethnic. Civilization flowed out of a great accumulation of spiritual, moral, and intellectual principles and ideas that a particular race at some given period in history might especially express. But Roosevelt insisted that greatness came from ideals and not from blood. "We Americans and you people of the British Isles alike," he told his audience, "need ever to keep in mind that among the many qualities indispensable to the success of a great democracy, and

second only to a high and clear sense of duty, of moral obligation, are self-knowledge and self-mastery." In public as in personal affairs, he declared, "though intellect stands high, character stands higher." It followed that problems, whether national or international in scope, ought to be approached in the "spirit of broad humanity, of brotherly kindness, of acceptance of responsibility." Referring to Western imperialism—in effect, to the world movement—he concluded that "in the long run there can be no justification for one race managing or controlling another, unless . . . in the interest and for the benefit of that race." What Roosevelt had striven to do in "Biological Analogies in History" was to identify, contemplate, and praise human purpose in social development.

Some three months later, on 31 August 1910, at Osawatomie, Kansas, in a setting very unlike the Sheldonian Theatre, the ex-president fired off one of the major political speeches in his long career, **"The New Nationalism."** Though a political speech, it was laced with the pragmatism of William James as transmitted to public uses by Herbert Croly and voiced by the premier public man of the time, Theodore Roosevelt. Croly, in *The Promise of American Life,* had insisted that government was but an instrument of the people, a tool to be used in bringing about socioeconomic reforms vital to the good health of the country. The Constitution as a frame of government was rejected as a limitation on what one generation could do to solve its problems. Specifically understood, constitutional government must become a living process of change and adaptation, with man's intellect the directing force for good. Croly had been much impressed by Roosevelt's conduct of the presidency and had drawn heavily upon it in writing *The Promise of American Life.* The book, in turn, helped TR crystallize his thinking as an advanced Progressive.

Early in the Kansas speech Roosevelt offered a quotation: "Labor is prior to and independent of capital. Capital is only the fruit of labor and could never have existed if labor had not first existed. Labor is superior to capital and deserves much the higher consideration." Such were the words not of a radical agitator, the ex-president announced with deliberate irony, but of Abraham Lincoln. He went on to define the great issue of 1910 as "the struggle of free men to gain and hold the right of self-government as against special interests." [**"The New Nationalism"**] This was nothing new, he said, but in a complex industrialized society it had assumed new forms and new meanings. He reminded his audience that the objective of any reform ought to be the enhancement of opportunities for individual citizens. The "square deal" did not stand for the dole but the right to work, a right ensured "free from the sinister influence or control of interests" through the agency of a powerful central government. Disposed to accept combinations in industry as "the result of an imperative economic law which could not be replaced by political legislation," Roosevelt thought that the individual would be served best "in completely controlling such combinations in the interests of public welfare." Control should extend over business corporations, the money system, the national natural resources—over wealth in whatever form. This must be done in the name of "national efficiency," as pragmatism itself had efficiency as a goal. The national government was thereby promoted as a popularly elected instrument of national efficiency, blending democracy and science.

"The New Nationalism" was a notable synthesis of Roosevelt's mature progressivism. At the same time it exhibited the main elements that generally describe his thought. The evolutionary component was evident in the assertion that combinations were the "result of an imperative economic law"; the pragmatic strain was revealed in a call for "national efficiency" that had to go beyond mere negative regulation of vested interests; and, finally, a traditional national purpose—"the object of government is the welfare of the people"—suffused the entire message.

The whole of Roosevelt's thinking as a public man, of which **"Biological Analogies in History"** and **"The New Nationalism"** are compacted expressions, is an instructive detail in the broad canvas of the American mind at mid-passage. The decades from 1858 to 1919, years marking TR's lifetime, were times of intellectual transition in America. The changes affecting thought were substantial, influencing happenings in the counting houses, the legislative halls, and the courts of law. If it is true that the American mind would never be the same again, it is equally proper to observe that by 1919 that mind had become an amalgam of the very new and the very old. The transition had been completed in the sense that the flow of applications of the new scientific hypotheses associated with the name of Darwin had sought out every corner and contour of the national experience. No area of individual or social significance escaped scientific interpretation. However, while the traditional ideas of the colonial and early national inheritance had been altered, adapted, and attenuated, they were far from effaced. What had occurred was a truly pragmatic version of truth-reality in the making; new ideas had been wedded to older concepts, creating a more vital synthesis.

The mid-nineteenth-century American mind had possessed a strongly traditional quality. This traditionalism was not without challenge and change in the early years, but as late as the Civil War, inherited, time-honored modes of thought and attitude commanded the adherence of most men. This was especially true of religion at a time when religious beliefs were widely held by Americans. At the center of this faith was supernaturalism, buttressed by a system of philosophical absolutism. The household that Theodore Roosevelt grew up in was permeated by a religious spirit, exceptional only in the degree of its commitment, for the senior Roosevelt was a genuinely pious, churchgoing, praying Christian. The finished fixity of the systems of faith and reason enjoyed by mid-century Americans like the Roosevelts found expression both in the development of the Constitution as the great law of the nation and in capitalistic enterprise based on the certainties of private property, the operation of the

two producing a mutually reinforcing effect. The Roosevelt family fortune, derived from trade and banking, rested squarely on the twin pillars of law and property, and rejoiced in heaven's approval. It was upon this traditional world of reassurance born of final answers that the new scientific hypotheses, pregnant with change, intruded. The year after Theodore Roosevelt's birth Darwin published *The Origin of Species*.

The Origin of Species has been called the most important book written in the nineteenth century. Whatever exaggeration may attach to this claim, its impact on American thought in Roosevelt's formative years was far-reaching. Darwin's book, with its principles popularized and applied to social conditions, delivered a grave blow to the supernaturalism that was central to American Protestant Christianity. As the inherited religious outlook yielded ground to new scientific teachings, much of the traditionalism of the American mind underwent a similar change. The allegiance of philosophers switched readily to evolutionary scientism and thence to pragmatism. The personalist ethic that had been part of the democratic-capitalistic impulse succumbed to the ravages of a relentless laissez-faire. The Constitution and the law, in turn, were made to do service in the working out of the nation's economic salvation.

Three ideas critical to American thought as it developed out of Darwinism fascinated Roosevelt's generation: changeability, progress, and a material order. Of the three, change and progress had formed part of American belief and experience from the first colonial foundations. No people had become more familiar with change and were more likely to accept it as a happy fact of life than were Americans. As for progress, the very word could be used to sum up national confidence in the national destiny. Progress in colonial America had become a reality even before progress was a philosophical postulate of the Enlightenment. Americans had been influenced by the fact and the philosophy of progress, their minds conditioned not merely to hope for human betterment but to demand it as their birthright. Their concept of progress, furthermore, had been keyed to individual success and to individual improvement, the social dimension being the sum of the well-being of individuals. Of all the features of America's past pointing the way to progress, none meant more to Theodore Roosevelt, or was to have greater impact on him, than the westward movement of the frontier. His zest for outdoor life and adventure had taken him to the Dakota country in the fall of 1883, and his experience there altogether enthralled him. He later was to speak of these western days as "the most important educational aspect of all my life." [**"Speech at Sioux Falls, S.D."**] In the West, in its history and actuality, Roosevelt was convinced he had found all that was best for America in nature and in society. To him it signified the free self-reliance of the individual and social progress for mankind, because the westward movement of superior peoples brought new lands under their dominion and their beneficence. There is something both paradoxical and sobering about Roosevelt's appreciation of the West. The very conquest would mean the eventual disappearance of the individual frontiersman and the assimilation of frontier populations into more complex social arrangements. But the two ideas: rugged individualism with its Darwinist overtones, and the welfare of mankind redolent of religious conviction, are suggestive of the persuasions that science and tradition continued to exert on him.

As social Darwinism supplied a new rationale for established ideas of change and progress, its acceptance by the American mind was hardly surprising. The stumbling block to a more complete victory for evolutionary thought was its third proposition, a material universe. Adherence to this concept, where adherence occurred, marked a dramatic break with tradition. Leading advocates of social Darwinism dismissed the claims of religion as unscientific, unverifiable, and therefore unworthy of their attention. The residue of traditional faith even of avowed evolutionaries could be considerable, nevertheless. John Fiske's advocacy of a theistic evolution in *Outlines of Cosmic Philosophy* illustrated the reluctance or the inability of some to cut loose completely from past intellectual moorings. This type of traditionalism was central to the view of Theodore Roosevelt. He saw Western man's history, especially since 1500, as an evolutionary process of the survival of the fittest and mastery by the superior races. He also believed that the mainspring of the evolutionary mechanism was character in individual men, and that the aggregate of this individual moral sense accounted for the superior race. Furthermore, the outcome of the evolutionary process was progress, invariably judged by him according to the norms of traditional ethics.

Pragmatism presupposed the same critical principles as social Darwinism. For similar historical reasons it proved congenial to the American mind. Pragmatism also encountered obstacles. The pragmatists differed from the Darwinists in their avoidance of a truculent challenge to ancient faiths, and their insistence on progress resulting from change that men could control and direct appeared more consistent with American history and the traditional spirit. While pragmatism was in fact a philosophy, it did not demand to become *the* philosophy of someone attracted to it. Pragmatism was readily utilized as an instrument of change by those who were generally satisfied with ethical values grounded in Scripture or on the rational nature of man. As instruments of reform, pragmatically inspired techniques might do yeoman service in the cause of maintaining the old moral order. For a "conservative as Progressive," for Theodore Roosevelt, this was the meaning of the Progressive movement.

Pragmatism was doubtlessly a more humane expression of scientific principles than social Darwinism. If its opposition to aspects of the traditional American mind was more subtle, it was also a philosophy better constituted to accommodate traditionalism, should the latter prove viable. After all, the ultimate test of the pragmatic dispensation was workability; a workable combination of the old with the new was among the first principles of prag-

matism. Roosevelt's mature public mind exhibited this distinction in **"The New Nationalism."** Progressive reforms, if they were better able to bring about greater individual fulfillment, were attractive applications of pragmatism. Individual fulfillment remained for Roosevelt the key to social improvement.

The public mind of Theodore Roosevelt represented a union of traditional beliefs and scientific theories. Coming together in his vibrant and aggressive personality, they constituted what may well be termed the "Rooseveltian ethic," for Roosevelt himself added a unique and powerful ingredient. The constituents were closely related but not necessarily of equal importance. Each worked at times to qualify the others, and each at a given moment might appear dominant. All were securely part of his outlook as he came of age politically; all remained permanently in his thought. His mind was an amalgam of the old and the new, combining loyalty to traditional morality with a respect for scientific progress that was largely characteristic of the Establishment of his generation. The claims of traditional ethics were as much a part of him as his admiration for Darwin and Huxley, "seekers after truth." Insofar as Roosevelt was guided by high principles, traditionalism was modified by social Darwinism. Inasmuch as his public philosophy owed some of its character to his response to a succession of actual problems, in his mature years it displayed elements properly associated with pragmatism as an intellectual instrument, as well as with political expediency.

Theodore Roosevelt was born in 1858 into a family deeply rooted in New York City's history, the place of his birth. His father, also called Theodore, was more a philanthropist than a businessman, but his considerable success in the marketplace enabled him to indulge his sense of responsibility for the less fortunate. TR's mother was Martha Bulloch, a Georgia belle who came north in 1853 after her marriage, though she remained Southern in spirit. The Civil War created some strain on the family. Once the conflict was over, the Roosevelt horizons were unclouded, and Teedie, as young Theodore was known in the family, grew up in a comfortable, regulated household presided over by his father. Later Roosevelt was to speak of his father as "the best man I ever knew," and a warm and loving relationship was part of the fact and memory of Theodore Roosevelt's growing up.

Education figured prominently in Roosevelt's youth. His father was keen to have his son instructed in the fundamentals of learning as well as in the new ideas of the scientific revolution. His education was an ongoing one; it originated at home, continued at school, and was not yet completed by the time Roosevelt became president in 1901. The formalities of that education began with Andrew Cutler on one end of the log when Cutler was hired in 1873 to prepare his young charge for the Harvard entrance examinations. Teedie was both a willing and an able student. His imagination and curiosity had been fired by the constant round of activities in his father's house, by travels to England, Europe, North Africa, and the

Middle East, and by a six-month residence in Dresden, where he learned something of the German language and culture—all this by the age of fifteen. In between these experiences he had been taught to read and write, mostly by tutors drawn from the family because of the uncertainties of his health. His father had been greatly concerned about the boy's physical well-being and had sternly but compassionately advised him "to make his body." "You have the mind but you have not the body," his father told him when he was about ten years old, "and without the body the mind can not go as far as it should." The result of this fatherly advice is well known. Theodore Roosevelt, from that moment, was the practitioner and advocate of "the strenuous life." There is no comparable episode that marks the beginning of Roosevelt's equal determination to make his mind.

He read extensively as a boy because the family was devoted to books, but his reading was commonplace in character. His father, noting his son's interest in natural history and wanting to occupy him during bouts of illness, gave him volumes by J. G. Wood, the English writer of popular books on nature. In this way and from observation and a collection of specimens, Teedie acquired an extraordinary amount of information about birds, animals, and flowers. He also read history, especially American history, and tales of adventure, including the writings of Cooper and Longfellow. In all of this there was too much of what interested the youngster and too little of an organized and rigorous approach to learning. He was able to read German well, for example, and do passably in French, but he had no grounding in Greek or Latin and had received no instruction in mathematics. It fell to Andrew Cutler to inculcate a method and to encourage a discipline, habits that were to become a permanent part of his life, as well as to accomplish the more mundane objective, passing the Harvard entrance examinations. Cutler's task, from the viewpoint of the tutor, proved both easy and satisfying. Roosevelt was the ideal student at the opposite end of the log. He prepared for eight different fields of examination, doing the minimum only in Greek. Special emphasis was given to Latin, history, mathematics, and elementary science. Roosevelt had to apply himself to these subjects, but he had little difficulty with German and French. In literature he needed neither introduction nor urging, but Cutler supplied proper guidance, while in botany and zoology he struck out on his own. Under Cutler's tutelage Roosevelt acquired the intellectual confidence necessary for him to make the most of Harvard.

The Harvard of the late 1870s was in the process of absorbing the initial educational reforms of President Eliot, making the school an interesting and an exciting place to be. By introducing the elective system to the undergraduate curriculum and developing graduate programs in various fields, Eliot sought to improve the educational experience of the college students and at the same time establish Harvard as an important university. Like others, Roosevelt profited directly from the elective system and indirectly from the enhanced intellectual at-mosphere. Despite the liberalizing efforts of Eliot, there were prescribed courses for freshmen and some required subjects for the second year as well. In the first year Roosevelt studied Greek and Latin literature and language, German, advanced mathematics, physics, and chemistry—an arresting blend of the knowledge of antiquity and the findings of modern science. In his sophomore year he took rhetoric, Anglo-American constitutional history, French, German, comparative anatomy and physiology, and botany. Roosevelt applied himself diligently to all these subjects and was among the best students in what was deemed a brilliant class. By his junior year he had hit full stride, taking nine subjects that totaled twenty hours of lectures and laboratory periods. Performing well in all courses, he excelled in political economy and zoology. These two disciplines represented diverging roads, one of which he would choose to follow as a life's work, while the other would remain an avocation. Several factors dissuaded Roosevelt from a scientific career. He was an "outdoor naturalist" at a time when natural science was exclusively a matter of the laboratory. Having fallen in love with Alice Lee and become determined to marry her as soon as possible after graduation from Harvard, he recognized the value of a career of large prospects consistent with the Lee family's position. Finally, his desire to keep up his father's name as a civic leader drew him toward some form of public life. This decision is clear enough in retrospect, but hardly so if one examines his choice of senior subjects, which included political economy and Italian, and geology and zoology. When he graduated in June 1880 he won "honorable mention" in natural science, was elected to Phi Beta Kappa, and was ranked twenty-first in a class of 177. In his autobiography, Roosevelt recalled that he "thoroughly enjoyed" Harvard but that "there was very little in way of actual studies which helped me in after life." The influence of the varied curriculum may well have been too elusive to be appreciated, but his study of history and science honed his mind as surely as the regimen of physical exercise had toughened his body. It was while a senior, for example, that he commenced his research on the naval war of 1812, the background of a book that would launch his career as a writer.

Looking beyond courses and grades and prizes, other considerations must be weighed in assessing the impact of the Harvard years on Theodore Roosevelt. The death of his father in 1877—"the best man I ever knew"—forced him to become more independent. He found the social life at college immensely appealing, and he was part of the extracurricular scene at the highest levels. His passion for Alice Lee, which was to lead quickly to marriage in 1880, thrust fresh responsibilities on him, completing his passage to manhood. Yet through it all, learning remained a critical element in his outlook, and Harvard confirmed his commitment to it. Books no longer meant withdrawal from the world as they may have during his sickly childhood, but "a reaching for a growing understanding" of the world and its people. He read literally hundreds of books over the course of the years and would later write them to describe an experience (*The Wilderness Hunter*), to analyze a historical event (*The Naval War of 1812*), and to celebrate a theory of history (*The Winning of the West*). Books about people were also to be part of Roosevelt's literary output: *Gouverneur Morris,* a founding father, *Thomas Hart Benton,* a frontier statesman, and *Oliver Cromwell,* a leader of moral purpose. According to Henry Adams, students of Roosevelt's day came to Harvard ignorant of all that men had thought and hoped, but while at Cambridge "their minds burst open like flowers at the sunlight of suggestion." Harvard had fertilized Roosevelt's mind, which burst forth in an impressive array of books and other writings over the course of the next several years. Yet his future was to involve much more than books, devoted as he was to them. His total education had served a dual purpose. In Cardinal Newman's phrase, the end of education is "fitness for the world," by which he intended neither instant social utility nor economic success. What was meant, rather, was an intellectual fitness, the mental capacity for life that alone makes a person substantially useful and successful. This was the result of Theodore Roosevelt's education, of which Harvard was a part.

The image of the frenetic Teddy Roosevelt has an unquestioned validity. He had other dimensions, one of which was given a vivid rendering in his first book, published when he was only twenty-four. *The Naval War of 1812* appeared in 1882. Edward Wagenknecht, in *The Seven Worlds of Theodore Roosevelt,* tends to dismiss the books as "hardly more than the work of a boy," yet "fair and soundly researched." It was a work, in fact, marked by patriotism but marred by jingoism. Some years afterward, and on the strength of this first book, Roosevelt was invited to do a study of "the naval operations between Great Britain and the United States, 1812-1815." This became volume six of William Laird Clowes's authoritative *The Royal Navy* (London, 1901). The later work is briefer than the original and, purged of much of its American bias, secured Roosevelt's place in the ranks of recognized naval historians.

The Naval War of 1812 had four editions by 1889 and was frequently reprinted thereafter. The book largely concerned naval battles. Maps were included to help the reader visualize the tactics employed, and various charts were presented, giving tonnage, armaments, and personnel attached to the ships in action. In these respects it was highly detailed if not greatly technical and a tribute to the author's respect for research. Roosevelt also proposed to use his study for larger purposes. He determined that the major disagreement between the United States and Great Britain was not so much over the neutral rights of ships and cargo as the impressment of American seamen by British captains. This problem led ultimately to the nature of citizenship, the question of *jus soli* or *jus sanguinis.* The rule of citizenship based on the choice of the individual was extremely important to the United States at the time, but it also held extensive implications in an era of increasing migrations from mother countries to colonies that eventually might achieve independence.

As Roosevelt wrote: "The principles for which the United States contended in 1812 are now universally accepted and those so tenaciously maintained by Great Britain find no advocate in the civilized world." In effect, the United States had vindicated an important element of international law by its naval victories.

Equally noteworthy in *The Naval War of 1812* was the germ of the idea that was to be developed by others into the new field of geopolitics, paralleling the increasing concern with the influence of global conditions on national interests. America would have its own great geopolitician in Alfred Thayer Mahan, who would take his place alongside Sir Halford John MacKinder in his time. Years later Kaiser Wilhelm II was as intrigued by Mahan's writings on sea power quite as much as by the heartland thesis. In the preface to the first edition of *The Naval War of 1812,* Roosevelt wrote of the rising awareness of the role of the American navy in world affairs. "At present people are beginning to realize that it is folly for the great English-speaking Republic to rely for defense upon a navy composed partly of antiquated hulks and partly on new vessels rather more worthless than the old. It is worthwhile to study with some care," he went on, "that period of our history during which our navy stood at the highest pitch of its fame; and to learn . . . from the past. . . ." There is a good bit of the spirit of navalism and the Navy League mentality in these thoughts, but his basic proposition was grounded in a substantive, scholarly interest in naval history.

An amplified statement of Roosevelt's navalism was embedded in the reviews he wrote of three of Mahan's books. The first and the most important of these dealt with *The Influence of Sea Power on History* and appeared in the *Atlantic Monthly* in 1890. Roosevelt praised Mahan's recognition of the enduring effects that sea power had had on the development of certain of the great nations of the world, and his understanding "of the deep underlying causes and connections between political events and naval battles." Mahan's consideration of the juxtaposition of land and sea, of the extent and density of populations, and of the character of a people and their government made *The Influence of Sea Power on History* a remarkably timely book. Furthermore, just as Mahan demonstrated from history the dangers of naval improvisation, so Roosevelt voiced his renewed demands for naval preparedness. In his review of Mahan's *The Influence of Sea Power on the French Revolution* (1893), Roosevelt stressed two factors in particular: the ubiquity of the Royal Navy as the soundest explanation of British victory, along with the willingness of the French to be satisfied with privateering. Privateering was simply a variation of improvisation. In 1897, as war seemed more and more likely, Roosevelt used the occasion of his critique of Mahan's *Life of Nelson* to speak out for skill and bravery as essentials to victory in battle. By this time he was the assistant secretary of the navy and these were hawkish words, but TR felt more comfortable in so warlike a pose because he had founded his views on naval history.

An ardent admirer and good friend of Captain Mahan, Roosevelt had an unexampled opportunity to put into practice many of the ideas he shared with Mahan when he was appointed assistant secretary of the navy in 1897. His chief was John Davis Long, a superannuated Massachusetts politician who had been given the Navy Department for services previously rendered the Republican party. Long's age and disposition virtually made TR "lord of the navy," and he was eager to introduce Mahan's thinking into navy tactics and strategy. He rightly judged Secretary Long to be "only lukewarm" about an enlarged navy and sought to enlist Mahan's help to convince the secretary of the "vital need for more battleships now." As assistant secretary he was especially the foe of improvisation. He studied reports from the French, German, and British navies, especially regarding new developments in ships and armaments, determined to improve his grasp of the technical details of his job. At the same time he insisted on viewing the navy as an instrument of a great power. What was needed, therefore, were not merely coastal defenses or torpedo boats, but battleships and lots of them to carry American greatness across the world. Reflecting his review of Mahan's study of Nelson, Roosevelt was prepared to alter one of the sacred traditions of the navy, promotion by strict seniority. Roosevelt argued that men must be promoted to command positions on their record, because they had been brave and skillful, and they had to be young enough to be creative and energetic. Mahan had argued this persuasively and Roosevelt understood him perfectly. TR wrote the Naval Personnel bill of 1898, which the Congress passed and under which there was the strong tendency for the best officers to advance rapidly while the less fit were encouraged to retire after twenty years of service. In numerous ways the navy was stamped with the distinctive brand of Roosevelt and Mahan intertwined. The remarkable consideration was, perhaps, how much Roosevelt did in the year or so he was assistant secretary. He knew what he wanted to do, what he felt had to be done, long before his actual appointment. He learned from a study of books and from discussions with knowledgeable navy people, relating his ideas on the navy to an enlarging historical rationale.

The Naval War of 1812 was a testament to Roosevelt's scholarly if somewhat ingenuous interest in the navy and its place in national history. As keen as this interest was, the fleet remained but a means to an end, which was American greatness. Over the next ten years TR devoted himself to further writings, including books about the wilderness as he encountered it, the frontier, the marvels of nature, and the conquest of the western territories by the American race. In these literary endeavors the West as a part of the ongoing American experience held his attention fast. He was in the process of maturing his views of modern history, and while he was prepared to rely on books to inform his judgments, he insisted that personal experiences, whenever possible, should be some part of the raw material on which he drew for historical understanding.

Once while touring Egypt in 1872, a fourteen-year-old Theodore Roosevelt wrote of standing atop a pyramid:

"To look out on the desert gives one somewhat the same feeling as to look over the North American Prairies." He had, to be sure, not then glimpsed the Great Plains, but his remark does suggest the significance of the West to him. Roosevelt said it best when addressing an audience at Colorado Springs in 1901:

> You and your fathers who built the West did even more than you thought, for you shaped thereby the destiny of the whole republic and as a necessary corollary profoundly influenced the course of events throughout the world.

Roosevelt was to go out to the Dakota country for the first time in 1883, and a romance was born. He bought a ranch, investing a goodly portion of his inheritance in the venture. When his young wife died in February 1884, within hours of his mother's passing, he instinctively sought out his Dakota ranch at Elkhorn for solace and distraction. He divided his time between eastern politics and western ranching down to the winter of 1886-87, when, because of some of the severest weather in memory, fully one-half of his cattle herd was lost. At that point he liquidated his holdings, but not before the West had left an indelible stamp.

Theodore Roosevelt included much of his experience of the West in his natural history trilogy: *Hunting Trips of a Ranchman* (1885), *Ranch Life and the Hunting Trail* (1888), and *The Wilderness Hunter* (1893). The first two of these volumes were written on the Elkhorn ranch. As much as he internalized about the West, Roosevelt, the author, was prepared to fall back on standard authorities to verify or improve his books. At Elkhorn, for example, he had seen fit to supply himself with T. S. Van Dyke's *Still Hunter,* Richard Dodge's *Plains of the Great West,* John Dean Caton's *The Antelope and Deer of America,* and Elliott Coues's *Birds of the Northwest.* Even as an outdoorsman Roosevelt was a scholar. In addition he drew from Burroughs, Parkman, and Thoreau, and especially from the journals of Lewis and Clark, of which he had made a thorough study. As he wrote Brander Matthews in 1888: "Mind you, I'm a literary feller, not a politician nowadays." It must be added that in these literary endeavors are to be found a number of salient general statements that illuminate Roosevelt's theory of history, and especially demonstrate his attraction to many of the tenets of social Darwinism.

The first of these books based on Roosevelt's western days, *Hunting Trips of a Ranchman,* was in the main an account of stalking the buffalo, the black-tailed deer, and the giant grizzly, and in his story of the hunt lies the great charm of the narrative. Yet there is more here than storytelling. For example, in the fate of the plains buffalo is a wider lesson, heavy with Darwinist accents:

> The rapid and complete extermination of the buffalo afforded an excellent instance of how a race that has thriven and multiplied for ages under conditions of life to which it has always fitted itself, by a process of natural selection continued for countless

generations, may succumb at once when these surrounding conditions are varied by the introduction of one or more new elements, immediately becoming the chief forces with which it has to contend in the struggle for life.

Indeed, the history of the West was a history of the change of nature by technology—largely for the good, as Roosevelt judged it. It was the long-range rifle, along with the advance of the cattle industry, that denied the Great Plains to the buffalo and enabled settlers to develop a frontier civilization.

Incidental to all this but especially fascinating to Roosevelt, was the evolution of the wood or mountain buffalo, which acquired habits widely different from those of the plains animal. His observations led him to note that the mountain buffalo had developed a keener sense of smell but had less sharp eyesight, and that the mountain variety grew longer and denser hair on a body that was more thickset. "As a result, a new race has been built up; and we have an animal far better fitted to 'harmonize with the environment.'" Roosevelt concluded that "the formation of the race is due solely to the extremely severe process of natural selection that has been going on among the buffalo herds for the last sixty or seventy years." This kind of personal observation of evolution made a lasting impression.

Roosevelt afforded evolution a wide application that encompassed race relations between the white man and the red man. He believed that a good deal of "sentimental nonsense" had been written about the white man's taking of land from the Indians. Admitting that gross wrongs had been committed due to the brutality of the frontier and not infrequently deception by government agents, he denied that the plains had belonged to the Indians in the first place. "The simple truth is that the Indian never had any real ownership of it at all." Just as no one thought of the white hunters who roamed the wilderness as owning any part of it, so neither should the Indians be deemed proprietors of the lands they moved across. The wars against the Indians had been merciless, but also "just and rational." "It does no good to be merciful to the few at the cost of the many," was the way Roosevelt summed up his attitude regarding the sufferings of the Indians.

In *Ranch Life and the Hunting Trail* the basic evolutionary thesis had a different appeal. Roosevelt treated the frontier as a version or portion of the great American melting pot. Concerning the cowboys he wrote: "It would be impossible to imagine a more typically American assemblage, for although there are always a certain number of foreigners, usually English, Irish or German, yet they have become completely Americanized." These cowboys were the vanguard of a permanent civilization on the plains, inasmuch as their employers, the stockmen, were "the pioneers of civilization and their daring made the after-settlement of the region possible." Both stockmen and cowboys alike were of the self-reliant breed who had proven their superiority over the Indians and the Mexi-

cans. The Stockmen's Association was the seed from which a self-governing West would grow, a process uniting Darwinism and democracy and leading on to progress. Roosevelt found that "the frontiersmen show their natural aptitude for organization . . . lawlessness is put down pretty effectively." For those who cared to read Roosevelt closely it was evident that his concern went beyond claw and fang, and that he discerned in the work of conquest and settlement the true measure of American history.

From a literary standpoint the best of the natural history trilogy is *The Wilderness Hunter*. Roosevelt had greatly matured as a writer, avoiding annoying repetitions and extravagant generalizations from the limited samples of his own experience. He was intent on his storytelling and was ready to share his expanding knowledge of forest and game. But in the preface to *The Wilderness Hunter* he once again attempted to enlarge the meaning of the life of the wilderness hunter:

> In hunting, the finding and killing of the game is after all but part of the whole. The free self-reliant adventurous life, with its rugged and stalwart democracy, the wild surroundings, the grave beauty . . . all of these unite to give the career of the wilderness hunter its peculiar charm. The chase is among the best of all natural pastimes, it cultivates that vigorous manliness for the lack of which, in a nation, as in an individual, the possession of no other qualities can possibly atone.

The hunter was the archetype of freedom and thus the best kind of citizen in Roosevelt's idealized democratic republic.

Francis Parkman, Theodore Roosevelt, and Frederick Jackson Turner—three American historians of the West—were three men tied together by circumstance and substance. It is not inappropriate to bracket Roosevelt with these renowned scholars whose work he much admired, for in *The Winning of the West* he, too, made a lasting contribution to the historical literature of the frontier. Roosevelt's opus—not the magnum opus he dreamed of writing—was first published in four volumes: one and two in 1889, three in 1894, and the final volume in 1896. Altogether Roosevelt carried the story down through the purchase of the Louisiana Territory in 1803. In taking up *The Winning of the West* today, nearly one hundred years from the appearance of the first volume, certain allowances have to be made. There is much (too much for contemporary tastes) of spread-eagle triumphalism both in what Roosevelt wrote and in how he wrote it. Too often he chose to see his function as that of storyteller, neglecting institutions in favor of the lives of the men who conquered the land. The result is a series of vignettes that becomes locked in memory largely because the men described were cast in the mold of heroes. Then, too, Roosevelt's dislike and distrust of Jefferson is troubling, though it may be well to remember that Jefferson's stature has been greatly enhanced by historians and others writing long after Roosevelt registered his opinions.

In his correspondence with Frederick Jackson Turner, in fact, he appeared prepared to soften his strictures. In a review of volume four Turner had scolded him for his harsh evaluation of Jefferson's conduct during the Citizen Genêt affair and pleaded for a more sober judgment. Roosevelt wrote in reply: "I am more and more inclined to think you are quite right as to the inadvisability of my taking the tone I did toward Jefferson. The trouble is," he explained, "that I meet so many understudies of Jefferson in politics and suffer so much from them that I am apt to let my feelings find vent in words." Based on his own admission, the conclusion has to be offered that Roosevelt allowed subjective considerations to bias his historical writings. It was a fair admission, honestly made, but it indicates a serious shortcoming in his work.

The strengths of Roosevelt as historian of the West clearly outweigh the deficiencies. Not only did he make significant use of manuscripts and archival materials, but he did so under conditions not calculated to make his searches routine, as he explained in the preface to volume one of *The Winning of the West*. For the reader's information he listed the sources he had consulted, with a brief description of each. Apart from research in the archives in Washington, carried out between 1889 and 1895 when he was serving as a civil service commissioner—and an active one at that—Roosevelt made visits to Nashville, various locations in Kentucky, and New York to consult sources. Friends and contacts sent him material for use from Canada and from California. Compared with his research for *Thomas Hart Benton* and that done by other historians of the time, Roosevelt's research efforts were quite respectable.

A second aspect of *The Winning of the West,* which grows directly from the wide use of original sources, is the depth of the accounts Roosevelt offered. He brought his readers in close contact with many of the individuals who were in the vanguard of frontier conquest and who otherwise would have gone unnoticed. He was nothing if not thorough, exhausting what sources he had access to. The result is a spirited account, yet one in which the author is willing to linger over detail. Roosevelt demonstrated that he was something other than an amateur historian at a time when historians were just becoming conscious of themselves as professionals. The American Historical Association—Roosevelt would serve as its president in 1912—was organized in 1884, and the enduring work of Turner, Beard, and others lay ahead. Whether Theodore Roosevelt would ever have ranked with the great historians, had he decided to be a writer of history rather than primarily a maker, is debatable. He was not unaware of the deficiencies of *The Winning of the West,* as well as the superficiality of his studies of Benton and Morris. He agreed with Turner on the need to search the Spanish, English and French archives about the treaties of Jay and Pinckney, for example, and had he become a fully professional historian, no doubt he would have worked to overcome his faults.

Beyond the historical apparatus expertly used, Roosevelt's standing as an historian derives from a willingness to offer a conception of history at once seminal and controversial. Let the very first paragraphs of *The Winning of the West* speak for him:

> During the past three centuries the spread of the English-speaking peoples over the world's waste spaces has been not only the most striking feature in the world's history, but also the event of all others most far-reaching in its effects and its importance.
>
> The tongue which Bacon feared to use in his writings, lest they should remain forever unknown to all but the inhabitants of a relatively unimportant insular kingdom, is now the speech of two continents. The Common Law which Coke jealously upheld in the southern half of a single European island, is now the law of the land throughout the vast regions of Australasia, and of America north of the Rio Grande. The names of the plays that Shakespeare wrote are household words in the mouths of mighty nations whose wide domains were to him more unreal than the realm of Prester John. Over half the descendants of their fellow countrymen of that day now dwell in lands which, when these three Englishmen were born, held not a single white inhabitant; the race which, when they were in their prime, was hemmed in between the North and the Irish seas, today holds sway over worlds whose endless coasts are washed by the waves of the three great oceans.

In view of the foregoing passage there can be small doubt of Roosevelt's perspective, his prejudice, and his confidence respecting the English-speaking peoples and their place in modern times.

In *The Winning of the West* Roosevelt was striving for an acceptable historical framework into which he could fit the whole range of history since 1500, and with which the events of American history from the first settlements could be rightly understood. In this he was not following the lead of Turner, but was breaking new ground very much on his own initiative. He dedicated the four volumes to "Francis Parkman To Whom Americans Who Feel Pride In The Pioneer History Of Their Country Are So Greatly Indebted." Thus he stood between Parkman and Turner as historian of the pioneers and the frontier. Perhaps not nearly so good a historian as Parkman, and surely nowhere close to Turner in influence, Roosevelt nonetheless is justly associated with them. His analysis contained adumbrations of the democratic persuasions of the westward movement as it sought to justify the expansion of one people at the cruel cost to another. To Roosevelt the westward tide was irresistible by either Indian or Mexican. As he explained himself to Turner in discussing the Louisiana Purchase: ". . . the very point which Henry Adams failed to make [was] that the diplomatic discussions to which he devoted so much space, though extremely interesting, . . . did not at all determine the fact that the transfer had to be made. It was the growth of the western settlements that determined this fact." What Roosevelt had done was to catch the cadence of western expansion, and he marched across four volumes of the American frontier experience in step with it.

Equally remarkable, Roosevelt's writing during the 1880s and 1890s was done while he continued to be directly or indirectly active in politics. He campaigned for Blaine for the presidency in 1884, stood for mayor of New York City in 1886, served on the Civil Service Commission from 1889 to 1895, and in the latter year began a stint as police commissioner of the City of New York. The quality of his writing may well have suffered by reason of his hectic public pace, but the quantity remains impressive. Though he wrote some quite ordinary books, as a consideration of *Thomas Hart Benton* and *Gouverneur Morris* will show, his need to relate contemporary politics to historical models through the device of books and essays affords compelling evidence of Roosevelt's instinctive reliance on learning.

During these years when Roosevelt was writing at such a furious rate, he was conscious of himself as a literary person. Less deliberately, at least in terms of an overarching philosophy, he was busy formulating a theory of history. The study of history became the intellectual bridge between Roosevelt's life of the mind and his active public career, and a necessary part of it was a study of the work of individuals who had helped create the present. Though attracted to the social Darwinist explanation of change and progress, TR was too much a traditionalist to ignore the feats of heroes. He therefore expected that contemporary public life could not be significantly improved without men of upright character and purpose. In writing *The Winning of the West,* he admitted that he had "always been more interested in the men themselves than in the institutions through and under which they worked." For someone of this disposition, "the great man" theory of history was a sore temptation.

Roosevelt attempted three biographies, lives of Thomas Hart Benton, Gouverneur Morris, and Oliver Cromwell. He appeared convinced that history was more than forces or cycles, and that progress came about because men sought it. Roosevelt believed in man because he believed in men. Of the three biographies, that of Benton was the best. It was, however, hastily written during the spring of 1886 while TR was on his Badlands ranch and deprived of even the most elementary library resources. At one point he wrote his friend, Henry Cabot Lodge, to ask assistance in getting some basic information about Benton's last years so that he might finish the manuscript and send it off to the publisher. What makes *Benton* noteworthy is its view of the senator as a westerner. Benton's efforts to make cheap land available to settlers, his appetite for as much North American territory as might be had to accommodate the expanding American race, and his advocacy of hard money in the style of another westerner, Andrew Jackson, gave Roosevelt ample reason to describe his subject in favorable terms. Furthermore, Benton was a nationalist at a time when

nullifiers and secessionists plied their views. Roosevelt thought such attitudes totally abhorrent and judged Benton to be a better American for having used his position and influence to thwart them.

Despite a prolific pen, writing was not an easy matter for Theodore Roosevelt. "Writing is horribly hard work to me; and I make slow progress," he confessed at the time he was at work on *Benton.* "I have got some good ideas . . . but I am not sure they are worked up rightly; my style is very rough and I do not like a certain lack of sequitur that I do not seem able to get rid of." Evelyn Waugh once described writing as putting words down on the page and pushing them one after the other, and Roosevelt's technique shared something of this mode. What carried him forward, what gave him the push, was his sheer enthusiasm, a habit that made him want to explain and to justify, in the case of a biography, the accomplishments of a historical figure with whom he was in sympathy. Thomas Hart Benton easily qualified in this respect, but Gouverneur Morris was less likable.

Gouverneur Morris was in the nature of an assignment by the editor of the American Statesman series, John T. Morse, Jr. Roosevelt would have preferred to write about Hamilton or, better still, Lincoln, but once he was into Morris he found him a more apt subject for his pen than, for example, John Jay. Roosevelt had something less than total enthusiasm for Morris, a man thoroughly elitist in temperament. One who could refer to the people as "poor reptiles who bask in the sun," and who could predict that "they will bite 'ere noon, depend on it," was out of touch with TR's democratic spirit, however conservative Roosevelt has been judged. Consequently the Morris book was marked by frequent digressions, some of them quite gratuitous. At the start of chapter six, "The Formation of the National Constitution," Roosevelt chided Morris for not foreseeing that even with the loss of the colonies Britain would remain a great power, "that from their loins other nations, broad as continents, were to spring, so that the South Seas should become an English ocean and that over a fourth of the world's surface there should be spoken the tongue of Pitt and Washington." Such commentary might be dismissed as silly except when taken as part of a continued awareness and support of the world movement of the English-speaking peoples, which, to Roosevelt's consternation, was about to be challenged by the Boers in South Africa. Neither the subject nor the author's literary reputation was well served by *Gouverneur Morris*.

The last of the biographical trilogy was *Oliver Cromwell.* It appeared in serial form in *Scribner's* magazine from January to June, 1900, and was published as a book by Scribner's that same year. *Cromwell* was described only half-facetiously by Arthur Hamilton Lee as "a fine, imaginative study of Cromwell's qualifications for the governorship of New York." TR was, of course, serving in that office when the biography came into print. *Oliver Cromwell* is best termed a character study rather than a formal biography. It is not clear why Roosevelt took up

Cromwell, of all possible subjects open to him. If he had discovered many of Cromwell's traits, both his strengths and weaknesses, in himself and felt compelled to write about them through a thinly disguised literary device, the process would be consistent with his preoccupation with history as a way of explaining the contemporary, whether a scene or person. His admiration for the Lord Protector was genuine. He once wrote approvingly of the embattled Boer farmers as "belated Cromwellians," going on to say, however, that it was absolutely essential to the world movement that English be spoken south of the Zambesi.

As for Cromwell, Roosevelt determined that his real historical importance lay in his establishment of political liberty. It was a half-wrought kind of liberty, because in victory Cromwell tied its enjoyment directly to religious tests. But once religious animosity had moderated sufficiently, freedom of conscience was allowed to develop under the law. In the course of his analysis Roosevelt displayed a good comprehension of the Whig version of English history and generally endorsed it, but he was acute enough to reject misinterpretations from the past. A perceptive distinction between Spanish and French Catholicism in the first part of the seventeenth century was one example of his rejection of stereotyping. More than anything else, *Oliver Cromwell* revealed the Roosevelt passion to publish, stemming from his belief that thought must result in action. He viewed scholarship in somewhat the same fashion. Writing in *The Outlook* in 1912 he contended that "scholarship that consists in mere learning but finds no expression in production, may be of interest and value to the individual himself . . . but unless it finds expression in achievement" is sterile. ". . . Scholarship is of worth chiefly when it is productive, when the scholar not merely receives or acquires, but gives." For Roosevelt, thoughts were not fulfilled unless they resulted in a tangible product. Having studied Cromwell he was intent on sharing his knowledge with others.

From 1923 to 1926 the Memorial edition of *The Works of Theodore Roosevelt*, edited by Hermann Hagedorn, was published in twenty-four volumes. Each set in the limited edition was numbered and signed by Edith Kermit Roosevelt. In his preface Hagedorn explained the organization of the numerous writings and observed that his aim had been "to arrange the material in a way that would make it as easy as possible for the reader to find out what Mr. Roosevelt's convictions were on any subjects; or haply just to browse in the green fields of his stimulating discourse." The learned Roosevelt is present in each of these volumes, but perhaps nowhere does he show to better advantage than in volume fourteen, *Literary Essays*. In the preface to that volume Brander Matthews included a short essay, "Theodore Roosevelt as a Man of Letters," replete with comments on the literary Roosevelt. Comparing Roosevelt and Benjamin Franklin, he found they differed in "that Roosevelt was an author by profession and Franklin an author by accident." Matthews held further that Roosevelt "wrote well because he had read widely and deeply—because he had

absorbed good literature for the sheer delight he took in it." He called TR "A normal human being" and candidly pointed out that Roosevelt "liked to celebrate himself and to be his own Boswell." But Matthews also noted that to TR, "life was more important than literature, and what he was forever seeking to put into literature was life itself." *Literary Essays* brings to life an extraordinary mixture in Roosevelt—"distinctly a man of letters as a man of action."

"Social Evolution," an essay suggested by Benjamin Kidd's book of the same title, exhibited an important moderation in Roosevelt's endorsement of evolutionary ideas as applied to society. He objected to any account of society that rested on the single postulate of natural selection because he was bound to reject the materialistic implications deriving from such a position. He also faulted Kidd because nowhere in his work was character granted a function in human affairs. Roosevelt espoused character as essential for the achievement of social progress. Character was "the mother who watches over the sick child; the soldier who dies at his post." Both these models portrayed actions informed by convictions. "We need intellect," Roosevelt wrote, "and there is no reason why we should not have it together with character, but if we must choose between the two, we choose character without a moment's hesitation." As for social evolution, the hypothesis that progress was greatest where competition was keenest was not substantiated by cultural realities. Were this so, he contended, "the European peoples standing highest in the scale would be the south Italians, the Polish Jews, the people who live in the congested districts of Ireland. As a matter of fact, however, these were the people who made the least progress. . . ." The conclusion Roosevelt reached, one he continued to advance in essays and speeches throughout his lifetime, was that man's spirit, and in a sense, therefore, man's moral self, was the central consideration in accounting for social improvement.

Theodore Roosevelt's appreciation of literature of the more conventional sort is illustrated in three selected essays, **"The Children of the Night," "The Ancient Irish Sagas,"** and **"Dante and the Bowery."** It is well known that when Theodore Roosevelt, Jr., on a White House visit from Harvard in 1905, showed his father Edwin Arlington Robinson's verse, the president was captivated. He asked his son to find out what he could about Robinson. Eventually the poet was invited to the White House for dinner, a sure sign of presidential approval. Roosevelt procured a sinecure for Robinson at the New York Customs House, since Robinson was virtually destitute when "discovered" by the Roosevelts. Feeling strongly that Robinson's work "should have attracted more attention," TR wrote to that effect in his essay that reviewed *The Children of the Night*, appearing in the *Outlook* in 1905. He found in the poems "an undoubted touch of genius . . . a curious simplicity and good faith. There is in them just a little of the light that never was on land or sea . . . it is not always necessary in order to enjoy a poem that one should be able to translate it into terms of mathematical accuracy. Those who admire the coloring of Turner . . . do not wish always to have ideas presented to them with cold, hard, definite outlines. . . ." Roosevelt said of the poem, "Luke Havergal," for example, that "I am not sure I understand the poem; but I am entirely sure that I like it." And what of "Richard Cory," which has found its way unerringly into so many school anthologies? For Roosevelt the poem spoke "a very ancient but very profound philosophy of life with a curiously local touch which points its keen insight." Roosevelt, the optimist, seems to have understood the man who went and put a bullet in his head. Commenting on another poem, "The Tavern," the president as critic again revealed his poetic inner self. In "The Tavern," he noted, Robinson "writes of what most of us feel we have seen; and then again of what we have only seen with the soul's eyes." No doubt Roosevelt felt a special kinship with the man who could write "The Wilderness," which told of nature as TR knew and loved it. The author of *The Wilderness Hunter* identified with the poet's words: "And the lonely trees around us creak the warning of the night wind . . . / The winds that blow the message they have blown ten thousand years." The President's terse, last comment, "this little volume, not verse but poetry," summed up his admiration for Robinson.

"The Ancient Irish Sagas" showed Roosevelt's fascination with the old Celtic text whose stories were just then being paraphrased in popular form by Lady Gregory and others. Just as he was later to praise the Abbey Theatre as "an extraordinary contribution to the sum of Irish literary and artistic achievement," he praised the sagas as the corresponding Celtic contribution to the corpus of ancient literature that the Germans, the French, and the English had helped to develop long ago. The contemporary Irish revival, in other words, owed a great deal to the new emphasis on the Cuchulain cycle and the Ossianic cycle. Such tales have much to tell the historian, thought Roosevelt, since they tend to portray life as it was lived in Erin in far-distant times. The greatness of these epics fell short of those of other peoples only because of the calamities and tragedies that befell Ireland. Roosevelt believed the Irish sagas truly remarkable in their treatment of women. Whereas women played no part at all in the "Song of Roland," and they were "alternately splendid and terrible" in the Norse and German stories, "it would be hard indeed to find among them a heroine who would appeal to our modern ideas as does Emer, the beloved of Cuchulain, or Deirdre, the sweetheart of the fated son of Usnach." In his rendering of the story line of the Cuchulain cycle Roosevelt consistently demonstrated his poetic sense, striving to catch in plain prose the spirit of the epic itself. For him the sagas possessed "extraordinary variety and beauty, in their exaltation of the glorious courage of men and of the charm and devotion of women, they contained a curious attraction of their own." Like the Irish players of the Abbey Theatre who sprang from the soil and dealt with things Irish, so the ancient sagas spoke of an authentic if irrecoverable Erin that was a meaningful but unappreciated part of Western civilization.

No less typical of Roosevelt, the man of letters, was his concern for poetry that made honest and imaginative use of the language of the marketplace, "today's market place—the Fulton Market" of New York, for example, and not the marketplace of Florence in the thirteenth century. This was the theme of **"Dante and the Bowery."** What infinite use Dante would have made of the Bowery!" he enthused. As he went on to explain, the nineteenth century was more apt than the thirteenth to boast of itself as being "the greatest of centuries," but except for its technology "it did not wholly believe in its boasting." Thus a nineteenth-century poet, striving to make a point, was likely to draw material from ancient or medieval times rather than his own. In America, only Walt Whitman dared to use anything like the Bowery, that is, "what was striking and vividly typical of the humanity around him." And even he, Roosevelt remarked, "was not quite natural in doing so, for he always felt he was defying the conventions and prejudices of his neighbors." The difference between Dante and Whitman was not so much between the artists themselves as their respective times. The conventions of Dante's century did not forbid him to use human nature just as he encountered it. Why not explore human nature by examples drawn from the Brooklyn Navy Yard as well as Piraeus, from Tammany no less than the Roman mob? TR urged. Dante had unhesitatingly used his contemporaries, or his immediate predecessors, alongside the great names passed on to him from antiquity, because the passions of men are the same in all ages, godlike or demoniac. Dante was "quite simply a realist," displaying the sort of realism that Roosevelt judged to be missing in all too much of the poetry of his day. "We do not express ourselves nowadays in epics at all," he lamented; "we keep the emotions aroused in us by what is good or evil in the men of the present in a totally different compartment from that which holds our emotions concerning what was good or evil in the men of the past." The ex-president was not so sure that given the peculiar character of his times it could have been otherwise. "One age expresses itself naturally in a form that would be unnatural and therefore undesirable, in another age," he admitted. Nevertheless, he wanted the contemporary artist to see, as had Dante, the "eternal qualities" in the people around us, remarking that Dante himself would have preferred it so.

Another of Roosevelt's literary essays was in the form of a review of *The Law of Civilization and Decay* by his good friend, Brooks Adams. Of the Adams thesis it may be enough to say that it held out the prospects of the decline of Western civilization because the imaginative, artistic, and warrior classes were being preempted by the economic man—of industry, capital, and trade. TR wanted instinctively to reject the thesis outright since it ran counter to his belief in progress. In fact, he granted Adams some occasional points but found the tone of the argument in favor of decay intolerable. A more telling indicator of Roosevelt's erudition may be the numerous historical and literary references that he made good use of in developing his position vis-à-vis Adams. These included the Crusades, the British conquest of India, the house of Rothschild, the Knights Templar, the fall of Constantinople, the blind Doge Dandolo, Macaulay, Thucydides, Alexander the Great, Henry VIII, the historians Froude and Henry C. Lea, the "pope Hildebrand," Emperor Henry IV, Philip Augustus, Philip the Fair, Froissart, Malthus, Erasmus, jacqueries, Timothy Pickering, Henry Adams, Louis XV, Louis Philippe, Marlborough, Wellington, Nelson, Grant, Lee, Henry George, and Edward Bellamy. It must be added quickly that this was not unusual. Roosevelt moved as easily from one century to another as from one culture to another; he approached millennia as readily as epochs. He wrote in such fashion not for the sake of display but because his wide reading encouraged him to express himself in such terms.

In Roosevelt the learned man overmastered the man of action frequently and with lasting effect. His presidency offered substantial evidence of this; learning was an operative factor once TR assumed office in September 1901. Viewed from this novel perspective an understanding of the Roosevelt presidency will not be altered in its broader outline. What is likely, however, is an enhanced appreciation of that presidency made possible by a fresh awareness of certain of his policies insofar as they were affected by his learning. With Roosevelt there was no touch of self-consciousness in mixing love of literature with love of political power. He was convinced that his understanding of society was enhanced by an understanding of the literature that society produced, that he was a better leader because he was better read.

Books aside, Theodore Roosevelt was well qualified for the presidency when he succeeded McKinley. In and out of politics for twenty years, he had been a state legislator, civil service and police commissioner, sub-cabinet officer, and one-term governor of what was the largest state in the nation, New York. "The Albany Apprenticeship," as it has been termed, was the most valuable part of his political education. Since it had come just before his election to the vice-presidency, he retained a feel for high-level administration. Roosevelt's military service in the Spanish-American War—he resigned as assistant naval secretary almost as soon as war was declared—earned him experience of a different kind that no doubt influenced his decisions as commander in chief. Characteristically, he wrote a book about his adventures, *The Rough Riders* (1899), another witness to his need to explain himself in a literary fashion. Roosevelt was at least as much a soldier as Andrew Jackson, but fell below the standards of Washington, Taylor, Grant, and, at a later time, Eisenhower. At heart TR was an amateur soldier; once the fighting was finished he was eager to return to politics, his natural milieu. Wooed in New York by reformers and the Republican machine alike to run for the governorship, he decided on machine support, convinced that he could be effective as a chief executive only with machine cooperation in the promotion of reform. Roosevelt and Thomas Collier Platt, the "easy boss" of the New York Republican organization, were almost completely opposite political types, yet there came to be an unlikely cordiality between the moral governor and the machine politico. Roosevelt was sufficiently successful as a reformer for Platt to want to move him out of Albany after a single term. Kicked upstairs to the vice-presidency in 1900, he turned out to be a darling of destiny. Assassination was a monstrous thing to Roosevelt, who once declared that the assassin stood on the pinnacle of evil fame, but he refused to be morbid about the circumstances of his elevation to the ultimate office. "Here is the task, and I have got to do it to the best of my ability; that is all there is about it," he confided to Henry Cabot Lodge within a week of his swearing-in. Despite his age, and possibly because of it, Roosevelt was confident of himself in body, mind, and spirit.

Progressivism at home and imperialism abroad made up the twin theme of American politics during Theodore Roosevelt's presidency. In his approach to and handling of specifics relating to these large matters, the impact of learning was discernible, but in different ways. In domestic affairs the influence was exerted more subtly, more as a presupposition of many of his undertakings. In foreign affairs, by contrast, the authority of learning was at once apparent. Reasons for this distinction are embedded in the intellectual tendencies of the late nineteenth century. Evolution and social Darwinism were very much in vogue, and for America the application of their principles to imperialist expansion was so pervasive it was almost involuntary. Yet on the political home front the philosophy of laissez-faire, reinforced by the same cult of competition, was being challenged outright by new attitudes looking toward reform and derived from a combination of traditional human values and practical measures. Many such measures could be tentatively identified with pragmatism. While it might be premature to describe any but a very few of Roosevelt's policies as consciously pragmatic before 1910, it remains useful to think of his practical measures as a reformer as influenced by a sense of pragmatism.

The best place to look for the force of learning in Roosevelt's domestic policies is in his assessment of character in the individual and thus in the race, a position easily discernible in his writings. In terms of American politics Roosevelt viewed character as the central element in reforming society. "No man can lead a public career really worth leading," he was to write later in his *Autobiography,* "no man can act with rugged independence in a serious crisis, nor strike out at great abuses, nor afford to make powerful foes, if he himself is vulnerable in his private character." This avowal of character meant that he was as sensitive as any behaviorist to the ills of American society and, as a result, was caught up in the Progressive movement. Though he might differ with many Progressives as to ultimate causes, one and all were disturbed by the same evils and frequently sought to overcome them by common methods, so that a distinction between them and the president (or ex-president) is not always understood. Indeed, it appears likely that, lacking Progressive support, Roosevelt could not have accomplished very much as a reform president. He managed at the same time to impart a strong, and popular, flavor of traditional morality to the general conception of what Progressivism stood for. The Progressive movement, despite its more radical possibilities, was to many very much in keeping with the old ways of thought in which nothing was more elemental than individual honesty and initiative. Roosevelt's understanding of the importance of the individual was a recurring aspect of his histories and his biographies, and received added emphasis in his biographical sketches of those he called "Men of Action."

The president put the case squarely in an article in the *Outlook,* written as he was about to leave the White House in 1909. "A nation must be judged in part by the character of its public men, not merely by their ability but by their ideals. . . ." In the series of character profiles, written over a period of years, he singled out Washington and Lincoln as the great American public men; he described them as "of the type of Timoleon and Hampden." Dealing with men of yesterday such as John Marshall and Andrew Jackson, he stressed qualities that he deemed made them great. Marshall "was in the best sense . . . a self-made man," "a hardworking Virginian who relied on his own reasoning," "entirely democratic . . . simple, straight forward and unaffected." Not all historians might agree with Roosevelt's evaluation of Marshall, but none would deny him the strong and determined nationalistic spirit that TR thought so praiseworthy. Jackson, in turn, "belonged to a stern and virile race, the Presbyterian Irish." He combined "physical prowess" with "the resolute determination to uphold the cause of order." Roosevelt judged that Jackson, as president, had done "much good and much evil." He strongly censured the introduction of the spoils system and believed Jackson's bank policy replaced a less-than-perfect system with an infinitely worse one, the wildcat state banks. What redeemed Jackson was that he "was emphatically a true American." In these accounts Roosevelt allowed himself heroes, but he was not uncritical of those he admired.

Lincoln was the great figure from the American past, Lincoln "the practical idealist." While in the midst of his presidency, Roosevelt wrote the preface to the Connoisseur's Federal edition of the writings of Lincoln, dated "Sagamore Hill, Sept. 22, 1905." In it he quoted from Lecky's fifth volume of *History of England.* Lecky contended that successful statesmen need not have the moral qualities of a hero or a saint; more worldly virtues would do: tact, knowledge of men, resolution, and the ability to meet emergencies. Lincoln, in Roosevelt's reading of history, exhibited the two sets of virtues that Lecky had represented as antithetical. For him Lincoln was "the wise and cautious radical," with TR again reflecting his own aspirations as a public figure through literary expression.

Roosevelt wrote of his admiration for a great many among his contemporaries, including John Hay, Leonard Wood, Booker T. Washington, Augustus Saint-Gaudens, John Muir, and Frederick Courtney Selous. What he ob-

served of these men provides a deeper awareness of traits he admired that, in general, were needed for a healthy society, or as Roosevelt would have insisted, "a strong nation." John Hay's blend of a "marked literary ability" with public service delighted him. He identified Leonard Wood with "boundless energy and endurance," while his conduct of colonial governance was untainted by "selfish interests, whether political or commercial." Roosevelt quoted Scripture in a tribute to Booker T. Washington: "What more doth the Lord require of these than to do justice and love mercy and walk humbly with thy God? He did justice to every man. He did justice to those to whom it was a hard thing to do justice," according to Roosevelt, who valued Washington's "friendship and respect . . . a patriot and an American." Admiration was not confined to public men of action, however. Praising the sculptor, Augustus Saint-Gaudens, he lauded his design of United States coins as both artistic and historically meaningful. The "pure imagination" of the piece of sculpture, "Silence," done for the Adams gravesite, greatly moved the President. Linked with Saint-Gaudens was John Muir, the naturalist, whom TR credited with preserving beauty of a different kind, "those great natural phenomena: wonderful canyons, giant trees, slopes of flower-spangled hillsides." And he saluted the big-game hunter, Frederick Courtney Selous, "a highly intelligent, civilized man," but "hard-bit who pushed ever northward the frontier of civilization" in Africa. The character of people with whom he found himself involved in his conduct of affairs while president had a considerable effect on Roosevelt. He was comfortable and cooperated with the honorable man, but was easily put off by one whose behavior he thought was wrong, as his handling of the anthracite coal strike of 1902 bears out.

The anthracite strike, a major test of the new president's leadership, was governed in its outcome by three personalities: Roosevelt himself, who acted as a facilitator pushing hard for a peaceful resolution of the impasse between the miners and the coal operators; John Mitchell, the chief of the coal miners' union; and George F. Baer, president of the Philadelphia and Reading Coal and Iron Company, the spokesman for the owners. Roosevelt's observation of the two antagonists in the fight helped to persuade him of the path he ought to take, that of neutrality but with his sympathies for the workers only thinly disguised, as well as the path he ought to avoid, that taken by President Cleveland in the Pullman strike of 1894 in using federal troops to break the strike. TR gained a healthy respect for Mitchell because of his dignified manner and never forgot the arrogance of Baer as an example of the worst of laissez-faire capitalism.

The issues in the strike centered around a worker demand for a 10 percent wage raise, improved working conditions, including reduced hours per shift, and recognition of the United Mine Workers as a bargaining agent for the workers. Some one hundred and forty thousand hard-coal miners were off the job from May until October, a time of year when consumption of coal was off peak. In the absence of public inconvenience, much less suffering, the strikers won considerable public support. In essence, what the workers wanted was to sit down and talk with the operators and thereby come to an agreement. In such a process there could be give and take, and recognition of the union would come about. The owners showed themselves intransigently opposed to discussion, with Baer uttering some of the most extreme statements ever made publicly in labor-management confrontation. He announced when talks were first proposed that anthracite mining was a business, not a religious, sentimental, or academic proposition. Some weeks later he was prompted to deliver his now infamous confession of faith: "The rights and interests of the laboring man will be protected and cared for—not by labor agitators, but by the Christian men to whom God in his infinite wisdom has given the control of the property interests of this country." Baer's attitude was to take its toll on events. Mitchell, in contrast, was totally reasonable. He long had taken the position that the strike could have been avoided if a conference of the two sides had been convened, and it could be ended if such a conference were held at once. Baer's towering self-righteousness was set off sharply by Mitchell's moderation.

Over the summer months of 1902, though the president kept an eye on the situation, there was little sense of urgency. This mood was certain to change as coal inventories fell and cold weather loomed just ahead. Ordinarily priced at $2.40 a ton, coal had gone to $6.00 a ton and predictions were that it might reach $30.00 with little to be had unless the miners were soon digging coal. Roosevelt saw the unhappy prospects for what they were. The difficulty was that under the Constitution he was powerless to act to benefit the community at large. At one point he complained of being at his wit's end over how to proceed. Undeterred by constitutional incapacity to act, he continued to explore possible options and to worry about the outcome. Most importantly, he never stopped discussing the crisis with those he trusted: Elihu Root, Murray Crane, Philander Knox, and Cabot Lodge. With his persistent sense of history he informed Crane, the governor of Massachusetts, "I felt that the crisis was not one in which I could act on the Buchanan principle of striving to find some Constitutional means for inaction. . . ." Roosevelt, being Roosevelt, wanted to do something.

In early October the president played his trump card, calling a conference of representatives of the operators and the miners to meet with him and his attorney-general, Knox, in Washington. Both Baer and Mitchell attended. Though the meeting failed to resolve the crisis, it succeeded in convincing Roosevelt that George F. Baer was a reprobate and John Mitchell an honorable man. In the course of the October conference Mitchell once more iterated the position of the workers: a series of talks between miners and owners whereby a compromise might be secured. Failing that, the union was willing to accept a presidentially appointed arbitration commission and to abide by its decision. Baer would have no part of such an arrangement. He accused Mitchell of fomenting anarchy and violence and defiance of the law, and went to the

length of berating Roosevelt for the very idea of having Mitchell in the same room as the president and himself. Roosevelt's sympathies were readily enlisted on the side of Mitchell and thus on that of the workers, though he was quick to assure J. P. Morgan that he would not allow himself to be swayed by such considerations. Of course Roosevelt was swayed by the behavior he had witnessed. Mitchell was a gentleman, Baer was not. These things mattered to TR, however much he might disavow their influence.

Meanwhile, the war of nerves continued. Roosevelt dispatched Elihu Root to New York for talks with Morgan about a renewed proposal for a presidential conference. He named General Schofield as the army officer who would be in charge of maintaining law and order in the coal fields, should the government have to seize the mines. He welcomed the offer of ex-President Grover Cleveland to have a part in any scheme of arbitration. All this amounted to the kind of pressure Baer could not resist indefinitely. Finally, on 11 October, agreement was reached on arbitration. The following March the commission voted a 10 percent wage raise for the miners along with some reduction in hours. While the union did not win formal recognition as a bargaining agent, the newly formed National Board of Conciliation was to have union representation. An important corner had been turned in the union's fight for legitimacy.

Historians have agreed that Roosevelt acted out of mixed motives in his handling of the anthracite strike: fear of social upheaval, Republican party political advantage, and a desire to be in the eye of the storm. But in no small measure the type of men who were party to the dispute helped to shape his judgments and, accordingly, to direct his actions. It seems altogether unlikely that, if Mitchell had been as arrogant and uncooperative as Baer, the president would have wanted to facilitate the kind of settlement that was reached. Mitchell's character made it easy for Roosevelt to blend the public welfare with the good of the workers to the advantage of his reputation as a "square deal" president. Roosevelt's long-harbored suspicions of the economic man were confirmed by the callous disregard for humanity that Baer personified. It was difficult, for the president, or for any third party, not to side against a man who, when reminded of the sufferings of the miners, retorted that the miners were not suffering, adding, "why, they don't even speak English."

Few remarks could have more offended Roosevelt's belief in the melting-pot thesis. In dealing with Baer, therefore, TR discovered not only an enemy of the miners, but an enemy of his vision of an America that took the various peoples who came to its shores and molded them into a single race. Once when writing about "true Americanism," he reviewed the history of immigration and settlement in America, a study that showed that to the successive waves of immigrant groups, America was "a matter of spirit, conviction, and purpose, not of creed or birthplace or language." The history of "the ancient republics of Greece, the medieval republics of Italy, and the petty

German states of the last century" showed what particularism could do. The contrast between these historical examples and events in the United States meant that America would not be allowed to succumb to this local or regional sentiment that centered in race or language. The ghetto mentality had no place in America as the strange peoples were gradually assimilated.

The *Northern Securities* case (1904), which was another presidential triumph in the name of progressivism, involved a play of personalities as had the coal strike, but with a difference. In the coal dispute Roosevelt was a third party, whereas in the litigation involving the giant railroad combination engineered by Morgan, E. H. Harriman, and James J. Hill, the president was an antagonist. In the eyes of the business world TR was both antagonist and troublemaker. Business had long enjoyed virtual freedom from governmental regulation. As competition gave way to consolidation, monopoly conditions were achieved by the giant trusts. As early as 1902 Roosevelt had ordered his attorney general to institute proceedings against the Northern Securities Company, which had managed to clamp a stranglehold on all freight traffic out of Chicago to the upper West. Such a railroad combination was an ideal target for Roosevelt's ambition to show himself an enemy of the malefactors of great wealth and a friend of the people. After all, the combination included some of the biggest names in the corporate and financial world: Morgan, Harriman, Hill with Kuhn, and Loeb and Company thrown in for added measure. No sooner had Philander Knox instituted the legal proceedings than Morgan paid a visit to Roosevelt in Washington and made his bid to put TR in his pocket. "If we had done anything wrong," he advised the president, "send your man to my man and they can fix it up." To Morgan, life was that simple.

Roosevelt was not above a little "fixing" of his own and in a way that was to bear on the *Northern Securities* case. In 1902 with the death of Justice Horace Gray, the president named Oliver Wendell Holmes, Jr., to the United States Supreme Court. TR sized up Holmes as a good Republican, the son of a worthy father with a gallant Civil War record, and a man with twenty years of valuable experience on the Supreme Judicial Court of Massachusetts, where he had established his reputation as a liberal and reform-minded judge. Looking ahead to the time when reform laws would be put to the judicial test at the national level, Roosevelt was convinced Holmes was the right man for the job. The Holmes appointment revealed both the president's belief in the centrality of individuals in the working out of complex problems and a great faith in the power of men to control events. To him, the issue in the *Northern Securities* case was clearcut: business had to be made responsible to the will of the people through the agency of government. From what he knew of the man, he thought Holmes would see the matter as he did.

The decision was handed down in 1904. The effort to apply the Sherman Anti-Trust Act to the railroad combination was upheld by a five to four vote. To Roosevelt's surprise and annoyance, Holmes had voted against the regulation of railroads and for big business. More importantly, the rather unpromising Sherman act had been used to curb railroad monopoly in the public interest. The decision marked a notable advance in the war on the trusts, and other successful suits followed soon thereafter. Looking back on the outcome, Roosevelt chose to remember the case in terms of the men who had been involved. He complained that he could have carved from a banana a judge with more backbone than Holmes had displayed. Writing to Owen Wister, he put his finger on the main issue, singling out James J. Hill, probably because of the latter's outspoken criticism of the decision: "Mr. Hill was doing what I thought wrong in the Northern Securities case," he told his friend. Roosevelt had met numerous wrong-headed men in life and in literature. Hill was a familiar type. TR also believed firmly that he knew what was right and what was wrong, and that there could be no difference between private and public ethical standards in the conduct of business. The railroad trust had been judged in technical violation of a law, but in Roosevelt's interior judgment the crux of the matter was that the railroad men had done wrong.

"Of all Roosevelt's constructive endeavors, the movement for conservation was most marked by sustained intellectual effort and administrative force." This is the estimate of William H. Harbaugh, who has written further that in no other public enterprise "did the President blend science and morality quite so effectively." The tribute, which sums up the thinking of contemporaries and historians alike, is well deserved. Had TR been born a century or more earlier, he might well have had an important place in the conquest of great continent. As it was, it fell to him to describe that conquest as a historian, and, as a public official, to preserve as much of the continent and its resources as possible "for generations yet unborn." The historical, the literary, and the public Roosevelt were again forged as one.

The fight for conservation turned out to be a difficult one, in the process of which TR learned anew the meaning of "special interest" and congressional stonewalling, as well as the high price often extracted of a man of principle. In the effort to make conservation an enduring national commitment and not simply a passing policy of his administration, Roosevelt put the issue above partisanship; as a good Republican, he did not find that easy. No doubt the final outcome was favorably influenced by the man Roosevelt worked with in the conservation fight, Gifford Pinchot, a man with the qualities he admired in his father and in his historical heroes. Pinchot was the knight-errant in Roosevelt's quest for the holy grail of conservation. Wealthy, well connected, and well educated at Yale and at the School of Forestry in Nantes, France, he was a man of action who himself guided his official behavior by the learning he had acquired through study and experience.

Pinchot was an easterner, as was Roosevelt, of course, determined to save the westerners from the effects of their continued reckless use of natural resources. Ironically, the Roosevelt-Pinchot conservation program alienated westerners, including many of the plain folk as well as the giant timber and mineral tycoons. To westerners of all ranks, government regulation was seen as interference with economic freedom. The president understood this attitude perfectly, while not agreeing with it. As he told one meeting of the Forest Congress in Washington in 1905: "In the old pioneer days the American had but one thought about a tree and that was to cut it down; and the mental attitude of the nation toward forests was largely conditioned on that." But as a learned Roosevelt had discerned long ago, the freewheeling West was a phase in the evolutionary process. As the West matured and grew more complex it had to be regulated for the welfare of the people there and for the nation of which the West was an organic part. Roosevelt was prepared to follow the lead of forest technology, which was learning of a specialized kind. The scientists had the practical knowledge and the president sought to work through them to save the natural resources of America. At the same time he insisted that his own insights about the West, his careful study of its ways, and his experience as a ranchman gave him a special warrant to speak out.

Throughout his presidency Theodore Roosevelt pushed hard for conservation reforms by means of laws, executive decrees, and state cooperation. He supported the Newlands bill aimed at the construction of irrigation and reclamation projects as early as December 1901. His attitude was distinctly nonpartisan. Roosevelt set aside national forest reserves, on one memorable occasion just a step ahead of a congressional effort to tie his hands, adding millions of acres to this natural treasure. He supported tree-planting experiments on federal lands, became an advocate of selective cutting, acted to support flood-control works, and called for and got legislation that reorganized the federal bureaucracy responsible for supervising the conservation program. This latter reform was one Roosevelt identified with especially. He spoke of the need for a corps of professional foresters—"a new profession, a profession of the highest usefulness; a profession as high as the profession of law, as the profession of medicine, as any other profession most ultimately connected with the highest and finest development of a nation"—to the Society of American Foresters in 1903. Whatever the reform, it devolved upon individuals of character, of knowledge, and of energy to frame the laws and make them effective. Under Pinchot's firm guidance the forestry service became an outstanding component of the civil service. What the president had expressed as hopes for the conservation of American natural resources were well on the way to fulfillment by the time he left office.

Looking back over the various administration-led attempts to regulate private economic interests for the social good, Roosevelt is often heard invoking what he called "the Puritan spirit." He recalled on one occasion that the Puritans were people who possessed a to remarkable degree the power of individual initiative and self-

help. Combined with these traits was practical common sense that taught them the wisdom of joining with others when it was necessary to get a job done. "The spirit of the Puritan . . . never shrank from the regulation of conduct if such regulation was necessary to the public weal." Roosevelt urged this spirit on the nation in his day. "The American people became firmly convinced of the need of control of the great aggregations of capital," he said, "especially when they had monopolistic tendencies." Using the Puritan past as a touchstone, the president argued that as the Puritans had found a certain degree of regulation appropriate to the requirements of the seventeenth century, so regulation, different but generically the same, was essential to effective government in the twentieth century. Roosevelt claimed that in this spirit of just regulation "we have shown there is no individual and no corporation so powerful that he or it stands above the possibility of punishment under the law." Underlying the justice of regulation was the Puritan spirit of order and discipline. This use of the Puritan experience looks like a straining on Roosevelt's part to thread the historical needle, a demonstration that he could stray beyond limitations imposed by lessons drawn from the past.

"I am, as I expected I would be, a pretty good imperialist." Roosevelt pronounced this verdict on himself to his English friend from Spanish-American War days, Arthur Hamilton Lee, while touring Africa in 1910. What were the sources of that imperialism of which he spoke so confidently? They ranged from some primordial urge to conquer coming from deep within him, through a belief in the superiority of America as the highest expression of contemporary Western civilization, to a commitment to improve the lot of mankind generally by playing both master and servant to "the lesser breeds without the law." It was strongly Kiplingesque: brutal, self-serving, self-sacrificing, uplifting, and romantic. That it was also intellectual was made evident through two distinct but intersecting principles. The more basic one was evolution; its derivative, the authority of Anglo-Americans as the most advanced race, was evidenced by their achievements. From time to time Roosevelt called upon these principles to explain and justify the sweep of modern history and to account for particular actions taken during his presidency, actions for which he was ultimately responsible and that identify him with imperialism.

Greatly taken with the leading scientific proposition of his era, the process of natural selection, or what he once called "the line of descent from protozoan to Plato," Roosevelt made a careful study of both evolution and its outgrowth, social Darwinism. Darwin and Huxley had "succeeded in effecting a complete revolution in the thought of an age," so that "the acceptance of the fundamental truth of evolution is quite as necessary to sound thinking as the acceptance of the fundamental truths of the solar system." Yet he inclined to set Darwin and his work in perspective. Writing to Oliver Wendell Holmes, Jr., in 1904, he allowed that Darwin was "the chief factor in working a tremendous revolution," going on to express the opinion that in the future Darwin would be read "just as we read Lucretius now; that is, because of the interest attaching to his position in history." Early results of his study of evolution, as already shown by his opinion of Kidd's *Social Evolution,* strictly qualified the function of natural selection by insisting on the function of character. He later expressed mature judgments along these lines in **"Biological Analogies in History."** Accordingly, Roosevelt put great reliance on the achievements of the Anglo-Americans that exemplified the place of character. Of these none stood higher than the establishment of self-governing communities at home and the lessons of self-rule that they offered to colonial peoples. Successful self-government by a community was the equivalent of character in the individual. It required the adapting of a political system to changing circumstances while keeping intact the eternal principles of justice and truth. Imperialism called not for the exportation of the American system of government, but the American spirit of government. Just as "it was Roman influence on language, law, literature, the governmental system, the whole way of looking at life" that had given Rome its historical significance, so the contributions of the American people would be judged. The frontiersmen had swept across a vast continent, carrying their ideals and building up a superior nation. The superiority thereby demonstrated justified a continuing westward movement across the Pacific as well as American domination of the Caribbean. Weaker peoples, the Filipinos in particular, were to be servant and served alike. Destiny and responsibility met in imperialism no less in the twentieth century than two thousand years before.

Roosevelt inherited an imperialistic state of affairs when he took office in 1901. His mind-set was one that approved, in general terms at least, the policies that had brought about American presence in the Pacific and ascendancy in the Caribbean. The particulars of the situation, and therefore what he was bound to deal with once he was president, were, however, the result of the McKinley way of doing things. In the Philippines the nationalist insurrection under Aguinaldo had been put down by early 1901, so that as a new president, Roosevelt was not beset by the problems arising from a vicious guerilla war. He had enthusiastically approved the use of force against the native nationalists, likening Aguinaldo to Sitting Bull, but he sincerely rejoiced that such difficult times had passed. As he had looked forward to the end of the conflict as vice-president, he had told William Howard Taft, who was serving as governor general of the Philippines, that "the military arm should literally be an arm directed by a civil head." Believing fully in civilian control of the military establishment, he was from the start of his time in office prepared to give to Taft, and to William H. Hunt in Puerto Rico, "the largest liberty of action possible and the heartiest support," knowing that Taft and Hunt were themselves committed to civilian supremacy in the Anglo-American tradition.

The attainment by the Filipino people of self-rule was one of the objectives of Roosevelt's policy toward the Islands. But he was equally convinced that it had to be a gradual process if it were to be a permanent achievement. "It is not a light task for a nation to achieve the temperamental qualities without which the institutions of free government are but an empty mockery. . . ." "Our people," he went on to underscore in his first annual message to Congress, "are now governing themselves because for more than a thousand years they have been slowly fitting themselves, sometimes consciously, sometimes unconsciously. What has taken thirty generations to achieve we can not expect to see another race accomplish out of hand." Having urged caution both on Congress and the Filipino people, the president nonetheless declared: "We hope to do for them what has never been done for any people of the tropics—to make them fit for self-government after the fashion of the really free nations." Meanwhile American occupation of the Islands was imperative, an occupation depending directly on the American army, the same force that had denied the Filipinos their independence.

Buried in the rhetoric and the reality of American control was the inherent contradiction in the proposal of any imperialistic power to make the conquered fit for self-rule. The more pronounced the success of preparation for independence, the less justification there was for continued occupation by the colonial power. Irrespective of how cordial relations between colonial power and colonial people might have been, the contradiction became the controlling factor. It was a contradiction that Roosevelt could not escape and was prepared to face.

The president insisted that his administration was encouraging in every way the growth of those conditions that made for self-government, but the Congress appeared to want to move faster in the matter than Roosevelt. The Cooper Act, which the President signed into law in July 1902, made the Islands an unincorporated territory and declared that all citizens of the Philippines should enjoy the protection of the United States. The law also provided for the safeguarding of individual rights and specified a census, to be taken in preparation for the election of a lower house of a Philippine legislature. The Cooper Act further called for a strong, independent judiciary with the right of appeal to the United States Supreme Court when the Constitution or any treaty was involved in a dispute. The census was completed in 1905, the elections took place in July 1907, and in October of that year the first Filipino Assembly came together.

With his pronounced Anglo-American affinity, Roosevelt was inclined to compare American imperialism with its British counterpart, judging the former to be superior. "We have done more for the Philippines than the English have done in Egypt," he wrote Lodge in April 1906, and "our problems . . . were infinitely more complex." He noted further that while the British appeared to be exploiting the Malay Settlements, the cardinal doctrine of American rule in the Philippines was to avoid all forms of such behavior. As far as Roosevelt was concerned, Leonard Wood in Moro country had a more difficult job than his counterparts in Malaya and he had done his job better. In the same vein he told Lodge that the "performance of Taft, like the aggregate performances of Wood, surpasses the performance of Lord Cromer" in Egypt. Whether boasting or representing the facts, such estimates sharpened the contradictions in benign imperialism. Roosevelt accordingly garnished his optimism with a touch of restraint, saying that it would be unwise to "turn the attention of the Filipinos away from the problem of achieving the moral and material responsibility requisite . . . and toward dangerous intrigues for complete independence." At the end of his presidency TR continued to insist that the Filipinos had made great progress but that national independence was unthinkable, not only because of his judgment about the political maturity of the people of the Islands, but also because of what Captain Mahan had called "the problem of Asia."

Fascination with China and the lure of the China trade continued to work their magic on American foreign policy once Roosevelt became president. Mahan's book, *The Problem of Asia* (1901), marked his full emergence as a geopolitical thinker and, with other of TR's friends, including Brooks Adams and the English diplomat, Sir Cecil Spring Rice, he anticipated that China would be the great imperialist prize of the new country. All these observers tended to agree that Russia was the lurking menace. "I think the Russians have got the Chinese now whenever they like," Spring Rice wrote Roosevelt as early as 1896; "when they command and drill the Northern Chinese they will be a pretty big power—such a power as the world has never seen." Only later did the president become fully convinced of the potential danger of the Russians to the American position in the Far East. The Boxer Rebellion in 1900 occasioned Roosevelt to write Arthur Lee: "The stupendous revolution now going on in China is an additional reason why we [America and England] should work together." Later the president would orchestrate the peace negotiations bringing an end to the Russo-Japanese War because he said he thought the war a senseless slaughter of gallant men (a lesson learned well in Cuba) and because a continuation of the conflict would derange the balance of Far Eastern power. The Philippine Islands had to figure in the construction of an American strategy for the area, so that the United States could hardly forego possession of this stepping stone to the Asiatic mainland.

Before Roosevelt was long in office he came to realize the impossibility of America's doing more than maintaining the status quo in the Orient. Balance of power became the watchword. In such a policy British cooperation was vital. The English-speaking peoples would have to act together. The Taft-Katsura Agreement of 1905, wherein Japanese hegemony in Korea was acknowledged by Washington and American preeminence in the Philippines was recognized by Tokyo, and the Root-Takahira Agreement of 1908, which saw each nation accept the status quo, were completely consistent with the Anglo-Japanese Naval Treaty of 1902, signaling the friendship of these two countries. The aggressive American attitude

of 1898-1901 was distinctly moderated by Roosevelt, who admitted, toward the close of his presidency, that the Philippine Islands, from a military standpoint, might be "our heel of Achilles."

During Roosevelt's ascendancy the United States became an active policeman in the Caribbean and the watchdog of much of the western hemisphere. Cuba, Venezuela, Santo Domingo, Colombia, as well as Canada, in the dispute over the location of the Alaskan boundary, were all made to feel the power of the United States at one time or another. This was a posture based on strength and it immediately suggests the evolutionary ethic of survival of the fittest, giving a scientific justification for the dictum that might makes right. Roosevelt's disdain for Latin Americans generally went undisguised. "The bandits of Bogota," "banana republics," and "nests of a wicked and inefficient type" were all phrases of his manufacture. The sense of superiority they spoke was towering. As Roosevelt once remarked to the German ambassador, von Sternburg, "if any South American State misbehaves toward any European country, let the European country spank it." These states were like children, to be disciplined by adult nations as required by circumstances. They had not evolved to a sufficient degree of political maturity to enable them to manage their own affairs, necessitating American supervision.

Given the American sense of mission to uplift the peoples of the Philippines, it is appropriate to inquire whether the supervision in the Caribbean was in any way benign, in intention if not in effect, and whence the intended good derived. When there was a softening of the evolutionary thesis in Roosevelt's thinking about South America, it was due more to a general sense of justice and fair play and had limited relationship to Roosevelt's intellectual commitments. But the impression persists that the Latin American aspects of Rooseveltian foreign policy retained a distinct emphasis on power that was, in considerable part, traceable to Roosevelt's evolutionary outlook. His apologists have contended that TR did not believe that "might makes right" but that "might makes right possible to achieve." This is an intriguing distinction that, while possibly exonerating the president from extreme charges against him as a blatant imperialist, still does not deny the resort to force that was characteristic of the ethics growing out of the evolutionary dispensation. Yet force was a fact of life long before evolutionist teaching in the nineteenth century. Roosevelt had recognized this fact of life in building his body as a youngster, in his adventures as a Dakota ranchman, and in his military experiences during the Spanish-American War. Meanwhile, evolution as a cosmic explanation of things became part of his intellectual makeup. His learned mind gave no resistance to it. As for the tenets of social Darwinism, as opposed to evolution, he found he could not always morally or intellectually accept them. If Colombia was manhandled during negotiations over the building of a canal at Panama, force was utilized as a means to an end, but not as an end in itself. The application of force would eventuate in a result useful to mankind. As the president confided to his son, Kermit, the interests of civilization must take precedence over those of a wildcat republic like Colombia. There were times to draw on a knowledge of history for guidance and, again, there were times when it was plainly better to make history.

Much the same argument can be offered in evaluating Roosevelt's uses of the Monroe Doctrine, though the president appears far more imaginative, or creative, in his reliance on that historic pronouncement. Before he became president, TR spoke often and with passion about maintaining the Monroe Doctrine intact and applauded the efforts of others, not excluding the Democrat, Grover Cleveland, to see that it was honored. Yet Roosevelt was practical enough (and just possibly incipiently pragmatic enough, in the strict use of that word) to grasp the idea that the Monroe Doctrine had to be a tool of American power rather than a mere frame of reference. To be limited in its utilization by inherited versions of what the doctrine meant, inhibited meeting the fresh kinds of problems arising from an alarming dependence by many South American states on large European loans. The Roosevelt Corollary to the Monroe Doctrine, which he enunciated in his annual message to Congress in 1904, was an extension of the meaning of the doctrine necessitated by new conditions. If pragmatic truth comes about by the wedding of old ideas with new ideas to produce new truth, then Roosevelt may well have been acting in a clearly pragmatic way. And if the test of the new truth was to be its workability, his policy in Santo Domingo, where the corollary was first applied, proved that it was eminently true. European creditors were satisfied and the western hemisphere continued inviolate. As for Santo Domingo, it had surely received a moral insult to its sovereign status, but, practically speaking, it was better off with Americans collecting customs than when Dominican officials undertook the task. An immature nation, it had to rely on a more advanced nation for its immediate welfare. Roosevelt's incipient pragmatism had closed the intellectual circle, which helps to explain Roosevelt's confidence in his Santo Domingo policy despite heavy criticism in the Congress and the press.

The demands of the presidency on Theodore Roosevelt were heavy. The nature of the office and the changes that were part of the era combined with TR's own passion for action, resulting in what was a hectic pace. He retained his fondness and friendship with learning, nonetheless. Occasionally he dipped his pen into the literary well, though mostly he was preoccupied with matters and papers of state. He wrote several review-essays, including **"The Mongols,"** a critique of *The Mongols: A History* by Jeremiah Curtin, and **"The Children of the Night."** He kindly wrote prefaces to *The Master of Game* by Edward, Duke of York and *Hunting the Elephant* by C. H. Stigand. **"The Ancient Irish Sagas"** appeared in the *Century Magazine* for January 1907.

During TR's days in the White House the doors were always open and through them came many distinguished men of learning and intellectual accomplishment. The president delighted in such visits and was as prepared to listen as he was eager to speak his own viewpoints on law, poetry, history, science, or whatever else his guests might like to discuss. Most of all he loved people who loved books. He had abiding personal friendships with James Bryce, Henry Fairfield Osborn, Owen Wister, Cecil Spring Rice, the brothers Adams, John Hay, Cabot Lodge, and G. O. Trevelyan, several of whom exchanged long and serious letters with him. A forty-thousand-word account of his Afro-European tour of 1909-10 in letter form to Trevelyan is an example of his rare gift as a raconteur. "Literary salon" would be too tame a description of the White House during Theodore Roosevelt's occupancy. It was more like a literary merry-go-round. And when there was a break in the action the president turned to books, classics and contemporary works alike, which, after his wife and family, were his dearest companions.

For all of that Roosevelt often has been dismissed as anti-intellectual. Henry F. Pringle in his Pulitzer Prize-winning biography of Roosevelt, a book that is distinguished by a lively but serious prejudice against its subject, has advanced the argument that Roosevelt was "far from an objective critic," judging literature "in the light of his own stern moral code." He certainly distrusted Zola and Tolstoy; and he rejected naturalism in literature as in bad taste at the very least. But he was ready to read these novelists, and if he dismissed them on moral grounds he did not proceed blindly or without what he considered substantial reason. As a critic of the *Kreutzer Sonata,* for example, all he really said was that Tolstoy had written a bad book.

Roosevelt was not reluctant to moralize about literature or history. In his 1912 address as president of the American Historical Association he insisted that "the greatest historian should also be a great moralist. It is no proof of impartiality to treat wickedness and goodness on the same level. . . . Carlyle offers an instance in point. Very few men have ever been a greater source of inspiration than Carlyle when he confined himself to preaching morality in the abstract." But the ex-president believed that Carlyle "was utterly unable to distinguish either great virtues or great vices when he applied his own principles concretely to history. His 'Frederick the Great' is literature of a high order. . . . But 'morality' therein jubilantly upheld is shocking to any man who takes seriously Carlyle's other writings in which he lays down different principles of conduct." Put very simply, the "morality he praised had no connection with the morality as understood in the New Testament."

Theodore Roosevelt left the high office of president on an upbeat note. He was determined to keep his 1904 decision not to seek a second successive elected term, and to this effect he openly favored Taft's nomination by the Republican party, thus heading off a possible stampede for Teddy. His plan was to retire gracefully to private life and to his house at Oyster Bay, Sagamore Hill, much as Jefferson had sought out Monticello a century before, confident that Taft would be elected and would continue to follow the basic policy line he had laid out. "There is something rather attractive, something in a way living up to the proper democratic ideal, in having the president go out and become absolutely without reservation a private man," was the way he summed it up for St. Loe Strachey, the editor of the *Spectator*. As he was only fifty-one at the time, in good health and with a zest for life, there was, however, the real problem of a suitable occupation. He believed it would be an "unpleasant thing to be pensioned and given some honorary position," but at the same time he rejected one or two lucrative offers because of his suspiciousness of the marketplace. Apart from his not being a wealthy man, the very thought of idleness was so repugnant that Roosevelt was keen on both counts to do some worthwhile work. His earlier experience as an author naturally pointed him in a literary direction. He contracted with Scribner's to do a book on his pending hunting trip to Africa, and on his return from the Afro-European tour of 1909-10 he accepted an offer from Lyman Abbott to be a contributing editor of the *Outlook*. In 1909 it appeared that Roosevelt's career in the overall might go from books to books with high offices sandwiched in between.

The final decade of Roosevelt's life was far from totally bookish. The impression is that he went about like a roaring lion, such as he had missed killing while on safari, and that books and what they suggested had been put aside altogether. His need to be at the center of public life drew Roosevelt inexorably to active politics as early as 1910, and to political disaster in 1912 when the Bull Moose cause, for all its nobility and glamor, foundered on the reality of the two-party system. Any chance for a nomination in 1916, when he would have been fifty-eight and electable, was squandered in 1912. Meanwhile, another chasm opened, threatening both career and reputation—the 1914 war. Roosevelt believed almost from the start that America should join Britain and France in the fight. By 1915 he had gone fully public in his shrill demands for American entry on the Allied side and in his overbearing assaults on President Wilson's policy of neutrality. Frustrated by his lack of power, Roosevelt at this stage appeared to reverse the dictum of Lord Acton. It was a want of power that corrupted the ex-president, to the point that he resorted to name-calling to vent his spleen: "the trouble with Wilson is that he is plain yellow." This was not the learned Roosevelt speaking.

Prescinding from the misfortunes of his public life, Roosevelt had a great deal to say in his postpresidential years. It is altogether remarkable that he was able to combine public outcry with literary productivity, and political action with reflective writing. His previously cited **"History as Literature"** comes to mind at once. Consider the date of this address to the American Historical Association: 27 December 1912. TR had finished the arduous Bull Moose campaign six weeks before, a campaign in which he had blanketed the country, survived gunshot wounds to the chest, and roared his defiance at the old guard of his beloved Republican party in a cause

he knew was lost. He took his defeat in stride but it cut him to the quick. Then in late December in Boston he gave his address to the AHA, an address that, although generally neglected over the years, contained some stunning observations. For all his insistence that the great historian must be moral, he believed strongly in science as a healthy influence on historical writing. Morality in historical writing "does not mean that good history can be unscientific; the great historian can do nothing unless he is steeped in science," he told his fellow historians. "He must accept what we know of man's place in nature. He must realize that men have been on this earth for a period of incalculable length." He saw no conflict between morality and science, in other words. Roosevelt's own scientific bent and training go a long way toward explaining the ease with which he made this accommodation. Much more memorable were the two additional notes he sounded that have a striking contemporary ring to them. "The great historian of the future will have easy access to innumerable facts [computer assisted?] and can not be excused if he fails to draw on the vast storehouses of knowledge [data banks?]." Furthermore, Roosevelt contended, the historian of the future must be able to distinguish between the usual and the unusual in this world of innumerable facts.

A second novel way in which the ex-president called for a new version of history had to do with the commonplaces of the past. The great historian "must be able to paint for us the life of the plain people, the ordinary men and women of the time of which he writes." "Nothing that tells of their life will be amiss to him: implements of labor, weapons of warfare, wills written, bargains made, songs that they sang as they feasted and made love." Nor were these observations simply to be made in passing. Roosevelt labored his injunction that "the historians deal with common things" and deal with them "so that they shall interest us in reading of them as our common things interest us as we live among them."

"History as Literature" was also remarkable for its final thoughts. After speculating on how the historian of the future would write about the nineteenth and early twentieth centuries in America, Roosevelt was prompted to make a prediction. The historian would tell "of the frontier, of course, but also of the portentous growth of the cities," "the far-reaching consequences of industrialization," and of the new race arising from the melting pot. And "The hard materialism of our age will appear, and also the strange capacity for lofty idealism which must be reckoned with by all who would understand the American character." Roosevelt's final paragraph is worth quoting as well:

> Those who tell the Americans of the future what the Americans of today and of yesterday have done will perforce tell much that is unpleasant. This is but saying they will describe the arch-typical civilization of this age. Nevertheless, when the tale is finally told, I believe that it will show that the forces working for good in our national life outweigh the forces working for evil, that with

many blunders and shortcomings, with much halting and turning aside from the path, we shall yet in the end prove our faith by our works, and show in our lives our belief that righteousness exalteth a nation.

In uttering these thoughts, the obvious fruit of reflection on the ultimate meaning and nature of the American experience, Roosevelt might well have been speaking to the audience of a much later time. For all its preachy overtones it constitutes an extraordinary commentary on American life and character. Composed and delivered in the aftermath of the 1912 election, it serves as a reminder that the learned Roosevelt was never that distant from the man of action.

TR's life during the whole of the 1909-19 decade may be characterized in the same way. While a contributing editor for the *Outlook* and in a private capacity as well, Roosevelt turned out journalistic and political pieces with no lasting value on a variety of subjects, but he also did some impressive work of a substantial nature. He brought out two books on travel, *African Game Trails* and *Through the Brazilian Wilderness,* his *Autobiography,* a collection of essays under the title, *A Book-Lover's Holiday in the Open,* and several deserving essays that contained reviews of important books of the day, including Arthur E. P. B. Weigall's *The Treasury of Ancient Egypt* (1911), Octavius Charles Beale's *Racial Decay* (1911), H. J. Mozans's *Woman in Science* (1914), and Henry Fairfield Osborn's *The Origin and Evolution of Life* (1918), the latter appearing just a year before his death.

Of all his contributions to the *Outlook* none stirred more controversy and none has been so widely used to misrepresent his attitude toward the arts than **"A Layman's View of an Art Exhibition,"** his critique of the famous New York Armory Art Show of 1913. It has been described as the towering protest of an influential philistine against modern art. And it is true that Roosevelt was unsparing in his hostility to cubism and other futuristic art forms. "Probably we err in treating most of these pictures seriously," he wrote. "It is likely that many of them represent in the painters the astute appreciation of the power to make folly lucrative which the late P. T. Barnum showed with his fake mermaid." To him "the lunatic fringe was fully in evidence." Roosevelt observed that he was struck by the "resemblance of some of the art to the work of the palaeolithic artists of the French and Spanish caves." The palaeolithics were "interesting samples of the strivings for a human form . . . stumbling effort [that] represented progress. . . . Forty thousand years later, when entered into artificially and deliberately, it represents only a smirking pose of retrogression, and is not worthy of praise." These and like comments on some of the modernist entries have marked Roosevelt as an enemy of art. Too little notice has been taken of what he found in the Armory show that moved him. "In some ways," he wrote,

> it is the work of the American painters and sculptors which is the most interesting in this collection,

and a glance at this work must convince any of the real good that is coming out of the new movement, fantastic though many of the developments of these new movements are. There was one note entirely absent from the exhibition and that was the note of the commonplace. There was not a touch of simpering, self-satisfied conventionality anywhere in the exhibition [of the Americans]. Any painter or sculptor who had in him something to express and the power of expressing it found the field open to him. He did not have to be afraid because his work was not along ordinary lines. There was no stunting or dwarfing, no requirement that a man whose gift lay in new directions should measure up or down to stereotyped or fossilized standards.

Specifically, he singled out "'Arizona Desert,' 'Canadian Night,' the group of girls on the roof of a New York tenement-house, the studies in the Bronx Zoo, the 'Heracles,' the studies of the Utah monument, the little group called 'Gossip' which has something of the quality of the famous fifteenth idyl of Theocritus, the 'Pelf' with its grim suggestiveness"—these and many more he found worthy of notice and respect. Without denying the virulence of the ex-president's dislike for much in modern art, it is wrong to remember him as an enemy of art or of all new directions in the art world.

Roosevelt's decision to write an autobiography, at least in its timing, resulted in a book satisfying neither for him nor for posterity. "I am having my hands full writing certain chapters of my past experience," he admitted frankly to his sister-in-law, Emily Carow. The whole project, in fact, started tentatively. When installments began appearing in the *Outlook* in February 1913, they were entitled "Chapters of a Possible Biography." The completed account was published in book form by the end of that year, Roosevelt having decided after all that it might be useful to have his version of events on the record. He faced two problems in recounting his life and public career. First, aware that he was writing what would be an important historical document, he wanted to be candid; conscious that such candor would offend any number of people still alive and active in politics, he was persuaded that he must be balanced and dispassionate in what he set down. The result is a story of a tepid kind in view of Roosevelt's personality, yet it also sounded more self-serving than it would have if it had provided a full, unrestricted version of things. The second was a more complicated problem. TR decided to end his biography as his presidency came to a close, not unlike General Grant, whose *Memoirs* went no further than Appomattox. The note of triumph was intended to produce a lingering effect in both accounts. For Roosevelt this meant that the whole new nationalism phase of his career, climaxing in the Bull Moose campaign, went unregarded. Still nurturing political hopes, Roosevelt decided it was best to say nothing of 1912, but the *Autobiography* is a poorer historical source as a result.

This truncated life suffered further, of course, from the fact that it was not to include the controversial role the ex-president took in the battle over American neutrality after 1914. Those were dark days, and even Roosevelt's more friendly biographers have been somewhat wary in their treatment. For all its extremism, Roosevelt's position was not totally indefensible, and it would have benefited him a great deal had he taken the opportunity to make some measured and formal statements in his own behalf, as distinct from the fulminations he uttered that have so warped his wartime image. As it turned out he was not vouchsafed the time required for this much-needed apologia.

Still, the *Autobiography* captured some of the variety and vitality of the man. It was a big book, as it had to be to accommodate the many-sided individual it described. It was a confident book, though there are hints of self-doubt from time to time. For all its deficiencies it added an important account to the historical record, which all too few presidents, either before or after TR, have attempted to do, except with the aid of ghost writers and rewriters and other adjuncts. At the very least it is certain that TR himself put pen to paper. Therefore, both contemporaries and historians have a better knowledge of the inner workings of a man whom Henry Adams once described as "pure act." The *Autobiography* also provides another major piece of evidence of Roosevelt's compulsion to resort to a standard literary form.

African Game Trails was a worthwhile book. Subtitled "An account of the African wanderings of an American hunter-naturalist," it was the product of knowledge, enthusiasm, courage, and a devotion to the written word. It is a big book, occupying nearly five hundred pages in volume 24 of the Memorial edition of Roosevelt's *Works*. With a sense of the romantic, TR signed the preface "Khartoum, March 15, 1910." One of the book's winning features is that one may open it at almost any page and enter into the adventure: stalking the rhino or the elephant, making the dangerous trek into the high grass country, or viewing the awesome natural settings. Roosevelt is so very much alive on the trail of game in Africa. But he is also the naturalist and the literate man. He is writing about hunting the giraffe, when he pauses to explain:

> The country in which we were hunting marks the southern limit of the "reticulated" giraffe, a form or species entirely distinct from the giraffe we had already obtained in the country south of Kenia. The southern giraffe has blotches with dark on a light ground, whereas this northern or northeastern form is of a uniform dark color on the back and sides, with a network or reticulation of white lines placed in a large pattern on this dark background. The naturalists were very anxious to obtain a specimen of this form from its southern limit of distribution, to see if there was any intergradation with the southern form, of which we had already shot specimens near its northern, or at least northeastern, limit. The distinction proved sharp.

A page or two later, Roosevelt describes the sighting of a rhino amid a great herd of zebra. As the purpose of the

day was not to hunt, he did not want to kill the rhino, which remained in a position obscuring the party's view of the zebra. TR wrote: "I did not wish to kill it, and I was beginning to feel about the rhino the way Alice did in the Looking Glass country, when the elephants 'did bother so.'"

Roosevelt believed that apart from great sport "with the noblest game in the world," he was making some contribution to scientific knowledge. He had offered the Smithsonian Institution specimens of what he proposed to shoot and several field naturalists and taxidermists were members of the party. What makes *African Game Trails* all the more extraordinary as an account of the expedition is that it was written during the trekking itself. For that reason the adventures recounted have an immediacy and a freshness that produce a winning effect. During one six-week stretch, Roosevelt managed to put down forty-five thousand words, often writing by camp fire and under adverse conditions of weather and fatigue. The contributions the expedition made to scientific knowledge, while not great, were valiantly done, and the literary Roosevelt, put to the severest of tests, passed with high marks.

The literary Roosevelt was revealed further in the "pigskin library." In planning the African trip, Roosevelt proposed to take a number of books with him for solace by night after having hunted the big cats by day. His sister Corinne Douglas collected copies of the books he wanted, and had them cut to pocket size and bound in pigskin as a protection against jungle rot. It is necessary to cite only a few of the items he took. The Bible and Shakespeare, of course, along with Homer's *Iliad* and *Odyssey*, headed the list. also included were Bacon's *Essays*, Lowell's *Biglow Papers*, Emerson's *Poems*, Milton's *Paradise Lost*, Dante's *Inferno*, Mark Twain's *Tom Sawyer* and *Huckleberry Finn*, as well as *Vanity Fair* by Thackeray and *Pickwick Papers* by Dickens. The pigskin library was never intended to be a listing of the world's great books. As Roosevelt wrote, there was no trace of dogmatism in preferring this book to that. It was a matter of personal choice: classics to reread as well as more contemporary novels, and poems to roll off the tongue. He conceded that he did not take scientific books "simply because as yet scientific books do not have literary value." Throughout his life Roosevelt had counted books among his friends, and some of those that were his best friends he wanted as companions.

Through the Brazilian Wilderness was Roosevelt's personal account of what was officially the "Expedicao Scientifica Roosevelt-Rondon." Invitations from the governments of Argentina, Brazil, and Chile to visit those countries brought Roosevelt to South America in 1913. Once there, he was encouraged both by his fellow explorer, Father John Zahm, and the Brazilian government to undertake an exploration of the interior of Brazil. It was to be a scientific expedition to gather information about plant and animal life as well as to learn more about the geography and geology of the area. During the course of the exploration, Roosevelt, accompanied by his son

Kermit, Colonel Rondon of the Brazilian army, and a small number of others from the general party, undertook to descend the River of Doubt to determine its location and how it flowed into the Amazon. This latter phase of the trip proved to be extremely dangerous. At one point the ex-president nearly died of infection and the accompanying high fever. That he persevered as an explorer is no more surprising than that he persevered as a writer. Under conditions far more severe than those encountered in Africa—for days the party was totally out of contact with the rest of the world and disasters lurked at every step—TR wrote his daily notes as the basis for his book, attired in head net and heavy gloves as protection against the insect stings that were a relentless fact of life. Two things were notable about the expedition. It led to a first-rate account of the adventure in which Roosevelt's modesty, courage, vulnerability, curiosity, and physical stamina were all visible; it was perhaps the most honest book in terms of himself that TR was to write. Second, the expedition was responsible for important scientific finds, geographic, geologic, and zoologic. In recognition of his work the ex-president was awarded the David Livingstone Centenary gold medal by the American Geographical Society. No less than a dozen separate bulletins and papers were issued by the Brazilian government on the basis of the findings of the expedition. In addition, specimens of birds and mammals, almost two thousand in all, were collected for the American Museum of Natural Science.

Roosevelt had clearly risked his life in this further try at "a great adventure." Very probably his health was undermined, as he suffered ailments off and on for the remainder of his life. He had taken the trip out of a sense of adventure, and equally out of a desire to advance scientific knowledge. What had happened in the course of his explorations had more than fulfilled his expectations on both counts. The Brazilian government named the great interior river that he had helped to locate "Rio Teodora," as a tribute to this North American friend and compatriot. Later Roosevelt delivered various lectures founded on his experiences to the National Geographic Society, the Royal Geographic Society, and the American Museum in New York. The Brazilian wilderness was a long way from the Adirondacks where in 1874 TR had made his first extensive scientific listing of summer birds. Yet there was a unity in his endeavors that combined these two treasure troves of nature. It was the unity of nature itself. Not surprisingly, he continued to probe nature and its ultimate secrets in his last intellectual efforts, offered in several essays and book reviews.

When **"Biological Analogies in History"** and **"History as Literature"** are added to the essays and several other pieces that Roosevelt wrote in the years 1909-19, it is an easy matter to appreciate the ongoing literary man in the sometime president. For all the allure and command of science he remained a humanist at heart, protesting not long before he died that the study of science must not be carried out at the expense of the study of man. But who was man, what was his purpose in the final accounting?

In **"Racial Decadence,"** Roosevelt addressed the then delicate subject of "deliberate sterility in marriage." It takes a preacher of great compassion and a writer of taste to delineate views on such a subject without giving offense. The critique of Octavius Charles Beale's book was somewhat lacking in subtlety, advocating without qualification an anti-materialistic version of human life. In his analysis, Roosevelt came to the causes of a declining birth rate directly and forcefully. It was due, in his judgment, to "coldness, to selfishness, to love of ease, to shrinking from risk, to an utter and pitiful failure in sense of perspective and in power of weighing what really makes the highest joy and to a rooting out of a sense of duty, in a twisting of that sense into improper channels." To a large extent he equated the salvation of society with the fulfillment of duty by the individual. Flowing from duty were warm generosity, a willingness to take risks in a good cause, a healthy perspective on pleasure, and procreation.

In **"Woman in Science"** the ex-president raised his voice in praise of women and of women in history and deplored the deprivations they had endured for whatever reason. Yet he did so largely on empirical and rational grounds, rarely evoking God or sentiment. Though he respected women in a chivalrous fashion, he developed his celebration of womanhood from sterner stuff. After viewing what he termed "the so-called arguments" used to keep women down, he recognized that in the first flush of emancipation women might exult in their newly won freedom. But he was confident that women would not "shirk their duties" "any more than the average man in a democracy would be less dutiful than the average man in a despotism." Nor did Roosevelt believe he was being especially avant-garde in taking this position, describing it, rather, as part of "the right thinking of the day." He agreed with the contemporary French writer Jean Finot that humanity would be happier when women enjoyed equality with men. No less for women than for men, duty was the paramount consideration. No doubt Roosevelt's wife, Edith, to him a model woman, was not far from his thoughts as he wrote **"Woman in Science."** The mother of five of his children, she was endowed with a fine mind, a resolute will, and a sense of femininity, a combination that made her both companion and confidante.

Modern man, moral and scientific, was the inheritor of an anthropological and a historical past. Roosevelt entitled his review of E. P. B. Weigall's book on pre-Christian Egypt, **"Our Neighbors, The Ancients."** He discovered ready similarities between ancient and twentieth-century people. Using Ikhnaton to make the point that ideals and realities often clash, he flayed the doctrinaire reformers of his day for their insistence on immediate and total change. In effect, the human race was a constant in the ever-changing circumstances of time and place. Virtue and vice remained the same, though epochs might be separated by thousands of years. The unity of the human experience meant much to the philosopher in Theodore Roosevelt.

The ex-president's last significant book review appeared in the *Outlook* just a year before he died. It was a critique of Henry Fairfield Osborn's *The Origin and Evolution of Life,* a book he pondered. Osborn stressed that the beginnings of life to a physicist like himself lay not in form but in energy. But he offered his views without any dogmatic inflections. Roosevelt appreciated this because, as he had to admit, he himself was without the requisite physicochemical knowledge to dispute the scientists. As he had done numerous times before, he endorsed the evolutionary thesis as readily as the principle of a heliocentric solar system or the Newtonian postulates about gravity. But in pondering Osborn's treatment of the beginnings of life Roosevelt was moved to state his qualification of human evolution in a singularly trenchant fashion:

> The tracing of an unbroken line of descent from the protozoan to Plato does not in any way really explain Plato's consciousness, of which there is not a vestige in the protozoan. There has been a non-measurable quality of actual creation. There is something new which did not exist in the protozoan. It has been produced in the course of evolution. But it is a play on words to say that such evolution is not creation.

In the contention between science and humanism that was perhaps the leading intellectual battle of his day, Theodore Roosevelt came down on the side of the traditional estimate of man, of woman, and of humankind.

No one is likely to deny to Roosevelt that whatever he did he did with flair. His writings were no exception, nor was the range of his pursuits or the confidence of his expression. Many times he wrote books or articles that appear to have no direct or immediately useful purpose. As has been suggested from time to time, he often wrote such literary pieces to organize his thinking in a general way rather than to advocate or justify a specific proposal or policy. Writing was part of his thought process to an unusual degree, but his flair too often worked to obscure this fact.

Roosevelt's style should not be taken as a model for other learned presidents, and specifically not for Taft or Wilson. Taft's writings were much less general, less wide of focus, and less interesting in consequence; much the same must be said of his mind. Wilson, on the other hand, possessed the professional qualities of Taft, but he wrote for more general audiences, conscious of his intention to instruct the reader. Taft, as a professor of law, brought something of that to his writings. Each of these presidents was unique, but TR had one special characteristic. He was the first in line. Being first in this remarkable series of learned individuals did not mean that it was easier for Taft and Wilson to follow in the presidency, but that it was more congruous that as learned men they should occupy the office. Roosevelt alone could not have revived the tradition of a learned presidency; Taft and Wilson, coming after, were no less essential. The three men, taken together, responded to the intellectual impulses of their age, imparting a fresh vigor to the presidency as it entered the twentieth century.

Daniel Aaron (essay date 1990)

SOURCE: "Theodore Roosevelt As Cultural Artifact," in *Raritan: A Quarterly Review,* Vol. 9, No. 3, 1990, 109-26.

[*In the following essay, Aaron charts the declining image and reputation of Roosevelt as a public figure.*]

Four gigantic presidential heads, the work of the American-born sculptor Gutzon Borglum, look out from the granite wall of South Dakota's Mt. Rushmore. Washington, Jefferson, and Lincoln cluster clubbably on their mountain eminence, but does the head of Theodore Roosevelt, replete with a cleverly simulated pince-nez, belong in this godlike company? Borglum thought so, and not merely because he believed in and practiced the Rooseveltian gospel of the "strenuous life" (Americans, he complained, didn't live vigorously enough) or because Roosevelt had been a personal friend. He simply considered him a great man, an "all-American President" under whose aegis two oceans had been linked and the United States transformed into a world power. Borglum saw nothing incongruous in wedging him between Thomas Jefferson, whom Roosevelt held in reserved contempt, and Abraham Lincoln, whose fondness for unclean stories Roosevelt deplored but whom he nonetheless revered.

The finished stone portrait of Roosevelt was dedicated in 1939. By that time his name had been pretty well preempted by the then occupant of the White House, his fifth cousin and husband of a favorite niece. In fact, Roosevelt's deflation had started even before his death in 1919, partly because his misalliance with the Progressives had disappointed Republican stalwarts and pleased only a vehement minority of the voters he had captivated during his glory years, the people, as he put it, "who make up the immense bulk of our Nation—the small merchants, clerks, farmers and mechanics." Rejected by party conservatives in his bid for the presidency in 1912, he went on a kind of political binge that distanced him from the middle-of-the-road consensus and left the radicals unconvinced of his sincerity. Just as George F. Babbitt, the eponymous hero of Sinclair Lewis's novel, rejoined the Good Citizens' League after his brief revolt against the credo of Zenith, so Roosevelt after his own insurgency happily returned to the Republican fold to spur the crusade against Woodrow Wilson, the IWW, and the "Bolsheviki." Had he lived he would certainly have blocked the presidential nomination of his antithesis, pliable Warren Gamaliel Harding, the "bloviating" senator from Ohio, whom he had seriously contemplated as a possible running mate in the 1920 elections.

Whether the man President Harding eulogized as the "mighty hunter" and "the most courageous American of all times" could have worked his old magic on an electorate fed up with moralistic harangues now seems unlikely. The epithets lavished upon him by his celebrators—"genial giant," "Colossus," "Cid of the West," "Great Heart," "Mr. Valiant," "the Lion"—had a comical ring in America's Babylonian twenties. He had always recoiled from what he took to be the cynicism of Henry Adams and Henry James; he hated irony and had harsh words for Mark Twain's dark novel, *A Connecticut Yankee in King Arthur's Court*. "There is nothing cheaper," he wrote in 1907, "than to sneer at and belittle great men and great deeds and great thoughts of a bygone time." Sentiments of this sort, not to mention his calls to civic duty, didn't thrive in the debunking atmosphere of the Jazz Age.

In that decade, Roosevelt's "gloriously simple world" disappeared. H. L. Mencken's portrait of him as a calculating, anti-democratic politician, the "national Barbarossa" philosophically akin to the Kaiser, set the tone for the negative reappraisals to come. Historians and social critics over the next twenty years did more than question his liberal credentials. They also detected in the words and attitudes of this "perfect *representative* of the middle class of prewar America" (so John Chamberlain dubbed him) the signs of an incipient native fascism. By the end of World War II, however, the hostile stereotypes of Roosevelt—the unmagnanimous adversary, militant imperialist, coiner of platitudes, slaughterer of innocent beasts—had begun to be qualified or rejected in biographies and monographs, especially after the publication of his letters in eight fat volumes.

A revised portrait of Roosevelt as the far-sighted pragmatist and constructive conservative suited the national temper of the 1950s. Even Edmund Wilson, who thirty years earlier had ranked him low in the scale of presidents, conceded in a review of Theodore Roosevelt's correspondence that he had been "unfairly eclipsed" by Woodrow Wilson and "Franklin D." Now he found that he could sympathize "to some extent with Roosevelt in his doctrine of 'practical politics,' his insistence that the uncompromising kind of reformer, who refused to yield anything to expediency, can never put through his reforms." Since Wilson wrote these words, revisionists, in redressing several decades of T.R. baiting, have moved far beyond his measured approval.

There is still no firm consensus, but I doubt that many historians today would quarrel with Oscar Handlin's summation of Roosevelt as "the first modern chief executive of the United States" or deny the efficiency of his administration. He has been called "the greatest activist in the history of the American presidency." Truly or not, he saw himself as the steward of the whole nation, preserver of its natural resources and its spiritual and bodily well-being. The series of regulatory acts passed by the Congress with his strong backing left displeased both radical reformers and Big Business, but not the public, receptive to Roosevelt's doctrine of "applied idealism" and content to stay in the middle of the road. His advocates especially commend his tactful and moderate diplomacy. They see him as the first president to deal confidently and comfortably with the heads of foreign powers, the first to ensure America's future role in global politics.

Roosevelt's stock continues to fluctuate on the political Exchange in an era of White House adventurism and Noriega's Panama, and his recent co-option by President Bush—who describes himself as "an Oyster Bay kind of guy" and surmises that he may "turn out to be a Teddy Roosevelt"—could send Republicans and Democrats alike back to their history books. Roosevelt was no Lincoln (I think his most ardent partisans would concede as much), but he was one of our more spectacular and entertaining presidents, the most obstreperously boyish (his enemies would say "insane" or "manic"), and for all of his thousands of personal letters and twenty volumes of packaged views about everything under the sun, not easy to plumb. Perhaps the sheer mass of memorabilia and conflicting commentary that has accumulated about him, much of it self-spawned, impedes discernment. From this detritus, would-be interpreters construct their own Roosevelts.

Mine is a pastiche drawn from many sources but chiefly from the letters. I see him as the scion of old money (though the terms *aristocrat* and *patrician* often applied to him seem to me malapropos), an American "gentleman" with a strongly developed civic sense, ambitious for glory but—perhaps because he had no need of it—disinclined to claw his way up the political ladder. He learned early to compromise, to accept small defeats on the way to larger victories, even if that sometimes demanded the repudiation of former allies and a certain amount of truckling, though never to the extent of frequenting barrooms or kissing proletarian babies. Probably no other American president loved his job so much, felt more pleased with himself (his expressions of humility have a hollow ring), or pursued his goals with greater insouciance. Uninhibited, politically canny, temperamentally optimistic, he was blessed with an untroubled faith in his own rectitude. He liked to fight and to win; no one ever questioned his physical courage. If Justice Holmes's comment on Owen Wister's gushing memoir of Roosevelt ("the talent he depicts is that of a first class megaphone and not of a statesman") sounds unfair, his judgment of the man who appointed him to the Supreme Court does not: "R. was more or less a great man no doubt but I think he was far from having a great intellect."

But I don't want to debate the pros and cons of T.R.'s presidency, to concede or dispute his greatness, or to contrast him invidiously with other American presidents. My interest here is his reputation and how he acquired it. Why was he once widely judged to be the greatest and best-known American of his day—indeed, the incarnation of America? What was it about him and his times that contributed to his acclaim?

I believe he had a lot to do with his translation into the American "superstructure." Before the onset of the professional image-makers (that is to say, roughly from his election to the New York State Assembly in 1881 until at least 1917, when he tried but failed to raise a division of troops to fight in France), Roosevelt served very effectively as his own press agent. He was the first ex-president to publish his autobiography. His political, historical, and literary writings, not to mention his voluminous correspondence, constitute among other things a campaign of self-promotion, a sustained "Song of Myself."

"I celebrate myself and sing myself," chanted Walt of Manahatta, "And what I assume you shall assume / For every atom belonging to me as good belongs to you." Roosevelt delivered a comparable message to the electorate, although I suspect he would have shared his atoms more reluctantly than the Good Walt did. Both were histrionic and self-loving, but in other ways the two singers were quite antithetical. Whitman envisioned an American democracy composed of all races and occupations, a union of loving comrades. Roosevelt's Americanism, though resistant to nativist bigotry, had little to do with equality and brotherhood. Rather, in Edmund Wilson's words, "it was a concept he had to invent as an antidote to those tendencies in American life he found himself sworn to resist," tendencies that might be subsumed in the words Anarchy and Slouch. Whitman the loafer was passive and mystical; he dissolved into the experiences of his countrymen. Roosevelt despised anything loose, disorderly, slack, lawless, soft. Both celebrated strenuous deeds, but Roosevelt, unlike Whitman, acted out his fantasies in the public glare, and the public took the uncommon man into its collective heart as it never did Whitman.

Mark Twain often noted the paradox of an America ostensibly attached to leveling principles yet enamored with rank. "Scoffing democrats as we are, we do dearly love to be noticed by a duke, and when we are noticed by a monarch, we have softening of the brain for the rest of our lives." At home, "precious collisions" with the rich and the well-born were no less treasured, especially if the one on high were affable and gracious. Roosevelt capitalized on his upper-class affiliations, his dress and accent, his cartoonable mannerisms. It didn't take him very long to learn that the very presence of a dude in the rough-and-tumble political arena attracted attention. And when that dude happened to be quick-witted, belligerent, and demonically energetic (someone said Teddy "used adjectives like hammers"), he was bound to stand out in the crowd of big-city machine politicos and populist "Jack-asses" from the west.

A Roosevelt biographer mentions his subject's "genius for publicity." Mark Twain, himself no slouch at self-promotion, made the same point less silkily at the end of Theodore Roosevelt's administration. "Mr. Roosevelt," he wrote then, but prudently didn't publish, "is the Tom Sawyer of the political world of the twentieth century; always showing off; always hunting for a chance to show off; in his frenzied imagination the Great Republic is a vast Barnum circus with him for a clown and the whole

world for an audience; he would go to Halifax for half a chance to show off, and he would go to hell for a whole one."

Twain's remark was flip and simplistic but not wildly beyond the mark. Other ironists felt the same way, appalled and exhausted by the supercharged Roosevelt, whose ideas seemed to spring from his nervous system. Henry Adams and his inner circle (Gore Vidal brings this out in his novel *Empire*) found him refreshing if often irritating, and as impressive in his way as a spouting geyser. Reporters chronicled his tireless round of horseback rides, walks, and rock climbs, his swimming, boxing, and shooting. The public delighted in his furious spasms of activity. Never before had there been a president who was such a provocative phrasemaker, such a fist-thumping, arm-waving, toothy jack-in-the-box, yet withal dignified, powerful, and purposeful—and a little dangerous, too.

Roosevelt did more than tolerate the larger-than-life image of himself; he cultivated it. Less visible was the T.R. whose intimates addressed him as "Theodore" (he disliked being called "Teddy"), who played tennis (but forbade photographers to take pictures of him in his sissy tennis clothes), dressed for dinner, and displayed an almost feminine sweetness towards his family and close friends. What the public saw Roosevelt wanted it to see: the broncobuster, soldier, hunter, crime fighter—the moral exemplar and protector of the national domain who reigned in an era of good feeling. E. L. Doctorow captures the Rooseveltian euphoria in his novel *Ragtime:*

> Patriotism was a reliable sentiment in the early 1900s. Teddy Roosevelt was President. The population customarily gathered in great numbers either out of doors for parades, public concerts, fish fries, political picnics, social outings, or indoors in meeting halls, vaudeville theatres, operas, ballrooms. There seemed to be no entertainment that did not involve great swarms of people. Trains and steamers and trolleys moved them from one place to another. That was the style, that was the way people lived. . . . Women were stouter then. They visited the fleet carrying white parasols. Everyone wore white in summer. Tennis racquets were hefty and the racquet faces elliptical. There was a lot of sexual fainting. There were no Negroes. There were no immigrants.

Omitted from this postcard vignette (besides Negroes and immigrants, as Doctorow notes) are riots, strikes, scandals, and exposés. Yet none of these disquieting signs seem to have tarnished T.R.'s luster. The nation was advancing, and he was leading the charge. Everything was "Bully!" The president was "De-lighted."

When he left office, Roosevelt had already become a national artifact, a popular possession. Henry Cabot Lodge, one of the crowd of well-wishers who saw him off on his African safari in 1909, assured the ex-president that the American people were following the "minute accounts of [his] progress" in the daily press "as if it were a serial story" and "with all the absorbed interest of a boy who reads 'Robinson Crusoe' for the first time."

Roosevelt kept this public well informed of his comings and goings. He rarely missed the chance to advertise his invariably newsworthy opinions. "What funnily varied lives we do lead, Cabot!" he had written to Lodge back in 1889. "We touch two or three little worlds, each profoundly ignorant of the others. Our literary friends have but a vague knowledge of our actual political work; and a goodly number of our sporting and social acquaintances know us only as men of good family, one of whom rides hard to hounds, while the other hunts big game in the Rockies." A decade later, the whole country was inescapably privy to selected portions of his political, social, and literary worlds. Each of his subpublics focused on a different Roosevelt: the politicians on the unpredictable and slippery office holder and seeker; the literary and scholarly community (historians, explorers, naturalists, museum people) on the reputedly omniscient polymath with a photographic memory.

Of the assorted "Teddys," a few in particular caught the fancy of his national audience and inflated the Roosevelt myth. I shall concentrate on two of them, the Hunter and the Soldier. I believe he cultivated these two images more assiduously than he did his other personae—the Christian Gentleman, the Practical and Sane Reformer, the Peacemaker, the Man of Letters, the Conservationist—all subsidiary roles comprehended by his conception of the Hunter and Soldier.

A 1919 cartoon of him shows the retired president seated in his den. Heads of wild beasts deck the walls. He looks uncomfortable in repose and appears about to stir. Is his unease a presentiment of what's to come? (Roosevelt confessed in his autobiography that he was devoted to *Macbeth* but indifferent to *Hamlet*.)

Half derisively, half affectionately, the newspapers reported his African expedition. Cartoons showed jungle animals running in terror at the mere rumor of Teddy's presence. In one spoof, a "man-chewing" tiger explains to a jealous cobra how he intends to face the barrage of snapping kodaks and yield up his "sinful soul with a mean snarl." Teddy in caricature is a comic figure, his huge teeth bared, no less animal than the buffalo, rhinoceros, elephants, zebras, and giraffes he relentlessly pursues.

Of all the big game he tracked and killed, the bear was probably most closely associated with his prowess and personality, thanks, in part, to the reporters and camera crews who accompanied him on his publicized bear hunts. Mark Twain wickedly parodied one of them. It culminated, according to the newspaper account he quoted, with the president dashing into a canebrake, dispatching the bear at twenty paces, and then gleefully hugging the guides. (In Twain's version, Roosevelt has slain an exhausted cow, despite her touching plea for mercy.) A short film of 1902 entitled *Terrible Teddy, the Grizzly King* reenforced the popular image of a feral

Nimrod. The president-elect appears on the screen in the company of two flunkeys, one carrying a sign reading "My Press Agent," the other "My Photographer." Teddy shoots his gun in the air and down falls a dead cat which he proceeds to stab with a knife. But it took a much publicized incident, in which Roosevelt allegedly spared a bear cub, to fuse the hunter irrevocably with his totem. Teddy's act of clemency, according to one account, inspired a Russian immigrant toymaker to create and market, with historic consequences, a stuffed bear modeled on the fortunate cub. A few years later, Teddy Bears were selling by the thousands, and "The Teddy Bear March" had become a popular song.

Another film, *The "Teddy Bears,"* made in 1907 at the height of Roosevelt's popularity, introduced a sinister tone into what was ostensibly a comedy. Based on the tale of Goldilocks and the Three Bears, the film ends suddenly and equivocally with the appearance of Teddy the Hunter. Teddy kills Momma and Papa Bear as they are chasing Goldilocks across snow-covered fields; then he leads Baby Bear off on a leash. *The "Teddy Bears"* underscored what I think was always latent in the newspaper cartoons and in the parodies about the man with the big scary teeth, glinting eyeglasses, and death-dealing gun—that for Roosevelt hunting was serious business. A photograph he had taken of himself in hunting gear, rifle and knife prominently displayed, his expression cold and judgmental, strengthens this supposition.

Clearly, as the thousands of words he devoted to the subject might suggest, he regarded hunting less as a leisure-class diversion than as a rite fraught with moral and social meaning. The accolade, "Mr. President, you are no tenderfoot," bestowed upon him by one of his guides, was a public testimonial to his manhood. Roosevelt equated the hunterly virtues—courage, honor, tenacity, a willingness to take risks and accept pain without whimpering—with civic virtues. He upheld the virile outdoor man, tested by exposure to wilderness conditions, as a salutary corrective to what he called the "unadulterated huckster or pawn-broker type" that flourished in the immigrant-infested urban east. Roosevelt's conservation measures, in the opinion of many his most lasting contribution, preserved for the nation vast areas of unspoiled nature, but he had more in mind than recreation for urban vacationers. He was giving unborn generations a taste of the character-building frontier experience that had toughened and tempered him. Conservation was tantamount to social regeneration, a hedge against creeping decadence.

For Roosevelt, hunterly and military virtues smoothly blended. "Only those are fit to live who do not fear to die and none are fit to die who have shrunk from the joy of life and the duty of life," reads one of his pronunciamentos inscribed on the walls of the Theodore Roosevelt Memorial in New York's American Museum of Natural History. "Aggressive fighting for the right is the noblest sport the world affords," is another. "If I must choose between righteousness and peace," it continues, "I choose righteousness."

The image of Roosevelt the Soldier for a brief time dominated the media no less compellingly than Roosevelt the Hunter. Between the early spring of 1898, when he formed his volunteer regiment of Rough Riders to fight the Spanish "dagoes" in Cuba, and the demobilization of his military "cowboys" in the late summer of that year, he became a national celebrity.

He resigned his position as Assistant-Secretary of the Navy and sought military combat, he assured his friends, not because he dreamed of glory. After all, he had "consistently advocated a warlike policy." Now it was time to practice what he preached if he expected to go anywhere in politics. "I have a horror," he said, "of the people who bark but don't bite." Moreover, he thought the war would speed American expansion in the Pacific and Caribbean and give the nation a much needed "moral lift." Privately he excoriated both "the timid and scholarly men in whom refinement and culture have been developed at the expense of all virile qualities" and "the big moneyed men in whose minds money and material prosperity have finally dwarfed everything else."

Roosevelt's confidences, private or public, must be studied with caution, for he wasn't one to examine his inmost feelings, much less to reveal them. "Father has depths of insincerity not even he has plumbed," Roosevelt's daughter, Alice, remarks in Gore Vidal's novel. At least this reader of Theodore Roosevelt's letters feels the force of the fictional Alice's observation. He wasn't two-faced, and he didn't speak with a forked tongue, but he was hard to pin down. The pupil of Admiral Mahan had a grasp of international power politics and was a sophisticated player of the diplomatic game. The evangelical nationalist read history romantically. He studied it for personal edification and faulted and praised mighty captains and men of power from the Romans until his own times. His judgments on Cromwell, Hamilton, Gouverneur Morris, Thomas Hart Benton, Andrew Jackson, Abraham Lincoln, and the military leaders of the Civil War are clues to his character and ambitions.

Nothing in Roosevelt's correspondence suggests a calculated policy to make political capital out of his military adventures. Still, the examples of Washington, Jackson, and Grant would hardly have escaped the amateur historian, and his negotiations with magazine publishers, even before he sailed for Cuba, to write up his experiences look as if he didn't intend to hide his light under a bushel. From the start, "nineteenth-century America's greatest master of press relations," as Edmund Morris calls him, scarcely missed a chance to use the correspondents (most notably Richard Harding Davis, whom he particularly favored) and the photographers. Newspapers churned out human interest stories about the First U.S. Volunteer Cavalry, three quarters of them recruited from the Rocky Mountain states, the rest made up of eastern polo-playing "blue-bloods," southern gentlemen, and a sprinkling of Mexicans and Indians. Needless to say, their leader, the Lieutenant-Colonel of this motley regiment, got more than his share of space. Whether he planned it or not, he was freighted for the White House at the conclusion of the "splendid little war."

For almost a decade thereafter, Roosevelt exhorted, educated, and entertained a national audience from what he called his "bully pulpit." Simply being president kept him on center stage, but the periodic spectacles he arranged—the signing of the Russian-Japanese peace treaty at Portsmouth, New Hampshire, the neat surgical operation without congressional assistance that separated Panama from Columbia, the dispatching of the "Great White Fleet" on its intimidating goodwill voyage around the world—guaranteed the president star billing. His transparently motivated rupture with Taft (whose nomination he had dictated) and his abortive presidential campaign on the Progressive Party ticket against the incumbent President Taft and Woodrow Wilson, the Democratic candidate, marked the beginning of his political decline.

Until then he had made his self-image the public's. He had spoken for this public and in its name blistered any interest group or party he considered "Wrong," that is to say any faction that in his view threatened to upset the national equilibrium by challenging his policy of balance and compromise. These included "swinish" corporations; "mushy," "Bedlamite," and "foolish" reformers; "vicious" trade unionists, socialists, and anarchists, and all such "vermin." He was most in tune with the old-stock citizenry of the lower and upper middle class whose traditional values were like his own. And he had a special affection for "ordinary citizens," by which he meant not the industrial working class, not the newer immigrants with whom he had only gingerly ties, but soldiers, policemen, boxers, and cowboys. He called them "splendid fellows" and treated them as his grown-up children.

When he left the White House, Roosevelt was generally respected as a capable chief executive and a responsible custodian of the nation. Once out of office, he thirsted for his old prerogatives. Defeated in his bid for the Republican nomination, he aligned himself with party malcontents and independents, the same political types he had castigated for almost thirty years as mollycoddles, pussyfooters, milk-and-water philanthropists, and "nice little men." He had stuck with the Grand Old Party, notwithstanding his quarrels with some of its managers, because it stood in theory for the conservative principles he favored. But now to the dismay of Republican loyalists, he zoomed off on an eccentric tangent to collaborate with men whose support would have embarrassed him only a few years earlier. He had moved from the political consensus into the "lunatic fringe" (his term), and although he remained a celebrity, a hero to the Teddyites, he had good reason to believe before the end of his life that the American people had grown a little tired of him.

If Roosevelt was out of touch with the country after 1912, the World War made him obsolete. I have concentrated on the Teddy Roosevelt whose bravura performances, dash, and style endeared him to a national claque. That figure has ossified into a period piece.

But there is a Theodore Roosevelt at odds with the artifact, a troubled and un-Teddyish personality. He shows lapses of self-confidence, and he is more vulnerable to the barbs of the satirists than he lets on. His antipathies and rages hint of unacknowledged guilt. He subjects himself to endless tests; he registers esthetic vibrations, feeds on plaudits, and is addicted to reading. This bookish Roosevelt gets his due in the press, but some deeper political instinct tells him to subordinate the cap and gown to the lariat and the rifle. So he neither parades his cultural preoccupations before the rank and file nor condescends to them. Nor does he hint of the gulf separating Theodore Roosevelt of Oyster Bay and Harvard's Porcellian from the worthy people he conscientiously serves.

Theodore Roosevelt was a latter-day representative of the old Federalist elite first dispossessed by Andrew Jackson and his sweaty democrats and later denied power by the major parties. Hopes that the Civil War would burn out the national rot and restore a civic-minded, gentlemanly minority to positions of influence were briefly entertained and quickly flattened. The good-government people ("Goo-Goos" or "Mugwumps," as stalwart Republicans contemptuously referred to them) carried little weight in party councils. High-minded aspirants to political office faced cheerless options. They could organize campaigns to elect honest candidates in state and local contests, knowing that the rascals would be back after the flurry of reform; or, like the sardonic Henry Adams, they could withdraw from the action and watch—and document—the downfall of the republic. They could concede their political impotence and take up some other vocation; or, and this was the most atypical of strategies, they could work with the party bosses who determined the outcome of elections and bide their time. Roosevelt wanted to rule instead of being ruled by his inferiors. That meant taking the plunge into machine politics and braving the warnings of his social peers that politics was a dirty game, one no gentleman ought to play.

He proved them wrong. He bearded the bruisers. And thanks to his unquenchable ego and boldness, well-placed allies, a widely publicized act of derring-do in a brisk war, and a fortuitous assassination, he found himself president of the United States. Brooks Adams, Henry's brother and the brother-in-law of Henry Cabot Lodge, Roosevelt's closest friend, hailed him as the new Caesar. "'Thou hast it now: King, Cawdor, Glamis, all—'" he wrote him. "The world can give no more. You hold a place greater than Trajan's, for you are the embodiment of a power not only vaster than the power of the Empire, but vaster than men have ever known." Roosevelt listened more attentively to Adams's historical scenarios than he would admit, but he also considered him a little cracked. Having already pondered Macbeth and rebuked Cromwell (while half forgiving him) for his dictatorial acts, he wasn't about to upset any apple carts. If the business tycoons and professional politicians questioned his soundness, informed conservatives claimed him rightly as one of their own. He might verbally whip the

Trusts and "the malefactors of great wealth," shake his finger at them, appeal to their patriotism, but he followed an expedient course.

Even when he appeared to have broken out of the traces between 1912 and 1916, consorting with ideologues and nostrum-mongers and sounding very radical indeed, his political philosophy hadn't significantly changed. He still believed in order at all costs, in an idealism sensibly constrained; and though he was exasperated by the greed, stupidity, and arrogance of the big capitalists, he continued to worry more about a surly and knavish working class and the possibility of class war.

A book published in Roosevelt's heyday inadvertently abstracted him into a social type. This was Thorstein Veblen's 1899 *The Theory of the Leisure Class,* a study in the customs, attitudes, and styles of behavior of America's leisured elite, its would-be patriciate. Veblen presented this well-heeled tribe as the preservers of "archaic traits" and "devout observances." Their barbarian rituals obviously served no useful purpose in modern industrial society, but paradoxically their very obsolescence made them reputable in American cultural and institutional life. Veblen noted in particular how the leisure class prolonged the "puerile phase" in its children's development by encouraging their "proclivity for exploits" and truculent athleticism.

Similarly, a great deal of make-believe, he observed, pervaded leisure-class sporting pastimes. The mildest of men who went out shooting were "apt to carry an excess of arms and accoutrements in order to impress upon their own imagination the seriousness of their undertaking." They were also prone "to a histrionic prancing gait and to an elaborate exaggeration of the motions, whether of stealth or of onslaught, involved in their deeds of exploit." Football as well was imbued with "a colourable make-believe of purpose." Just as hunters systematically slaughtered their prey in the name of wholesome outdoor recreation and nature worship, so college football purportedly built strong bodies and fostered "a manly spirit." In reality, Veblen dryly asserted, that popular sport bore the same relation to physical culture "as the bull-fight to agriculture," and far from inculcating good fellowship and self-sacrifice, it encouraged a ferocity and predatory cunning that were readily adaptable to business or military enterprise.

Reading Veblen's deadpan sociological satire with Theodore Roosevelt in mind, one is reminded time and again of his sentiments and tastes, of his letters to Harvard football captains, for example, or his celebration of the fighting instincts, his eagerness for battle, and his frequent recourse in speaking and writing to the metaphors of war. Again, Roosevelt's pleasure in bloody Icelandic sagas and his wish that "The Battle Hymn of the Republic" (in which God is the "Him" of Battle) would become the national anthem are consistent with Veblen's profile of the martial socialite chieftain presiding over the sanguinary rites of his class.

In a discerning review of Veblen's book, William Dean Howells noted the insatiable appetite of ordinary Americans "for everything that relates to the life removed from work, from the simple Republican idea." The Roosevelt who in exalted moments conflated peaceful habits with besotted materialism and whose most cherished memories were of war and the chase became for them a figure of absorbing fascination. He lived their daydreams and touched their hearts and minds so long as he stayed in the limelight toward which he was tropistically drawn. Not long after his ouster from "the corridors of power," he dwindled in the public eye, and although never without champions while he lived, or thereafter for that matter, he never again assumed Mt. Rushmore proportions in the popular imagination.

Today his labors seem less herculean than his dazzled supporters perceived them to be. No public policy of lasting importance is attached to his name, save perhaps his conservation legislation which in our environment-conscious age seems more important than it did in his. Roosevelt the expansionist sent the fleet around the world and engineered the securing of the Panamanian isthmus and the construction of the canal ("by far the most important action I took in foreign affairs," he wrote); but (and to his deep regret) no major domestic crisis or foreign war tested him to the extreme. He wrote no outstanding state paper or literary work. To be sure, the same could be said of all but a few American presidents, but then not many of them were reputedly blessed with such splendid and diverse talents or shared his Icarian aspirations.

What's still arresting about him has less to do with the artifact, the posturing Teddy Roosevelt of the cartoons, than with his tenderer double who occasionally emerges in his letters and books, one who could drop the remark that the Dakota Badlands looked the way Poe sounded, or compare the extinction of the carrier pigeon to the destruction "of all the works of some great writer." "Charming" was the word often applied to him, a curious term for the thickset, hand-crushing monologuist but understandable to a reader of his correspondence. His tough carapace, like Hemingway's, protected a sensibility evidenced in moments of passivity, very rare with him, when nature (bird songs, plains, mountains, forests, and the like) imposed on him rather than the other way around. Walt Whitman detected such moments in Roosevelt's western reminiscences. They showed "a little touch of the dude," Whitman told Horace Traubel, but when Roosevelt looked and listened, he "realized" the alluring contours and spirit "of that wild Western life" and got "pretty near the truth."

During Theodore Roosevelt's incumbency, the White House acquired an imperial tone, but it wasn't dull or parochial or vulgar. It became a place where civilized company gathered at the behest of an energetic and cultivated host. Driven by an ungovernable curiosity, his range of interests and concerns exceeded those of all other presidents, Jefferson excepted. He reached out to men and women who wrote and said things that appealed to him, and he strained to stay abreast of the world's work. Can the same be said (and I include the second Roosevelt and John F. Kennedy) of the previous or subsequent occupants of the White House?

When Theodore Roosevelt died, according to one of his contemporaries, "it was as though the wind had fallen, a light had gone out, a military band had stopped playing." He had been on display for almost forty years, a public-spirited man ablaze with good intentions, self-absorbed if not introspective, and totally devoid of skepticism. He remained attractively and unattractively boyish until the end. In the Wilson years, his behavior was mischievous and vindictive. He withheld his sympathies from anything alien to his ancestral pieties, whether it was the muck raked up by reformers or the import of Tolstoy's "decadent" *Kreutzer Sonata*. He was broad, not deep. He liked happy endings, and he closed his ears to reports from the pit. He doesn't really belong on the granite mountain top with the titans.

Marcus Klein (essay date 1994)

SOURCE: "Easterns, Westerns, and Private Eyes," in *Easterns, Westerns, and Private Eyes: American Matters, 1870-1900,* The University of Wisconsin Press, 1994, pp. 78-87.

[*In the following essay, Klein discusses the figure of the cowboy as portrayed in various works by Roosevelt.*]

Imperialism was a principle. In his Foreword to the 1900 edition of his *The Winning of the West,* Theodore Roosevelt would justify the invasion of Cuba in 1898 as an extension, to the east, of the western continental expansion which in turn, he said, "has been the central and all-important feature of our history." In the four large volumes of the book itself, 1889-1896, he had elaborated the theme of the inevitability of "race expansion," the most striking instance of which in all of time had been that of the English-speaking peoples. "It is, indeed," he had said, "a warped, perverse, and silly morality which would forbid a course of conquest that has turned whole continents into the seats of mighty and flourishing civilized nations. . . . In its results, and viewed from the standpoint of applied ethics, the conquest and settlement by the whites of the Indian lands was necessary to the greatness of the race and to the well-being of civilized mankind." "This great continent," he had said, "could not have been kept as nothing but a game-preserve for squalid savages." In 1860 the author of *Seth Jones* had paused in his narrative to observe that "when the Anglo-Saxon's body is pitted against that of the North American Indian, it sometimes yields; but when his mind takes the place of contestant, it *never* loses," but Roosevelt would be less moping. "The warlike borderers who thronged across the Alleghenies," he reflected, and "the restless and reckless hunters, the hard, dogged, frontier farmers, by dint of grim tenacity, overcame and displaced Indians,

French, and Spaniards alike, exactly as, fourteen hundred years before, Saxon and Angle had overcome and displaced the Cymric and Gaelic Celts."

And if Roosevelt with his "abnormal energy" (in Henry Adams's phrase) brought a special forcefulness to the argument, his views here were not unique. Eventually he himself would discard the term "Anglo-Saxon race," but prior to the turn of the century he was speaking for respected and advanced theory, which brought science (with German university pedigree) to Manifest Destiny, and which had impressive supporters. Roosevelt, says the historian Thomas G. Dyer, had absorbed ideas of Anglo-Saxon and/or Teutonic superiority from his teachers including Nathaniel Southgate Shaler, at Harvard, and John Burgess, at Columbia. Shaler was a geologist, historian, and naturalist who, in Dyer's words, "enthusiastically accepted notions of white supremacy, innate black immorality, and the desirability of slavery as an instrument of necessary racial 'adjustment' ." Roosevelt the historian corresponded regularly with such other Anglo-Saxonists as Henry Fairfield Osborn, director of the Museum of Natural History in New York, David Starr Jordan of Stanford, Senator Henry Cabot Lodge, Rudyard Kipling, Sir George Trevelyan, and Edward Alsworth Ross (who had invented the term "race suicide"), and advanced his own refinements. Like Shaler, he was a Lamarckian and therefore in particular he was able to entertain the idea of not only an "Anglo-Saxon race" but a distinct "American race". And it followed from observation, for both Nathaniel Shaler and Roosevelt that, again in Dyer's words, Americans were "quicker witted and more adaptable to change than the other white 'races'."

It followed that in the story of the winning of the west, the idea of an "American race" discovered its seemingly inevitable expression, while in Teddy Roosevelt the idea found not only its most energetic proponent but its natural bard. No matter indeed where he might have come upon the idea for itself, first or later, Roosevelt knew that idea both for itself and in its poetry, the latter especially, and for the particular reason that he had lived it, or almost had.

The period covered by *The Winning of the West* was for the most part the late eighteenth century, only. At the end of volume 4 Roosevelt had not got much beyond the Louisiana Purchase. But if obviously it was homework that gave him the basic narrative, nonetheless and with whatever seeming whimsy, perhaps impudence, he tended to confirm history by reference to personal experience. He knew the *type* of the frontiersman, so he said, and the type did not change. In the footnotes, where he might have claimed scholarly authority, as often as not he cited personal acquaintance. Did Daniel Boone once remain alone in the wilderness for three months? Such endurance was to be expected of the type, for "in 1880, two men whom I knew wintered to the west of the Bighorns, 150 miles from any human beings," going nine months without seeing a white face, and "last winter (1887-88) an old trapper, a friend of mine in the days when he hunted

buffalo, spent five months entirely alone in the mountains north of the Flathead country." Did Daniel Boone refer once to *Gulliver's Travels?* Frontiersmen were *likely* to be readers, and "the better men among them appreciate really good literature quite as much as any other class of people. In the long winter evenings they study to good purpose books as varied as Dante, Josephus, Macaulay, Longfellow, Parton's 'Life of Jackson,' and the Rollo stories—to mention only volumes that have been especial favorites with my own cowboys and hunters".

He had gone to the West in September of 1883, at the age of twenty-six, for personal reasons, following upon personal tragedy. His mother and his wife had died, within twelve hours of each other. He owned two ranches in the Dakota Territories. Like many of his wealthy young friends, he had invested in western land. He went now to his ranches needing time and distance, but he stayed on, living on one or the other of the ranches for a period of almost three years, actually working as a ranch owner and cattle boss; later, therefore, when he referred to the authority of his personal experience, he had it.

At the time of this first trip to the West he was also already a recognized historian, and therefore had his additional authority, while still in his twenties. His first historical work, *The Naval War of 1812,* had been published in 1882. Also while yet in his twenties he was a recognized naturalist and "ethnologist," and as well, further, was already something of a political leader. He was a rising star in the New York State Assembly.

On the other hand, and just because of who he was and probably inevitably, his discovery of the West, both in the first instance and later, was directed by concerns other than discovery just for itself. Now and later when TR spoke of the West, he spoke to the East, and for the sake of the East. By birth, upbringing, milieu, as well as by his several careers, he was as eastern a person as one could be, for all of the western costuming early and late. He addressed himself to that Eastern Establishment to which he himself belonged more certainly than almost anybody. He was an eighth-generation New Yorker on his father's side. Had he happened to have been born in Georgia, on his mother's side he would have been a sixth-generation Georgian. He was heir to very substantial if not extravagant old money. His natural habitat was old family. Of Teddy's first wife's father, his friend Owen Wister was to say, in his biography of Roosevelt, "Henry Lee was one of those fine Americans with Colonial traditions who knew how to be rich," and while the statement was not appropriate to TR himself, it suggested a state of mind with which certainly he would have been very familiar. At the time he went West he was already the apostle for the strenuous life, but the quarrel with luxury reasonably was addressed to his own class and was within the family. When he famously said, "A life of slothful ease, a life of that peace which springs merely from lack either of desire or of power to strive after great things, is as little worthy of a nation as of an individual. . . . When men fear work or fear righteous war, when women fear motherhood, they tremble on the brink of doom"—it was to the men of the Hamilton Club of Chicago that he was speaking. Inevitably it was as an easterner in excellent social standing that he discovered the West, as it was as an easterner whose expectation as well as destiny it was to rule, that he created his version of the West and the westerner.

His friend Wister would later say, in the biography, that Roosevelt had been the pioneer in taking the cowboy seriously. Whether or not so, and no matter how much or little the cowboy whom Roosevelt put into print and whom for the rest of his life he valorized resembled any actual cowboy, he did discover in this livestock attendant an emblem of national importance and did compose a remarkably complex, seductive, and durable figure.

Whatever his intentions and presumptions, nonetheless there can be no doubting the immediacy of Roosevelt's response to the West. He wrote two books about his experience in the Dakotas, *Hunting Trips of a Ranchman,* published 1885, and *Ranch Life and the Hunting Trail,* published 1888. As a writer Roosevelt was more fluent than he was eloquent, but there were moments in those books when the composition was quite wonderfully fresh, vital, and engaged. Given the personal circumstances, perhaps the West was at this point dogmatically redemptive for him. In any event, he thrilled to the sight of the animals he hunted—the water-fowl, the grouse, white-tail and black-tail deer, antelope, mountain sheep—and described them with the talents and enthusiasm of the naturalist he was. He could take the life of the West to himself so intimately as to find it tasty: "Elk tongues are most delicious eating," he would advise, in the first of the two books, "being juicy, tender, and well flavored; they are excellent to take out as a lunch on a long hunting trip." He found to his great delight that the Bad Lands, for all that they deserved to be called such, as he thought, were open and in many places still untouched. He was as delighted by that fact as had been Mark Twain coming upon a virgin shore of Lake Tahoe.

Nor was it as a frontiersman or conquering Anglo Saxon that he himself arrived in the West. The West was for Roosevelt what it was for others particularly of his class: a pastoral, a garden, a picnic. For Roosevelt as for others, the West of the 1880s was already a fatally established refuge for status. In the seventies and eighties the trip to the Far West had become something of an acceptable alternative to the Grand Tour, except that it might be more expensive. "The number of Harvard graduates alone that appeared on the cattle frontier is ample testimony," says the historian Gene M. Gressley, "to the fact that long hours were spent in the Hasty Pudding Club by scions of wealthy families romanticizing the West as a place for adventure." By the time Roosevelt went to the West, in 1883, two transcontinental railroads had already been completed. The Pullmans were in service, as were the grand resorts in the West where wealthy men played polo on mustangs. The West in this aspect was an interlude between an immediate past and an immediate future,

rather than being a frontier, and rapidly was becoming only a locale for imagination.

Obviously the West was doomed, despite the fact that some areas of it were still untouched. Moreover, and more potentially perturbing, the specific agent of doom was eastern money in the possession of eastern family and power, carrying with it eastern ideas of order and polity and history, which was to say everything that Teddy Roosevelt himself represented. He himself was the agent of the destruction of the West, even in fact according to his own speculations about the future of the West.

Therefore seemingly, and after such knowledge, with great wit Roosevelt altered the tense and mood of his immediate observations of the West. That which was before him he regarded in future perfect. For all of the apparent immediacy of his delight, from the very first, in 1885, the West in his perception became a locale where displacement was natural law. His was a storied West, doom becoming a part of the story. The white hunters and trappers had expelled the Indians, so Roosevelt observed, who themselves had driven out the game. Now the cattle ranchers were displacing the hunters but would in their turn soon be forced from the land by new settlers. In *Hunting Trips* he reflected, "For we ourselves and the life that we lead will shortly pass away from the plains as completely as the red and white hunters who have vanished from before our herds." The buffalo had already disappeared, and the elk were at the point of extinction. "The free, open-air life of the ranchman," he said, "the pleasantest and healthiest life in America, is from its very nature ephemeral. The broad and boundless prairies have already been bounded and will soon be made narrow." He was not against fencing but, he said, at age twenty-seven, he hoped against hope that he himself would not live to see it.

The West was by this much a locale for high melancholy. No doubt that the West had its aggressive reality, but at the same time it was also a kind of confirming fiction, and was one very much like the reigning fiction of the antebellum South, as indeed Roosevelt perceived. His fellow ranchers, he said in *Hunting Trips of a Ranchman,* were men who had a stake in the country having invested their wealth in it. They constituted "a class whose members were in many respects closely akin to the old Southern planters." They had the manners and the moral authority of the old Southern planters, and that was to imply that his fellow ranchers as well shared their poignancy, that namely of a defeated aristocracy.

Cowboys, too, Roosevelt observed in *Ranch Life and the Hunting Trail,* although they came from anywhere, prevailingly were southerners, as might be considered to be appropriate beyond the mere fact of the matter, because southerners were better candidates than other Americans for a role of proud and sure defeat. If Roosevelt was serious about cowboys, no doubt he was so because he discovered in them an image of something he wanted to discover. Clearly he considered that they were the knights errant of the West. They were the personnel of a lost cause, miraculously surviving to carry on for a while and to be an emblem for a blighted age, about to be swept up into the dominating theme of disappearances, but meanwhile constituting a revelation. They were cause for joy and sorrow, being reminders of the line of the heroes. They had displaced the plainsman and the mountain man of an earlier era. "In the place of these heroes of a bygone age, the men who were clad in buckskin and who carried long rifles, stands," said Roosevelt, in *Hunting Trips,* "or rather rides, the bronzed and sinewy cowboy, as picturesque and self-reliant, as dashing and resolute as the saturnine Indian fighters whose place he has taken; and, alas that it should be written! he in his turn must at no distant time share the fate of the men he has displaced. The ground over which he so gallantly rides his small, wiry horse will soon know him no more, and in his stead there will be the plodding grangers and husbandmen."

The glamour of the figure was intricate with knowledge of defeat near at hand. The cowboy was a temporary staving-off of what one knew, according to the lessons of contemporary events in the East, and in the North, to be the likely death of the tradition of the heroes. The cowboy was that which was imperilled by modern times and by the East, which two quantities were synonymous.

The cowboy was an antique hero, equipped to be just that with the necessary and complex qualifications of looks, manner, vigor, race, and silence. "They are mostly of native birth," Roosevelt discovered, in *Hunting Trips,*

> and although there are among them wild spirits from every land, yet the latter soon become undistinguishable from their American companions, for these plainsmen are far from being so heterogeneous a people as is commonly supposed. On the contrary, all have a certain curious similarity to each other; existence in the west seems to put the same stamp upon each and every one of them. Sinewy, hardy, self-reliant, their life forces them to be both daring and adventurous, and the passing over their heads of a few years leaves printed on their faces certain lines which tell of dangers quietly fronted and hardships uncomplainingly endured. They are far from being as lawless as they are described; though they sometimes cut queer antics when, after many months of lonely life, they come into a frontier town in which drinking and gambling are the only recognized forms of amusement, and where pleasure and vice are considered synonymous terms. On the round-ups, or when a number get together, there is much boisterous, often foul-mouthed mirth; but they are rather silent, self-contained men when with strangers.

Also, they wore a costume which was "both picturesque and serviceable," consisting of a broad felt hat, a flannel shirt with a bright silk handkerchief loosely knotted around the neck," trousers tucked into high-heeled boots, "shaps," and a large-calibre revolver, which had further implications. Such figures might excite wonder in New

York, or even Chicago, as in fact they would do. They were distinctive, and somewhat flaunting (the handkerchief), and not a little ominous (the revolver), but finally they were a race apart.

They also, in fact, had a bad reputation, which in some ways Roosevelt reinforced. A few years earlier no lesser than the president of the United States, Chester A. Arthur, had also taken cowboys seriously; in 1881 in one of his addresses to the Congress he had referred to the numbers of "armed desperadoes known as 'Cowboys'" who were terrorizing Arizona. Now in Roosevelt's version they were still a company of armed men who, if rather silent and self-contained when with strangers, by that same bearing discouraged friendship, but for Roosevelt they seemed to be also alluring even when wicked. In any event he presented the wicked with attributes which would prove to be the basic enduring stuff of legend. In *Ranch Life* he would say that he had known "'bad men,' or professional fighters and man-killers [who] are, of course, used to brawling, and are not only sure shots, but, what is equally important, able to 'draw' their weapons with marvelous quickness. . . . These desperadoes always try to 'get the drop' on a foe—that is, to take him at a disadvantage before he can use his own weapon."

The cowboys were incongruous except in their own habitat, but then the place itself was less exotic than it was admonishing. The West might be a rapidly passing fancy, but it was also a demonstration of an ultimate truth of things containing implications for true social organization and evolution. "The whole existence [of ranch life] is patriarchal in character," said Roosevelt in *Ranch Life,* and was "the life of men who live in the open, who tend their herds on horseback, who go armed and ready to guard their lives by their own prowess, whose wants are very simple, and who call no man master." "Ranching," he said, "is an occupation like those of vigorous, primitive pastoral peoples, having little in common with the humdrum, workaday business world of the nineteenth century; and the free ranchman in his manner of life shows more kinship to an Arab sheik than to a sleek city merchant or tradesman." And: "The struggle for existence is very keen in the far West," he would say, "and it is no place for men who lack the ruder, coarser virtues and physical qualities." In the West law, too, was crude but was emphatic, and it too apparently was attractive to the ex-legislator from the state of New York. He took it upon himself to serve for a time as an under-sheriff in the Dakotas. Together with a couple of his cowboys, he had once captured a trio of horse thieves and had had his picture taken with them—but it is to be noted as well that he had taken care to preserve his station. His own morals certainly were better than those of the horse thieves, but just as importantly so were his tastes. He made note of his horse thieves' reading habits. They owned dime novels and "the inevitable 'History of the James Brothers'" and, surprisingly, "a large number of more or less drearily silly 'society' novels, ranging from Ouida's to those of The Duchess and Augusta J. Evans," while he at this moment, on the trail, was reading *Anna Karenina.*

No doubt Roosevelt discovered in his cowboys such qualities as he wanted to discover for his own sake for this moment, but in so doing he also did create a figure which for the whole of his public life would be a symbol of not only personal but national recuperation. His own astonishing popularity would in the future go quite beyond politics. "'Great-heart!' Roosevelt! Father of men!'" would cry out Vachel Lindsay; similarly, no other president of the United States could have inspired anything like "Teddy Bears." Not that it was only his association with cowboys, early and continued, that made him to be tonic for a nation, but the cowboy connection undoubtedly added another quantity to the heartiness.

The cowboy was health and restoration.

Thus the regiment of Roosevelt's "Rough Riders" in 1898 would be popularly known to be a meeting of East, in a Rooseveltian version, with West, also in a Rooseveltian version, issuing in the legend of San Juan Hill. The regiment was made up of a number of eastern "swells" together with a greater number of actual cowboys from the Southwest, in a proportion of approximately one to two, and it was remarked on all sides that they got along very well together. The explicit lesson in that was that this fellowship was both right and was fertile for heroism. They were brothers after all, long lost from each other. The cowboy had returned. The cowboy was the measure of these certain easterners, who did now measure up to family obligation. It was pointed out that while the easterners were students and clubmen, they were also athletes and trained sportsmen and finally therefore were entitled to the company they kept.

Thus during the years of the presidency, Roosevelt repeatedly confronted eastern propriety with western virtue. In his *Autobiography* he recalled the day at the White House when an old friend from the cow camps had happened to drop by just before lunch while he was entertaining Lord Bryce, and he had said to his friend, "Remember, Jim, that if you shoot at the feet of the British Ambassador to make him dance, it would be likely to cause international complications." Thus, just as his distant predecessor James K. Polk had installed Nathaniel Hawthorne in the Custom House at Salem, so Roosevelt appointed Pat Garrett collector of the customs at El Paso. Pat Garrett was an old friend who had shot Billy the Kid, and patronage in a high sense was still in order. In the late summer of 1903 Roosevelt went to Colorado. There, once, caparisoned presidentially in top hat and frock coat, so he wrote to John Hay, he ate his grub at the tail end of a chuck wagon, and relished the joke of it.

That the cowboy virtues were also proper political virtues, he well knew from particular experience. In *Ranch Life and the Hunting Trail* he recalled the occasion in 1886 when the cowboys on his ranches had volunteered to join the ranch owners in a private cavalry to fight off the Indians in the neighborhood, proving that in the West *comitatus* endured. Or the model was feudal and chivalric. It was decided ultimately that the task of the defense fell to the owners, but nevertheless the sentiments of the cowboys were much appreciated. Nor were his cowboys isolated from events in the republic at large. To the contrary, they followed events with a passion. Roosevelt recalled that they had been eager to obtain reports of the riot in Haymarket Square in Chicago in 1886, and that they followed the trials of the Anarchists. "The day that the Anarchists were hung in Chicago," he remembered, "my men joined with the rest of the neighborhood in burning them in effigy."

There was a lesson here for a time of misrule, written into an entertainment.

FURTHER READING

Biography

Burton, David H. *Theodore Roosevelt*. New York: Twayne Publishers, Inc., 1972, 236 p.
  Endeavors "to discover in Roosevelt's mind, in his thought, and in his values . . . truths about him which either have been ignored, or more commonly, misunderstood."

Harbaugh, William Henry. *The Life and Times of Theodore Roosevelt*. New York: Collier Books, 1967, revised edition, 540 p.
  Biography designed for the general reader, based upon primary sources and scholarly appraisals of his career.

Putnam, Carleton. *Theodore Roosevelt, Volume One: The Formative Years 1858-1886*. New York: Charles Scribner's Sons, 1958, 626 p.
  Describes Roosevelt's youth, incorporating new material from his family, such as his father's diaries and a previously unavailable eight-volume collection of his letters.

Vidal, Gore. "Theodore Roosevelt: An American Sissy." In *The Second American Revolution and Other Essays (1976-1982)*, pp. 209-23. New York: Random House, 1982.
  Anecdotal and satirical essay on Roosevelt.

Criticism

Blum, John Morton. *The Republican Roosevelt*. Cambridge, Mass.: Harvard University Press, 1965, 170 p.
  Interpretive summary of Roosevelt's political career.

Braden, Waldo W. "Theodore Roosevelt." In *American Orators of the Twentieth Century: Critical Studies and Sources*, edited by Bernard K. Duffy and Halford R. Ryan, pp. 353-59. New York: Greenwood Press, 1987.
  Discusses Roosevelt's speech-making and rhetoric.

Cordingly, Nora E. "Extreme Rarities in the Published Works of Theodore Roosevelt." *Papers of the Bibliographical Society of America* 39, No. 1 (1945): 20-50.
> Examines several rare literary works and fragments by Roosevelt.

Cutright, Paul Russell. *Theodore Roosevelt: The Making of a Conservationist*. Urbana: University of Illinois Press, 1985, 286 p.
> Explores Roosevelt's youthful exploits and writings as a naturalist.

Ferguson, Charles W. "Roosevelt—Man of Letters." *Bookman (New York)* 64, No. 6 (February 1927): 726-29.
> Review of *The Works of Theodore Roosevelt* that praises his writings on humanism and naturalism.

Fischer, Robert and James T. Gay. "A Post-mortem of Theodore Roosevelt in Historical Writings, 1919-1929." *Mid-America: An Historical Review* 56, No. 3 (July 1974): 139-59.
> Overview of the largely adulatory literature on Roosevelt from the 1920s.

Friedenberg, Robert V. *Theodore Roosevelt and the Rhetoric of Militant Decency*. New York: Greenwood Press, 1990, 209 p.
> Includes the texts of Roosevelt's significant speeches preceded by a critical analysis.

Gatewood, Willard B., Jr. *Theodore Roosevelt and the Art of Controversy: Episodes of the White House Years*. Baton Rouge: Louisiana State University Press, 1970, 294 p.
> Collection of essays on Roosevelt's responses "to diverse issues which attracted attention in the Progressive Era"—the status of African-Americans, the role of organized labor, federal patronage of the arts, and other questions.

Gould, Lewis L. *The Presidency of Theodore Roosevelt*. Lawrence: University Press of Kansas, 1991, 355 p.
> Details President Roosevelt's public activities while in office.

Grantham, Dewey W., Jr. "Theodore Roosevelt in American Historical Writing, 1945-1960." *Mid-America: An Historical Review* 43, No. 1 (January 1961): 3-35.
> Surveys literature on Roosevelt from the post-WWII era.

Morris, Edmund. "As a Literary Lion, Roosevelt Preached What He Practiced." *Smithsonian* 14, No. 8 (November 1983): 86-95.
> Anecdotal study of Roosevelt's literary exploits and the contemporary critical reception of his work.

Mowry, George E. *The Era of Theodore Roosevelt, 1900-1912*. New York: Harper & Row Publishers, 1958, 330 p.
> Evaluates Roosevelt's personality, activities, and political impact in the early years of the twentieth century.

Oliver, Lawrence J. "'On Deck' with Roosevelt during the Campaign for American Cultural Independence." In *Brander Matthews, Theodore Roosevelt, and the Politics of American Literature, 1880-1920*, pp. 112-44. Knoxville: University of Tennessee Press, 1992, 254 p.
> Investigates Roosevelt's role in the development of a culturally American literature.

Weber, Carl J. "Poet and President." *New England Quarterly* 16, No. 4 (December 1943): 615-26.
> Recounts Roosevelt's correspondence with the poet Edwin Arlington Robinson.

Additional coverage of Roosevelt's life and career is contained in the following sources published by Gale Research: *Contemporary Authors*, Vol. 115; *Dictionary of Literary Biography*, Vol 47.

Max Weber

1864–1920

German sociologist, economist, and political theorist.

INTRODUCTION

Regarded as one of the founders of modern sociological thought, Weber has had an immense impact on social science in the twentieth century, especially in the United States, and was one of the first to construct a systematic, methodological approach to the study of human behavior in society. Basing his conclusions on the comparative study of nearly all the major world cultures, Weber analyzed the economic, political, intellectual, historical, and religious factors that contribute to modern social realities. Among his major contributions to the field of sociology are his assessments of modern bureaucracy, his study of the nature of charismatic leadership throughout world history, his models of rational and non-rational social behavior based upon his theory of "ideal types," and his examination of the circumstances that made the growth of western capitalism possible. As part of the latter, Weber's *Die protestantische Ethik und der Geist des Kapitalismus* (1904-05, *The Protestant Ethic and the Spirit of Capitalism*) has had a profound effect on the study of the ethical and religious dimensions of economic issues. Weber's other significant achievements include the elevation of comparative and empirical research in sociology and the related integration of *wertfreiheit,* or value-neutrality, as the ideal for field. Weber's work in the realms of economics and political science is likewise highly valued, especially as it indicates his role in German political life during the early years of the twentieth century.

Biographical Information

Weber was born in Erfaut, Germany, on April 21, 1864. His father was a prosperous lawyer involved in German political circles and his mother was a religious woman who nonetheless emphasized the importance of secular education. Weber received classical instruction in his youth and later attended the University of Heidelberg to study law, history, and economics. He left the university briefly in 1883 to serve in the German army, but returned to his studies the following year, first at the University of Berlin and later at Göttingen. Passing the bar in 1886, Weber practiced law for a time, and in 1889 completed his doctoral thesis on the rise of medieval trading companies. A second dissertation, an agrarian history of the ancient world, appeared in 1891 and earned Weber the widespread admiration of his colleagues. The following year he undertook a renowned study of the economic conditions common among peas-

ants in Prussia. He married Marianne Schnitger, his distant cousin, and later his biographer, in 1893. Weber accepted a professorship in economics at Freiburg University in 1894 and later a position as economics chair at the University of Heidelberg. Incapacitated in 1897 after his father's death, Weber suffered from an extreme depression and nervous illness for several years, though he had largely recovered by 1902. The next period of his life saw an increased literary production including his editorship and frequent contributions to the *Archiv für Sozialwissenschaft und Sozialpolitik* (*Archive for Social Science and Social Policy*). For the next fifteen years Weber devoted himself to the research and composition of his *Wirtschaft und Gesellschaft: Grundriss der verstehenden Soziologie,* 1922 (known in English as *Economy and Society: An Outline of Interpretive Sociology*), which included his studies of the great eastern religions and cultures. He returned to a professorship at the University of Munich in 1918 while writing *Economy and Society*, a massive work that was left incomplete due to his death from pneumonia on June 14, 1920.

Major Works

Taken as a whole, Weber's works on sociology and economics detail a nearly systematic development, encompassing the great cultures and religions in world history. His early works, though narrower in scope, adumbrate many of the themes that occupied his greatest writings, *Economy and Society* and the *Gesammelte Aufsätze zur Religionssoziologie* (1920-21). *Die römische agrargeschicte in ihrer bedeutung für das staats und privatrecht* (1891, *The Agrarian Sociology of Ancient Civilizations*) illustrates Weber's approach to structural and comparative history as a means of uncovering the facts relating to modern sociology. In his well-known *The Protestant Ethic and the Spirit of Capitalism* Weber argues that the Protestant Reformation was an important step in the increasing rationalization of western civilization and demonstrates the connection between the values of Protestantism and the rise of capitalism in Europe. The work also inspired Weber to study the sources of capitalism and the reasons why similar systems had failed to develop in eastern cultures. For his *Gesammelte Aufsätze zur Religionssoziologie*, Weber studied the religions of Hinduism, Buddhism, Confucianism, Taoism, and ancient Judaism, evaluating the relation of each to the development of rationalization in the modern era. In addition, Weber assessed the characteristics of modern bureaucracy by evaluating conditions found in China, India, and Imperial Rome. His masterwork, *Economy and Society*, contains a system of extraordinary depth and breadth, combining historical and comparative sociological research and analysis. Weber elucidates his concept of the "ideal type," a construct used for evaluating individuals and societies across huge spans of time, and explains his methodology predicated on the ideal of value-neutrality. As for his economic writings, a series of lectures entitled *Wirtschaftsgeschicte: Abriss der univer-salen Sozial und Wirtschaftsgeschicte* (1923) reflect his systematic, empirical, and comparative approach to the subject.

Critical Reception

Weber's worldwide influence on the field of sociology is perhaps second only to that of Karl Marx, and may be even more pervasive in the Unites States. Likewise, those who have criticized the specifics of his theories almost never fail to acknowledge his seminal contributions to social science. His importance is also borne out by the growing number of English translations of his works. Also, the controversies that Weber's conclusions have sparked continue among sociologists just as the methods of study and analysis that he devised endure.

PRINCIPAL WORKS

Entwicklung des Solidarhaftprinzips und des Sondervermögens der offenen Handelsgesellschaft aus den Haushalts und Gewerbegemeinschaften in den italienischen Städte (sociology) 1889

Zur Geschichte der handelsgesellschaften im mittelalter: Nach südeuropäischen Quellen (sociology) 1889

Die römische agrargeschichte in ihrer bedeutung für das staats und privatrecht [*The Agrarian Sociology of Ancient Civilizations*] (sociology) 1891

Die Verhältnisse der Landarbeiter im ostelbischen Deutschland (sociology) 1892

Die Börse (sociology) 1894

Der Nationalstaat und die Volkswirtschaftspolitik (sociology) 1895

Die "Objektivität" sozialwissenschaftlicher und sozialpolitischer Erkenntnis (sociology) 1904

Die protestantische Ethik und der Geist des Kapitalismus [*The Protestant Ethic and the Spirit of Capitalism*] 1904-05

Parlament und Regierung im neugeordneten Deutschsland: Zur politischen Kritik des Beamtentums und Parteiwesens (sociology) 1918

Wissenschaft als Beruf [*Science as a Vocation*] (lecture) 1918

Politik als Beruf [*Politics as a Vocation*] (lecture) 1919

Das antike Judentum [*Ancient Judaism*] (sociology) 1920-21

Gesammelte Aufsätze zur Religionssoziologie (sociology) 1920-21

Hinduismus und Buddhismus [*The Religion of India: The Sociology of Hinduism and Buddhism*] (sociology) 1920-21

Konfuzianismus und Taoismus [*The Religion of China: Confucianism and Taoism*] (sociology) 1920-21

Gesammelte politische Schriften (sociology) 1921

Die rationalen und soziologischen Grundlagen der Musik [*The Rational and Social Foundations of Music*] (sociology) 1921

Gesammelte Aufsätze zur Wissenschaftslehre (sociology) 1922

Religionssoziologie [*The Sociology of Religion*] (sociology) 1922

Wirtschaft und Gesellschaft: Grundriss der verstehenden Soziologie [*Economy and Society: An Outline of Interpretive Sociology*] (sociology) 1922; revised edition, 1956

Wirtschaftsgeschichte: Abriss der universalen Sozial und Wirtschaftsgeschichte [*General Economic History*] (economics) 1923

Gesammelte Aufsätze zur Sozial und Wirtschaftsgeschichte (sociology) 1924

Gesammelte Aufsätze zur Soziologie und Sozialpolitik (sociology) 1924

Jugendbriefe (letters) 1936

Essays in Sociology (sociology) 1946

Schriften zur theoretischen Soziologe, zur Soziologie der Politik und Verfassung (sociology) 1947

Aus den Schriften zur Religionssoziologie: Auswahl (sociology) 1948

The Methodology of the Social Science (sociology) 1949

Soziologie, weltgeschichtlich Analysen, Politik (sociology) 1955

Staatssoziologie (sociology) 1956

CRITICISM

Peter M. Blau (essay date 1962)

SOURCE: "Critical Remarks on Weber's Theory of Authority," in *The American Political Science Review,* Vol. LVII, No. 2, June, 1963, pp. 305-16.

[*Originally delivered as a lecture at the Annual Meeting of the American Political Science Association in 1962, the following essay examines the role of authority and bureaucracy in Weber's sociology.*]

Max Weber has often been criticized for advocating a *wertfrei,* ethically neutral approach in the social sciences and for thereby denying to man, in the words of Leo Strauss, "any science, empirical or rational, any knowledge, scientific or philosophic, of the true value system." On the other hand, Carl Friedrich points out that Weber's "ideal-type analysis led him to introduce value judgments into his discussion of such issues as bureaucracy." There is some justification for both these criticisms. Indeed, a characteristic of Weber's work is that it can be and has been subjected to opposite criticisms, not only in this respect but also in others. Historians object to his disregard for the specific historical conditions under which the social phenomena he analyzes have taken place, which sometimes leads him to combine historical events that occurred centuries apart into a conception of a social system. Sociologists, in contrast, accuse him of being preoccupied with interpreting unique historical constellations, such as Western capitalism, instead of studying recurrent social phenomena which make it possible to develop testable generalizations about social structures. His methodology is attacked as being neo-Kantian, but his concept of *Verstehen* is decried as implying an intuitionist method. While his theories are most frequently cited in contradistinction to those of Marx, they have also been described as basically similar to Marx's.

The fact that Weber's work can be attacked on opposite grounds is due to his position in the development of so-cial thought and, in particular, to his methodological and theoretical orientation. Weber is one of the fathers of modern sociology. His contribution to the development of this new discipline undoubtedly has been more significant than Comte's or Spencer's and second in importance only to that of Durkheim. Implicitly in his theoretical analyses and explicitly in his methodological writings, he outlined a new approach to the study of social life that helped to differentiate sociology from the other social sciences. He formulated the new approach in contradistinction to various existing alternatives. It was at variance with the idealistic tradition from which Weber himself derived as well as with Marx's materialism; with positivism, utilitarianism, and social Darwinism as well as with the Enlightenment philosophy of natural rights. The task he set for sociology is to interpret historical and social occurrences in terms of the prevailing value orientation that give them their meaning without imposing the investigator's value judgment on them. In short, the substantive aim is a value-free study of value complexes in societies. The methodological aim is a generalizing science of historical phenomena and processes.

One reason, then, why contradictory criticisms advanced against Weber's theory are often both valid is that the new approach he charted is a multiple synthesis which conflicts in some material respects with the various theses as well as the antitheses from which it derived. A more specific reason, as we shall see, is that Weber's method of analysis, notably his ideal-type construct, has limitations that leave his procedure wide open to a variety of criticisms. A final reason is that Weber's substantive theories tend to focus on conflicting social forces, which makes them subject to criticism from opposite perspectives; thus his analysis stressed the role of economic interests not enough for the Marxist and too much for the idealist.

Despite Weber's great concern with the forces that order and organize social life and integrate social systems (which, however, probably has been exaggerated in Parsons' interpretation of his theories), he did not view social structure as a functionally unified *Gestalt* but as a complex pattern governed by opposing forces and hence in continual flux. His overall conception of reality is perhaps most strongly influenced by Hegel's philosophy, as Bendix suggests. He usually proceeds by developing contrasting social types, only to show that both or all of them can be found in the same empirical situation, creating a dynamic potential for change. Notwithstanding his emphasis on the unrelenting forces of rationalization and bureaucratization, he also calls attention to the intermittent eruption of charismatic leaders and movements, thereby contradicting the linear conception of change his other analysis seems to imply. He is intrigued by the paradoxical consequences of social life. The most famous example is his conclusion that, although Confucianism approves and Puritanism disapproves of the pursuit of material welfare, Confucianism did not but Puritanism did promote the spirit of capitalism. Impatient with the oversimplification necessarily involved in subsuming empirical reality under a few general concepts, he constructed several pairs of concepts to examine the same contrast from slightly different perspectives, such as *wertrational* and *zweckrational,* substantive and formal rationality, charisma and bureaucracy. This dialectical and multifocused approach makes Weber's analysis rich and full of fascinating insights, but it also makes his theories somewhat unsystematic and open to diverse criticisms.

The purpose of this paper is to examine critically Weber's theory of authority. After briefly summarizing the main concepts and analysis, a methodological criticism of Weber's procedure and some substantive criticisms of this theory will be presented.

I. THE CONCEPT OF AUTHORITY

Power is defined by Weber as a person's ability to impose his will upon others despite resistance. He distinguishes two basic types of power, the domination of others that rests on the ability to influence their interests, and the domination that rests on authority, that is, the power to command and the duty to obey. Weber does not explicitly consider coercive power in his analysis of domination, nor does he deal with such forms of personal influence as persuasion, but it is convenient to clarify his concept of authority by contrasting it with these opposite extremes.

A fundamental criterion of authority "is a certain minimum of voluntary submission." An army commander may impose his will upon the enemy, but he does not have authority over enemy soldiers, only over his own, since only the latter obey his commands because they are duty-bound to do so, while the former merely yield to the coercive force of his superior arms. Since authority entails voluntary compliance with the superior's directives, it obviates the need for coercive force or for sanctions. Resort to either positive incentives or coercive measures by a person in order to influence others is *prima facie* evidence that he does not have authority over them, for if he did their voluntary compliance would serve as an easier method of control over them.

Voluntary obedience is not a sufficient condition for authority, however, since other forms of personal influence also rest on willing compliance. In persuasion, for example, one person permits the influence of another to influence his decisions or actions. Authority is distinguished from persuasion by the fact that people *a priori* suspend their own judgment and accept that of an acknowledged superior without having to be convinced that his is correct. The subordinate in an authority relationship "holds in abeyance his own critical faculties for choosing between alternatives and uses the formal criterion of the receipt of a command or signal as his basis for choice." In Weber's words, the "ruled" act as if they "had made the content of the (ruler's) command the maxim of their conduct for its own sake."

Authority, then, involves unconditional willing obedience on the part of subordinates. It is not easy, however, to distinguish authority by these criteria from other forms of control. The slaves who blindly obey their master although he does not use a whip, for fear that he may do so, are not very different from the soldiers who obey their commander or the officials who obey their bureaucratic superior, since they too know that the superior may otherwise invoke sanctions to penalize them. But if we consider the slave's obedience to be *voluntary* compliance, then the distinction between this concept and coercion loses all its meaning. Many borderline cases exist, according to Weber, both because the distinction is an analytical one and because coercion or other forms of control often later develop into authority. For this transformation to occur, however, a belief system must emerge that socially legitimates the exercise of control, and this legitimating value system furnishes the final and basic distinguishing criterion of authority. We speak of authority, therefore, if the willing unconditional compliance of a group of people rests upon their shared beliefs that it is legitimate for the superior (person or impersonal agency) to impose his will upon them and that it is illegitimate for them to refuse obedience.

Before turning to the three types of authority Weber differentiates, let us briefly note some problems raised by his central concept. Authority denotes imperative control, from which there is no easy escape, yet a major criterion of it is voluntary compliance. While I may have stressed the voluntary element in authority more than Weber does himself, I have done so deliberately to call attention to the implicit paradox between voluntarism and authoritarian control, since by making it explicit we can hope to clarify it. Weber ignores this paradox, despite his interest in paradoxical phenomena, because his focus on types of legitimacy leads him to take the existence of legitimate authority for granted and never systematically to examine the structural conditions under which it emerges out of other forms of power.

Another problem concerns the specific referent of Weber's concept of authority. When he presents his abstract definitions, he seems to refer to authority in interpersonal relations. In his analysis of empirical situations, on the other hand, he is concerned with political systems or institutions, such as feudalism. Moreover, in his analysis of historical cases where he applies and develops his concepts he sometimes treats them as concrete types and sometimes as analytical elements. Feudalism, for example, can hardly be considered an analytical element that can be found in all kinds of historical situations, but charisma can be, and Weber sometimes, although not always, treats it as an analytical element. To ignore the important methodological difference between these two kinds of concepts confuses the analysis. These difficulties stem from Weber's abstract conception of action and from the particular procedure he employed to derive generalizations about historical reality.

II. TYPES OF AUTHORITY

The distinctive feature of authority is a belief system that defines the exercise of social control as legitimate. Three types of authority are consequently distinguished by Weber on the basis of differences in the legitimating belief systems that validate them.

The first type is authority legitimated by the sanctity of tradition. In "traditional authority" the present social order is viewed as sacred eternal, and inviolable. The dominant person or group, usually defined by heredity, is thought to have been pre-ordained to rule over the rest. The subjects are bound to the ruler by personal dependence and a tradition of loyalty, and their obedience to him is further reinforced by such cultural beliefs as the divine right of kings. All systems of government prior to the development of the modern state would seem to exemplify traditional authority. Although the ruler's power is limited by the traditions that legitimate it, this restriction is not severe, since some arbitrariness on the part of the ruler is traditionally expected. Generally, traditional authority tends to perpetuate the *status quo* and is ill suited for adaptation to social change; indeed, historical change undermines its very foundation. The spirit of traditional authority is well captured in the phrase, "The king is dead—long live the king."

The values that legitimate "charismatic authority," Weber's second type, define a leader and his mission as being inspired by divine or supernatural powers. The leader, in effect, heads a new social movement, and his followers and disciples are converts to a new cause. There is a sense of being "called" to spread the new gospel, a sense of rejecting the past and heralding the future. Devotion to the leader and the conviction that his pronouncements embody the spirit and ideals of the movement are the source of the group's willing obedience to his commands. Charismatic leaders may appear in almost any area of social life—as religious prophets, political demagogues, or military heroes. Indeed, an element of charisma is involved whenever a person inspires others to follow his lead. Charismatic authority usually acts as a revolutionary force, inasmuch as it involves rejection of traditional values and a rebellion against the established order, often in reaction to a crisis. There is also an anarchistic streak in charismatic movements, a disdain for routine tasks and problems of organization or administration, since the leader's inspiration and the sacred mission must not be profaned by mundane considerations. For Weber, the innovating spirit of charisma is symbolized by Christ's words, "It is written . . . , but I say unto you. . . ."

The third type, "legal authority," is legitimated by a formalistic belief in the supremacy of the law whatever its specific content. The assumption is that a body of legal rules has been deliberately established to further the rational pursuit of collective goals. In such a system obedience is owed not to a person—whether traditional chief or charismatic leader—but to a set of impersonal principles. These principles include the requirement to follow directives originating from an office superior to one's own, regardless of who occupies this higher office. All organizations that have been formally established—in

contrast to the organizations of social life that have slowly emerged in the course of history or that have spontaneously erupted—illustrate legal authority structures. The prototype is the modern government which has a monopoly over the legitimate use of physical coercion, and the same principles are reflected in its various executive agencies, such as the army, and also in private corporations, such as a factory. While superiors have authority over subordinates, the former as well as the latter are subject to the authority of the official body of impersonal regulations. Legal authority may be epitomized in the phrase, "A government of laws, not of men."

At one point, Weber outlines these three plus a fourth type of belief that legitimates a social order, namely, "rational belief in an absolute value [which creates the legitimacy] of 'Natural Law.'" This fourth type of legitimate *order,* however, is not included in the subsequent more detailed analysis of legitimate *authority,* while the other three are. Does this imply that Weber considered a *wertrationale* orientation toward natural rights a possible basis of political institutions but not a basis of political authority? He makes no explicit statements to help us answer this question.

Although his typology of authority involves three main types and not two, it also reveals the Hegelian practice of Weber to refine concepts by juxtaposing opposites; only it entails a more complex combination of contrasts. The traditional authority which maintains the *status quo* is defined by contrast with two dynamic forces that threaten it, the revolutionary ideals advocated by a charismatic leader, and the rational pursuit of ends guided by abstract formal principles in disregard of historical tradition and time-honored convention. The personal submission to a charismatic leader is defined in juxtaposition with two impersonal forces that tend to undermine it in the course of historical developments, the crystallization of the revolutionary movement into a traditional order, and its bureaucratization into a rational formal organization. The formal acceptance of legal principles as authoritative is characterized in contradistinction to two irrational forces which must be overcome for such formal rationality to be realized, the power of tradition, and the power of charisma. Extrapolation from these contrasts yields two important features of each authority system. The power of tradition is neither rational nor strictly personal. (While there are personal elements in traditional authority, analytically traditionalism should be considered an impersonal force.) The power of charisma is dynamic and nonrational. The power of rational law, finally, is impersonal and dynamic.

Weber's extensive analysis of authority structures follows somewhat different directions in the case of each type. His discussion of traditional authority focuses upon differences between sub-types, notably between patrimonialism and feudalism. Although "both types have in common rulers who grant rights in return for military and administrative services," patrimonialism is an extension of the patriarchal authority of the master over his household to include a group of dependent officials, whereas feudalism originates in a contract between independent knights and an overlord. "If a knight enters the service of a ruler, he remains a free man; he does not become a personal dependent like the patrimonial retainer."

In his analysis of charismatic authority, on the other hand, Weber is not concerned with different sub-types or with historical antecedents but primarily with subsequent developments. He traces in detail the ways in which charisma tends to become routinized in the course of time and to develop into traditional or bureaucratic institutions. The personal significance of the leader makes charismatic structures inherently unstable.

Weber's discussion of legal authority deals both with the historical conditions that led to its development and with its implications for subsequent developments, but there is again a difference in focus. In his treatment of charisma, his concern is with its transformation into *other* systems. In his treatment of legal rationality, however, his concern is with the way in which *this* system increasingly penetrates all institutions and becomes more fully realized throughout society. In short, Weber's theory encompasses only the historical processes that lead from charismatic movements to increasing rationalization and does not include an analysis of the historical conditions and social processes that give rise to charismatic eruptions in the social structure. He has no theory of revolution.

Weber's concept of bureaucracy occupies a central place in his analysis of legal authority, since a bureaucracy is the prototype of a social structure that is formally organized in terms of the principles of legal rationality and authority. The various characteristics of bureaucracy stipulated by Weber are well known: officials are assigned specialized responsibilities; they are appointed to positions on the basis of technical expertness and expected to pursue a lifelong career; offices are organized into a hierarchy of authority and responsibility; operations are governed by a formally established system of rules and regulations; written documents of all official actions are maintained; and officials are expected to maintain impersonal detachment in their dealings with clients and subordinates—to name only the most important ones. Weber indicates the interdependence between these organizational attributes, and he stresses that this combination of attributes maximizes rational decision-making and administrative efficiency. He seems to have designed the ideal-type bureaucracy in a deliberate attempt to describe how a large number of men must be organized in order to promote administrative efficiency in the rational pursuit of given objectives. Optimum rationality and efficiency appear to be the criteria in terms of which the ideal type intentionally differs from empirical bureaucracies.

III. THE IDEAL TYPE

Before criticizing Weber's method of analysis, a few words must be said about his basic approach and the

important methodological contribution he has made. His aim, as previously mentioned, was an objective generalizing science of historical reality, where the meaning of social actions is interpreted in terms of their relationships to prevailing values. Important as economic forces were in his thinking—note how preoccupied he is with problems of Western capitalism—he considered them as well as all historical processes and social patterns in need of interpretation by a more basic principle, namely, the spirit of a community which gives all social life its meaning. While this basic conception reveals the influence of German idealism, Weber's reformulation of it is under the influence of materialistic philosophy. He conceived of the spirit of a society or of an age not as a supernatural force but as a common value orientation that is reflected in the prevailing, observable beliefs and actions of people. Besides, his interest centered on the interplay between these spiritual values and material conditions of existence, particularly the class structure. If he held that the development of modern capitalism was contingent on the ethical values of Calvinism, for example, he also showed that the nature of religious values depends on the class position of the status group in which they originate: in the case of Protestantism, the urban middle class. More dialectical than the one-sided idealism of Hegel or the one-sided materialism of Marx, he viewed the historical process as governed by the conflicts and combinations between spiritual ideals and material conditions.

In one respect, according to Weber, the method of sociology is unlike that of the natural sciences and like that of social philosophy. Since values give social life its meaning, it is not enough to show that two social conditions occur together or that one produces the other. It is also necessary to interpret these observations in terms of existing values. This is the gist of Weber's concept of *Verstehen,* as I understand it. In another respect, however, the method of sociology parallels that of the natural sciences and contrasts with that of history. Sociology is a generalizing science. Although every historical event is unique, the sociologist must ignore these unique aspects of social events and subsume them under general categories or types in order to generalize about them. Even if history furnishes us only with one instance of a social system, as in the case of modern capitalism, Weber treated it as an ideal type in an attempt to explain its development by deriving generalizations about it rather than by interpreting the configuration of historical conditions that led up to it. This procedure was his solution to the issue posed in the German *Methodenstreit,* notably by Dilthey, Windelband, and Rickert.

The ideal type is an abstraction that combines several analytical elements which appear in reality not in pure form but in various admixtures. In actual bureaucracies, for example, officials are not completely impersonal, not all official business is recorded in writing, and the division of responsibilities is not always unambiguous. To be sure, the ideal type does not correspond to any empirical case or to the average of all cases, but it is intentionally designed in this form, as Weber stresses. It is not a substitute for empirical investigation of historical situations but a framework for guiding the research by indicating the factors to be examined and the ways in which the observed patterns differ from the pure type.

A criticism of the ideal type advanced by Schelting is that implicit in Weber's procedure are several different constructs. The two basic ones are the individualizing ideal type, which refers to a specific social system that occurred only once in history, such as Western capitalism, and the generalizing ideal type, which refers to a category that includes many social systems of the same kind, such as bureaucracy. In my opinion, Weber's use of the same procedure in the analysis of these different problems was quite deliberate. He tried to extend Rickert's conception and break through the dilemma posed by Windelband's postulate that one cannot generalize about unique events by treating Western capitalism, a unique historical phenomenon, as if it were a general type, that is, just as he treated bureaucracy. The attempt, however, is doomed to failure. One case cannot yield a general principle. For, as the very term implies, a generalization must refer to more than one case. But how can we possibly know that it does if there is only one case to examine? The relevant requirement of a generalizing science is that it abstracts those elements of unique occurrences that many have in common, thereby transforming them into non-unique cases in terms of the conceptual scheme and making it possible to subsume them under general categories. This is not accomplished by Weber's very different procedure of abstracting those elements of a historical system that reveal its most distinctive features in pure form. The analytical category and the ideal type are two entirely different abstractions from reality. Had Weber selected a few distinctive elements of modern capitalism that it has in common with other economic systems, he could have derived a generalization about the analytical elements of religious systems that promote these characteristic features of capitalism. But he was too interested in the unique aspects of Western capitalism to formulate his problem in this sociological manner, and his ideal type is no adequate substitute for doing so.

The generalizing ideal type is also subject to criticism. Parsons notes that it implies a fixed relationship between various elements, say, specification of responsibility and legal rationality—although these elements may in fact vary independently of one another. Friedrich's objections are that the ideal type is neither derived by systematic induction from empirical observations nor by deduction from more abstract concepts and that it implicitly led Weber to introduce value judgments into his analysis. Bendix points out that the procedure of constructing ideal types obscures the very contradictions, conflicts, and compromises in which Weber was especially interested.

A fundamental shortcoming of the ideal type, which underlies many criticisms of it, is that it is an admixture of conceptual scheme and hypotheses. Take the ideal type of bureaucracy. In part, it is a conceptual scheme which calls attention to the aspects of organizations that should be included in the investigation, and which supplies criteria for defining an actual organization as more or less bureaucratized. In addition, however, Weber indicates that these characteristics tend to occur together, that certain historical conditions promote them (such as a money economy), and that the specified characteristics and, in particular, their combination increase administrative efficiency. These are not elucidations of concepts but statements of fact which are assumed to be correct. Whereas concepts are not subject to empirical verification, hypothesized factual relationships are. Only empirical research can ascertain, for instance, whether authoritarian management and impersonal detachment, singly and in combination, always promote administrative efficiency, as predicted, or whether they do so only under certain conditions, or perhaps not at all. But what bearing would such empirical findings have on the ideal type? If we modify the type in accordance with the empirical reality, it is no longer a pure type, and if we do not, it would become a meaningless construct. Since the ideal type confuses statements that have different significance for empirical investigation and theoretical inference, it has serious limitations compared to analytical conceptual schemes.

Ignoring that Weber's analysis of bureaucracy is assumed to represent an ideal type, it can still be considered a sophisticated conceptual scheme and a set of interrelated hypotheses, which furnish guidelines for the study of bureaucracies of various kinds, and which can be refined on the basis of research as well as conceptual clarification. In Weber's ideal bureaucracy, for instance, the official's legal authority rests on technical expertness, but in actual bureaucracies, the professional standards of the expert often come into conflict with the administrative requirements of the managerial official, even if the two are the same person. Professional and bureaucratic authority must be distinguished, as Parsons and Gouldner point out, to clarify some of the central issues and conflicts in today's organizations which tend increasingly to be both professionalized and bureaucratized. Another problem is the specification of conditions under which the bureaucratic characteristics Weber delineated further operating efficiency. To cite only one illustration, it is highly questionable that strict lines of authority in an organization have the same significance for effective administration in a hospital as in an army, or in a country where an egalitarian ideology prevails as in Weber's imperial Germany. To refine Weber's theory by the investigation of such problems entails dispensing with the notion of the ideal type.

IV. ELABORATION OF THE CONCEPTION OF AUTHORITY

Turning now to a substantive analysis and clarification of Weber's conception of authority, the focus is on some issues his theory has not resolved. The first question is posed by the description of authority as voluntary imperative control. How can compliance be imperative if it is voluntary? The second problem is that of the origins of authority, especially of the processes through which other forms of power become transformed into legitimate authority. Closely related is a third issue, namely, that of the structural conditions that give rise to authority systems, of the existential determination of the beliefs that legitimate authority.

Authority often originates in other forms of power; for example, the conqueror later becomes the king. In a bureaucracy, with which I am most familiar, and which I therefore shall use as an illustration, the situation is somewhat more complex. The legal contract into which officials enter by becoming members of a bureaucracy legitimates the authority of superiors over subordinates. Although employees assume the contractual obligation to follow managerial directives, the scope of the formal authority that has its source in the legal contract is very limited. The legal authority of management to assign tasks to subordinates is rarely questioned—there is willing compliance—but this legal authority does not and cannot encourage willingness to work hard or to exercise initiative. Managerial responsibilities require more influence over subordinates than that which rests on their legal obligations.

The bureaucratic manager has the official power of sanction over his subordinates, a typical manifestation of which is the civil service efficiency rating, on which the career chances of officials may depend. He may use his sanctioning power directly to impose his will upon subordinates. Such domination does not, strictly speaking, involve the exercise of authority, since his orders are followed to avoid penalties or attain rewards rather than simply because doing so is an accepted duty. An alternative strategy is for the manager to try to expand the scope of his influence over subordinates by obligating them to follow his directives and requests. This strategy involves essentially relinquishing some of his official power in exchange for legitimate authority.

The official position and power of the bureaucratic manager give him opportunities to furnish services to subordinates and, thereby, create social obligations. His superior administrative knowledge, on the basis of which he presumably was promoted, enables him to train newcomers and advise even experienced officials in difficult cases. His managerial status gives him access to top echelons and staff specialists, making it possible for him to channel needed information to subordinates and, what is of special importance, represent their interests with the higher administration or the legislature. In brief, he has many occasions to benefit subordinates and win their appreciation. His formal prerogatives and powers make it possible for him to earn their good will merely by not exercising them—for instance, by not enforcing an unpopular no-smoking rule. The manager who discharges his responsibilities by refraining from resort to his coercive powers and by devoting effort to benefiting subordinates obligates them to himself. The advantages they derive from his mode of supervision obligate them to reciprocate by willingly complying with his demands and requests.

This type of personal influence over *individual* subordinates does not constitute the exercise of authority in the specific Weberian sense either. For authority requires social legitimation. Only the shared values of a social collectivity can legitimate the power or influence of a superior and thus transform it into authority. The bureaucratic superior whose managerial practices further the *collective* interest of subordinates creates joint social obligations. Hence, the group of subordinates has a common interest in remaining under this manager and maintaining his good will, which finds expression in shared feelings of loyalty to him and in group norms making compliance with his directives an obligation enforced by the subordinates themselves. The prevalence of such a normative orientation among subordinates legitimates the superior's authority over them.

The distinguishing criterion of authority suggested here is that structural constraints rooted in the collectivity of subordinates rather than instruments of power or influences wielded by the superior himself enforce compliance with his directives. To discharge its joint obligations to the superior, the group of subordinates is under pressure to make compliance with his directives part of the common norms, which are internalized by its members, and which are socially enforced by them against potential deviants. Such normative constraints require even the individual who does not feel personally obligated to the superior to submit to his authority. This conception helps to resolve the paradox posed by the definition of authority as a form of social control that is both voluntary and imperative. Voluntary social action is never devoid of social constraints. From the standpoint of the collectivity of subordinates, compliance with the superior's directives is voluntary, but from the standpoint of the individual subordinate it is the result of compelling social pressures. The compliance of subordinates in authority relationships is as voluntary as our custom of wearing clothes.

Let us recapitulate the main points of the argument and somewhat refine them. Authority usually has its source in other forms of power, specifically, in a situation where a group of people are dependent in vital respects on one person (or another group). Their dependence enables him to coerce them to do his bidding. He can, however, use his power and the resources from which it derives— whether these are superior physical force, wealth, knowledge, or charisma—to furnish services to subordinates and thus obligate them to follow his directives, which makes it unnecessary for him to coerce them. In this manner, coercive power is transformed into personal influence. If the superior's actions advance the common interests of subordinates and make them collectively obligated to him, a further transformation tends to occur as group norms enforce compliance with his directives to repay the joint obligations to him. This is the process by which personal influence turns into legitimate authority. The influence of one individual over another in a pair relationship cannot become legitimate authority, because only the shared norms of a collectivity can legitimate social control and only the collective enforcement of compliance makes the compliance independent of the superior's personal influence over the individual subordinate. But once an authority system has become institutionalized, it can find expression in apparently isolated pairs. A father exercises authority over an only child, since culturally defined role expectations, which are enforced by members of the community, such as teachers and neighbors, constrain the child to obey his father. Such institutionalized authority is typically supplemented by other forms of influence.

The power of sanction formally invested in the bureaucratic official has paradoxical implications for authority. In terms of the conception advanced, the direct use of sanctions by a manager to compel subordinates to carry out his orders does not constitute the exercise of authority. Quite the contrary, it shows that his directives do not command their unconditional compliance. It is this official power of sanction, on the other hand, that makes subordinates dependent on the bureaucratic superior, and this dependence, in turn, is the ultimate source of his authority over them. This paradox is not confined to bureaucracy but is characteristic of all power: its use to coerce others destroys its potential as a source of authority over them. What is distinctive about the bureaucratic case is that the instruments with which an official readily can extend his authority over subordinates beyond the narrow confines of the legal contract are placed into his hands by the formal organization.

In general, a situation of collective dependence is fertile soil for the development of authority, but its development is contingent on judicious restraint by the superior in the use of his power. If he alienates subordinates by imposing his will upon them against their resistance, they will obey only under duress and not freely follow his lead. If, on the other hand, he uses some of his power to further their collective interests, the common experience of dependence on and obligation to the superior is apt to give rise to shared beliefs that it is right and in the common interest to submit to his command, and these social values and the corresponding social norms of compliance legitimate and enforce his authority over them, as has been noted. In brief, coercive power and authority are alternative forms of social control, which are incompatible, but which both have their roots in conditions of collective dependence.

The question arises, what are the various kinds of collective dependence in which authority has its ultimate source? Weber calls attention to the importance of "the *monopoly* of the *legitimate* use of physical force" for the power of the state. The transformation of this coercive power by political values and norms produces political authority. Note that this type cuts across Weber's distinction between legal and traditional authority, since traditional political structures as well as rationalized legal ones ultimately rest on the force of arms. The dependence of the followers on a charismatic leader, in contrast, is due to their ideological convictions. Their firm belief in the mission the charismatic leader represents and symbolizes makes his approval and disapproval more important to them than any other sanctions. This is similar to the dependence created by any personal attachment, such as a boy's infatuation with a girl, except that the ideology makes an entire collectivity dependent on the leader and is, therefore, an essential condition for the development of charismatic authority. A very different source of domination is technical knowledge (real or attributed; quackery will do if superstition gives it credence), which makes people who suppose they need it dependent on a person. Socially acknowledged superior competence may be considered the basic source of professional authority. Finally, people are dependent on others for their material well-being, notably on their employer and his representatives. This dependence gives rise to managerial authority.

The purpose of presenting these types is not to make a claim for a definitive typology of authority but merely to illustrate that a classification on the basis of the dependency conditions in which authority is rooted does not yield the same types as Weber's classification in terms of legitimating beliefs. Although differences in these legitimating value systems have significant implications for social systems, as Weber's analysis shows, a theory of authority should also come to grips with the structural conditions in which it originates.

V. DEMOCRACY AND BUREAUCRACY

What is the referent of Weber's concepts of authority? In some discussions, he appears to deal with three analytical principles that underlie conformity—convention, ethics, and law. At other times, he seems to refer to political systems—traditional political institutions, revolutionary movements, and modern governments based on rational law. (The limitations of the ideal type may be responsible for Weber's switching between these different conceptualizations.) If his analysis is considered an approach to a theory of political institutions, it is amazing that it does not include a systematic treatment of democracy or the general conception of sovereignty, its locus and its distribution. Democracy is subsumed under the legal order, although Weber makes it clear that a legal order is not necessarily democratic. On the contrary, the prototype of the legal order is the autocratic bureaucracy. "Experience tends universally to show that . . . the monocratic variety of bureaucracy . . . [is] capable of attaining the highest degree of efficiency and is in this sense formally the most rational means of carrying out control over human beings." It is this kind of unsupported and questionable value judgment that Friedrich undoubtedly has in mind when he states that Weber's discussions of bureaucracy "vibrate with something of the Prussian enthusiasm for the military organization."

Weber examines the relationship between democracy and bureaucracy from several perspectives, but he never systematically differentiates the two concepts in the manner in which he distinguishes the legal order from the two other types of authority structures. One theme in Weber's analysis is the paradoxical relationship between the two institutions. Some legal requirements further democracy as well as bureaucracy, such as the principle of "equal justice under law," and the emphasis on technical knowledge rather than inherited status prerogatives (achieved instead of ascribed status), both of which help produce a levelling of status differences. Nevertheless, "'democracy' as such is opposed to the 'rule' of bureaucracy, in spite and perhaps because of its unavoidable yet unintended promotion of bureaucratization." A major reason for this is that bureaucracy concentrates power in the hands of those in charge of the bureaucratic apparatus and thereby undermines democracy.

A related problem with which Weber is concerned is the contrast between political and bureaucratic domination. Under the rule of law, as Bendix notes, "success in the struggle for power becomes manifest in decisive influence upon the enactment of binding rules. To exercise such decisive influence a politician must contend with others like himself in the competition for votes, in political organizations, and in the legislative process of enacting laws and supervising their execution." Political power is apparently viewed as containing elements of the two opposite prototypes, economic power which rests on constellations of interests and authority which rests on beliefs in its legitimacy. Power in the political struggle results from the manipulation of interests and profitable exchanges—for example, of commitments or "spoils" for votes—and does not entail legitimate authority of protagonists over one another. Success in this struggle, however, leads to a position of legitimate authority. The political struggle occurs not only among politicians but also between them and the executives of bureaucratic organizations to prevent the latter from exploiting their dominant administrative position to usurp political power. A final complication arises in mass democracies, where the political struggle is carried out through large party organizations which tend to become bureaucratized, with the result that the conflict between political and bureaucratic principles manifests itself again in the struggle between the politician who directly appeals to the voters and the regular party official, once more creating the danger that democratic processes become submerged by bureaucratic considerations.

These brief excerpts show that Weber discusses the differences and interrelations between democracy and bureaucracy extensively; nevertheless, he never makes a systematic analytical distinction between them. Let me attempt to draw such an analytical distinction. Two reasons why men organize themselves and others and form an association can be distinguished. First, their purpose may be to settle on common courses of actions, on objectives to be collectively pursued. Second, their purpose may be to implement decisions already agreed upon or accepted, to work together on attaining given objectives. There are other reasons for establishing a social association, for instance, giving common expression to shared values, as in religious congregations, but the discussion

here is confined to the first two kinds. The principle of organization must be adapted to its purpose.

If men organize themselves for the purpose of reaching common agreement on collective goals and actions by some form of majority rule, they establish a democratic organization. The specific mechanisms and institutions through which the democratic rule of the majority is effected can differ widely and pose important problems in a large social structure. Whatever the particular institutional solution to these problems, however, the fundamental principle that is expected to govern a democratic organization is freedom of dissent. For tomorrow's majority will not be able to emerge unless today's majority—and, indeed, every majority—relinquishes the right to suppress dissenting minorities, however extremist their views.

If men organize themselves and others for the purpose of realizing specific objectives assigned to or accepted by them, such as winning a war or collecting taxes, they establish a bureaucratic organization. The exact form best suited for such an organization depends on a variety of conditions, including notably the kinds of skills required for the tasks. Strict lines of authority, for example, are probably not conducive to the exercise of responsibility and initiative in a research organization. In any case, the fundamental principle that is expected to govern the specific character and administration of a bureaucratic organization is that of administrative efficiency, that is, the achievement of specified objectives at minimum cost.

In sum, the differentiating criteria between democracy and bureaucracy proposed are whether the organization's purpose is to settle on common objectives or to accomplish given objectives, and whether the governing principle of organizing social action is majority rule rooted in freedom of dissent or administrative efficiency. The distinction is an analytical one, since many organizations have the dual purpose of first deciding on collective goals and then carrying out these decisions. As a result, the two principles come into conflict. Unions are a typical example. Democratic freedom of dissent and majority rule are often set aside in the interests of administrative efficiency and effective accomplishment of union objectives. Even if Michels erred in considering this process inevitable, it is undoubtedly prevalent. Another illustration is the tendency of party bosses to circumvent primaries and other democratic processes in the interest of building an efficient machine for winning elections. Although some specific conflicts may be due to corrupt or domineering union or party officials, there is a fundamental organizational dilemma which is independent of individual motives. Democratic decisions are futile without an administrative apparatus strong enough to implement them, but the requirements of administrative efficiency frequently are incompatible with those of democratic decision-making—if only because one organization cannot be governed by two distinct ultimate principles of social action.

In our political system, we have attempted to resolve this dilemma by separating the process of deciding on collective goals and the process of accomplishing these goals into two distinct sets of political institutions—the party and election machinery and the legislative branch of the government, on the one hand, and the executive branch of the government, on the other. The former institutions are expected to be governed by majority rule and freedom of dissent, while the latter are expected to be governed by administrative efficiency. Democratic values demand not only that political objectives be decided by majority rule but also that they be implemented by the most effective administrative methods, that is, by executive agencies whose operations are governed by the principle of efficiency and not by majority opinion. Despite the institutional separation, however, the fundamental dilemma between democracy and bureaucracy recurrently reasserts itself, especially in the form of demands for suppressing freedom of dissent in the interest of national security.

VI. CONCLUSIONS

This paper has presented a critical review of Weber's theory of authority and bureaucracy. The ideal-type procedure Weber used in his analysis has been criticized for failing to differentiate between conceptual elaborations and hypotheses concerning the relationship between facts, and also for confusing the distinction between analytical attributes of social systems and prototypes of the social systems themselves. The substantive theory has been criticized for focusing primarily on the beliefs that legitimate authority while neglecting to conceptualize systematically the structural conditions that give rise to it. Finally, the lack of a systematic theory of democracy as well as of revolution was noted, despite the prominent part these two problems play in Weber's thinking and writing. Having focused in the paper deliberately on what appear to be limitations of Weber's theory, I would like to close by putting these criticisms into proper perspective.

Perhaps the most difficult task for a scholar is to develop a new approach to the study of reality, a new conception and perspective that fundamentally changes the development of theory and research in a discipline for generations to come. It is no exaggeration to say that Weber was one of the rare men who has done just this. He has shaped the course of sociology, not alone but together with a few others, and it would not be what it is today had he not lived. It is the fate of every scientist, but particularly the great innovator who blazes new trails and points in new direction, that his very success in clearing the path for others makes his own work soon appear crude and obsolete. While this does not hold true for the philosopher, it does for the social scientist, and Weber clearly and self-consciously was a social scientist rather than a philosopher. Much of Marx's work seems crude today; so does much of Freud's; and if much of Weber's does too, as I have suggested, it is because he belongs to this august company.

Hans H. Gerth (essay date 1964)

SOURCE: "Max Weber's Political Morality," in *Max Weber's Political Sociology: A Pessimistic Vision of a Rationalized World,* edited by Ronald M. Glassman and Vatro Murvar, Greenwood Press, 1984, pp. 29-38.

[*Originally presented as a lecture at Hokkaido University in Japan in 1964, the following essay discusses Weber's thoughts on the major political movements of the twentieth century, most notably fascism and totalitarianism.*]

Since World War II, Max Weber has become as influential and controversial as Karl Marx was before the conversion of the latter's thought into dogma by one-party socialist states. Karl Jaspers, the psychiatrist and existentialist philosopher, saw in Weber "the philosopher of our time." Others have called him the bourgeois Marx. If labels are necessary in this age of slogans, we might call him "the Jeremiah of Imperial Germany."

Ever since his visit to the United States in 1904, Weber deeply feared that Germany, and hence Europe, might well become divided under the respective influences or suzerainty of the United States and Russia. Yet "his existence," to quote Jaspers again, "was support for all those who face the future without illusions, who are active while life is granted them and who are hopeful so long as not all is lost."

Germany is a country with a history of repression, discontinuities and the forgetfulness of its own past. When in 1959 the German Sociological Society celebrated the first half century of its existence, not a single paper was devoted to its founder and most preeminent member. But at the 15th meeting of the Society, in May 1963, a storm of controversy raged over Max Weber and his legacy. Talcott Parsons celebrated Max Weber as the debunker of illusionist habits of thought and as a sociological realist without ideologies. Wolfgang Mommsen, the author of *Max Weber und die Deutsche Politik,* on the other hand, criticized Weber for being a theoretician of "national" and "power" politics. Mommsen thus implied that a politics not concerned with power is possible. It is indeed one of the liabilities of an impotent German liberalism to dichotomize and polarize *Gesinnungspolitik* and *Machtpolitik,* the politics of conscience and power. The latter was attributed to an evil Bismarck and the former to a morally superior but politically impotent liberalism. Mommsen is reported to have surpassed even Raymond Aron, who in his criticism evaluated Weber as a social Darwinist justifying imperialism and the plebescitarian rule of a charismatic leader. Weber allegedly thus prefigured fascism and Hitlerism.

Similarly Herbert Marcuse tended to telescope history by stating "the seizure of power by the bourgeois class means the democratization of the still pre-bourgeois state. The political immaturity of the German middle classes, however, raises a cry for caesarism. Democracy corresponding to capitalistic industrialization threatens to tilt into plebescitarian dictatorship; bourgeois rationality calls forth irrational charisma."

As in the case of Marx, one can, a few decades after his death, read into Weber's work diametrically opposed points of view. Some intellectual historians and ideologists take the position that, since this is true, they can avail themselves of whatever is useful in their predecessors' work for their own use and consign the rest of the work to oblivion. Thus Nikolai Bukharin, in his text *On Historical Materialism,* acknowledged the "mass of valuable" material Weber's work provided him.

Against Marxism, Weber raised the essential objection that Marxism was reductionist, that it views and interprets all cultural phenomena as being expressive of and determined by economic processes and class struggle. Weber rejected this view and maintained the position of causal pluralism in the attempt to explain social and structural phenomena. As an example, Weber argued that European feudalism arose in response to the threat of the armies of crusading Arabian horsemen invading France from Spain.

Weber attributed the rise of the economic basis of feudalism, i.e. economically expendable, rent-based manorial landlords, to the extensive confiscation of church lands by Charles Martell. Martell did this for military reasons. He needed an army of economically expendable but self-equipped knights. These were to displace the then current peasant militia.

In arriving at such an explanation, Weber used the concept of an "unanticipated totality," the idea of structural whole, an ideal type of feudal society, which had specified "requirements." He thus posited a teleological com-pletion of the dimensions entertained in his initial concept.

The same historical phenomenon can be seen as the product of an infinite number of causes, all of which in their own right lead together often to unwilled and unanticipated consequences from the standpoint of their original intentions. Yet when we look backward from the known result, we can see, as in the case of the rise of feudal society, the concatenation of a series of causes leading to a common result. In a purely causal analysis, a thousand and one senseless events, decisions, ideas and subjective intentions would seem to lead to utterly fortuitous and contingent results. And in a purely teleological perspective these would serve the purely unitary *ex post facto* ends of the theorist.

This teleological perspective stood behind Christian teleological faith as it was secularized by Hegel in his philosophy of history and his *Phenomenology of the Mind.* Hegel felt himself to be contemplating the end of history, which he conceived as the progress of man toward reason and freedom. Hence, with the French Revolution and, later, the British Reform Bill of 1832, little of

qualitative importance remained to happen before the end of history was achieved. Time, i.e. history, was fulfilled: the World Spirit had all but completed its work.

This Hegelian way of thinking entailed two assumptions. A distinction was made between mere intelligence and reason. Mere intelligence meant only insight into the value of instrumental efficiency and the concatenations of cause and effect. Mere intelligence entails only the knowledge of segments, aspects, of reality and never a conception of the totality of man's fate and experience. Knowledge of the totality requires, under this mode of thought, more than segmental causes of events: It requires an understanding of the meanings of man's estate as a whole.

Hegelian philosophy was, in addition, not oriented to cosmology and nature, not to the objective time of the celestial universe but to time as man experiences it in human history; in his life cycle and in the time spans of social collectivities, including the family, national states and social and cultural systems. It is the time of human memory and hope. While the objective time of the celestial universe is often called chronometric time, time as experienced is called "Kairos," historical time, i.e., the time of human decision. Thus nations have their own heroic time and stretches of time when nothing essential seems to happen or even when time seems to shrink and stand still. During crucial time periods, as during revolutions and war, when national identity and cohesion seems to be at stake, very much seems to happen in so short a time period that time looms large in memory and in the collective organization of memory that is historiography.

Weber, following these aspects of the Hegelian legacy and absorbing a century of work in German social science, saw the diverse causal chains of history culminating in two master trends, rationalization and bureaucratization.

Progressive rationalization had led to industrialism and to the formation of large-scale bureaucracies in increasingly complex business organizations and in the nation state. The latter was the framing organization of the unitary territorial political organization.

He conceived of capitalism as embodying two central dimensions. The first was based upon the organization of legally free labor oriented to the profitable production of goods and in their exchange in a market. Secondly, he saw capitalism as a preindustrial and universal phenomenon oriented to and depending upon political opportunities for profit. The first type accounted for the institutionalization of man's workaday life. It required, Weber emphasized, a rationally calculable and enforceable law, a dynamic technology and science and, hence, the elimination of magic and the dissolution of kinship cohesion.

Weber was convinced that the emergence of capitalism could not be adequately explained in terms of purely economic factors such as the availability of precious metals during the age of discovery and the availability of free labor through the dispossession of the English yeomanry during the enclosure movement when landlords shifted from crop raising to the grazing of sheep.

Weber felt a specific type of man was necessary for modern capitalism to emerge, one who was sober, rational-minded and given to hard work. Magical gifts of grace, i.e., religious dualism in standards had to be abolished in favor of a single standard of Puritan asceticism and to devotion to a workaday life in order to remake the world. Ostentation derived from, among other things, success at work had to be depreciated. This included the devaluation of luxurious living, the reinvestment of funds in rent-yielding landed estates, in race horses, and the purchases of Italian violins during the grand tours of the scions of aristocratic families. What counted was profitable reinvestment in productive enterprises. Piety was the god-willed service to give homeless men and vagrants the god-willed opportunity to prove themselves in their daily life as god-fearing servants pursuing their calling.

Weber's still controversy-provoking study, *The Protestant Ethic and the Spirit of Capitalism,* served, at the beginning of the century, to make essentially these points. His comparative studies of Ancient Eastern civilizations, especially of India, China and the Near East, seemed to fortify his thesis. While in the Oriental civilizations, some individual factors were more favorable to the development of capitalism than in Europe, there was always one or more essential factor lacking. Especially lacking was the training of men for an ascetic vocational way of life in the workaday world.

In contrast to this rational workaday capitalism with its demand for sober rationality, political capitalism, Weber's alternative type of capitalism was age-old and could be found throughout history all over the world. Political capitalism is oriented to securing profit opportunities from government. Examples are the "tax farmers" of ancient Rome, the privileged chartered company like Warren Hastings' East India Company, the venture and booty capitalism of Pizzaro, Columbus, the Fuggers, Cecil Rhodes and the purveyors and purchasers of American government during the Civil and post-Civil War era. Political capitalism, Weber felt, was in his era staging a grandiose revival on the basis of industrialism.

Weber, in the style of classical liberalism, separated politics and economics. He was, however, convinced that the merger of politics and economics was unavoidable in eras of chronic warfare. He further feared that this merger would continue during his time with no accountability to publicly elected and sufficiently strong parliamentary leaders. He strongly criticized emerging romantic glorifications of the "corporate state." He thus criticized fascism before it emerged. "Propagandists of anti-parliamentary ideas," he wrote,

> fancy that the state would then be the wise agent controlling business. The *reverse* holds. The bankers

and capitalist entrepreneurs, so much hated by them, would become the unrestrained masters of the state. Who in the world is the state besides this cartel machinery of large and small capitalists of all sorts, organizing the economy when the state's policy-making function is delegated to their organizations? . . . The profit interest of capitalistic producers represented by cartels would then exclusively dominate the state.

To Weber, the only practical way of organizing an industrialized nation under a democratic constitution was through the competition between the complex bureaucracies of corporate capitalism and mass organized trade unions, farmers and congeries of other class interest groups, all under a rational civil service controlled by a relatively strong and competitively selected party leadership. It is often forgotten in our telescoping of time that Weber wished to see a powerful executive leader in control over the army who was supported by the only party with strength in 1919, the Social Democratic Party. Weber knew Friedrich Ebert, the saddle maker from Heidelberg who became the first President of the Weimar Republic. Weber's concern was to make the office of President strong enough to safeguard the newly achieved democratic constitution. He also wished the German Republic to have a sufficiently strong central core to ensure national cohesion at a time when the particularism of the separate states of Germany threatened to dismember the nation. Finally, Weber hoped to safeguard Germany from Russian domination. Karl Marx considered Russia to be the main menace. This posture of both Weber and Marx was in the tradition of the democratic liberalism of 1848 and was opposed to the policy of Bismarck and the Junkers.

Weber's attitude to the executive reflects the change in German liberalism away from such older models as British constitutionalism and French parliamentary democracy to that of the American solution of presidential responsibility. This, in turn, reflected Weber's conception of democracy. Weber considered the personal regime of the Kaiser a great misfortune and a primary cause of policy blunders contributing to the imperialist division of the world.

In 1919 Weber examined German political life with a critical eye in order to assess the prospects of democracy. He was a monarchist who felt that hereditary kingship had the advantage of removing the center of national identification from competitive struggles for party leadership. He was a nationalist when young, but ended as a left-wing liberal and as a politically homeless man. He sympathized with the socialists without being a socialist, yet he criticized them for lacking imagination and passion. He dismissed the communists for lacking political realism and, despite their heroic, utopian but self-deluding posture, for wishing to transfer Leninist conceptions of politics into the entirely different political context of Germany.

When the Berlin Soviet, the council of workers and soldiers, was constituted, the soldiers of Potsdam voted for their officers as delegates. The soldiers were peasants and, accordingly, monarchists, conservative and god-fearing haters of Rosa Luxemburg and Karl Liebknecht, the founders of the German Communist Party. Their delegates were not even allowed access to the speaker's platform at the meetings of the Berlin Soviet. Weber considered their slogan, "a united front of workers and soldiers," a deceptive imposition based upon the Russian situation as applied to a German context which had radically different class and loyalty constellations.

The election results in Germany as recorded in the census volumes, published since 1871, would record the relative success of democratic monarchist parties during the 1920s and even during the great depression. These would bear out the conclusion that Weber had a more realistic appreciation of the facts of German political life than that of even high-minded communist intellectuals. One of these was Ernest Toller, who returned from the war in which he, a Jew from Silesia, had volunteered. Toller was a talented communist poet and playwright who in a short time became famous. At the end of the war, when the Communist Party established a Soviet Republic in Bavaria, Toller was its President. A Bavarian regiment returning from France made short shift of the Bavarian Soviet Republic. A thousand Bavarian communists were convicted by a military tribunal and executed. Toller was one of those arrested. Max Weber addressed the military tribunal and succeeded in snatching Toller from the fusillade.

Thomas Mann and Rainer Maria Rilke made depositions for Toller and French socialists pleaded on his behalf, but the soldiers of the tribunal had undoubtedly never heard of Mann and Rilke, nor would they be impressed by French socialists. Weber, on the other hand, donned his officer's uniform and presented himself to the tribunal as an officer of the Imperial Army. He surely knew how to address them. Weber wrote to his wife Marianna, "I had hardly spoken more than ten minutes when the tribunal broke out into laughter. I knew I had won."

Weber as a young man had been a first-rate jurist, and served in the Berlin courts. He knew how to prepare and plead a case; and Toller's death sentence was commuted to confinement in a fortress. In 1933, Toller fled Germany and came to the United States via Holland, but committed suicide in despair in 1939. Toller was one of the many veterans who were students before whom Weber delivered his famous lecture, **"Politics as a Vocation."**

The Toller defense is only one incident that demonstrates Weber's freedom from anti-Semitism. His circle at Heidelberg included Georg Lukacs, Emil Lederer and Georg Simmel. He repeatedly fought against anti-Semitism and pan-Germanic ideologies on the public platform, in the press and before the German Sociological Association; and he repeatedly opposed the social Darwinist racist interpretations of the events of the time. He considered race, the constancy of nature, a reductionist

idea infinitely worse than the reductionism of such Marxists as Karl Kautsky. The latter, Weber allowed, adduced at least a meaningful, changeable order of things into intellectual discourse.

Yet, as we have noted, Weber argued that propositions about causal significance of economic factors had to be determined in their respective situations. As a total explanation of man's estate, economic determinism was to him simply metaphysics.

Weber's overwhelming fear from 1904 onward was that "world power might be divided between the decrees of Russian officials on the one hand and the conventionalism of Anglo-Saxon society on the other with, perhaps, a dash of Latin reason thrown into the latter. To divide world power thusly meant to control the future of cultural development."

The impending defeat of Germany caused Weber to re-read the Bible and to write his essays on Ancient Judaism. Weber saw King Solomon's aspirations to act on the stage of world politics with an economically weak base as a vanity comparable to the Kaiser's megalomania during the post-Bismarck period of his "personal regime." The great prophets of doom of the fourteenth to eighth centuries B.C. therefore intrigued Weber especially. In them he discovered the birth of conscience, the inner-directed man. Unlike Freud, he saw this internal mechanism as an acquisition of the mind emerging in a specific historical and social situation of anguish and not as the product of an archaic, prehistoric past based upon the supposed frustration of a band of brothers-in-crime, committing patricide while vying for the love of their mother and subsequently creating the incest taboo.

The Old Testament prophets, whom Weber identified with, acted as solitary men in the name of God. They served as the conscience of their people and their time. They found the inner strength to stand up against false prophets who made their living off religion and who did not have the religious conviction necessary to sacrifice themselves, if need be, for it. John the Baptist made such a sacrifice in the face of the temptations of a dancing Salome. Von Hoffmannsthal and Richard Strauss placed the drama of the prophet and his temptress on the opera stage during this period of Weber's life. But Weber identified most with Jeremiah, the prophet of doom. He envisioned, in anguish, in **"Politics as a Vocation,"** the future of his people as one of a "polar night of darkness."

Yet Weber did not believe in hero worship, nor in Russian savior. He felt that the age of prophecy was forever past as that of charioteering military heroes and heroism. Similarly he believed that charismatic heroes and saviors belonged to preindustrial societies that had neither rational bureaucracies nor democracies.

Weber felt that revolutionary "cult of reason" taken by Robespierre during the French Revolution was the last genuine form of charisma that had emerged in charisma's fateful course through history. Neither Bismarckism nor Bonapartism appeared to him as genuine charisma. Weber considered modern charisma to be a deception, an apolitical appearing phantasmagoria created by despotic men who were out of step with the demands of an age that was in the process of fundamental democratization. These processes included the downward leveling of feudal nobilities into agrarian capitalists who retained feudal pretensions. It included the upward rise of a broad, literate level of working men in an age of bureaucratic industry and mass armies.

Weber was vehemently opposed to academic men who increasingly exploited their privileged academic positions as pulpits for political prophecies and world views. In the face of this trend Weber advocated the "value neutrality of science." He fought against special pleading in the classroom before captive audiences of intellectually helpless and disarmed students. Weber attempted to separate the role of scholar from that of political man.

Dying in 1920, he was spared the nightmare of the great depression, the rise of totalitarian fascism and Nazism with their personality cults of il Duce and Der Fuehrer and their despotic armies and total war.

He died with these words on his lips: "The real thing is the truth."

Guenther Roth (essay date 1964)

SOURCE: "Political Critiques," in *Scholarship and Partisanship: Essays on Max Weber*, by Reinhard Bendix and Guenther Roth, University of California Press, 1970, pp. 55-69.

[*Originally delivered as a lecture at a meeting of the American Sociological Association in 1964, the following essay articulates major objections to Weber's sociopolitical views, concluding that Weber sought to reconcile through his work the tension between opposing theoretical stances.*]

Max Weber has been a major target for a series of critiques aimed at political sociology in general, if not at most of social science. These critiques either use a sociological approach for political purposes or deny altogether the present rationale of political sociology and to some extent even the viability of Western pluralist society. Because Weber had a highly articulate view of politics and took his stand on political issues that have remained controversial to this day, it is not always easy to distinguish specific critiques of Weber's politics and scholarship from the general implications for political sociology. There is considerable room for different historical interpretations; it is, of course, also possible to put different accents on the definition of politics. At any rate, my intent is not a historical defense of Weber but a review of critiques so far as they seem to bear on the *raison d'être* of political sociology. In my judgment, this rationale is

imperiled if Weber's insights into the nature of politics are denied.

Since sociological analysis properly endeavors to look at the world dispassionately or, more correctly, from a "theoretical" perspective, in the strict contemplative sense of the word, it must appear relativist and Machiavellian to all those who, for ideological reasons, cannot recognize any dividing line between political sociology and political ideology. Weber emphatically insisted on such a distinction. He always made it clear that he did not claim scientific support for his political views. Of course, in his political writings he drew on his sociological learning; he also put concrete political issues into the universal historical context with which his studies were concerned. But since his political critics refuse to distinguish between his scholarship and his politics, they can quote sociological statements—his or anyone else's—as articulations of political views.

A SOCIOLOGICAL ETHIC

The vehemence of various critiques must be attributed not only to Weber's insistence on a scholarly study of power and authority, but also to his own political decision that politics is the art of the possible—a rational craft. Here, indeed, is a connection between Weber's sociological work and his political commitment, which may be said to imply a sociological ethic: it was sociological because he considered it empirically indisputable that recurrent ideological conflict was as basic a fact of social life as the impossibility of reconciling any Is with any Ought, so far as large-scale social structures were concerned; it was an ethic because he advocated moral stamina in the face of these "iron" facts. His recognition of the realities of power was not identical with the glorification of the state and of *Realpolitik* by many of his contemporaries. Rather, his views were the secular counterpart of the age-old Christian dualism revived as a major literary topic by Dostoevsky and Tolstoy, about whom Weber planned to write a book. Those who would remain pure and innocent must stay out of politics altogether, yet even this is not entirely safe, since values may be compromised by a refusal to act; witness the pacifists who refuse to fight the enemies of humanitarianism. Whoever enters politics encounters the need to exercise power, and this implies ethical as well as political compromise.

These sociological insights did not shake Weber's resolve that man should act decently toward his fellow man, even if there was no absolute supernatural or scientific justification for it. For him this was a simple rational affirmation of the humanitarian element in Western civilization. He had no illusions about the dark side of progress, and this was one reason for his aversion to abstract moralizing. He was convinced that responsible political leadership cannot afford to adhere to moralistic, legalistic or any other kind of ideological absolutism, since these are inherently self-defeating. His sociological ethic was thus a latter-day version of Stoic philosophy in that virtuous conduct was more important than any notion of ultimate salvation in a this-worldly or other-worldly millennium—and only in this ethical sense was Weber a Machiavellian.

This anti-ideological insistence on measure has provoked the true believers in political panaceas, Left, Right, and Center. Accordingly, the ideological critiques of Weber have come mainly from three quarters: Marxism, Nazism, and Natural Law with its liberal and conservative wings. In the United States, advocates of moralistic liberalism, which is rooted in a strong natural-rights tradition, have been especially provoked by Weber. Many of the other attacks, however, seem at first sight to refer to another land and another time. Most of the participants in the extended debate were born in Germany; many left involuntarily, some on their own initiative; some returned; and some merely studied there. (As I proceed, it should become clear that more is involved than a mere quarrel between Germans, ex-Germans, Germanophiles, and Germanophobes.)

The three ideologies are substantively opposed to one another, but they are all instances of an "ethic of good intentions" or "ultimate ends" (*Gesinnungsethik*) and, methodologically, they all resort to historical reductionism. To be sure, Marxism does not recognize the existence of absolute values in the sense of natural rights (a self-interested bourgeois postulate), but it adheres dogmatically to a correspondence theory of concept and object, maintaining that only critical, dialectical concepts can express the "truth." Nazism, in turn, was an "ethic of good intentions" only in the most formal sense.

THE MARXIST CRITIQUE

Not surprisingly, the only Marxist critiques that warrant attention have come from writers who opposed Communist totalitarianism from the outside or who eventually clashed with party orthodoxy from the inside. Among the latter, Georg Lukács was the only writer on sociology in the Moscow of the Stalinist purges who approached serious scholarship. At the time he kept himself busy—and out of the way—with an attempt to construe German intellectual history as a road to irrationalism leading from Schelling to Hitler via Weber and all other major German sociologists.

Despite important political and philosophical differences among these Marxist writers, their views on Weber appear very similar:

(1) Weber refused to accept the dialectical idea of potentiality; he studied the facts of social life and tried to extrapolate future trends instead of measuring reality against the great possibilities postulated by Marx's theory of human nature.

(2) Epistemologically, this was due to the fact that Weber was a Neo-Kantian, adhering to the belief that the phenomenal world can be conceptualized in many different ways.

(3) Therefore, Weber postulated a universe of conflicting values among which no scientific choices are possible; this opens the way to irrationalism, leading directly to imperialism and ultimately to fascism. For if Weber denies the truth of Marxism and is too much of a secular relativist to subscribe to outmoded religious metaphysics, he must perforce take the nationalist and militarist nation-state as his major political and even moral reference.

(4) Weber's mode of thinking was typically bourgeois, insensitive to the truth that capitalism has been the most extreme exploitation of man. In class defense, men like Weber and George Simmel—both capitalist rentiers and parasites, "objectively" speaking—view social reality in formalized terms, conceiving of capitalism as a system of rational calculation based on the abstract medium of money. Significantly, Weber is also concerned with the "spirit" (*Geist*) of capitalism and its affinity to the Calvinist ethic. But in his most detached scholarly work, **Economy and Society**, an "orgy of formalism" in its casuistic definitions of types of action and of domination, Weber reveals the depravity, the *Ungeist*, of capitalist society.

(5) Weber's interest in a comparative study of social structure and ideology "reflects" the imperialist interests of the capitalist countries; it is "expansionist" sociology.

Most of these charges clearly apply to contemporary American social science as well. In spite of their basic optimism, most American social scientists are skeptical of the idea of potentiality, have been vaguely Neo-Kantian, and have focused on the methodological and conceptual elaboration of their disciplines—hence have been guilty of "positivistic formalism." Moreover, American social science tends to appear as a defensive Cold War instrument, in view of its increasing interest in newly developing countries.

THE NAZI CRITIQUE

In general, the Nazi critique has been even less sophisticated than the Marxist critique, but there are also some striking parallels. Exceptions to the rule of ignorance and incompetence were Carl Schmitt, the renowned and notorious political scientist and constitutional expert, and the forgotten Christoph Steding, the unfulfilled hope of Nazi philosophy. Both men share two features with the Marxists mentioned above: they held substantially the same opinion of positivistic sociology—except for the race issue—and they were prominent but politically marginal ideologists. I shall limit myself to Steding, who was more direct and typical than the elusive and more capable Carl Schmitt.

Steding made a limited effort to conform to some of the canons of scholarship in his Ph.D. dissertation of 1932 on Max Weber's politics and science, in which he asserted their identity and found Weber's notion of charismatic leadership very congenial. Steding's major concoction, begun on a Rockefeller Foundation grant in the early thirties, grew into a violent attack on the "disease of European culture." Mixing historical fact and paranoid fantasy, he argued that this disease originated with the Westphalian Peace of 1648 when the Western European nation states established a balance of power that made an effective *Reich* impossible and hence vitiated a universalist political and cultural order that would have restored philosophic realism. The age of neutralism arrived and championed the liberal theory of the laissez-faire state, philosophical nominalism and value-free sociology.

In vivid organic imagery, Steding showed that the "disease carriers" that threatened the Reich were located in the Rhein valley; Weber had suggested that terms like "nation," *"Nationalgefühl,"* or *"Volk"* were not really applicable to "neutralized" areas like Switzerland, Alsace-Lorraine, Luxemburg and Liechtenstein, for which opposition to "militarist" Germany provided a strong basis of their sense of political community. The old Calvinist territories of Switzerland and the Netherlands became the cornerstones of the hostile wall of Rhenish cities which had been Free Imperial cities or anti-Prussian court residences. Basle was the preferred domicile of Jacob Burckhardt and Friedrich Nietzsche, the two most formidable intellectual enemies of the Reich in the last third of the nineteenth century; the old universities of Freiburg, Heidelberg, and Marburg excelled in "quasi-Calvinist" and "quasi-Jewish" Neo-Kantianism; the old court residence Darmstadt was the home of several figures of the charismatic George circle, which was suspect because of its esthetically refined vision of a Third Reich; the trade and university centers of Frankfurt and Cologne, which pioneered institutes for economic and sociological research, provided the link to Amsterdam.

In this context Max Weber and Thomas Mann appear as the last two outstanding and personally admirable representatives of bourgeois civilization in its terminal stage of decadence and fatal disease—exactly as they do for the Marxists. Their work is the last achievement of the bourgeois spirit: it is capitalist, urban, abstract, nominalist, neutralist, Neo-Kantian and, for Steding, of course, "Jewish" by association.

As in the Marxist perspective, there is no basic difference between Imperial Germany and the Weimar Republic: both are capitalist societies. The personnel and the personalities are largely the same: William II and Weber, his stormiest critic, appear akin in their haste, nervousness and imperialist posturing, lacking a real power-drive. But Weber and Thomas Mann are also acknowledged to have been more perceptive than most other members of their class. Their support of parliamentary government made them ideological spokesmen or symbols of the Weimar Republic, the spirit of which, alas, was that of Locarno—another "neutralist" locality.

Christoph Steding and his Marxist counterparts read their sociologists with malicious care so as to use sociological insights as political weapons and turn the tables on We-

ber, Simmel and other members of the Generation of 1890. Both Steding and the Marxists adhere to a vulgar sociology of knowledge, an all too easy and superficial notion of correspondence between ideas and social structure. The facts are sometimes correct, but the political conclusions arbitrary. Thus, Steding points out that Weber became interested in Confucianism only after Germany took over Kiaochow in 1898. Weber wrote ***Ancient Judaism*** and some of his most passionate political essays in the midst of the turmoil of the First World War, when he felt like a lonely prophet. Steding, the proud peasant son, also charged Weber with the inability of the decadent to finish their work and to defend their political interests successfully. Yet, ironically, he died at the age of 35 in 1938, before finishing his long and rambling work, and the two most notorious Nazi henchmen, Himmler and Heydrich, who considered using his book as a major indoctrination text, perished within a few years, eliminating for the time being this kind of threat to the social sciences.

THE NATURAL-RIGHT CRITIQUE

In reaction to the rise of totalitarian Nazism and Communism some prominent writers have urged a return to natural right, which posits a natural or rational hierarchy of values. Adherents believe that this hierarchy can be discovered by philosophic reflection or intuition, or that it has been revealed to man. But because this latter-day revival of natural right is so obviously a reactive phenomenon, it has a strong instrumental or functionalist admixture. Those of Weber's critics who more or less fall back on natural rights have either stressed philosophical implications or they have been concerned primarily with political consequences, especially with the course of German history.

Politico-philosophical critiques. The attacks on this level have been carried in particular by Leo Strauss and Eric Voegelin. For them, Weber is the greatest and most typical representative of modern social science. "No one since Weber," says Strauss, "has devoted a comparable amount of intelligence, assiduity, and almost fanatical relativism." According to Strauss and Voegelin, science should be understood no longer positivistically, but again ontologically as the search for *prima principia*. "Whoever does not believe in the devotion to the basic problem of the social sciences. Whatever may have been his errors, he is the greatest social scientist of our century." But Weber helped lead social science into the "morass of oneness of truth cannot help but succumb to a chaos of random values. Without the acceptance of natural rights, relativism and its dialectical counterpart, totalitarian absolutism, appear inevitable."

Like the Marxists and Steding, Voegelin develops a formula identifying the forces of evil in history. Instead of focusing on the capitalist spirit of inhuman rationality and neutrality, he attacks the whole "gnostic search for a civil theology," for a perfect order on earth. For Voegelin, the Nazis' belief in the Third Reich, and the

Marxists' hopes for a classless society after the Revolution, are gnostic fantasies about the millennium. Their very attempt to create total goodness by their own definition is bound to turn government into a force of total evil. Furthermore, gnosticism is not just a matter of totalitarianism but is typical of Westernization in general, a global process that is continuing in the United States and Western Europe.

Positivistic gnosticism has destroyed political science proper: methods have subordinated relevance, useless facts are accumulated, objectivity is equated with the exclusion of value judgments. In this scheme Weber occupies a transitional position. He was a "positivist with regrets," who tabooed classic and Christian metaphysics. Voegelin finds it revealing that Weber neglected these two traditions in his vast comparative studies of the affinity between status groups and ethical ideas. If he had not shied away from them he would have discovered there "the belief in a rational science of human and social order and especially of natural law. Moreover, this science was not simply a belief, but was actually elaborated as a work of reason." Weber's positivism made him see history as a process of rationalization, whereas modern history was actually a downfall from the grace of reason—in the light of the *scientia prima*. Because Weber did not recognize natural right, he had to demonize politics. Only his ethics of responsibility was a rational counterforce. Voegelin concedes that Weber made a stronger effort than all other positivists to turn social science in a meaningful direction, but since Voegelin adopts a Christian dualism, he feels compelled to reject Weber in the end.

For Strauss, too, the troubles of recent history have been due basically to the denial of natural right. Its rejection is tantamount to nihilism, and in Weber's case it led to "noble nihilism." Since American social science largely agrees with Weber's relativism, it has become something of a German aberration (says the German philosopher):

> It would not be the first time that a nation, defeated on the battlefield and, as it were, annihilated as a political being, has deprived its conquerors of the most sublime fruit of victory by imposing on them the yoke of its own thought. Whatever might be true of the thought of the American people, certainly American social science has adopted the very attitude toward natural right which, a generation ago, could still be described, with some plausibility, as characteristic of German thought.

This is an extreme statement, which may have been advanced for its shock value. But Strauss is fair enough to denounce the *reductio ad Hitlerum,* the assertion that Weber's thinking led to fascism. This kind of reductionism has been typical of the historical critique associated with moralistic liberalism.

The critique of moralistic liberalism. American liberals have traditionally shown exasperation with the reverses of democracy abroad. Moreover, their pragmatist background has made them especially skeptical toward German idealism and to a lesser extent toward historical materialism, another German product. Times have changed, however, since 1935 when Ellsworth Faris rejected Pareto from implied moral premises, without conceding any utility whatever to Pareto's political sociology. But many liberals still tend to distrust the detached sociological study of power and of nondemocratic systems of government, except Communism and Nazism—the most extreme negations of liberalism they fit into a moralistic black-white scheme. Until very recently, at least, there were few studies of the growing number of authoritarian governments not just as variants of Fascism or Communism but as different types of domination, age-old or brand-new. This traditional distrust may also explain some of the uneasiness toward Weber's insistence on the facts of power and toward his nationalism which at best is regarded as a characteristic he shared with most scholars of his generation, especially Durkheim. Moreover, the experience of Nazism provides a powerful moral perspective on German history and makes it hard to be fair to past generations.

The interest among American social scientists, first in fascism and then in totalitarianism in general, was shared and stimulated by German political exiles. In reflecting upon the rise of Nazism, some writers began to view Weber, not so much as a direct Nazi forerunner, but as a symptom of things to come. This concern has now been taken up by a new generation of German scholars. Intent on understanding the causes of the German catastrophe, some of them have been so preoccupied with the political interpretation of Weber that they tend to lose sight not only of his scholarly intentions and achievements but also of the rationale of sociology. Weber, a major argument goes, emphasized too strongly the instrumental instead of the inherent value of democracy—that is, democracy as decreed by natural law. He advocated charismatic leadership in the face of bureaucratization, and therefore favored the direct election of the president of the Weimar Republic, a constitutional provision that proved fatal in 1933. Hence the conclusion: Neither from the viewpoint of natural rights nor from that of pragmatic compromise does Weber's position provide reliable support for a pluralist system in which mundane group interests must continually be readjusted, a task that can be accomplished best with a minimum of charismatic excitement.

Related to these arguments is another kind of historical reductionism, which assumes a downfall from the Age of Reason. A number of younger German writers, holding a natural-rights position at least for polemical purposes, have construed an ideological line leading to Nazism which runs, for example, from Kant's formalistic Categorical Imperative, through Ranke's view of states and peoples as historical individualities, through the legal positivism since the 1860's, to Weber's sociological definition of politics and the state, and from there to Carl Schmitt's theory of politics as friend-foe relations—only one last step removed from Hitler's views and crimes. In the same fashion, other writers have tried to trace the rise of totalitarian democracy from Rousseau's general will, through Saint-Simon's technocratic elite and Marx's theory of the class struggle, to Lenin's democratic centralism—only one last step removed from Stalin.

The tracing of such ideological lineages is a challenging and fascinating task, but it is also very difficult, since the scholar must do justice to the individual's subjective intentions and to the complexities of historical reality; he must avoid a facile theory of antecedents, stepping stones, and parallels, since it is in the nature of politics that differences of degree in belief and action are critical (the rule of the lesser evil). With regard to Max Weber before fascism, Ernst Nolte has brilliantly balanced the account.

SUBJECT INTENT AND OBJECTIVE CONSEQUENCES

There is no effective protection against the misuse of ideas, against their deterioration into ideological coins and political weapons. The doctrine of natural rights, too, has been susceptible to political misuse, not least in this century. Ideas always have unintended consequences, and sociology largely lives off this fact. Weber himself showed the possible relations between the Protestant ethic and the spirit of capitalism. But he was never concerned with declaring Calvin or Baxter responsible for the materialism of the capitalist era, or Karl Marx, for the intransigence of the labor movement. His grasp of historical reality protected him from subscribing to any Devil theory of history.

Since my main interest is not an historical defense of Weber, I shall merely summarize some of the factors to be taken into consideration in this context:

(1) Weber insisted on realism in politics because the politically dominant Right adhered to idealist and romanticist notions to provide motive and cover for irresponsible power politics.

(2) Weber insisted on realistic politics also because for decades the sterile left-wing liberal opposition of Imperial Germany stuck to "principles" regardless of political feasibility.

(3) He insisted that he was patriotic as anybody else because (before 1918) he could not hope to exert any influence at all on the German Establishment unless he turned its own values against it by repeatedly pointing out that Imperial Germany and its ruling groups violated national ideals and national interests.

(4) He insisted on value-neutrality in the classroom because the nationalist historian Treitschke and similar "professors" of ideological creeds indoctrinated students from the rostrum.

(5) He insisted it was the university's business to make the students face the logical consequences of their beliefs because most of his listeners were middle- and upper-class students predisposed to nationalist sentiments.

(6) He insisted, finally, on an ethic of responsibility and of the politically possible (while conceding the abstract honorableness of an ethic of good intentions) because in 1919 the ideologists of the Right and the Left were interested in anything but the creation of parliamentary government in Germany.

It is true that national welfare was Weber's ultimate political yardstick, since he considered himself a political man, not a theologian or philosopher—two very different types, who are not forced to operate within a given political unit. Constitutional problems were secondary to national welfare only in this abstract regard, not in the realm of practical politics or of sociological analysis. Weber gave much more thought to the instrumentalities of parliamentary government than almost anybody else, including the Left, during the last decade of the Empire. His only hope for public effectiveness lay in the persuasiveness of the technical arguments for parliamentary government; the Empire's history had proven that ideological appeals for parliamentarism were in vain.

Political critiques of Weber can to some extent be considered merely the price a scholar must be prepared to pay for entering the political arena and exposing himself to the crude vehemence of political controversy. Most social scientists since Weber's time have refrained from playing the dual role of scholar and political man, but the critiques reviewed here illustrate that this does not guarantee protection. On the one hand, adherents of Marxism, Nazism, and Natural Law have not only refused to recognize any dividing line between ideology and sociology, but they have also shown a common tendency toward a historical reductionism which is a challenge to serious scholarship. On the other, political sociologists are liable to provoke political opposition by dealing with the facts of national power and domestic group interests. This makes them controversial in their professional roles and ultimately makes it impossible for them to avoid taking an explicit political stand. Weber's scholarly canons and his sociological ethic were a major attempt to cope with this perennial tension.

Reinhard Bendix (essay date 1970)

SOURCE: "Sociology and the Distrust of Reason," in *Scholarship and Partisanship: Essays on Max Weber*, by Reinhard Bendix and Guenther Roth, University of California Press, 1970, pp. 84-105.

[*The following essay, originally read as the Presidential Address to the 65th Annual Meetings of the American Sociological Association in 1970, examines Weber's essay "Science as a Vocation" and the late-twentieth century disillusionment with science.*]

Historical Perspectives and Sociological Inquiry as the theme of an American sociological convention would have been incongruous twenty years ago. It is not so today. We meet amidst upheaval directly affecting the academic community. The social sciences and sociology in particular are at the center of the storm. The freedom to do scholarly work has been questioned when it is not directed to problems considered "relevant" by the critics. In this setting we must demonstrate to those willing to listen that great issues of the day can be examined with that combination of passionate concern and scholarly detachment which is the hallmark of reasoned inquiry in our field.

But there are those unwilling to listen. Detachment and analysis as hitherto practiced, and almost regardless of content, appear to them fatally impaired because they feel that even in the midst of great wealth they must live by an ethic of social despair. Here is one expression of this sentiment, taken from the privately circulated manuscript of a sociologist who is a respected member of a university faculty.

> Time is short; we cannot wait years for research to give us impregnable theses. America's academia fiddles while the fires are burning. Where are the studies of the new corporate power, of the Defense Department, of the military-industrial complex, of the new bureaucracies, of Vietnam? American academics are prisoners of liberal democratic ideology. Even as the chains rust, they do not move. A new current of reason and passion is arising in America— outside of its conventional institutions. The current of reason must flow faster to create an image of reality and hope for the future, for a ruling class in despair will soon reach for some other kind of ideology, and all that is left for the American establishment is "patriotism," that is fascism.

In this view the evils of the world loom so large that only those energies are employed legitimately which attack these evils head on. By that standard much or most scholarship fails.

You will say they are a minority. This is true. But the social despair that motivates this minority also moves larger numbers, perhaps at a distance but still significantly. Why do the few who feel moved by social despair evoke such resonance among the many?

In posing this question I am mindful of several contributions. The sharp rise in student unrest during recent years has been analyzed in terms of generational conflict. Lewis Feuer has amassed evidence on this theme from far and wide and on this basis delineated the symptoms of student protest. Bruno Bettelheim has provided us with "a psychograph of adolescent rebellion." His emphasis, like that of Kenneth Keniston and Bennett Berger, is on an age-cohort of anxiety. In modern society there is a prolonged period of dependence between childhood and adult responsibility. In effect youths are permitted very early sexual experience. But when on that or other bases they claim or expect the independence of adults, education prolongs their dependence and an automated technology makes them feel obsolete. Edward Shils has analyzed the resulting protest in terms of a utopian fantasy of

plenitude, a belief in the sacredness of immediate experience, and the consequent attack on all boundaries of discipline, institutions and authority.

I have learned much from these and related analyses. But I also note that they end rather regularly with an appeal to the people over thirty. We are called upon to "stand firmly by the traditions of teaching, training, and research as the proper task of universities"; we should "not allow ourselves to be swept away by the desire to be 'with it', to relive our lost youth or to prolong our fading youth." I agree, but I ask myself whether this is enough. The literature on student protest often gives the impression of having been written by kindly uncles whose air of concern or sympathy and whose analytical stance give one no intimation of mortality. But we are mortal. When the value of scholarship is in question, an analysis confined to the protest of youth will appear patronizing. It will miss the fact that the protest expresses not only the disquiet of the children but also the growing uncertainty of their parents. In the midst of a crisis of legitimacy we must try once again to interpret the values we cherish and understand why our adherence to them has become ambivalent.

In addressing myself to this task I shall first characterize the belief in science that has become the central legitimation of universities. Second, I shall examine the attack on the value of academic scholarship which the great critics of modern civilization launched during the nineteenth century. Third, I want to show that, in the twentieth century, Western culture has been marked by a changed sensibility in the arts, which has increased the distrust of reason. Fourth, I will make reference to political aspects of this distrust of reason, especially by examining the rhetorical use of the term "fascism." Fifth, I shall note the greater institutional vulnerability of universities owing to the changed role of science since the Second World War. Finally, I shall offer an assessment of the problems facing sociology in a period when the belief in progress through knowledge has been impaired and the legitimacy of scholarship is in question.

THE BELIEF IN SCIENCE

The belief in science has remained remarkably consistent from the time of its first articulation in the seventeenth century to our own day. Francis Bacon wanted to inspire men with confidence that knowledge enhances human power. "Nature to be commanded must be obeyed; where the cause is not known the effect cannot be produced." He attacked the zealots who opposed science because they feared for religious faith and state authority.

> . . . surely there is a great distinction between matters of state and the arts (science) . . . In matters of state a change even for the better is distrusted, because it unsettles what is established, these things resting on authority, consent, fame and opinion, not on demonstration. But arts and sciences should be like mines, where the noise of new works and further advances is heard on every side. . . .

By the mid-nineteenth century, the "noise of new works" was on all sides and scientists could speak with the confidence of great success.

For a representative statement we may turn to the physiologist Helmholtz who considered the purposes of the university in terms of the relation between the natural sciences and all other disciplines. In 1862, he noted the specialization and frequent incomprehension among the several disciplines and asked whether it made sense to have them continue in the same institution of learning. Helmholtz compared the disciplines in terms of the way in which they achieved their results and noted—as so many have since—the greater precision in the natural sciences and the greater richness and human interest in the *Geisteswissenschaften*. The latter have a higher and more difficult task and contribute to order and moral discipline. But in respect of method they can learn much from the sciences proper.

> Indeed I believe that our time has already learned a good many things from the natural sciences. The absolute, unconditional respect for facts and the fidelity with which they are collected, a certain distrust of appearances, the effort to detect in all cases relations of cause and effect, and the tendency to assume their existence—[all this] distinguishes our time from earlier ones and seems to indicate such an [exemplary] influence [of the natural sciences].

The progress achieved through the advancement of science appeared to justify this position of the natural sciences as the model. Scientific knowledge is power and increases "the benefit and use of life." Helmholtz made two reservations only, as an aside. The scientist must become increasingly narrow in his specialization and "each student must be content to find his reward in rejoicing over new discoveries." Implicitly, all other qualities of the human mind were diminished.

For a contemporary statement it is perhaps best to recall the thesis of C. P. Snow that "the intellectual life of the whole of Western society is increasingly being split into two polar groups." World War II and the postwar years had been a period of unprecedented scientific advance and unprecedented public support of science. As a former research scientist Snow shared the resulting buoyancy of the scientific community. But as a writer sensitive to the critiques of science he put the case of science more sensitively than most. Everyone, he says, is aware of human tragedy at the individual level. Scientists certainly are. "But there is plenty in our condition which is not fate, and against which we are less than human unless we do struggle . . . As a group, the scientists . . . are inclined to be impatient to see if something can be done: and inclined to think that it can be done, until it's proved otherwise. That is their real optimism, and it's an optimism that the rest of us badly need." Snow contrasts this scientific creed with the cultural pessimism of literary intellectuals, whom he calls "natural Luddites." Ever since the industrial revolution men of letters have stood uncompre-

hending at the tremendous advances of science and technology, unable or unwilling to see that the age-old scourges of hunger and poverty could be relieved only in this way.

The history of the belief in science still needs to be written, but the three examples I have cited are prominent enough. The commitment to scientific work makes sense if there is hope that in the long run the constructive uses of knowledge will prevail. Science presupposes a belief in the perfectibility of man; it does not flourish amidst preoccupation with its own potential evil. These are among the reasons why the scholar is freed of purposes extraneous to his inquiry, and why the institutional immunities of the university were considered legitimate.

THE ROMANTIC CRITIQUE

We accept these beliefs and institutional arrangements as long as we cherish the pursuit of knowledge. But during the last two centuries the legitimacy of this pursuit has been challenged repeatedly by appeals to the imagination and to authentic experience. Generational revolts have reflected this conflict of values between reason and the "poetry of life." Such revolts have erupted in movements of liberation during the nineteenth century and in radical movements at the end of World War I, during the Depression, and in the 1960's. Conflicts over the belief in reason are a major characteristic of Western civilization.

Schopenhauer, Kierkegaard, Nietzsche, Marx, and Freud are among the great iconoclasts of the last century. All of them questioned the autonomy of knowledge and asserted that knowledge is inseparable from its preconditions, whether these are called will, commitment, will to power, class situation, or libidinal sublimation. On this basis all five deny the possibility of scholarly detachment, and some deny that scientific knowledge is desirable at all.

Two distinct premises are involved. To Schopenhauer, Kierkegaard, and Nietzsche the search for knowledge appears as an arid suppression of life; they seek a true way to knowledge through Indian mysticism, or religious experiences, or a cultural regeneration by men larger than life. For these writers the sickness of our time is a deadened feeling and a mediocrity of spirit of which the universities are an especially glaring manifestation. Their attack on scholarship is part of a more general critique of culture.

By contrast, Marx and Freud believe in the pursuit of knowledge and its promise of emancipation, at the same time that they reject academic scholarship. According to Marx, universities are involved in the contentions of society and their claim to be above the battle is false. For him, true awareness of history requires a critique of the ideological foundation of scientific work. And this awareness is achieved through a unity of theory and practice only to be found in revolutionary movement, not in universities. By a similar reductionism Freud considers every intellectual position in terms of its function in the "psychic economy" of the individual. The quest for knowledge cannot escape this psychological process, just as for Marx it cannot escape the historical process. Hence the path to knowledge in psychology lies in a heightened awareness of self, induced by the analysis and control-analysis of psychoanalytic training. This extramural recruitment and training of psychoanalysis is as incompatible with academic psychology as Marx's unity of theory and practice is incompatible with academic sociology.

Whereas Marx and Freud believed in the pursuit of knowledge and its promise of emancipation, Schopenhauer or Kierkegaard, who revolted against the Enlightenment, believed in neither. Shelley's *Defence of Poetry* (1821) puts the case with great lucidity. Science and reason are distinguished from poetry and the imagination. The poets, says Shelley, "have been challenged to resign the civic crown to reasoners and mechanics" and he acknowledges that these have their utility. The banishment of want, the security of life, the dispersal of superstition, and the conciliation of interests are utilities promoted by the calculating faculty. This is of value as long as it remains confined to "the inferior powers of our nature." But poetry and imagination represent another, higher utility. "The great secret of morals is love; or a going out of our own nature, and an identification of ourselves with the beautiful which exists in thought, action, or person, not our own. A man, to be greatly good, must imagine intensely and comprehensively; he must put himself in the place of another and of many others; the pains and pleasures of his species must become his own." The great difficulty is that in scientific and economic systems of thought "the poetry . . . is concealed by the accumulation of facts and calculating processes." Certainly, the sciences have enlarged our "empire over the external world." But in proportion as the poetical faculty is wanting, the sciences have also circumscribed the empire of the internal world. Here is Shelley's own summation:

> We want the creative faculty to imagine that which we know; we want the generous impulse to act that which we imagine; we want the poetry of life: our calculations have outrun conception; we have eaten more than we can digest. . . . The cultivation of poetry is never more to be desired that at periods when, from an excess of the selfish and calculating principle, the accumulation of the materials of external life exceed the quantity of the power of assimilating them to the internal laws of human nature.

It could not have been said more soberly.

But the romantic protest was not frequently sober. The praise of art was linked with a promethean image of the poet as godlike, rising above mere humanity and achieving ends which nature is incapable of achieving by herself. These views from Shaftesbury and Goethe to Carlyle and Nietzsche meant, as Novalis put it, that "poets know nature better than scientists." Such sentiments have a close kinship to attacks on the abstractions characteristic of all academic work. For Nietzsche all scientists were

plebeian specialists and the worst enemies of art and artists. Kierkegaard made the central theme of his work the primacy of living over reflecting. Philosophy deals with man in general only and thus is a treason to life. What matters is man's personal situation and his vital relation to God. In calling for more life and less thought, for more poetic imagination and less abstract reason, the romantics also attacked considerations of utility and the idea of material progress. Since the eighteenth century, scores of writers have elaborated the notion that the division of labor turns men into fragments, strangling their capacities and stultifying their emotions. This sentiment has implied an irrationalist, antiscientific stance so frequently since the industrial revolution that C. P. Snow is quite correct when he refers to literary intellectuals as "natural Luddites."

Yet the romantic protest of the nineteenth century was still bound up with the conventions of feeling and language that are the bases of discourse in ordinary life as well as in scholarship. By contrast, since before World War I a new sensibility in the arts has increasingly rejected that universe of discourse. The form and content of artistic expression have questioned the values of Western industrial civilization to such an extent that today the "Luddism" of literary intellectuals jeopardizes the legitimacy of academic pursuits and of much else besides. I can do little more here than sketch some tendencies that provide a ready arsenal for attacks upon universities and scholarship.

SUBJECTIVISM AND THE LOSS OF LANGUAGE

It is convenient to start with the generation of scholars and writers born in the 1850's and 1860's who were on the average a bit over forty around 1900. The classic writers of modern sociology belong to this generation. Beyond all the differences dividing them, men like Freud, Durkheim, Weber, Pareto, Park, Thomas, Cooley, and Mead are discernible as a group by their common concern with the subjective presuppositions of thought. This increased self-consciousness could easily become self-defeating. With Dilthey, for example, self-consciousness led to a skeptical relativism, while in the work of Sorel it produced a radical commitment in thought and action to overcome that relativism. Yet men like Freud, Durkheim, and Weber, while making room for this new awareness, fought "every step of the way to salvage as much as possible of the rationalist heritage."

Max Weber's essay **"Science as A Vocation,"** written just half a century ago, is a document of this generation. It represents a careful blend of rationalist convictions and romantic sensibility. Like the great rationalists before him, but with none of their optimism, Weber commits himself to the scientist's calling. For him science is the affair of an intellectual aristocracy. It demands concentration, hard work, inspiration, and the passionate devotion to a task that can only be accomplished if all extraneous considerations are excluded. Increasing knowledge can enhance the "technical mastery of life." It helps us to perfect methods of thought and to achieve intellectual clarity about the relation of means and ends. Weber stated these goals with deliberate restraint. Like the great romantic iconoclasts before him, he viewed the ideal of progress through knowledge with profound skepticism. The very achievements of science have "chained [us] to the idea of progress." For every scientific achievement poses new questions and calls for investigations that will lead to the quick obsolescence of the scholar's contribution. Weber states: "It is not self-evident that something subordinate to such a law [of progress] is sensible and meaningful in itself. Why does one engage in doing something that in reality never comes, and never can come, to an end?" Tolstoy attacked science because for men on this endless frontier death has no meaning; the logical goal of progress would be man's immortality. But in fact the scientific world view leaves the meaning of life and death undefined. Thus stating his case Weber deliberately rejected the idea that youth could find leadership and authentic experience in the universities.

Those academicians who want to assume the role of leader should engage in it where they can be challenged politically. Nor can the university teacher provide experience in the sense in which the churches offer it to the believer. Let those who search for authenticity learn that the individual who simply fulfills the exacting demands of the day, if he has found himself, expresses the creative spark that is within him. Weber addressed these remarks to a generation which rejected his own skeptical commitment to the Enlightenment tradition. The young men of the 1920's, like their age-mates in the years before World War I, demanded experience and action rather than words. Their drive had culminated in the enthusiasm with which they greeted the outbreak of war in 1914, and with which they were joining extremist movements of the Right or Left in 1918 to 1920.

But meanwhile imaginative writers had begun to explore the possibilities of relativism in a world without values, further helping to undermine the legacy of the Enlightenment still viable in men like Freud or Weber. The arts may have little direct bearing on science or scholarship, except where they destroy the notion of competence. However, their development in the twentieth century jeopardized the standards of discourse on which all academic work is based. The nature of this jeopardy is conveyed by two interrelated tendencies of modern art: the retreat from intelligibility and the emergence of a radical subjectivism. As Saul Bellow put it in *Mr. Sammler's Planet:* "When people are so desperately impotent, they play that instrument, the personality, louder and wilder."

Some nineteenth-century writers anticipated these developments. The German poet Novalis (1772-1801) wrote of poetry as a defense against ordinary life, a magical union of fantasy and thought, a productive language which like mathematics is a playful world of its own, intelligible only to a few. Novalis was read in France. Many of these elements are elaborated by Baudelaire, whose poems are

deliberately impersonal so that they can express every possible human emotion, preferably the most extreme. Baudelaire uses the term "modernity" to refer to the ugliness of large cities, their artificiality and sinfulness, their loneliness in large crowds, their technology and progress. He despised advertising, newspapers, the tide of a leveling democracy. But modernity also meant to him that these and other features of modern civilization result in a profusion of evil, decay, poverty, and artifice which fascinates the poetic imagination. Baudelaire and the many who followed him have had a desperate urge to escape this reality. Most of them were unbelievers with a religious longing. For them poetry became a magical incantation, designed to cast a spell rather than reveal a meaning. To this end fantasy decomposes the whole created world and by reordering the component parts out of the wellsprings of human experience fashions a new world of its own.

A retreat from meaning and coherence is evident in this orientation. When the poet does not want to recognize the existing world, ordinary themes and objects lose their relevance. Instead, style and sound are the prevalent means of expression at the expense of meaning. The poet has no object, says one writer. Pure poetry must be devoid of content so that the creative movement of language can have free rein, says another. A third speaks of formal tricks maintaining the verve of style; nothing is interrelated either thematically or psychologically, everything is nailed up rather than developed. Writers like Rimbaud, Apollinaire, Saint-John Perse, Yeats, Benn, search for a "new language" which is tantamount to the destruction of grammatical rules and rhetorical order. The spirit of this endeavor is beautifully expressed in T. S. Eliot's "East Coker." The poet is

> Trying to learn to use words, and every attempt
> Is a wholly new start, and a different kind of
>   failure . . .
>   And so each venture
> Is a new beginning, a raid on the inarticulate . . .

And in "Burnt Norton" Eliot writes that "words strain, crack and sometimes break, under the burden, under the tension."

Where language thus loses its communicative power, a radical subjectivism comes into its own, much as in painting and sculpture a free experimentation with colors and forms followed the classical ideal of representation. In his study of poetry, Friedrich refers to this tendency as "dictatorial fantasy." Rimbaud had said that memory and the senses are only food for the creative impulse; the world which the poet leaves will no longer resemble its former appearance, because artistic fantasy has cruelly disfigured it. Baudelaire, Mallarmé, Garcia Lorca, Proust, and Benn expressed similar ideas. In *The Counterfeiters* by André Gide, Edouard intends to write a novel which will be a sum of destructions, or a "rivalry between the real world and the representation of it which we make to ourselves. The manner in which the world of appearances imposes itself upon us, and the manner in which we try to impose on the outside world our own interpretation—this is the drama of our lives."

In the main this drama has been "resolved" by a radical subjectivism of the artist. Not only language has been destroyed, but persons and objects as means and ends of creative activity. In the futurist manifesto of 1909 the rejection of language and of the human subject are linked directly. The author, Marinetti, argues for the destruction of syntax, the elimination of adverbs and adjectives, and the serial listing of nouns, in order among other things to destroy the ego in literature. "People are completely stupefied by libraries and museums, and they are subjected to a terrible logic and science. Man is no longer interesting. Therefore, one has to eliminate people from literature." A parallel destruction of the object is evident in a comment of Picasso's. "I noticed that painting has a value of its own, independent of the factual depiction of things. I asked myself, whether one should not paint things the way one knows them rather than the way one sees them . . . In my pictures I use the things I like. I do not care, how things fare in this regard—they will have to get used to it. Formerly, pictures approached their completion in stages . . . A picture used to be a sum of completions. With me a picture is a sum of destructions."

Here then is the paradox of the development I have sketched. Since the later Nineteenth century modern art has been characterized increasingly by a retreat from meaning and coherence. That is to say, an ethics of social despair has led by circuitous routes to self-created, hermetic worlds of pure subjectivity in which neither the old romantic ideal of the human personality nor the objects and themes of ordinary experience have a recognized place or meaning. Thus, in the dominant culture of the West a type of sensibility has developed which reacts to the world as a provocation, and which is hostile to intellectual positions that retain a belief in the constructive possibilities of knowledge for all their questioning of fundamentals. In this way, the ground was prepared for protests which are based on

> the view that every human being simply by virtue of his humanity is an essence of unquestionable, undiscriminatable value with the fullest right to the realization of what is essential in him. What is essential is his sensibility, his experienced sensation, the contents of his imagination, and the gratification of his desires. Not only has man become the measure of all things; his sentiments have become the measure of man.

Here is a statement which exemplifies this interpretation:

> We are fed reason in order to give an inferiority complex to the rest of our emotions and senses. . . .

> We are trapped in a philosophical system of cause and effect. Rationality binds the mind and restricts the soul. It might even destroy the brain cells. We need to be liberated. We should be constrained no

longer by possible rational consequences. We should begin to allow other emotions to dictate our actions.

There is an "elective affinity" between a changed sensibility in the arts and the sectarian modes of protest which are inspired by a mystique of plenitude and subjectivism.

There is as well a political dimension to which brief reference must be made.

THE RHETORIC OF FASCISM

I emphasize the transformation of artistic sensibility for two reasons. The retreat from intelligibility and its radical subjectivism have long since prepared the ground for a distrust of reason among the educated middle class, including members of faculties as long as their own field is not in question. Also I emphasize the affinity between this changed sensibility and current student protests because I see little evidence that these protests have arisen from communist or fascist doctrines. To be sure, Bolshevism after the Russian Revolution of 1917 and the Nazi movement before and after 1933 launched a concerted attack upon the universities as bastions of false claims to scholarly objectivity. For example, A. A. Bogdanov declared in 1918 that with the exception of the social sciences transformed by Marxism "all the present sciences are bourgeois [though] not in the sense that they defend the interests of the bourgeoisie directly. [They are bourgeois] in that they have been worked out and presented from the bourgeois standpoint, in that they are suffused by the bourgeois Weltanschauung and as such have a bourgeoisifying influence. . . ." Bogdanov also added that all teaching and research must be transformed from the proletarian standpoint and based thenceforth on the "living, brotherly cooperation between teachers and students, rather than on authority and intellectual subjugation." Overtones reminiscent of current protest themes will be noted, yet I believe that these are distinct.

The rhetorical use of the word "fascism" helps to characterize the situation in which we find ourselves. Students proclaim that the Establishment is fascist, and critics over thirty reciprocate by calling the protesters fascists or, as Jürgen Habermas had it, "left fascists." There is no clearer indication of mutual incomprehension. What does this mean? Let me take each side in turn, though, of course, there is much diversity I must ignore.

Broadly speaking, "fascism" is for some students, some faculty members, and not a few writers an expressive term of utter derogation. It has a proven shock value for the older generation when applied to democratic institutions or indeed any aspect of industrial society. The term is also a potent weapon for a policy of escalation. Agitation may lead to police action, which proves that the regime is repressive like fascism. But if agitation does not lead to this result, then the question is raised: What did we do wrong? Since the regime is "objectively fascist" and the police was not called, the strategy of protest must have been at fault. There is no entry into this circle of a self-fulfilling prophecy.

Note the ethic of social despair that lies behind the provocation. Time has run out. No landing on the moon can assuage the prospect of a nuclear holocaust. The liberation movements around the world and the race problem at home have exposed the hypocrisy of the Western claim to liberty, justice, and equality. The invasion of Czechoslovakia and the manifest inequalities and repressions of Soviet society have exposed the hypocrisy of the Communist claim to represent the people and end the exploitation of man by man. Faced with ultimate horrors and proximate evils, protest draws once more on the arsenal of cultural pessimism with its total rejection of competition, efficiency, the division of labor, considerations of utility, and the whole world of technology. Last but not least is the visible tarnishing of the old promise of the Enlightenment, that knowledge is power for the benefit and use of life.

In the face of these massive evils, the first and sometimes the only response is to see everything as connected with everything else, and to call this web of iniquity fascism. Thus, universities, a central institution in a technological society, are a prime target. Their values of dispassionate inquiry and free discussion, of tolerance for ambiguity and diversity, presuppose an ethic of social hope, that means, a freedom to choose and to wait, to discuss and deliberate. To the protester this appears utterly incommensurate with the dire threats confronting us. An academia "which fiddles while the fires are burning" appears as actually engaged in an insidious "fascist repression," for discussion delays decision, and words are seen as a smoke screen for inaction. All the values of scholarship turn to dross: tolerance is repressive, objectivity or neutrality serve the "system," lectures become an abuse of authority, and indeed scholarship which uses abstract terms, as it must, "crumbles in the mouth like mouldy fungi," which phrase helped to initiate the change of sensibility I have traced. At one level or another a good many people respond positively to these sentiments, faced as they are with a world of local wars and international stalemates in which the threat of nuclear destruction hangs over every move.

On the other hand there are the liberals, young or old, who are outraged by these attacks upon the values of civilization. To be sure, conservatives rather than liberals call for law and order. But as the legal system is dragged into the vortex of political polarization, "fascism" comes to be used by liberals as a term of alarm at the deliberate abandon with which standards of academic and democratic civility are flouted. It is a term of abuse against those who reject tolerance, discussion, and the rule of law—or in an academic setting against those who reject free inquiry, the quest for objectivity, and the civilities of academic deliberation. It refers as well to the all-or-nothing perspective which fails to distinguish between authority and oppression, normal national interest

and violent aggression, political compromise and political corruption.

Liberals believe that the indiscriminate and immoderate attack upon all social and political conventions and upon traditional values is profoundly unpolitical. The liberals see protesters frequently attacking not only political abuses and empty pretensions, but the very institutions that protect their right to protest. To liberal critics it is clear that protesters are blind to the ways in which their activities consolidate opinion on the far right. But this characterization is answered by the protesters by saying that nothing else can be done, since ordinary politics have brought us to this impasse. Theirs is a sectarian mode of protest outside of time, of political calculation, and of technical efficiency.

Indeed, it is outside of ordinary communication when one considers how declamation has crowded out discussion. With or without drugs "the mystic finds himself exploring every negative experience in order to make possible his return to the world of a 'total' human being." Meanwhile, his more activist brother develops a cult of distant savior-leaders like Mao or Che, identifies with populist causes everywhere, and unites with others in a desperate, if superficially euphoric, rejection of his own civilization. In their indiscriminate attack upon social and political conventions the protesters begin to resemble intellectuals of the Weimar Republic, who were equally sweeping in their condemnations. Walter Laqueur has dubbed this the "Tucholsky Complaint" after the German satirist of the 1920:

> Tucholsky and his friends thought that the German Judge of their day was the most evil person imaginable and that the German prisons were the most inhumane; later they got Freisler and Auschwitz. They imagined that Stresemann and the Social Democrats were the most reactionary politicians in the world; soon after they had to face Hitler, Goebbels, and Goering. They sincerely believed that fascism was already ruling Germany, until the horrors of the Third Reich overtook them.

In a book entitled *Deutschland, Deutschland über Alles,* Tucholsky said "no" to everything except the landscape of Germany. But at least he despaired of a society without democratic traditions. Some recent critics like Herbert Marcuse simply despair of civilization altogether—without telling us how they would live without it.

Today, discussion within the academic community is gravely impaired by the distrust of reason of the present generation of dissenters. This rise of irrationalism in the cultural sphere is due in part to a failure of the national political community. In their relations with the young generation the universities cannot tackle issues like the Vietnam war, race relations, or the uses of technology which the political leadership has so far failed to resolve. The universities should not be asked to make the attempt. Nevertheless, protesters and politicians have misused the universities as a convenient battleground without immediate and obvious disadvantage to themselves. They have done so in part, because we are faced with a crisis of legitimacy within the walls of academe.

THE CHANGED ROLE OF SCIENCE

Agonizing questions are raised concerning the purposes to be served by a quest for knowledge wherever it may lead. When scientists help to create powers of destruction which threaten civilization, the authority of scholarship is placed in jeopardy, because the belief in progress through knowledge is impaired.

Strictly speaking, the uses of knowledge and the conditions that facilitate its pursuit are extraneous concerns. As Don Price has stated: "Science has achieved its great power by insisting on defining for itself the problems it proposes to solve, and by refusing to take on problems merely because some outside authority considers them important. But that power, and the precision of thought on which it depends, is purchased by a refusal to deal with many aspects of such problems." The power referred to is the capacity to advance knowledge. But the capacity to define problems autonomously depends upon authority. And this autonomous authority has become more difficult to maintain in recent decades.

The role of science has changed. Scientific research in World War II and its culmination in the military and peaceful employment of atomic energy produced a marked rise in the authority of the scientific community. In his report to the president in 1945, Vannevar Bush spoke for that community when he argued strongly that basic scientific research is indispensable for the nation's welfare in war and peace. Remember: only a year later Bernard Baruch declared that we tremble with fear as we think of the power science has put at our disposal, but science does *not* show us how we can control the dangers inherent in that power. Nevertheless, for a time, the positive claims of science were accepted very generally. Between 1953 and 1966, gross national product in the United States doubled, but total funds for basic research increased more than six times. During the same period the federal government increased its support of basic research from one half to two thirds of the national total. In the five-year period from 1959-60 to 1963-64, federal support of research in universities more than doubled.

In the last twenty-five years science has become very prominent; even the social sciences have advanced, albeit at a great distance. Clark Kerr, in his Godkin lectures, has analyzed the resulting changes in academic decision-making. By offering projects, federal agencies exert a subtle but potent influence upon the directions which research at universities will take. They affect the allocation of funds and space and hence the establishment of priorities. As extramural research funds become a major portion of a university's research budget, many scholars are prompted to shift their identification and loyalty from their university to the grant-giving agency. Increased emphasis on research through extramural funds entails a

shift of resources to graduate, at the expense of undergraduate, education, and to the employment of research personnel without faculty status. Projects, costly facilities, and program planning introduce a new managerial dimension. Scientists who launch a series of projects can become caught up in the apparatus they have helped to create, and may be deflected permanently from what they would prefer to do if they still had a free hand. Thus the earlier autonomy of science and of universities is in doubt just at the time when the destructiveness of weapons and the dangerous side effects of modern technology have become urgent concerns.

In addition, the demands on the educational system have increased greatly. In 1939/40 50 percent of those aged 17 were high-school graduates. By 1967/68 that percentage had risen to 74. During the same period college enrolments and the total number of college degrees increased by a factor of four and the number of higher degrees by a factor of seven. Nor is it a question of numbers alone. Increasingly, politicians, administrators, the general public, and not a few scientists, who should know better, have called upon the university to help solve the race problem, the urban crisis, generational conflict, pollution, the arms race. Scientists are called upon to be responsible for the application of their increasing knowledge at the same time that questions are raised whether the consequences of science are still beneficial. These and other demands subject the universities to a barrage of expectations which they cannot possibly fulfill. From being a method of inquiry to answer carefully delimited questions, science has been turned into a fetish with which to interpret the world, advise politicians, examine the future, provide an education, and entertain the public.

A crisis of legitimacy results whenever in critical periods the very claims of authority are used to question its justification. The claim is that "basic research performed without thought of practical ends" is indispensable for the nation's welfare. But this claim has led to public support for science, which undermines the freedom of scientists from practical ends. The claim has also led to uses of knowledge which have a destructive potential that appears incompatible with welfare. In their eagerness to advance knowledge scientists have made claims for the unequivocal beneficence of their results. Inadvertently, they have contributed to the distrust of reason which is upon us.

THE PLACE OF SOCIOLOGY

Ordinarily we do not think of science and scholarship as bases of authority. But knowledge has an authority of its own, and I have tried to show why the legitimacy of that authority is now in question. Protest aimed at the foundations of academic institutions has found considerable resonance among people ostensibly committed to the life of the mind. What then of sociology?

Like all academic disciplines sociology depends on the existence of a scholarly community. A modern university comprises a congeries of such communities. Teachers and students in the different disciplines may communicate little or not at all. But while they live with their different interests and obligations, all of them can share an interest in the advance of knowledge—an advance facilitated by independent inquiry, free discussion, and academic self-government. When this shared interest is in doubt, more is at stake than spurious talk about an academic community. For when the legitimacy of the pursuit of knowledge is questioned, discourse itself is threatened by a withdrawal of affect. Let me spell this out in relation to sociology.

As in other disciplines, scholarship in sociology depends on communication concerning the findings and methods of study. In this context every statement made invites consent and helps to define the circle of those who agree, while to some extent marking off those who do not. We are all familiar with the feeling of dismay and anxiety, or with the displays of aggression, when such agreement is not achieved. We are also familiar with the school- or clique-building tendencies that arise from this desire for consensual validation. Accordingly, the twin principles of toleration and free discussion are more difficult to achieve within disciplines than in the university at large. Indeed, there is more to discuss within disciplines than between them, and withdrawal of affect within disciplines threatens discourse quite directly.

Many sociologists aspire to bring their field of study to the status of a science of society. To an extent this is salutary. The aspiration to engage in empirical inquiry is an indispensable bulwark against speculations which are complacent towards idiosyncrasies and take a lofty view of the merely factual. Yet today sociologists as scientists face a crisis of legitimacy. The destructive possibilities of knowledge and the diminished autonomy of science have prompted a questioning of premises which is bound to affect a discipline whose scientific aspirations are well ahead of its achievements. Moreover, sociologists of this persuasion should have noted the antihumanistic impulse of their model all along. It appears that the qualities of the scientific mind have been extolled at the expense of philosophical breadth and historical perspective, of literary distinction and aesthetic sensibility, of moral imagination and the cultivation of judgment. To be sure, much has been gained in the process. But a sociology that takes the natural sciences as its model also falls heir to a tradition in which these other qualities are at a discount.

At the same time we are all aware that in our discipline there have always been those who thought science not enough, who believed that the cultivation of judgment and moral sensibility was indispensable for sociology as a scholarly discipline. Such cultivation provides a bulwark against the dangers of scientism, against the preoccupation with techniques for their own sake, and against the unthinking denigration of contextual understanding. At the same time, sociologists of this persuasion are committed to empirical inquiry, broadly conceived. But today they, also, face a crisis of legitimacy. For the destructive

possibilities of the distrust of reason, with its craving for authenticity and relevance, are evident once again. Hence the plea for more cultivation of judgment and sensibility in sociology should be made with care. A humanistic sociology which takes the distrust of reason as its model thereby undermines its own existence.

To me the tensions and debates between the scientific and the humanistic impulses appear as the foundation of modern sociology. Twenty years ago I wrote an essay on social science and the distrust of reason. My purpose then was to contrast an unreflective faith in science with the tradition of critical self-scrutiny reaching from Francis Bacon to Sigmund Freud. I wanted to warn that methodological preoccupations not be permitted to encroach on substantive concerns, lest we do harm to our discipline. In the meantime there have been notable attempts to redirect our efforts, to which I have tried to contribute. Hence today I would emphasize that the distrust of reason is not furthered by scientism alone. It consists also in a consciousness of crisis, an ethic of despair, and a call for action which do away with learning and deliberation altogether. I think sociology is as endangered by this retreat from meaning and coherence as it was by spurious analogies from the natural sciences.

Still, we are also enriched by the creative interplay of the traditions that have formed us. Their constructive use depends upon faith in the possibilities of human reason. Those who would destroy that use and that faith would not long survive in a world in which the ideals of reasoned inquiry have been abandoned. As long as we do not go back to the caves in anticipation of holocausts to come, learning has a creative role to play in the human community. It can do so only in universities which exist in the society and for it, and which provide institutional protection for learning in order to perform their mission.

Carl Mayer (essay date 1973)

SOURCE: "Max Weber's Interpretation of Karl Marx," in *Social Research*, Vol. 42, No. 4, 1973, pp. 701-19.

[*In the following essay, which was originally presented as a lecture at the University of Constance in 1973, Mayer contends that Marx's theories only became an important element of Weber's work after his illness from 1899 to 1902.*]

More than thirty years ago, Albert Salomon published an essay in which he asserted not merely that Max Weber's work could be understood only if seen against the background of Karl Marx but also that Weber's work itself was the product of an intense, life-long preoccupation with Marx. This assertion is not literally correct. In the first phase of Weber's scientific work—prior to his illness of 1899-1902—Marx's work meant little to him. What he did, before 1900, was to utilize the categories in Marx's system in a unique manner for his own investigations (for examples, in the fascinating little study of the social causes of the decline of the ancient world). Beyond this, he spoke of the shattered scientific system of Marx, which was then being hammered dogmatically into the minds of the German workers.

There is no trace of an actual critical analysis of Marx. Weber was influenced by other sources: Mommsen in the field of Roman agrarian history; Meitzer for the history of the Germanic agrarian structure; the exponents of historical economics for his socio-political essays. However, this changed completely in the second phase of his productivity, when he started to develop the theoretical-methodological foundations for his further work, simultaneously throwing himself into the immense materials for his investigations into the sociology of religion. The beginnings of this work made it necessary for him to deal with Marx. His biographer, Marianne Weber, reported that in 1918 he presented the results of his studies in the sociology of religion in Vienna under the title **"The Positive Critique of the Materialist Conception of History."** What is the result of this critical discussion of Marx?

Not the only, but the predominant opinion of the interpreters of Weber's work is the following: On the one hand, in spite of all differences in detail, there is no refutation of Marx by Weber in terms of basic methodological-theoretical positions. On the other hand, there exists far-reaching accord in the substantive analysis of the themes identical in both: the structure of what has been called the modern world; its development; and its consequences. To cite two entirely different writers who have expressed radical opinions in this regard: Schumpeter, in his book *Democracy, Socialism and Capitalism,* writes: "The whole of the facts and the arguments of Max Weber fit perfectly into the system of Marx." Another author, Lichtheim, insisted a few years ago that Max Weber's work could easily be transposed into the terminology of Marx's system.

It is important that the same thesis has been advanced by Gerth and Mills, whose views largely dominated the Weber interpretation in the United States and, as far as I can see, also exercised a great influence in the postwar interpretation of Weber in Germany. To be sure, in recent years Weber has been further interpreted, not only in regard to Marx but also to Nietzsche. But the basic thesis, as for example by Baumgarten and Mommsen, remains: Whether the problems of Weber coincide with those of Marx—that is, whether in the interpretation of modern capitalism there is identity in principle.

I shall attempt, by a comparative analysis of the key positions of Weber and Marx, to make this thesis the subject of my discussion.

It seems to me that there are two possible ways to achieve this goal. The first way is the exact comparison between Marx's and Weber's respective analyses of the origin of the character and the consequences of modern capitalism. This has been done in an exemplary manner by Karl Lowith. It would be pointless to simply repeat his investigations here. Nor would this be particularly fruitful if one does not accept all of Lowith's assertions. The other possible method is a comparison of those fundamental methodological-theoretical principles which we find in Marx's and Weber's work respectively. This is what I wish to do today, and I shall develop my position in five points. Before I enter upon the analysis itself, however, I wish to make a prefatory comment, lest what I am about to say be misunderstood.

Such a comparative analysis makes sense only if we take Weber's explicit or implicit interpretation of Marx as its basis. We must relegate to the background the question of whether Weber's interpretation of Marx is adequate. I shall deal with this question briefly at the end of these considerations. Now to the five points which will serve to articulate my topic.

THE PROBLEM OF IDEOLOGY

The first point concerns the structure of social systems and the problem of ideology. We approach this from the simplest vantage point: We all know that Marx (whether or not this was a particularly happy choice of expression) differentiated between the socalled substructure and the superstructure of a social system. By substructure, he designated both the so-called productive forces and the social relations of production built upon them. The term "productive forces" has to be understood in its broadest sense; not merely in the sense of the technology of a given society, but also as embracing nature, science, technique, and the division of labor. By social relations of production, again, Marx understands the social relationships which develop among the different members of the society on the basis of these productive forces. To put it briefly (and juridically) he means by this the conditions of ownership on which the class structure, ultimately the political order, and the solutions of the power problem are based. For Marx, the substructure or basis—occasionally also called "reality"—is specifically a combination of productive forces and social relations of production of a very complex nature.

On the other side, there is the phenomenon of the so-called superstructure, which Marx divides into two levels. The first is the low level of conceptions or theories which people develop in regard to the social order. The second is the higher, abstract level of ultimate conceptions of the nature of man, the nature of the world, metaphysics, religion, the symbolic world, and the like. The decisive problem I am aiming at is the question of the relationship between the substructure and the superstructure. To express Marx's point of view, we may say that the superstructure, in relation to the substructure, consists of ideology. We have the opposition of two concepts: reality, as represented by the substructure, and ideology, as represented by the superstructure. It is important, in the face of the very complex and heterogeneous use of the concept of ideology, to clarify what Marx means by it. He understands two things by this conception, which, it seems to me, he denotes with great precision.

On one hand, ideology means that the notions people have, on the upper or lower levels of thinking, do not have autonomous sources but are dependent upon the substructure. To quote Marx's famous dictum: It is not consciousness which determines existence, but existence which determines consciousness. How Marx conceives this in detail is problematic. We find concepts such as "product," occasionally even "expression of being" (*Ausdruck des Seins*). However, it is clear that ideology means the absence of any autonomy of man's ideas.

There is, however, also a second significance to Marx's concept of ideology: Ideas (that is, consciousness in the broadest meaning of the term) are not only dependent upon existence but they reflect this existence inadequately and, as a result, there comes about what we know as "false consciousness"—that is, ideologies. In other words, the superstructure does not rest securely upon the substructure. The reason for this can, of course, be found in the special antinomic structure of social reality which is expressed in classes and the class struggle. Let us take examples of Marx's use of the concept of ideology. Marx's own thinking was much influenced by the then classical British economists—consider the great influence of Ricardo on the Marxian system. Marx is perfectly willing to admit that classical economic theory represents the appropriate, theoretically accurate expression of the given social relationships. What he criticizes and unmasks as ideology is that, in his opinion, classical economics made an absolute out of categories which were appropriate to a specific social system, and distorted them into "natural" categories of timeless validity. Here, according to Marx, the ideologization of theoretical economics takes shape. Or, to take a second, even more important example, which already played a role for the early Marx: the problem of religion or of metaphysical systems. Marx does not claim that the conceptions men have of the ultimate meaning and purpose of life are necessarily false. What he does say is that such conceptions (which we may find, for example, in the Christian religion or in idealistic philosophy) can be false wherever they transform temporally valid categories into eternally valid categories. To put it another way, they have succumbed to the fallacy of hypostatization. It is this hypostatization which forms the basis for Marx's conception of the nature of religion, especially the essence of Christianity and its critique (Feuerbach).

Now the conclusions from this very brief first consideration. For Marx, science is in the position not only to describe the structure of social systems but to determine and explain this structure in its particular combination; that is, to demonstrate especially that what is accepted as an externally valid viewpoint is merely transcendental illusion. But just as Kant can reveal the transcendental illusion of metaphysics, Marx too accepts that science can unmask the transcendental illusion of ideologies. But it cannot get rid of them, because they are a necessary element whose function resides in the dominating classes' need for ideology in order to conceal their interests. The obliteration of ideology is the task of revolu-tionary action. The demonstration of the ideological character of the superstructure is the task of scientific theory. Marx believed he had solved this scientific problem.

What is Weber's position in this regard? Needless to say, it is evident that Weber recognized the problem of the sub- and superstructure (as well as the relationship between them). Weber too, in his substantive analyses, thinks in such concepts as "real" and "ideal" factors; Weber too is familiar with the problem of the ideologies—that is, the embellishment of originally adequate ideas, their distortions in the transcendental illusion previously mentioned. But here we come to the first point of disagreement. The decisive difference for Weber is this: For all his acknowledgment of the relation between the sub- and superstructure, for all his acceptance of the significance of ideologies as expressions of special interest, the ultimate sources of the ideas forming the superstructure *are* autonomous and cannot be derived from "social existence."

Weber does not accept Marx's assertion that social existence determines consciousness. To be sure, he does not claim that consciousness determines existence. But he says that the final and ultimate source of metaphysics, of religions and mythologies, cannot be derived from social existence; they are of autonomous origin.

If this is so, then Weber is confronted by a very serious and difficult problem: How to explain the connection between substructure and superstructure, between real and ideal factors. At any rate, he cannot revert to monocausality, to merely causal interpretation which is not removed when one speaks of "reciprocal effects" (*Wechselwirkung*) in Marx. This does not mean a thing. How can Weber solve this problem after he closed the path Marx had opened up, the path of causal and direct derivation?

Weber provides no systematic treatment of this problem. But in his general sociology of religion, there are hints of attempts to deal with it. The fundamental concepts of his approach appear in various sections of his work, without giving us any certainty as to what he means. However, it finds its real significance in the systematic sociology of religion in the concept of elective affinity (*Wahlverwandschaft*). Weber does not think in terms of mutual causalities but in concepts of elective affinities—that is, in most general terms, elective affinities between existence and consciousness. This is, of course, not the place to deal with this problem in a detailed and adequate way. But let us say this much: In his systematic sociology of religion, Weber makes the following construction. He takes social groups and strata, asks what their special interests are. Then he inquires, in a second process of his investigations, what naturally adequate world view, what general view regarding the nature of the world and of man, follows from them. So for the peasant, the worker, the positively or negatively privileged middle classes, etc. And then he takes a final, third step, and asks to what extent (to use one of Max Scheler's expressions) these relatively natural aspects of the world conform to or conflict with the autonomously evolved religious system and the theological constructions of philosophical-metaphysical speculation, how much they help or hinder these, etc.

The concept of elective affinity, furthermore, is known in literature. You will find it in Goethe's works; interestingly enough, you will also find it in the beginnings of chemistry with its notion of attraction and repulsion among the elements. Weber makes this concept productive for the solution of the problem of the relationship between super- and substructure, of the real and ideal spheres, which Marx seems to have solved in his concept of ideology. However one regards this Weberian solution, it differs fundamentally from that of Marx. We can approach this difference in yet another way: We can say that Marx's system is characterized by a *monism* of access (*Zugang*); Weber's by a fundamental *dualism*. For Weber, to use a more current expression, there is an "ontological difference" between the real and the ideal sphere.

THE PROBLEM OF SOCIAL ACTION

The second point I wish to consider concerns the problem of the explanation of social change and the problem of action in general and social action in particular. Just as, for Marx, economics determines the structure of the society, so too it determines the changes which appear in this area. The economic changes are the ones (according to Marx in his famous passage in the introduction to the *Critique of Political Economy*) which, slowly or rapidly, pull along the enormous superstructure of ideologies and transform it. To be sure, Marx was cognizant of the fact that economic structures and changes are the results of human action. He was equally aware of the fact that economic changes by themselves do not bring about changes in the social body, but that this is possible only by means of human action. But—and this I believe to be the crucial point in the comparison with Weber—for Marx, human actions, however necessary, are merely a dependent, not an independent, variable. They are organs, means, methods to bring about changes.

How does Weber approach this point of the explanation of what we today designate by the somewhat colorless term "social change"? Weber is of course aware of the tremendous significance of economic changes, if one takes this expression only in the broad sense of changes in a specific society. He knows as well as Marx—there is no difference here—that changes, of course, can only be brought about by action, the actions of people or of groups of people. The decisive difference: For Weber, action cannot be derived from existence. It represents an independent variable. Action is not merely the product of the conditions and their changes; the action, so to speak, stands on its own feet. This, again, is not to say that social changes can be explained exclusively by the actions of people, as perhaps in the "great men" theory of history. It means, rather, that Weber sees the problem as

a dualistic one, as an interplay of objectively given economic facts (in this case of social changes) *and* the reactions of people to them in the most differing ways. We have two groups of factors, and we must take both in their relative independence and then attempt to explain their interrelation.

Weber does not give us any substantive answer to the question, how does this interplay take place? There are, however, various modifications. First of all, Weber's theory tells us that social change is to be understood as the product, the result of the dialectic between objective givenness and subjective action. But this is not all. We still have to consider a second point. There is, for Weber, in regard to the problem of social change, an *extraordinary* form of action. There is the common, natural, normal action, and then there is an extraordinary, abnormal, unusual action. For this form of action Weber coined the term "charisma" (in a different context, to be sure, but this isn't the place to go into that). There are people who act in an extraordinary manner. It is Weber's thesis that essentially qualitative changes, historically, take place in differing social systems if there is something like "charismatic"—that is to say, extraordinary—action.

Whether the exponents of this extraordinary action are adventurers (the significance of the adventurer for the development of capitalism is one of Weber's special subjects) or whether they are prophets or founders of religions (and this is very carefully analyzed by Weber) who introduce a new law beyond the limits of the traditional—this is irrelevant. What is decisive is the significance of the extraordinary action for the phenomenon we call "social change."

Why is this the case? Weber, in contrast to Marx, sees the change of social systems not as normal, natural, and matter-of-course but as unnormal and problematic, because in all social systems the element of tradition has a decisive place. This creates the problem of how traditionally similar, repetitive actions can be interrupted.

In the place of determinism of action, Weber puts indeterminism. This means, however, that science is not in a position to directly make prognoses regarding whether and in what manner social change can take place. This is in contrast to Marx, who believed that science cannot tell whether and in what direction men actually act but, on the basis of his theory of social change, that science can tell what form this action must take in order to be correct. For Weber, it is impossible to explain the problem of correct action scientifically. For Marx, it is possible. This is one of the basic positions of his entire system.

THE PROBLEM OF THE DIALECTIC

A brief word with regard to the third point I wish to consider. It concerns the question of social dynamics and the problem of the dialectic. In contrast to the questions I have dealt with in the second point, it is not here a matter of the causes of social dynamics but of the law of social dynamics. In English we refer to it as "patterns of social change." As far as Marx is concerned, the basic feature of his system is the factor of internal and external contradiction, or the mutual conflicts of the diverse social elements ensuing from conflict. The law of development is nothing other than dialectic (*die im Konflikt angelegte Dialektik*). This dialectic expresses itself in the following way: First, the conflict is only latently and potentially present and hidden by a relative harmony of interests. Then it becomes actual. It continues to rise, finally reaching a point where it puts the existence of the society in question. That is the revolutionary situation which can only be solved by the creation of a new social system. Whether or not this transformation from one social system to another takes place externally, in a revolutionary form, is of little importance.

Weber too saw the problem of social conflict in its significance for the social dynamic. If one wishes to classify, Weber belongs, with Marx, to the group of theorists of conflict, not to that aggregation of theorists of harmony. To that extent, there is agreement with Marx. The difference between Marx and Weber begins with the significance which is ascribed to the fact of conflict. First, it is by no means taken for granted by Weber that the conflict itself develops an inner dialectical dynamic in the manner I have described. A society, in other words, can very well continue to exist, no matter how much it is shaken by conflict, if the traditions continue to carry their greater weight. Second, the conflict may be solved within a social system. That is at least a theoretical possibility. Only in rare cases comes about that transition to a new social system which Marx regarded as normal.

Naturally, this has far-reaching consequences for the interpretation of the theory of the dynamic of social systems. Summarizing, we can place the positions of both men in opposition to each other: Marx's theory of the dialectic of conflict, Weber's theory of the different possibilities of resolving a given conflict.

THE PROBLEM OF EVOLUTION

The fourth point I wish to deal with is the most difficult among these considerations. It concerns the relationship of the different social systems to one another within the dynamic process of history. Here we do not occupy ourselves with the question of the inner dynamic of any social system, but with the question of the dynamic connection of the differing given types or stages of society. This includes the problem of evolution.

It has been claimed that Marx could not possibly have been a theorist of evolution because he preaches revolution. It has also been said that Marx, in principle, cannot be a theorist of evolution because he teaches the dialectic of conflict. Both objections, however plausible they seem, do not appear to be correct to me.

The contrast between evolution and revolution is not a genuine antinomy. The process of evolution may well

make use of revolution as an organ. As concerns the second point, I believe a sharp division must be made between Marx's teachings regarding the inner dynamic of a social system and the dynamic interconnections among different social systems. My thesis is—and on this I am in agreement with Schumpeter—that Marx used the dialectic as a principle of explaining the inner dynamic of a society, but in order to explain the sequence of different social systems he used the scheme of evolutionary theory. This, at least, applies for the following decisive considerations which constitute evolutionary theory.

First, every social system is potentially preformed in the antecedent social system. Marx, as you know, used the image of the womb of the old society from which the new society is born. Second, each system follows the antecedent one necessarily, for the antecedent system not only creates the conditions for its successor but is also its cause. Third, every system in the evolutionary sequence is a higher form than its antecedent, not only in its degree of technical differentiation but definitely in a general sense: it represents a higher stage of development morally, intellectually, politically, economically, and technically. Marx is indeed the most severe critic of the modern capitalist system. But do not forget that no one else has spoken of it in such positive terms. It is absolutely impossible to separate this positive element from the critical element. The criticism refers to the fact that capitalism is not yet socialism, containing merely its potentiality. The praise consists in the assertion that capitalism, so far, represents the highest stage of development in the history of social systems.

It is interesting to see that Weber, too, occasionally uses the evolutionary scheme. Thus, in a fascinating study of the structure of late antiquity, he traced the emergence of the feudalism that came to full flower in the Middle Ages. But it would be erroneous to conclude from this that Weber was an evolutionist. He was not an evolutionist in the same sense in which Marx was. In fact, he radically rejected the three decisive characteristics of evolutionary theory, to the extent to which they are used in the social domain. That is, he rejected the thesis of the preformation of a later society in the society immediately preceding; he rejected the thesis of the necessity of developmental stages; and he emphatically rejected the notion that technically more differentiated societies are of higher value in other spheres too—politically, intellectually, and morally. How, Weber asks, could one possibly value the modern world more highly than the world of classical antiquity? This, for him, is simply impossible— at any rate, impossible on the basis of a scientific analysis. For Marx it is possible, because he is an evolutionist.

THE SCOPE OF SCIENCE

And now let us come to the final point. I shall attempt to put it as briefly as possible. This concerns the meaning and purpose of historical-social development and the scope of scientific analysis. The word "development" here is to be taken in an entirely colorless, formal sense.

For Marx, these concerns took the form of the problems of the ultimate goal toward which history is heading and the ultimate meaning which manifests itself in historic development. We know that he believed he could answer both these questions, not in the manner of speculative philosophers or utopian socialists but with the authority of science. Science, he believed, could give clear and objectively valid answers to the questions of the ultimate aim and meaning of history.

Why? For Marx, it was established that the history of the human species has its immanent aim and realizes its own purpose innately. It is, I believe, important that Marx found the final stage and the crowning of history to be socialism: this is the application of the theory for the specific situation of the present. The decisive aspect here is that Marx does not preach socialism but represents it as the necessary ultimate goal of history.

In this area he differs from evolutionism, which proclaims an ever increasing, infinite progress. He gives history a definite terminal point: What characterizes socialism is, in the end, that essentially nothing further happens. Similarly, Marx answers concretely the problem of the purpose of history. This problem is answered in the confrontation of the essential freedom of man with alienation, or in the confrontation between domination and freedom from domination.

The decisive difference between Weber and Marx is not in the details but in the fundamentals. It lies in this: Quite aside from the question of socialism vs. capitalism, domination vs. freedom from domination, Marx asserts on principle what Weber totally rejects—that science is in a position to answer the question of the ultimate aim of social history and its meaning. For Weber, this lies beyond the province of science. Here, of course, is the origin of the famous principle of value neutrality in Weber's sociology and in science in general. (I shall not deal with this distinction here.) For Weber, science is not qualified to answer questions concerning the aim and meaning of history. One can approach this problem only speculatively. In this respect, Weber does not see a difference between Marx and the other speculative systems but only a formal identity. Marx did not answer, with scientific authority, questions the utopian socialists had posed speculatively. The difference between utopian and so-called scientific socialism disappears.

RESULT AND SOCIOLOGICAL PERSPECTIVE

The thesis which has dominated the Marx-Weber discussion asserts that there may be differences in detail but no differences in principle. Speaking negatively, it seems to me that this thesis has to be reversed: Aside from the fact that the way the problem is put is similar, it is correct to say that there is agreement in many essential details, but there is a fundamental difference in regard to the decisive methodological positions with which we are confronted in the social sciences.

In this short address I have attempted to represent the problem, not to elucidate it critically or to ask who was right, Marx or Weber. Must we decide in favor of one or the other? One could perhaps make an attempt, as Peter Berger has done in an interesting but, I believe, ultimately impossible way, to combine Marx's and Weber's sociology of religion. Or is there perhaps a third way out of this thicket? The question of a critical comparison of Marx and Weber lies beyond the scope of these considerations. I merely wish to prepare the ground for such a critical analysis, and then to make two negative observations suggesting how I believe this problem must be approached.

It has often been said by Marxists, especially in our time, that whatever Weber may have said and whatever he may have thought of his position, Weber fundamentally misunderstood Marx. Weber's analysis, it has been said, is a criticism of vulgar Marxism. Or rather, Weber's critique concerns the "vulgar," not the "genuine," Marx. This position was particularly developed when, after Weber's death, Marx's early writings became increasingly accessible to us, and particularly after the discovery of the famous/notorious Paris fragments on "Political Economics and Philosophy." It has been said that only the interpretation of this manuscript can give us a genuine understanding of Marx, whereas Weber's interpretation, together with many interpretations from the Marxist camp itself (consider Kautsky, Plekhanov, Labriola, etc.) all concern vulgar Marxism and do not represent the genuine Marx.

In this connection, two things are interesting: First, there is no doubt that the rediscovery of Marx's early writings has given the study of Marx a new impetus. The question is, however, whether this impetus has put us in a position to find the key to an understanding of Marx. The editors of Marx's early writings, in 1932, expressed the hope that now, finally, there was the possibility of understanding Marx as he understood himself, and that now the completely sterile controversies of the later Marxists were obviated.

If one considers the literature in this field, one must regretfully admit that these expectations have not come true. There is, first of all, the greatest difference of interpretation concerning the young Marx. Consider those who interpreted the young Marx as nothing more than a reverse Hegelian, or the attempts to bring the young Marx into the vicinity of phenomenology, as Marcuse did. The fact is that today there is still no unity regarding the correct interpretation of the early writings of Marx. Even less is there agreement on the decisive problem, namely, the relationship between the early and the later Marx. To a large extent, only the latter was Max Weber's basis.

Opposed to the notion that there is a unity in Marx's life work to which the early writings give us a key, there is for example Althusser's thesis that there is a fundamental contradiction between the younger and the older Marx. The older Marx is not the continued development, the articulation of the younger Marx, but totally supersedes him. In Althusser's view, for example, it is possible to interpret Marx in terms of modern structuralism. However, I cannot go into those questions here.

A word must be said regarding the extent to which these discussions, these new aspects of Marx studies have affected Weber's understanding of Marx. Let me render my opinion in three statements. First, I am of the opinion that there is an inner continuity between the early and the late Marx. I cannot prove this here; I am merely communicating it. I am also of the opinion that a fundamental problem is always present, like a red thread, throughout all of Marx's analyses: How does the unavoidable alienation of man come about, and how is it overcome again? This is the basis of the problem of alienation which is so much under discussion.

Second, there is no doubt that Weber did not see this aspect of Marx's scientific theory—at least not sufficiently. This is hardly surprising, since the decisive works were not accessible at the time, and the few comments regarding the fetishistic character of merchandise in capitalist society neither dealt with the problem sufficiently nor clarified it. But is that to say, as those who accuse Weber of vulgar Marxism often do, that Weber's implicitly or explicitly stated theses regarding the most essential principles of Marx's methodology are fallacious? They require shoring up; they need the support of a philosophical anthropology, such as that found in Marx. But they are essentially correct.

Third, a further objection with which the exponents of Marxism reproach Weber goes in the exactly opposite direction. They do not claim that Weber misunderstood Marx. Rather, they resort to the so-called "sociology of knowledge" in the conventional sense of the term—that is, the sociology of ideas, including those ideas which find their theoretical expression in science. They look for proof that Weber's position does not represent any science at all but was rather, Marxistically speaking, an ideology. Can it be that Weber's work represents an enormously complex expression of his bourgeois limitations (since he, as you know, described himself as bourgeois)? Does he merely express the typical obtuseness of the modern middle-class citizen who cannot recognize the truth? It is impossible to treat here the problem of the sociology of knowledge in this area. But I would like to mention two points with which sociology of knowledge must occupy itself. First, is it possible that, from the social origins of a scientific work, one can draw conclusions regarding its objective validity? And two, if this is the case, what are the social conditions under which science (*Wissenschaft*) is at all possible?

CONCLUSION

These are the two questions which I believe must be posed if we wish to consider this objection to Weber specifically. Weber himself developed the counterthesis that the problem of the social genesis and the question of the validity of scientific investigation are totally different questions. It seems certain to me that the question, what are the social conditions which make science possible in the first place, requires an answer quite different from the Marxist one.

There remains the problem "Marx and Weber"—that is, "Marx or Weber"—to be answered factually on the basis of their work. There are two problems. One, if I understand it correctly, it is the task of the social sciences in general and of sociology specifically to explain and describe the surrounding social reality. Thus, the question is: Who gives us the better key to the description and understanding of social phenomena, Marx or Weber? It is certain that we can learn very little from Marx as regards the descriptive part. For description is at home in the realm of a social phenomenology. Weber has a tremendous amount to tell us in this area, even though I haven't treated this at all. As concerns the question of explanation (the origins, nature, or consequences of a social reality) in its different aspects, we ask ourselves whether Weber's or Marx's categories are more helpful to us in grasping our surrounding social reality, be it in its historic origins or its present condition. Who gives us better information as to the origin of those historic consequences of the modern world, especially of modern capitalism? Who gives us better information regarding the question of the better explanation of those social problems directly involving us, such as the problems of the capitalist and socialist social systems? This is the question which, I believe, must be posed, and the answer to which depends on how one relates to Marx or Weber.

Finally, one must pose a methodological question, or to use Weber's phrase, a question which concerns methodology as theory of science (*Wissenschaftslehre*). What are those philosophical-epistomological principles upon which science may be established? For Marx, undoubtedly, these principles were definitively laid down by Hegel. Marx, throughout all his transformations, methodologically remains a Hegelian. One could demonstrate this very neatly on the basis of his evolutionism and his dialectic. Weber, on the other hand, is a Kantian. Weber believes that the fundamental philosophical-epistemological problems which social science poses can be solved only on the basis of Kant's epistemology, that is, his critique of knowledge. Kant asked, how is science possible, referring to natural science. Weber asked, how is science possible—referring to social science. Both answer the question positively, by presenting the possibility and the limits of science. The fundamental problem on this level, which is posed with the confrontation of Marx and Weber, is the problem of Hegel vs. Kant, or Kant vs. Hegel.

Dirk Käsler   (essay date 1979)

SOURCE: "Methodological Writings," in *Max Weber: An Introduction to His Life and Work,* translated by Philippa Hurd, Polity Press, 1979, pp. 174-96.

[Originally published in German in 1979, the following essay examines the three main tenets supporting Weber's methodology.]

[If] we speak of Weber's methodology today, we mean for the most part those methodological observations which originally appeared separately in periodicals and which were published posthumously in 1922 by Marianne Weber under the title *Gesammelte Aufsätze zur Wissenschaftslehre* (*Collected Essays on Scientific Methodology*). We must realize that these collected texts consisted of casual projects and commissioned work, which for the most part remained fragmentary.

The condition of this source material is in part reasonable for the controversy that divides previous interpretations into two camps; one promotes unity in Weber's scientific doctrine, the other argues for diversity. Both positions were able to put forward good arguments. Doubtless Weber's methodological position itself was defined in the course of decades of research, which for him always took top priority, and as a result his own changes in position must be discussed. On the other hand, many cogent arguments can be settled without necessarily reducing the consequent discussion to one, uniform scientific doctrine.

Moreover, we must realize that Weber's own works on the methodology of the social sciences are connected very closely to their historical background. One set of texts were critical discussions of other contemporary authors, and thus a comprehensive understanding is impossible without knowledge of the writings under discussion. Equally all these contemporary debates and controversies took place within a philosophical context handed down by tradition and amid current social changes, particularly in the contemporary politics of the sciences. The formation and gradual institutionalization of the social sciences—sociology among others—provides an important backdrop to Weber's methodological project. In this condensed sketch of Weber's statements on sociological method, we can only include the historical background in an incomplete form. Equally we will not have the space to discuss both the continuities *and* the breaks in Weber's sketches.

Weber's work was organized in a way which befitted an important theorist in the methodology of modern sociology, thanks basically to three methodological concepts which we shall discuss below. These are:

1 The concept of *Verstehen,* or 'understanding'.

2 The concept of the 'ideal-type'.

3 The postulate of 'freedom from value-judgement' (*Werturteilsfreiheit*).

THE CONCEPT OF *VERSTEHEN* OR 'UNDERSTANDING'

Seen from the perspective of today's scientific sociology, the formation of 'interpretive sociology' (*verstehende Soziologie*) appears as an extremely important development which has had wide-reaching effects up to the present day. If we look back at the previous different manifestations and stages of this development, it is possible to recognize the division (albeit relatively arbitrary) of all existing sociological theories into three tendencies—interpretive, functionalist and reductionist. A similar analytical structure is thus made possible for the contents of all research areas in sociology: for action theory and systems theory as well as for all 'intermediary' concepts as, for example, role theory, reference group theory and theories of institutionalization.

It is remarkable that after a lengthy period of relative insignificance in the face of functionalist approaches, the interpretive orientation has at the present time regained considerable international importance. Trends like symbolic interactionism, ethnomethodology, ethnosociology, phenomenology, etc., have recaptured an important role in international sociological discourse. And as part of this, the persistent references to Weber, albeit frequently critical, are noticeable even when his work generally only constitutes their historical point of departure.

In view of today's extremely wide-reaching scientific and theoretical discussion, above all on the relationship between 'understanding' (*Verstehen*) and 'explanation' (*Erklären*), it becomes particularly necessary to comprehend Weber's original position. It is here in particular that clichés and misunderstandings have taken root; for one thing they attempt to tie Weber down exclusively to the interpretive method by presenting him as the 'father of interpretive sociology', and for another they misconstrue 'interpretation' as a method which involves empathy or intuition, both somewhat vague and arbitrary qualities.

In our presentation of Weber's position, we will refer to his later texts (1913-19), in particular to the **'Conceptual Exposition'** and the **'Basic Concepts in Sociology'** in *Economy and Society,* in spite of the fact that he had already tackled the problem of the interpretive approach much earlier.

In our previous discussion of his **'General Sociology'** [in *Max Weber: An Introduction to this Life and Work*] we were proceeding from Weber's definition of empirical sociology, according to which it is the science 'concerning itself with the interpretive understanding of social action and thereby with a causal explanation of its course and consequences'. The interpretive understanding of 'social action' as the object domain of Weber's sociology leads to an investigation into the determining effects of *meaning*. Weber defines his interpretive sociology as an empirical sociology of the understanding of meaning (*Sinn-Verstehen*). Its methodological procedure cannot be separated from a causal analytical procedure. Moreover Weber makes explicit an internal connection between the two heuristic strategies. It is precisely this relationship which, according to Weber, establishes the character of sociology as a discipline orientated towards reality.

Thus as we have already explained, 'meaning' is not intended as some pre-formed ideality but as one real, determining factor in human action. At this point the central premise of every interpretive approach emerges: the actor attaches a 'meaning' to his or her action and this 'meaning' acts at the very least as a contributory determinant to the action. Thus any scientific attempt to analyse human action requires the inclusion of meaning in an *explanation* of social phenomena.

From this basis Weber distinguishes terminologically between 'direct observational understanding' (*aktuelles Verstehen*) and 'explanatory understanding' (*Motivationsverstehen*).

Accordingly 'direct observational understanding' is

'direct rational understanding of ideas';

'direct observational understanding of irrational emotional reactions'; and 'rational observational understanding of actions'.

Motivational or 'explanatory understanding' similarly enquires into the symbolic quality of observable action, but goes one stage further by aiming beyond the understanding of the intended meaning towards an explanation of the manifest action. This is achieved by situating the action within a 'context', i.e. 'rational understanding of motivation, which consists in placing the act in an intelligible and more inclusive context of meaning'. Weber arrives at his definition of 'explanation': 'Thus for a science which is concerned with the subjective meaning of action, explanation [*Erklären*] requires a grasp of the complex of meanings in which an actual course of understandable action thus interpreted belongs'.

The introduction of the concept of a 'context of meaning' sheds light on that problematic which has frequently led to misunderstandings. Weber proceeds from the 'subjective' meaning of individual actors, but the relativizing formula of the subjectively 'intended' meaning makes it clear that Weber recognizes that this meaning does not have to be the meaning which *actually* determines the relevant action, and that the individual does not have to be *conscious* of his/her 'real', *actually* effective motives for his/her action.

The differentiation we have discussed above between different methodological ways of grasping meaning made it clear that Weber tends particularly towards conceptually constructed, pure types ('ideal types') of different meanings. Just as Weber, in his 'general sociology' had reached the category of '(legitimate) order', from the individual acting subjects via the concepts of 'social action' and 'social relations' he moves up from the construct of a 'subjectively intended meaning' to socially mediated 'contexts of meaning'. Lurking within these are all *intersubjectively* compulsory (i.e. according to his definition) 'valid' measures of meaning and value within a society, measures towards which individual actors and

social groups are oriented. In other words even the (supposedly) subjective meaning is a *social* meaning, i.e. a meaning which is reciprocal, and oriented towards and mediated by order. 'Action which is specifically important for interpretive sociology is behaviour which

1 in terms of the subjectively intended meaning of the actor refers to the *behaviour of others*.

2 is in its course *in part determined* by this meaningful reference, and thus

3 can be *explained* by the interpretation of this (subjectively) intended meaning.

Even if this position were not formulated unambiguously in the **'Basic Concepts in Sociology'**, it can still be seen in Weber's entire material work. His investigations into the social order of Antiquity or those on the sociology of religion leave no doubt that the concept of socially constructed meaning is one of Weber's basic conceptions. Weber is always concerned to present meaning as being *communicable*. However, communicability is always already social and intersubjective and is expressed in changeable, symbolic forms.

To summarize, we can distinguish three variations on the interpretation of the concept of meaning in Weber's work, all of which can be grasped by the method of *Verstehen*:

1 Meaning as *cultural significance,* i.e. as 'objectified' meaning in a 'world of meanings'.

2 Meaning as *subjectively intended meaning* which is intersubjectively comprehensible and communicable.

3 Meaning as *functional meaning* which is influenced by objective contexts, is intersubjectively mediated and is of functional significance for social processes of change.

If we look, for example, at Weber's investigations into the cultural significance of Protestantism, all these variations can be seen. In these studies, Protestantism can be grasped as the 'world of meanings' under investigation, in which acting individuals and groups interacting with one another seek to realize subjective frameworks of meaning and projects for action. This action, thus defined as 'meaningful', had in turn a function in the origin of capitalism. Only through this could a certain religious meaning influence capitalism so strongly that it had a functionally adequate ('adequate on the level of meaning') effect on this economic form. The religious world of meanings was functional to the capitalist order and vice versa; the level of mediation was, as we have seen, the social, 'meaningful' action of individuals and groups.

Overlying Weber's differentiation of the concept of meaning and the method of *Verstehen,* there is another factor: Weber expressly stresses the *complementarity* of *Verstehen* and 'causal explanations'. 'The "understanding" of a context must always still be monitored as far as possible by the otherwise usual methods of causal inclusion, before an interpretation—however obvious—becomes the valid "understandable explanation".' Weber fought vehemently against those contemporary attempts, particularly by Wilhelm Dilthey and his followers, to create a specific method of the 'human sciences' (*Geisteswissenschaften*) out of a concept of *Verstehen* which comes from individual experience, intuition and empathy. On the contrary, Weber seeks neither a natural-scientific nor a human-scientific foundation or method for his sociology, but a *social scientific* one. In this method, 'meaningful' interpretations of a concrete relationship are despite all the 'evidence' only 'hypotheses by imputation' which require 'verification'.

> Causal chains into which instrumentally (*zweck-rational*) oriented motivations are inserted by interpretive (*deutend*) hypotheses are directly . . . accessible by statistical inspection and . . . are thus accessible via (relatively) acceptable proof of their validity as 'explanations' (*Erklärungen*). Conversely, statistical data . . . wherever they suggest the result or consequences of behaviour . . . are only 'explained' to us when they are also meaningfully interpreted in a concrete instance.

Here we arrive at a substantive definition of Weber's methodological linkage between *Verstehen* and *Erklären*. Following his demand for an explanatory control on *Verstehen,* he asserts, 'Thus interpretation in terms of rational purpose possesses the greatest degree of certainty (*Evidenz*). By a purposively rational disposition we mean one which is exclusively oriented towards means conceived (subjectively) as adequate for attaining goals which are unambiguously understood'. Although, as we have seen, Weber expressly emphasizes that such an instrumentality of social action is a 'limiting case', he introduces as a kind of yardstick the concept of a 'rationality of correctness' (*Richtigkeitsrationalität*) in the sense of a rationality of means and ends.

This apparent discrepancy between 'subjective' intention and 'objective' verification disappears if one looks at the pragmatic research justification Weber gives. For his *empirical* sociology, whatever degree of 'rationality of correctness' an action has is an 'empirical question'. But Weber is in no way insinuating that actual human social behaviour can be determined predominantly instrumentally: 'Looking at the role which "non-instrumental" (*zweckirrational*) affects and "emotional situations" play in human action . . . one could equally well assert the exact opposite'. However to be able to achieve understanding (*Verstehen*) and explanation (*Erklären*) which can be controlled, Weber introduces the idealtypical borderline case of the *supposed* validity, i.e. the hypothetical validity of absolute instrumentality and of a 'rationality of correctness'. In other words, he asks how the action would have taken place, *supposing* this rationality had actually operated. Such a *Verstehen* means not only investigating the subjectively intended meaning of the actor or actors, but at the same time measures the degree of deviation from a constructed 'type of correctness' (*Richtig-*

keitstyp). Weber confirms this kind of typification in instrumental complexes of meaning in his aim of reaching a maximum of non-ambiguity and conceptual precision. With this strategy, Weber wants to rid the 'interpretive' method of its 'intuitionist' character. He wants to create an intersubjectively verifiable method, with the aid of which the social relations of people and groups, both with regard to their (supposed) subjective creation of meaning, and including socially and culturally imparted and determined orders of value and structural conditions can be both 'understood' *and* 'explained'.

THE CONCEPT OF THE 'IDEAL-TYPE'

In our presentation of Weber's work we encounter *throughout* one methodological concept with which Weber is inextricably linked—the concept of the *ideal-typical procedure*. No other theme in Weber's works on the methodology of the social sciences has aroused such a widespread discussion—a discussion which has lasted until today. In this, as in any *isolated* discussion of Weber's methodological writings, the *instrumental* significance of this concept is, for the most part, not acknowledged, and this has led to considerable misunderstandings.

In fact, however, the concept of the ideal-typical procedure is inextricably linked to the material part of Weber's work: we have shown that crude outlines of this concept are already recognizable in his **Habilitation** thesis of 1891. As late as 1904, Weber made use of a defined methodological concept of the ideal-typical method, although we shall not go into the inconsistencies between the earlier and the later formulations here.

When he took over the *Archiv* in 1904, Weber defined the main exercise of the journal as 'breathing scientific synthesis' into the extensive subject matter of scientific analyses. In tackling this exercise, Weber sees one procedure in particular as being suitable:

> We shall have to consider the expression of social problems from *philosophical* viewpoints to a much greater extent, as in the form of research—called *theory* in a more narrow sense—of our special area: the formation of clear concepts. Although we are far from thinking that it is valid to squash the riches of historical life into formulae, we are still overwhelmingly convinced that only clear, unambiguous concepts can smooth the way for any research that wishes to discover the specific importance of social and cultural phenomena.

This intention to form 'unambiguous concepts' is the driving idea behind Weber's formulation of the ideal-typical procedure. The development of this method evolved against the background of several scientific and theoretical—and also frequently scientific and political—discourses and developments. Both the so-called *Methodenstreit* between the historical and the theoretical tendencies in political economy (Gustav Schmoller versus Carl Menger) as well as the controversy within the framework of the schools of 'neo-idealism' (Wilhelm

Dilthey, Edmund Husserl, Georg Simmel) and 'neo-Kantianism' (Heinrich Rickert, Rudolf Stammler, Wilhelm Windelband) are the contexts from which Weber formulated his own concept. It is clear from this that neither the concept of 'ideal-type' nor the ideal-typical method were Weber's 'invention'. the idea of a certain methodological procedure linked to the ideal-typical method emerged from a broad discussion which had begun long before Weber's contributions and which carried on after his death—partly without regard to his suggestions. This discussion, which can be characterized through the names of its main participants—Droysen, Lamprecht, von Below, Dilthey, Windelband, Rickert, Schmoller and Hintze—centred around the determination of the scientific character of *historical writing*.

And as in controversies like political history versus cultural history, individual history versus circumstantial history etc., this discussion was about the conflict between the 'natural sciences' which were becoming ever more important, and the established 'human sciences' (*Geisteswissenschaften*), which were beginning to feel threatened. The controversies of the time were made all the more violent and uncompromising by the fact that political and economic power positions played a role alongside theoretical and methodological problems.

In this intellectual controversy in Germany at the turn of the century, Dilthey, Windelband and Rickert, among others, made the concept of *Verstehen* the starting point for the division between natural and human sciences. *Verstehen* was to designate that specific method by means of which one could seek out knowledge of the particular, the individual and the unique, i.e. the alleged sphere of the human and cultural sciences, in which no *laws* could operate as in the natural sciences.

Weber's essay of 1904 on **'"Objectivity" in Social Science and Social Policy'**, was to represent the fulfilment of Weber's intention in taking over the *Archiv,* and it appeared in the same first volume of the new series as the 'Preface'. It came up against the fixed positions which stemmed from the idea of a constitutive and unchangeable division of problem areas and of the relevant sciences. In his interpretation both of *Verstehen* and the ideal-typical method in the context of this debate, Weber wanted to correct those historians who thought that the multiplicity and perpetual modification of historical circumstances did not permit the application of fixed and precise concepts. As he totally agrees with the view of reality as an unordered 'chaos', he pushes the demand for 'sharp' concepts all the more forcibly.

> But the unstructured multiplicity of the *facta* in no way proves that we should construct woolly *concepts,* but the reverse: that *sharp* ('ideal-typical') concepts must be *applied* correctly, not as schemata to assault the historical given, but to be able to determine the . . . character of a phenomenon with its help: i.e. to indicate *to what extent* the phenomenon approximates to one or another 'ideal-type'.

Weber's overriding concern was to explain the 'cultural meaning' of historical facts in order to establish some conceptual order in the 'chaos', not to undertake a reconstruction of the past with the help of lists of facts and data. His programmatic demand was as follows: 'We seek knowledge of an historical phenomenon, meaning by historical: significant *in its individuality (Eigenart)*'. The point of reference for Weber's own essay on the scientific analysis of the cultural importance of the 'unstructured multiplicity of the *facta*' was, as we saw from the presentation of his work, that Western process of rationalization, whose various manifestations, causes and effects he pursued.

Thus it is the prime task of the ideal-type to incorporate hypothetically the chaotic multiplicity of individual phenomena into an 'ideal' i.e. an *ideational* course of events. Ideal-types for Weber, are 'ideal' in two respects: on the one hand, they are always based on a concept of logical and ideational perfection and they pursue this through many considerations to a conceivable extreme; on the other hand, they are also related to 'ideas' i.e. they are 'analytical constructs' (*Gedankenbilder*), thus are plans for thought (*Gedanken*). The accentuation and synthesis of certain elements and moments of observable reality orients itself towards 'ideas', which are interpreted as crucial for the behaviour of people and groups.

Again and again Weber refuses to see the 'true content' of history or its 'essence' in the ideal-types he develops. He warns repeatedly of the danger of hypostatizing ideal-types as the real, driving forces in history. When he speaks of the 'analytical accentuation of certain elements of reality' he means on the one hand that the ideal-types must be extracted from historical reality, and on the other, that a cosmos of ideational contexts, internally lacking in contradiction, is created by accentuation, to the point of creating a utopian situation. The fact that for ideal-types reality is never taken into consideration, makes them into an exclusively formal instrument for the intersubjective, discursive understanding of historical reality, while this instrument must have the attributes of logical consistency and inner non-contradiction.

At least on the textual basis of the 'objectivity' essay, ideal-types present this heuristic aid to understanding historical phenomena from the viewpoint of its cultural significance. In Weber's last phase, in his work on the first part of *Economy and Society,* we can see his efforts to found a universal historical sociology with the aid of ideal-typical concepts which would be valid across time. We encounter this intention, and particularly the strategy he put forward of a 'procedure of measuring distance' away from the absolute ends-means-rationality of *Richtigkeitsrationalität* when Weber first propounds the concept of *Verstehen*.

Both these positions—chronologically and in content separable from one another—led to the distinction between 'historical' and 'sociological' idealtypes. The former aimed more at the cultural determination of certain historical phenomena, and the latter had an atemporal, systematic character. From his own suggested 'model' of ideal-typical variants, Weber suggests a tripartite and four-part structure. The only clear point to emerge from this is that Weber in no way envisaged the concept of 'ideal-types' as unitary and this caused numerous contradictions in the interpretation controversy.

To summarize our discussion we can draw up the following five points:

1 The ideal-type is a *genetic concept,* i.e. it releases from a collection of attributes those that are regarded as originally essential for certain 'cultural meanings'. As such its context should be reconstructed in a 'pure' way.

2 The ideal-type is itself *not a hypothesis,* but it can indicate the direction for the formation of hypotheses. Thus it is not 'falsifiable' by checking-up on historical reality: a too restricted 'adequacy' to empirical circumstances and for a particular line of enquiry, however, compel the continual development of *new* ideal-typical constructions.

3 The ideal-type serves as a *heuristic means* to guide empirical research, while it formulates possible viewpoints for the interpretation of social action by oneself and others. A strategy should thereby be made possible which classifies the interminable, meaningless multiplicity of empirical data by reference to an ideational ('ideal') context. The usefulness of an ideal-typical construction is measured by its 'success' in helping understanding.

4 The ideal-type is used in the *systematization* of empirical-historical reality, in that its distance from the typified construction is 'measured' interpretatively. The ideal-type is a *construction*—but this construction is derived from reality and is constantly examined against reality, by using the 'imagination' and the nomological knowledge of the researcher. The continual reconstruction and new development of ideal-types should enable an approach to purely nomothetical and ideographical methods, and to purely causally explanatory and purely individualizing interpretive methods. It should also *mediate* one method via the other.

5 The results which are produced with the aid of the ideal-typical procedure for the explanation and interpretation of historical phenomena underpin a *process of re-interpretation* which is never-ending. The social sciences belong to those disciplines 'to which eternal youth is granted . . . to which the eternally onward flowing stream of culture perpetually brings new problems. At the very heart of their task lies not only the transciency of *all* ideal types *but* also at the same time the inevitability of *new* ones'. Here we must point out a principal hypothesis of this procedure: the success of the ideal-typical ordering of historical reality depends on the degree of concordance between the formation of types and concepts of the actors in the given social context, and the formation of types

and concepts of the scientists who are investigating these contexts.

THE POSTULATE OF 'FREEDOM FROM VALUE-JUDGEMENT' (*WERTURTEILSFREIHEIT*)

The so-called 'value-judgement dispute' is an extremely difficult phenomenon to define in the history of science and cannot be reduced to a controversy in a special discipline about a specific, unambiguously localizable problem. The multiple problems which were fought over in this 'dispute' are not merely related to certain sciences like political economy or sociology but they engage with the *basic determination of any scientific knowledge.* As difficult as it is to determine the actual 'beginning' of this controversy, it is easy to assert that Weber's relevant works were the decisive points of contact for the discussion which has lasted until today particularly his essays **'"Objectivity" in Social Science and Social Policy'**, 1904, **'The Meaning of "Ethical Neutrality" in Sociology and Economics'**, 1917, and the text of his lecture **'Science as a Vocation'**, 1919.

If the reception of *The Protestant Ethic* and the methodological concepts of *Verstehen* and the ideal-type were frequently the occasion for the creation and perpetuation of misunderstandings, Weber's conception of 'freedom from value-judgement' underwent the most thorough distortion through misunderstanding and trivialization. But this fact cannot be traced back merely to different 'interests', but equally to the extremely complex structure of the situation in which Weber formulated his position. For a comprehensive understanding, and thus for an exhaustive discussion, we must examine at least four contextual areas which partly intersect, namely

1 The philosophical background

2 The theoretical background

3 The organizational background

4 The position and political self-consciousness of German science at the turn of the century

Within the scope of [*Max Weber: An Introduction to His Life and Work*] we can only give a very cursory survey of each area.

1 To reconstruct the philosophical background, what is important is the deep crisis in Europe's historical and social consciousness which took place during the twenty-five years before the First World War. In shorthand, this crisis is known as the 'crisis of historicism'. Despite considerable differences in position among the main participants in the argument at that time, particularly Hermann Cohen, Wilhelm Dilthey, Wilhelm Windelband, Heinrich Rickert, Max Weber, Ernst Troeltsch and Friedrich Meinecke, they shared a common denominator in their *critique of positivism*. Initiated by a variety of shake-ups in the positivist conception of the world and of

humanity in general—for example by Freud, Jung, Nietzsche, Bergson, Baudelaire, Dostoevski and Proust—the fiction of a rationally ordered world was plunged into confusion, and the gulf between the world of being and the world of meaning was seen increasingly as unbridgeable. From this viewpoint, which was frequently clothed in the garb of *Kulturkritik* and cultural pessimism, the question emerged of whether a science of history or society would ever be possible. A few historians and sociologists were inclined to think that human subjectivity and irrationality would considerably restrict any science in its explanatory and prognostic value.

Some participants in the discussion of method at the turn of the century, particularly Dilthey, Windelband, Rickert, Meinecke and Troeltsch, who believed in a *meaning of history,* directed their efforts against this 'relativism' and pessimism. Moreover, this belief was frequently linked to a conviction in the basic rightness of the German *political* development since 1870-1.

Precisely in order to avert relativism in all areas, these scientists sought an examination of the methodological and epistemo-theoretical foundations of the science of history. To understand Weber's position in *this* context, we need to understand two very different positions in this epistemological and theoretical discussion. First, the south-west German school of neo-Kantianism represented by Windelband and Rickert, and second, the position of Dilthey. Weber was fundamentally influenced by both groups, personally and theoretically. In part he took over their frameworks of questioning and reached, via an *attempt at mediation* between the opposing positions, his own orientation, which would become of considerable importance for the following debates—in spite of or even because of the many misunderstandings and foreshortenings. A comprehensive understanding of Weber's position is not possible without knowledge of how these arguments progressed.

2 The theoretical background means those contexts of argument which dealt with the *orientation of the German political economy* in the last third of the nineteenth century. The representatives of 'classical' political economy, in particular Wilhelm Roscher, Bruno Hildebrand and Karl Knies as the so-called 'older historical school', had already, around 1850, tried to establish the basis for a historically oriented political economy, which was directed towards empirical science, in order to check the contemporary influence of the prevailing naturalistic and positivistic currents.

As a consequence of changes caused by political influences, particularly through an increased state intervention in economic policy, these concepts of the 'younger historical school' were taken up once again by their acknowledged leader, Gustav Schmoller. In particular the idea of having to include the historical dimension of economic processes was of crucial importance. The close connection of the 'younger school' with practical economic policy led to the institutionalization of the dia-

logue of science and politics in the *Verein* in 1872. We will be investigating this briefly in the next section.

During the dispute with the 'younger school', the eighties brought that discussion which has gone down in the history of German economic policy as the *Methodenstreit* and which can be classified by the two names of Gustav Schmoller and Carl Menger.

In his 1883 work *Untersuchungen über die Methode der Sozialwissenschaften and der politischen Ökonomie insbesondere,* Menger differentiates the sciences into three groups: historical, theoretical and practical. Accordingly, the historical disciplines are directed towards the understanding of the individual, the theoretical disciplines towards extracting generalities from phenomena, and the practical disciplines are concerned with what should be, with what one must do to attain certain goals for people. In the *theoretical* mode of research that Menger ascribes to himself, he distinguishes between two variants: the *empirical-realistic direction* that wants to establish real types; and an *exact direction* that wants to set up strict laws, comparable to 'laws of nature'.

In the same year, Schmoller responded with an article entitled *'Zur Methodologie der Staats- und Sozialwissenschaften'.* In it he emphasized the intrinsic value of the *descriptive* procedure, because with the aid of 'the descriptive experiences of all kinds, the classification of phenomena which improves the formation of concepts, the typical rows of phenomena and their context of causes can be more clearly recognized in their entire scope'. According to Schmoller, the progress of science did not lie in a further distillation of the precepts of the old dogmatism which have been investigated again and again. Whoever proceeded from hypotheses would only get hypothetical sentences to which one would then try to give the appearance of strict scientific method by using the adjective 'exact'.

Carl Menger felt personally attacked by Schmoller's critique and responded violently to it the same year. In all this it was largely ignored that from the beginning Menger had suggested a mediating position which amounted to acknowledging *both* positions, the theoretical *and* the historical. However, the contemporary controversies between 'positivism' and 'historicism', between 'natural sciences' and 'cultural, or rather, human sciences' forced the adoption of frequently simple, dichotomized polarizations. In any case, they effected a systematic reflection on the methodological foundations in *all* sciences, and particularly in disciplines which were not organized like the natural sciences.

Weber, who engaged with the *Methodenstreit* in the most intensive way once again took up his position as a *mediator.* He wanted to detach the controversy from its connection with problems of political economy alone, and to place it in the context of the discussion which we have described as the 'philosophical background'. Weber was influenced greatly by the debate over the relationship between the 'human sciences' and the 'natural sciences', as led by Windelband and Rickert, and this brought him to formulate his concept of a 'science of reality' (*Wirklichkeitswissenschaft*).

3 Both the philosophical as well as the theoretical background to Weber's concept of freedom from value-judgement meant discussions which were carried out largely in a literary way. Those discussions which were and are described as the actual 'value-judgement dispute' nevertheless found *organizational* 'stages' on which these debates were performed—especially the *Verein,* and for Weber in particular the *Deutsche Gesellschaft für Soziologie.*

After the turn of the century three 'fractions' of the *Verein*'s membership, who were made up predominantly of academics, high-ranking civil servants, journalists, trade-unionists, bankers and entrepreneurs became roughly distinguishable. These were a 'left wing', the so-called 'academic socialists' (*Kathedersozialisten*), comprising Brentano, Sombart, Naumann, Harms and Max and Alfred Weber among others; a 'centre' of Schmoller, Gneist, Nasse and others; and a 'right wing' of Wagner, von Philippovich and others. At the Mannheim conference of 1905 on 'The relationship of the cartels to the state', the discussions became very heated at some of Schmoller's demands for the control of the cartels. These discussions provoked Schmoller to the point of threatening resignation, if the left wing—Naumann in particular—persisted in pursuing its 'materialistic demagogy'. In these initiatory, highly polemical arguments over the understanding of theory and method in the *Verein,* and indeed of the *Verein* itself, the left wing demanded that theory and method be made the objects of discussion, while the right wing wanted to prevent such discussions and saw the main task of the *Verein* as influencing practical social policy—because of which, the themes had to be of a 'practical nature'. Schmoller, in his role as integrator and mediator, strove to keep the *Verein* as a forum for the discussion and publicizing of *science,* which could, however, also influence practical social policy. Weber, meanwhile, still very much kept his distance from these affairs.

The 'value-judgement dispute' broke out in its totality at the Vienna conference of 1909, at which Eugen von Philippovich, Weber's predecessor in the Freiburg chair, and as representative of the 'Austrian School' gave the first purely scientific-theoretical paper in the history of the *Verein,* on **'The Essence of National Economic Productivity'**. He presented a survey which charted the history of ideologies and raised the challenges which lie in the concept of national economic productivity. Sombart, Max Weber and Gottl von Ottlilienfeld criticized the scientific uselessness of the concept of productivity as it might hide proper evaluations, and particularly since it was increasingly mixed with the concept of 'national prosperity'. Weber began his vehement campaign against 'a mixture of science and value-judgement' and saw 'the work of the devil in the intermingling of pre-

scriptive notions in scientific questions . . . work which has frequently richly provided for the *Verein*'. Von Zwiedineck-Südenhorst, Spann, Goldscheid and Neurath spoke out against Weber's position (Tönnies being on his side) in the course of the lively debates. For reasons of *Verein* policy, they demanded, a *fundamental discussion,* both on the problematics of 'value-judgements' in the *Verein*'s proceedings, as well as on the economic character of the political economy, should be postponed until the 1911 sitting in Nuremburg. However, at this sitting, Weber's initial proposal was as follows: 'I would like to suggest that the question of whether we have to exclude value-judgements here or not, or whether they are justifiable in principle, and of how far their exclusion is practicable, be presented once by the *Verein* committee as a special issue on the agenda'.

In preparation for this special conference, a circular letter was sent out in 1912 at Weber's instigation to the committee members asking them to take up positions. Out of the fourteen authors of the published paper, Epstein, Eulenburg, Rohrbeck and Neurath adopted Weber's position; Hartmann, Wilbrandt, Schumpeter, Spann and Oldenberg turned out to be reconcilable with Weber's position, and only Goldscheid, Hesse, Oncken, Spranger and von Wiese took up more or less overt opposition. The committee meeting on 5 January 1914 from which the publicized positions took the lead and which fifty-two members attended, produced no result and brought the standpoints no closer together. Apart from Sombart, Weber could scarcely find any other advocates for his approach among the younger and middle generations.

The outbreak of the First World War did not completely interrupt the work of the *Verein,* but it did put an end to the value-judgement discussion. Weber revised his written position in 1912 and published the new version in 1917 in the journal *Logos* with the title **'The Meaning of "Ethical Neutrality" in Sociology and Economics'**. That Weber was still willing to continue working in the *Verein* in spite of what had happened, is shown by his election to deputy chairman in September 1919.

The second organizational 'stage' on which the 'value-judgement dispute' was played out, and which we need to know about to understand Weber's position in more than a fragmentary way, was the *Deutsche Gesellschaft für Soziologie* (German Society for Sociology), in the foundation of which Weber took a considerable, initiatory part in 1909. Precisely because of his experiences in the *Verein,* Weber tried to avoid the possible repetition of what were in his opinion unprofitable disagreements. To do this, he suggested on the occasion of his 'invitation' to found the *Gesellschaft*

> The *Gesellschaft* should . . . have a purely objective, scientific character. It follows from this that *any* kind of political, socio-political, socio-ethical, or any other kind of propaganda for *practical* aims or ideals within or under the name of the *Gesellschaft* must be *excluded*. The *Gesellschaft*

may only serve the research of facts and their contexts.

Weber's demand was preserved in paragraph one of the Society's statute, which said:

> The aim [of the *Deutsche Gesellschaft für Soziologie*] is to promote sociological knowledge by the arrangement of purely scientific investigations and enquiries, by the publication and support of purely scientific works and by the organization of German sociology conferences to take place periodically. It will give equal space to all scientific directions and methods of sociology and will reject the representation of any practical (ethical, religious, political, aesthetic etc.) goals.

The embittered controversies at the two initial sociology conferences in 1910 and 1912, particularly the arguments with Rudolf Goldscheid on the principle of freedom from value-judgement led to Weber's disappointment and resignation, and to his ultimately leaving the *Gesellschaft* in 1913. Weber saw himself as 'a Don Quixote of an allegedly unfeasible principle'.

4 These three backdrops to the so-called 'value-judgement debate' must be connected to the general position and the—particularly political—self-consciousness of German science in the years before the First World War, if we are to reach a comprehensive understanding from which to derive any adequate evaluation of Weber's position. Such a discussion can, in this book, only serve to highlight certain details.

If the Bismarck years brought stormy developments in the natural sciences to the German university system, these processes nevertheless did not effect any far-reaching identity-crisis in the human sciences. The dominant position of the historians was maintained and the established disciplines and their representatives, basically because of a prevailing liberal-nationalist attitude, kept a fundamental consensus with the political system. However, in time, currents emerged which were called *Kulturkritik* (critique of civilization) and 'cultural pessimism', which began to doubt the legitimacy of the political and social order, from the perspective of the 'social question'. The extremely popular writings of Paul de Lagarde and Julius Langbehn, in particular, began to give space to a fundamental critique of the kind of 'false science' that could only confirm the facts, when by contrast the 'ultimate goal' of 'true science' was to formulate value-judgements. They saw something equally untrue in the 'objectivity' of science, 'like that modern humanism, which says that all human beings are of equal value.' Such demands for an *evaluative science* were thus not only 'a matter taken up by German youth—and a youth that was not spoiled, not badly educated, not prejudiced' but between 1890 and 1914, such views spread more and more widely. George Hinzpeter, Wilhelm II's tutor, complained at the German state school conference in 1890 that 'personal, spiritual development' had once been considered as 'the highest goal worth aiming at'.

Meanwhile, however, education was merely regarded as 'the means to successful participation in the wild struggle for existence'. In 1902, Friedrich Paulsen stated that the task for German universities was to represent 'in their entirety something like the public conscience of the people with a view to good and evil in politics'.

Such statements, which amounted to demands to create, with the support of the German universities, a conflict-free, ideologically identical society out of German Wilhelminian life were not only taken from instances of (educational) policy, but fell on fertile ground in the universities themselves as can be seen in the activities of the *Euken-Bund*.

The four contextual areas we have sketched outline the background against which Weber tried to determine his own position. Since these debates stretched across the period from 1890 to 1920, a knowledge of all relevant works in which he discussed the problem of 'values' and 'evaluations' is vital for an *exact* representation of Weber's position. We shall leave out the modifications of his position in the course of discussion and will try to elaborate the general arguments.

As a way in, we can look at the *interpretations* of Weber's approach which have been current until today. Accordingly, Weber's demand attests to a 'freedom from value-judgement' for the (social) sciences:

> Social scientists must refrain from all evaluating statements, either all the time, or in the practice of their profession, or when they publish the results of their work.
>
> Social scientists must not take on any kind of aesthetic or moral evaluations; 'evaluations' in the sense of distinguishing between true and false are allowed.
>
> Social scientists must not be politically active.
>
> All conceivable ethical and political absolute values, like freedom, equality, and justice are of equal value; science must therefore not accord a higher rank to one over another.
>
> Values and evaluations of social actors are not the subject of the social sciences.

Weber's approach is covered by *none* of these interpretations. Basically it is divided into two mutually detachable arguments: (1) the demand for 'freedom from value-judgement' (*Werturteilsfreiheit*) in the narrow sense; and (2) the problem of 'relevance to values' (*Wertbeziehung*).

The demand for 'freedom from value-judgement' in the narrow sense

On the first level, Weber's demand for freedom from value-judgement meant

> the intrinsically simple demand that the investigator and teacher should keep unconditionally separate

the establishment of empirical facts (including the 'value oriented' conduct of the empirical individual whom he is investigating) and *his* own practical evaluations, i.e. his evaluation of these facts as satisfactory or unsatisfactory . . . These two things are logically different and to deal with them as though they were the same represents a confusion of entirely heterogeneous problems.

This 'postulate . . . which they often misunderstand so gravely' and which caused 'unending misunderstanding' and the 'completely sterile dispute', was set up by Weber as a reference to the 'professorial prophecy' which was not uncommon in his time. With explicit reference to university teachers like Treitschke, Theodor Mommsen and Schmoller, Weber condemns the propagation of practical-political ideals in the lecture hall from the lectern, and demands as the 'absolute minimum', as 'a precept of intellectual honesty', the suppression of personal prophecy and the announcement of a *'Weltanschauung'*.

> Today the student should obtain, from his teacher in the lecture hall, the capacity: (1) to fulfill a given task in a workmanlike fashion; (2) definitely to recognize facts, even those which may be personally uncomfortable, and to distinguish them from his own evaluations; (3) to subordinate himself to his task and to repress the impulse to exhibit his personal tastes or other sentiments unnecessarily.

Only in this way could the 'self-importance', the 'fashionable "cult of the personality" [in] the throne, public office or the professorial chair' which could prejudice the matter, be combatted.

> An unprecedented situation exists when a large number of officially accredited prophets do not do their preaching on the streets, or in churches or other public places or in sectarian conventicles, but rather feel themselves competent to enunciate their evaluations on ultimate questions 'in the name of science' in governmentally privileged lecture halls in which they are neither controlled, checked by discussion, nor subject to contradiction.

Weber expressly emphasizes that the 'distinction between empirical statements of fact and value-judgements' which he demands, is *difficult* and even that he himself has offended against this distinction. Even so, Weber does not dispute the fact that the choice of theme and the selection of subject matter already involves 'evaluations'. Moreover, he stresses that this does *not* imply 'that empirical science cannot treat "subjective" evaluations as the subject matter of its analysis—(although sociology depend[s] on the contrary assumption)'.

Thus on the 'first level' of Weber's postulate of 'freedom from value-judgement' *in science,* he asserts that 'evaluations', in the sense of assessments as 'objectionable' or 'approvable', must be *separated* from statements of empirical facts and circumstances. If a scientist cannot or will not forgo such an evaluation, he must separate his personal standpoint, for which he may not claim any *scientific* legitimation, from the description of facts, both with respect to his discourse partners and with respect to *himself*. Science for Weber is a *'professionally* run "vocation" . . . in the service of the self-consciousness and awareness of factual contexts, and not a gift of grace for seers and prophets, bestowing cures and revelations, or an element of the thoughts of sages and philosophers on the *meaning* of the world'.

The problem of 'relevance to values'

Weber's essential, deep concern goes far beyond what we have just looked at and touches a basic problematic in all sciences, but particularly in all social sciences. This is a question of the 'relevance' and relation of the results of scientific research to the 'values' of the researcher.

Because Weber stresses that the evaluations that lie at the heart of the actions of the individual—whether scientist or the observed acting subject—must not be accepted as 'fact', but can be treated 'as the object of scientific criticism', the question emerges of *how* empirical disciplines based on the science of experience can settle this task. It is thus a matter of investigating each 'evaluation' with respect to its 'individual social [and historical] conditions', which for Weber can only be possible through an *understanding explanation (verstehendes Erklären)*. This has

> high scientific importance: (1) for purposes of an empirical causal analysis which attempts to establish the really decisive motives of human actions; and (2) for the communication of really divergent evaluations when one is discussing with a person who really or apparently has different evaluations from one's self.

In determining this task Weber sees that

> the real significance of a discussion of evaluations lies in its contribution to the understanding of what one's opponent—or one's self—really means—i.e., in understanding the evaluations which really and not merely allegedly separate the discussants and consequently in enabling one to take up a position with reference to this value.

Because the 'understanding' (*Verstehen*) of another's evaluations does *not* mean its approval, a scientific investigation of each value which might possibly collide with another becomes both possible *and* necessary.

Although Weber inclines towards and proceeds from an acknowledgement of a 'polytheism' of ultimate values, and that between values 'it is really a question not only of alternatives between values but of an irreconcilable death-struggle, like that between "God" and the "Devil"' (and here there can be no relative measures or compromises), Weber, representing the viewpoint of a 'collision of values', resists the insinuation of 'relativism' with great resolve.

To be able to deal with values and evaluations in an empirical way, Weber puts forward four functions for a scientifically productive 'discussion of value-judgements':

> (a) The elaboration and explication of the ultimate, internally 'consistent' value-axioms, from which the divergent attitudes are derived . . .

> (b) The deduction of 'implications' (for those accepting certain value-judgements) which follow from certain irreducible value-axioms, when the practical evaluation of factual situations is based on these axioms alone . . .

> (c) The determination of the factual consequences which the realization of a certain practical evaluation must have . . . Finally:

> (d) the uncovering of new axioms (and the postulates to be drawn from them) which the proponent of a practical postulate did not take into consideration . . .

Such a method of researching 'value-judgements' which constructs *ideal-types,* in which the analysis of ideas of value, the specification of suitable means and combinations of means for chosen purposes ('values'), the assessment of prospects for success, the assertion of the secondary effects of the available means, the estimation of the 'costs' of the sought-after values and the estimation of the compatibility (in a logical as well as a practical sense) of different values which lie at its centre—such a method displays its 'relevance' to values. With reference to Rickert, Weber uses the concept of 'relevance to values', meaning 'the philosophical interpretation of that specifically scientific "interest" which determines the selection of a given subject matter and the problems of an empirical analysis'. This concept, which is extremely important for the sociology of science, points to the fact that 'cultural (i.e., evaluative) interests give purely scientific work its direction'.

Here, Weber uses again the concept which he formulated in 1904: 'epistemological interest' (*Erkenntnisinteresse*). Then, he was concerned to emphasize the *constructedness* of a certain perspective from which one could approach the particular object under investigation. He wrote on his own 'socio-economic' perspective:

> The quality of an event as a socio-economic phenomenon is not something which is 'objectively' attached to the event. Rather it is determined by the direction of our epistemological *interest,* as it emerges from the specific cultural meaning which we attribute to the event concerned in the individual case.

If the (social) scientist wants to approach his or her object of investigation, he or she must do it from the perspective of certain values which the surrounding culture offers. Without such a value-loaded perspective, reality remains an unordered chaos of the multiplicity and contradiction of facts and phenomena. Already, the infinite complexity of reality makes a simple 'description' of events impossible. If, in scientific knowledge, it is a question of discovering the contexts of causation, one needs a knowledge-motivated interest from which one can derive a desire to 'understand' and 'explain' social and historical reality. The task of the cultural sciences, among which sociology numbers, is, according to Weber, to research the reality and operation of 'meaning' and 'significance'. There is no possibility of 'objective' treatment for this task, but merely a research selection by means of 'value-ideas', in which 'culture' is regarded as a particular case.

> From the standpoint of the *human being,* 'culture' is a finite section of the senseless infinity of world events, furnished with meaning and sense . . . A transcendental precondition of any *cultural science* is *not* that we find a certain 'culture', or even any 'culture' *valuable,* but that we are cultural *beings,* gifted with the capacity and the will to take up a conscious *position* with regard to the world and to give it a *meaning.* Whatever this meaning may be, it will lead us to *judge* certain phenomena of human interaction in life on the basis of this meaning, and to take up a position in the face of it which is (positively or negatively) *significant.*

'Epistemological interest' and 'value ideas' establish the 'relevance to values' between the researcher and the object of research, and are of great importance for the results of the research. *Which* 'value ideas' are selected as determining research and knowledge is not a subjective, arbitrary matter for the individual scientist.

> *What* becomes the object of the investigation and how far this investigation stretches into the infinity of causal relationships is determined by the value-ideas which govern the researcher and his epoch . . . For scientific truth is only that which *desires* to be valid for everyone who *wants* the truth.

This *intersubjectively* determined and controlled choice of research ideas and interests is the basis for a continuing *process of change.* With the change in 'cultural problems', i.e. in the 'dominant value-ideas', the points of view by which research is carried out are also changing. This amounts to the 'eternal youth' of all historical disciplines 'to which the eternally progressing stream of culture supplies continually new problems'.

If the 'starting points' of the cultural sciences remain 'variable far into the boundless future', there is however, *'progress'* in scientific-cultural research. It lies in a continual process of formation and reformation in scientific *concepts,* i.e. the 'ideal-types' with which the inexhaustible reality must be grasped.

> The history of the sciences of social life is and remains a continual fluctuation between the attempt to order facts ideationally through the formation of concepts . . . and the formation of concepts from scratch . . . It is not the incorrectness of the attempt to form conceptual systems *in the first*

place which is expressed here, but the fact that in the sciences of human culture the formation of concepts depends on the posing of the problems, and that the latter is altered alongside the content of culture itself. The relationship of concept and conceptualized in the cultural sciences makes the transitoriness of every such synthesis unavoidable.

To emphasize intersubjective restraint and the control of social-scientific research and to postulate an accumulation of conceptual knowledge changes nothing in the basic transitoriness and fluctuation of all social-scientific 'epistemology'. Decades before the formulation of the concept of 'paradigmatic change' in the sociology of science, Weber recognized the fundamental importance of fixing knowledge to 'value-ideas' and 'epistemological interests', and of their permanent 'revolutionizing'.

> But at some time or another the complexion changes: the significance of unreflectedly realized viewpoints becomes uncertain, and one loses one's way in the growing darkness. The light of the great cultural problems has moved on. Then science too prepares itself to change its position and its conceptual apparatus and to look down from the heights of ideation on to the stream of activity.

John Owen King III (essay date 1983)

SOURCE: "American Apocalypse: Max Weber," in *The Iron Melancholy: Structures of Spiritual Conversion in America from the Puritan Conscience to Victorian Neurosis,* Wesleyan University Press, 1983, pp. 289-322.

[*In the following essay, King discusses Weber's struggle with the alienation and moral stringency of Puritanism as evidenced in* The Protestant Ethic and the Spirit of Capitalism.]

> If my own activity does not belong to me, if it is an alien compulsive activity, to whom does it belong? To a being other than myself. Who is this being? The gods?
>> [Karl Marx, from the "economic-philosophic manuscripts" of 1844, in the translation of Norman O. Brown]

> The religious root of modern economic humanity is dead; today the concept of the calling is a *caput mortuum* in the world.
>> [Weber, *General Economic History* (1919-20)]

Puritanism gave expression to a struggle of soul so widespread within the writings of even ordinary men and women that by the end of the nineteenth century, historians—focusing like Royce on the development of cultural consciousness—could argue that the seventeenth century had given birth to the self. In Max Weber's argument, Puritanism had created the idea of personality. Radical Protestantism had pulled the self from webs of custom and had broken the bonds of ritual and ceremony, Weber argued, thereby placing the self alone, like Bunyan's Christian, to pursue its course as an individual. To live

without even a semblance of works, to stand alone before God in a state of predestination, to forego the intercession of others such as patriarchs and priests, demanded, for Weber, a wholeness of person that other Protestant churches never conceived of requiring. The aloneness also demanded an incredible amount of work. Weber's portrait stands necessarily as an ideal, and his Puritan as an ideal type, but in itself his argument re-created the idea that Puritanism had given birth to a new character— and in capitalism to a new economy. With Freud, Weber created the understanding that a particular type of modern personality had come into being, a personality that defined—most particularly, Weber thought—the ethic of America.

Weber, at the close of *The Protestant Ethic,* then brought this new personality to its end. The worldly ascetic ethic that he had set upon its course found itself, at the end of its progress, strangled in a cage of its own ironic making. Weber left a nation to wonder at its works:

> The Puritan wanted to work in a calling; we are forced to do so. For when asceticism was carried out of monastic cells into everyday life, and began to dominate worldly morality, it did its part in building the tremendous cosmos of the modern economic order. This order is now bound to the technical and economic conditions of machine production which to-day determine the lives of all the individuals who are born into this mechanism, not only those directly concerned with economic acquisition, with irresistible force. Perhaps it will so determine them until the last ton of fossilized coal is burnt. In Baxter's view the care for external goods should only lie on the shoulders of the "saint like a light cloak, which can be thrown aside at any moment." But fate decreed that the cloak should become an iron cage.

It was Weber who, more than any modern scholar, composed a nation convulsing in its own mechanism. A new nation, having given up all works as a help in its salvation, had created a work before which it finally stood estranged.

Puritanism had in fact given unique expression to the self's individuality when churches enjoined men and women to articulate their lives. Discursively, a revolution had occurred when sectarian groups of English men and women, loosely gathered under the term of Puritan, had separated in various degrees from the Anglican Church and, as sects, now sought a definition for those who had chosen to covenant together. As opposed to the sects of radical Protestantism, it was birth and family, when coupled with certain ceremonial observances and a ritual adherence to creeds, that had defined membership within a church, whether Anglican or Catholic. Puritanism had set itself against this automatism of time and geographic location as fully as it had opposed other apparent "works." Puritanism had placed these spiritual locations within the self, giving to each person the necessity of defining, through a process of articulation, his or her own time and place of membership within the body of Christ.

Puritanism had thus required a voluntary search undertaken across an internal space, the profession of an individual experience of conversion that alone, in the words spoken, defined the fellowship of Christ.

No term defined this character that the Puritan had given expression to until, for the opening of the twentieth century, Weber offered his phrase of "the Protestant ethic." American Victorian intellectuals such as James, Royce, and Putnam, writing within a practice of Puritan confession, and searching for meanings to renew the idea of spiritual conversion, offered perspectives that ranged from neurology to psychoanalysis to speak of their own and their nation's personality. Weber brought this discursive practice to completion by speaking now of an ethic. Writing within a developing European sociology, he turned to a question of religious consciousness and culture. By the end of the 1920s, when his writing began to appear in America, particularly within the guiding hands of Talcott Parsons of Harvard, the son of a Congregational minister, his work came to define the American character. When joined with the writings of Freud, Weber's work also came to define the type of mechanistic psychopathology that such a character was said to possess. By enwrapping a cultural psychology around a people, Weber gave time and space to the internal of Protestant psychomachy. Most particularly, Weber placed an ascetic ethic upon America and then drew the irony of the ethic out. He brought America through the course of a conversion, to its end in a new alienation. The psychological struggle that English Puritans had, upon their first migration, placed upon the New England landscape, giving place to their own psychomachy, Weber gave to the whole of the nation's history.

WORK AND PERSON

Max Weber's biography and scholarship have become woven together in such a way that his life and writing form—as in the context of modernity from the seventeenth century on they only can form—a single plain of text. His character as an author, in other words, is to give meaning or provide significance for his work. His writing stands not as an anonymous text akin to a medieval narrative, or as a text that Michel Foucault views as without authorial intent, but as scholarship with a self—Weber's own Protestant character—as referent. Revealed as nervously exhausted or neurotic in the Victorians' forming word, Weber himself has become an expression of the Protestant ethic. The "rosy blush" of his Enlightenment, his sanguine figure of history, is seen as consumed in the coals of his own particular production, burned in the humor, as it were, of his melancholy. "Weber," then, has become a plain of discourse of self and script working together, himself a piece of Protestant psychopathology. His writing has become expansive enough to include the "fable" of the author, the modern writer, in Roland Barthes's words, who "inscribes himself in his text as one of his characters."

One portion of this writing, recorded by Weber's wife Marianne, exemplifies the destruction that Weber gave to the Protestant ethic: "I am bone-tired. . . . I accomplish almost *nothing* aside from my lectures; one to two hours a day, then it doesn't go anymore." Weber was writing from Munich in the summer of 1919, explaining to a friend that he felt exhausted and lay under a terrible strain. "Work," he wrote, "is coming along very modestly—one to two hours a day. I am astonishingly worn out, my head is in bad shape. But it will work out. . . . I am preparing [a new edition of] the 'Protestant Ethic' for publication, then I shall take up the 'Economic Ethic.' After that the Sociology." The new edition did come out and other work as well, including two lectures that Weber had presented on the sanctity of vocation. If he rested, however, and felt "tolerably well," remaining to walk in a forest at six o'clock in the morning, bathing in a sunlight "so wonderful" and "calm," then his lingering stood as an "escapade" that came only with cost—"the cost of tremendous laziness; the 'Spirit of Capitalism' is hardly making any progress in addition to the lectures!"

The following spring Weber again expressed his "nervous exhaustion." Now he "had to pay," his wife Marianne explained, "for his extraordinary intensity." Some mention was given of a cardiac spasm—"The machine," as Weber told visitors, "wouldn't work anymore"; lying on his sofa "unable to work," he occupied himself with the meaning of death. In these months preceding his death, in other words, Weber is to be seen as completing the dismantling of his own machinelike works.

Marianne Weber's biography (the source of much that scholars repeat of Weber's personality)—the words of Weber chosen, the intermingling of private letters, scholarship, and past remembered phrases spoken only to Marianne and now printed as dialogue—testify to a confessional discourse. These memories, even contemporary letters so often considered directly reflective of an author's personality, work together with the formal texts that Weber wrote to reveal the character or the cultural spirit of Protestantism. The great amount of psychoanalytically informed scholarship given to uncovering the Protestant character—modern scholarship that began in 1932 when Erich Fromm joined *The Protestant Ethic* with Freud's essay on "Character and Anal Eroticism"—reveals that the pathology of a Protestant or "Puritan ethic" remains significant enough to become rewritten and extended.

A discursive field that had opened in the seventeenth century with the Puritans' disclosure of their own melancholy, has broadened, becoming a whole field of writings on Protestant cultural psychopathology. The presence is this text, however, from which persons can make sense; it is not hidden forces that persons reveal themselves in their writings or a culture that expresses itself in its books, as though writing lies above nature, simply absorbing and marking lower or material forces. This type of cultural discourse, including the fact that an author's life does become interwoven with his own printed words, completes itself in relation to other texts and within a textual region, a "geo-graphy"; the discourse remains universal. It remains to be used, however, by persons who have chosen to write about themselves.

It is inappropriate, then, to speak of a new critical approach to writing, including some versions of structuralism, when writing is used to fashion meaning from lives. Clearly, Christian culture—most especially, one might think, Puritanism, in the sense of the broad publication that Puritanism demanded of the Word—has read lives as it has considered lives composed. ("These *are* the words . . . which were written in the law . . . , and *in* the prophets, and *in* the psalms, concerning me.")

WORK AND TEXT

In employing discourse as an interpretant drawing together oppositions such as personal author and formal text, Michel Foucault seeks the embodied text in a function that as a practice relates author and writing, inserting the one into the other.

> It is not possible to reexamine . . . the privileges of the subject? Clearly, in undertaking an internal and architectonic analysis of a work (whether it be a literary text, a philosophical system, or a scientific work) and in delimiting psychological and biographical references, suspicions arise concerning the absolute nature and creative role of the subject. But the subject should not be entirely abandoned. It should be reconsidered, not to restore the theme of an originating subject, but to seize its functions, its intervention in discourse, and its system of dependencies.

Literary critical theory has thus posed the issue to historians as to what constitutes an "author," a "work," and a "text." Turning the question into a matter for the history of ideas, Foucault writes: "The coming into being of the notion of 'author' constitutes the privileged moment of *individualization* in the history of ideas." "Certainly it would be worth examining how the author became individualized in a culture like ours, what status he has been given." Foucault speaks of a "reversal" that "occurred in the seventeenth or eighteenth century. Scientific discourses began to be received for themselves. . . . The author-function faded away. . . . By the same token, literary discourses came to be accepted only when endowed with the author-function." Reconstructing Foucault's essay, three points may be said to follow. First, that "it is not enough to declare that we should do without the writer (the author) and study the work in itself." Second, that the "work" remains a "problematic"—what is to be made, for example, of pieces of writing "left behind" or of disjointed markings that a critic collects and claims constitute a significant text? Third, that the authority newly given to literary texts newly creates a critical function, most typically that of psychologism:

> Nevertheless, these aspects of an individual which we designate as making him an author are only a projection, in more or less psychologizing terms, of the operations that we force texts to undergo, the connections that we make, the traits that we establish as pertinent, the continuities that we recognize, or the exclusions that we practice. All these operations vary according to periods and types of discourse.

The psychoanalytic interpretation of a text, say, is itself a historical location—not a way that may be universally used to get at a particular text, but a part of the modern text that the analyst reads.

In the arguments of Foucault, pathological revelation emerges within historically delimitable fields, and thus one works not to recover a universal unconsciousness but to understand how traditions of writing and intellectual assemblages of thought make things like an unconsciousness appear sensible. One does not return, therefore, from a reflective reading like the cultural recovery of texts, the American approach of myth and symbol, to the older, more rarefied history of ideas, for such a return would erase whatever discursive practice is present, here one of spiritual confession that holds a work and person together. The practice of writing autobiography is to be broadly defined, then, to include a writing like Marianne Weber's biography of her husband and even bits of private letters. This makes for a "field of the text" in which an author can work. In the pathology that Weber expressed of the Protestant ethic, and which he formed as a cultural character, he was not reflecting but making his nature; he was reworking writings of psychopathology inherent in a practice of religious confession. He was forming a composition of himself that reflects a certain "pre-text" and the sense he could produce from that. He was composing his ethic much as the Puritan divines he read had done, placing his melancholy both in his books and in the writing that he was making of his life.

The composition that Marianne Weber offered in her biography continues: Weber's depression momentarily lifted, and writing to Marianne in April of 1920, Weber said that once again he was becoming what she had always feared, "this constantly 'working' grumpy *Ehemann* [husband]. Otherwise everything is going well. . . . Except work. . . . That'll come, too. It has to!" By June, however, Weber became mildly delirious. He was occupied now with "fantasies" or with ideas that he had finally begun working as he thought he should. He remembered an earlier collapse in the last months of 1897, his moment of severest depression when, as Marianne earlier wrote, "he was overloaded with work, [and] an evil thing from the unconscious underground of life stretched out its claws toward him. One evening, after the examination of a student at which he had, as always, worn himself out, he was overcome by total exhaustion, with a feverish head and a strong feeling of tension." It was during that depression that Weber had also lain on the sofa he was resting upon now, examining the same patterns of the paper on the wall, "'but at that time,'" he said, "'I was able to think and I struggled with the good Lord.' . . . Did he feel remorse or have any feelings of guilt? He thought it over and said first hesitantly and then definitely: No." This time the final diagnosis was pneumonia, and Weber died quietly that spring.

Within Marianne Weber's reconstruction of her husband's death, Weber dies from more than a lung infection. Marianne offers the sense that Weber quite literally labored to death, suffering his final collapse for the same reason that the "breakdown" of twenty-two years earlier was said to have occurred, from a nervous exhaustion deriving from a scholar's vast labors. Weber becomes caught within the "irresistible force" that he had described within the most famous of his passages, in the end of his jeremaid, *The Protestant Ethic,* as determining "the lives of all . . . born into this mechanism." "Today the spirit of religious asceticism—whether finally, who knows?—has escaped from the cage. But victorious capitalism, since it rests on mechanical foundations, needs its support no longer. The rosy blush of its laughing heir, the Enlightenment, seems also to be irretrievably fading, and the idea of duty in one's calling prowls about in our lives like the ghost of dead religious beliefs." His rational ascetic had built such an incredible machine that it had estranged its own motives. The irony for Marianne Weber was now "this complete halting," as she wrote of her husband, "of the precious machine."

Marianne Weber's published biography mirrors Weber's completion: lines on pages are graphically set and justified in print to describe the mechanics that had failed to justify. Marianne stands as interpreter to Weber as the interpreter stands to Christian in *The Pilgrim's Progress:* "stay (said the *Interpreter,*) till I have shewed thee a little more, and after that, thou shalt go on thy way. So he took him by the hand again, and led him into a very dark room, where there sat a Man in an Iron Cage." Marianne offers Biblical meaning for this sight of the cage—the spiritual promise entailed in acknowledging one's bondage and affliction: "For he hath broken the gates of brass, and cut the bars of iron in sunder."

Marianne's narrative reflects neither a collapse of *fin de siècle* society nor, in the image of Ferdinand Töennies that Weber himself closely followed, an objective historical alienation, or a transition from *Gemeinschaft* to *Gesellschaft.* Her narrative expresses something other than what Weber had sought along with his generation of European scholars, the consciousness of society that H. Stuart Hughes has discussed so well: a *Weltanschauung,* a *Geist,* a collective consciousness or unconsciousness that, as a cultural personality, is thought of as either reflecting or informing productive modes and nature. What is evidenced is material, but it is itself a way of writing. What is expressed is discourse, the text of such psychologism itself.

The structure of conversion entails an irony: first, establishing a process of salvation as a path charted to heaven, and then, tearing the process apart. The steps of conversion become, in Stanley E. Fish's phrase, "self-consuming artifacts." The consumption reflects the Calvinist demand that the self and its works be displayed before the works become the waste they are. As Fish culls from a close reading of *The Pilgrim's Progress* (leaving aside the whole of Bunyan's own self-recorded obsessional

life), no progress occurs in the sense that no relation exists for Christian between the geographic distance he covers and linear time. There is no way of saying just where Christian is, no more than there are actual historical locations in Weber's ironic text of Protestantism. In that text, Weber moves his ascetic as he moved himself: first from an obsessively constructed monastery to the world, and then to the ascetic's ending in a "compulsion" of high capitalism. Weber folds his text back upon itself, in other words, back to beginnings in other cells of despair. What has begun in a cage ends there, for in the end, progress is erased in order to create a timeless space for faith.

With Weber, a writing of Puritan conversion has broadened to become a whole cultural narrative. The narrative weaves culture with self to the extent of composing Weber's life just as he had worked to compose himself, writing of himself within the language that Puritanism offered, the measures of conversion against which Weber could "de-scribe" himself, or write from, thereby making his life "work." His writing becomes a testament: the "storie of those things, whereof we are fully persuaded." "And he began . . . , and interpreted unto them in all the Scriptures the things which were *written* of him."

This formation of personality argues the use of a typology, for the composing and the reading of a life is accomplished in relation to past texts. A person fulfills "prescriptions" when he discovers his self in writing. Through the words of interpreters, Weber provides a most important example of using writing in just this manner:

> During the course of his studies in ancient Judaism, in 1916 and 1917, he was profoundly moved by the analogies he saw between the situation of the ancient Hebrew peoples and modern Germany. It was not only the public and historical situation he saw as parallel; in the personality of many prophets and in their irregular and compulsive psychic states, particularly of Jeremiah, Weber saw features he felt resembled his own. When he read passages of this manuscript to his wife, she was touched in immediately seeing that this reading was an indirect analysis of himself.

What Weber described from Jeremiah were "compulsive acts," "compulsion," and the possibility "of a specific 'personality type'" involving "emotional depressions and *idées fixes,*" the last, again, a psychiatric phrase for obsessions. What he valued from Jeremiah concerned "a strong devaluation of all ritual," a reaction against "massive ritualism," above all a "magic" analogous here to a "machine." What he celebrated of the Yahwe prophets stood "superior" to magic and ritual law: the "'call,'" the "*berith*-conception," "this workaday ethic."

> Perhaps it was only in this fashion that Weber, who since childhood was incapable of directly revealing himself, could communicate his own self-image. Thus, what was most personal to him is accessible and at the same time hidden by the objectifications of his work.

Here in texts reflecting themselves—Weber's manuscript, Marianne Weber's biography, a commentary on the biography by Hans Gerth and C. Wright Mills, and then returning to read Weber's *Ancient Judaism*—sense is made of Weber; and Weber, through the prophetic writings, could make sense of himself. The revelation remains "direct," for rather than hiding himself, Weber was making an understanding of himself, here in past scripts. His "work and person" become related not in an interior boring to explain the production of an author's pen but, again, in an exterior delimitation.

WEBER'S COLLAPSE

Weber completed *The Protestant Ethic* after he had made a visit to America in 1904. In America, he wrote, one could observe certain matters "in their most massive and original shape." He completed the essay after a tour through Oklahoma and then through Chicago, this last an industrial wilderness ("the whole tremendous . . . like a man whose skin has been peeled off and whose intestines are seen at work"). And he completed the essay after he had spoken with William James and read James's *Varieties of Religious Experience*.

In those lectures, again, James had moved his religious genius through a process of conversion. He had taken his saint from once-born innocence through panic fear and crisis, a conviction of sin or melancholy, and then offered a step of wordly ascetic discipline, the building of a personal and social economy of saintliness. James had then ended by crossing work out. Having inserted himself into his own narrative ("William's melancholy about the universe is due to bad digestion [the disbelievers will say]—probably his liver is torpid"), and having described himself as coming out of the "wilderness," by which he meant America, and into the "dreamland" of Edinburgh, James spoke in "Conclusions" of a "kind of aimless weather, doing and undoing, achieving no proper history, and leaving no result." Nature, he finished, "appears to cancel herself," crossing herself out.

Weber re-created this spiritual movement. Among the first writings Weber published following six years of incapacitating depression, his essay on the Protestant ethic was meant to end his own sighting of terror. The essay, which demands the saint's removal from self-imposed seclusion, was begun after Weber's own massive collapse of 1897.

After his father's death in the summer of 1897, Weber had become severely depressed. In Freudian terms, he had begun a long struggle with work inhibition. Unable to teach or to write, he had left his university, gone in and out of asylums, and had attempted long vacations. With the little energy that he said remained, he began to study religious values of rationality. In an early passage of his *Protestant Ethic* he wrote of a Pietist's "mental concentration," "strict economy," "cool self-control"—attitudes that his depression had seemingly dashed.

During his collapse, Weber pulled within himself. His hands shook, his back ached, his nerves jangled at small noises, his sleep suffered. He spoke of exhaustion, broken nerves, and an inability to speak. "The inability to speak is purely physical, the nerves break down, and when I look at my lecture notes I simply can't make sense of them." "All mental functions and a part of the physical ones fail him," his wife wrote. "If he nonetheless forces them to work, chaos threatens him, a feeling as though he could fall into the vortex of an overexcitement that would throw his mind into darkness." His doctor prescribed hydrotherapy.

Others variously debated the reason for Weber's depression, seeking the natural causes for what was taken as a physical collapse. As Mary James had thought of her son William during his crisis, and as Christiana thinks of her husband prior to Christian's leaving the City of Destruction behind, so Weber's mother considered him quite simply a hypochondriac. Weber and the doctors he consulted attributed the illness to overwork, the alienists' then favored way of making sense of such breakdowns. In 1892 Weber himself had spoken of working too much: "an overestimation of my capacity to work." But now, five years later, with the death of his father having presumably shattered his world, Weber still labored to manage the smallest details of his life. He failed and, in the words of Marianne, interpreted an acute irritability over some minor points of vacation planning "as a sign of nervous exhaustion. . . . On the return trip the strained organism reacts with an illness. Weber becomes feverish and feels threatened." With a "strong feeling of tension," Weber collapsed at the age of thirty-one. He was one of James's "sporadic adult cases."

This is the age of crisis that Erik Erikson's great men suffer—an experience, it is supposed, that should normally erupt in adolescence. Here the legal fear and conviction of sin of the Puritans is translated into the melancholic crisis of the Victorian intellectual. Weber, given an extended leave of absence from his university, remained nearly incapacitated for almost seven years, until 1904.

It becomes a matter of further interpretation if one moves past the physical explanation of Weber's collapse to seek not structural configurations but genetic causations. One may move, in other words, from the organic (overwork) to the Oedipal. One may place the Oedipal struggle either within the context of Weber's family or, more ambitiously, within the field of a whole European generational battle. Coincidentally and almost wondrously in Freud's own terms, Weber's father had died shortly after a bitter quarrel with his son, a quarrel involving Weber's mother. Weber's own illness followed. Strains do appear to have existed within the Weber household, for the piety and the quiet religiosity of Weber's mother more than once clashed with his father's genteel yet autocratic living. Weber himself spoke of matters that had "completely alienated" him from his father, and spoke too of the guilt that he attributed to a seemingly fatal decision, one that involved a vacation the mother was to spend with her son, that he had finally made to defend his mother before his father's demands.

Contradictions marked the Weber household as well, where, in a post-Freudian interpretation, one may read parental behavior as confusing Weber as much as creating his anger. If the piety of the mother did clash with the anger and moodiness of the father, then the confrontation could only have contributed to Weber's doubts, doubts that come with the inability of any child to take sides easily while parents collide. Within the evidence of parental conflict, Weber found a contradiction in his father's behavior. His father, he wrote, "was always sanguine," and yet his "mood was often subject to sudden change from little external cause." Such whimsical moods could again create doubt and only be feared—here, the capriciousness that left a "painful impression" on the mother that the son had to consider.

The ability to face out uncertainty, which remains at the heart of Weber's celebration of Puritanism, is the ability to engage the image of one's world as a jungle, the tangle created for the child, Andras Angyl argues, by conflicting and seemingly chaotic parental moods and decisions. For Angyl, such an image lies in the eye of a fearful, compulsive person, one who in terror would try to order nature completely. It is an ascetic effort such as Weber tried, one that in American literature (in *Walden,* for example) eventually suffers its own collapse.

In the years of his breakdown Weber, in his reflection, was indolently living off the resources of his family and university. In his own term he had suffered an "emotional depression," one that he believed, or that his doctors informed him, only time and rest could cure. Weber hoped to regain a discipline through another physic by working his way out from the erratic moods that he said his father and now he himself experienced. "We may tolerate no fantastical surrender to unclear and mystical moods in our souls," Weber later wrote. "For when feeling rises high, you must fetter it, to be able to steer with sobriety." After the worst period of his depression, Weber began to study asceticism as a form "opposite" to "a positively hysterical character." He looked to an ethic of "strict and temperate discipline"—"the systematic life of holiness of the Puritan." He spoke now of those engaged "in the ascetic struggle for certainty."

If overwork is irresponsive to other than a somatic interpretation of a breakdown and appears, especially for the psychoanalytically informed historian, too naive a cause for Weber's melancholic depression, work may nevertheless become as significant as Oedipal drives by becoming itself a full sign. If one abandons the search for the cause of psychopathology and studies instead the formation of a discursive plain of description, then meaning becomes attached to objects rather than revealed by them. Meaning is not simply found, but becomes a historically variable social production. Rather than searching Weber's unconsciousness, one watches as he manipulates his own work, which includes his own writing, within conventions to make a meaningful account of himself. Foucault, in speaking of "commentary"—a process of interpretation that says that something else (a remainder) has yet to be deciphered, that something still lies hidden behind the text—writes: "Is it not possible to make a structural analysis of discurses that would evade the fate of commentary [that of an infinite regression of interpretations, especially a regression of psychological interpretations] by supposing no remainder, nothing in excess of what has been said, but only the fact of its historical appearance." Foucault seeks neither a disembodied history of ideas nor a psychologically revealed reading of history—neither a timeless form nor an as yet unrevealed text, neither a universal aesthetic nor an author's hidden intention—to center a history of thought, but the arrangements that persons make between words and things. The question is how persons make an interpretation that draws together the object and the sign, the signified and the signifier. Foucault watches as interpreters point to what is behind the lines of texts, saying, as if to Christian, what for all time is meant. He watches, then, for the transformations of this interpretation as the relation made between things spoken and things said to have been thought changes:

> What counts in the things said by men is not so much what they may have thought or the extent to which these things represent their thoughts, as that which systematizes them from the outset, thus making them thereafter accessible to new discourses and open to the task of transforming them.

Following his depression, Weber used familiar schedules to carve a certain economy out of his bewilderment. He set the significance of his labor against the "chaos" and the "vortex" that his illness had expressed. He structured his life carefully after his visit to America. He worked only six hours a day, while at the same time he refused the emotional entanglements of public lectures and social occasions and minimized his relationships with family and friends. Though he complained of slowness, as James incessantly did, following his depression Weber produced a great volume of his most important writing. The depression, in other words, expressed the end of a cycle through which Weber had moved: an intense grasp for assurance which, when the grasp failed, could bring the sense of impending disaster.

Weber's personal mechanics are to be found within an extended text—a writing that moves from his own reported words to those words as explicated within secondary texts. "If I don't work until one o'clock [in the morning] I can't be a professor," Weber told his wife in 1894. When he was a student in 1884-85, Marianne Weber wrote: "he continues the rigid work discipline, regulates his life by the clock, divides the daily routine into exact sections for the various subjects, saves in his way." Weber described the function his work was to serve during the decade preceding his depression:

> When I had finally come to an inner harmony [through marriage] after years of a nasty sort of

agony, I feared a deep depression. It has not occurred, to my mind, because, through continual work I did not let my nervous system and brain come to rest. Quite apart from the natural need for work, therefore, I am most unwilling to allow a really marked pause in my work; . . . I can't risk allowing the present composure . . . to be transformed into relaxation.

Weber routinized himself, to such an extent that he has become the exemplum of his own ascetic character type. He then probed for the meaning of the magic that he thought his routine contained. He considered, that is, the mechanics of himself, the signification of his own working.

WEBER'S OBSESSIVE ACTIONS

Weber's habits of labor, along with the descriptions that he gave of himself and those provided by others—accounts of his conscience and forceful temperament—resemble the type of character that Freud was calling compulsive. These stand as the architectonics of a particular self-formation, however—behavior that signaled for Freud a character type, and for Weber an ethic. Neither considered the formation irrational; indeed, Weber viewed the repression required to hold such an ethic in place as a sign of productive activity. For Freud, the significance remained the same, at least as regarded the work that his character type performed. Freud found a crossing stratum running beneath the character, however, the faults of which could erupt and break into the overlying character, cutting his type into a neurosis: an obsessive-compulsive malaise. For the ill-productive labors that distinguish the neurosis, or again the behavior that Freud referred to as "obsessive actions," such as meticulously performed ceremonies, Freud sought unconscious significance. He sought to read the obsessive action by looking for reflective evidence of the unconscious wish that the action represented, symbolized, stood for, or replaced. The ideational manipulations that also distinguished the neurosis—thoughts the neurotic himself gave little significance to, except that he possessed them often in fear—also appeared to Freud to hold hidden meaning: to represent, in fact, an actual reverse of the moralistic character that the obsessive enjoyed. Freud could view the obsessions along with the compulsive acts as distorted signs or refractions of the unconscious desire that the neurotic, like a primitive, actually implied. Freud linked the neurotic and the primitive, for whether in the form of compulsions and obsessions or of totem and taboo, the same chains of significance were repressed: the attempt, through such works, to control a deed of primordial violence.

For Freud, repression never expressed the willful endeavor that it did for Weber. Weber is often held apart from Freud, as indeed he held himself, speaking as he did for what he thought of as the efficacy rather than sickness of repression. Weber nevertheless adhered to a similar discursive architecture. He also presented an underlying irrationality—his "other-worldly" ascetic—a psychological formation that gives significance to the reversal of meaning that his wordly ascetic enjoys. Weber defined

his Puritan, and his own Protestant temperament, by this otherworldly difference, "psychological peculiarities" that run parallel to his this-worldly ethic. Behind the Protestant and his capitalist material production sits this peculiar psychological cell, its door slammed tight. Within the writing he made of himself, however, these irrationalities were opened, and Weber is revealed in the pathology these otherwordly eruptions entail.

Weber's depressions were unproductive enough, "irrational" within the terms he set for that word. Such depressions for Weber were akin to a mystic's or a hysteric's emotive elations and collapse, or to a Catholic's cycle of sin and expiation. Then, too, the question remained of the irrationality behind his ascetic's life, the pathology of "magic," that is, that his Protestant ascetic so adamantly opposed.

Weber was called neurotic, and his depressions are proof enough of that. As his own writing unfolds, however, it becomes apparent that Weber considered more than depression and more than the loosely defined "hysteric" moods that he so feared as undercutting his life. The symptoms other than depression that bothered Weber in a clinical sense have remained unknown, though evidence is present—or rather presented—in an extended public text. Weber was using his work to defend himself from depression and perhaps from sex (his closest psychological observer has argued that Weber left his marriage to Marianne unconsummated). Although Marianne Weber destroyed a document in which her husband described his symptoms for a psychiatrist, she did record that Weber likened his troubles to those of Jeremiah. In his study of ancient Judaism, again, Weber found in Jeremiah a mental pathology that he thought resembled his own.

It is more correct to say that Weber produced from his reading in Jeremiah a mental pathology that gave significance to his suffering. Otherwise ill-defined behavior could be focused by becoming historically significant. Jeremiah offered Weber a text that he could read his life into, as the words impressed and made sense to him. One is tempted to say that in piecing together certain works—Marianne's own *Max Weber* and portions of Weber's *Ancient Judaism*—one has uncovered a hitherto concealed symptom in Weber. This of course has not occurred; rather one has, in the very assembling of texts—in a reading of *Ancient Judaism* now in the light of Marianne's biography—read a discursive field. One has redefined what is to be meant by a text, extending the definition from an enclosed book temporally defined by a publishing date (a date hard enough to define in relation to Weber's own rewritings and complex publishing history) to a set of books, one of Weber's self and the other of Weber's scholarship. A new temporal definition now encloses a wider field. This new text, by intermingling self and theology in a confession of a small piece of mental pathology, forms a spiritual autobiography.

For Freud, obsessions and compulsions buried their significance in the unconsciousness, becoming themselves but distorted reflections of the violence such magical acts replaced. For Freud, such acts (like taboos) guarded the consumed father, and defended sons through the sons' use of incredibly precise ritual detail. For Weber, such rituals pointed consciously to ethical questions of law and faith. Rituals of otherwise confusing significance pointed consciously to questions as to whether the self had enwrapped itself in irrationalities, or whether it could emerge from such magic into disinterested vocations, into callings bonded to faith. As Weber wrote in **"The Social Psychology of the World Religions"**:

> Things have been quite different where the religiously qualified . . . have combined into an ascetic sect, striving to mould life in this world according to the will of God. To be sure, two things were necessary before this could happen in a genuine way. First, the supreme and sacred value must not be of a contemplative nature. Second, such a religion must, so far as possible, have given up the purely magical or sacramental character of the *means* of grace [magical asceticism]. For these means always devalue action in this world . . . and they link the decision about salvation to the success of processes which are *not* of a rational everyday nature. . . . The religious virtuoso can be placed in the world as the instrument of a God and cut off from all magical means of salvation. At the same time, it is imperative for the virtuoso that he "prove" himself before God, as being called *solely* through the ethical quality of his conduct in this world. This actually means that he "prove" himself to himself as well.

Not "merely ceremonious, ritualist, and conventional particulars," not "senseless brooding and events and long[ing] for the dreamless sleep," but a rational affirmation of the world through work confirms salvation—"methodical and rationalized routine-activities of workaday life in the service of the Lord. Rationally raised into a vocation, everyday conduct becomes the locus for proving one's state of grace."

In his portrayal of the **"Psychological Peculiarities of the Prophets,"** Weber described Jeremiah as a prophet combatting magic, visions, and "dream interpretations," a clear enough reference to Weber's opinion of Freud. Jeremiah lived as a speaker rather than as a passive or emotional seer, a prophet who felt compelled to speak:

> One meets with compulsive acts, above all, with compulsive speech. Jeremiah felt split into a dual ego. He implored his God to absolve him from speaking. Though he did not wish to, he had to say what he felt to be inspired words not coming from himself. Indeed his speech was experienced by him as horrible fate. . . . Unless he spoke he suffered terrible pains, burning heat seized him and he could not stand up under the heavy pressure without relieving himself by speaking. Jeremiah did not consider a man to be a prophet unless he knew this state and spoke from compulsion rather than "from his own heart."

Weber called some of Jeremiah's acts compulsions as well: the wearing of an iron yoke, the smashing of a jug,

the burying of a belt, the later digging up the belt's putrid remains—"strange activities thought to be significant as omens." Weber refused interpretation, however; indeed, he refused the "act of interpretation *per se*," the "obscure and ambiguous" signs that pointed only to the prophet as type, to *his* mission as an interpreter. The significance of the prophet lay not in the meaning but in the possession of his signs, in his calling which used unfathomable signs to erase magical significance. There existed in the prophet's images of iron—iron pans, iron yokes, iron horns—and the eating of filth, motifs of hardness and decay. Images also formed of bonds and destructions: the wearing of yokes, the smashing of vessels, the decay of belts, the inflicting of bodily wounds—prophetic demands for tearing apart constructions or for tasting decay, for being, as it seemed, within a cage besmeared with dirt, caught in the machinations of a design that barely contained the filth behind.

Whatever one means by "compulsion" or the obverse word "obsession," it becomes clear that Weber considered the prophet as necessarily driven—indeed, as vocationally defined—by these alien drives, himself forced to act like any running machine. Marx gave such alienation to the end of the capitalist consciousness. Weber gave the compulsion to the mouth of anyone crying from such a hell, here from Israel's own "bureaucratic machine." This is not to be considered evidence of a malaise that Weber suffered: "This is not the place," he wrote, "to classify and interpret, as far as that is possible, the various physiological, and possibly pathological states of the prophets. Attempts made thus far . . . are not convincing. It affords, furthermore, no decisive interest for us." But the compulsion becomes a meaningful text in that for Weber it could make sense by uniting his symptoms with those of the prophet with whom he so identified. In the midst of his own estrangement, Weber stood like Jeremiah, this "prophet of doom," "ridiculed, threatened, spit upon"— an image that Weber at times gave to himself and that his Puritan, standing in the midst of a great American desert, had also given to himself.

Weber continued his analysis. He declared that for a prophet such as Jeremiah there had never existed the wish to lose control or to reside in mystic vision or, for that matter, to dream dreams or hear mysterious voices. Rather, as for Weber's Puritan, a drive had started toward "clarity and assurance." This quest for assurance and the rigidity involved came at the expense of, or held beneath it, behavior that, unlike the vague compulsive acts mentioned above, better delineates in Weber's reading a mental disorder. Like the sociologist just prior to his long depression—when Marianne recorded that every small thing seemed in need of control, and Weber grasped to order the smallest particulars of his world—so the prophet had fretted over the minutiae of life: "The typical prophet apparently found himself in a constant state of tension and of oppressive brooding in which even the most banal things of everyday life could become frightening puzzles, since they might somehow be significant."

Significance becomes attached haphazardly as words and things normally scattered now link themselves in incredible chains of signs. Portents, meanings, omens, all could be located, in Weber's frame of reference, beyond the limits of a normal grammar, within a swirl of colliding sounds and interpretations. Moving now, however, in the sections of his text from "psycho-patholo(gy)" to "prophetic ethic," Weber stressed a way out of endless interpretation. The prophet now refuses to use "magical compulsion" to relieve his confusion, meaningless rituals that for Weber had come in the face of meaningless signs. Weber's prophet turns instead to an early form of occupation that for Weber faithfully replaces the magic: a productive work, calling, or vocation that effaces both magic and depression. For the prophet, the calling—not immaterial ritual—combats sin and, most important, frightening obsessions, compelled ideas that like the acts can pain while they still preoccupy and absurdly cement a mind: "Jeremiah's tender soul suffered grievously from emotional depressions and *idées fixes*," Weber finally concluded, "but he disciplined himself by force of his calling to a desperate heroism."

Earlier Weber had written of his own work as a defense against depression. Now, in addition, he was writing of work as defending against an *idée fixe,* one of the less ambiguous phrases in turn-of-the-century psychiatry. It was one of the most common terms for an obsession—the hurtful, criminal, or blasphemous expression that one cannot banish from the mind. Weber had identified himself with an ancient text, if not with his Puritans' conceiving of their own melancholy, then with the malaise of the prophet for whom the Puritans so often spoke. He was reconstructing Jeremiah, and constructing himself, in modern terms within the oldest of prophetic psychomythologies.

Weber's reading, then, is to declare a psychopathology for any religionist who tries to make signs that are not common sense. Weber made Jeremiah's words unreadable, quite the opposite of Freud's approach to such ritual in *Totem and Taboo.* If words and things, meanings and materials, or sounds and conceptions—even such obvious signs as an iron yoke and putrid remains—fail to hold together through the interpretation of symbolism (what a sign represents), then the interpreter's production of meaning can itself become significant, rather than the interpreter's use of a particular sign. Meanings that become attached to banal everyday accidents, significance that is given to absurd intruding thoughts, worked for Weber as the psychological peculiarities of Old Testament prophets compelled by the Law. The prophet acts only through magical forces playing upon him from without. Weber, of course, attached significance to all this. The unreadable text he made a readable sign. He wrote of the inefficacy of such law itself, the unproductive labors that had been required for the law's interpretation. He wrote of the entangling alliances that persons make between words and things, immaterial productions that enchain persons in ritual circles of magic and superstition. Such expressions, repeated to the self while fixed in

the mind, make for senseless acts performed again and again as if holding the self in check. Weber's reading of this text as a pathology, and his making a sign of that, allowed him to create a difference for Jeremiah. The reading allowed Weber to hold work or the calling against irrational compulsion, since the rationality of work, as a vocation, had erased such immaterial production. The psychopathology Weber spoke of—this particular piece of mental pathology of the *idée fixe* and the compulsive act that otherwise hold little significance—assumed incredible proportions by defining that which the prophet, as later Weber's Puritan, had worked against: the ritual law that precedes the giving up to faith, the prophetic Law of the Old Testament that had to be closed before the opening could be made into callings undertaken only in faith. For a moment in time in the protostruggle of Jeremiah, then in the opening light of the Reformation, rationality held no magic. Work remained unpossessed of the demonology that a later capitalism would, ironically, re-embrace, the commodity fetish and estranged labor that Marx, for example, portrayed.

THE WORLDLY ASCETIC ETHIC

Erik Erikson has written of this movement in the life of his great men, extending Weber's text: a movement, again, from "works" to "work" or from "vow" to "vocation." When Erikson writes of man's reliance on magic—meaning, in particular, a neurotic's reliance on superstition—to control his world, he stresses the damage which occurs to one's sense of wholeness and identity:

> The dangers to man's identity posed by a confused realism allied with a popular demonology are obvious. The influences from the other world are brought down to us as negotiable matter; man is able to learn to master them by magical thinking and action. But momentary victories of magic over an oppressive superreality do not, in the long run, either develop man's moral sense or fortify a sense of the reality of his identity on this globe.

When Weber wrote of man's use of ritual to atone for sin, he stressed the same point, arguing that the periodic relief of fear which superstition allows opposes the formation of a "total personality pattern":

> The vouchsafing of grace always entails the subjective release of the person in need of salvation; it consequently facilitates his capacity to bear guilt and . . . largely spares him the necessity of developing an individual planned pattern of life based on ethical foundations. The sinner knows that he may always receive absolution by engaging in some occasional religious practice or by performing some religious rite. It is particularly important that sins remain discrete actions against which other discrete deeds may be set up as compensations or penances. Hence, value is attached to concrete individual acts rather than to the total personality pattern which has been produced by asceticism.

Weber returned to Germany from America in 1904 and completed his greatest essay, *The Protestant Ethic and the Spirit of Capitalism*. "Stimulation and activity of the brain without mental strain is the only means of healing," he remarked upon the end of his American travel. He thought his health now good and felt he could, in 1904, complete things that he had formerly thought impossible.

Weber composed the *"innerweltliche Askese,"* the life of monastic virtue to be led beyond one's own self-imposed chamber, by describing an asceticism requiring that one construct some sort of "disenchanted" view. This was to be Weber's scientific ethic in which "no mysterious incalculable forces come into play, but rather . . . [one in which] one can in principle, master all things by calculation. This means the world is disenchanted"—freed, that is, from magical interpretations. As Weber would use this science to free inquiry, so he felt that his inner-worldly ascetic had freed himself from "spirits," "magical means," "mysterious powers," creating the world view to which, Weber wrote, early radical Protestantism had given completion.

> That great historic process in the development of religions, the elimination of magic from the world which had begun with the old Hebrew prophets and, in conjunction with Hellenistic scientific thought, had repudiated all magical means to salvation as superstition and sin, came here to its logical conclusion. The genuine Puritan even rejected all signs of religious ceremony at the grave and buried his nearest and dearest without song or ritual in order that no superstition, no trust in the effects of magical and sacramental forces on salvation, should creep in.

Weber desired to study empirically this new rationality in man, an attempt, as he thought, to hold the demonic by the throat.

Weber gave his most eloquent expression of this consciousness in the years 1904 and 1905, when he published *Die protestantische Ethik und der 'Geist' des Kapitalismus*. The essay was an opening expression for a new discipline that Weber called a *"Religionssoziologie."* The term was his own. Beyond looking at a single religious form in terms of its social and economic behavior (and indeed, though Weber denied it, looking at Protestantism in terms of its "neurology and psychology" as well), Weber's essay provided the image of the *"protestantische Ethik"* itself, for that phrase was neither current in the vocabulary nor, as yet, was it reified. In a moment of clarity, as Marianne remembered, Weber conflated history and crystalized themes, drawing together already abstracted types (Pietism, Puritanism, asceticism, sect) until, for the opening of this century, his ideal type was made. The sociologist had formed his ethic by offering a whole economy as *Geist,* arguing the existence of a historically unique spirit of labor and restraint. The Protestant ethic, Weber imagined, existed as a singular quest for "rational" behavior.

Rationality was not a new expression. When sorted out and conceptually seized, however, rationality, as Foucault writes, calls for an other. Rationality requires a reversal of image (as in a camera obscura) or a farther nature or frontier. Like Henry Adams's pile of coal hidden behind the dynamo, rationality demands a difference. If placed in time and given origin (the Reformation), then, whether as a new mechanics, a Protestant ethic, a Cartesian graph, or simply a "machine," rationality requires a parallel, foreign history that offers the other side to the taxonomic sheet and its grid. The irrational too therefore begins, rising with the eruption of the self, both faults of which Weber plotted to the seventeenth century and measured with the new autobiographies upon which he relied. One should not view it as a matter of mere interest, then, that economic rationality received its most thorough sifting by a scholar psychologically revealed.

Weber constructed his essay on the Protestant ethic by equating "capitalism" with "worldly asceticism," choosing the latter term to emphasize the restraint and renunciation that any enormous enterprise requires. The first term, capitalism, remained in one sense merely a device, a convenient expression for the production that such an ascetic discipline had created. Capitalism arose, Weber wrote in the most powerful of his images (other than that of the iron cage itself), when asceticism emerged from its cell, when the Reformation carried the order of the monastery—the first institution that Weber believed man had run according to the dictates of time, efficiency, and ritual perfection—to the marketplace.

> Christian asceticism, at first fleeing from the world into solitude, had already ruled the world which it had renounced from the monastery and through the Church. . . . Now it strode into the marketplace of life, slammed the door of the monastery behind it, and undertook to penetrate just that daily routine of life with its methodicalness, to fashion it into a life in the world, but neither of nor for this world.

This image commands Weber's essay and draws an irony for his reader: this removal from the chamber (as Emerson had demanded in his *Nature*) and the slamming of the chamber's door behind, then the entry into a strange arena—most pre-eminently, for Weber, America—which awaits to become a new cage.

Weber's finest psychological interpreter, Arthur Mitzman, has argued that *The Protestant Ethic* begins "those years when [Weber's] theoretical defense of the ascetic code began to crumble." Mitzman equates Weber's worldly ascetic with the authoritarianism of Weber's father, the iron cage that becomes, in literal translation, the "housing hard as steel." It is the house, that is, of the father. This reading, however, demands that the critic equate two of the three types of capitalism of which Weber wrote—the ascetic Protestant and the high—and ignore Weber's description of the Puritan saint as, most particularly, "anti-authoritarian." The equation—simply saying that Weber was writing about "capitalism"—remains analogous to the reading that Erich Fromm made in 1932 when, in an influential essay, Fromm equated the whole of the "Protestant ethic" with the acquisitive character of Freud's anal compulsive character type. Fromm made the link despite Weber's opening remarks that "the impulse to acquisition, pursuit of gain, of money, of the greatest possible amount of money, has in itself nothing to do with capitalism"—that is, with Weber's idea of an ascetic capitalism. Weber's Puritan was not given to "hoarding." Both readings, however, are not simply misreadings; as modern psychological readings, they have informed a good deal of popular discourse on the Protestant ethic—important (and, one should think, almost inevitable) discourse, in that these additions take the Protestant or "Puritan ethic" back to earlier psychological charges, back to Robert Burton's *Anatomy of Melancholy,* for example, and to the Puritans' own charges against themselves as the slandered and sick of the world.

In terms of a specific expression of obsessional psychopathology—whether of melancholy in the seventeenth-century understanding or of *"Zwangsneurose"* in Freud's formulation—the Puritan spiritual autobiography had opened the self to expressions of a ritually encumbered conscience, the *Grace Abounding to the Chief of Sinners* that Weber knew to be the pre-eminent example. The "meere excrementall" of the melancholy humor had interworked themes of psychopathology and theology by using obsessional ideation as a sign of the irrational satanic temptation waiting at the edge of spiritual conversion, the temptation Satan used to create false impressions of the conscience of sin which, along with the ritual acts, expressed a merely legal fear and a legal way of getting out of sin. Obsession, again a rare point of psychopathology, had become a way to distinguish such fear from a conscience of sin as sin, or to know of that which was not true sorrow. The attempt ritually to rid the self of its fear defined the kind of estranged works the self undertook prior to accepting the sacrifice of Christ.

Weber drew this writing to completion not by disparaging his Protestant ascetic but by unfolding its irony. His worldly ascetic saint, having rid himself of magic and having combatted doubt as but another form of temptation (one works simply for the work there is to do), begins to create wealth, making goods quite against his own intentions. As Weber quoted from John Wesley:

> "For religion must necessarily produce both industry and frugality, and these cannot but produce riches. But as riches increase, so will pride, anger, and love of the world in all its branches. How then is it possible that Methodism, that is, a religion of the heart, though it flourishes now as a green bay tree, should continue in this state? For the Methodists in every place grow diligent and frugal; consequently they increase in goods. Hence they proportionately increase in pride, in anger, in the desire of the flesh, the desire of the eyes, and the pride of life. So, although the form of religion remains, the spirit is swiftly vanishing away. Is there no way to prevent this—this continual decay. . . ."

Weber's saint creates the machines and thereby the materials of his own destruction, so that in the end he finds himself lost as to the meaning of the ethic that had brought about his labor. The alienation comes as a new temptation: unintended vanity in which, as in Vanity-Fair, there sits a new cage.

The Protestant Ethic, then, becomes expressive not of Weber's turn against his own "work asceticism" of which Marianne wrote, but of a narrative movement of conversion. Weber is to be seen as leaving a certain irrational work behind—his crisis and depression, certainly, and perhaps particular obsessional manipulations. He is to emerge from this enclosed chamber, psychopathologically wrought, to write of the Puritans' calling not as a means but as an expression of their faith. From "the ascetic death-in-life of the cloister," he brings his Puritan out of ill-productive works akin to the works (and ill work) of his own crisis and depression. He brings his Puritan from an asceticism that can strive for such control that men are, in effect, incapacitated—an estrangement against which, in text, both Weber and his Puritan work.

As Weber wrote, such an estrangement is a "magical asceticism" that demands a host of encumbering devices. It requires the otherworldly production of things like fastings, chastisements, mortifications, taboos, petty rituals, precise ceremonies, prayers, chants, sanctioned thoughts—behaviors all of which disallow the production of rational material labor. In an assumption that grounds the whole of Weber's argument as to why the Protestant chose to work ascetically, the guilt of all men must in one way or another be relieved. Guilt must somehow be read or understood. At times Weber looked almost nostalgically to Catholicism and its periodic use of oral confessions and priests (whom he considered magicians) to relieve guilt. He considered Catholicism as organically relieving such pressure by mating the person to the natural rhythms of his environment, matching sin and repentance to the movements of the seasons, making for a cyclical as opposed to a linear (or Puritan) text of salvation. A pragmatic question evolved, however, as to the "productivity" of such cyclical labor. And a psychological question emerged as to the "personality" of the magical worker himself.

Magic, ritual law, and taboo appeared to Weber as a "fear-ridden punctiliousness," "a mental alienation," a "slave-liked dread." Weber wrote of relieving guilt through a "methodical compulsion of the gods," and in words close to Freud's study of compulsion in his anthropology of totem and taboo, he wrote of the ceremonies of eating a sacred totem. Such practices created the "incredible irrationality of . . . painfully onerous norms," practices, for example, of those in "a fraternal community" who were attempting to placate a god. "Within this complex," Weber concluded, "there is little differentiation between important and unimportant requirements; any infraction of the ethic constitutes sin." Freud deemed such a complex neurotic; Weber considered such labors estranged. Marianne attributed obsessionally careful be-havior to her husband, at least as regarded the banalities of Weber's incessant planning prior to his collapse—again, not symptomatic evidence, but a sign of that which Weber had set himself to work against by composing his writing on rationality. It "is perfectly obvious," Weber reiterated, "that economic rationalization would never have arisen originally where taboo had achieved such massive power."

Whenever Weber explained the rise of "rational" work processes, he emphasized this importance of being re-lieved from magic, however ironic such an emphasis for "high capitalism" and its fetishes would appear. Weber used the idea in a variety of forms. In part, the release from magic allowed for economically rational deci-sions—such mundane choices as the location of a factory without reference to the place of spirits and demons. More significantly, however, Weber stressed the author and the authority to be given to work, for when he con-trasted the Puritan's productivity with what he saw as the Confucian's mere ceremony, he again emphasized the encumbrance that any magic style entailed. Caught in a "magical coercion of spirits and deities"—in a "vestigal ritualism" that Weber's Puritan considered "impudent blasphemy"—buried in observances and in obscure is-sues of law, the Confucian lives without an "inward core" or an "autonomous value position." He lacks "a 'unified personality,' a striving which we associate with the idea of personality. Life remained a series of occurrences. It did not become a whole placed methodically under a transcendent goal." Weber opposed such piecemeal "ritual" to the "rational-ethical." He opposed this "merely apparent" of magic to the "real." The key becomes the release from "works": for those bound "hand and foot," rational ascetic prophecies could effect freedom by re-leasing the self from magic.

In *The Protestant Ethic,* Weber wrote that this "radical release of magic from the world allowed no other psycho-logical course than the practice of wordly asceticism." The decomposition of magic that the Reformation em-phasized removed the types of devices other psychologi-cal formations could use to relieve stress. Without priestly intermediaries, for example, or confessions and penances, the Protestant faced his God and his sin di-rectly. He had turned magic, that is, into a transparent sign, providing magic with no significance at all. With the Catholic cycle of sin and expiation removed, the Prot-estant had no other recourse but to live a linear working life unrelieved of pressure. Though Weber denied that psychology or psychiatry could unravel the Protestant ethic, he nevertheless argued that it was the "psychologi-cal sanction" or the "psychological effect" of Calvinism that distinguished the ethic. The doctrine of predestina-tion disallowed works, but work, the hopeful proof of salvation—more properly, the sign—became a labor of grace. Logically, fatalism should have become the only outcome of predestination, but "on account of the idea of proof the psychological result was precisely the oppo-site." All men required some assurance of salvation, and

some way to work out their guilt, and thus one's work represented not the means of grace but the signification, "the technical means, not of purchasing salvation, but of getting rid of the fear of damnation." Work became a whole endeavor singularly written—authored, for the first time in history, by a unified "personality."

Again, the Puritans' signification of grace is expressed not in isolated contents, discrete signs, or "single good works"—not in a work bound like an enclosed book—but in a whole faith running through to infinity. The Calvinist had found himself forced to forego the "planless and unsystematic character" of those who could magically undo whatever transgression they thought they had com-mitted. Thus they had replaced this doing and undoing, or the periodic acts of thought and behavior of undoing vio-lence that Freud placed at the center of his obsessional neurosis, with the constancy of the calling. The Puritans had allowed the self its own writing. The book of God stood absolutely prescribed: its word was made transpar-ent, therefore the book could never be opened to anxious, intermediate, and peculiar interpretations.

If one held grace to be other than plainly read, then one did leave the world open to doubt that only magic could periodically unravel. The ascetic labor Calvinism in-duced, as Weber wrote after his depression, eradicated doubt along with the magical sign: "it is held to be an absolute duty to consider oneself chosen, and to combat all doubts as temptations of the devil, since lack of self-confidence is the result of insufficient faith, and hence of imperfect grace." Never, for Weber, had the Puritans simply worked their way out, bargaining around unfath-omable questions, no more than they had remained in states of abject doubt, anguishing over themselves as psychological peculiarities. The combatting of "tempta-tions" nevertheless demanded that the temptations be-come fixed or conceptually defined as signs of the "irra-tional impulses" that the self was working against. The impulses needed to be expressed as the alienation, or the satanically induced other, that the self was holding itself against. Weber argued that asceticism first defined this estrangement by holding the body apart from its Creator. Monastic asceticism combatted depression along with the confusion that Weber's own exhaustion had itself only magnified. But only worldly asceticism provided self-identity, the sense of constancy and worth that Weber himself struggled to attain.

It becomes, then, not merely a psychologism to move between Weber and his texts; such a reading is almost demanded. It is demanded discursively, for even if one seeks an impersonal text, psychologism presents itself from the seventeenth century on as a universal text, giv-ing to narrative literature, for example, an author, while opening up the author psychologically within the newly popular autobiographical literature. Fascinated with types, Weber viewed his sociologies as studying such shifting patterns of consciousness. He was honing his analysis here to this point of the self, his concern being, as he said, with the historical formation of the "psychological sense" of personality that he believed his Puritan had, for the first time in history, achieved.

The achievement came as the Puritan removed himself from singular acts of contrition. Weber pitted the new personality against such "compensations," for personality came only with the ethical wholeness provided by Luther's *Beruf* or calling. William James argued the same, though never by so precisely locating the movement in history. James pitted the "automatic or semi-automatic composition" of the Hebrew prophets ("We have distinct professions of being under the direction of a foreign power, and serving as its mouthpiece") against "the teachings of the Buddha, of Jesus, of Saint Paul . . . of Luther, of Wesley." "And it always comes," James had quoted in the *Varieties* from another source, speaking in the main of Jeremiah, "in the form of an overpowering force from without, against which he struggles, but in vain"—"some strong and irresistible impulse," that is, "coming down upon the prophet, determining his attitude to the events of his time." The attitude strikes at the time when the Law appears about to fall, crushing the old toward creating the new. Topologically it becomes the space experienced for passing from Law to faith; typologically it becomes the juxtapositions that one makes of the Testaments.

Weber struck out against his own manner of working only when he held that his work had become like a magic or "talisman." One may read Weber, however, as using much of his work as a form of ritual. He undertook incredibly precise studies to organize his world—perhaps to control the unpredictability of his emotions, perhaps to defend against the fact of his father's "killing," or perhaps to combat doubts instilled in childhood as to whether his world was sanguine or punishing. Weber fled not in the first and most readable instance from the sex of marriage or from an Oedipal reaction, but from the self-doubt any emotional entanglement could bring, doubt that work as a carefully performed ceremony could end. When minutely performed, labor could clear one's mind as one might clean a room. Weber worked carefully. He paused, rearranged, digressed, added clauses, reservations, balance, refusing to write freely as if he might let some unpredictable emotion show. Until the defense broke and depression ensued, scientific labors allowed Weber to mechanize his life, which Weber well knew and which he took as a sign.

Clearly, to the end of his life Weber strove to return to the thoroughness of what he called the "malignant growth" of his footnotes. The form of his labor expressed a prolonged quest to grasp and control every facet of his learning. The attempt, of course, gave Weber his genius, but his circumspection could further confusion, for in the multiplicity of sides, a chaos of reflections could blind a reader. Those who have translated Weber's German testify that his writing expresses a need for such mastery that at times his words evolve into a private, almost magical or totemic language, as if Weber were attempting to preserve his knowing through codes of secrecy. He

never apologized for this; he simply said that he wished his reader to labor as hard as he, to bring them, as it seemed, through his own travail.

Doubt could also encourage the resolution of the world into predictable patterns, the figurations that Weber applied to history. These are the "ideal types" or structures that could make every block and being of the world fit for Weber and perform as they were supposed to perform. Weber opposed such structures to one such type: patriarchalism's "free arbitrariness." It was asceticism that functioned to order patriarchialism along with other dangerously chaotic expressions. More than any religious form, asceticism strove to "devalue" the world. It banished "the peculiar irrationality of the sexual act," for example, along with the capriciousness of patriarchs, the demonology of magicians and artists, or anyone who worked with uncontrollable powers or emotions. Protestant asceticism, and the scientific devaluation that Weber proposed Protestantism had created along with capitalism, was, again, anti-authoritarian. It opposed monarch and priest, and it opposed the closed texts of a dogma's chambers, the study of life through circular, ratiocinative signs. In all, ascetic prophecies demanded the release from the affections that ended in entanglements: "The sib has had to fear devaluation by the prophecy. Those who cannot be hostile to members of the household, to father and mother, cannot be disciples." The text, of course, is the New Testament.

THE END OF THE WORLDLY ASCETIC IDEAL

For a moment in history, grace was attained. Now, in the larger text that Weber gave to his Protestant ethic, the new work and its rationalism is to end itself in a terror, or more mundanely, in "sport." Ascetic renunciation ends in the mechanization and the fetishism of high capitalism. Adumbrations of Weber's theme appeared in 1904 in letters he wrote to his mother. He gave expression to an America transposing itself from an ascetic community of various sects into a Chicago. Weber's ascetic, in other words, fails to contain the forces within itself—in Oklahoma, for example, the "stench" and "smoke" and "numerous clanging railways," and in the fact of "lawyers" that Weber wrote about in quotes. The "boiling heat of modern capitalistic culture" was transforming America, changing the physiognomy of the nation. Weber stood as a prophet viewing the sins of a newly foreign nation. His European tongue was an appropriate emblem.

When Weber looked to America, he celebrated only remains—the vitality of the Oklahoma town he visited, for example, that was about to decay. "It is a shame," he had written his mother, but "within one year everything will appear here as in Oklahoma City, i.e., as in every other city in America. WITH FURIOUS SPEED EVERYTHING THAT COULD HAMPER CAPITALISTIC CIVILIZATION IS SMASHED." America's high capitalism had thoroughly rationalized itself. It was introducing systems of standardized bookkeeping, aptitude testing, and a factory discipline that

Weber saw as symbolizing the nation's compulsion for scientific management.

Upon his return to Germany, in completion of his essay, in the final, most famous paragraphs, Weber spoke of the iron closing on the West, particularly on the United States. "The Puritan wanted to work in a calling; we are forced to do so"—forced as if by some external power. Of course the exigencies of the machine itself existed, along with the cloak of external goods that fell now as "an iron cage [*ein stahlhartes Gehause*]." An "economic compulsion" had replaced ascetic labor. Like Marx, Weber destroyed the work of capitalist production through an irony, finding in high capitalism the same magic estrangement of other-worldly ascetic enclosure. Unlike Marx, Weber wrote now in timeless frames. He turned his text, as Freud was turning *Totem and Taboo,* from a chronicle of history to literature, ending outside of history in myth. He was fastening rebeginnings.

It was as though Weber were drawing for his reader timeless psychological conclusions, offering again Bunyan's portrayal of the iron cage of despair in the midst of the "Profits" of Vanity-Fair:

> Chr. *For what did you bring yourself into this condition?*
>
> *Man*. For the Lusts, Pleasures, and Profits of this World; in the enjoyment of which, I did promise my self much delight: but now even every one of those things also bite me, and gnaw me like a burning worm.

The Puritan had rejected Vanity Fair, so Weber argued, but in a modern economy the lusts, temptations, and fears reappeared. In an ambiguous statement, Weber appeared to join the entrapment to a new psychology—a secular Pauline psychology expressing the end of the inner calling and the beginning of the external compulsion of work in a high economy. As predestination could slip into mere fatalism, Weber wrote, so "there is a non-religious counterpart . . . , one based on a mundane determinism":

> It is that distinctive type of guilt and, so to speak, godless feeling of sin which characterizes modern man. . . . It is not that he is guilty of having done any particular act, but that by virtue of his unalterable idiosyncracy he "is" as he is, so that he is compelled to perform the act in spite of himself, as it were—this is the secret anguish that modern man bears.

In an economy without sanctions for work, persons felt inexplicable sin. They felt "inhuman," compelled to act in spite of themselves as if coerced by another. Weber worked the irony of his history by twisting his ethic into a spiritually barren renunciation of the self to specialized, totemic labor, "mechanized petrification." Compulsion, the neurotic possession of but a few, still symbolized an appropriate nature. With the performance of penances seemingly to atone, and a fear of one's eternal damnation, no other neurosis so openly displayed the guilt that

presumably underlay other neurotic structures as well. In compulsion the guilt becomes consciously felt, and the form of a strange act can retain its significance. Weber conceived his ascetic ideal out of such agony—too far removed, it seemed, to work any longer as a step in a morphology of national conversion. Ahead nothing awaited except a desiccated bureaucracy, the "Specialists without spirit" coveting the graph.

As Weber witnessed the travail, he did offer the promise—the faith that could begin in such wastes. ". . . they burn soft coal. When the hot, dry wind from the deserts of the southwest blows through the streets, and especially when the dark yellow sun sets, the city looks fantastic. [He was speaking of Chicago and its "endless filth."] In broad daylight one can see only three blocks ahead—everything is haze and smoke, the whole lake is covered by a huge pall of smoke." "It is an endless human desert." "All hell had broken loose." "On the billboards there was a poster proclaiming CHRIST IN CHICAGO," Marianne remembered. "Was this brazen mockery? No, this eternal spirit dwells there, too." From all this, Marianne concluded, Weber had returned, "conscious [now] of the reserves of energy that had slowly accumulated." For Weber, his genius expressed enough of a testament to the efficacy of such a hell. Weber thus brought America to its end, choked in its new world. In such deserts life began, in the forty years of national exile, or in the forty days of the temptations of Christ.

WORK AND DEATH

In a suspicion too of the completeness of any work at hand, Roland Barthes distinguishes a "work" from a "text." Barthes holds the text as an infinity, almost as an analogue of faith. "In other words, *the text is experienced only in an activity, a production.* It follows that the Text cannot stop, at the end of a library shelf, for example; the constitutive movement of the Text is a traversal . . . : it can cut across a work, several works." A text, then can cut across works—this crossing, for Barthes, being the only completion.

As Barthes's translator quotes in other regards, poststructuralism becomes a matter of deconstructing "Law." A critical despair of sterility appears, of order and ritual structures ("It is as if," Weber wrote, ". . . we were deliberately to become men who need 'order' and nothing but order, who become nervous . . . if for one moment this order wavers"). A "Protestant ethic" woven in script and in the figure of an author's life demonstrates Barthes's aim, to make of the work, that is, an "imaginary tail."

Edward Said locates this violence within the earliest of structural expressions, works that for him remain totemic rituals for "cutting down" nature to size, carving out in desperation too much rationality in an intensity of structuralist industry. For Said, such writing becomes an "economy of means that renders every detail," closed orders the anxiety of which can be opened only in a dispersion of signs, in a realization of the buried irony, in a "beginning," then, again.

This expresses Weber's text, and Freud's in *Totem and Taboo*. For the post-structural critic, critical method becomes this text, as critic and subject reflect themselves; for Joseph Riddel, writing of the themes of beginnings in American literature, it is a language that "must build a machine to bridge the abyss its questioning repeatedly opens up, a machine that turns out to be the sign itself of the abyss."

Like Freud, Weber had constructed a mechanics of personality interplaying (or for Freud, masking) the depths of a specific psychopathology. The personality represents the most rigidly structured of the Freudian character types and of David Shapiro's "neurotic styles." Like Said's early structuralist, the neurotic structure possesses its own violent potential, one for cutting at the bars of its mechanical repression. Unlike Freud, Weber offered the personality as a historically unique formation. It is fairly argued that Weber recovered his Protestant ethic from American manuscripts, the archives of which he searched, as well of course from Luther and to a lesser extent from Calvin. In its renewing frontiers enclosed now by mechanism, and in the land provided—blank as it had appeared, and waiting for Puritan inscription—America presented the space for the development of Weber's iron cage. Now, as Weber wrote, his own work was breaking down.

Mechanism fails to work, having first been built before a demonic sight. The end appears when the technologically contrived plays the work out. For Barthes, this becomes the nature of a text, "its motto the words of the man possessed by devils," or "legion," "play," something never compulsively enclosed. The text expresses Thoreau's "deep cut on the railroad" composed as a winter sand and mechanics exploding in an arrival of spring, and of a garden left in decay, the miles, as Thoreau said, of his garden's rows. The text expresses the labor of William James, who for all his will wrote in the end of letting go, of the mind that would "strike work" again in a crossing out. This becomes the narrative movement of psychomachy that Weber recomposed. As Barthes entitles his own essay, the movement becomes one "from work to text."

Within an American literature that holds itself within spiritual narrative forms, such structures, as Leo Marx writes, work as tight buildings that authors leave in depression, factory ships that end in their own destruction, rafts that explode in the middle of their pilgrims' passage, banks of sand that erupt in an explosion from the bowels of the earth in spring. Weber's cage reflects the decomposition Henry Adams made of his own dynamo displayed at a Paris exposition. Within Bunyan's narrative, the waste is displayed when Christian is smeared with dirt and placed within his own cage before he can leave Vanity Fair behind. The narrative begins in the sealing of the self in methodical devices, in the ritual bathings of a Thoreau, in strange ascetic manipulations, in the whole neurotic primitivism that Freud gave to totem and taboo. There follows a wordly ascetic and then an opening to nature, a cutting out there of economical forms, the linear structure enfolding back with the arrival then of terror. In a moment of realization of what the self has committed, the structure turns, and in uncovering the trope of its irony, falls apart. Life begins now in the perfectly random dispersion of Adams's entropic void.

For the American audience who would receive his writing, Weber's importance lay in re-creating this theme of the nation's spiritual journey. America had become an archetypal reference, Weber thought, for all of what he wanted his ethic to say. In the years in which Freud was writing to America, uncovering an "especially revealing" money complex that obsessed the nation, filthy lucre of coin and dirt, Weber was also writing of what Freud called the "transformations" of American values, of turnings or tropes, of which the most significant is irony.

By creating a desert of ritualization, Weber offered a timeless cycle of death and birth. Works vanish at the point of faith, and ritualization is self-destructive, the machine being defined by its waste and insanity, paradigmatic oppositions of metal and dirt, effort and collapse, with America to become this narrative of wilderness turning to iron. "Wilderness" and "iron," as Hayden White points out, possess the same root. The soil of America becomes this site of bewildering rationalizations, the land of the highest capitalism where the demonics of the machine are most visibly displayed. This penetration of nature, this machine in the garden (in Professor Marx's apt phrase), this cutting for Weber of organic forms with the edge tools that Emerson had described, with the calculation or "understanding" that Emerson had then denied, calls for an interpreter. The interpreter points to the lines of iron that have carved a graph from nature, and then to the terror crawling out from behind those lines. He points, as Bunyan or William James did, to the meaning of such "steps" or "progress," to the terror waiting when one makes such a satanic machine. As Marianne Weber to her husband or as Max Weber to himself, the interpreter points to the fear waiting when one attempts one's own conversion, making the self a progressive machine by writing the lines of the way to God as if the text were not already prescription, that is, preordained. The absolute Calvinist demand of the Protestant sects that Weber studied—beyond the capitalism created or the work performed or the contracts drawn—drew his interest, centered his essay, and in his own declaration of the mechanist's grip, brought him within the demonic of Puritan conversion. The debate enjoined, the "Weber thesis" and the question how a scholar could ever have celebrated—as Weber clearly did—the horror of the compulsion his worldly ascetic came to display, resolve before the understanding that Weber was rewriting the most radical of Puritan texts. He looked to the signs of the terrors of America, claiming that birth—for Emerson, "reason"—came at the end of the understanding (*Verstehen*) within sight of the cage. In alienation came the waters of separation, and the creation then of saints.

Anthony T. Kronman   **(essay date 1983)**

SOURCE: "Modernity," in *Max Weber,* Stanford University Press, 1983, pp. 166-88.

[In the following essay, Kronman explains Weber's reaction to and interpretation of the trends in modern social life.]

Beneath its richly detailed surface, Weber's ***Rechtssoziologie*** exhibits a surprising consistency and unity of purpose. Throughout, Weber is concerned with a single subject—the development of the institutions and forms of thought most characteristic of the modern legal order. 'Our interest', he remarks, 'is centred upon the ways and consequences of the "rationalization" of the law, that is, the development of those juristic qualities which are characteristic of it today.' Whether he is discussing modes of legal analysis, techniques of adjudication, or the forms of contractual association, Weber's fundamental aim is to give an account of those aspects of the present legal order that distinguish 'our contemporary modes of legal thought' from those prevailing in the past.

In this respect, the *Rechtssoziologie* parallels Weber's writings on authority, religion and economic action, all of which also reflect his predominant interest in the structure and meaning of modern social life. Each of his sociological investigations seeks to explain some distinctive component of modern European civilization—legal-rational authority, bureaucratic administration, capitalist production or the uniquely disenchanting Judeo-Christian conception of god as a supra-mundane, personal lord of creation. Indeed, it would not be too far-fetched to describe the entire *corpus* of Weber's substantive writings as a sociology of modernity. The *Rechtssoziologie* is only a part of this larger enterprise. To appreciate its full significance, one must view it in this wider context as a contribution to Weber's general theory of modernity, as one aspect of his lifelong obsession with the meaning of modern social life.

MODERNITY AND RATIONALITY

According to Weber, the institutions of modern society are distinguished by their high degree of rationality. What he means by the term 'rationality' is not always clear; nevertheless, despite his own ambiguous use of the concept, Weber's substantive writings all rest on the assumption that modern occidental culture exhibits a 'specific and peculiar rationalism' which distinguishes it from earlier forms of social life. What gives this 'modern occidental form' of rationality its 'special peculiarity'?

The beginnings of an answer can be found in the following passage from Weber's well-known essay, '**Science as a Vocation**'.

> Scientific progress is a fraction, the most important fraction, of the process of intellectualization which we have been undergoing for thousands of years

and which nowadays is usually judged in such an extremely negative way. Let us first clarify what this intellectualist rationalization, created by science and by scientifically oriented technology, means practically.

> Does it mean that we, today, for instance, everyone sitting in this hall, have a greater knowledge of the conditions of life under which we exist than has an American Indian or a Hottentot? Hardly. Unless he is a physicist, one who rides on the streetcar has no idea how the car happened to get into motion. And he does not need to know. He is satisfied that he may 'count' on the behaviour of the streetcar, and he orients his conduct according to this expectation; but he knows nothing about what it takes to produce such a car so that it can move. The savage knows incomparably more about his tools. When we spend money today I bet that even if there are colleagues of political economy here in the hall, almost every one of them will hold a different answer in readiness to the question: How does it happen that one can buy something for money—sometimes more and sometimes less? The savage knows what he does in order to get his daily food and which institutions serve him in this pursuit. The increasing intellectualization and rationalization do *not,* therefore, indicate an increased and general knowledge of the conditions under which one lives.

> It means something else, namely, the knowledge or belief that if one but wished one could learn it at any time. Hence, it means that principally [in principle] there are no mysterious incalculable forces that come into play, but rather that one can, in principle, master all things by calculation. This means that the world is disenchanted. One need no longer have recourse to magical means in order to master or implore the spirits, as did the savage, for whom such mysterious powers existed. Technical means and calculations perform the service. This above all is what intellectualization means.

If one asks what makes the streetcar's complicated mechanism intelligible—even if it is not actually understood by those who ride it—the answer would seem to be that its operation can be comprehended, at least in principle, because the streetcar itself was made by human beings acting in accordance with a plan and on the basis of known scientific principles. The same is true of the monetary system and the exchange process; these, too, are the products of purposeful human action, of many human beings acting in deliberately coordinated, though not necessarily cooperative, ways.

This idea can be extended to other important aspects of modern social life. Legal-rational bureaucracies, for example, administer laws which are acknowledged to be the deliberate creations of human beings; indeed, it is the artificiality of these laws—the fact that they have been intentionally posited or promulgated—which establishes their validity and grounds the authority of those who administer them. Similarly, the method of juristic analysis that Weber considered most developed from a purely rational point of view treats the legal significance of events as a human artifact, a product of the various meanings that different individuals assign to them rather than an intrinsic characteristic of the events themselves. In an analogous fashion, the Judeo-Christian conception of ethical personality and the contemporary (Weberian) form of existentialism inspired by it view the human soul itself as something that must be formed in accordance with a plan and that possesses meaning and value only insofar as it displays a deliberately imposed shape of this sort. Finally, even the modern capitalist economy may be viewed as a human artifact to the extent that it rests upon a network of voluntary, purposive contracts rather than prescriptive status relationships thought to be part of a fixed, natural order. Whether one is describing the nature of political authority, the forms of legal interpretation, the meaning of religious ideals or the structure of economic life, the beliefs and institutions that define modern European civilization all rest upon the idea implicit in Weber's streetcar example, the idea that what appears to confront the individual as a given datum (his material circumstances, his political, legal and economic relationships and even his own soul) is in reality a human invention, something that has been deliberately created or arranged by human beings and which therefore belongs to the world of artifacts. It is its artificiality that makes modern social life comprehensible; we can understand its institutions, despite their complexity, because they have been constructed by human beings for reasons or purposes we ourselves can grasp and that need only be recalled for the institutions to become intelligible.

In **'Science as a Vocation',** Weber contrasts our world—characterized, he claims, by an 'increasing intellectualization and rationalization' of life in all its departments—with the world of the savage, a world filled with 'mysterious incalculable forces' that must be implored by 'magical means'. If the rationalism of our world is ultimately attributable to the fact that our tools, techniques and institutions are all purposeful human inventions (and known to be such), the mysterious forces that haunt the world of the savage reflect a condition which is just the opposite of this: these forces are mysterious, in some ultimate sense, because they present themselves to the savage as a fateful datum. The powers that confront the savage are not of his own making; they are, in his own eyes, inhuman powers belonging to the world as it is revealed to him in experience, a *locus* of independent forces. Although it is possible for the savage to achieve (or believe he has achieved) some measure of control over these powers by means of various magical techniques, the control they yield is always tenuous and incomplete, and often entirely illusory. In the final analysis, the limited efficacy of the savage's magic is to be explained by the fact that it aims to control a foreign power, a power that can never be completely understood, even in principle, because—unlike a streetcar or the modern system of economic exchange—it is not itself the product of purposeful human action.

This basic characteristic is reflected in each of the institutions and modes of thought (political, legal, religious and economic) that Weber associates, in a general way, with pre-modern society. All forms of traditional authority, for example, rest on the assumption that social norms, far from being human artifacts, belong to a permanently fixed order and form part of an uncreated, preexisting world in which individuals are assigned a place by the fateful circumstances of their birth. In this view, relations of domination are unalterable facts of life, like the characteristics of age and sexual identity on which they rest. To the extent that pre-modern forms of economic activity are carried on within the framework of a household (whether large or small) and are oriented toward the satisfaction of traditionally stereotyped, statusbased needs, the same can be said of them as well: the circumstances and goals of all such activities appear to those engaged in them to be conditions fixed by nature or God or immemorial custom rather than the product of a deliberately established economic scheme of the kind every purposive contract might be said to constitute.

The same is true in the legal sphere. Primitive or magical forms of adjudication are not subject to intellectual control. The judgment of an oracle, unaccompanied by supporting reasons, is a fateful decree which men, with their limited powers of comprehension, must accept but can never understand. Only when human beings assume the role played by divine powers in all oracular forms of lawmaking and begin giving reasons for their decisions—thereby transforming legal judgments into human artifacts—can the adjudicatory process itself be subjected to intellectual control and in this sense rationalized.

The world of the savage, of the traditional master, of magic and oracular adjudication is above all else a world of *fateful* events and relationships. It is the idea of fate—of what is given to men as a fixed condition of their existence—that best expresses the central, defining quality of this world, a world that provides a home for man and yet confronts him as a fate or destiny rather than the product of his own purposeful activity. In this world, even his most human achievements—the social arrangements under which he lives—belong to a comprehensive, unbroken and unalterable natural order. By contrast, wherever man turns today, he sees only himself, only the artifacts of his own creative industry; today we live in a world that has been humanized and in this sense disenchanted.

The disenchantment of the world, the result of an historical process that 'has continued to exist in occidental culture for millenia', reflects the revolutionary change in perspective produced by the view that human society is an artifact rather than a fateful datum. Only when social relationships and institutions are viewed in this way do they lose their mysteriousness and become fully comprehensible, at least in principle. The social world in which we live today is transparent to reason because it is our own human creation: as Hobbes observed, a scientific understanding of the organization of society is possible precisely because society is itself a human artifact—

something of which we are, in his words, both the matter and the maker. It is this Hobbesian thought—echoed in the writings of many other philosophers including Vico, Kant, Hegel and Marx—that underlies Weber's conception of the 'modern occidental form' of rationality and the age-old 'process of disenchantment' that has defined the historically unique career of Western culture.

Anyone familiar with Weber's writings knows, however, that his view of modernity was more complex and ambiguous than what I have said might suggest. The ambiguity in Weber's conception of modernity is most strikingly revealed by his paradoxical assertion that the very process of rationalization which has produced the belief that 'one can, in principle, master all things by calculation', itself represents a fateful destiny. In **'Science as a Vocation',** Weber speaks of the *'fate'* of scientific work, reminds us of the 'fundamental fact' that we are *'destined* to live in a godless and prophetless' age and warns that 'it is weakness not to be able to countenance the stern seriousness of our *fateful* times.' The 'tremendous cosmos of the modern economic order' itself represents an 'iron cage' whose construction has been decreed by 'fate', the same 'inescapable fate' that underlies the 'sober fact of universal bureaucratization' in the political sphere. This idea runs, like an undercurrent, through all of Weber's writings: modernity means enlightenment and greatly enhanced possibilities for human control, but it also means the increasing domination of fateful forces, among which he includes reason itself.

Weber's emphasis on the fatefulness of modernity is indeed paradoxical. Fate means: what is inexplicable and cannot be controlled; but since Weber himself equates reason with control (control in principle), it is difficult to understand how reason can itself be a fate, how the process of rationalization can be regarded as one that, in some sense or other, is beyond our individual and collective powers of control. To the extent the disenchantment of the world has unleashed forces that today dominate us as a fate, it cannot be said to have unambiguously increased the rationality of social life. When Weber says that 'the fate of our times is characterized by rationalization and intellectualization and, above all, by the "disenchantment of the world"', he implies that the rationalization is less complete or unqualified than it might seem, that the modern world is dominated by peculiar irrationalities of its own—different, to be sure, from those that conditioned the magical experience of the savage or the traditional world of the Abrahamite peasant who 'stood in the organic cycle of life', but equally beyond human comprehension and control. What did Weber believe these peculiarly modern irrationalities to be?

FATE AND THE LOSS OF AUTONOMY

This question is more difficult than might appear. The reason for the difficulty is that Weber uses the concept of fate to describe two quite different aspects of the rationalization process. Each use in turn suggests a particular critique of modern social life, but these critiques are

themselves different and indeed antithetical. Weber's insistence on the fatefulness of reason thus has an ambiguity of meaning which reveals an underlying ambivalence in his attitude toward the most basic features of modern European civilization.

The first of the two meanings that Weber gives to the concept of fate is most clearly revealed in those passages in which he describes the 'substantially irrational' consequences of modern capitalism—in particular, the enervating system of shop discipline imposed by capitalist entrepreneurs in an effort to achieve a 'maximum of formal rationality in capital accounting'.

> No special proof is necessary to show that military discipline is the ideal model for the modern capitalist factory, as it was for the ancient plantation. However, organizational discipline in the factory has a completely rational basis. With the help of suitable methods of measurement, the optimum profitability of the individual worker is calculated like that of any material means of production. On this basis, the American system of 'scientific management' triumphantly proceeds with its rational conditioning and training of work performances, thus drawing the ultimate conclusions from the mechanization and discipline of the plant. The psychophysical apparatus of man is completely adjusted to the demands of the outer world, the tools, the machines—in short, it is functionalized, and the individual is shorn of his natural rhythm as determined by his organism; in line with the demands of the work procedure, he is attuned to a new rhythm through the functional specialization of muscles and through the creation of an optimal economic of physical effort. This whole process of rationalization, in the factory as elsewhere, and especially in the bureaucratic state machine, parallels the centralization of the material implements of organization in the hands of the master. Thus, discipline inexorably takes over ever larger areas as the satisfaction of political and economic needs is increasingly rationalized. This universal phenomenon more and more restricts the importance of charisma and of individually differentiated conduct.

This passage has a sharply critical tone—could have come from Marx's *Paris Manuscripts*—and it seems clear that Weber considers the 'functional specialization' of the human animal in accordance with the work requirements of the modern factory to be one of the most costly consequences of the capitalist system of production. What is not made clear is why the growth of discipline associated with the rationalization of the production process should be viewed as anything more than a cost that must be incurred to obtain the benefits, such as increased material prosperity, that capitalism offers—a price it is arguably rational to pay so long as the benefits of capitalism outweigh its costs. Weber at times seems to imply that the deliberate mechanization of the human worker in the capitalist factory is substantively irrational because it imposes costs on the worker that are not taken into account in calculating the overall profitability of the enterprise. If that were so, however, the irrationality of shop discipline could be eliminated by making its costs explicit, and by deciding whether the harm it does to the 'psychophysical apparatus' of the individual worker is justified by the increase in productivity and consequent rise in material well-being that such discipline makes possible.

There is, however, a second and more troubling sense in which capitalist shop discipline is irrational. The defining characteristic of modern capitalism is its high degree of calculability, and calculability implies control. Although it can never eliminate all risk or contingency, increased calculability reduces the mysteriousness of economic life by permitting its most fundamental processes—the production and exchange of goods—to be deliberately designed and monitored by human beings. One consequence of capitalist discipline, however, is a loss of control on the part of workers. Above all else, factory discipline means a loss of autonomy for the individual worker, a reduction in his ability to control the conditions of his own employment. This follows inevitably from the entrepreneur's effort to maximize the profitability of his enterprise by adjusting the 'apparatus' of his human workers to the demands of the inanimate objects on and by means of which they perform their various functions. In a capitalist factory, workers are required to sacrifice their own psychophysical independence and to subordinate themselves to the inhuman rhythm of the machine (which Weber elsewhere describes as 'mind objectified'). For the capitalist worker, the machine is a kind of fate to which he must deliver himself—even though, for the entrepreneur, it represents a powerful instrument of control. To achieve maximum control over his own enterprise, a capitalist factory owner must impose a discipline on his workers that deprives them of the control they would otherwise have over the conditions of their employment and even their own selves. Shop discipline is substantively irrational in the sense that it requires some to give up their self-control so that others may increase theirs. Describing its consequences in this way underscores the extent to which the regimentation of factory life represents a departure from the rationalizing tendencies of capitalism as a whole.

It is possible to view the distributional effects of capitalist production in a similar light. A modern capitalist exchange economy rests upon a complex web of purposive contracts. The utilities that are exchanged in an economy of this sort are transferred through the free agreement of the parties—not in satisfaction of status-based obligations of service and support, as was often the case in the past. Weber emphasizes, in particular, the freedom of the capitalist labour contract: before he can appropriate the labour of his workers, a factory owner must contract for the right to do so by entering an agreement which they are, in theory, entirely free to reject. The contractual freedom that an individual today enjoys in defining his economic relationships with others significantly increases his power of control, his ability to determine, for himself, the interests and even the way of life he shall pursue.

This increase in control may, however, lose much of its meaning if an individual lacks the material resources to make his decisions effective, if his choices are in a practical sense narrowly limited because he can afford to make only a few of them. 'The great variety of permitted contractual schemata and the formal empowerment to set the content of contracts in accordance with one's desires and independently of all official form patterns, in and of itself by no means makes sure that these formal possibilities will in fact be available to all and everyone. Such availability is prevented above all by the differences in the distribution of property as guaranteed by law.'

These differences render pointless, for some, the very freedom on which the capitalist order is predicated. Like the intensified discipline of the capitalist factory, the inequalities in wealth created and sustained by the principle of effective demand—'the ability of those who are more plentifully supplied with money to outbid the others'—entail a loss of control for the disadvantaged. For those who lack the resources to 'make use of [their legal] empowerments', this loss of control transforms the formal freedom of contractual association on which the capitalist order is based into an 'iron cage' that guarantees the preservation of existing disparities in wealth.

In the concluding paragraph of the *Rechtssoziologie,* Weber describes the analogous loss of control that has resulted from the rationalization of the legal order.

> Whatever form law and legal practice may come to assume under the impact of these various influences [Weber has just concluded a discussion of the 'anti-formal tendencies' in modern law] it will be inevitable that, as a result of technical and economic developments, the legal ignorance of the layman will increase. The use of jurors and similar lay judges will not suffice to stop the continuous growth of the technical elements in the law and hence of its character as a specialists' domain. Inevitably, the notion must expand that the law is a rational technical apparatus, which is continually transformable in the light of expediential considerations and devoid of all sacredness of content. This fate may be obscured by the tendency of acquiescence in the existing law, which is growing in many ways for several reasons, but it cannot really be stayed. All of the modern sociological and philosophical analyses, many of which are of a high scholarly value, can only contribute to strengthen this impression, regardless of the content of their theories concerning the nature of law and the judicial process.

According to Weber, 'the notion must expand that the law is a rational technical apparatus', a tool for achieving certain social, political and economic ends that have been chosen on the basis of 'expediential considerations'. He implicitly contrasts this instrumental conception of law with one that ascribes a sacred meaning of some sort to the legal order: modern law is 'devoid of all sacredness of content', and tends increasingly to be viewed as a tool whose value depends entirely on its success in furthering whatever extra-legal goals we happen to have set for ourselves. In this respect, it resembles the 'fully developed bureaucratic apparatus', a form of administration that enjoys a 'purely *technical* superiority' over every other and 'compares with other organizations exactly as does the machine with the non-mechanical modes of production'.

What this instrumental conception of law expresses, above all else, is the belief that law is a deliberately created artifact, a human invention designed for human ends. Before it can come to be viewed in this way, however, the legal order must be disenchanted and this requires that law be conceived as a product of human legislation. The instrumentalism that predominates today thus presupposes the acceptance of a positivistic conception of law. Acceptance of this idea is also critical to the growth of 'the technical elements in the law and hence of its character as a specialists' domain'. A science of law is possible only if the principles that underlie the legal order—that determine its general structure and define the relationship between its parts—are fully accessible to human understanding. The principles in question can attain this kind of intelligibility, however, only on one condition—that they are themselves conceived, in a positivistic fashion, as rules deliberately formulated by human beings and intentionally employed by them in the construction of the legal order. Modern law resembles Weber's streetcar; we all know that it is fully intelligible in principle and accept the idea of a science of law even though its actual workings are unfamiliar to us. This is because the law is our own human creation. By contrast, primitive law is filled with the same mysterious forces that dominate other aspects of pre-modern life, forces that cannot be mastered except by 'recourse to magical means'. The elaborate techniques of dispute resolution that Weber associates with primitive law are in reality a species of magic which lacks the one distinguishing characteristic of all true science—intellectual control. Primitive law, like primitive life in general, must reckon with 'incalculable forces' that exceed human powers of comprehension; only after these forces have been banished and the responsibility for law-making assumed by human beings, can the legal order be subjected, even in principle, to intellectual control. And only after such control has been achieved can the law be treated as a 'rational technical apparatus' administered by experts in a scientific fashion.

The rationalization of the law has undoubtedly increased the control we have over our own social life. At the same time, however, it has also inevitably increased 'the legal ignorance of the layman', thereby strengthening his dependency on specialists. Legal specialists, in the broadest sense, are a universal phenomenon and have played a role of some sort in every legal system of which we are aware (including even the most primitive ones). Today, however, legal specialists play a larger and more significant role than they have in the past; indeed, Weber describes the increasing importance of legal experts as a 'fate' that 'cannot really be stayed'. For the non-expert,

this development entails a loss of control. To an ever greater degree, the layman today requires the assistance of a legal specialist in arranging his personal and commercial affairs, and since he is often not in a position to evaluate, even on purely instrumental grounds, the advice he has been given, he is frequently forced to rely on his legal counsellor for advice of a more substantive nature concerning the ends he ought to set for himself—the things he should care about and strive to attain. In this way, the growing dependence of the layman on legal experts threatens his autonomy in a critical respect by limiting his ability to determine, for himself, the goals that give his conduct direction and meaning.

The transformation of the law into a 'technically rational apparatus' has therefore had the same paradoxical result as the rationalization of other aspects of modern life. We no longer regard the legal order as a medium in which incomprehensible powers declare themselves and determine our destinies, but view it, instead, as a powerful tool for the advancement of human ends, as a device for expanding the deliberate control we exercise over our own social arrangements. At the same time, however, the rationalization of the law has limited individual autonomy by subjecting the layman to an increasing dependence on legal specialists—a consequence that parallels the similar loss of autonomy in the capitalist factory and modern bureaucratic organization (which Weber describes, in a remarkable passage, as a form of 'objectified intelligence' that 'together with the inanimate machine . . . is busy fabricating the shell of bondage which men will perhaps be forced to inhabit some day, as powerless as the fellahs of ancient Egypt'). The modern legal order, too, represents a 'shell of bondage', an 'iron cage' in which the individual's power of self-control is increasingly limited by the continuous and irreversible growth of 'the technical elements in the law'—a process that resembles (indeed, is merely one aspect of) the 'irresistible advance of bureaucratization' characteristic of modern political and economic life.

Weber describes the increasing 'legal ignorance of the layman' and his growing dependence on experts in the same way that he describes the progress of bureaucratic organization and market-oriented capitalism—as a 'fate'. In this way, he draws our attention to what he considered their common and most paradoxical feature, the fact that in each case men find the control they are able to exercise over their lives increasingly limited by institutions of their own making. In the past, the control a man had over his life was narrowly bounded by forces that were, or were experienced as being, inhuman in character and origin. Today, by contrast, the forces that constrain the individual and limit his power to determine for himself the kind of life he shall have are, to a degree previously unimaginable, forces that have been deliberately created and set in motion by human beings. It is this fact, more than any other, which distinguishes the special fatefulness of modern society. We live in a world dominated by institutions that we ourselves have made, yet which imprison us in an 'iron cage'. We have, in short, constructed our own 'shell of bondage', a shell whose permanence and indestructability are only enhanced by the fact that it is 'as austerely rational as a machine'. It is the paradox of this self-imposed unfreedom that Weber often appears to have in mind when he speaks of the fatefulness of the process of intellectualization which has liberated mankind from the 'mysterious incalculable forces' that have hitherto dominated his existence—but only by substituting for them a prison of his own construction. A man found the Archimedian point, Kafka says in a parable, but used it against himself; he was permitted to find it only on this condition.

FATE AND THE DECLINE OF LEADERSHIP

In 1917, near the end of his life, Weber wrote a long and revealing essay with the title, **'Parliament and Government in a Reconstructed Germany'**. The essay is in large part devoted to specific political problems facing Germany at the time. It also contains, however, some of Weber's most general observations regarding the nature of modern society and, in particular, the rationalization of political life produced by what he terms 'the irresistible advance of bureaucratization'. At one point in the essay, a question is raised concerning the character of leadership in bureaucratic organizations. According to Weber the bureaucratization of party politics and of the state's administrative machinery has meant the 'elimination of political talent' and the gradual weakening of those institutions, such as parliamentary government, which in the past have encouraged responsible political leadership and nurtured its development. Similarly, in the economic sphere, the exercise of genuine entrepreneurial leadership has been made increasingly difficult by the rationalization of the firm—a result that Weber believed would only be exacerbated by the nationalization of economic resources under a programme of state socialism. In both realms, 'the directing mind or "moving spirit"'—the politician in one case and entrepreneur in the other—has been replaced by the bureaucratic official with his characteristic 'civil-service' mentality.

> The difference [between the bureaucrat and the leader] is rooted only in part in the kind of performance expected. Independent decision-making and imaginative organizational capabilities in matters of detail are usually also demanded of the bureaucrat, and very often expected even in larger matters. The idea that the bureaucrat is absorbed in subaltern routine and that only the 'director' performs the interesting, intellectually demanding tasks is a preconceived notion of the literati and only possible in a country that has no insight into the matter in which its affairs and the work of its officialdom are conducted. The difference lies, rather, in the kind of *responsibility*, and this does indeed determine the different demands addressed to both kinds of positions. An official who receives a directive which he considers wrong can and is supposed to object to it. If his superior insists on its execution, it is his duty and even his honour to carry it out as if it corresponded to his innermost conviction and to demonstrate in this fashion that

his sense of duty stands above his personal preference. It does not matter whether the imperative mandate originates from an 'agency', a 'corporate body' or an 'assembly'. This is the ethos of *office*. A political leader acting in this way would deserve contempt. He will often be compelled to make compromises, that means, to sacrifice the less important to the more important. If he does not succeed in demanding of his master, be he a monarch or the people: 'You either give me now the authorization I want from you, or I will resign,' he is a miserable *Kleber* [one who sticks to his post]—as Bismarck called this type—and not a leader. 'To be above parties'—in truth, to remain outside the realm of the struggle for power—is the official's role, while this struggle for personal power, and the resulting personal responsibility, is the lifeblood of the politician as well as of the entrepreneur.

According to Weber, the increasing rationalization of social life threatens to bring about a uniform 'domination by the "bureaucratic spirit" to the disadvantage of real leaders', leaders with 'political ambition and the will to power and responsibility'. Instead of such leaders one finds bureaucratic office-holders, men who possess the expertise required to implement political and economic programmes, but whose 'mentality' or 'spirit' prevents them from exercising genuine leadership. 'If a man in a leading position is an "official" in the spirit of his performance, no matter how qualified—a man, that is, who works dutifully and honourably according to the rules and instruction—then he is as useless at the helm of a private enterprise as of a government.' The rule of officials, of professional civil servants who have neither the desire nor the strength to be held personally accountable for their decisions, 'unavoidably increases in correspondence with the rational technology of modern life'; in this sense, the increasing dominance of the 'civil-service mentality of the official' is an inevitable consequence of 'the irresistible advance of bureaucratization', a process that itself represents the 'unambiguous yardstick for the modernization of the state'.

This is the second sense in which Weber uses the concept of fate: it is our fate to live in a world in which responsible leadership, of any sort, is increasingly rare. The very conditions that today promote the intellectualization of social life discourage all forms of leadership except those based upon a mass following whose trust and faith have been won through popular demagoguery, a type of leadership that in Weber's view is 'always exposed to direct, purely emotional and irrational influence' and whose basic tendency is to frustrate, rather than promote, the formation of consistent, continuous and—above all else—responsible political programmes. Today, according to Weber, our public life is dominated by the apolitical bureaucrat and the irresponsible caesarist demagogue; this is our fate and we must struggle, as best we can, to preserve a few remnants of responsible leadership while recognizing that in doing so we set ourselves against a centuries-old process of rationalization that only the naïve can hope to reverse. Even socialism is subject to these same rationalizing forces: although 'a progressive elimination of private capitalism is theoretically possible', the abolition of capitalism would not mean 'the destruction of the steel frame of modern industrial work', but only 'that also the *top management* of the nationalized or socialized enterprises would become bureaucratic.'

Why is the spirit of true leadership, as Weber conceives it, necessarily antithetical to the mentality of the bureaucratic official? Weber's fullest answer is to be found in his essay, **'Politics as a Vocation',** where he gives a detailed account of the personal qualities required in a political leader. There are, he says, 'three pre-eminent qualities [which] are decisive for the politician: passion, a feeling of responsibility, and a sense of proportion.' A leader must first of all have passion: unlike the bureaucratic official, he must be passionately devoted to a cause, and to 'the god or demon who is its overlord'. The 'proper vocation' of the bureaucrat is 'impartial administration'. He is therefore forbidden to do 'precisely what the politician, the leader as well as his following, must always and necessarily do, namely, *fight*. To take a stand, to be passionate—*ira et studium*—is the politician's element, and above all the element of the political *leader*.'

The passion that distinguishes the true political leader from the bureaucrat is not, however, a 'sterile excitation, a "romanticism of the intellectually interesting", running into emptiness devoid of all feeling of objective responsibility.' No matter how strongly it is felt, mere passion 'does not make a politician, unless passion as devotion to a "cause" also makes responsibility to this cause the guiding star of action.' In this respect, the conduct of the politician

> is subject to quite a different, indeed, exactly the opposite, principle of responsibility from that of the civil servant. The honour of the civil servant is vested in his ability to execute conscientiously the order of the superior authorities, exactly as if the order agreed with his own conviction. This holds even if the order appears wrong to him and if, despite the civil servant's remonstrances, the authority insists on the order. Without this moral discipline and self-denial, in the highest sense, the whole apparatus would fall to pieces. The honour of the political leader, of the leading statesman, however, lies precisely in an exclusive *personal* responsibility for what he does, a responsibility he cannot and must not reject or transfer.

To feel a responsibility of this sort, however, a politician needs the third of the three qualities that Weber identifies—a sense of proportion.

> This is the decisive psychological quality of the politician: his ability to let realities work upon him with inner concentration and calmness. Hence his *distance* to things and men. 'Lack of distance' *per se* is one of the deadly sins of every politician. It is one of those qualities the breeding of which will condemn the progeny of our intellectuals to

political incapacity. For the problem is simply how can warm passion and a cool sense of proportion be forged together in one and the same soul? Politics is made with the head, not with other parts of the body or soul. And yet devotion to politics, if it is not to be frivolous intellectual play but rather genuinely human conduct, can be born and nourished from passion alone. However, that firm taming of the soul, which distinguishes the passionate politician and differentiates him from the 'sterilely excited' and mere political dilettante, is possible only through habituation to detachment in every sense of the word . . . Therefore, daily and hourly the politician inwardly has to overcome a quite trivial and all-too-human enemy: a quite vulgar vanity, the deadly enemy of all matter-of-fact devotion to a cause, and of all distance, in this case, of distance towards one's self.

Only if he overcomes his vanity by maintaining a distance towards himself can the politician avoid the constant danger 'of becoming an actor as well as taking lightly the responsibility for the outcome of his actions and of being concerned merely with the "impression" he makes.' Vanity, and the lack of objectivity that it encourages, 'tempts [the politician] to strive for the glamourous semblance of power rather than for actual power', an attitude which represents, in Weber's words, a 'sin against the lofty spirit of his vocation'.

> Although, or rather just because, power is the unavoidable means, and striving for power is one of the driving forces of all politics, there is no more harmful distortion of political force than the parvenu-like braggart with power, and the vain self-reflection in the feeling of power, and in general every worship of power *per se*. The mere 'power politician' may get strong effects, but his work leads nowhere and is senseless.

For the work of the politician to have any meaning at all, it must be continuously informed by a conception of the programme or goal in whose service he places himself; the true politician, according to Weber, will always be prepared to sacrifice his own interests for the sake of his cause, in a spirit of passionate detachment. To do this, however, a man must be 'not only a leader but a hero as well, in a very sober sense of the word . . . Only he has the calling for politics who is sure that he shall not crumble when the world from his point of view is too stupid or too base for what he wants to offer. Only he who in the face of all this can say "In spite of all!" has the calling for politics.'

The intensity of his commitment and the courage he displays in maintaining his 'sense of proportion'—his distance from men and things and even himself—distinguish the experience and conduct of a leader from that of a mere dilettante and set him apart from those who do not have a calling for politics. This fact is of utmost importance: it is not the substance or content of the goal he has chosen for himself that makes someone a leader—a politician, according to Weber, 'may serve national, humanitarian, social, ethical, cultural, worldly or religious ends'—but the spirit in which he makes his choice and attempts to implement it. The politician not only has a goal, he is passionately devoted to it; and he pursues his goal while struggling against the temptations of vanity—which requires the courage and strength of character to keep his own human impulses at a distance.

To make a choice or commit oneself to a cause is not necessarily to do so with passion and courage; these are qualities that any particular commitment, whether shortlived or longlasting, may or may not possess. Since courage and passion are qualities that do not accompany every choice, they must owe their existence to some aspect of a person's character—some part of his soul—other than the will, understood simply as the power of affirming or disaffirming, the power of saying 'yes' to one thing and 'no' to another. Every choice necessarily involves the exercise of this power, but for a choice to possess the special qualities that distinguish a genuine leader's commitment to his cause from the 'sterile excitation' of the political dilettante, something more is required. Courage and passion are qualities that must be brought *to* the choices we make and although it is by no means clear where these qualities come from or how they are to be summoned, there is nothing in the simple act of choice itself that determines their existence or non-existence. The true politician is distinguished by the fact that he is able, for whatever reasons, to draw upon powers in his soul quite different from the general capacity, which he shares in common with other men, for making choices and setting ends. What is decisive, in this respect, is a 'trained relentlessness in viewing the realities of life, and the ability to face such realities and to measure up to them inwardly.' He who possesses this ability is, in Weber's phrase, a '*mature* man' (whether he is young or old in a chronological sense), and it is this quality that we find 'genuinely human and moving' in the actions of such an individual when, with a full sense of responsibility for the consequences of his conduct, he 'reaches the point where he says: "Here I stand; I can do no other."'

The qualities that Weber emphasizes in describing the prerequisites for responsible political leadership—the leader's passionate devotion to his cause, and his courageous self-discipline in maintaining a sense of proportion by resisting the distorting influence of ordinary human vanity—are present either not at all or in a much altered form in the ideal bureaucrat. The perfect bureaucrat, the one who fully lives up to the demands of his vocation, executes his duties with complete impassivity and in a spirit of disinterested neutrality. In contrast to the politician, the bureaucrat strives to eliminate all passion from his work since passion is a personalizing force—passion is the feeling we have for those things that matter to us personally—and it is the bureaucrat's fundamental responsibility to administer the law without regard to his own personal concerns (as distinct from the objective requirements of the legal order, as he conceives them). A genuine politician, on the other hand, identifies in a personal sense with his own programme—it is *his* cause and he takes responsibility for it.

Weber recognizes that the civil servant's tasks, like the politician's, sometimes requires 'moral discipline and self-denial'—as, for example, when he is asked to execute an order that he considers wrong and nevertheless strives to do so 'exactly as if the order agreed with his own conviction'. But the courage required of a politician is different and more demanding, for a politician must be prepared to do something that no bureaucrat need ever do, at least in the performance of his official duties: he must ask others to make sacrifices in order to further a cause for which he alone is personally accountable. Every politician, if he aspires to genuine leadership, must accept the terrible burden this implies, a burden far greater than that associated with even the most extreme acts of *self*-sacrifice. The need for courage cannot be avoided in the struggles of political life; a bureaucrat, by contrast, is not required to be a hero in Weber's sense in order to perform his task (although his work, like that of anyone with a principled vocation, may give him an opportunity to display a heroic devotion to his calling).

There is, however, another and even more fundamental difference between the political leader and the bureaucrat. According to Weber, modern bureaucratic organization 'has usually come into power on the basis of a leveling of social and economic differences', and inevitably accompanies '*mass democracy*'. The leveling tendencies of bureaucratic administration and its close connection with modern mass democracy derive from what Weber calls its 'characteristic principle'—the 'abstract regularity of the exercise of authority, which is a result of the demand for "equality before the law" in the personal and functional sense . . .' When a civil servant issues a command or makes a decision, he does so not in his own name, but in the name of the law; the authority he claims for his official acts is independent of any personal quality he himself happens to possess. Both the bureaucrat issuing an order and the person to whom the order is issued are bound by the system of 'intentionally established' norms that justify the command in question; these norms constitute, in Weber's phrase, an 'impersonal order' to which even the person exercising authority is subject.

Officeholder and private citizen owe obedience to this impersonal legal order only insofar as its rules have been deliberately established by an organization of which each is a member. In their capacity as members of such an organization, the bureaucrat exercising authority and the person subject to his command are 'equals before the law'. Leadership, by contrast, is importantly non-egalitarian. The 'warm passion' and 'cool sense of proportion' that must be 'forged together in one and the same soul' if a man is to be a responsible leader—if he is, in Weber's words, 'to be allowed to put his hand on the wheel of history'—are qualities that are not distributed equally among men. Men differ in the extent to which they possess the 'preeminent qualities' needed for political leadership and hence in their ability to live up to the demands of politics; only he who is able to combine passion and courage in the way Weber suggests can sustain his commitment in the face of the world's stupidity and preserve a sense of responsibility while struggling against both the temptations of vanity and 'the diabolic forces lurking in all violence'. To have a calling for politics, one must have a 'knowledge of [the] tragedy with which all action, but especially political action, is truly interwoven' and be able to act without denying this knowledge or collapsing under its weight. Politics requires an inward strength which only a few men possess and the true leader—the leader who is 'more than a narrow and vain upstart of the moment'—is therefore, in the most literal sense, an *extraordinary* individual, a 'hero . . . in a very sober sense of the word'.

Nothing could be more alien to the leveling democratic spirit of bureaucratic rule with its characteristic principle of equality before the law. A genuine political leader not only reminds us that men are differentially endowed with respect to those personal qualities that are necessary for responsible leadership, he also insists, up to a point, that these same qualities give him the right—a right others do not have—to make demands on himself and his followers. Every true politician, in Weber's sense, feels himself to be an 'innerly "called" leader of men' and finds in this feeling the legitimation for his demand that others, too, make sacrifices on behalf of the cause which is 'the guiding star' of his action. To this extent, all true political leadership has a personal quality that sharply differentiates it from the impersonal authority of the civil servant—indeed, that contradicts the egalitarian premises of bureaucratic rule. 'The devotion of [a leader's] disciples, his followers, his personal party friends is oriented to his person and to its qualities.' This explains why the 'irresistible advance of bureaucratization' poses a threat to the continued exercise of responsible leadership: wherever the bureaucratic spirit prevails, the demands a leader makes on his followers must appear suspect since they are in part legitimated by the possession of extraordinary personal qualities not shared by others. The increasingly bureaucratic world in which we live is a world that has no room for heroes—not for accidental reasons but because bureaucracy itself is predicated upon an egalitarian conception of legitimacy that does not allow us to recognize, as a source of authority, the exceptional personal qualities which all heroism reveals.

The meaning of this last point should perhaps be stated more precisely. To say that our world no longer has room for political heroes does not mean that individual acts of heroism are impossible, but only that we lack confidence in, and to some extent view as illegitimate, the institutions that historically have served as recruiting grounds for political leaders. The very idea of an institution whose fundamental purpose is to foster and reward leadership in Weber's sense must appear suspect from the standpoint of an anti-heroic bureaucratic ethic. According to Weber, the gradual decay of these institutions—in particular, those associated with parliamentary politics—has weakened the conditions necessary for responsible leadership and encouraged a shift in the method of choosing leaders towards what he calls 'the *caesarist* mode of selection', the selection of leaders through mass acclama-

tion achieved by means of demagoguery and tending, at the extreme, to the 'irrational mob rule typical of purely plebiscitary peoples'. To counteract this tendency, which he considered a consequence of 'active mass democratization', Weber argued that faith must be restored in those institutions that in the past have been training grounds for political heroes. This requires, however, that we affirm the value of leadership and hence take a stand against the levelling spirit of bureaucratic rule that increasingly dominates every aspect of our public and private lives. If we do not, we can expect to live in a world divided between the bureaucrat and the plebiscitarian demagogue. This is our fate, a fate that cannot be avoided so long as the responsible heroism which Weber considered the highest form of politics continues to seem an embarrassment from the perspective of the egalitarian ideals that underlie our bureaucratic civilization.

WEBER'S AMBIVALENT CRITIQUE OF MODERNITY

The peculiar rationality of modern European civilization is to be explained by the fact that its political and economic institutions are deliberately created artifacts which are, in principle at least, intelligible to the human beings who have made them. In Weber's view, however, the rationalization of modern society itself represents a kind of fate or destiny. One encounters this idea in each of Weber's works, including the *Rechtssoziologie* (whose final paragraph characterizes the transformation of the legal order into a 'rational technical apparatus' as an inevitable development that 'cannot really be stayed'). Weber's description of the rationalization process as a fateful destiny seems to be a contradiction in terms: reason means understanding and control, while fate implies a domination by uncontrollable powers. How can reason itself be a fate? This is the fundamental question that any reader of Weber is eventually led to ask.

I have attempted to clarify Weber's concept of fate by describing the two different ways in which he uses it. Weber sometimes uses the concept of fate to describe the loss of individual autonomy that has accompanied the rationalization of political, legal and economic life. Today, we live in a self-imposed shell of bondage 'as austerely rational as a machine', with little control over the forces that determine our material opportunities, work conditions and legal status. It is to the paradox of this self-created unfreedom that Weber is sometimes referring when he speaks of the fatefulness of the intellectualization process. However, Weber often uses the idea of fate to describe a different aspect of modern European civilization—the relentless expansion of the 'bureaucratic spirit', with its profoundly anti-heroic ethic and horror of all personal privilege. This, too, represents an irresistible fate, one that means, above all else, the elimination of real leaders with 'political ambition and the will to power and responsibility'.

Each of these two ways of understanding the fatefulness of the rationalization process—as the paradoxical loss of control that has accompanied the triumphal spread of reason itself or as the disappearance of heroes from a bureaucratically levelled world—provides the foundation for a critique of modern society. Although Weber did not develop either critique in a systematic fashion, there are hints—or more accurately, chronic eruptions—of each in his writings. The first of these two critiques is suggested by certain passages in the *Rechtssoziologie* and by his analysis of the substantive irrationalities of modern capitalism. It can be summarized in the following way: The modern legal order is predicated upon the related ideas of freedom and equality. Today, individuals are free to construct their own legal relationships through voluntary contractual arrangements with others, and consider themselves entitled to equal treatment before the law, regardless of their status or class position. However, despite the very extensive formal freedoms which the modern legal order confers on every individual, material circumstances—in particular, the distribution of wealth and the conditions of work—deprive these formal freedoms of their meaning or value. Freedom and equality cannot be realized in a concretely meaningful sense until property has been redistributed and work routines reorganized so as to eliminate, or at least reduce, the disparities of wealth and the inhuman discipline associated with the capitalist system of production. There must therefore be a fundamental alteration in the material conditions under which individuals exercise their formal freedoms if the egalitarian ideal that justifies these freedoms is actually to be achieved.

This first critique, which Weber states sympathetically without ever actually endorsing, is of course most often associated with the Marxist left, which helps to explain why some Marxist writers have regarded Weber as a cautious fellow-traveller, a materialist who could never quite rid himself of his idealist tendencies. However, it is not the Marxist overtones of this first critique that I want to emphasize, but rather its basic acceptance of equality and autonomy as moral ideas. Someone who accepts this first critique believes that redistribution of wealth and abolition of the factory system are necessary to establish conditions under which individual freedom can flourish to a degree not possible in a society based upon market-oriented capitalism. To this extent, advocates of Weber's first critique embrace the ideal of individual autonomy and disagree with apologists for the existing order only in maintaining that material conditions must be rearranged if a meaningful degree of autonomy is to be secured for everyone. The capacity for autonomous action that will be liberated by a change in material conditions is one that every man possesses and has an equal right to exercise, subject to a similar right in others. Because it celebrates the notion of autonomy as a moral ideal and endorses an egalitarian conception of society, the first critique of modernity implicit in Weber's writings marks an extension or development, rather than a repudiation, of the normative principles that underlie the modern bureaucratic order at its deepest level.

The same cannot be said for Weber's second critique of modern society. This critique challenges rather than sup-

ports the ideal of impersonal equality and seeks to rehabilitate the legitimacy of personal leadership in a world dominated by the levelling tendencies of bureaucratic rule. The egalitarian ideal on which the bureaucratic order rests is threatened by the appearance of a leader with courage and passion and a sense of responsibility. A true leader feels entitled, by virtue of his own extraordinary qualities, to call on his followers to make the sacrifices he believes they must; nothing could be further from the attitude of the bureaucratic official who seeks, so far as possible, to eliminate everything strictly personal from his dealings with peers and clients and to perform his duties in a spirit of studied passionlessness. The bureaucrat is devoted, above all else, to the principle that every citizen is equal before the law, regardless of the distinctive personal qualities he happens to possess: from the perspective of the ideal bureaucrat, qualities of this sort can never be a basis for the exercise of authority. A leader, on the other hand, is an extraordinary man who demands to be recognized as such and claims the right to rule others on the ground that only he has both the passion and courageous self-discipline required to lead them, in a responsible way, toward the goal he champions. Every genuine leader draws attention—by his actions and the claims he makes on his followers—to those personal qualities that set him apart as a leader of men and that justify, in the eyes of those devoted to him, the often strenuous demands he makes in the name of his cause. Weber's second critique of modern society insists on the need for responsible leadership in political affairs and hence on the necessity of counteracting the growth of a bureaucratic spirit incapable of tolerating the claims to personal authority which the exercise of genuine leadership always entails. The point of this critique is not to emphasize the extent to which the egalitarian ideals of the legal-rational bureaucratic order remain unfulfilled, but to question these ideals themselves in a fundamental respect. To this extent, it represents a deeper or more radical critique of modern society than the first one.

If the first critique of modern society implicit in Weber's writings is broadly suggestive of the criticisms developed by Marx and his followers, the second parallels, in many respects, the critique of modern society that Nietzsche offers, especially in his later writings. Weber's account of political leadership in **'Politics as a Vocation'** reminds one of many similar passages in Nietzsche's own writings and his deliberate use of Nietzschean phrases seems calculated to draw attention to the similarity in their views. In his account of political leadership, Weber stresses the same personal qualities that Nietzsche does—courage, passion, self-discipline, a heightened sense of responsibility, a distance from oneself and the world—and emphasizes (again, as Nietzsche does) the rarity of these qualities and the anti-democratic consequences of treating their possession as a justification for the exercise of authority. Anyone who accepts the democratic principle of equal respect for persons—as the bureaucratic official and Marxist critic of modern society both do—will reject and perhaps even regard as offensive Weber's limited endorsement of Nietzsche's ideas. Similarly, anyone who is sympathetic to Nietzsche's critique of modern society, as Weber obviously was, will dismiss the Marxist programme of reconstructing the material foundations of society in order to achieve a fuller and more meaningful freedom for everyone as a symptom of our disease rather than its cure.

Between these two positions, and the different critiques of modern society they imply, no reconciliation is possible since one embraces egalitarian ideals while the other challenges them. That Weber, at least in a limited and tentative way, adopted both positions reflects an ambivalence in his own attitude toward modern society and the process of rationalization that he took to be its defining characteristic. Weber was by no means a spokesman for the virtues of contemporary European civilization, despite the fact that he made its institutions the point of departure for all his sociological and historical investigations and devoted a lifetime to explaining their development and meaning. But the two criticisms of modernity implicit in his writings—to which his frequent, indeed obsessive, use of the idea of fate provides an important clue—point in different directions and express fundamentally different attitudes toward the egalitarian ideal associated with formal legal rationality and bureaucratic rule. There is, in this regard, something in Weber's writings that can almost be described as an intellectual (or moral) schizophrenia, an oscillation between irreconcilable perspectives that helps to explain why he has found supporters as well as detractors on both the Left and Right.

Whether these two critiques of modernity are justifiable and if so, how one is to choose between them, are questions that lie beyond the limits of this book. In concluding, I shall attempt only to close the circle of my argument by clarifying the connection between the ideas developed in this chapter and the main themes of the book as a whole.

I have called Weber's theory of value positivistic in order to underscore his belief that every value is a posit, the product of a deliberate choice or decision on the part of the individual whose value it happens to be. This theory is to be contrasted with all those that ascribe to the world an inherent meaning or value of its own, a value that antedates the choices and commitments of individual human beings. According to Weber, the very concept of value has no meaning apart from the acts of choice that alone generate norms, norms which the objective 'world-process' can never yield. This positivistic theory of value is the one Weber defends in his methodological writings. It also provides the implicit foundation for his discussion of: the three pure types of authority, the nature of formal legal rationality, the forms of contractual association, modern capitalism, and the Judeo-Christian conception of God.

In addition, Weber's theory of value is associated with a particular conception of personhood. I have defended this claim on independent philosophical grounds, but Weber's own writings—for example, his account of the difference between status and purposive contracts and his description of the Judeo-Christian ideal of ethical personality—suggest that he was himself aware of the connection between these ideas. The conception of personhood associated with Weber's positivism gives prominence to the power of choice exercised in every value-creating act; for this reason, I have called it a will-centred conception of personhood. To be a person, to be qualified to participate in the moral life of the species, one must, on this view, be endowed with the power of deliberate choice—with a capacity for purposeful action or action in accordance with the conception of a rule. Only those beings who possess such a capacity are persons, and Weber's own positivistic theory of value implies that no other quality or characteristic of human beings can have an intrinsic worth of its own—as distinct from the worth it acquires by being affirmed or disaffirmed through an act of choice. Because the capacity for purposeful action is a necessary and sufficient condition for personhood and because it is distributed on a species-wide basis, no human being can be more of a person or have a fundamentally different moral status than any other. The concept of personhood associated with Weber's positivistic theory of value is profoundly egalitarian.

Of the two critiques of modern society implicit in Weber's writings, the first, which emphasizes the loss of individual control resulting from the rationalization of social life, is consistent with the will-centred conception of personhood that I have just described. To be sure, Weber's first critique recognizes—indeed, insists upon—the important influence that material conditions (the distribution of wealth, nature of work, etc.) have on the exercise of human freedom; but it also treats the idea of freedom as the standard against which all social arrangements and programmes of reform are to be evaluated from a moral point of view. It is entirely consistent with this view to assert that human beings have the right to be recognized as persons and enjoy the moral status they do—a status that entitles each individual to a real or effective freedom as great as anyone else's—just because they are autonomous beings with a capacity for purposeful action. Indeed, to the extent that it has been defended on philosophical grounds, the first critique of modern society implicit in Weber's work has typically been justified by an appeal to just such a will-centred conception of the person. In any case, even if the critique in question can be defended on other grounds, it is certainly consistent with Weber's own theory of value and the conception of personhood implied by it.

By contrast, Weber's second critique of modernity challenges this conception. The true leader is set apart from other men by virtue of his special personal qualities—his passion, courage and ability to resist the temptations of vanity by maintaining what Weber calls a 'sense of proportion'. Every political leader chooses a goal of some sort as his 'guiding star', but it is not this choice alone that distinguishes him from other men. Rather, it is the spirit in which the choice is made, the special qualities of character that he displays in making his commitment, which set the leader apart. Even if each of us chooses his own values, some do so with greater passion, courage, steadfastness and modesty than others; these are qualities that are not evenly distributed among men, as the capacity for purposeful action, understood in the most general sense, might be said to be. They are therefore qualities that must be thought of as having their foundation in a part of the soul other than the choosing part, the part that establishes a person's value commitments by affirming some norms and disaffirming others, since there is nothing in the exercise of this capacity alone that can account for the difference between heroes or leaders, on the one hand, and ordinary men on the other. In short, every genuine leader is distinguished by personal qualities not shared by other men, qualities that are rooted in or expressive of some part of the soul other than the will, understood in an abstract sense as the faculty of choice.

From the standpoint of the leader, the possession of these qualities is itself a ground or warrant for the exercise of authority: a genuine leader feels entitled to make special demands on his followers because his courage and self-discipline endow him with a sense of responsibility they do not share. This view is incompatible, however, with a will-centred conception of personhood. For someone who believes that the special qualities of the leader give him a right to exercise authority over others, the possession of a capacity for purposeful action can at most be a necessary but not sufficient condition for determining the moral status of an individual—for deciding what he may rightly demand from others and owes them in return. It is also necessary to ask, on this view, whether the individual in question possesses the special qualities of character that set the true leader apart from ordinary men. A leader is justified in doing things that ordinary men are not and in this sense has a status or identity fundamentally different from theirs. It is uncertain what alternative idea of personhood is implied by the acknowledgement of such differences, but Weber's own will-centred conception must either be abandoned or modified in essential respects if one ascribes inherent value to personal qualities, like passion and courage, in the way his notion of responsible leadership invites and perhaps requires.

That such an incompatibility exists does not mean we must reject Weber's positivistic theory of value; it only means that Weber was himself more uncertain in his commitment to this theory and the conception of personhood associated with it than might appear. Weber's uncertainty is reflected in the ambivalence of his critique of modern society, which as we have seen is really two critiques pointing in different directions, only one of which is consistent with a will-centred conception of the person. Weber never confronted the ambivalence in his criticisms of modern society, and we can only guess how he would have responded if he had. Perhaps he would have said that these are questions for a professional philosopher, a title he emphatically denied for himself.

Despite his disclaimer, Weber's writings are informed by a powerful philosophical intelligence, and I have written [*Max Weber*] to clarify the neglected philosophical dimension of his work. Anyone who reflects on Weber's critical account of modern rationalism must eventually confront the questions raised in this chapter. To pursue these questions further, however, would lead us into the domain of moral philosophy. But for those who make the effort, the writings of Max Weber will remain a source of insight and inspiration. No one has thought about these matters on the same scale, or with the same passion as Weber and the fact that his work raises disturbing philosophical questions that it fails to answer is the best proof of his achievement as a philosopher.

Vatro Murvar   (essay date 1983)

SOURCE: "Max Weber Today: An Introduction to a Living Legacy," in *Max Weber Today: An Introduction to a Living Legacy: Selected Bibliography*, Max Weber Colloquia and Sumposia, 1983, pp. 1-30.

[*In the following essay, Murvar discusses major issues in the critical literature on Weber's writings.*]

Max Weber (1864-1920) is generally recognized as one of the major figures in sociological, political and economic theory. Comparisons of his intellectual and scientific legacy with the thought of Machiavelli, Hobbes, Rousseau, Marx, Tocqueville, Keyes and other have been commonplace. Moreover, the extraordinary impact of Weber's interdisciplinary, historical-comparative, however fragmented, achievements has increased to an unprecedented degree as more of his unfinished opus has become available in more adequate translations. In Germany an international academic project is underway to trace the original sequence of his writings in order to reflect more accurately all the aspects of his intellectual growth. It will result in the publication of his restructured collected works. This will hopefully eliminate all the existing confusion not only in relation to the German originals but also especially concerning the numerous carved-out and piece-meal translations in foreign languages.

Today this legacy poses the following questions, which, of course, by the very nature of this type of research cannot be answered at present. How far will this process of recovery and rediscovery extend? What are the consequences of this explosion of interest in Weber? Does it suggest that the growing stature of Weber will challenge or diminish the impact of other major theorists who sharply disagree with his basic methodological and theoretical propositions? Is a synthesis between Weber's theoretical approach and alternative theoretical perspectives possible, or do the contradictions between Weber's legacy and competing perspectives rule out the possibility of a convergence? One can easily imagine some lively controversies generated by the present dominant schools of thought.

If Weber is firmly established as one of the classics, then the frequent fate of the classics is his burden too: elevation on a pedestal, being transformed from a scientifically and intellectually significant living reality into an historical image without contemporary relevance. Ritualistic genuflection before the legitimation-bestowing authority replaces the genuine willingness to take the author seriously. Weber has not entirely escaped this for there are books and articles aplenty in which references to him amount to no more than lip service.

While being often mentioned and seldom read is one of the classics' vicissitudes, another is that of being the subject of a flood of interpretations and reinterpretations. To be sure the line between legitimate and illegitimate variants is not always easy to draw. This difficulty notwithstanding, it can be said that Weber has been misinterpreted with remarkable thoroughness and frequency, moreover, some of the misinterpretations have enjoyed considerable longevity, so much so as to become orthodoxy.

Misinterpretations of his original work can be found in all areas: from epistemology, sociology of knowledge and art, to political and economic sociology, to sociology of law, revolution, religion, and ideology. Some are located within a very specific context involving too many details, the others are popularized as journalistic cliches and political slogans. Most likely every specialist within various areas of Weber's opus has his own list of "favorite" misinterpretations. Only some brief, general and rather oversimplified samples that are naturally confined to the editor's area of interest are presented here.

In the last two decades it has been repeatedly pointed out with documented references by some respected authorities (who are otherwise listened to)

—that Weber's celebrated typology of ruler ship and legitimacy on the whole ought to be utilized as an open-ended scheme and not to be confined to only three types per usual;

—that this typology of rulership can not be analytically separated from the corresponding typology of legitimacy, however, some continue to work only with one while ignoring the other;

—that the concept of bureaucracy in general can not be identified with the legal-rational type as it is commonly done;

—that Weber insisted on the need to differentiate various types of bureaucracy: his considerable writings on bureaucracy analyze hierocratic, patrimonialist, post-revolutionary, post-charismatic, usurpational and other types of bureaucracy and contain frequent references to bureaucratic river- and city-kingdoms;

—that the type of legal-rational bureaucracy can not be identified with the type of modern patrimonialist bureaucracy as it is regularly assumed by the many proponents of various convergence theories and especially those focusing on the Soviet Union;

—that in Weber's opus there are several types of rationality and processes of rationalization (Chinese, Islamic, Japanese, etc.) instead of one type (Western) as it is usually taken for granted;

—that bureaucracy and patrimonialism can not be taken out of context and declared a dichotomy as it is recently being done;

—that neither bureaucracy nor charisma can be taken out of contest and contrasted as if there is nothing else in Weber's entire typology because bureaucracy is one of the major means used by practically all rulerships and, of course, charisma as well as patrimonialism are basic types of rulership and legitimacy;

—that Weber's concept of charisma is not another simplistic great-man-theory of history as it is frequently interpreted and then dismissed, indeed, he duly emphasized extraordinary societal crises as one of the three basic prerequisites for a successful charismatic movement;

—that Weber did not ignore informal actual relationships thereby limiting himself to formal structures only for he wrote several large sections on informal structures/relationships, however, the authors continue with the same unwarranted assumptions.

These commonly held misinterpretations in only one major area illustrate the magnitude of the problem. But above and beyond it, there is a wealth of more complex misconceptions covering several interdependent areas from which only two particular but strikingly different illustrations will suffice here:

First, it has been repeatedly argued (Bendix, Simey, Freund and others) that Weber can *not* by any stretch of imagination be considered an evolutionist, organicist, stage-theorist, etc. Indeed, it was documented that just the opposite is true: he was a consistent and sharp critic of these persistent theoretical trends. Although this has been to no avail. Subsequent publications continue to repeat the very same misconceptions.

Secondly, Weber's approach to and understanding of modern economic structures was early recognized by scholars of divergent persuasions as being scientifically neutral. Alvin Gouldner rejected the assumptions that Weber is "at bottom anti-socialist," and that his views are an ideology, "serviceable for the survival of capitalism". His theories, Gouldner insists, are not an ideology in the first place, but they cut two ways, not one. Weber's position "is not anti-socialist alone nor anti-capitalist alone, it is both. In the final analysis its political slogan becomes 'a plague on both your houses'." Discussing the emergence and disconcerting growth of bureaucracies in modern political machineries, Richard Pipes explains the reasons for Weber's firmness: "Neither capitalism nor socialism was in a position to reverse this trend, since they too were succumbing to bureaucratization." Bureaucracies' persistent undermining and ultimate non-delivery of the ideological programs and goals as a major aspect of excessive rationalization is one of Weber's basic themes. In spite of all this, still today Weber is frequently imputed to defend and apologize for either capitalism or socialism, and according to the writer's value-preference he is then labeled "Marx of the Bourgeoisie," bourgeois ideologist, anti-socialist or socialist, anti-capitalist, the most sophisticated up-to-date Marxist, etc.

It has not been generally appreciated or even noticed that Weber's opus was a torso, and that at least two different sets of reasons account for the alleged incompleteness. His protracted illnesses and then his early death prevented him from executing his projected volumes on political power structures and legitimizing religious doctrines of Talmudic Judaism, Islam before and after the tenth century, and Medieval Catholicism. This is well-known, of course. But also in Weber's opus there are several major theoretical and methodological gaps which were deliberately left open-ended, because in his judgment there was not sufficient evidence at the time to warrant a sound theoretical foreclosure. This is a most significant quality of his work, consistent with his entire intellectual and scientific legacy, however, it is not sufficiently appreciated as such. Thus the potentially enormous resources of sociological, political science, and economic theory in Weber's open-ended and incomplete opus remained largely unexplored and unexploited.

Another fundamental proposition is that Weber's legacy does not call for a discipleship, instead he demanded of his posterity substantive criticism. Disciples are needed when dogmas are present in a system of ideas and, when dogmas are present, the system becomes a closed system whatever the original intentions of the systemfounder. Disciples have to perform a most vital function if the system is to survive: they defend, propagate, apologize, interpret, and re-interpret the dogmas. Weber offers no dogmas; therefore he does not have nor need a discipleship. Any bona fide "disciple" here disregards his "master's" wishes. Instead, Weber worried whether or not posterity would take him seriously enough to criticize and reject any of his conceptual tools or theoretical propositions that could not be accepted or modified. With a few exceptions the Weber scholars of today have not received his opus as a fixed and revered treasure as has been the case with the discipleship of some great masters. The social scientists and humanists interested in Weber's intellectual and scientific legacy have to utilize Weber's work as a living document to be added to.

Research is by definition an unending process and data collected thereby are constantly liable to varying corrections. "The stream of immeasurable events flows unendingly towards eternity." And Weber continued: "The cultural problems which move men form themselves ever anew and in different colors, and the boundaries of that area in the infinite stream of concrete events which acquires meaning and significance for us, i.e., which becomes an 'historical individual,' are constantly subject to change." Consequently at times Weber avoided on principle extracting from insufficient data, especially historical-comparative data, formal conceptualizations and definitions to compete with all the other existing ones, particularly when a definition or concept in his opinion would be arbitrary premature or confined to limited data. Repeatedly Weber expressed this position. It is, therefore, hard to understand why his statements and practices of self-limitation, chosen by design, not by neglect, were overlooked by those who criticize him precisely for this distinctive virtue as if it were a major failure. Weber's inclination to leave numerous and apparently sound theoretical propositions open-ended considerably lessens the possibility of his successors' building unwarranted social-scientific systems and, even less, of creating ideological blueprints, however attractive.

During and after World War I, in those few years before his death in 1920, Weber became deeply convinced (and bitterly disappointed) that the humanist expectations for growth of liberty in the world, based on President Wilson's 14 points, the creation of the League of Nations, and the general optimism that the past war would be the last one ever, would not be fulfilled. Instead, on the basis of some evidence which perhaps escaped others, Weber almost prophetically visualized the mushrooming growth of non-democratic, non-legal/rational, non-pluralistic, (and without explicitly using this label) patrimonialist regimes around the world. These tendencies in the post-war period would spread and intensify oppression, the inevitable, undesirable result being more oppressed peoples on this earth, no matter whether they were peasants and industrial workers, national and religious minorities, or entire nonstate nations—majorities within their own national territory under foreign occupation.

Still today to insist that in Weber's search for an explanation of these discouraging trends toward loss of freedom and the growth of patrimonialism in the modern world there is an overwhelming indebtedness of his to Hobbes, Machiavelli, Nietzsche and/or Darwin is obscene and it is so no matter who the accusers are. How sorely mistaken they are is demonstrated in many of his controversial propositions which were given wide publicity in his time and provoked a great deal of hostility against him, but are almost entirely forgotten in our time.

Weber's abhorrence of oppression everywhere applies, perhaps most intensively, to the German oppressors as well: the Kaiser, the Junkers, the industrialists separately and the entire German power establishment in general. As Baumgarten testifies, "power, typically German power, was the actual object of hatred, of Weber's national self-hatred."

In 1911 in a letter to Graf Keyserling, Weber wrote that the Germans are not a civilized nation or people with a refined politically sophisticated culture simply because "we never have had the nerve to behead one of our monarchs," as the civilized nations have, presumably France, England, and others. He felt that such an emotional experience in the German cultural heritage would have been a good lesson for all the future rulers of Germany. During the war Weber publicly attacked the Kaiser and at the same time ridiculed the concept of master-race (*Herrenvolk*): "We are not a master race for we put up with our monarch." Even this so typical of Weber's biting sarcasm was taken out of context and misinterpreted by some as an endorsement of the German "master-race" ideology.

The first President of the German Bundesrepublic after World War II Theodore Heuss recalls how many leading intellectuals and statesmen of Weber's era were profoundly shaken by Weber's continuous and implacable attacks against Wilhelm II, not only during but even after the war when Weber himself too said that it was not "gentlemanly" to use "harsh" words against the deposed monarch. Heuss also said that modern readers still will be shocked with Weber's rage (*die grimmige Wut*)—nary any word expresses it—when he, who in those fatal years was so basically disturbed with the German foreign policy, attacked the decision-makers in German (Prussia's) domestic policies.

With the accusation that "Max Weber is a disgrace to the nation" people from the right and left cancelled subscriptions to the journals and newspapers in which Weber criticized Chancellor Bismarck and the German politicians and industrialists. However, according to Heuss *Die Frankfurter Zeitung* always welcomed whatever Weber wished to say: it became Weber's "organ."

As reported by Heuss there was also an emotional confrontation between Weber and General Ludendorff, a celebrated war hero, after he refused Weber's request to voluntarily submit himself to an investigation of war activities by the victorious Allied forces, even though Weber believed that Ludendorff would be fully vindicated. Later Ludendorff told Baumgarten that Weber was a traitor to his country.

German public opinion was also deeply angered by Weber's position in one national issue of extreme emotional intensity: the future of Alsace and Lorraine—a perennial bone of contention between Germany and France. Weber's views here were not conditioned by his alleged psychic needs to exhibit continuous pathological hostility against his country's establishment, but were dictated by his humanist conscience and formed on solid scientific evidence which reflected a particularly significant aspect of his legacy, human rights and nonstate submerged nations. Rejecting a consensus of the German scholars on this issue, Weber agreed with the French philosopher Ernest Renan that the majority of the objectively significant attributes of the quest for nationhood clearly in his mind identified Alsace and Lorraine as French in spite of the German ethic origin and the use of the German language as the mother-tongue by most of its people.

In spite of all this evidence still today very much current are the assumptions of Weber's alleged German imperialism and chauvinism, contempt for democracy, hostility against Polish workers and Poland, and, especially of his rampant russophobia.

Deeply committed to his personal values of liberty, basic human rights, and self-determination for all nations, Weber paid to the Russian liberation movement a touchingly eloquent tribute:

> Never has a liberation movement been carried out under such difficult circumstances after all and never with such a high measure of almost reckless readiness for martyrdom as the Russian, . . . (Tr. by this editor.)

In the same article written after the 1905 revolution Weber expressed his fears that the prospects for the success of the Russian liberation movement were not too promising, but he warned his German readers not to assume that this was due to the alleged "Russians' immaturity for constitutional government," as it was fashionable to believe in Germany. Any future failure would be entirely ascribed to the unusually harsh conditions of political life under despotism in Russia. Weber also attacked the cynicism of the German establishment who in their reactionary insensitivity for long-range relationships preferred an unstable Russia as an easy prey for German imperialist purposes. Again in 1917 he spoke of his "very strong sympathies for the Russian liberation movement."

Probably Weber's "russophobia" accusers were misguided by his vehemence and the caustic language and style he used almost regularly when discussing not only the Russian but also the German ruling elites and their imperialistic politics. His articles on Russia, some of which are lengthy and largely untranslated, are evidently considered by themselves alone for his criticism directed against the Russian ruling circles, Tsarist and post-Tsarist, has never been compared with his more devastating attacks against the German imperialistic establishment and its defenders of before and during World War I. Also, some of his remarks on Russian development were taken entirely out of the context in which he had at the same time expressed his admiration for what he called the Russian liberation movement, namely the various revolutionary groups, however conflicting they were with each other. This practice of omission is almost common even among those who rejected the unwarranted accusations of Weber's russophobia.

In his Russian studies as well as elsewhere Weber on the basis of the fundamental human rights and rights to the national self-determination endorsed independence for Finland, Poland, Ukraine, Croatia, Ireland and other submerged or nonstate nations of his era.

Weber's alleged pessimism concerning the future of liberty and rationality among humankind, projected through an oversimplified but catchy image of the "iron cage" mentality, is plainly journalistic overkill that persists. It just shows how popularized images and labels work miracles, not only commercially, but academically too. Perhaps because of the longevity of these established images, Weber's extraordinarily valuable criticism of certain myths still cherished by some is not enjoying the same currency or degree of fashionableness. The sharply critical evaluations of the "beatitudes of economic self-development" as illusionary, written by Weber seventy years ago and supported by ample evidence today (thus obliterating most of the current modernization theories) are only rarely noticed (in an occasional book review, e.g., Roth), until recently (Zaret; Barker; Lee and Munch; Lee).

. . . [Attempts] were made in 1965 and 1971 (German and English editions respectively) to explain how such misunderstanding of Weber's fundamental politico-philo-sophical values originated in the first place and why it is hard to eradicate them. "Weber writes as a lawyer, an advocate of certain political courses of action or strategy," and consequently, Deutsch argues, "it often appears that Weber employed the rhetoric of the power-politics of 1916 in order actually to persuade his readers to modera-tion. . . . Above all, Weber constantly proposed moderate aims, not exaggerated ones." Deutsch reiterates that the age of Weber was characterized by an ever increasing glorification of German claims to world leadership and that Weber was not part of it for he rejected the idea of German hegemony most emphatically:

> "Only the balance between the great powers guarantees the freedom of the smaller nations." (Deutsch quotes Weber). And again: the Germans were fighting the overrunning of the world by the Russians and the Anglo-Saxons. . . . It is the classical aim of a balance between the powers, including Germany, in contrast to the newer dream of a German world-hegemony, cherished by the extreme nationalists of his day.

That is nationalism, Deutsch said, but it is not unlimited power-politics. "It is perhaps no more than just, not to ignore how much separates Weber also from the extreme nationalism and power-worship of so many of his con-temporaries." Contrary to frequent accusations, Weber has not reduced, Baumgarten said, parliamentarism and democracy to mere tools of the nation's greatness and this national greatness was *not* for Weber the supreme absolute value:

> The ideal of "the greatness of the nation" was on the contrary conditionally qualified. So little is it true that he thought of democracy as the sum of a number of tools, that the greatness of a nation in the modern world only consisted for him to the extent to which this nation developed real democracy.

Finally to Baumgarten, "Weber's concept of power was oriented not to Nietzsche nor to Darwin, let alone to the concept of the 'master-race'." Against frequently re-peated incorrect judgments that Weber recognized no il-legitimate power Arndt said: "When he investigates the

legitimacy and explains its three kinds, he is questioning the justification of power." Arndt argues that "in Weber's eyes" there is plenty of illegitimate power. While this can easily be seen in history, Arndt asks, "What did Weber meet within his own times?"

> What he found was an unlawful handling of power by officials who understood nothing about politics. Thus Germany's condition up to 1914, and again after 1917, was worsened by the fact that the military leadership, the supreme army command, unlawfully took over political leadership, the leadership of the Reich.

Recognizing that "Weber often stood in his own way," that some of his unfortunate decisions were "due to a personal and political bias, not a scientific judgment," Arndt affirmed that to Weber "there is no value in power alone." He added that Weber's misfortune was that his single definitions eventually became isolated, "for in-stance the inadequate definition of the state as the com-munity which successfully claims for itself within a cer-tain sphere the monopoly of legitimate physical force." This definition was an "attempt to approach the phenom-enon of 'state' under the postulate of value-freedom." What Weber really wished to define was the nation-state in its international relations with other nation-states, and *not* the "state" in relation to its own citizens. This, in-deed, inadequate definition was labeled "positivistic" and in the light of it Weber was eventually declared a mem-ber of the positivist school. It became unjustly famous through innumerable quotations as *the* definition. As a classic example of proverbial lip service it was used out of context, of course, by many who did not cite anything else from Weber. And to reiterate, this definition was a preliminary attempt by Weber to reflect the empirical reality of the phenomena of almost universal human mis-ery of experience with power. Deutsch said that in Aron's paper there is a definition of power, "which aligns Weber with Machiavelli and Hobbes." But it is not only Aron: some commentators do the same in a much more exag-gerated fashion than he and this entire approach repre-sents a gross oversimplification that ignores some other conceptual elements in Weber's multifaceted con-ceptualization of power. And these other conceptual ele-ments, especially in his later writings, seem to converge toward a quite different definition of power. This will be explored in the Editor's symposium in press.

Since the tension between liberty and legitimation of power—the only opening to foster growth of human free-dom and an elusive goal at best—captivated Weber's entire personality there is a glimpse of eternal truth in Arndt's comment: "In wrestling with this problem Weber should be seen as a political pedagogue, not as a political practitioner." Weber, indeed, wanted people everywhere (not only the Germans) to be political people, not in the sense of the dreadful "political education" as practiced in totalist, patrimonialist societies of today, but *political* in their unceasing watch over the seductiveness of power and willingness to personal sacrifice in order to stop abuses of power. Weber expressed his fear, as Arndt said, "out of his doubts about Germany. His direction was always towards disenchantment, de-ideologizattion, towards awareness, the rational and reasonable."

THE RECEPTION OF WEBER'S OPUS ABROAD

Outside Germany, especially in the English speaking world, the reception of partially carved pieces from Weber's opus in different periods of time by various translators who perhaps could not be expected to agree on common terminology is a lamentable story.

The first translated work of Weber appeared in 1927, the second in 1930, and the rest of the carvings commenced to trickle in in the late 1940s. Only in 1968 *The Economy and Society, E&S,* which is generally considered to be the major work of Weber, became available in English. Tenbruck's argument that *E&S* is not his principal work seems fully applicable only to Part I of *E&S.* Part I consists of 180 pages which were written, edited and proofread by Weber shortly before his death in 1920. It is too technical and taxonomic with far too many outline-like subdivisions with little text and superficially it may appear as an armchair scholar's hair-splitting enterprise. In contrast to it, the much larger Part II was written in rough-draft form between 1911 and 1914 and never revised. It offers a wealth of empirical evidence collected toward the discovery of developmental processes and formulation of theoretical propositions.

But irrespective of the question of whether or not *E&S* is Weber's principal work, which remains moot, *E&S* is still today in many instances cited purely perfunctorily. Usually only one general reference is made to entire chapters, however, in one perhaps "record" case one single reference was made to Chs. 9-13 with a total of 210 pages without reacting to or even touching upon the actual subject-matter of its long and substantive chapters (Skocpol). Perhaps 15 years is not enough time for the slow-moving, comfortably-situated academic establishment to respond to the challenge of new materials.

As already noted, not only Weber's Russian studies but also other significant pieces remained untranslated, e.g., certain parts of what Tenbruck considers the principal work of Weber, *Die Wirtschaftsethic der Welt-religionen,* a collection of essays that were originally published in several segments in the Archiv für Sozialwissenschaft und Sozialpolitik, 1915-1919.

The very first work to be translated in English in 1927 was a posthumous transcription of Weber's last course of lecture notes compiled by his students, *General Economic History, GEH*. This in many respects unquestionably superb work for some inexplicable reasons did not capture attention or provoke any intellectual excitement for over a half-century. Randall Collins in a lecture at the Max Weber Colloquia and Symposia at the University of Wisconsin-Milwaukee called *GEH* "perhaps Weber's finest work" and some agreed, but it still remains almost

unknown and citations from it are very rare. There is a second British edition and now a new third American edition of *GEH,* (Cohen). Things may start happening now.

In glaring contrast to the almost total neglect of *GEH,* the next translated work in 1930, *The Protestant Ethic and the Spirit of Capitalism, PE&SC,* received a follow-up of immense proportions which seem entirely and absolutely unwarranted. Apparently Weber himself had serious problems in attempting to revise and finalize it for he accomplished a revision of one segment only. Even the label "Protestant" in the title of *PE&SC* is a misnomer, because the issue there is the uniquely Calvinist doctrinal deviation in interpreting the doctrine of predestination which was not shared by the other branches of doctrinal Protestantism. Finally, there is a substantive body of persistent criticism of *PE&SC* from the very beginning which is well summarized by Runciman.

The inexplicable near-obsession with this relatively inferior piece in comparison with other of Max Weber's writings is correlated with the fact that Weber, total Weber, is still celebrated or dismissed by too many academic persons entirely on the basis of this work alone as though he had not written anything else. In most undergraduate and too many graduate classes the only work ever discussed is the *PE&SC* and the textbooks duly service this well-established norm. This damaging image of Max Weber as a One-Book-Author remains almost ineradicable at the present.

There are a number of plausible speculations to explain what went wrong in this series of seemingly never-ending publishing disasters surrounding *PE&SC.* Some attribute this primarily to the originally Calvinist religious background of the early dominant upper classes in colonial and post-1776 liberated America. Its leadership perhaps found the rather novel Calvinist interpretation of the basic Christian value-system, especially the doctrine of predestination, useful for the legitimacy and perpetuation of its power and as a source of legitimation it was very much alive when *PE&SC* hit these shores. Many who were involved with *PE&SC* admit in their biographical sketches and even in conversations that their solid Calvinist family background is somehow correlated to the fascination they always experienced with *PE&SC*. In one of his last letters (written in 1979) Parsons, the son of a Calvinist divine, said somewhat possessively:

> Naturally, [the receiving of] this paper occasions a great many complex reverberations for me since I was after all the translator of *The Protestant Ethic*. It is interesting that now, nearly sixty years after the publication of that translation, the focus of attention on Weber's thesis has recently been coming to be more intensive than at almost any time. This phenomenon might be the occasion for an essay in the sociology of knowledge. Of course, we have been met with sweeping statements . . . that "the Protestant Ethic is dead." But it seems to be a very lively corpse indeed.

What is dead? That particular ethical doctrine and practice among the contemporary Americans OR the seemingly unstoppable avalanche of literature on *PE&SC* is dead? Parsons was wrong if he had in mind the latter, because no one ever predicted that the avalanche will mercifully stop in any forseeable future.

Instead of placing *PE&SC* within the context of the scholarly pursuits of Weber's intellectual era in Germany and Western Europe to which he kept responding, a total misconception of the purposes of this work created a popular and artificially controversial issue dividing those engaged in it into two hostile camps with plenty of hagiolatry and demonology respectively.

The criticism here is not to deny that *PE&SC* may still generate some other possibly useful sociological theoretical propositions as occasionally happens and that there will be some desirable additional by-products. In spite of his extensive disagreement with Weber on several political issues, Otto Hintze offered in considerable detail a truly admirable evaluation of Weber's actual purposes and basic propositions in *PE&SC*. Hintze's extensive efforts in interpreting Weber's opus remained untranslated and with a few exceptions largely unnoticed.

Weber's propositions in *PE&SC* appear very tentative and certainly never dogmatic; they are much less affirmative than the numerous followers and critics have claimed. His original intent was to suggest a comparative-*historical* inquiry into why certain economic experiences in the Calvinist-creed dominated societies of *the seventeenth century,* especially in Geneva, Switzerland, the Netherlands, Scotland, the Puritan Bible Commonwealth in Massachusetts Bay and perhaps some other places, did not occur anywhere outside these societies. It was strictly a study *of seventeenth century historical materials* designed to serve as an experimental balloon to be shot down if anything similar to it would be found in Confucianism, Islam, Catholicism or elsewhere.

However, under no circumstances should this historical inquiry into *seventeenth century limited localities* be utilized as a respectable scientific "thesis" when investigating the economic attitudes of various American groups in the twentieth century, there being such a thing as social change.

At least half-a-century after the Calvinist hierocracy of Massachusetts Bay disintegrated, the popular writings of Benjamin Franklin show most eloquently how totally, already in his day, the age of the Founding Fathers, the "secularization" or "Americanization" of most of the ingredients of the old, originally Calvinist doctrine was completed. Needless to say that neither Franklin nor the other Founding Fathers of the new republic were Christians, but deists of the French enlightenment's vintage, however, they were all enthusiastic promoters of the new creed. It became then inevitably an all-American national societal creed, the source of the legitimation for the new republic and of the future American dream, eagerly embraced not only by the Calvinist Protestants, but also by all the non-Calvinist Protestants (Episcopalians, Lutherans and others) as well as by the other non-Protestant Christians (Catholics) and all the non-Christians (Jews, Confucianists, and others). At the certain point in the process of the transformation from a "religious" to a "social" ethic the Calvinist theologians dropped the religious core of the original Calvinist creed, the doctrine of predestination, as too embarrassing for the modern age.

In a complete disregard of all this, the literature on "Weber's Thesis," i.e., Weber's One and Only Thesis was furiously engaged in the statistical testing of the attitudes toward money-making and business orientation in general between Protestant (sic!) and Catholic college students in the twentieth century U.S.A. Ever since 1930 several hundred of these statistical studies have been produced and keep coming. Many of them found out that there is indeed a difference between the Protestant and Catholic students and Weber was profusely glorified: the others, equally numerous, discovered that there is no difference and Weber or "Weber's Thesis" was summarily dismissed as irrelevant. With his presidential address to one of the sociological societies "to tell you all you wanted to know" about *PE&SC,* a maverick sociologist entered the picture "in the negative." In response to criticism by this Editor and others he cordially said that he learned his lesson and would stay out of the fracas. However, a few years later he delivered another lecture, "Max Weber, Eat Your Heart Out," which documented with extended statistical research that, indeed, there is no difference between Catholics and Protestants in their basic economic motivations, activities and successes.

If one is permitted to express somewhat tartly the retentiveness of this *fata morgana* "conflict," it appears that some segments of the American establishment, academic and otherwise, still welcome "Weber's Thesis" as solid proof of their unique original contribution to the American heritage, while other perhaps more recently added segments and still not totally secure in it, are eager by rejecting "Weber's Thesis" to prove that their impact is just as significant and that their Americanization is just as complete as any other segment of the establishment.

Finally, there is another, perhaps major, misconception related to the impact of *PE&SC,* which should be reported here. In the very last sentences Weber said:

> But it is, of course, not my aim to substitute for a one-sided materialistic an equally one-sided spiritualistic causal interpretation of culture and of history. Each is equally possible, but each, if it does not serve as the preparation, but as the conclusion of an investigation, accomplishes equally little in the interest of historical truth. [Footnote:] I should have thought that this sentence and the remarks and notes immediately preceding it would have sufficed to prevent any misunderstanding of what this study was meant to accomplish, and I find no occasion for adding anything.

Over a half-century ago this statement was available, of course, with the rest of **PE&SC** and indeed should have "suffced to prevent any misunderstanding of what this study was meant to accomplish." Notwithstanding this Weber was and still is, perhaps slightly less frequently now, accused of deliberately creating an idealistic interpretation of history and society with the allegedly sole purpose of tearing down the philosophy of materialistic monism with its materialistic/economic interpretation. All this occurred in spite of his precise statement above, his firm and persistent rejection of Hegel's philosophy of idealistic monism, and his general acceptance of and orientation toward Kantian solutions in the multifaceted controversies of Kant vs. Hegel and their respective legacies.

Rogers Brubaker (essay date 1984)

SOURCE: "Weber's Moral Vision," in *The Limits of Rationality: An Essay on the Social and Moral Thought of Max Weber*, George Allen & Unwin, 1984, pp. 91-112.

[*In the following essay, Brubaker examines the underlying philosophy of ethics in Weber's works.*]

Weber presents himself as an empirical scientist, not as a moral philosopher. It is true that he has no moral philosophy in the traditional sense. He elaborates no rules of individual conduct, harbors no vision of an ideal society. And the standard terms of moral argument—good, right, ought, should—are conspicuously absent from his vocabulary. Yet the whole of his scientific work is informed by a fundamentally moral impulse—by a passionate concern with the 'fate of man' in contemporary capitalist civilization (Löwith). This concern is embodied in Weber's empirical interpretation of modernity in terms of its 'specific and peculiar rationalism' and in his moral response to this rationalized world. The former I have explored in the preceding chapters; the latter—the set of ideas and ideals comprising Weber's moral response to modernity—I explore in this [essay].

Weber's moral thought is highly idiosyncratic, and it invites criticism in a number of respects. In this [essay], however, my aim is neither to criticize nor to defend Weber's views but simply to reconstruct them from his very sketchy remarks on the subject and to present them in a clear and systematic manner. I focus on his conception of the nature and limits of moral rationality, and on his view of the relation between the freedom and moral rationality of the individual and the supra-individual rationality of the modern social order.

THE ETHIC OF PERSONALITY: FROM PHILOSOPHICAL ANTHROPOLOGY TO MORAL PHILOSOPHY

Weber's fact-value distinction is perhaps his best known contribution to moral philosophy. Echoing Hume, who was the first to question the legitimacy of deriving 'ought' from 'is', Weber insists on the absolute logical heterogeneity of empirical propositions and normative judgments. This distinction, however, is more likely to obscure than to clarify the status of Weber's own moral ideals. For these *ideals* are derived from certain *ideas* about the nature of man—ideas that are at once empirical and normative. These ideas make up Weber's philosophical anthropology, his conception of the essence of human being, of what it is that distinguishes human life from other natural processes.

At the heart of Weber's philosophical anthropology is the concept of meaning. Meaning is the essential property of human action; it is what distinguishes human actions from other natural events. Not all human behavior is meaningful, but conduct that is not meaningful is not specifically human; such conduct has more in common with non-human natural events than with meaningful action.

Meaning is intrinsically linked with rationality. Although Weber does not attempt to define 'meaning', he does delimit the domain of meaningful action through two kinds of examples: paradigmatic cases and borderline cases. Paradigmatic of unambiguously meaningful action are the two types of rational action: means-ends rational (*zweckrational*) and value-rational (*wertrational*) action. These have in common a self-consciousness on the part of the actor about his action: in both cases the actor knows what he is doing and does it deliberately. *Zweckrational* action is guided by the actor's conscious weighing of his ends, the various possible means to these ends, and the probable secondary consequences of employing these means. Similarly, *wertrational* action is marked by the 'clearly self-conscious formulation of the ultimate values governing the action and the consistently planned orientation of its detailed course to these values'. Paradigmatically, then, meaningful action is action that is rational in the sense of deliberately planned and consciously guided.

The outer limits of meaningful action are marked by two borderline cases: traditional and affectual behavior. In contrast to the two types of rational action, these have in common the actor's relative lack of conscious awareness of and deliberate control over his conduct. The degree of awareness and control—and thus the degree of 'meaningfulness' of traditional and affectual behavior—varies from case to case. On the one hand, strictly traditional behavior is 'very often a matter of almost automatic reaction to habitual stimuli'. Similarly, purely affectual behavior may take the form of an 'uncontrolled reaction to some exceptional stimulus'. In these cases, conduct passes from the domain of meaningful action—and thereby from the domain of truly human action—to the realm of merely reactive behavior. On the other hand, an actor may deliberately and self-consciously persist in traditional patterns of action, or he may deliberately decide to release consciously experienced emotional tension in a certain way. In these cases conduct is no longer purely traditional or purely affectual: it has an important rational component and is therefore meaningful.

Action is meaningful, then, in so far as it is rational, meaning consciously guided. Freedom, too, is intrinsically linked with rationality:

> We associate the highest measure of an empirical 'feeling of freedom' with those actions which we are conscious of performing rationally—i.e., in the absence of physical and psychic 'coercion,' emotional 'affects' and 'accidental' disturbances of the clarity of judgment, in which we pursue a clearly perceived end by 'means' which are the most adequate in accordance with the extent of our knowledge.

Rational action, then, is at the same time free and meaningful action. Together, these qualities distinguish human actions from other events in nature. *Truly human action is rational, free and meaningful; natural events are non-rational, unfree and devoid of meaning.*

Not all human conduct, of course, is rational, free and meaningful; much, indeed most human behavior falls below the threshold of the truly human. Thus consciously meaningful action is only a 'marginal case': 'In the great majority of cases actual action goes on in a state of inarticulate half-consciousness or actual unconsciousness of its subjective meaning'. Some human conduct—the behavior of the insane, for example—shares fully the non-rationality, unfreedom and meaninglessness of natural events; most falls somewhere in between the poles of the truly human and the merely natural. Weber's conception of *truly* human action is thus not a conception of *typically* human action: it is a polar concept, an ideal-typical limiting case.

Weber's conception of the truly human applies not only to individual actions but also to human life as a whole. Just as it is meaning that distinguishes a truly human individual action from an event in nature, so it is meaning that distinguishes a truly human life from a chain of natural events. A human life, like an individual action, is meaningful in so far as it is consciously guided, i.e. in so far as it is rational, in the broadest sense of this term. And just as a consciously guided individual action is a free action, so too a consciously guided life—and only such a life—can be considered free.

Meaning, rationality and freedom, however, have a different significance in reference to a human life as a whole than they do in reference to a single action. Morally neutral when applied to a single action, they become morally charged when applied to life as a whole. Thus for an individual action to be meaningful, it is sufficient that it be consciously oriented to some purpose, however insignificant. Swatting a fly is every bit as meaningful, in itself, as rescuing children from a burning building. A meaningful action can just as well be morally indifferent or even blameworthy as morally praiseworthy. A meaningful life, in contrast, is one endowed with *dignity* and thereby, in Weber's view, with moral worth. Meaning and moral dignity derive from the systematic integration of individual actions into a unified life pattern based on certain fundamental values. A life that lacks this systematic unity is not a meaningful life, even if it is composed of a string of meaningful actions.

Rationality, too, is a concept that is morally neutral on the level of individual action but morally charged on the level of life as a whole. While the rationality of an individual action may depend solely on the appropriateness of the means to a single given end, whatever its value and whatever its relation to other ends, the rationality of a life as a whole depends on the coherence of an individual's ends and values, the constancy over time with which he pursues these ends and values, and the clarity of his self-understanding. The rationality of an individual action, in short, may be no more than a matter of efficiency; the rationality of a complete life, on the other hand, is always a matter of *integrity*.

Freedom, finally, has a deeper and richer meaning when applied to life as a whole than it does when applied to an individual action. For a single action to be free, it is sufficient that it be uncoerced by physical or psychic factors beyond the agent's conscious control. Life as a whole, in contrast, has the potential to be free not in the merely negative sense of being uncoerced, but in the positive sense of being *autonomous*, i.e. guided by norms of the individual's own making.

Weber's philosophical anthropology is summed up in his conception of *personality*. (Personality, for Weber, is not a psychological but a philosophical concept.) The qualities that distinguish a truly human action from an event in nature—meaning, rationality and freedom—converge in this conception:

> The freer the action . . . i.e. the less it has the character of a natural event, the more the concept of personality comes into play. The essence of personality lies in the constancy of its inner relation to certain ultimate values and life-meanings, which, in the course of action, turn into purposes and are thus translated into teleologically rational action.

Here Weber presents personality as a methodological ideal type. Only in so far as individuals have personalities can science genuinely understand individuals and their actions. Natural events, however regular, can never be 'understood', in Weber's special sense of this term, for they have no intrinsic meaning. They can be explained by being subsumed under general laws, but they cannot be understood in terms of their meaning. To the extent that human lives remain natural events, they too can be explained but not understood. But to the extent that individuals become personalities, their lives cease to be mere events in nature; they become consciously guided, meaningful, and therefore understandable. Personality, then, is what distinguishes the truly human and the merely natural from the point of view of science: the truly human personality and his actions are understandable; the 'natural' man and his conduct are not.

But personality is also what distinguishes the truly human and the merely natural from the point of view of moral philosophy: personality is a moral ideal as well as a methodological ideal type. Weber regards as *'objectively valuable* [his emphasis] those innermost elements of the "personality", those highest and most ultimate value judgments which determine our conduct and give meaning and significance to our life'. The morally charged qualities that distinguish a truly human life from an event in nature—dignity, integrity and autonomy—are inherent in the concept of personality. Thus Weber emphasizes the 'dignity of the "personality"', which 'lies in the fact that for it there exist values about which it organizes its life'. Integrity, too, is bound up with the idea of personality, for personality is constituted by the *'constancy* of its inner relation to certain ultimate values and life-meanings' (emphasis added). Autonomy, finally, derives from the individual's deliberate shaping of his own personality through his choice of the ultimate values and meanings that are to structure his life-activity.

Personality, however, is a purely formal moral ideal. To become a personality, an individual must be committed to certain fundamental values, but he need not be committed to any particular values. Any value or complex of values to which the individual can consciously and consistently orient his existence is as good as any other. More broadly, Weber's philosophical anthropology and moral philosophy as a whole are purely formal. Every truly human life, according to Weber, has the same form: it is oriented to some central value or complex of values. Weber affirms this *form* as a central moral ideal: every person, in his view, *should* orient his life to some central value. But while the form of the truly human life is fixed, the content varies widely: the central values to which life can be oriented range from purely personal values 'within the sphere of the person's "individuality"' to suprapersonal intellectual, cultural, moral, religious, social or political values. And within any one of these domains—within the political domain, for example—there is a plurality of irreconcilably opposed ultimate value positions to which an individual can orient his life. Weber's philosophical anthropology is silent about what the content of the truly human life is, and his moral philosophy is silent about what this content should be.

Despite its formal character, Weber's ethic of personality imposes arduous demands on individuals. To be a personality, one must systematically unify the whole of one's existence. To consistently observe certain standards in one's external conduct is not enough: one's ultimate value-orientation, whatever its substantive content, must inform inner bearing as well as external conduct. Such thoroughgoing unity does not come naturally: it can be achieved (or rather approached: to be a personality is not a goal that one can achieve once and for all, but an ideal that one can at best approximate) only through a continuous and strenuous conscious effort. For only through vigilant awareness and active exertion can the individual progress from a 'natural' to a 'truly human' state, from a life governed by the chaotic impulses of his raw, unformed, given nature to one governed by the co-

herent values and meanings of his consciously formed personality.

In the rigor of its demands, Weber's ethic of personality is a heroic ethic, an aristocratic ethic, an ethic of virtuosi—to use terms he himself employs. Weber distinguishes explicitly between 'heroic' and 'average' ethics, for example, in a letter criticizing a pseudo-Freudian attempt to construe mental health as a moral ideal:

> All systems of ethics, no matter what their substantive content, can be divided into two main groups. There is the 'heroic' ethic, which imposes on men demands of principle to which they are generally *not* able to do justice, except at the high points of their lives, but which serve as signposts pointing the way for man's endless *striving*. Or there is the 'ethic of the mean', which is content to accept man's everyday 'nature' as setting a maximum for the demands which can be made.

A heroic ethic may well start from a 'pessimistic assessment of the "nature" of the average man'. Unlike the ethic of the mean, however, it is not content to accept this average nature as normatively valid, as setting a limit to the ethical demands that can 'reasonably' be made. Instead, it imposes on men arduous demands that can be realized only by the select few and only 'at the high points of their lives'. In this sense, Weber's is clearly a heroic ethic.

A radical bifurcation of humanity is implicit in this aristocratic moral philosophy. The mass of men are condemned to the meaninglessness of a merely natural existence; only the ethical virtuosi are privileged to lead a truly human existence. No special dignity inheres in human nature as such. As Walter Kaufmann (1967) has written about Nietzsche's moral philosophy, to which Weber's bears a striking resemblance:

> such dignity is not *gegeben* but *aufgegeben,* not a fact but a goal that few approach . . . to raise ourselves above the senseless flux, we must cease being merely human, all-too-human. We must be hard against ourselves and overcome ourselves; we must become creators instead of remaining mere creatures.

In Weber's as well as Nietzsche's moral vision, few succeed in becoming creators of their personalities, in bestowing meaning and dignity on their lives; most remain mere creatures, mired in the meaningless flux of the merely natural. And for the latter, in Weber's as in Nietzsche's moral universe, there is no redemption.

THE LIMITS OF MORAL RATIONALITY

There is a disturbing paradox at the heart of Weber's moral philosophy. The truly human life is one that is guided by reason. To live a life informed by reason, an individual must become a personality. To become a personality, he must commit himself to certain fundamental values. But this commitment, though it is the foundation of every personality, and thus of every rational life, cannot itself be guided by reason, for in Weber's view there is no rational way of deciding among the plurality of conflicting possible value commitments. Every rational life, in short, is founded on a non-rational choice.

This paradox arises from the disjunction between the *anthropological* perspective on reason that informs the normative strand of Weber's moral philosophy and the *logical* perspective on reason that informs his metaethical views. Anthropologically understood, reason is a distinctively human power of conscious self-formation. Through the exercise of reason, an individual can transform unconscious impulses and semi-conscious habits into conscious purposes, integrate these purposes into a systematic life plan, and in this way consciously shape and create a personality out of the tangle of contradictory impulses that comprise raw, unformed human nature. This broad anthropological understanding of reason underlies Weber's normative ethic. Grounded in a conception of the distinction between rational man and irrational nature (including raw human nature), this ethic bids men become personalities and thereby realize their true humanity through the exercise of reason. It is by virtue of his unwavering commitment to reason in this anthropological sense that Weber can be understood as an advocate of the values of the Enlightenment and, in particular, as a defender of moral rationality.

Conjoined with Weber's essentially anthropological ethic of self-realization through reason, however, is a metaethical theory emphasizing the narrowly limited moral significance of reason. The perspective that informs this metaethical theory is that of logic, not philosophical anthropology; reason is conceived narrowly as a power of determining empirical truths and making logical deductions, not broadly as a self-formative power. Reason in this restricted sense can resolve moral disagreements that are based on factual disagreements, and it can criticize inconsistencies in moral argument. Fully rational and conclusive moral argument, however, is impossible in principle. To be sure, actions can be justified in terms of value judgments, and particular value judgments in terms of more general ones. But every such chain of reasoning eventually reaches some ultimate value judgment or value-orientation that cannot be rationally (i.e. empirically or logically) justified. There is an irreducible plurality of conflicting ultimate values, and among these the individual must simply choose.

Both Weber's normative ethic and his metaethical theory emphasize the central moral significance of choice. But while the one conceives choice as a conscious, deliberate, commitment-founding, personality-forming and in these respects rational event, the other conceives choice as unguided by criteria and therefore non-rational. It is thus because rationality has both a broad anthropological sense and a narrow logical meaning in Weber's thought that a rational (in the anthropological sense) and therefore truly human life can be held to depend on a non-rational (in the logical sense) and therefore arbitrary choice.

In its emphasis on the moral significance of choice, Weber's moral thought displays a marked affinity with that of existentialism. This affinity is comprised by a shared conception of man as a self-creating being, a shared emphasis on the limits of moral rationality, and a shared conception of autonomy as a central moral ideal.

For existentialist thinkers, as for Weber, man makes himself, forms his own nature, creates his own personality through his choices. The central doctrine of existentialism, according to Alisdair Macintyre (1967), is that 'men do not have fixed natures that limit or determine their choices, but rather it is their choices that bring whatever nature they have into being'. Similarly, Weber claims that 'life as a whole, if it is not to be permitted to run on as an event in nature but is instead to be consciously guided, is a series of ultimate decisions through which the soul . . . chooses its own fate, i.e. the meaning of its activity and existence'.

A second theme common to Weber and existentialist thinkers is that the most fundamental choices are necessarily nonrational. For while rational choice—choice governed by criteria—is possible, there are various conflicting criteria of rationality. These criteria must themselves be chosen, and *this* choice cannot be a rational one.

The final and most crucial similarity between the moral thought of Weber and that of existentialist thinkers is their overriding concern with autonomy. In Kant's classic formulation, autonomy is the condition of being subject only to self-created and self-imposed obligations; heteronomy, in contrast, is the condition of being subject to obligations that one has not created. This morally charged opposition between autonomy and heteronomy persists in the moral thought of Weber and the existentialists, but the connection established by Kant between autonomy and rationality is severed. For Kant, autonomy resides in the rule-making of the 'rational will'—a will that can adopt as its own ruling principles only maxims that can be universalized. Universality is a necessary and sufficient condition of the rationality—and thus the rightness—of a moral principle; autonomous moral legislation is thus purely rational, having nothing to do with arbitrariness or choice. For Weber and the existentialists, in contrast (and for Nietzsche, whose ideas deeply influenced their work), autonomy resides not in the formulation of universal laws but in the value-creating activity of a will unconstrained by any criteria—except, in Weber's case, by the criterion of self-consistency. Autonomous moral legislation depends on criterionless choice.

MORAL CHOICE IN THE MODERN WORLD

Despite his proto-existentialist emphasis on criterionless choice, Weber remains committed to moral rationality as an ideal—and not only to reason in the anthropological sense but to the moral significance of logical and scientific rationality. This commitment to moral rationality is manifest in his conception of the role of science in what might be called moral education (though Weber does not use this expression): a strictly rational enterprise that helps individuals 'gain clarity' about their choices. For Weber as well as for existentialist thinkers, ultimate choices are necessarily non-rational, for they cannot be guided by any objective criteria (since choice-guiding criteria must themselves be chosen). But for Weber there is none the less an element of rationality in choice. For while fundamental choices cannot be rationally governed, they can be rationally *framed*. Choice situations, that is, can be rationally analyzed, and the logical implications and empirical consequences of the various possible choices can be specified. Choice occurs, in short, between rationally delineable alternatives. It is this rational analysis of choice situations that is in Weber's view the task of moral education, for it permits individuals to gain clarity about their choices, and thus to choose in full awareness of what they are embracing and of what they are forgoing.

Moral education employs both empirical and philosophical analysis to help individuals gain clarity about their choices. Empirical analysis, to begin with, can call attention to what Weber calls 'inconvenient facts'—facts that do not fit individuals' party opinions or personal world-views. To make students acknowledge such facts is in Weber's view 'the primary task of a useful teacher'; it is not a 'mere intellectual task' but a genuine 'moral achievement'. More generally, empirical analysis can help individuals gain clarity about particular socioethical problems by specifying the probable consequences—especially those that are unintended but none the less scientifically foreseeable—of alternative courses of action. Such analysis often reveals that some ends can be achieved only with morally dubious means, or that the realization of a desired end entails undesirable secondary consequences. When this is the case, moral education can confront the individual with the necessity of choosing between the end and the unavoidable means, or between the end and the undesired secondary consequences. But while the teacher, as moral educator, can help the individual to recognize *that* he must choose, he cannot help the individual to determine *how* he must choose: moral education, as Weber conceives it, is strictly formal.

While empirical analysis helps individuals gain clarity about their evaluative response to particular problems of social life, philosophical analysis helps them gain clarity about their value-orientations—about the meaning and structure of their lives as a whole. Philosophical analysis does this by forcing individuals to consider the relations between their evaluative stands on particular socio-ethical issues and the 'ultimate *weltanschauliche* position[s]' from which such particular evaluations can be consistently derived:

> we [teachers] can and should state: In terms of its meaning, such and such a practical stand can be derived with inner consistency, and hence integrity, from this or that ultimate *weltanschauliche* position. Perhaps it can only be derived from one such fundamental position, or maybe from several, but it cannot be derived from these or those other

positions. Figuratively speaking, you serve this god and you offend the other god when you decide to adhere to this position . . . Thus we can . . . force the individual, or at least we can help him, to give himself an *account of the ultimate meaning of his own conduct* . . . [A] teacher who succeeds in this . . . stands in the service of 'moral' forces; he fulfills the duty of bringing about clarity and a sense of responsibility.

Clarity and responsibility are intrinsically linked; together they are a precondition of genuine moral autonomy. For only responsible ultimate value choices, only those made in full awareness of their logical implications, have moral dignity and contribute to moral development; all other choices are simply arbitrary acts, incapable of furthering the development of autonomous moral personality.

Moral education is not confined to the classroom: it embraces all activities that help individuals gain clarity about the choices they face. Thus Weber's interpretation of modern society in terms of its peculiar rationality falls within the province of moral education, for it elucidates what is in Weber's view the fundamental moral problem of modernity: the problem of how individuals can preserve their true humanity—their autonomy, dignity and integrity—in the modern rationalized world.

From the point of view of the basic moral task of individuals—to develop autonomous personalities—the pervasive rationalization of social life poses a triple threat. First, the scientific disenchantment of the world makes more arduous the task of defining the meaning of life—a task that is a precondition for becoming a personality. For with the development of the scientific view of the world as a structure of causal relationships, it become increasingly difficult to conceive of the world as having an objective meaning. As a result, it is less and less likely that the individual will be able to derive the meaning of his life from any generally accepted conception of the meaning of the world as a whole. Instead, the individual is thrown back on his own resources. Starting from scratch, each individual must create anew the meaning of his own life. The task of forging on one's own an integral life-meaning is an arduous one, and one to which many individuals fail to measure up, allowing their lives instead 'to run on as an event in nature'.

Secondly, the rationalization of the modern economic and political order endangers human freedom. Though modern capitalism is dependent on formally free labor, it is the locus of a powerful though impersonal form of coercion, employing as a sanction the 'loss or decrease of economic power and, under certain conditions . . . the very loss of one's economic existence':

> The private enterprise system transforms into objects of 'labor market transactions' even those personal and authoritarian-hierarchical relations which actually exist in the capitalistic enterprise. While the authoritarian relationships are thus drained of all

normal sentimental content, authoritarian constrain not only continues but, at least under certain circumstances, even increases. The more comprehensive the realm of structures whose existence depends in a specific way on 'discipline'—that of capitalist commercial establishments—the more relentlessly can authoritarian constraint be exercised within them, and the smaller will be the circle of those in whose hands the power to use this type of constraint is concentrated and who also hold the power to have such authority guaranteed to them by the legal order.

An even more serious threat to freedom, according to Weber, is posed by the apparently inexorable extension of bureaucratic control over social life. Characterizing bureaucracy as 'that animated machine . . . busy fabricating the shell of bondage which men will perhaps be forced to inhabit some day, as powerless as the fellahs of ancient Egypt', Weber asks: 'How can one possibly save *any remnants* of "individualist" freedom?'

The final—and most insidious—threat posed by the process of rationalization to the development of autonomous moral personality derives from the increasing predominance of the instrumentally rational (*zweckrational*) orientation of action (Mommsen, 1974). While the ever-widening reach of the formally rational mechanisms of capitalism and bureaucracy threatens to curtail individual freedom from without, the steady diffusion of the *zweckrational* orientation threatens to subvert individual autonomy from within. This idea is not explicitly developed by Weber, but it is implicit in the structure of his moral thought.

The threat to individual autonomy posed by the increasing salience of *Zweckrationalität* is not readily apparent. *Zweckrationalität* appears to maximize individual freedom: the individual with a purely *zweckrational* orientation is by definition unhampered by the constraints of tradition, strong emotion, or ultimate value commitments. Yet this individual is free only in a purely negative sense. Consider two individuals. One is the embodiment of pure *Zweckrationalität*. He is committed to no ultimate values and carried away by no violent emotions; he observes no customs, follows no habits, and abides by no rules—except, of course, the rules of marginal utility. He does nothing without a conscious decision, and every decision involves a similar calculation. He takes stock of his wants, orders them according to urgency, calculates the cost of satisfying them, predicts the secondary repercussions of pursuing them, and weighs costs against benefits—all without reference to ultimate values. The second individual, in contrast, does not simply consult his 'given subjective wants' in order to decide how to act. Instead, he derives his ends from his value commitments. He possesses a personality—a concept, it will be recalled, that 'entails a constant and intrinsic relation to certain "values" and "meanings" of life, "values" and "meanings" which are forged into purposes and thereby translated into rational-teleological action'. This individual consciously strives to shape his life in accordance with his chosen ultimate value commitments.

Which individual is freer? The first individual, to be sure, is not bound, as is the second, by any ultimate value commitments, and is thus completely unfettered in his decisions. But in a deeper sense the first individual is less free. For he does not really choose his ends; his agenda of ends is in fact determined by his given subjective wants—by his 'raw' nature rather than by his consciously formed personality. In Kant's language, the first individual, far from being free, is at the beck and call of inclination: 'reason merely supplies a practical rule [in this case, the principles of marginal utility] for meeting the need of inclination'. *Given* wants guide the first individual in his selection of ends; *chosen* ultimate values guide the second. Only the second individual is autonomous in Weber's sense. For autonomy does not connote the radical 'freedom from inner bonds' (*inneren Ungebundenheit*) that characterizes pure *Zweckrationalität*, but rather the capacity of an individual to create his own moral personality by committing himself to certain ultimate values and meanings and organizing his life around them. Pure *Zweckrationalität*, in short, is morally dangerous because it is incompatible with genuine autonomy.

Faced with this threefold threat to the development of autonomous moral personality, the individual must make a fundamental choice. On the one hand, he may decide to reject the modern rationalized world. Thus, for example, instead of struggling on his own to create a meaning for his life, he may consciously and deliberately make the necessary 'sacrifice of the intellect' and 'return to the old churches, whose arms are opened widely and compassionately for him'. Instead of working to defend individual freedom *within* the modern rationalized politico-economic order, he may seek freedom *from* this rationalized world and strive to realize his fundamental values in the interstices of the modern social order, in those spheres of social life, such as the 'brotherliness of direct and personal human relations', that have remained relatively untouched by the dynamic of rationalization. Or instead of trying to combine a commitment to ultimate values with the rational calculation of consequences involved in the *zweckrational* orientation of action, he may reject *Zweckrationalität* completely in favor of pure *Wertrationalität* (value-rationality) and orient his action to the realization of some absolute value or unconditional demand, paying no heed to the probable consequences of his action.

On the other hand, the individual may accept—indeed affirm—the modern rationalized world as the arena in which he will strive to become a personality. This is what Weber himself chooses to do, though he acknowledges the dignity of the conscious, deliberate, internally consistent decision to reject this world and argues that such a decision cannot be rationally criticized. Aware that the modern world harbors grave moral dangers, Weber sees it as offering at the same time a unique moral opportunity—the opportunity to achieve the special kind of dignity he associates with the 'ethic of responsibility' (Schluchter). This dignity attaches above all to the politician who, forced to consider the use of morally dubious means to realize important ends, is 'aware of a responsibility for the consequences of his conduct and really feels such responsibility with heart and soul'. But the ethic of responsibility is not a specifically political ethic; it is rather an extremely general ethical orientation applicable to many domains of social life.

Weber defines the ethic of responsibility in opposition to the ethic of conviction (*Gesinnungsethik*). They differ decisively with respect to what Weber calls the 'very first question' of ethics:

> (a) whether the intrinsic value [*Eigenwert*] of ethical conduct—the 'pure will' or the 'conscience' [*Gesinnung*] as it used to be called—is sufficient for its justification, following the maxim of the Christian moralists: 'The Christian acts rightly and leaves the consequences of his action to God'; or (b) whether the responsibility for the foreseeable—as possible or probable—consequences of the action is to be taken into consideration . . . Both [points of view] invoke ethical maxims. But these maxims are in eternal conflict—a conflict which cannot be resolved by means of ethics alone.

The believer in an ethic of conviction, who takes the former attitude, considers the foreseeable consequences of his action ethically irrelevant; the believer in an ethic of responsibility, who takes the latter attitude, considers them ethically relevant in the highest degree, and feels personally responsible for them. The conflict between these two ethical orientations, Weber argues, 'cannot be resolved by means of ethics alone'. Each individual must resolve it for himself through an extra-ethical choice.

The choice between an ethic of conviction and an ethic of responsibility is ultimately a choice between two modes of rationality. Here again we encounter the central paradox of Weber's moral philosophy: in order to live a rational (meaning consciously guided) life, an individual must make a criterionless and in this sense non-rational choice between two irreconcilably opposed modes of rationality. To choose to be guided by an ethic of conviction is to adopt a purely *wertrational* (value-rational) orientation: it is to act, according to Weber's definition of *Wertrationalität*, which could serve equally well as a definition of the ethic of conviction, on the basis of a 'conscious belief in the unconditional, intrinsic value (*Eigenwert*) of some ethical, esthetic, religious or other form of behavior as such, independently of its consequences'. Adopting an ethic of conviction thus entails the unreserved rejection, as ethically barren, of all rational reckoning of means and ends, all calculating of consequences—the rejection, in short, of the central elements of rational purposeful (*zweckrational*) action. To choose to be guided by an ethic of responsibility, on the other hand, is to commit oneself to precisely these central elements of *Zweckrationalität*. It is to reason in terms of means and ends; to 'give an account of the foreseeable results of one's action'; to 'rationally weigh not only means against ends but ends against secondary

consequences and finally also the various possible ends against one another', as Weber puts it in his definition of *Zweck-rationalität*.

Yet the ethic of responsibility is *not* identical with pure *Zweckrationalität*. For pure *Zweckrationalität*, as I argued above, precludes any reference to ultimate value commitments: ends are determined by the urgency of an individual's 'given subjective wants' and by the ease of satisfying them, not by their 'worth' from the point of view of a system of ultimate values. The ethic of responsibility, on the other hand, is not merely compatible with a commitment to ultimate values, but demands just such a commitment. For responsibility is empty unless it is responsibility to some 'substantive purpose', unless it is informed by 'passionate devotion to a "cause"'.

Far from being identical with pure *Zweckrationalität*, the ethic of responsibility can best be understood as an attempt by Weber to integrate *Wertrationalität* and *Zweckrationalität*, the passionate commitment to ultimate values with the dispassionate analysis of alternative means of pursuing them. Thus Weber argues that the politician must weld 'warm passion' to a 'cool sense of proportion'—must combine passionate devotion to a cause with the 'ability to let realities work upon him with inner concentration and calmness'. Put somewhat differently, the ethic of responsibility is an attempt by Weber to integrate reason in the anthropological sense with scientific rationality. Reason in the anthropological sense, it will be recalled, is the distinctively human power to give meaning and dignity to one's life by adhering to a central value-orientation; while scientific rationality, as it relates to action, is the power to act on the basis of empirical knowledge of the causal relations linking ends, means and secondary consequences. The ethic of responsibility requires on the one hand that the development of personality through the exercise of reason in the anthropological sense be disciplined by the cool skepticism of scientific rationality so as to maximize the chances of actually realizing the values to which one is committed. It requires, in short, that ends determined in a *wertrational* manner be pursued with means selected in a *zweckrational* manner. On the other hand, the ethic of responsibility requires that scientific rationality serve reason in the anthropological sense, that the calculating attitude of *Zweckrationalität* be subordinated to the pursuit of ends chosen in a *wertrational* manner. For scientific rationality alone affords no basis for the conduct of life; in and of itself, like pure *Zweckrationalität*, it is ethically barren. Only by integrating the *wertrational* and *zweckrational* orientations, by joining reason in the anthropological sense to scientific rationality, can an individual live a truly human life *within* the modern rationalized world.

WEBER'S MORAL TEMPERAMENT

To choose between an ethic of conviction and an ethic of responsibility, then, is to choose between two modes of rationality: between pure *Wertrationalität* and a synthesis of *Wert-* and *Zweckrationalität*. The choice cannot itself be a rational one, for it is precisely the criteria of rationality that must be chosen. Weber's own allegiance to the ethic of responsibility—and thus to a synthesis of *Wert-* and *Zweckrationalität*—reflects his deeply ambivalent attitude toward the processes of rationalization that have shaped and that continue to shape modern Western culture. Weber recognizes that the modern social world harbors grave moral dangers—dangers that arise directly from its specific and peculiar rationality. The 'tremendous cosmos of the modern economic order', based on the purely formal rationality of the market, 'determine[s] the lives of all the individuals who are born into this mechanism, not only those directly concerned with economic acquisition, with irresistible force'. Bureaucracy, because of its unsurpassable technical rationality the 'only really inescapable power', threatens to develop a stranglehold over all of social life, condemning man to 'social impotence'. Modern science, construing the world as a causal mechanism, has eroded older conceptions of the world as a meaningful cosmos and thereby saddled individuals with the arduous task of creating meaning for the world on their own. And the permeation of *Zweckrationalität* into all domains of social life threatens to take place 'at the expense of any commitment to ultimate values', thus 'ethically neutralizing' the world. In view of these serious threats to the development of autonomous moral personality—threats that are inherent in the modern rationalized social world—Weber acknowledges the dignity of those who deliberately reject this world in order to lead their lives outside the domain of the rationalized institutional orders.

Yet while he recognizes the legitimacy of a stance of uncompromising rejection of the modern world, Weber is himself committed to a radically this-worldly moral perspective: committed, that is, to struggling to lead a truly human life within the modern rationalized world. Like the Puritan ascetic, whom he so movingly portrays in his studies of religion, Weber too 'affirms individual rational activity within the institutional framework [*Ordnungen*] of the world, affirming it to be his responsibility as well as his means for securing certification of his state of grace'. More precisely, he affirms the ethical significance of rational action 'within the institutions of the world but in opposition to them'. This ethos of engaged opposition, of responsible struggle, is crystallized in his attitude toward bureaucracy. Appalled by 'the idea that the world should be filled with nothing but those cogs who cling to a little post and strive for a somewhat greater one', Weber does not ask how it is possible to escape from the bureaucratized realms of life. Instead, he identifies the 'central question' as 'what we have to *set against* this [bureaucratic] machinery, in order to preserve a remnant of humanity from this parcelling-out of the soul, from this exclusive rule of bureaucratic life ideals' (quoted in Mitzman, 1971).

The moral life, for Weber, is framed by a series of tensions: between ultimate values and recalcitrant reality, between warm passion and a cool sense of proportion, between ends and means, between *Wertrationalität* and *Zweckrationalität*, between reason in the anthropological sense and scientific rationality, between idealistic striving and realistic adaptation to the possible—between, in sum, the ethically rationalized personality, committed to certain standards of *substantive* rationality, and the ethically neutral social world, governed by mechanisms of purely *formal* rationality. These tensions can be definitively resolved in two ways: by abandoning one's ideals, one's ultimate value commitments, and learning to adjust or adapt to the world as it is (and to oneself as one happens to be) in a purely *zweckrational* manner; or by denying the significance of what Benjamin Nelson (1971) has called the 'social reality principle', by rejecting a concern with the consequences of one's action and striving to realize one's values in a purely *wertrational* manner. Weber rejects the first way of resolving the tensions on principled grounds as incompatible with the core requirement of a truly human life—that the individual give his life a coherent meaning and direction by committing himself to certain ultimate values and orienting his action to their realization; he rejects the second way of resolving them on personal grounds as indicative of an inability to 'bear the fate of the times like a man'. For Weber himself, or for any individual committed to struggling to realize ultimate values within the modern rationalized world, the tensions can never be resolved: they constitute the enduring framework within which all moral conduct takes place.

What Raymond Aron has called a 'metaphysics of struggle', part Darwinian, part Nietzschean, lies at the foundation of Weber's thought. Weber repeatedly emphasizes the inevitability of conflict—among nations, among classes, among individuals, and, not least, within each individual. Moreover, he affirms the value—the 'productivity', in Löwith's expression—of conflict and contradiction. 'The highest ideals', for Weber, are formed only in the struggle with other ideals', the highest personalities only 'in the struggle against the difficulties which life presents'.

In his emphasis on the inevitability of conflict and tension in social life, Weber stands allied in moral temperament with his contemporary Sigmund Freud. Both reject conceptions of a happy and harmonious social existence as illusory and disdain the impulse toward reconciliation and reunion as immature. Both combine an unwavering commitment to scientific rationality with a keen awareness of its limited moral significance. Both aim to advance individual autonomy, to help individuals 'reach heightened levels of self-conscious free choice' (Levine) through a strenuous 'training in lucidity' (Rieff). At the center of their austere moral visions is not a new type of society but a new type of individual: one who harbors neither nostalgia for a golden past nor hope for a redeeming future but who, possessing a 'trained relentlessness in viewing the realities of life', is able to measure up to the 'demands of the day'.

Dennis Wrong   (essay date 1984)

SOURCE: "Marx, Weber, and Contemporary Sociology," in *Max Weber's Political Sociology: A Pessimistic Vision of a Rationalized World,* edited by Ronald M. Glassman and Vatro Murvar, Greenwood Press, 1984, pp. 69-81.

[In the following essay, Wrong explains the influence of Marxist theory on Weber's thought.]

The failure of our multiple particular researches conducted with increasingly precise and complex methods to cumulate into a coherent overall vision of the world largely accounts for the immense flowering of interest in recent years in the so-called classical sociologists. This new interest has been especially pronounced in the cases of Marx and Weber, both of whose work was preeminently historical in focus, guided by what the Marxist philosopher Karl Korsch called the "principle of historical specificity."

A major theme of recent discussions of Weber has been his relation to Marx and Marxism, discussions that have revised the simplistic view of Weber as an "idealist" critic of Marxist "materialism" based on *The Protestant Ethic and the Spirit of Capitalism,* the first of Weber's major writings to be translated into English and to become widely known. The Parsonian interpretation of Weber exaggerated the differences from Marx in many areas and sometimes tended to present Weber as a kind of anti-Marx. One of the first overviews of Weber's sociology in English antedating Parsons's 1937 discussion in *The Structure of Social Action* was that of Albert Soloman, whose writings on Weber are largely remembered for his description of Weber as the "bourgeois Marx" and his later claim that Weber's sociology was "a long and intense dialogue with the ghost of Karl Marx." The label retains a certain appositeness, but the characterization of Weber's sociology is not really tenable. Weber's stature in the Anglo-American world has become so great that Marxists and neo-Marxists today are prone to try to assimilate him to Marx, seeing him as expanding upon a number of themes first adumbrated by Marx which have become more salient in this century, such as the greater bureaucratization of capitalism and the state and their increasing interpenetration. This perspective was ably presented by Hans Gerth and C. Wright Mills in their introduction to the first book-length selection in English of Weber's sociological writings, which appeared in 1946. In more recent versions, one sometimes detects an inclination to dispose of Weber by annexing him to an essentially Marxist outlook, but that Weber and Marx are less at odds than was formerly believed, at least at the level of their substantive interpretations, seems to me to be undeniable.

Some Marxists of a doctrinaire cast of mind, unable simply to dismiss Weber as a bourgeois ideologue—though efforts to do so continue—have tried to cope with him by claiming that his most valuable ideas are directly borrowed from Marxism. On the other hand, disillusioned Marxists or neo-Marxists, whose hopes have been irretrievably shaken by two world wars, the creation in Russia and elsewhere of new political and social tyrannies in the name of Marxism, and the stolidly non-revolutionary temper of the working class in capitalist countries, have often tended to cannibalize Weber, drawing heavily on his vision while reformulating it in more congenial neo-Marxist or Hegelian terms. I have in mind particularly the original Frankfurt School theorists. As Raymond Aron, the man who introduced Weber into France, wrote of Herbert Marcuse's famous attack on Weber at the 1964 Heidelberg conference honoring the centennial of Weber's birth:

> Have events proved Max Weber wrong . . . ? It is quite obvious that they have borne him out, as even Herbert Marcuse admits. . . . Herbert Marcuse cannot forgive Max Weber for having denounced in advance as a utopia something that up to now has indeed turned out to be utopian: the idea of a liberation of man by the modification of the system of ownership and a planned economy.

That is what sticks in the craw of Marxists to this day even more than Weber's ironic definition of himself as a "class-conscious bourgeois." For he engaged Marxists on their very own terrain with superior intellectual resources, often reached similar conclusions about past and contemporary history, and yet unreservedly rejected their historical optimism. Marxism, even in the complex and subtle variants that are influential in Western universities today, remains a political faith affirming the unity of theory and practice, however unconsummated that unity is presently conceded to be by "Western" Marxists shorn of any illusions about the oppressive practice of all existing Communist states. Although Weber died just a few years after the Bolshevik seizure of power, he foresaw almost immediately that it would prove to be a historical disaster for the Russian people, producing "mounds of corpses."

Weber was equally blunt in rejecting the revolutionary means as well as the utopian ends cherished by Marxism: "He 'who wishes to live as modern man,' even if this be 'only in the sense that he has his daily paper, railways, electricity, etc.,' must resign himself to the loss of ideals of radical revolutionary change: indeed he must abandon 'the *conceivability* of such a goal.'" Recent events in France in 1968, in Chile and Portugal in the 1970s, and the appearance of what has come to be called "Eurocommunism" have in different ways powerfully confirmed this conclusion. Today's "Marxists of the chair," a species at long and welcome last becoming established in the American university, often expound a Marxism that owes more to non-Marxist thought than to the original doctrine. In particular, the eschatological hopes invested in the proletariat have been considerably diluted or abandoned to the point where some latter-day self-described Marxist theoreticians remind one of the death-of-God theologians who made a brief stir in the 1960s. They have tacitly accepted the diagnosis of modern industrial civilization that Weber advanced with weak but unsurpassed clarity over sixty years ago. Yet Marx remains for them an iconic figure while Weber continues to arouse their ambivalence.

Western Marxists who long ago rejected the world of the Gulag Archipelago often remain reluctant even to acknowledge that world as *a* form of Marxist "praxis," if not the only imaginable one. Self-declared Marxists, after all, rule states containing over a third of the world's population, whereas Weberians control no more than a few professorships. An American Marxist professor once complained to me rather bitterly of an eminent colleague: "He thinks it fine to love Tocqueville, but you're not supposed to love Marx." Such an attitude was certainly not uncommon in American sociology until fairly recently, but I could hardly refrain from remarking—though I did refrain—that in the world at large people have been killed for not loving Marx, or for not loving him in the prescribed way. To be sure, people have also been killed for loving him, though not quite as many; the numbers in both cases, however, run to the millions. But no one has ever been killed for not loving Tocqueville or Max Weber.

Twenty years ago I described Max Weber as "the one great man we sociologists can plausibly claim as our own," a judgment with which I concur if anything more than ever today. But the word *plausibly* was deliberately inserted in the statement with Marx in mind, for it is possible to deny that Marx was essentially or fundamentally a sociologist but not that he was a great man who, whatever the fate of the movements launched in his name, achieved an encompassing grasp of wide swaths of human history without sacrificing, like so many of his contemporaries and his own epigoni, concrete detail to the conceptual demands of an abstract scheme. In reaction against such schemes, Weber was deeply suspicious of wide-ranging developmental theories, but the scope and depth of his own historical work achieves as much as Marx's does the level of universal history. Marx and Weber are therefore likely to continue to be linked together less as antipodal figures than as sources of inspiration for the large-scale comparative historical sociology toward which the more ambitious social scientists in a number of countries are increasingly moving now that the view that the natural sciences present an appropriate model for the social sciences to emulate has been epistemologically dethroned.

The present revival of broad comparative history which recognizes both Marx and Weber as ancestors is an interdisciplinary project involving both sociologists and historians who have overcome the traditional barriers that have long divided them. In its fidelity to the actual historical record, the new comparative history even at its most ambitious bears little resemblance to the all-embracing systems of such nineteenth-century sociologists as Comte and Spencer, who tried to impose abstract nomological straitjackets on the disorderly and variegated materials of actual history. If we turn, however, to the discipline of sociology as presently conceived in the United States, Weber's influence is considerably more pervasive than that of Marx.

Let us assess Weber's impact on American sociology, considering it in relation to the established specialties of the field rather than according to the natural lines of di-

vision in his work that have been carefully drawn by recent Weber scholars.

FORMAL ORGANIZATIONS

It is scarcely an exaggeration to say that the very existence of formal organizations as a specialty stems from Weber's conception of bureaucracy. Weber, of course, did not invent the concept of bureaucracy: Hegel and Marx used it, Saint-Simon at least implied it, and such nineteenth-century novelists as Gogol, Balzac and Dickens (not to speak of Kafka early in the present century) satirized it. Weber's achievement was to extend it from the realm of government to other areas of social organization, to identify bureaucratization as a master trend in modern society, and—most important to American sociologists—to define it formally as a generic type of social structure. American social scientists took the Weberian model as a point of departure for the empirical observation and analysis of a huge variety of special-purpose organizations which, not surprisingly, were often found to deviate from the attributes of the model.

Apart from legitimating a new field of empirical research, the early users of Weber's concept were actuated by two extrasociological aims. First, the Weberian model could be used to defend the welfare state of the New Deal—and even the idea of "socialism"—against its conservative political opponents, who made an epithet of "bureaucrat" in their diatribes against "red tape," desk-warming civil servants feeding at the public trough and the like. Weber's emphasis on the *efficiency* of bureaucracy as a means to the achievement of clearly defined collective goals served as a defense against its detractors: "The decisive reason for the advance of bureaucratic organization has always been its purely technical superiority over any other form of organization. The fully bureaucratic mechanism compares with other organizations exactly as does the machine with nonmechanical modes of production." At the same time, Weber's insistence that bureaucratization was not confined to government but encompassed the corporate economy as well drew the sting from the arguments of the defenders of "free enterprise" against state intervention in the economy.

A second aim, following from the first, was to reformulate the idea of bureaucracy in order to make it less incompatible with the American democratic and egalitarian ethos. This involved divesting the Weberian concept of its heavy emphasis on hierarchical authority, impersonal relations and the suppression of individual initiative. The accounts by the Harvard industrial sociologists of the emergence of an "informal structure" of social relations in large organizations, modifying and bypassing the formally prescribed rules and lines of authority, were widely employed for this purpose. Weber's relative neglect of "staff" as opposed to hierarchical "line" positions in organizations and his failure to discuss the collegial ties central to the professions were also stressed in this connection, especially by Talcott Parsons.

These uses and modifications of Weber's model tended to ignore the duality of his own outlook toward bureaucracy as, on the one hand, an indispensable rational instrumentality under the conditions of modern life, and, on the other, as a "living machine" which "in union with the dead machine . . . is laboring to produce the cage of that bondage of the future to which one day powerless men will be forced to submit like the fellaheen of ancient Egypt." American liberal democratic social scientists found Weber's historical pessimism, based on the fear of a trend toward total bureaucratization, no easier to stomach than did Marxists. The "counterculture" of the 1960s, on the other hand, has given far greater resonance to Weber's despair over the "iron cage" of modern society, though it often assumed oppositional stances that he would have regarded as sentimental and unrealistic.

Indeed, the negative side of Weber's view of bureaucracy has in recent years almost completely overshadowed the positive side. What one writer has called "bureaucracy baiting" has become as characteristic of the left as of the right. Bureaucracy is presented as an implacable force opposing both personal freedom and popular democracy. Weber's emphasis on the essential passivity of bureaucracies, their availability to any political leaders strong and determined enough to use them, is ignored in this view. Nor has the possibility of combining democratic leadership and control with a reliable and efficient civil service, advocated by Weber in the last few years of his life, received anything like the attention given to his more pessimistic statements about the spread of bureaucratization.

SOCIAL STRATIFICATION

Marx, of course, long ago placed classes and class structures at the very center of sociological and historical analysis, and his views have loomed large in most theoretical discussion ever since. However, the Weberian triad of status, wealth and power is indispensable to the study of social inequality and class structure, although the interdependences among the three are as important a subject of investigation as the distinction itself. This has not always been recognized by American sociologists, whose quick acceptance of the triad was not free of selective distortion. The concept of "status group" is sometimes employed as a counter to the economically based Marxist concept of class, although Weber never contended that status groups were *more* important in modern society than classes, which he, like Marx, grounded in the economy, merely that they were distinguishable. Weber's emphasis on status was also sometimes invoked in support of a quite different use of the term: its equation with the prestige rankings of individuals or positions (usually occupations derived by the favored methods of survey research). But Weber wrote of status *groups,* not of status as an attribute of individuals or positions, and he did not identify status groups with a rank-order reflecting an underlying consensus on values in society. Far from implying consensus, conflict between status groups was in Weber's view just as prevalent as class conflict.

POLITICAL SOCIOLOGY

Nearly all of the classical sociologists were concerned at some level with politics, even though—or perhaps because—the hallmark of the sociological perspective, as it arose in the nineteenth century was to claim historical, causal and normative priority for society over the state. This, in conjunction with the later almost simultaneous development of political science as a discipline, retarded the emergence of political sociology as a sociological specialty.

Like formal organizations and social stratification, political sociology began to emerge as a specialty not long after publication of the first translations of Weber's sociological writings. (His many commentaries on the political issues of his time remain untranslated, as does Mommsen's important study of his political views.) Weber's concept of legitimation, his threefold typology of legitimate authority, his definitions of the state and of power and his treatment of bureaucracies as power structures (which influenced his contemporary, Robert Michels) have had a far-reaching effect on the theoretical formulations of political scientists as well as political sociologists. Weber alone of the "classical" sociologists, including Marx, did not treat the state and politics as secondary phenomena subordinate to autonomous "social forces." Of nineteenth-century social thinkers, only Tocqueville bears comparison with Max Weber in this respect, and his insights were less systematically developed. Traditional Marxism, like its bourgeois counterparts, has a dusty Victorian ring and has required strong infusions from later thinkers, including Weber, in order to retain the appearance of relevance to our time, not to speak of its embarrassments in confronting the record of the movements and regimes it has itself inspired. Max Weber of all the classical sociologists seems most to be our contemporary, for the troubled history of the twentieth century has cast doubt, to put it mildly, on the classical ascription of primacy to the social over the political. Totalitarianism has merely deviated furthest in achieving the complete ascendancy of the latter over the former.

The three specialities influenced by Weber that I have reviewed are all primarily concerned with social organization. If a sociology of economic life ever develops as a recognized specialty, it will join them in owing a large debt to Weber. The sociology of culture rather than of social organization is a larger component of the other specialties in which Weber's influence has been great. He is with Durkheim one of the two major theorists of the sociology of religion. Without reducing religious ideas to simple reflections of the social location of the classes and communities that upheld them, he explored their intimate connection with the concrete situations in which their creators and carriers found themselves. Weber was formally educated in the law and his earliest scholarship dealt with legal institutions. Since much of it remains untranslated, or has been translated only recently, his influence on the sociology of law, especially in comparative historical scholarship, is bound to increase. His writings on the sociology of music and of architecture are major contributions to these undeveloped fields.

Weber does not easily lend himself to the categorizations favored by writers of textbooks and taxonomists of sociological theories. Specious though such pedagogic labeling often is, at least a modicum of plausibility exists for calling Marx a "conflict theorist," Durkheim and Parsons "functionalists" or "consensualists," and various other people "exchange" or "phenomenological" or "symbolic interactionist" theorists. Weber fails to fit under any of these familiar rubrics or under those that stress epistemological standpoints ranging from strict positivism to pure hermeneutics. *Historicist* perhaps suits him best, but most sociologists have felt uncomfortable with the label. Their historical knowledge, especially in America, has usually been limited, and in Weber they confront a man whose works, in Mommsen's words, "display an abundance of historical knowledge which has so far not been surpassed by anyone else, with the possible exception of Arnold Toynbee." American sociologists have often regarded sociology as a kind of intellectual short-cut providing nomological formulae under which historical particulars can be subsumed, thus eliminating the necessity of understanding them directly in their complex particularity. Weber's vast and detailed knowledge seems to reproach sociologists for their hubris, especially since he makes little claim to derive from it universal generalizations, in contrast to Toynbee's "challenge and response" theory of civilization, which can be identified with a familiar tradition of theorizing and criticized for its vague, metaphorical character.

But Max Weber was more than a scholar of prodigious learning. Even his most specialized and objective writings communicate an underlying tension and moral passion, a "pathos of objectivity" in Gerth and Mills' incisive phrase. Moreover, he never confined himself to "scholarship as a vocation" but was constantly drawn to politics even if in the end his career as a political man was abortive. Thus he demands to be assessed according to the ultimate values that gave his life and work a unity despite the apparent fragmentation of his omnivorous intellectual concerns.

There is much justification for regarding Weber as an existentialist *avant la lettre*. To his close friend, Karl Jaspers, Weber himself was an existentialist hero, and Jaspers claimed that his own existentialist philosophy was inspired by the example of Weber as "the man who embodied human greatness," who "lived in the only way possible for a man of integrity in those times; breaking through all illusory forms he disclosed the foundations of human Existenz." Weber's indebtedness to Nietzsche, generally regarded now as one of the fathers of existentialism, has been increasingly recognized by his more recent interpreters. Weber's conception of the relationship between values and knowledge can now be seen as much more existentialist than positivist. His insistence on "value freedom" or "ethical neutrality" as a prerequisite for any social science worthy of the name has long been

upheld by American sociologists as the first commandment of their calling. Younger sociologists involved in the protest movements of the 1960s attacked value neutrality as a self-serving defense of professional interests, as an excuse for political indifference and simply as a sham violated in the actual research of many who proclaimed it. Neither side in this rancorous dispute, now thankfully showing signs of moving to higher intellectual ground, did justice to Weber's position, whether in claiming to affirm it or to reject it.

Weber did not argue for the exclusion of value judgments from social science because he regarded them as blind, irrational eruptions of human emotion posing a threat to the majestic authority of pure science. It was rather the other way around: He wished to preserve values as the realm of individual freedom subject to the dignity of responsible choice uncoerced by the constraints of the world of fact revealed by science, even in the face of a full and stoical awareness of these constraints. This was, of course, a Kantian position reflecting Weber's neo-Kantian philosophical heritage. But Weber differed from the Kantians in denying that there were objective values on which rational consensus was possible. He insisted rather that there was a plurality of irreconcilable values, that the world was one of "warring gods" and that to align oneself with one of the gods meant to deny the claims of another who might be equally attractive and powerful. This position is existentialist or Nietzschean rather than Kantian: We are condemned to the often painful and even tragic choice between rival values, and we cannot slough off the burden of choice by claiming that it is not ourselves but the world as understood by science that dictates our conduct.

For politics, Weber favored an "ethic of responsibility" in preference to an "ethic of intention" (or of "absolute ends" as it has often—misleadingly, I think—been translated). An ethic of responsibility takes into account the consequences and further ramifications of realizing a particular end and also appraises an end in terms of the costs of attaining it. Empirical knowledge therefore enters into the consideration of ends to be pursued regardless of their status in some "ultimate" scheme of values. Here Weber places less of an existentialist emphasis on the autonomy and irreducibility of the choice of ends and gives weight to the interaction of ends and means and their frequent interchangeability, treating knowledge and values as complementary rather than as sealed off from one another.

It is impossible to confront Weber without a sense of the man behind the work. He is the only one of the classical sociologists who has been the subject of a psychobiography, whose life and character have been made into a cultural symbol in a brilliant if tendentious study by a literary scholar, and whose love letters, no less, are shortly to be published. Even Marx's life and personal history have not attracted comparable interest, largely because Marx's message was ultimately an affirmative one embraced by an entire movement whereas the tension and ambivalence of Weber's thought points in the direction of personal stoicism rather than collective commitment. The spell cast by the passion and the pathos Weber projects has been a source of irritation to his critics.

Donald MacRae, a proper Scotsman, who has written a little book deliberately intended to "demystify" Weber, remarks that "practically all that is written on Weber is written in awe," with the result that "when one is knocking one's forehead on the floor one's vision is certainly limited and probably blurred."

Why then Weber's continuing spell? I write unashamedly from within the circle of the bewitched, also as one who in middle age feels historical nostalgia for the time of his parents' childhood, the years of Weber's manhood, and, moreover, as one with little inclination to apologize for his own "bourgeois values." Part of the answer lies in one remark of Donald MacRae's with which I can agree: "Our century has apparently dedicated itself, only halfknowingly, to acting out the ideas and dreams of [early twentieth-century Europe] in deadly earnest." By the late 1970s we are perhaps entitled to conclude that the acting out has almost ended. This too is a source of Weber's relevance, for he anticipated the trajectories of our belief, disbelief and unbelief. A world of "specialists without vision and sensualists without heart" today sounds painfully more like a description of the way we live now than like the possible future described by Weber in 1905. And we have had a good deal of unsatisfactory experience with the "entirely new prophets" and "great rebirth of old ideas and ideals" that he expected to arise in reaction to the world of modernity. although the imperatives facing us are scarcely the same, we are unable to improve upon his conclusion that "nothing is gained by yearning and tarrying alone" and that what remains is for us to "set to work and meet the 'demands of the day,' in human relations as well as in our vocation."

Hans-Ulrich Derlien (essay date 1991)

SOURCE: "Beaurocracy in Art and Analysis: Kafka and Weber," in *Journal of the Kafka Society of America,* Nos. 1-2, 1991, pp. 4-16.

[In the following essay, Derlien examines the Weberian influence in the works of Franz Kafka.]

Sociology of literature is based upon the assumption that literary fiction, through the personal concern of the artist, reflects societal conditions. Yet, surprisingly little sociological work has been undertaken to analyze the reflection in literature of bureaucracy as a social phenomenon—at least in the German speaking countries. Elsewhere the administrative novel as a special genre has been extensively discussed (Egger 1959; Kroll 1965; Savage 1965; McCurdy 1973) and anthologies edited (Coser 1963; Holzer, et al. 1979) to teach the sociology of bureaucracy through literature. This neglect of the bureaucratic contents of German literary fiction in gen-

eral, and of Franz Kafka's in particular, is all the more astonishing as Kafka's older contemporary Max Weber (1864-1920) is commonly regarded as the leading sociological theorist of bureaucracy. In literature departments, on the other hand, bureaucracy is usually not dealt with as a literary motif (Frenzel 1976a; 1976b); the main currents of Kafka interpretation are transcendental and psychological while the bureaucratic aspects in Kafka's work are regarded as marginal, although his novels owe a great deal of their grotesque impact on the reader to such bureaucratic settings. Only recently has the bureaucratic paradigm been applied to Kafka, while additional parallels to Weber have been developed by German literature specialists.

While other novelists view bureaucracy predominantly from the outside and through the perspective of the individual confronted with repressive parts of the state apparatus (police, military, judicial branch), Kafka displays an unusually differentiated insight into the internal mechanisms and the social functioning of bureaucracy. This makes it worthwhile to first elaborate Kafka's treatment of bureaucracy by applying Weberian categories. Approaching Kafka through literary sociology will bring to the fore a far reaching congruency of the conceptualization of bureaucracy in his major novels, *The Trial* and *The Castle,* with Weber's model of bureaucracy. Second, with the immanent parallels given, it is tempting to investigate to what extent Kafka's way of treating bureaucracy reflects his personal office experience. Contrary to outright critics of bureaucracy, its evaluation tends to remain hidden with sophisticated authors like Kafka. Therefore, the assessment of bureaucracy, which Kafka the artist and Max Weber the social scientist posit, is to be compared-the latter contrary to his emphasis on value-freedom in sociological analysis. Finally, I shall relate Kafka and Weber in yet another way by following two clues that point to an—albeit indirect—biographical relationship between both men. The literary approach, the sociological approach, and the sociology of literature approach focus on Kafka's bureaucratic experience as well as on his exposure to Weber's analysis, appear to justify the claim that bureaucracy must be attributed more weight in interpreting and understanding Kafka than is customarily the case.

KAFKA'S WORK IN WEBERIAN
PERSPECTIVE

There is hardly another author in the world of literature whose work appears so deeply colored by features of the bureaucratic state apparatus. This is indicated by the technical nature of the titles of most of Kafka's short stories and novels, for example: "Report to an Academy," "The Penal Colony," "The Judgment," *The Trial* and *The Castle.* Kafka, like no writer before or after him, uses core institutions of the modern state as the scenery for his novels; the penal colony, the judicial court, and the castle as the center of bureaucratic power are all, in a Weberian sense, the agents of political domination in everyday life and exercise a monopoly of physical power over civil society as the distinctive feature of the modern state.

Kafka's characters and protagonists are taken from the professions; country doctor, salesman, military officers, managing bank director, surveyor and—most prominently in the two novels under consideration—civil servants of various ranks, and the law professions. The author's imaginary counterparts, although not civil servants specifically, nevertheless also belong to the historically new professional service class, such as the managing director and surveyor who serve, or aspire to serve, in private and public bureaucratic organizations.

Weber's Model of Bureaucracy

In order to convey to the reader the richness of Kafka's observations on bureaucracy I shall systematize the material by applying the characteristics of Max Weber's ideal type of bureaucracy. This ideal type is an abstraction of features which distinguish the modern type of legal/rational political domination from traditional (feudal or patrimonial), as well as from the unstable form of charismatic domination. Legal/rational domination relies on professional (contrary to honorary) personnel who receive monetary rewards, are specifically trained, employed full-time, appointed, and promoted according to objective criteria (performance or seniority) instead of being elected or selected according to social origin. This configuration is historically juxtaposed to the feudal rule of landlords, to whom the office is just an annex to their estate from which they make their living. In bureaucracies, the monarch or parliament have appropriated all means of production (as, for instance, opposed to the custom of self-equipment in traditional communal society); thus the office is financially and physically separated from the household, instead of alimenting civil servants in the palace. The bureaucratic apparatus is characterized by a hierarchy of command, and monocratic decision-making has replaced collegial decisions in chambers. Decision-making follows formal regulations within specialized areas of jurisdiction, instead of producing voluntary ad hoc decisions in all matters coming up to officials who happen to be available. This formalization renders political domination calculable for society as well as for the ruler. Furthermore, communication is basically written and recorded so that monitoring is possible through the hierarchy and by external control agencies. In the course of the historical formation of the bureaucratic structure, civil servants develop as a distinct social class with their own code of honor and professional role understanding, including disciplined work and impersonal decision making. This model of legal/rational domination can be applied to the picture Kafka paints in both *The Trial* and *The Castle,* and these bureaucratic dimensions can be found in his works. It is not to judge their empirical adequacy, for this would do injustice to Weber's ideal type which exaggerates reality, as well as to Kafka, who of course transcends reality through irony.

The Categories of the Weberian Model Applied

Josef K. and K. are mostly confronted with subordinate officials of the lowest status: messengers, the usher, clerks, K.'s two undisciplined assistants, the schoolmaster in *The Castle,* servants in the bank, an official thrasher, and warders. As the protagonist in both novels, initially at least, has no personal experience with the higher strata of officials, it is through these subaltern characters and civil figures that he forms his first image of court and castle bureaucrats. Only occasionally does the protagonist himself observe the social life of the bureaucrats and technical procedures, such as the early morning circulation of files in *The Castle* (ch. 19). In order to achieve a still higher degree of objectivity, Kafka even deviates from his typical approach of viewing the world through the protagonist's subjective perspective; instead, he has other characters (the village mayor, the attorney, and the portraitist) give K. lectures on hierarchical communication, departmental specification of jurisdictions, or the decision-making process. This occurs most impressively in chapter 5 of *The Castle* and chapters 7 and 8 of *The Trial.*

The separation of private household and public office, which is important in Weber's historical account of the emergence of European states and bureaucracies, does not yet appear fully developed in Kafka's bureaucratic world. Even higher civil servants have beds in their offices (at least in *The Castle*), and on the subaltern level the private living room is often used for official purposes. Indeed, officials receive clients while lying in bed: so do the village mayor and other officials in *The Castle* (Erlanger, Bürgel) when working at night. K. and his fiancée are still asleep in the classroom, which serves as their bedroom, when the children and the teacher enter. The official portraitist has a bed in his room in the court (Josef K. even has to climb over it). When Josef K. visits the court, he is disoriented because he finds the courtroom hidden in a multistory house and has to enter it through a private flat. Offices are also situated under the roof, where the laundry is drying.

Closely related to the separation of office from household is the monetary payment of officials. Only under this condition, in Weber's view, can political control over the "staff of domination" be fully exercised, because officials without property are totally dependent. That is to say, they do not have the potential to become self-controlling in such a way as that of the nobility in premodern society. Again, Kafka's bureaucracy does not measure up to the "fully developed" Weberian type. In particular the lowest ranks depend upon receiving natural goods as remuneration and thus often live in the office building like K. after his degradation to school clerk. Furthermore, monetary payment is so low that officials in *The Trial* turn corrupt—an aspect which fills Josef K., the principled and explicitly incorruptible bank director, with disgust. It is also this factor which exposes the female characters to the sexual harassment of the officials, because they cannot afford to attract their hate by denying them favors. The consequences are fatal, as the case of the Barnabas family (Amalia) shows.

In turn, full-time employment is not the rule. Only the higher echelons are professional civil servants and are in a position to devote themselves fully to office work, while the servicemen often keep having a private basis of subsistence (Barnabas as a shoemaker); indeed, the honorary village mayor does his official paperwork merely during evening hours. The typical layman administration [*Dilettantenverwaltung*], which Weber likes to contrast with the professional bureaucracy, is accurately depicted through the mayor in *The Castle* by his sloppy file keeping and irregular work on incoming proceedings. He also needs the village teacher for communication and seeks his wife's advice.

Professional training is implied for the higher officials in the novels; they are obviously jurists. In *The Trial,* a law student is helping the investigative judge and envisions a future career as a state attorney. As the higher officials are generally not individually characterized but are displayed as examples of the functionary type without a biography, there is no need for Kafka to elaborate; juridical training had become the rule for higher civil service in the Habsburg empire from the middle of the 19th century.

Striving for career advancement along formalized patterns is a more visible aspect of bureaucratic life in the writings of Kafka. Josef K. is afraid of the competition from the deputy director of his bank when his own professional attention is increasingly distracted by the trial. The thrasher, who punishes the warders, as well as the warders themselves, are afraid of losing their promotions. In general, however, the concern is less with advancement in an established career as with entering a career or a position, be it K.'s unsuccessful attempt to be employed as a surveyor, or Barnabas the messenger's hope to become elevated to the status of a full-time servant.

Hierarchy appears in the novels in various forms. First, there is the hierarchy of offices: in the court system, as well as between the village administration and the Castle offices where the hierarchy runs from K.'s servicemen through K. (school clerk), the teacher, the mayor, the village secretary in the Castle (Bürgel), Erlanger, and finally, Klamm. The way the higher offices function is normally not transparent for lower officials and the protagonists. Higher echelons also appear to be following different rules and decision criteria. Second, the characters of the stories act in hierarchical interpersonal relationships, with the higher officials not being directly accessible for lower members of the system. K. requires some time and advice to discover this hierarchical order. Third, the social order corresponds to the hierarchy of offices: subordinate officials are poor and hardly distinguishable from K. vis-à-vis their social conduct. Only when they are on an official mission are they distinct: Barnabas, having brought a letter, displays a dirty shirt when dropping his fine coat. Subordinate servants, even in the court, can be distinguished only by wearing signs on their collars and bright buttons, while they are indistinguishable from the clients in any other respect. Furthermore, the state/Castle officials gather socially in a particular pub, the "Herrenhof", while the villagers drink beer in the "Brückenhof," the only place K. is permitted to go. Klamm, representing the top of the hierarchy, is even separated by a room of his own in the "Herrenhof." As K. initially does not understand or accept the special status of the officials and the private/public role distinction, he starts observing Klamm secretly and tries to establish contacts by using personal relations.

Discipline—in Weber's perspective the product of an increasingly methodical conduct of life (and rationalization in general) culminating in devotion to one's calling—is a dimension which sets apart the higher officials from their servants and subjects who still follow a traditional mode of life. Subalterns, too, are characterized by inactivity, both in the sense of completely depending upon orders and of sluggishness in executing given orders. They also do not sufficiently concentrate on their jobs, but are easily distracted and follow private objectives: while K. himself does not get up in time from his bed in the classroom, his two assistants are constantly fooling around. Obviously, they have not undergone professional training to assist the surveyor. However, we also find that the investigative judge in *The Trial* is keeping pornographic material in his dirty manual. In general, though, the higher officials are featured as being completely absorbed in their office work. They handle cases in a principled manner, interpret the law from a higher perspective than the subordinate courts, observe their departmental boundaries, and exert themselves by working even through the night, therefore having to sleep in their offices. The protagonists learn from people familiar with Klamm or Sortini that these higher officials are suffering from the burden of their duties, are nervous and permanently tired owing to a chronic lack of sleep. These dysfunctional consequences of excessive office work contrast with the masters' social behavior in that they turn angry, and even vengeful, when clients disturb their administrative work. In their secluded office life they appear "like children," such as when they are struggling for their share of the files in the morning. When they are out of the office and no longer bound by discipline, sexual greed and reckless personal exploitation of female service personnel give the officials almost human traits. Office routines appear to have shaped the personalities of the higher civil servants; they dislike appearing in public, abhor light, and are easily irritated by the slightest changes in exterior arrangement of the work place. K. and Josef K. suspect the officials of hiding and avoiding contact with them.

The typically bureaucratic impersonality of official/client relations, deriving from written communication, formal decision programs, status differences, specialization, and internal controls, is almost completely missing in Kafka's novels. Momus, the village secretary of the Castle, of course, emphasizes that claiming the report is his duty, but seemingly understands K.'s resistance and is trying to persuade K. (with the help of the pub's landlady). In general, too much of Josef K.'s and K.'s sought after success depends on personal relations occasionally backed by bribery, than impersonality in Weber's sense. What at first glance could appear as impersonal conduct of the higher officials is simply a lack of interest in the case and the person being investigated. Officials mostly act impersonally in that they hardly show signs of emotions like despair, hate, rage, or love.

Division of labor, demarcation of jurisdictions, and specialization within an office and between horizontally and vertically arranged authorities, between lower and higher courts as well as within the Castle and among various reviewing agencies, are well described in both of the novels. Here we come across phenomena such as departmental identification and selective perception, instances of filtering information in hierarchical and boundary-crossing communication, and deadlocks in the decision-making process as when K.'s record gets lost and he is consoled that it is bound to turn up one indefinite day, or when contradictory decisions arrive as to his employment.

Communication and decision-making processes structured by hierarchy and area of jurisdiction are, in particular, extensively dealt with by Kafka. Between hierarchical offices, written communication is predominant and confusion arises when the mayor cannot find the letter concerning K.'s case. Higher courts will receive the records of lower courts and review the cases on the basis of the records without entering the stage of information gathering, but are likely to arrive at completely different decisions without informing the lower courts about their decisions and reasoning. Another feature of vertical communication consists of written reports to higher echelons and offices. In *The Castle,* K. is asked by Klamm's village secretary Momus (who cannot specify the purpose), to give account of his activities for a report to the Castle. Momus has to admit that the report will probably never be read by the superiors, but insists that the procedure be carried through. Communication between client and authority appears particularly pathological as higher officials are existentially removed from "real life" in a spatial as well as intellectual respect. In their offices they do not know what is going on in the world and what motivates people. They are not familiar with the particularities of an individual case like K.'s. What is not represented in the records does not exist for them. In *The Trial,* Josef K. complains that the officials lack contact with the citizens and have no sense of human relations; the judges, therefore, have to rely on the attorney and ask his advice on how to assess a case. Stating his point in written form would not help Josef K. with the court, as he is certainly advised by his attorney. In contrast to inter-agency communication, the client/office relationship decisively depends on face-to-face contacts and informal networks, and induces Josef K. to manipulate the social fabric at the price of becoming dependent on boundary persons such as Frieda and Barnabas, or Dr. Huld and Titorelli. Conversely, the letter K. intermediately receives from Klamm praises surveying work K. has never

done and is arbitrarily interpreted by the mayor. Written reports and statements are necessarily a selective mirror of real life or would be endless and infinitely detailed. This consideration is explicitly outlined in *The Trial,* and it makes Josef K. abstain from the necessarily "endless, accurate description of all deeds and events of his entire life", which could be of relevance for the court to recognize his innocence. K., too, refuses to give Momus a "detailed account of today's afternoon" (ch. 9), because he does not see what purpose it is to serve other than to disappear into the registry. As Josef K. does not know what he is accused of, he is lacking criteria of relevance for a statement, and as K. is not given an explanation relating the purpose of the report in his case, he refuses to cooperate.

Deviation of Kafka's Bureaucracy from the Model

The difference between the picture Kafka draws and the Weberian model is partly rooted in the fact that Kafka's bureaucracy is not of the legal/rational type shaped by the concept of *Rechtsstaat,* but obviously represents the older patrimonial bureaucracy. The lack of formal decision-making rules (including external juridical controls of the bureaucracy) has been noted above. It should be added that impersonality—literally the treatment of a client without respect to his (particularly ascribed) social status—juridically presupposes the principle of equal rights for all citizens. It is precisely this aspect of *Rechtsstaat* which is missing. As the absence of external controls accounts for the disinterested manner in which K.'s case is handled, and for his employment being ultimately a matter of patrimonial grace, the missing standard of equal treatment causes the very personal way the protagonists try to promote their cases. This is the reason why they ultimately existentially depend on the goodwill of the officials even in procedural matters of the Castle administration and the court. Equally, secrecy of operation and ambiguity of decision-making standards are properties not contained in the Weberian ideal type of legal/rational domination. In both novels, the protagonists do not manage to see through the system, not even after receiving insider instructions. Their subjective individual rationality, grounded in common sense and experience of their own professions as banker and geographer respectively, is confronted with the rationality of a system they do not understand; the more so as the decision-premises of court and castle are unknown, and the charge against Josef K. and the seriousness of the need to employ a surveyor, respectively, are kept in the dark and rules and regulations of the "machine"—a metaphor used in *The Penal Colony*—are not transparent.

Nevertheless, the features of bureaucracy displayed in Kafka's novels can be related to all of the Weberian dimensions of bureaucracy. Thus far, we have shown little more than the depth at which Kafka deals with bureaucracy and the heuristic value of Weber's model in analyzing the text of an artist. That Kafka's bureaucracy deviates from the historically "fully developed" type of bureaucracy, to a certain extent, is also a reflection of bureaucratic reality during the Habsburg monarchy. It is also, of course, an artistic device.

KAFKA'S OFFICE EXPERIENCE AS A
REFERENCE POINT OF INTERPRETATION

How does this wealth of sociological and, in particular, bureaucratic observation combine with the main currents of Kafka interpretations which almost completely neglect this aspect of the work? Do the deviations from the ideal type just illustrated, typical of Kafka's technique of running counter to the reader's expectations, remind one of the technique of estrangement [*Verfremdung*] Bertolt Brecht was later to employ? The artistic peculiarities of style and composition, which make Kafka a forerunner of expressionism as well as surrealism, were bound to induce competing interpretations as to the meaning of his works and the message Kafka wanted to convey.

> The typical Kafka text derives much of its powerful effect from the intensity with which it simultaneously invites and frustrates interpretation. (Bernheimer)

Be it the metaphysical interpretation as in Kafka's struggle with God and for justice (Brod), be it the biographical interpretation referring to Kafka's conflict with his father personified in the supreme court or Klamm, whose approval and acceptance he is longing for but does not achieve due to his failure to live up to his father's standards of physical, professional, and marital success (Canetti; Binder)—these interpretations pay far too little attention to the obvious reflection of Kafka's professional experience as a bureaucrat. While many biographical aspects are recognized as simple transpositions in the novels, surprisingly the bureaucratic contents reflecting Kafka's personal experience in the state related Bohemian Workers' Accident Insurance Agency are not taken at face value. Already Max Brod had conceded:

> It is clear that Kafka received a great deal of his knowledge of the world and of life as well as his skeptical pessimism from his office experience, from his contact with the laborers suffering from injustice, from the dragging official routine, and the stagnating life of the records. Entire chapters of the (two) novels take their shell, their realistic cover from the milieu experienced in the . . . Insurance Agency. (Max Brod; my translation)

It was writers like Musil, Döblin, Tucholsky, and Brecht who appreciated the bureaucratic contents of Kafka's works as early as the 1930's; Brecht even drew a parallel between Kafka's institutional allegories and the coming of the Nazi system with its insecure legitimacy, absolutist, and terrorist state apparatus. Furthermore, it is remarkable that in the Soviet Union Kafka was read as an author depicting the bureaucratic universe of that society, and illuminating the individual's exposure to bureaucratic powers. Obviously, interpretation is shaped by the sociopolitical situation of the reader and his or her idealist or materialist intellectual background.

Hermsdorf has edited the official documents Kafka produced during his short career in the semi-state insurance agency. Several of the points which have been made above with reference to the Weberian model are underpinned by Hermsdorf. For instance, that reports are not read was Kafka's office experience: he officially complained that not all annual reports about accidents and risks in the factories could be read by the insurance agency. Kafka was concerned about it, and he very much tried to improve the dangerous machines in the factories. These events were later to be described as the complicated execution machine in "The Penal Colony." Furthermore, decisions of the agency were, in fact, based on incomplete information without contact with the firms and inspection of the sites. Not only are the titles of the officials in the novels the same as those used in the agency, but even the Italian names of some of the characters, such as Titorelli, Sortini, and Sordini point to Kafka's experience as a substitute in the private Assicurazioni Generali in 1907! In projecting his physical symptoms (sleeplessness, irritability) onto his characters, Kafka was attempting to distance himself from the office and the alienation caused by the division of labor. After all, he had already left the agency when he finished *The Castle* in 1922.

Weeks has convincingly argued that K.'s struggle to establish his terms of employment in *The Castle,* and the general poverty of the subaltern officials, reflect the demands of the lower civil servants' movement (1909-13) for better salary and job security in the civil service order during the Habsburg monarchy. Kafka was still an untenured apprentice in the agency (1908-10), when a new code began to regulate the status of public employees. These were kept a level apart from the civil servants, prohibited from the provision of room and board, and received a salary decided on only after a probationary period. Kafka, thus, strongly depended on the approval of his superiors, and had to apply several times for salary increases. In 1913 he became an active member of the recently founded professional organization of Jewish officials.

Furthermore, the problem of being accepted as a surveyor in *The Castle* probably reflects the situation of Jews in the Habsburg empire (as in imperial Germany) vis-á-vis being admitted to government service. That Kafka, a professional jurist, ended up in the Workers' Insurance Agency is typical, because Jews were only admitted to state *related* offices of a non-authoritative nature. But even there it was difficult to get a job. Kafka managed to be accepted because the father of a school mate held a leading position there. Indeed, among several hundred employees there were only two Jews (Binder). In *The Castle,* K., at the end of his confrontation with the village mayor (ch. 5), insists on equal rights, stating "I do not want a gift of grace from the castle, but my right."

Kafka was able not only to adopt the perspective of the subaltern stratum in the office he was familiar with from the beginning of his career, but also had gathered experience in higher echelons; this becomes visible particularly in his last novel, *The Castle.* By 1913 he had advanced so far in the hierarchy that he was superior to 30 clerks, and in 1920 he was promoted to secretary of the agency (section head), a rather responsible position which involved conceptual work and representation of the agency in the law courts. Therefore, his picture of Klamm in *The Castle* could well mirror his own role understanding (Binder 1979).

Besides his experience in the Workers' Insurance Agency, Kafka was also contemplating his entrepreneurial activity, which is seldom commented on. Between 1911 and 1917 he had functioned as a silent partner (with his father's capital) in an asbestos firm, an enterprise that finally failed. Albach (1968) has drawn attention to the peculiar character of entrepreneurs in Kafka's early short stories; they are regularly not in control of the economic process, but rather its victim, thus objectifying Kafka's anxiety and subjectively felt burden of entrepreneurial responsibility in the person of the bank manager Joseph K. or Gregor Samsa in *Metamorphosis.*

Maybe the large range of potential associations allowed for by Kafka's metaphors occasionally stimulates far-fetched interpretations of details. In the last resort, this is probably the very distinction between artistic and analytical work. Nevertheless, in view of Kafka's rich bureaucratic experience condensed in the novels, alternative approaches which take into account Kafka's profession, his training as a jurist, and his thorough historical reading (including a 1906 oral examination in the history of law), should also be envisioned to provide an understanding of the novels.

KAFKA'S AND WEBER'S EVALUATION OF BUREAUCRACY

If we assume that Kafka's novels are not merely grand metaphors for transcendental or psychological problems, but at least can be additionally regarded to mirror the author's serious personal concern about his position and function as a public official, it is legitimate to look for Kafka's evaluation of bureaucracy as a social phenomenon.

Although the immediate impression of his personal suffering from office work could lead us to conclude that bureaucracy is negatively evaluated, this would be too simple an answer. On the contrary, there are various dimensions along which Kafka's evaluation of bureaucracy can be summarized.

Functional Criticism

As a bureaucratic insider of the Workers' Accident Insurance Agency, and as a citizen who often had to apply for a passport, Kafka is critical about the social distance between citizens and authorities, about filtering processes in hierarchical decision-making, and about the fictional basis of decisions relying on insufficiently read reports. Furthermore, Kafka is functionally critical of the judicial

system of his time with regards to personal biases and secrecy. As we have seen, he even attacks corruption. The author through the perspective of Josef K., takes the standpoint of the goal-rational actor confronted with bureaucracy's pathologies. On this level of analysis, McDaniel is correct in pointing out the difference between Kafka's view and Max Weber's so-called effectiveness-thesis stressing precision, continuity, discipline, thoroughness, reliability, universal applicability, and performance as criteria of effectiveness. However, this argument is too unsophisticated with respect to Kafka and to Weber. In fact, both authors are ambivalent in their judgements. There can be no doubt that Kafka, when taking the point of view of the organization, would subscribe to Weber's emphasis on precision, discipline, and reliability. In *The Castle,* these possibilities of bureaucracy are underlined by informants to K.; the system's perspective, which is not K.'s perspective, emphasizes positive aspects, while K. perceives the social costs accruing to the individual official, such as tiredness or signs of alienation in general, and to the client.

Formal versus Substantive Rationality

At this point of the analysis, both Kafka and Weber tend to employ the machine-metaphor, and thereby draw our attention to the merely formal rationality of the system. This implies the paradox that a formally rational system produces substantively irrational results—a fact that is fervently expressed by Kafka:

> Having listened to the explanation of the mayor, how the Castle's bureaucracy functions, the following dialogue develops:
>
> Mayor: ". . . doesn't the story bore you?"
>
> "No", said K., "it entertains me."
>
> Then the mayor: "I do not tell it for your entertainment."
>
> "It entertains me merely in that I get an insight into the ridiculous entanglement that eventually decides about the existence of a man," said K. (my trans.)

A similar scene is contained in *The Trial,* when Josef K. argues with the thrasher punishing the two warders who had misbehaved when Josef K. was searched at the beginning of the story:

> Had I known they were to be punished or even that they could be punished, I would not have told their names. I do not believe they are guilty. The organization is guilty. Guilty are the high officials. . . . If you had a high judge under your rod, K. said . . . indeed I did not prevent you from thrashing, on the contrary, I gave you money so that you gained power for a good purpose.
>
> What you say sounds credible, the thrasher said, but I won't let you bribe me. I am employed in order to thrash, thus I thrash. (my trans.)

These dialogues indicate what is known in organizational sociology as *goal displacement,* and hint at the inclination of the apparatus to produce results or deeds that are substantively irrational. Kafka also realizes that achieving substantive rationality depends upon the high officials' capability to define reasonable goals for the system. But the higher officials hide themselves, and the top ranks of the Castle are even empty. However, the bureaucratic machine, universally applicable as it is (Weber), functions to implement all sorts of tasks, no matter how well they are legitimized or what consequences they bring about.

Those social scientists who are not familiar with Weber's political writings, and (even worse) interpret the ideal type of bureaucracy as a prescriptive model, will probably be surprised to learn that Max Weber, too, was an acid, at times even outrageous, critic of the politico-administrative machinery of the German empire (particularly in 1917), because he was aware that the system produced irrational results. Apolitical as he is said to have been in life, Kafka, as a writer, nevertheless calls the systemic rationality of the Habsburg monarchy into question. However, he did not go as far as Weber, who considered confronting the Kaiser in court. Rather, he seems to have tried to survive under the given circumstances and to subject himself to the system's formal rationality. In *The Trial,* Josef K. is considering his situation:

> Almost every defendant, even very simple people, begins to deliberate at the very beginning of the trial how to improve the system, and in this respect they often waste time and courage, which otherwise might have been better used. It is simply best to accept the given circumstances. (my trans.)

In succumbing to this device and excluding considerations of absolute justice and substantive rationality from his pondering, he seems to persuade himself:

> There was no guilt. The trial was nothing else than a big business of the sort he experienced in the bank.

What the outright political attack was for Weber, the satire was for Kafka. Ernst Fischer reports that Kafka's friends burst out in laughter when he read to them the beginning of *The Trial,* specifically the passage where Josef K. considers legitimizing himself to the warders by producing his bicycle driver's license.

Anthropological Criticism

Apart from functional criticism from the point of view of the individual and doubts about the rationality of bureaucracy when perceived as a system, Kafka (and Weber) embarked on a third level of critical evaluation which could be called the anthropological dimension. As a result of the Occidental process of increasing formal rationalization of all of life's spheres, Weber not only observed the "disenchantment of the world" and the "Zerfall

kultureller Selbstverständlichkeiten," but also saw the "iron cage" of a bureaucratized world replace traditional ways of life and shape personality. For instance, in a political statement, made together with his brother Alfred at the 1909 Vienna meeting of the "Verein für Sozialpolitik," Weber complained that the needs of bureaucracy brought about the "Berufs- und Diplom-Mensch" [professional person with a university degree]:

> A dreadful idea that the world one day would consist of nothing but professors . . . even more dreadful is the vision that the world shall be filled with nothing but those small wheels (of a machine) . . . people clinging to their tiny positions and aiming at a somewhat bigger little position. . . . What can we do to oppose this machinery in order to spare a remainder of humanity from this parceling out of the soul, from this rule of bureaucratic ideals of life?

He envisioned this specialized, professionally trained, functionally adapted type would replace the "Kulturmensch." Where Weber's aristocratic individualism clashed with the upcoming professional man, Kafka experienced this conflict in coming to terms with his role as a fiction writer. On one hand he had to earn his living through office work, on the other hand he aspired to be an artist. Reducing office hours was the compromise. Although in his later years Kafka was well aware that he personally needed the bureaucratic subsistence of life and the relieving office routine, he complained in a letter to Milena that:

> with respect to his inherent traits he was an official, thus a member of the gutter class [Auswurfklasse] of the European professional man [Berufsmensch]. (Binder 1976, my trans.)

Is it not a striking parallel that Kafka resembles Weber even in the wording? Should there be more than "Wahlverwandtschaft" between Kafka's and Weber's conceptualization and evaluation of bureaucracy?

INTELLECTUAL AND BIOGRAPHICAL
RELATIONSHIPS

Although Weber died in 1920 and Kafka in 1924, Kafka was still 20 years Weber's junior; and though the two never met, they were connected biographically by two influential mutual acquaintances: Alfred Weber, Max's younger brother, and Otto Gross, one of Freud's first disciples.

Otto Gross (1877-1920) turned Freud political and his sexual anarchism brought him in touch with the Bohemian scene in Schwabing and in Berlin. Not only was Kafka acquainted with Gross and inclined to cooperate in a planned journal "Letters for Fighting the Will to Power," Otto Gross's father, the criminologist professor Hans Gross, was one of Kafka's academic teachers in Prague from 1902 to 1905. In 1913, the long smoldering father-son conflict escalated after Otto Gross had played a dubious role in two suicides and become dependent on drugs; he was taken into custody by the Berlin police on the personal request of his father from Austria. This incident caused wide-spread public protest in literary circles and it is assumed that it inspired Kafka in writing "The Penal Colony." Not merely did he compare the death machine to apparatuses used in asylums, some analysts even attribute to the Gross affair the enigmatic introductory sentence of *The Trial*: "Somebody must have slandered Josef K."

In 1907, Gross had submitted an article to Weber's *Archiv für Sozialwissenschaft und Sozialpolitik* on the liberation of women which provoked an annihilating letter of rejection by Weber. Nonscholarly reasons might have caused Weber's scorn, for Gross had practiced his theory with female acquaintances in Weber's social environment. Nevertheless, Otto Gross's forced hospitalization drew even Max Weber into action: Professor Gross had claimed guardianship over Otto's son, basically on the ground that Frieda Gross had retreated from civil society to a colony of anarchists in Ascona. Characteristic for Max Weber's personality, he traveled to Ascona in 1914 to help Frieda Gross, his wife's schoolfriend, to defend her maternal rights against her father-in-law. Taken the acquaintance between Gross and Kafka, it is not unlikely that Kafka had some familiarity with the sociologist Max Weber.

The second biographical connection is less indirect and could well have had a bearing on Kafka's evaluation, if not conceptualization of bureaucracy. Max's younger brother Alfred Weber was professor of sociology at Prague University during 1904-1907 and even awarded Kafka the Juris Doctor degree on 18th of June 1906, as Wagenbach discovered. This, however, was only a formal procedure of introduction to the rector of the university, as in those days one was not obliged to write a doctoral thesis. Although A. Weber cannot be regarded as Kafka's academic supervisor and Kafka did not attend Weber's lectures, Kafka was probably familiar with Weber's ideas from what Max Brod, an admirer of Alfred Weber's, told him. Even more directly, Kafka must have been exposed to Max Weber's sociology of religion, which extensively treats ancient Judaism. Max Brod asked him to read a draft of a chapter he had written in 1920 which dealt with Weber's theory. Brod and Kafka debated over this chapter by exchanging letters. On the other hand, there can be no doubt that Alfred drew on the body of knowledge and the evaluations he shared with Max, including those on bureaucracy. Last but not least, as a jurist Kafka underwent training in legal positivism, acquired knowledge in the history of law and had at least a sketchy overview of the state apparatus. Although Weber's seminal work on bureaucracy was not published early enough for Kafka to have read it, we may assume that Kafka knew some of the sources of Max Weber who was also a jurist by training. Albach, furthermore, assumes that Kafka might also have become acquainted with Sombart's and Weber's works about the entrepreneur and capitalism in his subsidiary field of "Nationalökonomie." Moreover, it is not unlikely that

Kafka followed A. Weber's statements after Weber had gone to Heidelberg University in 1907. For instance, he could have read about the Weber brothers' contribution to the 1909 meeting of the "Verein für Sozialpolitik," from which I quoted above. This is particularly likely, as Alfred Weber had played a leading role in Prague's public life during 1907 and returned there on several occasions. Most importantly, though, Kafka is more than likely to have studied the article "The Official" by Alfred Weber (1910), which appeared in the *Neue Rundschau,* a journal Kafka regularly read. Lange-Kirchheim has conclusively proved on a linguistic basis that Kafka, in writing "The Penal Colony" in 1913, took metaphors (in particular the notion of bureaucracy as a technical apparatus) from this article that condemned and ridiculed the mentality of civil servants in line with M. Weber's statement of 1909. In "The Penal Colony," Kafka alludes to the quasi-religious image that was widely attributed to state bureaucracy in the Austrian and German empires and which A. Weber coined as "Staatsmetaphysik."

The Weberian influence on "The Penal Colony" is also of some general importance for Kafka's literary production. Lange-Kirchheim argues that the story constitutes a turning point in Kafka's opus: the leitmotif of law-guilt-punishment after 1917 became transposed from the hitherto dominant intra-family-constellation as in *The Judgement* and *The Metamorphosis* into a societal frame of reference (state, society, history). The father, henceforth, is replaced by the impersonal authority of the "apparatus" as in *The Trial* and *The Castle*—thus constituting a theoretical reorientation from psychology to sociology.

CONCLUSION

Kafka, like no other German language novelist of the 20th century, wove the notion of bureaucracy into his fiction (especially in *The Trial* and *The Castle*). My thesis is that this could have more to do with Kafka's office experience than is generally acknowledged. Furthermore, a Weberian influence on his conceptualization and evaluation of bureaucracy is likely. That main stream literary science and the established Kafka experts have, so far, not elaborated upon the bureaucratic imagery of Kafka's work could have resulted from a lack of familiarity with bureaucracy, and a preoccupation with the idealist tradition.

The parallels with, and divergences from, Max Weber's model or ideal type of bureaucracy are complemented by Kafka's largely congruent assessment of bureaucracy. Although it is ambivalent and originates from his differentiated understanding (functional, systemic, anthropological), as well as from his personal experience with bureaucracy, such an antithetical appreciation can also be found in Max Weber's work when we pay attention to the paradox of formal and substantive rationality and take into account his political writings.

The amazing congeniality of Kafka and Weber as to analysis and evaluation of bureaucracy can certainly be understood from the intellectual currents of the "Zeit-geist" and a common intellectual background including juridical training, interest in the sociology of religion, and psychoanalysis. However, the two-albeit indirect-biographical linkages between Kafka and Weber, through Otto Gross and Alfred Weber, undoubtedly raise the immanent parallels of the artist's and the analyst's treatment of bureaucracy well beyond a mere "Wahlverwandtschaft."

Bryan S. Turner (essay date 1996)

SOURCE: "Logic and Fate in Weber's Sociology," in *For Weber: Essays on the Sociology of Fate,* second edition, SAGE Publications, 1996, pp. 3-28.

[*In the following essay, Turner discusses Weber as a neo-Kantian thinker, and contrasts his sociological ideas with those of Karl Marx.*]

With the development of various radical movements in the social sciences in the 1960s and 1970s, Marxists became increasingly insistent on demonstrating the presence of a sharp dividing line between conventional sociology and Marx's theory of society. In mounting a critique of the claims of sociology to a scientific status, Marxists have frequently selected Max Weber's sociology as the principal illustration of the limitations of sociological reasoning or of its irreducible ideological underpinnings. Weber appears to have come to the forefront of this debate because sociologists themselves have claimed that Weber provides the only valid reply to Marx's analyses of socio-economic relationships. Weber's studies of social class, state and religion have been treated from the time of their publication as decisive alternatives to the historical materialism of Marx and Engels. In addition, Weber's neo-Kantian epistemology has often been treated as the most appropriate epistemological foundation for a discipline which wants to be simultaneously value-neutral and value-relevant. Weber's epistemology can thus be approached as the principal alternative to the post-Hegelianism of Marx's dialectical materialism. According to Carl Mayer, the 'fundamental problem on this level, which is posed with the confrontation of Marx and Weber, is the problem of Hegel vs. Kant, or Kant vs. Hegel'. Alternatively, other commentators have argued that the fundamental divorce between Weberian sociology and Marxist science is to be found in neither substantive fields of research nor in epistemology, but in the political consequences of Weber's historical pessimism. Since Weber regarded capitalist technology and relations of production as the 'fate' of our times, he dismissed the notion that socialism could produce an alternative to capitalist rationalisation of the means and conditions of production as purely utopian. By contrast, Marcuse claimed that Weber's pessimistic sense of 'destiny' merely generalised the 'blindness of a society which reproduces itself behind the back of the individuals, of a society in which the law of domination appears as objective technological law'.

There is, consequently, massive disagreement over Weber's status as a social theorist. On the one hand, Weber pro-vides the 'paradigm of a sociology which is both historical and systematic.' On the other hand, Weber's sociology is motivated by his commitment to the capitalist system, the German state and blind opposition to revolutionary Marxism. By accepting the 'fate' of capitalist domination, Weber in fact provides a justification for exploitation and imperialism under the guise of a value-free sociology. Although there is fundamental disagreement over the validity and political implications of Weber's sociology (and hence of 'bourgeois sociology' *in toto*), there is also a curious agreement over the characterisation of the content of Weber's epistemology and substantive sociology. Both conventional sociology and Marxism concur that Weberian sociology *is* neo-Kantian. Four aspects of Weber's sociology are typically cited as evidence of Weber's dependence on Kantian philosophy. First, there is Weber's fundamental divorce between factual statements and judgments of value. While science may be useful in the selection and development of appropriate means, it cannot help us in determining what ends are important and valuable. In the last analysis, our empirical knowledge of the world is irrelevant in the field of moral choice. Second, there is the strong nominalism of Weber's approach to such general sociological concepts as 'state', 'status group' or 'corporation'. Weber's *verstehende soziologie* (interpretative sociology) treats all these 'collectivities' as 'solely the resultants and modes of organisation of particular acts of individual persons, since these alone can be treated as agents in a course of subjectively understandable action.' This nominalist position is closely related to the third aspect of Weber's neo-Kantian epistemology, namely Weber's subjectivism. There are various aspects of Weber's subjectivism. At the most general level, the significance and meaning of reality is not given empirically, but is rather imposed on existence by the action of human will. For example, Weber defines 'culture' as 'a finite segment of the meaningless infinity of the world process, a segment on which human *beings* confer meaning and significance.' In his typology of social action, Weber distinguishes between behaviour and social action in terms of the subjective meanings which are imposed on action and the subjective meanings which arise from social interaction. Sociology is the science which aims at 'the interpretive understanding of social action in order thereby to arrive at a causal explanation of its course and effects.' Fourth, the neo-Kantianism of Weber's epistemology is evidenced by Weber's rejection of objective, general, causal laws in sociological explanations. From Weber's viewpoint, the rich empirical complexity of history and social organisation could never be reduced to a set of finite laws. Sociology could properly construct typologies and general classifications, but its explanations of social action would always be expressed in terms of probable outcomes.

Once the description of Weber's sociology as neo-Kantian is accepted, it then becomes possible to formulate a nice opposition between Marx and Weber. Those Marxists who have been strongly influenced by the structuralism of French Marxism, especially Louis Althusser and Etienne Balibar, have argued that while Marx had a clear notion of the central role of objective structural determination, Weber reduces the objective structures of economic and political relations to interpersonal, human subjectivity. One particularly powerful version of this argument occurs in the work of Paul Q. Hirst. In this interpretation, Weber's sociology involves subjective reductionism because all 'social relations are reduced to the plane of inter-subjective relations.' Marx's historical materialism, by contrast, presupposes the independence of objective conditions which are not dissolved by a Weberian commitment to the freedom of individual will. This contrast is particularly marked in Marx's arguments about the primacy of productive relations over relations of circulation and consumption. Marx's economic arguments in this area 'are based on a conception of social relations as objective social forms irreducible to the actions and thoughts of human subjects.'

In attempting to achieve a demarcation line between Marx and Weber in terms of a contrast between the meaningful social actions of individuals and the independent, deterministic role of objective social structures, the Marxist exegesis has often followed the interpretation of Weber by Talcott Parsons. For example, John Lewis in presenting a Marxist critique of Weber's subjectivism refers to Parsons's *The Structure of Social Action* as 'the authoritative work' which is 'a first-rate and indispensable exposition'. To some extent, the Marxist and Parsonian interpretation of Weber's sociology intersect because it is central to Parsons's thesis that Weber's neo-Kantianism represents a major break with the rationalism and reductionism of classical positivism, pointing sociology in the direction of a voluntaristic theory of action which gives full weight to the importance of freedom of will in the choice of means and ends to goals. In Parsons's approach to Western sociology, therefore, Weber represents a major turning point in the breakdown of positivism and the emergence of the concept of normatively oriented action. Parsons consequently emphasises the difference between Marx and Weber in terms of the latter's concentration on meaningful action, values, subjectivity and choice. Although Marx and Weber agreed about the task of providing an account of modern capitalism as the *sine qua non* of any valid social theory, Weber provided 'a new anti-Marxian interpretation of it and its genesis.'

There has been, of course, considerable criticism of Parsons's contention that not only Weber, but also Durkheim and Pareto, were forced to abandon positivism in its entirety in favour of a voluntaristic theory of action. Parsons has overstated the importance of values in Durkheim and consequently neglected Durkheim's dependence on Saint-Simon rather than Auguste Comte. In the case of Weber, Parsons has understated Weber's pivotal interest in domination. These critical commentaries on Parsons's view of the history of sociological theory are a necessary and important corrective to Parsons's tendency to interpret all sociologists in such a manner that they prefigure Parsons's own interest in integration on the basis of common values. The problem of the

Hobbesian basis of social order was not the common concern of classical sociology. At the same time, however, Parsons recognised what he regarded as a Marxian legacy in Weber's pessimistic view of human freedom under capitalist conditions.

The point of Parsons's argument in *The Structure of Social Action* is to show that the rationalist, reductionist positivism of nineteenth-century sociology collapsed under the weight of its own analytical problems as a metatheoretical foundation for sociology as a theory of action. Hence Parsons does not regard Weber as unambiguously voluntaristic in his analysis of social, meaningful action. There is a deterministic feature of Weber's sociology in that, while Weber's position is 'fundamentally a voluntarist theory of action,' he did not wish to deny the significance of non-subjective factors (heredity and environmental) as conditions of ultimate values and actions. This recognition of the non-subjective constraints on action is particularly evident in Weber's characterisation of capitalism. Parsons argues that in the 'descriptive aspect of this treatment of capitalism' Weber was 'in close agreement with Marx'. Parsons's statement of the nature of that agreement is particularly interesting. By emphasising the compulsive aspects of the capitalist system, Weber produced

> a thesis concerning the determination of individual action within the system, namely that the course of action is determined in the first instance by the character of the situation in which the individual is placed, in Marxian terminology, by the 'conditions of production.'

The precise location of this thesis of the compulsion of individual action by the capitalist system is ironically in *The Protestant Ethic and the Spirit of Capitalism*, which was first welcomed (by Hans Delbruck, for example) as an anti-Marxist tract. It is worth quoting in full the deterministic element of Weber's position to which Parsons specifically draws our attention:

> The capitalist economy of the present day is an immense cosmos into which the individual is born, and which presents itself to him, at least as an individual, as an unalterable order of things in which he must live. It forces the individual, in so far as he is involved in the system of market relationships, to conform to capitalistic rules of action. The manufacturer who in the long run acts counter to these norms, will just as inevitably be eliminated from the economic scene as the worker who cannot or will not adapt himself to them will be thrown into the street without a job.

Both phenomenological commentaries, following Alfred Schutz, and Marxist viewpoints, following Louis Althusser, have persistently understated Weber's deterministic view of capitalist relations and overstated the apparent subjectivism of Weber's methodological essays. . . . In their interpretation of Marx, Hindess and Hirst argue that we must not be seduced by the overt, obvious meaning of Marx's texts. In order to read Marx, we must attempt a symptomatic reading (*lecture symptomale*) which uncovers the deeper problematic which informs the overt meaning. Furthermore, we should not treat the whole corpus of Marx's writing as of equal value since the later scientific texts (such as *Capital*) are separated from the early work by an epistemological break which occurred around 1857. The ideological object of analysis of the early Marx, namely human subjectivity, was replaced by the scientific object of the structure of modes of production. The inconsistency of Hindess and Hirst centres on the fact that when they come to perform a 'reading' of Weber they completely abandon these epistemological principles in favour of taking the overt meaning of Weber's methodological texts for granted. They do not identify different stages and problematics in Weber's sociology. They perform not a symptomatic, but a literal, reading in assuming that Weber's substantive studies, for example, actually embody his stated methodological principles. In fact, Weber's analyses of 'social formations' adhere far more closely to a Marxist structuralism than they do to *verstehen* principles. As Rex points out, there are at least four separate phases in Weber's development associated with the successive influence of Rickert, Dilthey, positivism and Simmel.

In stressing the subjectivism of Weber, Hirst, in particular, ignores the centrality of the theme of compulsion, fate and irony in human actions. It is odd that a sociologist who is allegedly committed to the centrality of human free will should persistently employ mechanist imagery in describing the interconnection between action, interest and ideas. For Weber, it is not ideas but 'material and ideal interests, directly govern men's conduct. Yet very frequently the "world images" that have been created by "ideas" have, like switchmen, determined the tracks along which action has been pushed by the dynamic of interest.' These mechanical metaphors follow directly from Weber's abiding interest in historical irony. It is too frequently forgotten that, while Weber is concerned with subjective meaning, he also realised that the effects of human actions are typically the obverse of human intentionality. This aspect of Weber's sociology has been somewhat inadequately conceptualised in functionalist terms as the 'unintended consequences of actions'. Weber 'retains a social determinism by emphasising charisma's routinisation' and thus it is through the notion of unintended consequences that Weber is able to show how charismatic loyalties are inevitably transformed into everyday routines under the sway of material interests.

However, the bland Mertonian conception of 'unanticipated consequences' and 'latent functions' does not capture the evil ambience of Weber's theory of routinisation. It is not simply that purposive actions have consequences which are not recognised by social actors; the outcome of human actions often work against social actors in such a way as to limit or reduce the scope of their freedom. Weber's sense of fate and evil in human history, his contrast between *virtù* and *fortuna*, results in a reversal of Bernard de Mandeville's optimistic moral philosophy: our private virtues are our public evils so that our per-

sonal striving for salvation works itself out in history as the iron cage of capitalist production. Whereas Adam Smith's 'invisible hand' and Wilhelm Wundt's 'heterogony of purposes' had attempted to identify benevolent trends in society, Weber's sense of the fatefulness of our times draws him to detect the underlying malevolence of social reality. The present is disenchanted and the future is a polar night. This aspect of Weber's historical pessimism has been referred to as a 'negative heterogony of purposes.' Weber's negativity leads him to assume that meaningful actions become meaningless and that morally impeccable actions become morally flawed. This aspect of Weber's sociology finds its ultimate moral substratum in 'the Calvinistic belief in the fall and total perversion of the human race, a fall and perversion so catastrophic that even men's goodness must in the end generate evil.'

While Weber appears overtly to adhere to a neo-Kantian view of human freedom within the noumenal reality of moral choices, Weber also adheres to what might be termed a Calvinistic problematic of evil logic. In reading Weber I am not struck *pace* Hindess and Hirst by the subjective freedom of the Weberian actor, but by the innumerable instances in which Weber's account of a particular historical process or an abstract model of social structure depends on the notion of an ineluctable logic of structure. The most frequently cited illustration of a Weberian logic in history is the process of rationalistation. In his classic study of rationalisation as the 'guiding principle' of Weber's whole sociology, Karl Loewith (1970) shows how rationality as a mode of life is a fateful inevitability, expressing itself not only at the level of political bureaucracy and industrial organisation but in sociology *per se*. Sociology is an effect of the process which it sets out to study. A further irony is that rationalistion of means results in the unintelligibility of ends which are no longer given by revelation or prophetic inspiration. For scientist and politician alike, the only honest response to this fate is one of moral resignation. For Loewith, therefore, the ultimate division between Marx and Weber is that Marx's view of human alienation is coupled with a sense of hope, while Weber's notion of rationalisation necessitates an 'unheroic' view of political possibilities.

At one level, therefore, the diversity of interpretations of Weber's sociology appears to result from the fact that Weber's sociology operates as a series of analytical tensions between choice and determinism, subjectivity and objectivity, contingency and logic. For Lukács and Marcuse, these tensions are themselves specific historical manifestations of the 'antinomies of bourgeois thought' which are transcended by Marxist *praxis*. In my view, these polarities are in fact merely different levels of analysis which have to be treated at different planes of sociological theory. To get at this point, we can do no better than quote Weber's statement of what sociology is about, namely:

> The type of social science in which we are interested is an *empirical science* of concrete *reality*

(*Wirklichkeitswissenschaft*). Our aim is the understanding of the characteristic uniqueness of the reality in which we move. We wish to understand on the one hand the relationships and cultural significance of individual events in their contemporary manifestations and on the other the causes of their being historically *so* and not *otherwise*.

Weber is concerned to demonstrate the logic of social action and social structure by showing, for example, how the logic of capital accumulation works itself out in history regardless of the subjective preferences of individual capitalists and workers or how the logic of prebendalism results in the arbitrary politics of what he calls 'sultanism' regardless of the 'good intentions' of vizierial reform. As we have seen, this logic of history is fateful, even demonic. However, the particular way in which sociological logic works itself out in history is subject to or influenced by the multiplicity of specific, contingent facts and relationships which happen to obtain in given societies and situations. We can express this relationship between sociological logic and historical contingency in two ways. First, for Weber, there often emerges an 'elective affinity' between ideas and material interests which plays a crucial role in influencing the particular direction of historical trends. In the sociology of religion, Weber demonstrates an 'elective affinity' between the Protestant calling and capitalist rationality, or between Muhammad's moral teaching and nomadism, or between the 'practical rationalism' of 'civic strata' and this-worldly asceticism. These contingent features of the lifestyle of certain social strata facilitated the logic of routinisation in a particular direction. The concept of 'elective affinity' (*Wahlverwandtschaft*) points to the great variety of ironic ways 'in which certain ideas and certain social processes "seek each other out" in history' (Berger).

A second and more precise formulation of this relationship between logic and contingency draws on a distinction between sociological generalisation and historical explanation. Guenther Roth argues that Weber's historical analysis involves three separate stages. In the configurational stage, Weber constructs a series of typologies or models with a particular historical content as distinct from the universal categories of sociology (such as the categories of social action). At the second level, we find Weber's developmental theories or 'secular' theories of long-term change and development, but these 'secular' theories are neither evolutionary nor predictive. These developmental theories attempt 'the description of the course and explanation of the genesis and consequences of particular historical phenomena' (Roth). At the third stage, Weber turns to situational analysis which tries to explain the particular timing of a historical event as the effect of 'secular' causation and situational contingency. This final level of analysis looks at the way in which certain historical constellations have 'come about not only by virtue of freely willed actions, organisational imperatives, the logic of the system and a plethora of social trends but also because of historical accidents' (Roth).

These two perspectives on the relationship between 'accident' (contingency) and 'logic' (the configurational and developmental) can be brought together by arguing that the particular ways in which the logic of the system and its secular trends work their way out historically is in terms of the elective affinities between developmental processes and contingent events or conditions. It is in these terms that Weber is able to assert both the peculiarities of given conditions for different societies and the presence of certain general societal 'secular' developments. For Weber, therefore, there are no general theories of the transformation of feudalism into capitalism and no general theory of the collapse of capitalism as a historical stage towards socialism, because the situational circumstances of given societies typically preclude any such application of law-like statements. However, certain contingent features of European society—their religious beliefs, legal norms, city organisation, technological development, political apparatus—contributed directly to the developmental rationality of capital accumulation. To express this relationship in another way, there is no necessary relationship between abstractly formulated economic structures and legal/political superstructures, because whether or not a contingently present set of religious (or other) beliefs has an affinity with economic production cannot be stated in advance. The social and economic pre-conditions for capitalist development in feudal England provide an interesting illustration of this issue for both Weber's and Marx's view of capitalist development. According to the general conditions favouring capitalist development in Weber's *General Economic History,* England is a deviant case. Weber acknowledges that England did not possess a gapless, systematic legal superstructure, that English cities did not, as on the continent, develop 'autonomous political ambitions' and that in England the Calvinistic calling was watered down by various strands of emotionalism, Arminianism and quietism in the Methodist, Baptists, and Quaker sects. The precise manner in which capitalist relations of production developed in England and the development of rationalisation in economic and political structures can only be determined by situational analysis into the conditions which favoured capitalist development despite, rather than because of, the nature of pre-capitalist social features in English society.

Having now provided a sketch of how I propose to interpret Weber's sociology in terms of the analysis of negative heterogony of purposes and in terms of a distinction between sociological logic and historical contingency, it is possible to return to the question of Weber's relationship to Marx. Just as Weber cannot be treated as merely a neo-Kantian sociologist of purposeful action, so, in the decades following the Second International, most writers on Marx have insisted that Marx's historical materialism cannot be reduced to technological determinism, that Marx did not treat the superstructure as simply a reflection of the economic base and that, in various ways, Marx placed human subjectivity and human agency at the centre of his view of history and social organisation. In denying Marx's economism, neo-Marxists came to concentrate on questions of epistemology (especially epistemological issues which derived from the neo-Kantian and neo-Hegelian philosophies of Simmel, Dilthey, Husserl and Croce). The classical focus on substantive questions of economics was partly replaced by a new interest in the superstructure (especially aesthetics and art rather than law and politics). Finally, Marx's optimism in revolutionary struggle gave way to a more 'realistic' but pessimistic assessment of working-class radicalism in late capitalism. These 'thematic innovations' (Anderson) in modern Marxism have had the peculiar consequence of making modern Marxist theory more, rather than less, like Weberian sociology. One of the objectives of this book is to show that attempts to destroy economistic versions of Marxism have often merely repeated Weber's own criticisms of the economism of Social Democratic Party theoreticians. However, it would be wrong to treat modern Marxism as a uniform movement. For example, not all modern interpretations of Marx agree in respect of the apparent subjective humanism of the Paris Manuscripts. If one puts great emphasis on the writings of the early Marx, then Marxism may indeed look rather like a subjectivist sociology in which it would be difficult to distinguish between a neo-Kantian humanism and a neo-Feuerbachian anthropology.

It is precisely in structural Marxism that awareness of this problem has been acute. As we have seen, Marxists who have been influenced by Althusser's formulation of historical materialism (Poulantzas, Hindess and Hirst) have attempted to reject any theory which reduces Marxism to economism or technological determinism or to some form of teleological evolutionism, but their rejection of these interpretations also involved a rejection of the early Marx and Marxist humanism. This position enables structural Marxists to contrast Weber's subjectivism ('the problematic of the subject') with Marx's science of the objective structures of modes of production, while also denying the determinism of technological versions of Marxist materialism. However, this theoretical position, which involves a distinction between the contingency of class struggles at the level of the social formation and the logic of relations of production at the level of modes of production, results in a close analytical parallel between Weber's developmental and situational analysis.

The central problem for Hindess and Hirst is to produce an account of how modes of production change without recourse to an essentialist teleology or to evolutionary determinism. According to this perspective, there is nothing within, for example, the feudal mode of production which results inevitably in its transformation (the non-reproduction of its conditions of existence) or which inevitably propels it towards the capitalist mode of production. The reproduction of the conditions of existence of the mode of production must be sought at the level of the social formation where they are determined by the conjunctural struggle between social classes. Accordingly,

> transition (and non-transition) can only be understood in terms of certain determinate conditions of the class struggle and as a possible outcome of

that struggle. 'Transitional conjuncture' refers to a condition of the social formation such that the transformation of the dominant mode of production is a possible outcome of the class struggle.

In any social formation in which the feudal mode of production is dominant, the non-reproduction of the conditions of existence of that mode is the contingent outcome of the class struggle between landlords and peasants over the variant conditions of rent (in kind, money or labour) and over the landlords' control of the labour process. There is no law which states as an iron necessity that the class struggle in feudalism will have a specific and decisive outcome in terms of the transition of the feudal mode. It follows from this argument that there can be 'no general theory of the transition in the sense of a specification of the general structure or process that must be followed in all particular cases of transition from one mode of production to another' (Hindess and Hirst). In other words, the developmental logic of modes of production (such as the law of the tendency of profit to fall in capitalism) is worked out at the social level in the contingent struggle between social classes which are determined at the level of production.

The criticisms which Hindess and Hirst subsequently developed against this formulation in *Mode of Production and Social Formation* reinforced rather than diminished the Weberian connotations of their view of social transformation. Their 'auto-critique' came to reject much of the Althusserian epistemological underpinning of *Pre-Capitalist Modes of Production* such as the distinction between abstract modes of production and concrete social formations. Hindess and Hirst now want to concentrate on a more complex range of class relations within given social formations. However, the way in which they now attempt to describe political and economic practices has a peculiarly Weberian dimension. For example, the possession of the means of production is now described as a 'capacity,' while political practice involves 'the calculation of effect.' Because politics involve a constant process of calculation and judgment of effects under political conditions which are constantly changing as a result of political practice, there can be no *general* knowledge of the political. The political activist has to make calculations in a conjuncture of uncertainty and in this respect the knowledge of the political scientist must be largely irrelevant. If this interpretation of the statement 'there can be no "knowledge" in political practice' (Hindess and Hirst, 1977) is correct, than it follows that there can be no general theory of political practice (which is a matter of calculations in a context of uncertainty) in the same way that there can be no general theory of the transition of a social formation (which is the outcome of contingent class struggle). As Weber believed, politics is about the exercise of power in which the outcome is probable not determinate. Despite constant references to 'determinate' relations of production and 'determinate' social class relationships, the effect of their epistemological critique has been to increase the importance of the notion of contingency in political and economic relationships.

Theoretical attempts to refine or to reject the alleged economism and technological reductionism of Marxism in both humanistic and structuralist neo-Marxism have had the peculiar consequence of making modern Marxism more, rather than less, like Weberian sociology. This unwilling merger can be seen in epistemological and theoretical terms, but it also takes place in substantive issues. when neo-Marxists have come to deal with issues where Marx's theory of society was apparently underdeveloped they have often been forced to confront Weber's sociology. This confrontation has been particularly significant in the analysis of the state, legal relationships, religion, agrarian sociology, race relations and bureaucracy. If modern Marxism and Weberian sociology appear to be forced into an unconscious or unwilling partnership, does this mean that much of Weberian sociology (such as Weber's sociology of religion) 'fits without difficulty into the Marxian scheme'? The answer to this sort of question depends on whether one believes that neo-Marxism is a radical departure from the historical materialism of Marx and Engels and on whether one argues that Weber was mounting a critique of Marxism rather than of Marx. Both of these questions play a large part in this study especially in the opening chapters. At this point, I shall simply turn to the question of Weber's relationship to Marx which will be greatly elaborated in subsequent sections.

We cannot approach the relationship between Marx and Weber in a unidimensional fashion. My commentary so far has been concerned with the analytical relationship between Marx's determinism and Weber's 'negative heterogony of purposes'. Whereas Weber's sense of the limitations of human freedom is closely bound up with his view of historical fate, Marx more characteristically connected human alienation with specific property relations. It would, however, be possible to develop the argument that Marx also possessed a pessimistic view of human purpose. There is, for example, Marx's famous observation in 'The Eighteenth Brumaire of Louis Bonaparte' that

> Men make their own history, but not of their own free will; not under circumstances they themselves have chosen but under the given and inherited circumstances with which they are directly confronted. The tradition of the dead generations weighs like a nightmare on the minds of the living.

Certain writers on Marx, like Shlomo Avineri for example, have argued that the ironic passages in Marx's view of history are inherited directly from Hegel's conception of the Cunning of Reason (*List der Vernunft*). There would be an obvious connection in this circumstance between Hegel's notion of historical fate and that of Weber's. Following the publication of James Steuart's *Inquiry Concerning the Principles of Political Economy,* Hegel came to believe that the task of philosophy was not to recapture the values of Greek civilisation in order to halt the regression of history, but to reconcile men to their contemporary fate by grasping the imminent principles of reason in the present. As Hegel poetically ex-

pressed this insight, 'To recognise reason as the rose in the cross of the present and thereby to enjoy the present is the rational insight which reconciles us to the actual.' Hegel's view of reconciliation with fate is, like Marx's, a far more active, hopeful doctrine than Weber's Calvinistic pessimism. These theoretical and philosophical linkages between Marx, Hegel and Weber cannot, however, be properly appreciated without a historical grasp of the relationship between Weber, Marx and Marxism.

Karl Marx died in London in 1883 when Weber was in the process of leaving his law studies at the University of Heidelberg to take up his military service at Strasbourg at the age of nineteen. In Weber's early manhood, specific works by Marx and Engels were not widely read or commented upon, but deterministic and economic interpretations of history were often fashionable among the German intelligentsia and educated bourgeoisie. By the 1880s *The Communist Manifesto, A Contribution to the Critique of Political Economy, Capital* (volumes I and II), *The Poverty of Philosophy, Anti-Dühring* and *The Origin of the Family, Private Property and the State* were all available in Germany. In addition, Weber would have been familiar with Marxist literature through writers like August Bebel, co-founder of the Social Democratic Party and author of *Die Frau and der Sozialismus* (1883). Other avenues for the influence of Marx and Engels on Weber included Werner Sombart (*Sozialismus und soziale Bewegung,* 1896 and *Der modern Kapitalismus,* 1902), Karl Kautsky (*Der Ursprung des Christentums,* 1908) and Levin Goldschmidt, professor of law at Heidelberg and Berlin. The influence of Marx and Marxism on Weber was not significant and continuous. As a general perspective on this relationship, Marianne Weber possibly overstated the case:

> Weber expressed great admiration for Karl Marx's brilliant constructions and saw in the inquiry into the economic and technical causes of events an exceedingly fruitful, indeed, a specifically new heuristic principle that directed the quest for knowledge (*Erkenntnistrieb*) into entire areas previously unilluminated. But he not only rejected the elevation of these ideas to a *Weltanschauung,* but was also against material factors being made absolute and being turned into the *common denominator* of causal explanations.

This commentary from Marianne Weber's biography did, however, reiterate Weber's own judgment of 'the great thinker' and of the problems of converting Marx's heuristic devices into an 'assessment of reality' in Weber's ' **"Objectivity" in Social Science and Social Policy'** from the *Archiv für Sozialwissenschaft und Sozialpolitik* in 1904.

The problem with this assessment is that Weber did not possess many of Marx's major works, which were not published until after Weber's death in 1920. The crucial feature of these lucanae in Weber's appreciation of the full extent of Marx's unpublished work is that it has been precisely the unpublished material which came to play such a dominant part in the reevaluation and reinterpretation of Marx's thought. These critical works included the *Economic and Philosophical Manuscripts* (1844), *Theses on Feuerbach* (1845), *The German Ideology* (1846), *Grundrisse* (1857-8) and *Remarks on Wagner* (1880). These texts provided the basis for arguments by Georg Lukács, Karl Korsch, Herbert Marcuse, Alfred Sohn-Rethel and István Mészaros pointing to the fact that iron laws of economic causation as the basis of a cultural superstructure were completely alien to Marx's dialectical thought. These new interpretations of the early *Manuscripts* and *Grundrisse* suggest that the theme of alienation is central to Marx, that Marx's break with Hegel was never absolute, that Marx was committed to a view of human praxis rather than inevitable material causes and consequently that the very idea of material laws is itself the manifestation of a reification in political economy. Weber's criticisms of Marxist materialism, therefore, cannot be criticisms of Marx's authentic theory.

The view that Weber had only a very partial understanding of Marx's complex view of economic relationships has been judicially stated by Mommsen. In general, Weber never approached Marx's materialist sociology 'in a systematic, let alone in a comprehensive way' and, to the extent that Weber did directly and specifically confront Marx's theory at first hand, this theoretical appraisal occurred late in Weber's intellectual career in *Economy and Society*. Weber's public lecture on '**Socialism**' (in *Gesammelte Aufsätze zur Soziologie und Sozialpolitik*) in 1918 to Austrian officers does provide direct evidence of Weber's attitude to Marx, but it cannot be accepted as a reliable guide, given its politically motivated content and the peculiarity of the circumstances. Weber's sources on Marx's original theoretical development were slight, unrepresentative and largely second-hand. This fact is sufficient warning against the view, originally expressed by Albert Salomon, that Weber's sociology can only be understood as a life-long debate with Karl Marx. What we must consider instead is Weber's political and theoretical opposition to institutionalised Marxism in the form of the Social Democratic Party in Germany.

With the demise of Bismarck's anti-Socialist legislation, the SDP became from 1890 onwards the largest and electorally the most successful socialist party in Europe operating within a parliamentary framework. The Erfurt Conference of 1891 committed the party to a revolutionary Marxist programme. This Marxist platform was strengthened by Karl Kautsky's editorship of the party's organ, the *Neue Zeit*. The electoral success of the party and the growing prosperity of the still backward German working class resulted in a gap between the revolutionary theory of the SDP leadership and the reformist, parliamentary socialism of its political practice. The goal of a proletarian dictatorship was submerged in the day-to-day championship of working-class demands within parliamentary democracy. There emerged, therefore, an obvious contrast between Kautsky's positivistic view of the inevitability of Marx's economic laws pointing to the inexorable victory of a revolutionary working class and the essentially limited objectives of practical politics (Plamenatz, 1954). By focusing on Marx's materialism as a scientific theory of economic laws providing a description of the 'facts' of the capitalist crisis, Kautsky was forced reluctantly into a position where Marx's moral critique of capitalism was divorced from science to become a largely residual feature of Marx's work., For Kautsky 'there appears occasionally in Marx's scientific work the impact of a moral ideal. But he always and rightly attempted to eliminate it so far as possible' (*Ethik und materialistische Geschichtsauffassung*). By accepting an implicit distinction between facts and values, Kautsky was forced into a general Weberian problem of the is-ought dichotomy in that one set of moral judgments can have no authority over any other set of moral opinions. Commitment to the Marxist critique of capitalism would thus become simply a matter of idiosyncratic preference.

For German and Austrian Marxists who were also steeped in *Lebensphilosophie* (philosophy of life) and *verstehende Geisteswissenschaft* (social science based on understanding and re-experiencing), Kautsky's positivism and its adjunct in fatalism were totally inadequate philosophical foundations on which to validate Marx's historical materialism. In Germany and Austria, the revisionist critique of Kautsky's orthodox Marxism came to borrow extensively from neo-Kantian philosophy in its attempt to rescue institutionalised Marxism from a positivist epistemology. Eduard Bernstein, who engaged in the theoretical debate of the relationship between Marxism and Darwinistic science, contrasted Kautsky's faith in a cataclysmic class war with what he took to be the facts of Germany in the 1890s, namely the increasing evidence of social order, economic prosperity and political security. Bernstein, however, also had to live through the bitter experience of fighting the reformist faction of the SDP which came to accept the entire programme of German imperialist expansion in 1914-18. Amongst the Austro-Marxists it was Max Adler who emphasised the continuity between the Kantian philosophy of active human consciousness and Marx's philosophy of social consciousness. For Adler, the inner connection between Marxism, sociology and social revolution is also

> a connection with classical German philosophy which, likewise, as a philosophy of social consciousness, can only be revolutionary. German classical philosophy always aspired to be a philosophy of action. But it could only achieve this idea; Marxism gave it the scientific knowledge that allowed it to realise this action historically. (*Der soziologische Sinn der Lehre von Karl Marx*, 1914)

In the perspective of Adler and Karl Renner, Marx's historical materialism was equated *tout court* with general sociology as an objective science of society equipped with a neo-Kantian epistemology, namely a science which occupied the space between natural science and idealist historiography.

Against this background of revisionist criticism of Kautsky's fatalistic positivism, Weber's criticisms of the Marxism of the SDP are not isolated and original objections, but part of the neo-Kantian opposition to an institutionalised Marxism which assumed that Marx's critique of capitalism could be assimilated without loss into a natural science model of social laws. Like the revisionists within Marxism, Weber objected to the conversion of Marx's concept of the laws of modes of production as a heuristic device into proven laws of empirical reality. Weber did not follow the neo-Kantian revisionist argument that Marxism represented the historical solution to the riddle of philosophy and action, values and reality. However, Weber's judgment of the hiatus between revolutionary philosophy and political reformism in the SDP was not wholly divorced from the revisionist position. Of course, Weber drew very different conclusions from this hiatus. For Weber, the German working class was politically immature and incapable of providing the German state with effective leadership. Weber was opposed to both the 'socially-minded' Christian of the Evangelical-Social Congress and to the secular socialists who believed that the material prosperity and political emancipation of the working class could be realised without a strong state. In the years before the First World War, Weber was convinced that the economic surplus created by capitalist development could not be secured without imperialist rivalry.

We can now state Weber's theoretical objections to the Marxism of the SDP in greater detail. While Weber accepted the heuristic value of historical materialism, he developed five general criticisms of Marxism. These were: (1) a rejection of all monocausal explanations of history and society in terms of ultimate causes as unscientific, (2) an assertion that the same economic base may have different legal and political superstructures, (3) a denial that socialism was a genuine alternative to the rationality of the market mechanism in capitalism and therefore that historical materialism and socialism were necessarily connected, (4) a critique of the theory of marriage and property as developed by Engels and Bebel, (5) a critical recognition of the logical incompatibility between Marxism as a deterministic science and Marxism as an ethical theory of human agency. The irony of neo-Marxist recoveries and revisions of the pristine theories of Marx and Engels is that they have often unwittingly reproduced Weber's neo-Kantian critique of the Marxism of the SDP.

One of the central problems of Marxism is to reconcile the centrality of human action and consciousness in Marx's Paris Manuscripts and *Theses on Feuerbach* with the apparent economic determinism of *Capital*. There are numerous subsidiary themes which flow from this paradox: humanistic versus scientific Marxism, *Lebensphilosophie* versus natural science, neo-Kantian epistemology versus positivism. This paradox is also behind many of the specific debates in modern Marxism concerning the relative autonomy of law and state from the economic base and concerning the status of 'social class'

in relation to 'mode of production'. In broad terms, there are two major solutions to this paradox in Marxism. On the one hand, the Austro-Marxists, Lukács and the Frankfurt School stress the continuity between classical German philosophy (Hegel and Kant) and Marx in order to argue that Marxism is a critical theory which transcends the epistemological dilemmas of bourgeois thought (especially positivistic sociology). On the other hand, Althusserian structuralism emphasises the break between Marx and classical German philosophy in order to show that Marxism (or more precisely, historical materialism) is a science of modes of production, but a science which cannot be reduced to a set of simple deterministic laws about the economy. This second option, as I have attempted to demonstrate, ends by showing that the effect of the mode of production is contingent on the complex effect of social class conflict on the conditions of existence of the mode of production. While it is more conventional to bring out the analytical relationship between Weber and the first Marxist solution (for example, between Weber and Lukács), there is in fact also a strong connection between Weber and structural Marxism on the grounds that Weber contrasted the logic of ideal type constructions and the fateful contingency of historical situations. On both counts, Max Weber has been an unwanted and largely incognito guest in modern Marxist debates about the real nature of Marx's historical materialism.

While I have been making some introductory observations on the analytical parallels between Weberian sociology and Marxism, I do not want to understate the enormous gulf which separates Weber from Marx and Marxism in political, ideological and ethical grounds. However, even if these assertions about the theoretical overlap between Weberian sociology and Marxism should prove to be unwarranted exaggerations, we would still be left with the paradox of substantive overlap between the empirical interests of Weberians and Marxists. In spite of all the methodological and theoretical differences, 'there exists far-reaching accord in the substantive analysis of the themes identical in both [Marx and Weber]: the structure of what has been called the modern world; its development; and its consequences' (Mayer). This 'far-reaching accord' in substantive characterisation of 'the modern world' is true both in general and in particular. There is an overlap between their view of capitalism as a dynamic and self-destructive system in comparison with the relative stability of feudalism and the stationariness of Oriental societies which is evident in Marx's Asiatic mode of production and Weber's prebendalism (Turner). Both Marx and Weber agreed that imperialism was not an accidental but necessary feature of capitalist growth. Their characterisations of the conditions by which classical slavery collapsed have many common features. In more recent debates, Weber's study of the agrarian problem in Germany which was published in the *Verein für Sozialpolitik* in 1892 (**'Die Verhältnisse der Landarbeiter im ostelbischen Deutschland'**) instigated the general debate in the SDP over the agrarian question and stimulated Kautsky's reply in his *Agrarian Question* (**Die Agrarfrage,** 1899).

In a similar fashion, developments within the Marxist theory of law have often directly or indirectly returned to analytical problems and substantive issues which lay at the centre of Weber's treatment of law-making and the nature of law in capitalist society. Just as Weber thought that religion in providing rational theodicies of the world had its own inner logic, so Weber attempted to show that the Western system of law, developing from a common Roman base, possessed its own internal logic which drove the law towards an increasingly gapless system of abstract rules. This autonomous process of legal rationalisation had, as a contingent fact, an 'affinity' with the requirements of the capitalist mode of production for a formal system of dependable law. By raising questions about the form and function of law, developments in Marxism with respect to the relative autonomy of the law from relations of production have often produced theoretical solutions which reflect aspects of Weber's treatment. While E. B. Pashukanis (1978) attempted to demonstrate that the form of law was intimately related to the commodity form in capitalism and therefore the form of law under socialism would be revolutionised, Karl Renner (1949) in 1929 attempted to show that the form of law was always neutral. For Renner, the social functions of law were dictated by historically given specific social class interests, but the form of law, such as the abstract form of a legal contract, could never be reduced to economic interests arising from the economic base. This issue of the relative autonomy of the law continues to play a prominent role in Marxist legal theory.

One reason for the continuing relevance of Weber's sociology for Marxism is that contemporary Marxism has been faced with the issue of whether 'late' capitalism has institutional and productive features which distinguish it sharply from the competitive capitalism of the nineteenth century. The increasing role of the state in production, the internationalisation of ownership and production, the decline of private capital and the emergence of a new middle class were aspects of capitalism to which Austro-Marxism specifically drew attention. In contemporary Marxism the analysis of monopoly capitalism has been the theoretical driving force behind the writing of Nicos Poulantzas, Elmar Altvater, Paul Baran, Paul Sweezy, Ralph Miliband and Ernest Mandel. By focusing on the Bismarckian state in the rise of German capitalism, the role of imperialism in advanced capitalism, the weakness of the German middle class and the rise of a new salariat, Weber's sociology predates many of these contemporary Marxist themes. Of course, the conventional criticism of Weber, in respect to Weber's analysis of social class for example, is that he concentrated on the market and the phenomenal forms of circulation rather than the relations of production which determine these surface institutions of the capitalist mode of production. In this respect, it could be argued that the capitalist mode of production has Marxist causes (the relations of production) and Weberian effects (Protestant religion, status groups, the market mechanism, plebiscitarian democracy). Even on these grounds, one could still claim that Weber provides a masterly, detailed description of the concrete reality of capitalist institutions. However, in my view the value of Weber's sociology goes far beyond this descriptive level on the grounds that Weber's concept of the logic of rationalisation operating independently of the will of agents is directly compatible with Marx's concept of the logic of modes of production.

It has become fashionable to combine the perspectives of Marx and Weber into a theory which attempts to show how social reality is continuously constructed by the social actions of individuals; social reality becomes alienated and reified by the forgetfulness of conscious agents. . . . [What] sociologists and Marxists have in common is a deterministic perspective of social reality whose structure and process has a logic independent of the will and consciousness of individual agents. The operation of this logic is, however, partly shaped and directed by the accidental or contingent features of sets of institutions which happen to be present in given societies. It is not a logical requirement of the capitalist mode of production that capitalists should possess Protestant beliefs. The fact that capitalists did espouse Protestantism rather than Catholicism gave a particular twist to the logic of capital accumulation. In this respect the logic of capital had an affinity with the internal rationalisation of Christian theodicy in its Protestant form. Weber's notion of fate, therefore, places Weberian sociology at the very centre of the sociological enterprise. Sociology's preoccupation with fatefulness can be summarised in the cynical aphorism that, if economics is about scarcity and choice, sociology is about why those choices cannot be realised.

FURTHER READING

Biography

Weber, Marianne. *Max Weber: A Biography*, translated and edited by Harry Zohn. New York: John Wiley & Sons, 1975, 719 p.

> Annotated English-language edition of Weber's life, written by his widow.

Bibliography

Kivisto, Peter and William H. Swatos, Jr. *Max Weber: A Bio-Bibliography*. New York: Greenwood Press, 1988, 267 p.

> Groups Weber's works by subject matter and notes works in English translation. Includes several introductory biographical and historical essays.

Murvar, Vatro. *Max Weber Today—An Introduction to a Living Legacy: Selected Bibliography*. Brookfield, Wisc.: Max Weber Colloquia and Symposia at the University of Wisconsin-Milwaukee, 1983, 129 p.

> Bibliography preceded by essays on Weber's contemporary influence.

Nordquist, Joan. *Max Weber: A Bibliography*. Santa Cruz, Calif.: Reference and Research Services, 1989, 80 p.
    Bibliography of primary and secondary sources, including contemporary reviews of Weber's works in translation.

Criticism

Albrow, Martin. *Max Weber's Construction of Social Theory*. Houndmills, England: Macmillan, 1990, 316 p.
    Analysis of Weber's theoretical system which includes an exploration of its intellectual and philosophical sources.

Bendix, Reinhard. *Max Weber: An Intellectual Portrait*. Garden City, N. Y.: Anchor Books, 1962, 522 p.
    Comprehensive survey of Weber's work designed to present his sociological system in a lucid form.

Burger, Thomas. *Max Weber's Theory of Concept Formation: History, Laws, and Ideal Types*. Durham, N. C.: Duke University Press, 1976, 231 p.
    Attempts "to interpret the central segment of Max Weber's writings on the methodology of the empirical sciences," specifically his concepts of ethical neutrality and the ideal type.

Collins, Randall. *Max Weber: A Skeleton Key*. Beverly Hills, Calif.: Sage Publications, Inc., 1986, 149 p.
    Summary and analysis of the key components in Weber's sociological thought.

Dronberger, Ilse. *The Political Thought of Max Weber: In Quest of Statesmanship*. New York: Meredith Corporation, 1971, 436 p.
    Discusses "the nature and consequences of Weber's political philosophy and his political career."

Giddens, Anthony. *Politics and Sociology in the Thought of Max Weber*. London: Macmillan Press Ltd., 1972, 64 p.
    Investigates the political dimension of Weber's sociological studies.

Honigsheim, Paul. *On Max Weber*, translated by Joan Rytina. New York: Collier-Macmillan Ltd., 1968, 155 p.
    Contains four essays on Weber, the largest of which, "Memories of Max Weber," occupies the bulk of the volume.

Jameson, Fredric. "The Vanishing Mediator; or, Max Weber as Storyteller." In *The Ideologies of Theory: Essays 1971-1896, Volume 2: The Syntax of History*, p. 3-34. Minneapolis: University of Minnesota Press, 1988.
    Structuralist and psychoanalytic study of Weber's concepts of charisma and the ideal type.

Loewenstein, Karl. *Max Weber's Political Ideas in the Perspective of Our Time*, translated by Richard and Clara Winston. Amherst: University of Massachusetts Press, 1966, 105 p.

Examines Weber's thoughts on German politics, post-WWI Europe, and the nature of political leadership throughout history.

Löwith, Karl. *Max Weber and Karl Marx*, translated by Hans Fantel. London: George Allen & Unwin, 1982, 112 p.
    Comparative analysis of Marx and Weber expressed in terms of Marx's idea of "alienation" and Weber's conception of "rationality." Includes a section on Weber's "critique of the materialist conception of history."

MacRae, Donald G. *Max Weber*. New York: The Viking Press, 1974, 111 p.
    Brief critical survey of Weber's life and works.

Mitzman, Arthur. *The Iron Cage: An Historical Interpretation of Max Weber*. New Brunswick, N. J.: Transaction Books, 1985, 337 p.
    Uses Weber's evolving world view as presented in his sociological theory to interpret "the psycho-social conditions in which the ideology of German imperialism developed around the turn of the century."

Mommsen, Wolfgang J. *Max Weber and German Politics 1890-1920*, translated by Michael S. Steinberg. Chicago: University of Chicago Press, 1984, 498 p.
    In-depth exploration of Weber's role in drafting the Weimar constitution and of his writings on German foreign policy, nationalism, and imperialism.

Rheinstein, Max. Introduction to *Max Weber on Law in Economy and Society*, edited by Max Rheinstein, translated by Edward Shils and Max Rheinstein, pp. xxv-lxxii. Cambridge, Mass.: Harvard University Press, 1954.
    Overview of Weber's sociology of law.

Roth, Guenther and Wolfgang Schluchter. *Max Weber's Vision of History: Ethics and Methods*. Berkeley: University of California Press, 1979, 211 p.
    Contains a series of essays on Weber's concepts of rationalization, value-neutrality, and charisma, as well as his ideas on religion and history.

Sahay, Arun, ed. *Max Weber and Modern Sociology*. London: Routledge & Kegan Paul, 1971, 111 p.
    Collection featuring papers relating to Weber's modern relevance, preceded by an introductory essay.

Turner, Stephen P. and Regis A. Factor. *Max Weber and the Dispute Over Reason and Value: A Study in Philosophy, Ethics, and Politics*. London: Routledge & Kegan Paul, 1984, 274 p.
    Traces the historical development of the debate over Weber's ideas on reason and the ethics of value.

Wrong, Dennis, ed. *Max Weber*. Englewood Cliffs, N.J.: Prentice-Hall, Inc., 1970, 214 p.
    Consists of brief chapters on the important concepts of Weber's thought, including his methodology, concept of rationalization, sociology of religion, theory

on bureaucracy, political sociology, and vision of history. Preceded by a lengthy introduction summarizing his work.

Additional coverage of Weber's life and career is contained in the following sources published by Gale Research: *Contemporary Authors,* Vol. 109.

Twentieth-Century Literary Criticism

Cumulative Indexes
Volumes 1-69

How to Use This Index

The main references

Calvino, Italo
1923-1985.....CLC 5, 8, 11, 22, 33, 39,
73; SSC 3

---

list all author entries in the following Gale Literary Criticism series:

BLC = *Black Literature Criticism*
CLC = *Contemporary Literary Criticism*
CLR = *Children's Literature Review*
CMLC = *Classical and Medieval Literature Criticism*
DA = *DISCovering Authors*
DC = *Drama Criticism*
HLC = *Hispanic Literature Criticism*
LC = *Literature Criticism from 1400 to 1800*
NCLC = *Nineteenth-Century Literature Criticism*
PC = *Poetry Criticism*
SSC = *Short Story Criticism*
TCLC = *Twentieth-Century Literary Criticism*
WLC = *World Literature Criticism, 1500 to the Present*

The cross-references

See also CANR 23; CA 85-88;
obituary CA 116

---

list all author entries in the following Gale biographical and literary sources:

AAYA = *Authors & Artists for Young Adults*
AITN = *Authors in the News*
BEST = *Bestsellers*
BW = *Black Writers*
CA = *Contemporary Authors*
CAAS = *Contemporary Authors Autobiography Series*
CABS = *Contemporary Authors Bibliographical Series*
CANR = *Contemporary Authors New Revision Series*
CAP = *Contemporary Authors Permanent Series*
CDALB = *Concise Dictionary of American Literary Biography*
CDBLB = *Concise Dictionary of British Literary Biography*
DLB = *Dictionary of Literary Biography*
DLBD = *Dictionary of Literary Biography Documentary Series*
DLBY = *Dictionary of Literary Biography Yearbook*
HW = *Hispanic Writers*
JRDA = *Junior DISCovering Authors*
MAICYA = *Major Authors and Illustrators for Children and Young Adults*
MTCW = *Major 20th-Century Writers*
NNAL = *Native North American Literature*
SAAS = *Something about the Author Autobiography Series*
SATA = *Something about the Author*
YABC = *Yesterday's Authors of Books for Children*

Literary Criticism Series
Cumulative Author Index

Abasiyanik, Sait Faik 1906-1954
See Sait Faik
See also CA 123

Abbey, Edward 1927-1989...... **CLC 36, 59**
See also CA 45-48; 128; CANR 2, 41

Abbott, Lee K(ittredge) 1947-...... **CLC 48**
See also CA 124; CANR 51; DLB 130

Abe, Kobo
1924-1993 .... **CLC 8, 22, 53, 81;**
DAM NOV
See also CA 65-68; 140; CANR 24; MTCW

Abelard, Peter c. 1079-c. 1142 ... **CMLC 11**
See also DLB 115

Abell, Kjeld 1901-1961........... **CLC 15**
See also CA 111

Abish, Walter 1931-.............. **CLC 22**
See also CA 101; CANR 37; DLB 130

Abrahams, Peter (Henry) 1919- ..... **CLC 4**
See also BW 1; CA 57-60; CANR 26;
DLB 117; MTCW

Abrams, M(eyer) H(oward) 1912-... **CLC 24**
See also CA 57-60; CANR 13, 33; DLB 67

Abse, Dannie
1923- ... **CLC 7, 29; DAB; DAM POET**
See also CA 53-56; CAAS 1; CANR 4, 46;
DLB 27

Achebe, (Albert) Chinua(lumogu)
1930- ... **CLC 1, 3, 5, 7, 11, 26, 51, 75;**
BLC; DA; DAB; DAC; DAM MST,
MULT, NOV; WLC
See also AAYA 15; BW 2; CA 1-4R;
CANR 6, 26, 47; CLR 20; DLB 117;
MAICYA; MTCW; SATA 40;
SATA-Brief 38

Acker, Kathy 1948- .... **CLC 45**
See also CA 117; 122; CANR 55

Ackroyd, Peter 1949-.......... **CLC 34, 52**
See also CA 123; 127; CANR 51; DLB 155;
INT 127

Acorn, Milton 1923-........ **CLC 15; DAC**
See also CA 103; DLB 53; INT 103

Adamov, Arthur
1908-1970 .... **CLC 4, 25; DAM DRAM**
See also CA 17-18; 25-28R; CAP 2; MTCW

Adams, Alice (Boyd)
1926- .... **CLC 6, 13, 46; SSC 24**
See also CA 81-84; CANR 26, 53;
DLBY 86; INT CANR-26; MTCW

Adams, Andy 1859-1935......... **TCLC 56**
See also YABC 1

Adams, Douglas (Noel)
1952- .... **CLC 27, 60; DAM POP**
See also AAYA 4; BEST 89:3; CA 106;
CANR 34; DLBY 83; JRDA

Adams, Francis 1862-1893....... **NCLC 33**

Adams, Henry (Brooks)
1838-1918 ...... **TCLC 4, 52; DA; DAB;**
DAC; DAM MST
See also CA 104; 133; DLB 12, 47

Adams, Richard (George)
1920- ...... **CLC 4, 5, 18; DAM NOV**
See also AAYA 16; AITN 1, 2; CA 49-52;
CANR 3, 35; CLR 20; JRDA; MAICYA;
MTCW; SATA 7, 69

Adamson, Joy(-Friederike Victoria)
1910-1980 .... **CLC 17**
See also CA 69-72; 93-96; CANR 22;
MTCW; SATA 11; SATA-Obit 22

Adcock, Fleur 1934-.............. **CLC 41**
See also CA 25-28R; CAAS 23; CANR 11,
34; DLB 40

Addams, Charles (Samuel)
1912-1988 .... **CLC 30**
See also CA 61-64; 126; CANR 12

Addison, Joseph 1672-1719......... **LC 18**
See also CDBLB 1660-1789; DLB 101

Adler, Alfred (F.) 1870-1937..... **TCLC 61**
See also CA 119

Adler, C(arole) S(chwerdtfeger)
1932- .... **CLC 35**
See also AAYA 4; CA 89-92; CANR 19,
40; JRDA; MAICYA; SAAS 15;
SATA 26, 63

Adler, Renata 1938-............. **CLC 8, 31**
See also CA 49-52; CANR 5, 22, 52;
MTCW

Ady, Endre 1877-1919........... **TCLC 11**
See also CA 107

Aeschylus
525B.C.-456B.C........ **CMLC 11; DA;**
DAB; DAC; DAM DRAM, MST

Afton, Effie
See Harper, Frances Ellen Watkins

Agapida, Fray Antonio
See Irving, Washington

Agee, James (Rufus)
1909-1955 .... **TCLC 1, 19; DAM NOV**
See also AITN 1; CA 108; 148;
CDALB 1941-1968; DLB 2, 26, 152

Aghill, Gordon
See Silverberg, Robert

Agnon, S(hmuel) Y(osef Halevi)
1888-1970 .... **CLC 4, 8, 14**
See also CA 17-18; 25-28R; CAP 2; MTCW

Agrippa von Nettesheim, Henry Cornelius
1486-1535 .... **LC 27**

Aherne, Owen
See Cassill, R(onald) V(erlin)

Ai 1947-................... **CLC 4, 14, 69**
See also CA 85-88; CAAS 13; DLB 120

Aickman, Robert (Fordyce)
1914-1981 .... **CLC 57**
See also CA 5-8R; CANR 3

Aiken, Conrad (Potter)
1889-1973 .... **CLC 1, 3, 5, 10, 52;**
DAM NOV, POET; SSC 9
See also CA 5-8R; 45-48; CANR 4;
CDALB 1929-1941; DLB 9, 45, 102;
MTCW; SATA 3, 30

Aiken, Joan (Delano) 1924-........ **CLC 35**
See also AAYA 1; CA 9-12R; CANR 4, 23,
34; CLR 1, 19; DLB 161; JRDA;
MAICYA; MTCW; SAAS 1; SATA 2,
30, 73

Ainsworth, William Harrison
1805-1882 .... **NCLC 13**
See also DLB 21; SATA 24

Aitmatov, Chingiz (Torekulovich)
1928- .... **CLC 71**
See also CA 103; CANR 38; MTCW;
SATA 56

Akers, Floyd
See Baum, L(yman) Frank

Akhmadulina, Bella Akhatovna
1937- .... **CLC 53; DAM POET**
See also CA 65-68

Akhmatova, Anna
1888-1966 .... **CLC 11, 25, 64;**
DAM POET; PC 2
See also CA 19-20; 25-28R; CANR 35;
CAP 1; MTCW

Aksakov, Sergei Timofeyvich
1791-1859 .... **NCLC 2**

Aksenov, Vassily
See Aksyonov, Vassily (Pavlovich)

Aksyonov, Vassily (Pavlovich)
1932- .... **CLC 22, 37**
See also CA 53-56; CANR 12, 48

Akutagawa, Ryunosuke
1892-1927 .... **TCLC 16**
See also CA 117; 154

Alain 1868-1951 .... **TCLC 41**

Alain-Fournier.................... TCLC 6
See also Fournier, Henri Alban
See also DLB 65

Alarcon, Pedro Antonio de
1833-1891 .... **NCLC 1**

Alas (y Urena), Leopoldo (Enrique Garcia)
1852-1901 .... **TCLC 29**
See also CA 113; 131; HW

Albee, Edward (Franklin III)
1928- ...... **CLC 1, 2, 3, 5, 9, 11, 13, 25,**
53, 86; DA; DAB; DAC; DAM DRAM,
MST; WLC
See also AITN 1; CA 5-8R; CABS 3;
CANR 8, 54; CDALB 1941-1968; DLB 7;
INT CANR-8; MTCW

Alberti, Rafael 1902-.............. **CLC 7**
See also CA 85-88; DLB 108

Albert the Great 1200(?)-1280.... **CMLC 16**
See also DLB 115

Alcala-Galiano, Juan Valera y
See Valera y Alcala-Galiano, Juan

Alcott, Amos Bronson 1799-1888 .. **NCLC 1**
See also DLB 1

Alcott, Louisa May
1832-1888 ..... **NCLC 6, 58; DA; DAB;
DAC; DAM MST, NOV; WLC**
See also AAYA 20; CDALB 1865-1917;
CLR 1, 38; DLB 1, 42, 79; DLBD 14;
JRDA; MAICYA; YABC 1

Aldanov, M. A.
See Aldanov, Mark (Alexandrovich)

Aldanov, Mark (Alexandrovich)
1886(?)-1957 .... **TCLC 23**
See also CA 118

Aldington, Richard 1892-1962 ...... **CLC 49**
See also CA 85-88; CANR 45; DLB 20, 36,
100, 149

Aldiss, Brian W(ilson)
1925- .... **CLC 5, 14, 40; DAM NOV**
See also CA 5-8R; CAAS 2; CANR 5, 28;
DLB 14; MTCW; SATA 34

Alegria, Claribel
1924- .... **CLC 75; DAM MULT**
See also CA 131; CAAS 15; DLB 145; HW

Alegria, Fernando 1918- .... **CLC 57**
See also CA 9-12R; CANR 5, 32; HW

Aleichem, Sholom .... **TCLC 1, 35**
See also Rabinovitch, Sholem

Aleixandre, Vicente
1898-1984 .... **CLC 9, 36; DAM POET;
PC 15**
See also CA 85-88; 114; CANR 26;
DLB 108; HW; MTCW

Alepoudelis, Odysseus
See Elytis, Odysseus

Aleshkovsky, Joseph 1929-
See Aleshkovsky, Yuz
See also CA 121; 128

Aleshkovsky, Yuz .... **CLC 44**
See also Aleshkovsky, Joseph

Alexander, Lloyd (Chudley) 1924- .. **CLC 35**
See also AAYA 1; CA 1-4R; CANR 1, 24,
38, 55; CLR 1, 5; DLB 52; JRDA;
MAICYA; MTCW; SAAS 19; SATA 3,
49, 81

Alexie, Sherman (Joseph, Jr.)
1966- .... **CLC 96; DAM MULT**
See also CA 138; DLB 175; NNAL

Alfau, Felipe 1902- .... **CLC 66**
See also CA 137

Alger, Horatio, Jr. 1832-1899 ..... **NCLC 8**
See also DLB 42; SATA 16

Algren, Nelson 1909-1981 .... **CLC 4, 10, 33**
See also CA 13-16R; 103; CANR 20;
CDALB 1941-1968; DLB 9; DLBY 81,
82; MTCW

Ali, Ahmed 1910- .... **CLC 69**
See also CA 25-28R; CANR 15, 34

Alighieri, Dante 1265-1321 .... **CMLC 3, 18**

Allan, John B.
See Westlake, Donald E(dwin)

Allen, Edward 1948- .... **CLC 59**

Allen, Paula Gunn
1939- .... **CLC 84; DAM MULT**
See also CA 112; 143; DLB 175; NNAL

Allen, Roland
See Ayckbourn, Alan

Allen, Sarah A.
See Hopkins, Pauline Elizabeth

Allen, Woody
1935- .... **CLC 16, 52; DAM POP**
See also AAYA 10; CA 33-36R; CANR 27,
38; DLB 44; MTCW

Allende, Isabel
1942- .... **CLC 39, 57, 97; DAM MULT,
NOV; HLC**
See also AAYA 18; CA 125; 130;
CANR 51; DLB 145; HW; INT 130;
MTCW

Alleyn, Ellen
See Rossetti, Christina (Georgina)

Allingham, Margery (Louise)
1904-1966 .... **CLC 19**
See also CA 5-8R; 25-28R; CANR 4;
DLB 77; MTCW

Allingham, William 1824-1889 ... **NCLC 25**
See also DLB 35

Allison, Dorothy E. 1949- .... **CLC 78**
See also CA 140

Allston, Washington 1779-1843 .... **NCLC 2**
See also DLB 1

Almedingen, E. M. .... **CLC 12**
See also Almedingen, Martha Edith von
See also SATA 3

Almedingen, Martha Edith von 1898-1971
See Almedingen, E. M.
See also CA 1-4R; CANR 1

Almqvist, Carl Jonas Love
1793-1866 .... **NCLC 42**

Alonso, Damaso 1898-1990 .... **CLC 14**
See also CA 110; 131; 130; DLB 108; HW

Alov
See Gogol, Nikolai (Vasilyevich)

Alta 1942- .... **CLC 19**
See also CA 57-60

Alter, Robert B(ernard) 1935- ...... **CLC 34**
See also CA 49-52; CANR 1, 47

Alther, Lisa 1944- .... **CLC 7, 41**
See also CA 65-68; CANR 12, 30, 51;
MTCW

Altman, Robert 1925- .... **CLC 16**
See also CA 73-76; CANR 43

Alvarez, A(lfred) 1929- .... **CLC 5, 13**
See also CA 1-4R; CANR 3, 33; DLB 14,
40

Alvarez, Alejandro Rodriguez 1903-1965
See Casona, Alejandro
See also CA 131; 93-96; HW

Alvarez, Julia 1950- .... **CLC 93**
See also CA 147

Alvaro, Corrado 1896-1956 .... **TCLC 60**

Amado, Jorge
1912- .... **CLC 13, 40; DAM MULT,
NOV; HLC**
See also CA 77-80; CANR 35; DLB 113;
MTCW

Ambler, Eric 1909- .... **CLC 4, 6, 9**
See also CA 9-12R; CANR 7, 38; DLB 77;
MTCW

Amichai, Yehuda 1924- ...... **CLC 9, 22, 57**
See also CA 85-88; CANR 46; MTCW

Amiel, Henri Frederic 1821-1881 .. **NCLC 4**

Amis, Kingsley (William)
1922-1995 ..... **CLC 1, 2, 3, 5, 8, 13, 40,
44; DA; DAB; DAC; DAM MST, NOV**
See also AITN 2; CA 9-12R; 150; CANR 8,
28, 54; CDBLB 1945-1960; DLB 15, 27,
100, 139; INT CANR-8; MTCW

Amis, Martin (Louis)
1949- .... **CLC 4, 9, 38, 62**
See also BEST 90:3; CA 65-68; CANR 8,
27, 54; DLB 14; INT CANR-27

Ammons, A(rchie) R(andolph)
1926- .... **CLC 2, 3, 5, 8, 9, 25, 57;
DAM POET; PC 16**
See also AITN 1; CA 9-12R; CANR 6, 36,
51; DLB 5, 165; MTCW

Amo, Tauraatua i
See Adams, Henry (Brooks)

Anand, Mulk Raj
1905- .... **CLC 23, 93; DAM NOV**
See also CA 65-68; CANR 32; MTCW

Anatol
See Schnitzler, Arthur

Anaya, Rudolfo A(lfonso)
1937- .... **CLC 23; DAM MULT, NOV;
HLC**
See also AAYA 20; CA 45-48; CAAS 4;
CANR 1, 32, 51; DLB 82; HW 1; MTCW

Andersen, Hans Christian
1805-1875 .... **NCLC 7; DA; DAB;
DAC; DAM MST, POP; SSC 6; WLC**
See also CLR 6; MAICYA; YABC 1

Anderson, C. Farley
See Mencken, H(enry) L(ouis); Nathan,
George Jean

Anderson, Jessica (Margaret) Queale
.... **CLC 37**
See also CA 9-12R; CANR 4

Anderson, Jon (Victor)
1940- .... **CLC 9; DAM POET**
See also CA 25-28R; CANR 20

Anderson, Lindsay (Gordon)
1923-1994 .... **CLC 20**
See also CA 125; 128; 146

Anderson, Maxwell
1888-1959 ...... **TCLC 2; DAM DRAM**
See also CA 105; 152; DLB 7

Anderson, Poul (William) 1926- .... **CLC 15**
See also AAYA 5; CA 1-4R; CAAS 2;
CANR 2, 15, 34; DLB 8; INT CANR-15;
MTCW; SATA 90; SATA-Brief 39

Anderson, Robert (Woodruff)
1917- .... **CLC 23; DAM DRAM**
See also AITN 1; CA 21-24R; CANR 32;
DLB 7

Anderson, Sherwood
1876-1941 .... **TCLC 1, 10, 24; DA;
DAB; DAC; DAM MST, NOV; SSC 1;
WLC**
See also CA 104; 121; CDALB 1917-1929;
DLB 4, 9, 86; DLBD 1; MTCW

Andier, Pierre
See Desnos, Robert

Andouard
See Giraudoux, (Hippolyte) Jean

Andrade, Carlos Drummond de . . . . . . **CLC 18**
See also Drummond de Andrade, Carlos

Andrade, Mario de 1893-1945. . . . . **TCLC 43**

Andreae, Johann V(alentin)
1586-1654 . . . . **LC 32**
See also DLB 164

Andreas-Salome, Lou 1861-1937. . . **TCLC 56**
See also DLB 66

Andrewes, Lancelot 1555-1626 . . . . **LC 5**
See also DLB 151, 172

Andrews, Cicily Fairfield
See West, Rebecca

Andrews, Elton V.
See Pohl, Frederik

Andreyev, Leonid (Nikolaevich)
1871-1919 . . . . **TCLC 3**
See also CA 104

Andric, Ivo 1892-1975 . . . . **CLC 8**
See also CA 81-84; 57-60; CANR 43;
DLB 147; MTCW

Angelique, Pierre
See Bataille, Georges

Angell, Roger 1920- . . . . **CLC 26**
See also CA 57-60; CANR 13, 44; DLB 171

Angelou, Maya
1928- . . . . **CLC 12, 35, 64, 77; BLC; DA;**
DAB; DAC; DAM MST, MULT, POET,
POP
See also AAYA 7, 20; BW 2; CA 65-68;
CANR 19, 42; DLB 38; MTCW;
SATA 49

Annensky, Innokenty (Fyodorovich)
1856-1909 . . . . **TCLC 14**
See also CA 110; 155

Annunzio, Gabriele d'
See D'Annunzio, Gabriele

Anon, Charles Robert
See Pessoa, Fernando (Antonio Nogueira)

Anouilh, Jean (Marie Lucien Pierre)
1910-1987 . . . . . . **CLC 1, 3, 8, 13, 40, 50;**
DAM DRAM
See also CA 17-20R; 123; CANR 32;
MTCW

Anthony, Florence
See Ai

Anthony, John
See Ciardi, John (Anthony)

Anthony, Peter
See Shaffer, Anthony (Joshua); Shaffer,
Peter (Levin)

Anthony, Piers 1934- . . **CLC 35; DAM POP**
See also AAYA 11; CA 21-24R; CANR 28,
56; DLB 8; MTCW; SAAS 22; SATA 84

Antoine, Marc
See Proust, (Valentin-Louis-George-Eugene-)
Marcel

Antoninus, Brother
See Everson, William (Oliver)

Antonioni, Michelangelo 1912- . . . . . **CLC 20**
See also CA 73-76; CANR 45

Antschel, Paul 1920-1970
See Celan, Paul
See also CA 85-88; CANR 33; MTCW

Anwar, Chairil 1922-1949 . . . . **TCLC 22**
See also CA 121

Apollinaire, Guillaume
1880-1918 . . . . **TCLC 3, 8, 51;**
DAM POET; PC 7
See also Kostrowitzki, Wilhelm Apollinaris
de
See also CA 152

Appelfeld, Aharon 1932- . . . . **CLC 23, 47**
See also CA 112; 133

Apple, Max (Isaac) 1941- . . . . **CLC 9, 33**
See also CA 81-84; CANR 19, 54; DLB 130

Appleman, Philip (Dean) 1926- . . . . . **CLC 51**
See also CA 13-16R; CAAS 18; CANR 6,
29, 56

Appleton, Lawrence
See Lovecraft, H(oward) P(hillips)

Apteryx
See Eliot, T(homas) S(tearns)

Apuleius, (Lucius Madaurensis)
125(?)-175(?) . . . . **CMLC 1**

Aquin, Hubert 1929-1977. . . . . **CLC 15**
See also CA 105; DLB 53

Aragon, Louis
1897-1982 . . . . . **CLC 3, 22; DAM NOV,**
POET
See also CA 69-72; 108; CANR 28;
DLB 72; MTCW

Arany, Janos 1817-1882. . . . . **NCLC 34**

Arbuthnot, John 1667-1735 . . . . **LC 1**
See also DLB 101

Archer, Herbert Winslow
See Mencken, H(enry) L(ouis)

Archer, Jeffrey (Howard)
1940- . . . . **CLC 28; DAM POP**
See also AAYA 16; BEST 89:3; CA 77-80;
CANR 22, 52; INT CANR-22

Archer, Jules 1915- . . . . **CLC 12**
See also CA 9-12R; CANR 6; SAAS 5;
SATA 4, 85

Archer, Lee
See Ellison, Harlan (Jay)

Arden, John
1930- . . . . . **CLC 6, 13, 15; DAM DRAM**
See also CA 13-16R; CAAS 4; CANR 31;
DLB 13; MTCW

Arenas, Reinaldo
1943-1990 . . . . . . **CLC 41; DAM MULT;**
HLC
See also CA 124; 128; 133; DLB 145; HW

Arendt, Hannah 1906-1975 . . . . . **CLC 66, 98**
See also CA 17-20R; 61-64; CANR 26;
MTCW

Aretino, Pietro 1492-1556 . . . . **LC 12**

Arghezi, Tudor. . . . . **CLC 80**
See also Theodorescu, Ion N.

Arguedas, Jose Maria
1911-1969 . . . . **CLC 10, 18**
See also CA 89-92; DLB 113; HW

Argueta, Manlio 1936- . . . . **CLC 31**
See also CA 131; DLB 145; HW

Ariosto, Ludovico 1474-1533. . . . . **LC 6**

Aristides
See Epstein, Joseph

Aristophanes
450B.C.-385B.C. . . . . **CMLC 4; DA;**
DAB; DAC; DAM DRAM, MST; DC 2

Arlt, Roberto (Godofredo Christophersen)
1900-1942 . . . . . **TCLC 29; DAM MULT;**
HLC
See also CA 123; 131; HW

Armah, Ayi Kwei
1939- . . . . **CLC 5, 33; BLC;**
DAM MULT, POET
See also BW 1; CA 61-64; CANR 21;
DLB 117; MTCW

Armatrading, Joan 1950- . . . . **CLC 17**
See also CA 114

Arnette, Robert
See Silverberg, Robert

Arnim, Achim von (Ludwig Joachim von
Arnim) 1781-1831 . . . . **NCLC 5**
See also DLB 90

Arnim, Bettina von 1785-1859. . . . **NCLC 38**
See also DLB 90

Arnold, Matthew
1822-1888 . . . . . **NCLC 6, 29; DA; DAB;**
DAC; DAM MST, POET; PC 5; WLC
See also CDBLB 1832-1890; DLB 32, 57

Arnold, Thomas 1795-1842 . . . . . . **NCLC 18**
See also DLB 55

Arnow, Harriette (Louisa) Simpson
1908-1986 . . . . **CLC 2, 7, 18**
See also CA 9-12R; 118; CANR 14; DLB 6;
MTCW; SATA 42; SATA-Obit 47

Arp, Hans
See Arp, Jean

Arp, Jean 1887-1966. . . . . **CLC 5**
See also CA 81-84; 25-28R; CANR 42

Arrabal
See Arrabal, Fernando

Arrabal, Fernando 1932- . . . **CLC 2, 9, 18, 58**
See also CA 9-12R; CANR 15

Arrick, Fran. . . . . **CLC 30**
See also Gaberman, Judie Angell

Artaud, Antonin (Marie Joseph)
1896-1948 . . . **TCLC 3, 36; DAM DRAM**
See also CA 104; 149

Arthur, Ruth M(abel) 1905-1979. . . . **CLC 12**
See also CA 9-12R; 85-88; CANR 4;
SATA 7, 26

Artsybashev, Mikhail (Petrovich)
1878-1927 . . . . **TCLC 31**

Arundel, Honor (Morfydd)
1919-1973 . . . . **CLC 17**
See also CA 21-22; 41-44R; CAP 2;
CLR 35; SATA 4; SATA-Obit 24

Arzner, Dorothy 1897-1979 . . . . **CLC 98**

Asch, Sholem 1880-1957 . . . . **TCLC 3**
See also CA 105

Ash, Shalom
See Asch, Sholem

Bashkirtseff, Marie   1859-1884 . . . **NCLC 27**

Basho
See Matsuo Basho

Bass, Kingsley B., Jr.
See Bullins, Ed

Bass, Rick   1958- . . . . **CLC 79**
See also CA 126; CANR 53

Bassani, Giorgio   1916- . . . . **CLC 9**
See also CA 65-68; CANR 33; DLB 128;
MTCW

Bastos, Augusto (Antonio) Roa
See Roa Bastos, Augusto (Antonio)

Bataille, Georges   1897-1962 . . . . **CLC 29**
See also CA 101; 89-92

Bates, H(erbert) E(rnest)
1905-1974 . . . . **CLC 46; DAB;**
DAM POP; SSC 10
See also CA 93-96; 45-48; CANR 34;
DLB 162; MTCW

Bauchart
See Camus, Albert

Baudelaire, Charles
1821-1867 . . . . **NCLC 6, 29, 55; DA;**
DAB; DAC; DAM MST, POET; PC 1;
SSC 18; WLC

Baudrillard, Jean   1929- . . . . **CLC 60**

Baum, L(yman) Frank   1856-1919 . . . **TCLC 7**
See also CA 108; 133; CLR 15; DLB 22;
JRDA; MAICYA; MTCW; SATA 18

Baum, Louis F.
See Baum, L(yman) Frank

Baumbach, Jonathan   1933- . . . . . . **CLC 6, 23**
See also CA 13-16R; CAAS 5; CANR 12;
DLBY 80; INT CANR-12; MTCW

Bausch, Richard (Carl)   1945- . . . . . . **CLC 51**
See also CA 101; CAAS 14; CANR 43;
DLB 130

Baxter, Charles
1947- . . . . **CLC 45, 78; DAM POP**
See also CA 57-60; CANR 40; DLB 130

Baxter, George Owen
See Faust, Frederick (Schiller)

Baxter, James K(eir)   1926-1972 . . . . **CLC 14**
See also CA 77-80

Baxter, John
See Hunt, E(verette) Howard, (Jr.)

Bayer, Sylvia
See Glassco, John

Baynton, Barbara   1857-1929 . . . . . **TCLC 57**

Beagle, Peter S(oyer)   1939- . . . . **CLC 7**
See also CA 9-12R; CANR 4, 51;
DLBY 80; INT CANR-4; SATA 60

Bean, Normal
See Burroughs, Edgar Rice

Beard, Charles A(ustin)
1874-1948 . . . . **TCLC 15**
See also CA 115; DLB 17; SATA 18

Beardsley, Aubrey   1872-1898 . . . . . **NCLC 6**

Beattie, Ann
1947- . . . . **CLC 8, 13, 18, 40, 63;**
DAM NOV, POP; SSC 11
See also BEST 90:2; CA 81-84; CANR 53;
DLBY 82; MTCW

Beattie, James   1735-1803 . . . . **NCLC 25**
See also DLB 109

Beauchamp, Kathleen Mansfield   1888-1923
See Mansfield, Katherine
See also CA 104; 134; DA; DAC;
DAM MST

Beaumarchais, Pierre-Augustin Caron de
1732-1799 . . . . **DC 4**
See also DAM DRAM

Beaumont, Francis
1584(?)-1616 . . . . **LC 33; DC 6**
See also CDBLB Before 1660; DLB 58, 121

Beauvoir, Simone (Lucie Ernestine Marie
Bertrand) de
1908-1986 . . . . **CLC 1, 2, 4, 8, 14, 31, 44,**
50, 71; DA; DAB; DAC; DAM MST,
NOV; WLC
See also CA 9-12R; 118; CANR 28;
DLB 72; DLBY 86; MTCW

Becker, Carl   1873-1945 . . . . **TCLC 63**
See also DLB 17

Becker, Jurek   1937- . . . . **CLC 7, 19**
See also CA 85-88; DLB 75

Becker, Walter   1950- . . . . **CLC 26**

Beckett, Samuel (Barclay)
1906-1989 . . . . . . **CLC 1, 2, 3, 4, 6, 9, 10,**
11, 14, 18, 29, 57, 59, 83; DA; DAB;
DAC; DAM DRAM, MST, NOV;
SSC 16; WLC
See also CA 5-8R; 130; CANR 33;
CDBLB 1945-1960; DLB 13, 15;
DLBY 90; MTCW

Beckford, William   1760-1844 . . . . **NCLC 16**
See also DLB 39

Beckman, Gunnel   1910- . . . . **CLC 26**
See also CA 33-36R; CANR 15; CLR 25;
MAICYA; SAAS 9; SATA 6

Becque, Henri   1837-1899 . . . . **NCLC 3**

Beddoes, Thomas Lovell
1803-1849 . . . . **NCLC 3**
See also DLB 96

Bede   c. 673-735 . . . . **CMLC 20**
See also DLB 146

Bedford, Donald F.
See Fearing, Kenneth (Flexner)

Beecher, Catharine Esther
1800-1878 . . . . **NCLC 30**
See also DLB 1

Beecher, John   1904-1980 . . . . **CLC 6**
See also AITN 1; CA 5-8R; 105; CANR 8

Beer, Johann   1655-1700 . . . . **LC 5**
See also DLB 168

Beer, Patricia   1924- . . . . **CLC 58**
See also CA 61-64; CANR 13, 46; DLB 40

Beerbohm, Max
See Beerbohm, (Henry) Max(imilian)

Beerbohm, (Henry) Max(imilian)
1872-1956 . . . . **TCLC 1, 24**
See also CA 104; 154; DLB 34, 100

Beer-Hofmann, Richard
1866-1945 . . . . **TCLC 60**
See also DLB 81

Begiebing, Robert J(ohn)   1946- . . . . . **CLC 70**
See also CA 122; CANR 40

Behan, Brendan
1923-1964 . . . . **CLC 1, 8, 11, 15, 79;**
DAM DRAM
See also CA 73-76; CANR 33;
CDBLB 1945-1960; DLB 13; MTCW

Behn, Aphra
1640(?)-1689 . . . . . . **LC 1, 30; DA; DAB;**
DAC; DAM DRAM, MST, NOV,
POET; DC 4; PC 13; WLC
See also DLB 39, 80, 131

Behrman, S(amuel) N(athaniel)
1893-1973 . . . . **CLC 40**
See also CA 13-16; 45-48; CAP 1; DLB 7,
44

Belasco, David   1853-1931 . . . . **TCLC 3**
See also CA 104; DLB 7

Belcheva, Elisaveta   1893- . . . . **CLC 10**
See also Bagryana, Elisaveta

Beldone, Phil "Cheech"
See Ellison, Harlan (Jay)

Beleno
See Azuela, Mariano

Belinski, Vissarion Grigoryevich
1811-1848 . . . . **NCLC 5**

Belitt, Ben   1911- . . . . **CLC 22**
See also CA 13-16R; CAAS 4; CANR 7;
DLB 5

Bell, Gertrude   1868-1926 . . . . **TCLC 67**
See also DLB 174

Bell, James Madison
1826-1902 . . . . **TCLC 43; BLC;**
DAM MULT
See also BW 1; CA 122; 124; DLB 50

Bell, Madison Smartt   1957- . . . . **CLC 41**
See also CA 111; CANR 28, 54

Bell, Marvin (Hartley)
1937- . . . . **CLC 8, 31; DAM POET**
See also CA 21-24R; CAAS 14; DLB 5;
MTCW

Bell, W. L. D.
See Mencken, H(enry) L(ouis)

Bellamy, Atwood C.
See Mencken, H(enry) L(ouis)

Bellamy, Edward   1850-1898 . . . . . . **NCLC 4**
See also DLB 12

Bellin, Edward J.
See Kuttner, Henry

Belloc, (Joseph) Hilaire (Pierre Sebastien
Rene Swanton)
1870-1953 . . . **TCLC 7, 18; DAM POET**
See also CA 106; 152; DLB 19, 100, 141,
174; YABC 1

Belloc, Joseph Peter Rene Hilaire
See Belloc, (Joseph) Hilaire (Pierre Sebastien
Rene Swanton)

Belloc, Joseph Pierre Hilaire
See Belloc, (Joseph) Hilaire (Pierre Sebastien
Rene Swanton)

Belloc, M. A.
See Lowndes, Marie Adelaide (Belloc)

Bellow, Saul
　1915- ...... **CLC 1, 2, 3, 6, 8, 10, 13, 15,**
　　25, 33, 34, 63, 79; DA; DAB; DAC;
　　DAM MST, NOV, POP; SSC 14; WLC
　See also AITN 2; BEST 89:3; CA 5-8R;
　　CABS 1; CANR 29, 53;
　　CDALB 1941-1968; DLB 2, 28; DLBD 3;
　　DLBY 82; MTCW

Belser, Reimond Karel Maria de 1929-
　See Ruyslinck, Ward
　See also CA 152

Bely, Andrey .... **TCLC 7; PC 11**
　See also Bugayev, Boris Nikolayevich

Benary, Margot
　See Benary-Isbert, Margot

Benary-Isbert, Margot 1889-1979 ... **CLC 12**
　See also CA 5-8R; 89-92; CANR 4;
　　CLR 12; MAICYA; SATA 2;
　　SATA-Obit 21

Benavente (y Martinez), Jacinto
　1866-1954 ..... **TCLC 3; DAM DRAM,**
　　　　　　　　　　　　　　　　　MULT
　See also CA 106; 131; HW; MTCW

Benchley, Peter (Bradford)
　1940- ..... **CLC 4, 8; DAM NOV, POP**
　See also AAYA 14; AITN 2; CA 17-20R;
　　CANR 12, 35; MTCW; SATA 3, 89

Benchley, Robert (Charles)
　1889-1945 .... **TCLC 1, 55**
　See also CA 105; 153; DLB 11

Benda, Julien 1867-1956 .... **TCLC 60**
　See also CA 120; 154

Benedict, Ruth 1887-1948 .... **TCLC 60**

Benedikt, Michael 1935- .... **CLC 4, 14**
　See also CA 13-16R; CANR 7; DLB 5

Benet, Juan 1927- .... **CLC 28**
　See also CA 143

Benet, Stephen Vincent
　1898-1943 ...... **TCLC 7; DAM POET;**
　　　　　　　　　　　　　　　　SSC 10
　See also CA 104; 152; DLB 4, 48, 102;
　　YABC 1

Benet, William Rose
　1886-1950 ...... **TCLC 28; DAM POET**
　See also CA 118; 152; DLB 45

Benford, Gregory (Albert) 1941- .... **CLC 52**
　See also CA 69-72; CANR 12, 24, 49;
　　DLBY 82

Bengtsson, Frans (Gunnar)
　1894-1954 .... **TCLC 48**

Benjamin, David
　See Slavitt, David R(ytman)

Benjamin, Lois
　See Gould, Lois

Benjamin, Walter 1892-1940 ...... **TCLC 39**

Benn, Gottfried 1886-1956 .... **TCLC 3**
　See also CA 106; 153; DLB 56

Bennett, Alan
　1934- ... **CLC 45, 77; DAB; DAM MST**
　See also CA 103; CANR 35, 55; MTCW

Bennett, (Enoch) Arnold
　1867-1931 .... **TCLC 5, 20**
　See also CA 106; 155; CDBLB 1890-1914;
　　DLB 10, 34, 98, 135

Bennett, Elizabeth
　See Mitchell, Margaret (Munnerlyn)

Bennett, George Harold 1930-
　See Bennett, Hal
　See also BW 1; CA 97-100

Bennett, Hal .... **CLC 5**
　See also Bennett, George Harold
　See also DLB 33

Bennett, Jay 1912- .... **CLC 35**
　See also AAYA 10; CA 69-72; CANR 11,
　　42; JRDA; SAAS 4; SATA 41, 87;
　　SATA-Brief 27

Bennett, Louise (Simone)
　1919- ..... **CLC 28; BLC; DAM MULT**
　See also BW 2; CA 151; DLB 117

Benson, E(dward) F(rederic)
　1867-1940 .... **TCLC 27**
　See also CA 114; DLB 135, 153

Benson, Jackson J. 1930- .... **CLC 34**
　See also CA 25-28R; DLB 111

Benson, Sally 1900-1972 .... **CLC 17**
　See also CA 19-20; 37-40R; CAP 1;
　　SATA 1, 35; SATA-Obit 27

Benson, Stella 1892-1933 .... **TCLC 17**
　See also CA 117; 155; DLB 36, 162

Bentham, Jeremy 1748-1832 ..... **NCLC 38**
　See also DLB 107, 158

Bentley, E(dmund) C(lerihew)
　1875-1956 .... **TCLC 12**
　See also CA 108; DLB 70

Bentley, Eric (Russell) 1916- .... **CLC 24**
　See also CA 5-8R; CANR 6; INT CANR-6

Beranger, Pierre Jean de
　1780-1857 .... **NCLC 34**

Berdyaev, Nicolas
　See Berdyaev, Nikolai (Aleksandrovich)

Berdyaev, Nikolai (Aleksandrovich)
　1874-1948 .... **TCLC 67**
　See also CA 120

Berendt, John (Lawrence) 1939- .... **CLC 86**
　See also CA 146

Berger, Colonel
　See Malraux, (Georges-)Andre

Berger, John (Peter) 1926- ...... **CLC 2, 19**
　See also CA 81-84; CANR 51; DLB 14

Berger, Melvin H. 1927- .... **CLC 12**
　See also CA 5-8R; CANR 4; CLR 32;
　　SAAS 2; SATA 5, 88

Berger, Thomas (Louis)
　1924- .... **CLC 3, 5, 8, 11, 18, 38;**
　　　　　　　　　　　　　　　　DAM NOV
　See also CA 1-4R; CANR 5, 28, 51; DLB 2;
　　DLBY 80; INT CANR-28; MTCW

Bergman, (Ernst) Ingmar
　1918- .... **CLC 16, 72**
　See also CA 81-84; CANR 33

Bergson, Henri 1859-1941 .... **TCLC 32**

Bergstein, Eleanor 1938- .... **CLC 4**
　See also CA 53-56; CANR 5

Berkoff, Steven 1937- .... **CLC 56**
　See also CA 104

Bermant, Chaim (Icyk) 1929- ...... **CLC 40**
　See also CA 57-60; CANR 6, 31

Bern, Victoria
　See Fisher, M(ary) F(rances) K(ennedy)

Bernanos, (Paul Louis) Georges
　1888-1948 .... **TCLC 3**
　See also CA 104; 130; DLB 72

Bernard, April 1956- .... **CLC 59**
　See also CA 131

Berne, Victoria
　See Fisher, M(ary) F(rances) K(ennedy)

Bernhard, Thomas
　1931-1989 .... **CLC 3, 32, 61**
　See also CA 85-88; 127; CANR 32;
　　DLB 85, 124; MTCW

Berriault, Gina 1926- .... **CLC 54**
　See also CA 116; 129; DLB 130

Berrigan, Daniel 1921- .... **CLC 4**
　See also CA 33-36R; CAAS 1; CANR 11,
　　43; DLB 5

Berrigan, Edmund Joseph Michael, Jr.
　1934-1983
　See Berrigan, Ted
　See also CA 61-64; 110; CANR 14

Berrigan, Ted .... **CLC 37**
　See also Berrigan, Edmund Joseph Michael,
　　Jr.
　See also DLB 5, 169

Berry, Charles Edward Anderson 1931-
　See Berry, Chuck
　See also CA 115

Berry, Chuck .... **CLC 17**
　See also Berry, Charles Edward Anderson

Berry, Jonas
　See Ashbery, John (Lawrence)

Berry, Wendell (Erdman)
　1934- .... **CLC 4, 6, 8, 27, 46;**
　　　　　　　　　　　　　　　　DAM POET
　See also AITN 1; CA 73-76; CANR 50;
　　DLB 5, 6

Berryman, John
　1914-1972 ...... **CLC 1, 2, 3, 4, 6, 8, 10,**
　　　　13, 25, 62; DAM POET
　See also CA 13-16; 33-36R; CABS 2;
　　CANR 35; CAP 1; CDALB 1941-1968;
　　DLB 48; MTCW

Bertolucci, Bernardo 1940- .... **CLC 16**
　See also CA 106

Bertrand, Aloysius 1807-1841 .... **NCLC 31**

Bertran de Born c. 1140-1215 ..... **CMLC 5**

Besant, Annie (Wood) 1847-1933 ... **TCLC 9**
　See also CA 105

Bessie, Alvah 1904-1985 .... **CLC 23**
　See also CA 5-8R; 116; CANR 2; DLB 26

Bethlen, T. D.
　See Silverberg, Robert

Beti, Mongo .... **CLC 27; BLC; DAM MULT**
　See also Biyidi, Alexandre

Betjeman, John
　1906-1984 .... **CLC 2, 6, 10, 34, 43;**
　　　　　　DAB; DAM MST, POET
　See also CA 9-12R; 112; CANR 33, 56;
　　CDBLB 1945-1960; DLB 20; DLBY 84;
　　MTCW

Bettelheim, Bruno 1903-1990 ...... **CLC 79**
　See also CA 81-84; 131; CANR 23; MTCW

Betti, Ugo 1892-1953 .... **TCLC 5**
See also CA 104; 155

Betts, Doris (Waugh) 1932-.... **CLC 3, 6, 28**
See also CA 13-16R; CANR 9; DLBY 82;
INT CANR-9

Bevan, Alistair
See Roberts, Keith (John Kingston)

Bialik, Chaim Nachman
1873-1934 .... **TCLC 25**

Bickerstaff, Isaac
See Swift, Jonathan

Bidart, Frank 1939-.............. **CLC 33**
See also CA 140

Bienek, Horst 1930-........... **CLC 7, 11**
See also CA 73-76; DLB 75

Bierce, Ambrose (Gwinett)
1842-1914(?) .... **TCLC 1, 7, 44; DA;**
DAC; DAM MST; SSC 9; WLC
See also CA 104; 139; CDALB 1865-1917;
DLB 11, 12, 23, 71, 74

Biggers, Earl Derr 1884-1933 ..... **TCLC 65**
See also CA 108; 153

Billings, Josh
See Shaw, Henry Wheeler

Billington, (Lady) Rachel (Mary)
1942- .... **CLC 43**
See also AITN 2; CA 33-36R; CANR 44

Binyon, T(imothy) J(ohn) 1936-.... **CLC 34**
See also CA 111; CANR 28

Bioy Casares, Adolfo
1914- .... **CLC 4, 8, 13, 88;**
DAM MULT; HLC; SSC 17
See also CA 29-32R; CANR 19, 43;
DLB 113; HW; MTCW

Bird, Cordwainer
See Ellison, Harlan (Jay)

Bird, Robert Montgomery
1806-1854 .... **NCLC 1**

Birney, (Alfred) Earle
1904- .... **CLC 1, 4, 6, 11; DAC;**
DAM MST, POET
See also CA 1-4R; CANR 5, 20; DLB 88;
MTCW

Bishop, Elizabeth
1911-1979 ...... **CLC 1, 4, 9, 13, 15, 32;**
DA; DAC; DAM MST, POET; PC 3
See also CA 5-8R; 89-92; CABS 2;
CANR 26; CDALB 1968-1988; DLB 5,
169; MTCW; SATA-Obit 24

Bishop, John 1935-................ **CLC 10**
See also CA 105

Bissett, Bill 1939-........... **CLC 18; PC 14**
See also CA 69-72; CAAS 19; CANR 15;
DLB 53; MTCW

Bitov, Andrei (Georgievich) 1937-... **CLC 57**
See also CA 142

Biyidi, Alexandre 1932-
See Beti, Mongo
See also BW 1; CA 114; 124; MTCW

Bjarme, Brynjolf
See Ibsen, Henrik (Johan)

Bjornson, Bjornstjerne (Martinius)
1832-1910 .... **TCLC 7, 37**
See also CA 104

Black, Robert
See Holdstock, Robert P.

Blackburn, Paul 1926-1971 ...... **CLC 9, 43**
See also CA 81-84; 33-36R; CANR 34;
DLB 16; DLBY 81

Black Elk
1863-1950 ..... **TCLC 33; DAM MULT**
See also CA 144; NNAL

Black Hobart
See Sanders, (James) Ed(ward)

Blacklin, Malcolm
See Chambers, Aidan

Blackmore, R(ichard) D(oddridge)
1825-1900 .... **TCLC 27**
See also CA 120; DLB 18

Blackmur, R(ichard) P(almer)
1904-1965 .... **CLC 2, 24**
See also CA 11-12; 25-28R; CAP 1; DLB 63

Black Tarantula
See Acker, Kathy

Blackwood, Algernon (Henry)
1869-1951 .... **TCLC 5**
See also CA 105; 150; DLB 153, 156

Blackwood, Caroline 1931-1996 ... **CLC 6, 9**
See also CA 85-88; 151; CANR 32;
DLB 14; MTCW

Blade, Alexander
See Hamilton, Edmond; Silverberg, Robert

Blaga, Lucian 1895-1961 .... **CLC 75**

Blair, Eric (Arthur) 1903-1950
See Orwell, George
See also CA 104; 132; DA; DAB; DAC;
DAM MST, NOV; MTCW; SATA 29

Blais, Marie-Claire
1939- .... **CLC 2, 4, 6, 13, 22; DAC;**
DAM MST
See also CA 21-24R; CAAS 4; CANR 38;
DLB 53; MTCW

Blaise, Clark 1940-.............. **CLC 29**
See also AITN 2; CA 53-56; CAAS 3;
CANR 5; DLB 53

Blake, Nicholas
See Day Lewis, C(ecil)
See also DLB 77

Blake, William
1757-1827 .... **NCLC 13, 37, 57; DA;**
DAB; DAC; DAM MST, POET; PC 12;
WLC
See also CDBLB 1789-1832; DLB 93, 163;
MAICYA; SATA 30

Blake, William J(ames) 1894-1969 ... **PC 12**
See also CA 5-8R; 25-28R

Blasco Ibanez, Vicente
1867-1928 .... **TCLC 12; DAM NOV**
See also CA 110; 131; HW; MTCW

Blatty, William Peter
1928- .... **CLC 2; DAM POP**
See also CA 5-8R; CANR 9

Bleeck, Oliver
See Thomas, Ross (Elmore)

Blessing, Lee 1949-.............. **CLC 54**

Blish, James (Benjamin)
1921-1975 .... **CLC 14**
See also CA 1-4R; 57-60; CANR 3; DLB 8;
MTCW; SATA 66

Bliss, Reginald
See Wells, H(erbert) G(eorge)

Blixen, Karen (Christentze Dinesen)
1885-1962
See Dinesen, Isak
See also CA 25-28; CANR 22, 50; CAP 2;
MTCW; SATA 44

Bloch, Robert (Albert) 1917-1994... **CLC 33**
See also CA 5-8R; 146; CAAS 20; CANR 5;
DLB 44; INT CANR-5; SATA 12;
SATA-Obit 82

Blok, Alexander (Alexandrovich)
1880-1921 .... **TCLC 5**
See also CA 104

Blom, Jan
See Breytenbach, Breyten

Bloom, Harold 1930-............. **CLC 24**
See also CA 13-16R; CANR 39; DLB 67

Bloomfield, Aurelius
See Bourne, Randolph S(illiman)

Blount, Roy (Alton), Jr. 1941-..... **CLC 38**
See also CA 53-56; CANR 10, 28;
INT CANR-28; MTCW

Bloy, Leon 1846-1917............ **TCLC 22**
See also CA 121; DLB 123

Blume, Judy (Sussman)
1938-... **CLC 12, 30; DAM NOV, POP**
See also AAYA 3; CA 29-32R; CANR 13,
37; CLR 2, 15; DLB 52; JRDA;
MAICYA; MTCW; SATA 2, 31, 79

Blunden, Edmund (Charles)
1896-1974 .... **CLC 2, 56**
See also CA 17-18; 45-48; CANR 54;
CAP 2; DLB 20, 100, 155; MTCW

Bly, Robert (Elwood)
1926- .... **CLC 1, 2, 5, 10, 15, 38;**
DAM POET
See also CA 5-8R; CANR 41; DLB 5;
MTCW

Boas, Franz 1858-1942.......... **TCLC 56**
See also CA 115

Bobette
See Simenon, Georges (Jacques Christian)

Boccaccio, Giovanni
1313-1375 .... **CMLC 13; SSC 10**

Bochco, Steven 1943-............. **CLC 35**
See also AAYA 11; CA 124; 138

Bodenheim, Maxwell 1892-1954 ... **TCLC 44**
See also CA 110; DLB 9, 45

Bodker, Cecil 1927-.............. **CLC 21**
See also CA 73-76; CANR 13, 44; CLR 23;
MAICYA; SATA 14

Boell, Heinrich (Theodor)
1917-1985 .... **CLC 2, 3, 6, 9, 11, 15, 27,**
32, 72; DA; DAB; DAC; DAM MST,
NOV; SSC 23; WLC
See also CA 21-24R; 116; CANR 24;
DLB 69; DLBY 85; MTCW

Boerne, Alfred
See Doeblin, Alfred

Boethius 480(?)-524(?) .... **CMLC 15**
See also DLB 115

Bogan, Louise
1897-1970 . . . . CLC **4, 39, 46, 93;**
DAM POET; PC **12**
See also CA 73-76; 25-28R; CANR 33;
DLB 45, 169; MTCW

Bogarde, Dirk . . . . CLC **19**
See also Van Den Bogarde, Derek Jules
Gaspard Ulric Niven
See also DLB 14

Bogosian, Eric 1953- . . . . CLC **45**
See also CA 138

Bograd, Larry 1953- . . . . CLC **35**
See also CA 93-96; SAAS 21; SATA 33, 89

Boiardo, Matteo Maria 1441-1494 . . . . LC **6**

Boileau-Despreaux, Nicolas
1636-1711 . . . . LC **3**

Bojer, Johan 1872-1959 . . . . TCLC **64**

Boland, Eavan (Aisling)
1944- . . . . CLC **40, 67; DAM POET**
See also CA 143; DLB 40

Bolt, Lee
See Faust, Frederick (Schiller)

Bolt, Robert (Oxton)
1924-1995 . . . . . CLC **14; DAM DRAM**
See also CA 17-20R; 147; CANR 35;
DLB 13; MTCW

Bombet, Louis-Alexandre-Cesar
See Stendhal

Bomkauf
See Kaufman, Bob (Garnell)

Bonaventura . . . . NCLC **35**
See also DLB 90

Bond, Edward
1934- . . . CLC **4, 6, 13, 23; DAM DRAM**
See also CA 25-28R; CANR 38; DLB 13;
MTCW

Bonham, Frank 1914-1989 . . . . CLC **12**
See also AAYA 1; CA 9-12R; CANR 4, 36;
JRDA; MAICYA; SAAS 3; SATA 1, 49;
SATA-Obit 62

Bonnefoy, Yves
1923- . . . . . . CLC **9, 15, 58; DAM MST,**
POET
See also CA 85-88; CANR 33; MTCW

Bontemps, Arna(ud Wendell)
1902-1973 . . . . CLC **1, 18; BLC;**
DAM MULT, NOV, POET
See also BW 1; CA 1-4R; 41-44R; CANR 4,
35; CLR 6; DLB 48, 51; JRDA;
MAICYA; MTCW; SATA 2, 44;
SATA-Obit 24

Booth, Martin 1944- . . . . CLC **13**
See also CA 93-96; CAAS 2

Booth, Philip 1925- . . . . CLC **23**
See also CA 5-8R; CANR 5; DLBY 82

Booth, Wayne C(layson) 1921- . . . . . CLC **24**
See also CA 1-4R; CAAS 5; CANR 3, 43;
DLB 67

Borchert, Wolfgang 1921-1947 . . . . . TCLC **5**
See also CA 104; DLB 69, 124

Borel, Petrus 1809-1859 . . . . NCLC **41**

Borges, Jorge Luis
1899-1986 . . . CLC **1, 2, 3, 4, 6, 8, 9, 10,**
13, 19, 44, 48, 83; DA; DAB; DAC;
DAM MST, MULT; HLC; SSC **4**; WLC
See also AAYA 19; CA 21-24R; CANR 19,
33; DLB 113; DLBY 86; HW; MTCW

Borowski, Tadeusz 1922-1951 . . . . . . TCLC **9**
See also CA 106; 154

Borrow, George (Henry)
1803-1881 . . . . NCLC **9**
See also DLB 21, 55, 166

Bosman, Herman Charles
1905-1951 . . . . TCLC **49**

Bosschere, Jean de 1878(?)-1953 . . . TCLC **19**
See also CA 115

Boswell, James
1740-1795 . . . . . . LC **4; DA; DAB; DAC;**
DAM MST; WLC
See also CDBLB 1660-1789; DLB 104, 142

Bottoms, David 1949- . . . . CLC **53**
See also CA 105; CANR 22; DLB 120;
DLBY 83

Boucicault, Dion 1820-1890 . . . . . . NCLC **41**

Boucolon, Maryse 1937(?)-
See Conde, Maryse
See also CA 110; CANR 30, 53

Bourget, Paul (Charles Joseph)
1852-1935 . . . . TCLC **12**
See also CA 107; DLB 123

Bourjaily, Vance (Nye) 1922- . . . . CLC **8, 62**
See also CA 1-4R; CAAS 1; CANR 2;
DLB 2, 143

Bourne, Randolph S(illiman)
1886-1918 . . . . TCLC **16**
See also CA 117; 155; DLB 63

Bova, Ben(jamin William) 1932- . . . . CLC **45**
See also AAYA 16; CA 5-8R; CAAS 18;
CANR 11, 56; CLR 3; DLBY 81;
INT CANR-11; MAICYA; MTCW;
SATA 6, 68

Bowen, Elizabeth (Dorothea Cole)
1899-1973 . . . . . . CLC **1, 3, 6, 11, 15, 22;**
DAM NOV; SSC **3**
See also CA 17-18; 41-44R; CANR 35;
CAP 2; CDBLB 1945-1960; DLB 15, 162;
MTCW

Bowering, George 1935- . . . . CLC **15, 47**
See also CA 21-24R; CAAS 16; CANR 10;
DLB 53

Bowering, Marilyn R(uthe) 1949- . . . CLC **32**
See also CA 101; CANR 49

Bowers, Edgar 1924- . . . . CLC **9**
See also CA 5-8R; CANR 24; DLB 5

Bowie, David . . . . CLC **17**
See also Jones, David Robert

Bowles, Jane (Sydney)
1917-1973 . . . . CLC **3, 68**
See also CA 19-20; 41-44R; CAP 2

Bowles, Paul (Frederick)
1910- . . . . CLC **1, 2, 19, 53; SSC 3**
See also CA 1-4R; CAAS 1; CANR 1, 19,
50; DLB 5, 6; MTCW

Box, Edgar
See Vidal, Gore

Boyd, Nancy
See Millay, Edna St. Vincent

Boyd, William 1952- . . . . CLC **28, 53, 70**
See also CA 114; 120; CANR 51

Boyle, Kay
1902-1992 . . . . . CLC **1, 5, 19, 58; SSC 5**
See also CA 13-16R; 140; CAAS 1;
CANR 29; DLB 4, 9, 48, 86; DLBY 93;
MTCW

Boyle, Mark
See Kienzle, William X(avier)

Boyle, Patrick 1905-1982 . . . . CLC **19**
See also CA 127

Boyle, T. C. 1948-
See Boyle, T(homas) Coraghessan

Boyle, T(homas) Coraghessan
1948- . . . . . CLC **36, 55, 90; DAM POP;**
SSC **16**
See also BEST 90:4; CA 120; CANR 44;
DLBY 86

Boz
See Dickens, Charles (John Huffam)

Brackenridge, Hugh Henry
1748-1816 . . . . NCLC **7**
See also DLB 11, 37

Bradbury, Edward P.
See Moorcock, Michael (John)

Bradbury, Malcolm (Stanley)
1932- . . . . CLC **32, 61; DAM NOV**
See also CA 1-4R; CANR 1, 33; DLB 14;
MTCW

Bradbury, Ray (Douglas)
1920- . . . . . CLC **1, 3, 10, 15, 42, 98; DA;**
DAB; DAC; DAM MST, NOV, POP;
WLC
See also AAYA 15; AITN 1, 2; CA 1-4R;
CANR 2, 30; CDALB 1968-1988; DLB 2,
8; INT CANR-30; MTCW; SATA 11, 64

Bradford, Gamaliel 1863-1932 . . . . . TCLC **36**
See also DLB 17

Bradley, David (Henry, Jr.)
1950- . . . . . CLC **23; BLC; DAM MULT**
See also BW 1; CA 104; CANR 26; DLB 33

Bradley, John Ed(mund, Jr.)
1958- . . . . CLC **55**
See also CA 139

Bradley, Marion Zimmer
1930- . . . . CLC **30; DAM POP**
See also AAYA 9; CA 57-60; CAAS 10;
CANR 7, 31, 51; DLB 8; MTCW;
SATA 90

Bradstreet, Anne
1612(?)-1672 . . . . . . LC **4, 30; DA; DAC;**
DAM MST, POET; PC **10**
See also CDALB 1640-1865; DLB 24

Brady, Joan 1939- . . . . CLC **86**
See also CA 141

Bragg, Melvyn 1939- . . . . CLC **10**
See also BEST 89:3; CA 57-60; CANR 10,
48; DLB 14

Braine, John (Gerard)
1922-1986 . . . . CLC **1, 3, 41**
See also CA 1-4R; 120; CANR 1, 33;
CDBLB 1945-1960; DLB 15; DLBY 86;
MTCW

Brammer, William 1930(?)-1978 .... **CLC 31**
See also CA 77-80

Brancati, Vitaliano 1907-1954..... **TCLC 12**
See also CA 109

Brancato, Robin F(idler) 1936- ..... **CLC 35**
See also AAYA 9; CA 69-72; CANR 11,
45; CLR 32; JRDA; SAAS 9; SATA 23

Brand, Max
See Faust, Frederick (Schiller)

Brand, Millen 1906-1980 .... **CLC 7**
See also CA 21-24R; 97-100

Branden, Barbara .... **CLC 44**
See also CA 148

Brandes, Georg (Morris Cohen)
1842-1927 .... **TCLC 10**
See also CA 105

Brandys, Kazimierz 1916- .... **CLC 62**

Branley, Franklyn M(ansfield)
1915- .... **CLC 21**
See also CA 33-36R; CANR 14, 39;
CLR 13; MAICYA; SAAS 16; SATA 4,
68

Brathwaite, Edward Kamau
1930- .... **CLC 11; DAM POET**
See also BW 2; CA 25-28R; CANR 11, 26,
47; DLB 125

Brautigan, Richard (Gary)
1935-1984 .... **CLC 1, 3, 5, 9, 12, 34, 42;**
DAM NOV
See also CA 53-56; 113; CANR 34; DLB 2,
5; DLBY 80, 84; MTCW; SATA 56

Brave Bird, Mary 1953-
See Crow Dog, Mary (Ellen)
See also NNAL

Braverman, Kate 1950- .... **CLC 67**
See also CA 89-92

Brecht, Bertolt
1898-1956 ...... **TCLC 1, 6, 13, 35; DA;**
DAB; DAC; DAM DRAM, MST; DC 3;
WLC
See also CA 104; 133; DLB 56, 124; MTCW

Brecht, Eugen Berthold Friedrich
See Brecht, Bertolt

Bremer, Fredrika 1801-1865 ..... **NCLC 11**

Brennan, Christopher John
1870-1932 .... **TCLC 17**
See also CA 117

Brennan, Maeve 1917- .... **CLC 5**
See also CA 81-84

Brentano, Clemens (Maria)
1778-1842 .... **NCLC 1**
See also DLB 90

Brent of Bin Bin
See Franklin, (Stella Maraia Sarah) Miles

Brenton, Howard 1942- .... **CLC 31**
See also CA 69-72; CANR 33; DLB 13;
MTCW

Breslin, James 1930-
See Breslin, Jimmy
See also CA 73-76; CANR 31; DAM NOV;
MTCW

Breslin, Jimmy .... **CLC 4, 43**
See also Breslin, James
See also AITN 1

Bresson, Robert 1901- .... **CLC 16**
See also CA 110; CANR 49

Breton, Andre
1896-1966 ...... **CLC 2, 9, 15, 54; PC 15**
See also CA 19-20; 25-28R; CANR 40;
CAP 2; DLB 65; MTCW

Breytenbach, Breyten
1939(?)- ...... **CLC 23, 37; DAM POET**
See also CA 113; 129

Bridgers, Sue Ellen 1942- .... **CLC 26**
See also AAYA 8; CA 65-68; CANR 11,
36; CLR 18; DLB 52; JRDA; MAICYA;
SAAS 1; SATA 22, 90

Bridges, Robert (Seymour)
1844-1930 .... **TCLC 1; DAM POET**
See also CA 104; 152; CDBLB 1890-1914;
DLB 19, 98

Bridie, James .... **TCLC 3**
See also Mavor, Osborne Henry
See also DLB 10

Brin, David 1950- .... **CLC 34**
See also CA 102; CANR 24;
INT CANR-24; SATA 65

Brink, Andre (Philippus)
1935- .... **CLC 18, 36**
See also CA 104; CANR 39; INT 103;
MTCW

Brinsmead, H(esba) F(ay) 1922- .... **CLC 21**
See also CA 21-24R; CANR 10; MAICYA;
SAAS 5; SATA 18, 78

Brittain, Vera (Mary)
1893(?)-1970 .... **CLC 23**
See also CA 13-16; 25-28R; CAP 1; MTCW

Broch, Hermann 1886-1951 .... **TCLC 20**
See also CA 117; DLB 85, 124

Brock, Rose
See Hansen, Joseph

Brodkey, Harold (Roy) 1930-1996 .. **CLC 56**
See also CA 111; 151; DLB 130

Brodsky, Iosif Alexandrovich 1940-1996
See Brodsky, Joseph
See also AITN 1; CA 41-44R; 151;
CANR 37; DAM POET; MTCW

Brodsky, Joseph
1940-1996 ... **CLC 4, 6, 13, 36, 50; PC 9**
See also Brodsky, Iosif Alexandrovich

Brodsky, Michael Mark 1948- ..... **CLC 19**
See also CA 102; CANR 18, 41

Bromell, Henry 1947- .... **CLC 5**
See also CA 53-56; CANR 9

Bromfield, Louis (Brucker)
1896-1956 .... **TCLC 11**
See also CA 107; 155; DLB 4, 9, 86

Broner, E(sther) M(asserman)
1930- .... **CLC 19**
See also CA 17-20R; CANR 8, 25; DLB 28

Bronk, William 1918- .... **CLC 10**
See also CA 89-92; CANR 23; DLB 165

Bronstein, Lev Davidovich
See Trotsky, Leon

Bronte, Anne 1820-1849 .... **NCLC 4**
See also DLB 21

Bronte, Charlotte
1816-1855 ..... **NCLC 3, 8, 33, 58; DA;**
DAB; DAC; DAM MST, NOV; WLC
See also AAYA 17; CDBLB 1832-1890;
DLB 21, 159

Bronte, Emily (Jane)
1818-1848 .... **NCLC 16, 35; DA; DAB;**
DAC; DAM MST, NOV, POET; PC 8;
WLC
See also AAYA 17; CDBLB 1832-1890;
DLB 21, 32

Brooke, Frances 1724-1789 .... **LC 6**
See also DLB 39, 99

Brooke, Henry 1703(?)-1783 .... **LC 1**
See also DLB 39

Brooke, Rupert (Chawner)
1887-1915 .... **TCLC 2, 7; DA; DAB;**
DAC; DAM MST, POET; WLC
See also CA 104; 132; CDBLB 1914-1945;
DLB 19; MTCW

Brooke-Haven, P.
See Wodehouse, P(elham) G(renville)

Brooke-Rose, Christine 1926- ...... **CLC 40**
See also CA 13-16R; DLB 14

Brookner, Anita
1928- .... **CLC 32, 34, 51; DAB;**
DAM POP
See also CA 114; 120; CANR 37, 56;
DLBY 87; MTCW

Brooks, Cleanth 1906-1994 ..... **CLC 24, 86**
See also CA 17-20R; 145; CANR 33, 35;
DLB 63; DLBY 94; INT CANR-35;
MTCW

Brooks, George
See Baum, L(yman) Frank

Brooks, Gwendolyn
1917- ...... **CLC 1, 2, 4, 5, 15, 49; BLC;**
DA; DAC; DAM MST, MULT, POET;
PC 7; WLC
See also AAYA 20; AITN 1; BW 2;
CA 1-4R; CANR 1, 27, 52;
CDALB 1941-1968; CLR 27; DLB 5, 76,
165; MTCW; SATA 6

Brooks, Mel .... **CLC 12**
See also Kaminsky, Melvin
See also AAYA 13; DLB 26

Brooks, Peter 1938- .... **CLC 34**
See also CA 45-48; CANR 1

Brooks, Van Wyck 1886-1963...... **CLC 29**
See also CA 1-4R; CANR 6; DLB 45, 63,
103

Brophy, Brigid (Antonia)
1929-1995 .... **CLC 6, 11, 29**
See also CA 5-8R; 149; CAAS 4; CANR 25,
53; DLB 14; MTCW

Brosman, Catharine Savage 1934-.... **CLC 9**
See also CA 61-64; CANR 21, 46

Brother Antoninus
See Everson, William (Oliver)

Broughton, T(homas) Alan 1936- ... **CLC 19**
See also CA 45-48; CANR 2, 23, 48

Broumas, Olga 1949- .... **CLC 10, 73**
See also CA 85-88; CANR 20

Brown, Alan 1951- .... **CLC 99**

Brown, Charles Brockden
1771-1810 .... NCLC 22
See also CDALB 1640-1865; DLB 37, 59, 73

Brown, Christy 1932-1981 .... CLC 63
See also CA 105; 104; DLB 14

Brown, Claude
1937- ..... CLC 30; BLC; DAM MULT
See also AAYA 7; BW 1; CA 73-76

Brown, Dee (Alexander)
1908- .... CLC 18, 47; DAM POP
See also CA 13-16R; CAAS 6; CANR 11, 45; DLBY 80; MTCW; SATA 5

Brown, George
See Wertmueller, Lina

Brown, George Douglas
1869-1902 .... TCLC 28

Brown, George Mackay
1921-1996 .... CLC 5, 48
See also CA 21-24R; 151; CAAS 6; CANR 12, 37; DLB 14, 27, 139; MTCW; SATA 35

Brown, (William) Larry 1951- ...... CLC 73
See also CA 130; 134; INT 133

Brown, Moses
See Barrett, William (Christopher)

Brown, Rita Mae
1944- ..... CLC 18, 43, 79; DAM NOV, POP
See also CA 45-48; CANR 2, 11, 35; INT CANR-11; MTCW

Brown, Roderick (Langmere) Haig-
See Haig-Brown, Roderick (Langmere)

Brown, Rosellen 1939- .... CLC 32
See also CA 77-80; CAAS 10; CANR 14, 44

Brown, Sterling Allen
1901-1989 .... CLC 1, 23, 59; BLC; DAM MULT, POET
See also BW 1; CA 85-88; 127; CANR 26; DLB 48, 51, 63; MTCW

Brown, Will
See Ainsworth, William Harrison

Brown, William Wells
1813-1884 .... NCLC 2; BLC; DAM MULT; DC 1
See also DLB 3, 50

Browne, (Clyde) Jackson 1948(?)-... CLC 21
See also CA 120

Browning, Elizabeth Barrett
1806-1861 ..... NCLC 1, 16; DA; DAB; DAC; DAM MST, POET; PC 6; WLC
See also CDBLB 1832-1890; DLB 32

Browning, Robert
1812-1889 ...... NCLC 19; DA; DAB; DAC; DAM MST, POET; PC 2
See also CDBLB 1832-1890; DLB 32, 163; YABC 1

Browning, Tod 1882-1962 .... CLC 16
See also CA 141; 117

Brownson, Orestes (Augustus)
1803-1876 .... NCLC 50

Bruccoli, Matthew J(oseph) 1931- .. CLC 34
See also CA 9-12R; CANR 7; DLB 103

Bruce, Lenny .... CLC 21
See also Schneider, Leonard Alfred

Bruin, John
See Brutus, Dennis

Brulard, Henri
See Stendhal

Brulls, Christian
See Simenon, Georges (Jacques Christian)

Brunner, John (Kilian Houston)
1934-1995 ..... CLC 8, 10; DAM POP
See also CA 1-4R; 149; CAAS 8; CANR 2, 37; MTCW

Bruno, Giordano 1548-1600 .... LC 27

Brutus, Dennis
1924- ..... CLC 43; BLC; DAM MULT, POET
See also BW 2; CA 49-52; CAAS 14; CANR 2, 27, 42; DLB 117

Bryan, C(ourtlandt) D(ixon) B(arnes)
1936- .... CLC 29
See also CA 73-76; CANR 13; INT CANR-13

Bryan, Michael
See Moore, Brian

Bryant, William Cullen
1794-1878 ..... NCLC 6, 46; DA; DAB; DAC; DAM MST, POET
See also CDALB 1640-1865; DLB 3, 43, 59

Bryusov, Valery Yakovlevich
1873-1924 .... TCLC 10
See also CA 107; 155

Buchan, John
1875-1940 .... TCLC 41; DAB; DAM POP
See also CA 108; 145; DLB 34, 70, 156; YABC 2

Buchanan, George 1506-1582 .... LC 4

Buchheim, Lothar-Guenther 1918- ... CLC 6
See also CA 85-88

Buchner, (Karl) Georg
1813-1837 .... NCLC 26

Buchwald, Art(hur) 1925- .... CLC 33
See also AITN 1; CA 5-8R; CANR 21; MTCW; SATA 10

Buck, Pearl S(ydenstricker)
1892-1973 .... CLC 7, 11, 18; DA; DAB; DAC; DAM MST, NOV
See also AITN 1; CA 1-4R; 41-44R; CANR 1, 34; DLB 9, 102; MTCW; SATA 1, 25

Buckler, Ernest
1908-1984 .. CLC 13; DAC; DAM MST
See also CA 11-12; 114; CAP 1; DLB 68; SATA 47

Buckley, Vincent (Thomas)
1925-1988 .... CLC 57
See also CA 101

Buckley, William F(rank), Jr.
1925- .... CLC 7, 18, 37; DAM POP
See also AITN 1; CA 1-4R; CANR 1, 24, 53; DLB 137; DLBY 80; INT CANR-24; MTCW

Buechner, (Carl) Frederick
1926- ...... CLC 2, 4, 6, 9; DAM NOV
See also CA 13-16R; CANR 11, 39; DLBY 80; INT CANR-11; MTCW

Buell, John (Edward) 1927- .... CLC 10
See also CA 1-4R; DLB 53

Buero Vallejo, Antonio 1916- ... CLC 15, 46
See also CA 106; CANR 24, 49; HW; MTCW

Bufalino, Gesualdo 1920(?)-........ CLC 74

Bugayev, Boris Nikolayevich 1880-1934
See Bely, Andrey
See also CA 104

Bukowski, Charles
1920-1994 .... CLC 2, 5, 9, 41, 82; DAM NOV, POET
See also CA 17-20R; 144; CANR 40; DLB 5, 130, 169; MTCW

Bulgakov, Mikhail (Afanas'evich)
1891-1940 .... TCLC 2, 16; DAM DRAM, NOV; SSC 18
See also CA 105; 152

Bulgya, Alexander Alexandrovich
1901-1956 .... TCLC 53
See also Fadeyev, Alexander
See also CA 117

Bullins, Ed
1935- .... CLC 1, 5, 7; BLC; DAM DRAM, MULT; DC 6
See also BW 2; CA 49-52; CAAS 16; CANR 24, 46; DLB 7, 38; MTCW

Bulwer-Lytton, Edward (George Earle Lytton)
1803-1873 .... NCLC 1, 45
See also DLB 21

Bunin, Ivan Alexeyevich
1870-1953 .... TCLC 6; SSC 5
See also CA 104

Bunting, Basil
1900-1985 .... CLC 10, 39, 47; DAM POET
See also CA 53-56; 115; CANR 7; DLB 20

Bunuel, Luis
1900-1983 .... CLC 16, 80; DAM MULT; HLC
See also CA 101; 110; CANR 32; HW

Bunyan, John
1628-1688 ...... LC 4; DA; DAB; DAC; DAM MST; WLC
See also CDBLB 1660-1789; DLB 39

Burckhardt, Jacob (Christoph)
1818-1897 .... NCLC 49

Burford, Eleanor
See Hibbert, Eleanor Alice Burford

Burgess, Anthony
CLC 1, 2, 4, 5, 8, 10, 13, 15, 22, 40, 62, 81, 94; DAB
See also Wilson, John (Anthony) Burgess
See also AITN 1; CDBLB 1960 to Present; DLB 14

Burke, Edmund
1729(?)-1797 ...... LC 7, 36; DA; DAB; DAC; DAM MST; WLC
See also DLB 104

Burke, Kenneth (Duva)
1897-1993 .... CLC 2, 24
See also CA 5-8R; 143; CANR 39; DLB 45, 63; MTCW

Burke, Leda
See Garnett, David

Burke, Ralph
See Silverberg, Robert

Camus, Albert
1913-1960 .... CLC 1, 2, 4, 9, 11, 14, 32,
63, 69; DA; DAB; DAC; DAM DRAM,
MST, NOV; DC 2; SSC 9; WLC
See also CA 89-92; DLB 72; MTCW

Canby, Vincent 1924-............. CLC 13
See also CA 81-84

Cancale
See Desnos, Robert

Canetti, Elias
1905-1994 ...... CLC 3, 14, 25, 75, 86
See also CA 21-24R; 146; CANR 23;
DLB 85, 124; MTCW

Canin, Ethan 1960-............. CLC 55
See also CA 131; 135

Cannon, Curt
See Hunter, Evan

Cape, Judith
See Page, P(atricia) K(athleen)

Capek, Karel
1890-1938 ...... TCLC 6, 37; DA; DAB;
DAC; DAM DRAM, MST, NOV; DC 1;
WLC
See also CA 104; 140

Capote, Truman
1924-1984 ...... CLC 1, 3, 8, 13, 19, 34,
38, 58; DA; DAB; DAC; DAM MST,
NOV, POP; SSC 2; WLC
See also CA 5-8R; 113; CANR 18;
CDALB 1941-1968; DLB 2; DLBY 80,
84; MTCW; SATA 91

Capra, Frank 1897-1991.......... CLC 16
See also CA 61-64; 135

Caputo, Philip 1941-.............. CLC 32
See also CA 73-76; CANR 40

Card, Orson Scott
1951- ...... CLC 44, 47, 50; DAM POP
See also AAYA 11; CA 102; CANR 27, 47;
INT CANR-27; MTCW; SATA 83

Cardenal, Ernesto
1925- .... CLC 31; DAM MULT,
POET; HLC
See also CA 49-52; CANR 2, 32; HW;
MTCW

Cardozo, Benjamin N(athan)
1870-1938 ....TCLC 65
See also CA 117

Carducci, Giosue 1835-1907...... TCLC 32

Carew, Thomas 1595(?)-1640........ LC 13
See also DLB 126

Carey, Ernestine Gilbreth 1908-.... CLC 17
See also CA 5-8R; SATA 2

Carey, Peter 1943-......... CLC 40, 55, 96
See also CA 123; 127; CANR 53; INT 127;
MTCW

Carleton, William 1794-1869...... NCLC 3
See also DLB 159

Carlisle, Henry (Coffin) 1926-...... CLC 33
See also CA 13-16R; CANR 15

Carlsen, Chris
See Holdstock, Robert P.

Carlson, Ron(ald F.) 1947-........ CLC 54
See also CA 105; CANR 27

Carlyle, Thomas
1795-1881 ...... NCLC 22; DA; DAB;
DAC; DAM MST
See also CDBLB 1789-1832; DLB 55; 144

Carman, (William) Bliss
1861-1929 .... TCLC 7; DAC
See also CA 104; 152; DLB 92

Carnegie, Dale 1888-1955 .... TCLC 53

Carossa, Hans 1878-1956........ TCLC 48
See also DLB 66

Carpenter, Don(ald Richard)
1931-1995 .... CLC 41
See also CA 45-48; 149; CANR 1

Carpentier (y Valmont), Alejo
1904-1980 .... CLC 8, 11, 38;
DAM MULT; HLC
See also CA 65-68; 97-100; CANR 11;
DLB 113; HW

Carr, Caleb 1955(?)-.............. CLC 86
See also CA 147

Carr, Emily 1871-1945............ TCLC 32
See also DLB 68

Carr, John Dickson 1906-1977 ...... CLC 3
See also CA 49-52; 69-72; CANR 3, 33;
MTCW

Carr, Philippa
See Hibbert, Eleanor Alice Burford

Carr, Virginia Spencer 1929-....... CLC 34
See also CA 61-64; DLB 111

Carrere, Emmanuel 1957- .... CLC 89

Carrier, Roch
1937- ... CLC 13, 78; DAC; DAM MST
See also CA 130; DLB 53

Carroll, James P. 1943(?)-......... CLC 38
See also CA 81-84

Carroll, Jim 1951- .... CLC 35
See also AAYA 17; CA 45-48; CANR 42

Carroll, Lewis .... NCLC 2, 53; WLC
See also Dodgson, Charles Lutwidge
See also CDBLB 1832-1890; CLR 2, 18;
DLB 18, 163; JRDA

Carroll, Paul Vincent 1900-1968.... CLC 10
See also CA 9-12R; 25-28R; DLB 10

Carruth, Hayden
1921- .... CLC 4, 7, 10, 18, 84; PC 10
See also CA 9-12R; CANR 4, 38; DLB 5,
165; INT CANR-4; MTCW; SATA 47

Carson, Rachel Louise
1907-1964 .... CLC 71; DAM POP
See also CA 77-80; CANR 35; MTCW;
SATA 23

Carter, Angela (Olive)
1940-1992 ...... CLC 5, 41, 76; SSC 13
See also CA 53-56; 136; CANR 12, 36;
DLB 14; MTCW; SATA 66;
SATA-Obit 70

Carter, Nick
See Smith, Martin Cruz

Carver, Raymond
1938-1988 .... CLC 22, 36, 53, 55;
DAM NOV; SSC 8
See also CA 33-36R; 126; CANR 17, 34;
DLB 130; DLBY 84, 88; MTCW

Cary, Elizabeth, Lady Falkland
1585-1639 .... LC 30

Cary, (Arthur) Joyce (Lunel)
1888-1957.............TCLC 1, 29
See also CA 104; CDBLB 1914-1945;
DLB 15, 100

Casanova de Seingalt, Giovanni Jacopo
1725-1798 .... LC 13

Casares, Adolfo Bioy
See Bioy Casares, Adolfo

Casely-Hayford, J(oseph) E(phraim)
1866-1930 .... TCLC 24; BLC;
DAM MULT
See also BW 2; CA 123; 152

Casey, John (Dudley) 1939-....... CLC 59
See also BEST 90:2; CA 69-72; CANR 23

Casey, Michael 1947-.............. CLC 2
See also CA 65-68; DLB 5

Casey, Patrick
See Thurman, Wallace (Henry)

Casey, Warren (Peter) 1935-1988... CLC 12
See also CA 101; 127; INT 101

Casona, Alejandro................. CLC 49
See also Alvarez, Alejandro Rodriguez

Cassavetes, John 1929-1989........ CLC 20
See also CA 85-88; 127

Cassian, Nina 1924- .... PC 17

Cassill, R(onald) V(erlin) 1919-... CLC 4, 23
See also CA 9-12R; CAAS 1; CANR 7, 45;
DLB 6

Cassirer, Ernst 1874-1945 .... TCLC 61

Cassity, (Allen) Turner 1929- .... CLC 6, 42
See also CA 17-20R; CAAS 8; CANR 11;
DLB 105

Castaneda, Carlos 1931(?)-......... CLC 12
See also CA 25-28R; CANR 32; HW;
MTCW

Castedo, Elena 1937-.............. CLC 65
See also CA 132

Castedo-Ellerman, Elena
See Castedo, Elena

Castellanos, Rosario
1925-1974 ...... CLC 66; DAM MULT;
HLC
See also CA 131; 53-56; DLB 113; HW

Castelvetro, Lodovico 1505-1571..... LC 12

Castiglione, Baldassare 1478-1529 ... LC 12

Castle, Robert
See Hamilton, Edmond

Castro, Guillen de 1569-1631........ LC 19

Castro, Rosalia de
1837-1885 ...... NCLC 3; DAM MULT

Cather, Willa
See Cather, Willa Sibert

Cather, Willa Sibert
1873-1947 .... TCLC 1, 11, 31; DA;
DAB; DAC; DAM MST, NOV; SSC 2;
WLC
See also CA 104; 128; CDALB 1865-1917;
DLB 9, 54, 78; DLBD 1; MTCW;
SATA 30

Cato, Marcus Porcius
234B.C.-149B.C............. CMLC 21

Catton, (Charles) Bruce
1899-1978 . . . . **CLC 35**
See also AITN 1; CA 5-8R; 81-84;
CANR 7; DLB 17; SATA 2;
SATA-Obit 24

Catullus c. 84B.C.-c. 54B.C. . . . . . **CMLC 18**

Cauldwell, Frank
See King, Francis (Henry)

Caunitz, William J. 1933-1996 . . . . . **CLC 34**
See also BEST 89:3; CA 125; 130; 152;
INT 130

Causley, Charles (Stanley) 1917-. . . . . **CLC 7**
See also CA 9-12R; CANR 5, 35; CLR 30;
DLB 27; MTCW; SATA 3, 66

Caute, David 1936-. . . . **CLC 29; DAM NOV**
See also CA 1-4R; CAAS 4; CANR 1, 33;
DLB 14

Cavafy, C(onstantine) P(eter)
1863-1933 . . . . **TCLC 2, 7; DAM POET**
See also Kavafis, Konstantinos Petrou
See also CA 148

Cavallo, Evelyn
See Spark, Muriel (Sarah)

Cavanna, Betty . . . . **CLC 12**
See also Harrison, Elizabeth Cavanna
See also JRDA; MAICYA; SAAS 4;
SATA 1, 30

Cavendish, Margaret Lucas
1623-1673 . . . . **LC 30**
See also DLB 131

Caxton, William 1421(?)-1491(?). . . . . **LC 17**
See also DLB 170

Cayrol, Jean 1911-. . . . . **CLC 11**
See also CA 89-92; DLB 83

Cela, Camilo Jose
1916- . . . . . **CLC 4, 13, 59; DAM MULT;
HLC**
See also BEST 90:2; CA 21-24R; CAAS 10;
CANR 21, 32; DLBY 89; HW; MTCW

Celan, Paul . . . . . . **CLC 10, 19, 53, 82; PC 10**
See also Antschel, Paul
See also DLB 69

Celine, Louis-Ferdinand
. . . . **CLC 1, 3, 4, 7, 9, 15, 47**
See also Destouches, Louis-Ferdinand
See also DLB 72

Cellini, Benvenuto 1500-1571 . . . . **LC 7**

Cendrars, Blaise . . . . **CLC 18**
See also Sauser-Hall, Frederic

Cernuda (y Bidon), Luis
1902-1963 . . . . **CLC 54; DAM POET**
See also CA 131; 89-92; DLB 134; HW

Cervantes (Saavedra), Miguel de
1547-1616 . . . . **LC 6, 23; DA; DAB;
DAC; DAM MST, NOV; SSC 12; WLC**

Cesaire, Aime (Fernand)
1913- . . . . **CLC 19, 32; BLC;
DAM MULT, POET**
See also BW 2; CA 65-68; CANR 24, 43;
MTCW

Chabon, Michael 1963- . . . . **CLC 55**
See also CA 139

Chabrol, Claude 1930- . . . . **CLC 16**
See also CA 110

Challans, Mary 1905-1983
See Renault, Mary
See also CA 81-84; 111; SATA 23;
SATA-Obit 36

Challis, George
See Faust, Frederick (Schiller)

Chambers, Aidan 1934- . . . . **CLC 35**
See also CA 25-28R; CANR 12, 31; JRDA;
MAICYA; SAAS 12; SATA 1, 69

Chambers, James 1948-
See Cliff, Jimmy
See also CA 124

Chambers, Jessie
See Lawrence, D(avid) H(erbert Richards)

Chambers, Robert W. 1865-1933. . . **TCLC 41**

Chandler, Raymond (Thornton)
1888-1959 . . . . **TCLC 1, 7; SSC 23**
See also CA 104; 129; CDALB 1929-1941;
DLBD 6; MTCW

Chang, Jung 1952- . . . . **CLC 71**
See also CA 142

Channing, William Ellery
1780-1842 . . . . **NCLC 17**
See also DLB 1, 59

Chaplin, Charles Spencer
1889-1977 . . . . **CLC 16**
See also Chaplin, Charlie
See also CA 81-84; 73-76

Chaplin, Charlie
See Chaplin, Charles Spencer
See also DLB 44

Chapman, George
1559(?)-1634 . . . . . **LC 22; DAM DRAM**
See also DLB 62, 121

Chapman, Graham 1941-1989 . . . . . . **CLC 21**
See also Monty Python
See also CA 116; 129; CANR 35

Chapman, John Jay 1862-1933 . . . . . **TCLC 7**
See also CA 104

Chapman, Lee
See Bradley, Marion Zimmer

Chapman, Walker
See Silverberg, Robert

Chappell, Fred (Davis) 1936-. . . . **CLC 40, 78**
See also CA 5-8R; CAAS 4; CANR 8, 33;
DLB 6, 105

Char, Rene(-Emile)
1907-1988 . . . . **CLC 9, 11, 14, 55;
DAM POET**
See also CA 13-16R; 124; CANR 32;
MTCW

Charby, Jay
See Ellison, Harlan (Jay)

Chardin, Pierre Teilhard de
See Teilhard de Chardin, (Marie Joseph)
Pierre

Charles I 1600-1649 . . . . **LC 13**

Charyn, Jerome 1937- . . . . **CLC 5, 8, 18**
See also CA 5-8R; CAAS 1; CANR 7;
DLBY 83; MTCW

Chase, Mary (Coyle) 1907-1981 . . . . . . **DC 1**
See also CA 77-80; 105; SATA 17;
SATA-Obit 29

Chase, Mary Ellen 1887-1973 . . . . . . **CLC 2**
See also CA 13-16; 41-44R; CAP 1;
SATA 10

Chase, Nicholas
See Hyde, Anthony

Chateaubriand, Francois Rene de
1768-1848 . . . . **NCLC 3**
See also DLB 119

Chatterje, Sarat Chandra 1876-1936(?)
See Chatterji, Saratchandra
See also CA 109

Chatterji, Bankim Chandra
1838-1894 . . . . **NCLC 19**

Chatterji, Saratchandra . . . . **TCLC 13**
See also Chatterje, Sarat Chandra

Chatterton, Thomas
1752-1770 . . . . **LC 3; DAM POET**
See also DLB 109

Chatwin, (Charles) Bruce
1940-1989 . . **CLC 28, 57, 59; DAM POP**
See also AAYA 4; BEST 90:1; CA 85-88;
127

Chaucer, Daniel
See Ford, Ford Madox

Chaucer, Geoffrey
1340(?)-1400 . . . . **LC 17; DA; DAB;
DAC; DAM MST, POET**
See also CDBLB Before 1660; DLB 146

Chaviaras, Strates 1935-
See Haviaras, Stratis
See also CA 105

Chayefsky, Paddy . . . . **CLC 23**
See also Chayefsky, Sidney
See also DLB 7, 44; DLBY 81

Chayefsky, Sidney 1923-1981
See Chayefsky, Paddy
See also CA 9-12R; 104; CANR 18;
DAM DRAM

Chedid, Andree 1920-. . . . . **CLC 47**
See also CA 145

Cheever, John
1912-1982 . . . . . . **CLC 3, 7, 8, 11, 15, 25,
64; DA; DAB; DAC; DAM MST, NOV,
POP; SSC 1; WLC**
See also CA 5-8R; 106; CABS 1; CANR 5,
27; CDALB 1941-1968; DLB 2, 102;
DLBY 80, 82; INT CANR-5; MTCW

Cheever, Susan 1943-. . . . . **CLC 18, 48**
See also CA 103; CANR 27, 51; DLBY 82;
INT CANR-27

Chekhonte, Antosha
See Chekhov, Anton (Pavlovich)

Chekhov, Anton (Pavlovich)
1860-1904 . . . . . **TCLC 3, 10, 31, 55; DA;
DAB; DAC; DAM DRAM, MST; SSC 2;
WLC**
See also CA 104; 124; SATA 90

Chernyshevsky, Nikolay Gavrilovich
1828-1889 . . . . **NCLC 1**

Cherry, Carolyn Janice 1942-
See Cherryh, C. J.
See also CA 65-68; CANR 10

Cherryh, C. J. . . . . **CLC 35**
See also Cherry, Carolyn Janice
See also DLBY 80

Chesnutt, Charles W(addell)
1858-1932 .... **TCLC 5, 39; BLC;
DAM MULT; SSC 7**
See also BW 1; CA 106; 125; DLB 12, 50,
78; MTCW

Chester, Alfred 1929(?)-1971....... **CLC 49**
See also CA 33-36R; DLB 130

Chesterton, G(ilbert) K(eith)
1874-1936 .... **TCLC 1, 6, 64;
DAM NOV, POET; SSC 1**
See also CA 104; 132; CDBLB 1914-1945;
DLB 10, 19, 34, 70, 98, 149; MTCW;
SATA 27

Chiang Pin-chin 1904-1986
See Ding Ling
See also CA 118

Ch'ien Chung-shu 1910- .... **CLC 22**
See also CA 130; MTCW

Child, L. Maria
See Child, Lydia Maria

Child, Lydia Maria 1802-1880 .... **NCLC 6**
See also DLB 1, 74; SATA 67

Child, Mrs.
See Child, Lydia Maria

Child, Philip 1898-1978 .... **CLC 19, 68**
See also CA 13-14; CAP 1; SATA 47

Childers, (Robert) Erskine
1870-1922 .... **TCLC 65**
See also CA 113; 153; DLB 70

Childress, Alice
1920-1994 .... **CLC 12, 15, 86, 96; BLC;
DAM DRAM, MULT, NOV; DC 4**
See also AAYA 8; BW 2; CA 45-48; 146;
CANR 3, 27, 50; CLR 14; DLB 7, 38;
JRDA; MAICYA; MTCW; SATA 7, 48,
81

Chislett, (Margaret) Anne 1943-.... **CLC 34**
See also CA 151

Chitty, Thomas Willes 1926-....... **CLC 11**
See also Hinde, Thomas
See also CA 5-8R

Chivers, Thomas Holley
1809-1858 .... **NCLC 49**
See also DLB 3

Chomette, Rene Lucien 1898-1981
See Clair, Rene
See also CA 103

Chopin, Kate
.... **TCLC 5, 14; DA; DAB; SSC 8**
See also Chopin, Katherine
See also CDALB 1865-1917; DLB 12, 78

Chopin, Katherine 1851-1904
See Chopin, Kate
See also CA 104; 122; DAC; DAM MST,
NOV

Chretien de Troyes
c. 12th cent. - .... **CMLC 10**

Christie
See Ichikawa, Kon

Christie, Agatha (Mary Clarissa)
1890-1976 ...... **CLC 1, 6, 8, 12, 39, 48;
DAB; DAC; DAM NOV**
See also AAYA 9; AITN 1, 2; CA 17-20R;
61-64; CANR 10, 37; CDBLB 1914-1945;
DLB 13, 77; MTCW; SATA 36

Christie, (Ann) Philippa
See Pearce, Philippa
See also CA 5-8R; CANR 4

Christine de Pizan 1365(?)-1431(?) .... **LC 9**

Chubb, Elmer
See Masters, Edgar Lee

Chulkov, Mikhail Dmitrievich
1743-1792 .... **LC 2**
See also DLB 150

Churchill, Caryl 1938-... **CLC 31, 55; DC 5**
See also CA 102; CANR 22, 46; DLB 13;
MTCW

Churchill, Charles 1731-1764........ **LC 3**
See also DLB 109

Chute, Carolyn 1947-............. **CLC 39**
See also CA 123

Ciardi, John (Anthony)
1916-1986 .... **CLC 10, 40, 44;
DAM POET**
See also CA 5-8R; 118; CAAS 2; CANR 5,
33; CLR 19; DLB 5; DLBY 86;
INT CANR-5; MAICYA; MTCW;
SATA 1, 65; SATA-Obit 46

Cicero, Marcus Tullius
106B.C.-43B.C............... **CMLC 3**

Cimino, Michael 1943-............ **CLC 16**
See also CA 105

Cioran, E(mil) M. 1911-1995...... **CLC 64**
See also CA 25-28R; 149

Cisneros, Sandra
1954- ..... **CLC 69; DAM MULT; HLC**
See also AAYA 9; CA 131; DLB 122, 152;
HW

Cixous, Helene 1937-............. **CLC 92**
See also CA 126; CANR 55; DLB 83;
MTCW

Clair, Rene....................... CLC 20
See also Chomette, Rene Lucien

Clampitt, Amy 1920-1994 .... **CLC 32**
See also CA 110; 146; CANR 29; DLB 105

Clancy, Thomas L., Jr. 1947-
See Clancy, Tom
See also CA 125; 131; INT 131; MTCW

Clancy, Tom..... CLC 45; DAM NOV, POP
See also Clancy, Thomas L., Jr.
See also AAYA 9; BEST 89:1, 90:1

Clare, John
1793-1864 .... **NCLC 9; DAB;
DAM POET**
See also DLB 55, 96

Clarin
See Alas (y Urena), Leopoldo (Enrique
Garcia)

Clark, Al C.
See Goines, Donald

Clark, (Robert) Brian 1932-....... **CLC 29**
See also CA 41-44R

Clark, Curt
See Westlake, Donald E(dwin)

Clark, Eleanor 1913-1996 .... **CLC 5, 19**
See also CA 9-12R; 151; CANR 41; DLB 6

Clark, J. P.
See Clark, John Pepper
See also DLB 117

Clark, John Pepper
1935- .... **CLC 38; BLC; DAM DRAM,
MULT; DC 5**
See also Clark, J. P.
See also BW 1; CA 65-68; CANR 16

Clark, M. R.
See Clark, Mavis Thorpe

Clark, Mavis Thorpe 1909- .... **CLC 12**
See also CA 57-60; CANR 8, 37; CLR 30;
MAICYA; SAAS 5; SATA 8, 74

Clark, Walter Van Tilburg
1909-1971 .... **CLC 28**
See also CA 9-12R; 33-36R; DLB 9;
SATA 8

Clarke, Arthur C(harles)
1917- .... **CLC 1, 4, 13, 18, 35;
DAM POP; SSC 3**
See also AAYA 4; CA 1-4R; CANR 2, 28,
55; JRDA; MAICYA; MTCW; SATA 13,
70

Clarke, Austin
1896-1974 ...... **CLC 6, 9; DAM POET**
See also CA 29-32; 49-52; CAP 2; DLB 10,
20

Clarke, Austin C(hesterfield)
1934- .... **CLC 8, 53; BLC; DAC;
DAM MULT**
See also BW 1; CA 25-28R; CAAS 16;
CANR 14, 32; DLB 53, 125

Clarke, Gillian 1937-............. **CLC 61**
See also CA 106; DLB 40

Clarke, Marcus (Andrew Hislop)
1846-1881 .... **NCLC 19**

Clarke, Shirley 1925-............. **CLC 16**

Clash, The
See Headon, (Nicky) Topper; Jones, Mick;
Simonon, Paul; Strummer, Joe

Claudel, Paul (Louis Charles Marie)
1868-1955 .... **TCLC 2, 10**
See also CA 104

Clavell, James (duMaresq)
1925-1994 .... **CLC 6, 25, 87;
DAM NOV, POP**
See also CA 25-28R; 146; CANR 26, 48;
MTCW

Cleaver, (Leroy) Eldridge
1935- ..... **CLC 30; BLC; DAM MULT**
See also BW 1; CA 21-24R; CANR 16

Cleese, John (Marwood) 1939- ..... **CLC 21**
See also Monty Python
See also CA 112; 116; CANR 35; MTCW

Cleishbotham, Jebediah
See Scott, Walter

Cleland, John 1710-1789 .... **LC 2**
See also DLB 39

Clemens, Samuel Langhorne 1835-1910
See Twain, Mark
See also CA 104; 135; CDALB 1865-1917;
DA; DAB; DAC; DAM MST, NOV;
DLB 11, 12, 23, 64, 74; JRDA;
MAICYA; YABC 2

Cleophil
See Congreve, William

Clerihew, E.
See Bentley, E(dmund) C(lerihew)

Clerk, N. W.
See Lewis, C(live) S(taples)

Cliff, Jimmy . . . . **CLC 21**
See also Chambers, James

Clifton, (Thelma) Lucille
1936- . . . . **CLC 19, 66; BLC;**
DAM MULT, POET; PC 17
See also BW 2; CA 49-52; CANR 2, 24, 42;
CLR 5; DLB 5, 41; MAICYA; MTCW;
SATA 20, 69

Clinton, Dirk
See Silverberg, Robert

Clough, Arthur Hugh 1819-1861 . . **NCLC 27**
See also DLB 32

Clutha, Janet Paterson Frame 1924-
See Frame, Janet
See also CA 1-4R; CANR 2, 36; MTCW

Clyne, Terence
See Blatty, William Peter

Cobalt, Martin
See Mayne, William (James Carter)

Cobbett, William 1763-1835 . . . . . **NCLC 49**
See also DLB 43, 107, 158

Coburn, D(onald) L(ee) 1938- . . . . . . **CLC 10**
See also CA 89-92

Cocteau, Jean (Maurice Eugene Clement)
1889-1963 . . . . **CLC 1, 8, 15, 16, 43; DA;**
DAB; DAC; DAM DRAM, MST, NOV;
WLC
See also CA 25-28; CANR 40; CAP 2;
DLB 65; MTCW

Codrescu, Andrei
1946- . . . . **CLC 46; DAM POET**
See also CA 33-36R; CAAS 19; CANR 13,
34, 53

Coe, Max
See Bourne, Randolph S(illiman)

Coe, Tucker
See Westlake, Donald E(dwin)

Coetzee, J(ohn) M(ichael)
1940- . . . . . . **CLC 23, 33, 66; DAM NOV**
See also CA 77-80; CANR 41, 54; MTCW

Coffey, Brian
See Koontz, Dean R(ay)

Cohan, George M. 1878-1942 . . . . . **TCLC 60**

Cohen, Arthur A(llen)
1928-1986 . . . . **CLC 7, 31**
See also CA 1-4R; 120; CANR 1, 17, 42;
DLB 28

Cohen, Leonard (Norman)
1934- . . . . **CLC 3, 38; DAC; DAM MST**
See also CA 21-24R; CANR 14; DLB 53;
MTCW

Cohen, Matt 1942- . . . . **CLC 19; DAC**
See also CA 61-64; CAAS 18; CANR 40;
DLB 53

Cohen-Solal, Annie 19(?)- . . . . **CLC 50**

Colegate, Isabel 1931- . . . . **CLC 36**
See also CA 17-20R; CANR 8, 22; DLB 14;
INT CANR-22; MTCW

Coleman, Emmett
See Reed, Ishmael

Coleridge, Samuel Taylor
1772-1834 . . . . . **NCLC 9, 54; DA; DAB;**
DAC; DAM MST, POET; PC 11; WLC
See also CDBLB 1789-1832; DLB 93, 107

Coleridge, Sara 1802-1852 . . . . . . **NCLC 31**

Coles, Don 1928- . . . . **CLC 46**
See also CA 115; CANR 38

Colette, (Sidonie-Gabrielle)
1873-1954 . . . . **TCLC 1, 5, 16;**
DAM NOV; SSC 10
See also CA 104; 131; DLB 65; MTCW

Collett, (Jacobine) Camilla (Wergeland)
1813-1895 . . . . **NCLC 22**

Collier, Christopher 1930- . . . . **CLC 30**
See also AAYA 13; CA 33-36R; CANR 13,
33; JRDA; MAICYA; SATA 16, 70

Collier, James L(incoln)
1928- . . . . **CLC 30; DAM POP**
See also AAYA 13; CA 9-12R; CANR 4,
33; CLR 3; JRDA; MAICYA; SAAS 21;
SATA 8, 70

Collier, Jeremy 1650-1726 . . . . **LC 6**

Collier, John 1901-1980 . . . . **SSC 19**
See also CA 65-68; 97-100; CANR 10;
DLB 77

Collingwood, R(obin) G(eorge)
1889(?)-1943 . . . . **TCLC 67**
See also CA 117; 155

Collins, Hunt
See Hunter, Evan

Collins, Linda 1931- . . . . **CLC 44**
See also CA 125

Collins, (William) Wilkie
1824-1889 . . . . **NCLC 1, 18**
See also CDBLB 1832-1890; DLB 18, 70,
159

Collins, William
1721-1759 . . . . **LC 4; DAM POET**
See also DLB 109

Collodi, Carlo 1826-1890 . . . . **NCLC 54**
See also Lorenzini, Carlo
See also CLR 5

Colman, George
See Glassco, John

Colt, Winchester Remington
See Hubbard, L(afayette) Ron(ald)

Colter, Cyrus 1910- . . . . **CLC 58**
See also BW 1; CA 65-68; CANR 10;
DLB 33

Colton, James
See Hansen, Joseph

Colum, Padraic 1881-1972 . . . . **CLC 28**
See also CA 73-76; 33-36R; CANR 35;
CLR 36; MAICYA; MTCW; SATA 15

Colvin, James
See Moorcock, Michael (John)

Colwin, Laurie (E.)
1944-1992 . . . . **CLC 5, 13, 23, 84**
See also CA 89-92; 139; CANR 20, 46;
DLBY 80; MTCW

Comfort, Alex(ander)
1920- . . . . **CLC 7; DAM POP**
See also CA 1-4R; CANR 1, 45

Comfort, Montgomery
See Campbell, (John) Ramsey

Compton-Burnett, I(vy)
1884(?)-1969 . . . . . **CLC 1, 3, 10, 15, 34;**
DAM NOV
See also CA 1-4R; 25-28R; CANR 4;
DLB 36; MTCW

Comstock, Anthony 1844-1915 . . . . **TCLC 13**
See also CA 110

Comte, Auguste 1798-1857 . . . . . . **NCLC 54**

Conan Doyle, Arthur
See Doyle, Arthur Conan

Conde, Maryse
1937- . . . . **CLC 52, 92; DAM MULT**
See also Boucolon, Maryse
See also BW 2

Condillac, Etienne Bonnot de
1714-1780 . . . . **LC 26**

Condon, Richard (Thomas)
1915-1996 . . . . **CLC 4, 6, 8, 10, 45;**
DAM NOV
See also BEST 90:3; CA 1-4R; 151;
CAAS 1; CANR 2, 23; INT CANR-23;
MTCW

Confucius
551B.C.-479B.C. . . . . **CMLC 19; DA;**
DAB; DAC; DAM MST

Congreve, William
1670-1729 . . . . **LC 5, 21; DA; DAB;**
DAC; DAM DRAM, MST, POET;
DC 2; WLC
See also CDBLB 1660-1789; DLB 39, 84

Connell, Evan S(helby), Jr.
1924- . . . . **CLC 4, 6, 45; DAM NOV**
See also AAYA 7; CA 1-4R; CAAS 2;
CANR 2, 39; DLB 2; DLBY 81; MTCW

Connelly, Marc(us Cook)
1890-1980 . . . . **CLC 7**
See also CA 85-88; 102; CANR 30; DLB 7;
DLBY 80; SATA-Obit 25

Connor, Ralph . . . . **TCLC 31**
See also Gordon, Charles William
See also DLB 92

Conrad, Joseph
1857-1924 . . . . **TCLC 1, 6, 13, 25, 43, 57;**
DA; DAB; DAC; DAM MST, NOV;
SSC 9; WLC
See also CA 104; 131; CDBLB 1890-1914;
DLB 10, 34, 98, 156; MTCW; SATA 27

Conrad, Robert Arnold
See Hart, Moss

Conroy, Donald Pat(rick)
1945- . . . **CLC 30, 74; DAM NOV, POP**
See also AAYA 8; AITN 1; CA 85-88;
CANR 24, 53; DLB 6; MTCW

Constant (de Rebecque), (Henri) Benjamin
1767-1830 . . . . **NCLC 6**
See also DLB 119

Conybeare, Charles Augustus
See Eliot, T(homas) S(tearns)

Cook, Michael 1933- . . . . **CLC 58**
See also CA 93-96; DLB 53

Cook, Robin 1940- . . . . **CLC 14; DAM POP**
See also BEST 90:2; CA 108; 111;
CANR 41; INT 111

Cook, Roy
See Silverberg, Robert

Cooke, Elizabeth 1948- . . . . **CLC 55**
See also CA 129

Cooke, John Esten 1830-1886 . . . . . **NCLC 5**
See also DLB 3

Cooke, John Estes
See Baum, L(yman) Frank

Cooke, M. E.
See Creasey, John

Cooke, Margaret
See Creasey, John

Cook-Lynn, Elizabeth
1930- . . . . **CLC 93; DAM MULT**
See also CA 133; DLB 175; NNAL

Cooney, Ray . . . . **CLC 62**

Cooper, Douglas 1960- . . . . **CLC 86**

Cooper, Henry St. John
See Creasey, John

Cooper, J(oan) California
. . . . **CLC 56; DAM MULT**
See also AAYA 12; BW 1; CA 125;
CANR 55

Cooper, James Fenimore
1789-1851 . . . . **NCLC 1, 27, 54**
See also CDALB 1640-1865; DLB 3;
SATA 19

Coover, Robert (Lowell)
1932- . . . . **CLC 3, 7, 15, 32, 46, 87;
DAM NOV; SSC 15**
See also CA 45-48; CANR 3, 37; DLB 2;
DLBY 81; MTCW

Copeland, Stewart (Armstrong)
1952- . . . . **CLC 26**

Coppard, A(lfred) E(dgar)
1878-1957 . . . . **TCLC 5; SSC 21**
See also CA 114; DLB 162; YABC 1

Coppee, Francois 1842-1908 . . . . . . **TCLC 25**

Coppola, Francis Ford 1939- . . . . **CLC 16**
See also CA 77-80; CANR 40; DLB 44

Corbiere, Tristan 1845-1875 . . . . . **NCLC 43**

Corcoran, Barbara 1911- . . . . **CLC 17**
See also AAYA 14; CA 21-24R; CAAS 2;
CANR 11, 28, 48; DLB 52; JRDA;
SAAS 20; SATA 3, 77

Cordelier, Maurice
See Giraudoux, (Hippolyte) Jean

Corelli, Marie 1855-1924 . . . . **TCLC 51**
See also Mackay, Mary
See also DLB 34, 156

Corman, Cid . . . . **CLC 9**
See also Corman, Sidney
See also CAAS 2; DLB 5

Corman, Sidney 1924-
See Corman, Cid
See also CA 85-88; CANR 44; DAM POET

Cormier, Robert (Edmund)
1925- . . . . **CLC 12, 30; DA; DAB; DAC;
DAM MST, NOV**
See also AAYA 3, 19; CA 1-4R; CANR 5,
23; CDALB 1968-1988; CLR 12; DLB 52;
INT CANR-23; JRDA; MAICYA;
MTCW; SATA 10, 45, 83

Corn, Alfred (DeWitt III) 1943- . . . . **CLC 33**
See also CA 104; CAAS 25; CANR 44;
DLB 120; DLBY 80

Corneille, Pierre
1606-1684 . . . . **LC 28; DAB; DAM MST**

Cornwell, David (John Moore)
1931- . . . . **CLC 9, 15; DAM POP**
See also le Carre, John
See also CA 5-8R; CANR 13, 33; MTCW

Corso, (Nunzio) Gregory 1930- . . . **CLC 1, 11**
See also CA 5-8R; CANR 41; DLB 5, 16;
MTCW

Cortazar, Julio
1914-1984 . . . . . . **CLC 2, 3, 5, 10, 13, 15,
33, 34, 92; DAM MULT, NOV; HLC;
SSC 7**
See also CA 21-24R; CANR 12, 32;
DLB 113; HW; MTCW

CORTES, HERNAN 1484-1547 . . . . . **LC 31**

Corwin, Cecil
See Kornbluth, C(yril) M.

Cosic, Dobrica 1921- . . . . **CLC 14**
See also CA 122; 138

Costain, Thomas B(ertram)
1885-1965 . . . . **CLC 30**
See also CA 5-8R; 25-28R; DLB 9

Costantini, Humberto
1924(?)-1987 . . . . **CLC 49**
See also CA 131; 122; HW

Costello, Elvis 1955- . . . . **CLC 21**

Cotter, Joseph Seamon Sr.
1861-1949 . . . . **TCLC 28; BLC;
DAM MULT**
See also BW 1; CA 124; DLB 50

Couch, Arthur Thomas Quiller
See Quiller-Couch, Arthur Thomas

Coulton, James
See Hansen, Joseph

Couperus, Louis (Marie Anne)
1863-1923 . . . . **TCLC 15**
See also CA 115

Coupland, Douglas
1961- . . . . **CLC 85; DAC; DAM POP**
See also CA 142; CANR 57

Court, Wesli
See Turco, Lewis (Putnam)

Courtenay, Bryce 1933- . . . . **CLC 59**
See also CA 138

Courtney, Robert
See Ellison, Harlan (Jay)

Cousteau, Jacques-Yves 1910- . . . . . . **CLC 30**
See also CA 65-68; CANR 15; MTCW;
SATA 38

Coward, Noel (Peirce)
1899-1973 . . . . **CLC 1, 9, 29, 51;
DAM DRAM**
See also AITN 1; CA 17-18; 41-44R;
CANR 35; CAP 2; CDBLB 1914-1945;
DLB 10; MTCW

Cowley, Malcolm 1898-1989 . . . . **CLC 39**
See also CA 5-8R; 128; CANR 3, 55;
DLB 4, 48; DLBY 81, 89; MTCW

Cowper, William
1731-1800 . . . . . . **NCLC 8; DAM POET**
See also DLB 104, 109

Cox, William Trevor
1928- . . . . **CLC 9, 14, 71; DAM NOV**
See also Trevor, William
See also CA 9-12R; CANR 4, 37, 55;
DLB 14; INT CANR-37; MTCW

Coyne, P. J.
See Masters, Hilary

Cozzens, James Gould
1903-1978 . . . . **CLC 1, 4, 11, 92**
See also CA 9-12R; 81-84; CANR 19;
CDALB 1941-1968; DLB 9; DLBD 2;
DLBY 84; MTCW

Crabbe, George 1754-1832 . . . . **NCLC 26**
See also DLB 93

Craddock, Charles Egbert
See Murfree, Mary Noailles

Craig, A. A.
See Anderson, Poul (William)

Craik, Dinah Maria (Mulock)
1826-1887 . . . . **NCLC 38**
See also DLB 35, 163; MAICYA; SATA 34

Cram, Ralph Adams 1863-1942 . . . . **TCLC 45**

Crane, (Harold) Hart
1899-1932 . . . . **TCLC 2, 5; DA; DAB;
DAC; DAM MST, POET; PC 3; WLC**
See also CA 104; 127; CDALB 1917-1929;
DLB 4, 48; MTCW

Crane, R(onald) S(almon)
1886-1967 . . . . **CLC 27**
See also CA 85-88; DLB 63

Crane, Stephen (Townley)
1871-1900 . . . . **TCLC 11, 17, 32; DA;
DAB; DAC; DAM MST, NOV, POET;
SSC 7; WLC**
See also CA 109; 140; CDALB 1865-1917;
DLB 12, 54, 78; YABC 2

Crase, Douglas 1944- . . . . **CLC 58**
See also CA 106

Crashaw, Richard 1612(?)-1649 . . . . . . **LC 24**
See also DLB 126

Craven, Margaret
1901-1980 . . . . **CLC 17; DAC**
See also CA 103

Crawford, F(rancis) Marion
1854-1909 . . . . **TCLC 10**
See also CA 107; DLB 71

Crawford, Isabella Valancy
1850-1887 . . . . **NCLC 12**
See also DLB 92

Crayon, Geoffrey
See Irving, Washington

Creasey, John 1908-1973 . . . . **CLC 11**
See also CA 5-8R; 41-44R; CANR 8;
DLB 77; MTCW

Crebillon, Claude Prosper Jolyot de (fils)
1707-1777 . . . . **LC 28**

Credo
See Creasey, John

Creeley, Robert (White)
1926- . . . . . **CLC 1, 2, 4, 8, 11, 15, 36, 78;
DAM POET**
See also CA 1-4R; CAAS 10; CANR 23, 43;
DLB 5, 16, 169; MTCW

Crews, Harry (Eugene)
1935- . . . . CLC 6, 23, 49
See also AITN 1; CA 25-28R; CANR 20;
DLB 6, 143; MTCW

Crichton, (John) Michael
1942- . . . . CLC 2, 6, 54, 90; DAM NOV,
POP
See also AAYA 10; AITN 2; CA 25-28R;
CANR 13, 40, 54; DLBY 81;
INT CANR-13; JRDA; MTCW; SATA 9,
88

Crispin, Edmund . . . . CLC 22
See also Montgomery, (Robert) Bruce
See also DLB 87

Cristofer, Michael
1945(?)- . . . . CLC 28; DAM DRAM
See also CA 110; 152; DLB 7

Croce, Benedetto 1866-1952 . . . . . . TCLC 37
See also CA 120; 155

Crockett, David 1786-1836 . . . . NCLC 8
See also DLB 3, 11

Crockett, Davy
See Crockett, David

Crofts, Freeman Wills
1879-1957 . . . . TCLC 55
See also CA 115; DLB 77

Croker, John Wilson 1780-1857 . . NCLC 10
See also DLB 110

Crommelynck, Fernand 1885-1970 . . CLC 75
See also CA 89-92

Cronin, A(rchibald) J(oseph)
1896-1981 . . . . CLC 32
See also CA 1-4R; 102; CANR 5; SATA 47;
SATA-Obit 25

Cross, Amanda
See Heilbrun, Carolyn G(old)

Crothers, Rachel 1878(?)-1958. . . . . TCLC 19
See also CA 113; DLB 7

Croves, Hal
See Traven, B.

Crow Dog, Mary (Ellen) (?)- . . . . CLC 93
See also Brave Bird, Mary
See also CA 154

Crowfield, Christopher
See Stowe, Harriet (Elizabeth) Beecher

Crowley, Aleister. . . . . TCLC 7
See also Crowley, Edward Alexander

Crowley, Edward Alexander 1875-1947
See Crowley, Aleister
See also CA 104

Crowley, John 1942- . . . . CLC 57
See also CA 61-64; CANR 43; DLBY 82;
SATA 65

Crud
See Crumb, R(obert)

Crumarums
See Crumb, R(obert)

Crumb, R(obert) 1943- . . . . CLC 17
See also CA 106

Crumbum
See Crumb, R(obert)

Crumski
See Crumb, R(obert)

Crum the Bum
See Crumb, R(obert)

Crunk
See Crumb, R(obert)

Crustt
See Crumb, R(obert)

Cryer, Gretchen (Kiger) 1935- . . . . . . CLC 21
See also CA 114; 123

Csath, Geza 1887-1919. . . . . TCLC 13
See also CA 111

Cudlip, David 1933- . . . . CLC 34

Cullen, Countee
1903-1946 . . . . . . TCLC 4, 37; BLC; DA;
DAC; DAM MST, MULT, POET
See also BW 1; CA 108; 124;
CDALB 1917-1929; DLB 4, 48, 51;
MTCW; SATA 18

Cum, R.
See Crumb, R(obert)

Cummings, Bruce F(rederick) 1889-1919
See Barbellion, W. N. P.
See also CA 123

Cummings, E(dward) E(stlin)
1894-1962 . . . . . . CLC 1, 3, 8, 12, 15, 68;
DA; DAB; DAC; DAM MST, POET;
PC 5; WLC 2
See also CA 73-76; CANR 31;
CDALB 1929-1941; DLB 4, 48; MTCW

Cunha, Euclides (Rodrigues Pimenta) da
1866-1909 . . . . TCLC 24
See also CA 123

Cunningham, E. V.
See Fast, Howard (Melvin)

Cunningham, J(ames) V(incent)
1911-1985 . . . . CLC 3, 31
See also CA 1-4R; 115; CANR 1; DLB 5

Cunningham, Julia (Woolfolk)
1916- . . . . CLC 12
See also CA 9-12R; CANR 4, 19, 36;
JRDA; MAICYA; SAAS 2; SATA 1, 26

Cunningham, Michael 1952- . . . . CLC 34
See also CA 136

Cunninghame Graham, R(obert) B(ontine)
1852-1936 . . . . TCLC 19
See also Graham, R(obert) B(ontine)
Cunninghame
See also CA 119; DLB 98

Currie, Ellen 19(?)- . . . . CLC 44

Curtin, Philip
See Lowndes, Marie Adelaide (Belloc)

Curtis, Price
See Ellison, Harlan (Jay)

Cutrate, Joe
See Spiegelman, Art

Czaczkes, Shmuel Yosef
See Agnon, S(hmuel) Y(osef Halevi)

Dabrowska, Maria (Szumska)
1889-1965 . . . . CLC 15
See also CA 106

Dabydeen, David 1955- . . . . CLC 34
See also BW 1; CA 125; CANR 56

Dacey, Philip 1939- . . . . CLC 51
See also CA 37-40R; CAAS 17; CANR 14,
32; DLB 105

Dagerman, Stig (Halvard)
1923-1954 . . . . TCLC 17
See also CA 117; 155

Dahl, Roald
1916-1990 . . . . . CLC 1, 6, 18, 79; DAB;
DAC; DAM MST, NOV, POP
See also AAYA 15; CA 1-4R; 133;
CANR 6, 32, 37; CLR 1, 7, 41; DLB 139;
JRDA; MAICYA; MTCW; SATA 1, 26,
73; SATA-Obit 65

Dahlberg, Edward 1900-1977. . . CLC 1, 7, 14
See also CA 9-12R; 69-72; CANR 31;
DLB 48; MTCW

Dale, Colin. TCLC 18
See also Lawrence, T(homas) E(dward)

Dale, George E.
See Asimov, Isaac

Daly, Elizabeth 1878-1967. . . . . CLC 52
See also CA 23-24; 25-28R; CAP 2

Daly, Maureen 1921-. . . . . CLC 17
See also AAYA 5; CANR 37; JRDA;
MAICYA; SAAS 1; SATA 2

Damas, Leon-Gontran 1912-1978 . . . CLC 84
See also BW 1; CA 125; 73-76

Dana, Richard Henry Sr.
1787-1879 . . . . NCLC 53

Daniel, Samuel 1562(?)-1619. . . . . . . LC 24
See also DLB 62

Daniels, Brett
See Adler, Renata

Dannay, Frederic
1905-1982 . . . . CLC 11; DAM POP
See also Queen, Ellery
See also CA 1-4R; 107; CANR 1, 39;
DLB 137; MTCW

D'Annunzio, Gabriele
1863-1938 . . . . TCLC 6, 40
See also CA 104; 155

Danois, N. le
See Gourmont, Remy (-Marie-Charles) de

d'Antibes, Germain
See Simenon, Georges (Jacques Christian)

Danticat, Edwidge 1969- . . . . CLC 94
See also CA 152

Danvers, Dennis 1947-. . . . . CLC 70

Danziger, Paula 1944- . . . . CLC 21
See also AAYA 4; CA 112; 115; CANR 37;
CLR 20; JRDA; MAICYA; SATA 36,
63; SATA-Brief 30

Da Ponte, Lorenzo 1749-1838. . . . NCLC 50

Dario, Ruben
1867-1916 . . . . . TCLC 4; DAM MULT;
HLC; PC 15
See also CA 131; HW; MTCW

Darley, George 1795-1846. . . . . NCLC 2
See also DLB 96

Darwin, Charles 1809-1882 . . . . . . NCLC 57
See also DLB 57, 166

Daryush, Elizabeth 1887-1977. . . . CLC 6, 19
See also CA 49-52; CANR 3; DLB 20

Dashwood, Edmee Elizabeth Monica de la
Pasture 1890-1943
See Delafield, E. M.
See also CA 119; 154

Daudet, (Louis Marie) Alphonse
1840-1897 .... **NCLC 1**
See also DLB 123

Daumal, Rene 1908-1944 .... **TCLC 14**
See also CA 114

Davenport, Guy (Mattison, Jr.)
1927- .... **CLC 6, 14, 38; SSC 16**
See also CA 33-36R; CANR 23; DLB 130

Davidson, Avram 1923-
See Queen, Ellery
See also CA 101; CANR 26; DLB 8

Davidson, Donald (Grady)
1893-1968 .... **CLC 2, 13, 19**
See also CA 5-8R; 25-28R; CANR 4;
DLB 45

Davidson, Hugh
See Hamilton, Edmond

Davidson, John 1857-1909 .... **TCLC 24**
See also CA 118; DLB 19

Davidson, Sara 1943- .... **CLC 9**
See also CA 81-84; CANR 44

Davie, Donald (Alfred)
1922-1995 .... **CLC 5, 8, 10, 31**
See also CA 1-4R; 149; CAAS 3; CANR 1,
44; DLB 27; MTCW

Davies, Ray(mond Douglas) 1944- .. **CLC 21**
See also CA 116; 146

Davies, Rhys 1903-1978 .... **CLC 23**
See also CA 9-12R; 81-84; CANR 4;
DLB 139

Davies, (William) Robertson
1913-1995 ..... **CLC 2, 7, 13, 25, 42, 75,
91; DA; DAB; DAC; DAM MST, NOV,
POP; WLC**
See also BEST 89:2; CA 33-36R; 150;
CANR 17, 42; DLB 68; INT CANR-17;
MTCW

Davies, W(illiam) H(enry)
1871-1940 .... **TCLC 5**
See also CA 104; DLB 19, 174

Davies, Walter C.
See Kornbluth, C(yril) M.

Davis, Angela (Yvonne)
1944- .... **CLC 77; DAM MULT**
See also BW 2; CA 57-60; CANR 10

Davis, B. Lynch
See Bioy Casares, Adolfo; Borges, Jorge
Luis

Davis, Gordon
See Hunt, E(verette) Howard, (Jr.)

Davis, Harold Lenoir 1896-1960.... **CLC 49**
See also CA 89-92; DLB 9

Davis, Rebecca (Blaine) Harding
1831-1910 .... **TCLC 6**
See also CA 104; DLB 74

Davis, Richard Harding
1864-1916 .... **TCLC 24**
See also CA 114; DLB 12, 23, 78, 79;
DLBD 13

Davison, Frank Dalby 1893-1970 ... **CLC 15**
See also CA 116

Davison, Lawrence H.
See Lawrence, D(avid) H(erbert Richards)

Davison, Peter (Hubert) 1928- ..... **CLC 28**
See also CA 9-12R; CAAS 4; CANR 3, 43;
DLB 5

Davys, Mary 1674-1732 .... **LC 1**
See also DLB 39

Dawson, Fielding 1930- .... **CLC 6**
See also CA 85-88; DLB 130

Dawson, Peter
See Faust, Frederick (Schiller)

Day, Clarence (Shepard, Jr.)
1874-1935 .... **TCLC 25**
See also CA 108; DLB 11

Day, Thomas 1748-1789 .... **LC 1**
See also DLB 39; YABC 1

Day Lewis, C(ecil)
1904-1972 .... **CLC 1, 6, 10;
DAM POET; PC 11**
See also Blake, Nicholas
See also CA 13-16; 33-36R; CANR 34;
CAP 1; DLB 15, 20; MTCW

Dazai, Osamu .... **TCLC 11**
See also Tsushima, Shuji

de Andrade, Carlos Drummond
See Drummond de Andrade, Carlos

Deane, Norman
See Creasey, John

**de Beauvoir, Simone (Lucie Ernestine Marie
Bertrand)**
See Beauvoir, Simone (Lucie Ernestine
Marie Bertrand) de

de Brissac, Malcolm
See Dickinson, Peter (Malcolm)

de Chardin, Pierre Teilhard
See Teilhard de Chardin, (Marie Joseph)
Pierre

Dee, John 1527-1608 .... **LC 20**

Deer, Sandra 1940-................ **CLC 45**

De Ferrari, Gabriella 1941-........ **CLC 65**
See also CA 146

Defoe, Daniel
1660(?)-1731 .... **LC 1; DA; DAB; DAC;
DAM MST, NOV; WLC**
See also CDBLB 1660-1789; DLB 39, 95,
101; JRDA; MAICYA; SATA 22

de Gourmont, Remy(-Marie-Charles)
See Gourmont, Remy (-Marie-Charles) de

de Hartog, Jan 1914- .... **CLC 19**
See also CA 1-4R; CANR 1

de Hostos, E. M.
See Hostos (y Bonilla), Eugenio Maria de

de Hostos, Eugenio M.
See Hostos (y Bonilla), Eugenio Maria de

Deighton, Len .... **CLC 4, 7, 22, 46**
See also Deighton, Leonard Cyril
See also AAYA 6; BEST 89:2;
CDBLB 1960 to Present; DLB 87

Deighton, Leonard Cyril 1929-
See Deighton, Len
See also CA 9-12R; CANR 19, 33;
DAM NOV, POP; MTCW

Dekker, Thomas
1572(?)-1632 ..... **LC 22; DAM DRAM**
See also CDBLB Before 1660; DLB 62, 172

Delafield, E. M. 1890-1943 .... **TCLC 61**
See also Dashwood, Edmee Elizabeth
Monica de la Pasture
See also DLB 34

de la Mare, Walter (John)
1873-1956 .... **TCLC 4, 53; DAB; DAC;
DAM MST, POET; SSC 14; WLC**
See also CDBLB 1914-1945; CLR 23;
DLB 162; SATA 16

Delaney, Franey
See O'Hara, John (Henry)

Delaney, Shelagh
1939- .... **CLC 29; DAM DRAM**
See also CA 17-20R; CANR 30;
CDBLB 1960 to Present; DLB 13;
MTCW

Delany, Mary (Granville Pendarves)
1700-1788 .... **LC 12**

Delany, Samuel R(ay, Jr.)
1942- .... **CLC 8, 14, 38; BLC;
DAM MULT**
See also BW 2; CA 81-84; CANR 27, 43;
DLB 8, 33; MTCW

De La Ramee, (Marie) Louise 1839-1908
See Ouida
See also SATA 20

de la Roche, Mazo 1879-1961 ...... **CLC 14**
See also CA 85-88; CANR 30; DLB 68;
SATA 64

Delbanco, Nicholas (Franklin)
1942- .... **CLC 6, 13**
See also CA 17-20R; CAAS 2; CANR 29,
55; DLB 6

del Castillo, Michel 1933- .... **CLC 38**
See also CA 109

Deledda, Grazia (Cosima)
1875(?)-1936 .... **TCLC 23**
See also CA 123

Delibes, Miguel .... **CLC 8, 18**
See also Delibes Setien, Miguel

Delibes Setien, Miguel 1920-
See Delibes, Miguel
See also CA 45-48; CANR 1, 32; HW;
MTCW

DeLillo, Don
1936- ..... **CLC 8, 10, 13, 27, 39, 54, 76;
DAM NOV, POP**
See also BEST 89:1; CA 81-84; CANR 21;
DLB 6, 173; MTCW

de Lisser, H. G.
See De Lisser, H(erbert) G(eorge)
See also DLB 117

De Lisser, H(erbert) G(eorge)
1878-1944 .... **TCLC 12**
See also de Lisser, H. G.
See also BW 2; CA 109; 152

Deloria, Vine (Victor), Jr.
1933- .... **CLC 21; DAM MULT**
See also CA 53-56; CANR 5, 20, 48;
DLB 175; MTCW; NNAL; SATA 21

Del Vecchio, John M(ichael)
1947- .... **CLC 29**
See also CA 110; DLBD 9

de Man, Paul (Adolph Michel)
1919-1983 .... **CLC 55**
See also CA 128; 111; DLB 67; MTCW

De Marinis, Rick 1934-.......... **CLC 54**
See also CA 57-60; CAAS 24; CANR 9, 25, 50

Dembry, R. Emmet
See Murfree, Mary Noailles

Demby, William
1922-..... **CLC 53; BLC; DAM MULT**
See also BW 1; CA 81-84; DLB 33

Demijohn, Thom
See Disch, Thomas M(ichael)

de Montherlant, Henry (Milon)
See Montherlant, Henry (Milon) de

Demosthenes 384B.C.-322B.C. .... **CMLC 13**

de Natale, Francine
See Malzberg, Barry N(athaniel)

Denby, Edwin (Orr) 1903-1983..... **CLC 48**
See also CA 138; 110

Denis, Julio
See Cortazar, Julio

Denmark, Harrison
See Zelazny, Roger (Joseph)

Dennis, John 1658-1734........... **LC 11**
See also DLB 101

Dennis, Nigel (Forbes) 1912-1989.... **CLC 8**
See also CA 25-28R; 129; DLB 13, 15;
MTCW

De Palma, Brian (Russell) 1940-.... **CLC 20**
See also CA 109

De Quincey, Thomas 1785-1859 ... **NCLC 4**
See also CDBLB 1789-1832; DLB 110; 144

Deren, Eleanora 1908(?)-1961
See Deren, Maya
See also CA 111

Deren, Maya .... **CLC 16**
See also Deren, Eleanora

Derleth, August (William)
1909-1971 .... **CLC 31**
See also CA 1-4R; 29-32R; CANR 4;
DLB 9; SATA 5

Der Nister 1884-1950........... **TCLC 56**

de Routisie, Albert
See Aragon, Louis

Derrida, Jacques 1930-......... **CLC 24, 87**
See also CA 124; 127

Derry Down Derry
See Lear, Edward

Dersonnes, Jacques
See Simenon, Georges (Jacques Christian)

Desai, Anita
1937-.......... **CLC 19, 37, 97; DAB;
DAM NOV**
See also CA 81-84; CANR 33, 53; MTCW;
SATA 63

de Saint-Luc, Jean
See Glassco, John

de Saint Roman, Arnaud
See Aragon, Louis

Descartes, Rene 1596-1650 ...... **LC 20, 35**

De Sica, Vittorio 1901(?)-1974 ..... **CLC 20**
See also CA 117

Desnos, Robert 1900-1945....... **TCLC 22**
See also CA 121; 151

Destouches, Louis-Ferdinand
1894-1961 .... **CLC 9, 15**
See also Celine, Louis-Ferdinand
See also CA 85-88; CANR 28; MTCW

de Tolignac, Gaston
See Griffith, D(avid Lewelyn) W(ark)

Deutsch, Babette 1895-1982 .... **CLC 18**
See also CA 1-4R; 108; CANR 4; DLB 45;
SATA 1; SATA-Obit 33

Devenant, William 1606-1649 ...... **LC 13**

Devkota, Laxmiprasad
1909-1959 .... **TCLC 23**
See also CA 123

De Voto, Bernard (Augustine)
1897-1955 .... **TCLC 29**
See also CA 113; DLB 9

De Vries, Peter
1910-1993 .... **CLC 1, 2, 3, 7, 10, 28, 46;
DAM NOV**
See also CA 17-20R; 142; CANR 41;
DLB 6; DLBY 82; MTCW

Dexter, John
See Bradley, Marion Zimmer

Dexter, Martin
See Faust, Frederick (Schiller)

Dexter, Pete
1943-......... **CLC 34, 55; DAM POP**
See also BEST 89:2; CA 127; 131; INT 131;
MTCW

Diamano, Silmang
See Senghor, Leopold Sedar

Diamond, Neil 1941-............. **CLC 30**
See also CA 108

Diaz del Castillo, Bernal 1496-1584 .. **LC 31**

di Bassetto, Corno
See Shaw, George Bernard

Dick, Philip K(indred)
1928-1982 .... **CLC 10, 30, 72;
DAM NOV, POP**
See also CA 49-52; 106; CANR 2, 16;
DLB 8; MTCW

Dickens, Charles (John Huffam)
1812-1870 ...... **NCLC 3, 8, 18, 26, 37,
50; DA; DAB; DAC; DAM MST, NOV;
SSC 17; WLC**
See also CDBLB 1832-1890; DLB 21, 55,
70, 159, 166; JRDA; MAICYA; SATA 15

Dickey, James (Lafayette)
1923-........ **CLC 1, 2, 4, 7, 10, 15, 47;
DAM NOV, POET, POP**
See also AITN 1, 2; CA 9-12R; CABS 2;
CANR 10, 48; CDALB 1968-1988;
DLB 5; DLBD 7; DLBY 82, 93;
INT CANR-10; MTCW

Dickey, William 1928-1994 ..... **CLC 3, 28**
See also CA 9-12R; 145; CANR 24; DLB 5

Dickinson, Charles 1951-......... **CLC 49**
See also CA 128

Dickinson, Emily (Elizabeth)
1830-1886 .... **NCLC 21; DA; DAB;
DAC; DAM MST, POET; PC 1; WLC**
See also CDALB 1865-1917; DLB 1;
SATA 29

Dickinson, Peter (Malcolm)
1927-.................... **CLC 12, 35**
See also AAYA 9; CA 41-44R; CANR 31;
CLR 29; DLB 87, 161; JRDA; MAICYA;
SATA 5, 62

Dickson, Carr
See Carr, John Dickson

Dickson, Carter
See Carr, John Dickson

Diderot, Denis 1713-1784 .... **LC 26**

Didion, Joan
1934-.. **CLC 1, 3, 8, 14, 32; DAM NOV**
See also AITN 1; CA 5-8R; CANR 14, 52;
CDALB 1968-1988; DLB 2, 173;
DLBY 81, 86; MTCW

Dietrich, Robert
See Hunt, E(verette) Howard, (Jr.)

Dillard, Annie
1945-.......... **CLC 9, 60; DAM NOV**
See also AAYA 6; CA 49-52; CANR 3, 43;
DLBY 80; MTCW; SATA 10

Dillard, R(ichard) H(enry) W(ilde)
1937-.................... **CLC 5**
See also CA 21-24R; CAAS 7; CANR 10;
DLB 5

Dillon, Eilis 1920-1994........... **CLC 17**
See also CA 9-12R; 147; CAAS 3; CANR 4,
38; CLR 26; MAICYA; SATA 2, 74;
SATA-Obit 83

Dimont, Penelope
See Mortimer, Penelope (Ruth)

Dinesen, Isak........ CLC 10, 29, 95; SSC 7
See also Blixen, Karen (Christentze
Dinesen)

Ding Ling........................ CLC 68
See also Chiang Pin-chin

Disch, Thomas M(ichael) 1940-... **CLC 7, 36**
See also AAYA 17; CA 21-24R; CAAS 4;
CANR 17, 36, 54; CLR 18; DLB 8;
MAICYA; MTCW; SAAS 15; SATA 92

Disch, Tom
See Disch, Thomas M(ichael)

d'Isly, Georges
See Simenon, Georges (Jacques Christian)

Disraeli, Benjamin 1804-1881 .. **NCLC 2, 39**
See also DLB 21, 55

Ditcum, Steve
See Crumb, R(obert)

Dixon, Paige
See Corcoran, Barbara

Dixon, Stephen 1936-..... **CLC 52; SSC 16**
See also CA 89-92; CANR 17, 40, 54;
DLB 130

Dobell, Sydney Thompson
1824-1874 .... **NCLC 43**
See also DLB 32

Doblin, Alfred .... **TCLC 13**
See also Doeblin, Alfred

Dobrolyubov, Nikolai Alexandrovich
1836-1861 .... **NCLC 5**

Dobyns, Stephen 1941-........... **CLC 37**
See also CA 45-48; CANR 2, 18

Doctorow, E(dgar) L(aurence)
1931- ..... **CLC 6, 11, 15, 18, 37, 44, 65;
DAM NOV, POP**
See also AITN 2; BEST 89:3; CA 45-48;
CANR 2, 33, 51; CDALB 1968-1988;
DLB 2, 28, 173; DLBY 80; MTCW

Dodgson, Charles Lutwidge 1832-1898
See Carroll, Lewis
See also CLR 2; DA; DAB; DAC;
DAM MST, NOV, POET; MAICYA;
YABC 2

Dodson, Owen (Vincent)
1914-1983 .... **CLC 79; BLC;
DAM MULT**
See also BW 1; CA 65-68; 110; CANR 24;
DLB 76

Doeblin, Alfred 1878-1957....... **TCLC 13**
See also Doblin, Alfred
See also CA 110; 141; DLB 66

Doerr, Harriet 1910- .... **CLC 34**
See also CA 117; 122; CANR 47; INT 122

Domecq, H(onorio) Bustos
See Bioy Casares, Adolfo; Borges, Jorge
Luis

Domini, Rey
See Lorde, Audre (Geraldine)

Dominique
See Proust, (Valentin-Louis-George-Eugene-)
Marcel

Don, A
See Stephen, Leslie

Donaldson, Stephen R.
1947- .... **CLC 46; DAM POP**
See also CA 89-92; CANR 13, 55;
INT CANR-13

Donleavy, J(ames) P(atrick)
1926- .... **CLC 1, 4, 6, 10, 45**
See also AITN 2; CA 9-12R; CANR 24, 49;
DLB 6, 173; INT CANR-24; MTCW

Donne, John
1572-1631 .... **LC 10, 24; DA; DAB;
DAC; DAM MST, POET; PC 1**
See also CDBLB Before 1660; DLB 121,
151

Donnell, David 1939(?)- .... **CLC 34**

Donoghue, P. S.
See Hunt, E(verette) Howard, (Jr.)

Donoso (Yanez), Jose
1924-1996 .... **CLC 4, 8, 11, 32, 99;
DAM MULT; HLC**
See also CA 81-84; 155; CANR 32;
DLB 113; HW; MTCW

Donovan, John 1928-1992 .... **CLC 35**
See also AAYA 20; CA 97-100; 137;
CLR 3; MAICYA; SATA 72;
SATA-Brief 29

Don Roberto
See Cunninghame Graham, R(obert)
B(ontine)

Doolittle, Hilda
1886-1961 ..... **CLC 3, 8, 14, 31, 34, 73;
DA; DAC; DAM MST, POET; PC 5;
WLC**
See also H. D.
See also CA 97-100; CANR 35; DLB 4, 45;
MTCW

Dorfman, Ariel
1942- .... **CLC 48, 77; DAM MULT;
HLC**
See also CA 124; 130; HW; INT 130

Dorn, Edward (Merton) 1929-... **CLC 10, 18**
See also CA 93-96; CANR 42; DLB 5;
INT 93-96

Dorsan, Luc
See Simenon, Georges (Jacques Christian)

Dorsange, Jean
See Simenon, Georges (Jacques Christian)

Dos Passos, John (Roderigo)
1896-1970 ...... **CLC 1, 4, 8, 11, 15, 25,
34, 82; DA; DAB; DAC; DAM MST,
NOV; WLC**
See also CA 1-4R; 29-32R; CANR 3;
CDALB 1929-1941; DLB 4, 9; DLBD 1;
MTCW

Dossage, Jean
See Simenon, Georges (Jacques Christian)

Dostoevsky, Fedor Mikhailovich
1821-1881 ...... **NCLC 2, 7, 21, 33, 43;
DA; DAB; DAC; DAM MST, NOV;
SSC 2; WLC**

Doughty, Charles M(ontagu)
1843-1926 .... **TCLC 27**
See also CA 115; DLB 19, 57, 174

Douglas, Ellen.................... CLC 73
See also Haxton, Josephine Ayres;
Williamson, Ellen Douglas

Douglas, Gavin 1475(?)-1522....... **LC 20**

Douglas, Keith 1920-1944 .... **TCLC 40**
See also DLB 27

Douglas, Leonard
See Bradbury, Ray (Douglas)

Douglas, Michael
See Crichton, (John) Michael

Douglas, Norman 1868-1952 ...... **TCLC 68**

Douglass, Frederick
1817(?)-1895 .... **NCLC 7, 55; BLC; DA;
DAC; DAM MST, MULT; WLC**
See also CDALB 1640-1865; DLB 1, 43, 50,
79; SATA 29

Dourado, (Waldomiro Freitas) Autran
1926- .... **CLC 23, 60**
See also CA 25-28R; CANR 34

Dourado, Waldomiro Autran
See Dourado, (Waldomiro Freitas) Autran

Dove, Rita (Frances)
1952- .... **CLC 50, 81; DAM MULT,
POET; PC 6**
See also BW 2; CA 109; CAAS 19;
CANR 27, 42; DLB 120

Dowell, Coleman 1925-1985........ **CLC 60**
See also CA 25-28R; 117; CANR 10;
DLB 130

Dowson, Ernest (Christopher)
1867-1900 .... **TCLC 4**
See also CA 105; 150; DLB 19, 135

Doyle, A. Conan
See Doyle, Arthur Conan

Doyle, Arthur Conan
1859-1930 .... **TCLC 7; DA; DAB;
DAC; DAM MST, NOV; SSC 12; WLC**
See also AAYA 14; CA 104; 122;
CDBLB 1890-1914; DLB 18, 70, 156;
MTCW; SATA 24

Doyle, Conan
See Doyle, Arthur Conan

Doyle, John
See Graves, Robert (von Ranke)

Doyle, Roddy 1958(?)- .... **CLC 81**
See also AAYA 14; CA 143

Doyle, Sir A. Conan
See Doyle, Arthur Conan

Doyle, Sir Arthur Conan
See Doyle, Arthur Conan

Dr. A
See Asimov, Isaac; Silverstein, Alvin

Drabble, Margaret
1939- .... **CLC 2, 3, 5, 8, 10, 22, 53;
DAB; DAC; DAM MST, NOV, POP**
See also CA 13-16R; CANR 18, 35;
CDBLB 1960 to Present; DLB 14, 155;
MTCW; SATA 48

Drapier, M. B.
See Swift, Jonathan

Drayham, James
See Mencken, H(enry) L(ouis)

Drayton, Michael 1563-1631........ **LC 8**

Dreadstone, Carl
See Campbell, (John) Ramsey

Dreiser, Theodore (Herman Albert)
1871-1945 .... **TCLC 10, 18, 35; DA;
DAC; DAM MST, NOV; WLC**
See also CA 106; 132; CDALB 1865-1917;
DLB 9, 12, 102, 137; DLBD 1; MTCW

Drexler, Rosalyn 1926- .... **CLC 2, 6**
See also CA 81-84

Dreyer, Carl Theodor 1889-1968.... **CLC 16**
See also CA 116

Drieu la Rochelle, Pierre(-Eugene)
1893-1945 .... **TCLC 21**
See also CA 117; DLB 72

Drinkwater, John 1882-1937...... **TCLC 57**
See also CA 109; 149; DLB 10, 19, 149

Drop Shot
See Cable, George Washington

Droste-Hulshoff, Annette Freiin von
1797-1848 .... **NCLC 3**
See also DLB 133

Drummond, Walter
See Silverberg, Robert

Drummond, William Henry
1854-1907 .... **TCLC 25**
See also DLB 92

Drummond de Andrade, Carlos
1902-1987 .... **CLC 18**
See also Andrade, Carlos Drummond de
See also CA 132; 123

Drury, Allen (Stuart) 1918-........ **CLC 37**
See also CA 57-60; CANR 18, 52;
INT CANR-18

Dryden, John
  1631-1700 .... **LC 3, 21; DA; DAB;
    DAC; DAM DRAM, MST, POET;
    DC 3; WLC**
  See also CDBLB 1660-1789; DLB 80, 101,
    131

Duberman, Martin 1930- .... **CLC 8**
  See also CA 1-4R; CANR 2

Dubie, Norman (Evans) 1945- ..... **CLC 36**
  See also CA 69-72; CANR 12; DLB 120

Du Bois, W(illiam) E(dward) B(urghardt)
  1868-1963 .... **CLC 1, 2, 13, 64, 96;
    BLC; DA; DAC; DAM MST, MULT,
    NOV; WLC**
  See also BW 1; CA 85-88; CANR 34;
    CDALB 1865-1917; DLB 47, 50, 91;
    MTCW; SATA 42

Dubus, Andre
  1936- .... **CLC 13, 36, 97; SSC 15**
  See also CA 21-24R; CANR 17; DLB 130;
    INT CANR-17

Duca Minimo
  See D'Annunzio, Gabriele

Ducharme, Rejean 1941- .... **CLC 74**
  See also DLB 60

Duclos, Charles Pinot 1704-1772 ..... **LC 1**

Dudek, Louis 1918- .... **CLC 11, 19**
  See also CA 45-48; CAAS 14; CANR 1;
    DLB 88

Duerrenmatt, Friedrich
  1921-1990 ...... **CLC 1, 4, 8, 11, 15, 43;
    DAM DRAM**
  See also CA 17-20R; CANR 33; DLB 69,
    124; MTCW

Duffy, Bruce (?)- .... **CLC 50**

Duffy, Maureen 1933- .... **CLC 37**
  See also CA 25-28R; CANR 33; DLB 14;
    MTCW

Dugan, Alan 1923- .... **CLC 2, 6**
  See also CA 81-84; DLB 5

du Gard, Roger Martin
  See Martin du Gard, Roger

Duhamel, Georges 1884-1966 .... **CLC 8**
  See also CA 81-84; 25-28R; CANR 35;
    DLB 65; MTCW

Dujardin, Edouard (Emile Louis)
  1861-1949 .... **TCLC 13**
  See also CA 109; DLB 123

Dumas, Alexandre (Davy de la Pailleterie)
  1802-1870 .... **NCLC 11; DA; DAB;
    DAC; DAM MST, NOV; WLC**
  See also DLB 119; SATA 18

Dumas, Alexandre
  1824-1895 .... **NCLC 9; DC 1**

Dumas, Claudine
  See Malzberg, Barry N(athaniel)

Dumas, Henry L. 1934-1968 ..... **CLC 6, 62**
  See also BW 1; CA 85-88; DLB 41

du Maurier, Daphne
  1907-1989 .... **CLC 6, 11, 59; DAB;
    DAC; DAM MST, POP; SSC 18**
  See also CA 5-8R; 128; CANR 6, 55;
    MTCW; SATA 27; SATA-Obit 60

Dunbar, Paul Laurence
  1872-1906 ...... **TCLC 2, 12; BLC; DA;
    DAC; DAM MST, MULT, POET; PC 5;
    SSC 8; WLC**
  See also BW 1; CA 104; 124;
    CDALB 1865-1917; DLB 50, 54, 78;
    SATA 34

Dunbar, William 1460(?)-1530(?) .... **LC 20**
  See also DLB 132, 146

Duncan, Dora Angela
  See Duncan, Isadora

Duncan, Isadora 1877(?)-1927 ..... **TCLC 68**
  See also CA 118; 149

Duncan, Lois 1934- .... **CLC 26**
  See also AAYA 4; CA 1-4R; CANR 2, 23,
    36; CLR 29; JRDA; MAICYA; SAAS 2;
    SATA 1, 36, 75

Duncan, Robert (Edward)
  1919-1988 .... **CLC 1, 2, 4, 7, 15, 41, 55;
    DAM POET; PC 2**
  See also CA 9-12R; 124; CANR 28; DLB 5,
    16; MTCW

Duncan, Sara Jeannette
  1861-1922 .... **TCLC 60**
  See also DLB 92

Dunlap, William 1766-1839 .... **NCLC 2**
  See also DLB 30, 37, 59

Dunn, Douglas (Eaglesham)
  1942- .... **CLC 6, 40**
  See also CA 45-48; CANR 2, 33; DLB 40;
    MTCW

Dunn, Katherine (Karen) 1945- ..... **CLC 71**
  See also CA 33-36R

Dunn, Stephen 1939- .... **CLC 36**
  See also CA 33-36R; CANR 12, 48, 53;
    DLB 105

Dunne, Finley Peter 1867-1936.... **TCLC 28**
  See also CA 108; DLB 11, 23

Dunne, John Gregory 1932- .... **CLC 28**
  See also CA 25-28R; CANR 14, 50;
    DLBY 80

**Dunsany, Edward John Moreton Drax
    Plunkett** 1878-1957
  See Dunsany, Lord
  See also CA 104; 148; DLB 10

Dunsany, Lord .... **TCLC 2, 59**
  See also Dunsany, Edward John Moreton
    Drax Plunkett
  See also DLB 77, 153, 156

du Perry, Jean
  See Simenon, Georges (Jacques Christian)

Durang, Christopher (Ferdinand)
  1949- .... **CLC 27, 38**
  See also CA 105; CANR 50

Duras, Marguerite
  1914-1996 .. **CLC 3, 6, 11, 20, 34, 40, 68**
  See also CA 25-28R; 151; CANR 50;
    DLB 83; MTCW

Durban, (Rosa) Pam 1947- .... **CLC 39**
  See also CA 123

Durcan, Paul
  1944- .... **CLC 43, 70; DAM POET**
  See also CA 134

Durkheim, Emile 1858-1917 ...... **TCLC 55**

Durrell, Lawrence (George)
  1912-1990 .... **CLC 1, 4, 6, 8, 13, 27, 41;
    DAM NOV**
  See also CA 9-12R; 132; CANR 40;
    CDBLB 1945-1960; DLB 15, 27;
    DLBY 90; MTCW

Durrenmatt, Friedrich
  See Duerrenmatt, Friedrich

Dutt, Toru 1856-1877 .... **NCLC 29**

Dwight, Timothy 1752-1817 ...... **NCLC 13**
  See also DLB 37

Dworkin, Andrea 1946- .... **CLC 43**
  See also CA 77-80; CAAS 21; CANR 16,
    39; INT CANR-16; MTCW

Dwyer, Deanna
  See Koontz, Dean R(ay)

Dwyer, K. R.
  See Koontz, Dean R(ay)

Dylan, Bob 1941- ...... **CLC 3, 4, 6, 12, 77**
  See also CA 41-44R; DLB 16

Eagleton, Terence (Francis) 1943-
  See Eagleton, Terry
  See also CA 57-60; CANR 7, 23; MTCW

Eagleton, Terry .... **CLC 63**
  See also Eagleton, Terence (Francis)

Early, Jack
  See Scoppettone, Sandra

East, Michael
  See West, Morris L(anglo)

Eastaway, Edward
  See Thomas, (Philip) Edward

Eastlake, William (Derry) 1917- ..... **CLC 8**
  See also CA 5-8R; CAAS 1; CANR 5;
    DLB 6; INT CANR-5

Eastman, Charles A(lexander)
  1858-1939 ..... **TCLC 55; DAM MULT**
  See also DLB 175; NNAL; YABC 1

Eberhart, Richard (Ghormley)
  1904- .. **CLC 3, 11, 19, 56; DAM POET**
  See also CA 1-4R; CANR 2;
    CDALB 1941-1968; DLB 48; MTCW

Eberstadt, Fernanda 1960- .... **CLC 39**
  See also CA 136

Echegaray (y Eizaguirre), Jose (Maria Waldo)
  1832-1916 .... **TCLC 4**
  See also CA 104; CANR 32; HW; MTCW

Echeverria, (Jose) Esteban (Antonino)
  1805-1851 .... **NCLC 18**

Echo
  See Proust, (Valentin-Louis-George-Eugene-)
    Marcel

Eckert, Allan W. 1931- .... **CLC 17**
  See also AAYA 18; CA 13-16R; CANR 14,
    45; INT CANR-14; SAAS 21; SATA 29,
    91; SATA-Brief 27

Eckhart, Meister 1260(?)-1328(?) .. **CMLC 9**
  See also DLB 115

Eckmar, F. R.
  See de Hartog, Jan

Eco, Umberto
  1932- ... **CLC 28, 60; DAM NOV, POP**
  See also BEST 90:1; CA 77-80; CANR 12,
    33, 55; MTCW

Eddison, E(ric) R(ucker)
  1882-1945 .... **TCLC 15**
  See also CA 109; 154

Edel, (Joseph) Leon 1907- ...... **CLC 29, 34**
  See also CA 1-4R; CANR 1, 22; DLB 103;
  INT CANR-22

Eden, Emily 1797-1869 .... **NCLC 10**

Edgar, David
  1948- .... **CLC 42; DAM DRAM**
  See also CA 57-60; CANR 12; DLB 13;
  MTCW

Edgerton, Clyde (Carlyle) 1944- .... **CLC 39**
  See also AAYA 17; CA 118; 134; INT 134

Edgeworth, Maria 1768-1849... **NCLC 1, 51**
  See also DLB 116, 159, 163; SATA 21

Edmonds, Paul
  See Kuttner, Henry

Edmonds, Walter D(umaux) 1903- .. **CLC 35**
  See also CA 5-8R; CANR 2; DLB 9;
  MAICYA; SAAS 4; SATA 1, 27

Edmondson, Wallace
  See Ellison, Harlan (Jay)

Edson, Russell .... **CLC 13**
  See also CA 33-36R

Edwards, Bronwen Elizabeth
  See Rose, Wendy

Edwards, G(erald) B(asil)
  1899-1976 .... **CLC 25**
  See also CA 110

Edwards, Gus 1939- .... **CLC 43**
  See also CA 108; INT 108

Edwards, Jonathan
  1703-1758 .... **LC 7; DA; DAC;
                        DAM MST**
  See also DLB 24

Efron, Marina Ivanovna Tsvetaeva
  See Tsvetaeva (Efron), Marina (Ivanovna)

Ehle, John (Marsden, Jr.) 1925- .... **CLC 27**
  See also CA 9-12R

Ehrenbourg, Ilya (Grigoryevich)
  See Ehrenburg, Ilya (Grigoryevich)

Ehrenburg, Ilya (Grigoryevich)
  1891-1967 .... **CLC 18, 34, 62**
  See also CA 102; 25-28R

Ehrenburg, Ilyo (Grigoryevich)
  See Ehrenburg, Ilya (Grigoryevich)

Eich, Guenter 1907-1972 .... **CLC 15**
  See also CA 111; 93-96; DLB 69, 124

Eichendorff, Joseph Freiherr von
  1788-1857 .... **NCLC 8**
  See also DLB 90

Eigner, Larry .... **CLC 9**
  See also Eigner, Laurence (Joel)
  See also CAAS 23; DLB 5

Eigner, Laurence (Joel) 1927-1996
  See Eigner, Larry
  See also CA 9-12R; 151; CANR 6

Einstein, Albert 1879-1955 .... **TCLC 65**
  See also CA 121; 133; MTCW

Eiseley, Loren Corey 1907-1977 ..... **CLC 7**
  See also AAYA 5; CA 1-4R; 73-76;
  CANR 6

Eisenstadt, Jill 1963- .... **CLC 50**
  See also CA 140

Eisenstein, Sergei (Mikhailovich)
  1898-1948 .... **TCLC 57**
  See also CA 114; 149

Eisner, Simon
  See Kornbluth, C(yril) M.

Ekeloef, (Bengt) Gunnar
  1907-1968 ...... **CLC 27; DAM POET**
  See also CA 123; 25-28R

Ekelof, (Bengt) Gunnar
  See Ekeloef, (Bengt) Gunnar

Ekwensi, C. O. D.
  See Ekwensi, Cyprian (Odiatu Duaka)

Ekwensi, Cyprian (Odiatu Duaka)
  1921- ...... **CLC 4; BLC; DAM MULT**
  See also BW 2; CA 29-32R; CANR 18, 42;
  DLB 117; MTCW; SATA 66

Elaine .... **TCLC 18**
  See also Leverson, Ada

El Crummo
  See Crumb, R(obert)

Elia
  See Lamb, Charles

Eliade, Mircea 1907-1986 .... **CLC 19**
  See also CA 65-68; 119; CANR 30; MTCW

Eliot, A. D.
  See Jewett, (Theodora) Sarah Orne

Eliot, Alice
  See Jewett, (Theodora) Sarah Orne

Eliot, Dan
  See Silverberg, Robert

Eliot, George
  1819-1880 ..... **NCLC 4, 13, 23, 41, 49;
              DA; DAB; DAC; DAM MST, NOV;
                                        WLC**
  See also CDBLB 1832-1890; DLB 21, 35, 55

Eliot, John 1604-1690 .... **LC 5**
  See also DLB 24

Eliot, T(homas) S(tearns)
  1888-1965 ..... **CLC 1, 2, 3, 6, 9, 10, 13,
              15, 24, 34, 41, 55, 57; DA; DAB; DAC;
              DAM DRAM, MST, POET; PC 5;
                                      WLC 2**
  See also CA 5-8R; 25-28R; CANR 41;
  CDALB 1929-1941; DLB 7, 10, 45, 63;
  DLBY 88; MTCW

Elizabeth 1866-1941 .... **TCLC 41**

Elkin, Stanley L(awrence)
  1930-1995 ...... **CLC 4, 6, 9, 14, 27, 51,
              91; DAM NOV, POP; SSC 12**
  See also CA 9-12R; 148; CANR 8, 46;
  DLB 2, 28; DLBY 80; INT CANR-8;
  MTCW

Elledge, Scott .... **CLC 34**

Elliot, Don
  See Silverberg, Robert

Elliott, Don
  See Silverberg, Robert

Elliott, George P(aul) 1918-1980..... **CLC 2**
  See also CA 1-4R; 97-100; CANR 2

Elliott, Janice 1931- .... **CLC 47**
  See also CA 13-16R; CANR 8, 29; DLB 14

Elliott, Sumner Locke 1917-1991 ... **CLC 38**
  See also CA 5-8R; 134; CANR 2, 21

Elliott, William
  See Bradbury, Ray (Douglas)

Ellis, A. E. .... **CLC 7**

Ellis, Alice Thomas .... **CLC 40**
  See also Haycraft, Anna

Ellis, Bret Easton
  1964- .... **CLC 39, 71; DAM POP**
  See also AAYA 2; CA 118; 123; CANR 51;
  INT 123

Ellis, (Henry) Havelock
  1859-1939 .... **TCLC 14**
  See also CA 109

Ellis, Landon
  See Ellison, Harlan (Jay)

Ellis, Trey 1962-................. **CLC 55**
  See also CA 146

Ellison, Harlan (Jay)
  1934- ...... **CLC 1, 13, 42; DAM POP;
                                    SSC 14**
  See also CA 5-8R; CANR 5, 46; DLB 8;
  INT CANR-5; MTCW

Ellison, Ralph (Waldo)
  1914-1994 .... **CLC 1, 3, 11, 54, 86;
              BLC; DA; DAB; DAC; DAM MST,
                        MULT, NOV; WLC**
  See also AAYA 19; BW 1; CA 9-12R; 145;
  CANR 24, 53; CDALB 1941-1968;
  DLB 2, 76; DLBY 94; MTCW

Ellmann, Lucy (Elizabeth) 1956-.... **CLC 61**
  See also CA 128

Ellmann, Richard (David)
  1918-1987 .... **CLC 50**
  See also BEST 89:2; CA 1-4R; 122;
  CANR 2, 28; DLB 103; DLBY 87;
  MTCW

Elman, Richard 1934-............. **CLC 19**
  See also CA 17-20R; CAAS 3; CANR 47

Elron
  See Hubbard, L(afayette) Ron(ald)

Eluard, Paul................. **TCLC 7, 41**
  See also Grindel, Eugene

Elyot, Sir Thomas 1490(?)-1546 ..... **LC 11**

Elytis, Odysseus
  1911-1996 .... **CLC 15, 49; DAM POET**
  See also CA 102; 151; MTCW

Emecheta, (Florence Onye) Buchi
  1944- .. **CLC 14, 48; BLC; DAM MULT**
  See also BW 2; CA 81-84; CANR 27;
  DLB 117; MTCW; SATA 66

Emerson, Ralph Waldo
  1803-1882 ..... **NCLC 1, 38; DA; DAB;
                DAC; DAM MST, POET; WLC**
  See also CDALB 1640-1865; DLB 1, 59, 73

Eminescu, Mihail 1850-1889 ..... **NCLC 33**

Empson, William
  1906-1984 .... **CLC 3, 8, 19, 33, 34**
  See also CA 17-20R; 112; CANR 31;
  DLB 20; MTCW

Enchi Fumiko (Ueda) 1905-1986.... **CLC 31**
  See also CA 129; 121

Ende, Michael (Andreas Helmuth)
  1929-1995 .... **CLC 31**
  See also CA 118; 124; 149; CANR 36;
  CLR 14; DLB 75; MAICYA; SATA 61;
  SATA-Brief 42; SATA-Obit 86

Endo, Shusaku
    1923-1996 .... CLC 7, 14, 19, 54, 99;
                                    DAM NOV
    See also CA 29-32R; 153; CANR 21, 54;
    MTCW

Engel, Marian 1933-1985......... CLC 36
    See also CA 25-28R; CANR 12; DLB 53;
    INT CANR-12

Engelhardt, Frederick
    See Hubbard, L(afayette) Ron(ald)

Enright, D(ennis) J(oseph)
    1920- .... CLC 4, 8, 31
    See also CA 1-4R; CANR 1, 42; DLB 27;
    SATA 25

Enzensberger, Hans Magnus
    1929- .... CLC 43
    See also CA 116; 119

Ephron, Nora 1941- .... CLC 17, 31
    See also AITN 2; CA 65-68; CANR 12, 39

Epicurus 341B.C.-270B.C. .... CMLC 21

Epsilon
    See Betjeman, John

Epstein, Daniel Mark 1948- .... CLC 7
    See also CA 49-52; CANR 2, 53

Epstein, Jacob 1956- .... CLC 19
    See also CA 114

Epstein, Joseph 1937-............ CLC 39
    See also CA 112; 119; CANR 50

Epstein, Leslie 1938- .... CLC 27
    See also CA 73-76; CAAS 12; CANR 23

Equiano, Olaudah
    1745(?)-1797 .... LC 16; BLC;
                                    DAM MULT
    See also DLB 37, 50

Erasmus, Desiderius 1469(?)-1536.... LC 16

Erdman, Paul E(mil) 1932- .... CLC 25
    See also AITN 1; CA 61-64; CANR 13, 43

Erdrich, Louise
    1954- .... CLC 39, 54; DAM MULT,
                                    NOV, POP
    See also AAYA 10; BEST 89:1; CA 114;
    CANR 41; DLB 152, 175; MTCW;
    NNAL

Erenburg, Ilya (Grigoryevich)
    See Ehrenburg, Ilya (Grigoryevich)

Erickson, Stephen Michael 1950-
    See Erickson, Steve
    See also CA 129

Erickson, Steve .... CLC 64
    See also Erickson, Stephen Michael

Ericson, Walter
    See Fast, Howard (Melvin)

Eriksson, Buntel
    See Bergman, (Ernst) Ingmar

Ernaux, Annie 1940- .... CLC 88
    See also CA 147

Eschenbach, Wolfram von
    See Wolfram von Eschenbach

Eseki, Bruno
    See Mphahlele, Ezekiel

Esenin, Sergei (Alexandrovich)
    1895-1925 .... TCLC 4
    See also CA 104

Eshleman, Clayton 1935-.......... CLC 7
    See also CA 33-36R; CAAS 6; DLB 5

Espriella, Don Manuel Alvarez
    See Southey, Robert

Espriu, Salvador 1913-1985........ CLC 9
    See also CA 154; 115; DLB 134

Espronceda, Jose de 1808-1842... NCLC 39

Esse, James
    See Stephens, James

Esterbrook, Tom
    See Hubbard, L(afayette) Ron(ald)

Estleman, Loren D.
    1952- ...... CLC 48; DAM NOV, POP
    See also CA 85-88; CANR 27;
    INT CANR-27; MTCW

Eugenides, Jeffrey 1960(?)- .... CLC 81
    See also CA 144

Euripides c. 485B.C.-406B.C. .... DC 4
    See also DA; DAB; DAC; DAM DRAM,
    MST

Evan, Evin
    See Faust, Frederick (Schiller)

Evans, Evan
    See Faust, Frederick (Schiller)

Evans, Marian
    See Eliot, George

Evans, Mary Ann
    See Eliot, George

Evarts, Esther
    See Benson, Sally

Everett, Percival L. 1956- .... CLC 57
    See also BW 2; CA 129

Everson, R(onald) G(ilmour)
    1903- .... CLC 27
    See also CA 17-20R; DLB 88

Everson, William (Oliver)
    1912-1994 .... CLC 1, 5, 14
    See also CA 9-12R; 145; CANR 20; DLB 5,
    16; MTCW

Evtushenko, Evgenii Aleksandrovich
    See Yevtushenko, Yevgeny (Alexandrovich)

Ewart, Gavin (Buchanan)
    1916-1995 .... CLC 13, 46
    See also CA 89-92; 150; CANR 17, 46;
    DLB 40; MTCW

Ewers, Hanns Heinz 1871-1943 ... TCLC 12
    See also CA 109; 149

Ewing, Frederick R.
    See Sturgeon, Theodore (Hamilton)

Exley, Frederick (Earl)
    1929-1992 .... CLC 6, 11
    See also AITN 2; CA 81-84; 138; DLB 143;
    DLBY 81

Eynhardt, Guillermo
    See Quiroga, Horacio (Sylvestre)

Ezekiel, Nissim 1924-............. CLC 61
    See also CA 61-64

Ezekiel, Tish O'Dowd 1943-....... CLC 34
    See also CA 129

Fadeyev, A.
    See Bulgya, Alexander Alexandrovich

Fadeyev, Alexander............... TCLC 53
    See also Bulgya, Alexander Alexandrovich

Fagen, Donald 1948-............. CLC 26

Fainzilberg, Ilya Arnoldovich 1897-1937
    See Ilf, Ilya
    See also CA 120

Fair, Ronald L. 1932-............. CLC 18
    See also BW 1; CA 69-72; CANR 25;
    DLB 33

Fairbairns, Zoe (Ann) 1948- .... CLC 32
    See also CA 103; CANR 21

Falco, Gian
    See Papini, Giovanni

Falconer, James
    See Kirkup, James

Falconer, Kenneth
    See Kornbluth, C(yril) M.

Falkland, Samuel
    See Heijermans, Herman

Fallaci, Oriana 1930-............. CLC 11
    See also CA 77-80; CANR 15; MTCW

Faludy, George 1913-............. CLC 42
    See also CA 21-24R

Faludy, Gyoergy
    See Faludy, George

Fanon, Frantz
    1925-1961 .... CLC 74; BLC;
                                    DAM MULT
    See also BW 1; CA 116; 89-92

Fanshawe, Ann 1625-1680......... LC 11

Fante, John (Thomas) 1911-1983 ... CLC 60
    See also CA 69-72; 109; CANR 23;
    DLB 130; DLBY 83

Farah, Nuruddin
    1945- ..... CLC 53; BLC; DAM MULT
    See also BW 2; CA 106; DLB 125

Fargue, Leon-Paul 1876(?)-1947 ... TCLC 11
    See also CA 109

Farigoule, Louis
    See Romains, Jules

Farina, Richard 1936(?)-1966 .... CLC 9
    See also CA 81-84; 25-28R

Farley, Walter (Lorimer)
    1915-1989 .... CLC 17
    See also CA 17-20R; CANR 8, 29; DLB 22;
    JRDA; MAICYA; SATA 2, 43

Farmer, Philip Jose 1918-........ CLC 1, 19
    See also CA 1-4R; CANR 4, 35; DLB 8;
    MTCW

Farquhar, George
    1677-1707 .... LC 21; DAM DRAM
    See also DLB 84

Farrell, J(ames) G(ordon)
    1935-1979 .... CLC 6
    See also CA 73-76; 89-92; CANR 36;
    DLB 14; MTCW

Farrell, James T(homas)
    1904-1979 .... CLC 1, 4, 8, 11, 66
    See also CA 5-8R; 89-92; CANR 9; DLB 4,
    9, 86; DLBD 2; MTCW

Farren, Richard J.
    See Betjeman, John

Farren, Richard M.
    See Betjeman, John

Fassbinder, Rainer Werner
　1946-1982 . . . . **CLC 20**
　See also CA 93-96; 106; CANR 31

Fast, Howard (Melvin)
　1914- . . . . **CLC 23; DAM NOV**
　See also AAYA 16; CA 1-4R; CAAS 18;
　　CANR 1, 33, 54; DLB 9; INT CANR-33;
　　SATA 7

Faulcon, Robert
　See Holdstock, Robert P.

Faulkner, William (Cuthbert)
　1897-1962 . . . . . **CLC 1, 3, 6, 8, 9, 11, 14,**
　　18, 28, 52, 68; DA; DAB; DAC;
　　DAM MST, NOV; SSC 1; WLC
　See also AAYA 7; CA 81-84; CANR 33;
　　CDALB 1929-1941; DLB 9, 11, 44, 102;
　　DLBD 2; DLBY 86; MTCW

Fauset, Jessie Redmon
　1884(?)-1961 . . . . **CLC 19, 54; BLC;**
　　DAM MULT
　See also BW 1; CA 109; DLB 51

Faust, Frederick (Schiller)
　1892-1944(?) . . . . . **TCLC 49; DAM POP**
　See also CA 108; 152

Faust, Irvin　1924- . . . . **CLC 8**
　See also CA 33-36R; CANR 28; DLB 2, 28;
　　DLBY 80

Fawkes, Guy
　See Benchley, Robert (Charles)

Fearing, Kenneth (Flexner)
　1902-1961 . . . . **CLC 51**
　See also CA 93-96; DLB 9

Fecamps, Elise
　See Creasey, John

Federman, Raymond　1928- . . . . . . **CLC 6, 47**
　See also CA 17-20R; CAAS 8; CANR 10,
　　43; DLBY 80

Federspiel, J(uerg) F.　1931- . . . . **CLC 42**
　See also CA 146

Feiffer, Jules (Ralph)
　1929- . . . . . . **CLC 2, 8, 64; DAM DRAM**
　See also AAYA 3; CA 17-20R; CANR 30;
　　DLB 7, 44; INT CANR-30; MTCW;
　　SATA 8, 61

Feige, Hermann Albert Otto Maximilian
　See Traven, B.

Feinberg, David B.　1956-1994 . . . . . **CLC 59**
　See also CA 135; 147

Feinstein, Elaine　1930- . . . . **CLC 36**
　See also CA 69-72; CAAS 1; CANR 31;
　　DLB 14, 40; MTCW

Feldman, Irving (Mordecai)　1928- . . . . **CLC 7**
　See also CA 1-4R; CANR 1; DLB 169

Fellini, Federico　1920-1993 . . . . . **CLC 16, 85**
　See also CA 65-68; 143; CANR 33

Felsen, Henry Gregor　1916- . . . . **CLC 17**
　See also CA 1-4R; CANR 1; SAAS 2;
　　SATA 1

Fenton, James Martin　1949- . . . . **CLC 32**
　See also CA 102; DLB 40

Ferber, Edna　1887-1968 . . . . **CLC 18, 93**
　See also AITN 1; CA 5-8R; 25-28R; DLB 9,
　　28, 86; MTCW; SATA 7

Ferguson, Helen
　See Kavan, Anna

Ferguson, Samuel　1810-1886 . . . . . **NCLC 33**
　See also DLB 32

Fergusson, Robert　1750-1774 . . . . **LC 29**
　See also DLB 109

Ferling, Lawrence
　See Ferlinghetti, Lawrence (Monsanto)

Ferlinghetti, Lawrence (Monsanto)
　1919(?)- . . . . **CLC 2, 6, 10, 27;**
　　DAM POET; PC 1
　See also CA 5-8R; CANR 3, 41;
　　CDALB 1941-1968; DLB 5, 16; MTCW

Fernandez, Vicente Garcia Huidobro
　See Huidobro Fernandez, Vicente Garcia

Ferrer, Gabriel (Francisco Victor) Miro
　See Miro (Ferrer), Gabriel (Francisco
　　Victor)

Ferrier, Susan (Edmonstone)
　1782-1854 . . . . **NCLC 8**
　See also DLB 116

Ferrigno, Robert　1948(?)- . . . . **CLC 65**
　See also CA 140

Ferron, Jacques　1921-1985 . . . **CLC 94; DAC**
　See also CA 117; 129; DLB 60

Feuchtwanger, Lion　1884-1958 . . . . . **TCLC 3**
　See also CA 104; DLB 66

Feuillet, Octave　1821-1890 . . . . . . **NCLC 45**

Feydeau, Georges (Leon Jules Marie)
　1862-1921 . . . . . **TCLC 22; DAM DRAM**
　See also CA 113; 152

Ficino, Marsilio　1433-1499 . . . . **LC 12**

Fiedeler, Hans
　See Doeblin, Alfred

Fiedler, Leslie A(aron)
　1917- . . . . **CLC 4, 13, 24**
　See also CA 9-12R; CANR 7; DLB 28, 67;
　　MTCW

Field, Andrew　1938- . . . . **CLC 44**
　See also CA 97-100; CANR 25

Field, Eugene　1850-1895 . . . . **NCLC 3**
　See also DLB 23, 42, 140; DLBD 13;
　　MAICYA; SATA 16

Field, Gans T.
　See Wellman, Manly Wade

Field, Michael . . . . **TCLC 43**

Field, Peter
　See Hobson, Laura Z(ametkin)

Fielding, Henry
　1707-1754 . . . . . . **LC 1; DA; DAB; DAC;**
　　DAM DRAM, MST, NOV; WLC
　See also CDBLB 1660-1789; DLB 39, 84,
　　101

Fielding, Sarah　1710-1768 . . . . **LC 1**
　See also DLB 39

Fierstein, Harvey (Forbes)
　1954- . . . . . **CLC 33; DAM DRAM, POP**
　See also CA 123; 129

Figes, Eva　1932- . . . . **CLC 31**
　See also CA 53-56; CANR 4, 44; DLB 14

Finch, Robert (Duer Claydon)
　1900- . . . . **CLC 18**
　See also CA 57-60; CANR 9, 24, 49;
　　DLB 88

Findley, Timothy
　1930- . . . . . . **CLC 27; DAC; DAM MST**
　See also CA 25-28R; CANR 12, 42;
　　DLB 53

Fink, William
　See Mencken, H(enry) L(ouis)

Firbank, Louis　1942-
　See Reed, Lou
　See also CA 117

Firbank, (Arthur Annesley) Ronald
　1886-1926 . . . . **TCLC 1**
　See also CA 104; DLB 36

Fisher, M(ary) F(rances) K(ennedy)
　1908-1992 . . . . **CLC 76, 87**
　See also CA 77-80; 138; CANR 44

Fisher, Roy　1930- . . . . **CLC 25**
　See also CA 81-84; CAAS 10; CANR 16;
　　DLB 40

Fisher, Rudolph
　1897-1934 . . . . **TCLC 11; BLC;**
　　DAM MULT
　See also BW 1; CA 107; 124; DLB 51, 102

Fisher, Vardis (Alvero)　1895-1968 . . . . **CLC 7**
　See also CA 5-8R; 25-28R; DLB 9

Fiske, Tarleton
　See Bloch, Robert (Albert)

Fitch, Clarke
　See Sinclair, Upton (Beall)

Fitch, John IV
　See Cormier, Robert (Edmund)

Fitzgerald, Captain Hugh
　See Baum, L(yman) Frank

FitzGerald, Edward　1809-1883 . . . . **NCLC 9**
　See also DLB 32

Fitzgerald, F(rancis) Scott (Key)
　1896-1940 . . . . **TCLC 1, 6, 14, 28, 55;**
　　DA; DAB; DAC; DAM MST, NOV;
　　SSC 6; WLC
　See also AITN 1; CA 110; 123;
　　CDALB 1917-1929; DLB 4, 9, 86;
　　DLBD 1; DLBY 81; MTCW

Fitzgerald, Penelope　1916- . . . **CLC 19, 51, 61**
　See also CA 85-88; CAAS 10; CANR 56;
　　DLB 14

Fitzgerald, Robert (Stuart)
　1910-1985 . . . . **CLC 39**
　See also CA 1-4R; 114; CANR 1; DLBY 80

FitzGerald, Robert D(avid)
　1902-1987 . . . . **CLC 19**
　See also CA 17-20R

Fitzgerald, Zelda (Sayre)
　1900-1948 . . . . **TCLC 52**
　See also CA 117; 126; DLBY 84

Flanagan, Thomas (James Bonner)
　1923- . . . . **CLC 25, 52**
　See also CA 108; CANR 55; DLBY 80;
　　INT 108; MTCW

Flaubert, Gustave
　1821-1880 . . . . **NCLC 2, 10, 19; DA;**
　　DAB; DAC; DAM MST, NOV; SSC 11;
　　WLC
　See also DLB 119

Flecker, Herman Elroy
　See Flecker, (Herman) James Elroy

Fredro, Aleksander 1793-1876..... NCLC 8

Freeling, Nicolas 1927- .... CLC 38
See also CA 49-52; CAAS 12; CANR 1, 17,
50; DLB 87

Freeman, Douglas Southall
1886-1953 .... TCLC 11
See also CA 109; DLB 17

Freeman, Judith 1946- .... CLC 55
See also CA 148

Freeman, Mary Eleanor Wilkins
1852-1930 .... TCLC 9; SSC 1
See also CA 106; DLB 12, 78

Freeman, R(ichard) Austin
1862-1943 .... TCLC 21
See also CA 113; DLB 70

French, Albert 1943- .... CLC 86

French, Marilyn
1929- .... CLC 10, 18, 60;
DAM DRAM, NOV, POP
See also CA 69-72; CANR 3, 31;
INT CANR-31; MTCW

French, Paul
See Asimov, Isaac

Freneau, Philip Morin 1752-1832.. NCLC 1
See also DLB 37, 43

Freud, Sigmund 1856-1939 .... TCLC 52
See also CA 115; 133; MTCW

Friedan, Betty (Naomi) 1921- ...... CLC 74
See also CA 65-68; CANR 18, 45; MTCW

Friedlander, Saul 1932- .... CLC 90
See also CA 117; 130

Friedman, B(ernard) H(arper)
1926- .... CLC 7
See also CA 1-4R; CANR 3, 48

Friedman, Bruce Jay 1930- .... CLC 3, 5, 56
See also CA 9-12R; CANR 25, 52; DLB 2,
28; INT CANR-25

Friel, Brian 1929- .... CLC 5, 42, 59
See also CA 21-24R; CANR 33; DLB 13;
MTCW

Friis-Baastad, Babbis Ellinor
1921-1970 .... CLC 12
See also CA 17-20R; 134; SATA 7

Frisch, Max (Rudolf)
1911-1991 ..... CLC 3, 9, 14, 18, 32, 44;
DAM DRAM, NOV
See also CA 85-88; 134; CANR 32;
DLB 69, 124; MTCW

Fromentin, Eugene (Samuel Auguste)
1820-1876 .... NCLC 10
See also DLB 123

Frost, Frederick
See Faust, Frederick (Schiller)

Frost, Robert (Lee)
1874-1963 .... CLC 1, 3, 4, 9, 10, 13, 15,
26, 34, 44; DA; DAB; DAC; DAM MST,
POET; PC 1; WLC
See also CA 89-92; CANR 33;
CDALB 1917-1929; DLB 54; DLBD 7;
MTCW; SATA 14

Froude, James Anthony
1818-1894 .... NCLC 43
See also DLB 18, 57, 144

Froy, Herald
See Waterhouse, Keith (Spencer)

Fry, Christopher
1907- ..... CLC 2, 10, 14; DAM DRAM
See also CA 17-20R; CAAS 23; CANR 9,
30; DLB 13; MTCW; SATA 66

Frye, (Herman) Northrop
1912-1991 .... CLC 24, 70
See also CA 5-8R; 133; CANR 8, 37;
DLB 67, 68; MTCW

Fuchs, Daniel 1909-1993 .... CLC 8, 22
See also CA 81-84; 142; CAAS 5;
CANR 40; DLB 9, 26, 28; DLBY 93

Fuchs, Daniel 1934- .... CLC 34
See also CA 37-40R; CANR 14, 48

Fuentes, Carlos
1928- ...... CLC 3, 8, 10, 13, 22, 41, 60;
DA; DAB; DAC; DAM MST, MULT,
NOV; HLC; SSC 24; WLC
See also AAYA 4; AITN 2; CA 69-72;
CANR 10, 32; DLB 113; HW; MTCW

Fuentes, Gregorio Lopez y
See Lopez y Fuentes, Gregorio

Fugard, (Harold) Athol
1932- .... CLC 5, 9, 14, 25, 40, 80;
DAM DRAM; DC 3
See also AAYA 17; CA 85-88; CANR 32,
54; MTCW

Fugard, Sheila 1932- .... CLC 48
See also CA 125

Fuller, Charles (H., Jr.)
1939- .... CLC 25; BLC; DAM DRAM,
MULT; DC 1
See also BW 2; CA 108; 112; DLB 38;
INT 112; MTCW

Fuller, John (Leopold) 1937- .... CLC 62
See also CA 21-24R; CANR 9, 44; DLB 40

Fuller, Margaret .... NCLC 5, 50
See also Ossoli, Sarah Margaret (Fuller
marchesa d')

Fuller, Roy (Broadbent)
1912-1991 .... CLC 4, 28
See also CA 5-8R; 135; CAAS 10;
CANR 53; DLB 15, 20; SATA 87

Fulton, Alice 1952- .... CLC 52
See also CA 116; CANR 57

Furphy, Joseph 1843-1912........ TCLC 25

Fussell, Paul 1924- .... CLC 74
See also BEST 90:1; CA 17-20R; CANR 8,
21, 35; INT CANR-21; MTCW

Futabatei, Shimei 1864-1909 ...... TCLC 44

Futrelle, Jacques 1875-1912 ...... TCLC 19
See also CA 113; 155

Gaboriau, Emile 1835-1873 ...... NCLC 14

Gadda, Carlo Emilio 1893-1973 .... CLC 11
See also CA 89-92

Gaddis, William
1922- ..... CLC 1, 3, 6, 8, 10, 19, 43, 86
See also CA 17-20R; CANR 21, 48; DLB 2;
MTCW

Gage, Walter
See Inge, William (Motter)

Gaines, Ernest J(ames)
1933- .... CLC 3, 11, 18, 86; BLC;
DAM MULT
See also AAYA 18; AITN 1; BW 2;
CA 9-12R; CANR 6, 24, 42;
CDALB 1968-1988; DLB 2, 33, 152;
DLBY 80; MTCW; SATA 86

Gaitskill, Mary 1954- .... CLC 69
See also CA 128

Galdos, Benito Perez
See Perez Galdos, Benito

Gale, Zona
1874-1938 ...... TCLC 7; DAM DRAM
See also CA 105; 153; DLB 9, 78

Galeano, Eduardo (Hughes) 1940-... CLC 72
See also CA 29-32R; CANR 13, 32; HW

Galiano, Juan Valera y Alcala
See Valera y Alcala-Galiano, Juan

Gallagher, Tess
1943- .. CLC 18, 63; DAM POET; PC 9
See also CA 106; DLB 120

Gallant, Mavis
1922- .... CLC 7, 18, 38; DAC;
DAM MST; SSC 5
See also CA 69-72; CANR 29; DLB 53;
MTCW

Gallant, Roy A(rthur) 1924- .... CLC 17
See also CA 5-8R; CANR 4, 29, 54;
CLR 30; MAICYA; SATA 4, 68

Gallico, Paul (William) 1897-1976 ... CLC 2
See also AITN 1; CA 5-8R; 69-72;
CANR 23; DLB 9, 171; MAICYA;
SATA 13

Gallo, Max Louis 1932-........... CLC 95
See also CA 85-88

Gallois, Lucien
See Desnos, Robert

Gallup, Ralph
See Whitemore, Hugh (John)

Galsworthy, John
1867-1933 ...... TCLC 1, 45; DA; DAB;
DAC; DAM DRAM, MST, NOV;
SSC 22; WLC 2
See also CA 104; 141; CDBLB 1890-1914;
DLB 10, 34, 98, 162

Galt, John 1779-1839 .... NCLC 1
See also DLB 99, 116, 159

Galvin, James 1951-............. CLC 38
See also CA 108; CANR 26

Gamboa, Federico 1864-1939...... TCLC 36

Gandhi, M. K.
See Gandhi, Mohandas Karamchand

Gandhi, Mahatma
See Gandhi, Mohandas Karamchand

Gandhi, Mohandas Karamchand
1869-1948 ..... TCLC 59; DAM MULT
See also CA 121; 132; MTCW

Gann, Ernest Kellogg 1910-1991.... CLC 23
See also AITN 1; CA 1-4R; 136; CANR 1

Garcia, Cristina 1958- .... CLC 76
See also CA 141

Gide, Andre (Paul Guillaume)
1869-1951 . . . . TCLC 5, 12, 36; DA;
DAB; DAC; DAM MST, NOV; SSC 13;
WLC
See also CA 104; 124; DLB 65; MTCW

Gifford, Barry (Colby) 1946- . . . . CLC 34
See also CA 65-68; CANR 9, 30, 40

Gilbert, W(illiam) S(chwenck)
1836-1911 . . . . . TCLC 3; DAM DRAM,
POET
See also CA 104; SATA 36

Gilbreth, Frank B., Jr. 1911- . . . . CLC 17
See also CA 9-12R; SATA 2

Gilchrist, Ellen
1935- . . . . CLC 34, 48; DAM POP;
SSC 14
See also CA 113; 116; CANR 41; DLB 130;
MTCW

Giles, Molly 1942- . . . . CLC 39
See also CA 126

Gill, Patrick
See Creasey, John

Gilliam, Terry (Vance) 1940- . . . . CLC 21
See also Monty Python
See also AAYA 19; CA 108; 113;
CANR 35; INT 113

Gillian, Jerry
See Gilliam, Terry (Vance)

Gilliatt, Penelope (Ann Douglass)
1932-1993 . . . . CLC 2, 10, 13, 53
See also AITN 2; CA 13-16R; 141;
CANR 49; DLB 14

Gilman, Charlotte (Anna) Perkins (Stetson)
1860-1935 . . . . TCLC 9, 37; SSC 13
See also CA 106; 150

Gilmour, David 1949- . . . . CLC 35
See also CA 138, 147

Gilpin, William 1724-1804 . . . . NCLC 30

Gilray, J. D.
See Mencken, H(enry) L(ouis)

Gilroy, Frank D(aniel) 1925- . . . . CLC 2
See also CA 81-84; CANR 32; DLB 7

Gilstrap, John 1957(?)- . . . . CLC 99

Ginsberg, Allen
1926- . . . . . . CLC 1, 2, 3, 4, 6, 13, 36, 69;
DA; DAB; DAC; DAM MST, POET;
PC 4; WLC 3
See also AITN 1; CA 1-4R; CANR 2, 41;
CDALB 1941-1968; DLB 5, 16, 169;
MTCW

Ginzburg, Natalia
1916-1991 . . . . CLC 5, 11, 54, 70
See also CA 85-88; 135; CANR 33; MTCW

Giono, Jean 1895-1970 . . . . CLC 4, 11
See also CA 45-48; 29-32R; CANR 2, 35;
DLB 72; MTCW

Giovanni, Nikki
1943- . . . . . . CLC 2, 4, 19, 64; BLC; DA;
DAB; DAC; DAM MST, MULT, POET
See also AITN 1; BW 2; CA 29-32R;
CAAS 6; CANR 18, 41; CLR 6; DLB 5,
41; INT CANR-18; MAICYA; MTCW;
SATA 24

Giovene, Andrea 1904- . . . . CLC 7
See also CA 85-88

Gippius, Zinaida (Nikolayevna) 1869-1945
See Hippius, Zinaida
See also CA 106

Giraudoux, (Hippolyte) Jean
1882-1944 . . . . TCLC 2, 7; DAM DRAM
See also CA 104; DLB 65

Gironella, Jose Maria 1917- . . . . CLC 11
See also CA 101

Gissing, George (Robert)
1857-1903 . . . . TCLC 3, 24, 47
See also CA 105; DLB 18, 135

Giurlani, Aldo
See Palazzeschi, Aldo

Gladkov, Fyodor (Vasilyevich)
1883-1958 . . . . TCLC 27

Glanville, Brian (Lester) 1931- . . . . . . CLC 6
See also CA 5-8R; CAAS 9; CANR 3;
DLB 15, 139; SATA 42

Glasgow, Ellen (Anderson Gholson)
1873(?)-1945 . . . . TCLC 2, 7
See also CA 104; DLB 9, 12

Glaspell, Susan 1882(?)-1948 . . . . . TCLC 55
See also CA 110; 154; DLB 7, 9, 78;
YABC 2

Glassco, John 1909-1981 . . . . CLC 9
See also CA 13-16R; 102; CANR 15;
DLB 68

Glasscock, Amnesia
See Steinbeck, John (Ernst)

Glasser, Ronald J. 1940(?)- . . . . CLC 37

Glassman, Joyce
See Johnson, Joyce

Glendinning, Victoria 1937- . . . . CLC 50
See also CA 120; 127; DLB 155

Glissant, Edouard
1928- . . . . CLC 10, 68; DAM MULT
See also CA 153

Gloag, Julian 1930- . . . . CLC 40
See also AITN 1; CA 65-68; CANR 10

Glowacki, Aleksander
See Prus, Boleslaw

Gluck, Louise (Elisabeth)
1943- . . . . CLC 7, 22, 44, 81;
DAM POET; PC 16
See also CA 33-36R; CANR 40; DLB 5

Gobineau, Joseph Arthur (Comte) de
1816-1882 . . . . NCLC 17
See also DLB 123

Godard, Jean-Luc 1930- . . . . CLC 20
See also CA 93-96

Godden, (Margaret) Rumer 1907- . . . CLC 53
See also AAYA 6; CA 5-8R; CANR 4, 27,
36, 55; CLR 20; DLB 161; MAICYA;
SAAS 12; SATA 3, 36

Godoy Alcayaga, Lucila 1889-1957
See Mistral, Gabriela
See also BW 2; CA 104; 131; DAM MULT;
HW; MTCW

Godwin, Gail (Kathleen)
1937- . . . . CLC 5, 8, 22, 31, 69;
DAM POP
See also CA 29-32R; CANR 15, 43; DLB 6;
INT CANR-15; MTCW

Godwin, William 1756-1836 . . . . . . NCLC 14
See also CDBLB 1789-1832; DLB 39, 104,
142, 158, 163

Goebbels, Josef
See Goebbels, (Paul) Joseph

Goebbels, (Paul) Joseph
1897-1945 . . . . TCLC 68
See also CA 115; 148

Goebbels, Joseph Paul
See Goebbels, (Paul) Joseph

Goethe, Johann Wolfgang von
1749-1832 . . . . . NCLC 4, 22, 34; DA;
DAB; DAC; DAM DRAM, MST,
POET; PC 5; WLC 3
See also DLB 94

Gogarty, Oliver St. John
1878-1957 . . . . TCLC 15
See also CA 109; 150; DLB 15, 19

Gogol, Nikolai (Vasilyevich)
1809-1852 . . . . NCLC 5, 15, 31; DA;
DAB; DAC; DAM DRAM, MST; DC 1;
SSC 4; WLC
See also CA 9-12R; CANR 17, 45; DLB 2;
DLBY 81

Goines, Donald
1937(?)-1974 . . . . CLC 80; BLC;
DAM MULT, POP
See also AITN 1; BW 1; CA 124; 114;
DLB 33

Gold, Herbert 1924- . . . . CLC 4, 7, 14, 42
See also CA 9-12R; CANR 17, 45; DLB 2;
DLBY 81

Goldbarth, Albert 1948- . . . . CLC 5, 38
See also CA 53-56; CANR 6, 40; DLB 120

Goldberg, Anatol 1910-1982 . . . . CLC 34
See also CA 131; 117

Goldemberg, Isaac 1945- . . . . CLC 52
See also CA 69-72; CAAS 12; CANR 11,
32; HW

Golding, William (Gerald)
1911-1993 . . . . CLC 1, 2, 3, 8, 10, 17, 27,
58, 81; DA; DAB; DAC; DAM MST,
NOV; WLC
See also AAYA 5; CA 5-8R; 141;
CANR 13, 33, 54; CDBLB 1945-1960;
DLB 15, 100; MTCW

Goldman, Emma 1869-1940 . . . . . . TCLC 13
See also CA 110; 150

Goldman, Francisco 1955- . . . . CLC 76

Goldman, William (W.) 1931- . . . . CLC 1, 48
See also CA 9-12R; CANR 29; DLB 44

Goldmann, Lucien 1913-1970 . . . . . . CLC 24
See also CA 25-28; CAP 2

Goldoni, Carlo
1707-1793 . . . . LC 4; DAM DRAM

Goldsberry, Steven 1949- . . . . CLC 34
See also CA 131

Goldsmith, Oliver
1728-1774 . . . . . . LC 2; DA; DAB; DAC;
DAM DRAM, MST, NOV, POET;
WLC
See also CDBLB 1660-1789; DLB 39, 89,
104, 109, 142; SATA 26

Goldsmith, Peter
See Priestley, J(ohn) B(oynton)

Gombrowicz, Witold
1904-1969 . . . . **CLC 4, 7, 11, 49;**
DAM DRAM
See also CA 19-20; 25-28R; CAP 2

Gomez de la Serna, Ramon
1888-1963 . . . . **CLC 9**
See also CA 153; 116; HW

Goncharov, Ivan Alexandrovich
1812-1891 . . . . **NCLC 1**

Goncourt, Edmond (Louis Antoine Huot) de
1822-1896 . . . . **NCLC 7**
See also DLB 123

Goncourt, Jules (Alfred Huot) de
1830-1870 . . . . **NCLC 7**
See also DLB 123

Gontier, Fernande 19(?)- . . . . **CLC 50**

Goodman, Paul 1911-1972. . . . **CLC 1, 2, 4, 7**
See also CA 19-20; 37-40R; CANR 34;
CAP 2; DLB 130; MTCW

Gordimer, Nadine
1923- . . . . **CLC 3, 5, 7, 10, 18, 33, 51, 70;**
DA; DAB; DAC; DAM MST, NOV;
SSC 17
See also CA 5-8R; CANR 3, 28, 56;
INT CANR-28; MTCW

Gordon, Adam Lindsay
1833-1870 . . . . **NCLC 21**

Gordon, Caroline
1895-1981 . . . **CLC 6, 13, 29, 83; SSC 15**
See also CA 11-12; 103; CANR 36; CAP 1;
DLB 4, 9, 102; DLBY 81; MTCW

Gordon, Charles William 1860-1937
See Connor, Ralph
See also CA 109

Gordon, Mary (Catherine)
1949- . . . . **CLC 13, 22**
See also CA 102; CANR 44; DLB 6;
DLBY 81; INT 102; MTCW

Gordon, Sol 1923- . . . . **CLC 26**
See also CA 53-56; CANR 4; SATA 11

Gordone, Charles
1925-1995 . . . . . **CLC 1, 4; DAM DRAM**
See also BW 1; CA 93-96; 150; CANR 55;
DLB 7; INT 93-96; MTCW

Gorenko, Anna Andreevna
See Akhmatova, Anna

Gorky, Maxim . . . . **TCLC 8; DAB; WLC**
See also Peshkov, Alexei Maximovich

Goryan, Sirak
See Saroyan, William

Gosse, Edmund (William)
1849-1928 . . . . **TCLC 28**
See also CA 117; DLB 57, 144

Gotlieb, Phyllis Fay (Bloom)
1926- . . . . **CLC 18**
See also CA 13-16R; CANR 7; DLB 88

Gottesman, S. D.
See Kornbluth, C(yril) M.; Pohl, Frederik

Gottfried von Strassburg
fl. c. 1210- . . . . **CMLC 10**
See also DLB 138

Gould, Lois . . . . **CLC 4, 10**
See also CA 77-80; CANR 29; MTCW

Gourmont, Remy (-Marie-Charles) de
1858-1915 . . . . **TCLC 17**
See also CA 109; 150

Govier, Katherine 1948-. . . . . **CLC 51**
See also CA 101; CANR 18, 40

Goyen, (Charles) William
1915-1983 . . . . **CLC 5, 8, 14, 40**
See also AITN 2; CA 5-8R; 110; CANR 6;
DLB 2; DLBY 83; INT CANR-6

Goytisolo, Juan
1931- . . . . . **CLC 5, 10, 23; DAM MULT;**
HLC
See also CA 85-88; CANR 32; HW; MTCW

Gozzano, Guido 1883-1916 . . . . **PC 10**
See also CA 154; DLB 114

Gozzi, (Conte) Carlo 1720-1806 . . **NCLC 23**

Grabbe, Christian Dietrich
1801-1836 . . . . **NCLC 2**
See also DLB 133

Grace, Patricia 1937-. . . . . **CLC 56**

Gracian y Morales, Baltasar
1601-1658 . . . . **LC 15**

Gracq, Julien. . . . . **CLC 11, 48**
See also Poirier, Louis
See also DLB 83

Grade, Chaim 1910-1982 . . . . **CLC 10**
See also CA 93-96; 107

Graduate of Oxford, A
See Ruskin, John

Graham, John
See Phillips, David Graham

Graham, Jorie 1951-. . . . . **CLC 48**
See also CA 111; DLB 120

Graham, R(obert) B(ontine) Cunninghame
See Cunninghame Graham, R(obert)
B(ontine)
See also DLB 98, 135, 174

Graham, Robert
See Haldeman, Joe (William)

Graham, Tom
See Lewis, (Harry) Sinclair

Graham, W(illiam) S(ydney)
1918-1986 . . . . **CLC 29**
See also CA 73-76; 118; DLB 20

Graham, Winston (Mawdsley)
1910- . . . . **CLC 23**
See also CA 49-52; CANR 2, 22, 45;
DLB 77

Grahame, Kenneth
1859-1932 . . . . **TCLC 64; DAB**
See also CA 108; 136; CLR 5; DLB 34, 141;
MAICYA; YABC 1

Grant, Skeeter
See Spiegelman, Art

Granville-Barker, Harley
1877-1946 . . . . . . **TCLC 2; DAM DRAM**
See also Barker, Harley Granville
See also CA 104

Grass, Guenter (Wilhelm)
1927- . . . . . **CLC 1, 2, 4, 6, 11, 15, 22, 32,**
49, 88; DA; DAB; DAC; DAM MST,
NOV; WLC
See also CA 13-16R; CANR 20; DLB 75,
124; MTCW

Gratton, Thomas
See Hulme, T(homas) E(rnest)

Grau, Shirley Ann
1929- . . . . **CLC 4, 9; SSC 15**
See also CA 89-92; CANR 22; DLB 2;
INT CANR-22; MTCW

Gravel, Fern
See Hall, James Norman

Graver, Elizabeth 1964-. . . . . **CLC 70**
See also CA 135

Graves, Richard Perceval 1945- . . . . **CLC 44**
See also CA 65-68; CANR 9, 26, 51

Graves, Robert (von Ranke)
1895-1985 . . . . . . **CLC 1, 2, 6, 11, 39, 44,**
45; DAB; DAC; DAM MST, POET;
PC 6
See also CA 5-8R; 117; CANR 5, 36;
CDBLB 1914-1945; DLB 20, 100;
DLBY 85; MTCW; SATA 45

Graves, Valerie
See Bradley, Marion Zimmer

Gray, Alasdair (James) 1934- . . . . . . **CLC 41**
See also CA 126; CANR 47; INT 126;
MTCW

Gray, Amlin 1946- . . . . **CLC 29**
See also CA 138

Gray, Francine du Plessix
1930- . . . . **CLC 22; DAM NOV**
See also BEST 90:3; CA 61-64; CAAS 2;
CANR 11, 33; INT CANR-11; MTCW

Gray, John (Henry) 1866-1934 . . . . **TCLC 19**
See also CA 119

Gray, Simon (James Holliday)
1936- . . . . **CLC 9, 14, 36**
See also AITN 1; CA 21-24R; CAAS 3;
CANR 32; DLB 13; MTCW

Gray, Spalding 1941-. . **CLC 49; DAM POP**
See also CA 128

Gray, Thomas
1716-1771 . . . . . . **LC 4; DA; DAB; DAC;**
DAM MST; PC 2; WLC
See also CDBLB 1660-1789; DLB 109

Grayson, David
See Baker, Ray Stannard

Grayson, Richard (A.) 1951-. . . . . . . **CLC 38**
See also CA 85-88; CANR 14, 31, 57

Greeley, Andrew M(oran)
1928- . . . . **CLC 28; DAM POP**
See also CA 5-8R; CAAS 7; CANR 7, 43;
MTCW

Green, Anna Katharine
1846-1935 . . . . **TCLC 63**
See also CA 112

Green, Brian
See Card, Orson Scott

Green, Hannah
See Greenberg, Joanne (Goldenberg)

Green, Hannah . . . . **CLC 3**
See also CA 73-76

Green, Henry 1905-1973 . . . . . **CLC 2, 13, 97**
See also Yorke, Henry Vincent
See also DLB 15

Green, Julian (Hartridge)   1900-
See Green, Julien
See also CA 21-24R; CANR 33; DLB 4, 72;
MTCW

Green, Julien . . . . CLC 3, 11, 77
See also Green, Julian (Hartridge)

Green, Paul (Eliot)
1894-1981 . . . . . . CLC 25; DAM DRAM
See also AITN 1; CA 5-8R; 103; CANR 3;
DLB 7, 9; DLBY 81

Greenberg, Ivan   1908-1973
See Rahv, Philip
See also CA 85-88

Greenberg, Joanne (Goldenberg)
1932- . . . . CLC 7, 30
See also AAYA 12; CA 5-8R; CANR 14,
32; SATA 25

Greenberg, Richard   1959(?)- . . . . CLC 57
See also CA 138

Greene, Bette   1934- . . . . CLC 30
See also AAYA 7; CA 53-56; CANR 4;
CLR 2; JRDA; MAICYA; SAAS 16;
SATA 8

Greene, Gael . . . . CLC 8
See also CA 13-16R; CANR 10

Greene, Graham
1904-1991 . . . . CLC 1, 3, 6, 9, 14, 18, 27,
37, 70, 72; DA; DAB; DAC; DAM MST,
NOV; WLC
See also AITN 2; CA 13-16R; 133;
CANR 35; CDBLB 1945-1960; DLB 13,
15, 77, 100, 162; DLBY 91; MTCW;
SATA 20

Greer, Richard
See Silverberg, Robert

Gregor, Arthur   1923- . . . . CLC 9
See also CA 25-28R; CAAS 10; CANR 11;
SATA 36

Gregor, Lee
See Pohl, Frederik

Gregory, Isabella Augusta (Persse)
1852-1932 . . . . TCLC 1
See also CA 104; DLB 10

Gregory, J. Dennis
See Williams, John A(lfred)

Grendon, Stephen
See Derleth, August (William)

Grenville, Kate   1950- . . . . CLC 61
See also CA 118; CANR 53

Grenville, Pelham
See Wodehouse, P(elham) G(renville)

Greve, Felix Paul (Berthold Friedrich)
1879-1948
See Grove, Frederick Philip
See also CA 104; 141; DAC; DAM MST

Grey, Zane
1872-1939 . . . . TCLC 6; DAM POP
See also CA 104; 132; DLB 9; MTCW

Grieg, (Johan) Nordahl (Brun)
1902-1943 . . . . TCLC 10
See also CA 107

Grieve, C(hristopher) M(urray)
1892-1978 . . . . CLC 11, 19; DAM POET
See also MacDiarmid, Hugh; Pteleon
See also CA 5-8R; 85-88; CANR 33;
MTCW

Griffin, Gerald   1803-1840 . . . . NCLC 7
See also DLB 159

Griffin, John Howard   1920-1980. . . . CLC 68
See also AITN 1; CA 1-4R; 101; CANR 2

Griffin, Peter   1942- . . . . CLC 39
See also CA 136

Griffith, D(avid Lewelyn) W(ark)
1875(?)-1948 . . . . TCLC 68
See also CA 119; 150

Griffith, Lawrence
See Griffith, D(avid Lewelyn) W(ark)

Griffiths, Trevor   1935- . . . . CLC 13, 52
See also CA 97-100; CANR 45; DLB 13

Grigson, Geoffrey (Edward Harvey)
1905-1985 . . . . CLC 7, 39
See also CA 25-28R; 118; CANR 20, 33;
DLB 27; MTCW

Grillparzer, Franz   1791-1872. . . . . . NCLC 1
See also DLB 133

Grimble, Reverend Charles James
See Eliot, T(homas) S(tearns)

Grimke, Charlotte L(ottie) Forten
1837(?)-1914
See Forten, Charlotte L.
See also BW 1; CA 117; 124; DAM MULT,
POET

Grimm, Jacob Ludwig Karl
1785-1863 . . . . NCLC 3
See also DLB 90; MAICYA; SATA 22

Grimm, Wilhelm Karl   1786-1859 . . NCLC 3
See also DLB 90; MAICYA; SATA 22

Grimmelshausen, Johann Jakob Christoffel
von   1621-1676 . . . . LC 6
See also DLB 168

Grindel, Eugene   1895-1952
See Eluard, Paul
See also CA 104

Grisham, John   1955- . . CLC 84; DAM POP
See also AAYA 14; CA 138; CANR 47

Grossman, David   1954- . . . . CLC 67
See also CA 138

Grossman, Vasily (Semenovich)
1905-1964 . . . . CLC 41
See also CA 124; 130; MTCW

Grove, Frederick Philip . . . . TCLC 4
See also Greve, Felix Paul (Berthold
Friedrich)
See also DLB 92

Grubb
See Crumb, R(obert)

Grumbach, Doris (Isaac)
1918- . . . . CLC 13, 22, 64
See also CA 5-8R; CAAS 2; CANR 9, 42;
INT CANR-9

Grundtvig, Nicolai Frederik Severin
1783-1872 . . . . NCLC 1

Grunge
See Crumb, R(obert)

Grunwald, Lisa   1959- . . . . CLC 44
See also CA 120

Guare, John
1938- . . . . CLC 8, 14, 29, 67;
DAM DRAM
See also CA 73-76; CANR 21; DLB 7;
MTCW

Gudjonsson, Halldor Kiljan   1902-
See Laxness, Halldor
See also CA 103

Guenter, Erich
See Eich, Guenter

Guest, Barbara   1920- . . . . CLC 34
See also CA 25-28R; CANR 11, 44; DLB 5

Guest, Judith (Ann)
1936- . . . . CLC 8, 30; DAM NOV, POP
See also AAYA 7; CA 77-80; CANR 15;
INT CANR-15; MTCW

Guevara, Che . . . . CLC 87; HLC
See also Guevara (Serna), Ernesto

Guevara (Serna), Ernesto   1928-1967
See Guevara, Che
See also CA 127; 111; CANR 56;
DAM MULT; HW

Guild, Nicholas M.   1944- . . . . CLC 33
See also CA 93-96

Guillemin, Jacques
See Sartre, Jean-Paul

Guillen, Jorge
1893-1984 . . . . . . CLC 11; DAM MULT,
POET
See also CA 89-92; 112; DLB 108; HW

Guillen, Nicolas (Cristobal)
1902-1989 . . . . CLC 48, 79; BLC;
DAM MST, MULT, POET; HLC
See also BW 2; CA 116; 125; 129; HW

Guillevic, (Eugene)   1907- . . . . CLC 33
See also CA 93-96

Guillois
See Desnos, Robert

Guillois, Valentin
See Desnos, Robert

Guiney, Louise Imogen
1861-1920 . . . . TCLC 41
See also DLB 54

Guiraldes, Ricardo (Guillermo)
1886-1927 . . . . TCLC 39
See also CA 131; HW; MTCW

Gumilev, Nikolai Stephanovich
1886-1921 . . . . TCLC 60

Gunesekera, Romesh . . . . CLC 91

Gunn, Bill . . . . CLC 5
See also Gunn, William Harrison
See also DLB 38

Gunn, Thom(son William)
1929- . . . . CLC 3, 6, 18, 32, 81;
DAM POET
See also CA 17-20R; CANR 9, 33;
CDBLB 1960 to Present; DLB 27;
INT CANR-33; MTCW

Gunn, William Harrison   1934(?)-1989
See Gunn, Bill
See also AITN 1; BW 1; CA 13-16R; 128;
CANR 12, 25

Gunnars, Kristjana   1948- . . . . CLC 69
See also CA 113; DLB 60

Gurganus, Allan
1947- . . . . CLC 70; DAM POP
See also BEST 90:1; CA 135

Gurney, A(lbert) R(amsdell), Jr.
1930- . . . . CLC 32, 50, 54; DAM DRAM
See also CA 77-80; CANR 32

Gurney, Ivor (Bertie) 1890-1937 . . . **TCLC 33**

Gurney, Peter
　See Gurney, A(lbert) R(amsdell), Jr.

Guro, Elena 1877-1913 . . . . **TCLC 56**

Gustafson, Ralph (Barker) 1909-. . . . **CLC 36**
　See also CA 21-24R; CANR 8, 45; DLB 88

Gut, Gom
　See Simenon, Georges (Jacques Christian)

Guterson, David 1956-. . . . . **CLC 91**
　See also CA 132

Guthrie, A(lfred) B(ertram), Jr.
　1901-1991 . . . . **CLC 23**
　See also CA 57-60; 134; CANR 24; DLB 6;
　SATA 62; SATA-Obit 67

Guthrie, Isobel
　See Grieve, C(hristopher) M(urray)

Guthrie, Woodrow Wilson 1912-1967
　See Guthrie, Woody
　See also CA 113; 93-96

Guthrie, Woody. . . . . **CLC 35**
　See also Guthrie, Woodrow Wilson

Guy, Rosa (Cuthbert) 1928-. . . . . **CLC 26**
　See also AAYA 4; BW 2; CA 17-20R;
　CANR 14, 34; CLR 13; DLB 33; JRDA;
　MAICYA; SATA 14, 62

Gwendolyn
　See Bennett, (Enoch) Arnold

H. D. . . . . **CLC 3, 8, 14, 31, 34, 73; PC 5**
　See also Doolittle, Hilda

H. de V.
　See Buchan, John

Haavikko, Paavo Juhani
　1931- . . . . **CLC 18, 34**
　See also CA 106

Habbema, Koos
　See Heijermans, Herman

Hacker, Marilyn
　1942- . . . . **CLC 5, 9, 23, 72, 91;**
　　　　　　　　　　　　　　　　DAM POET
　See also CA 77-80; DLB 120

Haggard, H(enry) Rider
　1856-1925 . . . . **TCLC 11**
　See also CA 108; 148; DLB 70, 156, 174;
　SATA 16

Hagiosy, L.
　See Larbaud, Valery (Nicolas)

Hagiwara Sakutaro 1886-1942 . . . . **TCLC 60**

Haig, Fenil
　See Ford, Ford Madox

Haig-Brown, Roderick (Langmere)
　1908-1976 . . . . **CLC 21**
　See also CA 5-8R; 69-72; CANR 4, 38;
　CLR 31; DLB 88; MAICYA; SATA 12

Hailey, Arthur
　1920- . . . . **CLC 5; DAM NOV, POP**
　See also AITN 2; BEST 90:3; CA 1-4R;
　CANR 2, 36; DLB 88; DLBY 82; MTCW

Hailey, Elizabeth Forsythe 1938-. . . **CLC 40**
　See also CA 93-96; CAAS 1; CANR 15, 48;
　INT CANR-15

Haines, John (Meade) 1924-. . . . . . . **CLC 58**
　See also CA 17-20R; CANR 13, 34; DLB 5

Hakluyt, Richard 155?-1616 . . . . **LC 31**

Haldeman, Joe (William) 1943-. . . . . **CLC 61**
　See also CA 53-56; CAAS 25; CANR 6;
　DLB 8; INT CANR-6

Haley, Alex(ander Murray Palmer)
　1921-1992 . . . . **CLC 8, 12, 76; BLC; DA;**
　　　DAB; DAC; DAM MST, MULT, POP
　See also BW 2; CA 77-80; 136; DLB 38;
　MTCW

Haliburton, Thomas Chandler
　1796-1865 . . . . **NCLC 15**
　See also DLB 11, 99

Hall, Donald (Andrew, Jr.)
　1928- . . **CLC 1, 13, 37, 59; DAM POET**
　See also CA 5-8R; CAAS 7; CANR 2, 44;
　DLB 5; SATA 23

Hall, Frederic Sauser
　See Sauser-Hall, Frederic

Hall, James
　See Kuttner, Henry

Hall, James Norman 1887-1951 . . . **TCLC 23**
　See also CA 123; SATA 21

Hall, (Marguerite) Radclyffe
　1886-1943 . . . . **TCLC 12**
　See also CA 110; 150

Hall, Rodney 1935- . . . . **CLC 51**
　See also CA 109

Halleck, Fitz-Greene 1790-1867 . . **NCLC 47**
　See also DLB 3

Halliday, Michael
　See Creasey, John

Halpern, Daniel 1945- . . . . **CLC 14**
　See also CA 33-36R

Hamburger, Michael (Peter Leopold)
　1924- . . . . **CLC 5, 14**
　See also CA 5-8R; CAAS 4; CANR 2, 47;
　DLB 27

Hamill, Pete 1935- . . . . **CLC 10**
　See also CA 25-28R; CANR 18

Hamilton, Alexander
　1755(?)-1804 . . . . **NCLC 49**
　See also DLB 37

Hamilton, Clive
　See Lewis, C(live) S(taples)

Hamilton, Edmond 1904-1977 . . . . . . **CLC 1**
　See also CA 1-4R; CANR 3; DLB 8

Hamilton, Eugene (Jacob) Lee
　See Lee-Hamilton, Eugene (Jacob)

Hamilton, Franklin
　See Silverberg, Robert

Hamilton, Gail
　See Corcoran, Barbara

Hamilton, Mollie
　See Kaye, M(ary) M(argaret)

Hamilton, (Anthony Walter) Patrick
　1904-1962 . . . . **CLC 51**
　See also CA 113; DLB 10

Hamilton, Virginia
　1936- . . . . **CLC 26; DAM MULT**
　See also AAYA 2; BW 2; CA 25-28R;
　CANR 20, 37; CLR 1, 11, 40; DLB 33,
　52; INT CANR-20; JRDA; MAICYA;
　MTCW; SATA 4, 56, 79

Hammett, (Samuel) Dashiell
　1894-1961 . . . . **CLC 3, 5, 10, 19, 47;**
　　　　　　　　　　　　　　　　　　　SSC 17
　See also AITN 1; CA 81-84; CANR 42;
　CDALB 1929-1941; DLBD 6; MTCW

Hammon, Jupiter
　1711(?)-1800(?) . . . . **NCLC 5; BLC;**
　　　　　　　　　DAM MULT, POET; PC 16
　See also DLB 31, 50

Hammond, Keith
　See Kuttner, Henry

Hamner, Earl (Henry), Jr. 1923- . . . **CLC 12**
　See also AITN 2; CA 73-76; DLB 6

Hampton, Christopher (James)
　1946- . . . . **CLC 4**
　See also CA 25-28R; DLB 13; MTCW

Hamsun, Knut . . . . **TCLC 2, 14, 49**
　See also Pedersen, Knut

Handke, Peter
　1942- . . . . **CLC 5, 8, 10, 15, 38;**
　　　　　　　　　　　　　　DAM DRAM, NOV
　See also CA 77-80; CANR 33; DLB 85,
　124; MTCW

Hanley, James 1901-1985 . . . **CLC 3, 5, 8, 13**
　See also CA 73-76; 117; CANR 36; MTCW

Hannah, Barry 1942-. . . . . . **CLC 23, 38, 90**
　See also CA 108; 110; CANR 43; DLB 6;
　INT 110; MTCW

Hannon, Ezra
　See Hunter, Evan

Hansberry, Lorraine (Vivian)
　1930-1965 . . . . . . **CLC 17, 62; BLC; DA;**
　　　　　　DAB; DAC; DAM DRAM, MST,
　　　　　　　　　　　　　　　MULT; DC 2
　See also BW 1; CA 109; 25-28R; CABS 3;
　CDALB 1941-1968; DLB 7, 38; MTCW

Hansen, Joseph 1923-. . . . . **CLC 38**
　See also CA 29-32R; CAAS 17; CANR 16,
　44; INT CANR-16

Hansen, Martin A. 1909-1955. . . . . **TCLC 32**

Hanson, Kenneth O(stlin) 1922- . . . . **CLC 13**
　See also CA 53-56; CANR 7

Hardwick, Elizabeth
　1916- . . . . **CLC 13; DAM NOV**
　See also CA 5-8R; CANR 3, 32; DLB 6;
　MTCW

Hardy, Thomas
　1840-1928 . . . . . . **TCLC 4, 10, 18, 32, 48,**
　　　53; DA; DAB; DAC; DAM MST, NOV,
　　　　　　　POET; PC 8; SSC 2; WLC
　See also CA 104; 123; CDBLB 1890-1914;
　DLB 18, 19, 135; MTCW

Hare, David 1947- . . . . **CLC 29, 58**
　See also CA 97-100; CANR 39; DLB 13;
　MTCW

Harford, Henry
　See Hudson, W(illiam) H(enry)

Hargrave, Leonie
　See Disch, Thomas M(ichael)

Harjo, Joy 1951- . . . **CLC 83; DAM MULT**
　See also CA 114; CANR 35; DLB 120, 175;
　NNAL

Harlan, Louis R(udolph) 1922- . . . . . **CLC 34**
　See also CA 21-24R; CANR 25, 55

Harling, Robert 1951(?)- · · · · · · · · · **CLC 53**
See also CA 147

Harmon, William (Ruth) 1938- · · · · · **CLC 38**
See also CA 33-36R; CANR 14, 32, 35;
SATA 65

Harper, F. E. W.
See Harper, Frances Ellen Watkins

Harper, Frances E. W.
See Harper, Frances Ellen Watkins

Harper, Frances E. Watkins
See Harper, Frances Ellen Watkins

Harper, Frances Ellen
See Harper, Frances Ellen Watkins

Harper, Frances Ellen Watkins
1825-1911 · · · · · · · · · · · **TCLC 14; BLC;**
DAM MULT, POET
See also BW 1; CA 111; 125; DLB 50

Harper, Michael S(teven) 1938- · · **CLC 7, 22**
See also BW 1; CA 33-36R; CANR 24;
DLB 41

Harper, Mrs. F. E. W.
See Harper, Frances Ellen Watkins

Harris, Christie (Lucy) Irwin
1907- · · · · · · · · · · · · · · · · · · **CLC 12**
See also CA 5-8R; CANR 6; DLB 88;
JRDA; MAICYA; SAAS 10; SATA 6, 74

Harris, Frank 1856-1931 · · · · · · · · **TCLC 24**
See also CA 109; 150; DLB 156

Harris, George Washington
1814-1869 · · · · · · · · · · · · · · · **NCLC 23**
See also DLB 3, 11

Harris, Joel Chandler
1848-1908 · · · · · · · · · · **TCLC 2; SSC 19**
See also CA 104; 137; DLB 11, 23, 42, 78,
91; MAICYA; YABC 1

Harris, John (Wyndham Parkes Lucas)
Beynon 1903-1969
See Wyndham, John
See also CA 102; 89-92

Harris, MacDonald · · · · · · · · · · · · · · · **CLC 9**
See also Heiney, Donald (William)

Harris, Mark 1922- · · · · · · · · · · · · · **CLC 19**
See also CA 5-8R; CAAS 3; CANR 2, 55;
DLB 2; DLBY 80

Harris, (Theodore) Wilson 1921- · · · · **CLC 25**
See also BW 2; CA 65-68; CAAS 16;
CANR 11, 27; DLB 117; MTCW

Harrison, Elizabeth Cavanna 1909-
See Cavanna, Betty
See also CA 9-12R; CANR 6, 27

Harrison, Harry (Max) 1925- · · · · · · **CLC 42**
See also CA 1-4R; CANR 5, 21; DLB 8;
SATA 4

Harrison, James (Thomas)
1937- · · · · · · · **CLC 6, 14, 33, 66; SSC 19**
See also CA 13-16R; CANR 8, 51;
DLBY 82; INT CANR-8

Harrison, Jim
See Harrison, James (Thomas)

Harrison, Kathryn 1961- · · · · · · · · · **CLC 70**
See also CA 144

Harrison, Tony 1937- · · · · · · · · · · · **CLC 43**
See also CA 65-68; CANR 44; DLB 40;
MTCW

Harriss, Will(ard Irvin) 1922- · · · · · · **CLC 34**
See also CA 111

Harson, Sley
See Ellison, Harlan (Jay)

Hart, Ellis
See Ellison, Harlan (Jay)

Hart, Josephine
1942(?)- · · · · · · · · · **CLC 70; DAM POP**
See also CA 138

Hart, Moss
1904-1961 · · · · · · **CLC 66; DAM DRAM**
See also CA 109; 89-92; DLB 7

Harte, (Francis) Bret(t)
1836(?)-1902 · · · · **TCLC 1, 25; DA; DAC;**
DAM MST; SSC 8; WLC
See also CA 104; 140; CDALB 1865-1917;
DLB 12, 64, 74, 79; SATA 26

Hartley, L(eslie) P(oles)
1895-1972 · · · · · · · · · · · · · · · **CLC 2, 22**
See also CA 45-48; 37-40R; CANR 33;
DLB 15, 139; MTCW

Hartman, Geoffrey H. 1929- · · · · · · · **CLC 27**
See also CA 117; 125; DLB 67

Hartmann von Aue
c. 1160-c. 1205 · · · · · · · · · · · · **CMLC 15**
See also DLB 138

Hartmann von Aue 1170-1210 · · · · **CMLC 15**

Haruf, Kent 1943- · · · · · · · · · · · · · **CLC 34**
See also CA 149

Harwood, Ronald
1934- · · · · **CLC 32; DAM DRAM, MST**
See also CA 1-4R; CANR 4, 55; DLB 13

Hasek, Jaroslav (Matej Frantisek)
1883-1923 · · · · · · · · · · · · · · · · **TCLC 4**
See also CA 104; 129; MTCW

Hass, Robert
1941- · · · · · · · · · **CLC 18, 39, 99; PC 16**
See also CA 111; CANR 30, 50; DLB 105

Hastings, Hudson
See Kuttner, Henry

Hastings, Selina · · · · · · · · · · · · · · · · **CLC 44**

Hatteras, Amelia
See Mencken, H(enry) L(ouis)

Hatteras, Owen · · · · · · · · · · · · · · · · **TCLC 18**
See also Mencken, H(enry) L(ouis); Nathan,
George Jean

Hauptmann, Gerhart (Johann Robert)
1862-1946 · · · · · · **TCLC 4; DAM DRAM**
See also CA 104; 153; DLB 66, 118

Havel, Vaclav
1936- · · · · · · · · · · · · · · · **CLC 25, 58, 65;**
DAM DRAM; DC 6
See also CA 104; CANR 36; MTCW

Haviaras, Stratis · · · · · · · · · · · · · · · · **CLC 33**
See also Chaviaras, Strates

Hawes, Stephen 1475(?)-1523(?) · · · · · **LC 17**

Hawkes, John (Clendennin Burne, Jr.)
1925- · · · · · · **CLC 1, 2, 3, 4, 7, 9, 14, 15,**
27, 49
See also CA 1-4R; CANR 2, 47; DLB 2, 7;
DLBY 80; MTCW

Hawking, S. W.
See Hawking, Stephen W(illiam)

Hawking, Stephen W(illiam)
1942- · · · · · · · · · · · · · · · · · · · **CLC 63**
See also AAYA 13; BEST 89:1; CA 126;
129; CANR 48

Hawthorne, Julian 1846-1934 · · · · · **TCLC 25**

Hawthorne, Nathaniel
1804-1864 · · · · · · · **NCLC 39; DA; DAB;**
DAC; DAM MST, NOV; SSC 3; WLC
See also AAYA 18; CDALB 1640-1865;
DLB 1, 74; YABC 2

Haxton, Josephine Ayres 1921-
See Douglas, Ellen
See also CA 115; CANR 41

Hayaseca y Eizaguirre, Jorge
See Echegaray (y Eizaguirre), Jose (Maria
Waldo)

Hayashi Fumiko 1904-1951 · · · · · · **TCLC 27**

Haycraft, Anna
See Ellis, Alice Thomas
See also CA 122

Hayden, Robert E(arl)
1913-1980 · · · · · · **CLC 5, 9, 14, 37; BLC;**
DA; DAC; DAM MST, MULT, POET;
PC 6
See also BW 1; CA 69-72; 97-100; CABS 2;
CANR 24; CDALB 1941-1968; DLB 5,
76; MTCW; SATA 19; SATA-Obit 26

Hayford, J(oseph) E(phraim) Casely
See Casely-Hayford, J(oseph) E(phraim)

Hayman, Ronald 1932- · · · · · · · · · · · **CLC 44**
See also CA 25-28R; CANR 18, 50;
DLB 155

Haywood, Eliza (Fowler)
1693(?)-1756 · · · · · · · · · · · · · · · · · **LC 1**

Hazlitt, William 1778-1830 · · · · · · **NCLC 29**
See also DLB 110, 158

Hazzard, Shirley 1931- · · · · · · · · · · · **CLC 18**
See also CA 9-12R; CANR 4; DLBY 82;
MTCW

Head, Bessie
1937-1986 · · · · · · · · · **CLC 25, 67; BLC;**
DAM MULT
See also BW 2; CA 29-32R; 119; CANR 25;
DLB 117; MTCW

Headon, (Nicky) Topper 1956(?)- · · · **CLC 30**

Heaney, Seamus (Justin)
1939- · · · · · · **CLC 5, 7, 14, 25, 37, 74, 91;**
DAB; DAM POET
See also CA 85-88; CANR 25, 48;
CDBLB 1960 to Present; DLB 40;
DLBY 95; MTCW

Hearn, (Patricio) Lafcadio (Tessima Carlos)
1850-1904 · · · · · · · · · · · · · · · · · **TCLC 9**
See also CA 105; DLB 12, 78

Hearne, Vicki 1946- · · · · · · · · · · · · · **CLC 56**
See also CA 139

Hearon, Shelby 1931- · · · · · · · · · · · · **CLC 63**
See also AITN 2; CA 25-28R; CANR 18,
48

Heat-Moon, William Least · · · · · · · · · **CLC 29**
See also Trogdon, William (Lewis)
See also AAYA 9

Hebbel, Friedrich
1813-1863 · · · · **NCLC 43; DAM DRAM**
See also DLB 129

Hichens, Robert S. 1864-1950 . . . . . **TCLC 64**
See also DLB 153

Higgins, George V(incent)
1939- . . . . **CLC 4, 7, 10, 18**
See also CA 77-80; CAAS 5; CANR 17, 51;
DLB 2; DLBY 81; INT CANR-17;
MTCW

Higginson, Thomas Wentworth
1823-1911 . . . . **TCLC 36**
See also DLB 1, 64

Highet, Helen
See MacInnes, Helen (Clark)

Highsmith, (Mary) Patricia
1921-1995 . . . . **CLC 2, 4, 14, 42;**
                    DAM NOV, POP
See also CA 1-4R; 147; CANR 1, 20, 48;
MTCW

Highwater, Jamake (Mamake)
1942(?)- . . . . **CLC 12**
See also AAYA 7; CA 65-68; CAAS 7;
CANR 10, 34; CLR 17; DLB 52;
DLBY 85; JRDA; MAICYA; SATA 32,
69; SATA-Brief 30

Highway, Tomson
1951- . . . . . **CLC 92; DAC; DAM MULT**
See also CA 151; NNAL

Higuchi, Ichiyo 1872-1896 . . . . **NCLC 49**

Hijuelos, Oscar
1951- . . . . **CLC 65; DAM MULT, POP;**
                             HLC
See also BEST 90:1; CA 123; CANR 50;
DLB 145; HW

Hikmet, Nazim 1902(?)-1963 . . . . **CLC 40**
See also CA 141; 93-96

Hildegard von Bingen
1098-1179 . . . . **CMLC 20**
See also DLB 148

Hildesheimer, Wolfgang
1916-1991 . . . . **CLC 49**
See also CA 101; 135; DLB 69, 124

Hill, Geoffrey (William)
1932- . . . **CLC 5, 8, 18, 45; DAM POET**
See also CA 81-84; CANR 21;
CDBLB 1960 to Present; DLB 40;
MTCW

Hill, George Roy 1921- . . . . **CLC 26**
See also CA 110; 122

Hill, John
See Koontz, Dean R(ay)

Hill, Susan (Elizabeth)
1942- . . **CLC 4; DAB; DAM MST, NOV**
See also CA 33-36R; CANR 29; DLB 14,
139; MTCW

Hillerman, Tony
1925- . . . . **CLC 62; DAM POP**
See also AAYA 6; BEST 89:1; CA 29-32R;
CANR 21, 42; SATA 6

Hillesum, Etty 1914-1943 . . . . **TCLC 49**
See also CA 137

Hilliard, Noel (Harvey) 1929- . . . . . **CLC 15**
See also CA 9-12R; CANR 7

Hillis, Rick 1956- . . . . **CLC 66**
See also CA 134

Hilton, James 1900-1954 . . . . **TCLC 21**
See also CA 108; DLB 34, 77; SATA 34

Himes, Chester (Bomar)
1909-1984 . . . . **CLC 2, 4, 7, 18, 58; BLC;**
                        DAM MULT
See also BW 2; CA 25-28R; 114; CANR 22;
DLB 2, 76, 143; MTCW

Hinde, Thomas . . . . **CLC 6, 11**
See also Chitty, Thomas Willes

Hindin, Nathan
See Bloch, Robert (Albert)

Hine, (William) Daryl 1936- . . . . **CLC 15**
See also CA 1-4R; CAAS 15; CANR 1, 20;
DLB 60

Hinkson, Katharine Tynan
See Tynan, Katharine

Hinton, S(usan) E(loise)
1950- . . . . **CLC 30; DA; DAB; DAC;**
                    DAM MST, NOV
See also AAYA 2; CA 81-84; CANR 32;
CLR 3, 23; JRDA; MAICYA; MTCW;
SATA 19, 58

Hippius, Zinaida . . . . **TCLC 9**
See also Gippius, Zinaida (Nikolayevna)

Hiraoka, Kimitake 1925-1970
See Mishima, Yukio
See also CA 97-100; 29-32R; DAM DRAM;
MTCW

Hirsch, E(ric) D(onald), Jr. 1928- . . . **CLC 79**
See also CA 25-28R; CANR 27, 51;
DLB 67; INT CANR-27; MTCW

Hirsch, Edward 1950- . . . . **CLC 31, 50**
See also CA 104; CANR 20, 42; DLB 120

Hitchcock, Alfred (Joseph)
1899-1980 . . . . **CLC 16**
See also CA 97-100; SATA 27;
SATA-Obit 24

Hitler, Adolf 1889-1945 . . . . **TCLC 53**
See also CA 117; 147

Hoagland, Edward 1932- . . . . **CLC 28**
See also CA 1-4R; CANR 2, 31, 57; DLB 6;
SATA 51

Hoban, Russell (Conwell)
1925- . . . . **CLC 7, 25; DAM NOV**
See also CA 5-8R; CANR 23, 37; CLR 3;
DLB 52; MAICYA; MTCW; SATA 1,
40, 78

Hobbes, Thomas 1588-1679 . . . . **LC 36**
See also DLB 151

Hobbs, Perry
See Blackmur, R(ichard) P(almer)

Hobson, Laura Z(ametkin)
1900-1986 . . . . **CLC 7, 25**
See also CA 17-20R; 118; CANR 55;
DLB 28; SATA 52

Hochhuth, Rolf
1931- . . . . . **CLC 4, 11, 18; DAM DRAM**
See also CA 5-8R; CANR 33; DLB 124;
MTCW

Hochman, Sandra 1936- . . . . **CLC 3, 8**
See also CA 5-8R; DLB 5

Hochwaelder, Fritz
1911-1986 . . . . . . **CLC 36; DAM DRAM**
See also CA 29-32R; 120; CANR 42;
MTCW

Hochwalder, Fritz
See Hochwaelder, Fritz

Hocking, Mary (Eunice) 1921- . . . . . . **CLC 13**
See also CA 101; CANR 18, 40

Hodgins, Jack 1938- . . . . **CLC 23**
See also CA 93-96; DLB 60

Hodgson, William Hope
1877(?)-1918 . . . . **TCLC 13**
See also CA 111; DLB 70, 153, 156

Hoeg, Peter 1957- . . . . **CLC 95**
See also CA 151

Hoffman, Alice
1952- . . . . **CLC 51; DAM NOV**
See also CA 77-80; CANR 34; MTCW

Hoffman, Daniel (Gerard)
1923- . . . . **CLC 6, 13, 23**
See also CA 1-4R; CANR 4; DLB 5

Hoffman, Stanley 1944- . . . . **CLC 5**
See also CA 77-80

Hoffman, William M(oses) 1939- . . . **CLC 40**
See also CA 57-60; CANR 11

Hoffmann, E(rnst) T(heodor) A(madeus)
1776-1822 . . . . **NCLC 2; SSC 13**
See also DLB 90; SATA 27

Hofmann, Gert 1931- . . . . **CLC 54**
See also CA 128

Hofmannsthal, Hugo von
1874-1929 . . . . **TCLC 11; DAM DRAM;**
                           DC 4
See also CA 106; 153; DLB 81, 118

Hogan, Linda
1947- . . . . **CLC 73; DAM MULT**
See also CA 120; CANR 45; DLB 175;
NNAL

Hogarth, Charles
See Creasey, John

Hogarth, Emmett
See Polonsky, Abraham (Lincoln)

Hogg, James 1770-1835 . . . . **NCLC 4**
See also DLB 93, 116, 159

Holbach, Paul Henri Thiry Baron
1723-1789 . . . . **LC 14**

Holberg, Ludvig 1684-1754 . . . . **LC 6**

Holden, Ursula 1921- . . . . **CLC 18**
See also CA 101; CAAS 8; CANR 22

Holderlin, (Johann Christian) Friedrich
1770-1843 . . . . **NCLC 16; PC 4**

Holdstock, Robert
See Holdstock, Robert P.

Holdstock, Robert P. 1948- . . . . **CLC 39**
See also CA 131

Holland, Isabelle 1920- . . . . **CLC 21**
See also AAYA 11; CA 21-24R; CANR 10,
25, 47; JRDA; MAICYA; SATA 8, 70

Holland, Marcus
See Caldwell, (Janet Miriam) Taylor
(Holland)

Hollander, John 1929- . . . . . . **CLC 2, 5, 8, 14**
See also CA 1-4R; CANR 1, 52; DLB 5;
SATA 13

Hollander, Paul
See Silverberg, Robert

Holleran, Andrew 1943(?)- . . . . **CLC 38**
See also CA 144

Hollinghurst, Alan 1954- . . . . **CLC 55, 91**
See also CA 114

Hollis, Jim
See Summers, Hollis (Spurgeon, Jr.)

Holly, Buddy 1936-1959 . . . . **TCLC 65**

Holmes, John
See Souster, (Holmes) Raymond

Holmes, John Clellon 1926-1988. . . . **CLC 56**
See also CA 9-12R; 125; CANR 4; DLB 16

Holmes, Oliver Wendell
1809-1894 . . . . **NCLC 14**
See also CDALB 1640-1865; DLB 1;
SATA 34

Holmes, Raymond
See Souster, (Holmes) Raymond

Holt, Victoria
See Hibbert, Eleanor Alice Burford

Holub, Miroslav 1923- . . . . **CLC 4**
See also CA 21-24R; CANR 10

Homer
c. 8th cent. B.C.- . . . . **CMLC 1, 16; DA;**
DAB; DAC; DAM MST, POET

Honig, Edwin 1919- . . . . **CLC 33**
See also CA 5-8R; CAAS 8; CANR 4, 45;
DLB 5

Hood, Hugh (John Blagdon)
1928- . . . . **CLC 15, 28**
See also CA 49-52; CAAS 17; CANR 1, 33;
DLB 53

Hood, Thomas 1799-1845 . . . . **NCLC 16**
See also DLB 96

Hooker, (Peter) Jeremy 1941- . . . . . . **CLC 43**
See also CA 77-80; CANR 22; DLB 40

hooks, bell . . . . **CLC 94**
See also Watkins, Gloria

Hope, A(lec) D(erwent) 1907- . . . . **CLC 3, 51**
See also CA 21-24R; CANR 33; MTCW

Hope, Brian
See Creasey, John

Hope, Christopher (David Tully)
1944- . . . . **CLC 52**
See also CA 106; CANR 47; SATA 62

Hopkins, Gerard Manley
1844-1889 . . . . **NCLC 17; DA; DAB;**
DAC; DAM MST, POET; PC 15; WLC
See also CDBLB 1890-1914; DLB 35, 57

Hopkins, John (Richard) 1931- . . . . . . **CLC 4**
See also CA 85-88

Hopkins, Pauline Elizabeth
1859-1930 . . . . **TCLC 28; BLC;**
DAM MULT
See also BW 2; CA 141; DLB 50

Hopkinson, Francis 1737-1791 . . . . . . **LC 25**
See also DLB 31

Hopley-Woolrich, Cornell George 1903-1968
See Woolrich, Cornell
See also CA 13-14; CAP 1

Horatio
See Proust, (Valentin-Louis-George-Eugene-)
Marcel

Horgan, Paul (George Vincent O'Shaughnessy)
1903-1995 . . . . . . **CLC 9, 53; DAM NOV**
See also CA 13-16R; 147; CANR 9, 35;
DLB 102; DLBY 85; INT CANR-9;
MTCW; SATA 13; SATA-Obit 84

Horn, Peter
See Kuttner, Henry

Hornem, Horace Esq.
See Byron, George Gordon (Noel)

Hornung, E(rnest) W(illiam)
1866-1921 . . . . **TCLC 59**
See also CA 108; DLB 70

Horovitz, Israel (Arthur)
1939- . . . . **CLC 56; DAM DRAM**
See also CA 33-36R; CANR 46; DLB 7

Horvath, Odon von
See Horvath, Oedoen von
See also DLB 85, 124

Horvath, Oedoen von 1901-1938. . . **TCLC 45**
See also Horvath, Odon von
See also CA 118

Horwitz, Julius 1920-1986 . . . . **CLC 14**
See also CA 9-12R; 119; CANR 12

Hospital, Janette Turner 1942- . . . . . **CLC 42**
See also CA 108; CANR 48

Hostos, E. M. de
See Hostos (y Bonilla), Eugenio Maria de

Hostos, Eugenio M. de
See Hostos (y Bonilla), Eugenio Maria de

Hostos, Eugenio Maria
See Hostos (y Bonilla), Eugenio Maria de

Hostos (y Bonilla), Eugenio Maria de
1839-1903 . . . . **TCLC 24**
See also CA 123; 131; HW

Houdini
See Lovecraft, H(oward) P(hillips)

Hougan, Carolyn 1943- . . . . **CLC 34**
See also CA 139

Household, Geoffrey (Edward West)
1900-1988 . . . . **CLC 11**
See also CA 77-80; 126; DLB 87; SATA 14;
SATA-Obit 59

Housman, A(lfred) E(dward)
1859-1936 . . . . . . **TCLC 1, 10; DA; DAB;**
DAC; DAM MST, POET; PC 2
See also CA 104; 125; DLB 19; MTCW

Housman, Laurence 1865-1959 . . . . . **TCLC 7**
See also CA 106; 155; DLB 10; SATA 25

Howard, Elizabeth Jane 1923- . . . **CLC 7, 29**
See also CA 5-8R; CANR 8

Howard, Maureen 1930- . . . . . **CLC 5, 14, 46**
See also CA 53-56; CANR 31; DLBY 83;
INT CANR-31; MTCW

Howard, Richard 1929- . . . . . . **CLC 7, 10, 47**
See also AITN 1; CA 85-88; CANR 25;
DLB 5; INT CANR-25

Howard, Robert Ervin 1906-1936 . . . **TCLC 8**
See also CA 105

Howard, Warren F.
See Pohl, Frederik

Howe, Fanny 1940- . . . . **CLC 47**
See also CA 117; SATA-Brief 52

Howe, Irving 1920-1993 . . . . **CLC 85**
See also CA 9-12R; 141; CANR 21, 50;
DLB 67; MTCW

Howe, Julia Ward 1819-1910 . . . . . **TCLC 21**
See also CA 117; DLB 1

Howe, Susan 1937- . . . . **CLC 72**
See also DLB 120

Howe, Tina 1937- . . . . **CLC 48**
See also CA 109

Howell, James 1594(?)-1666 . . . . **LC 13**
See also DLB 151

Howells, W. D.
See Howells, William Dean

Howells, William D.
See Howells, William Dean

Howells, William Dean
1837-1920 . . . . **TCLC 7, 17, 41**
See also CA 104; 134; CDALB 1865-1917;
DLB 12, 64, 74, 79

Howes, Barbara 1914-1996 . . . . **CLC 15**
See also CA 9-12R; 151; CAAS 3;
CANR 53; SATA 5

Hrabal, Bohumil 1914- . . . . **CLC 13, 67**
See also CA 106; CAAS 12

Hsun, Lu
See Lu Hsun

Hubbard, L(afayette) Ron(ald)
1911-1986 . . . . **CLC 43; DAM POP**
See also CA 77-80; 118; CANR 52

Huch, Ricarda (Octavia)
1864-1947 . . . . **TCLC 13**
See also CA 111; DLB 66

Huddle, David 1942- . . . . **CLC 49**
See also CA 57-60; CAAS 20; DLB 130

Hudson, Jeffrey
See Crichton, (John) Michael

Hudson, W(illiam) H(enry)
1841-1922 . . . . **TCLC 29**
See also CA 115; DLB 98, 153, 174;
SATA 35

Hueffer, Ford Madox
See Ford, Ford Madox

Hughart, Barry 1934- . . . . **CLC 39**
See also CA 137

Hughes, Colin
See Creasey, John

Hughes, David (John) 1930- . . . . . . **CLC 48**
See also CA 116; 129; DLB 14

Hughes, Edward James
See Hughes, Ted
See also DAM MST, POET

Hughes, (James) Langston
1902-1967 . . . . . **CLC 1, 5, 10, 15, 35, 44;**
BLC; DA; DAB; DAC; DAM DRAM,
MST, MULT, POET; DC 3; PC 1;
SSC 6; WLC
See also AAYA 12; BW 1; CA 1-4R;
25-28R; CANR 1, 34; CDALB 1929-1941;
CLR 17; DLB 4, 7, 48, 51, 86; JRDA;
MAICYA; MTCW; SATA 4, 33

Hughes, Richard (Arthur Warren)
1900-1976 . . . . . . **CLC 1, 11; DAM NOV**
See also CA 5-8R; 65-68; CANR 4;
DLB 15, 161; MTCW; SATA 8;
SATA-Obit 25

Hughes, Ted
1930- . . . . **CLC 2, 4, 9, 14, 37; DAB;**
DAC; PC 7
See also Hughes, Edward James
See also CA 1-4R; CANR 1, 33; CLR 3;
DLB 40, 161; MAICYA; MTCW;
SATA 49; SATA-Brief 27

Johnson, Benjamin F. of Boo
See Riley, James Whitcomb

Johnson, Charles (Richard)
1948- . . . . **CLC 7, 51, 65; BLC;**
DAM MULT
See also BW 2; CA 116; CAAS 18;
CANR 42; DLB 33

Johnson, Denis 1949- . . . . **CLC 52**
See also CA 117; 121; DLB 120

Johnson, Diane 1934- . . . . **CLC 5, 13, 48**
See also CA 41-44R; CANR 17, 40;
DLBY 80; INT CANR-17; MTCW

Johnson, Eyvind (Olof Verner)
1900-1976 . . . . **CLC 14**
See also CA 73-76; 69-72; CANR 34

Johnson, J. R.
See James, C(yril) L(ionel) R(obert)

Johnson, James Weldon
1871-1938 . . . . **TCLC 3, 19; BLC;**
DAM MULT, POET
See also BW 1; CA 104; 125;
CDALB 1917-1929; CLR 32; DLB 51;
MTCW; SATA 31

Johnson, Joyce 1935- . . . . **CLC 58**
See also CA 125; 129

Johnson, Lionel (Pigot)
1867-1902 . . . . **TCLC 19**
See also CA 117; DLB 19

Johnson, Mel
See Malzberg, Barry N(athaniel)

Johnson, Pamela Hansford
1912-1981 . . . . **CLC 1, 7, 27**
See also CA 1-4R; 104; CANR 2, 28;
DLB 15; MTCW

Johnson, Robert 1911(?)-1938 . . . . . **TCLC 69**

Johnson, Samuel
1709-1784 . . . . . **LC 15; DA; DAB; DAC;**
DAM MST; WLC
See also CDBLB 1660-1789; DLB 39, 95,
104, 142

Johnson, Uwe
1934-1984 . . . . **CLC 5, 10, 15, 40**
See also CA 1-4R; 112; CANR 1, 39;
DLB 75; MTCW

Johnston, George (Benson) 1913- . . . **CLC 51**
See also CA 1-4R; CANR 5, 20; DLB 88

Johnston, Jennifer 1930- . . . . **CLC 7**
See also CA 85-88; DLB 14

Jolley, (Monica) Elizabeth
1923- . . . . **CLC 46; SSC 19**
See also CA 127; CAAS 13

Jones, Arthur Llewellyn 1863-1947
See Machen, Arthur
See also CA 104

Jones, D(ouglas) G(ordon) 1929- . . . . **CLC 10**
See also CA 29-32R; CANR 13; DLB 53

Jones, David (Michael)
1895-1974 . . . . **CLC 2, 4, 7, 13, 42**
See also CA 9-12R; 53-56; CANR 28;
CDBLB 1945-1960; DLB 20, 100; MTCW

Jones, David Robert 1947-
See Bowie, David
See also CA 103

Jones, Diana Wynne 1934- . . . . **CLC 26**
See also AAYA 12; CA 49-52; CANR 4,
26, 56; CLR 23; DLB 161; JRDA;
MAICYA; SAAS 7; SATA 9, 70

Jones, Edward P. 1950- . . . . **CLC 76**
See also BW 2; CA 142

Jones, Gayl
1949- . . . . **CLC 6, 9; BLC; DAM MULT**
See also BW 2; CA 77-80; CANR 27;
DLB 33; MTCW

Jones, James 1921-1977 . . . . **CLC 1, 3, 10, 39**
See also AITN 1, 2; CA 1-4R; 69-72;
CANR 6; DLB 2, 143; MTCW

Jones, John J.
See Lovecraft, H(oward) P(hillips)

Jones, LeRoi . . . . **CLC 1, 2, 3, 5, 10, 14**
See also Baraka, Amiri

Jones, Louis B. . . . . **CLC 65**
See also CA 141

Jones, Madison (Percy, Jr.) 1925- . . . **CLC 4**
See also CA 13-16R; CAAS 11; CANR 7,
54; DLB 152

Jones, Mervyn 1922- . . . . **CLC 10, 52**
See also CA 45-48; CAAS 5; CANR 1;
MTCW

Jones, Mick 1956(?)- . . . . **CLC 30**

Jones, Nettie (Pearl) 1941- . . . . **CLC 34**
See also BW 2; CA 137; CAAS 20

Jones, Preston 1936-1979 . . . . **CLC 10**
See also CA 73-76; 89-92; DLB 7

Jones, Robert F(rancis) 1934- . . . . **CLC 7**
See also CA 49-52; CANR 2

Jones, Rod 1953- . . . . **CLC 50**
See also CA 128

Jones, Terence Graham Parry
1942- . . . . **CLC 21**
See also Jones, Terry; Monty Python
See also CA 112; 116; CANR 35; INT 116

Jones, Terry
See Jones, Terence Graham Parry
See also SATA 67; SATA-Brief 51

Jones, Thom 1945(?)- . . . . **CLC 81**

Jong, Erica
1942- . . . . **CLC 4, 6, 8, 18, 83;**
DAM NOV, POP
See also AITN 1; BEST 90:2; CA 73-76;
CANR 26, 52; DLB 2, 5, 28, 152;
INT CANR-26; MTCW

Jonson, Ben(jamin)
1572(?)-1637 . . . . . . **LC 6, 33; DA; DAB;**
DAC; DAM DRAM, MST, POET;
DC 4; PC 17; WLC
See also CDBLB Before 1660; DLB 62, 121

Jordan, June
1936- . . . . . **CLC 5, 11, 23; DAM MULT,**
POET
See also AAYA 2; BW 2; CA 33-36R;
CANR 25; CLR 10; DLB 38; MAICYA;
MTCW; SATA 4

Jordan, Pat(rick M.) 1941- . . . . **CLC 37**
See also CA 33-36R

Jorgensen, Ivar
See Ellison, Harlan (Jay)

Jorgenson, Ivar
See Silverberg, Robert

Josephus, Flavius c. 37-100 . . . . . . **CMLC 13**

Josipovici, Gabriel 1940- . . . . **CLC 6, 43**
See also CA 37-40R; CAAS 8; CANR 47;
DLB 14

Joubert, Joseph 1754-1824 . . . . **NCLC 9**

Jouve, Pierre Jean 1887-1976 . . . . . . **CLC 47**
See also CA 65-68

Joyce, James (Augustine Aloysius)
1882-1941 . . . . **TCLC 3, 8, 16, 35, 52;**
DA; DAB; DAC; DAM MST, NOV,
POET; SSC 3; WLC
See also CA 104; 126; CDBLB 1914-1945;
DLB 10, 19, 36, 162; MTCW

Jozsef, Attila 1905-1937 . . . . **TCLC 22**
See also CA 116

Juana Ines de la Cruz 1651(?)-1695 . . . **LC 5**

Judd, Cyril
See Kornbluth, C(yril) M.; Pohl, Frederik

Julian of Norwich 1342(?)-1416(?) . . . . **LC 6**
See also DLB 146

Juniper, Alex
See Hospital, Janette Turner

Junius
See Luxemburg, Rosa

Just, Ward (Swift) 1935- . . . . **CLC 4, 27**
See also CA 25-28R; CANR 32;
INT CANR-32

Justice, Donald (Rodney)
1925- . . . . **CLC 6, 19; DAM POET**
See also CA 5-8R; CANR 26, 54;
DLBY 83; INT CANR-26

Juvenal c. 55-c. 127 . . . . **CMLC 8**

Juvenis
See Bourne, Randolph S(illiman)

Kacew, Romain 1914-1980
See Gary, Romain
See also CA 108; 102

Kadare, Ismail 1936- . . . . **CLC 52**

Kadohata, Cynthia . . . . **CLC 59**
See also CA 140

Kafka, Franz
1883-1924 . . . . **TCLC 2, 6, 13, 29, 47, 53;**
DA; DAB; DAC; DAM MST, NOV;
SSC 5; WLC
See also CA 105; 126; DLB 81; MTCW

Kahanovitsch, Pinkhes
See Der Nister

Kahn, Roger 1927- . . . . **CLC 30**
See also CA 25-28R; CANR 44; DLB 171;
SATA 37

Kain, Saul
See Sassoon, Siegfried (Lorraine)

Kaiser, Georg 1878-1945 . . . . **TCLC 9**
See also CA 106; DLB 124

Kaletski, Alexander 1946- . . . . **CLC 39**
See also CA 118; 143

Kalidasa fl. c. 400- . . . . **CMLC 9**

Kallman, Chester (Simon)
1921-1975 . . . . **CLC 2**
See also CA 45-48; 53-56; CANR 3

Kaminsky, Melvin 1926-
See Brooks, Mel
See also CA 65-68; CANR 16

Kerry, Lois
See Duncan, Lois

Kesey, Ken (Elton)
1935- ...... **CLC 1, 3, 6, 11, 46, 64; DA; DAB; DAC; DAM MST, NOV, POP; WLC**
See also CA 1-4R; CANR 22, 38; CDALB 1968-1988; DLB 2, 16; MTCW; SATA 66

Kesselring, Joseph (Otto)
1902-1967 ..... **CLC 45; DAM DRAM, MST**
See also CA 150

Kessler, Jascha (Frederick) 1929- .... **CLC 4**
See also CA 17-20R; CANR 8, 48

Kettelkamp, Larry (Dale) 1933- .... **CLC 12**
See also CA 29-32R; CANR 16; SAAS 3; SATA 2

Key, Ellen 1849-1926 .... **TCLC 65**

Keyber, Conny
See Fielding, Henry

Keyes, Daniel
1927- .... **CLC 80; DA; DAC; DAM MST, NOV**
See also CA 17-20R; CANR 10, 26, 54; SATA 37

Keynes, John Maynard
1883-1946 .... **TCLC 64**
See also CA 114; DLBD 10

Khanshendel, Chiron
See Rose, Wendy

Khayyam, Omar
1048-1131 .... **CMLC 11; DAM POET; PC 8**

Kherdian, David 1931- .... **CLC 6, 9**
See also CA 21-24R; CAAS 2; CANR 39; CLR 24; JRDA; MAICYA; SATA 16, 74

Khlebnikov, Velimir .... **TCLC 20**
See also Khlebnikov, Viktor Vladimirovich

Khlebnikov, Viktor Vladimirovich 1885-1922
See Khlebnikov, Velimir
See also CA 117

Khodasevich, Vladislav (Felitsianovich)
1886-1939 .... **TCLC 15**
See also CA 115

Kielland, Alexander Lange
1849-1906 .... **TCLC 5**
See also CA 104

Kiely, Benedict 1919- .... **CLC 23, 43**
See also CA 1-4R; CANR 2; DLB 15

Kienzle, William X(avier)
1928- .... **CLC 25; DAM POP**
See also CA 93-96; CAAS 1; CANR 9, 31; INT CANR-31; MTCW

Kierkegaard, Soren 1813-1855.... **NCLC 34**

Killens, John Oliver 1916-1987..... **CLC 10**
See also BW 2; CA 77-80; 123; CAAS 2; CANR 26; DLB 33

Killigrew, Anne 1660-1685.......... **LC 4**
See also DLB 131

Kim
See Simenon, Georges (Jacques Christian)

Kincaid, Jamaica
1949- .... **CLC 43, 68; BLC; DAM MULT, NOV**
See also AAYA 13; BW 2; CA 125; CANR 47; DLB 157

King, Francis (Henry)
1923- .... **CLC 8, 53; DAM NOV**
See also CA 1-4R; CANR 1, 33; DLB 15, 139; MTCW

King, Martin Luther, Jr.
1929-1968 .... **CLC 83; BLC; DA; DAB; DAC; DAM MST, MULT**
See also BW 2; CA 25-28; CANR 27, 44; CAP 2; MTCW; SATA 14

King, Stephen (Edwin)
1947- .... **CLC 12, 26, 37, 61; DAM NOV, POP; SSC 17**
See also AAYA 1, 17; BEST 90:1; CA 61-64; CANR 1, 30, 52; DLB 143; DLBY 80; JRDA; MTCW; SATA 9, 55

King, Steve
See King, Stephen (Edwin)

King, Thomas
1943- ..... **CLC 89; DAC; DAM MULT**
See also CA 144; DLB 175; NNAL

Kingman, Lee .... **CLC 17**
See also Natti, (Mary) Lee
See also SAAS 3; SATA 1, 67

Kingsley, Charles 1819-1875 ..... **NCLC 35**
See also DLB 21, 32, 163; YABC 2

Kingsley, Sidney 1906-1995 .... **CLC 44**
See also CA 85-88; 147; DLB 7

Kingsolver, Barbara
1955- .... **CLC 55, 81; DAM POP**
See also AAYA 15; CA 129; 134; INT 134

Kingston, Maxine (Ting Ting) Hong
1940- .... **CLC 12, 19, 58; DAM MULT, NOV**
See also AAYA 8; CA 69-72; CANR 13, 38; DLB 173; DLBY 80; INT CANR-13; MTCW; SATA 53

Kinnell, Galway
1927- .... **CLC 1, 2, 3, 5, 13, 29**
See also CA 9-12R; CANR 10, 34; DLB 5; DLBY 87; INT CANR-34; MTCW

Kinsella, Thomas 1928- .... **CLC 4, 19**
See also CA 17-20R; CANR 15; DLB 27; MTCW

Kinsella, W(illiam) P(atrick)
1935- .... **CLC 27, 43; DAC; DAM NOV, POP**
See also AAYA 7; CA 97-100; CAAS 7; CANR 21, 35; INT CANR-21; MTCW

Kipling, (Joseph) Rudyard
1865-1936 ..... **TCLC 8, 17; DA; DAB; DAC; DAM MST, POET; PC 3; SSC 5; WLC**
See also CA 105; 120; CANR 33; CDBLB 1890-1914; CLR 39; DLB 19, 34, 141, 156; MAICYA; MTCW; YABC 2

Kirkup, James 1918- .... **CLC 1**
See also CA 1-4R; CAAS 4; CANR 2; DLB 27; SATA 12

Kirkwood, James 1930(?)-1989 ...... **CLC 9**
See also AITN 2; CA 1-4R; 128; CANR 6, 40

Kirshner, Sidney
See Kingsley, Sidney

Kis, Danilo 1935-1989 .... **CLC 57**
See also CA 109; 118; 129; MTCW

Kivi, Aleksis 1834-1872 .... **NCLC 30**

Kizer, Carolyn (Ashley)
1925- ..... **CLC 15, 39, 80; DAM POET**
See also CA 65-68; CAAS 5; CANR 24; DLB 5, 169

Klabund 1890-1928 .... **TCLC 44**
See also DLB 66

Klappert, Peter 1942- .... **CLC 57**
See also CA 33-36R; DLB 5

Klein, A(braham) M(oses)
1909-1972 .... **CLC 19; DAB; DAC; DAM MST**
See also CA 101; 37-40R; DLB 68

Klein, Norma 1938-1989 .... **CLC 30**
See also AAYA 2; CA 41-44R; 128; CANR 15, 37; CLR 2, 19; INT CANR-15; JRDA; MAICYA; SAAS 1; SATA 7, 57

Klein, T(heodore) E(ibon) D(onald)
1947- .... **CLC 34**
See also CA 119; CANR 44

Kleist, Heinrich von
1777-1811 .... **NCLC 2, 37; DAM DRAM; SSC 22**
See also DLB 90

Klima, Ivan 1931- ..... **CLC 56; DAM NOV**
See also CA 25-28R; CANR 17, 50

Klimentov, Andrei Platonovich 1899-1951
See Platonov, Andrei
See also CA 108

Klinger, Friedrich Maximilian von
1752-1831 .... **NCLC 1**
See also DLB 94

Klopstock, Friedrich Gottlieb
1724-1803 .... **NCLC 11**
See also DLB 97

Knapp, Caroline 1959- .... **CLC 99**
See also CA 154

Knebel, Fletcher 1911-1993 .... **CLC 14**
See also AITN 1; CA 1-4R; 140; CAAS 3; CANR 1, 36; SATA 36; SATA-Obit 75

Knickerbocker, Diedrich
See Irving, Washington

Knight, Etheridge
1931-1991 .... **CLC 40; BLC; DAM POET; PC 14**
See also BW 1; CA 21-24R; 133; CANR 23; DLB 41

Knight, Sarah Kemble 1666-1727 ..... **LC 7**
See also DLB 24

Knister, Raymond 1899-1932...... **TCLC 56**
See also DLB 68

Knowles, John
1926- ...... **CLC 1, 4, 10, 26; DA; DAC; DAM MST, NOV**
See also AAYA 10; CA 17-20R; CANR 40; CDALB 1968-1988; DLB 6; MTCW; SATA 8, 89

Knox, Calvin M.
See Silverberg, Robert

Knox, John c. 1505-1572 . . . . **LC 37**
See also DLB 132

Knye, Cassandra
See Disch, Thomas M(ichael)

Koch, C(hristopher) J(ohn) 1932- . . . **CLC 42**
See also CA 127

Koch, Christopher
See Koch, C(hristopher) J(ohn)

Koch, Kenneth
1925- . . . . **CLC 5, 8, 44; DAM POET**
See also CA 1-4R; CANR 6, 36; DLB 5;
INT CANR-36; SATA 65

Kochanowski, Jan 1530-1584 . . . . **LC 10**

Kock, Charles Paul de
1794-1871 . . . . **NCLC 16**

Koda Shigeyuki 1867-1947
See Rohan, Koda
See also CA 121

Koestler, Arthur
1905-1983 . . . . **CLC 1, 3, 6, 8, 15, 33**
See also CA 1-4R; 109; CANR 1, 33;
CDBLB 1945-1960; DLBY 83; MTCW

Kogawa, Joy Nozomi
1935- . . . . . . **CLC 78; DAC; DAM MST,**
MULT
See also CA 101; CANR 19

Kohout, Pavel 1928- . . . . **CLC 13**
See also CA 45-48; CANR 3

Koizumi, Yakumo
See Hearn, (Patricio) Lafcadio (Tessima
Carlos)

Kolmar, Gertrud 1894-1943 . . . . . . **TCLC 40**

Komunyakaa, Yusef 1947- . . . . . . **CLC 86, 94**
See also CA 147; DLB 120

Konrad, George
See Konrad, Gyoergy

Konrad, Gyoergy 1933- . . . . . . **CLC 4, 10, 73**
See also CA 85-88

Konwicki, Tadeusz 1926- . . . . . **CLC 8, 28, 54**
See also CA 101; CAAS 9; CANR 39;
MTCW

Koontz, Dean R(ay)
1945- . . . . . . **CLC 78; DAM NOV, POP**
See also AAYA 9; BEST 89:3, 90:2;
CA 108; CANR 19, 36, 52; MTCW;
SATA 92

Kopit, Arthur (Lee)
1937- . . . . . **CLC 1, 18, 33; DAM DRAM**
See also AITN 1; CA 81-84; CABS 3;
DLB 7; MTCW

Kops, Bernard 1926- . . . . **CLC 4**
See also CA 5-8R; DLB 13

Kornbluth, C(yril) M. 1923-1958 . . . . **TCLC 8**
See also CA 105; DLB 8

Korolenko, V. G.
See Korolenko, Vladimir Galaktionovich

Korolenko, Vladimir
See Korolenko, Vladimir Galaktionovich

Korolenko, Vladimir G.
See Korolenko, Vladimir Galaktionovich

Korolenko, Vladimir Galaktionovich
1853-1921 . . . . **TCLC 22**
See also CA 121

Korzybski, Alfred (Habdank Skarbek)
1879-1950 . . . . **TCLC 61**
See also CA 123

Kosinski, Jerzy (Nikodem)
1933-1991 . . . . **CLC 1, 2, 3, 6, 10, 15, 53,**
70; DAM NOV
See also CA 17-20R; 134; CANR 9, 46;
DLB 2; DLBY 82; MTCW

Kostelanetz, Richard (Cory) 1940- . . **CLC 28**
See also CA 13-16R; CAAS 8; CANR 38

Kostrowitzki, Wilhelm Apollinaris de
1880-1918
See Apollinaire, Guillaume
See also CA 104

Kotlowitz, Robert 1924- . . . . **CLC 4**
See also CA 33-36R; CANR 36

Kotzebue, August (Friedrich Ferdinand) von
1761-1819 . . . . **NCLC 25**
See also DLB 94

Kotzwinkle, William 1938- . . . **CLC 5, 14, 35**
See also CA 45-48; CANR 3, 44; CLR 6;
DLB 173; MAICYA; SATA 24, 70

Kowna, Stancy
See Szymborska, Wislawa

Kozol, Jonathan 1936- . . . . **CLC 17**
See also CA 61-64; CANR 16, 45

Kozoll, Michael 1940(?)- . . . . **CLC 35**

Kramer, Kathryn 19(?)- . . . . **CLC 34**

Kramer, Larry 1935- . . **CLC 42; DAM POP**
See also CA 124; 126

Krasicki, Ignacy 1735-1801 . . . . **NCLC 8**

Krasinski, Zygmunt 1812-1859 . . . . **NCLC 4**

Kraus, Karl 1874-1936 . . . . **TCLC 5**
See also CA 104; DLB 118

Kreve (Mickevicius), Vincas
1882-1954 . . . . **TCLC 27**

Kristeva, Julia 1941- . . . . **CLC 77**
See also CA 154

Kristofferson, Kris 1936- . . . . **CLC 26**
See also CA 104

Krizanc, John 1956- . . . . **CLC 57**

Krleza, Miroslav 1893-1981 . . . . **CLC 8**
See also CA 97-100; 105; CANR 50;
DLB 147

Kroetsch, Robert
1927- . . . . **CLC 5, 23, 57; DAC;**
DAM POET
See also CA 17-20R; CANR 8, 38; DLB 53;
MTCW

Kroetz, Franz
See Kroetz, Franz Xaver

Kroetz, Franz Xaver 1946- . . . . **CLC 41**
See also CA 130

Kroker, Arthur 1945- . . . . **CLC 77**

Kropotkin, Peter (Aleksieevich)
1842-1921 . . . . **TCLC 36**
See also CA 119

Krotkov, Yuri 1917- . . . . **CLC 19**
See also CA 102

Krumb
See Crumb, R(obert)

Krumgold, Joseph (Quincy)
1908-1980 . . . . **CLC 12**
See also CA 9-12R; 101; CANR 7;
MAICYA; SATA 1, 48; SATA-Obit 23

Krumwitz
See Crumb, R(obert)

Krutch, Joseph Wood 1893-1970 . . . . **CLC 24**
See also CA 1-4R; 25-28R; CANR 4;
DLB 63

Krutzch, Gus
See Eliot, T(homas) S(tearns)

Krylov, Ivan Andreevich
1768(?)-1844 . . . . **NCLC 1**
See also DLB 150

Kubin, Alfred (Leopold Isidor)
1877-1959 . . . . **TCLC 23**
See also CA 112; 149; DLB 81

Kubrick, Stanley 1928- . . . . **CLC 16**
See also CA 81-84; CANR 33; DLB 26

Kumin, Maxine (Winokur)
1925- . . . . . **CLC 5, 13, 28; DAM POET;**
PC 15
See also AITN 2; CA 1-4R; CAAS 8;
CANR 1, 21; DLB 5; MTCW; SATA 12

Kundera, Milan
1929- . . . . **CLC 4, 9, 19, 32, 68;**
DAM NOV; SSC 24
See also AAYA 2; CA 85-88; CANR 19,
52; MTCW

Kunene, Mazisi (Raymond) 1930- . . . **CLC 85**
See also BW 1; CA 125; DLB 117

Kunitz, Stanley (Jasspon)
1905- . . . . **CLC 6, 11, 14**
See also CA 41-44R; CANR 26; DLB 48;
INT CANR-26; MTCW

Kunze, Reiner 1933- . . . . **CLC 10**
See also CA 93-96; DLB 75

Kuprin, Aleksandr Ivanovich
1870-1938 . . . . **TCLC 5**
See also CA 104

Kureishi, Hanif 1954(?)- . . . . **CLC 64**
See also CA 139

Kurosawa, Akira
1910- . . . . **CLC 16; DAM MULT**
See also AAYA 11; CA 101; CANR 46

Kushner, Tony
1957(?)- . . . . **CLC 81; DAM DRAM**
See also CA 144

Kuttner, Henry 1915-1958 . . . . **TCLC 10**
See also CA 107; DLB 8

Kuzma, Greg 1944- . . . . **CLC 7**
See also CA 33-36R

Kuzmin, Mikhail 1872(?)-1936 . . . . **TCLC 40**

Kyd, Thomas
1558-1594 . . . . **LC 22; DAM DRAM;**
DC 3
See also DLB 62

Kyprianos, Iossif
See Samarakis, Antonis

La Bruyere, Jean de 1645-1696 . . . . . . **LC 17**

Lacan, Jacques (Marie Emile)
1901-1981 . . . . **CLC 75**
See also CA 121; 104

Laclos, Pierre Ambroise Francois Choderlos
de 1741-1803 . . . . **NCLC 4**

La Colere, Francois
See Aragon, Louis

Lacolere, Francois
See Aragon, Louis

La Deshabilleuse
See Simenon, Georges (Jacques Christian)

Lady Gregory
See Gregory, Isabella Augusta (Persse)

Lady of Quality, A
See Bagnold, Enid

La Fayette, Marie (Madelaine Pioche de la Vergne Comtes 1634-1693 . . . . . . **LC 2**

Lafayette, Rene
See Hubbard, L(afayette) Ron(ald)

Laforgue, Jules
1860-1887 . . . . **NCLC 5, 53; PC 14; SSC 20**

Lagerkvist, Paer (Fabian)
1891-1974 . . . . **CLC 7, 10, 13, 54; DAM DRAM, NOV**
See also Lagerkvist, Par
See also CA 85-88; 49-52; MTCW

Lagerkvist, Par . . . . **SSC 12**
See also Lagerkvist, Paer (Fabian)

Lagerloef, Selma (Ottiliana Lovisa)
1858-1940 . . . . **TCLC 4, 36**
See also Lagerlof, Selma (Ottiliana Lovisa)
See also CA 108; SATA 15

Lagerlof, Selma (Ottiliana Lovisa)
See Lagerloef, Selma (Ottiliana Lovisa)
See also CLR 7; SATA 15

La Guma, (Justin) Alex(ander)
1925-1985 . . . . **CLC 19; DAM NOV**
See also BW 1; CA 49-52; 118; CANR 25; DLB 117; MTCW

Laidlaw, A. K.
See Grieve, C(hristopher) M(urray)

Lainez, Manuel Mujica
See Mujica Lainez, Manuel
See also HW

Laing, R(onald) D(avid)
1927-1989 . . . . **CLC 95**
See also CA 107; 129; CANR 34; MTCW

Lamartine, Alphonse (Marie Louis Prat) de
1790-1869 . . . . . **NCLC 11; DAM POET; PC 16**

Lamb, Charles
1775-1834 . . . . . . **NCLC 10; DA; DAB; DAC; DAM MST; WLC**
See also CDBLB 1789-1832; DLB 93, 107, 163; SATA 17

Lamb, Lady Caroline 1785-1828 . . **NCLC 38**
See also DLB 116

Lamming, George (William)
1927- . . . . **CLC 2, 4, 66; BLC; DAM MULT**
See also BW 2; CA 85-88; CANR 26; DLB 125; MTCW

L'Amour, Louis (Dearborn)
1908-1988 . . . . **CLC 25, 55; DAM NOV, POP**
See also AAYA 16; AITN 2; BEST 89:2; CA 1-4R; 125; CANR 3, 25, 40; DLBY 80; MTCW

Lampedusa, Giuseppe (Tomasi) di . . . **TCLC 13**
See also Tomasi di Lampedusa, Giuseppe

Lampman, Archibald 1861-1899 . . **NCLC 25**
See also DLB 92

Lancaster, Bruce 1896-1963. . . . . . . **CLC 36**
See also CA 9-10; CAP 1; SATA 9

Lanchester, John . . . . **CLC 99**

Landau, Mark Alexandrovich
See Aldanov, Mark (Alexandrovich)

Landau-Aldanov, Mark Alexandrovich
See Aldanov, Mark (Alexandrovich)

Landis, Jerry
See Simon, Paul (Frederick)

Landis, John 1950- . . . . **CLC 26**
See also CA 112; 122

Landolfi, Tommaso 1908-1979. . . **CLC 11, 49**
See also CA 127; 117

Landon, Letitia Elizabeth
1802-1838 . . . . **NCLC 15**
See also DLB 96

Landor, Walter Savage
1775-1864 . . . . **NCLC 14**
See also DLB 93, 107

Landwirth, Heinz 1927-
See Lind, Jakov
See also CA 9-12R; CANR 7

Lane, Patrick
1939- . . . . **CLC 25; DAM POET**
See also CA 97-100; CANR 54; DLB 53; INT 97-100

Lang, Andrew 1844-1912 . . . . **TCLC 16**
See also CA 114; 137; DLB 98, 141; MAICYA; SATA 16

Lang, Fritz 1890-1976 . . . . **CLC 20**
See also CA 77-80; 69-72; CANR 30

Lange, John
See Crichton, (John) Michael

Langer, Elinor 1939- . . . . **CLC 34**
See also CA 121

Langland, William
1330(?)-1400(?) . . . . . . **LC 19; DA; DAB; DAC; DAM MST, POET**
See also DLB 146

Langstaff, Launcelot
See Irving, Washington

Lanier, Sidney
1842-1881 . . . . . . **NCLC 6; DAM POET**
See also DLB 64; DLBD 13; MAICYA; SATA 18

Lanyer, Aemilia 1569-1645 . . . . . . **LC 10, 30**
See also DLB 121

Lao Tzu . . . . **CMLC 7**

Lapine, James (Elliot) 1949- . . . . **CLC 39**
See also CA 123; 130; CANR 54; INT 130

Larbaud, Valery (Nicolas)
1881-1957 . . . . **TCLC 9**
See also CA 106; 152

Lardner, Ring
See Lardner, Ring(gold) W(ilmer)

Lardner, Ring W., Jr.
See Lardner, Ring(gold) W(ilmer)

Lardner, Ring(gold) W(ilmer)
1885-1933 . . . . **TCLC 2, 14**
See also CA 104; 131; CDALB 1917-1929; DLB 11, 25, 86; MTCW

Laredo, Betty
See Codrescu, Andrei

Larkin, Maia
See Wojciechowska, Maia (Teresa)

Larkin, Philip (Arthur)
1922-1985 . . . . **CLC 3, 5, 8, 9, 13, 18, 33, 39, 64; DAB; DAM MST, POET**
See also CA 5-8R; 117; CANR 24; CDBLB 1960 to Present; DLB 27; MTCW

Larra (y Sanchez de Castro), Mariano Jose de
1809-1837 . . . . **NCLC 17**

Larsen, Eric 1941- . . . . **CLC 55**
See also CA 132

Larsen, Nella
1891-1964 . . . . **CLC 37; BLC; DAM MULT**
See also BW 1; CA 125; DLB 51

Larson, Charles R(aymond) 1938-. . . **CLC 31**
See also CA 53-56; CANR 4

Larson, Jonathan 1961(?)-1996 . . . . . **CLC 99**

Las Casas, Bartolome de 1474-1566. . **LC 31**

Lasker-Schueler, Else 1869-1945 . . **TCLC 57**
See also DLB 66, 124

Latham, Jean Lee 1902-. . . . . **CLC 12**
See also AITN 1; CA 5-8R; CANR 7; MAICYA; SATA 2, 68

Latham, Mavis
See Clark, Mavis Thorpe

Lathen, Emma . . . . **CLC 2**
See also Hennissart, Martha; Latsis, Mary J(ane)

Lathrop, Francis
See Leiber, Fritz (Reuter, Jr.)

Latsis, Mary J(ane)
See Lathen, Emma
See also CA 85-88

Lattimore, Richmond (Alexander)
1906-1984 . . . . **CLC 3**
See also CA 1-4R; 112; CANR 1

Laughlin, James 1914- . . . . **CLC 49**
See also CA 21-24R; CAAS 22; CANR 9, 47; DLB 48

Laurence, (Jean) Margaret (Wemyss)
1926-1987 . . . . **CLC 3, 6, 13, 50, 62; DAC; DAM MST; SSC 7**
See also CA 5-8R; 121; CANR 33; DLB 53; MTCW; SATA-Obit 50

Laurent, Antoine 1952- . . . . **CLC 50**

Lauscher, Hermann
See Hesse, Hermann

Lautreamont, Comte de
1846-1870 . . . . **NCLC 12; SSC 14**

Laverty, Donald
See Blish, James (Benjamin)

Lavin, Mary
1912-1996 . . . . **CLC 4, 18, 99; SSC 4**
See also CA 9-12R; 151; CANR 33; DLB 15; MTCW

Lavond, Paul Dennis
See Kornbluth, C(yril) M.; Pohl, Frederik

Lawler, Raymond Evenor 1922- .... **CLC 58**
See also CA 103

Lawrence, D(avid) H(erbert Richards)
1885-1930 .... **TCLC 2, 9, 16, 33, 48, 61;
DA; DAB; DAC; DAM MST, NOV,
POET; SSC 4, 19; WLC**
See also CA 104; 121; CDBLB 1914-1945;
DLB 10, 19, 36, 98, 162; MTCW

Lawrence, T(homas) E(dward)
1888-1935 .... **TCLC 18**
See also Dale, Colin
See also CA 115

Lawrence of Arabia
See Lawrence, T(homas) E(dward)

Lawson, Henry (Archibald Hertzberg)
1867-1922 .... **TCLC 27; SSC 18**
See also CA 120

Lawton, Dennis
See Faust, Frederick (Schiller)

Laxness, Halldor .... **CLC 25**
See also Gudjonsson, Halldor Kiljan

Layamon fl. c. 1200- .... **CMLC 10**
See also DLB 146

Laye, Camara
1928-1980 .... **CLC 4, 38; BLC;
DAM MULT**
See also BW 1; CA 85-88; 97-100;
CANR 25; MTCW

Layton, Irving (Peter)
1912- .... **CLC 2, 15; DAC; DAM MST,
POET**
See also CA 1-4R; CANR 2, 33, 43;
DLB 88; MTCW

Lazarus, Emma 1849-1887 .... **NCLC 8**

Lazarus, Felix
See Cable, George Washington

Lazarus, Henry
See Slavitt, David R(ytman)

Lea, Joan
See Neufeld, John (Arthur)

Leacock, Stephen (Butler)
1869-1944 .. **TCLC 2; DAC; DAM MST**
See also CA 104; 141; DLB 92

Lear, Edward 1812-1888 .... **NCLC 3**
See also CLR 1; DLB 32, 163, 166;
MAICYA; SATA 18

Lear, Norman (Milton) 1922- ...... **CLC 12**
See also CA 73-76

Leavis, F(rank) R(aymond)
1895-1978 .... **CLC 24**
See also CA 21-24R; 77-80; CANR 44;
MTCW

Leavitt, David 1961-... **CLC 34; DAM POP**
See also CA 116; 122; CANR 50; DLB 130;
INT 122

Leblanc, Maurice (Marie Emile)
1864-1941 .... **TCLC 49**
See also CA 110

Lebowitz, Fran(ces Ann)
1951(?)- .... **CLC 11, 36**
See also CA 81-84; CANR 14;
INT CANR-14; MTCW

Lebrecht, Peter
See Tieck, (Johann) Ludwig

le Carre, John .... **CLC 3, 5, 9, 15, 28**
See also Cornwell, David (John Moore)
See also BEST 89:4; CDBLB 1960 to
Present; DLB 87

Le Clezio, J(ean) M(arie) G(ustave)
1940- .... **CLC 31**
See also CA 116; 128; DLB 83

Leconte de Lisle, Charles-Marie-Rene
1818-1894 .... **NCLC 29**

Le Coq, Monsieur
See Simenon, Georges (Jacques Christian)

Leduc, Violette 1907-1972 .... **CLC 22**
See also CA 13-14; 33-36R; CAP 1

Ledwidge, Francis 1887(?)-1917 ... **TCLC 23**
See also CA 123; DLB 20

Lee, Andrea
1953- ..... **CLC 36; BLC; DAM MULT**
See also BW 1; CA 125

Lee, Andrew
See Auchincloss, Louis (Stanton)

Lee, Chang-rae 1965- .... **CLC 91**
See also CA 148

Lee, Don L. .... **CLC 2**
See also Madhubuti, Haki R.

Lee, George W(ashington)
1894-1976 .... **CLC 52; BLC;
DAM MULT**
See also BW 1; CA 125; DLB 51

Lee, (Nelle) Harper
1926- .... **CLC 12, 60; DA; DAB; DAC;
DAM MST, NOV; WLC**
See also AAYA 13; CA 13-16R; CANR 51;
CDALB 1941-1968; DLB 6; MTCW;
SATA 11

Lee, Helen Elaine 1959(?)- .... **CLC 86**
See also CA 148

Lee, Julian
See Latham, Jean Lee

Lee, Larry
See Lee, Lawrence

Lee, Laurie
1914- .... **CLC 90; DAB; DAM POP**
See also CA 77-80; CANR 33; DLB 27;
MTCW

Lee, Lawrence 1941-1990 .... **CLC 34**
See also CA 131; CANR 43

Lee, Manfred B(ennington)
1905-1971 .... **CLC 11**
See also Queen, Ellery
See also CA 1-4R; 29-32R; CANR 2;
DLB 137

Lee, Stan 1922- .... **CLC 17**
See also AAYA 5; CA 108; 111; INT 111

Lee, Tanith 1947- .... **CLC 46**
See also AAYA 15; CA 37-40R; CANR 53;
SATA 8, 88

Lee, Vernon .... **TCLC 5**
See also Paget, Violet
See also DLB 57, 153, 156, 174

Lee, William
See Burroughs, William S(eward)

Lee, Willy
See Burroughs, William S(eward)

Lee-Hamilton, Eugene (Jacob)
1845-1907 .... **TCLC 22**
See also CA 117

Leet, Judith 1935- .... **CLC 11**

Le Fanu, Joseph Sheridan
1814-1873 .... **NCLC 9, 58; DAM POP;
SSC 14**
See also DLB 21, 70, 159

Leffland, Ella 1931- .... **CLC 19**
See also CA 29-32R; CANR 35; DLBY 84;
INT CANR-35; SATA 65

Leger, Alexis
See Leger, (Marie-Rene Auguste) Alexis
Saint-Leger

**Leger, (Marie-Rene Auguste) Alexis
Saint-Leger**
1887-1975 .... **CLC 11; DAM POET**
See also Perse, St.-John
See also CA 13-16R; 61-64; CANR 43;
MTCW

Leger, Saintleger
See Leger, (Marie-Rene Auguste) Alexis
Saint-Leger

Le Guin, Ursula K(roeber)
1929- ...... **CLC 8, 13, 22, 45, 71; DAB;
DAC; DAM MST, POP; SSC 12**
See also AAYA 9; AITN 1; CA 21-24R;
CANR 9, 32, 52; CDALB 1968-1988;
CLR 3, 28; DLB 8, 52; INT CANR-32;
JRDA; MAICYA; MTCW; SATA 4, 52

Lehmann, Rosamond (Nina)
1901-1990 .... **CLC 5**
See also CA 77-80; 131; CANR 8; DLB 15

Leiber, Fritz (Reuter, Jr.)
1910-1992 .... **CLC 25**
See also CA 45-48; 139; CANR 2, 40;
DLB 8; MTCW; SATA 45;
SATA-Obit 73

Leibniz, Gottfried Wilhelm von
1646-1716 .... **LC 35**
See also DLB 168

Leimbach, Martha 1963-
See Leimbach, Marti
See also CA 130

Leimbach, Marti .... **CLC 65**
See also Leimbach, Martha

Leino, Eino .... **TCLC 24**
See also Loennbohm, Armas Eino Leopold

Leiris, Michel (Julien) 1901-1990 ... **CLC 61**
See also CA 119; 128; 132

Leithauser, Brad 1953- .... **CLC 27**
See also CA 107; CANR 27; DLB 120

Lelchuk, Alan 1938- .... **CLC 5**
See also CA 45-48; CAAS 20; CANR 1

Lem, Stanislaw 1921- .... **CLC 8, 15, 40**
See also CA 105; CAAS 1; CANR 32;
MTCW

Lemann, Nancy 1956- .... **CLC 39**
See also CA 118; 136

Lemonnier, (Antoine Louis) Camille
1844-1913 .... **TCLC 22**
See also CA 121

Lenau, Nikolaus 1802-1850 ...... **NCLC 16**

L'Engle, Madeleine (Camp Franklin)
1918- .... **CLC 12; DAM POP**
See also AAYA 1; AITN 2; CA 1-4R;
CANR 3, 21, 39; CLR 1, 14; DLB 52;
JRDA; MAICYA; MTCW; SAAS 15;
SATA 1, 27, 75

Lengyel, Jozsef 1896-1975.......... **CLC 7**
See also CA 85-88; 57-60

Lenin 1870-1924
See Lenin, V. I.
See also CA 121

Lenin, V. I. .... **TCLC 67**
See also Lenin

Lennon, John (Ono)
1940-1980 .... **CLC 12, 35**
See also CA 102

Lennox, Charlotte Ramsay
1729(?)-1804 .... **NCLC 23**
See also DLB 39

Lentricchia, Frank (Jr.) 1940-...... **CLC 34**
See also CA 25-28R; CANR 19

Lenz, Siegfried 1926-............ **CLC 27**
See also CA 89-92; DLB 75

Leonard, Elmore (John, Jr.)
1925- ..... **CLC 28, 34, 71; DAM POP**
See also AITN 1; BEST 89:1, 90:4;
CA 81-84; CANR 12, 28, 53; DLB 173;
INT CANR-28; MTCW

Leonard, Hugh................... **CLC 19**
See also Byrne, John Keyes
See also DLB 13

Leonov, Leonid (Maximovich)
1899-1994 .... **CLC 92; DAM NOV**
See also CA 129; MTCW

Leopardi, (Conte) Giacomo
1798-1837 .... **NCLC 22**

Le Reveler
See Artaud, Antonin (Marie Joseph)

Lerman, Eleanor 1952-............ **CLC 9**
See also CA 85-88

Lerman, Rhoda 1936-............ **CLC 56**
See also CA 49-52

Lermontov, Mikhail Yuryevich
1814-1841 .... **NCLC 47**

Leroux, Gaston 1868-1927....... **TCLC 25**
See also CA 108; 136; SATA 65

Lesage, Alain-Rene 1668-1747...... **LC 28**

Leskov, Nikolai (Semyonovich)
1831-1895 .... **NCLC 25**

Lessing, Doris (May)
1919- ..... **CLC 1, 2, 3, 6, 10, 15, 22, 40,
94; DA; DAB; DAC; DAM MST, NOV;
SSC 6**
See also CA 9-12R; CAAS 14; CANR 33,
54; CDBLB 1960 to Present; DLB 15,
139; DLBY 85; MTCW

Lessing, Gotthold Ephraim
1729-1781 .... **LC 8**
See also DLB 97

Lester, Richard 1932-............ **CLC 20**

Lever, Charles (James)
1806-1872 .... **NCLC 23**
See also DLB 21

Leverson, Ada 1865(?)-1936(?) .... **TCLC 18**
See also Elaine
See also CA 117; DLB 153

Levertov, Denise
1923- ...... **CLC 1, 2, 3, 5, 8, 15, 28, 66;
DAM POET; PC 11**
See also CA 1-4R; CAAS 19; CANR 3, 29,
50; DLB 5, 165; INT CANR-29; MTCW

Levi, Jonathan................... **CLC 76**

Levi, Peter (Chad Tigar) 1931-..... **CLC 41**
See also CA 5-8R; CANR 34; DLB 40

Levi, Primo
1919-1987 .... **CLC 37, 50; SSC 12**
See also CA 13-16R; 122; CANR 12, 33;
MTCW

Levin, Ira 1929- ..... **CLC 3, 6; DAM POP**
See also CA 21-24R; CANR 17, 44;
MTCW; SATA 66

Levin, Meyer
1905-1981 .... **CLC 7; DAM POP**
See also AITN 1; CA 9-12R; 104;
CANR 15; DLB 9, 28; DLBY 81;
SATA 21; SATA-Obit 27

Levine, Norman 1924-............ **CLC 54**
See also CA 73-76; CAAS 23; CANR 14;
DLB 88

Levine, Philip
1928- .... **CLC 2, 4, 5, 9, 14, 33;
DAM POET**
See also CA 9-12R; CANR 9, 37, 52;
DLB 5

Levinson, Deirdre 1931-.......... **CLC 49**
See also CA 73-76

Levi-Strauss, Claude 1908- .... **CLC 38**
See also CA 1-4R; CANR 6, 32; MTCW

Levitin, Sonia (Wolff) 1934- .... **CLC 17**
See also AAYA 13; CA 29-32R; CANR 14,
32; JRDA; MAICYA; SAAS 2; SATA 4,
68

Levon, O. U.
See Kesey, Ken (Elton)

Levy, Amy 1861-1889.......... **NCLC 59**
See also DLB 156

Lewes, George Henry
1817-1878 .... **NCLC 25**
See also DLB 55, 144

Lewis, Alun 1915-1944........... **TCLC 3**
See also CA 104; DLB 20, 162

Lewis, C. Day
See Day Lewis, C(ecil)

Lewis, C(live) S(taples)
1898-1963 ..... **CLC 1, 3, 6, 14, 27; DA;
DAB; DAC; DAM MST, NOV, POP;
WLC**
See also AAYA 3; CA 81-84; CANR 33;
CDBLB 1945-1960; CLR 3, 27; DLB 15,
100, 160; JRDA; MAICYA; MTCW;
SATA 13

Lewis, Janet 1899- .... **CLC 41**
See also Winters, Janet Lewis
See also CA 9-12R; CANR 29; CAP 1;
DLBY 87

Lewis, Matthew Gregory
1775-1818 .... **NCLC 11**
See also DLB 39, 158

Lewis, (Harry) Sinclair
1885-1951 ..... **TCLC 4, 13, 23, 39; DA;
DAB; DAC; DAM MST, NOV; WLC**
See also CA 104; 133; CDALB 1917-1929;
DLB 9, 102; DLBD 1; MTCW

Lewis, (Percy) Wyndham
1884(?)-1957 .... **TCLC 2, 9**
See also CA 104; DLB 15

Lewisohn, Ludwig 1883-1955...... **TCLC 19**
See also CA 107; DLB 4, 9, 28, 102

Leyner, Mark 1956-.............. **CLC 92**
See also CA 110; CANR 28, 53

Lezama Lima, Jose
1910-1976 .... **CLC 4, 10; DAM MULT**
See also CA 77-80; DLB 113; HW

L'Heureux, John (Clarke) 1934-.... **CLC 52**
See also CA 13-16R; CANR 23, 45

Liddell, C. H.
See Kuttner, Henry

Lie, Jonas (Lauritz Idemil)
1833-1908(?) .... **TCLC 5**
See also CA 115

Lieber, Joel 1937-1971............ **CLC 6**
See also CA 73-76; 29-32R

Lieber, Stanley Martin
See Lee, Stan

Lieberman, Laurence (James)
1935- .... **CLC 4, 36**
See also CA 17-20R; CANR 8, 36

Lieksman, Anders
See Haavikko, Paavo Juhani

Li Fei-kan 1904-
See Pa Chin
See also CA 105

Lifton, Robert Jay 1926-.......... **CLC 67**
See also CA 17-20R; CANR 27;
INT CANR-27; SATA 66

Lightfoot, Gordon 1938-.......... **CLC 26**
See also CA 109

Lightman, Alan P. 1948- .... **CLC 81**
See also CA 141

Ligotti, Thomas (Robert)
1953- .... **CLC 44; SSC 16**
See also CA 123; CANR 49

Li Ho 791-817.................... **PC 13**

Liliencron, (Friedrich Adolf Axel) Detlev von
1844-1909 .... **TCLC 18**
See also CA 117

Lilly, William 1602-1681.......... **LC 27**

Lima, Jose Lezama
See Lezama Lima, Jose

Lima Barreto, Afonso Henrique de
1881-1922 .... **TCLC 23**
See also CA 117

Limonov, Edward 1944-.......... **CLC 67**
See also CA 137

Lin, Frank
See Atherton, Gertrude (Franklin Horn)

Lincoln, Abraham 1809-1865..... **NCLC 18**

Lind, Jakov .... **CLC 1, 2, 4, 27, 82**
See also Landwirth, Heinz
See also CAAS 4

Loxsmith, John
   See Brunner, John (Kilian Houston)

Loy, Mina .... **CLC 28; DAM POET; PC 16**
   See also Lowry, Mina Gertrude
   See also DLB 4, 54

Loyson-Bridet
   See Schwob, (Mayer Andre) Marcel

Lucas, Craig 1951-............... **CLC 64**
   See also CA 137

Lucas, George 1944-.............. **CLC 16**
   See also AAYA 1; CA 77-80; CANR 30;
   SATA 56

Lucas, Hans
   See Godard, Jean-Luc

Lucas, Victoria
   See Plath, Sylvia

Ludlam, Charles 1943-1987..... **CLC 46, 50**
   See also CA 85-88; 122

Ludlum, Robert
   1927- ... **CLC 22, 43; DAM NOV, POP**
   See also AAYA 10; BEST 89:1, 90:3;
   CA 33-36R; CANR 25, 41; DLBY 82;
   MTCW

Ludwig, Ken.................... **CLC 60**

Ludwig, Otto 1813-1865......... **NCLC 4**
   See also DLB 129

Lugones, Leopoldo 1874-1938..... **TCLC 15**
   See also CA 116; 131; HW

Lu Hsun 1881-1936 ...... **TCLC 3; SSC 20**
   See also Shu-Jen, Chou

Lukacs, George .... **CLC 24**
   See also Lukacs, Gyorgy (Szegeny von)

Lukacs, Gyorgy (Szegeny von) 1885-1971
   See Lukacs, George
   See also CA 101; 29-32R

Luke, Peter (Ambrose Cyprian)
   1919-1995 .... **CLC 38**
   See also CA 81-84; 147; DLB 13

Lunar, Dennis
   See Mungo, Raymond

Lurie, Alison 1926-........ **CLC 4, 5, 18, 39**
   See also CA 1-4R; CANR 2, 17, 50; DLB 2;
   MTCW; SATA 46

Lustig, Arnost 1926-.............. **CLC 56**
   See also AAYA 3; CA 69-72; CANR 47;
   SATA 56

Luther, Martin 1483-1546........ **LC 9, 37**

Luxemburg, Rosa 1870(?)-1919.... **TCLC 63**
   See also CA 118

Luzi, Mario 1914-................. **CLC 13**
   See also CA 61-64; CANR 9; DLB 128

L'Ymagier
   See Gourmont, Remy (-Marie-Charles) de

Lynch, B. Suarez
   See Bioy Casares, Adolfo; Borges, Jorge
   Luis

Lynch, David (K.) 1946-.......... **CLC 66**
   See also CA 124; 129

Lynch, James
   See Andreyev, Leonid (Nikolaevich)

Lynch Davis, B.
   See Bioy Casares, Adolfo; Borges, Jorge
   Luis

Lyndsay, Sir David 1490-1555 ...... **LC 20**

Lynn, Kenneth S(chuyler) 1923-.... **CLC 50**
   See also CA 1-4R; CANR 3, 27

Lynx
   See West, Rebecca

Lyons, Marcus
   See Blish, James (Benjamin)

Lyre, Pinchbeck
   See Sassoon, Siegfried (Lorraine)

Lytle, Andrew (Nelson) 1902-1995 .. **CLC 22**
   See also CA 9-12R; 150; DLB 6; DLBY 95

Lyttelton, George 1709-1773........ **LC 10**

Maas, Peter 1929- .... **CLC 29**
   See also CA 93-96; INT 93-96

Macaulay, Rose 1881-1958 ..... **TCLC 7, 44**
   See also CA 104; DLB 36

Macaulay, Thomas Babington
   1800-1859 .... **NCLC 42**
   See also CDBLB 1832-1890; DLB 32, 55

MacBeth, George (Mann)
   1932-1992 .... **CLC 2, 5, 9**
   See also CA 25-28R; 136; DLB 40; MTCW;
   SATA 4; SATA-Obit 70

MacCaig, Norman (Alexander)
   1910- ..... **CLC 36; DAB; DAM POET**
   See also CA 9-12R; CANR 3, 34; DLB 27

MacCarthy, (Sir Charles Otto) Desmond
   1877-1952 .... **TCLC 36**

MacDiarmid, Hugh
   .... **CLC 2, 4, 11, 19, 63; PC 9**
   See also Grieve, C(hristopher) M(urray)
   See also CDBLB 1945-1960; DLB 20

MacDonald, Anson
   See Heinlein, Robert A(nson)

Macdonald, Cynthia 1928-...... **CLC 13, 19**
   See also CA 49-52; CANR 4, 44; DLB 105

MacDonald, George 1824-1905..... **TCLC 9**
   See also CA 106; 137; DLB 18, 163;
   MAICYA; SATA 33

Macdonald, John
   See Millar, Kenneth

MacDonald, John D(ann)
   1916-1986 .... **CLC 3, 27, 44;**
                     DAM NOV, POP
   See also CA 1-4R; 121; CANR 1, 19;
   DLB 8; DLBY 86; MTCW

Macdonald, John Ross
   See Millar, Kenneth

Macdonald, Ross..... **CLC 1, 2, 3, 14, 34, 41**
   See also Millar, Kenneth
   See also DLBD 6

MacDougal, John
   See Blish, James (Benjamin)

MacEwen, Gwendolyn (Margaret)
   1941-1987 .... **CLC 13, 55**
   See also CA 9-12R; 124; CANR 7, 22;
   DLB 53; SATA 50; SATA-Obit 55

Macha, Karel Hynek 1810-1846.. **NCLC 46**

Machado (y Ruiz), Antonio
   1875-1939 .... **TCLC 3**
   See also CA 104; DLB 108

Machado de Assis, Joaquim Maria
   1839-1908 ..... **TCLC 10; BLC; SSC 24**
   See also CA 107; 153

Machen, Arthur.......... **TCLC 4; SSC 20**
   See also Jones, Arthur Llewellyn
   See also DLB 36, 156

Machiavelli, Niccolo
   1469-1527 .... **LC 8, 36; DA; DAB;**
                    DAC; DAM MST

MacInnes, Colin 1914-1976...... **CLC 4, 23**
   See also CA 69-72; 65-68; CANR 21;
   DLB 14; MTCW

MacInnes, Helen (Clark)
   1907-1985 ..... **CLC 27, 39; DAM POP**
   See also CA 1-4R; 117; CANR 1, 28;
   DLB 87; MTCW; SATA 22;
   SATA-Obit 44

Mackay, Mary 1855-1924
   See Corelli, Marie
   See also CA 118

Mackenzie, Compton (Edward Montague)
   1883-1972 .... **CLC 18**
   See also CA 21-22; 37-40R; CAP 2;
   DLB 34, 100

Mackenzie, Henry 1745-1831 .... **NCLC 41**
   See also DLB 39

Mackintosh, Elizabeth 1896(?)-1952
   See Tey, Josephine
   See also CA 110

MacLaren, James
   See Grieve, C(hristopher) M(urray)

Mac Laverty, Bernard 1942-....... **CLC 31**
   See also CA 116; 118; CANR 43; INT 118

MacLean, Alistair (Stuart)
   1922-1987 .... **CLC 3, 13, 50, 63;**
                      DAM POP
   See also CA 57-60; 121; CANR 28; MTCW;
   SATA 23; SATA-Obit 50

Maclean, Norman (Fitzroy)
   1902-1990 .... **CLC 78; DAM POP;**
                    SSC 13
   See also CA 102; 132; CANR 49

MacLeish, Archibald
   1892-1982 .... **CLC 3, 8, 14, 68;**
                      DAM POET
   See also CA 9-12R; 106; CANR 33; DLB 4,
   7, 45; DLBY 82; MTCW

MacLennan, (John) Hugh
   1907-1990 .... **CLC 2, 14, 92; DAC;**
                    DAM MST
   See also CA 5-8R; 142; CANR 33; DLB 68;
   MTCW

MacLeod, Alistair
   1936- .... **CLC 56; DAC; DAM MST**
   See also CA 123; DLB 60

MacNeice, (Frederick) Louis
   1907-1963 ...... **CLC 1, 4, 10, 53; DAB;**
                    DAM POET
   See also CA 85-88; DLB 10, 20; MTCW

MacNeill, Dand
   See Fraser, George MacDonald

Macpherson, James 1736-1796 ...... **LC 29**
   See also DLB 109

Macpherson, (Jean) Jay 1931-...... **CLC 14**
   See also CA 5-8R; DLB 53

MacShane, Frank 1927-.......... **CLC 39**
   See also CA 9-12R; CANR 3, 33; DLB 111

Macumber, Mari
   See Sandoz, Mari(e Susette)

Marivaux, Pierre Carlet de Chamblain de
1688-1763 .... **LC 4**

Markandaya, Kamala .... **CLC 8, 38**
See also Taylor, Kamala (Purnaiya)

Markfield, Wallace 1926-.......... **CLC 8**
See also CA 69-72; CAAS 3; DLB 2, 28

Markham, Edwin 1852-1940 ...... **TCLC 47**
See also DLB 54

Markham, Robert
See Amis, Kingsley (William)

Marks, J
See Highwater, Jamake (Mamake)

Marks-Highwater, J
See Highwater, Jamake (Mamake)

Markson, David M(errill) 1927- .... **CLC 67**
See also CA 49-52; CANR 1

Marley, Bob .... **CLC 17**
See also Marley, Robert Nesta

Marley, Robert Nesta 1945-1981
See Marley, Bob
See also CA 107; 103

Marlowe, Christopher
1564-1593 ..... **LC 22; DA; DAB; DAC;**
     DAM DRAM, MST; DC 1; WLC
See also CDBLB Before 1660; DLB 62

Marlowe, Stephen 1928-
See Queen, Ellery
See also CA 13-16R; CANR 6, 55

Marmontel, Jean-Francois
1723-1799 .... **LC 2**

Marquand, John P(hillips)
1893-1960 .... **CLC 2, 10**
See also CA 85-88; DLB 9, 102

Marques, Rene
1919-1979 ...... **CLC 96; DAM MULT;**
     HLC
See also CA 97-100; 85-88; DLB 113; HW

Marquez, Gabriel (Jose) Garcia
See Garcia Marquez, Gabriel (Jose)

Marquis, Don(ald Robert Perry)
1878-1937 .... **TCLC 7**
See also CA 104; DLB 11, 25

Marric, J. J.
See Creasey, John

Marrow, Bernard
See Moore, Brian

Marryat, Frederick 1792-1848 .... **NCLC 3**
See also DLB 21, 163

Marsden, James
See Creasey, John

Marsh, (Edith) Ngaio
1899-1982 ...... **CLC 7, 53; DAM POP**
See also CA 9-12R; CANR 6; DLB 77;
MTCW

Marshall, Garry 1934-........... **CLC 17**
See also AAYA 3; CA 111; SATA 60

Marshall, Paule
1929- .... **CLC 27, 72; BLC;**
     DAM MULT; SSC 3
See also BW 2; CA 77-80; CANR 25;
DLB 157; MTCW

Marsten, Richard
See Hunter, Evan

Marston, John
1576-1634 ...... **LC 33; DAM DRAM**
See also DLB 58, 172

Martha, Henry
See Harris, Mark

Martial c. 40-c. 104 .... **PC 10**

Martin, Ken
See Hubbard, L(afayette) Ron(ald)

Martin, Richard
See Creasey, John

Martin, Steve 1945-.............. **CLC 30**
See also CA 97-100; CANR 30; MTCW

Martin, Valerie 1948-............ **CLC 89**
See also BEST 90:2; CA 85-88; CANR 49

Martin, Violet Florence
1862-1915 .... **TCLC 51**

Martin, Webber
See Silverberg, Robert

Martindale, Patrick Victor
See White, Patrick (Victor Martindale)

Martin du Gard, Roger
1881-1958 .... **TCLC 24**
See also CA 118; DLB 65

Martineau, Harriet 1802-1876.... **NCLC 26**
See also DLB 21, 55, 159, 163, 166;
YABC 2

Martines, Julia
See O'Faolain, Julia

Martinez, Jacinto Benavente y
See Benavente (y Martinez), Jacinto

Martinez Ruiz, Jose 1873-1967
See Azorin; Ruiz, Jose Martinez
See also CA 93-96; HW

Martinez Sierra, Gregorio
1881-1947 .... **TCLC 6**
See also CA 115

Martinez Sierra, Maria (de la O'LeJarraga)
1874-1974 .... **TCLC 6**
See also CA 115

Martinsen, Martin
See Follett, Ken(neth Martin)

Martinson, Harry (Edmund)
1904-1978 .... **CLC 14**
See also CA 77-80; CANR 34

Marut, Ret
See Traven, B.

Marut, Robert
See Traven, B.

Marvell, Andrew
1621-1678 ...... **LC 4; DA; DAB; DAC;**
     DAM MST, POET; PC 10; WLC
See also CDBLB 1660-1789; DLB 131

Marx, Karl (Heinrich)
1818-1883 .... **NCLC 17**
See also DLB 129

Masaoka Shiki .... **TCLC 18**
See also Masaoka Tsunenori

Masaoka Tsunenori 1867-1902
See Masaoka Shiki
See also CA 117

Masefield, John (Edward)
1878-1967 .... **CLC 11, 47; DAM POET**
See also CA 19-20; 25-28R; CANR 33;
CAP 2; CDBLB 1890-1914; DLB 10, 19,
153, 160; MTCW; SATA 19

Maso, Carole 19(?)- .... **CLC 44**

Mason, Bobbie Ann
1940- .... **CLC 28, 43, 82; SSC 4**
See also AAYA 5; CA 53-56; CANR 11,
31; DLB 173; DLBY 87; INT CANR-31;
MTCW

Mason, Ernst
See Pohl, Frederik

Mason, Lee W.
See Malzberg, Barry N(athaniel)

Mason, Nick 1945-.............. **CLC 35**

Mason, Tally
See Derleth, August (William)

Mass, William
See Gibson, William

Masters, Edgar Lee
1868-1950 ...... **TCLC 2, 25; DA; DAC;**
     DAM MST, POET; PC 1
See also CA 104; 133; CDALB 1865-1917;
DLB 54; MTCW

Masters, Hilary 1928-........... **CLC 48**
See also CA 25-28R; CANR 13, 47

Mastrosimone, William 19(?)-...... **CLC 36**

Mathe, Albert
See Camus, Albert

Matheson, Richard Burton 1926- ... **CLC 37**
See also CA 97-100; DLB 8, 44; INT 97-100

Mathews, Harry 1930-.......... **CLC 6, 52**
See also CA 21-24R; CAAS 6; CANR 18,
40

Mathews, John Joseph
1894-1979 ...... **CLC 84; DAM MULT**
See also CA 19-20; 142; CANR 45; CAP 2;
DLB 175; NNAL

Mathias, Roland (Glyn) 1915-...... **CLC 45**
See also CA 97-100; CANR 19, 41; DLB 27

Matsuo Basho 1644-1694........... **PC 3**
See also DAM POET

Mattheson, Rodney
See Creasey, John

Matthews, Greg 1949-............ **CLC 45**
See also CA 135

Matthews, William 1942-......... **CLC 40**
See also CA 29-32R; CAAS 18; CANR 12;
DLB 5

Matthias, John (Edward) 1941-..... **CLC 9**
See also CA 33-36R; CANR 56

Matthiessen, Peter
1927- .... **CLC 5, 7, 11, 32, 64;**
     DAM NOV
See also AAYA 6; BEST 90:4; CA 9-12R;
CANR 21, 50; DLB 6, 173; MTCW;
SATA 27

Maturin, Charles Robert
1780(?)-1824 .... **NCLC 6**

Matute (Ausejo), Ana Maria
1925- .... **CLC 11**
See also CA 89-92; MTCW

McLuhan, (Herbert) Marshall
1911-1980 .... **CLC 37, 83**
See also CA 9-12R; 102; CANR 12, 34;
DLB 88; INT CANR-12; MTCW

McMillan, Terry (L.)
1951- .... **CLC 50, 61; DAM MULT,
NOV, POP**
See also BW 2; CA 140

McMurtry, Larry (Jeff)
1936- .... **CLC 2, 3, 7, 11, 27, 44;
DAM NOV, POP**
See also AAYA 15; AITN 2; BEST 89:2;
CA 5-8R; CANR 19, 43;
CDALB 1968-1988; DLB 2, 143;
DLBY 80, 87; MTCW

McNally, T. M. 1961- .... **CLC 82**

McNally, Terrence
1939- ... **CLC 4, 7, 41, 91; DAM DRAM**
See also CA 45-48; CANR 2, 56; DLB 7

McNamer, Deirdre 1950-......... **CLC 70**

McNeile, Herman Cyril 1888-1937
See Sapper
See also DLB 77

McNickle, (William) D'Arcy
1904-1977 ..... **CLC 89; DAM MULT**
See also CA 9-12R; 85-88; CANR 5, 45;
DLB 175; NNAL; SATA-Obit 22

McPhee, John (Angus) 1931- ...... **CLC 36**
See also BEST 90:1; CA 65-68; CANR 20,
46; MTCW

McPherson, James Alan
1943- .... **CLC 19, 77**
See also BW 1; CA 25-28R; CAAS 17;
CANR 24; DLB 38; MTCW

McPherson, William (Alexander)
1933- .... **CLC 34**
See also CA 69-72; CANR 28;
INT CANR-28

Mead, Margaret 1901-1978........ **CLC 37**
See also AITN 1; CA 1-4R; 81-84;
CANR 4; MTCW; SATA-Obit 20

Meaker, Marijane (Agnes) 1927-
See Kerr, M. E.
See also CA 107; CANR 37; INT 107;
JRDA; MAICYA; MTCW; SATA 20, 61

Medoff, Mark (Howard)
1940- .... **CLC 6, 23; DAM DRAM**
See also AITN 1; CA 53-56; CANR 5;
DLB 7; INT CANR-5

Medvedev, P. N.
See Bakhtin, Mikhail Mikhailovich

Meged, Aharon
See Megged, Aharon

Meged, Aron
See Megged, Aharon

Megged, Aharon 1920-............ **CLC 9**
See also CA 49-52; CAAS 13; CANR 1

Mehta, Ved (Parkash) 1934-....... **CLC 37**
See also CA 1-4R; CANR 2, 23; MTCW

Melanter
See Blackmore, R(ichard) D(oddridge)

Melikow, Loris
See Hofmannsthal, Hugo von

Melmoth, Sebastian
See Wilde, Oscar (Fingal O'Flahertie Wills)

Meltzer, Milton 1915- .... **CLC 26**
See also AAYA 8; CA 13-16R; CANR 38;
CLR 13; DLB 61; JRDA; MAICYA;
SAAS 1; SATA 1, 50, 80

Melville, Herman
1819-1891 ..... **NCLC 3, 12, 29, 45, 49;
DA; DAB; DAC; DAM MST, NOV;
SSC 1, 17; WLC**
See also CDALB 1640-1865; DLB 3, 74;
SATA 59

Menander
c. 342B.C.-c. 292B.C......... **CMLC 9;
DAM DRAM; DC 3**

Mencken, H(enry) L(ouis)
1880-1956 .... **TCLC 13**
See also CA 105; 125; CDALB 1917-1929;
DLB 11, 29, 63, 137; MTCW

Mendelsohn, Jane 1965(?)- .... **CLC 99**
See also CA 154

Mercer, David
1928-1980 ...... **CLC 5; DAM DRAM**
See also CA 9-12R; 102; CANR 23;
DLB 13; MTCW

Merchant, Paul
See Ellison, Harlan (Jay)

Meredith, George
1828-1909 .. **TCLC 17, 43; DAM POET**
See also CA 117; 153; CDBLB 1832-1890;
DLB 18, 35, 57, 159

Meredith, William (Morris)
1919- .. **CLC 4, 13, 22, 55; DAM POET**
See also CA 9-12R; CAAS 14; CANR 6, 40;
DLB 5

Merezhkovsky, Dmitry Sergeyevich
1865-1941 .... **TCLC 29**

Merimee, Prosper
1803-1870 .... **NCLC 6; SSC 7**
See also DLB 119

Merkin, Daphne 1954-............ **CLC 44**
See also CA 123

Merlin, Arthur
See Blish, James (Benjamin)

Merrill, James (Ingram)
1926-1995 .... **CLC 2, 3, 6, 8, 13, 18, 34,
91; DAM POET**
See also CA 13-16R; 147; CANR 10, 49;
DLB 5, 165; DLBY 85; INT CANR-10;
MTCW

Merriman, Alex
See Silverberg, Robert

Merritt, E. B.
See Waddington, Miriam

Merton, Thomas
1915-1968 .. **CLC 1, 3, 11, 34, 83; PC 10**
See also CA 5-8R; 25-28R; CANR 22, 53;
DLB 48; DLBY 81; MTCW

Merwin, W(illiam) S(tanley)
1927- ...... **CLC 1, 2, 3, 5, 8, 13, 18, 45,
88; DAM POET**
See also CA 13-16R; CANR 15, 51; DLB 5,
169; INT CANR-15; MTCW

Metcalf, John 1938-............. **CLC 37**
See also CA 113; DLB 60

Metcalf, Suzanne
See Baum, L(yman) Frank

Mew, Charlotte (Mary)
1870-1928 .... **TCLC 8**
See also CA 105; DLB 19, 135

Mewshaw, Michael 1943-.......... **CLC 9**
See also CA 53-56; CANR 7, 47; DLBY 80

Meyer, June
See Jordan, June

Meyer, Lynn
See Slavitt, David R(ytman)

Meyer-Meyrink, Gustav 1868-1932
See Meyrink, Gustav
See also CA 117

Meyers, Jeffrey 1939- .... **CLC 39**
See also CA 73-76; CANR 54; DLB 111

Meynell, Alice (Christina Gertrude Thompson)
1847-1922 .... **TCLC 6**
See also CA 104; DLB 19, 98

Meyrink, Gustav .... **TCLC 21**
See also Meyer-Meyrink, Gustav
See also DLB 81

Michaels, Leonard
1933- .... **CLC 6, 25; SSC 16**
See also CA 61-64; CANR 21; DLB 130;
MTCW

Michaux, Henri 1899-1984 ...... **CLC 8, 19**
See also CA 85-88; 114

Michelangelo 1475-1564........... **LC 12**

Michelet, Jules 1798-1874...... **NCLC 31**

Michener, James A(lbert)
1907(?)- .... **CLC 1, 5, 11, 29, 60;
DAM NOV, POP**
See also AITN 1; BEST 90:1; CA 5-8R;
CANR 21, 45; DLB 6; MTCW

Mickiewicz, Adam 1798-1855 ..... **NCLC 3**

Middleton, Christopher 1926-...... **CLC 13**
See also CA 13-16R; CANR 29, 54;
DLB 40

Middleton, Richard (Barham)
1882-1911 .... **TCLC 56**
See also DLB 156

Middleton, Stanley 1919-........ **CLC 7, 38**
See also CA 25-28R; CAAS 23; CANR 21,
46; DLB 14

Middleton, Thomas
1580-1627 .... **LC 33; DAM DRAM,
MST; DC 5**
See also DLB 58

Migueis, Jose Rodrigues 1901-..... **CLC 10**

Mikszath, Kalman 1847-1910 ..... **TCLC 31**

Miles, Josephine (Louise)
1911-1985 .... **CLC 1, 2, 14, 34, 39;
DAM POET**
See also CA 1-4R; 116; CANR 2, 55;
DLB 48

Militant
See Sandburg, Carl (August)

Mill, John Stuart 1806-1873 .. **NCLC 11, 58**
See also CDBLB 1832-1890; DLB 55

Millar, Kenneth
1915-1983 .... **CLC 14; DAM POP**
See also Macdonald, Ross
See also CA 9-12R; 110; CANR 16; DLB 2;
DLBD 6; DLBY 83; MTCW

Millay, E. Vincent
See Millay, Edna St. Vincent

Millay, Edna St. Vincent
1892-1950 . . . . . **TCLC 4, 49; DA; DAB;
DAC; DAM MST, POET; PC 6**
See also CA 104; 130; CDALB 1917-1929;
DLB 45; MTCW

Miller, Arthur
1915- . . . . **CLC 1, 2, 6, 10, 15, 26, 47, 78;
DA; DAB; DAC; DAM DRAM, MST;
DC 1; WLC**
See also AAYA 15; AITN 1; CA 1-4R;
CABS 3; CANR 2, 30, 54;
CDALB 1941-1968; DLB 7; MTCW

Miller, Henry (Valentine)
1891-1980 . . . . **CLC 1, 2, 4, 9, 14, 43, 84;
DA; DAB; DAC; DAM MST, NOV;
WLC**
See also CA 9-12R; 97-100; CANR 33;
CDALB 1929-1941; DLB 4, 9; DLBY 80;
MTCW

Miller, Jason 1939(?)- . . . . **CLC 2**
See also AITN 1; CA 73-76; DLB 7

Miller, Sue 1943- . . . . . **CLC 44; DAM POP**
See also BEST 90:3; CA 139; DLB 143

Miller, Walter M(ichael, Jr.)
1923- . . . . **CLC 4, 30**
See also CA 85-88; DLB 8

Millett, Kate 1934- . . . . **CLC 67**
See also AITN 1; CA 73-76; CANR 32, 53;
MTCW

Millhauser, Steven 1943- . . . . **CLC 21, 54**
See also CA 110; 111; DLB 2; INT 111

Millin, Sarah Gertrude 1889-1968 . . **CLC 49**
See also CA 102; 93-96

Milne, A(lan) A(lexander)
1882-1956 . . . . **TCLC 6; DAB; DAC;
DAM MST**
See also CA 104; 133; CLR 1, 26; DLB 10,
77, 100, 160; MAICYA; MTCW;
YABC 1

Milner, Ron(ald)
1938- . . . . . **CLC 56; BLC; DAM MULT**
See also AITN 1; BW 1; CA 73-76;
CANR 24; DLB 38; MTCW

Milosz, Czeslaw
1911- . . . . **CLC 5, 11, 22, 31, 56, 82;
DAM MST, POET; PC 8**
See also CA 81-84; CANR 23, 51; MTCW

Milton, John
1608-1674 . . . . . . **LC 9; DA; DAB; DAC;
DAM MST, POET; WLC**
See also CDBLB 1660-1789; DLB 131, 151

Min, Anchee 1957- . . . . **CLC 86**
See also CA 146

Minehaha, Cornelius
See Wedekind, (Benjamin) Frank(lin)

Miner, Valerie 1947- . . . . **CLC 40**
See also CA 97-100

Minimo, Duca
See D'Annunzio, Gabriele

Minot, Susan 1956- . . . . **CLC 44**
See also CA 134

Minus, Ed 1938- . . . . **CLC 39**

Miranda, Javier
See Bioy Casares, Adolfo

Mirbeau, Octave 1848-1917 . . . . . . **TCLC 55**
See also DLB 123

Miro (Ferrer), Gabriel (Francisco Victor)
1879-1930 . . . . **TCLC 5**
See also CA 104

Mishima, Yukio
. . . . . . **CLC 2, 4, 6, 9, 27; DC 1; SSC 4**
See also Hiraoka, Kimitake

Mistral, Frederic 1830-1914 . . . . . . **TCLC 51**
See also CA 122

Mistral, Gabriela . . . . **TCLC 2; HLC**
See also Godoy Alcayaga, Lucila

Mistry, Rohinton 1952- . . . . . . **CLC 71; DAC**
See also CA 141

Mitchell, Clyde
See Ellison, Harlan (Jay); Silverberg, Robert

Mitchell, James Leslie 1901-1935
See Gibbon, Lewis Grassic
See also CA 104; DLB 15

Mitchell, Joni 1943- . . . . **CLC 12**
See also CA 112

Mitchell, Joseph (Quincy)
1908-1996 . . . . **CLC 98**
See also CA 77-80; 152

Mitchell, Margaret (Munnerlyn)
1900-1949 . . . . . . **TCLC 11; DAM NOV,
POP**
See also CA 109; 125; CANR 55; DLB 9;
MTCW

Mitchell, Peggy
See Mitchell, Margaret (Munnerlyn)

Mitchell, S(ilas) Weir 1829-1914 . . **TCLC 36**

Mitchell, W(illiam) O(rmond)
1914- . . . . . . **CLC 25; DAC; DAM MST**
See also CA 77-80; CANR 15, 43; DLB 88

Mitford, Mary Russell 1787-1855 . . **NCLC 4**
See also DLB 110, 116

Mitford, Nancy 1904-1973 . . . . **CLC 44**
See also CA 9-12R

Miyamoto, Yuriko 1899-1951 . . . . . **TCLC 37**

Mo, Timothy (Peter) 1950(?)- . . . . . . **CLC 46**
See also CA 117; MTCW

Modarressi, Taghi (M.) 1931- . . . . . . **CLC 44**
See also CA 121; 134; INT 134

Modiano, Patrick (Jean) 1945- . . . . . **CLC 18**
See also CA 85-88; CANR 17, 40; DLB 83

Moerck, Paal
See Roelvaag, O(le) E(dvart)

Mofolo, Thomas (Mokopu)
1875(?)-1948 . . . . **TCLC 22; BLC;
DAM MULT**
See also CA 121; 153

Mohr, Nicholasa
1935- . . . . . **CLC 12; DAM MULT; HLC**
See also AAYA 8; CA 49-52; CANR 1, 32;
CLR 22; DLB 145; HW; JRDA; SAAS 8;
SATA 8

Mojtabai, A(nn) G(race)
1938- . . . . **CLC 5, 9, 15, 29**
See also CA 85-88

Moliere
1622-1673 . . . . . **LC 28; DA; DAB; DAC;
DAM DRAM, MST; WLC**

Molin, Charles
See Mayne, William (James Carter)

Molnar, Ferenc
1878-1952 . . . . . **TCLC 20; DAM DRAM**
See also CA 109; 153

Momaday, N(avarre) Scott
1934- . . . . . **CLC 2, 19, 85, 95; DA; DAB;
DAC; DAM MST, MULT, NOV, POP**
See also AAYA 11; CA 25-28R; CANR 14,
34; DLB 143, 175; INT CANR-14;
MTCW; NNAL; SATA 48;
SATA-Brief 30

Monette, Paul 1945-1995 . . . . **CLC 82**
See also CA 139; 147

Monroe, Harriet 1860-1936 . . . . . . **TCLC 12**
See also CA 109; DLB 54, 91

Monroe, Lyle
See Heinlein, Robert A(nson)

Montagu, Elizabeth 1917- . . . . **NCLC 7**
See also CA 9-12R

Montagu, Mary (Pierrepont) Wortley
1689-1762 . . . . **LC 9; PC 16**
See also DLB 95, 101

Montagu, W. H.
See Coleridge, Samuel Taylor

Montague, John (Patrick)
1929- . . . . **CLC 13, 46**
See also CA 9-12R; CANR 9; DLB 40;
MTCW

Montaigne, Michel (Eyquem) de
1533-1592 . . . . . . **LC 8; DA; DAB; DAC;
DAM MST; WLC**

Montale, Eugenio
1896-1981 . . . . **CLC 7, 9, 18; PC 13**
See also CA 17-20R; 104; CANR 30;
DLB 114; MTCW

Montesquieu, Charles-Louis de Secondat
1689-1755 . . . . **LC 7**

Montgomery, (Robert) Bruce 1921-1978
See Crispin, Edmund
See also CA 104

Montgomery, L(ucy) M(aud)
1874-1942 . . . . **TCLC 51; DAC;
DAM MST**
See also AAYA 12; CA 108; 137; CLR 8;
DLB 92; DLBD 14; JRDA; MAICYA;
YABC 1

Montgomery, Marion H., Jr. 1925- . . **CLC 7**
See also AITN 1; CA 1-4R; CANR 3, 48;
DLB 6

Montgomery, Max
See Davenport, Guy (Mattison, Jr.)

Montherlant, Henry (Milon) de
1896-1972 . . . . **CLC 8, 19; DAM DRAM**
See also CA 85-88; 37-40R; DLB 72;
MTCW

Monty Python
See Chapman, Graham; Cleese, John
(Marwood); Gilliam, Terry (Vance); Idle,
Eric; Jones, Terence Graham Parry; Palin,
Michael (Edward)
See also AAYA 7

Moodie, Susanna (Strickland)
1803-1885 . . . . **NCLC 14**
See also DLB 99

Mooney, Edward 1951-
See Mooney, Ted
See also CA 130

Mooney, Ted . . . . **CLC 25**
See also Mooney, Edward

Moorcock, Michael (John)
1939- . . . . **CLC 5, 27, 58**
See also CA 45-48; CAAS 5; CANR 2, 17,
38; DLB 14; MTCW

Moore, Brian
1921- . . . . . . **CLC 1, 3, 5, 7, 8, 19, 32, 90;**
DAB; DAC; DAM MST
See also CA 1-4R; CANR 1, 25, 42; MTCW

Moore, Edward
See Muir, Edwin

Moore, George Augustus
1852-1933 . . . . **TCLC 7; SSC 19**
See also CA 104; DLB 10, 18, 57, 135

Moore, Lorrie . . . . **CLC 39, 45, 68**
See also Moore, Marie Lorena

Moore, Marianne (Craig)
1887-1972 . . . . **CLC 1, 2, 4, 8, 10, 13, 19,**
47; DA; DAB; DAC; DAM MST, POET;
PC 4
See also CA 1-4R; 33-36R; CANR 3;
CDALB 1929-1941; DLB 45; DLBD 7;
MTCW; SATA 20

Moore, Marie Lorena 1957-
See Moore, Lorrie
See also CA 116; CANR 39

Moore, Thomas 1779-1852 . . . . **NCLC 6**
See also DLB 96, 144

Morand, Paul 1888-1976 . . **CLC 41; SSC 22**
See also CA 69-72; DLB 65

Morante, Elsa 1918-1985 . . . . **CLC 8, 47**
See also CA 85-88; 117; CANR 35; MTCW

Moravia, Alberto . . . . . . **CLC 2, 7, 11, 27, 46**
See also Pincherle, Alberto

More, Hannah 1745-1833 . . . . **NCLC 27**
See also DLB 107, 109, 116, 158

More, Henry 1614-1687 . . . . **LC 9**
See also DLB 126

More, Sir Thomas 1478-1535 . . . . **LC 10, 32**

Moreas, Jean . . . . **TCLC 18**
See also Papadiamantopoulos, Johannes

Morgan, Berry 1919- . . . . **CLC 6**
See also CA 49-52; DLB 6

Morgan, Claire
See Highsmith, (Mary) Patricia

Morgan, Edwin (George) 1920- . . . . . **CLC 31**
See also CA 5-8R; CANR 3, 43; DLB 27

Morgan, (George) Frederick
1922- . . . . **CLC 23**
See also CA 17-20R; CANR 21

Morgan, Harriet
See Mencken, H(enry) L(ouis)

Morgan, Jane
See Cooper, James Fenimore

Morgan, Janet 1945- . . . . **CLC 39**
See also CA 65-68

Morgan, Lady 1776(?)-1859 . . . . . **NCLC 29**
See also DLB 116, 158

Morgan, Robin 1941- . . . . **CLC 2**
See also CA 69-72; CANR 29; MTCW;
SATA 80

Morgan, Scott
See Kuttner, Henry

Morgan, Seth 1949(?)-1990 . . . . **CLC 65**
See also CA 132

Morgenstern, Christian
1871-1914 . . . . **TCLC 8**
See also CA 105

Morgenstern, S.
See Goldman, William (W.)

Moricz, Zsigmond 1879-1942 . . . . . **TCLC 33**

Morike, Eduard (Friedrich)
1804-1875 . . . . **NCLC 10**
See also DLB 133

Mori Ogai . . . . **TCLC 14**
See also Mori Rintaro

Mori Rintaro 1862-1922
See Mori Ogai
See also CA 110

Moritz, Karl Philipp 1756-1793 . . . . . . **LC 2**
See also DLB 94

Morland, Peter Henry
See Faust, Frederick (Schiller)

Morren, Theophil
See Hofmannsthal, Hugo von

Morris, Bill 1952- . . . . **CLC 76**

Morris, Julian
See West, Morris L(anglo)

Morris, Steveland Judkins 1950(?)-
See Wonder, Stevie
See also CA 111

Morris, William 1834-1896 . . . . **NCLC 4**
See also CDBLB 1832-1890; DLB 18, 35,
57, 156

Morris, Wright 1910- . . . **CLC 1, 3, 7, 18, 37**
See also CA 9-12R; CANR 21; DLB 2;
DLBY 81; MTCW

Morrison, Chloe Anthony Wofford
See Morrison, Toni

Morrison, James Douglas 1943-1971
See Morrison, Jim
See also CA 73-76; CANR 40

Morrison, Jim . . . . **CLC 17**
See also Morrison, James Douglas

Morrison, Toni
1931- . . . . **CLC 4, 10, 22, 55, 81, 87;**
BLC; DA; DAB; DAC; DAM MST,
MULT, NOV, POP
See also AAYA 1; BW 2; CA 29-32R;
CANR 27, 42; CDALB 1968-1988;
DLB 6, 33, 143; DLBY 81; MTCW;
SATA 57

Morrison, Van 1945- . . . . **CLC 21**
See also CA 116

Morrissy, Mary 1958- . . . . **CLC 99**

Mortimer, John (Clifford)
1923- . . . . . . **CLC 28, 43; DAM DRAM,**
POP
See also CA 13-16R; CANR 21;
CDBLB 1960 to Present; DLB 13;
INT CANR-21; MTCW

Mortimer, Penelope (Ruth) 1918- . . . . **CLC 5**
See also CA 57-60; CANR 45

Morton, Anthony
See Creasey, John

Mosher, Howard Frank 1943- . . . . . . **CLC 62**
See also CA 139

Mosley, Nicholas 1923- . . . . **CLC 43, 70**
See also CA 69-72; CANR 41; DLB 14

Mosley, Walter
1952- . . . . . **CLC 97; DAM MULT, POP**
See also AAYA 17; BW 2; CA 142

Moss, Howard
1922-1987 . . . . **CLC 7, 14, 45, 50;**
DAM POET
See also CA 1-4R; 123; CANR 1, 44;
DLB 5

Mossgiel, Rab
See Burns, Robert

Motion, Andrew (Peter) 1952- . . . . . **CLC 47**
See also CA 146; DLB 40

Motley, Willard (Francis)
1909-1965 . . . . **CLC 18**
See also BW 1; CA 117; 106; DLB 76, 143

Motoori, Norinaga 1730-1801 . . . . **NCLC 45**

Mott, Michael (Charles Alston)
1930- . . . . **CLC 15, 34**
See also CA 5-8R; CAAS 7; CANR 7, 29

Mountain Wolf Woman
1884-1960 . . . . **CLC 92**
See also CA 144; NNAL

Moure, Erin 1955- . . . . **CLC 88**
See also CA 113; DLB 60

Mowat, Farley (McGill)
1921- . . . . . . **CLC 26; DAC; DAM MST**
See also AAYA 1; CA 1-4R; CANR 4, 24,
42; CLR 20; DLB 68; INT CANAR-24;
JRDA; MAICYA; MTCW; SATA 3, 55

Moyers, Bill 1934- . . . . **CLC 74**
See also AITN 2; CA 61-64; CANR 31, 52

Mphahlele, Es'kia
See Mphahlele, Ezekiel
See also DLB 125

Mphahlele, Ezekiel
1919- . . . . . **CLC 25; BLC; DAM MULT**
See also Mphahlele, Es'kia
See also BW 2; CA 81-84; CANR 26

Mqhayi, S(amuel) E(dward) K(rune Loliwe)
1875-1945 . . . . **TCLC 25; BLC;**
DAM MULT
See also CA 153

Mrozek, Slawomir 1930- . . . . **CLC 3, 13**
See also CA 13-16R; CAAS 10; CANR 29;
MTCW

Mrs. Belloc-Lowndes
See Lowndes, Marie Adelaide (Belloc)

Mtwa, Percy (?)- . . . . **CLC 47**

Mueller, Lisel 1924- . . . . **CLC 13, 51**
See also CA 93-96; DLB 105

Muir, Edwin 1887-1959 . . . . **TCLC 2**
See also CA 104; DLB 20, 100

Muir, John 1838-1914 . . . . **TCLC 28**

Newman, John Henry
1801-1890 .... **NCLC 38**
See also DLB 18, 32, 55

Newton, Suzanne 1936- .... **CLC 35**
See also CA 41-44R; CANR 14; JRDA;
SATA 5, 77

Nexo, Martin Andersen
1869-1954 .... **TCLC 43**

Nezval, Vitezslav 1900-1958 ..... **TCLC 44**
See also CA 123

Ng, Fae Myenne 1957(?)-.......... **CLC 81**
See also CA 146

Ngema, Mbongeni 1955- .... **CLC 57**
See also BW 2; CA 143

Ngugi, James T(hiong'o)........ **CLC 3, 7, 13**
See also Ngugi wa Thiong'o

Ngugi wa Thiong'o
1938- ..... **CLC 36; BLC; DAM MULT,
NOV**
See also Ngugi, James T(hiong'o)
See also BW 2; CA 81-84; CANR 27;
DLB 125; MTCW

Nichol, B(arrie) P(hillip)
1944-1988 .... **CLC 18**
See also CA 53-56; DLB 53; SATA 66

Nichols, John (Treadwell) 1940- .... **CLC 38**
See also CA 9-12R; CAAS 2; CANR 6;
DLBY 82

Nichols, Leigh
See Koontz, Dean R(ay)

Nichols, Peter (Richard)
1927- .... **CLC 5, 36, 65**
See also CA 104; CANR 33; DLB 13;
MTCW

Nicolas, F. R. E.
See Freeling, Nicolas

Niedecker, Lorine
1903-1970 .... **CLC 10, 42; DAM POET**
See also CA 25-28; CAP 2; DLB 48

Nietzsche, Friedrich (Wilhelm)
1844-1900 .... **TCLC 10, 18, 55**
See also CA 107; 121; DLB 129

Nievo, Ippolito 1831-1861 .... **NCLC 22**

Nightingale, Anne Redmon 1943-
See Redmon, Anne
See also CA 103

Nik. T. O.
See Annensky, Innokenty (Fyodorovich)

Nin, Anais
1903-1977 ..... **CLC 1, 4, 8, 11, 14, 60;
DAM NOV, POP; SSC 10**
See also AITN 2; CA 13-16R; 69-72;
CANR 22, 53; DLB 2, 4, 152; MTCW

Nishiwaki, Junzaburo 1894-1982 .... **PC 15**
See also CA 107

Nissenson, Hugh 1933-.......... **CLC 4, 9**
See also CA 17-20R; CANR 27; DLB 28

Niven, Larry .... **CLC 8**
See also Niven, Laurence Van Cott
See also DLB 8

Niven, Laurence Van Cott 1938-
See Niven, Larry
See also CA 21-24R; CAAS 12; CANR 14,
44; DAM POP; MTCW

Nixon, Agnes Eckhardt 1927-...... **CLC 21**
See also CA 110

Nizan, Paul 1905-1940.......... **TCLC 40**
See also DLB 72

Nkosi, Lewis
1936- ..... **CLC 45; BLC; DAM MULT**
See also BW 1; CA 65-68; CANR 27;
DLB 157

Nodier, (Jean) Charles (Emmanuel)
1780-1844 .... **NCLC 19**
See also DLB 119

Nolan, Christopher 1965-.......... **CLC 58**
See also CA 111

Noon, Jeff 1957-.................. **CLC 91**
See also CA 148

Norden, Charles
See Durrell, Lawrence (George)

Nordhoff, Charles (Bernard)
1887-1947 .... **TCLC 23**
See also CA 108; DLB 9; SATA 23

Norfolk, Lawrence 1963-.......... **CLC 76**
See also CA 144

Norman, Marsha
1947- .... **CLC 28; DAM DRAM**
See also CA 105; CABS 3; CANR 41;
DLBY 84

Norris, Benjamin Franklin, Jr.
1870-1902 .... **TCLC 24**
See also Norris, Frank
See also CA 110

Norris, Frank
See Norris, Benjamin Franklin, Jr.
See also CDALB 1865-1917; DLB 12, 71

Norris, Leslie 1921-.............. **CLC 14**
See also CA 11-12; CANR 14; CAP 1;
DLB 27

North, Andrew
See Norton, Andre

North, Anthony
See Koontz, Dean R(ay)

North, Captain George
See Stevenson, Robert Louis (Balfour)

North, Milou
See Erdrich, Louise

Northrup, B. A.
See Hubbard, L(afayette) Ron(ald)

North Staffs
See Hulme, T(homas) E(rnest)

Norton, Alice Mary
See Norton, Andre
See also MAICYA; SATA 1, 43

Norton, Andre 1912- .... **CLC 12**
See also Norton, Alice Mary
See also AAYA 14; CA 1-4R; CANR 2, 31;
DLB 8, 52; JRDA; MTCW; SATA 91

Norton, Caroline 1808-1877...... **NCLC 47**
See also DLB 21, 159

Norway, Nevil Shute 1899-1960
See Shute, Nevil
See also CA 102; 93-96

Norwid, Cyprian Kamil
1821-1883 .... **NCLC 17**

Nosille, Nabrah
See Ellison, Harlan (Jay)

Nossack, Hans Erich 1901-1978 ..... **CLC 6**
See also CA 93-96; 85-88; DLB 69

Nostradamus 1503-1566........... **LC 27**

Nosu, Chuji
See Ozu, Yasujiro

Notenburg, Eleanora (Genrikhovna) von
See Guro, Elena

Nova, Craig 1945-.............. **CLC 7, 31**
See also CA 45-48; CANR 2, 53

Novak, Joseph
See Kosinski, Jerzy (Nikodem)

Novalis 1772-1801 .... **NCLC 13**
See also DLB 90

Nowlan, Alden (Albert)
1933-1983 .. **CLC 15; DAC; DAM MST**
See also CA 9-12R; CANR 5; DLB 53

Noyes, Alfred 1880-1958 .... **TCLC 7**
See also CA 104; DLB 20

Nunn, Kem 19(?)-................ **CLC 34**

Nye, Robert
1939- .... **CLC 13, 42; DAM NOV**
See also CA 33-36R; CANR 29; DLB 14;
MTCW; SATA 6

Nyro, Laura 1947- .... **CLC 17**

Oates, Joyce Carol
1938- ..... **CLC 1, 2, 3, 6, 9, 11, 15, 19,
33, 52; DA; DAB; DAC; DAM MST,
NOV, POP; SSC 6; WLC**
See also AAYA 15; AITN 1; BEST 89:2;
CA 5-8R; CANR 25, 45;
CDALB 1968-1988; DLB 2, 5, 130;
DLBY 81; INT CANR-25; MTCW

O'Brien, Darcy 1939-............. **CLC 11**
See also CA 21-24R; CANR 8

O'Brien, E. G.
See Clarke, Arthur C(harles)

O'Brien, Edna
1936- .... **CLC 3, 5, 8, 13, 36, 65;
DAM NOV; SSC 10**
See also CA 1-4R; CANR 6, 41;
CDBLB 1960 to Present; DLB 14;
MTCW

O'Brien, Fitz-James 1828-1862... **NCLC 21**
See also DLB 74

O'Brien, Flann... **CLC 1, 4, 5, 7, 10, 47**
See also O Nuallain, Brian

O'Brien, Richard 1942-.......... **CLC 17**
See also CA 124

O'Brien, Tim
1946- .... **CLC 7, 19, 40; DAM POP**
See also AAYA 16; CA 85-88; CANR 40;
DLB 152; DLBD 9; DLBY 80

Obstfelder, Sigbjoern 1866-1900... **TCLC 23**
See also CA 123

O'Casey, Sean
1880-1964 ...... **CLC 1, 5, 9, 11, 15, 88;
DAB; DAC; DAM DRAM, MST**
See also CA 89-92; CDBLB 1914-1945;
DLB 10; MTCW

O'Cathasaigh, Sean
See O'Casey, Sean

Ochs, Phil 1940-1976............. **CLC 17**
See also CA 65-68

O'Connor, Edwin (Greene)
  1918-1968 .... **CLC 14**
  See also CA 93-96; 25-28R

O'Connor, (Mary) Flannery
  1925-1964 .... **CLC 1, 2, 3, 6, 10, 13, 15,
    21, 66; DA; DAB; DAC; DAM MST,
    NOV; SSC 1, 23; WLC**
  See also AAYA 7; CA 1-4R; CANR 3, 41;
    CDALB 1941-1968; DLB 2, 152;
    DLBD 12; DLBY 80; MTCW

O'Connor, Frank .... **CLC 23; SSC 5**
  See also O'Donovan, Michael John
  See also DLB 162

O'Dell, Scott   1898-1989 .... **CLC 30**
  See also AAYA 3; CA 61-64; 129;
    CANR 12, 30; CLR 1, 16; DLB 52;
    JRDA; MAICYA; SATA 12, 60

Odets, Clifford
  1906-1963 .... **CLC 2, 28, 98;
    DAM DRAM; DC 6**
  See also CA 85-88; DLB 7, 26; MTCW

O'Doherty, Brian   1934- .... **CLC 76**
  See also CA 105

O'Donnell, K. M.
  See Malzberg, Barry N(athaniel)

O'Donnell, Lawrence
  See Kuttner, Henry

O'Donovan, Michael John
  1903-1966 .... **CLC 14**
  See also O'Connor, Frank
  See also CA 93-96

Oe, Kenzaburo
  1935- ..... **CLC 10, 36, 86; DAM NOV;
    SSC 20**
  See also CA 97-100; CANR 36, 50;
    DLBY 94; MTCW

O'Faolain, Julia   1932- ...... **CLC 6, 19, 47**
  See also CA 81-84; CAAS 2; CANR 12;
    DLB 14; MTCW

O'Faolain, Sean
  1900-1991 .... **CLC 1, 7, 14, 32, 70;
    SSC 13**
  See also CA 61-64; 134; CANR 12;
    DLB 15, 162; MTCW

O'Flaherty, Liam
  1896-1984 .... **CLC 5, 34; SSC 6**
  See also CA 101; 113; CANR 35; DLB 36,
    162; DLBY 84; MTCW

Ogilvy, Gavin
  See Barrie, J(ames) M(atthew)

O'Grady, Standish (James)
  1846-1928 .... **TCLC 5**
  See also CA 104

O'Grady, Timothy   1951- .... **CLC 59**
  See also CA 138

O'Hara, Frank
  1926-1966 .... **CLC 2, 5, 13, 78;
    DAM POET**
  See also CA 9-12R; 25-28R; CANR 33;
    DLB 5, 16; MTCW

O'Hara, John (Henry)
  1905-1970 .... **CLC 1, 2, 3, 6, 11, 42;
    DAM NOV; SSC 15**
  See also CA 5-8R; 25-28R; CANR 31;
    CDALB 1929-1941; DLB 9, 86; DLBD 2;
    MTCW

O Hehir, Diana   1922- .... **CLC 41**
  See also CA 93-96

Okigbo, Christopher (Ifenayichukwu)
  1932-1967 .... **CLC 25, 84; BLC;
    DAM MULT, POET; PC 7**
  See also BW 1; CA 77-80; DLB 125;
    MTCW

Okri, Ben   1959- .... **CLC 87**
  See also BW 2; CA 130; 138; DLB 157;
    INT 138

Olds, Sharon
  1942- ..... **CLC 32, 39, 85; DAM POET**
  See also CA 101; CANR 18, 41; DLB 120

Oldstyle, Jonathan
  See Irving, Washington

Olesha, Yuri (Karlovich)
  1899-1960 .... **CLC 8**
  See also CA 85-88

Oliphant, Laurence
  1829(?)-1888 .... **NCLC 47**
  See also DLB 18, 166

Oliphant, Margaret (Oliphant Wilson)
  1828-1897 .... **NCLC 11**
  See also DLB 18, 159

Oliver, Mary   1935- .... **CLC 19, 34, 98**
  See also CA 21-24R; CANR 9, 43; DLB 5

Olivier, Laurence (Kerr)
  1907-1989 .... **CLC 20**
  See also CA 111; 150; 129

Olsen, Tillie
  1913- ..... **CLC 4, 13; DA; DAB; DAC;
    DAM MST; SSC 11**
  See also CA 1-4R; CANR 1, 43; DLB 28;
    DLBY 80; MTCW

Olson, Charles (John)
  1910-1970 ..... **CLC 1, 2, 5, 6, 9, 11, 29;
    DAM POET**
  See also CA 13-16; 25-28R; CABS 2;
    CANR 35; CAP 1; DLB 5, 16; MTCW

Olson, Toby   1937- .... **CLC 28**
  See also CA 65-68; CANR 9, 31

Olyesha, Yuri
  See Olesha, Yuri (Karlovich)

Ondaatje, (Philip) Michael
  1943- .... **CLC 14, 29, 51, 76; DAB;
    DAC; DAM MST**
  See also CA 77-80; CANR 42; DLB 60

Oneal, Elizabeth   1934-
  See Oneal, Zibby
  See also CA 106; CANR 28; MAICYA;
    SATA 30, 82

Oneal, Zibby .... **CLC 30**
  See also Oneal, Elizabeth
  See also AAYA 5; CLR 13; JRDA

O'Neill, Eugene (Gladstone)
  1888-1953 ...... **TCLC 1, 6, 27, 49; DA;
    DAB; DAC; DAM DRAM, MST; WLC**
  See also AITN 1; CA 110; 132;
    CDALB 1929-1941; DLB 7; MTCW

Onetti, Juan Carlos
  1909-1994 .... **CLC 7, 10; DAM MULT,
    NOV; SSC 23**
  See also CA 85-88; 145; CANR 32;
    DLB 113; HW; MTCW

O Nuallain, Brian   1911-1966
  See O'Brien, Flann
  See also CA 21-22; 25-28R; CAP 2

Oppen, George   1908-1984 .... **CLC 7, 13, 34**
  See also CA 13-16R; 113; CANR 8; DLB 5,
    165

Oppenheim, E(dward) Phillips
  1866-1946 .... **TCLC 45**
  See also CA 111; DLB 70

Origen   c. 185-c. 254 .... **CMLC 19**

Orlovitz, Gil   1918-1973 .... **CLC 22**
  See also CA 77-80; 45-48; DLB 2, 5

Orris
  See Ingelow, Jean

Ortega y Gasset, Jose
  1883-1955 ..... **TCLC 9; DAM MULT;
    HLC**
  See also CA 106; 130; HW; MTCW

Ortese, Anna Maria   1914- .... **CLC 89**

Ortiz, Simon J(oseph)
  1941- .... **CLC 45; DAM MULT,
    POET; PC 17**
  See also CA 134; DLB 120, 175; NNAL

Orton, Joe .... **CLC 4, 13, 43; DC 3**
  See also Orton, John Kingsley
  See also CDBLB 1960 to Present; DLB 13

Orton, John Kingsley   1933-1967
  See Orton, Joe
  See also CA 85-88; CANR 35;
    DAM DRAM; MTCW

Orwell, George
  ..... **TCLC 2, 6, 15, 31, 51; DAB; WLC**
  See also Blair, Eric (Arthur)
  See also CDBLB 1945-1960; DLB 15, 98

Osborne, David
  See Silverberg, Robert

Osborne, George
  See Silverberg, Robert

Osborne, John (James)
  1929-1994 ..... **CLC 1, 2, 5, 11, 45; DA;
    DAB; DAC; DAM DRAM, MST; WLC**
  See also CA 13-16R; 147; CANR 21, 56;
    CDBLB 1945-1960; DLB 13; MTCW

Osborne, Lawrence   1958- .... **CLC 50**

Oshima, Nagisa   1932- .... **CLC 20**
  See also CA 116; 121

Oskison, John Milton
  1874-1947 ..... **TCLC 35; DAM MULT**
  See also CA 144; DLB 175; NNAL

Ossoli, Sarah Margaret (Fuller marchesa d')
  1810-1850
  See Fuller, Margaret
  See also SATA 25

Ostrovsky, Alexander
  1823-1886 .... **NCLC 30, 57**

Otero, Blas de   1916-1979 .... **CLC 11**
  See also CA 89-92; DLB 134

Otto, Whitney   1955- .... **CLC 70**
  See also CA 140

Ouida .... **TCLC 43**
  See also De La Ramee, (Marie) Louise
  See also DLB 18, 156

Ousmane, Sembene   1923- .... **CLC 66; BLC**
  See also BW 1; CA 117; 125; MTCW

Ovid
43B.C.-18(?) . . . **CMLC 7; DAM POET; PC 2**

Owen, Hugh
See Faust, Frederick (Schiller)

Owen, Wilfred (Edward Salter)
1893-1918 . . . . . **TCLC 5, 27; DA; DAB; DAC; DAM MST, POET; WLC**
See also CA 104; 141; CDBLB 1914-1945; DLB 20

Owens, Rochelle 1936-. . . . . **CLC 8**
See also CA 17-20R; CAAS 2; CANR 39

Oz, Amos
1939- . . . . **CLC 5, 8, 11, 27, 33, 54; DAM NOV**
See also CA 53-56; CANR 27, 47; MTCW

Ozick, Cynthia
1928- . . . . **CLC 3, 7, 28, 62; DAM NOV, POP; SSC 15**
See also BEST 90:1; CA 17-20R; CANR 23; DLB 28, 152; DLBY 82; INT CANR-23; MTCW

Ozu, Yasujiro 1903-1963 . . . . **CLC 16**
See also CA 112

Pacheco, C.
See Pessoa, Fernando (Antonio Nogueira)

Pa Chin . . . . **CLC 18**
See also Li Fei-kan

Pack, Robert 1929-. . . . . **CLC 13**
See also CA 1-4R; CANR 3, 44; DLB 5

Padgett, Lewis
See Kuttner, Henry

Padilla (Lorenzo), Heberto 1932-. . . **CLC 38**
See also AITN 1; CA 123; 131; HW

Page, Jimmy 1944-. . . . . **CLC 12**

Page, Louise 1955-. . . . . **CLC 40**
See also CA 140

Page, P(atricia) K(athleen)
1916- . . . . **CLC 7, 18; DAC; DAM MST; PC 12**
See also CA 53-56; CANR 4, 22; DLB 68; MTCW

Page, Thomas Nelson 1853-1922. . . . **SSC 23**
See also CA 118; DLB 12, 78; DLBD 13

Paget, Violet 1856-1935
See Lee, Vernon
See also CA 104

Paget-Lowe, Henry
See Lovecraft, H(oward) P(hillips)

Paglia, Camille (Anna) 1947-. . . . . . . **CLC 68**
See also CA 140

Paige, Richard
See Koontz, Dean R(ay)

Pakenham, Antonia
See Fraser, (Lady) Antonia (Pakenham)

Palamas, Kostes 1859-1943 . . . . **TCLC 5**
See also CA 105

Palazzeschi, Aldo 1885-1974 . . . . **CLC 11**
See also CA 89-92; 53-56; DLB 114

Paley, Grace
1922- . . . . **CLC 4, 6, 37; DAM POP; SSC 8**
See also CA 25-28R; CANR 13, 46; DLB 28; INT CANR-13; MTCW

Palin, Michael (Edward) 1943-. . . . . **CLC 21**
See also Monty Python
See also CA 107; CANR 35; SATA 67

Palliser, Charles 1947-. . . . . **CLC 65**
See also CA 136

Palma, Ricardo 1833-1919. . . . . . . **TCLC 29**

Pancake, Breece Dexter 1952-1979
See Pancake, Breece D'J
See also CA 123; 109

Pancake, Breece D'J. . . . . **CLC 29**
See also Pancake, Breece Dexter
See also DLB 130

Panko, Rudy
See Gogol, Nikolai (Vasilyevich)

Papadiamantis, Alexandros
1851-1911 . . . . **TCLC 29**

Papadiamantopoulos, Johannes 1856-1910
See Moreas, Jean
See also CA 117

Papini, Giovanni 1881-1956. . . . . . **TCLC 22**
See also CA 121

Paracelsus 1493-1541. . . . . **LC 14**

Parasol, Peter
See Stevens, Wallace

Pareto, Vilfredo 1848-1923 . . . . **TCLC 69**

Parfenie, Maria
See Codrescu, Andrei

Parini, Jay (Lee) 1948-. . . . . **CLC 54**
See also CA 97-100; CAAS 16; CANR 32

Park, Jordan
See Kornbluth, C(yril) M.; Pohl, Frederik

Parker, Bert
See Ellison, Harlan (Jay)

Parker, Dorothy (Rothschild)
1893-1967 . . . . **CLC 15, 68; DAM POET; SSC 2**
See also CA 19-20; 25-28R; CAP 2; DLB 11, 45, 86; MTCW

Parker, Robert B(rown)
1932- . . . . . . **CLC 27; DAM NOV, POP**
See also BEST 89:4; CA 49-52; CANR 1, 26, 52; INT CANR-26; MTCW

Parkin, Frank 1940-. . . . . **CLC 43**
See also CA 147

Parkman, Francis, Jr.
1823-1893 . . . . **NCLC 12**
See also DLB 1, 30

Parks, Gordon (Alexander Buchanan)
1912- . . . **CLC 1, 16; BLC; DAM MULT**
See also AITN 2; BW 2; CA 41-44R; CANR 26; DLB 33; SATA 8

Parnell, Thomas 1679-1718 . . . . **LC 3**
See also DLB 94

Parra, Nicanor
1914- . . . . . . **CLC 2; DAM MULT; HLC**
See also CA 85-88; CANR 32; HW; MTCW

Parrish, Mary Frances
See Fisher, M(ary) F(rances) K(ennedy)

Parson
See Coleridge, Samuel Taylor

Parson Lot
See Kingsley, Charles

Partridge, Anthony
See Oppenheim, E(dward) Phillips

Pascal, Blaise 1623-1662 . . . . **LC 35**

Pascoli, Giovanni 1855-1912 . . . . . . **TCLC 45**

Pasolini, Pier Paolo
1922-1975 . . . . **CLC 20, 37; PC 17**
See also CA 93-96; 61-64; DLB 128; MTCW

Pasquini
See Silone, Ignazio

Pastan, Linda (Olenik)
1932- . . . . **CLC 27; DAM POET**
See also CA 61-64; CANR 18, 40; DLB 5

Pasternak, Boris (Leonidovich)
1890-1960 . . . . . . **CLC 7, 10, 18, 63; DA; DAB; DAC; DAM MST, NOV, POET; PC 6; WLC**
See also CA 127; 116; MTCW

Patchen, Kenneth
1911-1972 . . . **CLC 1, 2, 18; DAM POET**
See also CA 1-4R; 33-36R; CANR 3, 35; DLB 16, 48; MTCW

Pater, Walter (Horatio)
1839-1894 . . . . **NCLC 7**
See also CDBLB 1832-1890; DLB 57, 156

Paterson, A(ndrew) B(arton)
1864-1941 . . . . **TCLC 32**
See also CA 155

Paterson, Katherine (Womeldorf)
1932-. **CLC 12, 30**
See also AAYA 1; CA 21-24R; CANR 28; CLR 7; DLB 52; JRDA; MAICYA; MTCW; SATA 13, 53, 92

Patmore, Coventry Kersey Dighton
1823-1896 . . . . **NCLC 9**
See also DLB 35, 98

Paton, Alan (Stewart)
1903-1988 . . . . . . **CLC 4, 10, 25, 55; DA; DAB; DAC; DAM MST, NOV; WLC**
See also CA 13-16; 125; CANR 22; CAP 1; MTCW; SATA 11; SATA-Obit 56

Paton Walsh, Gillian 1937-
See Walsh, Jill Paton
See also CANR 38; JRDA; MAICYA; SAAS 3; SATA 4, 72

Paulding, James Kirke 1778-1860. . **NCLC 2**
See also DLB 3, 59, 74

Paulin, Thomas Neilson 1949-
See Paulin, Tom
See also CA 123; 128

Paulin, Tom. **CLC 37**
See also Paulin, Thomas Neilson
See also DLB 40

Paustovsky, Konstantin (Georgievich)
1892-1968 . . . . **CLC 40**
See also CA 93-96; 25-28R

Pavese, Cesare
1908-1950 . . . . . **TCLC 3; PC 13; SSC 19**
See also CA 104; DLB 128

Pavic, Milorad 1929-. . . . . **CLC 60**
See also CA 136

Payne, Alan
See Jakes, John (William)

Paz, Gil
See Lugones, Leopoldo

Pinkwater, Daniel Manus 1941- . . . . **CLC 35**
See also Pinkwater, Manus
See also AAYA 1; CA 29-32R; CANR 12,
38; CLR 4; JRDA; MAICYA; SAAS 3;
SATA 46, 76

Pinkwater, Manus
See Pinkwater, Daniel Manus
See also SATA 8

Pinsky, Robert
1940- . . **CLC 9, 19, 38, 94; DAM POET**
See also CA 29-32R; CAAS 4; DLBY 82

Pinta, Harold
See Pinter, Harold

Pinter, Harold
1930- . . . . . **CLC 1, 3, 6, 9, 11, 15, 27, 58,
73; DA; DAB; DAC; DAM DRAM,
MST; WLC**
See also CA 5-8R; CANR 33; CDBLB 1960
to Present; DLB 13; MTCW

Piozzi, Hester Lynch (Thrale)
1741-1821 . . . . **NCLC 57**
See also DLB 104, 142

Pirandello, Luigi
1867-1936 . . . . . . **TCLC 4, 29; DA; DAB;
DAC; DAM DRAM, MST; DC 5;
SSC 22; WLC**
See also CA 104; 153

Pirsig, Robert M(aynard)
1928- . . . . **CLC 4, 6, 73; DAM POP**
See also CA 53-56; CANR 42; MTCW;
SATA 39

Pisarev, Dmitry Ivanovich
1840-1868 . . . . **NCLC 25**

Pix, Mary (Griffith) 1666-1709 . . . . **LC 8**
See also DLB 80

Pixerecourt, Guilbert de
1773-1844 . . . . **NCLC 39**

Plaidy, Jean
See Hibbert, Eleanor Alice Burford

Planche, James Robinson
1796-1880 . . . . **NCLC 42**

Plant, Robert 1948- . . . . **CLC 12**

Plante, David (Robert)
1940- . . . . **CLC 7, 23, 38; DAM NOV**
See also CA 37-40R; CANR 12, 36;
DLBY 83; INT CANR-12; MTCW

Plath, Sylvia
1932-1963 . . . . . **CLC 1, 2, 3, 5, 9, 11, 14,
17, 50, 51, 62; DA; DAB; DAC;
DAM MST, POET; PC 1; WLC**
See also AAYA 13; CA 19-20; CANR 34;
CAP 2; CDALB 1941-1968; DLB 5, 6,
152; MTCW

Plato
428(?)B.C.-348(?)B.C.. . . . . **CMLC 8; DA;
DAB; DAC; DAM MST**

Platonov, Andrei . . . . **TCLC 14**
See also Klimentov, Andrei Platonovich

Platt, Kin 1911- . . . . **CLC 26**
See also AAYA 11; CA 17-20R; CANR 11;
JRDA; SAAS 17; SATA 21, 86

Plautus c. 251B.C.-184B.C. . . . . **DC 6**

Plick et Plock
See Simenon, Georges (Jacques Christian)

Plimpton, George (Ames) 1927- . . . . . **CLC 36**
See also AITN 1; CA 21-24R; CANR 32;
MTCW; SATA 10

Plomer, William Charles Franklin
1903-1973 . . . . **CLC 4, 8**
See also CA 21-22; CANR 34; CAP 2;
DLB 20, 162; MTCW; SATA 24

Plowman, Piers
See Kavanagh, Patrick (Joseph)

Plum, J.
See Wodehouse, P(elham) G(renville)

Plumly, Stanley (Ross) 1939- . . . . . . **CLC 33**
See also CA 108; 110; DLB 5; INT 110

Plumpe, Friedrich Wilhelm
1888-1931 . . . . **TCLC 53**
See also CA 112

Poe, Edgar Allan
1809-1849 . . . . **NCLC 1, 16, 55; DA;
DAB; DAC; DAM MST, POET; PC 1;
SSC 1, 22; WLC**
See also AAYA 14; CDALB 1640-1865;
DLB 3, 59, 73, 74; SATA 23

Poet of Titchfield Street, The
See Pound, Ezra (Weston Loomis)

Pohl, Frederik 1919- . . . . **CLC 18**
See also CA 61-64; CAAS 1; CANR 11, 37;
DLB 8; INT CANR-11; MTCW;
SATA 24

Poirier, Louis 1910-
See Gracq, Julien
See also CA 122; 126

Poitier, Sidney 1927- . . . . **CLC 26**
See also BW 1; CA 117

Polanski, Roman 1933- . . . . **CLC 16**
See also CA 77-80

Poliakoff, Stephen 1952- . . . . **CLC 38**
See also CA 106; DLB 13

Police, The
See Copeland, Stewart (Armstrong);
Summers, Andrew James; Sumner,
Gordon Matthew

Polidori, John William
1795-1821 . . . . **NCLC 51**
See also DLB 116

Pollitt, Katha 1949- . . . . **CLC 28**
See also CA 120; 122; MTCW

Pollock, (Mary) Sharon
1936- . . . . **CLC 50; DAC; DAM DRAM,
MST**
See also CA 141; DLB 60

Polo, Marco 1254-1324 . . . . **CMLC 15**

Polonsky, Abraham (Lincoln)
1910- . . . . **CLC 92**
See also CA 104; DLB 26; INT 104

Polybius c. 200B.C.-c. 118B.C. . . . . **CMLC 17**

Pomerance, Bernard
1940- . . . . **CLC 13; DAM DRAM**
See also CA 101; CANR 49

Ponge, Francis (Jean Gaston Alfred)
1899-1988 . . . . . **CLC 6, 18; DAM POET**
See also CA 85-88; 126; CANR 40

Pontoppidan, Henrik 1857-1943 . . . **TCLC 29**

Poole, Josephine . . . . **CLC 17**
See also Helyar, Jane Penelope Josephine
See also SAAS 2; SATA 5

Popa, Vasko 1922-1991 . . . . **CLC 19**
See also CA 112; 148

Pope, Alexander
1688-1744 . . . . . . **LC 3; DA; DAB; DAC;
DAM MST, POET; WLC**
See also CDBLB 1660-1789; DLB 95, 101

Porter, Connie (Rose) 1959(?)- . . . . . **CLC 70**
See also BW 2; CA 142; SATA 81

Porter, Gene(va Grace) Stratton
1863(?)-1924 . . . . **TCLC 21**
See also CA 112

Porter, Katherine Anne
1890-1980 . . . . . . **CLC 1, 3, 7, 10, 13, 15,
27; DA; DAB; DAC; DAM MST, NOV;
SSC 4**
See also AITN 2; CA 1-4R; 101; CANR 1;
DLB 4, 9, 102; DLBD 12; DLBY 80;
MTCW; SATA 39; SATA-Obit 23

Porter, Peter (Neville Frederick)
1929- . . . . **CLC 5, 13, 33**
See also CA 85-88; DLB 40

Porter, William Sydney 1862-1910
See Henry, O.
See also CA 104; 131; CDALB 1865-1917;
DA; DAB; DAC; DAM MST; DLB 12,
78, 79; MTCW; YABC 2

Portillo (y Pacheco), Jose Lopez
See Lopez Portillo (y Pacheco), Jose

Post, Melville Davisson
1869-1930 . . . . **TCLC 39**
See also CA 110

Potok, Chaim
1929- . . . . **CLC 2, 7, 14, 26; DAM NOV**
See also AAYA 15; AITN 1, 2; CA 17-20R;
CANR 19, 35; DLB 28, 152;
INT CANR-19; MTCW; SATA 33

Potter, Beatrice
See Webb, (Martha) Beatrice (Potter)
See also MAICYA

Potter, Dennis (Christopher George)
1935-1994 . . . . **CLC 58, 86**
See also CA 107; 145; CANR 33; MTCW

Pound, Ezra (Weston Loomis)
1885-1972 . . . . . . **CLC 1, 2, 3, 4, 5, 7, 10,
13, 18, 34, 48, 50; DA; DAB; DAC;
DAM MST, POET; PC 4; WLC**
See also CA 5-8R; 37-40R; CANR 40;
CDALB 1917-1929; DLB 4, 45, 63;
MTCW

Povod, Reinaldo 1959-1994 . . . . **CLC 44**
See also CA 136; 146

Powell, Adam Clayton, Jr.
1908-1972 . . . . **CLC 89; BLC;
DAM MULT**
See also BW 1; CA 102; 33-36R

Powell, Anthony (Dymoke)
1905- . . . . **CLC 1, 3, 7, 9, 10, 31**
See also CA 1-4R; CANR 1, 32;
CDBLB 1945-1960; DLB 15; MTCW

Powell, Dawn 1897-1965 . . . . **CLC 66**
See also CA 5-8R

Powell, Padgett 1952- . . . . **CLC 34**
See also CA 126

Power, Susan . . . . **CLC 91**

Rabelais, Francois
1483-1553 . . . . . LC 5; DA; DAB; DAC;
DAM MST; WLC

Rabinovitch, Sholem   1859-1916
See Aleichem, Sholom
See also CA 104

Rachilde   1860-1953 . . . . TCLC 67
See also DLB 123

Racine, Jean
1639-1699 . . . . LC 28; DAB; DAM MST

Radcliffe, Ann (Ward)
1764-1823 . . . . NCLC 6, 55
See also DLB 39

Radiguet, Raymond   1903-1923 . . . . TCLC 29
See also DLB 65

Radnoti, Miklos   1909-1944 . . . . TCLC 16
See also CA 118

Rado, James   1939- . . . . CLC 17
See also CA 105

Radvanyi, Netty   1900-1983
See Seghers, Anna
See also CA 85-88; 110

Rae, Ben
See Griffiths, Trevor

Raeburn, John (Hay)   1941- . . . . CLC 34
See also CA 57-60

Ragni, Gerome   1942-1991 . . . . CLC 17
See also CA 105; 134

Rahv, Philip   1908-1973 . . . . CLC 24
See also Greenberg, Ivan
See also DLB 137

Raine, Craig   1944- . . . . CLC 32
See also CA 108; CANR 29, 51; DLB 40

Raine, Kathleen (Jessie)   1908- . . . CLC 7, 45
See also CA 85-88; CANR 46; DLB 20;
MTCW

Rainis, Janis   1865-1929 . . . . TCLC 29

Rakosi, Carl . . . . CLC 47
See also Rawley, Callman
See also CAAS 5

Raleigh, Richard
See Lovecraft, H(oward) P(hillips)

Raleigh, Sir Walter   1554(?)-1618 . . . . LC 31
See also CDBLB Before 1660; DLB 172

Rallentando, H. P.
See Sayers, Dorothy L(eigh)

Ramal, Walter
See de la Mare, Walter (John)

Ramon, Juan
See Jimenez (Mantecon), Juan Ramon

Ramos, Graciliano   1892-1953 . . . . . TCLC 32

Rampersad, Arnold   1941- . . . . CLC 44
See also BW 2; CA 127; 133; DLB 111;
INT 133

Rampling, Anne
See Rice, Anne

Ramsay, Allan   1684(?)-1758 . . . . LC 29
See also DLB 95

Ramuz, Charles-Ferdinand
1878-1947 . . . . TCLC 33

Rand, Ayn
1905-1982 . . . . . . CLC 3, 30, 44, 79; DA;
DAC; DAM MST, NOV, POP; WLC
See also AAYA 10; CA 13-16R; 105;
CANR 27; MTCW

Randall, Dudley (Felker)
1914- . . . . . CLC 1; BLC; DAM MULT
See also BW 1; CA 25-28R; CANR 23;
DLB 41

Randall, Robert
See Silverberg, Robert

Ranger, Ken
See Creasey, John

Ransom, John Crowe
1888-1974 . . . . CLC 2, 4, 5, 11, 24;
DAM POET
See also CA 5-8R; 49-52; CANR 6, 34;
DLB 45, 63; MTCW

Rao, Raja   1909- . . . CLC 25, 56; DAM NOV
See also CA 73-76; CANR 51; MTCW

Raphael, Frederic (Michael)
1931- . . . . CLC 2, 14
See also CA 1-4R; CANR 1; DLB 14

Ratcliffe, James P.
See Mencken, H(enry) L(ouis)

Rathbone, Julian   1935- . . . . CLC 41
See also CA 101; CANR 34

Rattigan, Terence (Mervyn)
1911-1977 . . . . . . CLC 7; DAM DRAM
See also CA 85-88; 73-76;
CDBLB 1945-1960; DLB 13; MTCW

Ratushinskaya, Irina   1954- . . . . CLC 54
See also CA 129

Raven, Simon (Arthur Noel)
1927- . . . . CLC 14
See also CA 81-84

Rawley, Callman   1903-
See Rakosi, Carl
See also CA 21-24R; CANR 12, 32

Rawlings, Marjorie Kinnan
1896-1953 . . . . TCLC 4
See also AAYA 20; CA 104; 137; DLB 9,
22, 102; JRDA; MAICYA; YABC 1

Ray, Satyajit
1921-1992 . . . CLC 16, 76; DAM MULT
See also CA 114; 137

Read, Herbert Edward   1893-1968 . . . . CLC 4
See also CA 85-88; 25-28R; DLB 20, 149

Read, Piers Paul   1941- . . . . . . CLC 4, 10, 25
See also CA 21-24R; CANR 38; DLB 14;
SATA 21

Reade, Charles   1814-1884 . . . . NCLC 2
See also DLB 21

Reade, Hamish
See Gray, Simon (James Holliday)

Reading, Peter   1946- . . . . CLC 47
See also CA 103; CANR 46; DLB 40

Reaney, James
1926- . . . . . . CLC 13; DAC; DAM MST
See also CA 41-44R; CAAS 15; CANR 42;
DLB 68; SATA 43

Rebreanu, Liviu   1885-1944 . . . . TCLC 28

Rechy, John (Francisco)
1934- . . . . CLC 1, 7, 14, 18;
DAM MULT; HLC
See also CA 5-8R; CAAS 4; CANR 6, 32;
DLB 122; DLBY 82; HW; INT CANR-6

Redcam, Tom   1870-1933 . . . . TCLC 25

Reddin, Keith . . . . CLC 67

Redgrove, Peter (William)
1932- . . . . CLC 6, 41
See also CA 1-4R; CANR 3, 39; DLB 40

Redmon, Anne . . . . CLC 22
See also Nightingale, Anne Redmon
See also DLBY 86

Reed, Eliot
See Ambler, Eric

Reed, Ishmael
1938- . . . . CLC 2, 3, 5, 6, 13, 32, 60;
BLC; DAM MULT
See also BW 2; CA 21-24R; CANR 25, 48;
DLB 2, 5, 33, 169; DLBD 8; MTCW

Reed, John (Silas)   1887-1920 . . . . . . TCLC 9
See also CA 106

Reed, Lou . . . . CLC 21
See also Firbank, Louis

Reeve, Clara   1729-1807 . . . . NCLC 19
See also DLB 39

Reich, Wilhelm   1897-1957 . . . . TCLC 57

Reid, Christopher (John)   1949- . . . . . CLC 33
See also CA 140; DLB 40

Reid, Desmond
See Moorcock, Michael (John)

Reid Banks, Lynne   1929-
See Banks, Lynne Reid
See also CA 1-4R; CANR 6, 22, 38;
CLR 24; JRDA; MAICYA; SATA 22, 75

Reilly, William K.
See Creasey, John

Reiner, Max
See Caldwell, (Janet Miriam) Taylor
(Holland)

Reis, Ricardo
See Pessoa, Fernando (Antonio Nogueira)

Remarque, Erich Maria
1898-1970 . . . . CLC 21; DA; DAB; DAC;
DAM MST, NOV
See also CA 77-80; 29-32R; DLB 56;
MTCW

Remizov, A.
See Remizov, Aleksei (Mikhailovich)

Remizov, A. M.
See Remizov, Aleksei (Mikhailovich)

Remizov, Aleksei (Mikhailovich)
1877-1957 . . . . TCLC 27
See also CA 125; 133

Renan, Joseph Ernest
1823-1892 . . . . NCLC 26

Renard, Jules   1864-1910 . . . . TCLC 17
See also CA 117

Renault, Mary . . . . CLC 3, 11, 17
See also Challans, Mary
See also DLBY 83

Roberts, Elizabeth Madox
1886-1941 . . . . TCLC 68
See also CA 111; DLB 9, 54, 102;
SATA 33; SATA-Brief 27

Roberts, Kate 1891-1985 . . . . CLC 15
See also CA 107; 116

Roberts, Keith (John Kingston)
1935- . . . . CLC 14
See also CA 25-28R; CANR 46

Roberts, Kenneth (Lewis)
1885-1957 . . . . TCLC 23
See also CA 109; DLB 9

Roberts, Michele (B.) 1949- . . . . CLC 48
See also CA 115

Robertson, Ellis
See Ellison, Harlan (Jay); Silverberg, Robert

Robertson, Thomas William
1829-1871 . . . . NCLC 35; DAM DRAM

Robinson, Edwin Arlington
1869-1935 . . . . TCLC 5; DA; DAC;
DAM MST, POET; PC 1
See also CA 104; 133; CDALB 1865-1917;
DLB 54; MTCW

Robinson, Henry Crabb
1775-1867 . . . . NCLC 15
See also DLB 107

Robinson, Jill 1936- . . . . CLC 10
See also CA 102; INT 102

Robinson, Kim Stanley 1952- . . . . . . CLC 34
See also CA 126

Robinson, Lloyd
See Silverberg, Robert

Robinson, Marilynne 1944- . . . . CLC 25
See also CA 116

Robinson, Smokey . . . . CLC 21
See also Robinson, William, Jr.

Robinson, William, Jr. 1940-
See Robinson, Smokey
See also CA 116

Robison, Mary 1949- . . . . CLC 42, 98
See also CA 113; 116; DLB 130; INT 116

Rod, Edouard 1857-1910 . . . . TCLC 52

Roddenberry, Eugene Wesley 1921-1991
See Roddenberry, Gene
See also CA 110; 135; CANR 37; SATA 45;
SATA-Obit 69

Roddenberry, Gene . . . . CLC 17
See also Roddenberry, Eugene Wesley
See also AAYA 5; SATA-Obit 69

Rodgers, Mary 1931- . . . . CLC 12
See also CA 49-52; CANR 8, 55; CLR 20;
INT CANR-8; JRDA; MAICYA;
SATA 8

Rodgers, W(illiam) R(obert)
1909-1969 . . . . CLC 7
See also CA 85-88; DLB 20

Rodman, Eric
See Silverberg, Robert

Rodman, Howard 1920(?)-1985 . . . . . CLC 65
See also CA 118

Rodman, Maia
See Wojciechowska, Maia (Teresa)

Rodriguez, Claudio 1934- . . . . CLC 10
See also DLB 134

Roelvaag, O(le) E(dvart)
1876-1931 . . . . TCLC 17
See also CA 117; DLB 9

Roethke, Theodore (Huebner)
1908-1963 . . . . . CLC 1, 3, 8, 11, 19, 46;
DAM POET; PC 15
See also CA 81-84; CABS 2;
CDALB 1941-1968; DLB 5; MTCW

Rogers, Thomas Hunton 1927- . . . . . CLC 57
See also CA 89-92; INT 89-92

Rogers, Will(iam Penn Adair)
1879-1935 . . . . . . TCLC 8; DAM MULT
See also CA 105; 144; DLB 11; NNAL

Rogin, Gilbert 1929- . . . . CLC 18
See also CA 65-68; CANR 15

Rohan, Koda . . . . TCLC 22
See also Koda Shigeyuki

Rohmer, Eric . . . . CLC 16
See also Scherer, Jean-Marie Maurice

Rohmer, Sax . . . . TCLC 28
See also Ward, Arthur Henry Sarsfield
See also DLB 70

Roiphe, Anne (Richardson)
1935- . . . . CLC 3, 9
See also CA 89-92; CANR 45; DLBY 80;
INT 89-92

Rojas, Fernando de 1465-1541 . . . . . . LC 23

Rolfe, Frederick (William Serafino Austin
Lewis Mary) 1860-1913 . . . . . . TCLC 12
See also CA 107; DLB 34, 156

Rolland, Romain 1866-1944 . . . . . . TCLC 23
See also CA 118; DLB 65

Rolle, Richard c. 1300-c. 1349 . . . CMLC 21
See also DLB 146

Rolvaag, O(le) E(dvart)
See Roelvaag, O(le) E(dvart)

Romain Arnaud, Saint
See Aragon, Louis

Romains, Jules 1885-1972 . . . . CLC 7
See also CA 85-88; CANR 34; DLB 65;
MTCW

Romero, Jose Ruben 1890-1952 . . . TCLC 14
See also CA 114; 131; HW

Ronsard, Pierre de
1524-1585 . . . . LC 6; PC 11

Rooke, Leon
1934- . . . . CLC 25, 34; DAM POP
See also CA 25-28R; CANR 23, 53

Roosevelt, Theodore 1858-1919 . . . . TCLC 69
See also CA 115; DLB 47

Roper, William 1498-1578 . . . . LC 10

Roquelaure, A. N.
See Rice, Anne

Rosa, Joao Guimaraes 1908-1967 . . . CLC 23
See also CA 89-92; DLB 113

Rose, Wendy
1948- . . . . CLC 85; DAM MULT; PC 13
See also CA 53-56; CANR 5, 51; DLB 175;
NNAL; SATA 12

Rosen, Richard (Dean) 1949- . . . . CLC 39
See also CA 77-80; INT CANR-30

Rosenberg, Isaac 1890-1918 . . . . . . TCLC 12
See also CA 107; DLB 20

Rosenblatt, Joe . . . . CLC 15
See also Rosenblatt, Joseph

Rosenblatt, Joseph 1933-
See Rosenblatt, Joe
See also CA 89-92; INT 89-92

Rosenfeld, Samuel 1896-1963
See Tzara, Tristan
See also CA 89-92

Rosenstock, Sami
See Tzara, Tristan

Rosenstock, Samuel
See Tzara, Tristan

Rosenthal, M(acha) L(ouis)
1917-1996 . . . . CLC 28
See also CA 1-4R; 152; CAAS 6; CANR 4,
51; DLB 5; SATA 59

Ross, Barnaby
See Dannay, Frederic

Ross, Bernard L.
See Follett, Ken(neth Martin)

Ross, J. H.
See Lawrence, T(homas) E(dward)

Ross, Martin
See Martin, Violet Florence
See also DLB 135

Ross, (James) Sinclair
1908- . . . . . . CLC 13; DAC; DAM MST;
SSC 24
See also CA 73-76; DLB 88

Rossetti, Christina (Georgina)
1830-1894 . . . . . NCLC 2, 50; DA; DAB;
DAC; DAM MST, POET; PC 7; WLC
See also DLB 35, 163; MAICYA; SATA 20

Rossetti, Dante Gabriel
1828-1882 . . . . . . NCLC 4; DA; DAB;
DAC; DAM MST, POET; WLC
See also CDBLB 1832-1890; DLB 35

Rossner, Judith (Perelman)
1935- . . . . CLC 6, 9, 29
See also AITN 2; BEST 90:3; CA 17-20R;
CANR 18, 51; DLB 6; INT CANR-18;
MTCW

Rostand, Edmond (Eugene Alexis)
1868-1918 . . . . . . TCLC 6, 37; DA; DAB;
DAC; DAM DRAM, MST
See also CA 104; 126; MTCW

Roth, Henry 1906-1995 . . . . . . CLC 2, 6, 11
See also CA 11-12; 149; CANR 38; CAP 1;
DLB 28; MTCW

Roth, Joseph 1894-1939 . . . . TCLC 33
See also DLB 85

Roth, Philip (Milton)
1933- . . . . . . CLC 1, 2, 3, 4, 6, 9, 15, 22,
31, 47, 66, 86; DA; DAB; DAC;
DAM MST, NOV, POP; WLC
See also BEST 90:3; CA 1-4R; CANR 1, 22,
36, 55; CDALB 1968-1988; DLB 2, 28,
173; DLBY 82; MTCW

Rothenberg, Jerome 1931- . . . . CLC 6, 57
See also CA 45-48; CANR 1; DLB 5

Roumain, Jacques (Jean Baptiste)
1907-1944 . . . . TCLC 19; BLC;
DAM MULT
See also BW 1; CA 117; 125

Rourke, Constance (Mayfield)
1885-1941 . . . . **TCLC 12**
See also CA 107; YABC 1

Rousseau, Jean-Baptiste 1671-1741 . . . **LC 9**

Rousseau, Jean-Jacques
1712-1778 . . . . **LC 14, 36; DA; DAB;**
DAC; DAM MST; WLC

Roussel, Raymond 1877-1933 . . . . . **TCLC 20**
See also CA 117

Rovit, Earl (Herbert) 1927- . . . . **CLC 7**
See also CA 5-8R; CANR 12

Rowe, Nicholas 1674-1718 . . . . **LC 8**
See also DLB 84

Rowley, Ames Dorrance
See Lovecraft, H(oward) P(hillips)

Rowson, Susanna Haswell
1762(?)-1824 . . . . **NCLC 5**
See also DLB 37

Roy, Gabrielle
1909-1983 . . . . **CLC 10, 14; DAB; DAC;**
DAM MST
See also CA 53-56; 110; CANR 5; DLB 68;
MTCW

Rozewicz, Tadeusz
1921- . . . . **CLC 9, 23; DAM POET**
See also CA 108; CANR 36; MTCW

Ruark, Gibbons 1941- . . . . **CLC 3**
See also CA 33-36R; CAAS 23; CANR 14,
31; DLB 120

Rubens, Bernice (Ruth) 1923- . . . **CLC 19, 31**
See also CA 25-28R; CANR 33; DLB 14;
MTCW

Rubin, Harold
See Robbins, Harold

Rudkin, (James) David 1936- . . . . . . **CLC 14**
See also CA 89-92; DLB 13

Rudnik, Raphael 1933- . . . . **CLC 7**
See also CA 29-32R

Ruffian, M.
See Hasek, Jaroslav (Matej Frantisek)

Ruiz, Jose Martinez . . . . **CLC 11**
See also Martinez Ruiz, Jose

Rukeyser, Muriel
1913-1980 . . . . **CLC 6, 10, 15, 27;**
DAM POET; PC 12
See also CA 5-8R; 93-96; CANR 26;
DLB 48; MTCW; SATA-Obit 22

Rule, Jane (Vance) 1931- . . . . **CLC 27**
See also CA 25-28R; CAAS 18; CANR 12;
DLB 60

Rulfo, Juan
1918-1986 . . . . **CLC 8, 80; DAM MULT;**
HLC
See also CA 85-88; 118; CANR 26;
DLB 113; HW; MTCW

Rumi, Jalal al-Din 1297-1373 . . . . **CMLC 20**

Runeberg, Johan 1804-1877 . . . . . . **NCLC 41**

Runyon, (Alfred) Damon
1884(?)-1946 . . . . **TCLC 10**
See also CA 107; DLB 11, 86, 171

Rush, Norman 1933- . . . . **CLC 44**
See also CA 121; 126; INT 126

Rushdie, (Ahmed) Salman
1947- . . . . . **CLC 23, 31, 55; DAB; DAC;**
DAM MST, NOV, POP
See also BEST 89:3; CA 108; 111;
CANR 33, 56; INT 111; MTCW

Rushforth, Peter (Scott) 1945- . . . . . **CLC 19**
See also CA 101

Ruskin, John 1819-1900 . . . . **TCLC 63**
See also CA 114; 129; CDBLB 1832-1890;
DLB 55, 163; SATA 24

Russ, Joanna 1937- . . . . **CLC 15**
See also CA 25-28R; CANR 11, 31; DLB 8;
MTCW

Russell, George William 1867-1935
See Baker, Jean H.
See also CA 104; 153; CDBLB 1890-1914;
DAM POET

Russell, (Henry) Ken(neth Alfred)
1927- . . . . **CLC 16**
See also CA 105

Russell, Willy 1947- . . . . **CLC 60**

Rutherford, Mark . . . . **TCLC 25**
See also White, William Hale
See also DLB 18

Ruyslinck, Ward 1929- . . . . **CLC 14**
See also Belser, Reimond Karel Maria de

Ryan, Cornelius (John) 1920-1974 . . . **CLC 7**
See also CA 69-72; 53-56; CANR 38

Ryan, Michael 1946- . . . . **CLC 65**
See also CA 49-52; DLBY 82

Rybakov, Anatoli (Naumovich)
1911- . . . . **CLC 23, 53**
See also CA 126; 135; SATA 79

Ryder, Jonathan
See Ludlum, Robert

Ryga, George
1932-1987 . . **CLC 14; DAC; DAM MST**
See also CA 101; 124; CANR 43; DLB 60

S. S.
See Sassoon, Siegfried (Lorraine)

Saba, Umberto 1883-1957 . . . . **TCLC 33**
See also CA 144; DLB 114

Sabatini, Rafael 1875-1950 . . . . . . **TCLC 47**

Sabato, Ernesto (R.)
1911- . . . . **CLC 10, 23; DAM MULT;**
HLC
See also CA 97-100; CANR 32; DLB 145;
HW; MTCW

Sacastru, Martin
See Bioy Casares, Adolfo

Sacher-Masoch, Leopold von
1836(?)-1895 . . . . **NCLC 31**

Sachs, Marilyn (Stickle) 1927- . . . . . **CLC 35**
See also AAYA 2; CA 17-20R; CANR 13,
47; CLR 2; JRDA; MAICYA; SAAS 2;
SATA 3, 68

Sachs, Nelly 1891-1970 . . . . **CLC 14, 98**
See also CA 17-18; 25-28R; CAP 2

Sackler, Howard (Oliver)
1929-1982 . . . . **CLC 14**
See also CA 61-64; 108; CANR 30; DLB 7

Sacks, Oliver (Wolf) 1933- . . . . **CLC 67**
See also CA 53-56; CANR 28, 50;
INT CANR-28; MTCW

Sade, Donatien Alphonse Francois Comte
1740-1814 . . . . **NCLC 47**

Sadoff, Ira 1945- . . . . **CLC 9**
See also CA 53-56; CANR 5, 21; DLB 120

Saetone
See Camus, Albert

Safire, William 1929- . . . . **CLC 10**
See also CA 17-20R; CANR 31, 54

Sagan, Carl (Edward) 1934-1996 . . . . **CLC 30**
See also AAYA 2; CA 25-28R; 155;
CANR 11, 36; MTCW; SATA 58

Sagan, Francoise . . . . **CLC 3, 6, 9, 17, 36**
See also Quoirez, Francoise
See also DLB 83

Sahgal, Nayantara (Pandit) 1927- . . . **CLC 41**
See also CA 9-12R; CANR 11

Saint, H(arry) F. 1941- . . . . **CLC 50**
See also CA 127

St. Aubin de Teran, Lisa 1953-
See Teran, Lisa St. Aubin de
See also CA 118; 126; INT 126

Sainte-Beuve, Charles Augustin
1804-1869 . . . . **NCLC 5**

Saint-Exupery, Antoine (Jean Baptiste Marie
Roger) de
1900-1944 . . . . **TCLC 2, 56; DAM NOV;**
WLC
See also CA 108; 132; CLR 10; DLB 72;
MAICYA; MTCW; SATA 20

St. John, David
See Hunt, E(verette) Howard, (Jr.)

Saint-John Perse
See Leger, (Marie-Rene Auguste) Alexis
Saint-Leger

Saintsbury, George (Edward Bateman)
1845-1933 . . . . **TCLC 31**
See also DLB 57, 149

Sait Faik . . . . **TCLC 23**
See also Abasiyanik, Sait Faik

Saki . . . . **TCLC 3; SSC 12**
See also Munro, H(ector) H(ugh)

Sala, George Augustus . . . . **NCLC 46**

Salama, Hannu 1936- . . . . **CLC 18**

Salamanca, J(ack) R(ichard)
1922- . . . . **CLC 4, 15**
See also CA 25-28R

Sale, J. Kirkpatrick
See Sale, Kirkpatrick

Sale, Kirkpatrick 1937- . . . . **CLC 68**
See also CA 13-16R; CANR 10

Salinas, Luis Omar
1937- . . . . . **CLC 90; DAM MULT; HLC**
See also CA 131; DLB 82; HW

Salinas (y Serrano), Pedro
1891(?)-1951 . . . . **TCLC 17**
See also CA 117; DLB 134

Salinger, J(erome) D(avid)
1919- . . . . . . **CLC 1, 3, 8, 12, 55, 56; DA;**
DAB; DAC; DAM MST, NOV, POP;
SSC 2; WLC
See also AAYA 2; CA 5-8R; CANR 39;
CDALB 1941-1968; CLR 18; DLB 2, 102,
173; MAICYA; MTCW; SATA 67

Salisbury, John
See Caute, David

Salter, James 1925- . . . . **CLC 7, 52, 59**
See also CA 73-76; DLB 130

Saltus, Edgar (Everton)
1855-1921 . . . . **TCLC 8**
See also CA 105

Saltykov, Mikhail Evgrafovich
1826-1889 . . . . **NCLC 16**

Samarakis, Antonis 1919- . . . . **CLC 5**
See also CA 25-28R; CAAS 16; CANR 36

Sanchez, Florencio 1875-1910 . . . . . **TCLC 37**
See also CA 153; HW

Sanchez, Luis Rafael 1936- . . . . **CLC 23**
See also CA 128; DLB 145; HW

Sanchez, Sonia
1934- . . . . . . **CLC 5; BLC; DAM MULT;**
PC 9
See also BW 2; CA 33-36R; CANR 24, 49;
CLR 18; DLB 41; DLBD 8; MAICYA;
MTCW; SATA 22

Sand, George
1804-1876 . . . . **NCLC 2, 42, 57; DA;**
DAB; DAC; DAM MST, NOV; WLC
See also DLB 119

Sandburg, Carl (August)
1878-1967 . . . . **CLC 1, 4, 10, 15, 35; DA;**
DAB; DAC; DAM MST, POET; PC 2;
WLC
See also CA 5-8R; 25-28R; CANR 35;
CDALB 1865-1917; DLB 17, 54;
MAICYA; MTCW; SATA 8

Sandburg, Charles
See Sandburg, Carl (August)

Sandburg, Charles A.
See Sandburg, Carl (August)

Sanders, (James) Ed(ward) 1939- . . . **CLC 53**
See also CA 13-16R; CAAS 21; CANR 13,
44; DLB 16

Sanders, Lawrence
1920- . . . . **CLC 41; DAM POP**
See also BEST 89:4; CA 81-84; CANR 33;
MTCW

Sanders, Noah
See Blount, Roy (Alton), Jr.

Sanders, Winston P.
See Anderson, Poul (William)

Sandoz, Mari(e Susette)
1896-1966 . . . . **CLC 28**
See also CA 1-4R; 25-28R; CANR 17;
DLB 9; MTCW; SATA 5

Saner, Reg(inald Anthony) 1931- . . . . **CLC 9**
See also CA 65-68

Sannazaro, Jacopo 1456(?)-1530 . . . . . . **LC 8**

Sansom, William
1912-1976 . . . . . . **CLC 2, 6; DAM NOV;**
SSC 21
See also CA 5-8R; 65-68; CANR 42;
DLB 139; MTCW

Santayana, George 1863-1952 . . . . . **TCLC 40**
See also CA 115; DLB 54, 71; DLBD 13

Santiago, Danny . . . . **CLC 33**
See also James, Daniel (Lewis)
See also DLB 122

Santmyer, Helen Hoover
1895-1986 . . . . **CLC 33**
See also CA 1-4R; 118; CANR 15, 33;
DLBY 84; MTCW

Santos, Bienvenido N(uqui)
1911-1996 . . . . . . **CLC 22; DAM MULT**
See also CA 101; 151; CANR 19, 46

Sapper . . . . **TCLC 44**
See also McNeile, Herman Cyril

Sapphire 1950- . . . . **CLC 99**

Sappho
fl. 6th cent. B.C.- . . . . **CMLC 3;**
DAM POET; PC 5

Sarduy, Severo 1937-1993 . . . . . . **CLC 6, 97**
See also CA 89-92; 142; DLB 113; HW

Sargeson, Frank 1903-1982 . . . . **CLC 31**
See also CA 25-28R; 106; CANR 38

Sarmiento, Felix Ruben Garcia
See Dario, Ruben

Saroyan, William
1908-1981 . . . . . **CLC 1, 8, 10, 29, 34, 56;**
DA; DAB; DAC; DAM DRAM, MST,
NOV; SSC 21; WLC
See also CA 5-8R; 103; CANR 30; DLB 7,
9, 86; DLBY 81; MTCW; SATA 23;
SATA-Obit 24

Sarraute, Nathalie
1900- . . . . **CLC 1, 2, 4, 8, 10, 31, 80**
See also CA 9-12R; CANR 23; DLB 83;
MTCW

Sarton, (Eleanor) May
1912-1995 . . . . **CLC 4, 14, 49, 91;**
DAM POET
See also CA 1-4R; 149; CANR 1, 34, 55;
DLB 48; DLBY 81; INT CANR-34;
MTCW; SATA 36; SATA-Obit 86

Sartre, Jean-Paul
1905-1980 . . . . **CLC 1, 4, 7, 9, 13, 18, 24,**
44, 50, 52; DA; DAB; DAC;
DAM DRAM, MST, NOV; DC 3; WLC
See also CA 9-12R; 97-100; CANR 21;
DLB 72; MTCW

Sassoon, Siegfried (Lorraine)
1886-1967 . . . . **CLC 36; DAB;**
DAM MST, NOV, POET; PC 12
See also CA 104; 25-28R; CANR 36;
DLB 20; MTCW

Satterfield, Charles
See Pohl, Frederik

Saul, John (W. III)
1942- . . . . . . **CLC 46; DAM NOV, POP**
See also AAYA 10; BEST 90:4; CA 81-84;
CANR 16, 40

Saunders, Caleb
See Heinlein, Robert A(nson)

Saura (Atares), Carlos 1932- . . . . **CLC 20**
See also CA 114; 131; HW

Sauser-Hall, Frederic 1887-1961 . . . . **CLC 18**
See also Cendrars, Blaise
See also CA 102; 93-96; CANR 36; MTCW

Saussure, Ferdinand de
1857-1913 . . . . **TCLC 49**

Savage, Catharine
See Brosman, Catharine Savage

Savage, Thomas 1915- . . . . **CLC 40**
See also CA 126; 132; CAAS 15; INT 132

Savan, Glenn 19(?)- . . . . **CLC 50**

Sayers, Dorothy L(eigh)
1893-1957 . . . . . **TCLC 2, 15; DAM POP**
See also CA 104; 119; CDBLB 1914-1945;
DLB 10, 36, 77, 100; MTCW

Sayers, Valerie 1952- . . . . **CLC 50**
See also CA 134

Sayles, John (Thomas)
1950- . . . . **CLC 7, 10, 14**
See also CA 57-60; CANR 41; DLB 44

Scammell, Michael . . . . **CLC 34**

Scannell, Vernon 1922- . . . . **CLC 49**
See also CA 5-8R; CANR 8, 24; DLB 27;
SATA 59

Scarlett, Susan
See Streatfeild, (Mary) Noel

Schaeffer, Susan Fromberg
1941- . . . . **CLC 6, 11, 22**
See also CA 49-52; CANR 18; DLB 28;
MTCW; SATA 22

Schary, Jill
See Robinson, Jill

Schell, Jonathan 1943- . . . . **CLC 35**
See also CA 73-76; CANR 12

Schelling, Friedrich Wilhelm Joseph von
1775-1854 . . . . **NCLC 30**
See also DLB 90

Schendel, Arthur van 1874-1946 . . . **TCLC 56**

Scherer, Jean-Marie Maurice 1920-
See Rohmer, Eric
See also CA 110

Schevill, James (Erwin) 1920- . . . . **CLC 7**
See also CA 5-8R; CAAS 12

Schiller, Friedrich
1759-1805 . . . . **NCLC 39; DAM DRAM**
See also DLB 94

Schisgal, Murray (Joseph) 1926- . . . . . **CLC 6**
See also CA 21-24R; CANR 48

Schlee, Ann 1934- . . . . **CLC 35**
See also CA 101; CANR 29; SATA 44;
SATA-Brief 36

Schlegel, August Wilhelm von
1767-1845 . . . . **NCLC 15**
See also DLB 94

Schlegel, Friedrich 1772-1829 . . . . **NCLC 45**
See also DLB 90

Schlegel, Johann Elias (von)
1719(?)-1749 . . . . **LC 5**

Schlesinger, Arthur M(eier), Jr.
1917- . . . . **CLC 84**
See also AITN 1; CA 1-4R; CANR 1, 28;
DLB 17; INT CANR-28; MTCW;
SATA 61

Schmidt, Arno (Otto) 1914-1979 . . . . **CLC 56**
See also CA 128; 109; DLB 69

Schmitz, Aron Hector 1861-1928
See Svevo, Italo
See also CA 104; 122; MTCW

Schnackenberg, Gjertrud 1953- . . . . . **CLC 40**
See also CA 116; DLB 120

Schneider, Leonard Alfred 1925-1966
See Bruce, Lenny
See also CA 89-92

Sexton, Anne (Harvey)
1928-1974 .... **CLC 2, 4, 6, 8, 10, 15, 53;
DA; DAB; DAC; DAM MST, POET;
PC 2; WLC**
See also CA 1-4R; 53-56; CABS 2;
CANR 3, 36; CDALB 1941-1968; DLB 5,
169; MTCW; SATA 10

Shaara, Michael (Joseph, Jr.)
1929-1988 .... **CLC 15; DAM POP**
See also AITN 1; CA 102; 125; CANR 52;
DLBY 83

Shackleton, C. C.
See Aldiss, Brian W(ilson)

Shacochis, Bob .... **CLC 39**
See also Shacochis, Robert G.

Shacochis, Robert G. 1951-
See Shacochis, Bob
See also CA 119; 124; INT 124

Shaffer, Anthony (Joshua)
1926- .... **CLC 19; DAM DRAM**
See also CA 110; 116; DLB 13

Shaffer, Peter (Levin)
1926- ..... **CLC 5, 14, 18, 37, 60; DAB;
DAM DRAM, MST**
See also CA 25-28R; CANR 25, 47;
CDBLB 1960 to Present; DLB 13;
MTCW

Shakey, Bernard
See Young, Neil

Shalamov, Varlam (Tikhonovich)
1907(?)-1982 .... **CLC 18**
See also CA 129; 105

Shamlu, Ahmad 1925- .... **CLC 10**

Shammas, Anton 1951-........... **CLC 55**

Shange, Ntozake
1948- .... **CLC 8, 25, 38, 74; BLC;
DAM DRAM, MULT; DC 3**
See also AAYA 9; BW 2; CA 85-88;
CABS 3; CANR 27, 48; DLB 38; MTCW

Shanley, John Patrick 1950-....... **CLC 75**
See also CA 128; 133

Shapcott, Thomas W(illiam) 1935-.. **CLC 38**
See also CA 69-72; CANR 49

Shapiro, Jane..................... **CLC 76**

Shapiro, Karl (Jay) 1913- .. **CLC 4, 8, 15, 53**
See also CA 1-4R; CAAS 6; CANR 1, 36;
DLB 48; MTCW

Sharp, William 1855-1905 .... **TCLC 39**
See also DLB 156

Sharpe, Thomas Ridley 1928-
See Sharpe, Tom
See also CA 114; 122; INT 122

Sharpe, Tom...................... **CLC 36**
See also Sharpe, Thomas Ridley
See also DLB 14

Shaw, Bernard................... **TCLC 45**
See also Shaw, George Bernard
See also BW 1

Shaw, G. Bernard
See Shaw, George Bernard

Shaw, George Bernard
1856-1950 ... **TCLC 3, 9, 21; DA; DAB;
DAC; DAM DRAM, MST; WLC**
See also Shaw, Bernard
See also CA 104; 128; CDBLB 1914-1945;
DLB 10, 57; MTCW

Shaw, Henry Wheeler
1818-1885 .... **NCLC 15**
See also DLB 11

Shaw, Irwin
1913-1984 .... **CLC 7, 23, 34;
DAM DRAM, POP**
See also AITN 1; CA 13-16R; 112;
CANR 21; CDALB 1941-1968; DLB 6,
102; DLBY 84; MTCW

Shaw, Robert 1927-1978 .... **CLC 5**
See also AITN 1; CA 1-4R; 81-84;
CANR 4; DLB 13, 14

Shaw, T. E.
See Lawrence, T(homas) E(dward)

Shawn, Wallace 1943- .... **CLC 41**
See also CA 112

Shea, Lisa 1953-................. **CLC 86**
See also CA 147

Sheed, Wilfrid (John Joseph)
1930- .... **CLC 2, 4, 10, 53**
See also CA 65-68; CANR 30; DLB 6;
MTCW

Sheldon, Alice Hastings Bradley
1915(?)-1987
See Tiptree, James, Jr.
See also CA 108; 122; CANR 34; INT 108;
MTCW

Sheldon, John
See Bloch, Robert (Albert)

Shelley, Mary Wollstonecraft (Godwin)
1797-1851 .... **NCLC 14, 59; DA; DAB;
DAC; DAM MST, NOV; WLC**
See also AAYA 20; CDBLB 1789-1832;
DLB 110, 116, 159; SATA 29

Shelley, Percy Bysshe
1792-1822 .... **NCLC 18; DA; DAB;
DAC; DAM MST, POET; PC 14; WLC**
See also CDBLB 1789-1832; DLB 96, 110,
158

Shepard, Jim 1956-............... **CLC 36**
See also CA 137; SATA 90

Shepard, Lucius 1947- .... **CLC 34**
See also CA 128; 141

Shepard, Sam
1943- .... **CLC 4, 6, 17, 34, 41, 44;
DAM DRAM; DC 5**
See also AAYA 1; CA 69-72; CABS 3;
CANR 22; DLB 7; MTCW

Shepherd, Michael
See Ludlum, Robert

Sherburne, Zoa (Morin) 1912-..... **CLC 30**
See also AAYA 13; CA 1-4R; CANR 3, 37;
MAICYA; SAAS 18; SATA 3

Sheridan, Frances 1724-1766........ **LC 7**
See also DLB 39, 84

Sheridan, Richard Brinsley
1751-1816 .... **NCLC 5; DA; DAB;
DAC; DAM DRAM, MST; DC 1; WLC**
See also CDBLB 1660-1789; DLB 89

Sherman, Jonathan Marc.......... **CLC 55**

Sherman, Martin 1941(?)- .... **CLC 19**
See also CA 116; 123

Sherwin, Judith Johnson 1936-... **CLC 7, 15**
See also CA 25-28R; CANR 34

Sherwood, Frances 1940-......... **CLC 81**
See also CA 146

Sherwood, Robert E(mmet)
1896-1955 ...... **TCLC 3; DAM DRAM**
See also CA 104; 153; DLB 7, 26

Shestov, Lev 1866-1938 .... **TCLC 56**

Shevchenko, Taras 1814-1861 .... **NCLC 54**

Shiel, M(atthew) P(hipps)
1865-1947 .... **TCLC 8**
See also CA 106; DLB 153

Shields, Carol 1935-......... **CLC 91; DAC**
See also CA 81-84; CANR 51

Shields, David 1956-.............. **CLC 97**
See also CA 124; CANR 48

Shiga, Naoya 1883-1971... **CLC 33; SSC 23**
See also CA 101; 33-36R

Shilts, Randy 1951-1994 .... **CLC 85**
See also AAYA 19; CA 115; 127; 144;
CANR 45; INT 127

Shimazaki, Haruki 1872-1943
See Shimazaki Toson
See also CA 105; 134

Shimazaki Toson................. **TCLC 5**
See also Shimazaki, Haruki

Sholokhov, Mikhail (Aleksandrovich)
1905-1984 .... **CLC 7, 15**
See also CA 101; 112; MTCW;
SATA-Obit 36

Shone, Patric
See Hanley, James

Shreve, Susan Richards 1939-...... **CLC 23**
See also CA 49-52; CAAS 5; CANR 5, 38;
MAICYA; SATA 46; SATA-Brief 41

Shue, Larry
1946-1985 ...... **CLC 52; DAM DRAM**
See also CA 145; 117

Shu-Jen, Chou 1881-1936
See Lu Hsun
See also CA 104

Shulman, Alix Kates 1932- ...... **CLC 2, 10**
See also CA 29-32R; CANR 43; SATA 7

Shuster, Joe 1914- .... **CLC 21**

Shute, Nevil..................... **CLC 30**
See also Norway, Nevil Shute

Shuttle, Penelope (Diane) 1947-..... **CLC 7**
See also CA 93-96; CANR 39; DLB 14, 40

Sidney, Mary 1561-1621 .... **LC 19**

Sidney, Sir Philip
1554-1586 ..... **LC 19; DA; DAB; DAC;
DAM MST, POET**
See also CDBLB Before 1660; DLB 167

Siegel, Jerome 1914-1996 .... **CLC 21**
See also CA 116; 151

Siegel, Jerry
See Siegel, Jerome

Sienkiewicz, Henryk (Adam Alexander Pius)
1846-1916 .... **TCLC 3**
See also CA 104; 134

Smart, Christopher
1722-1771 . . . **LC 3; DAM POET; PC 13**
See also DLB 109

Smart, Elizabeth 1913-1986. . . . . . . **CLC 54**
See also CA 81-84; 118; DLB 88

Smiley, Jane (Graves)
1949- . . . . **CLC 53, 76; DAM POP**
See also CA 104; CANR 30, 50;
INT CANR-30

Smith, A(rthur) J(ames) M(arshall)
1902-1980 . . . . **CLC 15; DAC**
See also CA 1-4R; 102; CANR 4; DLB 88

Smith, Adam 1723-1790. . . . . **LC 36**
See also DLB 104

Smith, Alexander 1829-1867 . . . . . **NCLC 59**
See also DLB 32, 55

Smith, Anna Deavere 1950- . . . . **CLC 86**
See also CA 133

Smith, Betty (Wehner) 1896-1972. . . **CLC 19**
See also CA 5-8R; 33-36R; DLBY 82;
SATA 6

Smith, Charlotte (Turner)
1749-1806 . . . . **NCLC 23**
See also DLB 39, 109

Smith, Clark Ashton 1893-1961 . . . . **CLC 43**
See also CA 143

Smith, Dave . . . . **CLC 22, 42**
See also Smith, David (Jeddie)
See also CAAS 7; DLB 5

Smith, David (Jeddie) 1942-
See Smith, Dave
See also CA 49-52; CANR 1; DAM POET

Smith, Florence Margaret 1902-1971
See Smith, Stevie
See also CA 17-18; 29-32R; CANR 35;
CAP 2; DAM POET; MTCW

Smith, Iain Crichton 1928- . . . . **CLC 64**
See also CA 21-24R; DLB 40, 139

Smith, John 1580(?)-1631 . . . . **LC 9**

Smith, Johnston
See Crane, Stephen (Townley)

Smith, Joseph, Jr. 1805-1844 . . . . **NCLC 53**

Smith, Lee 1944- . . . . **CLC 25, 73**
See also CA 114; 119; CANR 46; DLB 143;
DLBY 83; INT 119

Smith, Martin
See Smith, Martin Cruz

Smith, Martin Cruz
1942- . . . . . **CLC 25; DAM MULT, POP**
See also BEST 89:4; CA 85-88; CANR 6,
23, 43; INT CANR-23; NNAL

Smith, Mary-Ann Tirone 1944- . . . . . **CLC 39**
See also CA 118; 136

Smith, Patti 1946- . . . . **CLC 12**
See also CA 93-96

Smith, Pauline (Urmson)
1882-1959 . . . . **TCLC 25**

Smith, Rosamond
See Oates, Joyce Carol

Smith, Sheila Kaye
See Kaye-Smith, Sheila

Smith, Stevie . . . . . . **CLC 3, 8, 25, 44; PC 12**
See also Smith, Florence Margaret
See also DLB 20

Smith, Wilbur (Addison) 1933- . . . . . **CLC 33**
See also CA 13-16R; CANR 7, 46; MTCW

Smith, William Jay 1918- . . . . **CLC 6**
See also CA 5-8R; CANR 44; DLB 5;
MAICYA; SAAS 22; SATA 2, 68

Smith, Woodrow Wilson
See Kuttner, Henry

Smolenskin, Peretz 1842-1885. . . . **NCLC 30**

Smollett, Tobias (George) 1721-1771 . . **LC 2**
See also CDBLB 1660-1789; DLB 39, 104

Snodgrass, W(illiam) D(e Witt)
1926- . . . . **CLC 2, 6, 10, 18, 68;
DAM POET**
See also CA 1-4R; CANR 6, 36; DLB 5;
MTCW

Snow, C(harles) P(ercy)
1905-1980 . . . . **CLC 1, 4, 6, 9, 13, 19;
DAM NOV**
See also CA 5-8R; 101; CANR 28;
CDBLB 1945-1960; DLB 15, 77; MTCW

Snow, Frances Compton
See Adams, Henry (Brooks)

Snyder, Gary (Sherman)
1930- . . **CLC 1, 2, 5, 9, 32; DAM POET**
See also CA 17-20R; CANR 30; DLB 5, 16,
165

Snyder, Zilpha Keatley 1927- . . . . . . **CLC 17**
See also AAYA 15; CA 9-12R; CANR 38;
CLR 31; JRDA; MAICYA; SAAS 2;
SATA 1, 28, 75

Soares, Bernardo
See Pessoa, Fernando (Antonio Nogueira)

Sobh, A.
See Shamlu, Ahmad

Sobol, Joshua . . . . **CLC 60**

Soderberg, Hjalmar 1869-1941 . . . . **TCLC 39**

Sodergran, Edith (Irene)
See Soedergran, Edith (Irene)

Soedergran, Edith (Irene)
1892-1923 . . . . **TCLC 31**

Softly, Edgar
See Lovecraft, H(oward) P(hillips)

Softly, Edward
See Lovecraft, H(oward) P(hillips)

Sokolov, Raymond 1941- . . . . **CLC 7**
See also CA 85-88

Solo, Jay
See Ellison, Harlan (Jay)

Sologub, Fyodor . . . . **TCLC 9**
See also Teternikov, Fyodor Kuzmich

Solomons, Ikey Esquir
See Thackeray, William Makepeace

Solomos, Dionysios 1798-1857 . . . **NCLC 15**

Solwoska, Mara
See French, Marilyn

Solzhenitsyn, Aleksandr I(sayevich)
1918- . . . . . . **CLC 1, 2, 4, 7, 9, 10, 18, 26,
34, 78; DA; DAB; DAC; DAM MST,
NOV; WLC**
See also AITN 1; CA 69-72; CANR 40;
MTCW

Somers, Jane
See Lessing, Doris (May)

Somerville, Edith 1858-1949 . . . . . . **TCLC 51**
See also DLB 135

Somerville & Ross
See Martin, Violet Florence; Somerville,
Edith

Sommer, Scott 1951- . . . . **CLC 25**
See also CA 106

Sondheim, Stephen (Joshua)
1930- . . . . **CLC 30, 39; DAM DRAM**
See also AAYA 11; CA 103; CANR 47

Sontag, Susan
1933- . . . . **CLC 1, 2, 10, 13, 31;
DAM POP**
See also CA 17-20R; CANR 25, 51; DLB 2,
67; MTCW

Sophocles
496(?)B.C.-406(?)B.C. . . . . . **CMLC 2; DA;
DAB; DAC; DAM DRAM, MST; DC 1**

Sordello 1189-1269. . . . . **CMLC 15**

Sorel, Julia
See Drexler, Rosalyn

Sorrentino, Gilbert
1929- . . . . **CLC 3, 7, 14, 22, 40**
See also CA 77-80; CANR 14, 33; DLB 5,
173; DLBY 80; INT CANR-14

Soto, Gary
1952- . . . . **CLC 32, 80; DAM MULT;
HLC**
See also AAYA 10; CA 119; 125;
CANR 50; CLR 38; DLB 82; HW;
INT 125; JRDA; SATA 80

Soupault, Philippe 1897-1990 . . . . . . **CLC 68**
See also CA 116; 147; 131

Souster, (Holmes) Raymond
1921- . . . **CLC 5, 14; DAC; DAM POET**
See also CA 13-16R; CAAS 14; CANR 13,
29, 53; DLB 88; SATA 63

Southern, Terry 1924(?)-1995 . . . . **CLC 7**
See also CA 1-4R; 150; CANR 1, 55;
DLB 2

Southey, Robert 1774-1843 . . . . **NCLC 8**
See also DLB 93, 107, 142; SATA 54

Southworth, Emma Dorothy Eliza Nevitte
1819-1899 . . . . **NCLC 26**

Souza, Ernest
See Scott, Evelyn

Soyinka, Wole
1934- . . . . **CLC 3, 5, 14, 36, 44; BLC;
DA; DAB; DAC; DAM DRAM, MST,
MULT; DC 2; WLC**
See also BW 2; CA 13-16R; CANR 27, 39;
DLB 125; MTCW

Spackman, W(illiam) M(ode)
1905-1990 . . . . **CLC 46**
See also CA 81-84; 132

Spacks, Barry (Bernard) 1931- . . . . . **CLC 14**
See also CA 154; CANR 33; DLB 105

Spanidou, Irini 1946- . . . . **CLC 44**

Spark, Muriel (Sarah)
1918- . . . . . **CLC 2, 3, 5, 8, 13, 18, 40, 94;
DAB; DAC; DAM MST, NOV; SSC 10**
See also CA 5-8R; CANR 12, 36;
CDBLB 1945-1960; DLB 15, 139;
INT CANR-12; MTCW

Spaulding, Douglas
See Bradbury, Ray (Douglas)

Spaulding, Leonard
See Bradbury, Ray (Douglas)

Spence, J. A. D.
See Eliot, T(homas) S(tearns)

Spencer, Elizabeth 1921-.......... **CLC 22**
See also CA 13-16R; CANR 32; DLB 6;
MTCW; SATA 14

Spencer, Leonard G.
See Silverberg, Robert

Spencer, Scott 1945-............. **CLC 30**
See also CA 113; CANR 51; DLBY 86

Spender, Stephen (Harold)
1909-1995 ...... **CLC 1, 2, 5, 10, 41, 91;**
DAM POET
See also CA 9-12R; 149; CANR 31, 54;
CDBLB 1945-1960; DLB 20; MTCW

Spengler, Oswald (Arnold Gottfried)
1880-1936 .... **TCLC 25**
See also CA 118

Spenser, Edmund
1552(?)-1599 .... **LC 5; DA; DAB; DAC;**
DAM MST, POET; PC 8; WLC
See also CDBLB Before 1660; DLB 167

Spicer, Jack
1925-1965 .... **CLC 8, 18, 72;**
DAM POET
See also CA 85-88; DLB 5, 16

Spiegelman, Art 1948-........... **CLC 76**
See also AAYA 10; CA 125; CANR 41, 55

Spielberg, Peter 1929-............ **CLC 6**
See also CA 5-8R; CANR 4, 48; DLBY 81

Spielberg, Steven 1947-........... **CLC 20**
See also AAYA 8; CA 77-80; CANR 32;
SATA 32

Spillane, Frank Morrison 1918-
See Spillane, Mickey
See also CA 25-28R; CANR 28; MTCW;
SATA 66

Spillane, Mickey .... **CLC 3, 13**
See also Spillane, Frank Morrison

Spinoza, Benedictus de 1632-1677 .... **LC 9**

Spinrad, Norman (Richard) 1940-... **CLC 46**
See also CA 37-40R; CAAS 19; CANR 20;
DLB 8; INT CANR-20

Spitteler, Carl (Friedrich Georg)
1845-1924 .... **TCLC 12**
See also CA 109; DLB 129

Spivack, Kathleen (Romola Drucker)
1938- .... **CLC 6**
See also CA 49-52

Spoto, Donald 1941-............. **CLC 39**
See also CA 65-68; CANR 11

Springsteen, Bruce (F.) 1949- ...... **CLC 17**
See also CA 111

Spurling, Hilary 1940-........... **CLC 34**
See also CA 104; CANR 25, 52

Spyker, John Howland
See Elman, Richard

Squires, (James) Radcliffe
1917-1993 .... **CLC 51**
See also CA 1-4R; 140; CANR 6, 21

Srivastava, Dhanpat Rai 1880(?)-1936
See Premchand
See also CA 118

Stacy, Donald
See Pohl, Frederik

Stael, Germaine de
See Stael-Holstein, Anne Louise Germaine
Necker Baronn
See also DLB 119

Stael-Holstein, Anne Louise Germaine Necker
Baronn 1766-1817 .... **NCLC 3**
See also Stael, Germaine de

Stafford, Jean 1915-1979... **CLC 4, 7, 19, 68**
See also CA 1-4R; 85-88; CANR 3; DLB 2,
173; MTCW; SATA-Obit 22

Stafford, William (Edgar)
1914-1993 ... **CLC 4, 7, 29; DAM POET**
See also CA 5-8R; 142; CAAS 3; CANR 5,
22; DLB 5; INT CANR-22

Staines, Trevor
See Brunner, John (Kilian Houston)

Stairs, Gordon
See Austin, Mary (Hunter)

Stannard, Martin 1947-........... **CLC 44**
See also CA 142; DLB 155

Stanton, Maura 1946- .... **CLC 9**
See also CA 89-92; CANR 15; DLB 120

Stanton, Schuyler
See Baum, L(yman) Frank

Stapledon, (William) Olaf
1886-1950 .... **TCLC 22**
See also CA 111; DLB 15

Starbuck, George (Edwin)
1931-1996 .... **CLC 53; DAM POET**
See also CA 21-24R; 153; CANR 23

Stark, Richard
See Westlake, Donald E(dwin)

Staunton, Schuyler
See Baum, L(yman) Frank

Stead, Christina (Ellen)
1902-1983 .... **CLC 2, 5, 8, 32, 80**
See also CA 13-16R; 109; CANR 33, 40;
MTCW

Stead, William Thomas
1849-1912 .... **TCLC 48**

Steele, Richard 1672-1729 .... **LC 18**
See also CDBLB 1660-1789; DLB 84, 101

Steele, Timothy (Reid) 1948-....... **CLC 45**
See also CA 93-96; CANR 16, 50; DLB 120

Steffens, (Joseph) Lincoln
1866-1936 .... **TCLC 20**
See also CA 117

Stegner, Wallace (Earle)
1909-1993 ... **CLC 9, 49, 81; DAM NOV**
See also AITN 1; BEST 90:3; CA 1-4R;
141; CAAS 9; CANR 1, 21, 46; DLB 9;
DLBY 93; MTCW

Stein, Gertrude
1874-1946 ...... **TCLC 1, 6, 28, 48; DA;**
DAB; DAC; DAM MST, NOV, POET;
WLC
See also CA 104; 132; CDALB 1917-1929;
DLB 4, 54, 86; MTCW

Steinbeck, John (Ernst)
1902-1968 ...... **CLC 1, 5, 9, 13, 21, 34,**
45, 75; DA; DAB; DAC; DAM DRAM,
MST, NOV; SSC 11; WLC
See also AAYA 12; CA 1-4R; 25-28R;
CANR 1, 35; CDALB 1929-1941; DLB 7,
9; DLBD 2; MTCW; SATA 9

Steinem, Gloria 1934-............. **CLC 63**
See also CA 53-56; CANR 28, 51; MTCW

Steiner, George
1929- .... **CLC 24; DAM NOV**
See also CA 73-76; CANR 31; DLB 67;
MTCW; SATA 62

Steiner, K. Leslie
See Delany, Samuel R(ay, Jr.)

Steiner, Rudolf 1861-1925 .... **TCLC 13**
See also CA 107

Stendhal
1783-1842 .... **NCLC 23, 46; DA; DAB;**
DAC; DAM MST, NOV; WLC
See also DLB 119

Stephen, Leslie 1832-1904 .... **TCLC 23**
See also CA 123; DLB 57, 144

Stephen, Sir Leslie
See Stephen, Leslie

Stephen, Virginia
See Woolf, (Adeline) Virginia

Stephens, James 1882(?)-1950...... **TCLC 4**
See also CA 104; DLB 19, 153, 162

Stephens, Reed
See Donaldson, Stephen R.

Steptoe, Lydia
See Barnes, Djuna

Sterchi, Beat 1949-.............. **CLC 65**

Sterling, Brett
See Bradbury, Ray (Douglas); Hamilton,
Edmond

Sterling, Bruce 1954-............. **CLC 72**
See also CA 119; CANR 44

Sterling, George 1869-1926 .... **TCLC 20**
See also CA 117; DLB 54

Stern, Gerald 1925- .... **CLC 40**
See also CA 81-84; CANR 28; DLB 105

Stern, Richard (Gustave) 1928-... **CLC 4, 39**
See also CA 1-4R; CANR 1, 25, 52;
DLBY 87; INT CANR-25

Sternberg, Josef von 1894-1969..... **CLC 20**
See also CA 81-84

Sterne, Laurence
1713-1768 ...... **LC 2; DA; DAB; DAC;**
DAM MST, NOV; WLC
See also CDBLB 1660-1789; DLB 39

Sternheim, (William Adolf) Carl
1878-1942 .... **TCLC 8**
See also CA 105; DLB 56, 118

Stevens, Mark 1951- .... **CLC 34**
See also CA 122

Stevens, Wallace
1879-1955 .... **TCLC 3, 12, 45; DA;**
DAB; DAC; DAM MST, POET; PC 6;
WLC
See also CA 104; 124; CDALB 1929-1941;
DLB 54; MTCW

Stevenson, Anne (Katharine)
1933- . . . . CLC **7, 33**
See also CA 17-20R; CAAS 9; CANR 9, 33;
DLB 40; MTCW

Stevenson, Robert Louis (Balfour)
1850-1894 . . . . . NCLC **5, 14; DA; DAB;**
DAC; DAM MST, NOV; SSC 11; WLC
See also CDBLB 1890-1914; CLR 10, 11;
DLB 18, 57, 141, 156, 174; DLBD 13;
JRDA; MAICYA; YABC 2

Stewart, J(ohn) I(nnes) M(ackintosh)
1906-1994 . . . . CLC **7, 14, 32**
See also CA 85-88; 147; CAAS 3;
CANR 47; MTCW

Stewart, Mary (Florence Elinor)
1916- . . . . CLC **7, 35; DAB**
See also CA 1-4R; CANR 1; SATA 12

Stewart, Mary Rainbow
See Stewart, Mary (Florence Elinor)

Stifle, June
See Campbell, Maria

Stifter, Adalbert 1805-1868 . . . . . . NCLC **41**
See also DLB 133

Still, James 1906- . . . . CLC **49**
See also CA 65-68; CAAS 17; CANR 10,
26; DLB 9; SATA 29

Sting
See Sumner, Gordon Matthew

Stirling, Arthur
See Sinclair, Upton (Beall)

Stitt, Milan 1941- . . . . CLC **29**
See also CA 69-72

Stockton, Francis Richard 1834-1902
See Stockton, Frank R.
See also CA 108; 137; MAICYA; SATA 44

Stockton, Frank R. . . . . TCLC **47**
See also Stockton, Francis Richard
See also DLB 42, 74; DLBD 13;
SATA-Brief 32

Stoddard, Charles
See Kuttner, Henry

Stoker, Abraham 1847-1912
See Stoker, Bram
See also CA 105; DA; DAC; DAM MST,
NOV; SATA 29

Stoker, Bram
1847-1912 . . . . TCLC **8; DAB; WLC**
See also Stoker, Abraham
See also CA 150; CDBLB 1890-1914;
DLB 36, 70

Stolz, Mary (Slattery) 1920- . . . . CLC **12**
See also AAYA 8; AITN 1; CA 5-8R;
CANR 13, 41; JRDA; MAICYA;
SAAS 3; SATA 10, 71

Stone, Irving
1903-1989 . . . . CLC **7; DAM POP**
See also AITN 1; CA 1-4R; 129; CAAS 3;
CANR 1, 23; INT CANR-23; MTCW;
SATA 3; SATA-Obit 64

Stone, Oliver (William) 1946- . . . . . . CLC **73**
See also AAYA 15; CA 110; CANR 55

Stone, Robert (Anthony)
1937- . . . . CLC **5, 23, 42**
See also CA 85-88; CANR 23; DLB 152;
INT CANR-23; MTCW

Stone, Zachary
See Follett, Ken(neth Martin)

Stoppard, Tom
1937- . . . . . . CLC **1, 3, 4, 5, 8, 15, 29, 34,**
63, 91; DA; DAB; DAC; DAM DRAM,
MST; DC 6; WLC
See also CA 81-84; CANR 39;
CDBLB 1960 to Present; DLB 13;
DLBY 85; MTCW

Storey, David (Malcolm)
1933- . . . . . CLC **2, 4, 5, 8; DAM DRAM**
See also CA 81-84; CANR 36; DLB 13, 14;
MTCW

Storm, Hyemeyohsts
1935- . . . . CLC **3; DAM MULT**
See also CA 81-84; CANR 45; NNAL

Storm, (Hans) Theodor (Woldsen)
1817-1888 . . . . NCLC **1**

Storni, Alfonsina
1892-1938 . . . . . TCLC **5; DAM MULT;**
HLC
See also CA 104; 131; HW

Stout, Rex (Todhunter) 1886-1975 . . . CLC **3**
See also AITN 2; CA 61-64

Stow, (Julian) Randolph 1935- . . CLC **23, 48**
See also CA 13-16R; CANR 33; MTCW

Stowe, Harriet (Elizabeth) Beecher
1811-1896 . . . . . NCLC **3, 50; DA; DAB;**
DAC; DAM MST, NOV; WLC
See also CDALB 1865-1917; DLB 1, 12, 42,
74; JRDA; MAICYA; YABC 1

Strachey, (Giles) Lytton
1880-1932 . . . . TCLC **12**
See also CA 110; DLB 149; DLBD 10

Strand, Mark
1934- . . CLC **6, 18, 41, 71; DAM POET**
See also CA 21-24R; CANR 40; DLB 5;
SATA 41

Straub, Peter (Francis)
1943- . . . . CLC **28; DAM POP**
See also BEST 89:1; CA 85-88; CANR 28;
DLBY 84; MTCW

Strauss, Botho 1944- . . . . CLC **22**
See also DLB 124

Streatfeild, (Mary) Noel
1895(?)-1986 . . . . CLC **21**
See also CA 81-84; 120; CANR 31;
CLR 17; DLB 160; MAICYA; SATA 20;
SATA-Obit 48

Stribling, T(homas) S(igismund)
1881-1965 . . . . CLC **23**
See also CA 107; DLB 9

Strindberg, (Johan) August
1849-1912 . . . . . . TCLC **1, 8, 21, 47; DA;**
DAB; DAC; DAM DRAM, MST; WLC
See also CA 104; 135

Stringer, Arthur 1874-1950 . . . . TCLC **37**
See also DLB 92

Stringer, David
See Roberts, Keith (John Kingston)

Strugatskii, Arkadii (Natanovich)
1925-1991 . . . . CLC **27**
See also CA 106; 135

Strugatskii, Boris (Natanovich)
1933- . . . . CLC **27**
See also CA 106

Strummer, Joe 1953(?)- . . . . CLC **30**

Stuart, Don A.
See Campbell, John W(ood, Jr.)

Stuart, Ian
See MacLean, Alistair (Stuart)

Stuart, Jesse (Hilton)
1906-1984 . . . . CLC **1, 8, 11, 14, 34**
See also CA 5-8R; 112; CANR 31; DLB 9,
48, 102; DLBY 84; SATA 2;
SATA-Obit 36

Sturgeon, Theodore (Hamilton)
1918-1985 . . . . CLC **22, 39**
See also Queen, Ellery
See also CA 81-84; 116; CANR 32; DLB 8;
DLBY 85; MTCW

Sturges, Preston 1898-1959 . . . . . . TCLC **48**
See also CA 114; 149; DLB 26

Styron, William
1925- . . . . CLC **1, 3, 5, 11, 15, 60;**
DAM NOV, POP
See also BEST 90:4; CA 5-8R; CANR 6, 33;
CDALB 1968-1988; DLB 2, 143;
DLBY 80; INT CANR-6; MTCW

Suarez Lynch, B.
See Bioy Casares, Adolfo; Borges, Jorge
Luis

Su Chien 1884-1918
See Su Man-shu
See also CA 123

Suckow, Ruth 1892-1960 . . . . SSC **18**
See also CA 113; DLB 9, 102

Sudermann, Hermann 1857-1928 . . TCLC **15**
See also CA 107; DLB 118

Sue, Eugene 1804-1857 . . . . NCLC **1**
See also DLB 119

Sueskind, Patrick 1949- . . . . CLC **44**
See also Suskind, Patrick

Sukenick, Ronald 1932- . . . . . CLC **3, 4, 6, 48**
See also CA 25-28R; CAAS 8; CANR 32;
DLB 173; DLBY 81

Suknaski, Andrew 1942- . . . . CLC **19**
See also CA 101; DLB 53

Sullivan, Vernon
See Vian, Boris

Sully Prudhomme 1839-1907 . . . . . . TCLC **31**

Su Man-shu . . . . TCLC **24**
See also Su Chien

Summerforest, Ivy B.
See Kirkup, James

Summers, Andrew James 1942- . . . . . CLC **26**

Summers, Andy
See Summers, Andrew James

Summers, Hollis (Spurgeon, Jr.)
1916- . . . . CLC **10**
See also CA 5-8R; CANR 3; DLB 6

Summers, (Alphonsus Joseph-Mary Augustus)
Montague 1880-1948 . . . . TCLC **16**
See also CA 118

Sumner, Gordon Matthew 1951- . . . . CLC **26**

Surtees, Robert Smith
1803-1864 . . . . NCLC **14**
See also DLB 21

Susann, Jacqueline 1921-1974 . . . . . . CLC **3**
See also AITN 1; CA 65-68; 53-56; MTCW

Terkel, Louis 1912-
See Terkel, Studs
See also CA 57-60; CANR 18, 45; MTCW

Terkel, Studs . . . . **CLC 38**
See also Terkel, Louis
See also AITN 1

Terry, C. V.
See Slaughter, Frank G(ill)

Terry, Megan 1932- . . . . **CLC 19**
See also CA 77-80; CABS 3; CANR 43;
DLB 7

Tertz, Abram
See Sinyavsky, Andrei (Donatevich)

Tesich, Steve 1943(?)-1996. . . . . . **CLC 40, 69**
See also CA 105; 152; DLBY 83

Teternikov, Fyodor Kuzmich 1863-1927
See Sologub, Fyodor
See also CA 104

Tevis, Walter 1928-1984 . . . . **CLC 42**
See also CA 113

Tey, Josephine . . . . **TCLC 14**
See also Mackintosh, Elizabeth
See also DLB 77

Thackeray, William Makepeace
1811-1863 . . . . **NCLC 5, 14, 22, 43; DA;**
DAB; DAC; DAM MST, NOV; WLC
See also CDBLB 1832-1890; DLB 21, 55,
159, 163; SATA 23

Thakura, Ravindranatha
See Tagore, Rabindranath

Tharoor, Shashi 1956- . . . . **CLC 70**
See also CA 141

Thelwell, Michael Miles 1939- . . . . . **CLC 22**
See also BW 2; CA 101

Theobald, Lewis, Jr.
See Lovecraft, H(oward) P(hillips)

Theodorescu, Ion N. 1880-1967
See Arghezi, Tudor
See also CA 116

Theriault, Yves
1915-1983 . . **CLC 79; DAC; DAM MST**
See also CA 102; DLB 88

Theroux, Alexander (Louis)
1939- . . . . **CLC 2, 25**
See also CA 85-88; CANR 20

Theroux, Paul (Edward)
1941- . . . . **CLC 5, 8, 11, 15, 28, 46;**
DAM POP
See also BEST 89:4; CA 33-36R; CANR 20,
45; DLB 2; MTCW; SATA 44

Thesen, Sharon 1946- . . . . **CLC 56**

Thevenin, Denis
See Duhamel, Georges

Thibault, Jacques Anatole Francois
1844-1924
See France, Anatole
See also CA 106; 127; DAM NOV; MTCW

Thiele, Colin (Milton) 1920- . . . . **CLC 17**
See also CA 29-32R; CANR 12, 28, 53;
CLR 27; MAICYA; SAAS 2; SATA 14,
72

Thomas, Audrey (Callahan)
1935- . . . . **CLC 7, 13, 37; SSC 20**
See also AITN 2; CA 21-24R; CAAS 19;
CANR 36; DLB 60; MTCW

Thomas, D(onald) M(ichael)
1935- . . . . **CLC 13, 22, 31**
See also CA 61-64; CAAS 11; CANR 17,
45; CDBLB 1960 to Present; DLB 40;
INT CANR-17; MTCW

Thomas, Dylan (Marlais)
1914-1953 . . . **TCLC 1, 8, 45; DA; DAB;**
DAC; DAM DRAM, MST, POET;
PC 2; SSC 3; WLC
See also CA 104; 120; CDBLB 1945-1960;
DLB 13, 20, 139; MTCW; SATA 60

Thomas, (Philip) Edward
1878-1917 . . . . . . **TCLC 10; DAM POET**
See also CA 106; 153; DLB 19

Thomas, Joyce Carol 1938- . . . . **CLC 35**
See also AAYA 12; BW 2; CA 113; 116;
CANR 48; CLR 19; DLB 33; INT 116;
JRDA; MAICYA; MTCW; SAAS 7;
SATA 40, 78

Thomas, Lewis 1913-1993 . . . . **CLC 35**
See also CA 85-88; 143; CANR 38; MTCW

Thomas, Paul
See Mann, (Paul) Thomas

Thomas, Piri 1928- . . . . **CLC 17**
See also CA 73-76; HW

Thomas, R(onald) S(tuart)
1913- . . . . **CLC 6, 13, 48; DAB;**
DAM POET
See also CA 89-92; CAAS 4; CANR 30;
CDBLB 1960 to Present; DLB 27;
MTCW

Thomas, Ross (Elmore) 1926-1995 . . **CLC 39**
See also CA 33-36R; 150; CANR 22

Thompson, Francis Clegg
See Mencken, H(enry) L(ouis)

Thompson, Francis Joseph
1859-1907 . . . . **TCLC 4**
See also CA 104; CDBLB 1890-1914;
DLB 19

Thompson, Hunter S(tockton)
1939- . . . . **CLC 9, 17, 40; DAM POP**
See also BEST 89:1; CA 17-20R; CANR 23,
46; MTCW

Thompson, James Myers
See Thompson, Jim (Myers)

Thompson, Jim (Myers)
1906-1977(?) . . . . **CLC 69**
See also CA 140

Thompson, Judith . . . . **CLC 39**

Thomson, James
1700-1748 . . . . . **LC 16, 29; DAM POET**
See also DLB 95

Thomson, James
1834-1882 . . . . . **NCLC 18; DAM POET**
See also DLB 35

Thoreau, Henry David
1817-1862 . . . . . **NCLC 7, 21; DA; DAB;**
DAC; DAM MST; WLC
See also CDALB 1640-1865; DLB 1

Thornton, Hall
See Silverberg, Robert

Thucydides c. 455B.C.-399B.C. . . . . **CMLC 17**

Thurber, James (Grover)
1894-1961 . . . . **CLC 5, 11, 25; DA; DAB;**
DAC; DAM DRAM, MST, NOV; SSC 1
See also CA 73-76; CANR 17, 39;
CDALB 1929-1941; DLB 4, 11, 22, 102;
MAICYA; MTCW; SATA 13

Thurman, Wallace (Henry)
1902-1934 . . . . **TCLC 6; BLC;**
DAM MULT
See also BW 1; CA 104; 124; DLB 51

Ticheburn, Cheviot
See Ainsworth, William Harrison

Tieck, (Johann) Ludwig
1773-1853 . . . . **NCLC 5, 46**
See also DLB 90

Tiger, Derry
See Ellison, Harlan (Jay)

Tilghman, Christopher 1948(?)- . . . . . **CLC 65**

Tillinghast, Richard (Williford)
1940- . . . . **CLC 29**
See also CA 29-32R; CAAS 23; CANR 26,
51

Timrod, Henry 1828-1867 . . . . **NCLC 25**
See also DLB 3

Tindall, Gillian 1938- . . . . **CLC 7**
See also CA 21-24R; CANR 11

Tiptree, James, Jr. . . . . **CLC 48, 50**
See also Sheldon, Alice Hastings Bradley
See also DLB 8

Titmarsh, Michael Angelo
See Thackeray, William Makepeace

Tocqueville, Alexis (Charles Henri Maurice
Clerel Comte) 1805-1859 . . . . . **NCLC 7**

Tolkien, J(ohn) R(onald) R(euel)
1892-1973 . . . . **CLC 1, 2, 3, 8, 12, 38;**
DA; DAB; DAC; DAM MST, NOV,
POP; WLC
See also AAYA 10; AITN 1; CA 17-18;
45-48; CANR 36; CAP 2;
CDBLB 1914-1945; DLB 15, 160; JRDA;
MAICYA; MTCW; SATA 2, 32;
SATA-Obit 24

Toller, Ernst 1893-1939 . . . . **TCLC 10**
See also CA 107; DLB 124

Tolson, M. B.
See Tolson, Melvin B(eaunorus)

Tolson, Melvin B(eaunorus)
1898(?)-1966 . . . . **CLC 36; BLC;**
DAM MULT, POET
See also BW 1; CA 124; 89-92; DLB 48, 76

Tolstoi, Aleksei Nikolaevich
See Tolstoy, Alexey Nikolaevich

Tolstoy, Alexey Nikolaevich
1882-1945 . . . . **TCLC 18**
See also CA 107

Tolstoy, Count Leo
See Tolstoy, Leo (Nikolaevich)

Tolstoy, Leo (Nikolaevich)
1828-1910 . . . . . . **TCLC 4, 11, 17, 28, 44;**
DA; DAB; DAC; DAM MST, NOV;
SSC 9; WLC
See also CA 104; 123; SATA 26

Tomasi di Lampedusa, Giuseppe 1896-1957
See Lampedusa, Giuseppe (Tomasi) di
See also CA 111

Tzara, Tristan
    1896-1963 ...... **CLC 47; DAM POET**
    See also Rosenfeld, Samuel; Rosenstock,
    Sami; Rosenstock, Samuel
    See also CA 153

Uhry, Alfred
    1936- ..... **CLC 55; DAM DRAM, POP**
    See also CA 127; 133; INT 133

Ulf, Haerved
    See Strindberg, (Johan) August

Ulf, Harved
    See Strindberg, (Johan) August

Ulibarri, Sabine R(eyes)
    1919- .... **CLC 83; DAM MULT**
    See also CA 131; DLB 82; HW

Unamuno (y Jugo), Miguel de
    1864-1936 ... **TCLC 2, 9; DAM MULT,**
                  NOV; HLC; SSC 11
    See also CA 104; 131; DLB 108; HW;
    MTCW

Undercliffe, Errol
    See Campbell, (John) Ramsey

Underwood, Miles
    See Glassco, John

Undset, Sigrid
    1882-1949 .... **TCLC 3; DA; DAB;**
                DAC; DAM MST, NOV; WLC
    See also CA 104; 129; MTCW

Ungaretti, Giuseppe
    1888-1970 .... **CLC 7, 11, 15**
    See also CA 19-20; 25-28R; CAP 2;
    DLB 114

Unger, Douglas 1952- .... **CLC 34**
    See also CA 130

Unsworth, Barry (Forster) 1930-.... **CLC 76**
    See also CA 25-28R; CANR 30, 54

Updike, John (Hoyer)
    1932- ...... **CLC 1, 2, 3, 5, 7, 9, 13, 15,**
            23, 34, 43, 70; DA; DAB; DAC;
            DAM MST, NOV, POET, POP;
                             SSC 13; WLC
    See also CA 1-4R; CABS 1; CANR 4, 33,
    51; CDALB 1968-1988; DLB 2, 5, 143;
    DLBD 3; DLBY 80, 82; MTCW

Upshaw, Margaret Mitchell
    See Mitchell, Margaret (Munnerlyn)

Upton, Mark
    See Sanders, Lawrence

Urdang, Constance (Henriette)
    1922- .... **CLC 47**
    See also CA 21-24R; CANR 9, 24

Uriel, Henry
    See Faust, Frederick (Schiller)

Uris, Leon (Marcus)
    1924- .... **CLC 7, 32; DAM NOV, POP**
    See also AITN 1, 2; BEST 89:2; CA 1-4R;
    CANR 1, 40; MTCW; SATA 49

Urmuz
    See Codrescu, Andrei

Urquhart, Jane 1949-........ **CLC 90; DAC**
    See also CA 113; CANR 32

Ustinov, Peter (Alexander) 1921- .... **CLC 1**
    See also AITN 1; CA 13-16R; CANR 25,
    51; DLB 13

Vaculik, Ludvik 1926- .... **CLC 7**
    See also CA 53-56

Valdez, Luis (Miguel)
    1940- ..... **CLC 84; DAM MULT; HLC**
    See also CA 101; CANR 32; DLB 122; HW

Valenzuela, Luisa
    1938- ... **CLC 31; DAM MULT; SSC 14**
    See also CA 101; CANR 32; DLB 113; HW

Valera y Alcala-Galiano, Juan
    1824-1905 .... **TCLC 10**
    See also CA 106

Valery, (Ambroise) Paul (Toussaint Jules)
    1871-1945 .... **TCLC 4, 15;**
                        DAM POET; PC 9
    See also CA 104; 122; MTCW

Valle-Inclan, Ramon (Maria) del
    1866-1936 ..... **TCLC 5; DAM MULT;**
                                    HLC
    See also CA 106; 153; DLB 134

Vallejo, Antonio Buero
    See Buero Vallejo, Antonio

Vallejo, Cesar (Abraham)
    1892-1938 .... **TCLC 3, 56;**
                        DAM MULT; HLC
    See also CA 105; 153; HW

Vallette, Marguerite Eymery
    See Rachilde

Valle Y Pena, Ramon del
    See Valle-Inclan, Ramon (Maria) del

Van Ash, Cay 1918- .... **CLC 34**

Vanbrugh, Sir John
    1664-1726 .... **LC 21; DAM DRAM**
    See also DLB 80

Van Campen, Karl
    See Campbell, John W(ood, Jr.)

Vance, Gerald
    See Silverberg, Robert

Vance, Jack .... **CLC 35**
    See also Vance, John Holbrook
    See also DLB 8

Vance, John Holbrook 1916-
    See Queen, Ellery; Vance, Jack
    See also CA 29-32R; CANR 17; MTCW

Van Den Bogarde, Derek Jules Gaspard Ulric
    Niven 1921-
    See Bogarde, Dirk
    See also CA 77-80

Vandenburgh, Jane .... **CLC 59**

Vanderhaeghe, Guy 1951- .... **CLC 41**
    See also CA 113

van der Post, Laurens (Jan)
    1906-1996 .... **CLC 5**
    See also CA 5-8R; 155; CANR 35

van de Wetering, Janwillem 1931- .. **CLC 47**
    See also CA 49-52; CANR 4

Van Dine, S. S. .... **TCLC 23**
    See also Wright, Willard Huntington

Van Doren, Carl (Clinton)
    1885-1950 .... **TCLC 18**
    See also CA 111

Van Doren, Mark 1894-1972..... **CLC 6, 10**
    See also CA 1-4R; 37-40R; CANR 3;
    DLB 45; MTCW

Van Druten, John (William)
    1901-1957 .... **TCLC 2**
    See also CA 104; DLB 10

Van Duyn, Mona (Jane)
    1921- .... **CLC 3, 7, 63; DAM POET**
    See also CA 9-12R; CANR 7, 38; DLB 5

Van Dyne, Edith
    See Baum, L(yman) Frank

van Itallie, Jean-Claude 1936-....... **CLC 3**
    See also CA 45-48; CAAS 2; CANR 1, 48;
    DLB 7

van Ostaijen, Paul 1896-1928 ..... **TCLC 33**

Van Peebles, Melvin
    1932- .... **CLC 2, 20; DAM MULT**
    See also BW 2; CA 85-88; CANR 27

Vansittart, Peter 1920-............ **CLC 42**
    See also CA 1-4R; CANR 3, 49

Van Vechten, Carl 1880-1964 ...... **CLC 33**
    See also CA 89-92; DLB 4, 9, 51

Van Vogt, A(lfred) E(lton) 1912-..... **CLC 1**
    See also CA 21-24R; CANR 28; DLB 8;
    SATA 14

Varda, Agnes 1928- .... **CLC 16**
    See also CA 116; 122

Vargas Llosa, (Jorge) Mario (Pedro)
    1936- .... **CLC 3, 6, 9, 10, 15, 31, 42, 85;**
            DA; DAB; DAC; DAM MST, MULT,
                                NOV; HLC
    See also CA 73-76; CANR 18, 32, 42;
    DLB 145; HW; MTCW

Vasiliu, Gheorghe 1881-1957
    See Bacovia, George
    See also CA 123

Vassa, Gustavus
    See Equiano, Olaudah

Vassilikos, Vassilis 1933-......... **CLC 4, 8**
    See also CA 81-84

Vaughan, Henry 1621-1695 .... **LC 27**
    See also DLB 131

Vaughn, Stephanie .... **CLC 62**

Vazov, Ivan (Minchov)
    1850-1921 .... **TCLC 25**
    See also CA 121; DLB 147

Veblen, Thorstein (Bunde)
    1857-1929 .... **TCLC 31**
    See also CA 115

Vega, Lope de 1562-1635 .... **LC 23**

Venison, Alfred
    See Pound, Ezra (Weston Loomis)

Verdi, Marie de
    See Mencken, H(enry) L(ouis)

Verdu, Matilde
    See Cela, Camilo Jose

Verga, Giovanni (Carmelo)
    1840-1922 .... **TCLC 3; SSC 21**
    See also CA 104; 123

Vergil
    70B.C.-19B.C..... **CMLC 9; DA; DAB;**
                DAC; DAM MST, POET; PC 12

Verhaeren, Emile (Adolphe Gustave)
    1855-1916 .... **TCLC 12**
    See also CA 109

Verlaine, Paul (Marie)
        1844-1896 .... **NCLC 2, 51;**
                                DAM POET; PC 2

Verne, Jules (Gabriel)
        1828-1905 .... **TCLC 6, 52**
        See also AAYA 16; CA 110; 131; DLB 123;
        JRDA; MAICYA; SATA 21

Very, Jones 1813-1880 .... **NCLC 9**
        See also DLB 1

Vesaas, Tarjei 1897-1970 .... **CLC 48**
        See also CA 29-32R

Vialis, Gaston
        See Simenon, Georges (Jacques Christian)

Vian, Boris 1920-1959 .... **TCLC 9**
        See also CA 106; DLB 72

Viaud, (Louis Marie) Julien 1850-1923
        See Loti, Pierre
        See also CA 107

Vicar, Henry
        See Felsen, Henry Gregor

Vicker, Angus
        See Felsen, Henry Gregor

Vidal, Gore
        1925- ..... **CLC 2, 4, 6, 8, 10, 22, 33, 72;**
                                DAM NOV, POP
        See also AITN 1; BEST 90:2; CA 5-8R;
        CANR 13, 45; DLB 6, 152;
        INT CANR-13; MTCW

Viereck, Peter (Robert Edwin)
        1916- .... **CLC 4**
        See also CA 1-4R; CANR 1, 47; DLB 5

Vigny, Alfred (Victor) de
        1797-1863 ..... **NCLC 7; DAM POET**
        See also DLB 119

Vilakazi, Benedict Wallet
        1906-1947 .... **TCLC 37**

Villiers de l'Isle Adam, Jean Marie Mathias
        Philippe Auguste Comte
        1838-1889 .... **NCLC 3; SSC 14**
        See also DLB 123

Villon, François 1431-1463(?) .... **PC 13**

Vinci, Leonardo da 1452-1519 ...... **LC 12**

Vine, Barbara .... **CLC 50**
        See also Rendell, Ruth (Barbara)
        See also BEST 90:4

Vinge, Joan D(ennison)
        1948- .... **CLC 30; SSC 24**
        See also CA 93-96; SATA 36

Violis, G.
        See Simenon, Georges (Jacques Christian)

Visconti, Luchino 1906-1976 ...... **CLC 16**
        See also CA 81-84; 65-68; CANR 39

Vittorini, Elio 1908-1966 ..... **CLC 6, 9, 14**
        See also CA 133; 25-28R

Vizinczey, Stephen 1933- .... **CLC 40**
        See also CA 128; INT 128

Vliet, R(ussell) G(ordon)
        1929-1984 .... **CLC 22**
        See also CA 37-40R; 112; CANR 18

Vogau, Boris Andreyevich 1894-1937(?)
        See Pilnyak, Boris
        See also CA 123

Vogel, Paula A(nne) 1951- .... **CLC 76**
        See also CA 108

Voight, Ellen Bryant 1943- .... **CLC 54**
        See also CA 69-72; CANR 11, 29, 55;
        DLB 120

Voigt, Cynthia 1942- .... **CLC 30**
        See also AAYA 3; CA 106; CANR 18, 37,
        40; CLR 13; INT CANR-18; JRDA;
        MAICYA; SATA 48, 79; SATA-Brief 33

Voinovich, Vladimir (Nikolaevich)
        1932- .... **CLC 10, 49**
        See also CA 81-84; CAAS 12; CANR 33;
        MTCW

Vollmann, William T.
        1959- ...... **CLC 89; DAM NOV, POP**
        See also CA 134

Voloshinov, V. N.
        See Bakhtin, Mikhail Mikhailovich

Voltaire
        1694-1778 ..... **LC 14; DA; DAB; DAC;**
                        DAM DRAM, MST; SSC 12; WLC

von Daeniken, Erich 1935- .... **CLC 30**
        See also AITN 1; CA 37-40R; CANR 17,
        44

von Daniken, Erich
        See von Daeniken, Erich

von Heidenstam, (Carl Gustaf) Verner
        See Heidenstam, (Carl Gustaf) Verner von

von Heyse, Paul (Johann Ludwig)
        See Heyse, Paul (Johann Ludwig von)

von Hofmannsthal, Hugo
        See Hofmannsthal, Hugo von

von Horvath, Odon
        See Horvath, Oedoen von

von Horvath, Oedoen
        See Horvath, Oedoen von

von Liliencron, (Friedrich Adolf Axel) Detlev
        See Liliencron, (Friedrich Adolf Axel)
        Detlev von

Vonnegut, Kurt, Jr.
        1922- ...... **CLC 1, 2, 3, 4, 5, 8, 12, 22,**
        40, 60; DA; DAB; DAC; DAM MST,
                        NOV, POP; SSC 8; WLC
        See also AAYA 6; AITN 1; BEST 90:4;
        CA 1-4R; CANR 1, 25, 49;
        CDALB 1968-1988; DLB 2, 8, 152;
        DLBD 3; DLBY 80; MTCW

Von Rachen, Kurt
        See Hubbard, L(afayette) Ron(ald)

von Rezzori (d'Arezzo), Gregor
        See Rezzori (d'Arezzo), Gregor von

von Sternberg, Josef
        See Sternberg, Josef von

Vorster, Gordon 1924- .... **CLC 34**
        See also CA 133

Vosce, Trudie
        See Ozick, Cynthia

Voznesensky, Andrei (Andreievich)
        1933- ...... **CLC 1, 15, 57; DAM POET**
        See also CA 89-92; CANR 37; MTCW

Waddington, Miriam 1917- .... **CLC 28**
        See also CA 21-24R; CANR 12, 30;
        DLB 68

Wagman, Fredrica 1937- .... **CLC 7**
        See also CA 97-100; INT 97-100

Wagner, Richard 1813-1883 .... **NCLC 9**
        See also DLB 129

Wagner-Martin, Linda 1936- ...... **CLC 50**

Wagoner, David (Russell)
        1926- .... **CLC 3, 5, 15**
        See also CA 1-4R; CAAS 3; CANR 2;
        DLB 5; SATA 14

Wah, Fred(erick James) 1939- ..... **CLC 44**
        See also CA 107; 141; DLB 60

Wahloo, Per 1926-1975 .... **CLC 7**
        See also CA 61-64

Wahloo, Peter
        See Wahloo, Per

Wain, John (Barrington)
        1925-1994 .... **CLC 2, 11, 15, 46**
        See also CA 5-8R; 145; CAAS 4; CANR 23,
        54; CDBLB 1960 to Present; DLB 15, 27,
        139, 155; MTCW

Wajda, Andrzej 1926- .... **CLC 16**
        See also CA 102

Wakefield, Dan 1932- .... **CLC 7**
        See also CA 21-24R; CAAS 7

Wakoski, Diane
        1937- .... **CLC 2, 4, 7, 9, 11, 40;**
                                DAM POET; PC 15
        See also CA 13-16R; CAAS 1; CANR 9;
        DLB 5; INT CANR-9

Wakoski-Sherbell, Diane
        See Wakoski, Diane

Walcott, Derek (Alton)
        1930- .... **CLC 2, 4, 9, 14, 25, 42, 67, 76;**
        BLC; DAB; DAC; DAM MST, MULT,
                                POET
        See also BW 2; CA 89-92; CANR 26, 47;
        DLB 117; DLBY 81; MTCW

Waldman, Anne 1945- .... **CLC 7**
        See also CA 37-40R; CAAS 17; CANR 34;
        DLB 16

Waldo, E. Hunter
        See Sturgeon, Theodore (Hamilton)

Waldo, Edward Hamilton
        See Sturgeon, Theodore (Hamilton)

Walker, Alice (Malsenior)
        1944- .... **CLC 5, 6, 9, 19, 27, 46, 58;**
        BLC; DA; DAB; DAC; DAM MST,
                MULT, NOV, POET, POP; SSC 5
        See also AAYA 3; BEST 89:4; BW 2;
        CA 37-40R; CANR 9, 27, 49;
        CDALB 1968-1988; DLB 6, 33, 143;
        INT CANR-27; MTCW; SATA 31

Walker, David Harry 1911-1992 .... **CLC 14**
        See also CA 1-4R; 137; CANR 1; SATA 8;
        SATA-Obit 71

Walker, Edward Joseph 1934-
        See Walker, Ted
        See also CA 21-24R; CANR 12, 28, 53

Walker, George F.
        1947- .... **CLC 44, 61; DAB; DAC;**
                                DAM MST
        See also CA 103; CANR 21, 43; DLB 60

Walker, Joseph A.
        1935- .... **CLC 19; DAM DRAM, MST**
        See also BW 1; CA 89-92; CANR 26;
        DLB 38

Walker, Margaret (Abigail)
        1915- .... **CLC 1, 6; BLC; DAM MULT**
        See also BW 2; CA 73-76; CANR 26, 54;
        DLB 76, 152; MTCW

Walker, Ted...................... **CLC 13**
  See also Walker, Edward Joseph
  See also DLB 40

Wallace, David Foster   1962-....... **CLC 50**
  See also CA 132

Wallace, Dexter
  See Masters, Edgar Lee

Wallace, (Richard Horatio) Edgar
  1875-1932 .... **TCLC 57**
  See also CA 115; DLB 70

Wallace, Irving
  1916-1990 ..... **CLC 7, 13; DAM NOV,**
                                    POP
  See also AITN 1; CA 1-4R; 132; CAAS 1;
  CANR 1, 27; INT CANR-27; MTCW

Wallant, Edward Lewis
  1926-1962 .... **CLC 5, 10**
  See also CA 1-4R; CANR 22; DLB 2, 28,
  143; MTCW

Walley, Byron
  See Card, Orson Scott

Walpole, Horace   1717-1797.......... **LC 2**
  See also DLB 39, 104

Walpole, Hugh (Seymour)
  1884-1941 .... **TCLC 5**
  See also CA 104; DLB 34

Walser, Martin   1927-............. **CLC 27**
  See also CA 57-60; CANR 8, 46; DLB 75,
  124

Walser, Robert
  1878-1956 .... **TCLC 18; SSC 20**
  See also CA 118; DLB 66

Walsh, Jill Paton .... **CLC 35**
  See also Paton Walsh, Gillian
  See also AAYA 11; CLR 2; DLB 161;
  SAAS 3

Walter, Villiam Christian
  See Andersen, Hans Christian

Wambaugh, Joseph (Aloysius, Jr.)
  1937- .... **CLC 3, 18; DAM NOV, POP**
  See also AITN 1; BEST 89:3; CA 33-36R;
  CANR 42; DLB 6; DLBY 83; MTCW

Ward, Arthur Henry Sarsfield   1883-1959
  See Rohmer, Sax
  See also CA 108

Ward, Douglas Turner   1930-....... **CLC 19**
  See also BW 1; CA 81-84; CANR 27;
  DLB 7, 38

Ward, Mary Augusta
  See Ward, Mrs. Humphry

Ward, Mrs. Humphry
  1851-1920 .... **TCLC 55**
  See also DLB 18

Ward, Peter
  See Faust, Frederick (Schiller)

Warhol, Andy   1928(?)-1987....... **CLC 20**
  See also AAYA 12; BEST 89:4; CA 89-92;
  121; CANR 34

Warner, Francis (Robert le Plastrier)
  1937- .... **CLC 14**
  See also CA 53-56; CANR 11

Warner, Marina   1946-............. **CLC 59**
  See also CA 65-68; CANR 21, 55

Warner, Rex (Ernest)   1905-1986.... **CLC 45**
  See also CA 89-92; 119; DLB 15

Warner, Susan (Bogert)
  1819-1885 .... **NCLC 31**
  See also DLB 3, 42

Warner, Sylvia (Constance) Ashton
  See Ashton-Warner, Sylvia (Constance)

Warner, Sylvia Townsend
  1893-1978 .... **CLC 7, 19; SSC 23**
  See also CA 61-64; 77-80; CANR 16;
  DLB 34, 139; MTCW

Warren, Mercy Otis   1728-1814... **NCLC 13**
  See also DLB 31

Warren, Robert Penn
  1905-1989 .... **CLC 1, 4, 6, 8, 10, 13, 18,**
    39, 53, 59; DA; DAB; DAC; DAM MST,
                       NOV, POET; SSC 4; WLC
  See also AITN 1; CA 13-16R; 129;
  CANR 10, 47; CDALB 1968-1988;
  DLB 2, 48, 152; DLBY 80, 89;
  INT CANR-10; MTCW; SATA 46;
  SATA-Obit 63

Warshofsky, Isaac
  See Singer, Isaac Bashevis

Warton, Thomas
  1728-1790 .... **LC 15; DAM POET**
  See also DLB 104, 109

Waruk, Kona
  See Harris, (Theodore) Wilson

Warung, Price   1855-1911........ **TCLC 45**

Warwick, Jarvis
  See Garner, Hugh

Washington, Alex
  See Harris, Mark

Washington, Booker T(aliaferro)
  1856-1915 .... **TCLC 10; BLC;**
                                DAM MULT
  See also BW 1; CA 114; 125; SATA 28

Washington, George   1732-1799...... **LC 25**
  See also DLB 31

Wassermann, (Karl) Jakob
  1873-1934 .... **TCLC 6**
  See also CA 104; DLB 66

Wasserstein, Wendy
  1950- .... **CLC 32, 59, 90;**
                          DAM DRAM; DC 4
  See also CA 121; 129; CABS 3; CANR 53;
  INT 129

Waterhouse, Keith (Spencer)
  1929-...................... **CLC 47**
  See also CA 5-8R; CANR 38; DLB 13, 15;
  MTCW

Waters, Frank (Joseph)
  1902-1995 .... **CLC 88**
  See also CA 5-8R; 149; CAAS 13; CANR 3,
  18; DLBY 86

Waters, Roger   1944-............. **CLC 35**

Watkins, Frances Ellen
  See Harper, Frances Ellen Watkins

Watkins, Gerrold
  See Malzberg, Barry N(athaniel)

Watkins, Gloria   1955(?)-
  See hooks, bell
  See also BW 2; CA 143

Watkins, Paul   1964-............. **CLC 55**
  See also CA 132

Watkins, Vernon Phillips
  1906-1967 .... **CLC 43**
  See also CA 9-10; 25-28R; CAP 1; DLB 20

Watson, Irving S.
  See Mencken, H(enry) L(ouis)

Watson, John H.
  See Farmer, Philip Jose

Watson, Richard F.
  See Silverberg, Robert

Waugh, Auberon (Alexander)   1939-.. **CLC 7**
  See also CA 45-48; CANR 6, 22; DLB 14

Waugh, Evelyn (Arthur St. John)
  1903-1966 ...... **CLC 1, 3, 8, 13, 19, 27,**
    44; DA; DAB; DAC; DAM MST, NOV,
                             POP; WLC
  See also CA 85-88; 25-28R; CANR 22;
  CDBLB 1914-1945; DLB 15, 162; MTCW

Waugh, Harriet   1944- .... **CLC 6**
  See also CA 85-88; CANR 22

Ways, C. R.
  See Blount, Roy (Alton), Jr.

Waystaff, Simon
  See Swift, Jonathan

Webb, (Martha) Beatrice (Potter)
  1858-1943 .... **TCLC 22**
  See also Potter, Beatrice
  See also CA 117

Webb, Charles (Richard)   1939-...... **CLC 7**
  See also CA 25-28R

Webb, James H(enry), Jr.   1946-.... **CLC 22**
  See also CA 81-84

Webb, Mary (Gladys Meredith)
  1881-1927 .... **TCLC 24**
  See also CA 123; DLB 34

Webb, Mrs. Sidney
  See Webb, (Martha) Beatrice (Potter)

Webb, Phyllis   1927-.............. **CLC 18**
  See also CA 104; CANR 23; DLB 53

Webb, Sidney (James)
  1859-1947 .... **TCLC 22**
  See also CA 117

Webber, Andrew Lloyd............. **CLC 21**
  See also Lloyd Webber, Andrew

Weber, Lenora Mattingly
  1895-1971 .... **CLC 12**
  See also CA 19-20; 29-32R; CAP 1;
  SATA 2; SATA-Obit 26

Weber, Max   1864-1920 .... **TCLC 69**
  See also CA 109

Webster, John
  1579(?)-1634(?) ...... **LC 33; DA; DAB;**
        DAC; DAM DRAM, MST; DC 2; WLC
  See also CDBLB Before 1660; DLB 58

Webster, Noah   1758-1843 .... **NCLC 30**

Wedekind, (Benjamin) Frank(lin)
  1864-1918 ...... **TCLC 7; DAM DRAM**
  See also CA 104; 153; DLB 118

Weidman, Jerome   1913-............ **CLC 7**
  See also AITN 2; CA 1-4R; CANR 1;
  DLB 28

Weil, Simone (Adolphine)
  1909-1943 .... **TCLC 23**
  See also CA 117

Weinstein, Nathan
See West, Nathanael

Weinstein, Nathan von Wallenstein
See West, Nathanael

Weir, Peter (Lindsay) 1944- .... **CLC 20**
See also CA 113; 123

Weiss, Peter (Ulrich)
1916-1982 .... **CLC 3, 15, 51;**
DAM DRAM
See also CA 45-48; 106; CANR 3; DLB 69,
124

Weiss, Theodore (Russell)
1916- .... **CLC 3, 8, 14**
See also CA 9-12R; CAAS 2; CANR 46;
DLB 5

Welch, (Maurice) Denton
1915-1948 .... **TCLC 22**
See also CA 121; 148

Welch, James
1940- ..... **CLC 6, 14, 52; DAM MULT,**
POP
See also CA 85-88; CANR 42; DLB 175;
NNAL

Weldon, Fay
1933- .... **CLC 6, 9, 11, 19, 36, 59;**
DAM POP
See also CA 21-24R; CANR 16, 46;
CDBLB 1960 to Present; DLB 14;
INT CANR-16; MTCW

Wellek, Rene 1903-1995.......... **CLC 28**
See also CA 5-8R; 150; CAAS 7; CANR 8;
DLB 63; INT CANR-8

Weller, Michael 1942- .... **CLC 10, 53**
See also CA 85-88

Weller, Paul 1958- .... **CLC 26**

Wellershoff, Dieter 1925-.......... **CLC 46**
See also CA 89-92; CANR 16, 37

Welles, (George) Orson
1915-1985 .... **CLC 20, 80**
See also CA 93-96; 117

Wellman, Mac 1945- .... **CLC 65**

Wellman, Manly Wade 1903-1986 .. **CLC 49**
See also CA 1-4R; 118; CANR 6, 16, 44;
SATA 6; SATA-Obit 47

Wells, Carolyn 1869(?)-1942 ...... **TCLC 35**
See also CA 113; DLB 11

Wells, H(erbert) G(eorge)
1866-1946 .... **TCLC 6, 12, 19; DA;**
DAB; DAC; DAM MST, NOV; SSC 6;
WLC
See also AAYA 18; CA 110; 121;
CDBLB 1914-1945; DLB 34, 70, 156;
MTCW; SATA 20

Wells, Rosemary 1943-........... **CLC 12**
See also AAYA 13; CA 85-88; CANR 48;
CLR 16; MAICYA; SAAS 1; SATA 18,
69

Welty, Eudora
1909- ...... **CLC 1, 2, 5, 14, 22, 33; DA;**
DAB; DAC; DAM MST, NOV; SSC 1;
WLC
See also CA 9-12R; CABS 1; CANR 32;
CDALB 1941-1968; DLB 2, 102, 143;
DLBD 12; DLBY 87; MTCW

Wen I-to 1899-1946 .... **TCLC 28**

Wentworth, Robert
See Hamilton, Edmond

Werfel, Franz (V.) 1890-1945 ..... **TCLC 8**
See also CA 104; DLB 81, 124

Wergeland, Henrik Arnold
1808-1845 .... **NCLC 5**

Wersba, Barbara 1932-.......... **CLC 30**
See also AAYA 2; CA 29-32R; CANR 16,
38; CLR 3; DLB 52; JRDA; MAICYA;
SAAS 2; SATA 1, 58

Wertmueller, Lina 1928- .... **CLC 16**
See also CA 97-100; CANR 39

Wescott, Glenway 1901-1987....... **CLC 13**
See also CA 13-16R; 121; CANR 23;
DLB 4, 9, 102

Wesker, Arnold
1932- .... **CLC 3, 5, 42; DAB;**
DAM DRAM
See also CA 1-4R; CAAS 7; CANR 1, 33;
CDBLB 1960 to Present; DLB 13;
MTCW

Wesley, Richard (Errol) 1945-....... **CLC 7**
See also BW 1; CA 57-60; CANR 27;
DLB 38

Wessel, Johan Herman 1742-1785 .... **LC 7**

West, Anthony (Panther)
1914-1987 .... **CLC 50**
See also CA 45-48; 124; CANR 3, 19;
DLB 15

West, C. P.
See Wodehouse, P(elham) G(renville)

West, (Mary) Jessamyn
1902-1984 .... **CLC 7, 17**
See also CA 9-12R; 112; CANR 27; DLB 6;
DLBY 84; MTCW; SATA-Obit 37

West, Morris L(anglo) 1916-..... **CLC 6, 33**
See also CA 5-8R; CANR 24, 49; MTCW

West, Nathanael
1903-1940 ..... **TCLC 1, 14, 44; SSC 16**
See also CA 104; 125; CDALB 1929-1941;
DLB 4, 9, 28; MTCW

West, Owen
See Koontz, Dean R(ay)

West, Paul 1930- .... **CLC 7, 14, 96**
See also CA 13-16R; CAAS 7; CANR 22,
53; DLB 14; INT CANR-22

West, Rebecca 1892-1983 .. **CLC 7, 9, 31, 50**
See also CA 5-8R; 109; CANR 19; DLB 36;
DLBY 83; MTCW

Westall, Robert (Atkinson)
1929-1993 .... **CLC 17**
See also AAYA 12; CA 69-72; 141;
CANR 18; CLR 13; JRDA; MAICYA;
SAAS 2; SATA 23, 69; SATA-Obit 75

Westlake, Donald E(dwin)
1933- .... **CLC 7, 33; DAM POP**
See also CA 17-20R; CAAS 13; CANR 16,
44; INT CANR-16

Westmacott, Mary
See Christie, Agatha (Mary Clarissa)

Weston, Allen
See Norton, Andre

Wetcheek, J. L.
See Feuchtwanger, Lion

Wetering, Janwillem van de
See van de Wetering, Janwillem

Wetherell, Elizabeth
See Warner, Susan (Bogert)

Whale, James 1889-1957 .... **TCLC 63**

Whalen, Philip 1923- .... **CLC 6, 29**
See also CA 9-12R; CANR 5, 39; DLB 16

Wharton, Edith (Newbold Jones)
1862-1937 ...... **TCLC 3, 9, 27, 53; DA;**
DAB; DAC; DAM MST, NOV; SSC 6;
WLC
See also CA 104; 132; CDALB 1865-1917;
DLB 4, 9, 12, 78; DLBD 13; MTCW

Wharton, James
See Mencken, H(enry) L(ouis)

Wharton, William (a pseudonym)
.... **CLC 18, 37**
See also CA 93-96; DLBY 80; INT 93-96

Wheatley (Peters), Phillis
1754(?)-1784 .... **LC 3; BLC; DA; DAC;**
DAM MST, MULT, POET; PC 3; WLC
See also CDALB 1640-1865; DLB 31, 50

Wheelock, John Hall 1886-1978.... **CLC 14**
See also CA 13-16R; 77-80; CANR 14;
DLB 45

White, E(lwyn) B(rooks)
1899-1985 .. **CLC 10, 34, 39; DAM POP**
See also AITN 2; CA 13-16R; 116;
CANR 16, 37; CLR 1, 21; DLB 11, 22;
MAICYA; MTCW; SATA 2, 29;
SATA-Obit 44

White, Edmund (Valentine III)
1940- .... **CLC 27; DAM POP**
See also AAYA 7; CA 45-48; CANR 3, 19,
36; MTCW

White, Patrick (Victor Martindale)
1912-1990 .. **CLC 3, 4, 5, 7, 9, 18, 65, 69**
See also CA 81-84; 132; CANR 43; MTCW

White, Phyllis Dorothy James 1920-
See James, P. D.
See also CA 21-24R; CANR 17, 43;
DAM POP; MTCW

White, T(erence) H(anbury)
1906-1964 .... **CLC 30**
See also CA 73-76; CANR 37; DLB 160;
JRDA; MAICYA; SATA 12

White, Terence de Vere
1912-1994 .... **CLC 49**
See also CA 49-52; 145; CANR 3

White, Walter F(rancis)
1893-1955 .... **TCLC 15**
See also White, Walter
See also BW 1; CA 115; 124; DLB 51

White, William Hale 1831-1913
See Rutherford, Mark
See also CA 121

Whitehead, E(dward) A(nthony)
1933- .... **CLC 5**
See also CA 65-68

Whitemore, Hugh (John) 1936-..... **CLC 37**
See also CA 132; INT 132

Whitman, Sarah Helen (Power)
1803-1878 .... **NCLC 19**
See also DLB 1

Whitman, Walt(er)
1819-1892 ..... NCLC 4, 31; DA; DAB;
DAC; DAM MST, POET; PC 3; WLC
See also CDALB 1640-1865; DLB 3, 64;
SATA 20

Whitney, Phyllis A(yame)
1903- .... CLC 42; DAM POP
See also AITN 2; BEST 90:3; CA 1-4R;
CANR 3, 25, 38; JRDA; MAICYA;
SATA 1, 30

Whittemore, (Edward) Reed (Jr.)
1919- .... CLC 4
See also CA 9-12R; CAAS 8; CANR 4;
DLB 5

Whittier, John Greenleaf
1807-1892 .... NCLC 8, 59
See also DLB 1

Whittlebot, Hernia
See Coward, Noel (Peirce)

Wicker, Thomas Grey 1926-
See Wicker, Tom
See also CA 65-68; CANR 21, 46

Wicker, Tom .... CLC 7
See also Wicker, Thomas Grey

Wideman, John Edgar
1941- .... CLC 5, 34, 36, 67; BLC;
DAM MULT
See also BW 2; CA 85-88; CANR 14, 42;
DLB 33, 143

Wiebe, Rudy (Henry)
1934- .... CLC 6, 11, 14; DAC;
DAM MST
See also CA 37-40R; CANR 42; DLB 60

Wieland, Christoph Martin
1733-1813 .... NCLC 17
See also DLB 97

Wiene, Robert 1881-1938........ TCLC 56

Wieners, John 1934-.............. CLC 7
See also CA 13-16R; DLB 16

Wiesel, Elie(zer)
1928- ...... CLC 3, 5, 11, 37; DA; DAB;
DAC; DAM MST, NOV
See also AAYA 7; AITN 1; CA 5-8R;
CAAS 4; CANR 8, 40; DLB 83;
DLBY 87; INT CANR-8; MTCW;
SATA 56

Wiggins, Marianne 1947-......... CLC 57
See also BEST 89:3; CA 130

Wight, James Alfred 1916-
See Herriot, James
See also CA 77-80; SATA 55;
SATA-Brief 44

Wilbur, Richard (Purdy)
1921- ... CLC 3, 6, 9, 14, 53; DA; DAB;
DAC; DAM MST, POET
See also CA 1-4R; CABS 2; CANR 2, 29;
DLB 5, 169; INT CANR-29; MTCW;
SATA 9

Wild, Peter 1940-................ CLC 14
See also CA 37-40R; DLB 5

Wilde, Oscar (Fingal O'Flahertie Wills)
1854(?)-1900 .... TCLC 1, 8, 23, 41; DA;
DAB; DAC; DAM DRAM, MST, NOV;
SSC 11; WLC
See also CA 104; 119; CDBLB 1890-1914;
DLB 10, 19, 34, 57, 141, 156; SATA 24

Wilder, Billy .... CLC 20
See also Wilder, Samuel
See also DLB 26

Wilder, Samuel 1906-
See Wilder, Billy
See also CA 89-92

Wilder, Thornton (Niven)
1897-1975 ...... CLC 1, 5, 6, 10, 15, 35,
82; DA; DAB; DAC; DAM DRAM,
MST, NOV; DC 1; WLC
See also AITN 2; CA 13-16R; 61-64;
CANR 40; DLB 4, 7, 9; MTCW

Wilding, Michael 1942-........... CLC 73
See also CA 104; CANR 24, 49

Wiley, Richard 1944-............. CLC 44
See also CA 121; 129

Wilhelm, Kate .... CLC 7
See also Wilhelm, Katie Gertrude
See also AAYA 20; CAAS 5; DLB 8;
INT CANR-17

Wilhelm, Katie Gertrude 1928-
See Wilhelm, Kate
See also CA 37-40R; CANR 17, 36; MTCW

Wilkins, Mary
See Freeman, Mary Eleanor Wilkins

Willard, Nancy 1936-........... CLC 7, 37
See also CA 89-92; CANR 10, 39; CLR 5;
DLB 5, 52; MAICYA; MTCW;
SATA 37, 71; SATA-Brief 30

Williams, C(harles) K(enneth)
1936- .... CLC 33, 56; DAM POET
See also CA 37-40R; CAAS 26; DLB 5

Williams, Charles
See Collier, James L(incoln)

Williams, Charles (Walter Stansby)
1886-1945 .... TCLC 1, 11
See also CA 104; DLB 100, 153

Williams, (George) Emlyn
1905-1987 ...... CLC 15; DAM DRAM
See also CA 104; 123; CANR 36; DLB 10,
77; MTCW

Williams, Hugo 1942-............. CLC 42
See also CA 17-20R; CANR 45; DLB 40

Williams, J. Walker
See Wodehouse, P(elham) G(renville)

Williams, John A(lfred)
1925- ... CLC 5, 13; BLC; DAM MULT
See also BW 2; CA 53-56; CAAS 3;
CANR 6, 26, 51; DLB 2, 33;
INT CANR-6

Williams, Jonathan (Chamberlain)
1929- .... CLC 13
See also CA 9-12R; CAAS 12; CANR 8;
DLB 5

Williams, Joy 1944-.............. CLC 31
See also CA 41-44R; CANR 22, 48

Williams, Norman 1952-.......... CLC 39
See also CA 118

Williams, Sherley Anne
1944- ..... CLC 89; BLC; DAM MULT,
POET
See also BW 2; CA 73-76; CANR 25;
DLB 41; INT CANR-25; SATA 78

Williams, Shirley
See Williams, Sherley Anne

Williams, Tennessee
1911-1983 ..... CLC 1, 2, 5, 7, 8, 11, 15,
19, 30, 39, 45, 71; DA; DAB; DAC;
DAM DRAM, MST; DC 4; WLC
See also AITN 1, 2; CA 5-8R; 108;
CABS 3; CANR 31; CDALB 1941-1968;
DLB 7; DLBD 4; DLBY 83; MTCW

Williams, Thomas (Alonzo)
1926-1990 .... CLC 14
See also CA 1-4R; 132; CANR 2

Williams, William C.
See Williams, William Carlos

Williams, William Carlos
1883-1963 .... CLC 1, 2, 5, 9, 13, 22, 42,
67; DA; DAB; DAC; DAM MST, POET;
PC 7
See also CA 89-92; CANR 34;
CDALB 1917-1929; DLB 4, 16, 54, 86;
MTCW

Williamson, David (Keith) 1942-.... CLC 56
See also CA 103; CANR 41

Williamson, Ellen Douglas 1905-1984
See Douglas, Ellen
See also CA 17-20R; 114; CANR 39

Williamson, Jack.................. CLC 29
See also Williamson, John Stewart
See also CAAS 8; DLB 8

Williamson, John Stewart 1908-
See Williamson, Jack
See also CA 17-20R; CANR 23

Willie, Frederick
See Lovecraft, H(oward) P(hillips)

Willingham, Calder (Baynard, Jr.)
1922-1995 .... CLC 5, 51
See also CA 5-8R; 147; CANR 3; DLB 2,
44; MTCW

Willis, Charles
See Clarke, Arthur C(harles)

Willy
See Colette, (Sidonie-Gabrielle)

Willy, Colette
See Colette, (Sidonie-Gabrielle)

Wilson, A(ndrew) N(orman) 1950- .. CLC 33
See also CA 112; 122; DLB 14, 155

Wilson, Angus (Frank Johnstone)
1913-1991 .. CLC 2, 3, 5, 25, 34; SSC 21
See also CA 5-8R; 134; CANR 21; DLB 15,
139, 155; MTCW

Wilson, August
1945- .... CLC 39, 50, 63; BLC; DA;
DAB; DAC; DAM DRAM, MST,
MULT; DC 2
See also AAYA 16; BW 2; CA 115; 122;
CANR 42, 54; MTCW

Wilson, Brian 1942-.............. CLC 12

Wilson, Colin 1931-............. CLC 3, 14
See also CA 1-4R; CAAS 5; CANR 1, 22,
33; DLB 14; MTCW

Wilson, Dirk
See Pohl, Frederik

Wilson, Edmund
1895-1972 .... CLC 1, 2, 3, 8, 24
See also CA 1-4R; 37-40R; CANR 1, 46;
DLB 63; MTCW

Literary Criticism Series
Cumulative Topic Index

This index lists all topic entries in Gale's *Classical and Medieval Literature Criticism, Contemporary Literary Criticism, Literature Criticism from 1400 to 1800, Nineteenth-Century Literature Criticism,* and *Twentieth-Century Literary Criticism.*

Topic Index

Topic Index

Topic Index

Cumulative Nationality Index

McCoy, Horace (Stanley) **28**
McKay, Claude **7, 41**
Mencken, H(enry) L(ouis) **13**
Millay, Edna St. Vincent **4, 49**
Mitchell, Margaret (Munnerlyn) **11**
Mitchell, S(ilas) Weir **36**
Monroe, Harriet **12**
Muir, John **28**
Nathan, George Jean **18**
Nordhoff, Charles (Bernard) **23**
Norris, Benjamin Franklin Jr. **24**
O'Neill, Eugene (Gladstone) **1, 6, 27, 49**
Oskison, John Milton **35**
Phillips, David Graham **44**
Porter, Gene(va Grace) Stratton **21**
Post, Melville Davisson **39**
Rawlings, Marjorie Kinnan **4**
Reed, John (Silas) **9**
Reich, Wilhelm **57**
Rhodes, Eugene Manlove **53**
Riggs, (Rolla) Lynn **56**
Riley, James Whitcomb **51**
Rinehart, Mary Roberts **52**
Roberts, Elizabeth Madox **68**
Roberts, Kenneth (Lewis) **23**
Robinson, Edwin Arlington **5**
Roelvaag, O(le) E(dvart) **17**
Rogers, Will(iam Penn Adair) **8**
Roosevelt, Theodore **69**
Rourke, Constance (Mayfield) **12**
Runyon, (Alfred) Damon **10**
Saltus, Edgar (Everton) **8**
Santayana, George **40**
Sherwood, Robert E(mmet) **3**
Slesinger, Tess **10**
Steffens, (Joseph) Lincoln **20**
Stein, Gertrude **1, 6, 28, 48**
Sterling, George **20**
Stevens, Wallace **3, 12, 45**
Stockton, Frank R. **47**
Sturges, Preston **48**
Tarbell, Ida M(inerva) **40**
Tarkington, (Newton) Booth **9**
Teasdale, Sara **4**
Thurman, Wallace (Henry) **6**
Twain, Mark **6, 12, 19, 36, 48, 59**
Van Dine, S. S. **23**
Van Doren, Carl (Clinton) **18**
Veblen, Thorstein (Bunde) **31**
Washington, Booker T(aliaferro) **10**
Wells, Carolyn **35**
West, Nathanael **1, 14, 44**
Whale, James **63**
Wharton, Edith (Newbold Jones) **3, 9, 27, 53**
White, Walter F(rancis) **15**
Wister, Owen **21**
Wolfe, Thomas (Clayton) **4, 13, 29, 61**
Woollcott, Alexander (Humphreys) **5**
Wylie, Elinor (Morton Hoyt) **8**

ARGENTINIAN
Arlt, Roberto (Godofredo Christophersen) **29**
Guiraldes, Ricardo (Guillermo) **39**
Lugones, Leopoldo **15**
Storni, Alfonsina **5**

AUSTRALIAN
Baynton, Barbara **57**
Franklin, (Stella Maraia Sarah) Miles **7**
Furphy, Joseph **25**

Ingamells, Rex **35**
Lawson, Henry (Archibald Hertzberg) **27**
Paterson, A(ndrew) B(arton) **32**
Richardson, Henry Handel **4**
Warung, Price **45**

AUSTRIAN
Beer-Hofmann, Richard **60**
Broch, Hermann **20**
Freud, Sigmund **52**
Hofmannsthal, Hugo von **11**
Kafka, Franz **2, 6, 13, 29, 47, 53**
Kraus, Karl **5**
Kubin, Alfred (Leopold Isidor) **23**
Meyrink, Gustav **21**
Musil, Robert (Edler von) **12, 68**
Perutz, Leo **60**
Roth, Joseph **33**
Schnitzler, Arthur **4**
Steiner, Rudolf **13**
Trakl, Georg **5**
Werfel, Franz (V.) **8**
Zweig, Stefan **17**

BELGIAN
Bosschere, Jean de **19**
Lemonnier, (Antoine Louis) Camille **22**
Maeterlinck, Maurice **3**
van Ostaijen, Paul **33**
Verhaeren, Emile (Adolphe Gustave) **12**

BRAZILIAN
Andrade, Mario de **43**
Cunha, Euclides (Rodrigues Pimenta) da **24**
Lima Barreto, Afonso Henrique de **23**
Machado de Assis, Joaquim Maria **10**
Ramos, Graciliano **32**

BULGARIAN
Vazov, Ivan (Minchov) **25**

CANADIAN
Campbell, Wilfred **9**
Carman, (William) Bliss **7**
Carr, Emily **32**
Connor, Ralph **31**
Drummond, William Henry **25**
Duncan, Sara Jeannette **60**
Garneau, (Hector de) Saint-Denys **13**
Grove, Frederick Philip **4**
Knister, Raymond **56**
Leacock, Stephen (Butler) **2**
McCrae, John **12**
Montgomery, L(ucy) M(aud) **51**
Nelligan, Emile **14**
Pickthall, Marjorie L(owry) C(hristie) **21**
Roberts, Charles G(eorge) D(ouglas) **8**
Scott, Duncan Campbell **6**
Service, Robert W(illiam) **15**
Seton, Ernest (Evan) Thompson **31**
Stringer, Arthur **37**

CHILEAN
Huidobro Fernandez, Vicente Garcia **31**
Mistral, Gabriela **2**

CHINESE
Liu E **15**
Lu Hsun **3**
Su Man-shu **24**
Wen I-to **28**

COLOMBIAN
Rivera, Jose Eustasio **35**

CZECH
Capek, Karel **6, 37**
Freud, Sigmund **52**
Hasek, Jaroslav (Matej Frantisek) **4**
Kafka, Franz **2, 6, 13, 29, 47, 53**
Nezval, Vitezslav **44**

DANISH
Brandes, Georg (Morris Cohen) **10**
Hansen, Martin A. **32**
Jensen, Johannes V. **41**
Nexo, Martin Andersen **43**
Pontoppidan, Henrik **29**

DUTCH
Couperus, Louis (Marie Anne) **15**
Frank, Anne(lies Marie) **17**
Heijermans, Herman **24**
Hillesum, Etty **49**
Schendel, Arthur van **56**

ENGLISH
Barbellion, W. N. P. **24**
Baring, Maurice **8**
Beerbohm, (Henry) Max(imilian) **1, 24**
Bell, Gertrude **67**
Belloc, (Joseph) Hilaire (Pierre Sebastien Rene Swanton) **7, 18**
Bennett, (Enoch) Arnold **5, 20**
Benson, E(dward) F(rederic) **27**
Benson, Stella **17**
Bentley, E(dmund) C(lerihew) **12**
Besant, Annie (Wood) **9**
Blackmore, R(ichard) D(oddridge) **27**
Blackwood, Algernon (Henry) **5**
Bridges, Robert (Seymour) **1**
Brooke, Rupert (Chawner) **2, 7**
Burke, Thomas **63**
Butler, Samuel **1, 33**
Byron, Robert **67**
Chesterton, G(ilbert) K(eith) **1, 6, 64**
Childers, (Robert) Erskine **65**
Collingwood, R(obin) G(eorge) **67**
Conrad, Joseph **1, 6, 13, 25, 43, 57**
Coppard, A(lfred) E(dgar) **5**
Corelli, Marie **51**
Crofts, Freeman Wills **55**
Crowley, Aleister **7**
Dale, Colin **18**
Delafield, E. M. **61**
de la Mare, Walter (John) **4, 53**
Doughty, Charles M(ontagu) **27**
Douglas, Keith **40**
Douglas, Norman **68**
Dowson, Ernest (Christopher) **4**
Doyle, Arthur Conan **7**
Drinkwater, John **57**
Eddison, E(ric) R(ucker) **15**
Elaine **18**
Elizabeth **41**
Ellis, (Henry) Havelock **14**
Field, Michael **43**
Firbank, (Arthur Annesley) Ronald **1**
Ford, Ford Madox **1, 15, 39, 57**
Freeman, R(ichard) Austin **21**
Galsworthy, John **1, 45**
Gilbert, W(illiam) S(chwenck) **3**
Gissing, George (Robert) **3, 24, 47**
Gosse, Edmund (William) **28**

Grahame, Kenneth **64**
Granville-Barker, Harley **2**
Gray, John (Henry) **19**
Gurney, Ivor (Bertie) **33**
Haggard, H(enry) Rider **11**
Hall, (Marguerite) Radclyffe **12**
Hardy, Thomas **4, 10, 18, 32, 48, 53**
Henley, William Ernest **8**
Hichens, Robert S. **64**
Hilton, James **21**
Hodgson, William Hope **13**
Housman, A(lfred) E(dward) **1, 10**
Housman, Laurence **7**
Hudson, W(illiam) H(enry) **29**
Hulme, T(homas) E(rnest) **21**
Hunt, Violet **53**
Jacobs, W(illiam) W(ymark) **22**
James, Montague (Rhodes) **6**
Jerome, Jerome K(lapka) **23**
Johnson, Lionel (Pigot) **19**
Kaye-Smith, Sheila **20**
Keynes, John Maynard **64**
Kipling, (Joseph) Rudyard **8, 17**
Lawrence, D(avid) H(erbert Richards) **2, 9, 16, 33, 48, 61**
Lawrence, T(homas) E(dward) **18**
Lee, Vernon **5**
Lee-Hamilton, Eugene (Jacob) **22**
Leverson, Ada **18**
Lewis, (Percy) Wyndham **2, 9**
Lindsay, David **15**
Lowndes, Marie Adelaide (Belloc) **12**
Lowry, (Clarence) Malcolm **6, 40**
Macaulay, Rose **7, 44**
MacCarthy, (Sir Charles Otto) Desmond **36**
Maitland, Frederic **65**
Manning, Frederic **25**
Meredith, George **17, 43**
Mew, Charlotte (Mary) **8**
Meynell, Alice (Christina Gertrude Thompson) **6**
Middleton, Richard (Barham) **56**
Milne, A(lan) A(lexander) **6**
Murry, John Middleton **16**
Noyes, Alfred **7**
Oppenheim, E(dward) Phillips **45**
Orwell, George **2, 6, 15, 31, 51**
Ouida **43**
Owen, Wilfred (Edward Salter) **5, 27**
Pinero, Arthur Wing **32**
Powys, T(heodore) F(rancis) **9**
Quiller-Couch, Arthur Thomas **53**
Richardson, Dorothy Miller **3**
Rohmer, Sax **28**
Rolfe, Frederick (William Serafino Austin Lewis Mary) **12**
Rosenberg, Isaac **12**
Ruskin, John **20**
Rutherford, Mark **25**
Sabatini, Rafael **47**
Saintsbury, George (Edward Bateman) **31**
Saki **3**
Sapper **44**
Sayers, Dorothy L(eigh) **2, 15**
Shiel, M(atthew) P(hipps) **8**
Sinclair, May **3, 11**
Stapledon, (William) Olaf **22**
Stead, William Thomas **48**
Stephen, Leslie **23**
Strachey, (Giles) Lytton **12**

Summers, (Alphonsus Joseph-Mary Augustus) Montague **16**
Sutro, Alfred **6**
Swinburne, Algernon Charles **8, 36**
Symons, Arthur **11**
Thomas, (Philip) Edward **10**
Thompson, Francis Joseph **4**
Van Druten, John (William) **2**
Wallace, (Richard Horatio) Edgar **57**
Walpole, Hugh (Seymour) **5**
Ward, Mrs. Humphry **55**
Warung, Price **45**
Webb, (Martha) Beatrice (Potter) **22**
Webb, Mary (Gladys Meredith) **24**
Webb, Sidney (James) **22**
Welch, (Maurice) Denton **22**
Wells, H(erbert) G(eorge) **6, 12, 19**
Williams, Charles (Walter Stansby) **1, 11**
Woolf, (Adeline) Virginia **1, 5, 20, 43, 56**
Yonge, Charlotte (Mary) **48**
Zangwill, Israel **16**

ESTONIAN
Tammsaare, A(nton) H(ansen) **27**

FINNISH
Leino, Eino **24**
Soedergran, Edith (Irene) **31**

FRENCH
Alain **41**
Alain-Fournier **6**
Apollinaire, Guillaume **3, 8, 51**
Artaud, Antonin (Marie Joseph) **3, 36**
Barbusse, Henri **5**
Barres, Maurice **47**
Benda, Julien **60**
Bergson, Henri **32**
Bernanos, (Paul Louis) Georges **3**
Bloy, Leon **22**
Bourget, Paul (Charles Joseph) **12**
Claudel, Paul (Louis Charles Marie) **2, 10**
Colette, (Sidonie-Gabrielle) **1, 5, 16**
Coppee, Francois **25**
Daumal, Rene **14**
Desnos, Robert **22**
Drieu la Rochelle, Pierre(-Eugene) **21**
Dujardin, Edouard (Emile Louis) **13**
Durkheim, Emile **55**
Eluard, Paul **7, 41**
Fargue, Leon-Paul **11**
Feydeau, Georges (Leon Jules Marie) **22**
France, Anatole **9**
Gide, Andre (Paul Guillaume) **5, 12, 36**
Giraudoux, (Hippolyte) Jean **2, 7**
Gourmont, Remy (-Marie-Charles) de **17**
Huysmans, Joris-Karl **7, 69**
Jacob, (Cyprien-)Max **6**
Jarry, Alfred **2, 14**
Larbaud, Valery (Nicolas) **9**
Leblanc, Maurice (Marie Emile) **49**
Leroux, Gaston **25**
Loti, Pierre **11**
Martin du Gard, Roger **24**
Mirbeau, Octave **55**
Mistral, Frederic **51**
Moreas, Jean **18**
Nizan, Paul **40**
Peguy, Charles Pierre **10**
Peret, Benjamin **20**
Proust, (Valentin-Louis-George-Eugene-) Marcel **7, 13, 33**

Rachilde **67**
Radiguet, Raymond **29**
Renard, Jules **17**
Rolland, Romain **23**
Rostand, Edmond (Eugene Alexis) **6, 37**
Roussel, Raymond **20**
Saint-Exupery, Antoine (Jean Baptiste Marie Roger) de **2, 56**
Schwob, (Mayer Andre) Marcel **20**
Sully Prudhomme **31**
Teilhard de Chardin, (Marie Joseph) Pierre **9**
Valery, (Ambroise) Paul (Toussaint Jules) **4, 15**
Verne, Jules (Gabriel) **6, 52**
Vian, Boris **9**
Weil, Simone (Adolphine) **23**
Zola, Emile (Edouard Charles Antoine) **1, 6, 21, 41**

GERMAN
Andreas-Salome, Lou **56**
Auerbach, Erich **43**
Benjamin, Walter **39**
Benn, Gottfried **3**
Borchert, Wolfgang **5**
Brecht, Bertolt **1, 6, 13, 35**
Carossa, Hans **48**
Cassirer, Ernst **61**
Doblin, Alfred **13**
Doeblin, Alfred **13**
Einstein, Albert **65**
Ewers, Hanns Heinz **12**
Feuchtwanger, Lion **3**
George, Stefan (Anton) **2, 14**
Goebbels, (Paul) Joseph **68**
Hauptmann, Gerhart (Johann Robert) **4**
Heym, Georg (Theodor Franz Arthur) **9**
Heyse, Paul (Johann Ludwig von) **8**
Hitler, Adolf **53**
Huch, Ricarda (Octavia) **13**
Kaiser, Georg **9**
Klabund **44**
Kolmar, Gertrud **40**
Lasker-Schueler, Else **57**
Liliencron, (Friedrich Adolf Axel) Detlev von **18**
Luxemburg, Rosa **63**
Mann, (Luiz) Heinrich **9**
Mann, (Paul) Thomas **2, 8, 14, 21, 35, 44, 60**
Mannheim, Karl **65**
Morgenstern, Christian **8**
Nietzsche, Friedrich (Wilhelm) **10, 18, 55**
Plumpe, Friedrich Wilhelm **53**
Raabe, Wilhelm **45**
Rilke, Rainer Maria **1, 6, 19**
Simmel, Georg **64**
Spengler, Oswald (Arnold Gottfried) **25**
Sternheim, (William Adolf) Carl **8**
Sudermann, Hermann **15**
Toller, Ernst **10**
Wassermann, (Karl) Jakob **6**
Weber, Max **69**
Wedekind, (Benjamin) Frank(lin) **7**
Wiene, Robert **56**

GHANIAN
Casely-Hayford, J(oseph) E(phraim) **24**

GREEK
Cavafy, C(onstantine) P(eter) **2, 7**

Nationality Index

TCLC 69 Title Index

ISBN 0-7876-1169-7

90000